Churchill

This book is due for return on or before the last date shown below.

1 4 APR 2016

Don Gresswell Ltd., London, N.21 Cat. No. 1208   DG 02242/71

Also by Clive Ponting

The Right to Know:
The Inside Story of the Belgrano Affair

Whitehall: Tragedy and Farce

Breach of Promise:
Labour in Power 1964–1970

Whitehall: Changing the Old Guard

Secrecy in Britain

1940: Myth and Reality

A Green History of the World

Churchill

CLIVE PONTING

SINCLAIR-STEVENSON

First published in Great Britain in 1994
by Sinclair-Stevenson
an imprint of Reed Consumer Books Ltd
Michelin House, 81 Fulham Road, London SW3 6RB
and Auckland, Melbourne, Singapore and Toronto

This paperback edition published by Sinclair-Stevenson in 1995

A CIP catalogue record for this book
is available at the British Library

ISBN 1 85619 573 2

Typeset by CentraCet Limited, Cambridge
Printed and bound in Great Britain by Mackays of Chatham plc

Contents

Contents

Acknowledgements

During the course of writing this book I have accumulated many debts of gratitude, in particular to my editor Christopher Sinclair-Stevenson for enthusiastically backing the idea for four years.

I should also like to thank Richard Stevenson of the Royal Society of Chemistry. When the Government, after condemning the current Iraqi Government for gassing its own population, withdrew a file from the Public Record Office about Britain's use of gas warefare in Iraq in the early 1920s, he generously transcribed his own notes made a few years ago, thereby enabling me to complete one part of the story of Churchill's obsession with the use of gas. I am also grateful to Julian Putkowski, who suggested one line of research to me which unfortunately proved nugatory but our correspondence and his expertise on the British Army greatly helped my understanding of the immediate post-First World War period.

My thanks also go to the staff of that nicest of all government departments – the Public Record Office – for their unfailing helpfulness during my long periods of research there.

Any student of Churchill will be in the debt of Martin Gilbert for his painstaking reconstruction of the details of Churchill's long career. Although my interpretation of Churchill's life is radically different from Gilbert's I would like to acknowledge my own debt to his work. Finally I would like to acknowledge the permission of C & T Publications to quote from the documents in the official biography of Winston Churchill.

Picture Credits

The author wishes to thank the following for the use of illustrations: Topham Picture Source; 1a, 10, 18, 19a, 23b, 24a, 26, 28, 30, 31, 32, The Broadwater Collection, Churchill College, Cambridge; 1b, 1c, 2, 3b, 4b, 5a, 6, 7b, 9, 11a, 12, 13, 15, 20b, 22b, 25a, Popperfoto; 4a, 5b, 16, 19b, The Imperial War Museum; 7a, 8, 11b, 20a, 24b, Hulton Deutsch; 14b, 17, 22a, The Keystone Collection; 14c, 27a, 29b, Camera Press; 21, 23a, 25b, 27b, 29a, The Press Photograph Collection, Churchill College, Cambridge; 14a. Photograph 3a is taken from *My African Journey* by Winston Churchill (published by Hodder & Stoughton, 1908)

I

Introduction

> The biography stands, fat and worthy-burgerish on the shelf,
> boastful and sedate: a shilling life will give you all the facts, a ten
> pound one all the hypotheses as well. But think of everything that
> got away, that fled with the last deathbed exhalation of the bio-
> graphee. What chance would the craftiest biographer stand against
> the subject who saw him coming and decided to amuse himself?
>
> (Julian Barnes, *Flaubert's Parrot*, 1984)

Although the days of the 'shilling life' and even the 'ten pound one'
are long past, the problems have remained the same. Winston
Churchill certainly saw his biographers coming and was determined
to mould the view that later generations would have of his life.
Churchill's close friend Brendan Bracken warned his doctor and
would-be biographer Lord Moran of the difficulties: 'Mind you, my
dear doctor, it's not going to be easy. You won't get much from his
letters. You see, Charles, Winston is preoccupied with getting the
record straight for posterity.'[1]

All politicians are interested in safeguarding and enhancing their
reputations but Churchill was obsessed more than any other this
century about the way his life would be interpreted. He wrote about
himself prodigiously – two volumes of autobiography; a semi-
autobiographical novel; a multi-volume history of the First World

War that is largely about his own role; a six-volume history of the Second World War that is really a set of memoirs; a collection of short portraits of his contemporaries that say almost as much about Churchill as about the subjects of the essays; and a vast number of newspaper articles that recycle much of this material but add other details about his life and opinions.

Churchill was also acutely aware from an early age of the power of words, and he went to great lengths to cultivate a resonant and readable style in his published works. Moreover Churchill's pre-eminent position in the post-war world has lent an authority to his works and an aura to his life. For these reasons Churchill's own interpretation of his life, and of many of the events through which he lived (particularly the Second World War), became widely accepted. In this biography I have deliberately avoided quotations from Churchill's own writing about himself except in a few instances. I believe that they tell us mainly what he thought about events, often many years after they occurred, and what he wanted other people to think about them, not necessarily what really happened or their true significance.

In addition to the literary output there is the vast Churchill archive (only partly published in the companion volumes to the official biography). It contains one of the most voluminous sets of private papers available for a modern life. It was deliberately created by Churchill, who hoarded virtually every letter he received and copies of most letters and papers he wrote, not just to enable him to write his own books, but also to influence the way in which future historians would write about his life. Caution needs to be exercised in using this material. Many of these documents were written with more than half an eye on history and were designed from the beginning to place Churchill's interpretation of events on record and to express opinions which could be quoted later. Frequently Churchill refused to put down certain things on paper because he thought they might damage his reputation. Some of his colleagues realised what he was doing at the time. For example, in September 1939 Neville Chamberlain, writing to his sister just over a fortnight after Churchill had joined his government, remarked that 'he continually writes me letters many pages long . . . of course I realise that these letters are for the purpose of quotation in the Book which he will write hereafter . . .'[2]

Churchill's official biography draws heavily on these papers (and quotes extensively from his published works). Any biography built mainly on a single set of papers will necessarily bias the interpretation of the life towards that of the biographee. As R. F. Foster has written in his brilliant re-interpretation of the life of Lord Randolph Churchill, English political biography has tended to become:

> the personal monument, founded on one collection of papers which have been laundered to whiteness (or at least a uniform shade of grey) ... There is a soothing quality about British historical biography which calms by dint of repetition. A prominent politician is assured of recurrent applications of biographical varnish, borrowing the texture of previous layers to build up a warm and glowing patina: reiteration of anecdotes, judicious but limited reappraisals of character, a general air of comfortable reassurance.[3]

Winston Churchill has been subject to this process as much, if not more, than most other politicians. His stature in the latter part of his life was such that few people were prepared to be publicly critical – the overwhelming majority were adulatory. Books were also written by people who had risen to a certain degree of fame alongside Churchill and they too had a strong interest in preserving a particular view of Churchill as a way of increasing their own importance.

In the last two decades there has been a vast amount of historical research into various events which form part of Churchill's life. This has changed our perception of these events but little of this has found its way into any re-assessment of Churchill's career. Indeed apart from the official life there has been only one completed biography of Churchill in the last twenty years. In this work I have had Foster's comments in mind. I have tried to portray Churchill without starting from a point which he himself helped to create. This book uses material from the Churchill papers (which are obviously essential) but also draws on the range of material that has become available in the last few decades, including both private and government archives and the work of numerous historians working in specialised areas. We are now nearly thirty years on from Churchill's death and half a century or more away from some of the most important episodes of his life. Our historical perspective has changed and it is possible to see his life in a different and much wider context.

It is against this background that I have sought to interpret Churchill's life. The result is perhaps a less soothing view than some other interpretations would suggest and it differs greatly from the one he preferred. But to quote Foster again: 'Piety is the besetting weakness of most biography, and a pious imputation of consistency the besetting fault of most political biography.'[4]

Part 1

AMBITION AND NEMESIS

1874–1915

2

Youth

Winston Leonard Spencer Churchill was born at Blenheim Palace on 30 November 1874, just seven and a half months after his parents, Lord Randolph Churchill and Jennie Jerome, were married in Paris. His birth was announced as premature and tactfully accepted as such by the local doctor from the nearby village of Woodstock. It is more likely that he was conceived when Lord Randolph and Jennie were together in Paris at the end of February for the marriage contract negotiations. A marriage between an eligible English aristocrat and an attractive American heiress was a fairly common feature of the late nineteenth century. Lord Randolph, then twenty-five years old, was the younger son of the seventh Duke of Marlborough and nineteen-year-old Jennie was the daughter of Leonard Jerome, who had made and lost more than one fortune speculating on the New York Stock Exchange. The marriage settlement provided Lord Randolph with a capital dowry of £50,000 (nearly £2 million at today's prices) and an income of £2,000 a year, which his father supplemented with another £1,100.

The Marlborough family badly needed the Jerome money. The first Duke of Marlborough had led the English armies to victory on the continent against the French during the War of the Spanish Succession in the early eighteenth century. In the course of the campaign he had looted large amounts of money from public funds and at the end of it had been rewarded, by a grateful Parliament, with the estate at Blenheim, a palace and a substantial endowment.

However by the middle of the nineteenth century the family fortunes were greatly reduced. Much of their inheritance had been squandered by a series of extravagant and dissolute Dukes – many of the family jewels and substantial properties in Wiltshire and Shropshire and the family farm at Blenheim had been sold. In the year of Winston Churchill's birth four square miles of Buckinghamshire were sold to a member of the Rothschild family for the then enormous sum of £220,000. The sales of land and property were to continue during his early years – more family jewels in 1875 and five years later the Sutherland library of rare manuscripts and books.

Despite the waning family fortunes, the Marlboroughs had maintained a style of life that was typical for members of the social élite. The seventh Duke, Winston's grandfather, had been a member of the Conservative governments of the late 1860s. His heir, Winston's uncle, the Marquess of Blandford, was a spendthrift womaniser even by Marlborough standards. The younger son, Lord Randolph, went to a fashionable preparatory school, then Eton, where he was nicknamed 'gooseberry' because of his large, staring eyes. Having failed to get into Balliol College at Oxford, he scraped into Merton after attending a crammer. Much of his time at university was spent on horseback and after graduating he spent the next four years travelling and mixing in society. Although the family favourite, because of Blandford's exceptionally wayward behaviour, he was regarded by his contemporaries as rude, arrogant, a snob and a heavy drinker. At the first opportunity in 1874 he stood for the family borough of Woodstock, where the voters, who numbered just 1,100, dutifully returned him as their Member of Parliament at the age of twenty-five.

It was just before Lord Randolph became an MP that he met Jennie Jerome during Cowes week. After only three days' acquaintance they became engaged. Jennie had come to the Isle of Wight as part of the usual round of fashionable social events. She was living in Paris at the time with her mother and two sisters. They had moved there in 1868 when the family had broken up after Leonard's numerous affairs and countless illegitimate children and had rapidly established themselves in the glittering society of Napoleon III's court. Jennie, who was beautiful, vivacious and devoted to a life of frivolity and pleasure, was a great success. With the collapse in 1870 of Napoleon's empire, marriage to an English aristocrat must have seemed a great attraction. That marriage though had to wait for Lord Randolph to be elected to Parliament and for the financial details to be settled – the latter proved difficult because Leonard Jerome had lost a considerable sum of money in the 1873 stock market crash. The Duke and Duchess of Marlborough travelled to Paris for the all-important financial negotiations, but did not stay on for the wedding on 15 April 1874 at the British Embassy because they did not, despite the money involved, approve of a match outside the restricted circle of the aristocracy. In return Jennie actively disliked her mother-in-law and hated Blenheim.

The newly married couple settled into a house in Mayfair paid for by Leonard Jerome and became prominent members of 'society', especially the group around the Prince of Wales (the future Edward VII) that was not well known for its austere style of life and high moral tone (the Prince probably had a brief affair with Jennie at this time). They spent money freely and lost more in gambling (by 1876 Lord Randolph was already having to raise a loan of £5,000). But unfortunately for their social standing Lord Randolph showed poor judgement in the way he became embroiled in a particularly sordid episode on his brother's behalf. Two years after Winston's birth he provoked a quarrel with the Prince over a lover Blandford and the Prince shared; following Lord Randolph's abortive attempt to black-mail the Royal Family, he was effectively exiled to Dublin for four years. The Duke of Marlborough was virtually forced to accept the Lord Lieutenancy of Ireland (at a personal cost of £30,000 a year) and take Lord Randolph as his secretary in order to remove him from London society.

Winston Churchill was therefore born into the small, immensely influential and wealthy circle that still dominated English politics and society. For the whole of his life he remained an aristocrat at heart, deeply devoted to the interests of his family and drawing the majority of his friends and social acquaintances from that élite. From 1876 to 1880 he was brought up surrounded by servants amongst the splendours of the British ascendancy in Ireland. Like virtually all children of the aristocracy, he was handed over to a wet nurse immediately after his birth and then, in January 1875, to a nanny, Mrs Everest. But Winston was a neglected child, even by the standards of aristocratic families of the time. He saw his parents only fleetingly and it was Mrs Everest who was to remain his main companion and friend until her death in 1895. She provided his only constant source of love and affection and after she had been dismissed in a particularly ungrateful way by the family in 1893 (she had to beg for money from her previous employer in order to survive) Winston sent her small sums of money, paid for a nurse and doctor in her last illness, helped provide her gravestone and even paid for the wreath that nominally came from his mother.

When the Conservatives lost the 1880 Election Churchill's grandfather resigned as Lord Lieutenant and the family moved back to London, although Lord Randolph was not reconciled with the Prince of Wales until 1884. Back in England Lord Randolph embarked on an erratic but sensational political career within the Conservative Party that made him Chancellor of the Exchequer within six years. One reason for such a frantic pace was his realisation that he did not have long to live. Within a few weeks of Winston's birth Lord Randolph was being treated by a London doctor for a mysterious illness – almost certainly the first signs of the syphilis that was to kill him at the age of forty-five. The disease was probably contracted from a chambermaid at Blenheim immediately after Winston's birth – it meant that Lord Randolph's and Jennie's marriage rapidly disintegrated. Indeed it is possible that Winston's younger brother, Jack, who was born in February 1880 and whose middle name was Strange, was fathered by John Strange Jocelyn, one of Jennie's many lovers in Dublin.

Lord Randolph was driven by extreme ambition and he had few, if any, principles to restrain his single-minded pursuit of power. As a backbencher he gained attention through his virulent attacks on Gladstone's Liberal government and his obstructive Parliamentary tactics. His allies, in what was known as the 'Fourth Party', were Sir Henry Drummond Wolff, a career diplomat and man about town; John Gorst, a barrister who thought he had been unfairly neglected by the party leadership; and occasionally Arthur Balfour, a nephew of Lord Salisbury (and later Prime Minister and colleague of Winston). The 'party' had no programme – its adherents simply pressed for a more active policy from the Conservative Party in opposition and sought fame for themselves. It was during this period that the label of 'Tory Democracy' was attached to Lord Randolph and his activities. It was one that Winston came to emphasise constantly when talking or writing about his father. In fact Lord

Randolph hardly ever used the term, never defined what it meant and was certainly not a believer in the concept. His speeches in the five years after 1880 were not about social reform – they were largely attacks on the Liberal Government and a defence of traditional institutions, especially the monarchy, the House of Lords and the established church. Indeed he was actively opposed to many measures of social reform. For example he condemned the Metropolitan Water Bill (that would have increased charges in wealthier areas in order to pay for water supplies for the poorest parts of the capital) as 'the wildest Socialistic doctrine'. He originally opposed the 1884 Reform Act that extended the right to vote and only changed his position when it was obvious that his Woodstock constituency would be abolished and he would have to stand in a seat with many more voters and therefore needed to increase his popularity.

In addition to his high-profile role on the backbenches he was also active within the Conservative Party's national organisation, using it as another vehicle for advancing his career. By 1884 he had pushed himself into the front rank of the Conservative leadership through his support for the National Union of local associations, though he had no intention of democratising power within the party and rapidly distanced himself from the organisation once he had achieved his aim – the promise of a Cabinet post in the next Conservative Government. In December of that year he left for a three month tour of India and on his return became Secretary of State for India in Lord Salisbury's Government. In another example of his lack of principles he at first leant towards the Irish Nationalists, and then later backed the Unionists in Ulster when it was obvious that the Liberals would split on the issue after Gladstone's espousal of Home Rule. By 1886 he was the effective Conservative leader in the Commons and after the Election in July he was appointed Chancellor of the Exchequer and also became the formal leader in the Commons in the new Conservative Government. But political success was not accompanied by personal popularity: Lord Randolph was widely seen by his colleagues as over-ambitious, difficult to work with, untrustworthy and unstable.

Throughout this period Lord Randolph's personal and family life was extremely difficult. For much of the period he and Jennie were still not admitted to the society around the Prince of Wales. Money remained a constant problem because of their extravagance. After

1883 they rented a large house near Marble Arch, bills remained unpaid and his solicitors had to raise loans worth £15,000. Then in July that year his father died and Blandford inherited the estate. The two brothers quarrelled almost immediately over the inheritance. In February 1884 Lord Randolph did manage to raise a loan of £31,000 secured on his inheritance due when his mother died, but that was soon spent. One of Lord Randolph's problems in raising money was that rumours about his state of health and its cause were widespread in the political and social world. (From March till October 1882 Lord Randolph was out of politics undergoing treatment for his illness and he spent the winter of 1882–3 in Nice with his mistress trying to regain his health.) He was ill again for much of 1885, being treated by his doctor with a standard cocktail of chemicals – potassium iodide and mercury (which were themselves poisonous) – in a vain attempt to arrest the progress of the syphilis. This treatment caused progressive debility, tremors and heart weakness, which had to be countered with digitalis. His increasing instability and rudeness made him both a political and a social liability. His marriage had virtually collapsed. Since 1881 Jennie had been carrying on a well-known affair with an Austrian diplomat, Count Kinsky, but there were numerous other affairs as well. Lord Randolph was living separately from her at the Carlton Club and also having affairs with a succession of different women. The couple were openly quarrelling and the marriage only survived because the stigma of divorce would have ruined Lord Randolph's career and their place in society.

The sort of life his parents were leading left them with little time to devote to their two children. Winston was sent to an expensive preparatory school, St George's at Ascot, just before his eighth birthday in November 1882. Until this point he had been educated by a governess and the transition to boarding school proved to be very difficult for him. Winston spent eighteen unhappy months at St George's, where he was usually towards the bottom of the class. His behaviour was bad and he was regularly flogged by a headmaster who seems to have taken particular pleasure in the process. He left the school at the end of the summer term in 1884, probably after complaints from Mrs Everest about his treatment there (his brother Jack was sent to a different school). In the autumn he moved to a smaller and cheaper establishment in Brighton run by two elderly spinsters, the Misses Thomson. Here he was much happier, although his behaviour remained poor. He was seen as negligent, slovenly and perpetually late (he kept the last characteristic for the rest of his life). His academic performance though began to improve. In later life Churchill always tried to give the impression that school had taught him little and he was largely self-educated. This was not the case. He was a bright pupil with a phenomenal memory – but he took little interest in subjects that did not stimulate him and so his academic record was patchy. By the time he left school at Brighton he was reading Herodotus in Greek, liked Virgil, knew French and was working on Euclid and also algebra. He had also learnt to ride and even took a brief interest in cricket – he went to see W. G. Grace bat at Hove – but for the rest of his life he hated all forms of organised sport apart from polo. Winston was not widely liked at school – he was stabbed in the chest by one boy during an argument and one of his life-long memories was of hiding behind a large tree while other boys threw cricket balls at him. For the rest of his life he could never understand people who thought that their schooldays had been the happiest time of their lives.

Although Winston was taken by his father for his first foreign holiday in 1883 (to Paris and Gastein in Austria) and they were with him during a very bad attack of pneumonia in March 1886, his relations with his parents remained distant and difficult. They found him badly behaved and much more difficult to handle than Jack. Jennie wrote to Lord Randolph during his trip to India: 'The children have both gone – I shall have Jack before Xmas as I cld not undertake to manage Winston without Everest – I am afraid that even she can't do it.'[1] When he stayed with his grandmother during the Christmas holidays in 1887, she reported to Jennie: 'Winston is going back to school today. Entre nous I do not feel very sorry for he certainly is a handful.'[2] In general Winston's parents avoided these problems by concentrating on their separate social and political lives and keeping away from him as much as possible. In the summer holidays he and Jack were either left at Blenheim or sent off to a seaside resort such as Cromer with a governess and Mrs Everest, while their parents went off on their own. Winston came to depend on a relation, Lady Wilton, who used to send him money and food parcels signed 'Deputy Mother', and he remained close to Mrs Everest, whom he once described to his mother as being 'in my mind associated more than anything else with *home*'.[3]

Most of Winston's early letters were pathetic attempts to try and make his parents take some interest in him. In July 1883 he wrote to his mother to ask her, together with Jack and Mrs Everest, to come to his school sports – only Mrs Everest went. In February 1884 he wrote, 'I am wondering when you are coming to see me? I hope you are coming to see me soon . . . You must send someone to see me.'[4] In June of that year he was complaining that he had only had one letter from her during the whole of the term. In December 1886 when Jennie did visit her son in Brighton she would not stay to see him in the school play, preferring to travel back to London to attend a dinner party. Winston's relations with his father were no better. In October 1885 he wrote to him: 'I cannot think why you did not come to see me, while you were in Brighton, I was very disappointed but I suppose you were too busy to come.'[5] A year later he again found out his father had been in Brighton when he saw a report of his speech in a newspaper and wrote, 'You never came to see me on Sunday when you were in Brighton.'[6]

It was shortly after this second failure to visit his elder son that Lord Randolph's political career collapsed in ruins through his own actions. His overwhelming ambition together with the knowledge that he had little time to live drove him on to try to replace Lord Salisbury as Prime Minister. But he seriously misjudged the strength of his political position and overplayed his hand. In December 1886, when the Government was involved in the usual annual argument over the level of defence expenditure, Lord Randolph wrote a resignation letter to the Prime Minister over what he saw as the failure to cut military and naval expenditure. It was a deliberate attempt to break up the Government and demonstrate his own indispensability. However Salisbury was delighted to accept the resignation – he had in fact wanted to get rid of his troublesome colleague for a long time and saw this as an ideal opportunity. In a second letter Lord Randolph widened the grounds of the dispute so as to try to bring down the Government with the aim of creating some form of alliance with the Liberals and Liberal Unionists. But there was to be no repeat of the political manoeuvrings of the previous year over Home Rule. Lord Randolph found no support among his colleagues – he had made himself far too unpopular. He was replaced by W. H. Smith (whom he hated for his middle-class origins) as Leader of the Commons and by Goschen as Chancellor.

Smith speculated about Lord Randolph's abrupt departure from the Cabinet to another colleague, Lord Cranbrook: 'the real truth is, I think, that it is not possible for him to yield his opinion or mould it so as to co-operate with his colleagues. He must rule . . .'[7] The state of his marriage can be deduced from the fact that Jennie first learnt of her husband's resignation when she read about it in a newspaper – even though she had been with him on the night of his second resignation letter to Salisbury. Lord Randolph's political career was now over; he never held office again and became an increasingly isolated and embittered backbencher as his health continued to deteriorate.

In the summer after Lord Randolph's resignation a decision had to be made about Winston's future schooling. His father decided on Harrow rather than the family school of Eton (Winston knew so little about his father that he had to ask him which school he had attended). Winston sat the entrance exam in March 1888 and passed. The amusingly recounted story in his memoirs (written in the late 1920s) of how he produced nothing but a large blot on an otherwise blank sheet is obviously untrue, part of the myth of his youthful ignorance which he created later in life. He started at Harrow in April 1888 at the age of thirteen and a half and immediately liked the school. In his first year he was in a small house run by his main tutor, Mr Davidson, and then moved to one under the headmaster, the Reverend J. E. C. Welldon, who was to put in much time and effort with Winston and remained in touch with him long after he left the school. The masters at Harrow found many of the same problems that had emerged earlier. His behaviour remained bad. At the end of his first term his housemaster reported to his father 'I do not think . . . that he is in any way *wilfully* troublesome: but his forgetfulness, carelessness, unpunctuality, and irregularity in every way, have really been so serious' as to call for a strong parental lecture. Nevertheless his teachers recognised that he had potential; his basic problem was lack of application. 'As far as ability goes he ought to be at the top of his form, whereas he is at the bottom.'[8] Winston's ability was shown in those subjects that did interest him. He memorised 1,200 lines of Macaulay's 'Lays of Ancient Rome' in order to win a prize and he was awarded the history prize two terms running. But he remained an unpopular boy and also demonstrated a tendency to be a bully if given the chance.

From an early age Winston had been fascinated by toy soldiers and he joined the cadet corps from the beginning of his time at Harrow and thoroughly enjoyed the life. Although his academic performance made Lord Randolph doubt his son's ability and determination to get to university, another socially acceptable course was possible. His father decided to capitalise on Winston's enthusiasm and allowed him to follow his strong inclination and join the Army class after eighteen months at Harrow. (The curriculum in this class was different from the rest of the school, ruling out university entrance, and was designed to prepare students for the Army examinations.) After a year in the Army class it was decided that Winston's mathematical abilities were not good enough for entrance to Woolwich, the training college for the artillery and engineers, and that he should concentrate on the Sandhurst exam for cavalry and infantry officers (which is where his family would have wanted him to serve anyway on social grounds). In November 1890 he passed the preliminary exam in all subjects.

Winston was as neglected by his parents at Harrow as he had been at his prep schools in Ascot and Brighton. After a year the headmaster felt obliged to write to Winston's parents suggesting that they should pay their first visit to him; neither did so for another six months. In June 1889 when Winston was ill in the school hospital suffering the after-effects of concussion he wrote three letters to his mother asking her to visit him but without success. A month later he made all the necessary arrangements and wrote to his father asking him to come to Speech Day adding, 'I shall be awfully disappointed if you don't come'. He begged his mother to use her powers of persuasion but neither of his parents came down to Harrow – less than an hour's journey from central London.[9] In the autumn of that year he wrote to his mother 'It is more than a fortnight since I heard from you. In fact I have only had one letter this term. It is not very kind of my darling mummy to forget all about me, not answer my epistles.'[10] In June 1891 he again tried to persuade a member of the family to attend Speech Day. His father was in South Africa and he guessed his mother would not come, so he asked for a substitute – his grandmother or an aunt – saying 'I shall be awfully "out of it" if no one comes.'[11] Later that month his expectations were more realistic, writing to his mother: 'It was a pity you could not come to see me on Sat. I did not expect you & so was not disappointed.'[12]

The one thing that his parents did give him was money. His regular allowance at the age of fifteen was fifteen shillings a week (£27 at current prices) – more than many people in Britain earned for a week's work. By 1891, when he very reluctantly spent the Christmas holidays with a family at Versailles to improve his French, he was receiving £1 a week. Winston's expenditure was profligate in keeping with the family tradition. By the age of fifteen he was smoking regularly and a year later he had started his life-long regular consumption of champagne. Not surprisingly he was normally in debt.

During his time at Harrow Winston developed two interests. The first, collecting butterflies, he kept up into his early life in the Army in India. The second was fencing; he became the public schools' champion in April 1892. By this time he was also working hard for the main Sandhurst examination, which he took in July of that year. Like most other candidates he failed at his first attempt but he was 390th out of 693 candidates and came eighteenth in English history. Overall he gained 5,100 marks when 6,500 were needed for success. His masters at Harrow thought he would succeed at the second attempt in November and Winston continued to work hard throughout the summer. In the examination he improved his marks by over 1,000 (being placed in the top ten in chemistry) and was only 351 marks short of the pass mark. Lord Randolph was already thinking of sending him into the City through the Rothschild bank (the main source of his loans) but the Reverend Welldon persuaded him to send his son to one of the recognised crammers as a last chance of securing the career he wanted. Winston's start at Captain James's establishment was delayed by a broken thigh, the result of a fall whilst on holiday, but hard work and a small increase in marks, just under 200 (including the highest mark in English history), enabled him to pass into Sandhurst at the third attempt. Since his mark was too low for the infantry, he was assigned to the less intellectual but more socially exclusive and expensive cavalry.

In August 1893 Winston left for a holiday in Switzerland before starting his life as an Army cadet. While on holiday he received a letter containing all Lord Randolph's feelings of bitterness and disappointment with his son's performance and prospects. Much of it was unfair and exaggerated, reflecting his own growing mental instability:

Never have I received a really good report of your conduct in your work from any master or tutor you had from time to time to do with. Always behind-hand, never advancing in your class, incessant complaints of total want of application . . . with all the advantages you had, and with all the abilities which you foolishly think yourself to possess . . . with all the efforts that have been made to make your life easy & agreeable & your work neither oppressive or distasteful, this is the grand result that you come up among the 2nd rate & 3rd rate class who are only good for commissions in a cavalry regiment . . . I shall not write again on these matters & you need not trouble to write any answer to this part of my letter, because I no longer attach the slightest weight to anything you may say about your own acquirements & exploits. Make this position indelibly impressed on your mind, that if your conduct and action at Sandhurst is similar to what it has been in the other establishments in which it has sought vainly to impart to you some education. Then that my responsibility for you is over. I shall leave you to depend on yourself giving you merely such assistance as may be necessary to permit of a respectable life. [sic][13]

Although Winston did reply, expressing his hopes for a new start, he was, not surprisingly, immensely depressed by his father's letter, coming as it did just after he had at last achieved his ambition of getting into the Army. Lord Randolph's utterly jaundiced view of his talents and prospects had a deep and long-lasting effect on his psychology. For most of his life he felt the need to prove himself to his father and show that the opinions expressed in this letter were wrong – it was one of the major forces behind his driving ambition. It was not until after the Second World War that he felt that he had finally disproved his father.

Winston started on his sixteen-month course at Sandhurst in September 1893 just before his nineteenth birthday. He found that others had withdrawn and he was now high enough up the list to join an infantry regiment (saving his father £200 a year). Lord Randolph, through his influence with the Commander-in-Chief, the Duke of Cambridge, succeeded in placing Winston with the prestigious 60th Rifles. Winston liked the life of a military cadet and particularly enjoyed dressing up in uniform (a pleasure he retained for the rest of his life). He began to mature rapidly and within a few weeks even Lord Randolph was impressed by the improvement in his performance, although he still refused him permission to travel to London during the term as most other cadets were allowed to do. By the end of the first term Winston was in the top twenty on the course.

He was now beginning to make his own social life, though still dependent on a generous allowance from his father. He moved easily in the world of the aristocracy and the wealthy, building on his family connections and his parents' numerous political and social contacts. He spent the Christmas holiday of 1893 on his own programme of country house visits and no longer complained of not spending the time with his parents. In the summer of 1894 for the first time he took part in the London 'season' of lunches, dinners, receptions and balls organised by various political and social hostesses and went on the accepted outings to events such as the Ascot and Goodwood race meetings. Later he again went on holiday to Switzerland, this time with Jack. He was also a regular visitor to the Empire theatre, a well-known haunt of prostitutes, and in November 1894 was one of the leaders of a small demonstration against its closure. The death of Blandford in 1892 at the age of forty-seven meant that Winston's cousin, universally known in society as 'Sunny', inherited the Dukedom. Winston was invited to Blenheim as a regular guest and greatly appreciated its splendour and the life of luxury available there. The family though were anxious to see Sunny produce an heir and so disinherit Winston. His grandmother the Duchess of Marlborough told Consuelo Vanderbilt, who married Sunny in 1896 (and brought a lump sum of $2.5 million and an annual income of $30,000 to replenish the family coffers), that she must produce a son 'because it would be intolerable if that little upstart Winston ever became Duke'.[14]

Winston, as a member of a highly political family, was also beginning to develop an interest in politics. In April 1893 he had gone to the House of Commons to hear Gladstone wind up the debate on the second Home Rule Bill. He also began to meet socially senior politicians of both parties such as Arthur Balfour, Herbert Asquith and Lord Rosebery. Lord Randolph was also prepared to take him to one or two political gatherings, for example to the Rothschilds' house at Tring, but discouraged him from developing any serious interest and repulsed Winston's suggestion that he might help him as an unofficial political secretary.

At the end of 1894 Winston passed out of Sandhurst twentieth in his class of 130. But by then Lord Randolph was living out the last ghastly months of his life. In the early summer of 1893 his doctor had diagnosed the early stages of general paralysis – the last and fatal stage of syphilis. It was not until November 1894, when he persuaded the family doctor to tell him the truth, that Winston was aware of the nature of his father's illness and its inevitable outcome. The doctor would have reassured him that syphilis was not congenital but it must have been a shock for Winston to realise for the first time the true nature of his family life and this new knowledge must have further complicated the already difficult relationship with his father. He also had to dissemble in public about the nature of Lord Randolph's illness even though many in the political and social world Winston inhabited had already guessed what was wrong. (The family kept Lord Randolph's syphilis secret for more than eighty years and the first volume of the official biography of Winston published in the late 1960s simply talks of mental illness.)

Lord Randolph's health, behaviour and financial position had been deteriorating for some time. After his political career had self-destructed in 1886 he turned increasingly to gambling at Monte Carlo and horse racing (keeping his own horses at Newmarket). Both were expensive hobbies and combined with stock market speculation left him a staggering £11,000 in debt to the Rothschilds by 1891. His other link to the bank was his advisory role – when he was in Government he had passed them Cabinet secrets. In 1891 Lord Randolph went to South Africa, ostensibly to find areas for working-class emigration but was actually financed by a syndicate close to Cecil Rhodes to look for gold. Although socially the visit was a disaster because of Lord Randolph's erratic behaviour, it turned out for once to be a good investment for him – he put in £5,000 which was worth £70,000 on his death.

By 1892 both Lord Randolph's health and finances were collapsing rapidly. He suffered from slurred speech, vertigo and palpitations and his appearances in Parliament, when he often forgot what he wanted to say, were embarrassing. His accumulating debts forced him to give up racing and also his house in Connaught Place and he moved in with his mother in Grosvenor Square. He still managed to share with a friend the cost of keeping up a house in Paris, where they could entertain their mistresses. Lord Randolph and Jennie spent some of the year together but she maintained a succession of affairs with other members of the aristocracy and when she was ill with typhoid in December 1892 Lord Randolph did not bother to return from his holiday in the Mediterranean.

By early 1894 Lord Randolph was passing through alternating phases of mania and euphoria. In consultation with his wife, his doctors decided that it would be best for him to go abroad for the last months of his decline. He left, together with Jennie and a doctor, for a round the world tour in June 1894, ostensibly to recover his health. The trip was a disaster: husband and wife did not get on (Jennie was particularly upset that her lover, Count Kinsky, chose this moment to get engaged to somebody else) and Lord Randolph's behaviour was such that he could hardly be let out in public. After visiting Canada they crossed the Pacific but in India Lord Randolph had to be constrained in a strait-jacket and the party hurried back to London where he fell into a coma and died in agony on 24 January 1895.

Lord Randolph left the income from his estate to Jennie and his capital investments to his two sons. The capital was worth over £75,000, thanks largely to his South African investment, but £70,000 of it was swallowed up by his debts to the Rothschilds. Winston and Jack were left with some £5,000 between them. It was enough to ensure that they could continue to live in some style, but it meant that they would have to work for a living (something Lord Randolph had never done).

Winston's reaction to his father's early death is difficult to judge as he wrote nothing about it at the time. Certainly he does not seem to have been overwhelmed by grief, and neither was Jennie. In many ways it was a liberation from a difficult, unsympathetic man with whom he had been unable to establish a close relationship but who nevertheless still dominated him. The first sign of this change was that Winston was able to achieve a major ambition and join the cavalry. He was an excellent horseman but Lord Randolph had consistently objected to the cavalry on grounds of expense. His mother used her influence with the Duke of Cambridge, together with a fabricated story about Lord Randolph's dying wishes, to ensure that Winston was transferred from the 60th Rifles to the socially exclusive and expensive 4th Hussars. Winston began his career as a cavalry officer in February 1895, a month after his father's death.

3

Ambition

The life of a junior cavalry officer at the end of the nineteenth century was hardly onerous. Leave amounted to five months a year, and officers were encouraged to spend the autumn and winter hunting. Churchill's time in the 4th Hussars was devoted largely to horse-riding, drill, playing polo, eating in the mess, and gambling and drinking in the evenings. Even when on duty at Hounslow, west of London, there was still plenty of time for an active social life in the capital. His fellow officers were rich and well-connected, and determined to maintain the social exclusivity of the regiment. He fitted easily into this world and shared its outlook: he was one of the ringleaders in forcing out of the regiment Alan Bruce (whom he had known at Harrow) because he had a private income of only £500 a year to live on in addition to his pay. As well as his pay and his own small resources Churchill had an allowance of £300 a year from his mother and she also gave him over £400 to help him purchase clothes, saddles and a second horse. Even so his style of life – satin racing jackets, a number of polo ponies and expensive clothes – meant that he was soon in debt. In his first two years in the Army he spent £144 (over £5,000 at today's prices) on clothes from just one tailor and the bill was not paid for nearly seven years. In the summer of 1895 the 4th Hussars were told that they would sail to India for a nine year posting in just over twelve months. The result was even more leave and Churchill was able to enjoy to the full the London season.

Although this period from February 1895 until he left for India in September 1896 appears, superficially, to be one of easy enjoyment of the pleasures available to a reasonably wealthy and well-connected young aristocrat, it was in fact a time when Churchill's character began to mature. During his early months in the Army he first began to suffer moods of acute depression leading occasionally to near suicidal feelings (which he called 'Black Dog'). He was always reluctant to stand on the edge of railway platforms or on balconies for fear of what he might do on a sudden impulse. These periods of severe depression (for which it is difficult to establish a cause without more information than that made public so far) were to continue at varying intervals and with varying degrees of intensity for the rest of his life. For a while Churchill seems to have found it difficult to find a way of coping with his psychological problems. He then gradually evolved, perhaps almost unconsciously at first, a remedy often adopted by people facing acute depression – hyperactivity. Until he finally retired in 1955 Churchill deliberately sought to ensure that his life was one of incessant activity. Throughout his life colleagues and friends were impressed by the intensity and variety of Churchill's activities and by his enormous capacity for work – but this largely reflected his own inner tensions and drives.

At this time Churchill also began to reflect more about the father whom he had hardly known. As a boy he had read his speeches avidly but now he began to study them in detail and memorise them; Lord Randolph became a model for his own career. The premature death of his father opened up a new avenue of ambition for Churchill. If Lord Randolph had had a normal life and political career it might well have stopped Winston entering politics – his father always actively discouraged his political interests. Even had he managed to persuade his father to change his mind, Churchill would have been in the shadow of a father who might have continued in active politics until the son was in his late forties, and few sons of politically important fathers have been able to carve out their own wholly successful careers. As it was, Churchill had the freedom to enter politics in his own way, yet also had the advantage of utilising his family's political connections.

Within a few months of joining the Army Churchill decided on a political career. He was already calculating that since a general election had just been held, he would have to wait four or five years. He wrote to his mother in August 1895:

> It is a fine game to play – the game of politics – and it is well worth waiting for a good hand before really plunging. At any rate – four years of healthy and pleasant existence, combined with both responsibility & discipline can do no harm to me – but rather good. The more I see of soldiering the more I like it, but the more I feel convinced that it is not my metier.[1]

If he was to become a politician he had to be careful to protect his public reputation. He was therefore worried about allegations concerning his behaviour in the 4th Hussars that were publicised in the press and even raised in Parliament. Some of these involved the forcing out of socially unacceptable officers (which were true) and the rigging of horse races and illicit gambling (which seem to have had some truth in them). Potentially the most damaging of all to Churchill, and one that would have wrecked his political career before it started, was that he was homosexual. He sued the father of the officer who made the allegation for the then enormous sum of £20,000 but quickly settled out of court for a mere £500. In a letter to his mother he commented that the allegations had to be stamped on quickly or 'it would be fatal to any future in public life for me'.[2]

In the five years after his father's death Churchill was as close to his mother as at any time in his life. She was then in her early forties, still attractive, still indulging in numerous affairs and, since she had no other interests, still living a very active social life. She was his main correspondent and he expected her to use every ounce of her influence to help him achieve his ambitions. He wrote to her just before he left for India: 'It is useless to preach the gospel of patience to me. Others as young are making the running now and what chance have I of ever catching up . . . you really ought to leave no stone unturned to help me at such a period.'[3] In pursuing his ambitions Churchill had many advantages, in particular his family's social and political connections, and he was determined to exploit them to the full.

As well as evidence of growing ambition there were also signs of increasing egoism. He had been unusually self-centred as a child but as an adult Churchill was dominated by a belief in his own uniqueness and destiny, combined with a marked lack of interest in other people and their views. His old headmaster cautioned him just before he left for India: 'Above all, my dear Churchill, think more of others than of yourself.'[4] His mother, passing on what the Reverend Welldon had said to her, warned about the 'habit (which is this case has cost you a great deal) of putting yrself so much forward'.[5] But these admonitions had no effect. He declared himself prepared to risk his life in the Army because, as he told his mother: 'I am so conceited that I do not believe the Gods would create so potent a being as myself for so prosaic an ending.'[6] A few months later he remarked to her 'I always had a good opinion of myself and plenty of ambition.'[7] He advised his unambitious brother 'You can't push too much in all things.'[8] Churchill's actions in the five years after 1895 were fuelled by his burning desire to enter politics as quickly as possible. In 1899, on the verge of standing for Parliament for the first time he admitted to his mother the all-consuming nature of his urge to succeed in politics: 'What an awful thing it will be if I don't come off. It will break my heart for I have nothing else but ambition to cling to.'[9]

The first manifestation of Churchill's determination to become a public figure as a preparation for entering political life and, at the same time, find a field of activity to counter his depression, came in the autumn of 1895 when, together with a fellow officer, Reggie Barnes, he decided to visit Cuba to investigate the war between the Spanish and the nationalist rebels. Family connections were vital in making the trip possible. Lord Randolph's old friend Sir Henry Drummond Wolff, now Ambassador in Madrid, arranged for the necessary visas and accreditation to the Spanish military forces. His mother arranged with her friend the editor of the *Daily Graphic* to publish a series of letters from Winston (Lord Randolph had written for the paper from South Africa only a few years earlier). Churchill and Barnes travelled to Cuba via New York where a former lover of Jennie, Congressman Bourke Cockran, looked after them and arranged the hire of valets. Churchill, like many other English people of his background, found Americans vulgar but full of great energy and freshness. The two officers spent just over ten days in Cuba attached to the staff of a Spanish general and were involved in one skirmish with the disorganised rabble that passed for the rebel army. But it was long enough for Churchill to write his first publication –

five articles for the *Daily Graphic*, for which he was paid a total of twenty-five guineas (about £900 at current prices).

Churchill was not happy about leaving for India in September 1896 for a protracted stay, regarding it as a 'useless and unprofitable exile'.[10] The idea of spending nine years as an ordinary regimental soldier in a quiet posting did not fit in with his political ambitions. When he arrived with the 4th Hussars at Bangalore in southern India he became part of the self-contained world of the British Raj, with its fine gradations of social status, a sharp division between military and civil elements and a highly complex and rigid code of behaviour. He shared a bungalow with two friends, Reggie Barnes and Hugo Baring; they each had a butler and two valets and a syce for each of their horses and they shared two gardeners, three water carriers, four washermen and one watchman. Regimental duties were light. Churchill normally rose at 5am, took parade an hour later, had his second breakfast, inspected the stables for an hour and from 10.45 until 4.15 in the afternoon had no formal duties. Then a game of polo was followed by drinks and dinner in the mess. He spent the middle of the day sleeping, writing, reading, collecting butterflies and tending the roses around the bungalow. Within a month of arriving Churchill was bored with India. He shared the contempt of virtually all other members of the Raj for Indian life and culture, regarding Indians as an inferior, uncivilised people who had no future but to be ruled by the English governing élite. At the same time he found the bulk of the English in India, particularly the non-aristocratic 'civil' administrators, vulgar and socially beneath him. Disillusioned, he wrote to his mother: 'I shall not stay out here long ... It is a poor life to lead and even its best pleasures are far below those obtainable in England. I meet none but soldiers and other people equally ignorant of the country and hear nothing talked but "shop" and racing.'[11]

Partly to keep himself busy, Churchill used much of the quiet period in the middle of the day to continue a process of self-education he had begun in England. After joining the Army he felt that he needed to broaden his reading, which had been too confined by the necessities of Army entrance exams. While in England he started to read some economics and philosophy and also Gibbon's *Decline and Fall of the Roman Empire* (which took him over a year to finish). In India he continued with Gibbon, embarked on Macaulay's history and essays and began a close study of twenty-seven volumes of the *Annual Register* from the mid-nineteenth century in order to develop his political opinions.

At this time he gradually formed his personal and political views, most of which he was to hold unwaveringly throughout his life. Like most of his contemporaries he believed in the supremacy of the white nations. His life in India seemed an obvious illustration of this fact as a few thousand Britons ruled over 200 million Indians. He accepted without question the greatness of the British Empire. He had grown up at a time when Queen Victoria had only recently been declared Empress of India, when the empire was continuing to expand through the acquisition of Egypt in 1882 and the spoils from the partition of Africa with other European states in the late 1880s. It was a time of self-confidence in Britain about the country's position in the world and its ability to continue to rule virtually a quarter of the globe. It was a confidence that Churchill fully shared. He was deeply influenced by a popular Victorian work – Winwood Reade's *The Martyrdom of Man*. This painted a picture of increasing European expansion, continual struggle and conflict between nations as they fought for supremacy (a reflection of prevailing Social Darwinist beliefs) and the role of great individuals in leading nations and empires through these conflicts. It was a heroic role in which Churchill could cast himself and Reade also reinforced his view that only war settled issues between nations and that it played an essential part in human progress.

It was in India that Churchill lost what little religious faith he ever had. He told his mother later: 'I do not accept the Christian or any other form of religious belief', and he developed a particular dislike of Catholicism and Christian missions.[12] His own beliefs were clear: 'I expect annihilation at death. I am a materialist – to the tips of my fingers.'[13] In public he felt it politic to go through the conventional rituals of the Anglican Church, though he tried to avoid such occasions as much as possible. Cynically he supported the role of the church in providing a socially conservative doctrine for the masses and in helping to provide social cohesion. Philosophically Churchill always had a dark view of life. He told his doctor in 1943 that 'Death is the greatest gift God has made to us'[14] and a decade later remarked to him: 'Bloody world, no human being would have come into it if he had known what it was like.'[15] As a consequence, although he could be quite emotional about some individual misfortune, human suffering in general left Churchill unmoved and he deliberately cultivated a sense of detachment. He wrote to his brother in 1898, 'The plague is going on merrily – 400 deaths a day in Bombay alone. The population is however superabundant.'[16] A year later, when the plague had claimed 70,000 lives, he wrote to Sir Algernon West, 'a philosopher may watch unmoved the destruction of some of those superfluous millions, whose life must of necessity be destitute of pleasure'.[17] In 1900 he wrote to a close friend, 'You must cultivate a little healthy selfishness and not suffer so acutely for other people's troubles. Babies deaths are the least sad of all partings.'[18]

As Churchill read to counter the boredom of life in Bangalore he also began to think about the questions in which he would be involved when he entered politics. He did this by making notes about issues raised in the various volumes of the *Annual Register*. His study of education policy led him to conclude that the introduction of compulsory primary education in 1870 had been 'precipitate' and 'a dangerous experiment'. He recognised that politically it was impossible to withdraw it now but felt that for the majority of people 'extensive education will be a doubtful blessing. It will excite desires which cannot be gratified and it will voice the desires in the language of discontent.' His own view was that education for the masses should only include 'reading and writing, the knowledge of sufficient arithmetic to enable the individual to keep his accounts; the singing of patriotic songs and a gymnastic course'.[19] Nearly sixty years later he told the Cabinet Defence Committee that despite the raising of the school leaving age to fifteen, boys should still be able to join the Royal Navy at thirteen because the 'educational aspect was not so important'.[20]

He also thought about the position of women in society. He was strongly opposed to women's suffrage on the grounds that:

> it is contrary to natural law and the practice of civilized states ... only the most undesirable class of women are eager for the right – those ... who discharge their duty to the state – viz marrying & giving birth to children – are adequately represented by their husbands ... I shall unswervingly oppose this ridiculous movement.[21]

Throughout his life Churchill was a strong believer in capital and corporal punishment. He wrote to his brother from New York in 1895 about the informality of dress and proceedings in American courts but added 'they manage to hang a man all the same, and that after all is the great thing'.[22] He told Lord Moran in 1956: 'I'm a hanger. It is one of the forms of death of which I have no horror.'[23] Indeed he always believed in the efficacy of public execution.

After just six months of regimental soldiering Churchill managed to negotiate some leave and left India to sail home in early May 1897. He hoped to stop off en route to report on the war between Greece and Turkey and the revolt on Crete. He was prepared to join whichever side his mother, using her influence with the King of Greece and the British Ambassador in Constantinople, could persuade to give him accreditation. Unfortunately for Churchill the war was over by the time he reached the Mediterranean. On his return to Britain he saw the head of Conservative Party organisation and made clear his desire to stand for Parliament. The party arranged for him to make his maiden political speech at Claverton Manor, near Bath, on 26 July. Churchill, quite naturally, made himself out to be his father's political heir by mixing 'Tory Democracy' – interpreted on this occasion as support for workmen's compensation and better housing – with a strong belief in Britain's imperial destiny. The nation, Churchill declared, needed to show 'by our actions that the vigour and vitality of our race is unimpaired and that our determination is to uphold the Empire that we have inherited from our fathers as Englishmen'. For Churchill 'Tory Democracy' was first about the Conservative Party and the empire, and only second about minor measures of social reform. He told his mother that 'a tory democrat is a tory first and a democrat after'[24] and wrote to his brother of 'this great Empire of ours – to the maintenance of which I shall devote my life'.[25]

While enjoying the social life of the London season, Churchill heard that a force of three brigades was being raised in India by General Sir Bindon Blood to put down one of the regular revolts by Pathan tribes on the north-west frontier. Churchill had met the general the previous year at the Duchess of Marlborough's house and extracted a promise from him that he could join any such punitive expedition. On the basis of this promise he set out for India again at the beginning of August but on arrival found that Sir Bindon had already filled all the places on his personal staff and that in the first instance he would only be able to accompany the Army as a correspondent. His mother had already arranged with the editor of the *Daily Telegraph* for the publication of his articles from the front and Churchill secured a month's leave to travel with the expedition. He was clear about his motives. He told his mother at this time, 'I have faith in my star – that is that I am intended to do something in the world.'[26] His correspondence with her also reveals that the reason for his eagerness to be associated with an active campaign was essentially political rather than military:

> It might not have been worth my while, who am really no soldier, to risk so many fair chances on a war which can only help me directly in a profession I mean to discard. But ... I feel that the fact of having seen service with British troops while still a young man must give me more weight politically – must add to my claims to be listened to and may perhaps improve my prospects of gaining popularity with the country.[27]

Churchill joined up with Sir Bindon Blood's force on the North West Frontier in September 1897. He was soon acting as an orderly officer to the general and was then attached to Brigadier Jeffreys, who was leading part of the Army into the Mamund valley. It was a brutal war; no prisoners were taken by either side – the British burnt many alive and were also using 'dum-dum' bullets. Churchill was in the thick of the fighting on many occasions and casualties were high – the British lost a tenth of the force either killed or wounded in one battle on 16 September. He was determined to be noticed, telling his brother, 'Being in many ways a coward – particularly at school – there is no reputation I cherish so keenly as to gain a reputation of personal courage.'[28] In order to achieve this on three occasions he rode his horse along the front of the skirmish line even though there was no conceivable military rationale for the move – he stopped when he was at last noticed. He confided in his mother: 'I rode on my grey pony all along the skirmish line where everyone else was lying down in cover. Foolish perhaps but I play for high stakes and given an audience there is no act too daring or too noble. Without the gallery things are different.'[29] Churchill achieved his goal when he was mentioned in despatches.

In mid-October Churchill was ordered back to Bangalore by the Army authorities. There he found that his mother had agreed, on advice from her military friends, that his letters about the expedition published in the *Daily Telegraph* should not bear his name. He was furious at the lost opportunity for publicity, telling her: 'I had written them with the design, a design which took form as the correspondence advanced, of bringing my personality before the electorate. I had hoped that some political advantage might have accrued.'[30] In his next letter home he wrote:

> If I am to do anything in the world, you will have to make up your mind to publicity and also to my doing unusual things . . . I regard an excellent opportunity of bringing my name before the country in a correct and attractive light . . . as lost. I have no doubt that I should make another one in the near future; but one cannot afford to throw away chances.[31]

In order to repair the damage done by the non-attribution of his letters, Churchill, once again experiencing the tedium of life in Bangalore, worked rapidly on a book about the campaign, averaging about five hours' writing a day and putting aside a half-completed novel in order to do so. He was determined to be the first to publish and beat his better qualified rival, Lord Fincastle, who had been on the campaign longer and who had won the Victoria Cross. His mother was also working tirelessly in London – she consulted her husband's old colleague, Arthur Balfour, who suggested using the literary agent A. P. Watt to place the book with a publisher, and she was also promoting it at every opportunity with her well-connected friends. In order to win the race for publication Churchill left the task of proof-reading to his uncle, Moreton Frewen, who turned out not to be up to the task. Although the book was generally well received when published by Longmans as *The Story of the Malakand Field Force*, the *Atheneum* in its review spoke of the 'punctuation of an idiot or of a school-boy in the lowest form'. The author was greatly upset that people might think it was his punctuation that was at fault and ever afterwards he kept a close personal eye on his books.

Churchill was to remain in India until June 1898 (his longest stay). At this time he visited the Viceroy in Calcutta and dined with the

Commander-in-Chief and made as many useful contacts as possible. After a great deal of effort he joined another frontier expedition – the Tirah field force – but it was disbanded before he saw any action. He also played polo and dabbled with the novel he had put aside to write the book on the Malakand expedition. He was not very popular with his fellow officers because he made it clear that he was determined to leave India and the 4th Hussars at the first opportunity. He told his grandmother after his return from the North West Frontier that 'I intend to stand for Parliament at the General Election – so that my sojourn abroad will not be indefinitely prolonged.'[32] However he felt that he needed to see more military action in order to increase his reputation before becoming a politician. Almost from the time of his arrival in India he had been trying to get a posting to Egypt, where British and Egyptian forces under Lord Kitchener were slowly advancing up the Nile to re-establish control over the Sudan, defeat the Dervish forces that had revolted in the 1880s and forestall the French in what was seen as a strategically vital area. In December 1896, soon after arriving in India, he had written to his mother: 'Two years in Egypt . . . with a campaign thrown in – would I think qualify me to be allowed to beat my sword into a paper cutter and my sabretache into an election address.'[33] From the end of 1897 Churchill was determined to get to Egypt during the next year. Virtually every letter to his mother asked her to use her influence to secure him a posting rather than leave him languishing in India, unable to secure the fame he so desperately wanted. On one occasion he urged her, 'Now I beg you – have no scruples but worry right and left and take no refusal.'[34] By early 1898 he came to the conclusion that he would have to take leave and go to Egypt as a correspondent despite the disadvantages involved: 'it is a poor way of doing it. All the risks – & none of the glory – or at least you have to take double chances to attract attention.'[35]

Churchill eventually left India on 18 June 1898 to take the three months' leave to which he was entitled after the Malakand campaign. When he arrived in London in July he found that his mother, despite all her efforts, had been unable to secure a posting to Egypt. Churchill at first concentrated on developing his political career. Whilst in India he had already written an election address and he was considering possible constituencies. Now he held long discussions with Conservative Party officials and made his second and third political speeches. Both were a great success. Then came a stroke of luck. The Prime Minister, Lord Salisbury, who had read Churchill's book and knew of his intention to stand for Parliament, asked him to come and discuss his prospects. At the end of the meeting Salisbury conventionally asked whether there was anything he could do to help and Churchill naturally seized the opportunity to try once more to secure a posting to Egypt. This time, with Salisbury's patronage and further family influence with the Adjutant-General, he was successful.

However, when Churchill arrived in Egypt, he found that he was far from welcome. Kitchener felt he was only there for selfish reasons and since he did not intend to stay in the Army he was taking a place that should have gone to a career officer. He also believed (rightly as it turned out) that Churchill intended to write about the campaign despite an assurance to the contrary given in London. (Churchill argued he was released from the promise because Kitchener had posted him to an English rather than an Egyptian regiment.) Churchill reciprocated his Commander-in-Chief's dislike describing him as 'a vulgar common man'.[36] When he joined up with his new regiment, the 21st Lancers, at Shabluka, Churchill was largely ostracised by his fellow officers and put in charge of the mess stores and other menial tasks. He had only been with the regiment a week when he took part in the battle of Omdurman. Although British forces were outnumbered by more than two to one in facing a collection of 60,000 natives, they had the Maxim gun and their opponents did not. The result was less a battle than wholesale slaughter. The British and Egyptian armies killed about 10,000 and wounded at least another 15,000 and suffered only forty-eight killed and 428 wounded themselves. Churchill positively relished playing a part, telling his mother, 'I have a keen aboriginal desire to kill several of these odious dervishes ... and I anticipate enjoying the exercise vy much.'[37]

Almost half the British casualties occurred during the charge by the 21st Lancers in which Churchill took part – the last of any British cavalry regiment in war. The regiment had been kept in reserve by Kitchener in order to round up the enemy when they were defeated. But, acting without instructions, they charged the enemy line, and having achieved nothing of any importance, were badly mauled and had to be withdrawn and replaced by an Egyptian regiment. Churchill's contribution was, after the charge, to shoot down five men in cold blood with his Mauser pistol loaded with dum-dum bullets. However the widespread killing of the wounded native troops, condoned by Kitchener, left Churchill feeling revolted. After the battle he was determined to return to England as soon as possible and asked his mother to arrange some more political meetings. First though he had to escort all the stores of the 21st Lancers back to base – a tedious task the regiment had been glad to leave to this interloper in their ranks. Churchill was well aware of his strictly limited and unwelcome contribution to the campaign, as he made clear writing to a military friend, Ian Hamilton, in India: 'I did not distinguish myself in any way – although as my composure was undisturbed my vanity is of course increased ... I am in great disfavour with the authorities here. Kitchener was furious with Sir E. Wood [Adjutant-General] for sending me out and expressed himself freely.'[38]

On the basis of his one month's participation in the campaign, initially on his brief return visit to England and later on the boat back to India, Churchill began a 1,000-page two-volume history entitled *The River War*. The first volume was an historical account of events in Egypt and Sudan leading up to the final campaign; it was the first real historical writing Churchill had ventured upon and its style was heavily influenced by his reading of Gibbon. The second volume dealt with the campaign itself. The underlying construction of the book anticipated the approach of Churchill's best-known historical works, that is it subtly placed the author at the centre of great historical events, at the fulcrum of the great forces of history as befitted a man of destiny. The book was extremely critical of Kitchener (when reissued in one-volume form after Churchill became an MP these criticisms disappeared). Although it received reasonably good reviews, it was thought to be far too long and some felt that Churchill's *obiter dicta* were too much – for example the *Saturday Review* (to which Churchill had contributed items on Cuba) commented: 'The annoying feature in the book is the irrepressible egoism of its author ... The airs of infallibility he assumes are irritating.'

Churchill arrived back in England from Egypt in early October 1898. He managed to fit in three political speeches, dinner with the Prince of Wales and some hunting with the Quorn before leaving for

India in early December. By this time he had already decided to leave the Army and only returned in order to take part in six weeks of polo tournaments with his regiment. When these were successfully completed, he resigned his commission at the end of March 1899 and left India. During the two and a half years his regiment had spent in India Churchill had been with them for less than eighteen months. Although he had taken no interest in Indian life and was never to return to the sub-continent, during this period he formed views on the future of India and the way in which Britain should govern the country that were to remain virtually unchanged for the rest of his life.

By the time Churchill returned to England his novel, which he had now finished and which he called *Savrola*, had been serialised in *Macmillan's Magazine* for a fee of £100 (it was published as a book early in 1900). The story is set in an imaginary Mediterranean country, Laurania, and the plot concerns a revolt led by Savrola. The reviews felt that it was crude, immature, weak in portrayal of character, with a mechanically handled love story but enlivened with plenty of fighting. The main interest of the novel lies in the character of Savrola himself, who is clearly an idealised portrait of the author. Savrola is a depressive with a bleak view of life – in a scene that takes place in an observatory he muses: 'the perfect development of life would end in death; the whole solar system, the whole universe itself would one day be cold and lifeless as a burnt-out firework'. An aristocrat who despises the middle class, he is driven by a sense of himself as a man of destiny. He believes he is working for the people but reflects:

> Was it worth it? The struggle, the labour, the constant rush of affairs, the sacrifice of so many things that make life easy, or pleasant – for what? A people's good! That, he could not disguise from himself, was rather the direction than the cause of his efforts. Ambition was the motive force and he was powerless to resist it.

In later life Churchill grew to dislike the book with its rather too obvious self-portrait and tried as much as possible to steer people away from it.

Churchill was now committed to a political career and bent on obtaining as early an entry as possible into Parliament. His own view of politics was clear-cut – he saw it as a field for personal ambition where personality was far more important than policy. He told his mother: 'In politics a man, I take it, gets on not so much by what he *does*, as by what he *is*. It is not so much a question of brains as of character & originality.'[39] Indeed from the start he did not see political principles as particularly important, writing a year before he became a candidate, 'I do not care so much for the principles I advocate as for the impression which my words produce & the reputation they give me.'[40] In one revealing sentence he lays bare two characteristics which had such a powerful influence on his political career – his political flexibility and his belief in the power of oratory. Although he was, by family tradition and connection, entering politics as a Conservative he saw his career in strongly personal rather than party terms.

By the spring of 1899 Churchill already had a number of constituencies in mind, but it was the death of one of the Conservative MPs for Oldham and the retirement of his colleague that provided the first opening. Churchill was selected as a candidate for this marginal seat (the Conservative majority was only a few hundred) along with a local trades unionist. (The two Liberal candidates in the by-election, Alfred Emmott and Walter Runciman, were later to be Churchill's colleagues in the Liberal Government.) Churchill's election address was little more than a collection of platitudes – he presented himself to the voters as a Conservative, a 'Tory Democrat', a Unionist, as against ritual in the Church of England and for compensation to the drink trade if their licences were revoked. During the short by-election campaign one of the main issues was the Clerical Tithes Bill, which was then passing through Parliament and was strongly opposed by the non-conformist churches. At the last moment, in a desperate attempt to get elected, Churchill repudiated this Government measure much to the chagrin of the party hierarchy. His action did not have the required effect. On 7 July the Liberals gained both seats on a swing of about two per cent and he was defeated by almost 1,300 votes.

Churchill was rescued from a wait for the General Election or another by-election by developments in southern Africa. There growing British hostility to the two independent Boer republics of Transvaal and Orange Free State, and a determination to ensure British hegemony in the area – led by the aggressive High Commissioner, Lord Milner, and actively supported by the Colonial Secretary, Joseph Chamberlain – seemed to be leading inevitably towards war. In September negotiations on the rights of the English population in the two states broke down and with war imminent, Churchill was asked by Lord Harmsworth the proprietor of the *Daily Mail* to act as a war correspondent. He used this offer to negotiate a better deal with the *Morning Post* – £250 a month for four months, plus expenses and retention of the copyright of the articles for later use in a book. Churchill sailed on 14 October (two days after the opening of hostilities) on board the *Dunnotar Castle* along with Sir Redvers Buller, the new Commander-in-Chief, and his staff. He was well equipped with guns, a servant, eighteen bottles of claret, six each of port, brandy and vermouth and eighteen bottles of whisky. On his arrival in Cape Town at the end of October, he was granted an interview with Lord Milner (thanks to an introduction from Lord Randolph's old friend Chamberlain) and promptly left by train for the front. He wanted to get to Ladysmith but the town was already under siege, so he spent nine days at Escourt in Natal, a stop on the railway line to Ladysmith, wining and dining the Army officers stationed there.

The initial fighting had not gone at all as the British expected and the Boers were on the offensive, taking control of British territory. On 15 November Churchill left Escourt on an armoured train commanded by an old friend from India, Captain Aylmer Haldane, who had been ordered to undertake a reconnaissance towards the Boer positions. The train ran into Boer units much quicker than expected and in attempting to retreat to Escourt it was ambushed and partly derailed. While others defended the train Churchill, ignoring his status as a correspondent, took control of the operations to help clear the derailed trucks. Two people were killed and ten wounded in the fighting and Churchill then took charge of the efforts to move the wounded on to the engine, which was able to escape to Escourt. Churchill went back to join the forces around the remaining stranded trucks and coaches which were under fierce fire. Heavily outnumbered, the British troops tried to escape but they and Churchill were eventually captured by the Boers. The prisoners were marched for two days across country and then taken by train to Pretoria, where the officers were held in an old school building.

As a civilian who had chosen to become embroiled in the fighting

Churchill was now in something of a dilemma. On the one hand he was keen to take advantage of his military exploits. He told Haldane as soon as they were captured that he was sure that his own heroism during the fight over the train would significantly enhance his chances of getting into Parliament. On the other hand accepting his fate as a prisoner of war might mean that he would miss the chance of becoming an MP for some months, possibly even years. He was determined to get out of captivity somehow and tried a variety of methods. He argued with the Boers that he was simply a correspondent. His most blatant series of lies was contained in a letter addressed to the Boer authorities on 26 November: 'I have consistently adhered to my character as a press representative, taking no part in the defence of the armoured train and being quite unarmed.'[41] (At the same time he was trying to persuade the British authorities to treat him as a military officer and so obtain his release in a possible exchange of prisoners.) He persuaded Haldane to perjure himself by testifying that Churchill had not taken part in the defence of the train. He was also prepared to give his parole to continue as a non-combatant or even to leave South Africa. The Boers, who were quite well aware of Churchill's activities on 15 November, refused at first to accept these tales or these offers. Not until 12 December did General Joubert decide that he would after all accept Churchill's word as a gentleman that he had taken no part in the train incident and release him. Ironically it was on that day, after nearly four weeks in captivity, that he escaped from the prison camp.

Churchill's actions during this escape remained controversial for decades – in the 1920s the Conservative MP Leo Amery (who had also been a press correspondent in the war) was to use them as an argument for not giving Churchill support in a highly publicised by-election and for not inviting him to join a Conservative Government – and they shed interesting light on his character. Conditions in the school at Pretoria were very relaxed: Churchill was able to write to all his friends (including the Prince of Wales) within days of being captured, there was no roll-call and the food was good. By early December Haldane had decided to escape together with a Sergeant-Major Brockie, who was posing as an officer in the camp and who could speak Afrikaans. When Churchill found out what they planned to do, he tried every argument he could think of to persuade them to let him join in. After much discussion Haldane, who felt a sense of

34

obligation towards Churchill for his efforts on the train, said he would not invite him to join the escape attempt because of opposition from Brockie (who thought Churchill was too prominent and would be missed too quickly), so Churchill invited himself. The plan Haldane and Brockie had devised was to hide in a latrine, jump over a perimeter wall, walk through Pretoria and on the outskirts of the town board a train heading for neutral Portuguese territory miles away. By way of preparation Haldane had obtained a street map, details of where the police were posted in the town and train times.

A first attempt was made on 11 December, but it failed because a sentry remained at his post near the selected latrine. All the next day Churchill, worried that the others might after all go without him, was in a state of high excitement and made it clear he was determined to go that evening. Haldane wanted to wait for the best possible opportunity for all three to escape. Early that evening Haldane and Churchill went over to the latrine and found the same problem as the night before. After a while they went back to the main courtyard to discuss the situation with Brockie. He too went to the latrine and came back and reported that there was still no chance of escape. Brockie and Haldane then went off to dinner. Churchill though went back and, seizing an opportunity when the sentry moved, climbed over the wall. Churchill waited, hiding in a bush and desperate for at least Brockie with his ability to speak Afrikaans to follow. Eventually his two companions found out what had happened. They came to the latrine but could not find an opportunity to cross the wall. Unable to go back Churchill then had no choice but to go on with the escape on his own.

The reaction among the other officers in the camp to his escape was bitter. They were subjected to a much harsher regime once his absence was discovered and Haldane in particular never forgave him for what had happened. Although he never criticised him in public, for the rest of his life Haldane refused to support Churchill's contentions about the escape. In his account Churchill glosses over much of what happened – he never attributes the plan to Haldane and Brockie and indeed misleadingly says they had no idea what to do once out of the prison. He never says that it was supposed to be a joint escape and implies that Haldane and Brockie were merely incidental and lacked his nerve in climbing the wall. When questions were raised during the 1900 General Election campaign about Churchill's behaviour during the escape, he wrote to Haldane asking him to vindicate him in public. Haldane refused.

In 1912, when he was engaged in a libel action with *Blackwood's Magazine* over his time as a prisoner, Churchill summoned Haldane to the Admiralty and asked him to give evidence at any trial that he had always acted fairly and properly. Haldane again refused, whereupon Churchill tried to blackmail him by threatening to call Haldane and Brockie (then dead) cowards for refusing to escape. Later Haldane was asked to agree to a statement that Churchill had not broken any agreement over the escape and that he was fully justified in his actions. Again Haldane refused. His true views were only made clear in a private memoir written just before his death. There he wrote: 'Had Churchill only possessed the moral courage to admit that, in the excitement of the moment, he saw a chance of escape and could not resist the temptation to take advantage of it, not realizing that it would compromise the escape of his companions, all would have been well.' Instead he felt that Churchill was too worried about his own reputation, would not admit that he had acted badly by his fellow escapees and then tried to cover up the affair in his own writings by describing it as a daring personal escapade and claiming all the credit. Sadly Haldane concluded that Churchill was 'a man of such splendid ability and brilliant parts, whom I once regarded as my friend, but whom, since the events recorded, I have never felt I could really trust'.[42]

When his companions were unable to escape Churchill decided to follow the plan they had drawn up. (In his account Churchill makes out that he worked out the plan on his own after he escaped.) He walked through Pretoria, found a suitable point outside the town to board a passing train and later that evening he was on his way towards Portuguese East Africa. But because of his impetuous actions he was without the opium tablets he normally carried and had no map, no proper food and no water. Early the next morning he was forced to jump off the train to try to find water. He had no idea where he was but hid up for the day before attempting to board another train that night. No train came by and he found it impossible to walk along the line because of the Boer guards posted at regular intervals. His escape bid was collapsing as he headed for what he thought was a native village to find shelter. The lights he had seen turned out to be a colliery and by luck the first house he went to was occupied by the English manager, John Howard. He, together with some friends, agreed to shelter Churchill. For the first three days he was secreted at the bottom of a mineshaft but he became ill and had to be moved to a hut on the surface. He was then put aboard a train hidden amongst cotton bales and escorted at a discreet distance by one of the local Englishmen who travelled on the train to deal with any problems. After a trouble-free journey Churchill reached Lourenço Marques, where he went to the British Consulate and was immediately put on a boat to Durban. His arrival there on 23 December, just eleven days after beginning his escape, came at the end of the most disastrous period of the war for Britain – 'Black Week' – a series of demoralising defeats at Stormberg, Magersfontein and Colenso caused mainly by military incompetence on a grand scale. Churchill was immediately acclaimed by the press as the heroic Briton who had outwitted the Boers. At last he had achieved the fame he sought.

Churchill returned immediately to the front to resume his interrupted role as a war correspondent, and was also made a lieutenant in the South African Light Horse. He covered the war for the next six months on behalf of the *Morning Post*, having decided, as he told a friend, that there was no political advantage in going back to England at this stage, rightly conjecturing that there would be no general election until the British had secured a series of victories. Those victories were gradually achieved in the first half of 1900 once the British were able to bring stronger forces to bear. Churchill was at the Battles of the Tugela River and Spion Kop but did not accompany the relief column into Ladysmith as he later described himself doing in *My Early Life* – he was some distance away and only arrived several hours after the relief. But there were plenty of genuine experiences for him to recount: the fighting against the Boers was hard and Churchill was often in the thick of it.

He was however already demonstrating some of the double standards about warfare he was to exhibit later in life. In his account of the Malakand campaign he noted without comment the use by British forces of dum-dum bullets against the natives and indeed used them himself at Omdurman. When the Boers used them he described them as 'illegal' and 'improper' and thought they illustrated their 'dark and spiteful' character, adding that a person who

37

was fully human would not use them.[43] Churchill accompanied Lord Roberts on his march through the Orange Free State (Roberts was reluctant to take Churchill along because of his earlier criticisms of Kitchener and only did so because of his friendship with Lord Randolph). He was also present at the entry into Pretoria at the beginning of June – a moment that seemed to mark the end of the war. In fact the conflict then entered its grimmest phase as the British war against the Boer guerrillas lasted another eighteen months and 26,000 women and children died while interned in British concentration camps. Churchill however had already decided to leave and he sailed from Cape Town a month after the capture of Pretoria.

In July 1900, only five days after his return, he was readopted as a Conservative candidate in Oldham. Parliament was dissolved in the middle of September and polling in Oldham took place on 1 October. As Churchill expected, the Conservative Government had decided to use the national mood of euphoria in a 'khaki election' and the Liberals were branded as pro-Boer and unpatriotic. Churchill exploited that theme to the full – his campaign was based on the slogan of 'A seat lost to the Government is a seat gained (or sold) to the Boers.' He was competing against the same Liberals as in the by-election the previous year and in a very close contest for the two seats (there were less than 400 votes between the four candidates), he came second, 222 votes behind Emmott but just ahead of Runciman. Overall the Government secured a Parliamentary majority of 134 seats. Thus after five years of single-minded exploitation of every opportunity, Churchill had achieved his immediate ambition of becoming an MP. A life of political activity and further avenues for his ambition were now opening up before him.

After the election and before he took his seat in Parliament, Churchill decided to exploit his fame in order to try to secure his financial future (MPs were not yet paid a salary). Given his financial situation, he certainly needed to do so. He had continued to spend money freely; he admitted to his mother 'there is no doubt that we are both you & I equally thoughtless – spendthrift and extravagant. We both know what is good – and we like to have it. Arrangements for paying are left to the future.'[44] (His mother had spent £14,000 of her inheritance in the first three years after Lord Randolph died – equivalent to £500,000 today.) His income had not kept pace with his expenditure although he had had some success with his writings. He had earned just over £2,000 from the *Morning Post* for his despatches from South Africa and he also earned over £1,000 for two books based on them – *London to Ladysmith via Pretoria* and *Ian Hamilton's March*. In addition, a friend of Lord Randolph, Sir Ernest Cassel, had been investing money for him on the Stock Exchange. It was Cassel's money and he bore the losses but gave Churchill the profits – £500 by 1900. His cousin, Sunny, Duke of Marlborough, also gave him £400 to cover his election expenses. But he had accumulated debts of over £1,000 while he was in the Army and his private income was gone – he had given up his allowance from his mother in July 1900 when she married George Cornwallis-West, who was almost half her age.

At the end of October 1900 Churchill embarked on a nationwide tour of lectures about the Boer War and his own adventures. By the end of November he had given twenty-nine and earned almost £3,800. He then travelled to the United States and Canada for another lecture tour. This made only £1,600; it did not prove as profitable as Churchill had hoped, largely due to the incompetence of his agent and a general lack of interest. Nevertheless in three months he had earned nearly £80,000 at today's prices. He was in Canada when he heard of the death of Queen Victoria. He left there on 2 February 1901 ready to take his seat in Parliament at the age of twenty-six. He was to be actively involved in British politics for the next fifty-four years.

4

Changing Sides

When Churchill entered Parliament in 1901 he was part of a highly undemocratic political system. The majority of adults still could not vote in general elections – all women were denied the franchise and about forty per cent of men were excluded and many others had more than one vote through additional business votes. Churchill, brought up in and benefiting from this system, never ceased to regard it as anything less than ideal. Thirty years later he was to write of British politics at this time as being 'a real political democracy, led by a hierarchy of statesmen . . . All this was before the liquefaction of the British political system had set in.'[1] In 1896 he had defended the British system against American democracy on the grounds that it made 'government dignified and easy – & the intercourse with foreign states more cordial'.[2] And in a book written in his first years as a minister he described Britain as having 'a Parliament elected on a democratic franchise'.[3]

In 1901 the structure of British politics still reflected the impact of the Liberal split over Irish home rule in 1886. Then the Liberal Unionists, led by Joseph Chamberlain, formed an alliance with the Conservatives and, apart from a brief Liberal interregnum in the early 1890s, had shared power with them ever since. For most of this period the Liberal Party was divided over the pace and extent of domestic reform and was then further divided over the war against the Boers. The Government which Churchill supported had been led by Lord Salisbury since 1895. Churchill had described him as 'an able and obstinate man, who joins the brain of a statesman to the delicate susceptibilities of a mule'.[4] It was a government of old, cautious and conservative men who hoped to administer the country as quietly as possible for the next five years or so. A majority of well over a hundred made this a readily achievable ambition. As one of over 300 Unionist backbenchers Churchill hoped to make a political impact that would quickly promote him into the Government ranks.

Churchill made his well-received maiden speech in the House of Commons on 18 February. The gallery was packed with his friends and relations and he spoke to a crowded house at 10.30pm, just after the radical and pro-Boer David Lloyd George had condemned the war. Maiden speeches are by convention uncontroversial and Churchill's was no exception. He too spoke mainly of the war, which he supported as a 'war of duty' but, in the one mild departure from convention, he also recognised the strength of Boer feelings, saying 'if I were a Boer I hope I should be fighting in the field' and arguing for leniency towards the enemy. In conclusion he made a special mention of his father, stating that he hoped to inherit his political mantle.

Churchill fitted in easily to the all-male world of high politics that revolved around the House of Commons (especially the smoking room), the clubs of St James's (he was a member of the Carlton and the Turf among others) and political dinner parties (throughout his life he was an avid diner-out). Churchill also enjoyed the regular country house week-ends (or longer visits during the summer recess), where many important decisions were taken, and the constant diet of political gossip and speculation. It was an age when personality was as important as policy. Churchill had supreme confidence in his own abilities and saw himself as above mere party politics – a man of destiny who could direct the lives of millions of ordinary people and shape the future of nations. He felt he was a political and military genius in the mould of his hero Napoleon and was anxious to demonstrate his qualities as soon as possible.

As Churchill had always intended, his personality soon made an impact on his contemporaries but that impression was almost universally hostile. The features that struck them most forcibly were a mixture of strong character, cleverness, ambition and his egocentricity. In 1880 Sir Charles Dilke had described Lord Rosebery in his diary as 'about the most ambitious man I had ever met'. Two decades later he added in the margin: 'I have since known Winston Churchill.'[5] The social reformer Beatrice Webb met Churchill over dinner and she found him a difficult man to like:

> Restless – almost intolerably so, without capacity for sustained and unexciting labour – egotistical, bumptious, shallow-minded and reactionary, but with a certain personal magnetism, great pluck and some originality – not of intellect but of character . . . Talked exclusively about himself . . . Bound to be unpopular – too unpleasant a flavour with his restless, self-regarding personality . . .[6]

The American politician, Henry Cabot Lodge, wrote to President Theodore Roosevelt about Churchill, saying, 'I have met him several times. He is undoubtedly clever but conceited to a degree which it is hard to express either in words or figures.'[7]

Many other comments testify to the fact that Churchill came across as overbearing, wearing people down by his refusal to stop talking about himself or politics, his two real interests in life. He did not seem interested in other people or what they thought and therefore found it difficult to make close personal relationships. Most people found him more congenial when he was depressed than when he was on top – then he was very difficult to like. What struck most of his contemporaries as remarkable was not the mere fact that Churchill wanted to succeed – most politicians on entering Parliament aim to make a name for themselves – in his case it was his inability to disguise his ambition or his expectation of greatness to come.

At this time Churchill was living in a flat in Mayfair paid for by his cousin Sunny. Here he re-created his father's study, complete with Lord Randolph's original furniture and personal possessions. He had a valet, as he did throughout his life, who was expected to dress and undress him, tie his shoelaces, knot his tie, turn on the bath taps (even when Churchill was in the bath), dry him afterwards and even turn his pillow for him before he went to sleep. At this stage he used to go everywhere in London by cab (later he had a chauffeur to drive him); he never travelled on a bus in his life, and travelled on the underground on only one occasion, when he promptly got lost. Socially he continued to move in the aristocratic circles with which he had been familiar since childhood.

Even as a backbencher Churchill's whole life was dominated by politics to the exclusion of almost all other interests – he himself called it a 'busy, selfish life'.[8] His only sporting interests were polo and hunting; he read little apart from official documents; he rarely went to the theatre (he saw *Hamlet* for the first time when in his late seventies); he took no interest in music apart from military bands and a little Gilbert and Sullivan; and his first visit to an art gallery came in his mid-forties. He was a freemason from 1901 till 1912, probably to help acquire contacts to further his all-consuming concern for rapid political advancement.

As a new MP Churchill took great pains to cultivate his perform-ance and his image. In order to monitor every reference to his activities he subscribed to a newspaper cutting agency. He carefully rationed his Parliamentary and public appearances and limited the topics on which he spoke in order to increase the impact of his contributions. He made only nine speeches in Parliament during 1901, partly because they took so long to prepare. Churchill was worried that he might forget what he wanted to say and so forced himself to memorise all his speeches – he was to remain uneasy about performing in the House of Commons and not until the 1920s did he feel he had mastered the House and its debating techniques. He also had to cope with a slight speech impediment, a tendency to lisp which he was able to control with practice (it was later in life that he cultivated his lisp in order to increase his distinctiveness). Like many politicians, Churchill was in part an actor – he rehearsed his speeches in front of a mirror in order to perfect the appropriate gestures and intonation. From the start, he was a great believer in the power of rhetoric; he wrote a long essay entitled *The Scaffolding of Rhetoric*, which makes clear his conviction that it constituted the main weapon and talent of a politician, because it was a way of obtaining power over people. But Churchill had to work hard to develop his rhetorical skills and always envied people like Lloyd George to whom the power of words seemed to come naturally.

During his first years as an MP Churchill seemed determined to replicate the early pattern of his father's life – repeated attacks on military expenditure and disruptive Parliamentary tactics. The poor performance of the British Army in the Boer War led to a number of different schemes being put forward for reforming various aspects of military organisation throughout the first decade of the century, culminating in Haldane's reforms under the Liberal Government after 1905. The first attempt was made by St John Broderick, the Secretary of State for War in Salisbury's Government. In March 1901 he proposed the creation of a six corps army which, in addition to defending India and the empire and keeping order at home, would be equipped for a small-scale intervention in a continental war. This would require the recruitment of 11,000 regular soldiers and 50,000 extra militia and volunteers, at a total cost of £3 million a year. It was almost inevitable that Churchill would attack the Government proposal since his father had, at least in public, resigned over excessive military expenditure and St John Broderick had been a junior minister at the War Office at the time. Churchill criticised the scheme on grounds of its expense and because it meant raising an army bigger than that required for imperial defence but still not big enough to intervene effectively on the continent. He began his attack with a public speech in Liverpool on 23 April and then put down an amendment against the scheme during the Commons debate on 13 May. But although he spoke in the debate (making a speech that had taken him six weeks to prepare and memorise), he did not press his objections and eventually voted with the Government against the opposition amendment. Nevertheless he continued to oppose the scheme over the next couple of years. Although this Parliamentary opposition had some influence in undermining Broderick's scheme, it was eventually sunk by the combined opposition of the Treasury, the King and senior Army officers and the impact of a Royal Commission report, which was highly critical of Broderick's performance during the Boer War and led to his transfer to the India Office.

Again seeking to retrace his father's steps, Churchill tried to create a latter-day 'Fourth Party' to ginger up a tired ministry (though from the Government benches unlike his father in the 1880s). His allies were Ian Malcolm, a friend of the family; Arthur Stanley, the younger son of the Earl of Derby; Lord Percy, the eldest son of the Duke of Northumberland; and Lord Hugh Cecil, the younger son of the Prime Minister. Together they formed a set known as the 'Hughlians' or 'Hooligans'. The grouping was partly social – they met every Thursday night for dinner, usually inviting a prominent politician as a guest (often a Liberal such as Rosebery, Grey or Asquith). In Parliament they used procedural devices to cause as much trouble as possible and make a name for themselves. Their strongest opposition was reserved for the Deceased Wife's Sister Bill, a piece of private member's legislation introduced in the spring of 1902. Lord Hugh Cecil, a devout Anglican, had strong theological objections to removing the ban on a widower marrying his wife's sister. Churchill's objections were entirely opportunistic. Indeed only five years earlier he had condemned the prohibition saying that it was 'useless but harmful' and that 'I should have no scruples in reversing it by legislation'.[9] Now he joined with his friends in Parliamentary wrecking tactics which ensured that the Bill removing the ban had to be withdrawn.

During 1902 Churchill made fewer speeches in the country and also gave fewer lectures (he had given fourteen in 1901 earning himself £690). In Parliament he concentrated on criticising military inefficiency and debating imperial matters, particularly the future of South Africa. He spent little time in his constituency and did not even visit Oldham between April and October 1902. For the first time he was appointed to a House of Commons committee. It dealt with the control of public expenditure and Churchill supported its recommendation to establish an Estimates committee to investigate the merits of Government spending proposals – predictably the Government rejected the idea. However developments during his second year as an MP transformed his political career. In July 1902 the Prime Minister, Lord Salisbury, retired and was replaced by his nephew, Arthur Balfour, an old friend of Lord Randolph. Churchill had earlier privately described Balfour as 'a languid, lazy, lackadaisical cynic',[10] but he clearly expected to be offered his first junior ministerial job. Moreover in the short term his personal finances needed the extra income a Government position would provide. One of his 'Hughlian' colleagues, Lord Percy, was given a post at the India Office, but Churchill was ignored. He had followed Lord Randolph's example but had not received Lord Randolph's reward.

Up to this point Churchill's political debut had been fairly predictable. After all, it is a fairly common ploy for backbenchers to make life difficult on certain selected issues for the Government they support in order to attract attention and encourage the offer of a ministerial post to ensure their silence. Churchill's well developed sense of self-esteem had been hurt by the lack of recognition to which he thought he was entitled and he also had to face another period on the backbenches and possibly no ministerial post before the next election. His restless mind began to look for other ways of achieving his ambitions. He had already been showing an interest in the idea of a political realignment. His hope was that a party of the centre could emerge and dominate the political scene (indeed this was to be a regular theme throughout his political life). He wanted an overwhelmingly strong political bloc that would be able to preserve the existing structure of society – again one of the themes of his career, reflecting his total opposition to all radicalism and later to socialism in particular.

Churchill was by no means the only one thinking along these lines. More senior politicians were already contemplating moves in this direction. The gap between the imperialist wing of the Liberal Party (men like Asquith, Grey and Haldane) and many Conservatives was not great and many Liberals considered dropping what seemed the increasingly outdated policy of Home Rule. With high politics still dominated by personal factors new combinations always seemed possible. Churchill was not senior enough to influence the discussions in 1901–2 which foundered on the reluctance of many Liberals, particularly Asquith, to break with the party. But he did encourage the former Liberal Prime Minister Lord Rosebery, with whom he was very close socially, to persevere and at one point was warned by his close political friends, especially Lord Hugh Cecil, not to break with the Conservatives until there was firm ground elsewhere. During the passage of the Government's Education Act of 1902 (which placed religious education on the rates to the outrage of non-conformists and the Liberal Party) he loyally supported the Government. This measure though ended any immediate chance of party realignment.

However, Churchill became increasingly attracted to the idea of a new opening in direct proportion to the way in which his ambitions within the Conservative Party seemed likely to remain unfulfilled. In October 1902 he wrote to Rosebery that his idea was for a

> Government of the Middle – the party wh[ich] shall be free at once from the sordid selfishness & callousness of Toryism on the one hand & the blind appetites of the Radical masses on the other.

One feature of this new perennial party of government that he did not stress, but others readily surmised, was of course that Churchill would be a member. The move was also the first sign of a tendency that was to dog Churchill throughout his career – his poor sense of political timing. He still hoped to find an opportunity to bring Rosebery together with Conservative politicians, saying to his would-be leader:

> There lies the chance of a central coalition ... The one real difficulty I have to encounter is the suspicion that I am moved by mere restless ambition: and if some definite issue – such as Tariff – were to arise – the difficulty would disappear.[11]

Rosebery's advice was that the time was not ripe for a new political departure. Nonetheless Churchill's 'restless ambition' soon found an opportunity to exploit – though the outcome was not a realignment but rather a strengthening of existing party divisions. It did, however, stem from the definite issue he had hoped for – the tariff. But he was to be one of only a small minority who changed sides over it.

Churchill grew up in a world where Britain, as the first industrialised nation, had practised, preached, and, initially at least, greatly prospered from free trade. But as other nations increased in industrial strength – and used import duties to protect their domestic industry – there were growing doubts as to the wisdom of maintaining this policy. The basic question of tariff reform – using import duties as a defensive measure against the growing threat from rapid industrial expansion in the United States and Germany in particular (but with the risk of provoking retaliatory measures) – was also linked to the question of how to handle relations with the Empire and the concept of imperial preference. (Imposition of a universal tariff would make it possible to give preferential treatment to the Empire and, according to proponents of this policy, thus help to bind together an increasingly disparate collection of overseas territories.) In this way the issue was linked with arguments about the need to bolster Britain's economic and strategic position at a time when the Empire was facing an increasing number of threats around the globe.

The introduction of tariffs would also create a new source of government revenue at a time when expenditure was rising rapidly (by over forty per cent since 1895) and when the likely burden of the defence reforms after the Boer War would mean further large increases. But what would be in effect a new tax had sensitive political and social implications. For some, tariffs were welcome as a way of avoiding substantial increases in income tax (which then fell on the upper and middle classes). But a universal tariff, or one on agricultural products (as needed to introduce imperial preference, since the overwhelming majority of Britain's imports from the empire were agricultural), would make this a highly regressive form of taxation – a tax on food would disproportionately penalise the poor. No tax on bread had been central to British politics since the repeal of the Corn Laws in 1846. Altogether the tariff was a political minefield and one that would raise strong public feelings, as the Conservative Government found when it first became embroiled in the issue in 1902.

In that year's budget the Chancellor of the Exchequer, Sir Michael Hicks Beach, imposed what he called a small 'registration duty' on imported wheat in order to provide extra money to finance war expenditure. Although in effect a tariff, this measure caused little immediate trouble. Churchill spoke in favour in Parliament, voted for it and defended it in public to his constituents, arguing that a tax on food was justified because 'it is the most convenient method of raising the money . . . and because unless the whole community bear a share in the burden of taxation, what check is there upon expenditure'.[12] Yet within a few months it was clear that the registration duty had opened a Pandora's box that eventually was to split the Conservative Party and Government. In June Joseph Chamberlain, the Colonial Secretary, raised the question of an imperial remittance of the duty and in the autumn proposed a specific exemption for Canada – and at this point the Cabinet appeared to endorse the idea. However in March 1903 the new Chancellor, Ritchie (a keen Free Trader who had succeeded Hicks Beach when Lord Salisbury resigned), repealed the 'registration duty', in a strongly pro-Free Trade speech in Parliament after threatening to resign in order to force the proposal through a divided Cabinet. Chamberlain, on his return from South Africa, widened the split and made it public with speeches in Birmingham and the House of Commons in May, setting out the arguments for tariff reform and suggesting that some of the extra revenue could be used to introduce old-age pensions as a way of ameliorating the social (and political) impact of food price rises.

In many ways Churchill might have been expected to support Chamberlain and tariff reform. He had backed the idea of food taxes and he was a strong believer in the Empire. But he was also highly conservative in his views and accepted the inherited orthodoxies of the Free Trade arguments without question. There were other considerations too. He represented a highly marginal seat in Lancashire, a bastion of free trade because of its dependence on world trade for its staple product – cotton. He had earlier told a constituent that he opposed the idea of an imperial trading area, saying that it was 'a fantastic policy to endeavour to shut the British Empire up in a ringed fence'.[13] But, as he had already admitted to Rosebery, he was looking for an excuse to defect from a party that seemed reluctant to recognise his talents, and the Liberals were solid in defence of Free Trade.

When Chamberlain began his campaign, Churchill wrote to the Prime Minister expressing his support for free trade and his conditional support for the party. He said that if Balfour disavowed Chamberlain, he 'would command my absolute loyalty', but he warned that if tariff reform became party policy 'I must reconsider my position in politics'.[14] He made his opposition to tariff reform clear in the House of Commons debate on 28 May, but on the socially and politically conservative grounds that it would disrupt the present pattern of politics and 'cause the lobbies to be crowded with the touts of protected industries'. (He had told Balfour that one of his main reasons for opposing tariff reform was that it would lead to the 'Americanization of British politics'.) After this debate, which exposed the growing division within Conservative ranks, the Cabinet agreed to treat tariff reform as an open question. They were powerless to prevent the development of organisations on both sides to fight for their respective policies. On 1 July Churchill was one of fifty-three Conservative MPs who held a meeting in the House of Commons and agreed to set up a Free Food League with Hicks Beach as chairman. But they were outnumbered by those supporting tariff reform (130 MPs attended their inaugural meeting), and had far less money and a much smaller constituency organisation.

Churchill had a difficult political game to play. Was his aim to try and stop tariff reform becoming Conservative policy, or did he want to use it as a reason for defection? If the former he needed to help by campaigning vigorously within the party, if the latter then he needed to define his breaking point with clarity. In practice Churchill fell neatly between these two incompatible approaches and did not carry out his eventual defection to the Liberals with either skill or tact. At first he seems to have hoped that tariff reform would be the issue that opened the way to the new party alignment he had favoured earlier. Immediately after the House of Commons debate in May, he wrote to encourage Rosebery to act: 'I am absolutely in earnest in this business & if by the aid and under the aegis of Beach we cannot save the Tory party from protection I shall look to you.'[15] Rosebery, as in the past, proved a broken reed and with a variety of excuses refused to make any move. In mid-July Churchill wrote to a prominent Free Trader: 'my idea is, and always has been, of some sort of central government being formed' – this time he hoped, equally without foundation, that the Duke of Devonshire might fulfil the role.[16]

Balfour had been trying hard to keep the party together by refusing to commit himself to either side but after a series of acrimonious discussions and attempted compromises the Government split in September 1903. Then, by a series of deft political moves and by not telling either side the full truth of what was going on, he managed to ensure that both the tariff reformers and the extreme Free Traders resigned from the Cabinet. In a speech at Sheffield at the beginning of October Balfour set out a policy of freedom to impose retaliatory tariffs in cases where other countries discriminated against Britain but no imperial preference. This failed to mollify Chamberlain (now on the backbenches) who began a national speaking tour and during the autumn seemed likely to sweep the Conservative Party along with him.

In early August Churchill received a unanimous vote of confidence from his constituency party, probably because of the strongly pro-free trade views in Lancashire. The Cabinet resignations in September and Chamberlain's campaign rapidly changed sentiment in the Oldham party. By mid-September the chairman of the local party was advising Churchill that his long-term prospects were doubtful and it might be better to look for a seat elsewhere before he was actually asked to go. At the beginning of October the local party did not ask him to support Chamberlain's position (which was not official party policy) but rather Balfour's compromise position on retaliatory tariffs and to make a declaration of loyalty to the party leader. Churchill refused to give such assurances.

At the beginning of November Churchill and Lord Hugh Cecil spoke in Birmingham, the Chamberlain heartland, in favour of Free Trade, but already there were strong differences between the two as the Conservative Free Traders became increasingly isolated within the party. Lord Hugh was not prepared, in any circumstances, to break with the Conservative Party and preferred to maintain his principles in the party his family had supported for generations. Many other Free Traders took the same view and refused to change sides on this one issue when they disagreed with the Liberals on virtually every other policy. However, the Liberals were rapidly gaining support in the country as the defenders of Free Trade and cheap food. Churchill was one of a very small minority of eleven MPs who did decide to defect to the Liberal Party. But Churchill wanted to negotiate with the Liberals before finally committing himself.

In 1900 Churchill had described the Liberals as 'prigs, prudes and faddists' and denounced the party as 'hiding from the public view like a toad in a hole, but when it stands forth in all its hideousness the Tories will have to hew the filthy object limb from limb'. Now on 24 October 1903 he drafted a letter to Lord Hugh, though it was never sent. In it he declared, 'I am an English Liberal. I hate the Tory party, their men, their words & their methods. I feel no sort of sympathy with them.' He said he was not prepared to be a martyr for his principles but wanted instead to support Free Trade 'in the ranks of that great party without whose instrumentality it cannot be preserved'. In addition he described the Liberals as the best refuge 'against the twin assaults of capital & labour'.[17] On 2 November when Churchill dined with his uncle Lord Tweedmouth, who had been the Liberal Chief Whip in the House of Commons, he sounded him out about the Liberal Party's position. Tweedmouth told him that the only way he would gain Liberal support was to stand as a Liberal and that some sort of halfway house (perhaps standing as a Free Trader) would not be sufficient. This reflected the strongly held views in the Liberal hierarchy. Encouraged by rapidly rising support in the country, a series of by-election successes and the deep split in their opponents' ranks, they saw no reason to pay any great price to obtain what the Liberal leader Campbell-Bannerman described as 'half a dozen doubtful or difficult recruits'.[18] In particular he viewed Churchill's defection as 'hardly worth any increase in complications'.[19] His view of the Free Traders was that 'they are in a cleft stick . . . we are under no necessity to go to them, and indeed cannot go to them: it is they who must come to us'.[20]

Churchill's next moves in December clearly indicate that his decision to defect had been taken, but he failed to make a clean break until he had agreed suitable terms with the Liberals. On 12 December he told his local party that he would not be their candidate at the next Election. He was privately convinced that the Conservatives would lose the marginal seat of Oldham (and probably the General Election too) and this only increased his determination to defect and find a new seat rather than face life out of Parliament. In a letter to Bourke Cochran in New York written on the day he told the local party of his decision he said: 'Oldham will most certainly return a Liberal and Labour member at the next election, both staunch Free Traders, so that I do not feel that I shall be losing a counter in the game if I look elsewhere.'[21] On 16 December the chairman of the local party (J. T. Travis-Clegg, himself a free-trader but also a party loyalist, who felt that Churchill had handled the local party very badly by not talking to them and rarely visiting the constituency), wrote to set out their position. Since Churchill had been elected as a Free Trader, they were willing for him to stay on as an MP until the next Election provided he did not campaign in Oldham against the views of the local party but they would choose a new candidate immediately if he voted against the Government. The day he received the chairman's letter Churchill wrote to the Liberal Chief Whip, Herbert Gladstone, asking for a meeting before Parliament reassembled. Two days later he wrote an open letter supporting the Liberal candidate in the Ludlow by-election. Churchill was also making enquiries through his uncle, Lord Tweedmouth, about possible Liberal seats and he knew that Birmingham, Sunderland and Scarborough were interested.

He then went on to have a series of private meetings with senior figures in the Liberal Party. Churchill lunched with Lloyd George for the first time on 31 December and found him very agreeable, although he disagreed with his views on religious education (Churchill never understood why this was an important issue for the

Liberals), the land question, trades unions and site value taxation. (Two years earlier he had described Lloyd George to the main Conservative organiser in Birmingham as 'a vulgar, chattering little cad'.)[22] A fortnight later he lunched with Herbert Gladstone to discuss possible seats; Gladstone emphasised that it was important that Churchill vote with the Liberals against the Government in the near future. It is probable that in this period Churchill obtained an understanding that, if he defected, he would be offered a post in any Liberal Government.

By early 1904 there were overt signs of the breach to come. The party could no longer tolerate such open gestures of defiance as Churchill's letter supporting a Liberal candidate while still remaining a nominal Conservative and at the end of January the Conservative whip was withdrawn. On 14 February, together with a number of other dissidents, he did what Gladstone had recommended and voted with the Liberals on a Free Trade motion. Ironically by this time the tariff reform issue was in decline – Chamberlain had failed to convert the Conservative Party and Balfour's temporising position had prevailed. By this stage Churchill was actively negotiating with a number of Liberal constituency parties. He rejected the idea of standing as a Liberal in Oldham (the majority of Conservatives who crossed the floor did stay in their constituencies), dismissed Birmingham as unwinnable because of the Chamberlain influence and saw a seat in Cardiff go to his cousin, Ivor Guest. By March a seat in Manchester North West, where the sitting Conservative MP was likely to retire, was the most likely option. Manchester, long the home of Free Trade sentiment, was an attractive proposition. At the end of March he sought to reassure Manchester Liberals of his credentials apart from Free Trade. Naturally he emphasised his record of opposition to increased expenditure on the Army but now included the Navy in the same category (in 1901 he had in fact argued for a higher priority for the Navy). He now also advocated retrenchment in Government expenditure 'upon strict Gladstonian principles'.

Given his open search for a Liberal seat it is hardly surprising that Churchill's position on the Conservative benches was rapidly becoming untenable. On 29 March there was a mass Conservative walkout when he rose to speak in the House of Commons but still he made no formal move to the Liberals. In the last week of April he was at last formally adopted as a Liberal candidate in Manchester North West. A month later, on 31 May, he finally sat on the opposition benches for the first time. He was not the first Conservative to do so, four others had preceded him and six others were to follow. But his timing and method had been poor. Days after he crossed the floor Churchill admitted to Lord Hugh Cecil that he may have mishandled the situation:

> as the Free Trade issue subsides it leaves my personal ambitions naked and stranded on the beach – & they are an ugly & unsatisfactory spectacle by themselves, though nothing but an advantage when borne forward with the flood of a great outside cause.[23]

Churchill was now a new, though prominent, backbencher in a party that had been out of office for nearly ten years and where party loyalists expected to be rewarded ahead of men like Churchill. To some extent though the leadership had an interest in rewarding Churchill in order to emphasise the Conservative split. Nevertheless he still had to work his passage, or at least be seen to be doing so. This he did in three ways. First he took up the causes of his prospective constituents in Manchester, in particular the interest of the strong Jewish community in objecting to the Aliens Bill, introduced in 1904, that would have restricted immigration. Churchill was one of those who campaigned strongly against it and Parliamentary pressure eventually led to its withdrawal. Second, he campaigned across the country on the Free Trade issue, speaking for example at the mass meeting held in Manchester on 4 June 1905 to celebrate the centenary of the birth of Richard Cobden, who had led the campaign against the Corn Laws. Third, Churchill engaged in vituperative attacks on his former colleagues. Not unexpectedly he attacked the new Secretary of State for War, Arnold-Foster, over his plans to reform the Army, even though they were different from those advocated by St John Broderick. Churchill also turned on the Prime Minister. He spoke of Balfour's 'gross, unpardonable ignorance' and strongly condemned the Government he had desperately wanted to join: 'To keep in office for a few more weeks and months there is no principle which the Government are not prepared to betray, and no quantity of dust and filth they are not prepared to eat.' Not surprisingly Churchill's attacks were deeply resented by his former colleagues and as a result he was beginning to build up a considerable head of personal animosity and distrust. This even spilled over into the social field: when he tried to join the Hurlingham Club to play polo, he was blackballed.

At this time Churchill's main literary activity was writing the official biography of his father. He first began work on it in 1902, but it had been agreed within the family several years beforehand that he would undertake the task. Churchill reached an agreement with Lord Randolph's literary executors (two senior Conservatives) in August giving them a veto over the publication of any documents that might injure the memory of Lord Randolph and both the Foreign Secretary and the Secretary of State for India vetted the text to ensure that no potentially damaging official information was revealed. Churchill wrote to most of his father's colleagues and friends seeking their help – some such as Chamberlain co-operated whereas others such as Balfour and Lord Rosebery claimed they had lost or mislaid their papers. Churchill was about to accept an offer of £4,000 from Longmans for the rights when Frank Harris, part-time literary agent, man about town and old friend of Lord Randolph's (who later wrote his own sexually explicit autobiography), intervened and negotiated a deal worth £8,000 from Macmillans.

Much of Churchill's time while he was on the backbenches was taken up with the biography, which was published in January 1906. It is a political biography on the grand Victorian scale – in two volumes and 1,000 pages long. Churchill chose to represent his father's career as a Greek tragedy. He portrays his father not as a man of ambition but as a man of principle who invented 'Tory Democracy' in the early 1880s. He argues that the 'Fourth Party' had a serious political purpose and that Lord Randolph, by ensuring the National Union a major part in Conservative policy making, was the man who had secured the long-term future of the party by giving it this popular base. Lord Randolph's resignation is seen as a supreme act of self-sacrifice, undertaken for the cause of public economy and as a result of deep political differences between Lord Randolph and Lord Salisbury rather than personal incompatibility or clashing ambitions. In the years after his resignation Lord Randolph is portrayed as someone at the height of his powers, with much emphasis on his moderation, consistency and ability to exert a major influence over Lord Salisbury's Government. Superficially it is a convincing portrait but it is one that bears little relation to reality.

It is not surprising that Churchill says nothing of the reasons for Lord Randolph's madness or of the state of his parents' marriage. But there are many other examples of omissions, deliberate mis-quotations and selective presentation of the evidence. For example, there is nothing about Lord Randolph's sympathies towards Home Rule in the early part of the 1885–6 political crisis and before he declared for Ulster and Unionism. His abandonment of the National Union in July 1884 in return for the offer of a place in the next Conservative government is also ignored. Churchill omits his father's speech at Oldham in September 1881 in which he argued for 'fair trade' and retaliatory tariffs and also leaves out his declarations in favour of ultra-Toryism, all of which were obviously incompatible with Churchill's own position at the time he was writing. Indeed the biography is written so that a sub-text emerges: if Lord Randolph had lived, he would, like his son, have finished up in the Liberal Party as the natural home of a 'Tory democrat'. This had nothing to do with the real Lord Randolph but everything to do with Churchill's political situation. At the time of its publication, when the true state of Lord Randolph's last years was known only to a few people, the biography was well received. It is well written but like so many official biographies of the time it is too long and too pious.

By the time the book was published Churchill was a Junior Minister in a Liberal Government. His gamble on the future of the Liberals had paid off. The Conservative Government slowly col-lapsed during 1905 and at the beginning of December Balfour resigned rather than call a general election. He did so because he suspected that the Liberal Party might split. Balfour was probably aware of the outlines of the deal between Asquith, Haldane and Grey (the leading Liberal imperialists) to force the sixty-nine-year-old Henry Campbell-Bannerman, an old-fashioned Gladstonian who had been leader since 1899, to go to the House of Lords under threat that they would otherwise refuse to take office. Campbell-Bannerman was much too astute a politician to be caught in such a trap and after he had bought off Asquith by offering him the post of Chancellor of the Exchequer the conspiracy collapsed and all three took office. Once the major posts had been allocated Campbell-Bannerman was able to see Churchill on 9 December and offer him the post of Financial Secretary at the Treasury under Asquith. Churchill refused because he felt he would not gain enough public attention under a boss in the House of Commons. He preferred the post of Junior Minister at the Colonial Office under the languid Lord Elgin where he would be the sole departmental spokesman in the Commons. Not that Churchill was happy with his position (he may have hoped for a post in the Cabinet) – when Lord Rosebery asked him whether he was satisfied with his job at the Colonial Office, Churchill replied, 'They bought me cheap'.[24]

A General Election was announced by Campbell-Bannerman on 16 December with polling spread out from 12 January to 8 February. Manchester was due to vote on 13 January but Churchill did not move north until 4 January for a short campaign. His opponent was a solicitor, William Joynson-Hicks, later his colleague in the Conservative Government from 1924–9. He campaigned mainly on the issue of Free Trade and won the North West division (which covered the centre of the city and the suburb of Cheetham Hill) with a majority over 1,200 votes. His victory was part of a complete Liberal and Labour sweep of Manchester and Salford. In the 1900 Election the Conservatives won eight of the nine seats, in 1906 they lost them all (even including Balfour's seat in Manchester East). This pattern was repeated across the country. Overall the Liberals gained 216 seats and the Conservatives and their Liberal Unionist allies, on a swing of over ten per cent, lost 245. This gave the Liberals a majority of 130 over all other parties and, in alliance with Labour and the Irish Nationalists, a majority of 356 over the Conservatives and Unionists. The electoral system had produced a highly distorted result – the Liberals received just under fifty per cent of the votes but won 400 seats (Seventy-one per cent of the total), whereas the Conservatives won forty-three per cent of the vote but only 157 seats. Nevertheless the Liberals, and Churchill, were going to be in power for a considerable period. Here was the chance that Churchill had always sought – the possibility of rapid promotion to the Cabinet and real power and fame.

5

Junior Minister

When Churchill joined the Colonial Office under Lord Elgin, he rapidly found that he and his superior had very different expectations and temperaments. Elgin had been a junior minister under Gladstone and then Viceroy in India between 1894 and 1899. By 1905 his wife was seriously ill and he wanted to spend as much time as possible with her at their home in Scotland. He disliked society and making speeches and took a relaxed view of his tasks at the ministry. Elgin had to cope with an ambitious junior who was determined to obtain a place in the Cabinet at the first opportunity; to this end he was not afraid of publicity and was prepared to work very hard. Elgin disliked Churchill's habit of exposing political differences on paper for officials to see, his tendency to get carried away by temporary enthusiasms and his desire to create work. But despite his generally relaxed approach, Elgin remained in charge of the department. He took the final decisions and often redrafted Churchill's proposed answers to Parliamentary questions. He took great care to manage Churchill tactfully and their personal relationship remained good. After his retirement Elgin looked back on their time together:

> When I accepted Churchill as my Under-Secy I knew I had no easy task. I resolved to give him access to all business – but to keep control (& my temper) . . . we have had no quarrel during the two and a half years, on the contrary he has again and again thanked

me for what he has learned and for our pleasant personal relations, and I have taken a keen interest in his ability and in many ways attractive personality. But all the same I know quite well that it has affected my position *outside the office* and the strain has often been severe.[1]

When Churchill took up his post, he chose as his Private Secretary Edward Marsh, an aesthete involved in many aspects of the arts world and also at the centre of the homosexual circle in Edwardian society. Almost immediately they became devoted to each other. Within a few years Churchill could write that 'Few people have been so lucky as me to find in the dull and grimy recesses of the Colonial Office a friend whom I shall cherish and hold to all my life.'[2] Churchill went to extraordinary lengths and broke the normal civil service rules to ensure that Marsh was transferred from department to department so as to be his private secretary in every ministerial post he held until 1929, and during the 1930s they were still in close touch.

The most pressing question that the Colonial Office and the Liberal Government had to resolve in imperial policy was the future of the former Boer republics of Transvaal and Orange Free State, which had been formally annexed by Britain in 1902. Decisions on their constitutional arrangements involved difficult questions about the degree of self-government to be granted and the amount of British as opposed to Boer influence. Intertwined with this problem was that of Chinese labour in the Transvaal mines, an emotive issue exploited by the Liberals in the recent Election campaign.

The Balfour Government regarded the revival of mining as vital to reconstruction after the war and in June 1904 had agreed to the importation of Chinese labour. By 1906 there were about 50,000 involved (constituting a third of the workforce in the mines). They were recruited on three-year contracts with forced repatriation at the end of the term. Their conditions were harsh: they lived in compounds; worked ten hours a day, six days a week for a minimum wage of two shillings a day; could not leave the compounds without a permit; could be flogged; had no access to the courts and could not own land or engage in any business. The Liberals had consistently opposed this policy as degrading for the workers and damaging to the prestige of the Empire. Once in office they were less willing to upset vested interests and abolish the cheap labour scheme outright. Within ten days the new Cabinet decided against the immediate repatriation of the Chinese pending a decision by an elected Transvaal assembly (which was some years away) and agreed to allow the importation of another 13,000 labourers from China under licences already issued. Churchill had little say in this decision but after the Election, when many Liberals had described the scheme as slavery, he was pressed in the House of Commons on whether the Government agreed with the use of the word. Ministers had in fact agreed that the Chinese were not held in slavery, but Churchill, in something of a quandary as he wanted to avoid disowning a number of Liberal candidates and MPs, was reduced to claiming that the contract could not be called slavery 'without some risk of termino-logical inexactitude'. This convoluted statement was greeted with derision by the opposition and used against Churchill on many subsequent occasions.

After the Election Churchill privately consulted the financier Alfred Beit (an old friend of Lord Randolph) and Frederick Cres-swell, a South African businessman, about the Government's policy before it was publicly announced in February 1906. He discovered that the mineowners no longer favoured importing more labour, preferring instead to increase mechanisation and allow the scheme to wither as the contracts of the current workers expired. It was a useful way out for the new administration and became Government policy. On 22 February Churchill announced the new policy in the House of Commons. The scheme was not to end immediately and current contracts for new imports could continue. The changes introduced were largely cosmetic. There would be a modification of the disciplinary regulations to remove what Churchill described as 'all danger of cruelty, impropriety or gross infringement of liberty'. In fact the changes were minimal – the flogging of Chinese labourers continued as it had since 1904. A voluntary repatriation scheme was introduced but the numbers involved were small – just over 750 in the first year, about one and a half per cent of the total. Churchill personally was not keen on this scheme. In March 1906 he told Lord Selborne, the High Commissioner, that he did not want to upset the industry, expressed the hope that no more than a few thousand would take advantage of the opportunity to return to China early and suggested that bringing in Indian labourers would be a better policy. Within the Colonial Office he minuted: 'The first result to a Chinaman of an application [for repatriation] should be *not* a free passage home, but a spell of hard work with no pay. Make that clear and there will be no unmanageable rush.'[3]

In January 1907 Churchill wrote to Selborne saying he was quite happy for a very easy running down of the scheme and was even prepared to allow some renewal of contracts, although no new importations could be permitted because of the Government's public commitments. (Despite sensitivities within the Liberal Party Churchill and the Colonial Office had no objection to indentured labour as such and actually introduced it, using Chinese labour again on Ocean Island in the Pacific in 1907 to mine phosphates.) The Chinese labourers eventually left the Transvaal after an elected government under the ex-Boer leader General Botha voted, partly on racial grounds, to end the contracts by 1910. (The Liberal Government had originally intended the scheme to end earlier but refused to veto this policy.)

The Liberal Government's decision to grant self-government to the Transvaal in 1907, in which Churchill played a considerable part, is often seen as a policy of great magnanimity, coming within five years of the end of the Boer War, and helping to reconcile the two white nationalities in South Africa. In practice the decision was taken for more complex reasons and with considerably less altruism. Once the immediate aftermath of the war was over it was obvious to the Balfour Government that some constitutional settlement in South Africa was inevitable. In April 1904 the Colonial Secretary Alfred Lyttleton wrote to the High Commissioner, Lord Milner, wondering whether the first steps towards a new form of government should be taken 'under your and our guidance' rather than leaving the initiative to 'men who seem very reckless of the essential interests of South Africa' (i.e. the Liberals).[4] Eventually in March 1905 Balfour's Cabinet agreed to the 'Lyttleton Constitution' for the Transvaal, which provided for an assembly with an elected majority but for executive government to remain in the hands of the High Commissioner, who would also be able to veto any act of the legislature. (In his maiden speech in 1901, Churchill had supported this position, arguing that there should be no early grant of self-government and that time should be allowed for immigration to produce a British majority in the Transvaal.) The constitution had not come into force by the time the Liberals took office. In December 1905 the new Cabinet decided to set up a committee of five chaired by the Lord Chancellor, Lord Loreburn (a radical), to agree the way ahead. Churchill was not a member of this committee, but obviously knew what was happening through Elgin and was also involved in the work the Colonial Office needed to do setting out options for the committee.

From the beginning the committee proceeded on the basis that a new start was required. They felt the Lyttleton Constitution was unworkable because it would inevitably mean conflict between the High Commissioner and the elected assembly. They did not there-fore favour implementing the Lyttleton Constitution even for a short period. Before the end of the year the committee had agreed informally on full self-government. By the end of January Colonial Office officials were working out the details of a constitution for the colony based on 'responsible government'. Churchill attended the last meeting of the Cabinet committee so that he could reflect their conclusions in a report, which the Cabinet considered in early February. At this meeting they formally agreed to scrap the Lyttleton scheme and set up an enquiry into a future constitution.

The Government took this line for a number of reasons. First, politically they wanted to make a clear break with the policy of their predecessors. Second, as Churchill wrote in a paper of early January, the Government wanted to keep control of events rather than allow the local population to dictate the pace:

> In the end, which may come quite soon, the Lyttleton Constitution will be recognised as unworkable, and we, or our successors, will be forced to concede full responsible self-government. The control of events will then have largely passed from our hands. We may not be able, without the employment of force, to prescribe the electoral basis of the new Constitution, or even to reserve the functions necessary to the maintenance of public order and the King's authority.[5]

Third, they wanted the British not the Boers to have the upper hand in the Transvaal. For Churchill one of the primary objectives was 'so to shape our policy as to keep the British party well together, and so to frame the Constitution as to give it a fair chance of securing the balance of power'.[6] This could be done, he recognised, by the British Government deciding on the voting system and the distribution of constituencies in such a way as to benefit the English-speaking inhabitants. If constituencies were allocated according to population then the Boers would have an advantage, because most of them were married: whereas if constituencies were allocated according to the number of voters, then the English would benefit, because more of them were unmarried workers rather than settlers. As Churchill put it, 'Everything depends on the basis selected. H.M.G. are therefore in the position of the Grand Elector.'[7]

The fourth and final reason for the Liberal Government's approach was that it did not want to accept responsibility for Chinese labour policy. As one Colonial Office official commented at the end of January:

> The declared object of H.M.G. is to refuse to accept responsibility for the continuation of the system of importation of Chinese labour into the Transvaal, and to throw responsibility upon the inhabitants of the Transvaal ... It would therefore be the wish of H.M.G. to escape all responsibility, by advising His Majesty to grant responsible government to the Transvaal at the earliest possible moment.[8]

Churchill put the same point in a more political form (and showed a keen awareness of his own likely problems at the despatch box) in his report of the Cabinet committee's conclusions at the beginning of February: 'the difficulties of the House of Commons situation may be considerable if H.M.G. are forced for a prolonged or indefinite period to be *responsible* for the day-to-day administration of the Chinese Labour Ordinance'.[9]

The Boer leader General Smuts came to London at the end of January 1906 in an attempt to influence the Government's decision and he saw Churchill, among others, on 26 January. But he could do little to affect an outcome already largely settled. The decision taken by the Cabinet on 16 February to scrap the Lyttleton Constitution and hold an enquiry was intended to convey the impression that the wishes of the Transvaal inhabitants would be taken into account. The enquiry, which was to look at the basis for constituencies and voting, was entrusted to the safe hands of Sir

Joseph Ridgeway, one of the few unsuccessful Liberal candidates in the recent Election. Churchill was absolutely clear that in the last resort the Boers could not be trusted and that the British Government would have to safeguard the political position of the English-speaking element:

> I would do strict justice to the Boers; but when we remember that 20,000 of their women and children perished in our concentration camps in the year 1901/2, is it wise to count too much upon their good offices in 1906? ... [the cabinet] while anxious to do what is fair and right between both races, while resolved not to lend themselves to anything like a trick, are absolutely determined to maintain ... a numerical majority of a loyal and English population.[10]

Churchill regarded these comments as so sensitive that he removed all copies of this paper from the Colonial Office files and the only remaining copy, which he had kept privately, was not put back until after his death.

The Ridgeway Report, which was ready in early July, provided the required answer – constituencies should be allocated on the basis of voters not population. The Boer leaders strongly objected to this formula but were overridden. Churchill was somewhat surprised to find that the Government was able to use such democratic arguments as 'one vote, one value' to support its case in the Transvaal. As he wrote in January, 'It is not often that democratic principles are helpful in Imperial Administration. When they are they should be cherished.'[11] Nevertheless the arguments deployed in the report were regarded by the Government as so sensitive that they decided against publication and when parts of it were leaked to the press, they stopped publication as 'contrary to the public interest'. The announcement of the new basis for the Transvaal constitution was made simultaneously by Elgin in the House of Lords and by Churchill in the Commons on 31 July, just before the end of the session.

A new constitution was drafted in the autumn of 1906 and approved by Parliament just before Christmas. The Government was convinced that the new arrangements they had devised would secure their aim of an English administration in the Elections due to be held in February 1907 – they expected to see an English majority of about ten in an assembly of sixty-nine. Churchill had assured the King in August 1906 that a Boer government was 'an utter imposs-ibility'.[12] This sanguine view was not borne out by events – with the English parties badly divided, the Boers won thirty-seven seats and an absolute majority. The Liberal Government had failed to gain its primary objective – avoidance of Boer domination of the Transvaal. It had always conceded that, if self-government were granted to Transvaal, then it would also have to be given to the other ex-republic – the Orange River Colony – where there was an automatic Boer majority. After 1907, the Government, faced with Boer control of both states, tried to convince itself, and claimed in public, that it had all along intended to be magnanimous to the defeated Boers and by granting self-government on favourable terms, integrate them into the imperial system; but it was not what they had really intended.

The missing element in all these discussions of the constitutional future of southern Africa was of course the position of the over-whelming majority of the population – the black, coloured and Indian people. Churchill, like most of his contemporaries, accepted without question the idea of the inherent superiority of white people. But his views on the subject were passionately held and more extreme than most of his colleagues. As he said later in life: 'Why be apologetic about Anglo-Saxon superiority. We are superior.'[13] As a boy, when he played toy soldiers with his brother Jack, Churchill always had the British Army while Jack had to make do with the native troops, which were not allowed to have artillery and doomed to lose. When he was in South Africa during the Boer War Churchill wrote to his mother that he was 'disturbed' by the news that some Cape Coloured troops had been used against the Boers, adding: 'We have done without the whole of the magnificent Indian Army for the sake of a "White Man's War"; surely it is unnecessary to employ Cape Boys now ... Personally I am conscious of a feeling of irritation that Kaffirs should be allowed to fire on white men.'[14]

During the Parliamentary discussion of the constitutional future of South Africa, Churchill told the House of Commons that he believed that the 'threat' from the African majority would bring the Boers and British together. He described the 'ever swelling sea of black humanity' on which the whites 'float somewhat uneasily' and added, 'This black peril, as it is called in the current discussion of the day, is surely as grim a problem as any mind could be forced to face.' He thought that some improvement was possible for the Indians (he asked his fellow MPs to remember 'the gulf which separates the African negro from the immemorial civilisation of India and China') but 'a proper status' for the blacks would be to 'preserve those large reservations of good, well watered land where the African aboriginal, for whom civilisation has no chance, may dwell secluded and at peace'.[15] (Churchill did not point out that the Africans, over seventy per cent of the population, had to live on just fourteen per cent of the land, and had been allocated the worst, driest parts that the whites did not want.) In the privacy of the Colonial Office Churchill also spoke of 'the black peril' which 'may indeed be a grave danger, perhaps – though remote – the gravest of all'.[16] In November 1906, when the Government in Transvaal proposed to introduce legislation to stop further Indian immigration, Churchill did not object to the principle, only to the possibility that the British Government might have to accept responsibility. He therefore counselled leaving the decision until full self-government was granted and the Transvaal Government could take the blame. Churchill viewed all black people as at best primitive children, at worst savages. When he opposed the extension of British control into the more remote parts of Nigeria, he commented that he did not see 'why these savage tribes should not be allowed to eat each other without restraint'.[17]

During his time at the Colonial Office Churchill was often prepared to challenge the judgement of the Governor on the spot, when the normal Colonial Office practice, endorsed by Elgin, was to support them. On occasions his challenges were successful. In January 1906 the Governor of Ceylon recommended that a guard on the railways should be dismissed for theft. Churchill read the papers and commented:

> Mr David is formally charged with one offence, and actually dismissed for another; for another upon which he has had no opportunity of defending himself, and concerning which the evidence – purely circumstantial – is admitted to be insufficient to sustain a prosecution . . . Our duty is to insist that the principles of justice and the safeguards of judicial procedure are rigidly, punctiliously and pedantically followed.[18]

He persuaded a reluctant Elgin to reopen the case and submit a series of questions to the Governor. Churchill wrote about the reply from the Governor which stood by the original recommendation that 'such a jumble of confused argument, such indifference to ordinary principles of justice and fair play are intellectually contemptible if not morally dishonouring'. Elgin asked him to remove this part of his minute from the file on the grounds that officials should not see such criticism of a Governor.[19] Churchill was eventually able to persuade Elgin to give David another trial and he was reinstated.

Churchill's handwritten comments scattered through the Colonial Office files show his love of resounding phrases (one declaimed, 'Authority is disgraced when it claims to stand with equal right upon caprice or reason'[20]), but demonstrate no consistent policy about the Empire as a whole; his interest lay rather in pursuing particular cases. Churchill was shocked by events in Natal where martial law was declared after two whites were killed by blacks – the Government executed two blacks and proposed to carry out twelve other executions. Churchill called Natal 'this wretched Colony – the hooligan of the British Empire' and sent a telegram requesting more information and a suspension of the executions.[21] He received his first education in the rights of the independent self-governing colonies when the Government resigned as a result of his interference. Only after London had confirmed the full responsibility of the Natal Government for internal affairs were the resignations withdrawn and the executions, followed by a large-scale campaign against the Zulus, went ahead. Whatever the rights and wrongs of this particular episode, it illustrates two features Churchill often demonstrated in government – a desire to act quickly and a reluctance to think through the implications.

In Parliament although he was generally highly successful some aspects of Churchill's performance also came under criticism. In the first half of 1906 he lost a battle with Elgin over the future of Ceylon's pearl fishery. Having been overruled by Elgin, who objected to Churchill's idea of introducing minimal state control, he proceeded (contrary to all traditions of collective responsibility) to criticise Elgin's decision in the House of Commons, saying: 'I think there are grave objections to the procedure which was followed and that the results have not been at all satisfactory.'[22] However, the occasion that did most to damage his reputation was his criticism of Lord Milner, the former High Commissioner in South Africa. Milner had given him considerable support when he arrived in Cape Town to cover the Boer War and speaking in Birmingham in July 1900 Churchill had described Milner in glowing terms: 'few British public servants in this century have been saddled with a heavier load of difficulty and responsibility ... Scarcely one has borne it with greater strength', and compared his possible loss as a greater blow to the Empire than the three military defeats of Black Week.

In March 1906 he launched an attack on Milner for his policy in South Africa, describing him as a 'guilty Parnell' – about the worst epithet it was possible to find in contemporary politics. He then contemptuously dismissed his achievements:

> The public service knows him no more. Having exercised great authority he now exercises no authority. Having held high employment he now has no employment. Having disposed of events which have shaped the course of history, he is now unable to deflect in the smallest degree the policy of the day ... Lord Milner has ceased to be a factor in public life.

Such language used by a junior minister in his early thirties about an imperial statesman was not appreciated by the House of Commons and even senior Liberals thought Churchill had gone too far. The Conservatives were even more furious about someone they already viewed as a renegade. Churchill's old enemy, Arnold-Foster, moved that his salary be reduced (a formal way of showing official censure by the Commons) for the use of 'embittered and empoisoned language'. Edward VII was moved to write to the Prince of Wales that Churchill was *almost more* of [a] cad in office than he was in opposition'.[23] Nevertheless in general Churchill was able to take full advantage of his position as the sole spokesman for the Government's colonial policy in the Commons at a time when it was a major political issue. He was an adept debater and understood how to present the Government's case in the most politically acceptable way. His combative performances were usually appreciated by the Liberals and his political stock rose accordingly.

At the Colonial Office Churchill was to become embroiled in the less salubrious side of the honours system, political influence and imperial policy through the activities of J. B. Robinson, a South African businessman. Robinson wanted to break the monopoly, controlled by his business rivals, for importing Chinese labour for the mines. His plan was to give one of his mines to Frederick Cresswell (Churchill's old confidant) for an experiment in using white contract labour. He approached Churchill in May 1906 to gain his support, arguing that imported white labour would not only solve the problem of Chinese labour but would also build up the English population in the Transvaal, which was what the Government wanted in order to keep the Boers out of power. Churchill backed the scheme enthusiastically; but Robinson wanted rewarding for his efforts, as Churchill reported to the Prime Minister:

> In return, he asked me if he did all this, whether the government would be grateful to him, and whether they would give him an honour (baronetcy I presume) . . . He added that he had subscribed to Liberal party funds at the last election . . . I do trust you will give most favourable consideration to this.[24]

Campbell-Bannerman was reluctant to act and so a week later Churchill wrote to him again, arguing that Robinson should be given an honour and suggesting that the Prime Minister should see Robinson and give him some reassurances about the scheme. It seems the two did meet.

Churchill then set to work helping Robinson establish the scheme. In June 1906 he both wrote and telegraphed to Lord Selborne, the High Commissioner in South Africa, to put strong pressure on him to help and also withdraw his objections to the recruiting organisation run by Robinson. By September this obstacle had been removed and Churchill then lobbied Sir Edward Grey, the Foreign Secretary, to get him to put pressure on the Portuguese Government to allow Robinson to recruit in Portuguese East Africa. Despite these efforts Robinson's scheme never flourished and he was unable to break the monopoly on labour imports. Nevertheless Robinson expected his reward but encountered reluctance over the deal. Lord Elgin told Churchill: 'I distrust him – & would rather not see him in our front rank.'[25] The Permanent Secretary at the Colonial Office, Sir Francis Hopwood, wrote to Churchill in November 1907:

J. B. Robinson has been to see me in a really furious passion, because he did not receive a baronetcy. He says that he spent enormous sums of money, to a great extent at the bidding of the Government, and that he understood from the Prime Minister, and also I gather from you, that it would be alright.[26]

It was not until Asquith became Prime Minister in early 1908 that Robinson was given his baronetcy. Later he was convicted in South Africa of fraudulent share dealing. In 1922, when Churchill was Colonial Secretary, Robinson tried to buy a peerage from Lloyd George for £30,000, but his unsavoury business record caused a storm of protest and Churchill's cousin, Frederick Guest, persuaded Robinson to withdraw his bid.

In September 1907 Churchill left for the Mediterranean and east Africa. The tour had been approved by Elgin as a private visit to shoot wild game but it rapidly developed into an official journey to assess various colonial problems. Despite this Churchill was still allowed to write regular tourist accounts for *Strand Magazine* (Marsh, who accompanied him, did the same for the *Manchester Guardian*) and he later produced a book – *My African Journey*. Altogether, after allowing for expenses, Churchill made a profit of about £1,200 from his tour on Colonial Office business. After travelling through France (visiting Army manoeuvres) and then Italy with the Duke of Marlborough, he stayed in Malta for a week, visiting a school and a prison and meeting local leaders. Then, travelling on *HMS Venus*, he went on to Cyprus, where he was met by large demonstrations calling for unity with Greece, and sailed down the Red Sea to Somaliland, where he spent a couple of days on the coast at Berbera. As a result of this lightning visit he recommended an end to attempts to control the barren interior (the Italians had already given up in their part of Somaliland). The Cabinet did finally adopt this policy in 1909, but it proved a total failure and a major expedition had to be mounted to re-establish control in 1920.

The main part of Churchill's tour began when he arrived at Mombasa at the end of October. He travelled by special train through Kenya (stopping on many occasions to 'hunt' local wildlife) and then by steamer across the lakes of Uganda. The last part of the journey was undertaken on foot, along the proposed railway route to the head of the Nile and then by boat again down river to Khartoum, where Churchill's servant died of dysentery, and finally to Egypt and the boat home. Churchill's time in east Africa brought his racism to the surface. In *My African Journey* he reflected on the right racial policy to be adopted in Africa. He wrote of 'the dreams and hopes of the negrophile, so often mocked by results and stubborn facts' and described the Kikuyu as 'these light-hearted, tractable, if brutish children'.[27] He saw the world divided into races of very different aptitudes – the Europeans naturally at the top, followed by Arabs and Indians and then at the bottom of the pile the Africans. He wrote of the Arabs in east Africa:

> Armed with a superior religion and strengthened with Arab blood, they maintain themselves without difficulty at a far higher level than the pagan aboriginals among whom they live ... I reflected upon the interval that separates these two races from each other, and on the centuries of struggle that the advance had cost, and I wondered whether the interval was wider and deeper than that which divides the modern European from them both.[28]

The policy he envisaged for the British Empire was based on strict segregation. The white colonies should restrict Asiatic immigration and in east Africa the highland areas should be reserved for white settlement. He was worried by the influx of Indian workers into east Africa and the threat of interbreeding – 'the confusion of blood, of manners, of morals' leading to 'the disintegration of the existing order of society' unless strict segregation was followed.[29] Indian immigration could be allowed to continue if the Indians did not 'teach the African natives evil ways' and they only settled 'in the enormous regions of tropical fertility to which [they are] naturally adapted'.[30]

While he was on the journey, Churchill bombarded the Colonial Office with a constant stream of telegrams, minutes and papers containing a host of suggestions about future policy. Because of his habit of jumping to conclusions very quickly, many of these were based on a misunderstanding of the facts – for example his proposals for the reform of the financial affairs of Cyprus. In the same way that he needed to keep himself busy at work, he could not let up when away from it. The Colonial Office had suffered from Churchill's habits during an earlier holiday in 1907. Sir Francis

Hopwood, the Permanent Secretary, complained, 'Churchill full of energy at Biarritz – he has been writing and telegraphing to me day by day – but almost nothing important.'[31] After the African journey Hopwood commented on the problem again to Elgin:

> He is most tiresome to deal with, and will I fear give trouble – as his father did – in any position to which he may be called. The restless energy, uncontrollable desire for notoriety, and the lack of moral perception, make him an anxiety indeed![32]

Within the Government Churchill's hard work and political energy, especially in the House of Commons, was becoming more widely appreciated, though there were still, understandably, doubts about his grasp of some issues and his real commitment to the Liberal Party and its ideas. John Morley, biographer of Gladstone and now Secretary of State for India, had taken a keen interest in Churchill from the time they first met in 1901 and acted as a sort of patron within the party. In early 1908 he described his protégé as:

> the most *alive* politician I have ever come across – only he has not got Chamberlain's breadth nor his sincerity of conviction. But for ceaseless energy and concentration of mind within the political and party field, they are a good match. [He has] a curious *flair* for all sorts of political cases as they arise, though even he now and then mistakes a frothy bubble for a great wave.[33]

Churchill was quickly seen as a candidate for early promotion. At the end of 1906 and in early 1907, after the failure of the Education Bill, a reshuffle was in prospect and Churchill was a candidate to replace Birrell at the Board of Education. Campbell-Bannerman, who had never been very keen on Churchill, wrote to Asquith that Churchill was a 'very recent convert, hardly justifying cabinet rise'[34] and to Birrell expressed admiration for Churchill's qualities but also set out some of the reservations old-fashioned Liberals still retained:

> W's promotion would be what the public might expect, and what the Press is already booming; he has done brilliantly where he is, and is full of go and ebullient ambition. But he is only a Liberal of yesterday, his tomorrow being a little doubtful ... Also, wholly

ignorant of and indifferent to the subject . . . Further anxious at all hazards to make a splash.[35]

Even Churchill's supporter John Morley thought that his ignorance of the religious aspects of education policy, which were at the heart of Liberal Party concerns, ruled him out. He wrote to the Prime Minister:

> I should say that the Bd of Edn. is literally the only post in the Govmt. (save the Woolsack) for which C. is essentially unfit and even unthinkable . . . The idea of him as umpire between Church and Chapel, and haggling over Syllabuses . . . would be both ridiculous and a *scandal*.[36]

Morley saw Churchill to explain the position, and he was passed over in favour of Reginald McKenna (the start of a long political feud between the two men).

Churchill was passed over again in March 1907 when Harcourt was promoted to the Cabinet. As compensation, he was made a Privy Councillor at the beginning of May. By the end of 1907, after Campbell-Bannerman had had two heart attacks, Churchill was expecting early promotion in the reshuffle that would follow his retirement, possibly keeping his job at the Colonial Office. Campbell-Bannerman had a further heart attack at the beginning of February and then contracted influenza. He remained an invalid at No 10 for two months, with Asquith waiting to succeed him (to a display of general indifference and some hostility from the Liberal Party). On 3 March Asquith discussed Churchill's position with the King; they agreed that Churchill could not sit in the Cabinet while being under Elgin and that he would have to wait for a proper vacancy to emerge.

Later in March Asquith, who had a higher opinion of Churchill than Campbell-Bannerman, promised him a position in the Cabinet when he became Prime Minister, possibly the Local Government Board. Churchill was far from happy with the prospect. On 14 March he wrote to Asquith arguing that he should stay at the Colonial Office on Elgin's departure. He claimed somewhat immodestly that 'During the past two years practically all the constructive action & all the Parliamentary exposition has been mine', and added,

'I have been fortunate to establish excellent relations in many quarters, which will not soon be recreated by another'. In this letter he also rejected the idea of replacing his increasingly insane uncle, Lord Tweedmouth, at the Admiralty. Nor did he want to go to the Local Government Board. He argued that he had no training in domestic politics, had never worked on a Bill and really only knew about military and colonial matters. He also felt that the Local Government Board, which had a well-deserved reputation in White-hall for being hidebound and extremely conservative, was the worst place in the Government and nowhere was 'more laborious, more anxious, more thankless, more choked with petty & even squalid detail, more full of hopeless and insoluble difficulties'.[37]

On 8 April Asquith wrote from Biarritz, where he had gone to kiss hands with Edward VII on his appointment as Prime Minister, to offer him a job on the domestic front – President of the Board of Trade in succession to Lloyd George. Churchill accepted. The appointment was to be upgraded to the level of Secretary of State but even so he was not entirely satisfied with the post. The courtier Lord Esher noted in his journal that Churchill 'does *not* want to succeed Lloyd George . . . "A gleaned field" he calls it.'[38] Nevertheless Churchill was now a member of the Cabinet at the very early age of thirty-three. It was a considerable political achievement and an even larger field for his vaulting political ambition was now opening up ahead of him.

6

Cabinet

Immediately after his appointment as President of the Board of Trade, Churchill had to fight a by-election in Manchester North West. At this time it was still necessary for ministers to do this whenever they took up a new post, although by convention they were normally unopposed. The depth of the Conservative Party's hostility to Churchill following his defection and subsequent Parliamentary attacks can be judged from their decision to contest Churchill's return. He was opposed by the same candidate as two years earlier – William Joynson-Hicks. This time, however, the tide of opinion was running against the Liberals – with the economy depressed they had lost half the seats they had defended in by-elections. On 23 April Churchill was defeated, among scenes of great local rejoicing, by just over 400 votes (a swing of six and a half per cent to the Conservatives).

It was now necessary to find a new constituency for Churchill. After discussions with party officials and Asquith, he opted for Dundee, a safe Liberal seat and cheap to fight. The sitting member was duly given a peerage and Churchill fought the ensuing by-election. He was opposed by a Labour candidate and an independent socialist prohibitionist, Edwin Scrymgeour. Against this attack from the left and in a radical constituency, Churchill too became more radical in his language, describing the Conservative Party as 'filled with old doddering peers, cute financial magnates, clever wirepullers, big brewers with bulbous noses. All the enemies of progress are

75

there – weaklings, sleek, slug, comfortable, self-important individuals.' Privately he disliked Dundee and objected to having to take account of its views: just before the start of the campaign he wrote: 'It is an awful hindrance to anyone in my position to be always forced to fight for his life & always having to make his opinions on national politics conform to local exigencies.'[1] Nevertheless on 9 May Churchill was returned with a comfortable majority of over 2,700 votes.

Churchill's letter about local politics was written to his future wife, Clementine Hozier. For his first seven years as a professional politician Churchill had remained single. The relationship with his mother had cooled once he had achieved his immediate ambition and entered Parliament, and after her second marriage. He was obsessed with work and politics, although he led an active social life among the aristocratic élite, staying with rich friends such as Sir Ernest Cassel (who was still speculating on the Stock Exchange on Churchill's behalf) and continuing to gamble heavily – he won £260 at Deauville in 1906 (worth over £9,000 at 1990 prices). In 1908, at the age of thirty-three with a place in the Cabinet and a salary of over £3,000 a year (worth just over £100,000 at current prices), he finally married. Miss Hozier was not the first woman that Churchill had considered marrying. He had already made at least three formal proposals and been rejected. His first had been to Muriel Wilson. His second was to Pamela Plowden, whom he had met in India and with whom he remained friendly until old age; she married Lord Lytton instead. Churchill was also rejected by Ethel Barrymore and newspaper speculation suggested he might marry Helen Botha, the daughter of General Botha, whom he met during the 1907 Colonial Conference. It also seems likely that Churchill was greatly attracted to Lady Gwendoline Bertie (known as 'Goonie') when she was being courted by his brother Jack, and a number of letters exist that hint at more than simple friendship between them. There are only cryptic references to his sexual activities in the published papers.[2] Despite the eligibility of his name and his political prospects, many women seem to have found him difficult and egocentric and were unwilling to subordinate themselves to his ambitions. In many ways Churchill was also not a particularly attractive figure. He was below average height (five feet six inches tall), with a large head (balding from an early age), a small hairless chest, small hands and feet, a less pronounced version of his father's large staring eyes, and smooth, soft skin (which he wrapped in silk underwear and bathed twice a day).

Churchill was first introduced to Clementine Hozier in 1904, when he said nothing and just stared at her. They met again at a society dinner in March 1908; Churchill talked entirely about himself (his invariable habit), recommended her to read his biography of Lord Randolph, said he would send her a copy but failed to do so. Their relationship improved when they met again a month later at Salisbury Hall (Churchill's mother's house) and Churchill wrote regularly when Clementine was away on the continent for six weeks. By August Churchill was ready to propose but was determined to do so at the family palace at Blenheim. Clementine arrived at Blenheim on 10 August and Churchill promised to show her the rose garden early the next morning. When he failed to get out of bed in time, Clementine nearly walked out on him, but eventually he persuaded her to accompany him to the rose garden where he proposed and was accepted.

Clementine's childhood had been even more difficult than Churchill's. Her mother was Lady Blanche Ogilvy, the eldest daughter of the Earl of Airlie, and so, like Churchill, Clementine was by birth well connected in aristocratic social circles. Lady Blanche had married Henry Hozier, a much older, divorced Guards officer, in 1878. The marriage was a disaster from the start and Lady Blanche engaged in a series of affairs – it was the one with Captain George Middleton of the 12th Lancers that led to the birth of her two daughters, Kitty in 1883 and Clementine in 1885. The marriage finally broke up after her husband found her in bed with the Conservative MP, Ellis Ashmead Bartlett. Lady Blanche then moved to Dieppe, the haunt of many English people exiled from society for their behaviour, where she continued her life of pleasure and gambling. Kitty, the favourite daughter, died at the age of sixteen and Clementine led a lonely life apart from her mother. Brought up largely by relations in London, she was a serious, unsophisticated child, with little money, who actively disliked her mother for her dissolute behaviour. Throughout her life she exhibited a strong puritanical streak and suffered from long periods of depression and psychosomatic difficulties. Clementine was first engaged to Sidney

Peel, a banker fifteen years older, but broke it off. In 1906 she did the same to Lionel Earle, a civil servant nearly twice her age. She was twenty-two when she agreed to marry Churchill.

After the engagement was formally announced on 15 August, Churchill seems to have been determined to press ahead with the marriage as quickly as possible. Clementine once again wanted to back out at the last moment, but was told by her family that she could not do so for a third time and let down a public figure such as Churchill. The marriage took place at St Margaret's, Westminster, on 12 September. Most of the Cabinet were away on holiday but Churchill's old Army friends, Sir Bindon Blood and Ian Hamilton, were present as was Lloyd George (he and Churchill discussed politics during the signing of the register in the vestry). The best man was Churchill's colleague from the days of the 'Hooligans' – Lord Hugh Cecil. (Churchill was always to remain attached to Lord Hugh and at the first opportunity on becoming Prime Minister in 1940 gave him a peerage in his own right 'to sustain the aristocratic morale'.[3]) The first night of the honeymoon was spent at Blenheim and the couple left for Italy and then Austria, where they stayed with another of Churchill's rich friends, Baron de Forest.

Although Churchill was to claim in his autobiography that he and Clementine lived happily ever after, this was in fact far from the case. Clementine certainly remained devoted to Churchill and put his political career before anything else and there was also a strong bond between them, but there were considerable difficulties. Churchill never hesitated to sacrifice his family life for his political career and he continued to pursue his established habits and other interests in the same way as before his marriage. He worked very long hours, dined out regularly and was often away travelling abroad, frequently leaving Clementine on her own. Within a year they were sleeping in separate bedrooms and breakfasting apart and Clementine usually went to bed long before Churchill. They often took separate holidays. On their first wedding anniversary Churchill was away attending German Army manoeuvres, to which he had invited himself, and Clementine was already accusing him of having an affair. At times Churchill recognised that he had not contributed much to the marriage, and in 1918 on their tenth anniversary, when he was once again away, he wrote: 'I reproach myself vy much for not having been more to you.' He seemed to acknowledge the lack of satisfaction that Clementine had derived from her married life when he went on to express his hope that 'future years may bring you serene and smiling days, & full & fruitful occupation. I think that you will find real scope in the new world opening out to women.'[4] The tone of the letter seems distant and Clementine too often found it difficult to communicate, saying: 'I don't argue with Winston, he shouts me down. So when I have anything important to say I write a note to him.'[5]

Clementine also took a strong dislike to many of Churchill's friends, in particular the rising Conservative barrister and MP F. E. Smith with whom Churchill had rapidly become close friends after 1906. Although they came from different parties, their views were not dissimilar and, more important, there was an underlying similarity of attitude – both were highly ambitious, brilliant speakers who saw politics as a field for personal advancement and, in the last resort, a game to be played for pleasure, and neither was over-scrupulous about the rules. Socially both loved the all-male political world of clubs and dinners and they shared a penchant for spending money, drinking heavily and smoking large cigars. For twenty years, even when divided by party feuds, Churchill regarded 'FE' as his one true friend. When FE died in 1930 at the age of fifty-eight, largely from the effects of alcohol abuse, Clementine wrote to his wife Margaret (whom she did like): 'Last night Winston wept for his friend. He said several times "I feel so lonely".'[6]

When Churchill joined the Cabinet in April 1908 he became involved in a much wider political field and for the first time had the opportunity to play a part in determining the Government's strategy. Despite its overwhelming majority in the House of Commons, the Liberal Government was in considerable political trouble. It had been elected in 1906 without a clear political programme and much of what it stood for reflected the political concerns of the nineteenth century – the preservation of Free Trade, a reversal of the 1902 Education Act, an attack on the brewing interest and a measure of reform in Irish government. They faced a huge Conservative majority in the unelected House of Lords quite prepared to use its powers to wreck legislation. Of the Government's nine major bills introduced since 1905 only three had reached the statute book. The Liberals were unable to decide whether to confront the Lords and if so on what issue.

When Asquith took over the Premiership in 1908 the Liberals hoped for a new political departure but it proved very difficult to make one. Philosophically the party was divided between those who still looked to the old laissez-faire liberalism of the nineteenth century and the minority who were attracted to the 'new liberalism' that was prepared, in some cases, to use Government intervention for social ends. By the end of the nineteenth century many of the old Liberal verities were almost indistinguishable from Conservatism and even the party's more progressive thinkers were finding it difficult to formulate a coherent alternative to both the prevailing economic orthodoxy and to socialism. Proposals for social reform were beginning to raise difficult questions about the role of the State. The Government was embarking on a few tentative steps in this area – for example with the provision of 1908 of old-age pensions on a modest, means-tested scale designed to eliminate the 'undeserving poor' – but the overall direction of its policy remained unclear.

Although Churchill was never a philosophical thinker about political issues, he brought a number of assumptions about society with him to his work at the Board of Trade, one of the key ministries in the social field. At the time of his appointment, he was, as he admitted to Asquith, ignorant of social issues. His political interests had been almost entirely confined to colonial and defence issues. He had been brought up and educated in a sheltered world of great privilege, where his only contact with the lives of ordinary people was with his servants. He had never questioned the immense inequalities in British society, where about a third of the population lived in poverty (defined as below the level necessary for the bare maintenance of physical health), subsisting on less food than was doled out in the workhouse to paupers; where a third of the national income went to just three per cent of the population; half of the nation's capital belonged to one-seventieth of the population; the average national wage was 29s a week and most people were unable to make provision for old age, sickness and unemployment. While he was still a Conservative John Morley had suggested Churchill should read Seebohm Rowntree's classic study of poverty in York. He produced a competent review of the book but his only worries were about the impact poverty might have on the quality of recruits into the armed forces and the implications this would have for British strategy. The experience of representing a relatively poor constituency did not arouse any campaigning fervour in him. When he visited Manchester in 1906 for the General Election and saw for the first time some of the slums in his constituency, all he could say to Edward Marsh was 'Fancy . . . living in one of these streets – never seeing anything beautiful – never eating anything savoury – *never saying anything clever*.'[7] In his new constituency of Dundee only three hotels and two private houses had water closets and the rest of the town had to use just fourteen public conveniences, but Churchill never commented on this state of affairs.

Churchill had a strictly limited view of the scope of social reform measures. They should be restricted to a few areas where 'improvement' might be possible but he ruled out any idea of a general reform of society – indeed throughout his life a major theme in his thinking was a concern about the stability of society and preservation of the existing order. Churchill's view of necessary change was needed was strongly influenced by the idea of 'national efficiency' – one of the most important trends of thought among the élite in Edwardian Britain. Highly influential Social Darwinist thinking, which Churchill fully accepted, suggested that nations were like species – in the international struggle only the fittest would survive. Britain seemed to be losing out in this struggle. Its industrial pre-eminence and share of world markets were passing to the United States and Germany and the Boer War had shown that its strategic position was weak and its defence organisation a shambles. To many, including Churchill, the only answer seemed to be a fairly drastic reorganisation of Britain to fit it for international competition. A stronger, more effective state would organise and direct society to a greater extent so as to improve its industrial and military strength. This implied not a more 'democratic' Britain but one where duty, discipline and direction would be far more important – people would have to put the aims of the State before their own personal preferences.

Churchill was particularly impressed by the social organisation achieved in the state that was increasingly becoming Britain's main rival – Germany. It is not surprising that German social organisation appealed to Churchill, because it embodied virtues and displayed achievements he admired; it was undemocratic, it had strong military traditions and, in order to preserve the existing structure of society and bring the workers to support the aims of the Government it had, in the 1870s and 1880s, built a State system to provide industrial workers with pensions and other benefits. (Churchill's later objections to German power came solely because of its perceived threat to British interests.)

Churchill wanted a similar degree of organisation in Britain to provide greater economic and military strength. He told the newspaper proprietor Lord Riddell: 'Our national life requires more organisation and more discipline.'[8] The State would provide some benefits for the working class, not as a measure of egalitarianism, but in order to reconcile them to the existing system and build their support for a more authoritarian society able to compete in every field with its rivals. He enthusiastically wrote about this vision of the future to Asquith in December 1908:

> There is a tremendous policy in Social organisation. The need is urgent & the moment is ripe. Germany with a harder climate and far less accumulated wealth has managed to establish tolerable basic conditions for her people. She is organised not only for war, but for peace. We are organised for nothing except party politics ... I say – thrust a big slice of Bismarckianism over the whole underside of our industrial system.[9]

Earlier in the year he had given Asquith a list of the measures he envisaged as necessary to achieve what he called 'the minimum standard'. On leaving school young people were to be 'disciplined and trained' until eighteen, boy labour was to be abolished, the Army was to provide longer careers, new labour exchanges would 'decasualise' certain trades, hours of labour would be regulated, the State would provide employment during depressions 'within certain limits and for short periods'. Finally 'underneath, though not in substitution for, the immense disjointed fabric of social safeguards & insurances which has grown up by itself in England, there must be spread – at a lower level – a sort of Germanised network of state intervention & regulation'.[10]

In 1909 he gave Lloyd George an idea of how the Board of Trade could operate in the economic and social field. Again he saw it as providing the impetus for more 'organisation' and in what was, in many ways, a far-seeing paper, he used military metaphors to explain how the Government could 'organise' the country more efficiently. The Board of Trade was to act as the 'intelligence department' of the Government, forecasting trade and employment in the regions so that the Government could allocate contracts to the most deserving areas. At the summit of this organisation and in parallel with the Committee of Imperial Defence to provide military planning there would be a Committee of National Organisation, chaired by the Chancellor of the Exchequer to supervise the economy.[11]

Churchill's interest in social organisation reflected not just his desire for a more 'efficient' Britain but also his political position. He did not always feel free to state publicly his real views about the greater organisation of the British State and society and often used the language of 'social reform' to portray a more benign image that was acceptable to radical Liberals. His use of language after 1908 reflected his need to become identified with a new cause. Free Trade, the reason for his own defection, was fading as a political issue and Churchill had no interest in other traditional Liberal issues such as education and temperance. Although it is remarkable, given his own alcohol consumption, that he was prepared to claim in a speech to the Welsh miners' gala at Porth in July 1908 that 'we ought to be glad that among the causes to which democracy has set its shoulder, is the noble cause of temperance'. Some Liberals had doubts about the sincerity of Churchill's sudden interest in social issues. Charles Masterman (later Churchill's Junior Minister at the Home Office) commented he was 'full of the poor whom he has just discovered. He thinks he is called by providence – to do something for them.'[12] Churchill adopted the rhetoric of the 'new liberalism', partly to increase his political standing, but without any worked-out programme or commitment to a greater degree of egalitarianism.

For much of his initial period at the Board of Trade Churchill was dealing with measures inherited from his predecessor Lloyd George or routine legislation to which the Government was already committed. In the first category was Lloyd George's Bill to create the Port of London Authority, which he piloted successfully through the House of Commons. In the second category was the Trade Boards Bill, based on the recommendations of a Select Committee. For Churchill the measure was acceptable as a generally agreed piece of social reform (it was supported by the Conservatives) to organise employers to create a minimum wage in restricted circumstances. It was designed to cover only 200,000 workers in just four carefully defined trades. Churchill himself felt that such State interference was only justified as 'exceptional measures to deal with diseased and parasitic trades' and should not be extended to industry as a whole.[13] Churchill was also responsible for the passage through the Commons of the Eight Hours Bill, which restricted the hours worked in mines, though it was actually drafted by Herbert Gladstone the Home Secretary. Although presented as a reforming measure, it was in reality a means of restricting output and so raising prices; as such it was supported by the mine owners. The limits Churchill placed on State intervention and his unwillingness to challenge vested interests can be judged from the discussions within the Government over a possible international labour conference, which some Liberal and Labour backbenchers had suggested should be held in London. The idea had the support of Herbert Gladstone, the minister responsible for policy in this area. Churchill was opposed to it. He recognised that the Government might gain prestige from sponsoring the event but felt that 'awkward questions' might be raised, particularly about child and female labour, and proposals made which 'it might be difficult & uselessly dangerous for the Govt to adopt in view of the powerful interests affected'.[14]

During 1908 it became increasingly clear that the most pressing question for the Government in the social field was unemployment, partly as numbers rose following the 1907 depression but also because of the inadequate administrative structure to deal with it. There were no statistics on the level of unemployment and most debate centred around a highly censorious attitude to the unemployed, who were widely seen as morally inferior men who should be subjected to some degree of compulsion, either in labour colonies or through emigration. As unemployment had nearly doubled since 1902 to about eight per cent, the existing system of poor law relief was unable to cope, mainly because the unemployed would not subject themselves to the poor law regime and the social stigma it entailed.

In the midst of the worst recession since 1879, the Government was under increasing pressure to take some action to deal with unemployment and the labour market. The immediate practical steps taken by the Cabinet in 1908 were small – a few naval shipbuilding orders were brought forward and £300,000 was allocated to relieve distress in the worst-affected parts of the country. It fell to Churchill, in conjunction with Lloyd George, who was now Chancellor of the Exchequer, to provide some ideas for longer-term measures that would convince the public that the Government could cope with the problem and at the same time defuse the issue of tariff reform, which the Conservatives were projecting as a panacea for unemployment. Eventually two ideas were chosen for action – labour exchanges and unemployment insurance – although both had other objectives in addition to the relief of unemployment.

Labour exchanges already existed in some parts of the country on a charitable basis but in February 1908 the local body administering the London system backed the creation of a national scheme and the Government could therefore proceed without incurring opposition from local and voluntary bodies. In helping to devise a national scheme run by the Board of Trade Churchill relied heavily on William Beveridge, who began his career in charity work and then became an expert in unemployment. In early 1906 Beveridge had drawn up outline plans for labour exchanges, though it was not until his visit to Germany in the autumn of 1907 that he was convinced the idea would really work – the Germans already had over 4,000 exchanges that filled over 1 million jobs a year. Churchill did not bring Beveridge into the Board of Trade; he had begun working for them in 1907 and had drafted the department's official evidence to the Royal Commission on the poor law.

Churchill used Beveridge not just because he was an expert on the technicalities involved but because their social views coincided very closely. Beveridge, like Churchill, was inspired less by philanthropic ideas than by a passion for efficiency and a hatred of waste – he wanted an organised labour market so that the State would receive the maximum possible benefit. In 1905 he spoke of the 'power of society as an organism to make itself fit to survive' and believed that the interests of the individual should be subordinated to those of the nation through 'a remorselessly unsentimental government and individual sacrifices for the future of the race'. His own views on the working class were harsh; he told his brother-in-law, R. H. Tawney: 'The well-to-do represent on the whole a higher level of character and ability than the working class because in the course of time the better stocks have come to the top.'[15] At a conference at the London School of Economics in 1906 he declared that those working in industry should retain all their civic rights but:

Those men who through general defects are unable to fill such a 'whole' place ... must become the acknowledged dependants of the state ... with the complete and permanent loss of all citizen rights – including not only the franchise but civil freedom and fatherhood. To those moreover, if any, who may be born personally efficient, but in excess of the number for whom the country can provide, a clear choice will be offered: loss of independence by entering a public institution, emigration or immediate starvation.[16]

Churchill's first paper on labour exchanges, put to the Cabinet in July 1908, was based almost entirely on one prepared by Beveridge. The proposal to create a national network of labour exchanges run by the Board of Trade (this was about the only point on which Churchill differed from Beveridge – the latter wanted a locally run scheme) was seen not in the context of necessary social reform or the creation of more jobs – indeed labour exchanges would not in themselves create any jobs at all. The exchanges were viewed as a way of improving the efficiency of the industrial system, providing 'intelligence' about the state of industry and saving economic waste through the more efficient use of labour. It was also hoped that exchanges would have a social and moral function since they would, as Churchill told the Cabinet, 'enable the idle vagrant to be discovered unmistakably and sent to an institution for disciplinary detention'.[17]

The details were agreed in the Cabinet's committee on unemployment during the autumn of 1908 and announced by Churchill on 17 February 1909. There would be a network of several hundred exchanges as part of a national reporting system on the labour market. Employers would be free to send in whatever jobs they wished; registration of the unemployed at the exchanges would be voluntary and no conditions about pay would be laid down; the individual would be told the rate and left free to choose, and trades unions would only be given the right to state what their normal rate for the job would be. During the summer Churchill held talks with the employers and the trades unions and throughout the consultation process was concerned to placate the employers as much as possible. The only concession he made to the unions was that a man was not to be penalised for refusing to accept a job at less than union rates, but he declined to give any assurances about the use of labour exchanges to provide labour to break strikes. Indeed he reassured the Engineering Employers Association and the Shipbuilding Employers Federation about the outcome:

> If anybody had said a year ago that the trades unions would have agreed to a government labour exchange sending 500 or 1,000 men to an employer whose men are out on strike ... [nobody] would have believed it all.[18]

Although presented as a way of relieving unemployment, Churchill's own view of the purpose of labour exchanges was made clear when he told the employers that what he wanted was 'a perfectly colourless, soulless piece of commercial mechanism' whose purpose was 'only to remove friction' in the labour market.[19] Indeed Churchill's proposals were so lacking in radicalism that they were supported by the Conservatives.

During the autumn of 1909 Churchill was heavily engaged in setting up the exchanges and in a major reorganisation of the Board of Trade (involving the creation of a Labour Department) to administer the new scheme. By February 1910, 61 exchanges were open and a year later the total had risen to 175 and by 1914 to 423, nearly all situated in converted buildings in the worst parts of towns (at the Treasury's insistence in order to save money). In the first year nearly one and a half million applications were registered. But the exchanges were far from being successful – jobs were found for only a quarter of the applicants. They never took over any other function than providing a place where a limited number of jobs were advertised; they did not help to organise the labour market and there is no evidence that they helped to create employment. They were strongly disliked by the trades unions, who suspected them of undercutting union rates and providing blackleg labour. Socially they were also divisive by creating two groups – those who found jobs through labour exchanges and those who did not.

Labour exchanges did, however, perform one important function for the Government when it came to set up a scheme for unemployment insurance – they provided the basis of a strictly limited definition of unemployment and a test of 'willingness to work' and therefore enabled the costs of the scheme to be kept as low as possible. Churchill took much of the lead on this subject in late 1908 and 1909, in conjunction with Lloyd George who had visited Germany to study their system of social insurance. This offered a model for a fundamental change of direction in Britain away from the original non-contributory State pension introduced earlier in the year. In a major speech in Swansea at the beginning of October 1908 Lloyd George outlined a comprehensive scheme for insurance for widows and orphans, sickness and unemployment. However Lloyd George and Churchill both tried to claim the credit for the scheme. Lloyd George later told the Liberal Chief Whip 'I had a weak moment . . . when Winston was at the Board of Trade. I told him of my plans. He promptly went off with them to his own Department; and got permission from Asquith to frame a Bill on the lines I had proposed, and to introduce it himself.'[20] In fact what Churchill advocated in the autumn of 1908 was an unemployment insurance scheme (which had no German precedent) separate from Lloyd George's wide-ranging scheme and which he wanted to introduce himself.

In the autumn of 1908 the Board of Trade began drafting proposals for unemployment insurance. The scheme was restricted to trades which suffered from cyclical unemployment (shipbuilding, engineering and construction) and excluded those in decline, those with a large amount of casual labour and those with substantial short-time working (such as mining and cotton spinning). It would cover therefore only about two million workers. Churchill's first ideas were that employees would contribute twice as much per week as the State and employers, that benefit would only be paid for a maximum of fifteen weeks and at a low enough rate to 'imply a sensible and even severe difference between being in work or out of work'.[21] Indeed he felt that in the long term the burden of contribution should fall on the employee and that 'the whole system will prove to be nothing more than wages-spreading'.[22]

In the draft Bill that Churchill produced in April 1909 employer and State contributions had increased but benefits had decreased and were to be calculated on a stiff sliding-scale over the fifteen weeks so that, as Churchill told the Cabinet, 'an increasing pressure is put on the recipient of benefit to find work'.[23] The scheme virtually amounted to a form of additional taxation because the level of employee contributions was calculated on the basis of an average of twenty-seven days' unemployment a year when the actual average was only seventeen and a half days. Many members of the Cabinet wanted to introduce some sort of moral enquiry into the fitness of the individual worker to receive such benefits. Churchill felt that this was not necessary and that the same objective could be attained through the strict link between contributions and benefits and because 'it would pay the insurance fund to keep always available a certain proportion of tame jobs as testers, which could be offered in doubtful cases, refusal to accept which would disqualify for benefit and thus relieve the fund'.[24] However Churchill's colleagues decided that this was not enough and included a provision that any workman discharged for misconduct or who left his job 'without just cause' was excluded from benefit for six weeks.

Churchill's attempt to introduce unemployment insurance separately from the comprehensive scheme failed. The Cabinet decided that there should be only one Bill and that the two schemes should be integrated, which had always been Lloyd George's intention. Some desultory consultations followed in the summer of 1909 when Churchill saw the employers' organisations and told them that they would be able to pass on their contributions to the scheme to their employees and that anyway it would be cheaper than making charitable contributions. Meanwhile Lloyd George had taken over the work on the scheme and found that much still needed to be done. The Cabinet did not reconsider the full insurance scheme until the spring of 1911 and the unemployment part, still applying to just a small number of skilled workers, did not begin collecting contributions until July 1912 and paying benefits until the beginning of 1913.

The scheme faced few problems during the boom years before the First World War – it had a surplus of over £3 million by then and had paid out only £500,000 in benefits – but could not cope with the mass unemployment of the 1920s; and the majority of workers then had to fall back on a revised version of the poor law. For Churchill the scheme always had a deeper social purpose than simply providing unemployment benefit – it was to help preserve the existing structure of society. He wrote in the *Daily Mail* on 16 August 1909:

> The idea is to increase the stability of our institutions by giving the mass of industrial workers a direct interest in maintaining them.

> With a 'stake in the country' in the form of insurances against evil days these workers will pay no attention to the vague promises of revolutionary socialism.

When the Cabinet had agreed in mid-1909 to postpone Churchill's separate unemployment insurance scheme, they were in the middle of an acute constitutional and political crisis over the 1909 budget. The origins of the crisis were both fiscal and political. The fiscal problem was that Government expenditure had been rising inexorably since the mid-1890s and although the Liberals had taken power as the party of Gladstonian retrenchment they had been not only unable to halt the rise but had contributed to it with measures such as old-age pensions and increased expenditure on the Royal Navy. The problem for the Government was to find additional sources of revenue that did not penalise their own middle-class supporters and which did not involve a tariff. The political problem was that by 1909 the Government had been unable to carry out large parts of its programme (notably on education and licensing) because of the use by the Conservatives of their majority in the House of Lords to veto Liberal measures and they were unwilling to fight a major constitutional battle in defence of what could be portrayed as narrow sectarian interests.

In early 1909 the Cabinet agreed a new political strategy was needed. They would introduce a budget containing new taxes which would enhance their progressive image as well as providing new sources of revenue. The peers would be left with the option of either accepting the new taxes or they would have to take the unprecedented step of rejecting the budget, thereby giving the Liberals ideal ground on which to fight an Election – the issue of abuse of power by the unelected chamber of Parliament. In the circumstances Lloyd George devised a politically astute budget. The centrepieces were a supertax on high incomes and the introduction of land taxes – a form of capital tax on landholdings. (Both would affect peers directly but could be presented as progressive and reformist measures to the majority of the population.) In practice the budget proposals were neither radical nor redistributive – the supertax and the land duties raised very little money, whereas the heavily increased alcohol and tobacco duties, which were highly regressive, did do so, and constituted a higher proportion of Government revenue than at any time since the emergency war budget of 1900. (In fact by 1914 taxation was almost as regressive as in 1905 – those earning £1 a week still paid a higher proportion of their earned income in tax than those on £50,000 and twice that of the 'middle classes' on £200–500 a year.) What the Conservatives objected to was not the levels of the new taxation but the principles involved in imposing them at all. Politically the new sources of revenue would undermine the case for tariff reform and socially they objected to taxation of land and wealth.

The Cabinet only reluctantly agreed to the new taxes during the course of fourteen meetings between the middle of March and the end of April. Given Churchill's political and social background, it is not surprising that he was one of those objecting. He had opposed the idea of a radical budget from the start and had tried to persuade Asquith at the end of 1908 that the Lords would not reject a budget and the Government should therefore plan on two more years of legislation before an Election. He probably calculated that such a course would give him greater political prominence than a Lloyd George-led campaign on the budget. In the Cabinet debates Churchill opposed the introduction of taxation of land ownership (he wanted death duties on landed estates to be levied only every twenty-five years) and was very reluctantly persuaded to go along with them. Lloyd George finally introduced the budget in the Commons on 29 April in a four-and-a-half-hour speech that failed to arouse any excitement.

Until July the tide of opinion seemed to be running against the budget and on 23 June at a meeting of Liberal MPs it was agreed to form a Budget League to open a propaganda campaign in the country. Haldane (Secretary of State for War) was to be president and Churchill chairman. A sub-committee was set up to liaise with Liberal newspapers and a large series of meetings organised, some using gramophone recordings of Asquith, Lloyd George and Churchill. The League's first meeting at Edinburgh on 17 July was a disaster for Churchill, who announced that if the Lords rejected the budget the Government would dissolve Parliament and fight an immediate General Election. Unfortunately for him the Cabinet had not actually agreed to such a policy. Asquith was outraged at Churchill's presumption in taking 'upon himself to say things which in their very character are impossible to consider until the occasion arises'.[25] At the Cabinet on 21 July Churchill apologised, saying rather lamely that he thought the Cabinet had agreed. He was formally rebuked, as Asquith later told the King, for 'purporting to speak on behalf of the Government' in a way that was 'quite indefensible and altogether inconsistent with Cabinet responsibility and Ministerial cohesion'.[26]

The public mood began to change after a speech by Lloyd George at Limehouse on 30 July delivering a strong attack on landlords and the aristocracy. The Government became more optimistic about its chances; they thought that the Lords would reject the budget and they started to plan on a General Election in January on a new electoral register. They therefore slowed up progress on the Finance Bill in the Commons so that rejection by the Lords would not come too early in the autumn. Meanwhile the Budget League was prospering and holding meetings up and down the country. Churchill raised £10,000 (£350,000 at today's prices) from J. K. Caird, a jute manufacturer in his Dundee constituency, and £15,000 from another businessman (J. C. Horsfall), who promptly received a baronetcy. Churchill also played a prominent part in the campaign, making a series of speeches across the country in which he castigated the Lords in vigorous terms. In June 1907 he had already described them as 'one-sided, hereditary, unpurged, unrepresentative, irresponsible and absentee'. In Leicester on 4 September he spoke of the conflict between 'a representative assembly and a miserable minority of titled persons who represent nobody, who are responsible to nobody and who only scurry up to London to vote in their party interests, their class interests and their own interests'. In Bristol two months later he spoke of the members of the Lords who thought 'they were the only persons fit to serve the Crown. They regard the Government as their perquisite and political authority as merely an adjunct to their wealth and titles.' Later at Leven he described the upper House as a 'played out, obsolete, anachronistic Assembly, a survival of a feudal arrangement'. (A decade later he was to defend the hereditary House to the Cabinet as securing 'the vital breathing space for consideration and for the more stable forces in the community to assert themselves'.[27])

The Conservatives agreed by September that they would reject the budget: although they did not expect to win the Election that would inevitably follow, the alternative of acquiescence seemed worse and they foresaw that the Liberals might well finish up dependent on Irish support and having to fight a second Election to resolve the constitutional issue. On 30 November the Lords finally rejected the budget by 350 votes to seventy-five. Two days later Asquith announced in the Commons that this action was 'a breach of the Constitution and a usurpation of the rights of the Commons' and an immediate Election was called. Churchill embarked on another countrywide speaking campaign, which the *Manchester Guardian* ranked with 'the one or two other great political pilgrimages in English Parliamentary History'. He spoke in Lancashire, Cheshire, Scotland, the Midlands and finally the West Country. His themes were an assault on the Lords, the need for their reform as a basis to secure further social reform and a defence of Free Trade. When the Election results were complete by early February 1910, Churchill was easily returned at Dundee with a majority of over 6,000, but in the country as a whole the Liberals had lost ground compared with 1906. They had just two more seats than the Conservatives and were dependent on the support of the forty Labour MPs and eighty-two Irish Nationalists to remain in power. Altogether the Conservatives had gained 105 seats on a swing of just over four per cent. As Churchill commented to Haldane, using an analogy from the life of his great hero Napoleon: 'Our victory – tho' substantial – is clearly Wagram not Austerlitz.'[28]

Although the Liberals were back in power they had no agreed plan on how to proceed with reform of the Lords. Before the Election Churchill had advised Asquith that they should 'avoid if possible any showing of one hand in detail before the election & fight on the general phrase of "smash the veto" or any other sober variant of that'.[29] Now they had to decide the sensitive issues of how to remove the absolute veto, what powers to retain and whether to reform the composition of the Lords. In order to do this the Government needed a guarantee that the King would, if necessary, create enough new peers to force the necessary legislation through the House of Lords. During the Election campaign Asquith hinted that he had such a guarantee – in fact he did not and the King had told him on 15 December that he would require a second Election before giving such a pledge. The Government could count on Labour support but needed to reach an agreement with the Irish Nationalists over the passage of the budget (which the Irish opposed because of the increase in duties on alcohol) and what was to be done about Home

Rule, which would be a political possibility if the absolute veto of the Lords was removed. For two months the Government argued about what to do in a tense political atmosphere, made worse by Asquith's admission to the Commons that he had no guarantee from the King. Churchill's position was clear. In two papers to the Cabinet in January and February he argued: 'The time has come for the total abolition of the House of Lords' and he wanted to see its replacement with an elected chamber with no power over finance and only a one year delaying power, with its membership confined to politicians of long standing.[30] Churchill's recommendations were not accepted and by the end of April the Government was committed to a Bill removing the Lords' powers over finance, giving them a three-year delaying power over other legislation, limiting parliaments to five years and only dealing with reform of the Lords at a later stage. If this Bill was defeated they agreed they would only fight a second Election on the basis of a guarantee from the King.

With the Government planning on a second Election in midsummer, King Edward VII suddenly died on 6 May and as the new King George V settled in to his new duties an atmosphere of compromise permeated politics. In this mood the Government and opposition agreed to a constitutional conference. In March the Liberal Chief Whip Elibank had suggested the idea of an inter-party conference to the then Prince of Wales and also mentioned the idea to Churchill, who immediately spoke in the Commons about the Crown and Commons being united against the Lords. His remark was premature and tactless as Elibank commented: 'This is Winston all over. In mining parlance, if he can jump another man's claim, you can trust him to do it.'[31] The conference met through the summer and autumn until its failure was finally admitted in early November. Churchill was not included in these talks – no doubt his presence was unacceptable to the Conservatives and he had also opposed the idea in Cabinet.

He was also on the margins of one of the most peculiar episodes of this period – Lloyd George's attempt to reach a political deal with some of the opposition in order to form a coalition government with an agreed programme, reflecting a desire in many political quarters to end what was seen as the sterility of party politics and agree on policies to improve 'national efficiency'. Lloyd George first wrote a paper on the subject in August 1910 and discussed it with Churchill at Criccieth at the end of September. Lloyd George suggested two options – an out-and-out radical programme or a coalition with the opposition. Churchill, unsurprisingly, plumped for the latter. Churchill talked about it to his great friend FE but was largely excluded from the complex talks in the autumn, again because he was *persona non grata* with the Conservatives. Churchill's main worry was that he would be excluded from office in any deal because of Conservative opposition. At first he tried to convince Lloyd George that he would support any remaining radical aspirations the latter might have, saying: 'if we stood together we ought to be strong enough either to import a progressive character to policy, or by withdrawal to terminate an administration which had failed in its purpose'.[32] In the autumn though, when he was staying with the Mastermans, he was ambivalent about the idea – attacking the concept of coalition when he thought he would be excluded but later 'was more and more passionate in favour of coalition, praising government by aristocracy and revealing the aboriginal and unchangeable Tory in him'.[33] Like the constitutional talks, Lloyd George's initiative collapsed in November.

Following the failure of the formal constitutional conference the Government called a second Election for December 1910. Once again Churchill set off on a gruelling tour across the country; he was pelted with mud and rotten fish in Colchester in almost the only violent incident of the campaign. All the effort came to very little. Overall the results almost exactly duplicated those of the January Election, though in Dundee Churchill suffered a swing of seven per cent to the Conservatives (the average in Scotland was one per cent). Once again the Liberals were dependent on Labour and Irish votes but their combined support meant there was an overwhelming majority in the House of Commons for reform of the Lords. Through the spring of 1911 the Bill to reduce the power of the Lords was passed by the Commons and subsequently mutilated by the Lords. Asquith drew up a list of nearly 250 people to be ennobled (including at least three Churchill nominees – his friend Abe Bailey (a South African businessman), his cousin John Churchill, and Sir John Gorst, who had lobbied Churchill for a peerage the previous year), but eventually the peers drew back from the confrontation and the Bill was passed in early August.

By the time that the crisis over the House of Lords reached its height Churchill had moved on from the Board of Trade. During his two years in that office his public profile had been high and he had played a prominent part in the long and tiring political campaign over the budget; he now expected to be duly rewarded. In December 1909 when he heard that a Cabinet reshuffle was likely, Churchill wrote to his colleague John Morley to tell him that he would not accept the Local Government Board since there was no interesting political work at hand except reform of the poor law (the immense administrative complexity involved did not attract Churchill) and he argued instead for the Admiralty, which he now regretted rejecting two years previously. After the Election Asquith wrote to Churchill from Cannes offering him 'one of our most delicate & difficult posts' – Chief Secretary in Ireland.[34] To offer an ex-unionist and the son of Lord Randolph (who in 1886 had proclaimed 'Ulster will fight and Ulster will be right') responsibility for introducing Home Rule was a deft political move by Asquith. Churchill, however, equally deftly declined the poisoned chalice and asked for either the Admiralty or the Home Office. On 14 February 1910 he became Home Secretary.

Churchill stayed only eighteen months at the Home Office. This short time proved to be one of his most difficult periods in office. It was also a period when, after an extraordinarily successful political career, rapid ascent to the Cabinet and to one of the most senior posts in the Government, questions began to be raised about his political future. To some extent his colleagues had never accepted the sincerity of his conversion to Liberalism and many waspish comments were made privately about his lack of commitment to his new party and Government. Asquith wrote to one of his most trusted confidants, Lord Crewe, in 1908: 'Lloyd George has no principles and Winston no convictions'.[35] Even as late as 1914 another member of the Cabinet could write to a colleague of 'this brilliant, unreliable Churchill who has been a guest in our party for eight & a half years'.[36] Lloyd George said of him, 'He is an artist and will provide what is suitable for his audience.'[37] In 1911 Churchill himself made an unguarded comment that supported the idea that personal ambition rather than political conviction was still his main motivation. The political correspondent and editor C. P. Scott recorded Churchill, stretched out on the settee in the billiard room of a

London club just after Bonar Law had replaced Balfour as Conservative leader, as saying:

> 'Every politician makes one great mistake in his life. I made mine when I left the Tory party. If I hadn't I should now be its leader.' 'That may be so' the friend replied, 'but you can't change sides twice.' Churchill leapt up as if he had been shot and shouted 'Not change sides twice!' in violent protest.[38]

Some of Churchill's colleagues were also alienated by his manner. Charles Hobhouse recorded in his diary just three months after Churchill joined the Cabinet: 'Winston Churchill's introduction to the Cabinet has been followed by the disappearance of that harmony which its members all tell me has been its marked feature' and he also noted that although he and Lloyd George had a good case for arguing for reduced expenditure 'personal discourtesy will not help them, and that is C's chief weapon'.[39] After Hobhouse had joined the Cabinet he wrote another portrait:

> Churchill is ill mannered, boastful, unprincipled, without any redeeming qualities except his amazing ability and industry. I doubt his courage to desert during a victorious cruise, but he would, without hesitation, desert a sinking ship.[40]

Asquith too, while fully recognising Churchill's political abilities (hard work, ability, and combativeness), distrusted the ease with which Churchill got carried away with a subject – he commented caustically on one of Churchill's minutes in February 1911: 'this is very characteristic, begotten by froth out of foam'.[41] One of Churchill's other habits, the tendency to indulge in long monologues, also alienated many of his Cabinet colleagues. Hobhouse recorded one of these frequent examples: 'Very long cabinet yesterday. We were favoured by addresses from Churchill on Education, Finance, Navy, Aviation and Electioneering and finally there was a general revolt summed up by the P.M. remarking that his views were pure "cynicism defended by sophistry." '[42] Nevertheless, whatever their doubts Churchill's colleagues had to recognise the political position he had created through hard work and ambition – he might be a difficult colleague to work with but they had to accept him.

During his time at the Home Office Churchill faced a number of difficult issues. One of them was the maintenance of public order during industrial disputes at a time when falling real wages and increased militancy within the trades union movement were causing a number of highly charged confrontations. During this period Churchill displayed characteristics that were exhibited many times later in his career – a thirst for action combined with pleasure in taking personal command of a crisis. He was also always deeply concerned about the maintenance of the current order in society, had little or no sympathy with organised labour if it was other than grateful for any small concessions that might be offered and was determined to confront any action that might, in his view, threaten that order. At the Board of Trade he had been responsible for attempts to arbitrate in industrial disputes. Unlike his predecessor Lloyd George, he had developed no contacts with union represent-atives and displayed no sympathy towards their case – most of his interventions were designed to help the owners gain the settlement they wanted, as for example in the Scottish coal dispute. Later in 1912 one of his Cabinet colleagues wrote of the coal strike: 'Winston violent for the Masters against the Men'.[43] To break that strike he told the Cabinet he wanted 'a strong course to induce men to come back to work by Gov protection', which would be provided by armed troops. One member commented, 'We all listened to such twaddle with impatience.'[44]

The first major dispute Churchill dealt with as Home Secretary was in the Newport Docks during May 1910. With the dockers on strike, the owners wanted to bring in outside labour to break the strike and the local magistrates, alarmed at the possibility of mass disorder, asked the Home Office to provide troops or police to protect the blacklegs. Haldane, who was acting Home Secretary because Churchill was away on holiday in Lugano, turned down their request and instead asked the Board of Trade to arbitrate. Agreement was reached but later repudiated by the owners. Churchill, who had hurried back to London to take charge, promptly authorised the use of 250 Metropolitan police, with 300 troops in reserve, to back the owners and protect the outside labour they brought in.

Six months later he was faced with another dispute in South Wales, this time in the Rhondda valley where a lock-out and strike following a conflict over pay rates for a difficult new seam led to a bitter ten-month war of attrition between the miners and owners. On 7 November mass pressure from the miners to close the local collieries caused panic among the magistrates and owners and the Chief Constable asked the regional military commander to send troops into the area. When Haldane, Secretary of State for War, found out about the planned deployment of troops he went to Churchill on 8 November and asked him to keep the troops in the background. The most provocative part of the deployment – the cavalry – was stopped at Cardiff. More rioting that day made Churchill change his mind and the infantry were allowed forward to Pontypridd and by 9 November were on patrol in Tonypandy and the neighbouring valleys. Churchill also sent 900 Metropolitan police and 1,500 officers from other forces to supplement the two squadrons of hussars and two infantry companies stationed in the area and the three further companies within thirty miles. Although the Army did not fire on the miners, as later myth alleged, the troops, under the command of General Macready, remained in the area for eleven months, supporting the police, and were at times deployed on the streets with fixed bayonets. Although Churchill would not allow the police and Army to act to protect imported blackleg workers as the owners wanted, he consistently refused to allow any enquiry into their conduct. It was also the first time the Army had been placed in overall control of law and order and under the direct authority of the Home Office rather than local magistrates. Churchill also introduced legislation to force local authorities to pay the bill whenever he chose to deploy troops or the police in industrial disputes but there was so much opposition he had to withdraw it.

The dispute where Churchill decided to use the military on the greatest scale was the dock and rail strike of August 1911. On 14 August troops were deployed in Liverpool, where the dockers were locked out, and fired on a crowd of workers. With many in the establishment believing the city was on the verge of revolution, Churchill moved *HMS Antrim* to the Mersey (eleven other ships were sent to other ports) to overawe the population, and troops at Aldershot were put on standby to move to London (the Guards Brigade was moved to the capital on 17 August). Then Churchill, who was convinced that the strike was financed by German money, sent an instruction to local Army commanders that they were not to wait for a request for assistance from local magistrates or authorities before deploying (as King's Regulations required) but were to use their own discretion – about 50,000 troops were used as a result. In a communiqué issued on 18 August Churchill hoped this action would be enough but added 'if not measures of an even larger scope will have to be taken promptly'. After a few localised incidents Churchill asked his officials to prepare a catalogue of every possible offence the strikers could commit, together with the charges that could be brought, which was to be sent to every Chief Constable 'in view of the outrages which have been committed on railways in the last few days'.[45] Throughout the country the Army was used to protect those still at work in an attempt to break the strike and inevitably there were clashes, protests and conflicting allegations. When incidents were raised with the Home Secretary, Churchill made no attempt to take a detached or balanced view. His attitude was openly partisan; in every case of a protest about police or military violence he simply accepted the official account and dismissed the version from the strikers. He refused to contemplate awarding any compensation for a mother whose child had been injured by the military and told his officials not to send him any protests from local strike committees, only those from local businessmen and magistrates. In the end it was Lloyd George who was able to settle the dispute rapidly on 19 August by persuading the owners to recognise the unions. Churchill immediately telephoned him to say he was sorry to hear of the settlement; he had wanted an open conflict followed by a clear defeat for the unions. Three days later Churchill justified the massive deployment of military force on Britain's streets with his usual powerful rhetoric. He told the Commons that in his view if the Government had not intervened in such strength in the north of England the strike 'would have hurled the whole of that great community into an abyss of horror which no man can dare to contemplate'.

When Churchill went to the Home Office he saw it as an opportunity to carry out a programme that he had believed in for many years – the better breeding of the British 'race'. Even before he entered politics he told his cousin, Ivor Guest: 'The improvement of the British breed is my political aim in life.'[46] For Churchill this programme was part of his ideas for improving the 'efficiency' of Britain. He was brought up in an age that believed the human population was divided into distinct races, and individuals and indeed nations were subject to the same laws as Darwin had discovered in the natural world – the struggle for survival leading to the survival of the fittest. This was common to many who were concerned about improving Britain's 'national efficiency' but to only a small fringe was the quality of the population important. Churchill was one of the few politicians to take a serious interest in the subject and his views were extreme even among the small group of people interested in social eugenics.

Churchill seized the opportunity to promote his views on 'improving the breed' and tackling 'degeneracy' while the Government was considering the report of the Royal Commission on the Care and Control of the Feeble-Minded, set up by the Balfour Government in 1904. The report declared that its aim was to deal with 'persons who cannot take part in the struggle of life owing to mental defect' and defined the 'feeble-minded' as those who might be capable of earning a living 'under favourable circumstances' but who were incapable '(a): of competing on equal terms with their normal fellows; or (b) of managing themselves and their affairs with ordinary prudence'. This definition of 'feeble-mindedness' covered an estimated 100,000 people who were very far from being lunatics but nevertheless the Royal Commission recommended they should be brought within the scope of the lunacy laws.[47]

The Government had taken no action on the report before Churchill became Home Secretary. He decided to give the subject a high priority. He circulated to his colleagues a lecture by Dr Tredgold, one of the advisers to the Royal Commission, entitled 'The Feeble-Minded: A Social Danger', pointing out that 'Dr Tredgold speaks from wide experience and with special authority . . . This address gives a concise and, I am informed, not exaggerated statement of the serious problem to be faced.'[48] The paper that Churchill's colleagues would have read, and which he endorsed so enthusiastically, painted an apocalyptic picture of impending social decline and disaster.

Tredgold's argument was that feeble-mindedness was only one stage of a disease that began with migraine and epilepsy and ended with insanity and dementia. The 100,000 people in this group made up the class of 'criminals, paupers and unemployables, prostitutes and ne'er do wells' who formed 'a very considerable proportion, if not the whole, of the social failures who actually impede the advance of the nation'. These people were breeding almost twice as fast as the national average and, if this were not checked, the time would come 'if it has not already come' when the nation would contain a 'preponderance of citizens lacking in the intellectual and physical vigour which is absolutely essential to progress' and which therefore 'must inevitably end in national destruction'. The problem facing the country was that in the natural world these inferior people would be eliminated but the modern state kept them alive and thereby destroyed 'many of those national characteristics which have made this country truly great'. Hence the vital importance of having social laws to ensure that the unfit did not propagate and interbreed with 'healthy' members of society and so 'lower the general vigour of the nation'. The conclusion was that it was essential to ensure 'that this great social evil is removed and that this tide of degeneracy is stemmed'.

As well as circulating this report to the Cabinet, Churchill also wrote privately to Asquith to stress the urgent need for Government action. His message was couched in strong terms:

> The unnatural and increasingly rapid growth of the feeble-minded and insane classes, coupled as it is with a steady restriction among all the thrifty, energetic and superior stocks constitutes a national and race danger which it is impossible to exaggerate . . . I feel that the source from which the stream of madness is fed should be cut off and sealed up before another year has passed.[49]

Churchill wanted to go far further than the Royal Commission, Dr Tredgold, his officials and other ministers in the Government in dealing with the 'feeble-minded'. No-one else contemplated anything more drastic than locking certain people away in institutions so that they could not raise families. Churchill however passionately advocated the forcible sterilisation of the 100,000 'mental degenerates'. He told his more cautious officials that it was 'bound to come some day'.

Within a month of taking office he obtained a booklet from a friend on 'The Sterilization of Degenerates', written by a Dr H. C. Sharp of the Indiana Reformatory, which, like some other American states at the time, allowed forcible sterilisation. Churchill carefully marked, in his usual blunt blue pencil, the passages about the legislation in Indiana and the operations that were carried out on both males and females. He instructed officials to examine the possibilities of introducing a similar scheme into Britain and asked them to check whether the Royal Commission had faced up to the problem of sterilisation. The Permanent Secretary at the Home Office, Sir Edward Troup, trying to be tactful, told Churchill that sterilisation might be effective but it was not practical politics. Churchill disagreed and after a couple of months returned to his original ideas. He told his still reluctant officials: 'I am drawn to this subject in spite of many Parliamentary misgivings', this time telling them firmly 'It must be examined' and asking them to produce specific ideas on techniques. In particular he asked, 'what is the best surgical operation?' and wanted to know what new legal powers would be needed.[50] When this detailed work was complete, he intended to send a paper to the Cabinet. Once again Churchill met a wall of resistance in the Home Office. One of its experts, Dr Donkin, argued for adopting a more 'humane' policy, saying that sterilisation was difficult to defend and detention a perfectly adequate substitute.

With the argument still unresolved, a case arose that seemed to Churchill to illustrate exactly why sterilisation and not just detention should be employed. Alfred Oxtoby of Sancton in the East Riding had been convicted of bestiality in June 1910 and was also suspected of indecently assaulting a girl of twelve. He was described by the local police as mentally inadequate and over-sexed. Churchill read the file closely and marked all the passages about Oxtoby's offences. He realised that he had no power at present to sterilise Oxtoby but wrote, 'This seems to be a case where a complete cure might be at once effected by sterilization. Can this never be done by consent?'[51] It fell to Dr Donkin to tell Churchill that sterilisation would not in fact remove Oxtoby's sexual drive and anyway he was too insane to give informed consent. Oxtoby was sent to Broadmoor although Churchill insisted that the case should be kept under review in the hope that sterilisation would become possible in the near future.

Churchill was also keen to introduce forced labour camps to deal with what he described as 'mental defectives'. This reflected his view that such camps were a suitable remedy for many at the bottom of society. He told the Commons on 10 February 1911 that 'as for tramps and wastrels there ought to be proper Labour Colonies where they could be sent for considerable periods and made to realise their duty to the State'. Within six weeks of becoming Home Secretary he asked officials to devise a scheme to be introduced quickly to apply the same ideas to the 'feeble-minded'. The proposals they put forward covered only the small number already in prison who were unable to cope with prison discipline because of their mental state. Churchill wanted a much more draconian scheme that would give him personally almost unlimited power over the lives of some individuals. Although he only wanted people to be sent to labour camps on the medical ground that they were 'feeble-minded', this definition was so widely drawn that it would, on Home Office estimates, cover about 20,000 convicted criminals. Under Churchill's scheme someone who committed a second offence of any description could, on the direction of the Home Secretary, be officially declared criminally weak-minded, and made to undergo a medical enquiry. If this enquiry endorsed the declaration, they could then be detained for as long as was thought suitable. Under this scheme therefore a person sentenced by a court to only a short period in jail could find themselves sent to a labour camp and detained for as long as the Home Secretary wanted.

Not content with developing this scheme Churchill returned to his ideas for sterilising the 100,000 or more 'feeble-minded', which he thought of as a more 'humane' policy than incarcerating them in institutions. He stated 'it is cruel to shut up numbers of people in institutions . . . for their whole lives, if by a simple surgical operation they could be permitted to live freely in the world without causing much inconvenience to others'. He told his officials in September 1910 that 'there must be a considerable class among the feeble-minded who might be allowed to live outside special institutions if only one could be sure that they did not continue to multiply in the next generation the evils from which we suffer so greatly in our own'. He criticised his officials for casting doubt on the hereditary transmission of degeneration, saying, 'A very large proportion of criminals are abnormal only in the weakness of their faculty of self-control. Surely that weakness is a defect definitely traceable in a great number of cases to parentage.' Churchill went on to argue that humanity was divided into three categories. Most people came in the category of the naturally honest and virtuous. There was then a very small group 'who use their intelligence from a definitely immoral standpoint'. In between were those 'whose human intelligence is so far defective as to deprive them of the average restraining power possessed by individuals' and it was this group 'that we should seek by sterilization of the unfit to prevent'.[52]

These pessimistic and disturbing views of humanity and the need to improve the quality of the British race were not revealed to a wider audience than a few select officials and ministers. Churchill could not convince his colleagues of the correctness of his views and the expediency of his measures. His Junior Minister at the Home Office, Charles Masterman, told him that what he wanted was simply politically impossible. Asquith was not prepared to publicly defend such ideas. A diluted version of the Royal Commission's report did form the basis of a Bill introduced into Parliament after Churchill left the Home Office. But it had to be even further watered down before it became law in 1913. Churchill's aim of improving the British 'race' by stopping 'mental degenerates' breeding by forcible mass sterilisation and incarcerating others in forced labour camps was to remain unfulfilled.

Churchill also took a close interest in prison conditions and although his attitudes show some relatively liberal ideas they were generally authoritarian. Within a few weeks of becoming Home Secretary he announced a new regime for suffragettes, after his officials had talked him out of his original idea of creating a special class of 'political prisoner'. Instead Churchill insisted on better conditions for those prisoners whose offence did not impugn their character and, most important, for people of 'good antecedents'.[53] His predecessor, Herbert Gladstone, wrote to Churchill to complain that the latter had simply purloined his ideas and refused to give him any credit. Churchill replied that he had thought up the ideas on his own, although within the Home Office he admitted that he had read all Gladstone's minutes on the subject. Gladstone was stung into replying:

> During the last three years the Suff[ragette] question came frequently before the Cabinet. The concession was never suggested by anyone, not even by you. In fact the only suggestion you made to me – last December – was that to safeguard Cabinet Ministers and their meetings, I should proceed to lock up the Suff[ragette]s

wholesale. I don't remember on that occasion any advocacy for the improvement of their prison treatment.[54]

Churchill introduced one other change immediately he took office. Forcible feeding of suffragettes on hunger strike had already begun and was justified not as a punishment but on medical grounds. Churchill disagreed, telling his officials that it 'is not a medical question. It is a question of policy.' He insisted that forcible feeding must begin within twenty-four hours of the start of a hunger strike, regardless of the medical circumstances.[55] After the suffragette demonstrations in November 1910 Churchill issued new instructions to the prison authorities: 'There is to be no squeamishness as to forcible feeding . . . the strictest discipline is to be maintained & on the least infraction of the rules punishment is to be enforced.'[56]

Four months later Churchill announced some small-scale reforms in the prison regime and the criminal law – periods of solitary confinement were limited to one month, time was allowed for people to pay fines and borstal provision was extended to those aged eighteen to twenty-one. He also reviewed, with FE's assistance and in great detail, eleven cases of people convicted of homosexual offences, reduced their sentences and issued new guidelines that would lead to lower sentences in the majority of cases involving homosexuality in future. In the autumn of 1910 Churchill also proposed to Asquith new legislation extending probation, abolishing imprisonment for debt and introducing suspended sentences for trivial offences involving less than one month in prison. But no time could be found in the legislative programme and Asquith did not agree with all the proposals.

Although Churchill wanted to limit the number of young people sent to prison, he also wanted to introduce a new regime of strict army-style discipline for such offenders. He proposed introducing twenty-eight days of hard drill (of the type reserved in the Army for those convicted of disciplinary offences) and consisting, in addition to the drill, of 'physical extension motions, Swedish gymnastics with or without dumb-bells' to be carried out at police stations where 'the training should be severe, and rigorous discipline preserved'. On a further offence youths would be sent to a 'modified borstal' and the aim should be 'to make this period extremely unpleasant, but disciplinary and instructive'.[57] Churchill was also still worried about tramps and vagrants, given his failure to establish labour camps for them and after some complaints from a few local poor law guardians that prison conditions were so much easier for tramps and beggars that they committed offences in workhouses in order to be sent to prison. These 'easier' conditions consisted of an extra two ounces of bread for breakfast and supper, and a pint of porridge or even eight ounces of suet pudding for dinner in prison instead of a pint of soup. Churchill decided that this slackness in the prison regime should be removed since he felt that existing conditions 'may be a sufficient punishment for the ordinary citizen who lapses, perhaps repeatedly, into theft or drunkenness [but] may for the tramp or vagrant . . . make prison a place of comfort'.[58]

As well as changing the conditions for suffragettes in jail, Churchill also issued new instructions on how their demonstrations were to be policed. Herbert Gladstone had told the Metropolitan Police that arrests were to be avoided for as long as possible. Churchill told the Chief Commissioner that 'women were to be arrested as soon as any defiance of the law had been committed . . . prompt arrest is essential'.[59] Despite these instructions the demonstrations in central London in November 1910 got out of hand and large numbers of women were roughly handled by the police. Churchill refused to hold an enquiry into police conduct despite hundreds of complaints of assault. He also stated in the House of Commons that 'No orders, verbal or written, emanating directly or indirectly from me were given' and claimed that he had merely given 'directions' to the police. When one of the London magistrates wrote on behalf of the Men's League for Women's Suffrage (a non-violent organisation) threatening to organise a corps of witnesses to give evidence against the police if there was further violence at suffragette demonstrations, Churchill wrote to him demanding a written explanation. Before this had been received he told his officials: 'my intention is that he should be dismissed forthwith from his post'.[60] The magistrate explained what was involved but Churchill felt he should not be a member of a pro-suffragette society and demanded he either withdraw the letter or be sacked. The letter was withdrawn but the magistrate chose to resign anyway. During these suffragette demonstrations a member of the Cabinet, Augustine Birrell, twisted his knee while escaping from some women demonstrators. He refused to prosecute because he had not been actually assaulted by the women. This did not satisfy Churchill. He wanted 'stringent police enquiries' to find those involved and then 'they are to be prosecuted with the full rigour of the law'.[61] Birrell had to insist that Churchill drop the matter.

It was not just on suffragette questions that Churchill took a remarkably close interest in individual criminal cases. He diligently read the 'Calendar of Prisoners' list from each Quarter Sessions, commented on particular cases and also intervened on an extraordinary and unprecedented scale with the administration of justice to try and achieve the result he wanted. (The extent of his interference was such that the Home Office files on the subject were originally closed for a century, treatment meted out to no other Home Secretary.) His exaggerated responses to certain cases were typical of his persistent tendency to become involved in subjects that were not really his responsibility and to leap to conclusions and take up extreme positions, often on limited information. His relations with his officials were clearly strained by his refusal to understand that it was not his job to act as judge and jury in individual cases.

In July 1910 for example he found out about the case of Annie Connolly, who had thrown pepper in the face of a neighbour after a row and some of the pepper had accidentally got into a baby's eyes causing conjunctivitis. Connolly was bound over for the sum of £5 to keep the peace. An outraged Churchill told Sir Edward Troup: 'It is in my opinion, one of the most brutal and unnatural crimes a woman could commit, and certainly six months imprisonment with hard labour was richly deserved.' The magistrate in the case was, according to Churchill, 'unfit to hold his position' and he demanded a report on his record and character before his removal from the bench. Troup admitted that the Home Office had occasionally intervened to secure a stiffer sentence but felt that he had to remind Churchill that 'the independence of the judiciary from the control of the executive is one of the cardinal principles of the constitution'. Churchill, unabashed, took up the case with the Lord Chancellor (not realising that magistrates in Lancashire were the responsibility of the Chancellor of the Duchy of Lancaster) and forced the Home Office to write to the magistrate concerned demanding an explanation for his decision. Churchill then wrote out a formal rebuke to the local magistrates for a 'lamentable failure of justice' since 'by discharging the prisoner without sentence [they] have allowed themselves to appear as condoning such an offence'. He wanted the rebuke published but was eventually persuaded by his officials not to do so.[62]

In the case of Edward Prinsep Churchill was horrified to discover that he had only been sentenced to three years in prison for stealing three pairs of boots. Since he had also committed other offences in the past, Churchill demanded to know 'on what principle has he not been charged as a habitual?' When it turned out that the local police had not pressed a more serious charge, Churchill remarked that he was appalled that Prinsep 'who was on the verge of a life sentence got off with 18 months' [sic] and sarcastically remarked that he was lucky his 'heinous' crimes were 'redeemed' by a Chief Constable who forgot the law.[63]

But Churchill's opinions on these matters were very variable. In the case of Henry Wilkins, a 'fence' sentenced to ten years after already serving an eight-year sentence for a similar offence, Churchill decided, against the advice of his officials and despite the fact that Wilkins had not appealed against his sentence, that this was too harsh a punishment: 'I still think the sentence excessive. Advise me how it can be mitigated.'[64] He wrote to the judge who tried the case demanding he justify the sentence. When the judge told him that it was the 'very worst case of receiving' he had come across in thirty-two years, Churchill backed down. He did not do so however in the case of Bessie Carter, who was serving a sentence for false pretences in Reading prison and was about to be released. Churchill intervened with the Chief Constable of Warwickshire and told him that it was his 'strong opinion' that he should not proceed with another warrant for her arrest on a similar charge. His reason was that she was mentally unstable but also that she came from a 'respectable family'. When the Chief Constable wrote to the Home Office to protest, Churchill commented: 'What does he mean by using such expression as "at a loss to understand" & "before taking further action"? His tone appears disrespectful & I am doubtful whether he shd be answered.' Sir Edward Troup eventually sent a letter rebuking the Chief Constable for daring to write in such a manner.[65]

Similarly in the case of Edward Leveson Churchill showed remarkable magnanimity. Leveson had been sentenced to five years for a fraud involving £4,000 (£140,000 at current prices) but with evidence that in total the sum involved amounted to over £100,000

(£3.5 million). Churchill received a petition from members of the Royal Navy, where Leveson had once served, saying that they were prepared to club together to give him some money so that he could go to Mexico to start a new life. Churchill felt that these were 'persons in whose statements confidence may be placed' and that since Leveson had served two years, which 'to educated men must amount to agony', he should be released. Such a decision though also involved freeing Leveson's accomplice – who had no influential friends and would not be given money to start a new life. Sir Edward Troup argued that the releases would be 'not in the public interest' but Churchill forced them through.[66]

Churchill's ability to hold inconsistent opinions on a single case is illustrated by the conviction of a habitual poacher, George Townsend, for having a gun and poaching. The magistrates, Home Office officials and lawyers all thought the evidence against Townsend on this particular charge was thin but sufficient. Churchill though, having come under pressure in the Commons where the case had been raised, simply ordered a free pardon. Troup told him: 'I do not think it is a case for a Free Pardon. The H.O. never deals with such cases on technical questions of evidence' but only on grounds of guilt or innocence, and pointed out that even Townsend had not claimed to be innocent. Churchill gave in and then in the Commons used the fact of Townsend's previous convictions as a reason why he should not intervene. Having dealt with the matter politically, he then forced embarrassed Home Office officials to write to the magistrates to tell them that the case should have been dismissed.[67]

When one of Lloyd George's meetings in the City of London was disrupted by pro-suffragette demonstrators, Churchill called for an immediate enquiry. This revealed that one of the organisers was a Victor Duval. Churchill had crossed swords with Duval earlier during one of his public meetings in Bristol and Duval had also had the temerity to approach Churchill and speak to him on the train from London. Churchill was determined to use all his influence against Duval. Without any supporting evidence he urged Sir Edward Troup to act: 'I have not the slightest doubt that he is highly paid for his action. You will know what steps should be taken to make sure that he is dealt with with adequate severity.' The Metropolitan Police were called in to investigate the pro-suffrage organisation founded by Duval but were unable to find any evidence they could use against him. Churchill was still not satisfied and, becoming increasingly emotional, issued a further set of instructions, claiming, 'The fact remains that an assassination with a Knife only could easily have taken place.' 'Effective measures' were to be taken against Duval, his 'circumstances and antecedents' were to be investigated by the police (he still expected to find that Duval and his friends were 'hired persons') and this information was to be given secretly to the magistrate in the trial before Duval's case came up so as to influence his sentence. Churchill concluded: 'The organisation of gangs of paid ruffians to make personal attacks on Ministers ought to be treated with the extreme rigour of the law.' Reports were duly produced on Duval, his wife and a close friend. Churchill was disappointed that nothing incriminating had been found but still called the prosecuting solicitor to the Home Office to discuss the case with him and asked him to secure 'exemplary sentences'. No doubt Churchill was further disappointed when Duval was only sentenced to seven days in prison.[68]

The most overtly dramatic moment of Churchill's time at the Home Office came in January 1911 when a gang of burglars (believed to be Latvians), who had shot three policemen and wounded two others during a break-in at a jeweller's shop in Houndsditch the previous month, were tracked down to a house in Stepney. It was the beginning of the notorious Sidney Street siege. At 10.45am on 3 January Churchill, who was still at home in Eccleston Square, was asked to approve the use of troops with rifles to deal with the burglars who were firing on police from the house. He agreed and arrived half an hour later at the Home Office where nothing more was known. Together with Edward Marsh he set off for Stepney, where he arrived just before midday and characteristically took charge of the operation – calling up artillery to demolish the house and personally checking on possible means of escape. When the house caught fire he ordered, probably with police consent, the fire brigade not to attempt to put it out. When the fire burnt itself out, two bodies were found and Churchill left the scene just before 3pm. His presence had been unnecessary and uncalled for – the senior Army and police officers present could easily have coped with the situation on their own authority. But Churchill with his thirst for action and drama could not resist the temptation. His intervention attracted huge publicity and for the first time raised in public doubts about Churchill's character and judgement, which some of his colleagues had already had in private, and which were to increase in the next few years.

Within a fortnight of the siege of Sidney Street Churchill circulated a draft Bill to the Cabinet to introduce harsh new laws against aliens. He had dropped a provision that he originally wanted giving the police the right to arrest any alien who had no obvious way of earning a living but had retained one that allowed an alien, if he could not find sureties for good behaviour, to be kept in prison until the Home Secretary, not the courts, was satisfied about his position. Churchill described this power as 'a fine piece of machinery'.[69] The Bill also contained what Churchill rather coyly described to his colleagues as 'two naughty principles' – a deliberate distinction between aliens and British subjects and the power to deport an alien merely on suspicion even though he had committed no criminal offence.[70] The Bill was introduced into the Commons by Churchill at the end of April but MPs refused to pass such an illiberal measure and it had to be withdrawn.

Behind the scenes Churchill was taking other measures to keep watch on aliens. In September 1911 the opposition raised the question of the need to compile a register of aliens. Churchill imperiously dismissed the suggestion: 'Neither will it be found possible to establish a system of registration for aliens . . . registration is not necessary and it would not be neither convenient or desirable.'[71] That speech was totally disingenuous. A year earlier he had himself raised the question of a register at a sub-committee of the Committee of Imperial Defence and by March 1911 the Home Office already had draft legislation prepared which authorised the setting up of a register covering large 'restricted areas' in the country. The head of MI5, Vernon Kell, liaised with Chief Constables and devised a form, which Churchill approved, for a return covering the name, residence, age, property owned and family particulars of any alien together with suspected acts of espionage and a wonderful all-embracing category of 'other circumstances of an unusual nature'.[72]

Churchill's contact with Kell over the aliens question was the beginning of his long and enthusiastic association with the world of intelligence. For the intelligence agencies (which the Liberal Government had only recently secretly established) the interception of mail was an important source of information. In 1911 Churchill changed the system for signing warrants to authorise this interception. Until then it had been considered a necessary safeguard for the Home Secretary to sign an individual warrant for each person whose mail was to be opened. Churchill introduced a much more flexible and open-ended system under which the Home Secretary could sign warrants covering certain categories of people and the intelligence agencies were able to include people in these categories without obtaining specific approval. Churchill also chaired a committee on the introduction of a form of press censorship for the first time in peace. In 1907 the Government had failed in an attempt to establish a legal system to censor the press before publication, although it did manage to pass the all-embracing Official Secrets Act in 1911. Churchill favoured more indirect means to 'secure in large measure that control which we so greatly desire'.[73] The scheme he devised relied on informal controls and Government advice to newspapers about what they should not publish, organised through the Admiralty and War Office Press Committee, a secret body that was the forerunner of the D-Notice Committee. This interest in and support for the intelligence agencies was one that Churchill would pursue more actively later in his career. But at the end of October 1911, after just eighteen months as Home Secretary, he moved to the Admiralty to undertake a series of reforms which senior members of the Government thought were essential if Britain's defence preparations were to be effective.

7

Admiralty

During his period at the Admiralty Churchill enjoyed to the full the perquisites of the job. As he told Asquith earlier, 'it is of course in its amenities & attractions much the most pleasant & glittering post in the Ministry'.[1] One of the 'amenities' was the First Lord's 'yacht', the *Enchantress* – in fact an ocean-going ship of 4,000 tons with a crew of over 100. Churchill used the *Enchantress* to take his family, friends and political colleagues on cruises around Britain and into the Mediterranean at public expense. The Churchill family also moved from Eccleston Square, which they had leased on moving from Churchill's Mayfair flat, to Admiralty House, the First Lord's official residence, and increased the number of their servants from five to nine. Their first child, Diana, had been born in July 1909 and immediately given to a wet nurse while Clementine spent many months recovering, first with her mother in Sussex and then in Cheshire with Lord Stanley's family (Clementine's cousins). The second child, Randolph, was born in May 1911 just before Churchill moved to the Admiralty. Churchill was away at Army camp with FE and other friends before the birth and afterwards Clementine recuperated at Seaford, with just a few visits from Churchill, and then in Bavaria with her sister-in-law Goonie. In February 1912 Clementine had a miscarriage and remained depressed throughout the summer. She found that she was unable to cope with the two children and they were left to the attentions of a series of inadequate nursery maids, growing up undisciplined, badly behaved and fractious.

Churchill saw little of his family. One problem was that Clementine did not like most of Churchill's political friends, in particular his cousins Ivor and Freddie Guest and Lloyd George, and she was looked down on by Asquith and his social circle. Another was that Churchill himself was still obsessed by work and political life and much of what little spare time he allowed himself was spent away from the family. He was active in the Queen's Own Oxfordshire Hussars where he was promoted to major without taking the necessary exam, through the influence of his friend Ian Hamilton at Southern Command. He was occasionally on manoeuvres with the Army but the Hussars were largely a social organisation and the officers were happy to spend their annual camp eating, drinking and riding in the grounds of Blenheim Palace. In 1911 Churchill and FE (who was also an officer in the Hussars) founded the 'Other Club', after Churchill was blackballed at the exclusive 'The Club'. Despite the bitter public differences between the parties it had a balance of party membership plus friends and relations of both FE and Churchill, including the Duke of Marlborough, the past and present private secretaries to the King, leading Army figures such as Kitchener and French, together with editors and owners of the press such as Garvin, Massingham, Riddell and Dalziell. It usually met once a fortnight during the Parliamentary session, though activity lapsed during the early part of 1914, probably because of the party disputes over the Government's proposals to grant home rule to Ireland. Churchill described the club to his cousin as 'a small intimate gathering of friends most of whom move in the same world. One does not want to go there to meet strangers.'[2]

Churchill was first involved in naval affairs during the major row that split the Cabinet in the winter of 1908–9 over naval spending. Here, for the first time, Churchill came up against the fundamental factor that was to shape all his political life – Britain's position as a great power was declining. Superficially the empire that Churchill had grown up with seemed the strongest power in the world. It stretched around the globe from Canada, through the West Indies, the tropical colonies of west and east Africa, the newly emerging dominion of South Africa to what was widely seen as the centre of the Empire – India – and then to the Far Eastern trading colonies of Singapore and Hong Kong and the white dominions of Australia and New Zealand. All these territories were linked by a series of island outposts and strategic ports and bases for the deployment of the Royal Navy. But this vast, sprawling Empire was not integrated politically, economically or strategically and it was a drain on Britain's very limited resources. An island of some forty milion people with an economy that was being rapidly overtaken by other powers, in particular the United States and Germany, could not find enough resources to ensure the defence of the Empire against a multiplicity of possible threats.

These problems first became apparent in decisions on naval policy. By the 1880s the old mid-nineteenth-century idea of the Pax Britannica was already dissolving. Until 1889, as a way of ensuring naval supremacy, it was British policy to maintain a fleet equal to that of the next two strongest powers combined. Then the requirement was redefined to take into account only the fleets of France and Russia, which were seen as Britain's likeliest enemies. By the end of the nineteenth century Britain had had to give up any idea of fighting the United States and therefore had to accept American domination of the western hemisphere. In 1902 the Anglo-Japanese alliance was signed as a way of protecting British possessions in the Far East, given the inability of the Royal Navy to deploy sufficient force in the area. This deteriorating strategic position was made worse by the German decision to begin building a fleet for action in the North Sea, whether as a defensive measure against the British fleet or with an aggressive aim was unclear. What was clear was that Britain could never afford to build a 'three-power' Navy capable of fighting France, Russia and Germany. Diplomatically too Britain's power was weakening. Alarmed at its isolation during the Boer War and facing a perceived threat to India from Russia, the Balfour Government decided to reach an entente with France, at first on colonial issues (but with implications for the European balance of power) to pave the way for a similar agreement with France's ally, Russia (something that was achieved by the Liberal Government in 1907).

Technological changes were also undermining the supremacy of the Royal Navy. The 1905 decision to begin constructing the first all-big-gun battleship (*HMS Dreadnought*), although inevitable given technical improvements, meant that Britain's existing 3:1 supremacy over the German fleet was effectively wiped out as construction concentrated on the new types. Now supremacy depended on the relative speed of ordering and construction, which in turn depended on the availability of national resources. In 1905 the Conservative Government had suggested an ordering programme of four dreadnoughts a year. Numbers were reduced by the Liberal Cabinet in 1906 and again the year after because the Germans did not begin building their own dreadnoughts until 1907. In December 1907 the Admiralty had itself suggested building only one dreadnought in 1908–9 because of Britain's wide lead. Indeed in 1909 Britain had four dreadnoughts and three smaller battlecruisers in service whereas no other nation had any, and by 1910 the Royal Navy still expected to have a seven to three lead over the Germans. Overall Britain's naval power still met the two-power standard because of the large losses the Russians had sustained during the 1904–5 war with Japan.

Six months after Churchill joined the Cabinet Reginald McKenna, First Lord of the Admiralty, proposed that the minimum construction for 1909–10 should be six dreadnoughts, with a possibility of moving to eight, which was the maximum industrial capacity. The arguments for this increase were based on some dubious assumptions about possible German building programmes that could give the Germans a theoretical 21:18 lead in dreadnoughts by 1912. The likely increase in expenditure was £6 million a year. The Admiralty, and in particular the First Sea Lord, Admiral 'Jacky' Fisher, were backed by the Conservative opposition and a virulent press campaign ('We want eight and we won't wait') based on the fear of Britain's supposed vulnerability. Most of the senior members of the Cabinet – Grey, Haldane, Asquith and Runciman – supported the Admiralty. Churchill was ranged unequivocally with the 'economisers' led by Lloyd George and including Morley, Loreburn, Burns and Harcourt, who argued that four dreadnoughts would be sufficient. Many in the political élite had their doubts about Churchill's motives in opposing increased defence spending. In July 1908 during the fight over the Army estimates, Lord Esher, a courtier who held no official position but who was constantly involved in defence planning, wrote that 'Winston wanted to push himself to the front of the Cabinet. He thinks himself Napoleon.'[3] And during the naval estimates dispute the King's Private Secretary, Lord Knollys, wrote to Esher: 'What are Winston's motives for acting as he does in this matter? Of course it cannot be from conviction or principle. The very idea of him having either is enough to make anyone laugh.'[4]

By the end of January 1909 the Cabinet was deadlocked. Churchill was convinced that the whole episode was attributable to 'a naval panic'[5] and, working closely with Rear Admiral Custance, an ex-head of naval intelligence, and an ex-naval architect, Sir William White (both members of the strong anti-Fisher group in the Navy who hoped to force his resignation if only four orders were placed), he was able to draft papers showing an unexpectedly impressive knowledge of the minutiae of British and German naval programmes. On 2 February he argued that the Germans would have to pay off older ships as the new dreadnoughts came into service and even if they reached equality in dreadnoughts by 1912, Britain would still have twenty-two more older battleships and twenty-seven more armoured cruisers than Germany. Churchill concluded: 'It cannot therefore be argued that national security is involved in the question ... No justification has in my view been shown for 6.'[6] The next day he wrote privately to Asquith arguing for an agreed long term naval building programme and accepting Grey's proposed compromise 'of 4 ships declared now, & 2 others later if in Oct circumstances require them' – in contradiction to his argument in Cabinet the previous day.[7] On 24 February the Cabinet agreed to order four dreadnoughts immediately and another four before the end of the financial year if necessary – even though Fisher himself thought six were needed at most. By July the Government confirmed that eight would in fact be ordered. Churchill was right when he thought it was all a naval panic – there was no acceleration in German building and no plans for one. (In April 1912, supposedly the time of maximum danger, Britain had seventeen dreadnoughts operational compared with a German force of nine.)

In 1908–9 Churchill also argued strongly that there was no real quarrel between Britain and Germany. In a major speech at Swansea on 14 August 1908 he gave his reasons:

I think it is greatly to be deprecated that persons should try to spread the belief in this country that war between Great Britain and Germany is inevitable. It is all nonsense ... There is no collision of primary interests – big, important interests – between Great Britain and Germany in any quarter of the globe ... there is no real cause of difference between them, and although there may be snapping and snarling in the newspapers and in the London clubs, these two great peoples have nothing to fight about, have no prize to fight for, and have no place to fight in.

Picking his words for his audience, he went on to praise working-class solidarity between nations because the working class had no quarrels, and he said of Germany 'we do not envy them their power and their prosperity'. At no point did he mention trade rivalry; he dismissed colonial rivalry as unimportant and he did not discuss the rise of the German Navy.

Within Government Churchill was largely excluded from important strategic debates until well into 1911. He, like most of the Cabinet, was not aware that a small inner group had in 1905–6 authorised detailed discussions with the French over how the British Army might intervene in any war against Germany. He was also excluded from the Cabinet committee on foreign policy that Asquith established in 1911. Churchill was made a member of the Committee of Imperial Defence when he became Home Secretary in 1910 but by then the committee had become no more than a co-ordinating body to resolve detailed technical questions rather than a supreme body to decide British strategy. Churchill first moved into this field during the Agadir crisis in the summer of 1911 when the despatch of the German gunboat *Panther* to the Moroccan port, in response to an extension of French influence in the area and demands for German colonial compensation elsewhere, raised the possibility of a European war. The British Government, as in the 1905–6 Moroccan crisis, found itself, in the last resort, siding with France though they refused to make any public commitment and continued to hope that a conference would resolve the crisis (which it eventually did in September).

On 21 July Lloyd George, with the approval of Asquith and Grey, made a belligerent speech at the Mansion House that was widely seen as a warning to Germany. It was, for the first time, a public defection from the radical camp by Lloyd George (he had been much less radical in private for years) and he was followed by his supporter, Churchill. The next day the journalist C. P. Scott noted in his diary a meeting with Lloyd George, Churchill and Elibank during which 'Churchill's only contributions to the discussion were highly rhetorical denunciations repeated at intervals of the insolence of Germany and the need of asserting ourselves and teaching her a lesson. Every question with him becomes a personal question.'[8]

A month later Churchill was present at a meeting of carefully selected senior ministers to decide British strategy if a decision were taken to intervene in a Franco-German war. Ministers found that defence planning was a shambles and that the Army and Navy were still intending to fight completely different wars. The Army planned to send 160,000 troops to fight on the left flank of the French to counter any German advance. The Royal Navy had made no plans to escort this force across the Channel and since 1906 had been planning a highly dubious series of raids on German ports and an operation to land the Army on the Baltic coast of Germany from where it would march on Berlin and end the war. The Royal Navy presentation of its case was poor and Asquith described its plans as 'puerile'.[9] Churchill described the Admiralty to Lloyd George as 'cocksure, *insouciant* and apathetic'.[10] The main consequence of this meeting was an agreement among senior ministers that the Admiralty needed a major shake-up and that Reginald McKenna, the First Lord, should be moved. After much lobbying from both Churchill and Haldane, Asquith chose Churchill, who exchanged offices with McKenna in late October 1911 amid universal hostility from the press. The *Spectator* argued that Churchill did not have 'the loyalty, the dignity, the steadfastness, and the good sense which make an efficient head of a great office. He must always be living in the limelight.' The *National Review* was even more abusive, describing him as 'a windbag', 'a political gambler of the worst type' and 'a self-advertising mountebank'.

The main reason for sending Churchill to the Admiralty was to establish a proper planning staff, along the lines of the General Staff created at the War Office, so that the Royal Navy could devise a coherent set of plans for a future war. Until 1911 such plans as existed remained in the head of the First Sea Lord. Churchill failed in this task and preferred to adopt a system that gave him substantial control and did not ruffle too many feathers among the admirals. Although an Admiralty War Staff was set up in January 1912 with operational, intelligence and mobilisation divisions, it did little more than combine the existing functions of the old intelligence, trade and ordnance divisions of the Admiralty. Although a Staff College was established, few good officers were prepared or encouraged to attend and so there were hardly any suitably trained officers in the War Staff. The major problem though was that the First Sea Lord refused to become a chief of staff because he felt it demeaned his office. The War Staff achieved little before 1914 and never developed the stature of the General Staff. In December 1911 Churchill proposed a wholesale take-over of the nation's war planning through a 'Naval War Circle' under his own chairmanship which would combine all Government departments engaged in strategic planning. Not surprisingly Asquith vetoed the idea.

In bringing about these and other changes at the Admiralty Churchill relied heavily on the now retired Admiral Fisher, who had been First Sea Lord from 1904 till 1910. Fisher had brought about reforms in training, equipment and manning although he resolutely opposed any form of war staff or coherent planning. He was an arrogant, difficult man, tactless, autocratic and stern with a streak of mania but someone who responded quickly to any affection. His actions and character had split the Royal Navy into two camps – his favourites and those he regarded as 'traitors'. Churchill had first become infatuated with Fisher when they met at Biarritz in 1907 and Fisher remained one of the few people who could make Churchill stop talking and listen – but they drifted apart following the row over the 1909–10 naval estimates. Fisher had re-established contact in 1910 after his retirement and within days of taking over the Admiralty Churchill had begun consulting him about appointments and policy. Altogether Fisher sent Churchill eight letters in eleven days and at one point Churchill was on the verge of asking him to come back as First Sea Lord but Asquith blocked the idea.

Churchill followed some of Fisher's advice about appointments and unleashed one of the most disruptive periods ever within the Admiralty. Within a week of taking over Churchill found that Fisher's successor as First Sea Lord, Admiral Wilson, would not agree to even a limited version of the war staff plan. Asquith agreed to his removal and Admiral Bridgeman was chosen as his replacement. Churchill made this choice on Fisher's advice: Bridgeman was thought to be pliable and an excellent front for the Second Sea Lord, Prince Louis of Battenberg. Fisher informed Churchill that Battenberg 'has no friends at all but you and me' and said of Bridgeman that 'he has no genius whatever for administration', but Churchill felt that he was 'a splendid sailor and a gentleman'.[11]

Bridgeman only lasted as First Sea Lord for a year. In October 1912 he complained about Churchill's style in running the Admiralty, in particular the way he issued orders without consultation, and he threatened to go to Asquith and the King if Churchill did not change his ways. On hearing this Churchill broke down in tears and talked about his poor health. (There were similar complaints from the Prime Minister of Canada about the way Churchill sent papers without the agreement of the Admiralty Board and Asquith eventually had to stop Churchill's drafts going to Canada.) There then followed an unseemly struggle between the two men. Churchill rather prematurely told Battenberg on 14 November that he was to take over as the new First Sea Lord. A fortnight later he suggested to Bridgeman that he should retire on health grounds (Churchill had probably been shown a private letter from Bridgeman to Battenberg in which he expressed worries about his health). Immediately afterwards Churchill saw Asquith and the King and obtained their agreement to the appointment of Battenberg. At the beginning of December when Bridgeman wrote to say that his doctors were happy for him to continue in office, it was too late and he was forced to go. In the middle of December Bridgeman leaked the details of his enforced resignation to an opposition newspaper. Churchill immediately wrote him a letter threatening that unless Bridgeman agreed to a statement that there was no disagreement on policy, he would publicise the fact that as Second Sea Lord Bridgeman had refused to make any proposals to improve naval pay, that as First Sea Lord he had rarely attended the Committee of Imperial Defence and that he had written to Battenberg about his ill-health. Bridgeman refused to agree to these terms and Churchill, in an attempt to defend himself, revealed these details in the Commons.

Churchill's relations with other senior admirals produced equally stormy episodes. In November 1913 Churchill intervened in a dispute over some land in the Medway area and ordered Captain Vivian of *HMS Hermes* to accept plans drawn up by one of his lieutenants rather than his own proposal. Vivian complained about Churchill's interference to Admiral Poore, Commander-in-Chief Nore, who immediately wrote a letter of complaint to Admiral Jellicoe, the Second Sea Lord. Churchill found out about Poore's complaint and ordered Jellicoe to show him any letter he received from Poore. Before doing so, Jellicoe sent Poore's letter back to be redrafted in a more tactful vein. Churchill again discovered what was happening and in a huge temper ordered the Post Office to intercept the letter and deliver it to him personally. Such an order was illegal but they complied. After reading the letter Churchill worked himself up into an even more furious temper and ordered Poore to haul down his flag. At this point, unable to stand any more, Battenberg told Churchill that all the members of the Admiralty Board were about to resign. The situation was saved through the intervention of Sir Francis Hopwood, the civil servant who was secretary to the board (Churchill had asked him to transfer from the Colonial Office). Poore was eventually persuaded to withdraw his letter of protest although, as Hopwood told the King: 'Winston would not be flattered if he knew the arguments used by the Naval Lords to keep the Commander-in-Chief from going. They were in short that he (Churchill) was so much off his head over the whole business that Poore need take no notice of it.'[12]

A month after this incident there was another episode scarcely calculated to endear Churchill to his naval colleagues. When Admiral Limpus, the British adviser to the Turkish Navy, sent Churchill a despatch that failed to satisfy Churchill's standards of English and his always acute sense of his own dignity, he was rebuked like a schoolboy: 'A flag officer writing to a member of the Board of Admiralty on service matters ought to observe a proper seriousness and formality. The letters should be well written or typed on good paper; the sentences should be complete and follow the regular English form . . . No one can be so busy as not to be able to cast a letter to a superior in a proper form.'[13]

One of Churchill's first tasks at the Admiralty, after his failure to establish a full war staff, was to deal with internal reform of the Royal Navy. The senior service was still characterised by a rigid social hierarchy, poor conditions of service and harsh discipline. About 2,000 men a year were deserting, a third resigned at the first opportunity and recruiting was extremely difficult. Since 1900, partly under Fisher's influence, there had been a few reforms – better food, provision of some part of the uniform by the Royal Navy, a suspension of the birching of boy seamen and in 1909 a major reform of naval prisons. The scandal of naval conditions became a major public issue in the autumn of 1911 with the publication of *Our Fighting Sea Men* by Lional Yaxley, the editor of a lower deck newspaper. Fisher introduced Yaxley to Churchill and as a result of their talk, and under increasing public pressure, Churchill set up a series of enquiries. One on the use of summary punishments by officers proposed some limited reforms – abolition of standing facing the paintwork as a punishment, removal of the general ban on card playing and introducton of better leave arrangements. Churchill had a tough time forcing even these limited reforms, together with improved treatment for petty officers, through the Navy.

In some areas, where he had strong personal opinions, Churchill was more reluctant to accept Fisher's and Yaxley's lead. He was not for instance prepared to radically change the social structure of the Navy. Between 1820 and 1900 just two men had been promoted from the lower deck to be officers. During his time as First Sea Lord Fisher had introduced a scheme to widen opportunities but it was still restricted to the older petty officer at the end of his career who could not rise beyond lieutenant. Service attitudes were well reflected by the *Naval and Military Record* which wrote in June 1910 that 'The British Navy has long obtained an ample supply of capable officers . . . without recruiting from the Democracy to any visible extent . . . we should view with grave apprehension any attempt to officer the fleet at all largely with men of humble birth.' Under Churchill the scheme for promotion from the ranks was widened slightly but only teetotallers and single men were allowed to apply (the latter restriction was to stop other officers' wives having to mix socially with lower-class people) but seniority was not antedated and this ensured that candidates could never be promoted to a senior rank. Not surprisingly very few petty officers applied. Immediately after this small concession was announced, Churchill suggested to Battenberg, as a 'counterpoise', a major drive to recruit more officers direct from public schools rather than through Dartmouth, the training college, so as to maintain social exclusivity.[14]

Another area where reform was overdue was pay and pensions, which had not been increased since 1853. Under considerable pressure Churchill announced in the Commons in July 1912 that increases would be forthcoming. He did not give a figure because he had not been able to obtain agreement within the Government. He was working with Yaxley on a scheme for a total increase of about

£500,000 a year based on an extra 4d a day for those who had served for six years. By November Churchill was forced to cut the increase to 3d a day after his tactics and presentation of his case failed to convince his colleagues. The stormy scene in Cabinet was described by Hobhouse: 'We had the usual display of bad manners and bad temper from Churchill . . . he stormed, sulked, interrupted like an ill-bred cub. The P.M. treated him admirably and finally reduced him to silence.'[15] The internal reforms introduced by Churchill, though important, were probably the minimum that the Admiralty could concede given the rising external pressure orchestrated by Yaxley and others.

The other major reform introduced in Churchill's time at the Admiralty was the introduction of oil instead of coal to fire ships' boilers. This had long been an objective for Fisher and by 1912 the Admiralty itself had virtually accepted the need for the change-over. With some difficulty Churchill persuaded Fisher to head a royal commission to investigate the subject – it was not to be an impartial enquiry; with Fisher in the chair the outcome was obvious. As expected, the report found that there were overwhelming advantages in using oil – higher speed, increased radius of action, easier refuelling and manpower savings – and recommended that a stockpile of four years' supplies should be established.

The decision was taken to change over gradually to oil and in June 1913 Churchill obtained the Cabinet's agreement to build up a war reserve of six months' supply. Implementation of the decision proved difficult. Great importance was attached to sources of supply – the Cabinet had agreed it should be based on long-term contracts but drawn from a wide geographical area and from sources under British control if possible. The Anglo-Persian Oil Company (which had a monopoly in central and southern Persia but was financially weak and under pressure from the Royal Dutch Shell group over concessions in Mesopotamia) suggested that the Government should take over the company in order to ensure a continuity of supplies under British control. In December Churchill and the Admiralty rejected the offer.

The Admiralty tried to negotiate long-term contracts, but did not want to deal with Shell because of its Dutch connections, and found that although Anglo-Persian were prepared to supply oil on a long-term basis at low cost, the company wanted substantial advance payments. This raised doubts about the wisdom of making such payments to a company in a precarious financial state. In July 1913 the Cabinet agreed that they should acquire 'a controlling interest in trustworthy sources of supply'[16] and Churchill announced this general policy to the Commons five days later. No details were given. Nine months of further negotiation led to a Government decision to take a majority shareholding in Anglo-Persian for £2.2 million, in return for a guaranteed supply of six million tons of oil over twenty years, though the latter contract was to remain secret from Parliament. The Navy's conversion to oil and the negotiations leading up to the nationalisation of what became BP were not a brilliant political coup engineered by Churchill personally. The idea of oil-fired ships had been pushed by Fisher for some time, and the original suggestion of a Government purchase of shares came from the company, was rejected in the first instance by Churchill and only carried out as a last resort when it became clear that the risks involved in making large advance payments to a shaky private company were too great.

The most difficult problems Churchill had to face at the Admiralty stemmed from Britain's declining ability to safeguard its own territory and the Empire given the resources it could make available for defence. Churchill was at the centre of the decision-taking process, together with some of his Cabinet colleagues. They needed to work out how much could be spent on naval construction and then how best to deploy the available ships. Churchill, like most of his colleagues, realised that the primary threat came from Germany and Britain might not have enough resources to provide adequate defences elsewhere. But any failure to do so posed difficult strategic and diplomatic questions.

After the resolution of the Agadir crisis there was what proved to be the last effort to regulate the competition in naval construction with Germany and reach some sort of political accommodation. Despite his earlier speeches about the lack of Anglo-German rivalry Churchill had now reversed his position and did his best to sabotage any chances of an agreement being reached. These were always slight – Germany wanted a pledge of British neutrality in a future war in return for minor naval cutbacks, whereas Britain wanted a substantial reduction in German naval construction in return for minor political concessions in Africa. The first informal contacts were made through Churchill's wealthy banker friend, Sir Ernest

Cassel, and the head of the Hamburg-Amerika line, Albert Ballin. Early in January 1912 Churchill refused to go to Berlin with Cassel to meet Ballin since he felt this would give the talks too official a tone, and he also ensured that Grey, the Foreign Secretary, did not go either. However, at the end of January Cassel did make the trip, taking with him a memorandum drafted by Churchill, Lloyd George and Asquith. Five days later the Cabinet, having been consulted for the first time, decided that Haldane, who had many contacts in Germany, should go for three days of official discussions. Although Churchill accepted this as a collective decision, in the middle of Haldane's visit he quite deliberately ruined the atmosphere for the talks with a speech in Glasgow in which he said that British construction would rise faster than any other country if this was necessary and he insultingly described the German fleet as 'a luxury'.

Haldane brought back with him a copy of the new German naval programme, and Churchill presented the Admiralty's analysis of the plan to the Cabinet. Germany had been building two dreadnoughts a year while Britain, in order to maintain a sixty per cent supremacy (the most that the Cabinet thought could be afforded), had been alternating between three and four a year. Now the Germans proposed to alternate between two and three, which would force the British to build five and four alternately if they were to keep their advantage in numbers. In addition the readiness of the German fleet was to be increased through the creation of a permanent third battle squadron. Desultory discussions continued through March and April but came to nothing. Churchill made a specious offer of a 'holiday' in naval construction – with the increased level of German construction to come it could only benefit Britain. It was inevitably rejected by Germany but served its political purpose in allowing Britain to make a pacific gesture. In the two years after 1912 there were other contacts between Britain and Germany but they were not taken seriously on either side and the two countries continued to build up their navies competitively.

Churchill inherited a situation at the Admiralty where for years major ships had been steadily withdrawn from around the world and stationed in Europe, mainly to counter the increasing German fleet. So far Britain had been able to maintain a considerable fleet in the Mediterranean, through which passed half of Britain's food supply and where a number of vital strategic interests such as the Suez

Canal and the crumbling Ottoman Empire were situated. At the end of 1904 the Mediterranean fleet was reduced from fourteen to eight, with eight battleships of the Atlantic fleet stationed at Gibraltar able to move in either direction, although this possible force of sixteen was reduced to twelve after 1907. The situation in the Mediterranean that Churchill had to face by 1912 had been worsened by the decision of Austro-Hungary and then Italy to start dreadnought construction, which meant that Britain's older battleships would be outclassed. After the failure of the talks with Germany, Churchill announced in the Commons on 18 March 1912 that Britain was formally abandoning a two-power naval standard and would only be able to maintain a sixty per cent advantage over Germany. In order to achieve even this limited superiority the Atlantic fleet would be moved from Gibraltar to home waters and the small, obsolete Mediterranean fleet moved from Malta to Gibraltar. The seemingly remorseless decline of British naval power was gathering pace.

This decision concentrated Britain's available strength against the main threat but left an ineffective British fleet in the Mediterranean. At the end of May Asquith and Churchill left for a cruise in the Mediterranean that was largely a holiday but which also involved a three-day conference at Malta to discuss future policy in the area. On their return to London Churchill put a major paper to the Cabinet. The crux of the problem was the overwhelming need for a fleet that could defeat Germany. As he had told Haldane in May: 'The actual point has been settled long ago by the brute force of facts. We cannot possibly hold the Mediterranean or guarantee any of our interests there until we have obtained a decision in the North Sea.'[17] His Cabinet paper argued that Britain could not afford to build a major fleet in the Mediterranean for many years if at all and that by 1915 there would be at least ten Austrian and Italian dreadnoughts rendering the current British fleet there obsolete. The crews from these ships were urgently needed to man better quality ships in home waters. Nor could Britain afford to engage in a naval race with Austria and Italy. The conclusion was stark: according to Churchill, 'the naval control of the Mediterranean is swiftly passing from our hands whatever we do' and Britain would have to adopt a role 'appropriate to the weaker naval power'.[18] The most that Britain could provide there in future would be two battlecruisers. The inevitable consequence was that Britain would have to reach an agreement with France over the disposition of their respective navies.

Churchill was rightly concentrating Britain's limited naval strength against the main threat (Germany) but his message of implied imperial weakness and declining power did not go down well with his Cabinet colleagues. For a month, from mid-June to mid-July, ministers and senior officials grappled with the dilemma. Churchill's main opponent was McKenna, his predecessor at the Admiralty – the two men shared a deep personal rivalry and strong mutual dislike. McKenna argued that Churchill's proposals would inevitably lead to a *de facto* alliance with France and that the only alternative was to build more ships and station eight dreadnoughts at Malta. Churchill responded that Britain could not afford such a programme (and a subsequent attempt to induce Canada to pay for three dreadnoughts collapsed). The crucial confrontation came at an all-day meeting of the Committee of Imperial Defence on 4 July. The atmosphere, according to Fisher, was tense: 'McKenna and Winston were tearing each other's eyes out the whole time.'[19] Both McKenna and Lloyd George felt that the Admiralty were allowing too great a margin of strength in the North Sea, but Churchill threatened to resign if his judgement was not accepted, and carried the day – ships would not move away from the area of the greatest threat. But in the longer term Churchill was forced to accept the CID compromise that once an adequate fleet in the North Sea had been created, Britain should have a fleet 'equal to a one-power Mediterranean standard excluding France' (which effectively meant Austria). Further concessions to Churchill's opponents followed. The Cabinet agreed, after four more difficult meetings, that Britain should maintain four battle-cruisers in the Mediterranean in the immediate future. During these meetings Churchill's tactics alienated his colleagues. When he again threatened to resign on 5 July, Hobhouse noted 'this ultimatum fell quite flat except that one or two muttered, as all felt, that they wished to goodness he would go' and on 10 July Churchill was again 'most abusive and insulting to McKenna'.[20] In fact Churchill ensured he got his way regardless of the Cabinet decision. In practice it took a year to find three ships and this total was not increased. By the end of 1913 Churchill told the Cabinet that there was no chance of sending any dreadnoughts to the Mediterranean for at least three years.

Having agreed in effect that it could no longer maintain a major fleet in the Mediterranean, the Government now had to reach an accommodation with France. The French too faced a difficult strategic problem, operating from two widely separated bases (Brest and Toulon) against two fleets – Germany and Austro-Hungary. Since 1895 the Mediterranean had increasingly become their main priority. Anglo-French naval discussions had been taking place intermittently and at a low level for years, and continued under Churchill. In early 1912 they agreed on respective patrol zones in the Atlantic and Mediterranean. In July 1912, four days before announcing to Parliament Britain's new naval dispositions, Churchill gave details to the French Naval Attaché and suggested higher-level staff talks. In September 1912 the French decided to concentrate their forces in the Mediterranean, where they would be the major naval power.

The question was now whether Britain should formalise the position and accept that only the French could protect British interests in the Mediterranean and, in return, that Britain would have to be responsible for defending the northern French coastline. Such a peacetime agreement would obviously entail some moral obligations if the French found themselves at war with Germany but with their fleet in the Mediterranean. Writing to Asquith and Grey in August 1912 Churchill tried to play down the commitments involved in any agreement:

> I am anxious to safeguard . . . our freedom of choice if the occasion arises, and consequent power to influence French policy before-hand. That freedom will be sensibly impaired if the French can say that they have denuded their Atlantic seaboard, and concentrated in the Mediterranean on the faith of naval arrangements made with us. This will not be true.[21]

While Churchill's argument was technically correct, in practice obligations were incurred. At the end of November 1912 the Cabinet agreed an exchange of notes with France. The two countries stated that the disposition of their fleets was an independent matter, but agreed to hold immediate discussions in the event of war.

Within three months of this agreement Britain had told France that while they would try to keep enough ships in the Mediterranean for 'a reasonable chance of success' against the Austrian fleet, they might have to withdraw even more ships to home waters, in which case the residue would come under French command in the event of war. Other agreements were made on patrolling the straits of Dover, the western Channel and the Far East, code books were exchanged and intelligence swapped about the German fleet. Although there was no legally binding treaty of alliance, Britain had, because of its naval weakness, been forced into a position where *de facto* it was militarily, and therefore diplomatically, intertwined with France. As Churchill had warned Grey in January 1912, relocation of the bulk of the British fleet to home waters to counter the German Navy would inevitably mean reliance 'on France in the Meditn, and certainly no exchange of system [the Anglo-French and Anglo-Russian ententes] would be possible, even if desired by you'.[22] Growing British weakness meant, as Churchill wrote in August 1912, that 'we have the obligations of an alliance without its advantages and above all without its precise definitions'.[23] The events of late July and early August 1914 were to show the truth of that remark.

The growing expense of maintaining Britain's naval strength embroiled the Cabinet in another prolonged and acrimonious dispute over the naval estimates for 1914–15. It began when Churchill submitted his draft estimates on 5 December 1913 asking for a total of £50.7 million, an increase of £3 million over 1913–14 and nearly twenty per cent above the level two years before. (The cost of the Navy had been only £22 million a year at the turn of the century.) When he moved to the Admiralty Churchill naturally forgot his strong campaign against increased naval expenditure. Even with the increased expenditure, it was proving very difficult to keep up the sixty per cent margin over Germany; in 1913 Churchill had only managed it by assuming three dominion ships (which were never built) and including two pre-dreadnoughts of the Lord Nelson class that were not up to modern standards. Under pressure, the Admiralty was considering reducing the margin required to fifty per cent.

Churchill hoped for powerful support from the Treasury for his proposals as Lloyd George had struck a bargain with him over the 1914–15 estimates – the Chancellor would support higher spending in the short term in return for Churchill's support for his land reform campaign and the promise of reductions in future. However, as the Government's ability to fund its social programmes without major tax increases seemed in doubt, the scene was set for a repeat of the row five years earlier over naval expenditure.

The main opposition to Churchill's proposals came from eight of the more radical members of the Cabinet – Samuel, Hobhouse, Pease, Runciman, Beauchamp, Simon, Harcourt and McKenna (despite the latter's advocacy of increased expenditure for the Mediterranean in 1912). Their objection was not just to the level of proposed expenditure but also to the ordering of four more dreadnoughts; they suggested two. When a concerted attack was launched on Churchill at the Cabinet meeting on 16 December, Lloyd George, as guardian of public expenditure, felt he had no alternative but to join those who sought economies. As Hobhouse noticed: 'An interesting feature . . . was LlG's repudiation of the bargain, which had evidently been come to between Churchill and himself, as soon as he saw others were prepared to fight Churchill.' Asquith supported Lloyd George and 'Churchill therefore protested his inability to carry on and went off characteristically *banging* the despatch box and door as he went out as loud as he could'.[24] Under pressure, he submitted marginally reduced estimates the next day but on 18 December told Asquith that he would resign if the order for four dreadnoughts was not accepted.

Churchill spent the New Year in Paris and returned to find that Lloyd George, in a pointed interview in the *Daily Chronicle* on 1 January, had reminisced about Lord Randolph Churchill's resignation over 'bloated and profligate' arms expenditure. Churchill defiantly upped the political stakes by submitting another set of revised estimates £2.5 million above his pre-Christmas figures. He also sent the Cabinet a paper arguing that Britain's position was under threat all over the world. It contained the following passage:

> we are not a young people with *an innocent record and* a scanty inheritance. We have engrossed to ourselves, in time when other powerful nations were paralysed by barbarism or internal war, an *altogether disproportionate* share of the wealth and traffic of the world. We have got all we want in territory, and our claim to be left in the unmolested enjoyment of vast and splendid possessions, *mainly acquired by violence, largely maintained by force*, often seems less reasonable to others than to us.[25]

This unflattering description of Britain's imperial past was too blunt for Churchill later in life – when he published the paper in *The World Crisis* in the 1920s he omitted all the phrases in italics.

For some members of the Cabinet who disliked Churchill this bid for increased naval expenditure was an ideal opportunity to attack him. Churchill's Permanent Secretary, Sir Francis Hopwood, reported to King George V's Private Secretary, Lord Stamfordham: 'The Fact is the Cabinet is sick of Churchill's perpetually undermining & exploiting its policy and are picking a quarrel with him. As a colleague he is a great trial to them.'[26] C. P. Scott reported that: 'Both he [Simon] and Lloyd George strongly of opinion that Churchill was only waiting for a favourable opportunity to leave the party.'[sic][27] But compromise was always likely – Churchill could not carry the rest of the Admiralty Board with him in favour of resignation and Lloyd George, despite his attack in the Cabinet before Christmas, was still willing to give him a way out by agreeing to an immediate increase in return for a commitment to reductions later. At first Churchill drafted a letter to Asquith refusing any idea of future reductions – 'it wd not be possible for me to give an assurance to Plt that the 1915–16 Estimates will not exceed those of 1914–15'[28] – but probably realising that this might cut off his eventual retreat did not send the letter. Within nine days he had done just such a deal with Lloyd George and shown it to Asquith. During a series of exhausting Cabinet meetings in the first ten days of February a compromise agreement was finally reached. Four dreadnoughts would be ordered and expenditure in 1914–15 would be £51.6 million (almost £1 million higher than Churchill's opening bid in December but just under £2 million lower than his revised figure in January) with a reduction to £49.5 million the next year. Parliament was to be given an assurance of a further reduction in 1915–16, though the amount would not be quantified. Whether the deal would have stood the test of time was never put to the trial.

During his spell at the Admiralty Churchill, as a member of the Cabinet, had to face two major political issues – votes for women and Home Rule for Ireland. The growing campaign for votes for women, with its militant wing that disrupted ministerial meetings, attacked ministers and committed acts of violence, split the Liberal Government. Asquith for example was opposed in principle to giving the vote to women whereas others such as Grey, Haldane and Lloyd

George were much more sympathetic to their case. Any attempt at legislation would also have to tackle other difficult issues about the franchise. Should women be given the vote on the same limited basis as men (which would probably favour the Conservatives) or should there be a massive extension of the franchise to encompass virtually all adults as part of a major reform of the voting system? The Cabinet was never able to agree on a coherent and consistent policy and as a result, despite a number of efforts, no legislation was passed before the outbreak of war. Churchill's stance was at best deliberately ambiguous, at worst downright hypocritical on the subject – in public he intimated that he would support votes for women at the right time and on the right basis whereas in private he was strongly opposed. In March 1904, while he was negotiating for a Liberal seat, he had actually voted in favour of enfranchisement. In the House of Commons on 12 July 1910 Churchill spoke out against a Bill giving partial enfranchisement to women, and justified his opposition by attacking the provision omitting most married women and hinting that he wanted a full adult vote at age twenty-five (which would have disenfranchised many men). Again in a speech in Dundee in December 1910 he told his constituents that he supported the principle of female suffrage.

In private Churchill's views had not changed from the total hostility he had shown to female suffrage in India fifteen years earlier. He did not believe there was a real grievance to be remedied. In a private memorandum he wrote, 'in principle the absolute sex barrier is illogical yet there is no great practical grievance'.[29] When he attacked the Bill omitting married women in July 1910, one of the campaigners for the Bill wrote to protest, warning him 'I shall further state that you said what was false when you gave the House to understand that you are in favour of adult suffrage. You told me that you are strongly opposed to the duplicated vote of married women.'[30] Churchill replied that he would favour adult suffrage 'at the proper time & circumstances' (both of which were left carefully undefined).[31]

When the question was discussed in the Cabinet in December 1911 he wrote to Lloyd George deploring the 'mawkish frenzy' with which the latter supported votes for women and warned him that if he and Grey pressed for the enfranchisement of '8,000,000 women [i.e. full adult female suffrage] *without a fresh appeal to the country* . . .

I could not find any good foothold for common action ... I could not go with you in a campaign ... which would not be for the good of the country'.[32] Churchill argued that 'the only safe and honest course is to have a referendum – first to the women to know if they want it, and then to the men to know if they will give it'.[33] This double referendum was unlikely to produce a result in favour, as Churchill told Asquith: 'it would probably get smashed wh again wd be a solution'.[34] Churchill also discussed the idea with the Conservative opposition through FE (who was also strongly opposed to female suffrage) in order to obtain their support and stop them pointing out the inconsistency of any Liberal support for a referendum on this issue whilst rejecting one on Home Rule.

As so often with Churchill his hostile stance was strongly influenced by his personal experiences. C. P. Scott reported that Churchill confessed he did not favour giving the vote to more than very select categories of women such as graduates and doctors (no more than 100,000 in total – the complete opposite of his public position), and noted 'he practically admitted that his present wrecking tactics are the outcome of resentment at the treatment he has received from the W.P.S.U.' (the Women's Political and Social Union).[35] Churchill objected to their tactics of harassing known opponents of women's suffrage. But the extent of his hostility to a general widening of the franchise was typical of his persistently élitist views on how the country should be governed. Churchill remained opposed to an extension of the vote to more men, indeed he wanted to raise the voting age to twenty-five. In January 1913 he opposed the idea of giving soldiers the vote fearing armed rebellion. He told the Cabinet that extending soldiers' votes would only stimulate a 'class campaign' for the improvement of soldiers' working conditions and that they would 'force their will on any point they care about sufficiently by the use of lethal weapons'.[36] He also told Lord Riddell that he was opposed to any general extension of the franchise: 'The truth is we already have enough ignorant votes and don't want any more.'[37] He was not in the Government when the decision was taken to extend the vote to virtually all men and women over thirty (introduced in 1918) but in 1928 he still insisted on recording a formal dissent from the Cabinet decision to extend the vote to women aged between twenty-one and thirty.

The removal of the absolute veto of the House of Lords in 1911 and the Government's dependence on Irish support meant that Home Rule legislation was inevitable. This posed difficult problems for Churchill. In his 1899 election address he declared 'I am a Unionist' and described home rule as this 'odious measure'. In February 1904 when the Conservative whip was withdrawn he reassured Balfour that 'As a Unionist Free Trader I am opposed to what is generally known as Home Rule.'[38] And two months later on his adoption as a Liberal candidate he said, 'I remain of the opinion that the creation of a separate Parliament for Ireland would be dangerous and impracticable.'[39] However by the time of the 1906 election Churchill, while remaining opposed to any 'separation' or anything 'likely to injure the effective integrity of the United Kingdom', was prepared to accept devolution on education, roads, public works and expenditure. Two years later during his unsuccessful by-election in Manchester, in an attempt to secure Irish votes, he went beyond official party policy and actually supported the idea of a Home Rule Bill in the next Parliament. Although Churchill had sidestepped the offer of taking on the responsibility for introducing Home Rule, he was nevertheless placed in the rather uncomfortable position of having to accept collective responsibility for a measure he had strongly and publicly opposed only a decade earlier.

In early 1912, under pressure from the Irish to legislate so that Home Rule could become law before the next General Election despite the opposition of the Lords, the Cabinet had to agree on a measure. They did so in a hurry and with little consideration of the various difficulties involved. The Bill they hastily endorsed was very close to Gladstone's second attempt in 1893: it conceded an Irish Parliament, but retained key powers in London (including defence, foreign policy, police, land purchase, pensions and national insurance) and it left the Irish dependent on a financial grant from the British Government. The crucial problem of Ulster, where there was overwhelming opposition from the Protestants to even limited rule from Dublin, was ignored. In February 1912 Churchill and Lloyd George proposed to exclude Ulster from the provisions of the Bill (in 1911 Churchill had proposed a complex system of 'home rule all round', with ten subsidiary legislatures in Britain; the scheme was rejected because administratively it would have been a nightmare and because there was no demand for it). Although Asquith probably backed the idea of excluding Ulster, he sided with the majority in the Cabinet who opposed making such a concession so early in the controversial passage of the Bill and at a time when the Conservatives were determined to completely wreck the measure. Wilful as ever, in a speech in the Commons on 30 April, Churchill went further than agreed Government policy in implying that Ulster could be treated as a special case.

In 1912 and again in 1913 the Home Rule Bill was passed by the Commons only to be rejected by the Lords. Churchill continued to drop hints in public that Ulster might be excluded, and discussed the problem privately with both Bonar Law (the new Conservative leader) and Austen Chamberlain, but neither the Government nor the opposition were prepared to compromise on this basis. The situation reached crisis point in the first half of 1914. Ulster was in almost open revolt and the Protestants planned to set up a separate administration once home rule became law. Their defiance of the law was openly supported by the Conservative opposition. The Home Rule Bill would shortly become law in accordance with the 1911 Parliament Act, despite the opposition of the Lords, and it still contained no exclusion for Ulster. It was not possible at this stage to incorporate such a provision in the Bill because it had to be identical with the original 1912 Bill. The Government would therefore need Conservative support to pass a separate Exclusion Bill through the Lords.

On 9 March Asquith told the Commons that the Government was willing to accept a six-year exclusion from the provisions of the Bill for Ulster (though probably only for four counties). The offer was rejected by the opposition and by the Ulster Protestants, who wanted permanent exclusion. The Government now faced the prospect of open rebellion in the province. They agreed that Churchill, who was well-known for his desire to meet some of the Protestants' demands, should make a tough speech. He did so at Bradford on 14 March, launching a violent and unrestrained attack on the Conservatives for their tactic of choosing which laws they would obey and arguing that the constitution only applied when they wanted it to. He said that the Government would not surrender to the threat of force, that there were 'worse things than bloodshed, even on an extended scale' and concluded 'let us go forward together and put these grave matters to the proof'.

Churchill's exact role and motives in what happened in the next fortnight will probably never be known accurately in the absence of detailed contemporary papers and accounts. Certainly the opposition believed that the Government, and Churchill in particular, were engaged in nothing less than a deliberate plot to provoke Ulster so that they could put down a 'rebellion' and establish military control. The evidence is inconclusive, but some of the political moves are known. On 11 March the Cabinet set up a small committee to co-ordinate the Government's response to the threat of civil disobedience and violence in Ulster. It soon fell under Churchill's domination – the chairman Lord Crewe became ill, Birrell, the Chief Secretary, played little part in its proceedings and Churchill easily swayed his friend Jack Seely, the Secretary of State for War. On 14 March the War Office were told to send instructions to the Commander-in-Chief in Ireland, General Sir Arthur Paget, to take precautions to safeguard arms depots in Ulster. Three days later Paget refused to move troops to the north since he believed that such action would precipitate a crisis. The Government now faced a critical situation with the Army not carrying out legitimate orders. That day the Cabinet committee agreed to send troops from the mainland to Ulster, Churchill ordered the Third Battle Squadron to sail from Gibraltar and hold manoeuvres at Lamlash, just seventy miles from Belfast, and the Royal Ulster Constabulary was put under the control of Churchill's colleague from Tonypandy days, General Macready.

Paget was summoned to a series of conferences at the War Office, Admiralty and No 10 on 18–19 March. Churchill was present at nearly all these meetings, but no full record was kept of what was decided. There were further military deployments as a result. Orders were issued for the Royal Navy to move troops and guns to Belfast, the Fourth destroyer flotilla was moved to the Lamlash area, where the main battle squadron was expected to arrive on 23 March. The use of the Navy ashore as troops was not ruled out and Churchill told one Army commander that if Belfast should fight then the 'fleet would have the town in ruins in twenty four hours'.[40] Paget was told that officers living in Ulster need not take part in operations but any others who refused to obey orders would be dismissed without a pension. He was given guidance on how to react in different situations but in a panic finished up giving his officers the chance to resign rather than obey orders. In the 3rd Cavalry Brigade at the Curragh fifty-eight officers decided to resign or be dismissed – this was the so-called Curragh 'mutiny'. On 21 March the Government seemed to lose its nerve – the main part of the fleet was ordered not to proceed to Lamlash and public assurances were given that the Army would only be used to protect lives and property. Over the next two days Churchill, according to Asquith, spoke of creating a 'temporary Army – *ad hoc*'.[41] Seely then went further than agreed statements of policy and said that the Army would not be used to crush opposition to home rule. On 25 March despite Churchill's attempt to protect his friend, the Cabinet decided that Seely's statement should be repudiated and he resigned.

The political problem of what to do about Ulster remained but the possibility of using military force to support Government policy had gone and the need to reach a compromise was much increased. The most charitable explanation is that the Government mishandled a delicate situation. There remains a suspicion though that the Government failed in its intention to establish military control over Ulster prior to implementing Home Rule with only a limited exclusion clause and that it may even have deliberately engineered a 'mutiny' in the Army as a pretext for intervening with the Navy and other forces. A year later Lord Crewe did say that Asquith had commented about the 'Ulster plot' that 'the plan had been to engineer a revolt in the Army, which a loyal Navy under Churchill were to suppress'.[42]

From April until the end of July the Irish crisis deepened as the passage of the Home Rule Bill neared and no agreement proved possible over the terms of any Ulster exclusion. Churchill was not closely involved in the negotiations with the Unionists – Asquith and Lloyd George took the lead for the Government. On 22 July Churchill did revert to his previous idea of 'home rule all round' as a way of imposing a solution on both the nationalists and Ulster, but it was rejected by the Cabinet as impracticable since they realised that the opposition would never agree. Two days later the last attempt at producing a compromise – the Buckingham Palace conference – broke up without agreement. It was unclear what the Government proposed to do next. Before they had time to decide they were swept up in the European crisis triggered by the assassination of the heir to the Hapsburg throne, Archduke Ferdinand, at Sarajevo and the subsequent Austrian ultimatum to Serbia. Within ten days Britain was at war and Churchill's preparations and policy at the Admiralty were to be put to the test.

8

War

The European crisis engulfed the Cabinet and Churchill with great speed. On 24 July (the day the Buckingham Palace conference on Ulster failed), when Austria sent its ultimatum to Serbia, Asquith wrote, 'Happily there seems to be no reason why we should be anything more than spectators'[1] and Churchill decided to spend a rare moment with his family, who were then on holiday at Cromer. Two days later, when Austria, strongly encouraged by Germany, which had its own reasons for not opposing a wider conflict, rejected the conciliatory Serbian reply and prepared to attack its neighbour, European war seemed probable. The systems of alliances and complex mobilisation timetables threatened to involve Russia, Germany and France and posed difficult questions for the British Government. That day (26 July), with Churchill still away from the Admiralty at Cromer, Battenberg issued orders (which Churchill subsequently confirmed) to stop the demobilisation of the fleet – an exercise had just been completed followed by a fleet review at Spithead.

Churchill returned to London immediately and on 27 July secured Asquith's approval to take the first of a series of precautionary war preparation measures. His personal reaction to events was a feeling of excitement at the prospect of war. He wrote to Clementine: 'Everything tends towards catastrophe & collapse. I am interested, geared up and happy. Is it not horrible to be built like that? The preparations have a hideous fascination for me. I pray God to forgive me for such fearful moods of levity.'² Asquith, in one of his letters to Venetia Stanley, his confidante and probable lover (he wrote to her two or three times a day, often while a Cabinet meeting was in progress), told her that Winston 'is all for this way of escape from Irish troubles, and when things looked better last night [a possible European conference], he exclaimed moodily that it looked after all as if we were in for a "bloody peace"! . . . But at this moment things don't look well, & Winston's spirits are probably rising.'³ On 28 July the Cabinet agreed that part of the fleet should sail to its war station at Scapa Flow in Orkney and the next day the rest of the fleet was sent north from Portland. On 30 July Churchill sacked the Commander-in-Chief of the Home Fleet and replaced him with Sir John Jellicoe. This action caused widespread resentment in the Royal Navy and Jellicoe himself sent Churchill six telegrams in three days protesting that he did not want to take command of the fleet in such controversial circumstances. In making this decision Churchill was heavily influenced by Fisher's enthusiastic but as it proved erroneous opinion that Jellicoe was the twentieth-century Nelson – in fact when he had his one chance to secure a major naval victory at Jutland he failed.

Meanwhile the Cabinet was trying to decide under what circumstances Britain might become involved in any European war. On 29 July they agreed that if Belgian neutrality were violated (almost certainly as part of a German attack on France), then the question to be faced was 'one of policy rather than of legal obligation' under the treaty guaranteeing Belgian neutrality.⁴ Churchill went along with that decision and told Charles Masterman that he did not see 'why we need come in if they only go a little way into Belgium'.⁵ But this did not mean that Churchill was opposed to Britain joining in a European war – indeed he was one of the strongest and most consistent advocates of such a course within the Cabinet. At first he had little support. On 31 July, the day after Russian general mobilisation was ordered, the Cabinet felt that public opinion would not allow Britain to support France and no commitments should therefore be given, although they recognised that a German invasion of Belgium might change that view. On 1 August, when Germany had still not responded to the Russian mobilisation, Churchill was unable to persuade his colleagues to agree to a full mobilisation of the fleet. Asquith described the Cabinet meeting to Venetia Stanley:

'Winston very bellicose & demanding immediate mobilisation . . . It is no exaggeration to say that Winston occupied at least half the time.'[6] That evening, after the German declaration of war on Russia, Asquith did agree to mobilisation.

The crucial Cabinet decisions were taken at two meetings on Sunday 2 August, when a German attack on France seemed inevitable. Ministers then found that their freedom was severely constrained not just by the diplomatic entente but also by the naval dispositions that followed the British decision to effectively withdraw from the Mediterranean in 1912. During the Cabinet meetings Churchill, Grey, Haldane and Crewe favoured British entry into the war and a strong minority opposed it. Eventually a compromise was reached. First, ministers agreed that 'a substantial violation' of Belgian neutrality would compel Britain to intervene in the war. Second, they accepted that with the majority of the French fleet in the Mediterranean Britain would have to give a guarantee to protect the northern French coast from German naval attack. The consequences of the decisions taken in 1912 were now coming home to roost. Although in 1912 Churchill had denied that Britain had moral obligations towards France he now argued they existed. That evening Churchill issued instructions to begin co-operation with the French Navy, including arrangements for joint codes, the opening of British naval bases for French use and joint surveillance of the German fleet.

With the Cabinet still divided about entry into the European war that now seemed inevitable, Churchill took his own political initiative. Anticipating the possibility of a substantial anti-war group resigning from the Cabinet, he envisaged bringing together a coalition of Liberals (under Asquith and Grey) and the Conservative Party, which had endorsed a pro-war position on the morning of 2 August. He invited the Conservative Leader Bonar Law (and FE) to dine with him (and Grey) that evening to plot a possible coalition. Bonar Law refused the invitation since he did not want to take sides in a Cabinet dispute and probably also because of the continuing Conservative hostility towards Churchill. The next day it was clear that Churchill's preparations were unnecessary. The German ultimatum to Belgium, foreshadowing imminent invasion, convinced all but two Cabinet members that Britain should join the war. Lloyd George later described the scene in the Cabinet room as the British ultimatum to Germany expired at 11pm on 4 August:

> Winston dashed into the room radiant, his face bright, his manner keen and he told us, one word pouring out on the other how he was going to send telegrams to the Mediterranean, the North Sea and God knows where. You could see he was a really happy man. I wondered if this was the state of mind to be in at the opening of such a fearful war as this.[7]

Asquith too described Churchill on the evening of 4 August as having 'got on all his war-paint' and 'longing for a sea-fight in the early hours of to-morrow morning'.[8]

With Britain now at war questions were immediately raised about the Admiralty's pre-war preparations in which Churchill had played a large part. Although Britain had been able to build more dreadnoughts than Germany in the years before 1914 (Germany also had a huge army to finance), the Royal Navy was in most respects inferior to its opponent, especially in tactical training and initiative. Churchill had continued Fisher's policy of limited modernisation – introducing oil-fired ships, developing naval aviation (he had even tried to learn to fly himself but lacked the aptitude) – but the Navy remained an archaic institution. Most important of all it was technically deficient: Germany, which had only begun to build a navy in the 1890s, produced equally good ships and guns and its equipment was superior in crucial areas such as armour, mines, torpedoes and shells. The British fleet, despite the fact that Germany had been its most likely opponent for the last decade, also lacked a proper operating base on the east coast to enforce the distant blockade that had been adopted as its war strategy.

Initially the fleet was spread out along the east coast of Scotland at Scapa Flow, Invergordon and Rosyth. Construction had only just begun on Rosyth dockyard and Scapa Flow was only an unprotected anchorage with no provision for fleet repair and maintenance. In general preparations for war were sadly deficient. There were no anti-submarine defences such as mines, nets and booms. When the Admiralty finally realised that German submarines had a far greater radius of action than British models, the fleet had to be moved secretly to safer anchorages well out of range, even though the new locations made it almost impossible to counter any German thrust into the North Sea. In early September the fleet was at Loch Ewe on the west coast of Scotland and in mid-October it was moved to Lough Swilly on the north coast of Ireland, while anti-submarine defences were hastily improvised at its supposed bases. It was on a visit to Loch Ewe on 17 September that Churchill took part in an episode reminiscent of a John Buchan novel. A light was seen coming from a house nearby and Churchill, convinced he had discovered a nest of German spies, led an armed party to the house, which turned out to belong to Sir Arthur Bignold, a seventy-five-year-old former Conservative MP. Churchill searched the house, ordered the dismantling of a searchlight and although nothing supicious was found on the premises, went on to order secret police investigations into the MP, his guests, friends and servants, again without result.

Churchill also accepted the disastrous received wisdom in the Admiralty that convoying merchant ships would not only bring no advantages but would actually increase ship losses. (Not until 1917, with British merchant trade on the point of collapse, was the Admiralty forced to change its mind.) Another tragic misconception held by Churchill at the beginning of the war was that the development of submarine warfare posed no threat to Britain's vital imports of food and raw materials. In December 1913 Fisher sent him a remarkably prescient paper forecasting the development of unrestricted submarine sinkings of merchant ships. Churchill, for once disregarding Fisher's advice, rejected the idea that any nation would adopt such tactics. In typically extreme language he declared:

> If there were a nation vile enough to adopt systematically such methods, it would be justifiable, and indeed necessary, to employ the extreme resources of science against them: to spread pestilence, poison the water supply of great cities, and, if convenient, proceed by the assassination of individuals.[9]

On the outbreak of war Churchill set up a 'War Group' in the Admiralty, consisting of himself, the First and Second Sea Lords and the Chief of War Staff, to exercise direct control over operations. The Admiralty had traditionally given little discretion to commanders on the spot but this new group centralised control even more. Its disadvantages were to be apparent in the opening engagement of the naval war, which took place in the Mediterranean, where the British were weak. The German battlecruiser *Goeben* was superior to any of the British ships in the area; it was supported by the *Breslau*, which had inferior firepower to the British light cruisers but was faster. The British commander, Sir Berkeley Milne, was known to be incompetent but had been appointed by Churchill mainly because of his influence at court. On 30 July he was instructed by Churchill that his primary objective was to aid the French in protecting troop transports from North Africa to France and that although he was to try and bring the *Goeben* to action he was not to engage superior forces. On 2 August Milne was ordered to shadow the *Goeben* and although Churchill wanted it attacked before the outbreak of hostilities, the Cabinet refused to agree. The Admiralty also ordered Milne to stop the German ships escaping from the Mediterranean, not suspecting that after the signature of the German-Turkish alliance on 2 August they would try to reach Constantinople. On 4 August the Admiralty further instructed Milne that the neutrality of Italy was to be 'rigidly' respected and that all ships were to keep at least six miles from the shore. All those confusing and contradictory orders were at the root of the subsequent fiasco.

On 4 August the *Goeben* shelled ports in Algeria and sailed to Sicily, outsteaming the British shadowing forces. Milne kept his ships to the west of Sicily, to stop an escape from the Mediterranean. The *Goeben* and *Breslau* went eastwards, feinted up the Adriatic and sailed towards Greece with *HMS Gloucester* just in touch. Admiral Troubridge, off Cephalonia with a force of cruisers and destroyers, decided not to engage the German ships because he had inferior forces (as the Admiralty orders allowed). On 8 August, with Milne in pursuit of the German ships, which were recoaling in the Aegean, the Admiralty issued instructions to commence hostilities against Austria (the telegram was a mistake, war was not declared until four days later) and so Milne turned his ships towards the Adriatic. The next day the Admiralty issued a countermanding order to continue the pursuit of the *Goeben* but by then it was too late and on 10 August the German ships passed through the Dardanelles and eventually reached Constantinople. Direct Admiralty control of operations had proved disastrous, but most of the blame was placed on the admirals in command. Although the Admiralty formally approved Milne's actions, he was never given another post and

Troubridge was condemned by a Board of Enquiry, subjected to a court-martial, acquitted, but like Milne never re-employed.

This incident was to be the first of a series of blows to the prestige of the British Navy. It was able to impose a distant blockade on Germany – the inferior German fleet was not prepared to fight a battle to try and break the stranglehold. But despite Churchill's continual hankering after offensive action, the Royal Navy did not have the power to take the initiative off the German coast where German submarines and mines would be most effective. The result was essentially a stalemate – no grand fleet action between opposing dreadnoughts as the public expected, only a series of low level skirmishes. The first small-scale action by the British on 28 August into the Heligoland Bight was successful – they sank three light cruisers and a destroyer without any losses. On 21 September Churchill, speaking in Liverpool, said that if the German Navy did not come out and fight 'it would be dug out like rats from a hole'. The very next day three old armoured cruisers – *HMS Cressy*, *HMS Hogue*, and *HMS Aboukir* – were sunk off the Dutch coast by the German submarine *U9* with the loss of nearly 1,500 men. Churchill later claimed that he did not see the Admiralty signal moving these ships from the Dogger Bank into the area where they were left wedged between the Dutch coast and a German minefield and vulnerable to submarines, but on the two previous days he had chaired meetings to discuss the deployment of these vessels. Churchill had in fact been concerned with their vulnerability, but to the threat from surface ships not submarines. Further disasters were to follow. On 16 October *HMS Hawke* was torpedoed off the coast of Scotland, and eleven days later the superdreadnought *HMS Audacious* was sunk. Fearing the impact on the public of more naval reverses, the news was concealed. On 31 October *HMS Hermes* was torpedoed off Calais. (Churchill had told the Cabinet a fortnight earlier that the Navy could no longer guarantee protection for troop transports in the Channel and that they might have to sail to St Nazaire in Brittany instead.)

Only three months into the war Churchill was facing a crisis of confidence in the Royal Navy, which had been widely expected to be Britain's war-winning weapon. The crisis was made worse by Churchill's own interventions in two areas – the creation of the Royal Naval Division and his activities in Antwerp in early October.

He had always been devoted to the interests of his family and saw no reason why he should not look after them while he was in office. For example as Home Secretary in 1910 he had fought a long battle with McKenna at the Admiralty over a report on his brother-in-law, Lieutenant William Hozier, who had been described as 'inexperienced and highly inefficient' by Captain Ryan of *HMS Mars*. Churchill successfully insisted that Hozier be transferred to another ship and that the offending passage be removed from his report but was unable to convince McKenna of the need to discipline Captain Ryan for daring to write the offending report about a well-connected officer. The outbreak of war increased his opportunities to ensure that his family and friends were favoured. He managed to obtain the post of special messenger at the War Office (a largely honorific but prestigious office) for his cousin, the Duke of Marlborough. (A year later he ensured he was appointed Lord Lieutenant of Oxfordshire.) He was less successful at first in finding a job for another cousin, Ivor Guest. He asked Asquith to make him Civil Lord at the Admiralty but Asquith refused to go along with such blatant nepotism, writing to Venetia Stanley: 'Ivor Guest is very unpopular, & the whole thing wd be denounced as a Churchill job. I thought & still think it inconsiderate of Winston to raise & press such a point at such a time.'[10] Churchill eventually ensured that Guest was made Lord Lieutenant of Ireland.

On 16 August Churchill embarked on the creation of the Royal Naval Division (RND). It was a highly anomalous body – an infantry division recruited from reservists trained for service at sea and taking its orders from the Admiralty. It was Churchill's idea and he treated it as virtually his own private army. It provided him with a new source of patronage for his friends and his friends' relations. Those serving in it included the Duke of Westminster (who lent Churchill a luxury car for most of the war), Baron de Forest, the stepfather of George Cornwallis-West (his mother's second husband), Arthur 'Oc' Asquith (son of the Prime Minister), two nephews of Bonar Law and, from the press, J. L. Garvin's son and Max Aitken's brother. In September, when the Oxfordshire Yeomanry, with Churchill's brother Jack and his other officer friends from pre-war days, was sent to Dunkirk, it was virtually incorporated into the RND – Churchill arranged for them to have RND armoured cars and requisitioned lorries and buses. At the end of September the

RND was stationed at Dunkirk and Lille, operating on the flank of the German forces in co-operation with the main British army. Churchill also used the RND as a way of becoming more closely involved with the land war where the small British Expeditionary Force under his friend Sir John French was operating on the left wing of the French armies. It was clear that the land war would not be decided quickly – the Germans had been repulsed by the French at the Marne and the two armies were now engaged in a complex series of manoeuvres as they tried to edge round each other while moving towards the coast. Churchill visited France four times in September alone. His behaviour was already beginning to annoy many of his colleagues, who felt that he should be in London concentrating on naval policy. The following month Churchill's mission to the Belgian port of Antwerp increased still further the doubts among his colleagues about his judgement and stability.

By 28 September Antwerp was under siege – though the Germans had only five inferior divisions against 145,000 trained Belgian troops they did have very heavy siege guns. The Government recognised the importance of Antwerp: Asquith wrote on 1 October that its fall would be 'a great moral blow to the allies' but added 'of course it would be idle butchery to send a force like Winston's little army there'.[11] That was exactly what was to happen. On 2 October Churchill was on his way to Dover for yet another visit to his troops at Dunkirk when he was recalled to London by Kitchener, who had become Secretary of State for War on the outbreak of war (Asquith was away in Cardiff making a speech). Kitchener supposed (wrongly) that the Belgians might evacuate Antwerp the next day, thereby exposing all the other vital Channel ports, and suggested that Churchill should go there, assess the situation and rally Belgian resistance while he tried to find some regular British troops as reinforcements – like Asquith he was opposed to sending the raw recruits of the RND. The Belgians agreed not to take any decisions until Churchill arrived, which he did at noon on 3 October. That day the Government agreed to send the Royal Marine Brigade. It was Churchill who insisted on adding the untrained troops of his own Royal Naval Division. The Belgians agreed to continue fighting to give time for the British reinforcements to arrive.

On 4 October, as 2,000 men of the Royal Marine Brigade arrived and his own recruits prepared to leave Dover, Churchill toured the city's defences. He then offered his resignation as First Lord of the Admiralty so that he could take command of all British forces in Antwerp, provided that he was given an appropriate rank and adequate staff. (He did not discover until after the war that Kitchener was prepared to agree to his request and make him a Lieutenant-General – when he did find out he commented, 'It was a sporting offer, and I was lucky not to be taken at my word.'[12]) Churchill's political colleagues had a different reaction and his offer to resign was greeted with 'roars of incredulous laughter' when Asquith read it out to the Cabinet the next day. Asquith immediately ordered him to return. Churchill told Kitchener that he wanted to 'continue my direction of affairs unless relieved by some person of consequence'.[13] Churchill had at this point virtually taken control of the defences of Antwerp from the Belgians and was giving orders on the tactical disposition of the troops. General Rawlinson at Ostend was immediately ordered to Antwerp to take command and relieve Churchill. Rawlinson arrived at 5pm on 6 October, a few hours after the Royal Naval Division. After spending just over three days in the city Churchill left Antwerp late on 6 October, just as the Belgians began the withdrawal of their field army to ensure that it was not captured when the city fell. He arrived back in London on 7 October and the next day Asquith reported: 'Poor Winston is very depressed, as he feels his mission has been in vain.'[14]

Churchill was right to feel depressed – his mission had indeed been a failure. Antwerp fell to the Germans three days later and thousands of British soldiers were captured. After the war he claimed that his intervention had prolonged resistance in the city for seven days, thereby helping to ensure that the other Channel ports were secured. In fact his visit did not materially change Belgian plans. On 3 October the Belgians said they would not start to withdraw for three days if the British sent reinforcements and guaranteed an evacuation corridor. Despite British failure to guarantee the latter, the Belgians did not begin evacuating the field army until late in the evening of 6 October (as previously planned). The Belgian assessment, conveyed to the British late on 2 October, was that they would probably be able to continue resistance in the city for about another six days – the surrender took place on 10 October. The price of Churchill's intervention was that the RND lost a total of 2,610 men, most of whom were either prisoners of war or interned in the neutral Netherlands.

Reaction to Churchill's adventure was highly critical and badly damaged his reputation. After talking to his son 'Oc', who was with the RND at Antwerp, Asquith wrote to Venetia Stanley that 'I can't tell you what I feel of the *wicked* folly of it all.' He thought the use of the professional Royal Marine Brigade was justified but 'nothing can excuse Winston (who knew all the facts) from sending in the two other Naval Brigades. I was assured that all the recruits were being left behind ... only about ¼ were Reservists, and the rest were a callow crowd of the rawest tiros, most of whom had never fired a rifle.' He hoped that Churchill would now give up 'the little circus' he was running at Dunkirk.[15] Lloyd George, according to his mistress Frances Stevenson, was 'rather disgusted' with Churchill who had 'behaved in a rather swaggering way when over there, standing for photographers and cinematographers with shells bursting near him, and promoting his pals on the field of action'.[16] Most of the Royal Navy was appalled by the activities of its political chief. Battenberg was on the point of resignation; Admiral Richmond wrote that 'it is a tragedy that the Navy should be in such lunatic hands at this time';[17] and Admiral Beatty, commander of the battlecruisers of the Home Fleet, told his wife that 'the man must have been mad to have thought he could relieve [it] ... by putting 8000 half-trained troops into it'.[18] The political truce between the parties was broken for the first time when Walter Long, a senior Conservative, wrote to *The Times* on 14 October strongly criticising Churchill. (Churchill put pressure on the Press Bureau to officially censor this criticism but its head, the Liberal, Sir Stanley Buckmaster, refused.) In private the Conservative Leader, Bonar Law, was also highly critical of the Antwerp affair, describing it as 'an utterly stupid business' and Churchill as having an 'entirely unbalanced mind'.[19]

The outbreak of war had revived Churchill's never very dormant military instincts and his hankerings after a career of action and glory. In 1911, when discussing the coming war with Lloyd George, he imagined himself commanding the British armies in the Middle East and returning in triumph. As a minister, he believed he had a vitally important role to play in devising military strategy. For example, a week after the outbreak of war Asquith wrote: 'we had a long Cabinet, in which a huge part of the talking was done by

Winston and Kitchener: the former posing as an expert on strategy'.[20] Antwerp fired Churchill's desire for military command. Immediately on his return he saw Asquith to discuss his future and the latter told Venetia Stanley that Churchill 'implored me not to take a "conventional" view of his future. Having, as he says, "tasted blood" these last few days . . . begs that sooner or later, & the sooner the better, he may be relieved of his present office & put in some kind of military command'. Asquith told him that he could not leave the Admiralty but Churchill scoffed at that, alleging that the naval war was practically over. Churchill declared, according to Asquith, that 'a political career was nothing to him in comparison with military glory' and despite only being a lieutenant in the Yeomanry he asked, after a long stream of invective about the quality of existing Army commanders, for the command of the new armies Britain was raising.[21] Asquith left him to grapple with naval policy.

At the Admiralty the most immediate effect of Antwerp was to increase the pressure on Churchill to produce a success after an almost unbroken series of failures. Public hysteria about the German background of Prince Louis of Battenberg was also rising and Churchill decided to take advantage of this to bring about yet another series of changes in the senior echelons of the Royal Navy. Aware of forthcoming press criticism of Battenberg, Churchill saw Haldane on 18 October and discussed with him how to handle the situation. Haldane advised that Battenberg should be sacked. On 20 October Churchill told Asquith that he wanted to dismiss Prince Louis and bring back the seventy-three-year-old Fisher from retirement to take his place. Fisher knew of his imminent recall on 21 October. Churchill saw the King to tell him of the changes on 27 October. The King was opposed not only to the sacking of one of his relatives but also to the appointment of Fisher. Churchill rejected his suggestions of Admirals Meux, Jackson and Sturdee as alternatives. He finally told Battenberg of his fate on 28 October and invited him to resign, which he did after asking to be made a privy councillor. The same day Lord Stamfordham, the King's Private Secretary, saw Asquith to tell him that the King could not support the reappointment of Fisher. Constitutionally Asquith had little choice but to back Churchill, although he told Venetia Stanley: 'I have some misgivings of my own, but Winston won't have anybody else.'[22] Reinstalling Fisher was to prove one of Churchill's costliest mistakes. It is difficult to see how he envisaged the two of them could work together over any sustained period unless he believed, as he hinted to Margot Asquith months later, that Fisher was by now so old and incapable that he would be easily dominated. Kitchener certainly expected them to quarrel and Admiral Beatty perceptively recorded his assessment a month after Fisher's appointment: 'The situation is curious – the two very strong and clever men, one old, wily and of vast experience, one young, self-assertive, with a great self-satisfaction but unstable. They cannot work together, they cannot both run the show.'[23]

The new combination at the Admiralty got off to a bad start with a British defeat at the Battle of Coronel off the coast of Chile. The Germans had a force of five light cruisers and five armed merchantmen operating as commerce raiders in the Pacific after the outbreak of war and the Admiralty were unable to put together an effective force to counter them. The main British ship was *HMS Canopus*, optimistically described by Churchill as 'a citadel around which all our cruisers in those waters could find absolute security'. In fact she was due to be scrapped in 1915, was very lightly armoured, manned by a largely untrained crew and only capable of a speed of twelve knots. The Admiralty did not criticise or countermand the commander on the spot, Admiral Cradock, when he split his small force and sailed into the Pacific to find the German ships. But six days later, suddenly awake to the dangers of the situation, they ordered more ships to the area and signalled Cradock not to engage until all his force was concentrated. It was already too late – Cradock was dead and his ships sunk.

When the news reached London, Asquith wrote soberly to the King, 'The Cabinet were of the opinion that this incident, like the escape of the *Goeben*, the loss of the *Cressy* and her two sister cruisers, and that of the *Hermes* last week is not creditable to the officers of the Navy.'[24] But privately he revealed his exasperation: 'As I told Winston last night (and he is not in the least to blame) it is time that he bagged something and broke some crockery.'[25] Lloyd George was less charitable about the allocation of responsibility: 'Churchill is too busy trying to get a flashy success to attend to the real business of the Admiralty. Churchill blames Admiral Cradock for the defeat in South America – the Admiral presumably having gone down with his ship & so unable to clear himself. This is characteristic of Churchill.'[26] Churchill and Fisher knew they had to act quickly to reverse yet another defeat. Churchill wanted to send two battlecruisers to hunt down the German ships but Fisher insisted on four – only later did Churchill admit that Fisher had been right. By luck the British force arrived at Port Stanley in the Falklands (where *HMS Canopus* had been deliberately sunk to become a fort) a day before the German ships. On 8 December Admiral Sturdee, in command of superior British forces, was able to achieve the only major British naval victory of the war: all the opposing German ships apart from the *Dresden* were eliminated.

The removal of four battlecruisers from home waters was part of a general slippage in British naval superiority. Churchill warned Beatty at the end of November 1914: 'You must all get the sixty-per-cent standard out of your minds.'[27] The German High Seas Fleet exploited the situation well. They carried out a small-scale bombardment of Great Yarmouth on 3 November and on 16 December mounted a major raid. The Admiralty were warned through their reading of German codes that a major operation was about to take place and Jellicoe was able to devise an effective plan to meet the German ships with a superior force. Nevertheless Scarborough was heavily bombarded (122 people were killed and 443 wounded) and through a series of errors and bad weather the German ships were allowed to escape. Churchill could do little to assuage the outbreak of public anger, although belatedly the battle-cruiser squadron was moved south from Cromarty to Rosyth so as to be nearer to any subsequent German raid. On 23 January 1915 intercepted signals showed that the German battlecruisers would leave that evening for a sortie towards the Dogger Bank. Churchill and his advisers at the Admiralty worked out how to intercept the force with Beatty's battlecruisers, which sailed from Rosyth before the German ships left port. But they forgot to alert Jellicoe and the main battleships further north at Scapa Flow until it was too late for him to intervene. The next day Beatty's superior force sank *Blucher* and damaged *Seydlitz* but in return *HMS Lion* was badly damaged. However the remaining German ships were allowed to escape: as Beatty admitted, 'everybody thinks it was a great success, when in reality it was a terrible failure'.[28]

The first six months of the war at sea had failed to produce a significant fleet action but submarine warfare, the use of mines and commerce raiding by the Germans did have an impact on British trade and fleet operations. Churchill and the Admiralty had little idea how to respond to this 'unorthodox warfare' apart from issuing instructions for harsher conditions of warfare themselves. On 22 October the Admiralty told the fleet: 'British Officers will be held responsible that the enemy gains no advantage by any exercise of humanity' and two months later ordered that 'any white flag hoisted by a German ship is to be fired on as a matter of principle'.[29] Churchill's move towards more extreme forms of warfare was also found in the air war. At the beginning of September 1914 Churchill insisted that the Admiralty should take control of home air defence even though it had few resources to carry out the task – there were no anti-aircraft guns and searchlights, the available aircraft were not able to climb high enough or fast enough to intercept German raiders and Churchill sent most of the aircraft to supplement his private army at Dunkirk. Soon after he took charge of air defence Churchill suggested starting the bombing of military targets in German towns in retaliation for the two bombs the Germans had dropped on Ostend but Grey at the Foreign Office rejected his proposal. At the end of December Fisher and Churchill were convinced that the Germans were about to start bombing London. Unable to provide a military response, they considered the possibility of announcing a policy of taking hostages or even shooting interned German civilians in Britain in the same numbers as British civilian casualties. The War Council decided to take no action.

Churchill was most unhappy with the lack of decisive action at sea and the rapidly developing stalemate. He searched around desperately for some form of offensive action. Admiral Richmond found him at the end of October in 'low spirits ... oppressed with the impossibility of *doing* anything ... He wanted to send battleships – old ones – up the Elbe, but for what purpose except to be sunk I did not understand.'[30] In this state of frustration Churchill came to advocate more and more strongly the traditional Admiralty policies for fighting Germany – the very ones he had scorned in 1911 before he took up his post: operations along the German coast. Even before the outbreak of war Churchill had written to Asquith suggesting violating the neutrality of a number of countries and seizing islands off the coasts of Sweden, Norway, Denmark and the Netherlands. Asquith had rejected the idea and the Admiralty staff view was that none of these islands was of great strategic value. Undaunted by this, during the first week of the war Churchill elaborated, in great detail, an operational plan to capture Ameland off the Dutch Frisian coast and turn it into what he called an 'advanced flotilla base' but he could arouse no-one else's interest in the scheme. He turned next to Fisher's old favourite, which had been dismissed by ministers as laughable and puerile in 1911 – a landing on the coast of Pomerania and a direct advance on Berlin. On 19 August, with Asquith's approval, Churchill wrote to the Russians about joint offensive operations in the Baltic once the German fleet had been defeated or the Kiel Canal blocked and suggested landing the Russian Army near Berlin. At the Cabinet two days later he 'propounded a Napoleonic plan of forcing the Danish passage with the help of the Greeks [sic] and convoying Russian troops to the coast off Berlin and making a *coup de théâtre*'.[31] This scheme fell through when the Russian armies advancing into East Prussia were overwhelmingly defeated by the outnumbered German forces.

Attention then turned to the possibility of capturing Heligoland, the massively fortified island at the entrance to the Elbe, Weser and Jade Rivers that Churchill had called 'almost impregnable' in 1913. Churchill put Admiral Wilson's plan to capture it to Jellicoe when he visited him at Loch Ewe in mid-September but Jellicoe was not prepared to risk the fleet in an attack on the Heligoland forts when all the advantages would lie with the shore-based guns. In November 1914 Churchill began detailed work on two other schemes for the capture of either the island of Sylt off the north-west coast of Schleswig or Borkum in the mouth of the Ems. At the beginning of December he managed to obtain War Council approval to investigate the possibility of seizing an advanced base, although Kitchener refused to promise any troops. Churchill's plan for the capture of Sylt was worked out in great detail on an hour-by-hour basis, even including how messenger pigeons should be used. As so often in the initial stages of his ideas, he was swept away with enthusiasm and Balfour, who though a member of the opposition acted as unofficial defence adviser, found that Churchill was 'in the mood which refuses to recognise even the most obvious difficulties' such as the fact that the Germans had probably developed effective defences.[32]

By the end of December Churchill had worked out an even more elaborate plan for the capture of Borkum using three infantry brigades, to be followed by the mining of German coasts and estuaries; an invasion of Schleswig-Holstein (which would be given to Denmark in return for their support and the use of Funen as a base); an advance to the Kiel Canal; the sending of the fleet into the Baltic to cut off German supplies from Scandinavia; and, almost inevitably, the *coup de grâce* – the landing of Russian troops on the coast for an advance on Berlin. Luckily none of the ideas got beyond the initial planning stage. They would have been militarily disastrous and in his enthusiasm for the plan Churchill seems to have paid no attention to how the islands were to be held, what countermoves were open to the Germans or the difficulties of operating for extended periods on long supply chains in areas dominated by the enemy and without an effective capability for amphibious operations. But these ideas were not passing fancies – Churchill returned to them again in July 1917 when he produced a massive report on how and why they should be carried out.

Churchill's search for possible offensive operations reflected a desire, shared by all his Cabinet colleagues (even though they rejected his chosen methods), to find a way out of the problems facing Britain a few months after the start of the war. The open warfare on the western front of the first two months had, by the end of 1914, degenerated into trench warfare as the allied and German armies constructed increasingly elaborate defences stretching from the sea to the Swiss border. Technology, in particular barbed wire, machine guns and the ability to move reserves quickly by rail, overwhelmingly favoured the defence and neither side had any practical ideas to break the deadlock. Britain had begun the war adopting its traditional strategy based on the primacy of naval warfare and blockade (the only area where it was at all dominant) and the despatch of a small army to the continent. Although some industry was diverted to war production, the aim was to disrupt normal financial and commercial life as little as possible. It was on this basis that Sir Edward Grey told the Commons on 3 August that it would cost Britain very little more to join the war than to stay out. Churchill shared these views. On 1 August he estimated that 'the naval war will be cheap – not more than 25 millions a year' (only a fifty per cent increase in the annual peacetime budget).[33] A week later he told the Admiralty to plan on a war lasting a year.

Ministers found very rapidly that this strategy was not sustainable. Once the Army was in France it had to be maintained and supplied and Britain found that it could not restrict itself to such a limited liability. Without thinking through the long-term implications in terms of manpower planning or industrial mobilisation, the Government, under Kitchener's influence (he was already planning on a three-year war), moved steadily towards building a continental army. The naval war was not proving to be cheap either. Instead of keeping within his estimate of £25 million a year, Churchill found that he had spent £360 million in the first eight months. British financial dominance was far less than in the nineteenth century and there were very real limits (that were to become painfully apparent within a couple of years) to Britain's ability to finance her allies, who were in an even more parlous state. Britain had joined the war not just to oppose the rise of German power or protect Belgium but also to preserve its own independence and status as a great power and to ensure that its traditional enemies (France and Russia), now its allies, did not emerge from the conflict overwhelmingly strong, and therefore a threat to British interests, if they were victorious. Kitchener and his colleagues hoped that the new armies they were building would come to a peak in 1917 when, with luck, not just Germany but also France and Russia would be on the point of exhaustion and Britain would be able to deliver the war-winning blow and dominate the ensuing peace conference. But Britain could not remain militarily quiescent until then.

In this atmosphere ministers at the end of 1914 began to search around for possible operations which at limited cost might secure sizeable benefits. The German overseas empire had been largely conquered, but there were other areas away from the military stalemate of the western front where it might be possible to use Britain's limited resources not just to increase the pressure on its opponents but also to secure long-term British interests. They were increasingly drawn to the idea of an initiative in the Balkans and the Near East, where since the beginning of November Britain had been at war with its old ally, Turkey. The decisions they made at the beginning of 1915 were to lead to naval and military disaster, the demise of the Liberal Government and the near ending of Churchill's political career.

9

Disaster at the Dardanelles

The escape of the *Goeben* and *Breslau* to Constantinople was one of the major influences behind the decision of the Turkish Government to join Germany and Austria in the war. Another was the British decision, under Churchill's influence, to seize, while Turkey was still neutral, two dreadnoughts she had been building in British shipyards without mentioning tiresome details such as compensation. On 29 October the Turkish Government allowed the two German ships to bombard the Russian Black Sea coast and after this attack on one of its allies the British Government had little alternative but to declare war, which it did on 4 November.

Even before Britain was at war with Turkey, Churchill was looking at the possibility of an assault on the Gallipoli peninsula as the first stage of an operation aimed at Constantinople. These plans, which were worked out with Kitchener and the War Office in early September, were based on one fundamental assumption – it was to be a joint military and naval expedition. As Britain did not have sufficient spare troops, the plan was for about 60,000 troops (either Greek or Russian) to capture the Gallipoli peninsula, seize the Turkish forts and allow British warships to sail through the Dardanelles (the long, narrow channel linking the Mediterranean and the Sea of Marmora) before going on to Constantinople. These ideas came to nothing largely because the Russians had no spare troops either and no decision could be reached on whether to entice the Greeks into the war when both they and Russia wanted Constantinople after the war. But the decision not to proceed also reflected the pre-war assessment of the difficulties of any operation at Gallipoli. In 1907 Britain had considered a possible war with Turkey over a boundary dispute in Sinai and although the Committee of Imperial Defence believed the seizure of Gallipoli and passage of the fleet through the Dardanelles would lead to the fall of the Turkish Government, they concluded that such an operation 'would involve a great risk and should not be undertaken if other means of bringing pressure to bear on Turkey were available'.[1] As early as 1890 ideas for a purely naval attack had been rejected by the Commander-in-Chief of the Mediterranean fleet as far too risky given the power and range of modern artillery, a view endorsed by the Admiralty in 1896. The Italians had tried a small-scale attack during their war with Turkey in 1912 but had failed and the French also rejected the idea in the autumn of 1914 as too risky.

Just before war was declared on Turkey Churchill asked for a re-assessment of the possibility of a purely naval attack on the Dardanelles forts. The Admiralty's conclusions were, as in the past, clear: 'A bombardment of the sea face of the Dardanelles Forts offers very little prospect of obtaining any effect commensurate with the risk to the ships.'[2] Despite this advice Churchill ordered a ten-minute naval bombardment of the forts when war was declared, a move which achieved little apart from alerting the Turks and their German advisers (if they needed alerting) to British objectives. For the rest of 1914 Churchill remained attracted by the idea. On 25 November at the first meeting of the new War Council, during a discussion of the defence of Egypt, Churchill and Fisher proposed a joint military and naval expedition against Gallipoli but Kitchener told his colleagues that no troops were available and all were agreed that a substantial military force was a prerequisite. In early December Asquith reported to Venetia Stanley that Churchill's 'volatile mind is at present set on Turkey & Bulgaria, & he wants to organise a heroic adventure against Gallipoli and the Dardanelles: to wh I am altogether opposed'.[3]

The question of operations against Turkey rose to the top of the agenda at the turn of the year as ministers grappled with the consequences of the deadlock on the western front and sought to find a viable strategy for 1915. Many in the Government wanted an outlet for British operations away from the western front where the

French dominated strategy because of the size of their army. Walter Runciman, the President of the Board of Trade, reported to his wife: 'The War Lords are sad at their stalemate, & Winston in particular sees no success for the Navy (& himself) anywhere.'⁴ And Asquith told Venetia Stanley: 'I am profoundly dissatisfied with the immediate prospect – an enormous waste of life and money day after day with no appreciable progress.'⁵ Ministers were desperate for a solution that avoided a long drawn-out bloody war involving the mass mobilisation of economies and societies. As new forces became available, they could be used for a return to a traditional British strategy of leaving ther allies to do the bulk of the land fighting while they concentrated on theatres elsewhere at lower cost. (Kitchener and the Army were always reluctant to agree to such a course, preferring instead to build up maximum forces in France.)

Attention turned to the superficially attractive area of the Balkans and Turkey. The British (and also the French) hoped that it would be possible to organise some sort of Balkan grouping that would be prepared to join in an attack on Turkey (in return for offers of Turkish territory) and eventually turn on Austro-Hungary too, where these states had territorial claims and various ethnic allegiances. Although Serbia had survived the first ineffectual Austrian attack, a renewed offensive in 1915 seemed likely to knock them out of the war without Britain and France having provided any effective support. Russia too was facing three enemies – Germany, Austro-Hungary and Turkey – and allied assistance, if passage through the Dardanelles and into the Black Sea could be obtained, or even better Turkey defeated and pressure put on Austro-Hungary in the Balkans, might be vital in keeping them in the war.

The benefits of mounting operations in the Balkans and against Turkey were, as Churchill always insisted, enormous. But the difficulties were equally enormous. Constructing a viable Balkan alliance given the rivalries and conflicting claims between the various states in the area would be extremely problematic. In addition Russia was not keen to encourage the territorial pretensions of some of these states, especially Greece, and Britain would have to take into account the views of such a powerful ally. Assuming such an alliance was constructed, the military effectiveness of these states was open to question. Although they had comparatively large armies, they had virtually no armaments industries to support them and would depend on allied supplies at a time when the allies were themselves extremely short and only beginning to gear up to wartime production.

The first proposal for a major shift in strategy came from Maurice Hankey, Secretary to the Committee of Imperial Defence before the war, now Secretary to the War Council and increasingly influential in strategic discussions. On 28 December he proposed accepting the deadlock in the west and concentrating on a land campaign against Turkey, bringing in Bulgaria and Greece and eventually attacking Austro-Hungary. On 1 January Lloyd George, worried that Serbia and Russia might be knocked out of the war in the coming year and feeling the need for some victories for public consumption at home, suggested two operations – an attack on Austro-Hungary, via a landing at Salonika and assistance to Serbia, and a landing on the Syrian coast to cut off Turkish troops attacking Egypt.

Churchill took part in this debate by circulating a paper to his colleagues on 29 December. In it he too looked for alternatives to what he graphically described as 'sending our troops to chew barbed wire in Flanders'. His proposals were a reworking of his old ideas for operations in the Baltic involving Denmark and Russia or capturing islands off the German coast, neither of which had found favour earlier on. After reading Hankey's paper he sent another note to Asquith going over the same ground and arguing for Navy-dominated operations in the North Sea and Baltic. He concluded perceptively by saying: 'The war will be ended by the exhaustion of nations rather than the victory of armies.'[6]

Despite his earlier interest in operations against Turkey, Churchill was not, at this stage, suggesting that these were the way to break the strategic deadlock. Yet within days he changed his mind and became the leading exponent of the idea. The catalyst for this change was an appeal on 2 January by the Russian Commander-in-Chief, Grand Duke Nicholas, for a 'demonstration' against Turkey in order to relieve the pressure on the Russian armies fighting in the Caucasus. (It proved a false alarm and within days the Russian armies there were on the offensive – a fact they were reluctant to disclose to their allies.) The British offered help after Kitchener and Churchill had consulted about the prospects. Kitchener's view was that 'the only place that a demonstration might have some effect in stopping reinforcements going east [i.e. the Caucasus] would be the Dardanelles' but he warned 'we shall not be ready for anything big for some months'.[7] On 3 January Fisher sent Churchill a plan (devised by Hankey) for a Greek assault on Gallipoli with 75,000 troops combined with a Royal Navy attack on the Dardanelles, a landing by British troops on the Asiatic side of the straits and a Bulgarian attack on Constantinople. It was a bold conception but unlikely to be realisable – Kitchener was unwilling to release the necessary troops from France and the Greeks would never allow the Bulgarians to capture Constantinople.

It was Churchill who transformed these ideas into a purely naval attack on the Dardanelles, against all the existing advice that such an operation was not feasible. He did so for a variety of reasons. He was attracted by the idea of a purely naval assault because, with no troops available in the foreseeable future, it seemed the only possibility of taking action. A purely naval operation would also compensate for the failure of the Navy to achieve much in the first months of the war and thereby revive his waning personal reputation. Temperamentally, as his earlier career had demonstrated on many occasions, he was always prone to be carried away by enthusiasm for an idea. He would refuse to acknowledge the difficulties involved and his domineering personality, combined with his overwhelming self-confidence and belief in his own ability, meant that he would rarely be deflected by contrary arguments. Almost overnight Churchill became a passionate advocate of a naval attack on the Dardanelles and remained so. Opposition, far from discouraging him, always seemed to spur him on. As Frances Stevenson, who followed Cabinet discussions closely in her role as Lloyd George's secretary and mistress, noted later: 'Churchill very unwisely boasted at the beginning, when things were going well, that he had undertaken it against the advice of everyone else at the Admiralty' and that it was 'entirely his own idea'.[8] Although he never, strictly speaking, overrode his professional advisers, he did not set out their doubts fairly to his colleagues and within the Admiralty he used his considerable political and administrative skills to get the outcome he wanted. In advocating such an attack Churchill was ignoring the very clear warning he himself had given the Cabinet four years earlier. Then he told his colleagues: 'It should further be remembered that it is no longer possible to force the Dardanelles, that nobody would expose a modern fleet to such perils.'[9]

Churchill's immediate problem was that he had to overcome or circumvent the Admiralty's negative views on a purely naval attack. On 3 January he therefore telegraphed to Vice-Admiral Sackville Carden, commanding naval forces off the Dardanelles, asking whether it was possible to force the Dardanelles by ships alone using older battleships, and adding a crucial qualification: 'the importance of the results would justify severe loss'. It was, as Churchill later admitted, a leading question designed to provoke a positive response. Carden was faced with a difficult military situation. The Dardanelles were forty-one miles long and four miles wide at their maximum but only three-quarters of a mile in the Narrows. The outer defences at the entrance to the straits consisted of two forts with twenty-seven guns. Beyond them lay the key to the operation – the intermediate defences up to the Narrows consisting of a hundred guns protecting a minefield and then the Narrows themselves, where there were eighty-eight guns and a swift current ideal for sowing mines. It was not therefore a matter of simply knocking out the forts with battleships; it was also necessary to clear the minefields which were defended by the forts. Minesweepers could not start on this operation until the forts were silenced and it was difficult for the battleships to operate if they still had to contend with the minefields.

On 5 January Carden replied cautiously and rather equivocally to Churchill's question by saying that an operation could not be rushed but the Dardanelles 'might be forced by extended operations with a large number of ships'. It was hardly a strongly positive response and it was not based on any coherently worked-out plan – it was merely a statement of possibilities. Only two weeks earlier Churchill had been less than impressed by Carden, a former superintendent of Malta dockyard, telling Fisher that 'he has never commanded a cruiser squadron, and I am not aware of anything that he has ever done which is in any way remarkable'.[10] Now he chose to interpret Carden's response as an endorsement of his proposal for a naval assault and he argued for placing trust in the judgement of the man on the spot. When he later came to defend his actions, Churchill always placed great weight on Carden's telegram, arguing that it justified a naval attack.

On 6 January Churchill told Carden, 'High authorities here concur in your opinion' and asked him to draw up a detailed plan. In fact the 'high authorities' consisted of Churchill himself – the Admiralty War Staff were not summoned to discuss the response and Fisher always denied that he had seen the telegram before it was sent. The previous day Admiral Jackson of the War Staff had written an appreciation of a possible operation at the Dardanelles, but Churchill did not see it before he replied to Carden. Jackson was very dubious about a naval attack. He expected heavy losses, thought that even if the fleet did fight its way through it would have to depend on an insecure line of communications until the forts were captured by troops, and felt it would be difficult to follow up the attack and secure decisive results. Although it was not spelled out in the paper, it was implicit that Jackson thought the use of troops was essential to success.

While Carden was devising his plan, the War Council met on 8 January to discuss future British strategy. Churchill did not at this stage reveal his interest in a naval attack on the Dardanelles. He still argued in favour of amphibious operations in the North Sea or the Baltic. This was probably a deliberate attempt to find out the position of Kitchener and the War Office on the availability of troops. Lloyd George argued for an attack on Austro-Hungary in the Adriatic or a landing in Syria. A War Office appreciation accepted that an attack on the Dardanelles could be important, but argued it had to be a combined attack involving the Navy and about 150,000 troops. All these operations were ruled out by Kitchener's announcement that no troops were available for operations outside France. With ministers desperate to find an alternative strategy, the scene was set for Churchill to exploit the position with his idea of a purely naval attack. Indeed Churchill at this time supported Kitchener's position (which reduced the possibility of a landing at Salonika or in Syria and therefore strengthened the case for a naval attack in Churchill's eyes) and he argued against any weakening of Britain's military effort on the western front. On 11 January he wrote to his old friend Field Marshal Sir John French, now Commander of the Expeditionary Force, saying that he was 'strongly against deserting the decisive theatre & the most formidable antagonist to win cheaper laurels in easier fields'.[11]

Carden's response to Churchill's request for a detailed plan was available in the Admiralty on 12 January. He suggested a four-phase attack which he estimated might take a month. In practice his plan amounted to no more than an unimaginative attempt to demolish the defences steadily. It contained no ideas on how to cope with the integrated defences of forts and minefields. Churchill later claimed that it 'made a great impression on everyone who saw it'. That was far from being the case. Key people in the Admiralty such as Admirals Jackson and Oliver were unimpressed. Fisher did show some enthusiasm for the attack, even suggesting using the newly commissioned *HMS Queen Elizabeth* to attack the forts on the grounds that it would be good gunnery training for the new crew. Privately Fisher had entertained doubts about a naval attack since the beginning of the year but had not expressed them. Churchill decided to press ahead.

On 13 January the War Council met again to continue its discussion of future strategy. A whole range of operations were considered. French argued for an attack on Zeebrugge and Lloyd George for an attack on Austria, probably through Salonika. Churchill opposed any diversion of troops to the latter area, saying, 'We ought not to go South until we are satisfied that we can do nothing in the North.'[12] Instead at the end of the meeting he embarked on an impassioned plea for a naval assault on the Dardanelles, painting a picture of the big guns of the battleships systematically eliminating the forts and the fleet sailing on to Constantinople. He envisaged using three new battleships and twelve pre-dreadnoughts. Admirals Fisher and Wilson who were present did not speak, no doubt feeling they could not raise some of the worries they had and contradict their political superior at such a meeting. The War Council evaded the problem of priorities by agreeing that planning should proceed for all the proposed operations – an advance on Zeebrugge, an attack in the Adriatic to try and bring Italy into the war on the allied side (a possible diversion of troops from the western front if the stalemate continued) and a possible operation in the Dardanelles. The precise wording was that 'The Admiralty should prepare for a naval expedition in February to bombard and take the Gallipoli Peninsula, with Constantinople as its objective.'

Having obtained endorsement in principle of a naval attack, Churchill used the next fortnight to build up pressure for a decision to go ahead. Work was immediately put in hand in the Admiralty and although Carden reported that the Turks had already sown eight lines of mines he was informed that the date for the operation had been set for 15 February. When he asked for more time to assemble the force, he was told that the date could not be changed for political reasons. On 19 January the Russians were informed of the forthcoming operation; having reassured them that it would be forced through, Churchill expressed the hope that once the outer forts had been reduced the two countries would be able to co-operate in operations against Constantinople. Churchill then turned to the French. An agreement signed two days after British entry into the war had given the French operational primacy in the Mediterranean and they were alarmed by the despatch of a large number of British ships to the area and the plans for a landing at Alexandretta in Syria, an area they regarded as falling within their sphere of influence. In order to counter French claims to control operations in the Dardanelles, Churchill insisted on Carden's deputy, De Roebuck, being made a Vice-Admiral so that he could retain command, as the most senior allied naval officer in the area, when Carden was absent. He told Fisher and Oliver, 'I cannot run the risk of the French obtaining command.'[13]

The French Minister of Marine, Augagneur, came to London for talks with Churchill on 26 January. They agreed on a division of responsibility in the eastern Mediterranean – Britain was to take the lead in Egypt and the Dardanelles and the French in Syria. When Churchill outlined the proposed naval attack, Augagneur expressed doubts – French intelligence had briefed him that it was unlikely to succeed. Churchill argued that ships could silence the forts and that the Turks would give in once the outer forts were demolished. He put his case in such a way as to convince Augagneur that the operation had the backing of the Admiralty, British ministers and the Russians. Churchill did not ask for a French naval attack but Augagneur said they would join in (to keep some influence over the British). The French had not examined the plan in detail and Augagneur did not consult his advisers, relying on the expectation that the British would take responsibility for any failure. These contacts were enough though for Churchill to tell his colleagues that the French backed the operation.

But Churchill still had to overcome objections within the Admiralty, and in particular from Fisher, to a purely naval attack. Fisher, always temperamental and difficult, was becoming increasingly unstable under the pressure of the work involved in fighting a major war Admiral Richmond wrote in his diary: 'In reality he does nothing: he goes home and sleeps in the afternoon. He is old & worn-out & nervous . . . a failing old man anxious for popularity.'[14] On 19 January Fisher wrote to tell Jellicoe that he was only staying on to try and protect him and that in reality he wanted to resign over the planned attack, adding: 'I don't agree with one single step taken.'[15] The next day Hankey saw Asquith on Fisher's behalf and Asquith concluded that Fisher was 'rather unbalanced' but that there was some truth in his complaints.[16] On 21 January Fisher wrote again to Jellicoe saying that 'I just abominate the Dardanelles operation, unless a great change is made and it is settled to be made a military operation, with 200,000 men in conjunction with the Fleet.'[17]

On 24 January, no doubt under Fisher's influence, Hankey circulated to the War Council a copy of a 1906 Committee of Imperial Defence assessment which came down against a purely naval assault on the Dardanelles. On 25 January Fisher sent Churchill a long paper setting out all his objections that he wanted circulated to the War Council. Churchill later claimed this was the first he knew of Fisher's objections – more likely it was the first he knew of their scale. Fisher argued that the first priority was to concentrate resources against Germany, not dissipate them in subsidiary areas, and to be ready for a major fleet action at any time. On the Dardanelles he wrote that 'I make no objection . . . if accompanied by military co-operation . . . and our permanent military occupation of the Dardanelles Forts'.[18] He wanted the Zeebrugge operation stopped too. The next day Churchill responded by writing to Asquith assuring him that the fleet was always able to defeat the German fleet and to Fisher reminding him that he had earlier agreed to operations at Zeebrugge and the Dardanelles and that he could not now withdraw. Under Churchill's influence, Asquith, though worried by the friction within the Admiralty, refused to circulate Fisher's paper of 25 January to the War Council, which therefore remained in ignorance of his objections.

The crucial decisions on the Dardanelles were taken on 28 January at the War Council. There were two developments before that meeting. Fisher, always an early riser unlike Churchill, wrote to him early in the morning intimating that he intended to resign over the Dardanelles but that he would not make his objections public. At a short meeting between Asquith, Churchill and Fisher before the War Council they agreed to cancel the Zeebrugge operation but that the Dardanelles operation should continue. Fisher did not argue against a naval assault on its merits, neither did he make it clear that he would resign if it went ahead. He seems to have thought that more time would be given for reflection.

Fisher was therefore surprised when the meeting of the War Council opened with a long description by Churchill of the proposed operation, which included the statement that both France and Russia approved and would co-operate. Fisher said he thought it had been agreed not to discuss the Dardanelles. When Asquith overruled him, Fisher got up from the table and prepared to leave the meeting. It took a long talk from Kitchener to persuade him to return. Churchill then admitted that the inner forts posed a real problem and that losses to mines were inevitable. But the meeting was swept along by his enthusiasm and the prospect of the benefits which seemed likely to be gained with success. The serious objections from Fisher and Admiral Wilson, who was also at the meeting, were never clearly raised and discussed.

After lunch Churchill saw Fisher privately to persuade him to agree to the attack. In *The World Crisis* Churchill argued that he was right to do so, yet in an unpublished draft he described it as 'my greatest mistake'. Fisher had an almost intuitive feeling that the operation was wrong but he allowed himself to be persuaded by Churchill's arguments, enthusiasm and eloquence and the line that if it failed the ships could always be withdrawn. Churchill had used this argument before, telling Kitchener on 20 January 'if we are checked at the Dardanelles we can represent that oper[ation] as a mere demonstration to cover the seizure of Alexandretta'.[19] In the afternoon, at a sub-committee of the War Council, Churchill together with Lloyd George argued that any troops that could be spared from the western front should be used at Salonika and not at the Dardanelles, which should remain a naval operation. The War Council reconvened at 6pm. There was a row over the possible withdrawal of troops from France, with Churchill again arguing that they should be used, if available, at Salonika not the Dardanelles. Kitchener refused to make any commitments and the issue was left unresolved. Following his talk with Fisher, Churchill simply announced that the Admiralty Board favoured an attack on the Dardanelles and the War Council then endorsed that decision. Churchill had finally obtained approval for the operation he wanted.

There is no doubt that a purely naval attack on the Dardanelles would not have taken place without Churchill's determination to force it through against a number of obstacles. Nor is there much doubt that the idea of attacking without a combined operation involving the Army was Churchill's. It is also clear that in taking this line he was going against his own earlier advice and that of others, including his closest senior professional advisers. Admiral Richmond commented in his diary: 'Winston, very, very ignorant, believes he can capture the Dardanelles without troops.'[20] On 10 February Hankey wrote to Balfour that 'From Lord Fisher downwards every naval officer who is in the secret believes that the Navy cannot take the Dardanelles position without troops. The First Lord [Churchill] still professes to believe that they can do it with ships.'[21] But if Churchill was the chief instigator, others cannot be exonerated. The dissenters within the Admiralty, despite the difficulties in the way of making their dissent known outside the Admiralty, never made clear the extent of their objections. Other ministers, and in particular Asquith as Prime Minister and Chairman of the War Council, failed to ensure that the doubters were given the opportunity to express their views and failed to subject the proposals to a proper degree of scrutiny.

Such a scrutiny would have revealed some very obvious flaws. First, it was far from certain that ships would be able to knock out forts, even without the complications of operating in mine-infested areas. Second, the role of the Turkish mobile field artillery was severely underestimated. Even at the end of February, after operations had started, Churchill reassured the War Council that the passage of the fleet 'could not be interfered with by field artillery'.[22] Third, even if the fleet itself was able to force a passage through the straits, how would unarmoured supply ships be able to use these waters unless the forts and mobile guns were permanently silenced, which meant using troops to hold the Gallipoli peninsula? Fourth, if the fleet did ultimately reach Constantinople what would happen then? Unless the Turkish Government decided to give in (and they actually planned to move to Anatolia and continue the war), all the effort would be nugatory. As the French Admiral Aubert wrote to his minister, Augagneur, after seeing the British plans, 'the beginning can be seen but the end cannot'.[23]

These difficulties were ignored or belittled largely because of British perceptions of the Turkish state as rotten. For this they had some justification. For most of the nineteenth century Turkey had been the 'sick man of Europe' and her defeat in the Balkan War and the revolution that brought the 'Young Turks' to power only seemed to confirm the verdict of the past. One recent episode also reinforced this generally unflattering assessment of Turkish military prowess and willingness to resist. Just before Christmas 1914 *HMS Doris* had demanded the destruction of the stores and railways at the port of Alexandretta. The local Turkish Governor agreed but only on condition that the British provided the explosives. It then turned out that the Turks had no experts to lay the charges so a Royal Navy officer had to do the job. (To save face Turks would not allow him to do so as a British officer and gave him a temporary commission in the Turkish Navy first.) The British were also in touch with opposition groups in Constantinople and expected to be able to bribe them to stage a revolt at the appropriate moment.

Attitudes were also coloured by racial overtones, to which Churchill, with his strong views about the division of the world into racial blocs and his contempt for Islamic people, was particularly prone. Turkey was seen as a fifth-rate native regime that would crumble the moment pressure from a white, world power was applied. All that was required therefore was something akin to a punitive colonial expedition against some upstart native regime, along the lines of the bombardment of Alexandria in 1882 that had led to the collapse of the Egyptian Government and the establishment of British control. Churchill clearly believed that a naval attack on the outer forts was probably all that would be required. As Turkish resistance would then crumble, troops would not be needed to take over the forts; the fleet could pass through the Dardanelles at its leisure and take control of Constantinople as the Turkish Government collapsed in disarray. As Churchill told the Dardanelles Commission enquiry into the subsequent fiasco:

> incidents are very frequent in history especially against Mahommedan or native troops, where the advance of a naval force or flotilla along a river or waterway behind the positions which these troops are holding, have [sic] led to a general retreat.[24]

The events of the next months were to show that these views were hopelessly sanguine.

Following War Council approval of the naval attack on 28 January, large forces were deployed to the eastern Mediterranean – *HMS Queen Elizabeth*, the battlecruiser *HMS Inflexible*, two pre-dreadnoughts, ten old battleships together with four old French battleships and a host of support ships. The allies took over the island of Lemnos as a base with the tacit approval of the technically neutral Greek Government. Although Churchill in his original telegram to Carden had spoken of his willingness to accept severe losses, new instructions were now issued on 5 February that the most modern ships were not to be risked, no ships were to sail in unswept waters and stating, 'it is not expected nor desired that the operations should be hurried to the extent of taking large risks and courting heavy losses'.

While Carden built up his forces for the attack, most of February was taken up with a bitter row within the Government over how to exploit the expected success of the naval attack and in particular whether the only new division in the Army (the 29th) should be diverted from the western front to the Mediterranean. Throughout this period Churchill stuck to his position that the naval attack would achieve success without the Army becoming involved. He did not contemplate a combined operation to capture the Gallipoli peninsula in conjunction with the planned naval attack, and was only prepared to envisage the use of troops to follow up a successful naval enterprise. At the beginning of February he refused to send out the complete Royal Naval Division – only 2,000 Royal Marines were to go to demolish the forts once the fleet had put them out of action. On 16 February the War Council had an informal meeting, at which it was agreed that the 29th Division would be available if required, since operations based on Salonika to support Serbia, for which it had been provisionally earmarked, were no longer likely. In addition, since the Turkish attack on Egypt had been repulsed, about 50,000 Australian and New Zealand troops stationed in Egypt could be used if necessary. That day Churchill also told the Cabinet that 'he would take full responsibility' for the Dardanelles operation.[25]

Two days later he wrote to Kitchener to try and persuade him to have substantial forces ready to take advantage of the expected naval success:

> immense advantages may be offered wh cannot be gathered without military aid either to seize the Gallipoli peninsula when it has been

evacuated, or to occupy Constantinople, if a revolution takes place. We shd never forgive ourselves if the naval operations succeeded and the fruits were lost through the army being absent.[26]

On the same day the French, who had also decided to send troops so as to have some influence over operations, queried whether the naval operation should await their arrival. Churchill was strongly opposed, telling Grey and Kitchener that the naval operations would 'proceed continuously' to lessen the time available for the Germans to send submarines, and adding that any lull would 'prejudice the moral effect in the Turkish capital'.[27]

At the War Council on 19 February, Kitchener, reluctant as ever to send troops away from the western front, argued that the 29th Division should be held back and that the Anzac troops in Egypt would be sufficient to deal with the Turks. Churchill, who still favoured a purely naval operation, told his colleagues that he was not asking for troops actually to be sent to the Dardanelles, but only that 'they should be within hail'.[28] On 24 February he told Carden how he saw the plan of campaign:

> The operation ... consists in forcing the Dardanelles without military assistance ... It is not proposed at this stage to use military force other than parties of Marines landed to destroy particular guns & torpedo tubes. On the other hand, if your operation is successful, we consider it necessary that ample military force should be available to reap the fruits.[29]

Meanwhile operations had begun and they were not going well. The bombardment of the outer forts started on 19 February; only six ships were involved and about three-quarters of the Turkish guns survived. The battleships found that they had to drop anchor in order to attack individual guns. To do this in the Narrows would be very dangerous. Bad weather then stopped further attacks for a week. The War Council discussed the situation on 24 February. Fisher had expressed his continuing opposition the day before to Lloyd George, telling him 'the Dardanelles [would be] futile without soldiers'.[30] Lloyd George then told the War Council that he 'hoped that the Army would not be required or expected to pull the chestnuts out of the fire for the Navy'. Balfour said that a naval failure would be 'very serious' and Grey described such an eventuality as 'morally equivalent to a great defeat on land'. Despite the failure of the instant Turkish collapse to materialise, Churchill remained optimistic, saying that all involved were absolutely committed to success.

The meeting of the council two days later on 26 February rapidly degenerated into a furious shouting match, largely brought on by Churchill. He asked for the immediate despatch of the 29th Division, declaring that he would disclaim responsibility for the consequences if they were not sent. But he told his colleagues that these troops were only required 'to occupy Constantinople and to compel a surrender of all Turkish forces remaining in Europe, after the fleet had obtained command of the Sea of Marmora'.[31] Asquith told Venetia Stanley that 'Winston was in some ways at his worst – having quite a presentable case. He was noisy, rhetorical, tactless, & temperless – or – full.' When Kitchener's arguments to retain the 29th Division in England were accepted, Asquith noted 'Winston's immense & unconcealed dudgeon'.[32] In many ways these arguments over the despatch of the 29th Division were irrelevant – with over 50,000 troops available in Egypt, an additional 18,000 would not be critical – the crucial question was how troops were used. On this point Churchill was still adamant that he did not want a joint expedition, despite growing doubts in both the Navy and Army and among his ministerial colleagues about the likely success of the naval operation.

Then for a short while the attack seemed to go well and Churchill scented a stunning victory. On the day of the row in the War Council news reached Churchill that the renewed attack had silenced the guns at the entrance to the Dardanelles. (More ominously on three occasions Royal Marines had attempted to land to disable the forts but they were driven off and the expected quick Turkish collapse was still proving elusive.) Carden decided to move on to the next stage of the attack. On 28 February Churchill gave an off-the-record briefing to the press, in which he made it clear that the attack was not a mere demonstration of force but a determined attempt to break through the Dardanelles and move on to Constantinople. In taking this line Churchill had deliberately increased public expectations and made it much more difficult to pull back. At the War Council of 3 March Churchill painted a picture of a joint Greek, Russian, British and

French army of 120–140,000 men ready to exploit success. The next day he told Kitchener, 'I wish to make it clear that the naval operations in the Dardanelles cannot be delayed for troop movements, as we must get into the Marmora as soon as possible in the normal course.'³³ The feeling that success could be imminent was encouraged by a signal from Carden, who told Churchill that he expected to be in the Sea of Marmora, and therefore on the verge of reaching Constantinople, within a fortnight given favourable weather.

Almost immediately events began to go wrong. On 4 March the Russians formally vetoed any Greek participation in an expedition to Constantinople. (The British Government had promised to let the Russians have the city after the war and the latter did not want to jeopardise the chance to secure their centuries-old aim, especially to a rival with an equally ancient claim.) On 5 March Carden began the most difficult part of the operation – the attack on the forts in the Narrows – even though not all the intermediate forts had been crippled. Attacks that day and the next both failed, as did minesweeping efforts on 6–7 March and further bombardments on 7–8 March. Churchill was still optimistic despite these failures. On 9 March he wrote to Jellicoe: 'Our affairs in the Dardanelles are prospering, though we have not yet cracked the nut.'³⁴ The next day he reassured the War Council that passage of the Straits by naval means alone was still feasible – 'there was no hurry; and some time might be necessary'.³⁵ He then spoke rhapsodically of the political and strategic problems that would need to be faced after the fall of Constantinople, looking ahead to the achievement of war aims against Germany and the terms of a possible peace settlement, including the future of the German colonies and the surrender of their fleet. (Churchill also no doubt saw himself as gathering the political and public plaudits as the architect of victory.)

On the same day (10 March) Churchill saw a telegram from Carden, which, for the first time, freely admitted the limitations of naval power in the Dardanelles: 'our experience shows that gunfire alone will not render forts innocuous'.³⁶ The whole basis on which the operation had been launched in January now seemed to be in doubt. With the minesweepers unable to operate during daylight because of the fire from the forts, Carden decided to resort to nighttime minesweeping operations. These were tried on four nights but on each occasion they failed. Churchill drafted a response to

Carden's telegram, which was agreed by Fisher; it urged bold action and stated that losses could be accepted. Then in typically Churchillian fashion it went on to give the commander on the spot detailed instructions on how to carry out operations. In accordance with Churchill's orders, Carden made one more attempt to remove the mines at night. Again this failed and on 15 March Carden, on the point of complete mental collapse, resigned his post and was replaced by his deputy, De Roebuck.

In London faith in the Dardanelles operation was fading rapidly and the blame was beginning to be placed on Churchill as its chief instigator. On 16 March Hankey told Asquith: 'As recently as the last meeting [i.e. 10 March] the War Council were informed by the First Lord [Churchill] that the navy still hoped and expected to get through the Dardanelles without the assistance of military forces. Now, however, as was anticipated by most naval officers who were acquainted with the locality, the fleet is held up by a combination of mines and howitzers.'[37] Asquith shared the growing scepticism, writing on 18 March: 'The Admiralty have been very over-sanguine as to what they cd do by ships alone.'[38] Kitchener was not hopeful of success any more and blamed Churchill, telling French that 'W.C. was too impulsive and headstrong and that he had driven Carden off his head'.[39] Churchill too was becoming nervous about the prospects facing him. As Esher reported: 'Winston is very excited and "jumpy" about the Dardanelles; he says he will be ruined if the attack fails.'[40]

This nervousness reflected yet another unsuccessful attack, this time by De Roebuck on 18 March, with by far the most serious consequences so far. The daytime attack on the forts in the Narrows involved eighteen battleships with their escorting vessels and was intended to clear the way for minesweeping overnight followed by a short-range attack on the forts to finally open the way to the Sea of Marmora. At first the operation seemed to go well. By 2pm some of the forts were silenced but then the French ship *Bouvet* sank within a minute of being hit by a mine with the loss of nearly all the crew. Minesweepers failed to clear the minefields under fire from mobile artillery. Three more major ships were then struck by mines and put out of action. Altogether about a third of the force was either sunk or disabled and De Roebuck abandoned the operation. The allies had only been able to knock out permanently two of the fourteen-inch guns and some of the smaller ones but none of those protecting

175

the minefields (though this was only known after the war). Churchill was always to argue, on the basis of a single intercepted message, that at this juncture the forts were on the edge of running out of ammunition and that a resumed attack would have been successful. The best evidence from Turkish, German and Austrian sources suggests that they had enough shells for probably three more attacks on a similar scale and the allies could not have withstood continuing losses at the rate suffered on 18 March.

At first De Roebuck seemed willing to renew the attack. At an Admiralty meeting on 19 March Churchill, Fisher and Wilson all agreed that losses were only to be expected and that four more ships should be sent out to reinforce De Roebuck. Later in the day the War Council also agreed to another attack if De Roebuck were willing. On 21 March De Roebuck sent an optimistic message to say that he thought the forts could be dominated for long enough for minesweeping to take place (contrary to the evidence of the attack three days earlier) and that he was reorganising his force so that some of the destroyers could act as minesweepers. That day Churchill told Asquith that he was 'fairly pleased' with the situation.[41] In fact his remaining hopes were about to be shattered.

On 10 March Kitchener had finally agreed that the 29th Division should be sent to the eastern Mediterranean to support any naval breakthrough. After considerable lobbying, Churchill was able to secure the appointment of his old friend General Sir Ian Hamilton as Commander of British Forces and of his brother Jack to Hamilton's personal staff. Hamilton left London without any precise instructions, though Kitchener was coming round to the view that the Army would have to capture the Gallipoli peninsula, and badly briefed – he had a 1912 report on the Turkish Army, a pre-war report on the Dardanelles defences and an out-of-date map. At a conference with Hamilton on 22 March on board his flagship *HMS Queen Elizabeth*, De Roebuck announced that he now thought he would have to fight all the way to Constantinople and that he could not get through without the help of the Army. There was little discussion of the options and Hamilton accepted that the Army would have to land. This could not be done before 14 April and until then operations would cease.

Churchill saw De Roebuck's telegram announcing these decisions on the morning of 23 March. He convened a meeting of the

Admiralty War Group and put before it a draft reply ordering De Roebuck to resume the attack on the forts at the earliest opportunity. A furious row developed and Fisher, together with other naval members who had all along had doubts about a purely naval attack, refused to allow Churchill's draft to be sent. Churchill then went to see Asquith and Kitchener, who both felt that De Roebuck should make another attempt but neither was prepared to override the judgement of the commanders on the spot or that of the Admiralty Board. The Cabinet met later in the day and, like the War Council, failed to provide any strategic direction, making no formal decision for or against a land campaign – it was simply assumed Kitchener and the War Office would get on with the necessary planning.

The next day Churchill, unable to force De Roebuck's hand, sent a message, to which Fisher only reluctantly agreed, asking for detailed reasons why another naval attack should not take place. The commander's reply finally ended Churchill's hopes. He said that the idea that the forts could be destroyed by gunfire had 'conclusively proved to be wrong' and that the mines could not be swept until infantry had captured the peninsula and destroyed the forts. On 27 March Churchill was forced, reluctantly, to agree with those conclusions. His influence over operations at the Dardanelles was now declining as the War Office took increasing control. But he was still trying hard to avert the consequences of failure and hankered after sending more naval reinforcements despite Fisher's strongly expressed concern that the Navy's ability to take on the German fleet was being eroded. Fisher warned Churchill on 5 April: 'You are just eaten up with the Dardanelles and can't think of anything else! D_n the Dardanelles! they'll be our grave!'[42]

Asquith, Kitchener, Churchill and Hankey held a meeting on 30 March and agreed to go ahead with an amphibious landing despite the risks involved. That decision was confirmed at another meeting on 6 April when Churchill, sanguine as ever, told his colleagues that he 'anticipated no difficulty' with the military operation.[43] It was a fateful decision, lightly taken. In the annals of British military incompetence Gallipoli ranks very high indeed. The planning of the operation and the build-up of forces were the worst since the Crimea, and security was virtually non-existent. Not that it took a genius on the opposing side to guess what the British might do. The Turks had begun reinforcing the Gallipoli peninsula in the autumn of 1914 and at the end of March had appointed a German land commander. Landings were made by British and Anzac forces on 25 April (ten days behind schedule) at two points – Cape Helles on the toe of the peninsula and Anzac beach thirteen miles north. Both were badly handled and inadequately co-ordinated and local commanders failed to follow through their initial successes. By 8 May, after 20,000 casualties had been suffered, it was clear that no more progress would be made without reinforcements; the fighting had developed into a small-scale replica of the war on the western front. The campaign initiated so optimistically and with such little thought in January had failed on both the naval and military fronts.

The failure of the Dardanelles operation was one element in the political crisis that broke in the second week of May 1915, and it played a major part in Churchill's downfall. Given the scale of the naval and military ignominy suffered at the Dardanelles and Gallipoli it was virtually inevitable that a scapegoat would be required. Despite the failure of strategic judgement at both War Council and Cabinet level and by Asquith and Kitchener in particular, it was reasonable for Churchill to be given this role. He was overwhelmingly responsible for initiating the operation and he would without any compunction have claimed the considerable political credit available if the naval attack had been successful and led to Turkey's withdrawal from the war. Military failure also released a powerful current of negative feelings about Churchill among the political élite that had been accumulating for a long time. It reflected the nature of his rise in politics over the previous fifteen years.

Churchill was a man who saw politics as a field for personal ambition and often expressed that view a little too clearly for his own good. He was widely regarded as having few principles at all beyond self-advancement, and his behaviour had often exasperated and alienated his colleagues. In the wake of the Dardanelles disaster when Churchill badly needed friends and supporters, virtually none were to be found. He was widely seen in the Liberal Party as an interloper who did not really believe in the principles of Liberalism. Although a prominent figure in the party, he was not viewed as a future leader. The view held of him by influential Conservatives was even worse. They had never really forgiven him for betraying his party, and his family traditions, in joining the Liberals for what many saw as purely selfish reasons of personal ambition. His subsequent behaviour, especially his attacks on his former colleagues, only added insult to injury.

In his seven years in Cabinet he had proved on many occasions a difficult, temperamental and insensitive colleague. Churchill's eloquence (often directed at his colleagues' areas of responsibility) was also carried to extreme lengths among fellow politicians also eager to have their say. By early 1915 many in the Cabinet were becoming extremely tired of Churchill. In the autumn of 1914 he had been fairly close, both politically and socially, to Asquith but the Prime Minister's views were changing, as he showed in an unflattering portrait drawn for Venetia Stanley in early February:

> He never gets fairly alongside the person he is talking to, because he is so much interested in himself and his own preoccupations & his own topics than in anything his neighbour has to contribute, that his conversation (unless he is made to succumb either to superior authority or to well-directed chaff) is apt to degenerate into a monologue. It is the same to a certain extent in Cabinet.[44]

During one argument Lloyd George was driven to tell Churchill: 'You will see the point ... when you begin to understand that conversation is not a monologue.'[45]

Among less senior members of the Cabinet opinions of Churchill could be even less flattering. Hobhouse wrote of him in late March:

> always in a hurry to be conspicuous; he turns out *memorabilia* on international law, shipbuilding, blockade running, labour problems, and other *disjecta membra*, by the basketful. Nervous, fretful, voluble, intolerably bumptious and conceited, he squanders our time and his own in increasing orations.[46]

After just two months' experience of the Cabinet the new Chancellor of the Duchy of Lancaster, Montagu, listed Churchill's failings to Asquith: 'impetuous & wrong-headed energy, little power of adaptability, great obstinacy, lack of principle & & – these are a few of the flowers from a luxuriant posy of abuse'.[47]

Asquith was prepared to recognise that Churchill did have talents useful in a politician, notably his rhetorical powers and his capacity for hard work, but he felt there was a fatal flaw in his personality.

He told his wife in February: 'Winston is intolerable. It is all *vanity* – he is devoured by vanity.'[48] His sad (and inaccurate) conclusion was: 'he will never get to the top in English politics, with all his wonderful gifts; to speak with the tongues of men & angels, and to spend laborious days & nights in administration, is no good, if a man does not inspire trust'.[49] The senior Conservative politician, Lord Selborne, was driven to essentially the same conclusion in the judgement he penned in a series of sketches of members of the War Cabinet: 'I would go out tiger shooting with him any time, but I would never trust him in the absence of the tiger, because the motive power is always "self" and I don't think he has any principles.'[50]

Churchill was at the centre of two developments that preceded the political manoeuvring that led to the formation of a coalition Government: the so-called 'shell scandal' on the western front and the acrimonious resignation of Fisher as First Sea Lord. The 'shell scandal' was a political bombshell hurled by Sir John French – it came in the form of a newspaper story published in *The Times* on 14 May in direct contradiction to the Government's assurances that the Army had sufficient ammunition. Churchill had a long record of acting in concert with French. His constant visits to him in France caused major problems with Kitchener, who suspected Churchill of intriguing behind his back (he and French were old enemies from the time of the Boer War). Churchill had been friendly with French for years (the latter was a member of the Other Club) and since the outbreak of the war he had kept him informed of developments in the Cabinet and War Council and in particular the arguments used by Kitchener. In December 1914 Kitchener was on the point of resignation because of Churchill's activities and Asquith formally warned Churchill to stop his visits unless he had Kitchener's permission.

The background to the 'scandal' was the stalemate on the western front. In the spring of 1915 unimaginative British assaults on the German positions were failing ignominiously. At Neuve Chapelle in March as many shells were fired as in the whole of the Boer War but without securing a breakthrough. To quash rumours of a lack of artillery shells (the generals were convinced, wrongly, that shells, if used in sufficient quantity, would enable them to batter their way through trench defences) on 20 April Asquith made a public statement (based on a briefing by Kitchener) that British forces had

1a Lord Randolph Churchill

1b Lady Randolph Churchill
and Winston

1c Winston during his time
at Harrow

2 Churchill with the 4th Hussars at Bangalore

3a & b Churchill after his escape from Pretoria

4a Churchill speaking in Manchester during the 1908 by-election

4b Churchill and Clementine at Aldershot 1910

5a The Sidney Street siege

5b Churchill as First Lord of the Admiralty
with the Duke of Marlborough

6a Churchill at one of his flying lessons

6b Churchill during one of his visits to the front in 1915

7a British preparations for the landing at Cape Helles
after the failure of the naval attack at the Dardanelles

7b Churchill with the Munitions Council – Armistice Day 1918

8a Churchill at March Past of the 47th Division, Lille.
(Edward Marsh is in the row behind Churchill to his left)

8b Churchill during the 1918 General Election campaign

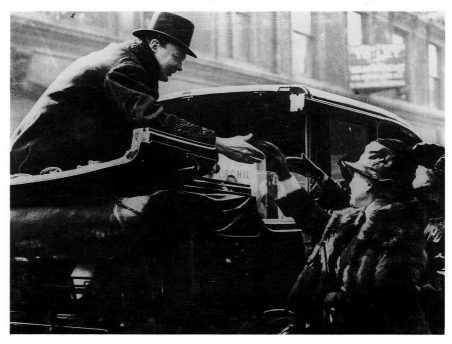

enough shells. The proprietor of *The Times*, Lord Northcliffe, was determined to pursue the Government on the issue and on 1 May he wrote to French suggesting that if French furnished one of his correspondents with a 'short and very vigorous statement' it would 'render the Government's position impossible'.[51] The failure of the assault on Aubers Ridge at the beginning of May (with even more casualties than at Neuve Chapelle) only exacerbated the issue.

Before joining French at his headquarters for the week-end of 8–9 May Churchill had been staying at the Ritz in Paris, not very well disguised as 'Mr Spencer', for talks with the Italians about naval operations if they joined the war on the allied side. Also present at BEF headquarters was Charles A'Court Repington, military correspondent of *The Times* and an old friend of Churchill, who had used him for many years to plant stories in the press. May Repington was given the story about the alleged shell shortage. French also sent his ADC, Captain Frederick Guest MP (Churchill's cousin), to London to tell Lloyd George, Balfour and Bonar Law, but significantly not Asquith, of the impending story. Exactly how Repington's story passed through military censorship is unclear but it appeared on 14 May. Churchill must have known what was happening while he was with French. Such moves might well have had his support, had he felt that the resulting political embarrassment could lead to formation of a coalition government. Political gossip for the previous six weeks (once the failure of the naval assault on the Dardanelles was clear) was full of stories of Churchill's intrigues, particularly with Balfour. For most of his political life he had hankered after coalitions and he may have felt that the best way of saving his career in the wake of the Dardanelles was through a major Government reconstruction – if so he was to be sadly disillusioned.

What Churchill could not have expected was that the furore over the shells shortage would coincide with an even worse one over Fisher's resignation and his role in it. On Churchill's return from France the question of the Dardanelles was once again at the top of the agenda within the Admiralty, reawakening Fisher's never very dormant fears that massive reinforcements would be sent, thereby weakening the fleet facing the Germans. With the Army unable to advance on the Gallipoli peninsula, Churchill was trying hard to revive the idea of a purely naval assault. On 11 May, after Churchill discussed with Fisher the idea of restarting minesweeping operations, the latter sent a minute to Asquith protesting. Later in the day Asquith reassured him that naval operations would not be begun without his approval, although Churchill only told him that he did not want to 'rush' the Dardanelles. Then on 12 May *HMS Goliath* was sunk with the loss of 570 men and Fisher forced Churchill to recall *HMS Queen Elizabeth*, although the latter insisted on replacing her with two older battleships and two monitor gunships. At this juncture Fisher was on the verge of resignation. He told Asquith he wished now that he had resigned at the War Council on 28 January when the Dardanelles had been initiated. However he agreed with Hankey not to go immediately, although he added ominously: 'I don't mean to explode my bomb without dead certainty it will act.'[52]

As had happened in Cabinet, Churchill's personal position was weakened by his arrogant behaviour and failure to co-operate with colleagues. When Fisher on 13 May demanded a formal end to operations at the Dardanelles, he had the backing of the other Sea Lords, who all felt that Churchill had usurped their authority by issuing telegrams and instructions without their consent. (He had deliberately chosen to interpret an 1869 Order-in-Council setting out his powers in the widest possible way, going far beyond the actions of his predecessors). Churchill deferred to the unanimous objections of his advisers although he still wanted to press De Roebuck into action. He told Fisher that he expected purely naval operations to be resumed within six weeks and asked him to stay on till they were completed. Fisher told Hankey that he thought Churchill was 'a determind mad Gambler'.[53]

On 14 May the War Council held a long, acrimonious and pessimistic meeting. The shell scandal had just broken and operations were deadlocked in both the west and east. It was agreed to ask Hamilton what further reinforcements he might need and this only added to Fisher's fears that more ships would be sent and a renewed naval attack undertaken. (If he had known that Churchill had told Asquith that he expected he would have to overrule Fisher on this point and take responsibility for another assault, Fisher's worst fears would have been confirmed.) That evening Churchill and Fisher discussed the scale of the naval reinforcements they were prepared to make available and appeared to reach agreement. After Fisher had gone to bed at his usual early hour Churchill worked on the details into the night (as was also usual with him) and added two submarines to the list of reinforcements, despite advice from Captain Crease, Fisher's secretary, that his boss would not agree and would probably resign. Churchill insisted on going ahead.

Fisher woke at 5am on Saturday 15 May to find four minutes from Churchill calling for more reinforcements than they had agreed the previous evening. This was too much for him. It showed Churchill as incorrigibly bent on having his way and he wrote his letter of resignation. It provoked a flurry of activity in political circles, aimed initially at trying to reverse Fisher's decision and avoid the scandal that would inevitably attach to a public rift at the Admiralty in the middle of a major operation. When Asquith learnt what had happened he wrote a terse letter to Fisher ordering him in the King's name to remain at his post. Fisher was eventually found locked in his room at the Charing Cross Hotel, where he was preparing to leave on the night sleeper bound for the Duke of Hamilton's house in Scotland. That afternoon Asquith saw Fisher and although he could not persuade him to change his mind prevailed upon him to stay in London. Churchill also wrote to Fisher appealing to him to stay. The arguments he deployed – that he had risked his career to bring Fisher back in the autumn of 1914 and that the resignation would let loose Conservative spite and be a major blow to the Gallipoli operation – were strange ones to use to Fisher.

Fisher replied to Churchill's letter on 16 May in one of his most emotional outbursts: 'YOU ARE BENT ON FORCING THE DARDANELLES AND NOTHING WILL TURN YOU FROM IT – NOTHING. I know you so well! . . . *You will remain* and I SHALL GO.' He thanked Churchill for his support but said that it was now 'a question beyond all personal obligations'.[54] He told McKenna that Churchill's letter the previous day had convinced him that he would go on and expand the Dardanelles operation. Churchill then wrote another letter trying to persuade Fisher not to go (Asquith would not accept the resignation without a statement of reasons) but Fisher refused to see Churchill. In the face of Fisher's determination Churchill turned his mind to the question of a successor and wanted to bring back Admiral Wilson, whom he had effectively sacked in 1911. He went down to Sutton Courteney, where Asquith was spending the day playing golf, to discuss possibilities.

The crucial political decisions about the Government's future took place on the morning of Monday 17 May, and Churchill was not involved. Early in the morning Bonar Law, the Conservative Leader, saw Lloyd George, who confirmed that Fisher was indeed resigning. They discussed the idea of a coalition Government, which both favoured. While Bonar Law consulted his two chief colleagues, Austen Chamberlain and Lord Lansdowne, Lloyd George went to see Asquith and they too agreed on the need for a coalition. Bonar Law and Asquith then met, formally agreed on a coalition and began a preliminary discussion about the distribution of offices. This rapid, seemingly casual decision taken by the two Leaders with little consultation marked the end of the last purely Liberal Government in British history. It is difficult to see the exact relationship between this decision and the shell crisis and Fisher's resignation; these two events may have been only the immediate pretext for a coalition that was decided on for other reasons. By May 1915 it was clear that the war was going to be prolonged and involve, as Churchill had remarked at the turn of the year, nations and not just armies. Economic mobilisation and possibly conscription would require a strong degree of national unity. The Liberal Government also faced an Election by the end of 1915 at the latest, which it expected to lose, and it could hardly ask for Conservative agreement to a postponement without offering to form a coalition. Bonar Law was reluctant to form a purely Conservative Government in wartime. Asquith, once he was convinced of the inevitably of coalition (which may have been some time before the actual crisis), acted quickly.

Despite his long adherence to the idea of coalition, its advent was a massive blow to Churchill's career. A fundamental Conservative demand was that he should leave the Admiralty. By now both Asquith and Lloyd George were quite willing to see Churchill in the role of scapegoat for the Dardanelles, a role which they felt he did in fact deserve. Lloyd George thought it was

the Nemesis of the man who has fought for this war for years. When the war came he saw in it the chance of glory for himself, & has accordingly entered on a risky campaign without caring a straw for the misery and hardship it would bring to thousands, in the hope that he would prove to be the outstanding man in this war.[55]

In the afternoon of 17 May ministers were surprised to receive a letter from Asquith asking for their resignations while a new Government was formed – it was the first most of them knew about a remaking of the Government. At this point Churchill still unaware of his deteriorating situation felt he was in a position to offer Asquith advice about the distribution of offices in the new Government, advice which was ignored. As for himself, he insisted: 'I will not *take* any office except a military department'; if this were not granted, his intention was to leave for the Army.

Fisher was still campaigning against Churchill. He wrote to Bonar Law that morning:

> I am absolutely unable to remain with W.C. (HE'S A REAL DANGER!) ... but W.C. MUST go at all costs! AT ONCE ... W.C. *is leading them all straight to ruin ... a very great national disaster is very near us in the Dardanelles.*[56]

In the afternoon intercepted signals suggested that the German fleet was putting to sea. Fisher refused to take command at the Admiralty and left operational control to Admiral Sir Frederick Hamilton, the Second Sea Lord. Asquith was furious and wrote to Balfour: 'Strictly speaking he ought to be shot: in any case it is a crime which ought not to be condoned, and still less to be rewarded.'[57] Any chance that Fisher had of influencing the outcome of the crisis caused by his resignation had ended.

Churchill still did not know about the Conservative veto on his staying at the Admiralty, nor of Asquith's and Lloyd George's real attitude towards him. But the papers on Tuesday 18 May began to change his views about his future. Most newspapers supported Fisher and there were strong personal attacks on Churchill's role in the affair. Early in the morning he wrote to Asquith saying that he would like to stay at the Admiralty because any move would by implication discredit his work and the Dardanelles operation. Nevertheless he hinted that he would take another office (perhaps the Colonies), a proposition which he had indignantly rejected when it was tentatively suggested by Lloyd George the previous afternoon. That evening he had a long discussion with his two Conservative friends, FE and Max Aitken, trying to see whether they could rally Conservative support for him. They had to tell him that he had no

Conservative support at all and they could not save him. Increasingly desperate, Churchill sent Bonar Law the next morning secret official telegrams on the Coronel and Falklands battles in an unavailing attempt to show that the public criticism was not justified.

That morning (19 May), Fisher, now clearly on the edge of mental derangement, sent an ultimatum to Asquith with his terms for remaining as First Sea Lord which were, if accepted, to be made public. Churchill was not to be in the Cabinet, Balfour was not to be at the Admiralty, there was to be a completely new Admiralty Board chosen by Fisher, who was also to have sole command over the disposition of the fleet and operations, with no war staff and the First Lord relegated to dealing mainly with 'parliamentary procedure'. Clearly no Government could have accepted such terms. They must have ended what little respect Asquith still had for Fisher. Churchill did not know of this ultimatum until after the war and still believed that striking a deal with Fisher might let him keep the Admiralty. On the evening of 19 May he approached Fisher through a junior minister, George Lambert, and offered him a place in the Cabinet if he would stay on as First Sea Lord. It was an extraordinary proposal and shows the depths of Churchill's desperation. Fisher rejected what was a hopelessly unrealistic proposal.

Feeling against Churchill was growing in all quarters. Jellicoe wrote to the Second Sea Lord that 'Winston Churchill is a public danger to the Empire'.[58] The Liberal politician Lord Beauchamp told the King's Private Secretary Lord Stamfordham (who passed the information to the King) that 'the feeling among his colleagues is that [Churchill] is primary cause of the trouble and should be the first to go instead of others who will lose their seats in Cabinet'[sic].[59] The King thought that Asquith should head a national government since 'only by that means can we get rid of Churchill from Admiralty. He is intriguing with French against K, he is the real danger.'[60] Others too thought that Churchill was involved not just in the Fisher resignation but also with the 'shell scandal'. A senior Liberal, W. M. R. Pringle, a close friend of Asquith, wrote to him to say that:

> a number of your supporters have been driven to the conclusion
> that the present crisis has been brought about by the actions of Mr.
> Churchill. I do not only refer to his differences with Lord Fisher
> but we believe that he was privy to the intrigue which resulted in

the Repington disclosures. In these circumstances we regard his presence in the Government as a public danger.[61]

On the same day (20 May) Lord Emott protested to Asquith about the rumours that Churchill might go to the Colonial Office, saying that 'he has neither the temperament nor manners to fit him for the post'.[62] And the next day Lord Beauchamp reported to Harcourt that as the Government's supporters watched the break-up of the administration 'the feeling in the Liberal Party against Churchill is very bitter in degree and increasing in extent'.[63]

On 20 May Asquith told Churchill clearly for the first time that he would not be staying at the Admiralty. Churchill was described by the newspaper owner Lord Riddell as 'worn out and harassed' and as having convinced himself that 'I am the victim of a political intrigue. I am finished.'[64] Churchill was so desperate that he persuaded Clementine to write an emotional letter to Asquith pleading for her husband's career. In the evening Churchill had a long talk with Bonar Law in a unavailing attempt to persuade him that he should stay at the Admiralty. Bonar Law told him what FE and Aitken had told him two days earlier – the Conservatives would not agree under any circumstanes. The following morning Churchill wrote a long letter to the Conservative Leader pleading for the new Cabinet to investigate the Dardanelles operation and then decide who should head the Admiralty (presumably with Churchill keeping the job until the investigation was complete). He also wrote an emotional appeal to Asquith. He argued that he could still make a success of the Dardanelles but if he was moved then the campaign might be abandoned and 'then on my head for all time wd be the blood of 30,000 brave men who have fallen . . . Let me stand or fall by the Dardanelles – but do not take it from my hands.' He then went on to claim, in complete contradiction to all the evidence he had of Conservative hostility, that: 'In the near future my aid to you in this strange government will be important: the political combination is one wh in the nature of things is extremely favourable to me.'[65]

Asquith had played his hand brilliantly and ruthlessly during the negotiations over the coalition. The Liberals retained all the key ministries – the Conservatives only obtained the Admiralty (Balfour), Colonies (Bonar Law), India (Austen Chamberlain) and the Local Government Board (Long). But he had sacked his close friend

Haldane without a word of apology. Now he told Churchill yet again that he could not stay at the Admiralty but that he still hoped to offer him a place in the Cabinet and suggested that he should take 'a large view' of the situation – something that it was rather easier for Asquith to do than Churchill. Churchill's second letter to Asquith on 21 May at last recognised the weakness of his political position. Instead of the bold declaration only four days earlier of a refusal to take anything but a military department he now capitulated totally and even offered an apology. He told Asquith: 'I am very sorry for yr troubles, and sorry to have been the cause of a situation wh has enabled others to bring them on you – I will accept any office – the lowest if you like – that you care to offer me.'[66] This wish at least was granted – Asquith finally offered him the sinecure office of Chancellor of the Duchy of Lancaster with a place in the War Council.

Within a week Churchill's political career had collapsed. His anger boiled over that evening when he bitterly criticised Asquith to Venetia Stanley for sacrificing him through lack of courage, friendship and loyalty. Churchill was never to forgive Asquith for his actions. There was a grain of truth in his complaint but Churchill had to a large extent brought his misfortunes on himself. His ambition, self-confidence and arrogance had left him with few friends in his hour of real political need. His judgement had been widely questioned for years before the disaster at the Dardanelles and his political opportunism meant that he had no solid base of party support on which to rely in a crisis. The events of May 1915 were in many respects the nemesis of his early career. As Frances Stevenson reflected when the political crisis was over: 'It seems strange that Churchill should have been in politics all these years, & yet not have the confidence of a single party in the country, or a single colleague in the Cabinet.'[67]

Part 2

RECOVERY AND DECLINE

1915–1938

10

The Wilderness

The whole of Churchill's adult life had been built around his political ambition. Now, in what must have seemed a ghastly repeat of his father's life, his career had been apparently smashed at an early age. He was disgraced, clinging on to a token appointment, at the age of forty. Many years earlier he told his colleague Walter Runciman that 'very few men are able to make more than one really bad mistake'.[1] Churchill had made that mistake. It was a shattering blow that left him deeply depressed, unable to see a way of rebuilding his career. Indeed worse was to come in the next few months as his career went further into decline. His best hopes were his comparative youth, which meant he had time to start again, together with his ambition, which was still driving him on. He never contemplated any other long-term career than politics.

His family life was also disturbed. They had to leave Admiralty House and find another home (their old house in Eccleston Square was still occupied by Sir Edward Grey). They moved to 41 Cromwell Road, which they shared with Goonie (Jack was at Gallipoli on Hamilton's staff). Most of their week-ends were spent at Hoe Farm near Godalming, which Churchill rented – it was not until the summer of 1917 that he bought a country house at Lullenden in Sussex, to be used for week-ends. Clementine, depressed herself, found it difficult to cope with Churchill's prolonged depression. The main problem for a man whose mental health was largely sustained by hyperactivity was that he had nothing much to do. Virtually all his time had been absorbed by politics and departmental work and he had no other interests to fill in the time. This void was at least partly filled when in the summer of 1915, at Hoe Farm, Goonie started Churchill on wha : was to become his main solace and pastime for the rest of his life – painting. He had been watching her paint and decided to try himself. For the first time he found something to interest him outside of politics and he rapidly became a skilful amateur painter (he held his first exhibition in 1921 under the pseudonym of Charles Morin), although the later value of his paintings probably owed more to his fame than their intrinsic merit.

Churchill took no interest in the work of the Duchy of Lancaster (mainly patronage) and left it in the safe hands of Lord Shuttleworth, the Lord Lieutenant, who had been a Liberal Chancellor himself in the 1880s. His personal staff consisted of his constant companion Edward Marsh and a shorthand writer; and his only achievement was to move the Duchy offices from the Strand to near Parliament, a more convenient base for what was left of his political life. As a face-saving gesture, Asquith had given Churchill a place on the Dardanelles Committee (which replaced the War Council as the body which was supposed to co-ordinate strategy) but his direct influence on decision making was minimal. He could give his opinion during discussions but it counted for little given the fact that he did not control an important department and his strategic judgement was tarred by failure. In public too he was widely associated with what was now becoming clear was a botched operation. He asked to go the Calais conference in July, which was to discuss future strategy with the French, but Asquith rejected his request. Later that month it seemed likely that he would be sent to Gallipoli to provide an assessment of the situation on the ground (Hankey was to accompany him to keep him under control) but when the Conservatives found out about the proposed expedition, they vetoed it and Hankey went on his own. It had become painfully clear that he was largely friendless at the top in politics. His relations with Asquith were cool at best; and, as he wrote to a friend, 'Between me and Ll G *tout est fini*.'[2] He devoted much of his energies to trying to salvage his tarnished reputation by circulating papers on Antwerp, the sinking of the three cruisers off the Dutch coast, Coronel and the Dardanelles to his Cabinet colleagues and even to sympathetic journalists like C. P. Scott of the *Manchester Guardian* but the effort was to no avail.

During the summer and autumn of 1915 Churchill was on the fringes of two important stategic and political decisions -- the future of operations at Gallipoli and the debate over the introduction of conscription. In early June despite the stalemate after the initial landings at Gallipoli, the new coalition Government decided to send three divisions as reinforcements so that a new assault could be tried. In early August the landings took place at Suvla Bay, just north of Anzac beach, and, demonstrating equal incompetence to the landings in April, failed dismally. Churchill saw his main object in this period as one of trying to see the operation through to success by backing it at whatever cost, in the hope that success might somehow redeem some part of his reputation. On 21 August, with the failure of the new landings evident, he wrote to Asquith, Kitchener and Balfour to suggest renewing the purely naval attack on the Dardanelles. Why Churchill thought it would succeed now when it had failed on many occasions before is unclear. His plea was rejected, as it was when he raised the matter twice more in October.

By the autumn the allies' overall strategic situation was deteriorating. A major German offensive in the east captured Warsaw, Austrian forces entered Belgrade and any remaining dreams of a Balkan confederation disintegrated when Bulgaria joined Austria and Germany, leading to the smashing of Serbia in the late autumn, which in turn left the pro-allied Rumania surrounded by hostile powers. The British had originally intended not to take part in any further offensives on the western front before 1916 but now agreed to participate in a French offensive in September. The attack at Loos cost about 200,000 British and French casualties without producing any significant gains. With failure on the western front and at Gallipoli the Government moved towards cutting its losses in the east. At one point Churchill did appear to agree with this approach – at the Dardanelles Committee on 19 August (when the new landings at Suvla Bay had obviously failed) he made the extraordinary proposal for a separate peace with Turkey on condition that the Straits were opened and their German advisers expelled. There was little chance of Turkey agreeing and Grey also pointed out that Britain's ally Russia could not agree to these terms either. A month later, after the Loos failure, Churchill advocated the opposite course of withdrawing ten divisions from France and landing them on the Asiatic side of the straits in another attempt to break the deadlock. As was now usual, his proposals were rejected by his colleagues.

Withdrawal from Gallipoli and the failure of the whole enterprise to knock Turkey out of the war was bound to further damage Churchill's reputation. He tried for some time to convince Asquith that he too would be tainted with the failure, but there was never much doubt that Churchill would be allotted the role of scapegoat by both the politicians and the public. In October General Sir Charles Monro (a man convinced that the western front was the decisive theatre) was sent out to report on the situation. He recommended withdrawal and the replacement of Hamilton as commander. Churchill was unable to save his friend, who was withdrawn in disgrace on 16 October and never given another command. The day before, Churchill wrote a long paper arguing for continuing the attack. Troops were in fact already being moved from Gallipoli to support the Anglo-French landing at Salonika (in neutral Greece) which failed to keep Serbia in the war. Gallipoli was finally evacuated in December and early January (when Churchill had left the Government) after the British, imperial and French troops had sustained over 200,000 casualties without achieving anything of military significance.

The second issue confronting the Cabinet was conscription: it was not new but it came up with greater urgency after the formation of the coalition. Although the Conservatives had no difficulty in accepting that the State should compel people to fight and direct labour into certain jobs, many Liberals were opposed on philosophical and political grounds to what they saw as a major betrayal of their principles; they preferred to try and fight the war without the mass mobilisation of economic and human resources. The problem for Asquith was to try and find a way of meeting the increasing manpower demands of the Army and munitions industries without breaking up the Government. Churchill never shared the agonies of many of his Liberal colleagues on the subject and on this issue remained close to his Conservative roots. Even before the outbreak of war he was privately moving towards supporting conscription. In 1912 he wrote to Lord Roberts, an old friend of Lord Randolph and commander in the Boer War who was running a major campaign for peacetime conscription, to say his views had changed. In 1900 he had been opposed, but 'I am disposed somewhat differently now towards it'.[3] He accepted without any difficulty the right of the State to conscript and his objections were entirely practical – there was insufficient support for it in peacetime. The next year he supported in Cabinet a Bill for compulsory military training in the Territorial Army but a majority of his colleagues were opposed.

Within three weeks of the outbreak of the war Churchill raised the issue of conscription in Cabinet. Kitchener retorted that it was not necessary; he already had more volunteers than the Army could handle (Kitchener wanted 700,000 men by April 1915 and 1 million volunteers had come forward by the end of 1914). In the circumstances the rest of the Cabinet could see no need to discuss the issue. Nevertheless they were subjected to what Asquith described as 'a long and rhetorical diatribe' from Churchill lasting for half an hour. One member recorded: 'we all sat and listened, much bored' and another described the scene thus:

> Winston wasted our time most atrociously today in pressing on our notice a premature scheme of conscription. He was both stupid and boring. Asquith contemptuous at first, but did not bear him down.[4]

Since Churchill was the earliest advocate of conscription in the Cabinet, it is perhaps surprising to find him taking an exactly opposite position in public in a speech given in his constituency on 5 June 1915. Then he extolled voluntary recruiting as 'one of the most wonderful and inspiring facts in the whole history of this wonderful island' and attacked conscription as 'unwise in the extreme' since it would only bring unsuitable people into the forces and moreover 'cast away this great moral advantage which adds to the honour of our Armies and to the dignity of our State'.

Whatever his high-blown rhetoric in public, Churchill was one of the strongest supporters of conscription in the coalition Government. In June he circulated a Bill to the Cabinet to conscript everyone in the country (male and female) who could then be directed to do any work the Government decided subject to a maximum of a six day week. Disobedience would lead to imprisonment. His ideas were savaged by Balfour. On 11 August along with Lloyd George and two

Conservatives, Curzon and Carson, he again argued strongly in Cabinet in favour of conscription. As a result he was made a member of the War Policy Committee set up four days later under the chairmanship of Lord Crewe to survey British economic and human resources for the long war that was now inevitable. The main report, ready in September, was non-committal. Since Kitchener still felt that voluntary recruiting was adequate, its main thrust was that Britain should be able to meet its obligation to provide seventy divisions throughout 1916 without introducing conscription. Churchill joined the three Conservatives on the committee in a dissenting report, which advocated an army of one hundred divisions throughout 1916 and the immediate imposition of conscription to achieve it. The resulting row badly split the Cabinet, with Churchill joining the group attacking Kitchener, Asquith and the direction of the war so far. For a time it seemed that Lloyd George might be prepared to lead the group in a coup against Asquith. Churchill hoped such a coup might revitalise his career, which probably explains why he wrote to Asquith on 4 October suggesting that Kitchener should leave the War Office and be replaced by Lloyd George. The tension was resolved because Lloyd George did not think the time propitious to replace Asquith and because a compromise was reached: Lord Derby was appointed as Director of Recruiting and it was announced that unless an unspecified number of volunteers registered by the end of March 1916 (the Government had in mind 500,000), conscription would be imposed.

The growing likelihood of the abandonment of the Gallipoli campaign and the resolution of the conscription crisis without Asquith's resignation seriously narrowed Churchill's political options. They were finally closed off with a reconstruction of the Cabinet committee overseeing strategic policy. By October there were growing complaints within the Government at Kitchener's handling of the Army and his refusal to involve his colleagues in decisions or give them vital information. Yet because of his over-inflated reputation and public standing it was almost impossible to sack him. He was first offered command of all armies outside France, which he refused, and then he was sent on what the politicians intended to be an extended fact-finding mission in the Near East. They agreed that during his absence they would replace the Dardanelles committee with a new smaller war committee that would exclude Kitchener. Unfortunately for Churchill it was also likely to exclude him too. At first he thought he would be included, basing his hopes on a highly ambiguous verbal agreement with Asquith. By the end of October he knew this was not the case. He would therefore be left as no more than the holder of a sinecure office with no scope for influencing the conduct of the war. Even if he could bring himself to accept such humiliation, it was likely he would be dropped from the Government altogether at the next reshuffle. Churchill decided to go before this happened and before the final decision was taken to evacuate Gallipoli in the hope that if he was out of office he might at least avoid some of the blame.

He wrote his first letter of resignation on 30 October but agreed that no action should be taken until after Asquith made his speech on the Dardanelles in the Commons on 2 November. The Prime Minister defended the operation in general terms but not Churchill specifically and, significantly, he failed to use any of the material Churchill had given him. The Dardanelles Committee met for the last time on 6 November and the new War Committee, consisting of Asquith, Lloyd George, Balfour, Bonar Law and McKenna, met for the first time on 11 November. The same day Churchill wrote another letter of resignation; Asquith accepted it on the 12th and their exchange of letters was published the next day. Churchill made his resignation speech in the Commons on 15 November. In it he naturally defended the Dardanelles and Gallipoli campaigns and still argued in favour of pushing on at Gallipoli. He blamed Fisher for most of the problems saying, in what was at best an over-simplification and at worst a travesty of the facts: 'I did not receive from the First Sea Lord either the clear guidance before the event or the firm support after which I was entitled to expect.' Then in a phrase that was to haunt him for years he described the naval attack at the Dardanelles as 'a legitimate gamble'. The speech did little to revive his tattered reputation.

Rather than staying on as an active backbencher Churchill decided to join the Army, an idea that had never been far from the front of his mind since the outbreak of the war, especially after Antwerp a year earlier. He had a clear idea of what he should do if he joined the Army, and it did not entail a return to regimental soldiering, despite his limited experience – four years as a cavalry lieutenant over fifteen years earlier. In early May 1915 (after the initial failure at Gallipoli but before the political crisis), sensing his career might be in trouble, he had written to his old friend French asking for his help. It is one of the few letters he wrote not to survive but in his reply French offered to find him a command in France. In June he turned down the offer from the GOC of Southern Command of the command of a battalion of his regiment, the Oxfordshire Hussars, partly because he wanted to stay in politics for a while but also almost certainly because he did not regard it as a sufficiently prestigious offer. At the beginning of September he discussed with Asquith the possibility of resigning and taking command of a brigade under French, with the likelihood of rapid promotion to General. The Prime Minister was happy with whatever French thought correct but when on 22 September the demand was upped to the command of a Corps with the rank of Major-General, he 'found the request a most embarrassing one, as he would like to get rid of Churchill, but could not offend the army'.[5] By October Churchill had increased his demands to being made Governor-General and Commander-in-Chief in east Africa, where the smaller German forces were defying inept British attempts to end the war there. Asquith was initially tempted but decided against it after worrying about the possible press reaction to a politician, in particular Churchill, being given the job.

Churchill, while remaining an MP, therefore left Britain for France on 18 November without a clear understanding of what his role in the Army was to be, although nominally he was going to join the Oxfordshire Hussars. The moment he landed at Boulogne he was taken by car to the headquarters of the BEF. Over dinner French suggested to his guest that he might like to be either one of his ADCs or command a brigade, with rapid promotion to General. Churchill chose the latter option, but felt that he ought to have at least a short spell in the trenches before taking command. The next day Lord Cavan, commander of the Guards division, was summoned and he agreed that Churchill should gain his experience with the socially exclusive Grenadiers. To compensate for life in the trenches French assured him that he had open access at any time to his headquarters for a room, bath and meals. Since he was also given the privilege of corresponding with Clementine via French's head-quarters, his letters, unlike those of other front-line officers, were not subject to censorship. Clementine was able to keep him well supplied with extra clothing, gourmet food and alcohol. Churchill was not made particularly welcome by the Grenadiers, who rightly regarded him as a temporary interloper in their private world, but the advantage of the attachment was that the Grenadiers only spent two days at a time in the front-line trenches compared with the six days endured by a normal regiment.

By the beginning of December, after two short spells in the trenches, Churchill returned to French's headquarters for a stay of nine days. French, suspecting that he was about to be sacked, suggested that his friend should immediately take over a brigade. Although he had spent less than a week in the front line, on 9 December Churchill was told he would be going to command 56th Brigade. During his brief time in France politics had never been far from his mind. On 27 November he had advised Clementine to keep in touch with important press owners and editors. After long talks with General Wilson, the latter reported that Churchill was openly discussing the overthrow of Asquith and that 'he was going to wait for Gallipoli and Salonika disasters and then jump in'.[6] On 7 December he received a letter from Curzon describing differences within the Cabinet over the Gallipoli evacuation and Churchill convinced himself that the breakup of the coalition was about to happen and that he ought to be back in London. On reflection he realised that it was too soon for his return, but his aims had not changed. On 15 December he wrote to Clementine that he was thinking of returning to the Commons early in the new year to try and remove Asquith and Kitchener, both of whom he now blamed for all the political and military failures: 'The hour of Asquith's punishment & K's exposure draws nearer. The wretched men have nearly wrecked our chances. It may fall to me to strike the blow. I shall do it without compunction.'[7]

Before he could make any political moves Churchill faced another disaster, this time in his military ambitions. On 14 December French was sacked as Commander of British Forces in France and replaced by Haig. On one level Churchill was pleased, because he disliked the alternative to Haig – General Robertson, who had risen through the ranks from private and who, according to Churchill, was no better than 'a footman & drops his aitches'.[8] However Haig, unlike French, was not a close friend and was not prepared to use his influence to promote Churchill far beyond the rank to which he was entitled based on his limited military experience. Asquith too was not happy with the sort of rapid promotion French had in mind and it was agreed that Haig should offer Churchill no more than the command of a battalion and the rank of Lieutenant-Colonel, which was his strict entitlement based on his experience, and no rapid promotion. This was not at all what Churchill had expected when he decided to join the Army in France nor did he relish the prospect of joining an ordinary regiment which, unlike the Grenadiers, would not contain people he regarded as his social equals. He objected to having to get by without any special treatment and influence but, he was left with no real alternative but to accept what was on offer. He made it clear to Clementine how much he objected to being treated as an ordinary citizen, complaining that there was little point in commanding a battalion. He went on:

> The risk and labour of such a task are vy heavy, & I am a special target for criticism. The appointment is no gift. With my rank & war services I cd have obtained it quite easily had I been an ordinary unknown officer. I shd be practically alone with 1000 amateur officers and untrained men, in a situation of much anxiety and no real scope.[9]

Churchill returned to London on 22 December in order to spend Christmas with his family and at the beginning of January 1916 he was back in France, where he learnt he had been put in command of the 6th Battalion of the Royal Scots Fusiliers.

Churchill arrived on horseback to join his battalion in a reserve area at Meteren near the Belgian border on 5 January, accompanied by two grooms and a large limber containing all his personal belongings, which included his own bath and boiler. At lunch on the first day he refused to speak to his junior officers and spent the time staring at them. They were, he told Clementine, 'small middle class Scotsmen'.[10] The battalion had been badly mauled in the futile battles of Loos and Ypres and morale was low. Churchill spent the next three weeks working hard to improve morale and efficiency before a spell in the front line.

The battalion moved forward on 24 January and took over a 200-yard stretch of trenches near Ploegsteert just over the Belgian border. It was a quiet section of line and the battalion was only to lose fifteen killed and 123 wounded in the next three months. They settled into a routine of six days in the front-line trenches and six days further back, though still under occasional artillery fire. Churchill set up his headquarters in a farm, led the occasional raid into no man's land at night, had one or two narrow escapes from exploding shells but generally took a fatalistic view that the chances of being killed in such a quiet sector were fairly low. He even found time to do some painting. He was with his battalion until 2 March when he returned to London on leave.

During January and February 1916, unusually for Churchill, politics receded in importance somewhat. Nearly all his regular letters to Clementine were filled with details of Army life instead of political intrigue. Yet he remained alert to the political situation. He met his old friend FE, together with Lloyd George, Max Aitken (later Lord Beaverbrook – with whom he became close for the first time in France) and Bonar Law on the night of 30–31 January. They naturally discussed politics and agreed informally that Asquith would have to go. From then on Churchill seems to have identified himself with them and to have hoped that if they mounted a coup against Asquith (whom he now regarded as his inveterate opponent), he might benefit politically. His leave in early March was designed to enable him to see people in the political world and plan his future course and so his family, whom he had not seen for two months, were expected to take a back seat.

The main event of his time in London was a speech in the Navy debate made from the opposition front bench. It was to further undermine his reputation and raise all the old doubts about his judgement. Churchill began with a strong attack on Balfour's time at the Admiralty since May 1915 and he spoke in general terms about his worries over the numbers of battleships and destroyers, the falling rate of ship construction and the increasing danger from submarines. He then undermined his whole case and provoked ridicule by demanding the recall of Fisher as First Sea Lord. In response Balfour demolished Churchill by simply repeating what his opponent had said about Fisher less than four months ago in his resignation speech. Asquith and Balfour also knew that Churchill had protested strongly about Fisher's appointment to the Admiralty Board of Inventions and Research in July 1915. On that occasion he had described him as 'a very old man, without the nerve to carry on war, not quite sane in moments of crisis, and perfectly unscrupulous'.[11] Even after this fiasco Churchill was still talking about staying in London to lead the opposition to the Government and he managed to have his leave extended so that he could speak in the Army debate. But he was told by Asquith on 9 March that his political position was hopeless and he really ought to return to France. Churchill did so on 13 March but his intention was to leave the Army and he left behind him a press release announcing the fact. He changed his mind on rejoining his battalion and had to hurriedly ask Clementine to withdraw the statement before publication.

Although he had decided not to leave the Army immediately, Churchill was clear it was only a matter of time before he would do so. On the day of his return to France he had convinced himself that Army life was not for him: 'my true war station is in the H of C' and a few days later he told Clementine that the only problem was how to present his return to politics in the most favourable light. It was, he wrote, simply a matter of 'when & on what grounds'.[12] Those advising Churchill at this juncture – Clementine, Archibald Sinclair (his second-in-command and a Liberal politician whom Churchill had promised to help find a constituency), his constituency chairman Sir George Ritchie, J. L. Garvin, editor of the *Observer*, and Sir Edward Carson, leader of the Ulster opposition to the pre-war Liberal Government – all advised against an early return. They all knew that despite Churchill's wishful thinking the Government was well-entrenched and unlikely to fall in the near future. They thought his return to active politics so soon after his resignation and after such a short stay in the Army would hardly improve his reputation.

Churchill's letters to Clementine after his return to France in mid-March are nearly all about politics rather than, as before, Army life. He was now more realistic about the weak hand he held but was still keen to play it rather than stay in the Army condemned to a life of routine soldiering among people he found socially beneath him. Assessing his chances, Churchill realised that Lloyd George represented his best hope of a return to government since Asquith had no reason to help him. He was not altogether confident that Lloyd George would help but through FE tried to remind his old colleague of some of the political debts he was still owed, in particular his help in defusing Conservative criticism and convincing FE to act as counsel for Lloyd George when he was embroiled in the Marconi share scandal before the war. Churchill was back in London on 19 April for a secret Commons session on the conduct of the war and wanted to stay on but was recalled to duty because his battalion was in the front line.

It was to be his last visit to France as an Army officer. At the end of April he learnt that the 6th and 7th Battalions of his regiment were to be amalgamated because of a shortage of men and that Lt Col Gordon of the 7th Battalion would command the new unit since he was a regular soldier. This was just the opportunity to quit that Churchill had wanted. He told Clementine, 'It is really a most fortunate and natural conclusion: & well worth waiting for.'[13] On 6 May Churchill's battalion entrained for a rest in reserve at Bethune before being sent to the slaughter on the Somme. Churchill left them the following day. He had been with the Army for under six months and had spent less than half that time in front-line conditions.

Churchill had now chosen the life of a backbencher in opposition to the coalition Government. He was returning to the House of Commons at a time when his reputation was at a low ebb. Although he spoke regularly, he was politically isolated and his interventions were ineffectual. He received only minimal co-operation from Carson and the Unionist War Committee that sought a more energetic war policy and he also found it difficult to criticise the work of the War Office after Kitchener's death in June because he depended on Lloyd George, the new Secretary of State, for political rehabilitation. He was still hated in Conservative circles and they made it abundantly clear that they were not prepared to work with him. Lord Derby told Lloyd George in August 1916: 'He has got a very attractive personality but he is absolutely untrustworthy as was his father before him.'[14]

It was a difficult time for Churchill as he realised that he could not change his mind again and return to the Army. The future must have seemed very bleak – he would have to continue as an impotent and unpopular backbencher. The timing of any return to government was largely out of his hands. He was still haunted by the Dardanelles and was desperate to restore his reputation by rehabilitating the operation he had been instrumental in launching. In the summer of 1916 Churchill thought that his chance to do so had at last arrived. Under increasing Parliamentary pressure to account for the disaster, the Government announced on 1 June that it would publish papers to explain the inception and conduct of the Dardanelles and Gallipoli campaign. Churchill, working closely with both Fisher and Hamilton (who shared his desire to clear their name), lobbied for publication of all the papers, seeing it as a way of vindicating himself by showing that others (particularly Asquith) were implicated. However, the Government had second thoughts about the damage that would be caused by exposing all its discussions in public and chose the safer route of a committee of enquiry. This was set up on 20 July, chaired by the aged and dying Lord Cromer.

Churchill spent nearly all his time between July and September preparing his evidence to the committee. He and Fisher agreed to concert their evidence and stand or fall together since exposing the differences within the Admiralty would help neither of them. Asquith refused access to the minutes of the War Council but Lloyd George helped by providing papers and FE advised him on how to present his case. Churchill rather naively believed that the whole process had been set up for his benefit and asked for the right to be present whenever the committee took evidence and to cross-examine all witnesses. Both requests were inevitably denied. Churchill's statement was ready by 8 September and he gave evidence at the end of the month. He accepted that he was 'the moving spirit' behind the Dardanelles operation[15] but naturally presented a case that put his own actions in the most favourable possible light, even though that meant on many occasions distorting events. According to Churchill's evidence all the plans were based on those of the commander on the spot and Admiralty advice. They were all approved in the regular way by the War Council and the French Government, and Fisher and the other admirals gave their assent at all stages. The operation was well-conceived and could have been called off at any stage and it was only not pushed through to final success because troops had become available for a combined operation.

After giving his evidence Churchill still felt that the committee was not carrying out the function he had allotted it – allowing him to clear his name. On 17 October he wrote to Cromer again asking to be given a privileged position and to be allowed to cross-examine witnesses and comment on all the evidence provided. His appeal was again rejected. In February 1917 he saw the first draft of the early sections of the report dealing with the Dardanelles and sent in his criticisms because he felt it did not sufficiently justify his actions. He also protested at the cuts made by the Government before the report was published, although he must have known that the evidence from for example the Director of Naval Intelligence could not be published during the war because it revealed the successful interception of German signals.

When the report was published in March 1917 Churchill found he had achieved some of his aims. It certainly made it clear that he did not take all the decisions and that people like Asquith and Kitchener had also been influential. But although the report squashed some of the wilder rumours about Churchill's role it did not clear him of all responsibility and neither did it take the view that the operation was, as Churchill put it, 'a legitimate gamble' – it was critical of the inception and planning of the whole campaign. Churchill spent six days preparing his speech for the subsequent Commons debate on 20 March. In it he argued that the criticism directed at him also involved others, he made detailed comments about the way the evidence was presented in the report and argued that final judgement should be suspended until all the evidence was available. Despite his efforts Churchill found that he had at best secured a draw over the work of the committee. He had not been vindicated. Doubts remained about his judgement and the inception of the campaign even if it was now clear that not all the blame could be heaped on his head.

The report of the committee was also important to Churchill because by early 1917 his political prospects had begun to improve, even though he had suffered another stunning disappointment at the end of 1916. During the autumn of that year criticism of Asquith's Government was rising as the position of the allies in the war deteriorated. The Somme offensive had been a disaster and had destroyed much of the carefully created British military strength for no recognisable gain. The Russians were in retreat, the French were nearing breaking point at Verdun, the Balkans were dominated by the Central Powers, Italy's contribution to the allies had been hard to detect, shipping losses were mounting, the Battle of Jutland had at best been a draw and Britain was rapidly approaching a financial crisis. There was widespread talk of a compromise peace. Unless all the work and losses of the previous two years were to be thrown away, a huge national effort would have to be made to mobilise every available resource. Asquith did not seem the man to do this and there was growing discontent with his leadership. With the Liberals still the largest party in the Commons only a Liberal could lead the coalition and Lloyd George was the obvious choice.

Churchill saw this as his opportunity. Ever since his resignation he had thought that a Lloyd George ministry would be his most likely route back to power. In mid-November 1916 C. P. Scott found Churchill in optimistic mood: 'I asked if in case George formed a ministry he could count on being included. He said he thought so – that George would desire it and that it would be in his interest.'[16] Churchill however was a mere spectator of the crisis that led to Asquith's resignation and replacement by Lloyd George in early December. By chance he was at a political dinner the night Asquith resigned and Lloyd George began the delicate task of distributing posts in the Government he expected to form. Max Aitken was delegated to tell Churchill that his old colleague could not include him in the new Government. At least four powerful Conservatives (Austen Chamberlain, Walter Long, Lord Robert Cecil and Lord Curzon) had made it clear that they would only join on condition that Churchill was excluded. Also the Conservative Leader, Bonar Law, had damningly told Lloyd George that Churchill was far more dangerous inside a government than outside it. The new Prime Minister could not afford to alienate the very men who were putting him into power. Churchill told Sinclair it was 'the downfall of all my hopes and desires'.[17]

Lloyd George shrewdly sent his confidant Lord Riddell to see Churchill shortly after the Government was formed. Riddell told him that there was no intention to keep him out of office permanently but that Lloyd George could do nothing until the Dardanelles report was published (and also, though this was left unsaid, until the Prime Minister's own political position was stronger). Churchill replied that he made no reproaches but Lloyd George's own conscience would tell him what to do – another oblique reference to the Marconi scandal and Churchill's help in getting him out of a tight spot. Lloyd George's initiative served to reduce the incentive for Churchill to ally himself with an embittered Asquith who had refused to serve under Lloyd George and was now leading the Parliamentary opposition to the coalition. (Asquith had tried to tempt Churchill with the extraordinary offer of a return to the Admiralty if he resumed the Premiership.)

Lloyd George's initiative worked. Churchill was politically quiescent during the first months of 1917 and his Parliamentary criticisms were much more muted and constructive. He saw Lloyd George fairly regularly and also remained close to FE, who had been promoted to Attorney-General, and his cousin Freddie Guest, who was now acting as Whip for those Liberals who supported the coalition. By early June, three months after publication of the Dardanelles committee report, Lloyd George felt politically strong enough to consider overriding continuing Conservative objections and recall Churchill. These objections were still very strong. Curzon warned the Prime Minister: 'It will be an appointment intensely unpopular with many of your chief colleagues . . . He is a potential danger in opposition. In the opinion of all of us he will as a member of the Govt be an active danger in our midst.'[18] Sir George Younger, Chairman of the Conservative Party, made a formal protest and the Central Council of the Conservative National Union passed a resolution that Churchill's recall would be 'an insult to the Army and Navy and an injury to the Country'.

Under this pressure Lloyd George hesitated for a while. In the end though the Conservatives were not prepared to stop the Prime Minister from having the colleagues he wanted. They also appreciated the political calculation behind the move. Churchill's recall, delayed until 16 July, was linked to that of Edwin Montagu, who was appointed Secretary of State for India, thereby depriving Asquith of two potential supporters. Churchill was given the much less prestigious post of Minister of Munitions, but by now he was grateful to accept whatever was offered. After over two years in the political wilderness and eighteen months out of office altogether Churchill was back in power.

The Fringes of Power

The bitter experience of the Dardanelles and his frustrating time in the wilderness did not change Churchill's character nor his way of dealing with his colleagues; neither did it undermine for long his tremendous self-confidence and firm belief that he was always right. At first though he was slightly more cautious, taken aback to discover that people were so hostile to him. Maurice Hankey saw Churchill just after his appointment as Minister of Munitions and noted in his diary:

> On the whole he was in a chastened mood. He admitted to me that he had been 'a bit above himself' at the Admiralty, and surprised me by saying that he had no idea of the depth of public opinion against his return to public life, until his appointment was made.[1]

But within a month many of the old complaints about his behaviour were being made. In the middle of August 1917 Lord Derby and the Chief of the Imperial General Staff, Robertson, backed by Curzon, were protesting to Lloyd George about Churchill's interference in their work. They were joined by the First Lord of the Admiralty, Sir Eric Geddes, who objected to Churchill involving himself in questions such as destroyer design, the use made of the 10th Cruiser Squadron and the manning of the fleet. Both Derby and Geddes threatened to resign unless Churchill was curbed. Lloyd George had a long talk with him and convinced him that he had to be more circumspect if he was to survive.

What had changed for Churchill was his position in Government. He was no longer part of the inner circle. He was not a member of the War Cabinet and he played no part in the crucial discussions on strategy and the conduct of the war. Even in his own field of responsibility he was often ignored. In March 1918 he sent a paper to the War Cabinet on the type of warfare likely if the war continued into 1919 but he was not invited to the meeting which discussed future strategy. Churchill was far from happy with this situation. In April 1918 he drafted a letter to send to Lloyd George arguing that 'the high policy of the State ought not to be settled by so narrow & unrepresentative a body as yr War Cabinet'.[2] He decided not to send the letter but a month later discussed the issue with the Prime Minister and afterwards sent him a letter saying 'I do not think the new system . . . of governing without a regular Cabinet is sound or likely to be successful'.[3] During the Second World War, when he was in Lloyd George's place, Churchill was to take the opposite view.

Churchill's exclusion reflected not just his weak political position and continued Conservative hostility but also the fact that the Ministry of Munitions was no longer of central political importance. The key decisions about the mobilisation of the economy and manpower resources had been taken before Churchill took office and the ministry now spent most of its time dealing with the administration of a complex armaments programme. Britain had entered the war hoping that normal economic and trade conditions could be preserved. The commitment to create a continental army and the scale of ammunition use meant that this policy could not be sustained. Neither the War Office nor the armaments industry was able to cope with such a rapid expansion. When the coalition Government was formed in May 1915 Lloyd George moved from the Treasury to the new Ministry of Munitions to direct the mobilisation of the economy for something approaching total war.

Under Lloyd George the structure of the ministry had been haphazard as he moved from solving one problem to another, bringing in businessmen (mainly from the armaments industry) to run particular departments and strongly resisting any attempts to impose normal Whitehall rules and staffing. The ministry grew rapidly as new functions were taken on – designing new munitions, supplying tanks, deciding policy on machine tools, developing Britain's mineral resources, allocating imports, and settling policy for the construction of such diverse items as railway supplies, motor engines and aircraft. In July 1916 there were eighteen departments and 5,000 staff, a year later fifty departments and 15,000 staff. Lloyd George's two immediate successors, Montagu and Addison, accepted that what the ministry needed, once the initial phase of growth was over, was a bureaucratic structure that would enable it to cope with running such a complex operation and they had begun to look at possible schemes though neither was there long enough to implement them.

Churchill decided that his first task was to turn the ministry into a normal Whitehall department with a coherent management structure. He brought in two civil servants from the Admiralty, Masterson-Smith, who had been one of his private secretaries there, and Sir Graham Greene, and between them they devised a scheme which Churchill implemented. This removed the power of the fifty semi-independent departmental heads and grouped them under ten members of a new Munitions Council responsible for policy on finance, design, steel and iron, materials, explosives, projectiles, guns, engines, labour policy and relations with allied governments (air and warfare departments were added later). The Munitions Council (acting rather like the Admiralty Board or the Army Board) would settle policy for the ministry and provide a structure for resolving internal disputes, replacing the previous unwieldy arrangement whereby it had been left to the minister to deal with differences between the fifty heads of department. The Council met regularly under Churchill's chairmanship in the second half of 1917 but most of its work was soon undertaken in a network of committees (seventy-five of them by the end of the war). At the same time more civil servants were moved into the ministry, its operating methods were brought into line with the Whitehall norm and its pay and staff grades made the same as the rest of the civil service. Churchill essentially presided over the bureaucratisation of the ministry and its development of routine procedures to replace the ad hoc methods of its initial phase.

On taking office Churchill found that the ministry was reaping the benefits from all the extra production facilities started by his predecessors in the previous two years. The problems he faced in 1917 were not those of constructing and expanding munitions production but rather of balancing the programme so as to make the optimum use of the resources available. Production was at a level that was difficult to increase given Britain's resources. From the end of 1917 Churchill found that it was necessary to cut imports because of the shipping shortage caused by Germany's successful submarine warfare. As a result steel production fell by fifteen per cent in 1918 and ammunition production by twenty per cent, leaving the British Army with lower levels of ammunition than the French. In 1918 production faced another major problem – too many miners had been called up into the armed forces and the resulting lower levels of coal production reduced steel output. Churchill was forced to plan on reducing ammunition production by another twenty per cent in 1919.

In order to compensate for these restrictions Churchill wanted to concentrate munitions production on high-technology items – tanks, aircraft and chemical warfare. He had been involved in early work on the tank when he was at the Admiralty. The idea of combining existing technologies (the internal combustion engine, armour plating and caterpillar tracks) into one machine had been around for some time. The initial stimulus came from Colonel Swinton, a War Office observer with the Army in France, who persuaded Hankey to push the concept within Whitehall, and work on prototypes began in the War Office in January 1915. Churchill also took up the idea enthusiastically but characteristically wanted his own programme in the Admiralty. His original idea for a vehicle that put down and picked up a 'bridge' for crossing trenches was rejected, but in late February 1915 he persuaded the Admiralty to spend £70,000 on building an experimental 'land ship' (it was Swinton who thought of the name tank). A month later Churchill agreed that eighteen prototypes should be built (six were to have wheels and twelve tracks). After he left the Admiralty they lost interest in financing what was obviously an Army project and only one of the prototypes was actually built. Churchill had therefore helped with some of the experimental work although the major work was undertaken by the War Office and Ministry of Munitions. Britain had the first tanks operational by 1916 although they were not used on a large scale until the Battle of Cambrai in 1917. As Minister of Munitions

Churchill remained enthusiastic about the new weapon and pushed hard for its wider and better use against obscurantist thinkers in the Army. By the summer of 1918 the Army had about 700 tanks, and Churchill envisaged a force of about 4,000 in 1919.

Another major new weapon of the war was aircraft. In 1914 Britain built fifty aircraft a month; by 1918 this had risen to an output of over 3,500 a month of vastly more technically complex machines and production was expected to rise still further in 1919. The technology in which Churchill placed greatest faith though was chemical warfare, which had first been used by the Germans in 1915. It was at this time that Churchill developed what was to prove a life-long enthusiasm for the widespread use of this form of warfare. In November 1917 he advocated its adoption on a massive scale, including for the first time production of gas bombs to be dropped by aircraft – this idea failed because it would involve the deaths of many French and Belgian civilians behind German lines and take too many scarce servicemen to operate and maintain the aircraft and bombs. By mid-1918 as much as a third of British artillery shells were filled with gas and Churchill planned to increase its use fivefold if the war went on into 1919. In April 1918 the Red Cross suggested restrictions on the use of gas. The French were prepared to accept them, but Churchill was totally opposed, telling his French opposite number, Loucheur, that the allies could manufacture more gas than the Germans and should therefore use it, adding: 'I am . . . in favour of the greatest possible development of gas-warfare.'[4] Churchill did not expect the war to end in 1918. In a paper for the War Cabinet in April of that year he argued that the campaign in 1919 should be dominated by high-technology warfare – the widespread deployment of tanks, large-scale bombing attacks on German civilians and the mass use of chemical warfare.

One of the most difficult problems Churchill faced as Minister of Munitions was labour relations. His experience in this field was limited and the views he expressed show how out of touch he was with the life of the majority of the population and how entrenched his opposition was to any form of effective and widespread labour organisation. In March 1915 he had believed that workers could be attracted into the munitions industries by an extremely one-sided deal. In return for the same rate of pay as elsewhere together with a bonus for 'diligent and regular work and good timekeeping' and 'a button of national service', they were to agree to the 'waiving of all Trade Union conditions hampering to production'.[5]

The new Ministry of Munitions found that the situation was much more complex than Churchill thought. Government control of the munitions industry (even including the construction of Government factories) meant that the ministry was inevitably drawn into questions of industrial organisation and labour relations. From the beginning in 1915 it introduced a series of radical measures: strikes and lockouts were made illegal, arbitration became compulsory, trades union restrictive practices were made illegal for the duration of the war, employees could not leave a job without a certificate and profits were limited. Later the ministry also regulated conditions of work, requiring employers to provide canteens, nurseries to help the increasing number of women workers and even housing in some cases. But the most difficult issue they had to grapple with was 'dilution'. As increasing numbers of workers, especially from skilled trades, joined the armed forces it was necessary to use more unskilled workers. Trades unions accepted this as inevitable during the war but they were determined that dilution should not continue in peacetime since it would destroy the position of the skilled worker.

When Churchill took office he faced a major problem following the report of a commission on industrial unrest. The unrest had a number of causes – rapid increases in the cost of living, the failure of wage rises to keep pace, the unequal distribution of food because of the inadequate rationing system, profiteering by firms, failure to consult the workers about changes in working conditions and anxiety about whether protected trades would continue to be protected as the demands of the Army for manpower went on increasing. In addition the unions wanted the abolition of the leaving certificate, which stopped skilled workers from changing jobs and increasing their pay. Churchill's predecessor, Christopher Addison, had already conceded abolition but in return the Government wanted controls to stop workers moving to private industry and bidding up wage rates and also to impose extensive 'dilution' in private industry. On 1 August Churchill chaired a conference at Central Hall: it gave the trades unions a chance to voice their strong opposition to the Government's ideas. After the conference Churchill wanted to go back on Addison's concession on leaving certificates and impose the new Government conditions on greater dilution as well. On 13

August, when he told the unions that he wanted more dilution of skilled labour, they withdrew from the negotiations. The next day he saw the employers, who did not support his stance. They were prepared to concede ending the leaving certificate in return for the introduction of new controls over the movement of labour. They were worried that Churchill's strategy would lead to confrontation with the unions, concessions and eventual abolition of the certificate without the controls that benefited the employers.

Once he knew the employers' views Churchill immediately changed his mind and agreed to drop the idea of dilution in private industry in order to secure controls on labour movement as the employers wanted. The provisions were stiff – any person unemployed for more than fourteen days without reasonable cause was liable to immediate call-up and employers were prohibited from poaching labour through inducements. Although Churchill had been forced to drop his original opposition to the abolition of leaving certificates and withdraw ideas for greater dilution, he insisted on dropping from the Bill other draft clauses that would have benefited the workers – compulsory consultation before the introduction of new working practices, restoration of the right to strike after the war and restoration of restrictive practices after the war.

Churchill remained passionately opposed to any restoration of the pre-war position of the trades unions – something the Government had promised on a number of occasions. Instead he suggested a general settlement after the war through a national conference to draw up a charter involving wages and conditions of production, although he never made clear what would be given in exchange for this concession of permanent 'dilution' by the trades unions. He thought that restoration of the pre-war position of the skilled worker 'would probably meet with the resistance of the great majority of the unskilled and women workers' but did not mention the huge benefit the employers would derive from using cheap, unskilled labour in place of more expensive skilled workers. He wanted to use the wartime concessions to permanently weaken the role of the trades unions and the position of the skilled worker. He could not understand that the 'restrictive practices' were the only way skilled workers could protect their interests against the much more powerful employers. Instead he could only argue, like the eighteenth-century liberal he really was, that restoration of pre-war working conditions would 'entrench a number of small and close corporations in restraint of trade'.[6]

In the autumn of 1917, with the greater mobility of labour that followed on from the abolition of leaving certificates, Churchill found that he was faced with more labour unrest over wages in sectors where piece-rates for many semi- and unskilled workers were higher than those for skilled workers. Early in October a bonus of twelve and a half per cent was introduced for the latter category, which Churchill wanted to restrict to 165,000 workers but which the War Cabinet agreed should apply to 250,000. It was soon clear, however, that Churchill had badly misjudged the situation and that this concession was insufficient. An increase across the board would have to be granted. Churchill so mishandled the negotiations with the trades unions on this issue that he had to be replaced by George Barnes, a Labour member of the Government, who secured a settlement in late January 1918. In general Churchill found himself unable to devise a coherent labour policy to deal with what was, admittedly, a highly complex situation. Although strongly opposed to the claims of organised labour, he did advocate a 100 per cent excess profits tax to stop business profiteering from the war. He put the suggestion forward at the War Cabinet meeting on 24 December 1917, but did not receive much support and dropped the idea.

As Minister of Munitions Churchill found that he had to face another aspect of Britain's decline as a world power, this time in the economic and financial field. In 1880, when Churchill was six, Britain produced nearly twenty-three per cent of the world's output of manufactured goods. By the outbreak of war this figure had fallen to thirteen per cent, below that of Germany and less than half that of the United States. British iron and steel production was less than half that of Germany and a quarter of United States' levels. Even at expanded wartime levels, British industry could not provide the armaments the armed forces needed and much had to be imported, mainly from the United States. In 1914 Kitchener had estimated that a total of $50 million worth of orders would be sufficient for three years of warfare. Yet in the first two years of the war alone Britain placed orders worth $20 billion. By the time Churchill returned to the Government about forty per cent of Britain's war production was being imported from the United States at a cost of $83 million a week.

The scale of this expenditure raised acute financial difficulties, made worse by the fact that Britain had had to take over responsibility for Russian and Italian purchases in the United States from September 1915 and also take on those of France after May 1916. All of these purchases had to be paid for from Britain's financial resources. At first selling off part of Britain's gold reserves was sufficient, but in August 1915 the first sales of British-owned securities had begun, followed two months later by the raising of the first British loan in the United States. By April 1917 it was clear that Britain had only enough gold and securities left to pay for about another ten weeks of supplies and that loans were becoming very difficult to raise – increasingly high interest rates had to be offered to tempt increasingly reluctant American financial institutions to invest. Britain's ability to continue the war was therefore in question if it could no longer afford to purchase munitions in the United States. In the autumn of 1916 the then Chancellor of the Exchequer, Reginald McKenna, had issued a grim forecast to his colleagues: 'by next June, or earlier, the President of the American Republic will be in a position, if he wishes, to dictate his own terms to us'.[7]

Britain and the allies were saved from a collapse in their war effort by the entry of the United States into the war in April 1917. But even so Britain's resources did run out. A week after Churchill became Minister of Munitions the Chancellor of the Exchequer, Balfour, had to issue a dire warning to the Americans: 'our resources available for payments in America are exhausted. Unless the United States Government can meet in full our expenses in the United States ... the whole fabric of the Alliance will collapse.'[8] The consequence was that the United States Government had to advance money to pay for allied war purchases, guarantee British loans in the United States, help support the pound on the foreign exchanges and lend the British Government about $180 million a week (producing a war debt of over $5 billion by the end of the war).

Churchill felt the impact of Britain's financial dependence on the United States in the munitions programme. The American Government insisted on the creation of an Allied Purchasing Commission in the United States, subordinate to its own War Industries Board which oversaw its armaments production. The United States was therefore able to decide which allied orders would be fulfilled and at what price, giving it an effective say over their military effort. The

American Government also forced the creation of an effective Inter-Allied Council to determine the relative priority of British, French and other allied orders to be placed through the new purchasing commission. Churchill was to spend much of his time in the last year of the war attending meetings of the Inter-Allied Council. In September 1918 it finally reached agreement on an allied production programme for 1919.

These long negotiating efforts helped to give Churchill the continuous workload he always strove for. After a few months as Minister of Munitions he moved into its headquarters, the old Metropole Hotel in Northumberland Avenue, and lived there rather than at home with Clementine. He also spent much time at the Ritz in Paris. Even so he still regretted the fact that he was not in control of military operations. In order to give himself the feeling of being near to military events he insisted on setting up a ministry headquarters at the requisitioned Château Verchocq to liaise with the nearby British military headquarters. There was little justification for this project apart from assuaging Churchill's sense of loss and satisfying his obsessive desire for constant stimulation. He described his life there to Clementine:

> I find each day lots to do, & lots to see ... In the mornings or afternoons I sit here quietly looking at my papers – or I can sally out in my car to some friend up the line. Or I can get someone I want to talk shop to, to come & dine here. Meanwhile the work arrives in steady consignments, & the telephone & aeroplane keep me in the closest touch. It is just the sort of life I like.[9]

Only once in his eighteen months as Minister of Munitions was Churchill even on the fringes of great events and even then special efforts were made to ensure that he was not able to influence decisions. After the collapse of the Russian war effort and the Bolshevik revolution in October 1917 the Germans were able to move troops to the west even before they forced the new Government to sign a humiliating peace. In March 1918 they launched an offensive designed to win the war before the full weight of the new American armies was brought to bear. Churchill was in France on one of his endless liaison visits when the German attack was launched on 21 March, but he was very quickly sent back to London.

On 24 March it was clear that the British 5th Army was broken and in full retreat across the Somme. The Germans had achieved the sort of breakthrough the allies had sought so unsuccessfully for the preceding three years.

That evening Churchill invited Lloyd George to dinner and tried to give him moral support and build up the Prime Minister's expectation, at one of the most crucial turning points of the war, that the allies would win through. Lloyd George kept in touch with Churchill over the next few days as the situation deteriorated further and appreciated his strength and determination. On 26 March the position was so serious that the allies finally agreed on a measure they (and particularly the British) had resisted for years – the appointment of a supreme commander, General Foch. Two days later, with the Germans on the point of opening a huge wedge between the British and French Armies, Lloyd George sent Churchill to France to see Foch and assess the situation. However, the moment that Bonar Law and Field Marshal Wilson (Chief of the Imperial General Staff) found out where Churchill was going, they forced Lloyd George to stop him interfering in military matters and so he was diverted to see Clemenceau, the French Premier, in Paris.

On 30 March Churchill accompanied Clemenceau on a visit to the front, where he met Foch and his deputy Weygand. When they arrived at British headquarters, Churchill was not allowed to join the discussion between Haig and the French Premier. After a visit to the front near Beauvais and dinner with Pétain, the Commander of the French Army, the pair returned to Paris convinced that the German attack was being held as the French moved up reinforcements to support the broken British 5th Army. Churchill went to the front again the next day and stayed on in Paris for three more days. Although he was excluded from the discussions on strategy, he felt better since he was at least on the edge of great events. When Lloyd George travelled to France for talks with Clemenceau on 3 April both he and Wilson insisted that Churchill was to take no part in the talks to decide the exact powers Foch would be given over the British and American armies. Churchill returned to London and the more mundane world of munitions supply that evening.

The Germans made a series of further attacks over the next months but they were of decreasing effectiveness. By August the allied armies were on the counter-attack and gradually they pushed the Germans back eastwards. In September Churchill still expected the war to go on into 1919 and possibly even until 1920. He, like many others, was therefore surprised at the speed of the German and Austrian collapse in October, which began with the disintegration of the Austro-Hungarian Empire and led to the German decision to sue for an armistice while their armies were still fighting on foreign soil, to the outbreak of revolution in both countries and to the end of the fighting in the west on 11 November.

The armistice brought to the surface important political issues that had been largely latent for the previous two years. When Lloyd George replaced Asquith as Prime Minister in December 1916, the latter had refused to serve under him and remained formal head of the Liberal Party. The party was divided between those who supported the new Government and those who went into opposition with Asquith. By the early summer of 1918 the division had hardened into a formal split as the two groups fought to control Liberal newspapers and party funds. Lloyd George's position was made up of almost equal parts of strength and weakness. As the leader who had seen Britain through the worst phase of the war to victory, his public position was unassailable. Yet the party organisation behind him was weak and he was heavily dependent on the Conservatives for support. The Conservatives and Lloyd George needed each other. Lloyd George knew that he had no alternative but to fight the post-war Election as leader of a coalition since reunion with the Liberals would leave Asquith as leader, and for their part the Conservatives knew that they had little choice but to support the victorious war leader they had put into power. In order to avoid competition in the General Election called for December 1918, Churchill's cousin, Freddie Guest, the coalition Liberal Whip, negotiated a deal whereby in most constituencies a 'coupon' would be issued to the candidate the Government identified as supporting the coalition. The 'coupon' was given to 364 Conservatives and 159 Liberals (together with eighteen anti-Labour National Democrats) so that if Lloyd George won the election he was bound to be dependent on the Conservatives to stay in office.

After he joined the Government Churchill naturally became part of the coalition Liberal organisation. On 6 November he, together with the other prominent coalition Liberals, dined at No 10 with Lloyd George. They had little choice but to go along with the decision to fight as a coalition and, although Churchill tried to make his support contingent on the abolition of the War Cabinet, a place for himself in the new Cabinet and some say over the distribution of offices in the new Government, he eventually had to settle for no firm promises on any of these objectives. Lloyd George would not be dictated to and simply told Churchill that he had to go along with the new arrangements. He pointed out that Churchill had after all accepted the coalition and his exclusion from the War Cabinet for eighteen months as the price of returning to government and had moreover advocated a coalition with the Conservatives for years. Lloyd George also reminded him that his treatment of Churchill had been far better than that he had received from Asquith.

Churchill received a 'coupon' and stood again at Dundee without any Conservative opposition. He was returned with a majority of over 14,000. His victory was part of a coalition landslide achieved in an intensely patriotic and anti-German atmosphere. The coalition won 526 seats in the Commons, whereas Labour, now the official opposition, had fifty-seven MPs and non-coalitionist Liberals were reduced to about twenty-five (and most of their famous figures, including Asquith, were defeated). But within the new Government the balance of power was clearly weighted in the Conservatives' favour, as 333 Conservative MPs were returned as against just 127 Liberals supporting Lloyd George.

Once polling was over Lloyd George began the task of reconstructing the Government. Churchill was just one of the pieces in a complex jigsaw. He still felt free to offer Lloyd George advice on how to form the new Government. For obvious reasons he still advocated the end of the War Cabinet and a return to pre-war arrangements of a Cabinet of about fourteen or fifteen members of whom half would be Conservatives. He suggested Milner should go the Colonial Office and Walter Long to the Admiralty, both of which Lloyd George accepted. Churchill thought either Rufus Isaacs or Edwin Montagu should go to the Treasury (Austen Chamberlain was appointed) although he told the Prime Minister 'there is a point about Jews wh occurs to me – you must not have too many of them'.[10] Churchill also objected to the creation of a permanent Ministry of Labour, believing it would help to create an atmosphere in which conditions of labour would be a legitimate area of concern for Government.

The question of what post Churchill should fill again proved contentious. The work of the Ministry of Munitions was now over – by the end of 1918 over 725,000 people had been discharged from munitions production, almost half of them becoming unemployed. Lloyd George wanted to keep Churchill in the Government and with a reasonably responsible post because at least nominally he was a supporter. However, continuing Conservative opposition and Churchill's own reputation meant that he could not be made a member of the War Cabinet. Churchill himself wanted to go back to the Admiralty as part of his political rehabilitation but Lloyd George convinced him that it was not possible. In the end Churchill had to settle for the War Office, which was combined with responsibility for air policy (both civilian and military) following the creation of an independent Royal Air Force in April 1918. Although the post had been important during the war, it was now less so and Churchill could hardly regard the move as promotion. He was still excluded from the War Cabinet and so unable to influence the most important questions occupying the Government for most of 1919 – the negotiations in Paris over the peace terms to be imposed on Germany and its allies and the attempt to create a new world out of the wreckage caused by the war. Churchill was expected instead to deal with the administrative difficulties of demobilising the largest army Britain had ever created and replacing it with a cheap peacetime alternative.

'The Only Remaining Specimen of a Real Tory'

When Churchill took up his new post at the War Office on 10 January 1919 he found that the British Army, amounting to over 3 million men, was scattered not just throughout the Empire but also across France, Belgium, Italy, Serbia, Russia, Greece and all the defeated powers. His immediate task was twofold – to continue the process of demobilisation and also to decide what size army would be required in the transition to peace and eventually in peacetime conditions.

The Army had discharged almost a million men since the armistice but the way in which it was done – according to a complex formula designed to release first those who were likely to gain civilian jobs rather than those who had served the longest and to keep those who had joined after the end of 1915 for the armies of occupation – was causing discontent. In January there were severe disturbances amounting to near mutiny among 10,000 men at Folkestone and a small mutiny at Calais at the end of the month (when Churchill had to remind Haig that he did not have the authority to shoot the three ringleaders). The new minister, whose first reaction on taking office was to stop all demobilisation, realised he would have to alter the system but he did not do so to the extent that he liked to claim afterwards and the new scheme was already being devised before he took office. Under these new arrangements those who enlisted in 1914–15 or who were aged thirty-seven and over or who had been promoted to Corporal or above would be due for release first, although Churchill emphasised that industrial priority would still apply 'in the large majority of cases'.[1] Nevertheless the new system, although it did not in fact speed up the rate of release, was rather nearer to a 'first in, first out' scheme and was enough to avoid any further major disturbances.

The scale of the Army's commitments had increased considerably from the pre-war era. On 17 January Churchill proposed to the War Cabinet that conscription should be retained for at least a further year and the Army should be kept at a strength of 1.2 million. His colleagues were dubious (mainly about the likely public reaction) and he had to travel to Paris to convince a sceptical Lloyd George, caught up in the peace negotiations. Eventually on 28 January the War Cabinet agreed to a continued period of conscription but insisted on a simultaneous announcement that it would end in April 1920. Army strength was not to rise above 900,000. Churchill wanted to keep conscription but in July 1919, under financial pressure, had to agree to it ending a month earlier than planned. He proposed a permanent peacetime army of 209,000 but this was rejected by his colleagues who insisted on returning to an army smaller than before 1914 despite the greater commitments, particularly in the Near East.

In the summer of 1919, after the German Government had with extreme reluctance signed the Treaty of Versailles, the Government had to decide the level and balance of peacetime defence spending. As Minister for the Army and Air Force Churchill naturally argued that the bulk of the cuts should fall on the Navy, although his views on the matter in the immediate post-war period show a degree of volatility unusual even by his standards. In May he wrote to Lloyd George arguing that there should be no new naval construction for many years and that Beatty should not be appointed as First Sea Lord until he agreed to these cuts. Two months later he advocated scrapping *Enchantress*, the First Lord's private yacht, which he had found so agreeable before the war. At the beginning of August he suggested that expenditure on the Navy should be set at about two-thirds of the pre-war level. These proposals implicitly accepted that Britain could not compete with the United States in naval strength and that naval supremacy would pass to the Americans, given their superior economic and financial strength and their large post-war construction programme. Eighteen months later, in February 1921, he wrote to Balfour that he strongly objected to losing naval supremacy to the United States and possibly Japan as well and he would not stay in a Government that agreed to such a policy. He now wanted, as in the pre-war naval competition with Germany, to build four battleships a year for a minimum of five years. Three months later he told the Cabinet that 'it would be a ghastly state of affairs if we were to drift into direct naval rivalry with the United States' and added later 'we have nothing to gain from such a competition and everything to lose'.[2]

It was in August 1919 that the Government, with Churchill playing an important role, decided the basis for future defence planning. At the beginning of the month Churchill argued for making general a rule he had already applied to the RAF, namely that there would not be a general war for five years and only the remotest possibility of one in the five years after that. At a Cabinet meeting on 5 August Churchill suggested applying what became known as the 'ten-year rule' to the armed forces. He was not present at a meeting six days later when Lloyd George, Bonar Law, Chamberlain and Milner agreed a total figure for defence spending for the next year and also a framework for the future that incorporated Churchill's idea of a minimum period of ten years' peace and this 'rule' became the basis of policy.

Churchill's application of strict financial limits on the RAF reflected his general attitude to the service and air power. Although he had strongly advocated the widespread bombing of German cities and civilians if the war had gone on into 1919, he now saw the Air Force as a small élite unit largely devoted to the cheap policing of the Empire. In early 1919 Trenchard, the head of the RAF whom Churchill had brought back to office, proposed a large peacetime force of 154 squadrons and 110,000 men. Churchill himself originally envisaged retaining about 100 squadrons but under financial pressure he proposed to spend only £13 million (out of an overall allocation of £75 million a year for the Army and Air Force) on the RAF which would only support a force of about forty squadrons. Nearly all of these were involved in policing the Empire – in November 1921 the RAF had only three squadrons based in Britain. Churchill also had to develop plans for civil aviation and his approach to this new field was very negative. When he brought back Trenchard, Churchill had demoted the then head of the RAF, Major-General Sir Frederick Sykes, whom he detested, by appointing him head of civil aviation, and allocating him a meagre six per cent of the already small RAF budget to spend on promoting the new form of travel. Churchill showed little enthusiasm for backing proposals for imperial air routes, either through the Near East or from Egypt to South Africa, and when he left he ministry at the beginning of 1921 British civil aviation was well behind its rivals.

One area of RAF affairs that did interest Churchill was the social background of the new service. He was determined to ensure that its officers were drawn from the same exclusive background and followed the same traditions as the Royal Navy and Army. In June 1919 he wrote a long paper setting out the policy the RAF should adopt. Officer recruits should be chosen 'by competitive examination, preferably from the public schools', because their most important characteristic should be 'the discipline and bearing of an officer and a gentleman' rather than their ability to fly aircraft. He wanted to create a social system akin to the regimental structure of the Army through the squadrons, which were to be the main unit of organisation 'possessing their own *esprit de corps* with good strictly managed messes, the officers of which know each other, and where there is a strong opinion on questions of behaviour'.[3] The RAF was also to train at least half its mechanics so that it did not become reliant on trades union members.

Although Churchill spent most of his time on War Office business, he gave his deputy for the RAF, Jack Seely (back in office after resigning over the Curragh 'mutiny' in 1914), little freedom. He did however allow Seely to undertake difficult tasks such as introducing the 1919–20 estimates in the Commons after he himself had been severely mauled over the Army estimates and did not want to repeat the experience. Seely resigned in November 1919 over Churchill's constant interference. Churchill, ever keen to promote the interests of his family, persuaded Lloyd George to appoint his cousin the Marquess of Londonderry as a replacement. Churchill wanted him because he was wealthy enough to subsidise the social functions of the War Office. When Churchill moved to the Colonial Office in January 1921 he asked Lloyd George to make Londonderry Secretary of State for Air or if not to transfer him to the Colonial Office where he could again pay for entertainment. Neither request was granted, although he did succeed in persuading Lloyd George to make his cousin Frederick Guest a privy councillor.

When Churchill took over the War Office in January 1919 he was convinced that one of his most vital tasks was to face down the threat of possible revolution in Britain. In the period of high inflation and unemployment brought on by the end of the war there was a series of strikes, which many in the Government (including Churchill), reading the weekly reports on subversive activity from Sir Basil Thomson, the Home Office Director of Intelligence, were convinced presaged revolution. At his very first meeting with Field Marshal Wilson, Chief of the Imperial General Staff, on 10 January Churchill said that he wanted to stop demobilisation and bring home what he called 'reliable troops' from the regiments drawn from the upper classes – the cavalry, yeomanry and home counties regiments. Churchill told the War Cabinet at the end of January that 'there should be a conflict to clear the air'. But the Government 'should be careful to have plenty of provocation before taking strong measures. By going gently at first, we should get the support we wanted from the nation, and the troops could be used more effectively.' They should therefore wait until 'some glaring excesses were committed'.[4]

Almost immediately troops and tanks were deployed on the streets of Glasgow to break a strike in support of demands for a forty-hour week. The strike leaders were arrested and convicted of incitement to riot and the strike was beaten. In July Churchill wanted to crush any attempted strike by the miners: 'This is the time to beat them. There is bound to be a fight. The English propertied classes are not going to take it lying down.'[5] Troops were again deployed in August, this time in Liverpool to defeat a local police strike. The greatest threat though appeared to come in September with a rail strike which the Government thought might be concerted with stoppages by the dockers and miners. Churchill was a leading member of the Cabinet Strike Committee – he was 'most energetic & talked more than anyone' according to Haig, who was present at the first meeting.[6] Churchill deployed 23,000 troops, with 30,000 more in reserve, to protect the railways and drive food lorries (he later discovered he had no legal power to do this). At the beginning of October the committee decided to create a Citizen Guard and Churchill offered military and naval personnel to act as recruiting officers. Later he backed proposals to set up the Guard on a permanent basis that were rejected by the police and Home Office. In the end the strike was settled by Lloyd George on the railwaymen's terms.

In January 1920 Churchill thought Britain was on the verge of revolution. A meeting of the Supplies and Transport Committee of the Cabinet, which was co-ordinating anti-strike measures, concluded that:

> the country would have to face in the near future an organised attempt at seizing the reins of Government in some of the large cities, such as Glasgow, London and Liverpool. . . . It was not unlikely that the next strike would commence with sabotage on an extensive scale.[7]

Wilson, who was at the meeting, recorded: 'It is truly a terrifying state of affairs & not one of them except Walter [Long] & Winston were prepared to put up a fight.'[8] Those at the meeting, Churchill, Long, Wilson and Beatty, all set off in a panic to see Lloyd George in Paris. He thought they were getting hysterical though he did agree that Wilson could retain in Britain eight battalions of infantry that were about to be sent to monitor the Silesian referendum. Lloyd George could be equally tough when he thought it necessary but on this occasion his views were well expressed by his friend and Deputy Secretary to the Cabinet, Tom Jones: 'What Churchill and co. forget is that there are other ways of averting discontent than with civil guards and the military.'[9] Although the Government took powers in March to allow them to issue arms to 'loyalists', the economic recovery throughout the year lessened discontent and when conditions deteriorated again the next year Churchill was no longer involved in the discussions.

Churchill's fear of revolution in part reflected his growing disenchantment with the post-war world and the threats he saw to his way of life. He had been brought up, and in the first part of his political life operated, in a system which was dominated as much by personality as policy and which, although divided over vital issues such as home rule, was essentially united on fundamental questions and the need to preserve the existing social and economic system. In this world Churchill had been quite happy to see politics as a field for personal ambition. Now the world was changing – revolutions had swept across Europe deposing the monarchies of Russia, Germany and Austro-Hungary. The privileged world that Churchill had known in his first forty-five years was also under threat from demands for social change, some of them violent. In addition the British Empire was under challenge internally, particularly in India, Egypt and Ireland. Although Churchill did not lose his ambitious instincts, politics for him now became a matter of organising resistance to change in many areas – revolution abroad, demands for a more equitable social and economic system at home and the desire for more self-government within the Empire. After 1918, and for the rest of his life, Churchill became more ideological in his approach to politics, more determined to preserve the world he had known in his youth from any alteration.

Domestically Churchill had never favoured the extension of the franchise to all adults and he was not a member of the wartime Government that gave the vote to the forty per cent of men who could not vote before 1918 and to women over thirty. As a result the electorate almost tripled in 1918, increasing from 7.7 million to 21.3 million. Although Labour won only fifty-seven seats in that Election, they received 2.5 million votes and became the official opposition. But in Churchill's eyes they were less a legitimate political party representing a large part of the country more a threat to the fabric of society – 'innately pledged to the fundamental subversion of the existing social and economic civilisation and organised for that purpose alone'. What is interesting here is his use of the word 'subversion' rather than, say, 'change'. As he told his Cabinet colleagues a few years later, he believed that members of the Labour Party 'espouse and proclaim doctrines fundamentally subversive not only of the State and of the Empire, but of economic civilisation. . . . I regard effectual resistance to Socialism – revolutionary or evolutionary – as a prime duty for those who wish to preserve the greatness of Britain . . . [and] avert the establishment of a Socialist tyranny . . . which will deprive us, not only of national greatness and prosperity, but of individual freedom.'[10] The Labour Party was therefore, as he told Lloyd George: 'a danger to society' and, as he told his constituents, 'unfit to govern the country' because they had 'made themselves into a class party, led by class leaders and fighting the balance of class interests in predominance over all other interests' and it would therefore be a very long time before they were fit 'to carry on the Government of the British Empire from an alternative but equally responsible standpoint'.[11] Trades unions were similarly excluded from any responsible role in society. In January 1922 he spoke in the Commons in favour of reducing expenditure on naval recruits because they were largely trades unionists and therefore 'could not be entirely relied upon to give loyal and devoted service'.[12]

Churchill had on many occasions in the past advocated a central coalition but now, with a divided and collapsing Liberal Party and the rise of Labour, it seemed to him more essential than ever. In a speech at the 1920 Club in January 1922 he attacked the 'old-fashioned' Liberalism of men like Asquith and Grey and compared it with the determination of the coalition to smash strikes and counter industrial unrest.[13] Two months later during the Loughborough by-election he defended the Lloyd George coalition as the only way of countering 'iron state regulation' and the 'crazy doctrines and anti-national sentiments of socialism'. Increasingly identified with the Conservative wing of the coalition, Churchill's reactionary tendencies became more apparent. At a dinner in Paris with Lloyd George, Bonar Law and others in January 1920 he severely criticised the Prime Minister's idea of a new world after the war, adding, 'You're not going to get your new world. The old world is a good enough place for me.' Lloyd George commented afterwards: 'Winston is the only remaining specimen of a real Tory.'[14]

Churchill's opposition to the rise of Labour went hand in hand with his visceral hatred of the October 1917 Bolshevik revolution. He saw little difference between the two. He said in a speech in London in 1925: 'Behind Socialism stands Communism, behind Communism stands Moscow, that dark sinister, evil power.' All the members of the coalition opposed Bolshevism but Churchill's language was almost pathological in its intensity and in the images he used; indeed his desire to exterminate Bolshevism was his main driving force at this period. Lloyd George's secretary Philip Kerr reported in January 1919 that 'he declares that the Bolsheviks are the enemies of the human race and must be put down at any cost'.[15] He told the House of Commons in May 1920: 'Bolshevism is not a policy; it is a disease. It is not a creed; it is a pestilence.' This image of Bolshevism as a disease was one of Churchill's favourites. In the *Evening News* in July 1920 he wrote of 'a poisoned Russia, an infected Russia, a plague bearing Russia'.[16] Nine years later in *The Aftermath* he described the Bolsheviks as 'swarms of typhus-bearing vermin'.[17]

The Bolsheviks were also a 'league of the failures, the criminals, the unfit, the mutinous, the morbid, the deranged and the distraught'.[18] In a speech at the Connaught Rooms in April 1919 they were a 'foul combination of criminality and animalism'. Animals were another favourite source of imagery. In a speech in Dundee in November 1918 Bolshevism was described as 'an animal form of Barbarism' and its adherents were 'troops of ferocious baboons amid the ruins of cities and the corpses of their victims' although the 'bloody and wholesale butcheries and murders [were] carried out to a large extent by Chinese executioners and armoured cars'. Again in a speech at the Mansion House in February 1919 he spoke of the 'foul baboonery' of Bolshevism (he later always referred to negotiations with the Soviet Government as shaking hands with 'the hairy baboon') although a month later the Bolsheviks were portrayed as vampires. Churchill also emphasised what he saw as the Jewish nature of Bolshevism. In private to Curzon the Foreign Secretary he described the Soviet Government as a 'tyrannic government of these Jew Commissars'[19] and even in public he called it 'a world wide communistic state under Jewish domination'.[20] In a public speech in Sunderland in 1920 he spoke of 'the international Soviet of the Russian and Polish Jew'. In April 1922 he drafted a letter to his friend FE, then at the Genoa conference with Lloyd George, in which he described the Bolsheviks as 'these Semitic conspirators'. On another occasion they were 'these cold Semitic internationalists' and he usually referred to Trotsky as Bronstein.

Churchill's move to the War Office in January 1919 gave him the opportunity to influence policy towards the Bolsheviks in a substantial way. He always claimed, rightly, that he did not initiate the allied intervention in Russia against the Bolsheviks, but he certainly took every possible opportunity to exploit the policy to try to overthrow the Bolshevik regime. That intervention had begun in the spring of 1918, shortly after the Bolsheviks seized power, in a desperate attempt to recreate some sort of eastern front against the Germans after the Bolshevik agreement to a separate peace at Brest-Litovsk. The main force was to be the Japanese moving west from Siberia to link up with a Czech and Slovak unit formed from Austro-Hungarian prisoners of war. The United States later joined the Japanese as did a small British unit. In May a larger British force landed at Murmansk and Archangel, nominally to protect war stores. By the summer of 1918 it was clear that the allies were fighting Soviet forces, at least on a small scale, and acting as a screen behind which 'white' forces could gather (other anti-Soviet forces were building up behind the remaining German armies in the south-west of the country).

Signature of the armistice in November raised the question of the continuing justification for the intervention in the internal affairs of another country. On 14 November the War Cabinet (Churchill was not present) decided to hold Murmansk and Archangel, to provide some help in Siberia, to assist Denikin, the white leader in southern Russia, and the new Baltic states, and to occupy Batum and Baku, which were thought to be close to vital British interests in the Near East. They justified the continuing intervention as a way of protecting those who had rallied to the allied side during the war – probably the most the public would support. This was in effect a middle course between a massive military expedition to overthrow the Bolsheviks and coming to terms with the revolutionary regime. But it was almost bound to end in failure because it gave enough aid to the whites to prolong the war but not enough to win it, which meant the British would eventually have to come to an agreement with the new Soviet Government.

At the first major meeting he attended on the subject – a War Cabinet meeting just before Christmas 1918 – Churchill argued for adopting a more clear-cut policy. He felt that small-scale intervention was no use. The Russians should either be left 'to stew in their own juice' and 'murder each other without let or hindrance' or Britain should adopt the policy he favoured. This was that the allies should intervene 'thoroughly, with large forces, abundantly supplied with mechanical appliances' supported by a major Government campaign to recruit a volunteer army for the purpose. Lloyd George however carried the meeting by arguing that although they might not like the Bolsheviks they nevertheless had support in Russia; and that Britain had no right to interfere in their internal affairs and anyway lacked the means to do so.[21]

To most of his colleagues, Churchill's belief that in the aftermath of the most horrific war the nation had known people would be prepared to support a massive campaign to conquer Russia and impose a government on the country showed his inability to understand the public mood, let alone the military realities. Some even suspected that Churchill was disappointed to have missed out on the direction of great campaigns during the war and was looking for an opportunity to display his talents. For more than a year this battle was to be refought in different guises. Churchill's advocacy of intervention in various forms to support the 'whites' left him isolated in the Government and whenever he took on Lloyd George he lost. He had no support from the coalition Liberals and although the Conservatives agreed with his views on Bolshevism, they agreed with Lloyd George on policy. Chamberlain as Chancellor felt Britain could not afford such a policy; Bonar Law could see no political attractions in intervention; Curzon had some sympathy as did Balfour but not for Churchill's more extreme support of the 'whites'. Wilson as CIGS was sympathetic but knew the Army had too much to do elsewhere. Almost the sole support Churchill received, apart from Walter Long at the Admiralty (who carried little weight politically), was from the more right-wing Conservative backbenchers.

For the first two months of 1919 Churchill still hoped it might be possible to send a large expedition to overthrow the Bolsheviks. He strongly opposed the allies' invitation to the different groups in Russia to meet on the island of Prinkipo off Turkey where they would be asked to settle their differences so that a Russian delegation could attend the peace conference. Churchill, convinced the Bolsheviks were a small minority who would be swept away easily, wanted instead a call for free Elections and when this inevitably failed, allied intervention to set up a democratic government. At Paris in January every Dominion Prime Minister refused to supply troops for intervention as did France, Italy and the United States. The allies, anxious to support the whites, were still floundering around unable to agree on a policy.

Lloyd George returned to London just before the deadline for the Prinkipo conference was about to expire. At the War Cabinet meeting on 12 February Churchill declared that the Bolsheviks were getting stronger and pressed for military action: 'If we were going to intervene, we should send huge forces there. He believed we ought to intervene.'[22] Lloyd George pointed out there was a slight practical problem – there weren't any large allied forces. The argument resumed the next day with Churchill favouring an allied declaration of war on the Bolsheviks. Lloyd George argued for only limited material support for the 'whites' on the basis that if they did not have enough popular support the allies could not save them. That evening the Prime Minister decided that he had to stay in Britain to deal with the industrial unrest and that Churchill should travel to Paris to discuss the issue the next day in the Supreme War Council before President Wilson left for the United States. Why Lloyd George chose Churchill for this delicate task given the latter's strong views is unclear, and his failure to provide him with a well-defined brief for the talks is even more inexplicable. It was to lead to turmoil in Paris and a major row between the two men.

At the Supreme War Council Churchill asked what would be done after the failure of the Prinkipo initiative (the deadline set for the opening of the talks was due to expire the next day and no Russian delegations had arrived). President Wilson suggested withdrawing all allied troops but when Churchill proposed using volunteers and experts and sending arms, munitions, tanks and planes, he did not positively veto the idea although in practice he was strongly opposed. He left to catch his boat before the issue was resolved. Churchill was determined to raise the matter again at the next meeting of the Council of 15 February and use the absence of a strict negotiating position to try and obtain the outcome he wanted.

At that meeting, after a presentation from the French Chief of Staff, General Alby, arguing that the Bolsheviks could be beaten (he was reflecting Foch's strong advocacy of all-out intervention), Churchill launched his ideas. He argued for getting rid of the Prinkipo scheme carefully to avoid antagonising the public. To achieve this a new, very one-sided proposal would be put forward, designed to be rejected by the Bolsheviks. They were to stop all attacks and withdraw five miles on all fronts. Only then would the 'whites' be asked to do the same. Meanwhile the allies, the states along the Russian border and the 'whites' would set up a council with political, economic and military sections and a general staff for co-ordinating action. This was to be the basis for action intended, as Churchill put it, to 'bring the Bolshevik regime to an end'.[23] It was, as he later admitted to Lloyd George, 'a plan for making war on the Bolsheviks, utilising every available resource'.[24] Although few among the allies had much sympathy for the Prinkipo scheme, no one supported Churchill's idea. The night before Balfour had hinted ambiguously he had some sympathy with Churchill, but he let him put the idea forward and then spoke against it at the council meeting.

Later that day Churchill sent two telegrams to Lloyd George outlining the scheme he had put forward. The Prime Minister, realising that Churchill had gone far further than intended, issued two warnings. The first messge told him 'not to commit us to any costly operations which would involve a large contribution of either men or money' and it repeated Lloyd George's view that if the 'whites' had support they would win but Britain could not save Russia from itself. The second message was even more explicit: 'Am very alarmed at your second telegram about planning war against the Bolsheviks. The Cabinet have never authorised such a proposal. They have never contemplated anything beyond supplying Armies in anti-Bolshevik areas.'[25] In order to ensure the defeat of Churchill's proposal, Lloyd George told his Private Secretary in Paris, Philip Kerr, to show the second telegram to Colonel House, President Wilson's closest adviser. Churchill, despite Lloyd George's instructions, continued to argue for his scheme. However his ideas were buried at the Supreme War Council meeting on 17 February in a discussion that was so acrimonious it was deleted from the minutes. He left for London furious that Lloyd George had gone behind his back to the Americans. For a long time afterwards he frostily addressed letters to him as 'My dear Prime Minister' instead of his usual 'My dear David'. Lloyd George was equally angry and wrote to Churchill only as 'Dear Secretary of State'.

Churchill's grandiose ideas for defeating the Bolsheviks had failed to get off the ground. None of the war-weary allies were interested in embarking on a huge military campaign to change the Russian Government. The Americans decided to withdraw their forces as soon as the spring thaw permitted, the French left Odessa in April, while the Japanese stayed in the most easterly part of Siberia, hoping they might be able to keep it permanently. Churchill though remained determined to do what he could to support the 'whites'. He secured a posting to Paris as military attaché for a friend from his time in the Army, Louis Spears, despite the strong opposition from the CIGS, Wilson, and the Ambassador, Lord Derby. Spears' role was to act as Churchill's personal emissary to the 'white' Russian leaders in Paris and as a source of intelligence for him. Churchill maintained strong, but unofficial, links with the 'white' leaders and reassured them that he would do all in his powers to help them. In January 1919 at a meeting in London he told Konstanin Nabokov, one of the 'white' leaders, that unless given categorical instructions to stop he would ensure that the War Office continued to give the 'whites' all possible supplies. At his first press conference as Secretary of State on 15 January Churchill said that his major policy was to keep up the size of the British armies in Russia.

He told Wilson in April that the supply of equipment to the 'white' Russian armies should be 'the first charge on all our resources'.[26] This policy did not cost much extra money because of the huge amount of surplus stores available after the war. (Churchill supplied just one of the 'white' armies – Denikin's in southern Russia – with 800 guns, 1.7 million rounds of ammunition, 6,000 machine guns, 200,000 rifles, 500 million rounds of small arms ammunition, 500,000 sets of uniforms and 12 general hospitals together with numerous lorries, cars and motor-cycles.) Churchill also kept in close touch with another 'white' leader in London, Boris Savinkov, who was regarded by the Foreign Office as 'most unreliable and crooked'.[27] He often made it clear in his dealings with the 'whites' that he did not agree with Government policy. In October 1919 for example he told Kolchak, the 'white' leader in Siberia, that he did not agree with the Government's policy of not recognising him as leader of the provisional Russian Government. For this he was rebuked by Lloyd George with a constitutional homily:

> It is very undesirable and quite contrary to the accepted traditions of Cabinet responsibility for a Minister to suggest that he holds a different view from that which has finally been adopted by the Cabinet of which he is a member and which he has himself accepted.[28]

Undeterred by such strictures, in May 1919 he instructed his officials in the War Office that aid to Kolchak and Denikin should not be limited to the amounts the Cabinet had agreed.

Churchill was unconcerned by the reactionary policies of all the white leaders and their intentions to restore the Czarist autocracy, reverse land reform and re-establish a Russian Empire that would include all the small independent states that had emerged on the borders of Russia during the revolution and civil war. When the Minister of Transport, Sir Eric Geddes, criticised the reactionary tendencies of the officers around Denikin, Churchill responded that 'he could not agree to the term "reactionary" being applied to a man who defended the lives of his wife and children'.[29] The all-important objective for him was the defeat of Bolshevism, and it led him to identify unquestioningly with the 'white' forces. He wrote in a uncirculated Cabinet paper at the end of 1919: 'It is a delusion to suppose that all this year we have been fighting the battles of the anti-Bolshevik Russians. On the contrary they have been fighting ours.'[30]

For Churchill everything (including treatment of the defeated Central Powers) should be subordinated to the fight against the Bolsheviks. On the evening before the armistice with Germany was to come into effect he warned the Cabinet of the need to maintain internal order in Germany because of his 'fear of the spread of Bolshevism'.[31] Two months later he suggested a virtual alliance with Germany and Austria against the Bolsheviks:

> It might be advisable to let the Germans know that if they were prepared to organise an Eastern Front against the ingress of Bolshevism, the Allied Governments would raise no objection. It was a matter for serious consideration whether we should not now decide to bolster up the Central Powers, if necessary, in order to stem the tide of Bolshevism.[32]

But, as had happened with his ideas for massive allied military intervention, his proposal found no support.

Churchill was therefore forced to fall back on what he always regarded as a second-best policy – exploiting the presence of British troops in Russia to the maximum extent possible to try and aid the 'whites'. Although Churchill always saw aid to Kolchak in Siberia and Denikin in the south as the best way of helping the 'whites', the only substantial British presence was at Murmansk and Archangel in the far north. In March the War Cabinet agreed that the troops there should be withdrawn before the onset of winter. After asking the commanders on the spot to request reinforcements, Churchill convinced his colleagues that the only way to withdraw was first to reinforce and then attack the Bolshevik forces in the area so as to enable evacuation to begin. Once he had received Lloyd George's approval for this scheme on 3 April, he immediately told the press that the military situation in northern Russia was very critical, the British force there was in danger (in fact there had been one attack in January which had easily been beaten off and the ground was now an impassable quagmire because of the spring thaw), and hinted that attack was the best form of defence.

On 9 April the War Office called for 8,000 trained troops to volunteer for what Churchill told his officials should be called 'the Rescue Force', a title he chose because it would 'in every way shield it from criticism and gain it support'.[33] Churchill had earlier told the Commons that conscripts would not be sent to Russia (privately the War Office did not believe they would obey such an order and were not prepared to put it to the test). Preparations now moved forward for a summer offensive. On 15 April the War Office sent orders to the new British commander, General Ironside, to advance up the Dvina River and attempt to make a junction with Kolchak's forces, which had begun moving westwards from Siberia. Once the 'white' forces building up behind the British troops were in contact with Kolchak, Ironside would be able to begin withdrawing.

If the British troops were to advance, Churchill wanted them to use every possible weapon including chemical warfare. In April he agreed that a new type of gas warfare (developed for use on the western front but not available before the end of the war) – a thermogenerator of arsenical dust that would penetrate all known types of protective mask – should be used, commenting 'of course I sh'd very much like the Bolsheviks to have it'[34] (and showing no concern for the effects on Russian civilians). 50,000 generators were sent to cover a five-mile front, together with 10,000 respirators for the British troops and twenty-five specialist gas officers to use the equipment. When news of this new form of warfare leaked out, Churchill defended himself in the Commons by trying to claim that Soviet forces were using gas. He said, 'I do not understand why, if they use poison gas, they should object to having it used against them. It is a very right and proper thing to employ poison gas against them.'[35] His statement was untrue. There is no evidence of Soviet forces using gas against British troops and it was Churchill himself who had authorised its initial use some six weeks earlier. Within a few weeks the British had begun developing the first ever gas bombs to be dropped from aircraft. At the end of August and in early September British DH9 bombers dropped 560 gas bombs on six different targets.[36]

On 26 April Churchill asked Lloyd George to recognise Kolchak as the 'Russian National Government' and three days later argued the case at the War Cabinet. Other members of the Government, appalled by the vast corruption and inefficiency around Kolchak and the openly reactionary aims of his movement, refused to do so. In fact Kolchak was shortly to retreat in front of the Red Army. Nevertheless on 11 June, with British forces reinforced and ready to move in northern Russia, Churchill told the War Cabinet that 'for the first time we proposed to depart from our present defensive policy [sic] and embark upon definite aggressive action against the Bolsheviks'.[37] The Cabinet agreed but on 17 June news arrived of a major reverse for Kolchak's troops and the plan collapsed on purely practical grounds. Churchill then tried to use the Czechs to achieve the same ends. When President Benes complained to Lloyd George about the lack of shipping to bring back the Czech forces still in Siberia, Churchill came up with a plan for 30,000 of them to fight their way from Siberia through to the British forces. Unfortunately for Churchill's ambitious ideas, the Czechs refused to fall in with his plan.

By the middle of June Ironside was convinced that his troops would not be able to advance very far. Conditions in the area were still bad and the 'white' Russian forces were suffering a series of mutinies (there were some in the British forces too); he recommended the British should withdraw after a small-scale attack on the Bolshevik forces to provide a breathing space in which to embark from the ports. On 29 July the Cabinet agreed to withdrawal and Ironside carried out his attack in early August, began withdrawing his forces at the end of the month and completed the task in early October. Churchill was bitterly opposed to the policy but powerless to stop it. In the summer of 1919 it was also clear that Kolchak would be beaten and on 25 July Churchill proposed to withdraw the remaining British forces in Siberia before they were caught up in fighting with the Red Army. Nevertheless he still wrote to Curzon (the Foreign Secretary) to try to stop British support for the pro-democratic and anti-Kolchak forces in Siberia.

In the summer of 1919 Churchill turned his attention to the 'white' forces in the Baltic area. The problem was that the interests of the 'whites', who wanted to recreate the Russian Empire, and the new states of Finland, Estonia, Latvia and Lithuania, who wanted to keep their independence, did not coincide. Churchill backed the 'whites' (even extreme reactionaries such as General Yudenitch) and objected to the small states negotiating with the Bolsheviks, who were prepared to recognise their independence. Much to Churchill's disgust, Britain gave only low-level support to Yudenitch and on 24 September the Cabinet agreed that the newly independent states should be left to decide on their own whether to come to terms with the Bolsheviks. The next day Churchill wrote a strong note of protest: he argued that such a decision would only help the Bolsheviks 'with whom on other parts of the front we are at war' and urged that they should instead develop a coherent plan since it 'would be much simpler, much safer, and, in the long run, much cheaper to continue to make war upon the Bolsheviks by every means in our power'.[38] During Yudenitch's last offensive in October, Churchill allowed British tank crews to fight with him and decided to send a British general once Petrograd fell. But Yudenitch was soon in full retreat.

During the late summer and autumn of 1919 Churchill pinned his hopes on General Denikin in southern Russia. By August his Cabinet colleagues were already tired of Denikin and the less than impressive results of British aid and intervention. Nevertheless, Churchill ensured the 'white' Russian leader was liberally supplied with surplus British equipment and food together with a military mission which actually manned tanks and planes in the front line. He also consistently backed Denikin in his attacks on Georgia, Azerbaijan and other states in the Caucasus area that were trying to establish their independence. As Denikin advanced towards Moscow in September and October, Churchill believed his dream of destroying the Bolsheviks was on the verge of coming true. He told Lloyd George on 20 September that the Bolsheviks were finished. A month later he made another optimistic assessment in a public letter: 'There are now good reasons for believing that the tyranny of Bolshevism will soon be overthrown by the Russian nation.' At this time he also came up with one of his most extraordinary proposals. He intended to go out to Russia as a roving ambassador, join Denikin as he entered Moscow and then help him draw up the new constitution for Russia. His hopes were once again shattered as yet another of the 'white' armies collapsed in front of a Bolshevik counter-attack. By the end of October Denikin too was in full retreat.

By the end of 1919 Churchill was even more isolated in Cabinet than before on the issue. In his Guildhall speech on 8 November

Lloyd George had already signalled an end to British intervention and a month later he agreed with Clemenceau that there were to be no more commitments to the 'white' forces. By the end of the year Archangel and Murmansk had been captured by Soviet forces, Kolchak was a prisoner in Siberia, Yudenitch was a refugee in Estonia and Denikin was about to be evacuated from the Crimea. Nearly all of Churchill's time during 1919 had been devoted to Russia – a whole wall in his office was covered with maps of the various campaigns and most of his correspondence was devoted to the subject. He had driven many of his colleagues, especially Lloyd George, to the point of distraction with his obsession. On 22 September, in a mood of absolute frustration, the Prime Minister wrote to complain of his repeated failure to take action on sorting out War Office administration and expenditure as expected:

> the first communication I have always received from you after these interviews related to Russia. I invited you to Paris to help me reduce our commitments in the East. You then produced a lengthy and carefully prepared memorandum on Russia. I entreated you on Friday to let Russia be for at least 48 hrs; and to devote your weekend to preparing for the Finance Committee this afternoon. You promised faithfully to do so. Your reply is to send me a four-page letter on Russia, and a closely printed memorandum of several pages – all on Russia. I am frankly in despair.[39]

Although Churchill's efforts to remove the Bolsheviks were effectively over by the end of 1919, for the remaining three years of the coalition's life he was to oppose all attempts to come to terms with the Soviet Union. At the end of January 1920 the Cabinet decided that realistically they had no alternative but to accept that the Bolsheviks ruled Russia for the foreseeable future and that they would therefore have to come to some sort of agreement. It was soon decided that the first step should be to open trade negotiations with the Soviet 'co-operatives', a move which could be defended in public as not recognising the Soviet Government as such. Lloyd George personally opened talks with two Soviet representatives Kamenev and Krasin in May (when Churchill made his remark about shaking hands with the hairy baboon). In practice they were political talks. By the end of June an outline trade agreement had been reached.

These discussions were then embroiled in the backwash from the Polish–Soviet war and an extraordinary episode in which elements in the British military seemed to contemplate a coup d'état.

By May 1920 Polish forces were far to the east of the line agreed by the allies as the eastern border of Poland (the Curzon line) and were attempting to set up a series of states between Poland and the Soviet Union. In mid-June the Red Army counter-attacked and by mid-August was in the outskirts of Warsaw. In mid-July Churchill asked the War Office to draw up plans for British military assistance to Poland, although the Cabinet's policy was that the Poles should try to obtain an armistice based on the Curzon line. On 28 July Churchill published an article in the *Evening News* in which he called for support for Poland, spoke of Germany as a 'dyke' against barbarism and suggested an alliance with her against the Soviets. Public reaction was almost universally hostile and Lloyd George disowned Churchill's views in the Commons on 2 August, saying that the article was 'not so much an expression of policy as a hankering'. Undeterred, Churchill produced a War Office paper, which was circulated to the Cabinet later in the month. He suggested that the best policy was to seek an entente with France and Belgium, review the worst parts of the Versailles Treaty, and secure Germany as part of a united front against the Soviets, leaving her with 'sufficient armed strength to keep order in her own country, and to meet the Red danger, which has overthrown Poland and is threatening the world'.[40] Churchill's view that Poland was already lost was proved wrong when on 13 August they launched their own offensive. This led to a rapid Soviet retreat and signature of the Treaty of Riga in October, under which the Soviets accepted a border over 100 miles east of the Curzon line and 3 million non-Poles were included in the new Polish state.

Lloyd George's willingness to open trade talks with the Soviet Government and his generally relaxed attitude to their activities seemed to some to place him in a dangerous quasi-Bolshevik camp. This atmosphere of distrust was heightened when intercepts of Soviet communications with the trade delegation in London revealed low-level interference in British politics and discreet funding of the *Daily Herald*. For some this confirmed their suspicions about the Prime Minister. The leader of this group was the CIGS, Field Marshal Sir Henry Wilson. A man with a violent distrust of all politicians, he wrote of Lloyd George in early 1920: 'I keep wondering if L-G is a traitor & a Bolshevist, & I will watch him very carefully.'[41] In May, after the Prime Minister would not use force against dockers who refused to load Army trucks bound for Ireland, Wilson's paranoia grew: 'I wonder, is L.G. allowing England to drift into Bolshevism on purpose?'[42]

On 17 August 1920 Churchill told Wilson that a strike by the Triple Alliance of trades unions (involving the railways, mines and docks) was inevitable. This was the threat the Government most feared – a near general strike and now combined with evidence of Soviet interference and the creation of local 'councils of action' that some thought looked like quasi-Soviets in the making. Wilson waited until Lloyd George departed on a three week holiday then the next day swung into action. He had already drawn up plans for what he described as 'war' against the councils of action (including stockpiling arms for issue to 'loyalists') and he now called a highly irregular meeting of senior generals and Sir Basil Thomson, the man responsible for anti-Bolshevik intelligence activity. The meeting identified Lloyd George and others as possible traitors. Wilson then went to see Churchill and told him about the meeting. The import of his message was clear: they wished to be loyal to the Government but they 'had a higher loyalty still to our King & to England'. Such talk was of course treasonable. Churchill did not object however. Indeed, according to Wilson, he virtually agreed with him, saying: 'it was quite true that L.G. was dragging the Cabinet step by step towards Bolshevism'.[43]

Later that day Churchill wrote to Lloyd George, Bonar Law and Balfour demanding action over the Soviet delegation in London. He also received a long hysterical letter from Wilson calling for a pre-emptive move against a revolutionary attempt by the workers. Churchill later forwarded this letter to some of his colleagues and associated himself with its sentiments. He told them that he wanted to bring to their notice the 'perturbation' caused to senior officers by 'a deliberate and dangerous conspiracy aimed at the main security of the state' but 'without any steps being taken to interfere with it'. He asked his colleagues to imagine what might result from the combination of 'the money from Moscow, the Kameneff-Krassin [sic] propaganda, the Council of Action, and something like a general strike, all acting and reacting on one another, while at the same time our military forces are at their very weakest'.[44] Wilson had persuaded Churchill to send this minute by telling him it was his chance to re-establish his political position and by alluding to the possibility of a military coup. According to Wilson's diary the two had the following exchange: 'I warned him that we Soldiers might have to take action if he did not & that in that case his position would be impossible. He agreed. He said he was "much worried about LGs attitude".'[45]

Wilson's hysteria faded in the next few days and Churchill concentrated on trying to get all the intelligence intercepts published (a move which would have made a substantial part of Britain's codebreaking ineffective in return for a short-term propaganda gain). He asked the intelligence agencies to consider the case for publication but even before he had received their report he told Lloyd George: 'No more deadly propaganda has ever come before me than this publication will make' and asserted that the threat of revolution was a more important consideration than any long-term effect on intelligence gathering.[46] Churchill then went off on holiday at the Duke of Westminster's estate at Mimizan in south-west France and in his absence Lloyd George was able to re-establish control of the Government. It was decided not to publish all the intercepts and not to expel the Soviet delegation and Lloyd George gave the latter a lecture about their behaviour.

Churchill protested about the trade talks continuing and took no part in them. His only, far from constructive, contribution came when he was consulted as part of a general trawl of departmental views: he suggested terms that would have meant the effective disarmament of the Red Army. On 16 November Churchill made one last effort to stop the trade deal, saying that the Soviet regime could not use their gold reserves to pay for British goods since it was bloodstained and stolen from the aristocracy. After two days of discussions the Cabinet voted to continue the trade talks – with only Churchill and two other members (Curzon and Milner) voting against. Having been persuaded by FE not to resign from the Government on the issue because he would only have the support of about thirty extreme right-wing Conservative MPs, Churchill told the Cabinet: 'Signing this agreement in no way alters the general position we have taken up . . . Ministers shall be free to point out the odious character of their regime. It seems to me you are on the high road to embrace Bolshevism [remarkably like his statement to Wilson in August]. I am going to keep off that and denounce them on all possible occasions.'[47] He did just that in a speech at Oxford the same night when he declared 'the policy I will always advocate is the overthrow and destruction of that criminal regime'. A trade deal with the Soviet authorities was finally signed in March 1921.

Churchill's last stand against Bolshevism during the life of the coalition came in March 1922 during preparations for the Genoa conference, at which it was expected that the allies would grant *de jure* recognition to the Soviet regime. Churchill threatened he would resign if such a step were taken. Austen Chamberlain told Lloyd George that Churchill would go 'because he was more Tory than the Tory ministers'.[48] Lloyd George thought he was 'a real wrecker' and 'obsessed by the defeat inflicted upon his projects by the Bolshevik armies'.[49] However as the Conservative members of the coalition did not relish being outflanked on the right by Churchill and as Lloyd George wanted to avoid a split, the Prime Minister suggested a compromise – full diplomatic recognition would be postponed, representatives would only be at chargé d'affaires level and action would only be taken in concert with their allies. However strong the case for granting some form of recognition to what was now an established regime, Churchill remained unhappy and made his views clear to the Cabinet: 'He was bitterly sorry that at a time of strong Conservative majorities in a country deeply devoted to the monarchy, it was proposed to accord this supreme favour and patronage to these people', a move which he thought was 'taking sides against Russia as a whole in favour of a band of dastardly criminals'.[50] In the end Churchill was spared from the decision whether to resign by the failure of the Genoa conference and the deal at Rapallo between Germany and the Soviet Union. Nevertheless in July Churchill once again told Lloyd George he would resign if the Soviet Government were recognised.

During his time at the War Office the other major question that Churchill had to face was the growing rebellion in Ireland against continued British rule. In August 1914 the question of Home Rule (and any possible exclusion of Ulster from its provisions) was postponed until after the war. The Easter rising in 1916 changed little and the Government continued with its policy of political inaction combined with mild coercion. In the December 1918 Election the older, more moderate Nationalists were swept away.

Sinn Fein, as the party which favoured total independence, won 73 seats, though its MPs refused to sit at Westminster and in January 1919 those not in jail formed a separate Irish parliament (the Dáil) and declared independence and war on Britain until the whole island was evacuated. Despite these developments Churchill was sanguine about the prospects. He told the Cabinet in February that he favoured the force feeding of Sinn Fein prisoners and that he 'did not contemplate any trouble in Ireland. In his view there was no place in the world where there was less danger at the present time.'[51]

For most of 1919 the Government did little while the situation continued to deteriorate. A political settlement was not considered by the Cabinet until the end of the year because signature of the last peace treaty, which would bring Home Rule into effect, was not likely for some years. A modified proposal was then developed involving two Home Rule parliaments (one for the majority and one for Ulster) and a council of Ireland as a fig-leaf for possible unification later. But the idea gained little support because under its provisions the British Government would retain so many powers that the Government in Dublin would have less than dominion status. Meanwhile republican groups were in control of most local councils and constituted the effective civil authority in many areas. The Irish Republican Army had enough local support and arms to mount a highly effective guerrilla campaign and even an attempted assassination of Viscount French, the Lord-Lieutenant, in December. Many police roles were being handed over to the Army but poor intelligence and training, limited numbers and inadequate co-operation with the police reduced the effectiveness of the military forces. The Government, with its strong Unionist majority, was not prepared to admit its increasing inability to govern Ireland nor did it recognise that a policy of repression was unlikely to build sufficient support for a compromise settlement. The sterility of its policy was to become increasingly apparent during 1920.

Churchill's comments on the Irish show a complete lack of understanding of the roots of a problem dating back centuries: he described the Irish troubles as part of 'a world-wide conspiracy against our country . . . [by] the rascals and rapscallions of the world who are on the move against us [and] designed to deprive us of our place in the world and rob us of victory'.[52] As the situation in Ireland continued to deteriorate in early 1920, the Government, with

Churchill playing a major role as the minister in charge of the Army, drifted into a policy of violence to try and stop an increasingly widespread rebellion. In April General Macready, whom Churchill knew well as the commander of the troops in the Rhondda in 1910–11, was appointed as military commander in Ireland and in May Churchill chose General Tudor as the commander of the Irish police. Neither appointment was a great success. Macready hardly moved outside of Dublin and had little idea of the problems of operations in a countryside increasingly controlled by the IRA, and Tudor proved to be a poor disciplinarian unable to bring the police under effective control. Both were strongly protected by Churchill and the Cabinet as violence mounted.

On 11 May 1920 the Cabinet agreed to increase the size of the army in Ireland and Churchill put forward the germ of the idea that was to lead to the notorious 'Black and Tans'. He suggested raising a force of 8,000 former soldiers to supplement the police. None of his colleagues was keen on the idea and when the War Office looked at the details they were immediately worried by the problem of the type of men likely to be recruited and how they would be disciplined. Churchill's initiative lapsed for the moment. At the end of May he proposed that the Government should now step outside the law and adopt a practice carried out by his hated opponents the Bolsheviks. He suggested setting up special tribunals that would dispense what was euphemistically described as 'summary justice' using military commanders not judges. In addition Churchill wanted to see people hung within a week of committing an offence and a general policy of 'making life intolerable in certain areas'.[53] His ideas were again rejected, as was his proposal a month later to start bombing and machine-gunning Sinn Fein gatherings from aeroplanes.

By this time (the end of July) law and order were breaking down across large areas of Ireland, and the Government was prepared to take more radical measures. They agreed to set up courts-martial to try capital cases (they could no longer get guilty verdicts from juries) and to begin recruiting volunteers to supplement the police (the Black and Tans). The policy that Churchill had long advocated was now being applied. The result was a vicious circle of increasing violence from the IRA and counter-violence from the police, Army and Black and Tans dubiously described as 'reprisals'. Churchill was a strong supporter of 'reprisals' (as were Lloyd George and some other Cabinet ministers). On 23 September Wilson wrote in his diary:

> Tudor made it very clear that the police and the Black and Tans ... are carrying out reprisal murders. At Bilbriggan, Thurles and Galway yesterday the local police marked down certain SFs as in their opinion the actual murderers or instigators and then coolly went and shot them without question or trial. Winston saw very little harm in this but it horrifies me.[54]

Churchill indeed told Wilson that he was quite happy for these unofficial but condoned reprisals to go on for a few years and he described the Black and Tans carrying them out as 'honourable and gallant officers'.[55] (In *The Aftermath*, published years later, Churchill stood by the Black and Tans and wrote of them as having been selected 'on account of their intelligence, their characters and their record in the War'.[56]) In November Churchill suggested going even further. He recommended to the Cabinet that they should agree to 'the substitution of regular, authorised and legalised reprisals for the unauthorised reprisals by the police and soldiers which are winked at and really encouraged by the Government'.[57] His colleagues thought the time not right for the introduction of official as opposed to unofficial State terrorism.

Even without these measures Churchill was optimistic about the outcome. He told Wilson on 16 November that 'we have nearly won in Ireland'.[58] He was to be proved wrong almost immediately. Five days later came 'Bloody Sunday' when the IRA killed twelve British intelligence officers and the Army responded by machine-gunning the crowd at a football match killing twelve people. On 28 November the IRA killed sixteen Army cadets. Nevertheless on 29 November Churchill assured Wilson that the Government would not introduce martial law. The very next day there were discussions about introducing martial law and Wilson reported a rapid *volte face*. 'Greenwood [Chief Secretary] inferred that he had always been in favour of it and so did Winston, their only doubt being whether we had enough troops! What amazing liars.'[59] On 1 December the Cabinet agreed to bring in martial law, which Greenwood and Churchill decided should be limited to four counties (extended to four more at the end of the month). At the beginning of 1921 the Government agreed to start official reprisals as Churchill had recommended in November. They were to last for five months as the Government tried to stamp out the IRA and the demand for independence. By the summer of 1921 it was apparent that the policy was futile and the Government began to edge very cautiously towards a policy of negotiation.

Almost as soon as the Government agreed to Churchill's policy of official terrorism he left the War Office and so did not have to carry it out. In February 1921 he became Colonial Secretary, a move which took him back to the area where he had begun his ministerial career just over fifteen years earlier. His two years at the War Office had not improved his reputation. Apart from reorganising the Army and RAF on a peacetime basis he had achieved little and most of his policies, especially the one to which he devoted nearly all his efforts in 1919 – the defeat of the Bolsheviks in Russia, had failed. He was seen as an extremist, moving speedily and deliberately to the far right of politics, as a warmonger because of his views over intervention in Russia, and as a man prone to take an unbalanced view of events because of his obsessive interest in certain subjects. Despite his earlier connection with Lloyd George his relations with the Prime Minister had been poor for most of the period. As he told Field Marshal Wilson in January 1921, he decided to accept the offer of the Colonial Office 'because he would not have lasted much longer in the WO owing to differences with LG'.[60] The new job was hardly promotion. He was not in charge of a major department and he was still excluded from the inner councils of the coalition. Nevertheless the range of problems the Colonial Office faced was enormous and the scope for Churchill's energy and initiative wide. Whether he would be able to devise constructive policies was another matter.

13

The Imperial Scene

The imperial scene that Churchill faced in 1921 was very different from the one that he had encountered fifteen years earlier. Then his main concern had been to bring the ex-Boer republics under British control. The rest of the task was largely a matter of day-to-day administration of an empire that seemed secure internally and externally. Now there were signs of revolt against British rule not just in Ireland but also in what were probably the two most important parts of the Empire – Egypt and India. He also had to produce a policy for governing the huge areas of the Near East which Britain had obtained for itself (under League of Nations auspices) from the defeat of the Ottoman Empire. New states had to be created and British control imposed but without involving any great expense at a time when the Government was under strong pressure to reduce public expenditure.

One of the firm foundations of Churchill's view of the world was his belief that Britain's status as a world power depended on the maintenance of the Empire. He was, therefore, clear about the policy to be adopted towards any desire for independence. He told the Cabinet in 1920: 'all demands to break away from the British Empire and British Crown should be perseveringly withstood'.[1] With his deeply held views about white supremacy, he simply never understood why other nations should want to rule themselves. To him such demands were perverse – Britain was not only entitled to rule the Empire but the British, as a civilised white race, were far better able to govern than other lesser breeds. His lack of understanding of and sympathy for the nationalist movements he was to face for the rest of his political career was well illustrated in his description (given to his constituents in 1922) of the campaigns for self-government in Egypt and India: 'millions of people hitherto sheltered by superior science and a superior law [showing] a desire to shatter the structure by which they live and to return blindly and heedlessly to primordial chaos'.[2]

Churchill first had to face nationalist pressures in Egypt, which was technically not part of the Empire (although Churchill always thought it was). In 1920 Milner (then Colonial Secretary and a strong imperialist) suggested that Britain should accept Egypt's nominal independence (which in theory had not ended with the British occupation in 1882) and in return demand a treaty that protected all her interests in the country. Churchill did not accept that this was a safe way of maintaining the British position in the long-term and objected to any negotiation with Egyptian nationalists and any acknowledgement that they might have a say in the country. He felt it would set a bad example in the Empire that would serve only to raise expectations elsewhere. He warned the Cabinet in August 1920: 'one can easily see that these proposals will become immediately the goal of Indian nationalism'.[3] He strongly opposed the Milner plan in Cabinet and voted against it in December 1920 but was in a minority.

In February 1921 the Cabinet agreed to open negotiations with Egypt (the responsibility of the Foreign rather than the Colonial Office) and Churchill again opposed the idea, telling Curzon, the Foreign Secretary, that he was 'not at all prepared to sit still & mute & watch the people of this country being slowly committed to the loss of this great and splendid monument of British administrative skill & energy'.[4] In July he told the Imperial Conference that Britain could not afford 'to let ourselves be pushed out of our position in Egypt by the continuance of local agitations'.[5] These 'local agitations' also included, as far as Churchill was concerned, any independent initiative by British politicians. When a delegation of Labour MPs visited Egypt to investigate conditions, Churchill was so incensed that he wrote to Curzon demanding that he withdraw their passports as a punishment.

Those on the spot found that the 'local agitation' was far harder to deal with than Churchill imagined. General Allenby, the High Commissioner, eventually proposed a treaty with Egypt which, while recognising independence, reserved four areas absolutely to Britain – the security of the Suez Canal, defence, protection of foreign interests and relations with the Sudan, and in practice Egyptian foreign policy would have to coincide with Britain's. Churchill failed to see that this represented in many ways a strengthening of Britain's position: while conceding domestic policy to the Egyptian Government, it would firmly entrench, with Egyptian consent, Britain's sole contol over every area that the Government thought important. What Churchill objected to was the principle that Britain's position in Egypt could in any way depend on Egyptian consent. He told Field Marshal Wilson in February 1922 that he would 'never agree' to the Allenby proposals and 'would fight to the end'.[6] Four days after that conversation he reluctantly accepted the Cabinet decision to agree to the Allenby plan.

If Churchill was on the fringes of the discussions over the future of Egypt, he was central to the decisions made elsewhere in the Near East. Here the Government was still driven by old imperial policies, especially safeguarding the route to India, although it had to use some novel expedients to achieve its ends. During the war Britain and France had agreed to a carve-up of the remains of the Ottoman Empire, giving France predominance in Syria and Britain supremacy elsewhere. The San Remo Treaty of 1920 officially endorsed this division although the French sphere of influence was reduced and Britain gained control of Mesopotamia and Palestine (later divided into Palestine and Trans-Jordan). The main constraint on imperial ambitions was that these territories were League of Nations mandates and so subject to some outside monitoring on the protection of the rights of the inhabitants and their eventual right to self-rule.

Churchill had already been involved in decisions on Mesopotamia as Secretary of State for War. In the autumn of 1919 there were still nearly 100,000 British and Indian troops there and Churchill wanted to reduce their numbers in order to save money. His problem was to secure from his colleagues a clear-cut decision about future policy. His worry was that in the absence of such a decision he would be left as the scapegoat if things went wrong. And there was plenty of scope for that to happen. There was no subordinate Arab administration on which the British could rely, and revolt in the Kurdish areas followed by a general rebellion against British rule in the summer of 1920 had to be put down by bringing in reinforcements from India, thus postponing the date for reducing the garrison. On two occasions in May and December 1920, in order to force his colleagues to make some decisions, he advocated withdrawing from the remoter areas and concentrating British control in the area around Baghdad, Basra and the oilfields, thereby cutting occupation costs by two-thirds. The problem was that this was simply not a realistic policy, because no coherent states could be created in the unoccupied parts in the north and the British area would be left without any defensible borders. In December 1920 he also backed a civil service plan to create a Middle East department in the Colonial Office to oversee British policy in the whole area. Then in February 1921 Lloyd George sent him to the Colonial Office largely to create the new department and co-ordinate British policy in the Middle East.

Churchill found that the outlines of a policy in Mesopotamia were already clear. The British intended to create an Arab kingdom, which would administer Mesopotamia under British guidance and provide an army (thus saving British costs) while meeting League of Nations susceptibilities about eventual self-government. The preferred candidate for the throne was Feisal, a son of Hussein, the head of the Sherifian dynasty, which ruled in Arabia and which had been under British tutelage for decades. Feisal's brother, Abdullah, was the candidate to rule Trans-Jordan, an arrangement Churchill contemptuously dubbed 'Hussein & Sons Ltd'.[7] On taking up his new office Churchill quickly decided that he should chair a conference of all British representatives in the Near East to decide future policy. He originally intended to go to Mesopotamia but settled instead on the greater comforts of Cairo.

The Cairo conference began in early March 1921 and within two days it had agreed that Feisal was, as Churchill told Lloyd George, the 'best and cheapest solution' to Britain's problems in Mesopotamia.[8] The conference then considered ways of reducing the cost of the garrison. Here Churchill felt 'no local interest can be allowed to stand in the way'.[9] Once Feisal was installed costs were expected to fall from about £30 million a year to only £6 million. The next problem was to put Feisal on the throne. Churchill was not prepared to allow a local assembly to meet and decide on their ruler, because of the risk that they might not choose Feisal. However, some popular element was necessary to satisfy the League of Nations, despite Churchill's view that their involvement and the whole idea of mandates was 'obsolescent rigmarole' and that the League would have collapsed within a couple of years.[10] The British authorities deported most of Feisal's opponents and after a rigged referendum of local notables in August 1921 he was duly installed as ruler of Mesopotamia.

The British achieved their objective of setting up a client regime in an artificial state ruling through the Sunni minority. However when they came to negotiate a treaty with Feisal, he proved less compliant than expected: he wanted a greater degree of independence and a direct agreement with Britain, avoiding any League of Nations involvement through its mandatory powers. Churchill had some sympathy with Feisal's objections to any League interference but in general found him tiresomely difficult and refused to take him seriously, asking his officials: 'Six months ago we were paying his hotel bill in London ... Has he not got some wives to keep him quiet?'[11] The Cabinet though decided in April 1922 that Feisal would have to accept the League of Nations mandate and after six months of further British pressure he finally did so.

Establishing Feisal's brother in Trans-Jordan proved much easier. No British troops, only the RAF, were to be based in the territory. Abdullah would govern the area in effect as a British puppet, in return for a subsidy of £180,000 a year. The creation of Trans-Jordan did however involve splitting the League of Nations mandate for Palestine. Churchill favoured this course because it tied in with his own strongly pro-Zionist sympathies. He believed absolutely in the Balfour declaration of November 1917, which favoured the creation of a 'Jewish National Home' in Palestine (although other conflicting assurances were given to the Arabs that this would not be at the expense of their rights). When Abdullah asked for an Arab ruler over the whole of the Palestine mandate, Churchill told him this was impossible. He did not explain that division of the mandate was essential in order to help the Zionists establish themselves in the smaller Palestine created once Trans-Jordan had been hived off.

Churchill had been sympathetic to Jewish people moving out of

Europe and establishing settlements within the Empire when he was first at the Colonial Office – then he had investigated Somaliland as a possible home for them. His positive attitude to Zionism in the 1920s also reflected his contempt for the Arabs. He seems to have seen the Jews as part of the European imperial enterprise to take over the land from a backward people who were, as he had written when in east Africa fifteen years earlier, inferior to white Europeans. Churchill had little sense of Arab history and culture (even after the Cairo conference he did not know the difference between the Sunni and Shi'a branches of the faith) and what he did know, he did not like. He told the Peel Commission that investigated British policy in Palestine that 'where the Arab goes it is often desert' and claimed that Palestine 'never will be cultivated by the Arabs'.

Churchill's view of the Arabs as a people who deserved to lose their home to more advanced Europeans was made quite clear in his evidence to the Peel Commission in the late 1930s. He described them as acting like a 'dog in a manger' and went on:

> I do not agree that the dog in a manger has the final right to the manger, even though he may have lain there for a very long time. I do not admit that right. I do not admit, for instance, that a great wrong has been done to the Red Indians of America, or the black people of Australia. I do not admit that a wrong has been done to these people by the fact that a stronger race, a higher grade race, or at any rate, a more worldly-wise race, to put it that way, has come in and taken their place.[12]

(Churchill realised that he had expressed himself rather too frankly and therefore wrote to Lord Peel to ensure that these remarks were not printed in the official evidence.) Churchill also gave individual Arabs short shrift. When he was staying at the Hotel Semiramis in Cairo for the conference, he objected to the management if any Arabs came into the hotel or even into the garden, and one of the participants has described how he 'talked impatiently to Arab deputations, as though his hearers were boys or minors, who understood nothing and were tiresome and perverse, and must have what was for their good told to them sharply'.[13]

Where Palestine was concerned, Churchill strongly endorsed the Balfour declaration which referred only to the civil and religious rights of the Palestinians and made no mention of any political rights. He was not prepared to grant the inhabitants any form of even limited self-government. This was because in 1922 Palestinian Arabs outnumbered Jews by 487,000 to 83,000. As far as Churchill was concerned, such institutions would have to wait until the Jews were a majority of the population. He told the Cabinet in August 1921, 'In the interests of the Zionist policy, all elective institutions have so far been refused to the Arabs.'[14] But if the small Jewish minority were ever to be a majority of the population there would have to be massive immigration. This was another reason for denying the Arabs any say in the administration of the mandate – he bluntly told an Arab and Christian delegation in August 1921: 'We intend to bring more Jews in. We do not intend you to be allowed to stop more from coming in.'[15] Churchill was quite clear about the scale of the immigration he envisaged. In August 1920 he wrote in the *Illustrated Sunday Herald* of Palestine containing 3–4 million Jews (a large proportion of the European Jewish population), who would of course be granted self-government within the British Empire like any other white dominion. It was therefore highly mendacious of Churchill during his visit to Jerusalem in March 1921 to reassure Abdullah that there was 'a great deal of groundless apprehension among the Arabs in Palestine' since they seemed to think hundreds of thousands of Jews would dominate the existing population – 'this was not only not contemplated, but quite impossible'.

Churchill's visit to Palestine in March 1921 after the Cairo conference encapsulates his one-sided attitudes very well. He grudgingly met Abdullah and an Arab delegation and when they asked why they should be forced to give up their country to Jewish settlers, he could only tell them that it was Government policy, and his own strongly held conviction, that the Balfour declaration should be implemented and nothing they could say would change that fact. He refused all social engagements with Arabs. When he met the Jewish delegation, he told them he supported their aims and hoped for their success. He had dinner with Zionist groups, inspected the new Hebrew university (where he said 'my heart is full of sympathy for Zionism') and visited Tel Aviv and the agricultural settlement of Rishon le-Zion. He implicitly recognised the Jews as the new rulers of the country when he told the Arab delegation, who represented the majority of the population, that they should deal direct with

Zionist organisations and not the British Government and accept the fact of Jewish domination. He advised them to share in the prosperity the Jews would bring, although he envisaged the local population as being no more than menial workers. His highly biased policy was shown quite clearly in June 1921 when he wrote to tell Samuel, the High Commissioner, that he was prepared to officially recognise Zionist bodies as part of the mandate but not Christian or Muslim organisations in order to 'avoid as far as possible crystallising distinction between Jews and non-Jews as such'![16]

In June 1921, following large-scale Arab riots against Britain's pro-Zionist policy, Churchill was forced to retreat on the speed at which Jewish immigration should proceed. In future it was not to be greater than the economic capacity of Palestine to absorb them (although this still implied a substantial rate and all his other pro-Zionist policies remained in place). He disliked having to make this concession and in 1937 told the Peel Commission that immigration should not be restricted in this way. Then his only criticism of the Jews was that they might have intermingled more with the Arabs, although he drew back in horror from any idea of 'the intermingling of the races by blood'.[17]

The cost of sustaining this pro-Zionist policy was high, as Churchill recognised. In August 1921 he advised the Cabinet that internal security in Palestine was a major problem because of continued Jewish immigration. He identified the cost of the British garrison as £3.3 million a year and stated that, 'It cannot be doubted that this expense is almost wholly due to our Zionist policy.'[18] Churchill was quite prepared to incur that cost in order to obtain his objectives, but elsewhere in the Empire he sought to find cheaper ways of keeping order. He was particularly keen on the use of the RAF rather than large Army garrisons. His interest in this policy had begun when he was responsible for air policy before he moved to the Colonial Office. He was strongly influenced by Trenchard and others in the RAF who were anxious to find a peacetime role and preserve the precarious independence the service had achieved only seven months before the end of the war. They claimed that the RAF would be able to keep order in remote parts of the Empire by bombing villages and rebel areas and it represented a cheaper option than having permanent Army garrisons and mounting large-scale punitive expeditions. Instead the Army would be relegated to protecting RAF bases.

During his search for ways of cutting the costs of occupying Mesopotamia Churchill became a firm advocate of using the RAF. In March 1920 he asked them to devise a scheme and advocated it strongly within Whitehall for the rest of the year. At the Cairo conference he was able to force the idea through as the long-term solution to bring occupation costs down. In August 1921 the Cabinet agreed Churchill's proposals to control Mesopotamia with eight RAF squadrons, armoured car companies, local Arab levies and a mix of British and Indian troops, all for an estimated £4 million a year (about one-seventh of the existing costs). The drawbacks of this policy were soon apparent. The RAF started bombing villages, and even machine-gunning women and children, as a way of enforcing a tax raising campaign. Churchill thought this was going too far (he even contemplated courts-martial for the pilots) and issued instructions that bombing was not to be used to raise taxes. In practice his instructions made no difference – the RAF were used to extend the control of the Feisal Government throughout the 1920s (the extension of tax raising to remote parts was central to that policy) and villages continued to be bombed and civilians killed. The same policy was also adopted in other remote parts of the Empire where control had always been difficult such as the North West Frontier and Somaliland.

Although Churchill had qualms about machine-gunning women and children from the air, he had no doubts about the use of chemical warfare by the RAF to establish control of these remote areas. After the end of the war he remained enthusiastic for the use of poison gas, telling the Cabinet in May 1920 that it 'should be definitely accepted as a weapon of war'.[19] But there was always an element of double standards in Churchill's thinking. When the Germans used it against British troops, he described it to Clementine as 'this hellish poison'.[20] When it was to be used against non-whites, it became justifiable, even benign. At he end of April 1919 the RAF asked for approval to use mustard gas in Mesopotamia (a gas that causes severe blistering, and in many cases blindness for two or three months and kills about ten per cent of those affected). Less than nine months after his earlier comment on its hellishness, Churchill wrote giving his approval to its use:

> I do not understand this squeamishness about the use of gas ... I am strongly in favour of using poisoned gases against uncivilised tribes. The moral effect should be so good that the loss of life should be reduced to a minimum ... Gases can be used which cause great inconvenience and would leave a lively terror and yet would leave no serious permanent affect on most of those affected.[21] (sic)

The RAF then found that gas bombs were not available (Churchill had decided to use most of them against the Bolsheviks), but during the 1920 rebellion in Mesopotamia he agreed to the Army sending 15,000 gas shells from Egypt for use against the rebels. Again he told Trenchard at this time that mustard gas could be used 'without inflicting grave injury' on its victims.[22]

In May 1919 Churchill also approved the use of gas during the campaign to subdue Afghanistan. When the India Office objected strenuously to such a policy, he wrote a strong rejoinder:

> The objections of the India Office to the use of gas against natives are unreasonable. Gas is a more merciful weapon than high explosive shell and compels an enemy to accept a decision with less loss of life than any other agency of war. The moral effect is also very great. There can be no conceivable reason why it should not be resorted to.[23]

Churchill was convinced that chemical warfare was not only highly effective against uncivilised natives ('the moral effect'), it was also more humane. He described it as firing 'a shell which makes the said native sneeze',[24] and when both the Mesopotamian administration and the RAF raised objections to chemical warfare, he responded that it was 'a scientific expedient for saving life wh shd not be prevented by the prejudices of those who do not think clearly'.[25] He was to remain enthusiastic for its use against non-whites, writing in 1927 to the then Secretary of State for War, Worthington-Evans, to congratulate him on sending out gas weapons for use against the Chinese nationalists in Shanghai.

During his spell at the Colonial Office Churchill also had to take crucial decisions about the future of Kenya, which he had visited during his African journey in 1907. Then, as a junior minister he had agreed that the highland parts of the country should be reserved for white settlement and had envisaged strict segregation being applied elsewhere to separate the whites, the increasing number of Indian immigrants and the Africans. In 1921–2 he was able to bring this vision to fruition against strong opposition from the India Office, which sought to protect the interests of the Indians against Churchill, who on every occasion supported the policies advocated by the white settlers.

Churchill first confirmed the earlier pledge that the highlands were to be exclusively white. Then he introduced strict residential segregation throughout the colony. A Bill to do this openly had been abandoned in 1918 and Churchill chose a more subtle route – public health regulations modelled on South African legislation passed in 1919. This approach was based on the premise that Indians suffered from what one official report called an 'incurable repugnance to sanitation and hygiene' and thereby lowered the already poor standards of the impressionable Africans still further.[26] Under Part XIII of Kenya's Public Health Act the Governor was able to reserve different areas of the country to different races on sanitation grounds. Churchill approved this provision in April 1921, after seeing the detailed plans for the restriction of Indian settlement and despite strong protests from the Indian community.

The political future of the colony was equally fraught. The Indians demanded equal political rights on the grounds that they were equal citizens of the Empire. Churchill refused to tolerate such claims. He supported the white settler position that there should not be a common franchise and that separate white and Indian electorates (nobody suggested the African majority might vote) should be established to ensure white domination despite their very small numbers (they were to be given twice as many representatives as the Indians). When Churchill discovered that the Europeans had created a secret military organisation to resist Indian claims and seize control of the country if they were granted, he accepted that they should not be coerced by use of African police or the King's African Rifles:

> Whatever the circumstances and whatever the provocation it would be madness to use black troops against the whites. Inter alia I should expect it to provoke an immediate revolution in South Africa which General Smuts would have to lead under penalty of being overthrown and the results to a British Government are obvious.[27]

Churchill's policy was that the whites should eventually run the colony. Kenya would be developed as 'a characteristically and distinctively British Colony evolving towards complete responsible self-government', i.e. white minority rule operating in a segregated society as in South Africa.[28] Churchill was adamant that Kenya was, as he told Montagu, Secretary of State for India, 'a white man's country' and he held firmly to the view: 'The Indians in East Africa are mainly of a very low class of coolies, and the idea that they should be put on an equality with the Europeans is revolting to every white man throughout British Africa.'[29] Montagu could only reply that Churchill's views were those of a 'European settler of a most fanatical type'.[30] It was Churchill's views that prevailed whilst he was at the Colonial Office and he tolerated no interference on behalf of the Indians (let alone the Africans).

Much of Churchill's time at the Colonial Office was taken up by the still unresolved problem of Ireland, where the policy he had advocated when at the War Office – violence and coercion – was beginning to run into the sand by the middle of 1921. Five months of official 'reprisals' and continuing IRA violence had produced no solution. The Government decided in late April to allow elections for the dominion Parliament of southern Ireland to go ahead. They rejected the idea of a truce during the campaign because the military thought it would help the Republicans. Churchill favoured a truce partly because he thought it would mean more anti-Republicans would stand and also because he did not think it would worsen the military situation and if necessary, he told his colleagues, 'we can break up this Irish parliament and revert to coercion'.[31] The Election resulted in an overwhelming Sinn Fein majority (they were only opposed in four constituencies) but they refused to take their seats.

The Government was now in a nasty dilemma. The Ulster Parliament was about to meet but in the south the only alternatives were either to adopt martial law in all twenty-six counties and govern without any elected institutions or to do a deal with Sinn Fein. On 2 June the Cabinet agreed to impose full martial law from 12 July and at this stage Churchill felt that the Black and Tans were proving to be highly successful – he told the Cabinet: 'on balance Tudor and his men were ... getting to the root of the matter quicker than the military'.[32] However when the Cabinet's Irish Committee (which did not include Churchill) looked at the implications of full martial law, they drew back and, using the King's speech opening the Belfast Parliament as an opportunity, made conciliatory gestures which led to a truce from 11 July – Churchill disliked the word truce because it implied military status for the IRA, but he accepted that for the moment military measures to suppress Irish republicanism had failed.

Lloyd George had four meetings with the Republican leader De Valera in July that opened the way to full-scale negotiations. The truce had left the Republicans in effective control of much of southern Ireland and the Government, by calling off the campaign of military repression, had tacitly accepted the need for an agreement. But they still wanted to hold Ireland to some form of dominion status with substantial British control. The Irish ideally wanted a republic but the process of negotiation was to drive some of them to accept dominion status, split the movement and lead to civil war. The first crucial issue for the Cabinet came in early September over the invitations to a conference on the future of Ireland. There were two alternatives: an unconditional invitation which would in theory leave open the possibility of granting republican status (though in practice the Government would never have accepted it) or a conditional one, where the Irish would have to accept in advance a settlement based on a state within the Empire and with the King as head of state. The latter alternative would almost certainly abort the negotiations before they had even begun. At an emergency Cabinet held in Inverness, near to where Lloyd George was on holiday, Churchill (described by one of the secretaries as 'breathing fire and slaughter') argued passionately against issuing an unconditional invitation saying that it 'would be to admit tacitly that the British Empire is an open question'.[33] On balance he preferred to reopen the war, arguing that it would be no worse than before. A majority of his colleagues disagreed and unconditional invitations were issued.

Lloyd George, in order to protect his political position, chose a strongly unionist negotiating team to join him in the discussions with the Irish, which opened in mid-October – Austen Chamberlain, FE (now Lord Chancellor and ennobled as Lord Birkenhead) and Churchill, whose anti-Irish and pro-Ulster views were becoming increasingly apparent. Churchill did not relish the process of what he saw as breaking up the Empire and, despite the impression he liked to create later, took little part in the talks. He chaired the sub-committee on naval and air defence, where he contemptuously rejected Irish claims that they should be responsible for their own defence and that they could be neutral in any conflict involving Britain, and he insisted on British control of strategic ports in Ireland. The details of the negotiations were left to Lloyd George and FE; they involved a complex series of compromises over the position of the Crown in the future Irish state, the oath the members of the Dáil would have to take, the process for demarcation of the Ulster boundary, fiscal autonomy, defence and treaty making powers. It was the first two issues that caused the greatest problem because the British wanted to keep a fig-leaf of monarchical and imperial powers in order to placate the Unionists.

Churchill was present at the final negotiating session on 5 December (where he made some concessions on defence issues) when Lloyd George finally persuaded the Irish delegation to sign an agreement which kept Ireland to a form of dominion status (though in practice the oath to the King was virtually meaningless and it did open the way to an eventual republic) and which contained only vague assurances about the treatment of the Ulster border and Britain's willingness to pressurise the Ulster Government into making compromises. Churchill's real views on the treaty are unclear. At the time he stood by it and he was to spend much of the next six months implementing it. Later he often tried to disown it. In 1925 over dinner with Beaverbrook he was reported as criticising Lloyd George 'very freely for the wicked Irish treaty and declares that the Coalition Government ought to have continued the war against Sinn Fein for another winter'.[34]

As Colonial Secretary, Churchill was given responsibility for the transfer of power to the new Irish Government and within a short period about half of the Irish administration was working for him as the job of the old Chief Secretary for Ireland unravelled. The actual process of the transfer of power was to be a tangled one. In early January 1922 the Dáil approved the agreement reached in London and a provisional Government led by Griffiths and Collins was set up to begin drafting a constitution in line with the agreement with Britain. However, De Valera rejected the agreement and led the movement for a full republic and a continuation of the war to achieve it. Churchill seems to have seen the position as analogous to South Africa after the Boer War. He cast Griffiths and Collins in the roles

of Botha and Smuts and expected them to bring about a reconciliation of southern Ireland and the Empire. But he never understood
the depth of Irish feeling on the issue of independence and therefore
remained disappointed, even hurt, when the Irish refused to fulfil
their allotted roles.

Within a few weeks the IRA had repudiated the provisional
Government and resumed raids into Ulster, and the south began the
slide towards civil war. Churchill steered through the Commons the
Bill to set up a provisional Irish Government, provide an Election on
the treaty and create a constituent assembly to ratify the new
constitution. Britain naturally backed the provisional government but
Churchill was worried about what would happen if the pro-republic
faction gained the upper hand. On 5 April he put a paper to the
Cabinet on what to do in these circumstances. He envisaged that
martial law would be declared and that if a Republican Government
were set up, British troops would protect the border with Ulster and
fall back on Dublin. A month later he told the Cabinet that he would
not supply the provisional Government with arms unless they
guaranteed to use them against the Republicans and that if necessary
he would continue to hold Dublin, which he called the 'English
capital', and convert it into a modern version of the medieval 'pale'.[35]

Churchill had also become as strong a supporter of Ulster as any
Unionist. In September 1912 he had foreseen problems if the
Protestants were allowed a free hand:

> There is not the slightest danger in my opinion of Protestants in
> Ulster being persecuted for their religion under a system of Home
> Rule. The danger is entirely the other way, *viz* – that the very
> strong and aggressive Protestant majority in parts of North East
> Ulster will maltreat and bully the Catholics in their midst.[36]

Now he forgot his earlier warning and strongly backed the Protestants. In April 1922 he formally approved the Special Powers Act
in Ulster, which suspended habeas corpus, removed any legal
protection against arbitrary search, seizure and imprisonment, introduced summary jurisdiction and gave powers to ministers to rule by
decree. IRA attacks on Ulster continued and there was a steadily
increasing Protestant pogrom against the Catholics. At the end of
May he blamed all the violence in Ulster on the IRA and Repub-

licans, without any evidence for such a claim and when the available evidence pointed to the Protestants being largely to blame. On 22 May in the Cabinet's Irish Committee he backed the creation of the armed 'B Specials' (in effect an armed Protestant militia) against the advice of General Macready who was in charge of Irish security policy. He also successfully resisted Lloyd George's attempt to set up a judicial enquiry into the Protestant-led outrages against the Catholics in the north.

At the beginning of June 1922 the two crises, in Ulster and in the south over the constitution, came together. On 27 May Churchill, having studied the draft Irish Constitution which the Law Officers advised was not compatible with the agreement made in December, wanted to order a stop to the Irish Elections. Lloyd George would not go that far and instead took charge of the negotiations with the Irish. He slowly persuaded them that they would have to make the constitution compatible with the agreement. Meanwhile Churchill was ready for tough measures, as he told the Irish Committee on 1 June: 'When we begin to act we must act like a sledgehammer, so as to cause bewilderment and consternation among the people of Southern Ireland.'[37]

With the negotiations poised at a delicate stage, just over sixty men from the south moved into the disputed border villages of Pettigo and Belleck. Craig, the Ulster Prime Minister, chose to regard this as an invasion of the north. Churchill, whose aunt Lady Leonie Leslie owned a 32,000 acre estate in the area, reacted by sending in 7,000 troops with artillery. He did not have Cabinet authority for the move and when Lloyd George tried to countermand the order, he threatened to resign. After a four-day battle, in which seven men from the south were killed and fifteen captured and British troops operated south of the border, the incident ended. Lloyd George was convinced that Churchill had deliberately over-reacted in order to try and wreck the talks with the Irish provisional Government, lead a campaign to reassert control over the south and place himself at the head of a pro-unionist Government. He told the Deputy Secretary to the Cabinet when it was all over that Churchill had acted like 'a chauffeur who apparently is perfectly sane and drives with great skill for months, then suddenly he takes you over a precipice ... there was a strain of lunacy. No Churchill was ever loyal. [He] is fancying himself as a leader of a Tory revolt.'[38]

If that was what Churchill intended, his hopes were soon dashed. Within ten days the problems over the Irish Constitution were solved. Although the Irish agreed that the King should be Head of State and that the Free State should be part of the Commonwealth, the British had allowed a statement that the Irish people were sovereign and in practice the monarchy was to be largely irrelevant as part of the Irish Government. On 16 June the Irish Election produced a large win for the pro-treaty party. Six days later Field Marshal Wilson (then acting as adviser to the Ulster Government) was assassinated by the IRA. The British Government decided to use this as an excuse to demand that the Irish Government attack the IRA forces holding the Four Courts area in Dublin (and thereby almost inevitably start a civil war). Churchill claimed there was a link between those holding the Four Courts and the killers of Wilson. When the Irish asked him to produce the evidence, he refused. With the Irish Government still considering what action to take, Churchill persuaded his colleagues to order General Macready to attack the Irish forces in the Four Courts. Macready did not carry out the order (ostensibly because British civilians in Dublin were not secure) and gave the Government time to change its mind. In doing so he probably averted a renewal of British–Irish hostilities. On 28 June Irish Government forces began the attack (which was inevitable without British prompting if they were to exercise effective control of the country) and within three days the Republican forces surrendered. The civil war, which the attack initiated, was to last for another year.

Churchill's last significant contribution on the Irish problem was to help ensure Protestant control of Ulster. In 1919 the coalition Government had insisted on introducing a system of proportional representation for local government in Ulster in order to ensure that the minority Catholic population were adequately represented. The Protestants saw this act as symbolic of resistance to their complete supremacy and introduced a Bill in the Ulster Parliament that removed the provision for PR and also gerrymandered constituency boundaries to ensure Protestant control. Churchill was told that he had the legal power to veto the Bill because it breached the Act setting up the separate Ulster Parliament. He rejected such advice and backed the Protestants. He allowed the Bill to become law over the protests of the Dublin Government. When he met their representatives, he mendaciously told them that PR had been abolished 'not to deprive the minority of its due representation' but solely on grounds of the extra expense involved.[39]

By the time the Irish problem was put into abeyance in the summer of 1922 the future of the coalition which had been created in 1916 and elected so overwhelmingly in 1918 was in doubt. To some extent it had always seemed a temporary and expedient alliance between the successful and popular wartime Prime Minister, now largely without a party, and the largest party in the country following the Liberal split. But it did have an underlying logic. For both the Liberal and Conservative élite that dominated British politics and Government the greatest threat they faced was the rise of Labour – by 1921 the TUC had 6.6 million members of which 4.5 million were affiliated to the Labour Party, which was not only the official opposition but also had a growing popular base. The main question the political élite faced was how to respond to that rise and how best to organise resistance so as to preserve the society and economy in which they believed. 'High politics' in the period 1918–24 was very largely concerned with finding answers to that question. It was not automatic that the political system that emerged after 1924 – a strong Conservative Party, a weakened Liberal Party in what turned out to be near terminal decline and the Labour Party as the main opposition – should be the outcome. A continuation of the coalition, some other form of central grouping or a more effective role for the Liberals were possibilities.

The political system within which Churchill had to operate at this time was therefore particularly fluid. His own position was far less so. Although he had been elected in 1918 as a Liberal supporting the coalition, his views and actions – fervid anti-Bolshevism, outright opposition to the claims of Labour, increasingly open support for Ulster – were driving him ever closer to the Conservatives. He also calculated that the chances of the Liberal Party reviving were slim, given the hostility between Asquith and Lloyd George, and that even if it did rally its political future was hardly rosy. He had no strong emotional or policy ties to the Liberal Party and had often hankered after a coalition as a way of forming a strong central conservative bloc in British politics. To a large extent the Lloyd George coalition provided exactly that. He was happy to see it survive and allow him to move closer to the Conservatives on virtually every issue while retaining his nominal Liberal affiliation. Nevertheless by this time there was little doubt that if a choice had to be made, he would choose the Conservatives rather than a Liberal Party which would probably be out of power and which might be tempted to co-operate in some way with Labour.

In early 1920 it seemed that the coalition might become permanent. Lloyd George favoured the idea (it was his best chance of staying in power), as did many Conservatives, and in March Bonar Law and Lloyd George agreed to talk with their respective parties about permanent fusion. On 16 March Lloyd George met other coalition Liberal ministers. Most, still attached to old Liberal ideas such as free trade and strict licensing for the drink trade, were opposed to the fusion proposals. Churchill, more attracted to Conservative ideas, was Lloyd George's sole supporter. Two days later the Prime Minister met coalition Liberal MPs and received a similarly hostile reception. Once this plan was dead, the coalition was bound to seem temporary, although the possibility of extending it through another election still remained open. Significantly, within ten days of the collapse of the fusion talks, Churchill was writing to Clementine about the possibility of leaving the Liberals and the 'difficult case' he would have to put to his constituency association.[40]

Churchill's personal position was far from strong at this time. He was still widely distrusted and few of his colleagues were impressed by his judgement. In September 1919 Lloyd George told the Liberal minister H. A. L. Fisher that 'Winston is a greater source of weakness than strength to the Gov – . . . he is like a Counsel that a solicitor employs not because he is the best man but because he would be dangerous on the other side'.[41] Four months later Lloyd George told his mistress: 'The worst feature of Winston . . . is his vanity! Everything that he does points to one thing – self.'[42] After working with Churchill for two years at the War Office, Field Marshal Wilson told his old boss Lord Derby, now Ambassador in Paris, that 'Winston is quite incapable of laying out a policy & then sticking to it, & that although he has his lucid & bright intervals these never continue for any length of time, & at other times he is frankly stupid in the mad things he does.'[43] His colleagues also continued to resent his almost constant interference in their affairs and his refusal to accept policies with which he disagreed. In May and June 1921 the Foreign Secretary, Lord Curzon, a martinet himself, complained on numerous occasions to Lloyd George about Churchill's speeches advocating a British-French-German alliance, his interference over Egypt and, as a last straw, his speaking at the Imperial Conference against renewing the Anglo-Japanese alliance when it was official policy at that time that it should be renewed. Austen Chamberlain endorsed these complaints and also showed the low political importance he attached to Churchill when he wrote to Curzon that he was right to 'profoundly resent his [Churchill's] constant & persistent interference. It goes far beyond anything that I at least have ever known in Cabinet even from the most important members of a Govt.'[44]

Some of these complaints in the summer of 1921 followed from Churchill's hostility and resentment towards Lloyd George after the resignation of the Conservative Leader Bonar Law, on grounds of ill-health, in March. Churchill wanted and expected to be made Chancellor of the Exchequer. He was out of the country (at the Cairo conference and then in Palestine) and although he hurried through the conference and his tour, when he arrived back in London the Cabinet reshuffle had taken place and left him where he was at the Colonial Office. Lloyd George probably had no intention of putting Churchill in charge of the Treasury, but his choice of the lightweight and relatively unknown Conservative, Sir Robert Horne, was taken as a personal insult by Churchill, who hated being subordinate to someone he regarded as a political inferior. He refused to speak to Lloyd George for a long time after this and he started to try to undermine all his policies – on Ireland, and on the coal strike among others. When Christopher Addison was forced to resign as Minister without Portfolio over inadequacies in the housing programme, Churchill pressed him to do the maximum possible damage to the Prime Minister even though Churchill himself had not shown the slightest interest before in either Addison or the housing programme. He told the editor of the *Daily Mail* at the end of May that he was 'fed up with Lloyd George'[45] and at the same time Frances Stevenson reported that Lloyd George was 'so sick with C I don't think he cares if he does go. Horne says Churchill is criticising the Government on Finance and Ireland in the Clubs & lobbies.'[46]

Despite the rift with Lloyd George Churchill had little choice but to stick with the coalition. He always preferred to be in office and there was no real alternative political home if he chose to resign. A move to the Asquithian Liberals looked like political suicide and went against all Churchill's increasingly Conservative instincts. His best chance was to stay in the Government but move even further towards the Conservatives, which he did throughout 1921 and 1922, particularly on the issues of Ireland and recognition of the Soviet Union. Others identified this tendency at the time. Lloyd George described Churchill to C. P. Scott in January 1922 as second-in-command of the coalition Liberals (the only other important figures – Addison, Montagu and Hewart – had left the Government for various reasons and the remainder were largely political non-entities) but pointed out that at heart he was 'not a Liberal; his sympathies were all with the Imperialists. But he was sound on free trade, almost fanatical.'[47] Beaverbrook wrote to Lloyd George in March 1922 of Churchill that 'his tendency is all to the Right and his principles becoming more Tory'.[48]

That these were correct assessments of Churchill's views was shown during the political discussions in December 1921. The Government seemed in a strong position (Conservative discontent had been contained at the party conference the previous month, a settlement had been reached on Ireland and the international situation looked reasonably stable after the convulsions of the immediate post-war period) and Lloyd George was keen to take advantage of the situation by calling an Election and fighting it as a coalition. On 19 December he consulted Chamberlain (as Conservative leader), Horne, FE and Churchill about the possibilities. Horne and FE favoured an early Election, Churchill was guarded and Chamberlain talked about consulting the party. When the five met again early in the new year for dinner it was clear that, although the coalition Liberals generally supported Lloyd George, opinion in the Conservative Party was against an early Election. This was a major blow to the Prime Minister's authority – he could not call an Election against the advice of the party that dominated the Government and so the coalition limped on with its future even more in doubt. After these talks Churchill favoured continuing the coalition and fighting the Election on that basis as the best way of resisting Labour. But if the coalition was going to break up, he wanted it to do so immediately. The Conservatives would then take office but, he argued, the coalition Liberals should continue to support them (rather than reunite with the Asquithians). Churchill hoped that he would be given a post in such a Government under Chamberlain even if Lloyd George were excluded and in this way his return to his old party would be accomplished relatively painlessly.

The coalition continued into 1922 and during the spring and early summer its position strengthened somewhat, with no obvious alternative available and an election not required before the end of 1923. But in June the scandal which revealed Lloyd George's extensive sale of honours to finance the coalition Liberals (the Asquithians controlled existing Liberal funds) seriously damaged his reputation and increased Conservative discontent. (The sale of honours was nothing new in itself; both major parties had done it for decades, but its public revelation was embarrassing.) By the time of the summer recess, which lasted from August to October, feeling in the Conservative Party against fighting the next election as a coalition was rising rapidly. To a large extent this reflected the view that the Conservatives could win on their own and that Lloyd George's attractions as the war leader were now rapidly waning. The affair that was to raise real doubts about his value as a leader and bring on the final crisis of the coalition revolved around events on the Asiatic shore of the Dardanelles.

The crisis stemmed from the peace treaty with Turkey (signed at Sèvres), which relegated the country to third-rate status by depriving it of control of the Straits and giving large parts of the Mediterranean coast and Anatolia to Greece and Italy as a reward for being on the winning side. The allies, lacking sufficient forces of their own, had to rely on the Greeks to enforce this policy, and had not reckoned with the power of renascent Turkish nationalism under the military leader Kemal (later known as Ataturk). In July 1921 a major Greek offensive in Anatolia failed and produced growing doubts in Britain and France about whether the Treaty of Sèvres could actually be enforced. Nevertheless both governments continued to back the Greeks and demand that the Straits should remain internationalised and Greek troops stay on in the old European parts of Turkey. Churchill was not happy with this pro-Greek policy for two reasons. First, he adopted the old British nineteenth-century policy of seeing Turkey as a bastion against Russia, now run by the despised Bolsheviks. Second, as Secretary of State for War and later at the colonies, he felt the security of Mesopotamia could be ensured in the cheapest way by coming to a deal with Turkey which reduced the threat to the northern parts of the new British protectorate. In March 1920 in a letter to Lloyd George and again in December 1920 in a paper to the Cabinet, Churchill unsuccessfully argued for a reorientation of British policy and conclusion of an agreement with the Turkish nationalists rather than continuing with the pro-Greek policy of trying to contain the reviving Turkey.

An almost complete Greek collapse in front of a Turkish offensive in August 1922 and the fall of Smyrna (Izmir) brought on the crisis. Constantinople and European Turkey were still under either international or Greek control and a 'neutral' zone on the Asiatic side of the Straits (where under the treaty of Sèvres no Turkish forces were allowed) was maintained by a small British force at Chanak. The question for the British Government was whether they were prepared, in the last resort, to fight Turkey to stop her entering the 'neutral' zone or crossing the Straits to re-establish control over the pre-war territory of Turkey. Churchill's first reaction was to reverse the policy he had adopted in the previous three years to argue along with Lloyd George for a policy of resistance to Turkish claims. Why he changed his mind is not clear. It was probably a mixture of politics (supporting Lloyd George) and his unwillingness, when it came to a direct confrontation, to see Britain having to compromise with an oriental power, particularly the one that had ruined his political career only seven years earlier. On 7 September he told the Cabinet: 'If the Turks take the Gallipoli peninsula and Constantinople we shall have lost the whole fruits of victory and another Balkan war would be inevitable.'[49] Even without Churchill's prompting the Cabinet was determined to maintain the Treaty of Sèvres and exclude Turkey from the threatened territories.

After the Greek collapse the first question the Cabinet had to resolve was how to stop the relentless Turkish advance from Anatolia. On 15 September Churchill argued for putting together an international force comprised of British, French, Greek, Serbian, Rumanian and Anzac troops to constitute a permanent garrison. The Cabinet agreed to send British reinforcements but Churchill's idea of an international force rapidly collapsed. France and Italy withdrew their troops from the area and when he appealed to the dominions only New Zealand and Newfoundland expressed any willingness to help. It was clear that if there was to be any resistance to Turkey, it would be a solely British effort. On 16 September, after lunch at No 10, Lloyd George and Churchill agreed a strong public note foreshadowing war with Turkey. At the Cabinet the previous day Churchill, in a bellicose mood, had argued for attacking the Turks the moment they entered the 'neutral' zone and not waiting till they attacked the British force at Chanak and he was ready to evacuate the whole of Mesopotamia in order to find enough troops to confront the Turks. The Cabinet took a more cautious line and agreed to wait until the Turks approached the British troops at Chanak.

Churchill was made chairman of the cabinet committee overseeing the detailed movement of troops and warships to the area but, as so often in a crisis, his opinions fluctuated wildly almost from day to day. On 19 September he argued in Cabinet for withdrawing the small British force from Constantinople, effectively allowing the ancient capital to fall to the Turks, and concentrating all troops at Chanak. On 23 September, with Turkish troops on the edge of the British fortifications at Chanak but carefully avoiding any hostilities, he argued that the loss of Chanak would effectively close the Straits to shipping and that the possibility of giving Turkey back Thrace (currently occupied by Greece) should be considered as part of a deal to keep the 'neutral' zone. He stuck to the view that Chanak should be held at all costs at the afternoon Cabinet meeting on 27 September. Four hours later he argued for giving up Chanak (and Constantinople) and concentrating all forces across the Straits at Gallipoli. Two days later he reverted to wanting troops to stay at Chanak as the key to the situation.

The mood in the Cabinet was increasingly belligerent, although an offer to negotiate with Kemal about the future of Thrace was made through the French. Maurice Hankey, the Cabinet Secretary, noted in his diary 'What Ll.G, Churchill and Birkenhead dread is that Mustapha Kemal will accept the conference.'[50] On 29 September the Commander of British Forces at Chanak, General Harrington, was instructed to deliver an ultimatum to the Turks – either they withdrew or British forces would attack. Later that day at a second meeting, Curzon argued for withdrawing the ultimatum but FE, Chamberlain and Churchill all supported it. Churchill was particularly bellicose, saying that he wanted Kemal to be taught a lesson and he was even prepared for an alliance with Greece (a policy he had vigorously opposed for three years). However, General

Harrington turned a Nelsonian eye to his instructions and did not issue the ultimatum. Instead he told the Cabinet that Kemal had given instructions not to provoke an incident and was willing to negotiate. Churchill led the Cabinet discontent over Harrington's failure to act and drafted a stiff reply which accepted Kemal's offer to negotiate (it could hardly be rejected) but upbraided the General for failing to carry out instructions (even though they would almost certainly have resulted in war). Churchill added, in a passage that has all the hallmarks of his own views, that the Cabinet did not believe that 'repeated concessions & submissions to victorious orientals is the best way to avert war'.[51]

Although negotiations began between Kemal and General Harrington, Churchill still expected a Turkish advance, a British withdrawal to Gallipoli and a slaughter of the Christian population in Constantinople. On 5 October he was in a minority of one in the Cabinet in arguing for fighting Turkey to keep her out of Thrace – most of the rest recognised that it was inevitable that in any revision of the peace treaty the territory would revert to Turkey. On 11 October agreement on all issues was reached with Kemal. Churchill was disappointed at the outcome. Hankey's diary records how he walked across St James's Park with Churchill towards the end of the crisis and noted that 'he quite frankly regretted that the Turks had not attacked us at Chanak' and felt that the agreement to allow Turkey into Thrace was 'humiliating' and the return of Turkey to Europe would lead to 'an infinity of troubles'.[52]

By the time the Chanak crisis was resolved the coalition was about to collapse. Although the Cabinet had been united in its policy of resistance, many Conservatives chose to regard the incident as an example of Lloyd George's unsuitability as a leader and a critical letter from the ex-leader Bonar Law in *The Times* on 7 October, appealing for peace and arguing that Britain could not act as policeman of the world on its own, reinforced that mood. In September Churchill had favoured an Election in October on a coalition basis, telling Balfour that 'absolute unity in the face of Labour is essential'.[53] At a meeting at Chequers on 17 September Lloyd George, Chamberlain, FE, Horne and Churchill agreed on an early Election in order to try and head off a Conservative revolt in favour of fighting as an independent party, which was expected to surface at a meeting of the National Union in mid-November. But by the time the Chanak crisis was resolved there was growing discontent within the Government itself, mainly among Conservative junior ministers such as Boscawen at Agriculture and Stanley Baldwin at the Board of Trade, over continuing the coalition.

On 15 October Lloyd George, Chamberlain, FE and Churchill agreed, over dinner at Churchill's house, to call an immediate General Election and that Chamberlain, in a bad misjudgement of his position and strength, would call a meeting of Conservative MPs at the Carlton Club to endorse that decision. The next day Churchill was incapacitated by pains in his side, which were diagnosed on 17 October as appendicitis. An operation, still a serious one in the 1920s, was carried out on 19 October. As Churchill came round from the anaesthetic, his mind was, as ever, concentrated on politics. In a semi-conscious state he asked about the result of the by-election at Newport and learnt it had been won by an independent Conservative against a coalition supporter. He had relapsed into unconsciousness when later that day Conservative MPs voted heavily against continuing the coalition. Lloyd George resigned immediately but Bonar Law was able to form a government including some members of the coalition Government. Curzon and Baldwin stayed on but most of its senior members such as Austen Chamberlain, FE, Balfour and Horne refused to serve. (Churchill later dubbed it the 'Second XI'.) Bonar Law then called an immediate General Election.

Churchill was recovering from his operation in a nursing home until 1 November and was therefore able to play little active part in his campaign in Dundee, which, like other coalition Liberals, almost certainly benefited from Lloyd George's campaign fund raised by the sale of honours. He was not opposed by a Conservative and ran as a Liberal and free trader, calling on 'Liberals and Conservatives to stand shoulder to shoulder against the Socialist-Communist forces'. He attacked Labour as 'inspired by class jealousy and the doctrines of envy, hatred and malice' and denounced his opposing candidates for distributing 'slimy and insidious propaganda' and belonging to a 'band of degenerate international intellectuals'. He lumped together Gallacher, the Communist candidate, and Morel, the Labour candidate, saying: 'Mr Gallacher is only Mr Morel with the courage of his convictions, and Trotsky is only Mr Gallacher with the power to murder those whom he cannot convince.' Clementine did much of the early campaigning for Churchill but she was widely disliked in Dundee for her obvious wealth and English upper-class attitudes. FE also spoke for Churchill, but he was drunk and his speech degenerated into an abusive personal attack on Morel. Churchill, who had paid little attention to his constituency in the last sixteen years, arrived a few days before polling, still recovering from his operation. On 13 Novmber he tried to make a public speech but he was shouted down and had to abandon the meeting.

The November Election was won overwhelmingly by the Conservatives, who obtained 327 seats against Labour's 142. In third place came the Liberals. They accounted for nearly a third of the vote but were badly split – Lloyd George's faction won forty-seven seats, the Asquithians forty and uncommitted members twenty-nine. For Churchill the Election was a personal disaster. In a landslide swing he lost by over 12,000 votes to the independent prohibitionist, Scrymgeour, who had first stood against him in 1908. The second seat went to Morel. The depth of the hostility to Churchill in Dundee can be judged from the fact that despite (or perhaps because of) his national fame and known policies, he came nearly 2,000 votes behind his unknown fellow coalition Liberal, Macdonel. He had already lost his position as a minister, and now, after twenty-two years as an MP, he was also out of Parliament.

14

Changing Sides – Again

Churchill was, surprisingly, quite relaxed about his defeat and exclusion from Parliament. The new Conservative Government had a majority of at least eighty (and probably more in most circumstances), and he calculated on it lasting for four or five years and felt therefore that he had plenty of time to work out a new political strategy. He knew where he wanted to be: it was just a question of how to get there. All his instincts, and all his actions in the past three years, made it certain, now that the coalition was over, that he would leave the Liberal Party and rejoin the Conservatives as the best way of becoming a minister again. His only problem was to manage the transition as smoothly as possible. That he fully intended at this point to leave the Liberals as soon as practicable is the best explanation of why, almost immediately after the Election, he turned down the offer from his old friend General Louis Spears to resign as coalition Liberal MP for Loughborough to enable Churchill to regain a seat in Parliament (and he turned down other offers too).

In fact Churchill's political luck was about to change yet again. After his initial seemingly unstoppable upward movement before 1910, his career had marked time, and it was difficult to see how he could advance further in the Liberal Party. The war, which Churchill thought would be his great opportunity, turned out to be a disaster for him. The Dardanelles almost ended his career altogether and his time in Government since 1917 had done little to resuscitate his reputation. Now the political fluidity brought on by the disintegration of the Liberal Party and the rise of Labour was, unexpectedly, to provide two further Elections in as many years, creating the opportunity for a relatively easy, if unprecedented, second defection back to the Conservatives and his promotion to the centre of a new Conservative Government.

Churchill left England at the end of November 1922 and spent the winter of 1922–3 near Cannes, working on his war memoirs, painting and relaxing. He did not return to London for more than a short visit until May 1923. Then on 4 May at the Aldwych Club he made his first political speech since his defeat at Dundee and used the opportunity to lay the foundations for his move to the Conservatives. As before, he used what he saw as the threat posed by Labour – 'a great vehement, deliberate attack upon the foundations of society' – to justify a supra-party alliance with 'the clear purpose of rallying the greatest number of persons of all classes . . . to the defence of the existing constitution' so as to resist 'the ceaseless advance and . . . victorious enforcement of the levelling and withering doctrines of socialism'. He specifically disagreed with Asquith's view that it was 'disgraceful for any Liberal to co-operate with any Conservative' and, unlike Lloyd George, he did not dissociate himself from the limited protectionist measures the coalition had taken under Conservative influence. He went on to argue that the Conservatives would not undo the achievements of the Liberal Government of which he had been a member – the 1911 Parliament Act was now accepted, Home Rule was being carried out, the franchise extension was settled and taxation was, according to Churchill, now on a democratic and progressive basis. The obvious conclusion to draw from this analysis of the situation, though not specifically stated in his speech, was that it was now possible for Liberals, without being inconsistent with their previous beliefs, to ally with the Conservatives against Labour.

In private Churchill chose to put it rather differently. He now convinced himself that he had always been a Conservative at heart and only an unfortunate set of circumstances had forced him to be a Liberal minister for most of the last seventeen years. He told Sir Robert Horne (Conservative Chancellor of the Exchequer under Lloyd George): 'force of circumstance has compelled me to serve with another party, but my views have never changed, and I should be glad to give effect to them by rejoining the Conservatives'.[1]

Churchill's main political activity for the rest of the summer was lobbying the Government on behalf of a consortium of oil companies. He was paid £5,000 (equivalent to about £100,000 at current prices) to represent the interests of Royal Dutch Shell and Burmah in their efforts to merge with the Anglo-Persian Oil Company, in which the Government had bought shares when Churchill was at the Admiralty. He put their case to the Prime Minister, the Board of Trade and the Admiralty, and also helped draft their formal submission to the Government. He also again rejected an offer, this time from the Caerphilly Association, to stand as a Liberal. His political plans for a move to the Conservatives were however unexpectedly thrown into disarray in the autumn.

In May 1923 Bonar Law had resigned because of ill-health (he was to die of cancer a few months later) and the relatively unknown Stanley Baldwin was now Prime Minister. Although the Government had a large majority, his political position was far from strong. The leading figures from the Lloyd George Government were still refusing to join him, leaving open the question of whether the coalition could be reconstructed at some point. A desire to reunite the Conservative Party was one of the main factors behind Baldwin's unexpected endorsement of protection in a speech he gave on 25 October. This speech threw the political world into turmoil. His subsequent decision, against the advice of the party machine and most of the Cabinet, to call an Election a few weeks later did so even more. First, his stance forced the Conservatives from the coalition, such as Austen Chamberlain and FE, back into the Conservative mainstream by throwing up the one issue on which they could not agree with the coalition Liberals. At the same time it forced the Liberals to reunite under Asquith's leadership, but using Lloyd George's money, for one last fight for their great inheritance from the nineteenth century – Free Trade. The coalition Liberals and Conservatives, including Churchill, did meet before the Election at Beaverbrook's house, but their discussion simply showed how difficult it would be in the new political situation for them to agree on any form of common action.

For Churchill, Baldwin's move was a political bombshell which exploded with devastating force under his plans for a move to the Conservatives. Having left the Conservatives on the issue of Free Trade twenty years earlier, he could hardly rejoin them on the basis of protection now. He was therefore forced back into the ranks of the Liberal Party, of which he was still a nominal member. But his actions in November 1923 show that he was nonetheless determined to leave the Liberals and rejoin the Conservatives. He was offered six possible seats including Manchester Exchange, close to the scene of his Free Trade triumph in 1906, and a good prospect since it was at the centre of the Lancashire Free Trade movement and a seat the Liberals actually won at the Election. He turned it down and refused to stand in any seat where he would be fighting a sitting Conservative MP. Having been forced to stand as a Liberal, Churchill for once in his life deliberately courted political defeat. The seat he opted for was the hopeless prospect of Leicester West, held by Labour (who also backed Free Trade), and which the coalition Liberals had failed to win a year earlier. In this seat it was much easier for Churchill to avoid the Free Trade issue and concentrate on the anti-Labour battle.

The December 1923 Election resulted in a massive Conservative loss – they emerged as the largest party but had only 258 seats. The Liberals gained seats and had 159 MPs but Labour, with about the same share of the vote, benefited from the electoral system and emerged in second place with 191 seats. Churchill was, as he expected, defeated easily in Leicester by over 4,000 votes. It left him free to make his move to the Conservatives once the political agenda had moved on from protectionism. In a highly uncertain Parliamentary situation Baldwin decided not to resign but to wait until Parliament assembled in January. The intervening period was one of intense political manoeuvring. Some wanted to remove Baldwin and reconstitute the coalition in a desperate attempt to avoid a Labour Government. Baldwin, prepared to play a longer game, wanted the Liberals to help Labour defeat the Conservative Government and so install a minority Labour Government, thereby, he reckoned, destroying their support among their generally conservative voters. The Liberals were in a dilemma. They could not ally with the Conservatives because of Free Trade and were therefore forced to contemplate a minority Labour Government. Asquith wanted to vote out the Conservatives, then defeat a Labour Government and take office himself as a minority government but with tacit Conservative support. Lloyd George preferred to support a minority Labour Government. They finished up with the worst possible choice –

supporting a minority Labour Government but without any agreement on general policy.

Churchill took no part in these discussions. His own position was clearcut – violent opposition to any support for a Labour Government or, as he preferred to call it, 'this Socialist monstrosity'.[2] On 18 January he made his stance clear in a letter to *The Times*. It effectively ended his connection with the Liberals. The minority Labour Government, about to take office pledged to a moderate, pragmatic policy in the Liberal tradition – no policy on unemployment, no nationalisation, Free Trade, tax cuts and a Liberal-style foreign policy – was described in terms suitable for the revolutions in Russia and Germany in 1917–18; it would in Churchill's words be 'a national misfortune such as has usually befallen a great state on the morrow of defeat in war'. He went on to paint a horrifying picture of the next Election with a 'Socialist Government actually holding the reins of power and the sole guarantee of law and order' and, presumably through intimidation on the streets, manipulating the vote to stay in office. Altogether it was an event which would 'cast a dark and blighting shadow on every form of national life and confidence'.

On 21 January the Liberals supported Labour in voting out the Baldwin Government and a minority Labour administration took office (though it actually contained two Conservative peers and ex-Liberals like Haldane). Having allowed the Liberals to incur the odium of supporting Labour, Baldwin announced three weeks later that he was dropping protection as a Conservative policy. The way was now conveniently open for Liberals, such as Churchill, who were opposed to support for Labour to move into the Conservative camp. With the Labour Government not expected to last long and after nearly fifteen months out of the political mainstream, Churchill was desperate to return to Parliament. He acted with a characteristic recklessness which, without a large slice of luck, could have severely jeopardised his chances of being accepted by the Conservatives.

On 22 February, just ten days after Baldwin's announcement on protection, Churchill discovered there was to be a by-election in the strongly Conservative seat of Westminister Abbey. The next day, after seeing Beaverbrook and Rothermere to obtain the support of their newspapers, he announced that he intended to stand as an independent candidate. He hoped that this would pre-empt the

Conservative organisation and lead them to support him. He then contacted Central Office and spoke to Baldwin in an attempt to get pressure brought on the local party. However, they would not be influenced and chose the son of the former member as the new candidate. Although the Conservative leadership were keen to see Churchill in the party as part of what they hoped would be a general Liberal defection, they were not prepared to force him through as a candidate at this stage. Austen Chamberlain wrote to FE to recommend patience (with the obvious intention that he should pass the message on to his close friend):

> We want to get him [Churchill] and his friends over, and although we cannot give him the Abbey seat, Baldwin will undertake to find him a good seat later on when he will have been able to develop naturally his new line and make his entry into our ranks much easier than it would be to-day. Our only fear is lest Winston should try and rush the fence.[3]

It was typical of Churchill that, notwithstanding these assurances, he should try to 'rush the fence'.

Without waiting to let his new line 'develop naturally', Churchill issued a statement on 2 March declaring that the current three-party system had to be ended (with the Liberals cast as the doomed party) and the Labour Government had to be brought down, and announcing that in order to achieve these aims he wanted to 'work effectually with the Conservative party in resistance to the rapid advance of Socialism'. Two days later he announced that he would stand as an anti-socialist candidate, because the Labour Government was a challenge to 'our existing economic and social civilisation', but not as one hostile to the Conservatives (although that party had its own candidate in what was a safe seat). It was a peculiar stance and one without any political logic except his own desire to re-enter Parliament at the first opportunity. The danger was that he would split the Conservative vote, let in Labour, and incur the justified wrath of large elements of the party he hoped to join.

Churchill was helped in his campaign by nine Conservative MPs, his cousin Freddie Guest (still nominally a Liberal) and a new companion from the newspaper world, Brendan Bracken. In his final speech of the campaign Churchill set out his ideas on how politics should now develop: he ruled out any idea of a Liberal-Conservative coalition and proposed instead a Conservative Party with a more 'liberal' wing. Once Churchill had no further use for the Liberal Party, he felt the country could equally well dispense with it. When polling took place on 19 March Churchill's luck held. Although he lost by just forty-three votes to the official Conservative, the badly split vote still left Labour 2,000 votes adrift. Although it postponed his return to Parliament, in many ways it was an ideal result. The Conservatives had held the seat, Churchill's own electoral strength as a Conservative in all but name had been demonstrated and the Asquithian Liberal had been humiliatingly defeated, coming bottom of the poll with a handful of votes.

Immediately after the by-election Churchill recommenced his negotiations with the Conservatives for a safe seat in the General Election that could not be far away. He saw Baldwin and spoke of bringing over to the Conservatives about thirty Liberal MPs and, as in his negotiations with the Liberals during his first defection, he tried to obtain a guarantee that any MPs who did cross the floor would not be opposed at the Election. In this he was not entirely successful but the shadow cabinet did agree, at the beginning of April, to consider each case on its merits. A few days later Churchill was able to persuade Alderman Salvidge, the boss of the Conservative machine in Liverpool, to invite him to speak at a Conservative Party meeting for the first time since 1903. Churchill's theme when he spoke was predictable – 'The Present Dangers of the Socialist Movement'. Interestingly though some of the speech was about protection and Churchill tried hard to give the impression that he was no longer a hard-line free trader. He criticised the Labour Government for trying to repeal some of the wartime 'McKenna duties' on luxury items and hinted that he favoured some form of imperial tariffs or preference. In the political sphere he once again argued that there was no longer a place for the Liberals – all those opposed to Labour must now support the Conservatives.

Although Churchill was well received in Liverpool, he found he would not be welcome as an MP in what was a strongly Protestant, Unionist local party because of his pre-war attitude to Ulster. He was also in contact with a number of Conservatives in the neighbouring seat to Westminster Abbey (St George's) and used their pressure for him to stand as blackmail with Baldwin to find him a suitable

Conservative seat elsewhere. His requirement was a cheap, safe seat near London. Between May and July he turned down offers from four seats to stand as a Conservative – two because they were in the provinces and two because they were not safe enough. He was also reluctant to stand where there would be a Liberal candidate and rejected Hackney North on those grounds. At the beginning of August Central Office suggested that either Epping or Richmond would meet his requirements. Churchill opened negotiations with the Epping constituency party and by early September, when it was confirmed that this was the best offer he was likely to get, accepted it even though there was to be a Liberal candidate. He made his first speech in the constituency on 3 October, five days before the Labour Government was defeated in the Commons and an Election was called for the end of the month.

Churchill was formally standing as a 'Constitutionalist' – a fig-leaf designed to help cover his political *volte face* from the Election only ten months earlier. But he endorsed all aspects of the Conservative programme – his Election address stated, 'I give my whole-hearted support to the Conservative Party' – and he singled out their anti-Soviet and anti-Labour line. In a campaign marked by a virulent attack on Labour and its supposed links with Moscow (the leak of the almost certainly forged 'Zinoviev' letter was part of that campaign) Churchill was able to indulge to the full his anti-socialist rhetoric. He tacitly compared Britain with Russia after the February 1917 revolution when he compared MacDonald with Kerensky – 'apologising behind the scenes to the wild, dark, deadly forces which had him in their grip'. Support for the Liberals was already in decline before the Election, and the Conservatives were largely successful in polarising the electorate, as Churchill wanted, into Labour and anti-Labour camps. The Liberal vote fell from almost thirty per cent of the total in December 1923 to under eighteen per cent and they lost 114 seats. Labour's share of the vote actually rose by three per cent but they lost over forty seats. The Conservative vote rose by over eight per cent and they had a net gain of 155 seats, giving them an overall majority in the new Parliament of over 200. Churchill was elected with a majority of nearly 10,000 over his Liberal opponent.

When Baldwin began to construct his government he was determined to demonstrate the unity of the party by including the former coalitionists who had excluded themselves from the 1922–4 governments. Austen Chamberlain went to the Foreign Office and FE to the India Office. Churchill was unsure whether he would be offered a job but there seems to have been little doubt in Baldwin's mind that he wanted him in the Government for two main reasons. First, it would deprive Lloyd George of his strongest potential ally and help ensure he would remain in the political wilderness (always an important consideration for Baldwin). Second, Baldwin, and many others, believed that it was preferable to have Churchill inside the Government rather than leading Conservative opposition from out-side. Austen Chamberlain, for instance, took the view 'if you leave him out he will be leading a Tory rump in six months time'.[4] Baldwin consulted Tom Jones, the Deputy Secretary of the Cabinet, whose opinion he greatly respected. Jones said, 'I would certainly have him inside, not out. He is incapable of being permanently loyal to anybody but Winston, and you must count on your loyal men to withstand him.'[5] Baldwin agreed with this view and when he saw Neville Chamberlain on 5 November, he confirmed that Churchill would be in the Government because 'he would be more under control inside than out'.[6]

The problem though was what post to give Churchill. Many of Baldwin's colleagues thought a return to the Colonial Office would be adequate reward but the Prime Minister wanted to put the strong imperalist Leo Amery there. The Admiralty was another possibility as was the Ministry of Health. However, Neville Chamberlain was keen to take the latter (rather than the Treasury which he was offered) so that he could be in charge of social policy. Baldwin and Chamberlain agreed there would be an outcry about Churchill's return whatever they did and that the difference between sending him to the Treasury and the Admiralty would not be great. Baldwin also felt Churchill was completely unsuitable to be in charge of social policy, as he told Tom Jones: 'it would be a good thing to keep him fully occupied with finance, which should not bring him very much into direct contact with Labour. Had he been at Housing he would constantly be in danger of getting at loggerheads with them.'[7] J. C. C. Davidson, a key man in the Conservative Party machine and a close confidant of Baldwin, thought the appointment was a stroke of genius and added picturesquely, 'you have hamstrung him so that his hairy heels are paralysed'.[8] Baldwin himself saw it as a test of Churchill's mettle, saying tersely, 'it would be up to him to be loyal, if he is capable of loyalty'.[9] When Churchill saw the Prime Minister on 5 November, he was agreeably surprised to be offered the Treasury (the post he had coveted in 1921 but which Lloyd George had refused to give him), although he might have been less flattered had he known some of the reasons behind the choice.

For much of the time that he was out of Parliament Churchill had concentrated on writing his war memoirs. He had begun the task in the winter of 1919, determined to be one of the first to publish an inside account of the war. In November 1920 he found literary agents to act for him and demanded they negotiate an advance of at least £20,000 (about £400,000 at today's prices) – he eventually made about £30,000 from the book. The first volume was published in April 1923 and it became an instant best-seller. It was followed by two other main volumes and, much later, by two additional works, *The Aftermath* and *The Eastern Front*, which were far less successful. The title – *The World Crisis* – was chosen by Churchill's American publishers, Scribner, in preference to his favourite – *The Great Amphibian*. (It is impossible to trace who first coined the *bon mot*, 'Churchill has written a book all about himself and called it *The World Crisis*', but Balfour is a strong candidate.)

In preparing his war memoirs Churchill adopted for the first time a technique that he was to keep for the rest of his life. He would read and select a number of documents for inclusion and then dictate the sections that were to surround these documents in the book. The result was prose style that was much nearer to his oratorical style – slightly archaic and florid but never dull. The problem with the book is that, like his later Second World War volumes, although it purports to be an objective history, it is in fact a set of memoirs designed to justify Churchill's actions, with the evidence carefully selected and edited to that end. Because Churchill was only engaged in the central direction of the First World War for a short period, this process is more obvious in *The World Crisis* than in the later war memoirs. After an introduction on the pre-war scene, two-thirds of the first volume deals with the 1914–15 period. Churchill's romantic and old-fashioned view of war, particularly war at sea, comes to the fore and he concentrates most of the attention on dramatic but relatively unimportant episodes such as the shelling of Scarborough rather than the less spectacular, but more significant elements such as the blockade, submarine warfare and mines. He is highly critical of Jellicoe and effusive in his praise of Beatty and blames the commanders on the spot for the failed operations in the first months of the war rather than the instructions he gave them – even here though he has to express himself cautiously because he appointed most of these men.

The bulk of the history is devoted to a defence of his actions at the Dardanelles, drawing on the evidence he submitted to the official commission. Nearly half the text comprises quotations from contemporary documents. But Churchill carefully selected only those which back up his arguments and he also deleted key sections of some of those that are included where they do not support his case – though he does not make the fact of these omissions clear to the reader. On many occasions his descriptions of his attitudes at the time do not coincide with contemporary accounts (then not available to the public). It is also possible to trace Churchill gradually improving his case through the successive drafts. For example in an early version he described the key telegram from Admiral Carden on 5 January suggesting that a naval operation might be possible as having 'produced a great impression upon my mind'. On reflection Churchill obviously thought that this left him too exposed as the sole progenitor of the disaster and so the published version was altered to read that the telegram 'produced a great impression upon everyone who saw it'.

In constructing his case Churchill often stretches the evidence to breaking point and beyond. He ignores for example his advocacy of other naval and amphibious operations such as Borkum, Zeebrugge or the Dutch islands in order to give the impression that the Dardanelles was consistently his single great strategic alternative. He also gives the impression that there was a consensus of military and naval opinion in favour of the Dardanelles when in fact there was a great deal of dissent, both open and secret, against the operation. His analysis of the long discussions about the possible use of the Army to back up the naval operation is also highly misleading. His own views (advocating use of military forces only to exploit a successful naval attack) are well concealed and at widely separate points in the book he both criticises Kitchener for not supplying the troops and De Roebuck for not asking for them. He argues that one or two extra divisions would have made all the difference and claims that the attainment of what were essentially tactical objectives on the

Gallipoli peninsula would somehow have transformed the strategic situation. He introduces the idea of 'fate' as deciding against the Dardanelles operation and chooses to overlook the large number of inherent flaws.

The third volume is much more objective, dealing as it does with the period after 1915 when Churchill was out of power. There is a good account of the Somme battles (though Passchendaele is virtually ignored) and an excellent account of comparative allied and German losses, and the reader is left in no doubt of Churchill's highly critical view of the type of warfare waged on the western front and the casualties it involved. Overall the main criticism of the work was shrewdly set out by John Maynard Keynes, in his review of *The Aftermath*. He identified a central theme running through Churchill's writing, and indeed in his view of life – 'his undoubted conviction that frontiers, races, patriotisms, even wars if need be, are ultimate verities for mankind, which lends for him a kind of dignity and even nobility to events, which for others are only a nightmare interlude, something to be permanently avoided'.[10]

The substantial advance Churchill obtained for *The World Crisis* was part of his growing wealth at this period. In early 1921, after the death of his cousin Lord Henry Vane-Tempest in a rail crash, he inherited an estate in Antrim worth in total about £60,000, which brought in an income of around £4,000 a year (about £80,000 at today's prices). In May 1922 he owned stocks and shares worth just over £60,000 (equivalent to well over £1 million). His brother Jack supervised his investments from his position in the firm of Vickers da Costa, although Churchill himself also paid close attention to the stock market. Some of his lucrative investments were in effect a one-way bet. A close friend, the South African millionaire businessman, Abe Bailey, guaranteed him against any loss on shares bought on his advice, and he also volunteered to buy any shares Churchill wanted to sell at whatever was the ruling price. Churchill also continued to spend money lavishly. He gambled regularly at the casinos at Monte Carlo, Deauville and Biarritz; he also bought a Rolls Royce and employed a chauffeur. At this period Churchill's heavy drinking became apparent for the first time, although it was not on the gargantuan scale it reached later in life. Whatever the psychological mainspring for his desire to drink, there is no doubt that he had an alcohol addiction problem – he drank throughout the day and in large quantities. He wrote to Clementine in April 1924: 'I drink champagne at all meals & buckets of claret and soda in between.'[11]

Churchill's greatest expense was incurred in property. On his return to London from the Army in 1916 the family lived in a succession of rented houses, although they did own a farmhouse at Lullenden in Sussex. When he became Secretary of State for War in 1919, he asked to be provided with an official residence in London. The Chancellor, Austen Chamberlain, rejected the request out of hand as unjustifiable and unprecedented and Churchill was therefore forced to sell the property at Lullenden to his old friend Sir Ian Hamilton and buy a London property – 2 Sussex Square, near Paddington Station, in early 1920. But as his wealth increased, Churchill hankered after a country property. At first he looked for a fruit farm of about 500–600 acres, but in 1921 spotted Chartwell in Kent, a run-down house with an estate of about eighty acres and a superb view across the Weald. The price was comparatively low because of the huge amount of work needed to modernise it, tackle the twin problems of dry rot and woodworm and also re-orientate it to take advantage of the view. Clementine took one look, disliked the house and vetoed its purchase.

In September 1922, with Clementine pregnant and away from London and the family, Churchill bought Chartwell without consulting her. The family could not move into the new house until Easter 1924 because of the extensive works required, which cost Churchill almost three times the £5,000 purchase price – a total investment of more than £600,000 at current prices. Although Clementine continued to hate Chartwell and never liked living there, for Churchill it was a great new focus for his desire for incessant activity – he was soon supervising works in the grounds on a grand scale (ponds and complex watercourses) and he also took up bricklaying and built a number of cottages himself. The rising Conservative politician, Samuel Hoare, reported wryly in February 1926 after a week-end at Chartwell: 'Winston seems blissfully happy over it all. He scarcely stopped talking the whole time, though occasionally Hugh Cecil talked at the same time.'[12]

Churchill was able to recoup part of the expenditure on Chartwell when he became Chancellor. This post did have an official residence (No 11 Downing Street) and the family moved there so that the house in Sussex Square could be sold for £10,750. Despite the expense incurred in buying and renovating Chartwell, Churchill lived in a grand style. He kept two horses in London so that he could ride in Rotten Row every morning (he had four horses altogether) and he also had a string of polo ponies until he gave up the sport in 1925 just after he was fifty. By the late 1920s there was a huge entourage of servants at Chartwell – apart from Churchill's valet, Clementine's maid and two secretaries, there were nine indoor servants (two maids in both the kitchen and pantry, two housemaids, a cook, nursery maid and an odd-job man) and six outdoor: three gardeners, a groom, a bailiff and a chauffeur. Churchill's attitude to his servants was summed up in a letter to Clementine: 'Servants exist to save one trouble, & shd never be allowed to disturb one's inner peace.' In addition to the capital expenditure on Chartwell and the payment of regular bills, Churchill planned to spend about £10,000 a year on miscellaneous 'living expenses'.

Churchill's decision to buy Chartwell in opposition to Clementine's clearly expressed views and without telling her (for which she never really forgave him) was symptomatic of the fragile state of their marriage. Although Churchill was to write a few years later in *My Early Life* that after his wedding he lived happily ever after, he knew that was not really the case. For Churchill, marriage and the family were never at the centre of his life. It provided a vital part of his life and he was always affectionate towards Clementine and his children, but he was too much of an egoist to subordinate it to his other interests. He saw the family as a useful base but expected it to look after itself when he had other things he preferred to do. Clementine clearly expected more from him than he was willing to give and so was disappointed with the marriage. For much of the time she was depressed and nervous, frequently difficult to deal with and subject to hysterical attacks. Although she remained devoted to furthering Churchill's political career, she liked very few of his friends and made her dislikes very clear. She found it virtually impossible to cope with the children and seems to have shown little affection towards them. They grew up under a succession of governesses. When the youngest child, Mary, was born in September 1922, Clementine's cousin Maryott White (known to the family as 'Moppett') was brought in as a full-time nanny and she and Mary lived separately from the rest of the family in a house in the grounds of

Chartwell. Mary was the only child to have a reasonably ordered childhood.

In the early 1920s the marriage seemed on the point of breaking down and Churchill and Clementine spent much of the time apart. Often Churchill acted as though he had very little, if any, consideration for Clementine's feelings. For much of the year he was engaged in a ceaseless round of activity in his department, in Parliament and at political lunches, dinners and clubs. It is surprising, therefore, that he and Clementine nearly always spent their holidays apart as well. For example in early 1920 Churchill went off with General Rawlinson for a hunting, shooting and painting holiday at the Duke of Westminster's estate at Mimizan, south of Bordeaux. That summer a family holiday had been arranged near Rugby specifically so that Churchill could play polo. Instead he spent the time in London and left his family in the country. Then in the first months of 1921 they were again apart – Clementine went to the south of France, to stay with Sir Ernest Cassel and then Lady Essex, just as Churchill returned to London from his holiday.

A series of tragedies hit the family later in the year. In April Clementine's only brother committed suicide in Paris and in June Churchill's mother died. The greatest blow came in August 1921 with the death of their then youngest daughter Marigold. Churchill and Clementine were, as was now usual, apart for the holidays – he was in London and she was staying with the Duke of Westminster at Eaton Hall. The children had been sent off with an inexperienced French governess to Broadstairs. There Marigold contracted a bad throat infection which turned to septicaemia and she died on 23 August, aged three. Within a fortnight Churchill had left Clementine alone in London and was on holiday with the Duke of Sutherland in Scotland.

In 1922 Churchill and Clementine seem to have deliberately kept apart. Early in the year all the children were ill and Clementine was still depressed by the death of Marigold, but Churchill was away on holiday in the south of France and did not return even when told of the situation. When he did come back to London, Clementine left almost immediately for her own holiday on the Riviera. For the whole of the summer of that year they were apart. In July Clementine was at Barnstaple and spent the next month at Frinton. Churchill went off to Deauville with Beaverbrook, moved on to Paris and then on to Mimizan and remained away for much of September. The next summer the pattern was much the same. Clementine spent some of the time at Cromer with the children while Churchill stayed in London working on *The World Crisis* by day and enjoying himself in the evening. At the end of August Clementine suffered one of her periodic nervous breakdowns and went to the house the family rented near Chartwell while renovations were underway. Churchill, who was there overseeing the works, immediately left for France, having invited himself as a guest on the Duke of Westminster's yacht. He returned to London briefly and then left to spend a month in France playing polo.

In the early part of 1924 the picture was similar. In February they spent a short time in Paris together but then separated – Churchill went to Mimizan and Clementine to the Riviera. Churchill returned to London but Clementine stayed on in the south of France. She came back briefly for the Abbey by-election but then left almost immediately for Dieppe while Churchill was at Chartwell. She made her feelings perfectly clear by staying away when the family officially moved into Chartwell. They again took separate holidays in the winters of 1925, 1926 and 1927.

Another crisis arrived in the summer of 1927. Clementine was ill yet again, this time following a traffic accident in June, but Churchill went off with Beaverbrook on his yacht to Amsterdam just before Clementine left to spend six weeks in Venice. She was still feeling depressed in Venice and asked him to come and join her. He pleaded that it would be too expensive (a rare argument for him to use) and that he had too much work to do at Chartwell. That this was a feeble excuse is shown by the fact that he immediately left for a shooting holiday in Scotland with his old friend the Duke of Westminster. Clementine again wrote pleading for him to come out to Italy. Churchill finally relented but it cannot have been the holiday she expected because he only stayed for ten days and was accompanied throughout by his companion Professor Lindemann. (Churchill had first met Lindemann through FE and the Duke of Westminster in the early 1920s and soon became deeply attached to the extremely wealthy, socialite professor of physics, who regarded all blacks, Jews and members of the working class as a form of sub-humans. Churchill was prepared to overlook the fact he was an extreme vegetarian and teetotaller.) After this brief and scarcely intimate reunion Clementine stayed away from Churchill until early November, moving on to Florence before returning to England.

Throughout the period that Churchill was Chancellor their movements suggest that the state of the marriage was still far from ideal. For Churchill though, as always, it was his political life that came first. Now that he had achieved one of his great ambitions and attained the office which his father had held, albeit briefly, he was not going to allow the family to interfere with his enjoyment of the great game of politics.

15

The Summit?

When Churchill went to the Treasury in November 1924 he had no experience of financial or economic matters and very little of domestic policy. He had taken virtually no interest in such questions and the only ideas on economic policy he was known to advocate were free trade and sound finance on Gladstonian principles. Apart from his short period at the Board of Trade and an even shorter time at the Home Office, his political career and interests had been devoted entirely to questions of defence and imperial policy. Although he had very clear political and social objectives, as became apparent in his budgets and his attitude to social reform, he was, unusually for him, lacking in self-confidence on economic policy and proved much more willing to accept conventional wisdom and follow the advice of the 'experts' around him, rather than insist, as he did so often in other areas, on his own ideas being implemented.

This tendency was very apparent in Churchill's decision to return to the gold standard at the 1914 rate. The issue arose at the very start of his Chancellorship and it had a profound impact both on the British economy and on his own policy during the remainder of his time at the Treasury. Britain had left the gold standard in 1914 as a wartime measure, but it was always assumed by the Treasury and by the City of London financial institutions that once the war was over Britain would return to the mechanism that had seemed so successful before the war in providing stability, low interest rates and a steady expansion in world trade. Even before the war was over, a committee

293

chaired by the retiring Governor of the Bank of England had looked at the transition to a peacetime monetary system. The committee assumed without question that there would be a return to the gold standard, with the pound restored to its 1914 parity of $4.85, and considered only the mechanics of the transition. They fully understood that because the value of the pound had fallen during the war a restoration of pre-war parity would involve deflating the economy, but they felt that this was a price that had to be paid to achieve an acceptable financial system.

During the chaotic conditions of the immediate post-war period the Lloyd George coalition did not take an early decision to restore the gold standard. A short-lived boom in 1919 was followed by a deflationary budgetary policy from 1920. Gross domestic product fell by six per cent, unemployment rose rapidly to twenty-three per cent of those insured by May 1921 and prices actually fell. The pound rose in value against the dollar – from $3.40 in February 1920 to $4.27 at the beginning of 1923. Between 1923 and the end of 1924 deflation continued, exports were below 1913 levels, imports rose and severe structural unemployment was experienced in Britain's key traditional industries – coal, shipbuilding, iron and steel, textiles and machine tools. Nevertheless the objective of a return to the gold standard remained, although the Government decided to wait until the complex and interlinked questions of war debt repayment and reparations were resolved. The short-lived Labour Government also accepted the goal of restoration, although when a Bank of England committee looked again at the question in June 1924, they were worried by the further rise of over ten per cent in the exchange rate that would be required to restore the 1914 parity and the effect this would have on the domestic economy.

When Churchill took office in late 1924 the general expectation was that the new Government would restore the gold standard and as a result the pound rose speculatively to something nearer its pre-war parity. Within a month of taking office the new Chancellor accepted the unchanged advice of his officials and of the Bank of England. He wrote to alert Baldwin to the implications of an imminent re-establishment of the gold standard:

> It will be easy to attain the gold standard and almost impossible to avoid taking the decision, but to keep to it will require a most strict

policy of debt repayment and a high standard of credit. To reach it
and have to abandon it would be disastrous.'[1]

He allowed detailed planning to go ahead on this assumption, which
inevitably raised expectations in the City and reduced any room for
manoeuvre he might have. Just after Christmas the Governor of the
Bank of England, Montagu Norman, was sent to the United States
to sound out opinion there. They felt the time was ripe for Britain to
rejoin the gold standard and that not to do so would be a major
blow; to help the process the US Government and banks were
willing to provide major credit facilities. By the middle of January
1925 the Bank of England concluded that the time was now right:
the circumstances were as good as they were ever likely to be, and
following the rise in the value of the pound since the Election, the
further adjustment required to reach the 1914 level (about six per
cent) was, in their view, comparatively small.

At the end of January, with a final decision now imminent,
Churchill sent his officials a paper containing a series of arguments
against restoration. At the same time he made it clear that he was
not opposed to a return to the gold standard, and he was doing no
more than testing the strength of the case and asking his officials to
set out the arguments in favour. The counter-arguments he put were
essentially that the gold standard was a relic of the past and that the
experience of the post-war period had shown it was perfectly possible
to maintain a stable and successful currency through a sound
financial policy and therefore there was no need to adopt gold as a
standard. In addition he argued that if the United States was so keen
for Britain to return to gold and it was so much in their interest,
then perhaps they should pay more towards it. Churchill also
expressed the worry that too much weight was being given to the
interests of the City of London. He wrote: 'The merchant, the
manufacturer, the workman and the consumer have interests which,
though largely common, do not by any means exactly coincide either
with each other or with the financial and currency interests. The
maintenance of cheap money is a matter of high consequence' and
the Government might be accused of having 'favoured the special
interests of finance at the expense of the special interests of
production'.[2]

The response to Churchill's paper made by Sir Otto Niemeyer of the Treasury ignored these questions and simply argued that as expectations had been aroused, it would be difficult not to go ahead. He suggested that in the long term the gold standard would be good for trade and stressed that it was important to restore the position of the London financial markets as soon as possible. In a strong minute designed to keep Churchill in line, Montagu Norman emphasised once again that all knowledgeable people expected a return and now was the best time. Churchill responded by quoting two more cautious views from Reginald McKenna, an ex-Chancellor now chairman of the Midland Bank, and from Barclays Bank. He also consulted Austen Chamberlain, another former Chancellor and chairman of the Treasury committee on restoration, who advised that the decision was inevitable.

These exchanges continued during February as preparations for restoration continued. Churchill was stirred into print again after reading Keynes' article in *The Nation* on 21 February entitled 'The Return towards Gold'. The next day he wrote to Sir Otto Niemeyer to raise another area of concern:

> The Treasury have never, it seems to me, faced the profound significance of what Mr Keynes calls 'the paradox of unemployment amidst dearth'. The Governor shows himself perfectly happy in the spectacle of Britain's possessing the finest credit in the world simultaneously with a million and a quarter unemployed.

Churchill thought it would be a 'terrible responsibility' if a strong pound and unemployment were connected. However he did not see an alternative and preferred to stay with the known, orthodox, policy:

> I do not pretend to see even 'through a glass darkly' how the financial and credit policy of the country could be handled so as to bridge the gap between a dearth of goods and a surplus of labour and I well realise the danger of experiment to that end.

Although he had rejected the idea of experimenting with alternative policies, he still felt uneasy about the likely consequences – 'I would rather see Finance less proud and Industry more content'[3] – but in the end he concluded that the Treasury and the Bank of England probably knew best.

Churchill, as an amateur in economic policy, could hardly be expected to devise a new approach and he was surrounded by officials at the Treasury who held firmly to the orthodox view. It is to Churchill's credit that he did think about a policy that would give less weight to the demands of the City and more to the needs of industry and employment. But he did not press his musings and misgivings further within the Treasury, having come up against Niemeyer's orthodox argument that stable finance was the only permanent solution to the problems of industry and would somehow lead eventually to better trade and more employment. Another sign of lurking doubts about the conventional wisdom was a dinner he organised on 17 March, where McKenna and Keynes confronted Niemeyer and Bradbury of the Bank of England. But in the end he approached the decision politically – he felt that all actions since the war had been aimed at eventual restoration and that he could not go back now. The final decision to go ahead was taken three days later at a meeting chaired by Baldwin, and it fell to Churchill to announce the decision in his budget speech.

In an atmosphere where there was a strong quasi-moral belief in the efficacy and rightness of gold, debt repayment and the mechanisms of the pre-1914 gold standard, there was never any real chance that a different policy would be adopted, especially since experience after the war of managed currencies, for example in Germany and Austria, was taken as a dire warning. The City was bent on re-establishing the financial pre-eminence it had lost during the war to New York and believed that restoration at the 1914 level was essential for this purpose. Churchill, despite lingering doubts about what he was being asked to do, did not have the necessary background, the intellectual ability or the willingness to challenge established orthodoxies. It is doubtful whether anyone else would have acted differently in his position. All the evidence presented by officials emphasised the benefits and minimised the problems of adjustment. What he failed to do was to press home his doubts and insist on his reluctant officials producing either a realistic assessment of the problems associated with the existing policy or alternative courses of action for consideration by the Cabinet. It is clear that the Treasury and the Bank of England did in fact expect problems in the real economy as a result of restoration of the 1914 level of the pound, but they thought these were a price worth paying.

The price was to become increasingly clear during Churchill's time at the Treasury. Britain's international position was far weaker in 1925 than it had been in 1914 and to overvalue sterling by at least ten per cent, which is what the 1925 decision did, was bound to exacerbate these problems. Britain took little part in the world boom from 1925 to 1929 (its share of world markets continued to fall), the balance of payments surplus recorded in 1924 disappeared and overpriced British exports were the first to suffer when world import demand fell drastically after 1929. Domestically the results were disastrous. The overvalued pound meant that costs had to be reduced in an unavailing attempt to keep exports competitive and this at a time when real wages were already below 1914 levels. Attempts to impose further wage reductions inevitably led to industrial disputes, lock-outs, strikes, rising unemployment (by seven and a half per cent between 1924 and 1929) and increased social strains. The overvalued pound made perhaps as many as 700,000 people unemployed. The impact showed up the 1925 decision for what it was – a banking and financial policy designed to benefit the City of London.

The decision to rejoin the gold standard at the 1914 rate ensured that Churchill's time at the Treasury was one of economic failure that turned into political failure. As the economic, social and political results of the policy became more clear (and as the prospect of fighting the next election on a poor economic record rapidly approached), Churchill became increasingly resentful about the advice he had been given. But even now he had no alternative to offer – he could only fume impotently. To ventilate his feelings he wrote two minutes, addressed to his Treasury officials, one in May 1927 and another in July 1928, full of recrimination (about 'their' policy, as though it was not his as well). There was, however, no suggestion that they should begin to devise an alternative – he continued to accept and implement the prevailing orthodoxy however much he protested his dislike of the results it produced:

> The Niemeyer attitude of letting everything smash into bankruptcy and unemployment in order that reconstruction can be built upon the ruins, is neither sound economics nor wise policy ... what is airily called 'cutting out the dead wood' means transferring vast masses of workmen and their families from productive industry to Poor Law ... I should think on the whole with 300,000 miners

unemployed we have cut out enough dead wood for the moment
... [the Treasury and Bank of England] have caused an immense
amount of misery by their pedantic handling of the problem. In
ruined homes, in demoralised workmen, in discouraged industry,
in embarrassed finances, in inflated debt and cruel taxation we have
paid the price.[4]

It seems a great pity that the power of Churchill's eloquence and the
cutting edge of his sarcasm were put to no better use than secretly
lambasting his advisers for the deprivation and misery suffered by
millions of unemployed.

Churchill's policy as Chancellor, particularly in the budgetary
field, was constrained not just by the decision to restore the 1914
value of the pound but also by inherited financial problems caused
by the war. Britain had entered the war in 1914 as financially the
strongest nation in the world (it had £4 billion of overseas investments, over forty per cent of the world's total) but by 1918 its
position had collapsed. The need, as Churchill discovered at the
Ministry of Munitions, to continue to buy a large part of Britain's
armaments in the United States and at the same time prop up the
disintegrating finances of its allies, created huge war debts. Britain
gave loans of £1.7 billion to its allies and borrowed almost £1.4
billion from the United States. In the long drawn out negotiations
on a post-war settlement of inter-allied debts (which Churchill was
still grappling with when he was Chancellor) Britain did relatively
badly, being left with a large debt to the Americans and much
smaller repayments from its continental allies. Domestically too
Britain's post-war financial position had seriously deteriorated. The
national debt rose from £650 million in 1914 to £7,435 million by
the end of the war. This meant that interest charges on the debt in
the 1920s were seventy per cent higher than total Government
spending in 1914 and were taking up over forty per cent of public
expenditure. The depressed state of the economy, largely caused by
the return to the gold standard, ensured that Government revenues
remained stagnant.

Churchill's room for manoeuvre as Chancellor was therefore
extremely limited. But, as a new arrival in the Conservative Party, he
was determined to make a major impression in his first budget and
keen to include measures with a strong appeal to Conservative

voters. Shortly after taking office he told Lord Salisbury that: 'the rich, whether idle or not, are already taxed in this country to the very highest point compatible with the accumulation of capital for further production'.[5] Despite the problem of low Government revenue he was determined to make the centrepiece of his first budget in the spring of 1925 a major reduction in income tax. In 1924 the majority of people did not pay income tax – only 2½ million people were liable and just 90,000 paid supertax. Any reductions would therefore be, as Churchill himself said, 'a class measure' designed to help the comfortably off and the rich.[6] Under pressure from Treasury officials, alarmed at the long-term consequences for Government revenues, he was forced to reduce the scale of cuts he originally wanted but even so the standard rate was reduced by 6d in the pound to 4s. in the pound and supertax was also cut. Other measures introduced in order to demonstrate his Conservative credentials were a tariff on silk and imperial preference on a few minor food imports.

Treasury officials, including the Permanent Secretary Sir Warren Fisher, thought that Churchill's first budget was a bad one: it gave too much away and so would cause problems in the next few years. Indeed Fisher told Neville Chamberlain that Churchill was 'a lunatic ... an irresponsible child, not a grown man' and complained that all the senior officials in the Treasury had lost heart – 'they never know where they are or what hare W.C. will start'.[7] Their judgement was proved right as Churchill struggled hard in his next four budgets to avoid a politically damaging rise in income tax. In 1926 he introduced a new betting tax, which he hoped would raise about £6 million a year, together with a tax on petrol and heavier taxes on cars and commercial vehicles. As a desperate expedient he brought forward the payment of beer duty so as to provide an extra £5 million in the 1926–7 financial year. The next year he again had to introduce a series of measures to avoid an income tax rise (which the Treasury thought should be about 2d in the pound). Tariffs on pottery and motor vehicle tyres were introduced and duties and taxes on matches, wine and tobacco were increased. For the first time the Road Fund (financed by vehicle licences and earmarked for road improvement) was raided and used simply as general taxation to help out revenues. Beer duty was brought forward yet again and, as another expedient to give a short-term boost to revenues, the date Schedule A income tax was due was advanced so as to give an increase of £14 million, but of course for one year only. The 1928 budget was strongly deflationary and also designed to benefit the comfortably off. Tax allowances for children were increased but this only benefited the minority who paid income tax. To increase revenue a duty on oil was introduced and the excise duty on British wine increased by fifty per cent.

1929 was the Election budget, but by this point Churchill had little room for injecting politically attractive proposals. He had made his large tax cut in 1925 and then exhausted expedients for bringing forward taxation in his next three budgets. All that remained was some minor juggling with different duties. New licence duties were introduced on alcohol and tobacco. The betting tax of 1926 was abolished (because it had proved unworkable). The only Election sweetener that Churchill could suggest to his colleagues was the abolition of the duty on tea – a measure he told the Cabinet he 'would not have dreamed of allowing ... except for Electoral reasons'.[8] He justified it in the House of Commons on the quaint grounds that 'no other comfort enters so largely into the budget of the cottage home'. In general Churchill's budgets were financially orthodox and mildly deflationary throughout his time in office. This policy only exacerbated the economic and financial problems caused by the overvaluation of the pound. They were also regressive in their impact, shifting taxation from the middle class and rich to the poor by lowering income tax for the few and increasing duties and taxes on major items of household expenditure. Politically too Churchill had once again 'rushed his fences'. In wanting to make too great an impact too early, he left himself with little to offer as the Election approached.

During his time as Chancellor, Churchill trimmed his own free trade ideas to make himself more acceptable to a Conservative Party increasingly moving towards some form of protection, despite their pledge in the 1924 Election not to increase taxes on food and not to introduce a general tariff. Before he joined the Government Churchill accepted tariffs to 'safeguard' certain key industries. (Informally he indicated that he would be content to see these applied to about half a dozen industries during the lifetime of the Parliament.) As Chancellor he reintroduced tariffs abolished by the Labour Government, introduced new ones on a few luxury items and in other areas such as tyres and even accepted some form of imperial preference on sugar and tobacco. But he was initially reluctant to contemplate any action that might lead to protection for the iron and steel industry. In the summer of 1925 he opposed the rising pressure for a 'safeguarding' enquiry on the grounds that the industry was so central to the economy that if a tariff was granted here it would soon be widened into a general tariff. In August 1928 though Churchill went along with his colleagues and accepted such an enquiry and, by implication, a tariff if it was recommended by the report as seemed inevitable. By now Churchill had effectively abandoned the cause of free trade. He decided that he could not, given his past record, publicly endorse the theoretical arguments for tariffs but would instead justify his new-found protectionism on pragmatic grounds. He told his Private Secretary in July 1928: 'I should not challenge the theoretical argument . . . but present it as a practical step necessitated by revenue requirements and likely to be beneficial to trade and employment.'[9]

Churchill had become Chancellor in 1924 because the strongest candidate for the post, Neville Chamberlain, chose to go to the Ministry of Health to embark on a series of changes in the field of social policy and the structure of local government. As the controller of public expenditure, Churchill became closely involved in these schemes. After less than three weeks in office Chamberlain put to the Cabinet on 26 November an extensive series of proposals covering the poor law, local authority rates, health insurance and the creation of local health authorities – in total twenty-five Bills in a programme lasting through three parliamentary sessions. Churchill was opposed to the whole approach. He told the Cabinet 'the Government should concentrate on a few great issues in the social sphere, such as the solution of the housing problem and an "all-in" insurance scheme rather than fritter away our resources on a variety of services'.[10] The Cabinet asked the two ministers to sort out their differences after the meeting.

Churchill met Chamberlain that afternoon and it soon became clear that he was pursuing a political agenda of his own. He thought Chamberlain's pension scheme would be 'a very heavy burden on employers . . . acceptance . . . would be rendered more easy if it were accompanied at the same time by a reduction in direct taxation'.[11] He wanted however to gain as much political credit as possible from any measures of reform by announcing the new scheme in his budget speech and leaving Chamberlain the tedious task of piloting the legislation through the Commons. Chamberlain recorded his impression of the meeting and of his colleague in his diary: 'It was curious how all through he observed how he was thinking of personal credit.' He concluded that the Chancellor was 'a man of tremendous drive and great imagination but obsessed with the glory of doing something spectacular which should erect monuments to him'.[12]

The pension scheme that Churchill and Chamberlain settled between them in the next few months was based on work that had been undertaken by the Baldwin Government in 1923 and continued in opposition. The aim was clear. The Conservatives opposed any attempt to extend the 1908 pension scheme introduced by the Liberal Government because it was non-contributory and therefore paid for out of general taxation – any extension on this basis would increase taxation (probably on Conservative supporters) and might even involve a capital levy. In the Conservative proposals developed in the winter of 1924–5, the 1908 scheme was transformed into a contributory pension scheme. New entrants paid the full cost of a bigger pension and also had to pay for over twenty per cent of what they would have received free if the 1908 scheme had continued. Eventually, as contributions rose, people would have to pay for everything – non-contributory pensions would be abolished. To partially compensate for this fundamental change the number of those eligible for the scheme was widened and a widows' pension of 10s a week (about £15 a week at 1990 prices) at age sixty-five was introduced immediately.

Churchill fully approved of the demolition of the pension scheme which he had supported when a member of the Liberal Government. He told the Cabinet committee dealing with the scheme that the principle that beneficiaries should pay almost the entire cost of their pensions was 'a good example of Conservative Social reform'.[13] Even so he objected to the cost that would fall to the Government. He wanted a scheme designed so that if wages rose so did contributions and in a slump, when there would be greater demands on the fund, benefits would be reduced. Similarly any break in contributions would lead to a major cut in benefits. He told Chamberlain in February: 'It is clear that I cannot undertake the burden you ask me to shoulder.'[14] He reduced the size of the State contribution to the scheme that had been suggested during the work of the previous

Conservative Government and he also wanted to make people aged sixty-five contribute for two years before they received any benefits under the scheme, although he had to give way on this point. The resulting scheme was very modest in scope – it cost £4 million a year and totalled less than six per cent of the amount spent on war pensions. As far as Churchill was concerned the scheme was intended to have the same social and political effect as his proposals for unemployment insurance in the pre-war Liberal Government: the avoidance of any major social and economic changes. Provision of pensions would, in his view, provide another incentive for the working class not to challenge the existing social structure – 'it must have the effect of attaching the mind of the people . . . It must lead to the stability and order of the general structure.'[15]

Churchill's social conservatism was also apparent during discussions within the Government in 1925 over changes to unemployment insurance. The scheme that Churchill had favoured as President of the Board of Trade had collapsed after the war because of large-scale structural unemployment, particularly among trades that were not covered by the scheme. A benefit (the 'dole') was first introduced for unemployed ex-servicemen, later extended to others and then made subject to a means-test in 1922. But as unemployment continued at high levels through the 1920s the Government became alarmed at the cost, and those subjected to the strict means-test found it highly demeaning. Churchill thought that far too many people were drawing the 'dole'. On 30 April 1925 he spoke in the Commons of the 'growing up of a habit of qualifying for unemployment relief' and the need for an enquiry. Three weeks later he told Tom Jones, the Deputy Secretary of the Cabinet, that 'there should be an immediate stiffening of the administration, and the position should be made much more difficult for young unmarried men living with relatives, wives with husbands at work, aliens etc'.[16]

Four months later he wanted to go even further. In a letter to Steel-Maitland, the Minister of Labour, he suggested that when the legislation to pay for the dole expired in 1926, rather than reduce the benefit, as most of his colleagues wanted to do, they should abolish it altogether. He wrote: 'It is profoundly injurious to the state that this system should continue; it is demoralising to the whole working class population . . . [it is] charitable relief; and charitable relief should never be enjoyed as a right.' In future, if Churchill had his way, the huge number of unemployed families would have to depend on private charity once their insurance benefits were exhausted. The Government might make some donations to charities but money would only be given to 'deserving cases' – Churchill did not elaborate on how they would be identified. Even so 'no person under, say, 25 shall receive such relief without doing a full days work, which of course the State would have to organise and pay for'. Churchill was convinced he was acting in the best interests of the unemployed. He told Steel-Maitland that by 'proceeding on the present lines we are rotting the youth of the country and rupturing the mainsprings of its energies'.[17] He hastened to reassure Baldwin the next day about his motivation: 'I am thinking less about saving the exchequer than about saving the moral fibre of our working classes.'[18]

Churchill did not get his way. The other members of the Government, regardless of any possible moral consequences, could not face the political impact of ending the 'dole' at a time when over a million people were out of work. Nevertheless he was able to achieve the objective he referred to as less important – reducing the cost to the Exchequer by cutting the level of benefits for the unemployed. In 1926 the Treasury's contribution to the health and unemployment schemes was reduced by eleven per cent (to save £2.5 million on the health scheme) and a Royal Commission recommendation to extend the schemes was ignored. In 1927 the unemployment benefit for single men was reduced by a shilling a week. The test that the unemployed had to pass was also stiffened: they now had to prove that they were 'genuinely seeking work' even if there were no jobs available. The Government was able to increase, as a matter of deliberate policy, the rejection rate from three per cent in 1924 to over eighteen per cent by 1927. In November 1925 he was also able to convince his colleagues that 'to the utmost extent possible Government unemployment relief schemes should be closed down' in order to save money.[19]

During his time at the Treasury Churchill also had the opportunity to express his views on other aspects of social policy. His lack of interest in education for the bulk of the population, which had been evident during his time in India thirty years earlier, resurfaced during a dispute within the Government in December 1925. He summed up his view of education in a letter to Baldwin: 'a Conservative

Education policy, instead of allowing the automatic growth of expenditure on primary education, ought surely to concentrate any additional aid from the Exchequer upon developing the higher forms and the cleverest pupils etc'.[20] Two years later Churchill took up some complaints from his friends in the hunting world. He told Treasury officials that he was worried by the fact that a number of extremely wealthy Americans who came to England for the hunting season and lived in what he described as 'the sporting counties' had been forced to sell their horses and leave the country. He wanted the tax laws changed to facilitate 'the use of this country for the temporary residence of wealthy Americans'.[21]

Churchill's idea of one policy for the élite and another for the masses was also openly expressed during discussions on gambling with the Home Secretary – his old opponent during his short spell as an MP in Manchester, Sir William Joynson-Hicks. Churchill wanted to introduce State-backed gambling on horses through the Tote because, after discussions with his friends in the exclusive Jockey Club, he believed that it would remove the worst elements from horse racing (off-course bookmakers), thereby ensuring that 'an altogether cleaner and healthier condition prevails'. However Churchill strongly disapproved of the mainly working-class sport of greyhound racing, which he called 'this new degeneracy'. He told the Home Secretary: 'I should like to see dog racing checked effectually in the near future.' He proposed a system of local authority licensing, which he thought would appease the anti-gambling lobby enough to allow his favoured sport of horse racing to be given State support through the Tote.[22] Even the strongly evangelical and puritanical Joynson-Hicks thought Churchill's ideas were going too far in their open discrimination between the two forms of racing and gambling. Churchill replied with total aplomb: 'If there is any subject in the world in which there may be one law for the rich and another for the poor, it is in regard to gambling.'[23]

Churchill's fear of social and political revolution, which had been so apparent in the early 1920s, was again to the fore during the General Strike of 1926. The origins of the strike lay in the mining industry, which had been in decline for some years because of falling productivity due to lack of investment by the owners and the loss of export markets – a problem brought to crisis point in the early summer of 1925 when the overvaluation of the pound on the return to the gold standard worsened an already serious situation. Both the owners and the miners' union rejected rationalisation of the industry through the closure of inefficient pits; the union wanted nationalisation and the owners wanted longer hours, wage cuts and the end of national bargaining as the way of reducing costs – a solution that ensured that all the costs of improving the industry's position fell on the workers. Under the threat of a coal strike in July 1925 the Cabinet agreed to a £10 million State subsidy for nine months while a Royal Commission produced a report on the industry. The main purpose of the subsidy was to buy time in which the Government could prepare for a possible general strike. Hankey wrote of the Cabinet's thinking: 'Many members ... think that the struggle is inevitable and must come sooner or later – the PM does not share this view. The majority of the Cabinet regard the present moment as badly chosen for the fight though conditions would be more favourable nine months hence.'[24]

Churchill had been with Baldwin when the Prime Minister suggested the idea of the subsidy to the TUC and he was put in charge of negotiating the details with the owners. His offer was so favourable to them that they accepted it straight away – there were to be no restrictions on reopening closed pits or receiving a subsidy for doing so, thereby increasing the amount of over-production. In the autumn Churchill insisted on public expenditure cuts equal to the subsidy. The report of the Royal Commission, published in March 1926, failed to deal with the immediate problem and with its recommendations managed to alienate all the parties involved. The owners disliked the idea of amalgamations, the Government objected to the suggested purchase of royalties by the State and the miners rejected the idea of wage cuts of at least ten per cent. The subsidy was also to end.

Although Baldwin announced the Government would accept the report if the owners and miners did (he could hardly do less and he was unlikely to have to carry out the pledge), the Government took no initiative for a month and left the two sides to fight over wage reductions. Even though the miners offered a reduction of 200,000 in the workforce to contract the industry and maintain wage levels, the employers wanted to cut wage levels and continue large-scale over-production. By the last week of April, with a lock-out threatened by the owners, the Government did intervene. But its proposals largely supported the owners and no pressure was put on them to reach a settlement. The idea of reorganisation was dropped and Baldwin backed wage cuts and an extension of the working week from the current statutory maximum seven-hour day. Once the lock-out started at the beginning of May the Government did enter into negotiations with the TUC, although their determination to secure an agreement by the miners to a pay cut before negotiations reopened with the owners ensured the talks would not be successful. These talks though did start to drive a wedge between the TUC and the miners. The TUC was more favourably disposed towards the Royal Commission report than the miners were, yet felt that it had little alternative but to support its fellow trades unionists. They drifted unenthusiastically into a general strike from 4 May after the Government chose to interpret a separate dispute at the *Daily Mail* as the start of an all-out TUC-backed strike and therefore broke off all negotiations until the strike was ended. The TUC ensured, however, that the strike was far from being general. One of its main preoccupations was to maintain essential services and the strike only covered transport, printing, iron and steel, building trades, engineers and electricians.

Churchill took no part in the negotiations with the miners and the TUC in the ten days before the strike. During this time he was described by his colleague, Neville Chamberlain, as 'getting frantic with excitement and eagerness to begin the battle'.[25] For Churchill this was indeed a battle, the moment when the open threat of revolution on the Soviet model had to be faced down. Three days into the strike he warned his colleagues who were discussing setting up a reserve constabulary: 'if we start arguing about petty details, we will have a tired-out police force, a dissipated army and bloody revolution.'[26] In this situation Churchill was prepared to support any firm action by the authorities, legal or otherwise. He wanted an indemnity to be issued to the armed forces so that they could take 'any action which they may find it necessary to take in an honest endeavour to aid the Civil Power' and felt such action should receive 'both now and afterwards the full support of His Majesty's Government'.[27] His colleagues blanched at the prospect of issuing a blank cheque to the armed forces to put down the strike and the King took the trouble to write to Baldwin to protest about Churchill's views.

Although the Government had been carefully developing its

contingency plans and organisation to deal with the strike, no decision was taken on Churchill's role until just before the strike began. On 27 April J. C. C. Davidson, Baldwin's close friend and key man within the Conservative Party organisation, was put in charge of Government propaganda. At the last moment he and Baldwin agreed that Churchill should help out in this area. As Baldwin put it: 'Well, it will keep him busy and stop him doing worse things . . . I'm terrified of what Winston is going to be like.'[28] On 3 May Davidson and Churchill met representatives of the Newspaper Proprietors Association, who informed them that no newspapers would be published the next day and suggested the Government should issue its own. Churchill outlined the Government's plans for a *British Gazette*. Later that day H. A. Gwynne, publisher of the high Tory *Morning Post*, wrote to Davidson to offer the use of its facilities. Davidson requisitioned the *Post*'s premises, the Argus press, a W. H. Smith warehouse, Phoenix Wharf for paper storage and the Bowater paper mill at Northfleet, which was guarded by the Army. Churchill also asked his friend Beaverbrook to provide a number of key skilled printing workers to ensure production was possible.

After the event Churchill always tried to give the impression that he was in charge of the *British Gazette* and that he masterminded Government propaganda during the strike. That was not the case. Editorial supervision was the responsibility of David Caird, the publicity officer at the War Office, and he had a direct line to Davidson at the Admiralty. Davidson was executive head of the operation; he was fully supported by Baldwin and in a position to censor much of what Churchill wrote. Though as Davidson commented wryly, these facts 'didn't stop him [Churchill] or FE from telling everybody that they were running the *British Gazette*, when they weren't'.[29] Although Davidson admitted that Churchill's drive 'was one of the major factors in the success of the *Gazette*'[30] his claim to instant expertise and his constant interference in every aspect of newspaper production soon caused a revolt among the staff. Early in the strike Davidson wrote to Baldwin about the disruptive effects of Churchill's behaviour:

> The failure to some extent in the details of distribution of the *British Gazette* has been due entirely to the fact that the Chancellor occupied the attention of practically the whole staff who would

normally have been thinking out the details . . . So long as he does not come to the *Morning Post* offices again tonight the staff will be able to do what it is there to do . . . I must depend on you, and the staff are relying on me, to find some means of preventing him coming . . . He thinks he is Napoleon, but curiously enough the men who have been printing all their life in the various processes happen to know more about their job than he does.[31]

Later in the strike there were similar complaints and appeals to Baldwin by Gwynne at the *Morning Post*.

Although Davidson censored much of what Churchill wrote, and some of his editorials were removed altogether, a good deal of the material in the *British Gazette* bore the distinctive stamp of Churchill's strong views. Many of the resonant phrases in the first issue suggest Churchillian influence: 'Nearly all the newspapers have been silenced by violent concerted action. And this great nation . . . is for the moment reduced in this respect to the level of African natives.' There had at this stage been no violence, and the racist comparison was certainly Churchill's, as was the description of trades unions as 'a vast political body, spending money to the end that the capitalist state may be overthrown'. It was no doubt Churchill who condemned the aims of the TUC as 'the virtual supercession of Parliament and . . . the foundation of our democratic freedom'. The strike was portrayed as a 'deliberate and organised assault upon the rights and freedom of the nation'. And there was the prospect of a 'reign of force . . . threatening the basis of ordered government and coming nearer to proclaiming civil war than we have been for centuries past'. After these effusions from Churchill his copy was kept under tight control in the remaining seven issues. They remained highly partisan – George Lansbury in the Commons was described as 'a wild Socialist, passionate and shouting' – and great prominence was given to a sermon by Cardinal Bourne supporting the Government. Only after a major argument was a more conciliatory one by the Archbishop of Canterbury printed on the back page without any comment. Churchill was strongly opposed to printing news of what became one of the most famous incidents of the strike – the football match between police and strikers at Plymouth. This did not fit in with the picture he wanted to portray of the country on the verge of violent revolution, but he was overruled by his colleagues.

During the strike Churchill consistently supported extreme action. Unlike many of his colleagues, particularly Baldwin, he was not worried about the atmosphere after the strike was over – he wanted the unions humiliated and thoroughly beaten so they would not be a 'threat' again. Even the solid Conservative Davidson was unhappy with an attitude which 'regarded the strike as an enemy to be destroyed . . . [Churchill] had it firmly in his mind that anybody who was out of work was a Bolshevik'.[32] On 7 May Churchill asked the Secretary of State for War, Worthington-Evans, to mobilise the Territorial Army to combat the strike, but the Cabinet refused to do so. Churchill immediately changed tack and suggested asking the TA to volunteer en masse to form an armed militia to take on the strikers. His colleagues would go no further than thinking about expanding the special constabulary but keeping it unarmed and under the control of the police. When it was decided to organise a food convoy from the London Docks (more as a show of strength by the Government than for any other reason), Churchill wanted a major military demonstration to overawe the strikers, envisaging an escort of tanks and armoured cars together with hidden machine gun nests along the route. He was again overruled by his more cautious colleagues.

Churchill favoured such measures because he believed, as he told Tom Jones, 'we were at war'.[33] His colleagues were also struck by this turn of thought. On 9 May Neville Chamberlain wrote to his wife that at the Cabinet committee meeting that morning overseeing the response to the strike 'some of us are going to make a concerted attack on Winston. He simply revels in this affair, which he *will* continually treat and talk of as if it were 1914. He interferes with everyone who has active work to do.'[34] Churchill also fully supported a Bill drawn up by other hard-line members of the Government which would have made any sympathetic strike illegal, frozen all union funds and stopped them expelling any member who refused to take part in a strike. By this stage though the strike was already beginning to disintegrate and the limited enthusiasm the TUC had shown for a general strike was rapidly disappearing altogether. After originally agreeing to introduce the Bill, the Cabinet had second thoughts and decided to wait. By 12 May the TUC gave in and left the miners to continue their dispute on their own. Churchill's fear of violent revolution had never borne any relation to the reality of a limited strike and moderate aims within the TUC.

The general strike had little impact on the course of the miners' dispute. The Government, while nominally staying independent, took action to strengthen the hand of the owners. They withdrew the offer of any further subsidy to the industry, gave no commitments on reorganisation, legislated to end the miners' entitlement to a maximum seven-hour working day and took the view that a wage cut of about ten per cent should precede any final settlement and any national minimum wage should have significant local variations, thus effectively destroying its rationale. Churchill supported this approach, telling Baldwin at the end of June that it ought to bring about a break-up of the miners' solid front.

Towards the end of August that started to happen as miners in the Midlands began to drift back to work. As Baldwin was on holiday at his favourite resort of Aix-les-Bains, Churchill was the senior minister left in London. He was therefore in charge, for about a fortnight, of talks with the miners. He was no more favourably inclined to their case than he had been earlier, but he was keen to see if he could not end the strike. Although he told Baldwin that he did not want any credit for doing so, it is difficult to believe that he was entirely unaware of the political benefits that would stem from finally ending the long dispute. He stuck with the tough terms the Government had elaborated earlier in the summer but in his search for a settlement, and in the face of total intransigence from the owners, he probably wanted to put more pressure on them than his colleagues did – they were quite content for the owners to secure an unconditional triumph.

Churchill first heard that the miners might welcome a settlement from Tom Jones, who had good contacts with the Labour movement. Jones dined at Chartwell on 25 August and Churchill saw the miners the next day but told them he would do nothing unless they had new proposals to make. Five days later he saw the owners and informed them that the Government supported their demand for longer hours and a pay cut but not the demand to end national wage bargaining. On 1 September Churchill met the Labour Leader, Ramsay MacDonald, at Chartwell, to discuss some ideas for a settlement; he agreed to try to reopen tripartite negotiations if MacDonald would put pressure on the miners. Two days later the two had another secret meeting, this time at Sir Abe Bailey's house in London. They agreed a formula in which the miners were to write to the Government accepting 'a reduction in labour costs', which in effect meant longer hours and less pay, while retaining a national agreement.

Churchill then took this formula to the owners to see if they would agree to continuing with some form of national wage negotiations (they had obtained everything else they wanted). Even if they accepted, he did not expect the negotiations to get very far, but thought it would then be possible to put greater pressure on the miners to settle. Meanwhile the absent Baldwin insisted that there could not be any tripartite negotiations – the talks must be direct between the miners and the owners. On 6 September the Cabinet Coal Committee agreed to make a general appeal for national negotiations, though some members thought that even this was going too far in putting pressure on the owners. Predictably the owners rejected any national negotiations – they knew they had virtually won the dispute and that the Government would not really pressurise them and were therefore content to wait until the miners surrendered. Baldwin returned to London and on 15 September convinced the Coal Committee (which probably needed little convincing) not to pressurise the owners. Churchill, having invested considerable personal effort in the negotiations, still hoped to get a settlement. He tried at the Coal Committee on 16 and again on 22 September to reopen the question but did not press it further against Baldwin's and his colleagues' objections.

By the end of the month Churchill had come to the same view as other ministers. On 28 September in a speech in the Commons he savagely attacked MacDonald and Lloyd George for supporting the miners. A few days later at the Coal Committee he suggested an ultimatum to the miners to accept within forty-eight hours, failing which the Government would withdraw completely from efforts to end the strike. The miners hung on for a few more weeks but eventually drifted back to work on the owners' terms. By then Churchill had little patience with either side. In a Cabinet paper at the beginning of November he criticised the owners for their intransigence and for only discovering the 'principle' of no national negotiations after the start of the strike and after the Government had abolished the seven-hour day. But most of his attack was directed at the miners – there were too many of them and their pay was too high. He objected to the Treasury paying out £250,000 in social welfare payments to provide food for miners' families on the grounds that this helped the miners themselves who, after six months on strike, were 'becoming gradually habituated to an indigent idleness'.[35] To force the miners back to work on the Government's terms he wanted to end all relief to their families within a week.

Churchill's views about trades unions and the threat of revolution had not changed. When the strike was over he wrote an open letter to the chairman of his constituency party, Sir James Hawkey, alleging that the miners could have had better terms by settling earlier (which was quite correct) but their refusal to do so was because 'the Moscow influence and the Moscow money have been powerful enough to drown the voice of reason & good feeling'. He re-stated his belief that there was an attempt underway to 'establish in this island a Socialist State in sympathy and alliance with Moscow'. As the mining communities tried to recover from the strike and its aftermath of even lower wages, Churchill would countenance no sympathy for their plight. In February 1927 he opposed any Government contribution to relieving distress in the mining areas, saying 'we must harden our hearts'.[36]

Before the miners' strike was over the Government was considering what revenge it would take against the trades unions for calling a general strike. Churchill was a member of the Cabinet committee set up to make proposals. In early 1925 he had written to Baldwin with a very one-sided suggestion. The finances of the Labour Party would be hobbled by introducing a provision that union members would have to contract in to the political levy rather than contract out to avoid it. (In 1911 Churchill had vehemently defended the principle of 'contracting in' in the House of Commons.) A general Government subsidy should be given to all Parliamentary candidates, which would help already wealthy Conservatives but with no guarantee of replacing the value of trades union help to the Labour Party. Baldwin opposed this proposal and even spoke in the Commons against a Conservative backbench attempt to introduce it. In the autumn of 1926 the Cabinet committee proposed a prohibition on any future general strike, limits on strikes in essential services, a ban on civil servants joining unions that were members of the TUC, compulsory ballots before strike action and registration of union rules.

Churchill felt that this did not go far enough. He returned to his idea for crippling the finances of the Labour Party and described the existing contracting-out system as 'a real and dangerous abuse'. He went on to argue that 'as we shall in any case encounter the violent hostility of the Labour Socialist Party, it is surely worth our while to do our work thoroughly in the general [sic] interest'. At the same time he wanted to repeal the 1906 Trade Union Act (passed when he was a member of the Liberal Government) which gave the unions legal immunity for their actions.[37] When his colleagues rejected these proposals as an attack on the very basis of trades unionism, Churchill, together with another hard-line member of the Cabinet, Lord Cave, the Lord Chancellor, insisted on their dissent being formally recorded in the minutes. Churchill returned to the attack in the new year while sailing with the fleet in the Mediterranean as the guest of his old friend Admiral Keyes (now Commander-in-Chief in the Mediterranean). He wrote to Baldwin again proposing a piece of political revenge through the end of the contracting-out system and a stiff Bill that would really cripple the trades unions and the Labour Party. He argued that 'even the most perfunctory will excite united Labour Opposition; that therefore we shd have a real Bill which rallies our own forces for the fight & wh when passed will have cut into the vitals of our enemies, & given them something to cry out for'.[38] This time Baldwin accepted Churchill's arguments (he was also under pressure from his backbenchers) and went back on his speech in the Commons in 1925 against forcing through contracting out. The 1927 Trade Disputes Act was a compromise that the Government hoped would give the Conservatives a short-term political gain (and a sense of revenge) but it did not cripple the trades unions or ruin the source of Labour Party funds as Churchill had hoped.

As Chancellor Churchill spent a considerable amount of time on defence and foreign policy issues. He emerged as a strong advocate of cuts in existing defence programmes and the need to plan on the basis that peace would last for decades to come. By the time he left office the Government had significantly reduced the capability of the armed forces and Britain's ability to mount a rearmament programme. During his time in the Lloyd George coalition he had actively supported the idea of the 'ten-year rule' – first introduced in 1919 – which put defence planning on the sensible basis that there would be no major war before 1929. But that decision had never really been enforced and neither had it reduced defence spending to pre-1914 levels as the Treasury had wanted. Indeed major new programmes had been agreed – a naval base at Singapore was to be built to counter the Japanese, RAF strength was to be built up to fifty-four squadrons for home defence against the French and the Navy's oil stocks were to rise so as to provide for a war against Japan. When Churchill took office in late 1924 he found that unless action was taken, spending on the armed forces would rise by another twenty per cent during the life of the new Government.

Churchill's first major argument was over naval expenditure. Here he was faced with the consequences of the Lloyd George Government's adherence to the Washington Treaty in 1922. Unable to afford a naval building race with the United States, the Government had gratefully seized on the suggestion from the Americans of naval limitations. The Royal Navy was no longer to be the largest navy in the world – the Government accepted a ratio in capital ships that gave them equality with the US and a small superiority over the Japanese. However at the same time the Americans insisted that the British, against the entreaties of most of the dominions, must abandon their alliance with the Japanese which, since 1902, had provided protection for the Empire in the Far East and the Antipodes. As a consequence Britain had to plan on a potentially hostile Japan, hence the proposed base at Singapore. The task of protecting Australia, New Zealand and the rest of the Empire ideally required a large fleet to be stationed in the Far East. The second-best solution was to send a large part of the fleet to Singapore in time of crisis. The dilemma of how to meet this commitment, without so denuding the fleet in home waters as to leave Britain vulnerable to a European threat to its homeland, was never resolved. Later, in another capacity, Churchill would face the final dénouement of the problem in 1940–2.

Now however Churchill got round the difficulty by arguing that there was no likelihood of war with Japan. With unfortunate lack of prescience he wrote to Baldwin a month after taking office arguing: 'Why should there be a war with Japan? I do not believe there is the slightest chance of it in our lifetime ... war with Japan is not a possibility any reasonable Government need take into account.' He wanted, therefore, all plans to be based on the assumption that 'no naval war against a first class Navy is likely to take place in the next twenty years' (i.e. not before 1946 at the earliest).[39] He expressed the same conviction to his friend Admiral Keyes, telling him in March 1925: 'I do not believe Japan has any idea of attacking the British Empire, or that there is any danger of her doing so for at least a generation to come.'[40]

Churchill went on to advise Baldwin that on current plans increased naval expenditure would take up all the extra Government spending that was likely to be possible during the lifetime of the Government and suggested that this would be electorally disastrous. The first stage of the fight with the Navy was over the estimates for 1925–6. The Admiralty wanted spending to be about £65 million a year in order to maintain what they identified as the absolute minimum cruiser strength of seventy – although their absolute minimum oscillated between ninety-two and fifty ships on different occasions. (Battleship numbers were fixed under the Washington Treaty so all the arguments were now over the next biggest class of ship.) The Treasury wanted to see annual spending at about £58–60 million. Baldwin, Churchill and the First Lord of the Admiralty, Bridgeman, an old friend of Baldwin's, eventually compromised on £60.5 million, with a possible extra £2 million once the building programme was settled.

The strategic basis for naval expenditure was referred to a committee chaired by Churchill's old friend FE. The Admiralty wanted to replace virtually all its warships within ten years as part of the largest peacetime building programme ever undertaken. Churchill argued for a more defensive strategy against Japan (at one point suggesting the Singapore base should not be built because it was too provocative) and for building sixteen cruisers in the next ten years instead of the forty-six the Admiralty wanted. The committee eventually recommended, and the Committee of Imperial Defence agreed, that plans should be based on no war with Japan for at least ten years, that Singapore should not be ready until 1936 and that Britain should not attempt to send a fleet equal to Japan's to the base. When the arguments over the future programme were renewed in the summer, Churchill first offered the Admiralty a firm construction programme, though it would not start for a year. At this stage he suggested only two cruisers to be built in 1925–6 financed by cuts elsewhere in the naval programme. With an irate Admiralty

Board and Bridgeman threatening to resign over his proposals, Churchill did not, unlike his father, push his case to the point of resigning – he realised his political position was too weak and resignation would not be popular within his new party. He eventually accepted that the Admiralty should order four cruisers in 1925–6, all to be paid for by savings elsewhere in the programme, and two in the next year.

The Admiralty's victory was a Pyrrhic one. In August 1925 Churchill convinced his colleagues to appoint a committee of three – the Colwyn Committee (including two ex-heads of the Treasury) – to investigate future defence expenditure. They recommended that total defence expenditure should not exceed £115 million a year (slightly more than a ten per cent cut on the existing level, but substantially more than that in future years when the services' plans for substantial growth were taken into account). In the spring of 1926 Churchill suggested to the Cabinet that the figure should actually be no more than £110 million (the figure the Treasury had wanted since the early 1920s). Eventually in July 1926 the Cabinet agreed to Churchill's lower figure and also suggested that overall defence expenditure should eventually fall to below £110 million. The new figure meant cutbacks all round. The Admiralty pro- gramme, particularly for cruisers, was reduced. In 1927 the Army was told to plan on no European war before 1937. The RAF programme was similarly reduced. When Churchill took office it was planning on a fifty-two squadron home defence force by 1929. In November 1925 Churchill argued that this aim should be deferred for eleven years and not completed until 1940. The committee chaired by FE compromised on a date of 1936 and when the Government left office there were thirty-one home defence squad- rons compared with the fifty-two planned when it took office.

When Churchill became Chancellor defence planning was on an incoherent basis – it was unclear whether or not the services were expected to be ready to fight a full-scale war by 1929 (the end of the original ten year period agreed in 1919). By 1927 he had been able to ensure, in a series of separate decisions, that all the services were planning on no war before the late 1930s at the earliest. It was in 1928 that Churchill decided to go further. He proposed to the Committee of Imperial Defence, which accepted his proposals on 5 July 1928, that 'it should be assumed, for the purposes of framing the Estimates of the Fighting Services, that at any given date there will be no major war for ten years'.[41] Now for the first time the ten-year rule was established on a permanent basis and, moreover, it was to be automatically rolled forward every day unless some special action was taken to revoke it. This was a fundamental change. Churchill proposed that the new permanent rule should start with the 1929–30 estimates then being drawn up by the Service departments – i.e. that defence planners should assume that there would be no major war before April 1940. By the time he left office in May 1929 no action had been taken to revise the rule for the 1930–1 estimates and the Government were therefore planning on no war before April 1941.

In line with his attitude on defence spending Churchill took an optimistic view of the European situation. He felt that Britain should not support France against Germany, he thought that Germany's eastern frontiers needed major alteration in her favour and he became increasingly anti-American. He opposed the policy adopted by the Foreign Secretary, Austen Chamberlain, of seeking a mutual guarantee of frontiers in western Europe between Britain, France and Germany, which culminated in the Locarno Treaty of 1925. His reason for thinking that Britain should refuse to give France any guarantee against German aggression was that he hoped without it France would be forced within a few years to make sweeping concessions to Germany. He thought there would be another Franco-German war at some point and was determined that Britain should, this time, remain isolated. He told Baldwin in February 1925 he did not 'accept as an axiom that our fate was involved with that of France' and he was even prepared to accept a German-dominated continent.[42] He told the Committee of Imperial Defence that no agreement with Germany was possible 'without a recasting of the arrangements of the Treaty of Versailles as far as the oriental frontiers of Germany are concerned'.[43] He thought this would have to be a 'substantial rectification' and would obviously involve the Czech Sudeten territory (which had a majority German population) and the Polish corridor to the sea at Danzig which split East Prussia from the rest of the country. But he reassured his colleagues that they had plenty of time to deal with these problems, probably more than their political lives – 'At worst there is a breathing space, measured by decades.'[44]

Churchill was also acutely conscious of Britain's declining power, particularly in relation to the economic and financial strength (and latent military power) of the United States. He told Clementine in November 1928, 'Poor old England [sic] – she is being slowly but surely forced into the shade.'[45] Three months earlier he spoke bitterly to a friend about the United States, saying that it was 'arrogant, fundamentally hostile to us, and that they wish to dominate world politics'.[46] He also thought 'they have exacted every penny owing from Europe; they say they are not going to help; surely they might leave us to manage our own affairs'.[47] He was, therefore, opposed to accepting naval parity with the United States (which as a member of the Lloyd George Government he had agreed to in the Washington Treaty of 1922) and was prepared to accept a naval race with them. He thought that by spending an extra £20–30 million a year on the Navy (this was five months before he successfully argued for making the ten-year rule permanent) it would be possible to have a navy the Americans would be unable to match – a calculation which seriously underestimated US economic strength and their ability to outbuild the UK. He was particularly worried about the threat the Americans posed to the Empire and was even prepared to contemplate war with the United States, something every British Government since the late nineteenth century had ruled out as totally impracticable and foolhardy given Britain's unprotected territories in the western hemisphere. He told his colleagues in July 1927:

> No doubt it is quite right in the interests of peace to go on talking about war with the United States being 'unthinkable'. Everyone knows that this is not true . . . We do not wish to put ourselves in the power of the United States. We cannot tell what they might do if at some future date they were in a position to give us orders about policy, say, in India or Egypt, or Canada.[48]

Although the Government failed to reach an agreement with the United States during the naval limitation talks at Geneva in 1927, it did not pay any attention to Churchill's wilder fantasies of confrontation.

By the summer of 1927, when Churchill was contemplating the possibility of war with the United States, the political fortunes of the

Government were on the wane despite their huge majority and their defeat of the General Strike. They had few ideas to offer and the Chancellor's economic policies, constrained as they were by the overvalued pound and mildly deflationary budgets, had failed to produce economic prosperity. Churchill searched around for a big idea that might rejuvenate their standing before the Election due in 1929. He believed he had found it with a proposal for a complete derating of industry and agriculture. When at the beginning of June 1927 he put the idea to Baldwin as the proposed centrepiece of the Government's programme for 1928, it looked deceptively simple. Industry and agriculture accounted for about a third of all rate payments – these were to be abolished and local authorities would be compensated for the loss of revenue by an increased Government grant. This increase in central government expenditure would be funded by cutting spending on the Navy (at the same time as he was proposing starting a naval race with the Americans), by introducing a new tax on all fuel and by a low profits tax on industry. It was a characteristically Churchillian scheme – a grand gesture that looked impressive superficially but when worked out in detail posed a whole host of problems. In effect the proposal was to completely change the basis of local government finance and at the same time provide a massive subsidy to the Government's supporters in industry and agriculture (which Churchill hoped might lessen the pressure for a tariff) at the expense of the general taxpayer. Quite why Churchill thought this would be electorally popular is unclear.

Baldwin gave his approval for Churchill to develop the scheme but without a commitment to include it in the 1928 legislative programme. Treasury officials were put to work and Churchill also brought in a backbench Conservative MP, Harold Macmillan, who was to become a protégé, mainly because he had the qualification Churchill always thought important in any MP or minister – a good war record. In December he outlined his ideas to Baldwin. The total relief to industry and agriculture would amount to £48 million a year (over £1 billion at 1990 prices). In its place a new fuel tax would bring in revenue of £24 million and a profits tax at five per cent would raise half that sum. That still left a large gap of £12 million. He offered no ideas on how to fill it except to hope that after 1931 increasing prosperity would provide enough extra revenue. The whole scheme was highly regressive in favouring industry at the expense of the consumer. But even after six months' work Churchill could provide no details on how the new system for financing local government would work. Indeed he had to make the damaging admission to Baldwin that he was out of his depth: 'Of course I know very little about the rating system ... I find it very difficult to understand.'[49]

Not surprisingly Baldwin was unimpressed by his Chancellor's grasp of the problem and began thinking about postponing the whole scheme until after the Election. Churchill was also under pressure from his colleagues, who were less than impressed too. At the beginning of 1928 he was forced to drop the idea of a profits tax because the Cabinet did not like the possible implications if such a tax were available to a future Labour government. With the proposed scheme already expected to be in deficit, the only option left was to abandon the grand simplicity of abolishing all rates and plan on leaving industry paying about a third of its current bills. On 20 January the Cabinet agreed to remit the scheme to a committee to consider whether it was practicable and if it could be introduced before the election. It was only later that Baldwin realised he made a mistake in allowing Churchill to chair the committee rather than doing the job himself. The committee recommended including a reference to the scheme in the King's speech for the 1928 session even though the details had not been settled.

It was in the early months of 1928 that the complexities of what Churchill was proposing started to become clear. The main opposition to the scheme came from Neville Chamberlain, who had spent three years working on a series of complex administrative reforms of local government finance and structure in order to concentrate local taxation and responsibility and was not keen to see this system replaced by Churchill's vaguely thought out proposals. Chamberlain also pointed out the danger from the Conservative Party's point of view in the scheme. By largely removing business interest in the level of rates and therefore in local government, it threatened increased Labour control. He also thought that Churchill, totally inexperienced in the field of local government, did not appreciate the sensitivities involved in his idea of raising nationally at a uniform level the new one-third rate that industry would pay and then distributing it from the Treasury to local authorities. At the end of March, Churchill had to concede that the reduced industrial rate should be raised by the local authorities as before. The committee also became embroiled in the complex question, which the Chancellor had not faced, of how to define who should pay the new lower rate – i.e. what consituted industry? In the end the scheme they devised provided for all agricultural land to be derated but there were huge anomalies in the new industrial rates – breweries paid the lower rate but dairies did not, manufacturers of whisky and golf balls were helped but builders were not. After a long row between ministers, railways were not derated (Churchill was both for and against this at different times) but they were given an equivalent subsidy from the Treasury provided they used it to reduce their freight rates to industry.

The scheme, which Chamberlain thought was now 'so utterly illogical, so complicated . . . that I could not imagine that it would not be torn to pieces at once',[50] was in the end agreed by the Cabinet, largely because of the momentum it had developed within Whitehall and because of the public commitment given to do something in this field. In 1928 the Government was only able to introduce legislation that initiated the process of surveying industries to be rerated. In the 1929 budget Churchill brought forward the proposed de-rating of agriculture (which was administratively much less complex) to April 1929 so that it would be in place before the general election in order to bolster Conservative support in rural constituencies. However, in the event Churchill's scheme made little political impact and it certainly did not turn into the Election winner he had envisaged in 1927.

By 1929 Churchill's political fortunes, which had improved markedly in the early years of the Government, were again in decline. Despite Baldwin's worries about Churchill's loyalty the period after the 1924 Election was probably the time when Churchill's colleagues complained least about his attitudes and interference. He realised that Baldwin was safely in power for five years and that there was no point in plotting against him. The better political strategy was to build up his credit within his new party in the hope that he might yet become leader. After his determined move to the right in politics between 1919 and 1924, it is hardly surprising that the journalist C. P. Scott recorded, after a political dinner in June 1925, that Churchill had 'professed himself entirely at home in the Tory Party'.[51] Churchill also still had hopes that other ex-Liberals would follow him. In January 1926 in a letter to his ex-colleague Sir Alfred Mond he forecast that their old leader Lloyd George would move 'steadily to the Left' and therefore all Liberals should join the Conservatives in order to fight against the 'common foe' – socialism and its allies.[52]

Even so doubts about Churchill remained. His relations with Baldwin were reasonably close but never warm, and the Prime Minister remained convinced that Churchill should not become leader of the party. Most of the senior figures in the party took the same view. After a year with Churchill in Government, Neville Chamberlain wrote in his diary that the more he knew Churchill the less he liked him. It was not that Churchill was a villain but that he was amoral. He had courage, a strong will and the power of oratory but, as so many others had found, he thought Churchill lacked judgement. All of this made him 'a very dangerous man to have in the boat. But I don't see how he could be got out of it safely now.'[53] Even Churchill's close friend of over twenty years, FE, commented he was 'often right, but my God, when he's wrong!!'[54]

One area where Churchill was increasingly successful was in performances in the House of Commons. Until the 1920s he had always prepared his speeches very carefully beforehand, unsure of his oratorical powers. Now he suddenly found a much greater ease and assurance and his speeches showed him at his rhetorical best. The improvement was noticed by all his colleagues, and particularly by Neville Chamberlain. He wrote to Lord Irwin (the Viceroy in India and later Lord Halifax) in August 1926: 'Winston constantly improves his position in the House and in the Party. His speeches are extraordinarily brilliant and men flock to hear him . . .' But there was still a strong note of reserve about Churchill's other capabilities: 'So far as I can judge they think of it as a show and they are not prepared at present to trust his character and still less his judgement.'[55] Two years later in another summary of the political scene Chamberlain was even more impressed by Churchill's oratory: 'To listen to him on the platform or in the House is sheer delight. The art of arrangement, the unexpected turn, the flashes of sparkling humour, and the torrent of picturesque adjectives combine to put his speeches in a class by themselves.'[56] Churchill's mastery of the Commons allowed him to relax more and stop being so aggressive and domineering in his behaviour. He even apologised to a Labour

MP for his criticisms when he found out the man was ill. As he moved into his mid-fifties he increasingly donned the mantle of elder statesman.

Despite Churchill's acclaimed speeches and his senior position as Chancellor, he still seemed an unlikely candidate for leader of the Conservative Party. His performance at the Treasury was less than impressive and he was widely blamed for the poor state of the economy and of the Government's political fortunes. Douglas Hogg, one of the main candidates, had ruled himself out by taking a peerage as Lord Chancellor, leaving Neville Chamberlain as the clear favourite to succeed Baldwin. If Chamberlain did succeed, it seemed unlikely that Churchill would ever become Leader or Prime Minister, on age grounds alone. In the autumn of 1928 Baldwin considered a possible government reshuffle before the Election. He planned to move Chamberlain to the Treasury and Churchill was to go to the India Office (if the opposition of the Viceroy could be overcome) or, if not, back to the Colonial Office. Baldwin then dropped the idea of a pre-Election reshuffle, but there seems little doubt that had the Conservatives won the 1929 Election, Churchill's political career was destined to fade following what would have been an obvious demotion. Just over four years at the Treasury would have been the summit of his political life.

The Government's chances of winning the Election did not look bright: unemployment was high, the economy was in the doldrums and a revived Liberal Party, now under the sole leadership of Lloyd George following the resignation of Asquith, was arguing for a large programme of public works. Churchill cynically dismissed unemployment as a political problem, because it only affected Labour areas. He told Beaverbrook in November 1928: 'Bad unemployment ... was confined to certain areas, which would go against the Government anyhow, but it was not sufficiently spread to have a universal damaging influence all over the country.'[57] Indeed he told his colleagues in late February 1929, when some members of the Cabinet were pressing for a more activist policy, that the British economic position was sound and that there was 'a more contented people and a better standard of living for the wage earners than at any other time in our own history'. He thought the Government should not allow itself to be 'disparaged abroad and demoralised at home' by the unemployment figures. This was because they did not represent genuine unemployment, only 'a special culture developed by the post-war extensions of the original Unemployment Insurance Act'. He also wrote of 200,000 'so-called miners' who were out of work as 'wisely shed' as part of a 'healthy process' in the coal industry. He thought the unemployment figures should only be published quarterly instead of monthly and added, 'it is to be hoped that we shall not let ourselves be drawn by panic or electioneering into unsound schemes to cure unemployment'.[58]

Nevertheless privately Churchill was not optimistic about the Government's chances. Earlier in February 1929 he had met Lloyd George to discuss Conservative-Liberal co-operation if Labour became the largest single party after the Election. He accepted Lloyd George's demand for electoral reform and a reconstruction of the Government; they compromised on an enquiry into tariffs, and agreed on a two-year pact to exclude Labour. Whether Churchill was acting with Baldwin's knowledge is not clear, but the talks demonstrated yet again that one of his prime political considerations was to keep Labour out of power at any cost. Lloyd George was just seeing who would offer him most for his support.

The 1929 Election was the first at which all adults in Britain could vote following the enfranchisement of nearly five million women between the ages of twenty-one and thirty. Churchill was totally opposed to this move. In March 1927 when the Cabinet considered what action to take he argued, consistent with his views first expressed in India in 1896, that there was no need to extend the franchise and that the affairs of the country ought not to be put into the hands of a female majority. In order to avoid giving the vote to all adults he was prepared to take the vote away from all men between twenty-one and thirty so as to equalise the voting age or, as a possible compromise, make twenty-five the age for voting. He lost the argument in Cabinet but asked for a formal note of dissent to be entered in the minutes. When the Bill giving women in their twenties the vote was considered in the Commons in March 1928, he deliberately absented himself so as to avoid voting against it in public and revealing his position.

During the winter of 1928–9 the Government argued about how it should fight the Election it had already decided to hold in May. Without any major policies of its own and realising it was unable to outbid the Liberals in a public works programme, it decided that it should rely on the 'safety first' line – stressing Labour as the unknown factor and the Conservatives as the tried and tested Government. Churchill naturally wanted a strong anti-Labour campaign. He told Baldwin in January that he should do 'everything to confront the electors with the direct choice between Socialism and modern Conservatism'.[59] He believed that if Labour were returned the country would face a widespread campaign of subversion. On 12 February he told the Anti-Socialist and Anti-Communist Union (one of his favourite organisations) gathered at the Queen's Hall that if Labour won 'they would be bound to bring back the Russian Bolsheviks, who will immediately get busy in the mines and the factories, as well as among the armed forces, planning another general strike'. And the Government would be manipulated by 'a small secret international junta'.

Churchill, like his colleagues, found the campaign difficult, given the uninspiring message the Government was putting forward. His Election broadcast on 30 April contained an awful collection of political clichés and mixed metaphors:

> We have to march forward steadily and steadfastly, along the highway. It may be dusty, it may be stony, it may be dull; it is certainly uphill all the way, but to leave it is only to flounder in the quagmires of delusion and have your coat torn off your back by the brambles of waste.

The outcome was a rout for the Conservatives. They lost 152 seats and their share of the vote fell by over eight per cent. Labour emerged as the largest party with 287 seats (twenty-seven more than the Conservatives), a gain of 136 seats, although their vote rose by less than four per cent. The Liberals increased their vote by almost six per cent but with the electoral system working against them gained only nineteen seats to make a total of fifty-nine. Churchill retained his safe seat, but his majority was cut in half to under 5,000.

At first Churchill, together with some of his colleagues, favoured not resigning and waiting until Parliament assembled to see if they could stay in power. But it was soon clear that after such an overwhelming defeat the Liberals were not going to prop up a rejected Conservative Government just to keep Labour out. Baldwin resigned on 4 June and four days later MacDonald became Prime Minister for the second time, again without having reached any formal agreement with the Liberals. For a few weeks Churchill still hoped that it might be possible to reach an agreement with Lloyd George. They met on 27 June and afterwards Churchill tried to frighten Baldwin, warning him that if the Conservatives became more protectionist then 'there can only be one result – very likely final for our lifetime, namely a Lib-Lab block in some form or other and a Conservative Right hopelessly excluded from Power'.[60] Some in the shadow cabinet, particularly the ex-coalitionists such as Austen Chamberlain, were prepared to contemplate a deal with Lloyd George but Baldwin, who deeply distrusted and feared the ex-Prime Minister, was not. Churchill met his ex-colleague again and afterwards told the shadow cabinet of Lloyd George's price for turning out Labour – some form of proportional representation and then another General Election. The Conservatives rejected the deal.

It was clear that the minority Labour Government was likely to be in power for some time. Churchill had now to adapt his political ambitions to a period of opposition. What he did not expect was that it would be over ten years before he returned to office.

16

Backbencher – the Diehard

After the defeat of the Conservative Government in the May 1929 election Churchill took a long time to assemble a political strategy for the period of opposition which followed. On 3 August he sailed from Southampton onboard the *Empress of Australia* bound for Canada and his third visit to the United States, after a gap of thirty years. He was accompanied by his son Randolph, his brother Jack and his nephew Johnny. Clementine was unhappy to be left behind with the younger children during the three months Churchill was away. For nearly the whole of those three months he was able to depend, as he did for most of holidays, on his rich friends to entertain him.

After Churchill made speeches in Montreal, Ottawa and Toronto, the party travelled across Canada in a luxurious private railroad car provided by Canadian Pacific – it had three bedrooms, four lavatories, two bathrooms, a sitting room, dining room and kitchen and was plentifully supplied with staff. In the first week of September they crossed the border to Seattle and drove to California. Churchill had to suffer the indignity of staying in two hotels at his own expense and, for once without servants, was at a loss how to pack his own clothes. Compensation arrived with a stay (arranged through Beaverbrook) at the palatial mansion of William Randolph Hearst, the newspaper tycoon. Then they moved on to stay in Los Angeles at the luxury Biltmore Hotel (paid for by a local businessman) where Randolph spent most of his time trying to seduce a succession of married women. Churchill moved back eastwards at the end of September, travelling to Chicago in the private railroad car of a millionaire friend from his time as Minister of Munitions, Charles Schwab. In Chicago he met another millionaire acquaintance made in the same way, Bernard Baruch (who also looked after Churchill's investments in the United States). He travelled to New York in Baruch's luxury railroad car and stayed at Baruch's house while he discussed his literary affairs with his agent.

Shortly after his return to England at the beginning of November came the great Wall Street stock market crash. Churchill had sizeable investments in the United States, which fell drastically in value. Finances were, for the next decade, to be a major constraint on his political activities – the need to earn money had to come first. After the May 1929 Election he had cast around for ways of making up the loss of his ministerial salary. He put out feelers through Lord Southborough, who as Sir Francis Hopwood had been Churchill's Permanent Secretary at the Colonial Office in 1905–8 and Civil Lord at the Admiralty before 1915. He found Churchill two directorships with companies owned by Lord Inchcape and involved in the storage and transport of coal (not an area in which Churchill was an expert). They were worth in total £2,000 a year (about £40,000 at today's prices) and he held them for the next ten years. Exactly how much Churchill lost in the stock market crash is not known. At the peak of the boom he was speculating with £20,000 (about £400,000 at current prices) advised by Sir Harry McGowan, the chairman of ICI, who managed Churchill's investments, was made a member of the Other Club in 1930 and later gave Randolph his first job on the firm's newspaper. Much of this money was lost or tied up in worthless shares that could not be sold.

Churchill therefore turned to writing to create additional income. He produced an abridged version of *The World Crisis* and a final part, *The Eastern Front*, but neither was a great success in either historical or financial terms. In 1930 he collected and polished a series of articles he had written about his time before entering Parliament and published them as *My Early Life*. In many ways it is probably his best book – it has good pace, a light touch and more irony as well as excellently told adventure stories. He even recounted some stories against himself, including one anecdote that wittily acknowledged that his preferred form of communication was the monologue.

Churchill described the scene at Government House in Poona when he was enjoying after-dinner brandy and port with Lord Sandhurst:

> His Excellency ... was good enough to ask my opinion upon several matters, and considering the magnificent character of his hospitality, I thought it would be unbecoming of me not to reply fully. I have forgotten the particular points of British and Indian affairs upon which he sought my counsel; all I can remember is that I responded generously. There were indeed moments when he seemed willing to impart his own views; but I thought it would be ungracious to put him to so much trouble; and he very readily subsided.

But a great deal of distortion is also apparent as he sought to fashion his early life into a story that he wanted people to believe. For example, the well-known anecdote about the Harrow entrance exam – that he produced nothing but an elaborate blot – is certainly untrue. His life in the Army and as a war correspondent also suffers from numerous embellishments. He describes for instance his entry into Ladysmith with the relief column after the 118-day siege as 'a thrilling moment' – in fact he was miles away with the 2nd Mounted Brigade under Lord Dundonald, and did not reach Ladysmith until after dark when the celebrations were over.

Churchill's main literary effort during this period was a biography of his ancestor, the first Duke of Marlborough. It had long been agreed within the family that he should undertake this task and the archives at Blenheim had been kept closed to historians so as to increase the value of what would be the 'official biography'. Churchill clearly expected the Conservatives to lose the Election because he signed a contract to deliver a two volume life in two years at the beginning of May 1929, three weeks before votes were cast. Altogether he received an advance of £15,000 for the British and empire rights and £5,000 for the US rights. He immediately engaged a research assistant, Maurice Ashley from Oxford University, together with military and naval experts to act as advisers. He also persuaded the Oxford historian, Keith Feiling, an expert on late seventeenth-century history, to come to Chartwell for a week and talk about the historical background he needed for the work. But long before his assistants looked at the papers, Churchill knew what sort of biography he would write – indeed he started dictating part of the work before research had even started. He told Ashley: 'Give me the facts and I will twist them the way I want to suit my argument.'[1]

For Churchill the biography was an act of devotion; an attempt to vindicate the family's name against the detractions of previous historians, in particular Macaulay. In correcting these earlier attacks in some areas it goes too far in others in an attempt to magnify Marlborough; it ignores important aspects of his character such as his greed and the highly dubious way in which his wealth was accumulated. Although Ashley drew on the Blenheim archives, they added little that was new to Marlborough's story, and Churchill did not use other important sources such as the Harley papers, and ignored those at Blenheim, such as the Sunderland papers, that dealt with the political side of Marlborough's career. The result was a book that was weak on the political side but good on the military aspects. This reflected Churchill's own peculiarly limited view of history – he told his Junior Private Secretary in 1940 that 'a lot of people talked a lot of nonsense when they said wars never settled anything; nothing in history was ever settled except by wars'.[2]

In addition Churchill's method of writing – the fact that he dictated the work to a series of secretaries – led to a rhetorical and florid style that often overwhelms the content. But his aim in the biography was clear. He remarked to Clementine just after starting work: 'reading the various current histories, I am pretty sure I can tell a tale which will rivet attention. They lack colour, structure and simplicity.'[3] The criticism of Churchill's work is that it is too simple (especially in terms of character) and too colourful. In writing as in politics, he could get carried away with an idea and take it to extremes with great relish and complete disregard for the complexities of a situation or an issue. In addition he fails to understand the society and politics of Marlborough's time and continually paints them as though they were similar to those of the late nineteenth century. For example he often refers to 'public opinion' and 'the mass of the nation' when such terms were completely inappropriate to apply to the late seventeenth century. Also he paints a highly romantic view of the past – it is history as Churchill would have liked it to be. On one occasion he writes that 'in the alehouses or upon the village greens ballads and songs expressed the popular sentiment against the French' and on another that 'the sense of common cause grew across the barriers of class, race, creed and interest in the hearts of millions of men'.

Churchill let the biography run out of control. Instead of the two volumes it sprawled across four and instead of being finished in two years, it was nine before the last volume was published. Although the first volume sold well when it was published in October 1933, contrary to Churchill's expectations it did not earn more than the advance. So he found himself committed to finishing a major project that could not earn him new money (he had already spent the advance). The later volumes did even less well and turned out to be a financial disaster for his publishers, Harrap. Churchill therefore needed, if he was to keep up the style of life he thought suitable for himself, to earn a considerable amount from journalism. Apart from supplying a succession of occasional pieces of topical journalism in various papers, he obtained a number of major contracts. In 1930 his agents negotiated a ten-year agreement with *Colliers* for six articles a year for an annual fee of £2,000. In August 1931 his closest friend Brendan Bracken persuaded the *Daily Mail* to pay £7,800 (about £150,000 at current prices) for weekly articles over the course of a year – in fact the paper did not like Churchill's material and took only one article a fortnight for six months. In the summer of 1932 Churchill's old acquaintance Lord Riddell, proprietor of the *News of the World*, suggested he write a series entitled 'Great Stories of the World Retold'. Eventually the series was extended to twelve stories and six of them were also sold to the *Chicago Tribune*.

Churchill, who had not read many of the stories he was to retell, employed his well-read ex-Private Secretary Edward Marsh to provide the material for him. For doing all the hard work he was paid the princely sum of £150 out of the £2,000 Churchill received for the first six articles. In order to keep up his output Churchill employed other ghost writers. Marshall Diston, a journalist, was used to rework a lot of old material to reappear in the *News of the World* as 'Great Men of our Time' – he was paid even less than Marsh, £15 an article. Diston also wrote another series for the same paper – 'Great Events of our Time' (for which Churchill was paid £5,000), an article on King George VI and three of the articles for *Colliers*. Bracken arranged for two of Churchill's articles about economics to be written by 'Otto' Clarke, later a permanent secretary in Whitehall, and Professor Lindemann wrote many of those on science. Churchill even dabbled in writing film scripts. Alexander Korda offered him £10,000 to write one about the reign of King George V to be released at the time of the silver jubilee in 1935. Unhampered by his complete lack of experience, Churchill was ready to lecture Korda on how to make films, but unfortunately his script, a highly romanticised view of early twentieth-century British history, was so poor that it could not be used. Korda gave him £4,000 anyway and Churchill reworked the material into a series for the *Daily Mail* (for which he was paid £2,500). Afterwards Korda continued to pay him a retainer of £2,000 a year although Churchill did nothing for the money. Korda was knighted in 1942.

On average Churchill earned about £12,500 a year from his literary activities in the early 1930s – about £250,000 at today's prices. He continued to spend money lavishly on a vast retinue of servants, large quantities of alcohol and food and entertaining at Chartwell. Despite a substantial income, supplemented by many gifts, such as a Daimler car, from rich friends, he was usually in debt and the local tradesmen at Chartwell went unpaid for long periods. By September 1933 he had an overdraft of £9,500 (about £200,000 today) and his friend Sir Abe Bailey helped him out by buying £3,500 worth of his shares at well above market rates.

All this work on journalism and books left little time for political activity. Six months before the end of the Conservative Government he had dinner with Beaverbrook. Churchill afterwards recounted the key part of the conversation to Clementine: 'My time wd come he [Beaverbrook] said the moment we got into Opposition. I rather agree.'[4] Three months after the Election he told Clementine that only the thought of becoming Prime Minister kept him in politics. The problem for Churchill was how to exploit the situation created by Baldwin's weak position after leading the Conservatives to two defeats in three Elections. To his dismay, on his return to Britain in November 1929, he found Conservative Party politics dominated by the issue of Empire Free Trade. It was a modern version of Joseph Chamberlain's campaign – an external tariff but not on imperial products, in particular food – and was being run by the two press barons, Lords Beaverbrook and Rothermere. For Churchill this was unfortunate – it was the one issue, given his need to maintain some consistency with his free trade past, on which it was most difficult for him to lead a revolt against Baldwin.

For most of 1930 Churchill concentrated on literary activities and took little part in the politics of Empire Free Trade. The part he did play though shows a disposition to push his leader into an extreme position where he might be defeated. At the shadow cabinet at the end of January 1930 Baldwin proposed to respond to the press campaign by adopting a policy of safeguarding industries on a large scale, some sort of imperial preference but no taxes on food. Churchill was happy to accept this stance. He did however suggest that Baldwin should launch an all-out offensive against the press, which was only likely to deepen the poltical divisions. In mid-February, when Beaverbrook and Rothermere suggested forming a new party to challenge the Conservatives, Churchill proposed to respond by engineering a wave of by-elections across the country to test public opinion. Baldwin and the party leadership rejected such a course as much too likely to lead to defeat for official party candidates. In October Churchill went along with Baldwin's acceptance of imperial preference with a ten per cent tariff on other imports. He was now prepared to endorse just about anything as long as it was not a tariff on meat and cereals – he told Baldwin he would support a quota on imported wheat, a general tariff on imported manufactures, an attack on dumping and restrictions on food imports. There was now little left of Churchill's free trade beliefs.

It was in the autumn of 1930 that Churchill thought he had found the issue he could use to bring down Baldwin – the future of the Empire. This was a natural issue for Churchill to exploit and one of the few on which he held consistent beliefs throughout his political life. He subscribed wholeheartedly to the view that the continuation of the Empire was essential to Britain's greatness and therefore Britain could, and should, hold and rule the Empire in its own interests without making any concessions to the aspirations of other peoples within it, and certainly not to their demands for some form of self-government. His views had been formed in his youth and they did not evolve with the passage of time. In September 1930 he expounded to Baldwin the roots of his attitudes: 'I was a child of the Victorian era, when the structure of our country seemed firmly set, when its position in trade and on the seas was unrivalled, and when the realization of the greatness of our Empire and of our duty to preserve it was ever growing stronger.'[5] He accepted that his view was 'narrow and limited': he wanted to see 'the British Empire preserved for a few more generations in its strength and splendour'.[6] Even in the case of Palestine, partly populated by European immigrants whose policies he strongly supported, he thought there should be no self-government for generations: 'The time to think about changing our policy is in another fifty or hundred years.'[7]

It was not just the British Empire that needed to be preserved – in Churchill's view all the white empires should be maintained. He told the readers of *Colliers* magazine in December 1932 that American withdrawal from the Philippines would mean the country 'would speedily sink into the primitive welter of Asiatic anarchy and misgovernment'.[8] After a visit to Morocco in the winter of 1935–6 he praised the French in the *Daily Mail*, writing: 'They have a purpose and are not ashamed of it. Their purpose is not to hand over the country to its inhabitants.'[9] What worried Churchill was that Britain did not have the strength of purpose he admired in the French. He saw his mission as being to help 'our Island out of the rotten state into which it has now fallen . . . I cannot understand why it is we should now throw away our conquests and our inheritance with both hands, through sheer helplessness and pusillanimity . . . My only interest in politics is to see this position retrieved.' He wanted an attack on the mood of what he called 'the miserable public' and 'a new and strong assertion of Britain's right to live and right to reign her Empire splendid and united'.[10]

Churchill was not alone in believing in the future of the Empire – that was accepted by virtually all politicians and the majority of the British public. But he was in a small minority in wishing to fight any and every attempt to change the status quo. He did not even envisage its development into the Commonwealth, opposing any legal recognition of the right of the white dominions to self-government. For Churchill, it was Britain's Empire and the dominions should recognise their subordinate position and place their interests after those of Britain. In November 1931 he spoke in the Commons against the Statute of Westminster that formally accepted the right of self-government in the dominions. He argued against throwing away 'necessary and proper' safeguards which retained ultimate British control in return for what he described as the 'valuenessness' of paper safeguards. He thought the time had arrived for 'calling a halt in these matters' and being 'resolute to preserve the lawful, practical essentials of Imperial structure' – i.e. formal British control of the dominions.[11]

At first Churchill believed that the issue on which to fight about the future of the Empire might be Egypt. His opposition to any change in the British position in the country, which had been clearly manifested during his time in the Lloyd George Government, had resurfaced again immediately after he became Chancellor. In December 1924 he seized the opportunity of what he hoped would be an imperially minded Conservative Government to try and undo the work of the Lloyd George Government, which he had opposed unsuccessfully at the time, in granting formal recognition of Egyptian independence while retaining all essential matters in British hands. He told Baldwin's Cabinet that the recent troubles in the country were entirely due to the fact that the nationalists thought Britain might leave. What was now needed was a clear demonstration of Britain's abililty to rule and if necessary a dismantling of the limited reforms enacted a few years earlier. He wrote: 'Our position in Egypt . . . has always rested on a fiction supported by force. . . . We must not deem ourselves incapable of exercising a complete control over the whole administration of Egypt . . . In order to carry out such a policy successfully, we must have a preserving will of our own.'[12] He was unsuccessful in this quest and thwarted again in November 1927 when he strongly opposed any increase in the Egyptian Army.

Churchill was stirred into action by a decision of the new Labour Government soon after it took power to recall his friend and fellow hard-line imperialist Lord Lloyd from his post as British representative in Egypt and to withdraw British troops to the Canal Zone. Any moves to lessen British control were regarded with horror by Churchill, who told audiences during his tour of Canada that the Egyptians were no more capable of self-government than they had been fifty years before when Britain took control. For him withdrawal of British troops from the bulk of the country into the Canal Zone would simply allow the Egyptians to produce chaos in their own country. He told Clementine, 'fortifying ourselves on the canal and leaving Egypt to go to hell will never last, will be followed by disorder and degeneration, and will lead to our resuming an abdicated responsibility, possibly after serious bloodshed'.[13] Worse still, he believed that any change in the status quo in Egypt would be a near mortal blow to the Empire: 'the removal of the British troops from Cairo to the Canal Zone will strike an immediate blow at our prestige throughout the East ... the once glorious episode of England in Egypt comes to an end'.[14] He tried to mount a Parliamentary campaign to support Lord Lloyd and halt any move by British troops but found little support. Moreover Baldwin, who thought Churchill's views were hopelessly out of date, and the party leadership gave no encouragement. By the autumn of 1929 his campaign had collapsed without ever really getting off the ground.

Churchill found the issue he was seeking almost as soon as the Egyptian issue flopped – the future of India. Before 1929 he had not involved himself closely in Indian affairs; he simply assumed that British rule would and should continue in much the same way as it had in the past. He had not been in the country for thirty years and his views, which had been reactionary even in the 1890s, had not changed. In 1897 he wrote to his mother: 'East of Suez Democratic reins are impossible. India must be governed on old principles.'[15] In May 1932 he told the Indian Empire Society 'democracy is totally unsuited to India'. For him the Indians were, as he told the Commons in June 1932, 'humble primitives' who were 'unable in 450,000 villages even to produce the simple organisation of four or five people sitting in a hut in order to discuss their common affairs'. Writing in *My Early Life* he spoke of England's 'high mission to rule these primitive but agreeable races'. He wanted the Indians to be told that 'we are there for ever'.[16] Churchill was not interested in learning more about the situation in India and resisted any attempt to challenge his views. In 1929 when the Viceroy, Lord Irwin, told him that his opinions were out of date and that he ought to meet some Indians in order to understand their views, he indignantly rejected the suggestion: 'I am quite satisfied with my views of India. I don't want them disturbed by any bloody Indian.'[17]

Since 1909 successive British Governments had embarked on a series of reforms of Indian administration and politics with the aim not of moving towards independence but of preserving British rule by developing a class of Indian collaborators who would have a vested interest in maintaining the Raj. In 1917 and 1919 Churchill, as a member of the Lloyd George Government, had reluctantly accepted the reforms developed by the Viceroy and Montagu, the

Secretary of State. Their intention was to increase Indian involvement in government – 'the gradual development of self-governing institutions with a view to the progressive realization of responsible government in India as an integral part of the British Empire' – whilst keeping a divided India made up of the central government, local assemblies and the princely states. But Churchill had not been consulted about the plans – which were not for a self-governing dominion (that privilege was reserved for whites) – and he did not approve of them at all. His view was clearly expressed to the Cabinet in February 1922:

> An idea was prevalent among many people, both in India and at home, that we were fighting a rearguard action in India, that the British *raj* was doomed, and that India would gradually be handed over to Indians. He was strongly opposed to that view of the situation. On the contrary we must strengthen our position in India ... He believed that opinion would change soon as to the expediency of granting democratic institutions to backward races which had no capacity for self-government.[18]

He wrote to his old sweetheart Pamela Lytton, who was then in India, that the policy of the Government should be 'to keep the flag flying & the prestige & authority of the white man undiminished' against 'the chatterboxes who are supposed to speak for India today'.[19]

As a member of the Baldwin Government Churchill fully supported the line taken by his friend FE as Secretary of State for India that there should be no more concessions to Indian opinion. His fears about what might happen in India went back to the mid-nineteenth century. In 1924 he wrote to FE opposing his plan to give Indian troops obsolete artillery because they might be used against the Europeans in any future mutiny. When the Committee of Imperial Defence endorsed the proposal in February 1925, Churchill wanted his formal dissent to be registered in the minutes. However he did support FE's decision to bring forward the ten-year review of Indian constitutional development, required under the 1919 reforms, so that the Conservative Government could nominate the members. After the Conservatives lost power, but before the ten-year review under the Liberal Lord Simon reported, the Viceroy Lord Irwin issued a declaration, agreed by the MacDonald Government and also by Baldwin (though without the full consent of his colleagues), that the aim of policy in India was to produce 'full responsible government' and eventually a 'full self-governing dominion' similar to the white dominions of Canada, Australia, New Zealand and South Africa.

From the start Churchill made it clear that he would never accept what he described as a 'criminally mischievous policy'.[20] He wrote to Irwin that dominion status was not 'in any way attainable or even approachable in any period which it is now profitable to consider'. If the Indians did not like this rejection, then a determined British Government should go back on all the reforms made since 1909 – 'we need not hesitate to resume in form as well as in fact the direct administration of every branch of the Indian services'.[21] This was governing India on 'old principles' with a vengeance. He told Irwin that the Empire and Parliament would rise up against the policy, that it would be the main issue at the next Election and the electorate would reject it too. (This was symptomatic of Churchill's continual misjudgement for the next six years of the real importance of Indian issues in British politics.) In support of his position he also produced the argument that dominion status should not be granted while there were still sixty million untouchables at the bottom of the caste system in India. While such concern for the underprivileged was touching, he had not applied similar principles when he had helped to devise a system in South Africa whereby a small white minority kept the overwhelming majority of the population in just as bad a condition as the untouchables, nor had he voiced concern over the condition of Africans (or Indians) in colonies such as Kenya.

In October 1930 Churchill joined the Indian Empire Society, a small group of ex-Indian civil servants, ex-Indian Army officers and a few MPs who were die-hards over the future of India. They had little support (24 MPs and about the same number of peers) but it was funded by Lady Houston, the wealthy widow of a shipping magnate, a fanatical anti-Communist and Fascist sympathiser. Soon after joining, in an entirely negative speech, Churchill denounced all the reforms in India since 1919 and argued that Government policy would put the Congress Party in control. If this happened he predicted all India's debts would be repudiated and German mercenaries would be brought in to establish Hindu control. Instead he wanted Congress forcibly broken up and all its leaders deported – 'Ghandi-ism will have to be grappled with and finally crushed.'

The major clash over the future of India did not come until the Round Table conference in London in November 1930, which brought together all the British parties and Indian representatives (but not Congress) to consider the report of the Simon Commission. Churchill had publicly opposed summoning the conference, believing that Indian representatives should not be involved in discussions about the future of India. At first the Conservatives' official position was to support the report of the Simon Commission, which suggested granting greater provincial autonomy in British India (the princely states were to remain outside the scheme) but with only an indirectly elected assembly and no responsible Government at the national level.

Then, when some of the Indian representatives at the conference suggested a federal solution, the most prominent member of the Conservative delegation, Samuel Hoare, recommended accepting it. This was not a move towards endorsing Indian aspirations. Such a solution would take years to negotiate through the tangle of different interests, religious, communal and princely. Meanwhile the status quo would continue. A federal scheme would also make Indian unity against the British virtually impossible and reduce the power of the Congress Party. The Viceroy would retain large powers, the Army would remain under British control, finance would be so organised that any Indian finance minister in a central government would only control twenty per cent of Government revenue. The federal government would not be fully responsible to, or removable by, an indirectly elected assembly. As Hoare told his colleagues, this plan 'made it possible to rescue British India from the morass into which the doctrinaire liberalism of Montagu had plunged it'. Under the scheme 'it is possible to give a semblance of responsible government and yet retain in our hands the realities and verities of British control'.[22] The shadow cabinet accepted this devious scheme and it was to become the basis of British Government policy for the next decade.

For Churchill, although he supported the idea of 'divide and rule', this attempt to tie up the Indians in knots and thereby preserve British control still went too far – it actually gave some unimportant extra powers to Indians. He was the only dissenter at the shadow cabinet meeting. He roundly denounced it to the Indian Empire Society as a 'hideous act of self-mutilation astounding to every nation in the world'. When the first phase of the Round Table Conference concluded in the middle of January 1931 with the federal scheme gaining strong support and agreement that Indian opinion should now be consulted, Churchill spoke of the 'frightful prospect . . . opened up so wantonly, so recklessly, so incontinently and in so short a time'.[23] The next day, 27 January, he resigned from the shadow cabinet.

He was convinced opinion was moving away from Baldwin and as long as a General Election was not called he expected to be successful in bringing him down as party Leader. Baldwin was at this time still under considerable pressure over Empire Free Trade and Churchill, now working closely with Lords Rothermere and Beaverbrook, hoped to add enough pressure over India to force him to resign. But his departure from the shadow cabinet did not have the impact within the Conservative Party, or the country, he anticipated. He grossly overestimated the extent of his support within the party, let alone within the electorate as a whole.

Part of his campaign over India was to present a lurid picture of what might happen if concessions were made to the Indians. He painted an apocalyptic scene, designed to stir up hatred with memories of the mutiny, of the British public demanding severe action once they saw white women and children 'in hourly peril amidst the Indian multitudes'. He also began a campaign of abuse against the leaders of the Congress Party, in particular Gandhi. In August 1930 he had called him a 'malevolent fanatic'; now in February 1931, with the Labour Government about to agree that Gandhi could take part in discussions on the future of India, he launched a vicious personal attack, calling him 'this malignant and subversive fanatic' and continuing:

> It is alarming and also nauseating to see Mr Gandhi, a seditious Middle Temple lawyer, now posing as a fakir of a type well-known in the East, striding half-naked up the steps of the Vice-regal palace . . . to parley on equal terms with the representative of the King-Emperor.

A month later he described Gandhi's followers and associates such as Nehru as 'Brahmins who mouth and patter principles of Western Liberalism and pose as philosophic and democratic politicians'.

His own proposals were entirely negative. Not only should Congress be smashed and its leaders exiled but, speaking in Manchester at the end of January, he demanded a British declaration that they would stay in India indefinitely. The basis on which they were to stay was also made clear. In mid-February he denounced the 1919 reforms saying that 'every service that has been handed over to Indian administration has been a failure'. He believed that the British could decide what to do without consulting the Indians and he wanted a return to nineteenth-century-style autocratic government without Indian participation: 'Our right and our power to restrict Indian constitutional liberties are unchallengeable ... We are free to call a halt ... to retrace our steps.'

Churchill was also working to ensure that his views became Conservative Party policy. He scored his greatest success at a meeting of the party's India Committee on 9 March. Working with his friend Lord Lloyd, he was able to gain acceptance for a motion that welcomed Baldwin's intention not to attend any Round Table conference held in India (which the Government did not intend anyway). He had hoped for outright opposition to attending any conference but had to compromise. Nevertheless the motion was seen as critical of Baldwin and a reversal of existing policy. Baldwin decided to strike back quickly in order to reassert his authority. He persuaded the Prime Minister, MacDonald, to hold a Commons debate on India on 12 March and used the opportunity to condemn the extremists in both India and Britain. He utterly undermined Churchill's position by quoting his own words during the debate on the Amritsar massacre in 1920. On that occasion, as a member of the Lloyd George Government, Churchill had made a strong attack on the policies of Brigadier Dyer in opening fire on an unarmed Indian crowd. In lofty statesman-like tones he had said:

> Our reign in India or anywhere else has never stood on the basis of physical force alone and it would be fatal to the British Empire if we were to try and base ourselves only upon it ... The British way of doing things ... has always meant and implied close and effectual co-operation with the people of the country.

The Tory die-hard was shown up as a one-time Liberal pragmatist. A deflated Churchill could no longer hope to rally support by an inflammatory Parliamentary performance. His response was weak – he could only call for a strong law and order policy in India.

The end of Churchill's hopes of toppling Baldwin came with the Westminster St George's by-election on 19 March, six weeks after his resignation. Duff Cooper was standing as a pro-Baldwin candidate against an Empire Free Trade candidate, Sir Ernest Petter, supported by Rothermere and Beaverbrook. On the night before polling Churchill spoke at an Albert Hall rally organised by the Indian Empire Society. He expressed support for Petter and attacked Baldwin for co-operating with the Socialist government. Duff Cooper's easy victory the next day re-established Baldwin's position as leader. Even if Baldwin had been forced to resign, it is doubtful whether Churchill would have been chosen as his replacement – his previous views on tariffs were anathema to many who agreed with his policy on India and Neville Chamberlain was still the most widely acceptable alternative.

Former Cabinet ministers of Churchill's seniority and experience might expect to become heavyweight figures even on the backbenches, but he had not only fallen out with the shadow cabinet, he was out of step with majority opinion in the party and associated with a cause that aroused no great public or Parliamentary concern. He began to devote more and more time to journalism and the biography of Marlborough, although he still attended the Commons from time to time to utter dire warnings about the future of India. On 13 May he said that Britain was simply creating a 'Hindu and Brahmin movement', superstition and greed would increase and the consequence would be 'the spoilation of millions of people'. On 9 July he described the riots that had affected parts of the sub-continent as an 'outbreak of primordial fury and savagery' which had unleashed 'animal and bestial instincts'. But with talks in India continuing between the Viceroy and Congress, Churchill's warnings made little impact. And his political hopes were about to suffer a worse setback.

By the summer of 1931 the minority Labour Government was facing severe political strains as it attempted to deal with the economic and financial consequences of worldwide recession and financial collapse. It seemed unlikely that it would survive for very long. On 21 July Churchill spent the week-end at Archie Sinclair's house. Also present were other outcasts of the political system – Lloyd George, Harold Nicolson, Brendan Bracken and Oswald

Mosley (the latter was at this time close to Churchill and had been made a member of the Other Club the previous year). Lloyd George, who was also discussing his possible participation in a Labour Government, surmised, correctly, that Baldwin and MacDonald would come together and form a coalition Government. His idea was that this group should then form the opposition and, within a short period, hopefully the Government. Those present agreed to keep in touch. It was hardly surprising therefore that in an article in the *Daily Mail* on 12 August Churchill should heap praise on Lloyd George, arguing that as a former national leader the country needed his help.

Churchill was in France when the anticipated political crisis broke in mid-August; it followed the Government's inability to agree on public expenditure cuts, mainly on unemployment benefit and social programmes, in order to gain the support of the international financial community in defending the pound. He hurried back to London and immediately began to argue strongly against any attempt by Baldwin to form a coalition with Labour. He also wanted to be on the spot to assess the chances of being offered a place in any new government. After three days in London he returned to France and wrote to Brendan Bracken on 23 August that he might be asked to take office. But when the National Government was formed the next day, he was not included, and it is doubtful whether Baldwin ever had any intention of bringing back one of his main critics and the man who had tried to remove him as leader only five months earlier. Churchill stayed on in France and virtually ignored politics. He did however send his son Randolph to see the ex-Labour minister who was already moving towards Fascism, Oswald Mosley, to discuss whether they could form a joint opposition to the new Government – Churchill felt he would benefit from Mosley's greater support among younger voters and MPs. The talks came to nothing.

In September, after the National Government had failed to achieve one of the major aims for which it had been formed – keeping the pound on the gold standard – there was a General Election. Churchill, as might be expected, saw this as a marvellous opportunity to finish off the divided Labour Party. In the *Daily Mail* on 6 October, blaming the financial crisis entirely upon socialism, he called on Liberals to support the National Government to ensure that socialism would 'cease to impede British progress for a good many years to come'. In the General Election the Conservatives won 473 seats, other supporters of the National Government over seventy and Labour was left with just fifty-two seats. Although Churchill had seen his general political objective achieved, the result seriously worsened his political situation. He was excluded from the coalition Government and Baldwin was unassailable as Conservative Leader. His chances of mounting a successful opposition from the back-benches were small, given the huge Government majority. His political strategy had failed and left him in the wilderness.

In the new Government the Conservatives took control of Indian policy with Samuel Hoare becoming Secretary of State. A much hard line approach was introduced. The Viceroy was stopped from taking part in talks with Gandhi while civil disobedience continued (he had held them earlier in the year in similar circumstances) and in early 1932 there was a crackdown on Congress – 40,000 members were arrested and general repression was imposed. The Government stuck with the federal scheme, refusing any Indian participation in Government until its complexities were sorted out and agreed between all parties (an outcome which seemed highly unlikely). Meanwhile behind the scenes Hoare worked slowly but steadily towards producing a scheme for future government but without any real consultation of Indian opinion. The old Labour Government/Irwin policy of trying to work towards a future political structure for India in consultation with the Indians was dead.

Churchill expressed satisfaction with the repressive policy – he told one of his few supporters in Parliament: 'I always said how easy it would be to crush Gandhi and the Congress.'[24] However the new approach had the effect of further undermining his position – politically the Indian issue was effectively dead for the moment. Some two months after the General Election, in early December 1931, he left Britain for a lecture tour of the United States designed to earn £10,000 (about £200,000 at current prices) plus another £8,000 for a series of articles for the *Daily Mail* about his impressions of America. A lucrative and popular tour, mainly on the theme of the need for Britain and the United States to stand together against Communism, might have helped to restore his spirits, but an unfortunate traffic accident intervened. Just after arriving in New York he looked the wrong way while crossing Fifth Avenue and was hit by a car. He suffered two cracked ribs, severe bruising and later an attack of pleurisy. He was detained in hospital for eight days, spent another two weeks in bed at the Waldorf-Astoria hotel and then went to the Bahamas for three weeks to rest before taking on a shortened lecture tour since he could not afford to cancel it entirely.

After his return to Britain in mid-March he concentrated on his writing and took little notice of politics while India was temporarily off the agenda. His main contribution was to attack the idea of a small extension of the electorate in India. In the *Daily Mail* on 30 June he argued condescendingly that the Indians had to spend their time struggling to exist and therefore Britain should not 'dump on their naked skinny shoulders the cost of this immense strange electioneering harlequinade'. In August he left for a tour of Marlborough's battlefields, but this time he had the misfortune to contract paratyphoid and had to stay in a sanatorium in Salzburg for two weeks. On his return he spent time convalescing at Chartwell but had to go to hospital with a relapse and a severe haemorrhage. He was too ill to attend the Conservative Party conference and move his resolution against 'the creation of a vast illiterate Indian electorate'.

Political activity on India picked up early in 1933 shortly before the Government's White Paper on constitutional changes was expected to be published. On 22 February a motion by the hard-line Conservative MP Sir Henry Page-Croft advocating a return to the proposals of the Simon Commission was defeated by 297:42 votes. Churchill supported Page-Croft and went along with the Simon idea of limited provincial self-government but no Indian involvement at the national level. Personally he preferred a tougher policy but accepted this as the best way of ensuring unity among the Government's opponents. This opposition was stronger within the Conservative Party than in Parliament. On 26 February the Conservative National Union only endorsed Government policy by 181:165 votes. On 14 March, when opponents in Parliament formed the India Defence Committee, Churchill was made a vice-president. Initially about fifty MPs and twelve peers joined, but over fifteen left when it became obvious that the hardliners would oppose the White Paper whatever was in it.

The Government's proposals to create a federal India were published on 17 March. It was a complex scheme designed to ensure that any change in India was very limited and very slow and that the country remained divided. The Cabinet had agreed to it as the best

347

way of keeping India in the Empire and maintaining British control, and Hoare had specifically reassured them that 'there was no great risk of a Congress majority'.[25] Churchill was not interested in the subtleties of the Government's scheme to abort progress towards a unified India under Congress control. As far as he was concerned the White Paper, as he said in a formal statement to the press, would 'strike the death-knell of the greatness of the British Empire'. He refused therefore to have anything to do with the proposals. The Government had decided, in order to delay progress as much as possible, to set up a Joint Select Committee comprised of MPs and peers to examine the White Paper plan before any legislation was introduced. The Conservative Chief Whip, Margesson, approached Churchill and offered him four places on the committee for opponents of the plan – a reasonable reflection of their strength in Parliament. Churchill however wanted eight places to the Government's twelve and objected strongly to any Indian assessors taking part in the work of the committee. When the Government rejected his demands, he refused to serve.

Churchill probably never wanted to take part in the work of the committee – he favoured ringing denunciations and outright opposition. Despite all the evidence to the contrary he was still convinced that he had enough strength to bring down the Government over the proposals. He told Baldwin's confidant J. C. C. Davidson: 'I warn you, I am going to lead a Midlothian Campaign against you, and the Government will be out. I am going to start in . . . the Free Trade Hall . . . I think we'll have the Government out in a fortnight.'[26] Churchill's vision of himself as the modern Gladstone was doomed to disappointment. His campaign got off to a bad start. In his Commons speech on the White Paper he attacked the handing over of some Government functions to Indians saying, 'every service which has been transferred to Indian hands has deteriorated markedly' through 'nepotism, corruption and inefficiency'. He then accused the Government of only promoting those in the Indian civil service who agreed with their views, but when he was asked to give examples he could not provide any. The speech was very badly received – Neville Chamberlain put Churchill's poor performance down to the three whiskys and soda he had drunk beforehand.

The Joint Select Committee was set up in early April without Churchill and efforts now concentrated on influencing Conservative

Party opinion. The Government were behind the creation of the pro-White Paper group – the Union of Britain and India – although they denied any links in public. Their opponents merged the India Defence Committee and the Indian Empire Society into the India Defence League, which had a local organisation in the constituencies and published over twenty pamphlets against the White Paper. Many of these productions were simply scaremongering, with their claims that if the Government's plans were implemented the Viceroy might one day be an Indian, the country might secede from the Empire, law and order might be under the political control of Indians and the pensions of Britons who had served in India might be confiscated. Despite these wild claims Churchill could not raise enough support within the party to defeat the Government. At the Central Council meeting on 28 June Baldwin argued against taking a vote while the Joint Committee was still examining the White Paper. When Churchill insisted on a vote, his speech was shouted down by the audience; and when it was put to the test, he lost by 856:356 votes. At the party conference he lost again by roughly the same margin.

Once again Churchill had seriously overestimated the importance of India as a political issue. If he could not convince even the naturally conservative members of his own party, many of whom had close ties with the old Indian Raj, then there was little chance of convincing the electorate as a whole. The future of India was not a topic to rally British public opinion in the early 1930s. Yet for five years it was the only political issue that really roused his interest. As might have been expected given his lack of interest in economic and social issues he completely disregarded the country's economic difficulties, mass unemployment and the acute hardship suffered by millions of people throughout the country. He offered no policy suggestions and no rhetoric attacking the Government for its economic record.

The way in which Churchill handled the Indian issue was hardly designed to increase support. Not only was he opposed to any proposals for change in India's constitutional arrangements, he wanted to turn the clock back and return to the old nineteenth-century way of governing the country. Yet Churchill himself believed that his views represented the wave of the future. He thought that the liberalism of the late nineteenth and early twentieth century, for which he had never had any real sympathy, was finished and that the trend was now towards more authoritarian states at home and more integrated empires (exactly the policy for 'national efficiency' he had tried to implement before the First World War). This was the road he believed Britain should follow, starting with a more tightly controlled Empire to enable it to compete with its rivals. He told Linlithgow, the new Viceroy, that 'your schemes are twenty years behind the times'.[27] Samuel Hoare identified this train in Churchill's thought when he wrote to the outgoing Viceroy:

> I believe that at the back of his mind he thinks that he will not only smash the Government but that England is going Fascist and that he, or someone like him, will eventually be able to rule India as Mussolini governs north Africa.[28]

This pro-authoritarian, anti-democratic way of thinking in fact dominated Churchill's outlook at this time.

Churchill was a great admirer of Mussolini, who had come to power in Italy in 1922. He welcomed both Mussolini's anti-Communism and his authoritarian way of organising and disciplining the Italians. In January 1927 he visited Italy on his way to a Mediterranean cruise with the Royal Navy. He wrote to Clementine about the great improvements under the dictator: 'This country gives the impression of discipline, order, goodwill, smiling faces. A happy strict school . . . The Fascists have been saluting in their impressive manner all over the place.'[29] On his return through Rome he met Mussolini and heaped praise on him at a press conference. He had been 'charmed' by his 'gentle and simple bearing' and praised the way 'he thought of nothing but the lasting good, as he understood it, of the Italian people'. He added that it was 'quite absurd to suggest that the Italian Government does not stand upon a popular basis or that it is not upheld by the active and practical assent of the great masses'. As for Communism, although Britain had 'not yet had to face this danger in the same deadly form' as Italy and had its own ways of dealing with the threat: 'If I had been an Italian, I am sure that I should have been whole-heartedly with you from the start to the finish in your triumphant struggle against the bestial appetites and passions of Leninism.' For the next ten years Churchill was to continue to praise Mussolini.

Some of the trends in British politics caused Churchill much concern. In the face of the gradual shift to greater democracy, at least in the sense of giving more people the vote, Churchill's aristocratic hauteur and distrust of the masses came out in private. As with India, he wanted to stay with the late nineteenth century state of affairs. He thought that universal suffrage 'deprives the House of Commons of the respect of the nation'. And in *My Early Life* he said: 'All experience goes to show that once the vote has been given to everyone and what is called full democracy has been achieved, the whole [political] system is very speedily broken up and swept away.'[30] In January 1931 he expressed his fear to his son Randolph that future historians would probably record 'that within a generation of the poor silly people all getting the votes they clamoured for they squandered the treasure which five centuries of wisdom and victory had amassed'.[31] Four years later he again expressed the view that national policy should not be dependent on the people. He wrote to Abe Bailey during the 1935 Election campaign: 'I think we ought to pull off a satisfactory majority but it is a fearsome thing to cast the whole future of this Empire on the franchise of so many simple folk.'[32]

Churchill therefore cast around for ways of countering the effects of democracy. In June 1930 he gave the Romanes Lecture at Oxford University on 'Parliament and the Economic Problem'. The first part was a conventional defence of the House of Commons as Churchill envisaged it – a debating chamber for the political and social élite. He went on to doubt 'whether institutions based on adult suffrage could possibly arrive at the right decision upon the intricate propositions of modern business and finance'. He then suggested a semi-corporatist, anti-democratic alternative that would have appealed to any authoritarian state in the Mussolini mould. There would be an 'economic sub-parliament' debating 'day after day with fearless detachment from public opinion'. It would consist of 'persons of high technical and business qualifications', although he did not elaborate on how they would be chosen and he naturally excluded any representatives from the trades unions. They would be joined by just 100 MPs, although how they would be chosen and whether they would be a majority in the new economic parliament was not made clear. Churchill was therefore proposing to remove economic and financial policy from the direct influence of democratic politics. As well as the benefits he thought would flow from leaving 'experts' to decide such policy 'with fearless detachment from public opinion', it would also have the advantage from Churchill's point of view of ensuring that any future Labour Government would never be able to carry out its economic plans because it would not be able to control the sub-parliament.

Churchill repeated these proposals during his rectoral address to the University of Edinburgh in March 1931 on 'The Present Decline of Parliamentary Government in Great Britain'. On this occasion he declared that the House of Commons was 'incompetent to deal with economic questions' and unable to take a 'steady, sober and far-sighted policy over a long period of years'. These suggestions for a solution to Britain's problems met with little response. In January 1934 Churchill suggested a different approach to dealing with what he saw as the problems caused by democracy. In an article in the *Evening Standard* he expressed his worry that with the advent of universal suffrage the political and social class to which he belonged was losing its control over affairs. In the near future he feared that what he called 'the responsible elements in the country' would lose 'all control both of the House of Commons and of the executive' and be replaced by 'a majority of inexperienced and violent men'. Indeed he thought that 'a universal suffrage electorate with a majority of women voters' would be unable to preserve the British form of government. His solution was to go back to the nineteenth-century system of plural voting – those he deemed suitable would be given extra votes in order to outweigh the influence of women and the working class and produce the answer he wanted at General Elections. He proposed to go on adding extra votes until: 'the total vote at the poll [is] representative of the pulling and driving power of the country instead of its more dependent and more volatile elements'.[33]

Until such a political system could be introduced Churchill had to continue to wrestle with the vagaries of policy making under democracy. And this produced a result over India that he continued to hate. In 1933, once he had lost the initial battle over the White Paper and refused to serve on the Joint Committee, he again detached himself from politics and concentrated on writing the biography of Marlborough – the first volume was just about to appear over two years late. During 1933 this was his overwhelming obsession – he wrote 308 letters on the subject of his distinguished ancestor and received over 420 – and much of the rest of his time was spent on his other literary activities. In the autumn, worried by Hoare's success in his evidence to the Joint Committee, Churchill did decide to appear himself. The decision was a mistake. He had not read the White Paper carefully and he was simply not interested in the intricacies of the proposals or the problems involved in suggesting alternatives. His opposition was sweeping and broad-brush. When he gave evidence he was soon in a tangle over the White Paper proposals and did not impress the committee with his understanding of Indian problems. One Conservative MP, Sir Hubert Carr, commented: 'Churchill's evidence was really rather a washout. He was good humoured and of course he is clever but as a witness on India I could not give him a more complementary adjective than "cunning".'[34]

The Joint Committee continued to take evidence during the autumn of 1933 and constructive opponents of the Government's plans, such as Austen Chamberlain, secured a number of changes that placed further obstacles in the path of Indian aspirations. Then, in April 1934, with the report due to be published shortly, Churchill thought he had found the issue that would seriously, perhaps even fatally, damage the Government. Lord Rothermere told him of information given to the *Daily Mail* that Hoare (Secretary of State for India) and Lord Derby (the leading Conservative in Lancashire) had put pressure on the Manchester Chamber of Commerce to alter its evidence to the Joint Committee and substitute a version more favourable to the Government. The allegations were printed in the paper on 1 April and a week later Churchill met the dissident members of the chamber who had given the information to the *Daily Mail* and obtained some additional documents from them. On 16 April he laid formal charges before the Commons.

Churchill accused Hoare and Derby of the 'high crime' of tampering with the evidence to be given to a select committee. Specifically he said they had seen the draft evidence before it was submitted, arranged for Derby to dine with leading members of the chamber in June 1933 in order to induce them to withdraw their evidence and eventually in the autumn substituted material that was more acceptable to Hoare. He demanded punishment of the 'utmost severity' – but whatever that might be, it was obvious that if his charges were proved Hoare would have to resign and the Government's Indian policy would be seriously damaged. In his initial response Hoare denied all Churchill's charges. He admitted to some contacts but argued that the dinner was simply routine and that he had only suggested changes in the evidence to help the chamber during its negotiations with Indian manufacturers. They had ignored his advice and only changed their evidence after their delegation returned from a visit to India in the autumn. Nevertheless Churchill had thrown down the gauntlet successfully. His charges were referred to the Commons Committee on Privileges for investigation.

In fact Churchill's allegations were true. In the spring of 1933 the chamber had been split between a faction that supported the India Defence League (they wanted to send a memorandum to the Joint Committee to demand the Government obtain greater preference for British goods in India under the new constitutional arrangements) and a more moderate group. At first the hard-line group prevailed but two of the moderate leaders told Hoare and Derby of the split. Hoare asked Derby to get the demand for a treaty to enshrine British commercial predominance (which would have been unacceptable to the Indians and might have wrecked the Government's proposals) removed from the memorandum. Hoare meanwhile stopped the offending memorandum being circulated to the committee even though it had technically been submitted, and Derby was able to ensure that the necessary changes were made. This was done before the mission to India returned although Derby suggested this should be given as the excuse for the changes. Hoare privately admitted the whole plot when he wrote to the Viceroy in November 1933, five months before Churchill made his charges: 'Derby has been exceedingly good with the Manchester Chamber of Commerce. He has induced them to withdraw a dangerous and aggressive memorandum that they had sent in to the Committee and that fortunately I had prevented from being circulated.'[35]

Churchill's problem was that the evidence he had was only circumstantial. The Government decided that it could not afford to allow Hoare to resign as the result of a scandal and so resolved to fight their way out of the corner in which Churchill had placed them, relying on a mixture of clever drafting and outright lies to see them through. Since they effectively controlled the Committee of Privileges (MacDonald the Prime Minister chaired it and Baldwin and the Attorney-General Inskip were also members together with four Government backbenchers and just three from the opposition), this was not too difficult. The Committee went through the motions of meeting sixteen times, taking evidence from fifteen members of the Chamber of Commerce and examining their records. Churchill tried to obtain the right to cross-examine all witnesses (just as he had with the Dardanelles Committee when he thought the exercise was mounted entirely for his benefit) but was refused on grounds of there being no precedent. MacDonald tried to bribe him with a mission as a special envoy to the dominions if he would drop the charges. He refused and gave evidence.

The Committee completed its Inquiry at the beginning of June 1934. The evidence given to it was suppressed, ostensibly on the grounds of protecting the confidentiality of the Chamber of Commerce. Churchill's hopes were dashed by a unanimous report predictably clearing Hoare and Derby – they had not put pressure on the chamber, simply offered them advice. The report was debated in the Commons a week later. Here Churchill made a major mistake. He was beaten, albeit unfairly, but he rejected the Speaker's advice that he should accept the report and disregarded other advice that he should simply ask for all the evidence to be published (the Government's main weakness). Instead his speech was an angry and sarcastic attack on the report; he refused to withdraw any of his charges and insisted that everything he had said was correct. He had seriously misread the mood of the Commons. Not only was he judged to have brought damaging and unsubstantiated charges but to have refused to accept he was wrong even after the inquiry. The atmosphere in the Commons was ugly and hostile and Churchill left before the end of the debate, humiliated. The episode served to further isolate him within the party. A fortnight later when he held a meeting in the Free Trade Hall not a single Manchester MP would appear on the platform with him.

Churchill's accusations had delayed the work of the Joint Committee on India for two months and it was then further held up by the summer recess. Once again he largely withdrew from active politics and he was away on a three week cruise in the Mediterranean when the Conservative Party conference in October endorsed the Government's position by the narrow margin of 543:520 votes. It was the nearest the die-hards ever came to defeating the Government. The Joint Committee reported later that month and the Cabinet accepted their amendments to the proposed constitutional arrangements for India. At the beginning of December, at a carefully orchestrated meeting, Baldwin obtained the approval of the Conservative Central Council to the proposals. The sceptics who had sought constructive amendments to the scheme now supported the Government. Churchill was in the minority as an extreme die-hard resistant to any change. He claimed that Britain was 'chloroformed by defeatism' and that the Government was deliberately 'sapping the foundations of our forefather's structures' but lost the vote 1,102:390.

In January 1935 Churchill was faced with a difficult dilemma – a conflict of loyalties between his family and his party. Randolph, without consulting Churchill or the India Defence League, stood as an anti-Government Conservative at the Liverpool Wavertree by-election. Churchill decided to accept the fait accompli; rather than disown him, he launched himself into Randolph's campaign. He returned to his old themes and attacked the Government because it was run by a Socialist (apparently a reference to Ramsay Macdonald) and had other ex-members of the Labour Party in it. At the height of the campaign he said 'this is not an election, it is a national uprising'. The result was unfortunate for the Conservatives and for the Churchills. Randolph took 10,500 votes from the official Conservative and allowed Labour to win the seat with a majority of 1,800. In Churchill's constituency there were resignations from the association in protest and three branches passed resolutions deploring his 'consistent opposition' to the Government and threatened that his actions at Wavertree posed a 'highly dangerous precedent' for a pro-Government Conservative to run in Epping in the next General Election.

Churchill had no more luck resuscitating India as a political issue or his reputation when the legislation to give effect to the modified White Paper proposals was going through Parliament in the first eight months of 1935. The Bill had 473 clauses and sixteen schedules and Hoare made over 600 speeches during its passage. But all this effort was simply going through a ritual. India had almost disappeared as an issue inside the Conservative Party after the Central Council vote in December 1934; and the die-hard opposition in the Commons could rarely muster more than about sixty MPs to vote against the Bill and so its passage was assured. Churchill doggedly kept up his outright opposition to the proposals. He was now becoming such an extremist that even some of his die-hard colleagues were deserting him. At the end of February Lord Salisbury wrote to a friend that Churchill had 'entirely lost his parliamentary touch' and that unless he changed his attitudes 'I doubt whether we will do anything in the House of Commons'. He refused to chair an Albert Hall meeting for Churchill because 'I am afraid I am not prepared to identify myself with Winston and the kind of speech which he will wish to make on that occasion'.[36]

The Government, by pressurising the BBC, had ensured that Churchill was largely kept off the radio for the previous four years. He was allowed to make a broadcast at the end of January 1935. In it he described the Bill as 'a monstrous monument of shame built by pygmies' which would deliver India to 'inefficiency, nepotism and corruption' in the hands of 'the most narrow, bitter and squalid vested interests and superstitions'. In the House of Commons he continued his forlorn opposition to the Bill throughout its passage, making a series of extremely negative and ineffectual speeches. His last opportunity came with the Third Reading on 4 June. In a bitter speech he condemned every aspect of the Government's proposals and rejected any plan to increase Indian participation in government – 'In the name of theoretical progress you have opened the door to practical retrogression.'

Once the Bill had passed through Parliament Churchill hastened to make his peace with the party both nationally and in his constituency. In a statement he made clear that he no longer had any quarrels over policy. Baldwin had now replaced MacDonald as Prime Minister and with a General Election due soon Churchill hoped that by calling off his campaign of dissent he would soon be back in government.

Backbencher – the Uncertain Call

In the first volume of his memoirs of the Second World War – *The Gathering Storm* – Churchill painted a highly biased picture of Government policy in the 1930s and his own role in opposing it. He portrayed the Government as criminally weak, refusing despite all the evidence to rearm until it was too late and determined to appease Germany when concerted action at any stage would have avoided war. He portrayed himself as being the prophet in the wilderness – the sole individual who appreciated what needed to be done but whose consistent and clear warnings were always ignored. Because he published his account first, Churchill's interpretation of the events of the 1930s and his own position became widely accepted among the public. In nearly every respect it is simplistic and frequently grossly misleading as well.

Churchill went into opposition to the leadership of the Conservative Party, and eventually the National Government, not over defence or foreign policy but over India. Until 1935 it was his outright opposition to constitutional reform in India that placed him in self-imposed exile. The longer his dissent continued and the more extreme his opposition became, the less likely he made his subsequent recall. From 1930 till 1935 India was almost his sole preoccupation in politics. He told the Viceroy in May 1933 (over three months after Hitler came to power): 'I do not think I should remain in politics, certainly I should take no active part in them, if it were not for India.'[1] Eighteen months later, in November 1934, after the Hitler dictatorship was firmly established and long after his first speeches calling for rearmament, he told his constituents that the two most important tasks facing the Conservative Party were, in his view, not foreign policy or rearmament, but his old favourites – 'first . . . to defeat the policy of abdication at the centre in India, and the second is to beat the Socialists.'[2]

During the 1920s there appeared to be few threats to peace. Many countries had come together after the war to form the League of Nations, pledged to respect international boundaries and to take collective action to deal with any aggressor. Nearly every country had signed the Kellogg-Briand pact renouncing force as a part of national policy. Germany under the Weimar Republic was increasingly integrated into the European concert after the Locarno Pact; the issue of reparations was contained if not resolved and in the Far East, Japan, now estranged from Britain after the ending of the alliance in 1922, seemed quiescent. It was here in the Far East not in Europe that the first threat arose to the post-war settlement and the League of Nations was challenged to implement its lofty ideal of collective action to secure international order. In September 1931 Japan invaded the Chinese province of Manchuria, rapidly established control and set up a puppet regime. After much prevarication and many misunderstandings, Britain and the United States failed to agree on joint action, and the League as a whole failed to find a way of removing Japan from Chinese territory, contenting itself instead with fine words.

Churchill did not support strong collective action by the League against the aggressor in this first major instance of the open flouting of the League's charter. In fact he admired Japan for its authoritarian and patriotic culture and supported it as the state most likely to secure order in the Far East against the increasing disintegration of the Chinese republic and the threat of Soviet expansion. On 17 February 1933 he told the Anti-Socialist and Anti-Communist Union:

> I do not think that the League of Nations would be well advised to have a quarrel with Japan . . . I hope we shall try in England to understand a little the position of Japan, an ancient state, with the highest sense of national honour and patriotism.

At the end of the month he openly supported Japan's position in Manchuria. He told his constituents: 'It is in the interests of the whole world that law and order should be established in Northern China.' He compared the disintegration of China to what would happen in India if the British left and said that he had 'no doubt whatsoever that the Northern Province of China, to which Japan gives a very considerable measure of orderly government, is the least unhappy of all the provinces of China at the present time'. He thought there would be no problem in securing British trade in the area and therefore there was no need for war.[3] In reacting to the first example of open agression Churchill's views were little different from those of the Government. To the extent that there was any difference, Churchill was more favourable to the aggressor because he saw no direct threat to British interests regardless of the open flouting of international law.

During his time in the Baldwin Government Churchill had opposed the Locarno pact negotiated by Austen Chamberlain. He did not support the concept of a collective guarantee of borders in western Europe, preferring that Britain should remain isolated from the continent and leave France to deal with Germany as they thought necessary. After 1929 Churchill remained an isolationist for many years. On 23 November 1932 he told the Commons that Britain should undertake no commitments in Europe that the United States would not support. Since the United States was not even a member of the League and took no interest in Europe's political quarrels, Churchill obviously intended that Britain should do likewise. Hitler's appointment as Chancellor in Germany on 30 January 1933 made no difference to this stance. A month later, speaking to his constituents, he reassured them that 'there is no likelihood of a war in which Great Britain would be involved' and he praised the foreign policy of the Government because 'they have very rightly refused to extend our obligations in Europe or elsewhere'.[5] In the middle of April 1933 he told the House of Commons that 'we have no right to meddle too closely in Europe'. He opposed any close association with France and thought Britain should be neutral in any future European war. On 14 March he told MPs: 'I hope and trust that the French will look after their own safety, and that we shall be permitted to live our life in our island without being again drawn into the perils of the continent of Europe' and reminded the House that 'we have to be strong enough to defend our neutrality'. He told Oxford University Conservatives that Britain needed to rearm but only to be 'safe in our Island Home'. Again on 12 August 1933 he told his constituents that Britain should be 'strong enough if war should come in Europe to maintain our effective neutrality, unless we should decide of our own free will to the contrary'.

This policy of isolation, no alliances and neutrality in any European war involving France and Germany continued to attract Churchill into the mid-1930s. In March 1934 in the Commons he again emphasised the importance of not undertaking commitments in Europe and not being dependent on other states: 'We must be free. We must preserve our full latitude and discretion of choice.' Even in July 1935, in an open letter that marked the end of his rebellion over India, he criticised Labour Party foreign policy because it would endanger peace in Europe by Britain 'meddling too much in foreign quarrels which it is beyond our power to heal'. This isolationist policy, refusal to be involved in European problems and contemplation of neutrality in a future war was the very opposite of resolute collective action against potential aggressors. This attitude was consistent with Churchill's views in the 1920s that France was quite strong enough to deter, and if necessary defeat, Germany without British help. He wanted to maintain that position so that Britain would not find it necessary to intervene in any quarrel. That was why he opposed equality of French and German armaments, one of the possible outcomes of the Geneva disarmament conference.

In the early 1930s Churchill largely restricted himself to his old themes of sniping at the Labour Government and building up the Soviet threat. On 13 May 1932 he spoke in the Commons about the major Soviet threat to peace: 'We must also remember that the great mass of Russia, with its enormous armies and its schools of ardent students of chemical warfare, poison gas and appliances, looms up all along the eastern frontier of Europe.' A fortnight later in the *Daily Mail* he argued that the small states of eastern Europe should undertake massive rearmament programmes in order 'to protect themselves from being submerged in a ferocious deluge from Russia'.[4] On 29 June 1931 he told the Commons that Britain had disarmed so much that it was 'extremely vulnerable' and that the Army was no more than a 'glorified police force'. He saw the main threat coming from the Soviet Union which was 'malignant and actively preparing for war'.

These criticisms of Britain's defences were a piece of dreadful hypocrisy and opportunism on Churchill's part. As Chancellor he had ensured that the ten-year rule became permanent and was rolled forward continuously unless specific action was taken to reverse the decision. While in office he had planned on no major war before April 1941 and to extend the no-rearmament policy into the 1930–1 financial year that had ended only three months before he made these criticisms. If Britain had indeed disarmed so much as to be 'extremely vulnerable' then Churchill himself bore a large measure of responsibility for that policy.

Such considerations did not prevent Churchill from launching a series of attacks on the Government for the reduced state of Britain's defences including a call in March 1933 for the end of the ten-year rule and the beginning of air rearmament. As a backbencher he was unaware that the Government had already abandoned the rule a year earlier, although because of Britain's severe economic and financial position in the midst of the worst recession for decades they decided in 1932 that they could not afford to finance an immediate rearmament programme. By the time that Churchill made his first major speech in the Commons about the state of Britain's air force and the need for rearmament – on 2 February 1934 – the Government had (in November 1933) agreed the order of priorities for Britain's rearmament and a top level committee in Whitehall had completed its report on the immediate deficiencies to be put right.

The problem the Government faced was one with which Churchill had been familiar for twenty-five years – inadequate economic and financial resources to defend a global empire against multiple threats – and which he was to face again in its final and almost fatal form between 1940 and 1942. The temporary reprieve granted Britain in the 1920s was disappearing as first Japan and then Germany under Hitler began to pose threats to British interests. In essence Britain was trying to control an empire that comprised about a quarter of the globe with less than ten per cent of the world's manufacturing output. In addition the Government had to cope with massive external and internal debts caused by the war together with a major trade slump. Britain's strategic position had also worsened significantly from that faced by the Liberal Government and Churchill before 1914. Instead of a single threat from Germany and an effective alliance with France and Russia, Britain now faced a potentially hostile Germany posing a threat to its homeland and a hostile Japan threatening the Far Eastern empire and the dominions of Australia and New Zealand, with help only from France badly weakened by the war. This double threat at opposite ends of the globe was to pose problems that were not resolved by any government, including Churchill's.

Beginning in 1933, soon after Hitler took power, the Government took a number of fundamental decisions that shaped the rearmament programme. First, they decided that the ultimate threat came from Germany but the immediate threat was from Japan (only a few years earlier Churchill had complacently assumed no such threat in his lifetime). Second, they decided to scrap Churchill's assumption that they would have at least ten years' warning of any conflict and prepare for a war in just six years' time – April 1939. It was vital to get this calculation right. If rearmament peaked too soon, the armed forces would have to fight with a large number of obsolete weapons when war did come; if it was too late, they would be unprepared. The Government reckoned that Germany would have to rebuild all three services from the minimal levels allowed under the Versailles Treaty and expand their armaments industry. All of this was bound to take time. In the event the Government's assumption proved correct. But there might well be periods in the early phases of the rearmament programme, as new weapons were being developed and new factories constructed, when preparations would seem slow and inadequate – the important point was to ensure that the climax of preparedness came at the right moment.

Having made its reappraisal, the Government embarked on a prodigious rearmament effort beginning in 1934. The first part of the programme was to put right the 'worst deficiencies' – which meant essentially implementing those plans that had been postponed by the Baldwin Government under Churchill's prompting and later by the 1929–31 Labour Government. The cost of this immediate programme was £93 million (over £2 billion at current prices). Rearmament was concentrated on the Air Force, in particular the bomber fleet, so as to try to provide a deterrent against any German action while the rest of the programme was still underway. The second phase was for expenditure of just over £1 billion in five years, later concentrated into four years and increased to £1.5 billion. To pay for it income tax was raised by over twenty per cent between 1934 and 1939 and a special Defence Loan funded. Overall Britian's defence expenditure rose from £103 million in 1932–3, when the ten year rule was abandoned, to £701 million a year by 1939 – an increase of 580 per cent. At first increases were about five per cent a year, but after 1936 they went up to over forty per cent a year. As a percentage of gross national product defence spending rose from three per cent in 1932–3 to eighteen per cent in 1939.

The problem for the Government was how much it said about its plans in the interim period. For diplomatic reasons it was impossible to acknowledge that Britain was planning for a possible war with Germany within six years. At home public opinion needed to be brought to face the possibility of another war so soon after the First World War with its appalling loss of life. On intelligence grounds the Government could not disclose its estimates of actual and likely German rearmament and it obviously could not explain in public the level of forces it was planning to build, thereby alerting the Germans. It was against this background that Churchill made his criticisms of the state of Britain's defences generally and its air capability in particular. They reflected his concern, partly due to his ignorance of the Government's plans, about the threat to British interests posed by a revitalised Germany and also his need to find a new political issue to exploit as his India campaign failed.

On 2 February 1934 he outlined the horrors of bombing and called for the RAF to be equal in size to the strongest European power. Just over a month later he claimed that within eighteen months Germany would be able to threaten London with massive bombing. The Government felt the need to respond and Baldwin declared in public what they had already accepted in private, that the RAF should have 'parity' with the German Air Force. At this time the Government was well aware from material provided by French intelligence that Germany was aiming at a front-line force of about 500 aircraft by about 1935, no bigger than the RAF. In July 1934 the Government's Industrial Intelligence Centre (IIC), based on accurate estimates of expanding German aircraft production, decided that the German Air Force would, by some time in 1936, be larger than the RAF. Churchill was promptly given an unofficial copy of the IIC report by the head of the centre, Desmond Morton.

He had first known Morton soon after the war when he found him a job in the intelligence services and they were now near neighbours in Kent. Churchill used the report as the basis for his speech in the Commons on 30 July when he declared that 'some time in 1936 Germany will be definitely and substantially stronger in the air than Great Britain'. He then went on to claim that Germany would establish such a lead in aircraft construction that Britain would never be able to overtake them. Churchill's points might have had greater impact if they had not been made a month after his terrible performance in the Commons over the report of the Privileges Committee on the Manchester Chamber of Commerce affair.

On 28 November, using further material from Morton, Churchill again gave the Commons a horrific picture of London under mass bombing. On this occasion he went further than before and claimed that the German Air Force 'is rapidly approaching equality with our own' and would be double the size of the RAF by 1937. Baldwin rightly rejected Churchill's claims of German parity in 1934–5. German front-line strength was known accurately because low-grade German Air Force codes were being deciphered with some ease at this time. However Baldwin went on to imply that parity would be maintained into 1936 (intelligence estimates suggested a German front line of 1,300 by the end of that year). This was a much more dubious point to sustain because British estimates in fact suggested a German lead by then in numbers but not quality, though not by the wide margin that Churchill suggested for 1937.

In making these claims (and the even wilder ones he was to make in early 1935) Churchill was ignoring some obvious facts about the state and role of the German Air Force. The Luftwaffe did not exist when Hitler took power in 1933 and an effective modern air force could not be created overnight from nothing. Pilots had to be trained, aircraft designed and factories built to produce them. From 1933 to 1936 the Luftwaffe was in reality a vast training camp as the officers who were to become pilots were drafted in from the Army for training, and the planes available to them were either obsolescent military machines or converted civilian models. Half the aircraft production programme agreed in 1934 was actually for trainers in order to produce pilots. The Luftwaffe was not even in a state to take part in operational manoeuvres until 1936 and modern aircraft did not begin to become available until then. In making his horrific speeches about the bombing of London Churchill was assuming that the Luftwaffe was planning to create an independent bombing force like the RAF and that it had the machines to carry out such a policy. In March 1935 he was to claim 'Practically the whole of the German bombing air force can reach London with an effective load'. Such claims were untrue. In fact the Luftwaffe was designed for close support of the Army. More important, in 1934–5 it did not have, and was not planning to build, a heavy bomber fleet. Given existing technology, in terms of the range and payload of aircraft, it was almost impossible for Germany to mount a bombing campaign against Britain without first capturing bases in the Low Countries and northern France.

Until the beginning of 1935 Churchill's claims about the size of the German Air Force were not wildly inaccurate, although he greatly exaggerated its potential effectiveness, relied too much on front-line strength and did not take account of the operational competence of each side. What he said was certainly not news to the Government. Then his claims began to lose touch with reality. On 19 March 1935 he told MPs that the Luftwaffe would, by the end of the year, 'be at least beween three and four times as strong as we are', and he implied this would be not just a matter of numbers but also of quality. Such a prediction – about a time only nine months away – was ridiculous and had no basis in fact. On 4 April in the *Daily Mail* he made another grossly exaggerated claim when he wrote that preparations to convert the whole of industry to munitions production have 'already been completed by every other country in the world to an extent and refinement which is at once astounding and alarming'. The idea that every country in the world except Britain was on the verge of all-out war production was patently untrue. It was not even an accurate assessment of Germany, which at this time was spending roughly six per cent of its national wealth on defence.

Churchill's claims about the rapid development of the Luftwaffe appeared to gain credibility when, during a visit by British ministers to Berlin on 25 March 1935, Hitler claimed that Germany had achieved 'parity' in the air with Britain. The British Government knew, from its reliable intelligence sources, that Hitler was lying but the Permanent Secretary at the Foreign Office, Sir Robert Vansittart, authorised the leak of the Hitler claim as part of his private campaign to increase defence preparations. Churchill accepted Hitler's claim as accurate and on 2 May in the Commons berated the Government for the slow pace of rearmament, declaring 'it cannot be disputed that both in numbers and in quality Germany has already obtained a marked superiority over our Home Defence Air Force'. Shortly afterwards, on 22 May, Churchill repeated his alarmist prediction of 19 March: 'by the end of the year, unless their rate of construction and development is arrested by some agreement, they will be possibly three, or even four, times our strength'.

During the debate on 22 May Baldwin admitted that his statement on 28 November that 'parity' would be maintained throughout 1936 could not now be sustained. This revision was based on the latest intelligence assessment about the Luftwaffe, which now estimated a front-line strength of 1,500 aircraft by April 1937. The Government had agreed RAF expansion to reach the same figure but for some time Germany would be stronger in the air than Britain. Baldwin's admission lent credence to Churchill's claims. Attention focused on the Government's error rather than on Churchill's gross exaggerations. (Germany never had had a front-line air force three or four times that of Britain, nor did it have a bigger front line by the end of 1935.) To inform Churchill how far out his claims were, on 19 September the Air Minister, Cunliffe-Lister, showed him a paper, based on British intercepts of German Air Force codes, which revealed that British and German front-line strengths were roughly equal, and that on some definitions of operational capability Germany was still behind. Morton, who was still giving Churchill advice, accepted these figures and other intelligence information that the pace of German expansion was beginning to slow down as they tried to produce effective squadrons out of a mass of newly trained pilots.

Churchill wrote a defensive reply to Cunliffe-Lister in which he insisted the Germans had superiority – on the basis of the number of pilots they were training. He never acknowledged the problems involved in creating an air force from scratch. Nevertheless, although he would not admit it, the sight of these highly secret Government papers did influence him. After the summer of 1935 his criticisms of the pace of Britain's air rearmament became much more muted and much less frequent and he no longer made exaggerated claims about German plans and capabilities. Cunliffe-Lister's aim in showing him these papers was thus achieved. Indeed many of Churchill's criticisms were now in private correspondence with the ministers concerned rather than in public. In the Commons he restricted himself to more general claims about Germany's plans and capabilities. On 23 April 1936 he said that Germany had spent £1 billion on armaments between March 1933 and June 1935, and another £800 million in 1935 alone. Indeed Churchill thought the figures should be even higher because he wanted to include the German road construction programme as military expenditure. Morton, relying on IIC information, thought his figures were highly exaggerated but Churchill was determined to use them. In the Commons debate on defence on 12 November 1936 he claimed that German front-line strength was already 1,500 aircraft, which Baldwin rightly challenged as being too high. Churchill also said: 'Germany has specialised in long-distance bombing aeroplanes ... her preponderance in that respect is far greater than any of these figures would suggest.' In fact Germany had done nothing of the sort. Luftwaffe bombers were two-engined machines optimised for Army support and the month before one of the Government's best informants on Luftwaffe policy had told them, quite accurately, that plans for a fleet of four-engined strategic bombers had been abandoned. At this time the RAF was drawing up specifications for the four-engined bombers that were to form the backbone of Bomber Command from 1942 on.

Despite the impression he liked to create later, Churchill was not a lone, or even the chief, voice calling for rearmament. His concerns were shared by many other MPs, the most important of whom was Austen Chamberlain, who had held almost every senior post in government and had been Foreign Secretary in the 1924–9 Government. After the Commons debate on defence on 20 July 1936 Baldwin agreed to meet a Parliamentary delegation to discuss the situation confidentially. As the opposition leaders refused to take part, it was only Conservatives who met Baldwin and his senior colleagues over two days at the end of the month. The delegation was led by Austen Chamberlain from the Commons and Salisbury from the Lords; Churchill was simply a senior member of the team. As might be expected, he spoke at enormous length about the RAF and the measures necessary to cope with the effects of bombing. The points raised by the delegation were examined in great detail by the Service departments. After the 11 November debate Baldwin saw the joint delegation again on 23 November. The Minister for Defence Co-ordination (Inskip) dealt with all the points raised at the July meeting. The meeting was not very productive, partly because Churchill insisted on getting sidetracked into detailed arguments about the level of RAF preparedness and how exactly to determine the front-line strength of the RAF and Luftwaffe. After this there were no more Parliamentary delegations and Churchill kept the few criticisms he made of the rearmament programme to private correspondence with ministers. The impression Churchill gave after 1936 was of a backbencher generally content with the Government's rearmament policy.

Although Churchill was to make a few very guarded public comments in 1937, he made no sweeping attacks on Britain's position in the air. Yet this was time when the disparity between the two air forces was at its greatest. Germany did have a larger front-line air force and their production was over twice the British level. The RAF had underestimated the size of air force the Germans were aiming for and it took time to modify British production plans. Also the British were waiting for the production of the modern designs agreed in 1934–5 to come on stream. But reacting to Churchill's exaggerated claims in 1934–5 would have been disastrous. If there had been a crash programme of expansion then the RAF would have consisted largely of obsolete biplanes by the late 1930s.

In March 1938 Churchill returned to the fray but not in public. He compiled a paper listing what he believed were Britain's shortcomings in the air. He pointed out for example that the new Hurricane and Spitfire fighters were only just coming into service. This was a statement of fact, but having refused to accept Morton's assurances that these aircraft were equal to German designs, he went on to assert that the Germans had developed new aircraft even though there was no evidence to substantiate such a claim. In private his exaggerations continued. He told the editor of the *News of the World* in June 1938 that the RAF was 'less than one-third of the German Air Force and the rate of production is at present less than one-third'.[6] In fact at this stage the RAF front line was about seventy per cent of the Luftwaffe (the RAF had more operational reserves) and production was about two-thirds of German levels. More important, the number of British and French front-line aircraft substantially outnumbered the Luftwaffe. British production levels were to reach equality with Germany in 1939 and were planned to substantially exceed them in 1940.

Churchill also had strong views about RAF recruitment and equipment. He always believed that officers should only be drawn from the right social background. During the expansion of the 1930s the RAF could only find the number of pilots it needed by training more sergeant pilots. He objected to this and wrote to Baldwin in July 1936 accusing the RAF of deliberately excluding the people he favoured, and commenting sharply, 'This is no time for class prejudice.'[7] Turning to the aircraft, he wrote to the Prime Minister Neville Chamberlain in March 1938 to criticise the design of the new British fighters:

> We have concentrated upon the forward-firing fixed-gun Fighter [Hurricane and Spitfire]. The latest developments increasingly suggest that hostile aircraft can only be engaged with certainty on parallel or nearly parallel courses, hence that the turret type of equipment will become paramount.[8]

If Churchill had had his way, Fighter Command would have been equipped with the Defiant, which had a rear turret that proved so ineffective against the enemy and so lethal for the crew that it had to be withdrawn from operations almost immediately serious fighting began in May 1940.

Churchill's criticisms of defence preparations became much more muted not just because he was shown official figures which disproved his wilder claims but also because he was involved in the work to devise an effective air defence system for Britain. His contribution was less than helpful. This involvement stemmed from a letter his friend Professor Lindemann had written to *The Times* in August 1934, almost certainly at Churchill's prompting, calling for a major scientific effort in this field. In the early autumn of 1934 Churchill and Lindemann had a meeting with Baldwin when he was on holiday at Aix-les-Bains. By the end of 1934 the Government had set up a scientific committee under Sir Henry Tizard of Imperial College to work on possible methods of air defence. In December the Secretary of State for Air, Lord Londonderry (Churchill's cousin), wrote to Lindemann to tell him about the Tizard committee and invited him to take part in its work. In January 1935 Lindemann replied that he and his friends (presumably Churchill) did not consider the Tizard committee suitable and he therefore refused to join.

When Baldwin became Prime Minister, he replaced Londonderry with Cunliffe-Lister, who was keen to defuse Churchill's criticisms. Baldwin therefore invited Churchill to join the Air Defence Research Committee (ADRC) chaired by Cunliffe-Lister. Churchill promptly agreed on condition Lindemann was made a member of the Tizard committee. Churchill was to remain a member of the ADRC until 1939 and use it as a base for lengthy correspondence with various members of the Government's defence planning team. Lindemann's time on the Tizard committee was much less happy – he was highly disruptive and difficult when his favoured solutions were criticised and this period marked the beginning of a long feud between the two scientists that lasted into the war. When Churchill and Lindemann joined the Government's efforts on air defence, great progress had already been made on the detection of aircraft by radio waves (which later became known as radar). Decisions were made at remarkable speed. The first experimental use of radar was demonstrated on 24 July 1935. The next day the ADRC agreed to go ahead with full development work and within six weeks had decided to build a chain of radar stations along the coast together with a research facility. Before the end of the year the Treasury had agreed to the building of the first four operational stations. It was this work that provided the essential foundations for Fighter Command's success in the Battle of Britain.

Churchill though was deeply unimpressed by radar and the speed with which the ADRC had acted. In a letter to the Minister for the Co-ordination of Defence in May 1936 he said 'on this no progress worth speaking of has been made' and was pessimistic about its chances: 'it is not likely to be perfected for a long time' – his best estimate was ten years before radar would be effective. Churchill was here repeating the views of Lindemann. The latter was keen to see the ADRC concentrate on his pet projects – aerial mines, night operations, infra-red detection and the science fiction idea of placing 'a cloud of substance in the path of an aeroplane to produce detonation'. In June 1936 Churchill circulated a paper to the ADRC, drafted by Lindemann, attacking Tizard over the lack of action on aerial mines. In fact work on the idea had started before Lindemann

joined the committee and it rapidly demonstrated the almost insuperable difficulties of dropping mines from above into the path of
aircraft. Churchill chose to interpret this rejection as a lack of
willingness to take action on air defence. Lindemann then
announced that he would fight the by-election for the Oxford
University Parliamentary seat on a platform of air rearmament (with
Churchill's support). This was the last straw for the other members
of the committee and their protests to Lord Swinton (as Cunliffe-
Lister had become) ensured the establishment of another research
committee minus Lindemann.

Churchill did not resign in support of his friend, preferring to
influence the Government from the inside. Under Lindemann's
influence Churchill remained unconvinced about radar and the
system devised to relay the information it provided to control rooms
from where the fighters were guided on to the bombers. Even after
a visit to Biggin Hill in July 1937, where he was shown in outline
how the system would work (and it lived up to expectations in 1940),
he was not impressed. By 1938 this highly complex system, at the
then frontiers of science and technology, was about to become fully
operational only three years after the first primitive demonstration of
its capabilities. Churchill still withheld all credit for this achievement.
In a letter to the Secretary of State for Air about the work of the
ADRC, he complained: 'I have never seen anything like the slow-
motion picture which the work of this committee has presented' and
'the final result is that we have nothing that will be of any effective
use in the next two years'.[9]

The Government's massive rearmament programme did not of
itself solve any of the difficult foreign policy questions that dominated
the 1930s. The international system was in an unstable state with
the United States and the Soviet Union both standing apart from
international affairs, particularly in Europe. Britain and France
therefore had to face an expansionist Japan in the Far East and a
renascent and increasingly rearmed Germany in Europe virtually
unaided. As Britain still tried to distance itself from Europe, the
French could only rely on the small, weak states created in eastern
Europe at Versailles as allies against Germany. It was generally
recognised that any attempt to produce a new settlement in Europe
would have to involve an adjustment to the Versailles Treaty to
rectify what were seen as its unjust and unsustainable provisions

9a British troops in Murmansk April 1919

9b Churchill reviews British troops, Cologne 1919

10 Churchill with the Prince of Wales, the future King Edward VIII

11a Churchill speaks in favour of Home Rule – Belfast 1912

b The 'Black and Tans' deploy for action 1921

12 Churchill campaigning for his return to Parliament in 1924

13 Churchill at Chartwell, 1924

a Churchill and 'FE'
deep in conversation

b 'The Prof': Frederick Lindemann,
later Lord Cherwell

14 Churchill with his colleagues and advisers

c Churchill as Chancellor of the Exchequer with Prime Minister Stanley Baldwin (centre)
and Foreign Secretary Austen Chamberlain (left)

15 Churchill leaves No 11 Downing Street
to deliver his first Budget speech (1925)

16a Churchill visiting his Epping constituency with Clementine (left) and Diana (centre)

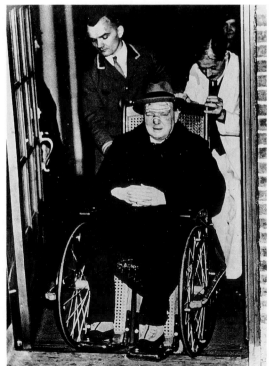

16b Churchill leaving hospital after his road accident in New York, December 1931

affecting Germany. The problem was how to achieve this while maintaining peace and security.

Like the Government, Churchill found it almost impossible to advocate a consistent and straightforward policy. He recognised that the Versailles settlement was unjust. In 1925 he had told the Committee of Imperial Defence that there could be no lasting agreement with Germany 'without a recasting of the arrangements of the Treaty of Versailles as far as the oriental frontiers of Germany are concerned' and he later made it clear that he had 'a substantial rectification' in mind.[10] On 23 November 1932 he told the Commons that these 'rectifications' in eastern Europe (he had in mind specifically the return of Transylvania from Rumania to Hungary and alterations to the Polish corridor to the sea at Danzig, which cut off East Prussia from the rest of Germany) should be made before the French disarmed – 'The removal of the just grievances of the vanquished ought to precede the disarmament of the victors.' Since both the British and French Governments were already thinking about rearmament there was no difference between their policies and Churchill's.

One way in which these grievances might be resolved would be through the League of Nations. In November 1933 Churchill advocated 'an attempt to address Germany collectively' through the League – one of the few occasions in which he endorsed the League's role in resolving disputes. His attitude to the League of Nations was to be highly inconsistent throughout the 1930s. When it was set up after the war, he did not expect it to last more than a few years and had no confidence in its ability to bring some order into the international system. He told the Committee of Imperial Defence in December 1924 that 'he had never considered that the League of Nations, in view of the present state of the world, was in a position to preserve peace'.[11] During the dispute with Japan over Manchuria he backed the Japanese in the first real test of the League's ability to resolve an international dispute and impose a collective solution on an aggressor state. Then in July 1934 he suddenly made a complete change of direction in favour of collective security – 'the League of Nations should be the great instrument upon which all those resolved to maintain peace should centre'.[12] In the same speech he made another equally astonishing volte face. Only two years earlier the Soviet Union had been considered the

373

main threat to peace, ready to sweep across eastern Europe. Now he supported its entry into the League, saying: 'Russia is most deeply desirous of maintaining peace.'

Churchill's new attachment to the League was put to the test within a year after the Italians invaded Abyssinia, and it was found wanting. As might have been expected, given his views of black people, he had little sympathy for one of the two last surviving independent African countries. He told the House of Commons on 24 October 1935 (three weeks after the start of the Italian invasion): 'No one can keep up the pretence that Abyssinia is a fit, worthy and equal member of a league of civilised nations.' His admiration for Mussolini was also unchanged. He told the Anti-Socialist and Anti-Communist Union in that he was 'the greatest lawgiver among living men' and wrote in the *Sunday Chronicle* just five months before the start of the invasion that he was 'a really great man'.[13] Like the Government, Churchill was caught in a dilemma between backing the League through effective sanctions to stop the Italian invasion, thereby providing a clear example of the effectiveness of collective security as a lesson to Germany, or coming to an agreement with Italy at the expense of Abyssinia in order to preserve her as a likely ally against Germany. The Government, under pressure from public opinion that wanted to back the League, vacillated and finally fell between two stools, alienating Italy without strengthening the League. Churchill was more consistent in wanting to reach a deal with Mussolini.

In the summer of 1935, when it seemed virtually certain that an Italian invasion would take place in the autumn, Churchill, along with Austen Chamberlain and opposition leaders, was consulted by the Government about what course to take. All apart from Churchill and Lloyd George advocated a policy of collective security through the League (sanctions of some sort) and based on Anglo-French co-operation. Churchill argued that Germany was the main enemy and therefore nothing should be done to alienate Italy. In his view France was unlikely to agree to more than mild economic sanctions and Britain should do no more than France. As he explained later: 'throughout this business I have strongly advised the Government not to try and take a leading part or to put themselves forward so prominently'. He explained the limits of his commitment to Hoare the Foreign Secretary and Anthony Eden his deputy: they were 'justified in going as far with the League of Nations against Italy as [they] could carry France' but he 'did not expect France would go very far'.[14]

Although Churchill made a strong speech at the City Carlton Club on 26 September aimed at deterring Mussolini from attacking Abyssinia, in private he was trying to suggest how an agreement might be reached. Two days after the speech he saw the Italian Ambassador and told him, as he reported to Vansittart (a strong supporter of Italy), that he hoped it would be possible 'to carry off something' in a meeting between Italy, France and Britain and then impose it on the League as a settlement of the dispute. Specifically Churchill said that he would support the 'claims of Italy to primacy in the Abyssinian sphere' and the 'imperative need for internal reform' in the country. He told Vansittart that he saw such a deal as 'the only chance of avoiding the destruction of Italy as a powerful and friendly factor in Europe'.[15] However at a League meeting in Geneva, under public pressure, the Government had taken a strong line in favour of collective security and sanctions if there was an Italian attack. Churchill disapproved of this policy. He wrote to Austen Chamberlain at the beginning of October, telling him: 'I am very unhappy. It would be a terrible deed to smash up Italy, and it will cost us dear . . . I do not think we ought to have taken the lead in such a vehement way.'[16]

The Government, having backed collective security, decided to call a General Election in order to benefit from the public mood. Although the Labour Party gained 100 seats more than in their catastrophic Electoral performance in 1931, the Government was returned with a majority of nearly 280. In *The Gathering Storm* Churchill castigated Baldwin for calling the Election and accused him of putting party before country. At the time he wrote to Baldwin supporting his decision to call the Election and was fulsome in his praise of the party leader. He told the Conservative Party conference on 4 October that Baldwin was 'a statesman who has gathered to himself a greater volume of confidence and goodwill than any public man I recollect in my long career'. The reason for Churchill's attitude was that he hoped for a recall to government. The India Bill had been passed and Churchill had called off his campaign of opposition. As far as he was concerned, his only reason for being in exile was gone – he never thought that his criticisms of the pace of rearmament were a bar to his return to Government. Unfortunately Churchill's warmth of feeling about Baldwin was not reciprocated. That summer the Prime Minister privately described Churchill as 'a military adventurer who would sell his sword to anyone'.[17]

Throughout the autumn Churchill behaved cautiously so as not to damage his chances of a recall. In the Commons debate three weeks after the invasion he spoke of German rearmament and referred to Abyssinia as 'a very small matter compared with the dangers I have just described'. He hoped there would be a satisfactory peace (at Abyssinia's expense) and then in a long rhetorical passage, designed to support the Government, he spoke of the need to build up the League of Nations (presumably to contain Germany). It was a speech of substantial illogicality and inconsistency, as other speakers in the debate pointed out. How could he support building up the League when he was advocating a deal with Italy at the expense of Abyssinia – the very country which the League was supposed to be supporting?

Churchill decided in October to plan a foreign trip so that he would not have to comment further on the crisis. He left on 10 December for Majorca and Barcelona accompanied by Clementine but she returned to the family for Christmas and Churchill went on to Morocco, where he discovered for the first time the delights of Casablanca and also of the surrounding countryside. He spent the time painting and writing and only returned at the end of January 1936 because of the death of King George V. He left Britain just in time. Within days news broke of the pact Samuel Hoare had negotiated secretly with his French opposite number, Pierre Laval, providing for the Italian take-over of part of Abyssinia. It was the policy that Churchill had favoured all along. Public reaction to this revelation of a cynical deal, at complete variance with the Government's stated aims of supporting the League and sanctions against Italy, was so hostile that the Cabinet decided to throw Hoare to the wolves and accept his resignation. Had Churchill been in the country he would have found it very difficult to attack the Hoare-Laval pact, given his record of trying to appease Italy in the previous months.

For a while the Government took a muted line in favour of the League while ensuring that no effective sanctions were imposed on Italy. Churchill had a low opinion of Anthony Eden, Hoare's replacement, describing him to Clementine as a 'light-weight'.[18] He continued to support the Government's reluctance to impose sanctions. Speaking in the Commons on 6 April, he rightly criticised the Government for falling between two stools but argued that they had been wrong to encourage Abyssinia and other countries at the League and urged that the existing sanctions should be dropped now that the Italian conquest was virtually complete. A fortnight later though he took a strange line in private when talking to his old acquaintance, Maurice Hankey, Secretary to the Cabinet. He advocated giving Italy an ultimatum to come to terms with the League or else Britain would close the Suez Canal, thereby cutting Italian communications with her forces in Somaliland and Abyssinia, a move which would very probably lead to war. At the same time he would also demand French co-operation, with the threat that if they refused 'we should ourselves come to terms with Germany'.[19] A month later he was publicly advocating a pact with Italy for Mediterranean defence.

Once the Italian occupation of Abyssinia was complete, Churchill wanted a swift end to the limited sanctions the League had imposed. He told his constituents on 8 May that they should not be continued just to hurt the Italian people – 'we have no right to go further along that path'. He was also now prepared to claim publicly that the Hoare-Laval pact was 'a very shrewd, far-seeing agreement' and only criticised Hoare for personally concluding the pact after his strong support for League action in September. After the affair his admiration for Mussolini was unchanged. In October 1937 he told the readers of the *News of the World*: 'It would be dangerous folly for the British people to underrate the enduring position in world-history which Mussolini will hold, or the amazing qualities of courage, comprehension, self-control and perseverance which he exemplifies.'[20]

At its second major test in imposing collective security Churchill had again failed to support the League of Nations. Yet despite this public lack of support he still envisaged that the League would have a role to play in containing the rise of Germany. Since 1933, like many other people, he had been alarmed at the consequences of Hitler's accession to power. He was critical of his internal policy, particularly the growing discrimination against the Jews, but less so about the clampdown on the opposition parties such as the Communists and Social Democrats. Churchill's rooted objection to a reviving Germany was a conventional one – the threat it might pose to British interests in the way Imperial Germany had done before the First World War. The problem for the Government, and for Churchill, was to recognise at what point Germany's claims for rectification of what he called her 'legitimate grievances' about the Versailles Treaty became unacceptable demands for a change in the balance of power in Europe. Although in retrospect, when writing his memoirs, Churchill found it easy to decide that Germany should have been opposed and challenged from Hitler's accession to power in 1933, and in that way war would have been avoided, at the time he found it far more difficult to decide on a policy.

One of Germany's grievances was the limitations imposed on her Navy under the Versailles Treaty. In July 1935 the Government reached an agreement with Germany allowing her to rebuild her fleet to thirty-five per cent of the British level. The British found this advantageous because it enabled them to calculate with some precision the size of fleet needed at home if the bulk of the Navy were sent to the Far East to counter Japan. At the time Churchill supported the treaty, calling it 'a separate agreement for ourselves, of a perfectly innocent character'.[21] Only later and in his memoirs did he criticise it as a unilateral renegotiation of the Versailles provisions (which it was). He was constrained at the time, as he was over the Abyssinian crisis, by his hope of a recall to Government. Similar considerations affected his initial reaction to Hitler's decision to take advantage of that crisis and move military forces into the Rhineland, which was a demilitarised zone under the Versailles Treaty. Much later Churchill declared that this was the point at which Britain and France should have acted firmly to remove German forces and bring down Hitler, thus at little cost saving the world from war. At the time he did not take this line. Writing in the *Evening Standard* on 13 March, six days after the German move, he praised the French for their restraint: 'instead of retaliating with arms, as the previous generation would have, France has taken the correct course by appealing to the League of Nations', and he called on Germany to respond by withdrawing voluntarily so as 'to open a new era for all mankind'.

In a debate in the Commons held on 9–10 March Churchill took a similarly restrained line. The new post of Minister for Defence Co-ordination was about to be created and he believed, wrongly, that he was a strong candidate. In his speech he largely ignored the

Rhineland crisis and concentrated instead on defending and encouraging the Government over rearmament. He spoke of the need for defence planning, praised the Government's recent White Paper on defence and commended Chamberlain's ability to control defence spending at the Treasury. Then, notwithstanding his earlier refusal to back the League over Abyssinia, he praised its possible role, saying that if it 'were able to enforce its decree upon one of the most powerful nations of the world found to be an aggressor, then its authority would be set upon so high a pedestal that it must henceforth be the accepted sovereign authority'.

The debate on the Rhineland was held over until 26 March while the Government consulted the other European powers, who all agreed not to take any action. By then Churchill knew that he would not be joining the Government, following the appointment of Sir Thomas Inskip, the Attorney-General, to the post he coveted. He therefore felt freer to take a more critical line in the Commons. He spoke of the deterioration in the international situation since 1931, the possibility of war, Hitler's triumph following his audacious move into the Rhineland and his now secure position in Germany. But he did not call for the use of force to expel German forces nor did he predict war if this was not done. He concentrated on the scale of German rearmament and, overlooking the makeshift nature of German policy and Hitler's determination for political reasons to meet domestic needs as well as military ones, described him as 'making the whole industry of the country an arsenal' and of the population becoming 'one great disciplined war machine'. He again ignored his own views over Abyssinia and called for the 'collective forces of the world' to be invested with 'overwhelming power'. It was a general warning of the potential threat from Germany but it contained little guidance on how to act.

Yet like many others Churchill still hoped that it would be possible to 'appease' Germany and reach a settlement. On 6 April in the Commons he called on the League to invite Germany 'to state her grievances and her legitimate aspirations' so that under the League's auspices 'justice may be done and peace preserved'. It was easy to make general calls for action but much harder to devise specific policies. Churchill himself was unclear about the way ahead. On 19 April he suggested to Maurice Hankey that the League should be used to encircle Germany from the Baltic to the Low Countries,

Switzerland and the Balkans, with the Royal Navy to be based in Soviet ports along the Baltic. He recognised that the British public would only approve of rearmament if it were part of the League's efforts for collective security but personally saw the League as no more than a fig-leaf for an old-fashioned alliance against Germany. On 25 May he wrote to his old friend Violet Bonham-Carter (Asquith's daughter) outlining a very different scenario. If Italy continued to defy the League then he advocated constructing a western pact of Britain, France, Belgium and Holland to deter Germany from attacking in the west. Then, like many of his contemporaries, he expected Hitler would turn eastwards and attack the Soviet Union, and he proposed that Britain should stand aside while his old enemy Bolshevism was destroyed: 'we should have to expect that the Germans would soon begin a war of conquest east and south and that at the same time Japan would attack Russia in the Far East. But Britain and France would maintain a heavily-armed neutrality.'[22] Standing by while members of the League were destroyed by Germany was hardly an example of collective security in operation.

Since his immediate chance of returning to government was now gone, Churchill felt free to engage in more open advocacy of the League as a means of collective defence and as a way of justifying rearmament. This brought him into contact with a number of people and organisations that had been advocating identical policies, together with resistance to Nazi Germany, for several years before he took them up. This fact was always a sensitive point in later years with Churchill. In *The Gathering Storm*, determined to give the impression he was a lone voice, he mentions none of the groups he worked with after the spring of 1936 and implies that he was acting on his own. In later years he also repeatedly tried to prevent the main financier of one of the groups from publishing a book on the subject, a battle he finally lost a few years before his death. In the middle of May 1936, after pressure from Vansittart at the Foreign Office, Churchill for the first time attended a lunch organised by the Anti-Nazi Council, a body formed in 1933 in which Hugh Dalton of the Labour Party and Walter Citrine of the TUC were prominent. The next month he was invited to join the New Commonwealth organisation, which advocated armed collective security through the creation of an international force controlled by the League. He did not respond until he had consulted Neville Chamberlain about the acceptability of the organisation and discovered that the Chancellor of the Exchequer was actually a member. Given this seal of approval, Churchill decided to join. He also began to take a limited part in the activities of an informal group known as the 'Focus for the Defence of Freedom and Peace'. This was a cross-party group of people who met occasionally over lunch to discuss international affairs and organise some meetings and the writing of pamphlets. Churchill found that members included Austen Chamberlain from the Conservatives, the ex-Foreign Secretary Arthur Henderson from Labour and his old friend Archibald Sinclair from the Liberals. The group had the moral support of Vansittart and the Foreign Secretary, Anthony Eden, spoke at its lunches.

In 1936 Churchill's views on collective security remained ambivalent. He told his constituents on 19 October that 'in the present state of the world collective security is no substitute for national self-defence.' In September he made a major speech in Paris in defence of democracy. The month before though he had refused to take part in the International Peace Conference in Brussels run by the man who had devoted most of the last fifteen years to the League – Lord Robert Cecil – and attended by major European figures such as Pierre Cot and Edouard Herriot from France, because he would have to appear on the same platform as Communists.

During the second half of 1936 Churchill made a series of speeches as part of a campaign in favour of collective security and the League. On 26 June he said: 'There is no reason to despair of collective security against the Aggressor. If a sufficient number of powerfully armed nations were ready to enforce economic sanctions, the Aggressor would in many cases have to submit or attack the combination.' On 12 November he made an attack in the Commons on the Government record on foreign policy and preparedness:

> The Government simply cannot make up their minds, or they cannot get the Prime Minister to make up his mind. So they go on in strange paradox, decided only to be undecided, resolved only to be irresolute, adamant for drift, solid for fluidity, all-powerful to be impotent. So we go on preparing more months and years – precious perhaps vital to the greatness of Britain – for the locusts to eat.

It was a brilliant debating speech but Churchill did not put forward an alternative policy. A fortnight later he presided over the New Commonwealth dinner at the Dorchester. On 3 December he was one of the principal speakers at an Albert Hall rally organised by Focus, presided over by Citrine and with twenty other MPs on the platform. In *The Gathering Storm* Churchill implied that this meeting was the last climactic event in his campaign. In fact it was intended to be the first of a series of rallies. The launch of the campaign was aborted because on the night of the Albert Hall rally news of the likely abdication of King Edward VIII broke. In the next few days, through a series of hasty and ill-thought-out actions, he was to destroy much of the credit he had built up since he had called off his campaign on India.

Churchill had long been a friend of Edward VIII. In the 1920s they had played polo together, they regularly dined together and Churchill wrote many of the King's speeches. He was consulted about the King's relationship with the American, Mrs Simpson, by the King's lawyer, Walter Monckton, in early July 1936. He advised that Mrs Simpson should not sue for divorce from her second husband because the case might involve the King and that she should not be invited to Balmoral. His advice was rejected and he was not consulted again. It was not until mid-November, immediately after Mrs Simpson was granted a *decree nisi* that the King formally told Baldwin of his intention to marry her. News of the King's intentions spread rapidly in political circles. The establishment, and later the country, was plunged into a constitutional crisis over the King's wish to marry whom he chose against the mainstream view that he could not marry a divorcee and remain on the throne.

The day after his interview with the King, Baldwin met a Parliamentary delegation to brief them on the crisis. Churchill refused to join, preferring to operate on his own because he backed the King. Through Beaverbrook and Rothermere, who were in touch with the King, he put forward his own solution to the dilemma – a morganatic marriage: the King would marry but Mrs Simpson would not become Queen; she would be made Duchess of Cornwall and the children of the marriage would not inherit the throne. This idea seems to have attracted the King because when he saw Baldwin on 25 November he spoke of public support for a morganatic marriage. Baldwin told the King that there was no such support among the public and certainly the political and religious establishment were strongly opposed to the idea.

On 26 November Baldwin saw the opposition leaders, Attlee and Sinclair, and, significantly, Churchill to discuss what might happen should the King reject the advice of his elected Government. Attlee and Sinclair promised that in these circumstances they would refuse to form an alternative Government thereby offering the King no way of avoiding the advice of the Government that he must abdicate if he wished to marry. Churchill gave a more ambiguous pledge to the effect that 'although his attitude was a little difficult, he would certainly support the government'.[23] Some members of the Cabinet such as Neville Chamberlain did not believe Churchill's pledge and thought he would support the King against the Government. Lord Zetland, Secretary of State for India, wrote to the Viceroy that if the Government resigned 'it seems that the King has been encouraged to believe that Winston Churchill would . . . be prepared to form an alternative Government'.[24]

On 2 December the King told Baldwin that he would marry whatever the consequences. The next day, as the news began to break to the public, Churchill had to be stopped by Citrine from making a long statement on the issue at the Albert Hall rally in support of collective security. On 4 December, with Baldwin's permission, he had a meeting with the King. He urged him not to abdicate and to take time to think, and reassured him that the Government would not dare resign if he simply asked for more time. He also told him that he objected to Baldwin's actions in getting the opposition leaders' agreement beforehand not to form a Government (significantly he did not include himself in this category despite his earlier meeting with Baldwin). According to the King, Churchill's final advice was 'You must allow time for the battalions to march.' The next day he wrote to the King about his intention to launch a campaign to rally support for him.

Churchill was deeply attached to the monarchy and to the hereditary principle. However, his view of the position of the monarch in Britain was perhaps better suited to the eighteenth-century than a twentieth-century democracy. Before making a move, he took advice from Professor J. H. Morgan, a former adviser to the India Defence League, on the possibility of his forming a government. Morgan's view was that if the King insisted on marrying and not abdicating, if Baldwin then resigned and Labour refused to form an alternative Government, the King could call on Churchill to form a Government. Because it would have so little support in Parliament, it would have to consist mainly of non-political figures, but it would nevertheless be the legal Government and entitled to ask for the dissolution of Parliament and to fight an election on the basis of supporting the King against the elected government. Morgan's view of how the royal prerogative could be used bore no relation to politics in a modern democracy.

On the day he received Professor Morgan's advice (5 December) Churchill issued a press statement. He had clearly accepted Morgan's interpretation of the constitutional position and he was seeking to prepare the ground for such action. First he appealed for delay, arguing that nothing could be done until Mrs Simpson's divorce was made absolute in April. A 'hastily extorted' abdication would be an 'outrage'. As he must have known of the King's determination to marry at any cost, it was highly misleading of him to go on to claim, as a way of postponing action, that the marriage 'may conceivably, for various reasons, never be accomplished at all'. He then stated: 'No Ministry has the authority to advise the abdication of the Sovereign.' It was also wrong, he argued, for the Government to seek assurances from the opposition that they would not form an alternative Government. If the King did not accept the advice of the elected Government, they could always resign.

Although he was lobbying hard with the dominions and with his old friend the Ulster Prime Minister, Lord Craigavon, Churchill soon found that this extreme monarchist view had little support apart from in the Beaverbrook and Rothermere press and from the Fascist leader Oswald Mosley. Moreover by 6 December it was also clear that the King was not prepared to fight on in a way that would enable Churchill to become Prime Minister – he had made up his mind to abdicate. Churchill now suggested he should stay on the throne but not marry, although he must have known that such advice would be unacceptable. It was on 7 December that Churchill demonstrated just how far he had misjudged the situation. Baldwin told the Commons that there would be no rushed abdication. Churchill, who had not bothered to read the copy of Baldwin's statement he had been given beforehand, jumped up and in emotional terms pleaded for delay. He was ruled out of order by the Speaker for trying to make a speech and shouted down by his fellow MPs, who believed he was simply acting for himself and not the King. *The Times* described it as 'the most striking rebuff of modern parliamentary history'. Baldwin's prestige soared and Churchill's collapsed. Even friends such as Robert Boothby disowned him.

> I knew that Winston was going to do something dreadful. I had been staying the weekend with him. He was silent and restless and glancing into corners. Now when a dog does that, you know that he is about to be sick on the carpet. It is the same with Winston. He managed to hold it for three days, and then comes up to the House and is sick right across the floor.

Harold Nicolson, one of his admirers, concluded sadly that 'he has undone in five minutes the patient reconstruction work of two years'.[25] Churchill tried belatedly to restore some credibility to his stance, by arguing on 19 December, the day the abdication was signed, that it was not now as hurried as it would have been a few days earlier. It was singularly unconvincing and his political position remained badly damaged by the whole affair.

The abdication crisis coincided with a particularly bad time for Churchill's finances and also with strains within the family, and both were to influence his political activities over the next two years. An invitation to travel to the United States on behalf of Focus on a well-paid lecture tour was withdrawn after his role over the abdication. In February 1937 he received the last of his annual £1,000 advances (totalling £5,000) for his projected book *A History of the English Speaking Peoples*, and could expect no more money until the manuscript was delivered in 1939. He had signed a contract for the history in November 1932 and his earlier historical adviser Keith Feiling was engaged in 1935 to produce the preliminary drafts of fourteen chapters, but with *Marlborough* still uncompleted Churchill could devote no time to finishing this task. He resorted to journalism: between 1936 and 1938 he wrote fortnightly for the *Evening Standard* at £70 a time, and after March 1937 (thanks to his new foreign agent – Imre Revesz, who later changed his name to Emery Reves) these articles were syndicated in twenty-two European papers, bringing the value of each article to about £150. Altogether in 1937 he wrote sixty-four articles for the press to help maintain his income.

In early 1937 Churchill was even thinking of selling Chartwell if an offer of about £25,000 was made. Then in March 1938 his share account plunged into debt after the American stock market collapsed again. In this crisis Chartwell was placed on the market, but rapidly taken off after Brendan Bracken was able to find a financier to bale out his affairs. Sir Henry Strakosch, a wealthy Moravian Jew, who had earlier given Churchill some highly dubious statistics about German rearmament, agreed to take over his share account, effectively write off the debts and indemnify him against any losses. The rescue benefited Churchill by £18,000 (about £350,000 at today's prices). The only known return Strakosch received was membership of the Other Club in 1939.

There was some similarity between the abdication crisis and the Churchill family's domestic crisis. However he showed considerably less sympathy when his daughter wanted to marry a twice-married man than he did towards King Edward VIII's problems. Sarah, always the most unconventional member of the family, had persuaded her parents to allow her to go on the stage in the autumn of 1935. There she met Vic Oliver, a comedian who was seventeen years older than her, twice married and with a mistress in New York. Almost immediately she told her parents that she intended to marry him. This was not at all the sort of man Churchill wanted his daughter to marry. When he met Oliver in February 1936, he refused to shake his hand and spent a long time bullying him, and he later described him to Clementine as 'common as dirt'.[26] He did everything he could think of to stop the affair. He hired a shady New York lawyer to investigate Oliver, his wives and mistress and tried to stir up trouble with the first wife, who was living in Vienna. Then, while Churchill was on holiday in the south of France, Sarah fled to New York. Randolph was despatched, in the full glare of publicity from the British and American media, to bring her back but failed. In December 1936 Sarah and Oliver were married in New York.

Of Churchill's other children, only Mary, growing up away from the family under the care of 'Moppett', caused no trouble in the family circle. Randolph, difficult as a child, had developed into an arrogant, loutish, aggressive individual who showed even less judgement and respect for other people's feelings than his father. Bent on a political career, he fought by-election after by-election as an unofficial candidate, often to the embarrassment of Churchill, and with a total lack of success. The relations between father and son were as bad as between Churchill and Lord Randolph. In the mid-1920s when Churchill learnt that Randolph wanted to leave Eton and go to Oxford he wrote to him that he was disappointed to learn 'how little you are using your abilities and opportunities at Eton. You will certainly not go to Oxford unless you show some aptitude and love for learning ... It would give me more pleasure to hear something creditable about you from your masters.' Randolph's housemaster had already said of him that 'He will never persuade himself that he is wrong, and becomes quite intolerable for everyone.'[27] Randolph did eventually go to Oxford – Professor Lindemann ensured him a place at his college. In 1931 Churchill paid off Randolph's large gambling debt of £600 even though he continued to maintain a large car and chauffeur. He told his son:

> I grieve more than is worth setting down to see you with so many gifts & so much good treatment from the world leading the life of a selfish exploiter, borrowing & spending every shilling you can lay yr hands upon, & ever increasing the lavish folly of yr ways. But words are useless.[28]

The quarrels between father and son grew worse during Randolph's by-election forays – Churchill told Clementine after one contest in 1934: 'he does not wish to consider any other interests but his own and we have had sharp words upon the subject'.[29] The periods of reconciliation were usually short-lived and their worst row occurred in February 1938 when Randolph accused his father of trying to curry favour with the Government by giving a small gift to the Secretary of State for War, Leslie Hore-Belisha. Churchill refused to speak for the rest of the meal, rejected Randolph's written apology and wrote to him that: 'I really did not & do not want such a thing to happen again. I do not see why at my age I shd be subjected to such taunts from a son I have tried to do my best for.'[30]

In 1932, Churchill's other daughter, Diana, had married the son of Churchill's financial supporter, Abe Bailey, at one of the big social events of the year. The service was held in St Margaret's, Westminster, and the Duke of Marlborough lent his house in Carlton Terrace for the reception. Diana's husband turned out to be an alcoholic and they were separated within a year. In September 1935 she married the rising Conservative politician, Duncan Sandys.

One of the reasons the children, in particular Diana, wanted to leave home at the first opportunity was that they found the atmosphere at Chartwell impossible. Churchill, deprived of power in the political world, imposed his will within the family circle. Life at Chartwell revolved around him and his demands. Family, servants, secretaries and researchers were all expected to fall in with his requirements, including his habit of not starting to dictate his books until long after dinner and continuing into the small hours of the morning. At mealtimes Churchill would hold forth at immense length in front of the family and his small band of sycophantic followers such as Bracken and Lindemann.

He was equally insensitive to others when he was on one of his regular holidays at the expense of wealthy friends – he virtually never took a holiday at his own expense. One less than impressed observer of Churchill at this time was the actor Peter Willes, who met him when they were both staying in the south of France in August 1933:

> At meals he just banged on and on, regardless of anybody else's interests or desire to talk; and if you weren't deeply involved in politics . . . he really was a most dreadful bore. All he seemed to do was smoke cigars, eat, drink and talk far more than anybody else, and never give a damn what anybody thought about him.[31]

The 1930s was also a time when Churchill's heavy drinking became a serious problem, probably as some form of compensation for the depression caused by his exclusion from power. A typical day's imbibing would begin in mid-morning with a whisky and soda and continue through a bottle of champagne at lunch, more whisky and soda in the afternoon, sherry before dinner, another bottle of champagne during dinner, the best part of a bottle of brandy after dinner, and would end with a final whisky and soda before going to bed. On occasions he drank even more than this. His friends were naturally worried: Rothermere even bet him £2,000 he could not give up alcohol during 1936. Churchill refused this bet, although he agreed to give up spirits for the year and won a revised bet of £600. He took the same amount of money off Rothermere for 1937 and 1938 but must have cheated, because at one dinner at Oxford in

May 1937 a fellow guest noted that Churchill refused all the wines but drank eleven whiskys and soda during the meal. Rothermere did not renew the bet for 1939.

The family problems, Churchill's drinking, his egotism and Clementine's bouts of depressions during the menopause meant that the state of the Churchills' marriage in the mid- and late-1930s was no better than in the past. They often lived apart – Churchill at Chartwell working on his books and articles, Clementine, who still disliked the house, staying at their flat in London and seeing her own friends. When in London Churchill did not stay at the flat but instead lived with Brendan Bracken. In December 1934 Clementine left for a five month cruise to the Dutch East Indies on Lord Moyne's yacht. On the boat she fell in love with Terence Philip, who was seven years her junior and almost certainly homosexual. Churchill wrote to her regularly but Clementine rarely replied, glad to be away from a life from which she gained little satisfaction. She continued to see Philip for two years after her return to Britain. Churchill and Clementine continued to take separate holidays. In the summer of 1935 Churchill rejected the idea of a joint holiday in Spain and went off on his own to the south of France. That winter Clementine started regular skiing holidays in Austria or Switzerland with her sister-in-law, Goonie, and her daughter Mary. Churchill normally went to the south of France at this time of the year. The relationship was so bad in the winter of 1936–7 after the abdication crisis and Sarah's marriage that Clementine was talking to her friends of divorce. The pattern of usually living apart and taking separate holidays continued for the remainder of the 1930s. When Clementine again went with Lord Moyne for a cruise to the West Indies in the autumn of 1938 (he spent his spare time chairing a Royal Commission on the islands), Churchill did not write to her for over a month and when he did, could not be bothered to write personally as before and the letters were dictated to his secretary.

Churchill's financial problems after 1936 restricted the amount of time he devoted to politics. Although he had expected a period of international crises, 1937 turned out to be tranquil for most of Europe. In January Lord Davies asked him to continue his support of the League with a regular series of public meetings throughout the year to help build public support for rearmament and collective security. Churchill refused, on the grounds that Davies tended to 'overrate the value of public meetings' and that a campaign would achieve little.[32] Within the Focus group Churchill did nothing but speak at the occasional lunch and left it to others to do the fund-raising and organising.

For many people the main foreign policy issue at this time was the Spanish Civil War, which had begun in August 1936 when a group of right-wing Army officers, led by General Franco, attempted to overthrow the legitimate republican government. As the revolt developed into a long-drawn-out and bitter conflict that increasingly involved Italy and Germany on behalf of the insurgents and the Soviet Union on the side of the Government, opinion was polarised between those who thought Fascism should be opposed at every opportunity and those who feared social revolution. In *The Gathering Storm* Churchill wrote, 'In this quarrel I was neutral'.[33] He was nothing of the sort. As might have been expected given his earlier views, all his sympathies were with Franco and the nationalist side. His military adviser on the Marlborough biography, Brigadier Packenham-Walsh, wrote in his diary after a visit to Chartwell in October 1937, 'Winston says at heart he is for Franco.'[34]

The articles Churchill wrote at this time made it very clear which side he supported. He was convinced that the civil war was the result not of an Army coup but of Communist intrigues. On 10 August 1936 he wrote of the Republican Government 'falling into the grip of dark, violent forces coming ever more plainly into the open, and operating by murder, pillage and industrial disturbances'. He described the legitimate Government and Republican side as 'a poverty stricken and backward proletariat demand[ing] the overthrow of Church, State and property and the inauguration of a Communist regime'. Against them stood the 'patriotic, religious and bourgeois forces, under the leadership of the army, and sustained by the countryside in many provinces . . . marching to re-establish order by setting up a military dictatorship'. Although he thought, as did the Government, that Britain should stay out of the quarrel, he concluded that 'revivified Fascist Spain in closest sympathy with Italy and Germany is one kind of disaster. A Communist Spain spreading its snaky tentacles through Portugal and France is another, and many will think the worse.'[35] For him the Communist threat was still uppermost in his mind. However, when he came to reprint an article on Spain dated 4 September 1936 in a book of collected speeches and writings, he removed the passage that said Britain 'must also discern and unmask the many false pretences under which Communism advances among her Continental friends, and even tries to rear its head at home' – by then he supported an alliance with the Soviet Union.

In the autumn of 1936 Churchill refused to shake hands with the Republic's ambassador in London, although he regularly saw Franco's representative and used propaganda he supplied on Government 'atrocities' in his articles. In these articles he usually referred to Franco's supporters as 'the anti-Red movement' and the legitimate Government as 'the Communist, Anarchist and Syndicalist forces'. There is also evidence of him applying double standards on the fighting. Massacres of civilians and prisoners were 'butcheries' when carried out by Republican forces, but he condoned Franco's decision 'to shoot a proportion of their prisoners taken in arms', saying they were not the same as the 'atrocities' committed by their opponents. In July 1937, speaking in the Commons, he called for recognition of Franco as the legitimate government, although privately he thought that the outcome of the war ought to be a restoration of the monarchy. In December 1938, with Franco just weeks away from final victory, Churchill underwent another of his remarkable changes of mind. He now recognised the dangers inherent in a Franco victory and backed the Republican Government, which he had abused for over two years. On 30 December he concluded, 'It would seem today the British Empire would run far less risk from the victory of the Spanish government than from that of General Franco.'

The main domestic political event of 1937 was the retirement of Stanley Baldwin and his replacement by Neville Chamberlain at the end of May. Churchill had deliberately stayed in Britain that month on the offchance that he might be invited to join the reconstructed Government, but he did not really expect an offer and his realism was justified. Nevertheless, as the most senior Conservative backbencher, he seconded Lord Derby's nomination of Chamberlain as party leader in a fulsome speech (a fact he forgot when writing *The Gathering Storm*). He also defended Chamberlain on his first appearance in the Commons as Prime Minister. Throughout 1937 he made almost no public criticisms of the Government. He welcomed the defence White Paper of February 1937 with its commitment to further increases in the rearmament programme, and he was in regular and helpful correspondence with Government ministers, in particular Eden at the Foreign Office and Hore-Belisha at the War Office.

The new Government began a review of Britain's strategic position, which had deteriorated significantly since rearmament plans were drawn up in 1933–4. Then it had been assumed that Italy would not be a hostile power. Indeed one of the official reports of November 1935 concluded:

> It is a cardinal requirement of our national and Imperial security that our foreign policy should be so conducted as to avoid the possible development of the situation in which we might be confronted simultaneously with the hostility of Japan in the Far East, Germany in the west and any power on the main line of communication between the two.[36]

That was why the Government (and Churchill) had been anxious to avoid alienating Italy over Abyssinia. But by 1937, as Italy drew ever closer to Germany the Government concluded that it would have to be treated as a possible enemy in any war.

Britain now had to face three threats spread across the globe but with only the economic, financial and military resources to at best deter, and if necessary fight, one of the potential enemies. It was a terrible dilemma. The chiefs of staff concluded in November 1937:

> We cannot forsee the time when our defence forces will be strong enough to safeguard our territory, trade and vital interests against Germany, Italy and Japan simultaneously. We cannot, therefore, exaggerate the importance, from the point of view of Imperial defence, of any political or international action that can be taken to reduce the number of our potential enemies or to gain the support of potential allies.[37]

Given this military advice the Government decided that diplomacy had to accompany rearmament and part of that effort would have to be an exploration of a possible accommodation with Italy or Germany that might avert war in the immediate future. (An immediate deal with Japan was ruled out because of her attack on China, which had begun in the summer of 1937.) A deal with Italy would have to recognise her conquest of Abyssinia but might improve the situation in the Mediterranean. As for Germany, although Hitler had rearmed the country, he had not threatened external aggression (the Rhineland crisis was regarded as an internal matter) and there was no reason to suppose that an expansionist programme was inevitable. Lord Halifax (as Churchill's old opponent over India, Lord Irwin, had become) was sent on a spurious hunting trip to Germany to open contacts in the autumn of 1937.

Churchill, like most of his contemporaries, did not condemn Hitler out of hand and did not foresee that he would inevitably lead Germany, Europe and the world to catastrophe. In 1937 in his book of collected essays entitled *Great Contemporaries*, he published a less fulsome assessment of Hitler than the one he wrote in 1935. Even so, while he attacked what he called 'the darker side of his work and creed' – his Jewish policy and internal repression – he praised what Hitler had achieved. On his rise to power he swallowed the Nazi propaganda line and wrote:

> the story of that struggle, cannot be read without admiration for the courage, the perseverance, and the vital force which enabled him to challenge, defy, conciliate or overcome, all the authority or resistances which barred his path.

Even after the violent internal purge of 1934, the suppression of all opposition and the setting up of concentration camps, he still seems to have hoped that Hitler would develop into a duplicate of Mussolini, whom he admired so much. He wrote:

> Although no subsequent political action can condone wrong deeds, history is replete with examples of men who have risen to power by employing stern, grim and even frightful methods, but who nevertheless, when their life is revealed as a whole, have been regarded as great figures whose lives have enriched the story of mankind. So may it be with Hitler.

On 17 September 1937 he could still write that 'One may dislike Hitler's system and yet admire his patriotic achievement. If our country were defeated I hope we should find a champion as indomitable to restore our courage and lead us back to our place among the nations.' Even as late as July 1938, when he was asked by the Nazi Gauleiter of Danzig whether German discriminatory legislation against the Jews would prevent an understanding with Britain, Churchill thought 'it was a hindrance and an irritation, but probably not a complete obstacle to a working agreement, though it might be to comprehension'.[38]

In 1937 the idea of coming to terms with Hitler was not something that Churchill ruled out. He, like the Government, was unsure about future developments in Germany, and he generally endorsed the Government's foreign policy. On 7 October 1937 he spoke at the Conservative Party conference at Scarborough. He took the opportunity to make it clear that his opposition to Government policy not just on India but also on rearmament was over and he also ringingly endorsed Chamberlain's foreign policy. He praised 'the great effort for rearmament' and continued:

> I used to come here year after year when we had some differences between ourselves about rearmament and also about a place called India. So I thought it would only be right that I should come here when we are all agreed . . . let us indeed support the foreign policy of our Government, which commands the trust, comprehension, and the comradeship of peace-loving and law-respecting nations in all parts of the world.

A week later in the *Evening Standard* he told his readers that 'War is NOT imminent'. He emphasised that dictators had to be dealt with from strength and that the Government was now in that position. Three or four years earlier he had been 'a loud alarmist' but despite the dangers the Government had taken action: 'great efforts are being made to meet them'. He did not think that the balance of armaments would continue to shift in favour of Britain and France and so now was indeed a good time to try and reach an agreement with Germany and Italy. He concluded with a biblical quotation: 'Agree with thine adversary quickly whilst thou art in the way with him.'[39]

Just before Christmas, in the Commons debate following Halifax's visit to Germany, Churchill expressed his confidence that the worst was now over. He felt convinced that the French and British forces 'in spite of their tardiness in making air preparations, constitute so vast and formidable a body that they will very likely be left alone undisturbed, at any rate for some time to come'.[40] Privately he told his old friend General Ironside (the Commander of British Forces at Murmansk in 1919) that Germany was unlikely to attempt any forceful action before 1940 and that the most likely threat in the intervening period came from Japan.

Churchill's optimistic mood, which reflected the fact that after nearly five years in power Hitler had made no move against his neighbours and the knowledge that rearmament had strengthened Britain's position in the meantime, was to be rudely shattered by the events of 1938. Indeed at the very moment that Churchill was suggesting an agreement with Germany and Italy, Hitler was outlining to his top advisers his plans for dismantling the remaining parts of the Versailles structure through pressure on his neighbours and if necessary war. The first crisis of the year though came within the British Government. The Foreign Secretary, Anthony Eden, resigned after a dispute with Chamberlain about whether and how to approach Italy, although equally important was a growing temperamental difference and animosity between the two. Speaking in the Commons on 22 February, Churchill made a careful and restrained speech, starting a process of distancing himself from the foreign policy of the Government, and mixing personal praise for Eden (unlike his view of him two years earlier) with a warning to the Government that at some point they would have to make a stand against the dictators. He did not offer a view as to when this point might arise. As for the Italians, he was still prepared to endorse appeasement. He said that if they would help Britain and France maintain Austrian independence 'I would go as far as any man in making concessions', though he thought the Italians would not help.

Events over the next couple of weeks indeed showed that Italy was prepared to stand by and watch Germany incorporate Austria into the Reich, contrary to the provisions of Versailles. Hitler, through a mixture of internal disruption provoked by the Austrian Nazi movement and bullying of the Austrian Government, managed to precipitate a peaceful *Anschluss*. Churchill, like the Government and most of his fellow politicians, found it difficult to decide how to react to what seemed to be a highly popular peaceful union of the two countries. During the ensuing debate in the Commons on 14 March he did not advocate the use of force to remove German forces from Austria. The only action he called for in the short term was discussion between diplomats at Geneva. The *Anschluss* did not qualify as the point at which to make a stand, but it changed Churchill's view of likely developments in the next few years. The optimism of the end of 1937 had disappeared and he believed there was now a pressing need for action, though not by Britain alone. He called for a 'grand alliance' to be built around Britain and France, although under the auspices of the League. He then called for a 'moral basis' for British policy. He did not define what this meant and it was in stark contrast with his *realpolitik* views over Manchuria and Abyssinia. He believed that if this new policy 'were sustained, as it would be, by the moral sense of the world; and if it were done in the year 1938 – and, believe me, it may be the last chance there will be for doing it – then I say you might even now arrest this approaching war'.

Later in the month he travelled to Paris and met various French politicians. In these meetings he advocated an Anglo-French military alliance and agreements with the states of eastern Europe and the Balkans. On 19 March the Soviet Union offered a four power conference involving Britain, France and the United States. The British Government rejected the idea and in a Commons debate on 24 March Churchill did not refer to the offer. Yet within a few weeks he called for an opening to the Soviet Union – the Bolshevik revolutionary state had been miraculously transformed from the source of all evil into a country that sought 'no military aggression upon its neighbours, a country whose interests are peace'. Under Churchill's revised view of affairs, the Soviet Union was to be part of a network of alliances involving the states of eastern Europe and the Balkans, although his comments did not acknowledge the obstacles to constructing such an alliance when many of the small states bordering the Soviet Union took a less sanguine view of its long-term aims than he now did.

It was in the debate on 24 March that Churchill, still reluctant to make specific suggestions on policy, made an impassioned plea. The speech is often portrayed, in retrospect, as a rallying cry to stand firm against the ruthless advance of the dictators. But at the time it must have been difficult to draw from it any very firm guidance as to what Britain should actually do. Like many of his speeches on India, it was about the need for Britain to go back to what he believed were its old values and ideals, to rediscover a glorious but mythical past:

Now is the time at last to rouse the nation. Perhaps it is the last time it can be roused with a chance of preventing war, or with a chance of coming through to victory should our efforts to prevent war fail. We should lay aside every hindrance and endeavour by uniting the whole force and spirit of our people to raise again a great British nation standing up before all the world; for such a nation, rising in its ancient vigour, can even at this hour save civilization.

Despite the fine rhetoric his own ability to rouse the House of Commons was in doubt. Many MPs objected to his habit (in part attributable his desperate need to make money from journalism) of only appearing in the chamber when he was to speak and leaving again rapidly without listening to other speeches in the debate. He had very few followers – Bracken, and occasionally Macmillan. He was shunned by the largest groups of dissenters over foreign policy within the Conservative Party centred around Eden (mainly younger MPs) and Amery (mainly the pro-imperialist group). Neither grouping wanted to have much to do with Churchill, who was regarded as far too unreliable and too willing to use others for his own ends. Nor was he particularly influential in the country – a book of his collected speeches and journalism, *Arms and the Covenant*, only sold about half its print run.

After the *Anschluss* the foremost foreign policy issue was the future of Czechoslovakia and in particular the Sudetenland, a German area given to the new state at Versailles in an attempt to provide it with defensible frontiers. Hitler was exploiting the grievances of the German population to back their demand for union with Germany, at a time when the *Anschluss* had made Czechoslovakia indefensible by placing German forces on three sides of the country. Although Britain (unlike France) had no treaty obligation to support Czechoslovakia, there was a case for upholding the 1919 settlement and resisting this new form of German expansionism. But there were also some strong reasons for not doing so, or at least not to the point of fighting a war. The British Government accepted that the Sudeten Germans had a legitimate grievance and that it would be difficult to oppose self-determination and fight to stop them joining Germany, if a free vote showed this was what they wanted. They were also advised by the chiefs of staff that Czechoslovakia's military position

397

was hopeless: 'No pressure that we and our possible Allies can bring to bear, either by sea, or land or in the air, could prevent Germany from invading and overrunning Bohemia and from inflicting a decisive defeat on the Czechoslovakian army.'[41] In order to liberate Czechoslovakia it would then be necessary to defeat Germany, with the probability that Italy and Japan would join the war. Neither Britain or France wanted to begin a world war over such an issue. They therefore resorted to diplomacy. The first British move was a 'mediation' mission designed to persuade the Czech Government to make enough concessions to their German minority to defuse the demand for union with Germany.

Churchill, who after many refusals was undertaking a national speaking tour organised by Focus and the League of Nations Union, endorsed the Government's approach to defusing the Czech crisis. In Sheffield on 31 May he said that outside support for Czechoslovakia meant that the Czech Government had to be 'all the more earnest to meet the legitimate grievances of the German people in their country'. He had earlier taken the same line when he entertained the Sudeten German leader, the Nazi Conrad Henlein, to lunch at his flat in London on 13 May. Although he warned Henlein against any attack on Czechoslovakia, they discussed a possible scheme of devolution for the region. Churchill endorsed the idea as a possible solution, and passed details to the Czech leader Jan Masaryk. At this point he was therefore actively supporting the efforts of the Chamberlain Government to persuade the Czechs to make substantial concessions over the future of the Sudetenland in the hope of preserving the country's integrity. On 18 August, in an article in the *Daily Telegraph*, he argued in favour of autonomy for the Sudeten Germans. On 27 August he told his constituents that the Czechs were 'doing their utmost to put their house in order' and an agreement that was 'not designed to compass their ruin as a state' was possible.

Nevertheless there were growing signs during August that such an agreement would not be possible and that Hitler might decide to use the Sudeten issue as a pretext to attack Czechoslovakia. At the end of the month Churchill suggested to Halifax, the Foreign Secretary, that there should be a joint note from Britain, France and the Soviet Union calling for a settlement and voicing a general warning to Germany about the consequences of any aggression. In the first week of September Henlein, after talks with Hitler, rejected the limited autonomy offer made by the Prague Government. So far Chamberlain's Government and Churchill had been united in a policy of putting diplomatic pressure on the Czechoslovak Government. On 7 September, in an editorial inspired by the Foreign Office, *The Times* suggested the cession of the Sudetenland to Germany. In a desperate attempt to avoid war, the Government was about to embark on the hazardous course of trying to persuade Hitler to accept a peaceful transfer of the Sudetenland and then pressurising the Czechoslovak Government into giving up part of their country. They accordingly refused to give the French any assurance of support so as to increase pressure on the Prague Government.

It was at this point that Churchill parted company with the Government's policy. On 9 September he went to No 10 and also saw Halifax. Both then, and two days later in similar meetings, he demanded that they support France and issue an immediate ultimatum declaring that any German attack on Czechoslovakia would mean war. Chamberlain, who was about to fly to his first meeting with Hitler (about which Churchill was unaware), never contemplated such action. Churchill first put his ideas to the public in the *Daily Telegraph* on 15 September, when he spoke of Czech resistance to a German attack lasting three to four weeks (which was probably optimistic) and suggested that this might lead to a 'crusade' against the aggressor (a rather romantic way of describing a European war). After his first meeting with Hitler, Chamberlain persuaded the French to accept the idea of a plebiscite in the disputed Sudeten region and an Anglo-French guarantee of the remainder of Czechoslovakia after the inevitable vote to join Germany. The French agreed to put joint pressure on the Czechs to accept. Churchill met Halifax on 19 September and was told that the French were reluctant to fight for the present Czech frontiers and against the principle of self-determination in the Sudeten region.

The next day Churchill left for Paris to try and undermine the British Government's policy by suggesting the French should take a firmer stand against the British proposals. (There is also some evidence that he was in touch with the Czechs advising them to stand firm because Chamberlain was about to fall.) In Paris he saw Paul Reynaud and George Mandel, two dissident members of the

French Cabinet, who had little influence. On his return he issued a press statement on 21 September condemning Anglo-French pressure for the dismemberment of Czechoslovakia. His policy was war unless Hitler backed down.

On 22 September, with Chamberlain at Bad Godesberg for his second meeting with Hitler, members of the various dissident groups on the Government side of the Commons met together for the first time at Churchill's flat to plan what to do. Hobbled by the fact that Parliament was not in session, they decided to wait and see what terms Chamberlain could negotiate. On 25 September the Cabinet refused to accept these terms – automatic transfer of the Sudetenland without a plebiscite – and prepared for war. Churchill saw Chamberlain and Halifax at No 10 the next day and urged an Anglo-French declaration of solidarity, possibly involving the Soviet Union too. The Government had already agreed to a formal Anglo-French alliance and war if Czechoslovakia were attacked. The dissidents met again that night. With the Government moving rapidly towards war, they talked at length but agreed nothing – it was difficult to see what they could do or demand; they were powerless. On 27 September the fleet was mobilised and Churchill issued a statement supporting the Government. When the Czechs complained to him about British pressure on them, he told them they could expect no more and slammed down the phone.

With war now imminent, Chamberlain announced to a stunned and joyful House of Commons, meeting for the first time during the crisis on 28 September, that Hitler had just accepted Mussolini's invitation to an international conference in Munich and that he would be flying immediately to take part. Churchill wished him 'God Speed' and issued a press statement. In it he recognised that the Munich conference would lead to the dismemberment of Czechoslovakia and so avoid war but warned that the danger to the democracies was not over and the balance of power was tipping against them. The next day he wanted to send a telegram to Chamberlain in Munich saying that any more pressure on the Czechoslovaks would lead to a Parliamentary revolt. Eden and Attlee, realising that the principle of carving up the country had already been conceded and that the argument was now only over the method, refused to agree. That evening there was a bitter row at the Other Club over the crisis and no agreement about what to do. The terms agreed at the Munich conference – occupation of the German areas of the Sudetenland almost immediately and a plebiscite elsewhere (a marginal concession by Hitler on the Godesberg terms) – and more important the avoidance of war, were greeted with huge relief throughout the country.

Churchill spoke towards the end of the three-day Commons debate on Munich. He followed the line taken by the Labour leader Clement Attlee, who said, 'We are in the midst of a tragedy. We have felt humiliation. This has not been a victory for reason and humanity. It has been a victory for brute force.' Churchill said, 'We have sustained a total and unmitigated defeat, and France has suffered even more than we have.' Like many others in the debate, he forecast the rapid end of what was left of Czechoslovakia but also expected a long process of British decline unless there was 'a supreme recovery of moral health and martial vigour' and the country took its 'stand for freedom'. He closed by warning, 'And do not suppose that this is the end. This is only the beginning of the reckoning.' It was a fine speech but the most important intervention in the debate came from a senior Conservative backbencher, Sir Sidney Herbert, making his last speech in the chamber. He protested about the threat of an Election from the Government Whips and a 'coupon' against those not supporting the Government – it was enough to stop any thoughts Chamberlain might have had of a quick Election to cash in on the mood of relief sweeping the country. The Conservative rebels, joined by Duff Cooper, the First Lord of the Admiralty who resigned over the Munich agreement, decided not to vote against the Government and just over twenty, including Churchill, abstained – it was about a quarter of the rebel strength over India.

Churchill was immensely disheartened by Munich although uncertain about what to do next. He wrote to Paul Reynaud that it was the worst defeat for Britain since 1783 and France since 1870. He even considered whether it might be best for Britain and France to do a deal with Hitler: 'The question now presenting itself is: Can we make head against the Nazi domination, or ought we *severally* to make the best terms possible with it – while trying to rearm? Or is a common effort still possible? . . . I do not know on what to rest today.'[42] He felt that the public mood was still too pro-Munich for any campaign to have an effect. He rejected the suggestion of a national speaking tour, saying, 'I am afraid that making speeches in the country no longer has the old effect' and reflected that his tour earlier in the year 'did not seem to produce the slightest result'.[43] He also turned down an invitation to speak at the Oxford Union.

One of the reasons for Churchill's caution about a public campaign was that he, like the other Munich dissenters, was under pressure within the party. Although he won a vote of confidence from his constituency association at the beginning of November by 100 votes to forty-four, there was still considerable opposition and disquiet and he had to proceed carefully against what he described as the 'dirty Tory hacks who would like to drive me out of the Party'.[44] He did not support the anti-appeasement candidate, A. D. Lindsay, at the Oxford by-election in November because he was standing against a Conservative (Quintin Hogg), even though the latter was strongly pro-appeasement. His one rebellion in the Commons was on a Liberal motion to create a Ministry of Supply to manage the rearmament programme: he called on fifty Conservatives to vote against the Government and force it to act. He was joined only by his two faithful followers, Bracken and Macmillan. Despite his earlier notes of dissent, it was the first time that Churchill had actually voted against the Government over rearmament or foreign policy.

At the end of 1938 Churchill was aged sixty-four years old and he appeared to be reaching the end of his career. It was ten years since he had been in government; his extremist views on India had been ignored; his warnings on rearmament had been overtaken, as he himself admitted, by the Government's major increase in defence spending; and his warnings about the threats facing Britain and the policies required to counter them lacked consistency and clarity. Within his own party and in Parliament he was isolated and largely ignored. Yet within eighteen months, in one of the most remarkable of modern political transformations, he was to achieve his life's ambition and become Prime Minister.

Part 3

TRIUMPH AND REJECTION

1939–1945

18

The Road to Power

For the first eight months of 1939 Churchill's main preoccupation was not politics or foreign policy but writing. He was due to deliver the manuscript of *A History of the English Speaking Peoples* by the end of the year and he badly needed the £12,000 he would then receive. A small army of research assistants was enlisted to write different parts of the book – Maurice Ashley (the Stuarts and Cromwell), John Wheldon (the Tudors), George Young (most of the early chapters), General Edmonds (American Civil War) and Alan Bullock (Australia and New Zealand), with William Deakin acting as Churchill's personal assistant. Churchill himself was writing furiously at the rate of over 1,000 words a day after August 1938 – by the outbreak of war over 530,000 words were written although not all of them had been finally revised. He also produced his usual crop of newspaper articles to earn immediate money, being careful, as usual, to clear all his articles about foreign countries with the Foreign Office to ensure that he did not embarrass the Government.

All this activity meant that he turned down virtually every speaking engagement he was offered, including two appeals from the League of Nations Union to lead a campaign to alert the public. He was also very loath to criticise the Government. Speaking in one of his rare appearances in the Commons on 21 February, he admitted that aircraft production was increasing rapdily, that 1939 would see 'a very great accretion to our defensive strength', which would equal Germany's front-line forces, and he supported 'the very great exertions' the Government was making on defence. He told his constituents on 10 March that he would 'cordially support' the Government's defence preparations and found 'much to approve' in its foreign policy. Although he did not withdraw any of the criticisms he had made of Munich, he added, 'I recognise, however, that the fact that the Prime Minister is known to be a sincere worker for peace has had a good effect upon the populations of the dictator countries.' At this time he had in his sights the post of Minister of Supply, the necessity for which the Government now accepted. Five days after this speech German troops occupied Prague and dismembered what remained of post-Munich Czechoslovakia. It was the first time Hitler had gone beyond his demands for a revision of the Versailles provisions affecting Germany. The day before the occupation Churchill, agreeing with the Government's policy, had argued there was no point in helping Czechoslovakia now when nothing had been done in the previous autumn: 'I agree entirely with those who think we should not intervene at the present time. We cannot. That is the end of it.'

After the rapid overthrow of the Munich agreement the backbench attack on the Government's foreign policy was carried out by Eden and his group. Churchill felt that the Government was now adopting the foreign policy he wanted, that public opinion was moving in his favour and that there was no need to be more than a constructive critic. On 22 March he told Margot Asquith that his relations with the Government were good and two days later he refused to sign an appeal for national service to be introduced when it was circulated by the Amery group of dissenters, on the grounds that the Government was already working on a scheme. (Conscription was introduced for the first time in peace on 24 April.) He did however, together with thirty other backbenchers, sign an appeal for a national government drawn up by the Eden group. He approved the guarantees given to Poland, Rumania and Greece at the end of March and told the Commons on 3 April that there was 'almost complete agreement' between him and the Government on foreign policy. He argued that Chamberlain was trying to build the 'Grand Alliance' against Germany which he had advocated and warned 'we cannot afford to fail . . . It has become a matter of life and death'.

Before making a speech in the Commons on 13 April he saw Chamberlain to reassure him his criticism was only constructive. He invited the Conservative Chief Whip, Margesson, to dinner after-wards and told him of his 'strong desire' to enter the Government. He said he was happy to work with Chamberlain, who had many admirable qualities, and expressed a preference for the Admiralty, or failing that a non-departmental job co-ordinating defence. He wanted Eden to be recalled too, although he told Margesson that he had more to offer than the former Foreign Secretary. Churchill's request was not met, and he was passed over when the Ministry of Supply was set up five days later. Nevertheless he was hopeful about his prospects. Expecting war within a few months, he felt confident that it would produce his recall. Meanwhile there was little he needed to do apart from wait on events which appeared to be moving in his favour. Demands in the newspapers for his recall were on the increase: Churchill was portrayed (understandably but not very accurately) as the man who had foreseen and warned about all that had happened. An opinion poll in the *News Chronicle* on 10 May showed fifty-six per cent wanted Churchill in the Government. But his general popularity was still low. Eden, with thirty-eight per cent support, was the most popular choice to replace Chamberlain when he retired – Churchill was backed by only seven per cent of those interviewed.

Churchill held strong views on warfare and modern technology, and was quite willing to make predictions about what war would be like when it came. He thought defences like the Maginot line would be highly effective and would make it 'very difficult indeed for the other army to break through . . . The idea that enormous masses of mechanical vehicles and tanks will be able to overrun these fortifica-tions will probably turn out to be a disappointment.' On equipment, he commented 'the tank has, no doubt, a great part to play; but I, personally, doubt very much whether it will ever see again the palmy days of 1918'.[1] Turning to the war at sea, he dismissed the idea that aircraft could sink ships: 'the air menace against properly armed and protected ships of war will not be of decisive character . . . even a single well-armed vessel will hold its own against aircraft'. He also dismissed the submarine: 'the undoubted obsolescence of the sub-marine as a decisive war weapon, should give a feeling of confidence and security so far as the seas and oceans are concerned to the western democracies'.[2] All these predictions were to be falsified by events.

The major question the British Government faced in the early summer of 1939 was whether to involve the Soviet Union in an alliance against Germany. Churchill, who for years had defended the states that bordered the Soviet Union as a bulwark against Bolshevism and had called on them to arm themselves to the maximum extent possible, expected them to suspend their distrust in the Soviet Union's intentions in 'an act of faith'.[3] He said that eastern Europe could not survive without 'the massive, solid backing of a friendly Russia' and Britain should 'get some of these brutal truths' into the heads of these countries. Britain should accept the Soviet offer of a triple alliance with France – 'What is wrong with this simple proposal?' he asked.[4] What was wrong with the proposal was that Germany and the Soviet Union had no common frontier and Soviet troops would therefore have to pass through Poland and the Baltic states to attack Germany and those Governments did not trust the Soviets to withdraw at the end of the war. Britain and France negotiated in a desultory fashion with the Soviet Union, but could not give them the assurance that Poland in particular would allow Soviet troops into the country because the Polish Government had refused pointblank.

Churchill took almost no part in the debate about this question after May. He did however express satisfaction with the Government's defence preparations. On 4 June he wrote 'all arrangements for enduring air attack have advanced' and 'it is, perhaps, not too much to say that by 1940 the British Air Force and the British nation will feel a great measure of confidence so far as the defence of the British island is concerned'.[5] In mid-August he took a trip to France to visit the French defences and then spent a short holiday at a château near Dreux. He left for London as planned on 23 August, the day the German-Soviet pact was announced (although not its secret clauses carving up the territory between them that gave the Soviets what Britain and France could not). War was now seen as inevitable. On 24 August Parliament was recalled and the next day Britain signed a formal alliance with Poland.

On 1 September Churchill was woken with the news of the German invasion of Poland. Later that day he saw Chamberlain at No 10 and agreed to join a small War Cabinet, from which the service ministers would be excluded. He himself expected to be made Minister without Portfolio. He offered Chamberlain his views on forming a wartime Government. It was not to be a national

Government. He suggested that Eden should be recalled and that the Liberals should be invited to join the Government but Labour should be excluded. For two days the Government tried desperately not to implement its alliance with Poland and to find a way of avoiding war. On the evening of 2 September, when the Government was denounced for its hesitations and was pushed into issuing an ultimatum to Germany, Churchill did not speak in the Commons. He did no more than write to Chamberlain asking where he stood and hoping for a firmer policy. In the Commons on 3 September, after Britain had declared war, he spoke of Chamberlain's previous efforts for peace as having been 'of the highest moral value'. He declared Britain now was at war not just for Poland but 'to save the whole world from the pestilence of Nazi tyranny'. Later in the day he again saw Chamberlain, who now proposed to bring the service ministers into a War Cabinet and offered Churchill the Admiralty. Eden was brought back outside the War Cabinet as Dominions Secretary, but neither the Liberals nor Labour were invited to join. Churchill went to the Admiralty at 6pm that night – he was back where he had been at the beginning of the last war against Germany.

The Government's worst fears about the forthcoming war were not realised – both Italy and Japan remained neutral. But even though it was fighting not a world war but a limited European war, with many of the combatants from twenty years earlier, such as Turkey, Russia and Belgium, not involved, Britain's position strategically and financially was weak. Within a week of joining the War Cabinet, Churchill had to face the problem that was to dominate British strategy, especially during his first nine months as Prime Minister in 1940 – the prospect of bankruptcy. British industry could not produce many of the armaments required by the war and many vital raw materials also had to be imported. As he had discovered during his time as Minister of Munitions in the First World War, most of this material had to come from the United States. Then too Britain had been on the edge of bankruptcy by mid-1917 as its dollar reserves and assets in the United States ran out. It was saved by the American Government backing its loans. Now American legislation prevented them from raising loans and obliged them to pay cash for everything. On 8 September the Chancellor, Sir John Simon, put a paper to his colleagues that was so secret no minister was allowed to retain a copy. It revealed that at most Britain had about £700 million it could spend in the United States and pointed out 'our total resources are vastly inferior' to the 1914 level. As more orders were placed, these reserves would rapidly be depleted. It contained a final ominous warning: 'It is obvious that we are in grave danger of our gold reserves being exhausted at a rate that will render us incapable of waging war if war is prolonged.'[6]

Allied strategy was based on fighting a three year war (though the gold and dollar reserves might not last that long). It made the assumption (which turned out to be false) that the German economy was already stretched to breaking point by their rearmament pro-gramme and would not survive the strains for very long. Britain and France agreed their best approach was to stay on the defensive in the first year, gradually building up their forces for limited operations in the second year and paving the way for a final assault, as the Germans collapsed, by the third year at the latest. Churchill shared these expectations of how the war would evolve in a paper he wrote on 23 August before he joined the Government. He wrote that the French agreed 'with the view I personally hold that time is now on our side, and that Hitler will be worse off next year than this'.[7] Once in office Churchill shared the widespread view that German morale was bad and would soon disintegrate. He reassured his colleagues on 19 September that Germany was short 'of certain vital materials, and some at least of their population was gravely disaffected . . . after a few months weaknesses would begin to show in the German military machine'.[8]

At the beginning of 1940 Churchill was even more optimistic that Hitler was already losing the war. He told an audience in Manchester that Germany was far weaker than in the First World War: 'I cannot rid my mind of the feeling that the Imperial Germany of 1914 was a stronger community than the Nazi Germany which now confronts us.' He fully endorsed the defensive Anglo-French strategy (includ-ing using the RAF to drop leaflets rather than bombs over Germany) and was sure that the war was moving inexorably in favour of the allies:

> I feel I was right in saying, in one of my earliest broadcasts, that, if we reached the spring without any interruption of our seaborne trade and without anything serious happening on land or in the air, we should in fact have gained the opening campaign of the war.

He added: 'Herr Hitler has already lost his best chance'.[9]

It was within this strategic framework that Churchill approached his task at the Admiralty. His way of working, many of the problems that he faced and the operations he suggested were remarkably similar to the first nine months of the First World War. As before, he wanted as First Lord to be involved in the direction and detail of operations and once again he spent many hours in the Map Room or the Duty Captain's office giving his opinions on which ships should be moved and directing operations whenever possible. The First Sea Lord he had to deal with was very different from 'Jacky' Fisher. Admiral Sir Dudley Pound was cautious, reserved and slightly deaf, with a tendency to fall asleep in meetings. He was determined not to have outright rows with Churchill and adopted instead a strategy of slowly undermining his wilder schemes, usually on grounds of practicality and lack of resources. In the end the two came to have a grudging respect for each other. But Churchill could still be impossibly difficult to work with. Admiral J. H. Godfrey, the Director of Naval Intelligence, recalled Churchill's methods:

> To get his own way he used every device and brought the *whole* battery of his ingenious, tireless and highly political mind to bear on the point at issue. His battery of weapons included persuasion, real or simulated anger, mockery, vituperation, tantrums, ridicule, derision, abuse and tears, which he would aim at anyone who opposed him or expressed a view contrary to the one he had already formed, sometimes on quite trivial questions.[10]

Churchill brought with him to the Admiralty Professor Lindemann, nominally in charge of a new statistical section but in practice acting as his general adviser on all matters. Many of Lindemann's interventions were far from helpful. With Churchill's patronage he forced through development of the Naval Wire Barrage, which was designed to bring down planes with wires – it was a complete failure. So was the machine that Churchill thought might be this war's equivalent of the tank – the trench cutting tank, also known as project 'White Rabbit Number 6'. 240 of these huge machines, each weighing 130 tons, eight foot high and eighty feet long, were ordered. They were designed to excavate a deep trench at one mile per hour and make what was described, perhaps rather optimistically, as a 'secret' penetration of enemy lines at night. None was ever used. Churchill also began to put together the small staff that would stay with him for the rest of the war – Captain Richard Pym, who organised his personal map room, and Lieutenant Commander 'Tommy' Thompson, his personal factotum. In February 1940 he started his 'Action This Day' minutes, although often action was not taken within this short deadline.

Churchill also took a close interest in the administration of the Navy. He forced through improved rest facilities at Scapa Flow. He personally interviewed three potential officer cadets who had been rejected on the snobbish grounds that one had a slight cockney accent and the other two were sons of a petty officer and an engineer in the merchant marine – all three were eventually accepted. When the Second Sea Lord informed him that the long-standing ban on coloured men enlisting as sailors was to be lifted (although measures were to be taken to ensure that none could become officers), he only agreed reluctantly: 'In practice much inconvenience would arise if this theoretical equality had many examples ... not too many of them please.'[11]

Behind much of this activity lay Churchill's desperate desire for publicity stemming from his political position. Having regained office when he was almost sixty-five, he knew that he had his last chance to become Prime Minister. He hoped to play the role of Lloyd George in the First World War and overthrow the Prime Minister if the war did not go well. He was therefore determined to take every opportunity to increase his personal standing. He kept tight control over all information given out by the Admiralty, reserving to himself the right to announce all good news. When Admiral Hallett, in charge of the press section, did release a favourable item of news on his own authority he was immediately sacked and sent to sea. To some extent he was lucky; with the RAF reduced to dropping leaflets over Germany and the Army inactive on the western front, only the Admiralty appeared to be taking much active part in the war. However, when there was a lack of good news Churchill was prepared to embroider it or even make it up in order to enhance his prestige. For example, in a broadcast on 12 November 1939 he claimed that 'the attack on the U-boats has been controlled and they have paid a heavy toll' – in fact just six out of the fifty-seven operational boats had been sunk and the Admiralty estimates available to Churchill also suggested a figure of less than ten per cent out of action. When he came to broadcast again on 20 January 1940 Churchill knew that no U-boats had been sunk since the beginning of December. Yet he assured his listeners it seemed 'pretty certain' that the Navy had sunk half the boats with which Germany had begun the war. Admiralty figures suggested nothing of the sort (nine out of fifty-seven sunk and all subsequently replaced by new construction – Churchill added sixteen 'probables' and ten more for luck). A month later he went further into the realms of fantasy. Within the Admiralty he claimed forty-five sunk and only twelve left operational, when Admiralty intelligence suggested forty operational boats remained. When Captain Talbot, in charge of anti-submarine warfare, dared to contradict Churchill's assertions he was told, 'Stop grinning at me you bloody ape!' and dismissed at ten minutes' notice.[12]

In dealing with the U-boat threat Churchill continued with his sanguine opinion formed before the war that they were no longer a menace. He therefore opposed the convoy system, wanting instead to reduce the number of escorts and concentrate on what he optimistically described as 'hunting packs' of destroyers to attack the U-boats while they were in transit. The results were almost a complete failure. Although merchant ship sinkings were, at about 100,000 tons a month, only an eighth of the horrendous figures for April 1917, when the U-boats almost broke Britain's supply line this was due to their lack of numbers (on average about fourteen at sea at any one time) rather than the Royal Navy's tactics – they rarely detected a U-boat and their attacks when they happened were largely ineffective: about a five per cent success rate. Lindemann influenced Churchill by giving him ill-thought-out figures on shipping losses suggesting that convoys had no effect – he failed to notice that virtually all the sinkings had occurred when ships were unescorted.

Although the Royal Navy had, unlike in 1914, immense superiority over a German navy it was largely on the defensive for the first months of the war, just as in 1914–15. The latter could only deploy two fast battleships, three 'pocket battleships', five cruisers and seventeen destroyers. Churchill paid his first visit to the fleet at Scapa Flow in the Shetlands in mid-September. He was less than impressed with what he saw – in many respects it was again the undefended anchorage of 1914. He wanted more blockships and nets. Before they could be deployed, a German U-boat slipped through the defences on 14 October and sank the battleship *HMS Royal Oak* (the carrier *HMS Courageous* had already been sunk off the west coast of Ireland). After this disaster the fleet moved, just as it did in 1914, to the west coast of Scotland. Churchill did not want it anchored in the Clyde because, he alleged, 'there are plenty of Irish traitors in the Glasgow area'.[13] But when he visited the area at the end of October he was persuaded to change his mind by the Commander-in-Chief. Even here the fleet was not out of danger and both *HMS Belfast* and *HMS Nelson* were badly damaged by mines. The fleet did not return to Scapa Flow until March 1940. Even then Churchill expressed concern about what might happen to his political reputation if there was another disaster – he told one admiral: 'They will hang us all if it happens again.'[14]

Despite their inferior numbers the German Navy took the initiative in the first months of the war. They deployed two pocket battleships – *Graf Spee* and *Deutschland* – as commerce raiders. By the beginning of October 1939 the British and French had eight groups of warships scouring the oceans trying to find them. By early December the *Graf Spee* had sunk ten merchantmen before it was finally caught by three British cruisers, which, although outgunned, managed to force her into Montevideo harbour for repairs. Churchill had tried to conduct this operation in detail from the Admiralty, based on signals that were six hours out of date, but was stopped by Pound. The *Graf Spee* was scuttled a few days later. Churchill ensured that this first naval success of the war was treated in spectacular fashion, and Commodore Harwood, in charge of the operation, became a firm favourite and was promoted far above his abilities later in the war.

For Churchill this was the real war at sea. Just as he had done in 1914, he objected to the less glamorous but far more important task of keeping open the sea lanes to maintain supplies and enforcing the blockade on Germany. He told Pound in early December 1939: 'I cd never be responsible for a naval strategy wh excluded the offensive principle, & relegated us to keeping open the lines of communication.'[15] Just three days after taking office, he reverted to his old favourite from the last war – a Royal Navy operation in the Baltic. It was, he told the admirals, 'the supreme naval offensive open to the Royal Navy'.[16] The idea was to force an entry into the Baltic, bring

Sweden, Norway and Denmark into the war and influence the Soviet Union. That was the theory; in practice the difficulties, which Churchill never wanted to address, were overwhelming. The fleet would need a base from which to operate, it would be permanently within range of German shore-based aircraft (always a weakness Churchill discounted) and highly vulnerable to submarine and mine attack in the shallow waters of the Baltic. Necessary modifications to the warships would take nine months, there were no protected anchorages in Sweden, favoured as the site for an operational base, and last but not least there was no evidence that the political benefits he expected to flow from the operation would in fact be forthcoming.

Pound, following his usual approach with Churchill, did not oppose him outright and planning began in the middle of September. Churchill brought back his old friend the Earl of Cork and Orrery from retirement to mastermind the operation. In the third week of November the operation was postponed until May because no ships were available but planning continued at Churchill's insistence. On 10 January Pound wrote to him at length highlighting all the problems; he warned that most of the ships involved would be sunk and pointed out: 'The loss of such a large proportion of our Fleet would be the surest inducement to either Italy or Japan to come in against us.'[17] He then set prerequisites for the operation that could not be met. Churchill finally gave in on 15 January. It had cost the Admiralty about £12 million (over £250 million at today's prices) in wasted modifications and a great deal of nugatory effort before Churchill could be dissuaded from an impracticable scheme. Churchill took his revenge on Captain Danckwerts, the Director of Plans, who wrote most of Pound's minutes – he, like other Admiralty casualties before him, was sacked and sent to sea.

With their armies sitting quietly on the western front, the allies turned to the area that fascinated Churchill, Scandinavia, as the scene for possible offensive operations. During the winter of 1939–40 they developed a number of highly dubious schemes that would have involved them in violating Norway's neutrality and brought them to the brink of war with the Soviet Union as well as Germany. Churchill was one of the main supporters of these ideas. Before the outbreak of war British planners had decided that Germany would be seriously affected by any disruption of iron ore traffic from the mines in northern Sweden. They thought this accounted for over eighty per cent of Germany's consumption and that interruption of suppies would end the war in a few months. This was a major misapprehension: the trade accounted for less than a third of German supplies, their stocks were high and forty per cent of German steel production was still going to civilian uses. Stopping the supplies would not rapidly bring Germany to its knees.

Churchill was told by the Admiralty about this intelligence assessment on 18 September and promptly raised it the next day at the War Cabinet. Characteristically he jumped in prematurely with an ill-thought-out plan. He wanted to mine Norwegian territorial waters to force the ore ships out into international waters where they could be stopped. In fact the Admiralty knew the ships left territorial waters at two points on their route anyway and wanted them intercepted off Narvik, the port from which they sailed – it was Churchill who was obsessed with the minefield idea. Apart from the obvious objections to violating Norwegian neutrality by mining her territorial waters, his initial proposals got nowhere because no ships left Narvik until later in the year when the Swedish ports became icebound. When he put a fully prepared paper to the War Cabinet at the end of the month, it contained no call for action and his colleagues simply took note of the idea.

The situation was transformed by the Soviet invasion of Finland at the end of November. This was yet another example of unprovoked aggression against a small state. (The Soviet Union had already stabbed Poland in the back and occupied the eastern half of the country in late September under the secret clauses of the German-Soviet treaty.) At first, despite his earlier outright resistance to the spread of Bolshevism and defence of the states of eastern Europe as a bulwark to protect the west, Churchill supported Soviet expansion. He took a highly pragmatic line at the War Cabinet on 16 October:

> No doubt it appeared reasonable to the Soviet Union to take advantage of the present situation to regain some of the territory which Russia had lost as a result of the last war . . . It was to our interests that the U.S.S.R. should increase their strength in the Baltic, thereby limiting the risk of German domination in that area. For this reason it would be a mistake for us to stiffen the Finns against making concessions to the U.S.S.R.[19]

It was left to Lord Halifax to remind Churchill that the Finns did have a right to defend their independence.

However the strong surge of public support for the Finns as, heavily outnumbered, they held off a hopelessly incompetent Soviet Army, and the chorus of demands to go to their assistance, made Churchill change his mind. For many Communism was still the ultimate enemy. Lord Cork and Orrery told Churchill on 5 December British help to Finland was 'a wonderful chance – and perhaps the last – of mobilising the anti-Bolshevik forces of the world on our side'.[19] Churchill was obviously sympathetic to this argument, because he told Pound six days later that Britain might be leading the crusade against Bolshevism alongside the man he admired so much – Mussolini: 'It may be that we may find ourselves at war with Russia, and Allies of Sweden, Norway, Finland and Italy.'[20]

On 16 December Churchill reopened the debate about Scandinavian iron ore by proposing to his colleagues mining the Swedish port of Lulea (how was not made clear) and possibly occupying Narvik and Bergen. He brushed aside any qualms about breaking international law with an extraordinary argument: 'small nations must not tie our hands when we are fighting for their rights and freedom. The letter of the law must not in supreme emergency obstruct those who are charged with its protection and enforcement.' He argued that the proposed move would be 'a major offensive operation of war' that would be a short cut to total victory since it would produce a 'crisis before the summer' in Germany, and possibly would even be 'immediately decisive'.[21] At the Military Co-ordination Committee four days later he argued that the allies should occupy the iron ore mines at Gallivare in Sweden, and, if necessary, fight the Soviet Union. In order to achieve this aim the Scandinavian countries might have to be invaded and occupied: 'we should make a friendly offer of assistance to the Scandinavian countries as was proposed by the French, but we should make it quite clear that whether they accepted it or not we should come in and take possession of the minefields [around Gallivare]'.[22]

The War Cabinet decided on 22 December that planning was becoming confused between an operation to stop the ore traffic, either by mining Norwegian territorial waters or sending destroyers in to capture the ore ships, and a wider operation to land with the consent of the Scandinavian countries (only Churchill was willing to ignore their opposition), occupy the orefields and possibly move on to assist Finland against the Soviet Union. Over Christmas and the New Year Churchill argued with the Prime Minister that occupying the iron ore mines 'may be the surest and shortest road to the end'.[23] He still wanted to combine the two operations by sending in destroyers (he had dropped the idea of sowing mines) and occupying part of Sweden and Norway. At the beginning of January the War Cabinet agreed to start planning for a large-scale occupation of Scandinavia and in the meantime, after consulting the governments involved, to enter Norwegian waters to stop the ore ships. Within the week there were outraged protests from Sweden and Norway at the contemplated violation of their neutrality. Churchill wanted to override their objections: 'The neutral countries could not be permitted to tie our hands . . . the only way of obtaining [their] co-operation would be . . . to make them more frightened of us than they were of Germany.'[24] The War Cabinet did not agree but planning went ahead for a possible wider occupation of Scandinavia if the Governments would consent.

While this planning continued, a small group of ministers, including Churchill, agreed that British intelligence should attempt to destroy the Swedish port of Oxelosund – the plan went badly wrong and those involved were captured. Churchill caused more stir among the neutrals with a broadcast on 20 January when he accused them of bowing to German pressure and not standing with the allies. Protests flooded in to the British Government and came from within it too when it was discovered that he had not cleared the text with the Foreign Office beforehand. On the same day Churchill wanted to respond to a Finnish appeal for help by sending aircraft and RAF crews to fight against the Soviet Union – his colleagues only agreed to send aircraft. He was present for the first time, but made no contribution, at the Supreme War Council meeting with the French on 5 February that agreed to intervene in Scandinavia. The Finns were to be asked to issue an 'appeal' for help, and Norway and Sweden would be asked to co-operate with the passage of troops.

In mid-February the War Cabinet discussed the details of a plan for assistance to Finland drawn up by the chiefs of staff. A substantial Anglo-French force would land at Narvik, go on to Gallivare, help the Finns and also occupy Stavanger, Bergen and Trondheim to pre-empt any German intervention. The inclusion of help for the

Finns was a way of gaining a foothold in Scandinavia. Churchill now raised again his previous idea of mining Norwegian waters and occupying Narvik, and planning was restarted on that too. On 23 February the Cabinet agreed to consult the opposition, the dominions, the United States and even the Scandinavians about the operation which Churchill believed was 'the main fulcrum on which the whole course of the war would turn'.[25] Even as they did so, the Finns opened secret talks with the Soviet Union on an armistice, which was eventually signed on 12 March. Before then, despite the repeated Scandinavian objections to the violation of their neutrality, the Government agreed to go ahead with a landing at Narvik and, if necessary, to use force to overcome Norwegian opposition. On 14 March, with the excuse for intervention now gone, the War Cabinet drew back, despite Churchill's pleas for an immediate expedition to Narvik – in his view 'our real objective was of course to secure possession of the Gallivare ore fields'.[26] He wrote to Halifax later that day: 'There never was any chance of giving effective help to Finland; but this hope – or rather illusion – might have been the means of enabling us to get to Gallivare.'[27] On 18 March Churchill made one last attempt to revive the idea of attacking in Scandinavia with a carrier-based aircraft attack on the Swedish port of Lulea to close it through torpedoing ships and sowing mines. The chiefs of staff were opposed and so were his political colleagues.

Despite these setbacks, the idea of attacking the Soviet Union, which had lain behind the plans to assist the Finns, was not dead. The French were keen to see attacks on the Soviet oil fields and operations in the Black Sea. Most of the British Government was sceptical, though at the Supreme War Council on 28 March Chamberlain accepted that bombing the Baku oilfields 'would have the double advantage of paralysing Russia's economic structure and effectively preventing her from carrying out military operations outside her own territory'.[28] Churchill was now one of the main proponents of attacking the Soviet Union. As early as October 1939 he had suggested to the Cabinet sending submarines into the Black Sea to sink Soviet ships taking supplies to Germany. On 23 March 1940 he advocated to Pound operations not just in the Baltic but also in the Black Sea and remarkably in the Caspian too. On 27 March he supported the French proposals for attacks in the Black Sea: 'two or three submarines would not only interrupt the Russian oil traffic in that sea, but would also have a terrifying moral effect on Russia'.[29] After much discussion nothing came of these ideas.

The Supreme War Council meeting on 28 March, which Churchill attended although he was asleep for much of the time, agreed to go ahead with mining Norwegian waters in early April. He explained to the Cabinet the next day that if the Germans reacted then troops would be ready to seize Narvik as well as Stavanger, Bergen and Trondheim and from Narvik they might advance to the Swedish frontier along the railway line. Approval was given for mining to start on 4 April. At this point the operation became tangled up in yet another ill-thought-out plan – Operation Royal Marine to drop mines in the Rhine and other German waterways. Churchill strongly supported this latter scheme, although it was held up throughout the winter of 1939–40 by design problems and the need to produce enough mines to sow around 2,000 a week to keep the waterways closed. On 6 March the Cabinet agreed to go ahead with 'Royal Marine' but by then the French had cold feet, fearing German retaliatory raids on aircraft factories, and wanted more time to disperse the industry. On 11 March Churchill went to Paris to obtain final French approval but finished up agreeing to their pleas to postpone it to at least mid-April. The French agreed at the 28 March meeting to go ahead in conjunction with the operations in Norway, but withdrew their agreement within a few days, largely because of political in-fighting within the Government. The British threatened to call off both operations and Churchill was again sent over to Paris to convince them to let both go ahead. He arrived in Paris on 4 April and within a few hours had been converted from strong advocacy of 'Royal Marine' to endorsement of the French position to postpone it yet again. He told the Cabinet the next day that he 'felt strongly that it would be a very great mistake to try to force the French to fall in with our wishes'.[30] The Cabinet had little alternative but to agree.

Nevertheless, despite this setback, the mining of Norwegian waters was due to start on 8 April (a little late because the ore traffic was virtually over with the coming of spring). Unfortunately for the allies Hitler had been aware of their interest in Scandinavia for some time and since the third week of February had been planning his own invasion. British intelligence received plenty of warnings of these plans from 11 March but they were discounted – Churchill in particular did not believe that Germany, with such a small navy, had the capability to invade Scandinavia. On 7 April RAF planes spotted the German fleet moving north out of the Baltic towards Norway. Britain, which for many months had been planning its own mining operation and a possible invasion, and with the added advantage of a superior fleet, ought to have been in a superb position to counter and defeat the Germans. Instead the Norwegian campaign turned into a fiasco of bad planning, indeterminate aims and shifting objectives that resulted in complete failure within three weeks. After the war, and in private, Churchill was prepared to admit his inglorious role: 'I certainly bore an exceptional measure of responsibility for the brief and disastrous Norwegian Campaign – if campaign it can be called.'[31]

Churchill made the first, and probably the decisive, mistake right at the beginning. Convinced that the German fleet was trying to sail into the Atlantic, he ordered the troops to disembark from the ships that were to sail to Norway (there was no time to unload the equipment) and also diverted the warships stationed off Narvik to protect the minelaying to look for the German fleet. On the evening of 8 April (with minelaying underway), at dinner with his fellow service ministers, he was reported as being 'very optimistic, delighted with mine laying and sure he had scored off the Germans'.[32] He woke up the next morning to find that he was facing not a second Jutland but a German invasion of Norway (Denmark had already been overrun). At a Cabinet meeting at 8.30am the chiefs of staff recommended landing in the far north at Narvik, which they thought the Germans had not occupied, while attacking at Bergen and Trondheim in central Norway. Churchill agreed. He thought 'no large forces would be required' at either Bergen or Trondheim and therefore the Narvik landing could go ahead as well.[33] However, by midday it was clear that the Royal Navy had allowed the Germans to slip through and land at Narvik. Churchill gave orders that the Navy were to fight their way into Narvik and Bergen. He was confident about the general situation, saying: 'Our hands are now free, and we could apply our overwhelming sea power on the Norwegian coast. We could liquidate their landings in a week or two.'[34] That afternoon he told a hastily summoned meeting of the Supreme War Council that British troops were sailing to Bergen and Trondheim and that 'the actual operation of clearing any Germans out of Narvik should not present any great difficulty'.[35] By the evening operations at Bergen and Trondheim had been abandoned and the Military Co-ordination Committee (now chaired by Churchill) agreed to concentrate their efforts on Narvik, although the chiefs of staff were told to take into account the possibility of landing British troops at Namsos and Andalsnes (500 miles south of Narvik).

On 10 April Churchill learnt that the naval attack on Narvik had been beaten off. Ill-trained and badly equipped troops were being re-embarked on to ships in Britain to try and take the port. His earlier optimism vanished. He told Pound 'we have been completely outwitted'.[36] The War Cabinet agreed to land at Narvik (still with the optimistic aim of going on to the Swedish iron ore fields) and to blame the neutrals for the growing disaster. Churchill did just that in his speech the next day in the Commons. It was judged to be a poor effort. One normally sympathetic MP reported:

> He starts off by giving an imitation of himself making a speech, and he indulges in vague oratory coupled with tired gibes. I have seldom seen him to less advantage . . . He hesitates, gets his notes in the wrong order, puts on the wrong pair of spectacles, fumbles for the right pair, keeps on saying 'Sweden' when he means 'Denmark', and one way and another makes a lamentable peformance.[37]

Later that day (11 April) two commanders were appointed for the Narvik operation – Churchill's friend the Earl of Cork and Orrery (with a special cipher for direct communication with him rather than with Pound) and General Mackesy for the Army. Mackesy was instructed to land thirty-five miles away from Narvik because the expedition was without artillery, engineers and transport, and the ships were so chaotically loaded that an opposed landing was out of the question. At the Military Co-ordination Committee Churchill agreed to planning going ahead for a later Trondheim attack but insisted 'no action should be taken' until the scale of the Narvik operation was clear.[38] Within hours he had changed his mind. About midnight, 'half-tight' according to one member of the naval staff, he dragged Pound, Newall (Chief of the Air Staff) and Phillips (Pound's deputy) round to see his old friend General Ironside, now Chief of the Imperial General Staff. Churchill wanted to divert half the

Narvik convoy to Namsos with the aim of 'staking out a claim'.[39] There was a major row but he got his way.

On 12 April at the War Cabinet Churchill did another volte-face – he now argued that 'it was not thought right to interrupt in any way the progress of operations against Narvik'.[40] Later in the day he kept to this line, that landings along the coast (such as at Trondheim) might be important politically but 'they should not be carried out at a cost of a diversion of effort from the Narvik expedition'.[41] That night Churchill told Ironside that any operations against Trondheim were just a diversion. The next day he again told his colleagues that if anything else was done before Narvik was captured there was a grave danger that 'we might find ourselves committed to a number of ineffectual operations along the Norwegian coast, none of which would succeed'.[42] That afternoon, with some of his colleagues favouring an attack on Trondheim, Churchill still wanted to stick with Narvik. In the evening he learnt that seven German destroyers had been sunk at Narvik and he became convinced that the port could easily be captured. Ignoring the warnings he had given his colleagues only hours before, at a military co-ordination meeting at 10.30pm that night he recommended a 'reconnaissance' the next day at Namsos (eighty miles north of Trondheim), followed by landings at Aalesund (150 miles south of Trondheim) on 16 April, with most of the ships for these operations to be diverted from Narvik. These two landings were to form a 'pincer' attack on Trondheim itself. He told the War Cabinet on 14 April that Trondheim was 'an even greater prize than Narvik' and the War Cabinet agreed to plan on landing there as soon as possible.

On 14–15 April British landings began along the Norwegian coast amid total confusion caused by the constant changes of mind during the previous week. The troops which landed at Namsos (half the convoy intended for Narvik) only had maps of Narvik and all their vehicles, some of their ammunition and their commander were still sailing to their original destination from which Churchill had diverted them. When they landed at Namsos they would have to advance for eighty miles over one road with no air cover. The troops landing further south at Andalsnes, perhaps rather predictably, only had maps of Namsos. By this stage Churchill was once again optimistic about their chances of success. Ironside found him on the night of 15 April, 'full of confidence in the strategical error that Hitler had made going into Scandinavia'.[43]

However, by now the chiefs of staff were in open revolt over Churchill's method (or lack of method) in running the campaign and the chaos that inevitably ensued from his constant changes of mind and reluctance to allow the defence chiefs to develop fully worked out options. As Ironside put it, 'We cannot have a man trying to supervise all military arrangements as if he were a company commander running a small operation to cross a bridge.'[44] Under pressure Churchill was forced to relinquish the chair of the Military Co-ordination Committee on 16 March and allow Chamberlain to take charge. He reluctantly admitted that this arrangement had 'got him out of a hole'. The chiefs of staff were advised to 'exercise the most rigid control over themselves and at all costs to keep their tempers' in order to avoid 'a first-class political row'.[45] They did so and under Chamberlain some order was restored to planning.

By now though it was too late to rescue the disastrous campaign, and Churchill continued to swing from one expedient to another as a route to success. At the 16 April meeting ministers agreed to concentrate on Trondheim as the main objective. For Churchill the landings at Namsos and Andalsnes were now, once again, diversions and he advocated withdrawing troops from Narvik to Trondheim. Narvik had still not been captured and the commander, Mackesy, was reluctant to assault the town given his inferior numbers (as a result of Churchill diverting half his forces elsewhere). On 17 April Churchill set out his priorities and hopes to Admiral Forbes, Commander-in-Chief Home Fleet: 'I regard the operations from Namsos and Andalsnes in the light of feints to confuse and distract the enemy in order that the blow may be delivered with full surprise and force at the centre [Trondheim]. All that has happened makes me sure that Hitler has made a grave strategic blunder in giving us the right, as we have always had the power, to take what we like on the Norwegian coast . . . I look forward to an increasingly vigorous campaign being fought along the Norwegian coast during the summer.'[46] On 19 April, after the chiefs of staff had rejected an assault on Trondheim by ships up a narrow thirty mile long fjord without air cover, Churchill recommended concentrating on Narvik again as the main operation. Though the next day he recommended reinforcing the landings at Namsos and Andalsnes and concentrating on Narvik with the objective of gaining control of the Swedish iron ore fields. After the War Cabinet meeting that day Ironside reflected: 'Winston is very apt to paint a rosy picture in his enthusiasm. He forgets all the administrative snags that exist and is run away with his own explanations.'[47]

By 21 April it was becoming clear in London that the Norwegian campaign was going disastrously wrong and Churchill's optimism of only four days earlier had been entirely misplaced. That morning the Cabinet agreed that Namsos and Andalsnes should not be reinforced and that the troops there would probably have to be evacuated because of the weight of German air attacks. Churchill admitted that withdrawal would be 'a very hazardous operation' and that the situation 'gave rise to some anxiety but was by no means desperate'.[48] That evening he changed his mind yet again and recommended to Chamberlain that they should now reinforce at Namsos and Andalsnes. The next day at the Supreme War Council in Paris the French were not told of the likely British intention to pull out from central Norway and Churchill changed his mind again and now recommended diverting all forces back to Narvik. General Ironside wrote in his diary: 'He is so like a child in many ways. He tires of a thing, and then wants to hear no more of it ... It is most extraordinary how mercurial he is.'[49]

Over the next two days things went from bad to worse. At Narvik a preliminary landing near the port was abandoned in a heavy snowstorm. Both the forces at Namsos and Andalsnes were under heavy German pressure and evacuation was now seen in London as inevitable. On the morning of 24 April Churchill suggested to Pound that with the 'pincers' to the north and south failing they should think again about a direct attack on Trondheim. In the evening at the military co-ordination meeting he suggested concentrating on Narvik. The next day both Chamberlain and Churchill agreed that withdrawal from central Norway was now inevitable, though Churchill still wanted an examination of a direct attack on Trondheim. That was called off on 26 April when the Cabinet agreed to evacuate Namsos and Andalsnes. The next day Churchill objected to this course on the grounds that it was politically damaging. Instead he advocated guerrilla warfare and 'leaving the troops now in Norway to put up the best fight they could, in conjunction with the Norwegians' and that 'it was better to condemn the force ashore to fight to the end'.[50] Ironside objected: 'I could not find any military reason for doing this. It was all political.'[51]

After a three-week campaign the British forces did not hold any of the important Norwegian ports; most of the country was in German hands and they were left clinging on to a small piece of land outside Narvik. (Troops were finally withdrawn from there at the end of May after Churchill had insisted they capture the town, at the cost of 150 lives, even though it was to be evacuated immediately afterwards.) British supremacy at sea had counted for little (the Germans were reading about half the Royal Navy's signals) and dynamic leadership on land combined with air supremacy had enabled the Germans to completely outwit the allies. Clearly explanations would be required and the military fiasco threatened to become a political crisis about the quality of British war leadership. These problems were uppermost in the minds of the Cabinet. On 26 April, the day evacuation of central Norway was agreed by the Cabinet, Ironside reported: 'they all, including the P.M., began making up stories they could tell the public and make out that our stroke against Trondheim was to put the Germans off Narvik'.[52] Two days later the story was the same: 'The War Cabinet were all very downcast and were thinking more of public opinion than of the military disaster.'[53]

The political and military situation at the end of April 1940 was remarkably similar to that in May 1915. In both cases after about nine months of war a botched military operation, largely brought about by Churchill's direction, produced a political crisis that led to the collapse of the Government and the creation of a national coalition. The difference was that the first time it almost ended Churchill's career; the second time it made him Prime Minister. That this would be the outcome of the 1940 crisis was in no way inevitable. Churchill was largely responsible for the Norwegian fiasco. On a conservative estimate, he changed his mind about the military objectives of the campaign at least fourteen times in less than three weeks. His way of taking decisions had led to open revolt within Whitehall and to his replacement as chair of the Miliary Co-ordination Committee after just eight days in charge. Yet none of this was known to the public and he was still regarded as the man who had been right in his warnings about the course of German policy. Most of the blame was heaped on Chamberlain, whose pre-war policy was judged to have failed and who was seen as an inadequate war leader.

Churchill was well aware of the strength of his political position and determined to exploit it to the full to become Prime Minister. On 24 April, the day it was clear that withdrawal from central Norway was inevitable, he drafted a letter to Chamberlain saying that he would not take back the chair of the Military Co-ordination Committee without extra powers that would in effect make him Minister of Defence and leave Chamberlain largely powerless as Prime Minister. He did not send the letter but instead saw Chamberlain that evening. He threatened that if Chamberlain did not agree he would 'go down to the House and say he can take no responsibility for what is happening'.[54] Chamberlain knew that he might not survive Churchill's resignation and therefore over the next few days a compromise over the future direction of war policy was worked out. It was finally agreed that Churchill would chair the Military Co-ordination Committee and would give guidance to the chiefs of staff and summon them as required. He was to have a small central staff, headed by Colonel Ismay, who would also sit on the Chiefs of Staff Committee. His fellow service ministers – Samuel Hoare (Air) and Oliver Stanley (War Office) – both objected to working under Churchill as a quasi-Minister of Defence but when they threatened to resign Chamberlain said that if they did he would go too and let Churchill become Prime Minister. They succumbed before this threat, but the new system had no time to work before the political crisis brought on by the Norwegian campaign ended the Chamberlain Government.

Once the news of the disaster in Norway filtered out to the public, political speculation in Whitehall and Westminster mounted. The Government machine was trying, with some justification, to put the blame on Churchill. Lord Dunglass (later Sir Alec Douglas-Home), Chamberlain's Parliamentary Private Secretary, was wondering 'whether Winston should be deflated' and another MP reported that 'the Whips are putting it about that it is all the fault of Winston who has made another forlorn failure'.[55] Churchill did not remain passive as these rumours went around. In the last ten days of April he was in close touch with the Parliamentary 'Watching committee' that wanted a more active prosecution of the war and was chaired by his colleague from the Indian campaign of the 1930s, Lord Salisbury.

He was also in contact with the opposition – both his old friend from the First World War, Sinclair, who was now leader of the small group of independent Liberals, and members of the Labour Party. The well-connected Conservative MP, 'Chips' Channon, reported on 25 April: 'Winston, it seems, has had secret conversations and meetings with Archie Sinclair, A.V.Alexander and Mr Attlee and they are drawing up an alternative government.'[56] On 1 April he noted: 'Tonight Churchill sat joking and drinking in the smoking room, surrounded by A.V.Alexander and Archie Sinclair, the new Shadow Cabinet.'[57]

Churchill was clearly paying his hand carefully – steering a difficult course between making it clear to the opposition that he was prepared to form a coalition Government and remaining superficially loyal to Chamberlain. But it was by no means inevitable that he would become Prime Minister if there was a full-blown political crisis. In early April much of the opinion within Parliament saw a return to power of Lloyd George as the most likely outcome. Many wondered whether Churchill had the capacity to be Prime Minister, not just in terms of his judgement and reliability under pressure but also because of his age (sixty-five) and general condition. On 2 April he had great difficulty finishing a speech in the Commons and had to be led away. One observer commented, 'It is times like these that age and excessive brandy drinking tell.'[58] He was obviously suffering from the effects the next morning because Ironside reported that at the first Military Co-ordination Committee meeting with Churchill back in the chair 'we found him very tired and sleepy and we hardly did anything at all'.[59]

Nor was Churchill overwhelmingly popular with the public – opinion polls still showed that twice as many people wanted Chamberlain as Prime Minister. The main strength of Churchill's position was that there was no obvious alternative within the Government except Lord Halifax, the Foreign Secretary. In this he was the beneficiary of Chamberlain's determination (like so many Prime Ministers) not to have an obvious replacement available. Most of his likely successors – Hoare, Inskip and Eden – had drifted out of the picture by 1939 and Churchill was quickly able, once he was back in Government, to establish himself as a strong candidate to succeed Chamberlain. This was one of the reasons why the Prime Minister was so reluctant to recall him before the outbreak of war. Like Lloyd George and

Baldwin before him, Chamberlain had included Churchill because he felt he would cause fewer problems inside the Government than if he were left outside. He wrote to his sister a fortnight after Churchill joined the Government: 'I can't say that I think W.C. has been particulary helpful though certainly he would have been a most troublesome thorn in our flesh if he had been outside.'[60]

The two day debate on the Norwegian campaign, which Chamberlain had been forced to concede, began on 7 May. It was still by no means clear that he would have to go, or, if he did, who would replace him. Chamberlain was in fact optimistic about surviving even if some of his supporters deserted him. The debate opened with poor speeches from the Prime Minister and Attlee and one from Sinclair that was clearly based on inside information, probably provided by Churchill. An old Navy friend of Churchill's, Sir Roger Keyes, appeared in full uniform to denounce the Government. The most effective speech came from the old imperialist hardliner, Leo Amery, who quoted Cromwell at Chamberlain, telling him 'You have sat too long for any good you have been doing. Depart, I say, and let us have done with you. In the name of God, go!' But the Government's opponents were still unsure what to do. Members of the 'Watching committee' meeting the next morning did not want to vote against the Government and the Labour opposition only decided at the last moment to insist on a formal vote of censure on the Government. On the second afternoon Chamberlain made the mistake of saying he had friends in the House, thereby helping to turn the vote into a personal one about his future rather than about the Government as a whole. Lloyd George called on Chamberlain to go and tried to exonerate Churchill from any blame. Churchill wound up the debate, defending the Norwegian campaign and calling for national unity. In the vote on the night of 8 May the Government's normal majority of about 200 fell to eighty-one. Overall forty-two Government supporters voted against Chamberlain and there were in total eighty-eight abstentions, although taking account of those away ill or on active service, the true figure was thirty-six.

The next day the politicians argued over the consequences of the vote. Chamberlain realised from the beginning that a national coalition was inevitable and that Labour would not agree to serve under him. The crucial question was, therefore, which Conservative politician should be called on to create that coalition. Most opinion within the establishment (including the King) wanted Halifax, as did Chamberlain and Margesson, the Conservative Whip in the Commons, who believed that the majority of the party favoured that outcome. (They decided that Halifax's peerage could be put into abeyance in order to allow him to sit in the Commons.) Within the Labour Party there was a large body of opinion in his favour, including Dalton, Morrison and Cripps. The problem for these people was that Halifax did not want to be Prime Minister. His Permanent Secretary, Sir Alexander Cadogan, noted on the morning of 9 May: 'He [Halifax] very gloomy – thinks PM will go and fears he (H.) may be asked to take over.'[61] That is exactly what happened when the two had a long meeting, but Chamberlain could not convince Halifax to agree.

Churchill was also discussing his position with his own entourage – Beaverbrook, Eden and Kingsley Wood (an ex-Chamberlain protégé who had defected). They told him that Chamberlain wanted Halifax to succeed and would ask him whether he would be prepared to serve under Halifax. They advised him not to answer the question (it would be difficult to refuse in the middle of a war). The crucial meeting that ensured Churchill became Prime Minister took place at 4.30 that afternoon at No 10. Those present were Chamberlain, Halifax, Margesson and Churchill. Chamberlain explained that he was sure he could not form a national government and the question was therefore who could? He probably suggested Halifax. Churchill, taking his friends' advice, kept quiet. Halifax then explained his own reluctance. He felt, rightly, that if Churchill remained in effective charge of operational decisions he would 'speedily become a more or less honorary prime minister' and that he was not the right man for the job. Halifax recorded in his diary that night 'the PM reluctantly, and Winston evidently with much less reluctance, finished by accepting my view'.[62] Almost immediately the Labour leaders, Clement Attlee and Arthur Greenwood, were called in. They were asked to join a national Government under Chamberlain. Attlee indicated that this was most unlikely. They were then asked whether they would serve under someone else. Attlee said he thought so but that he would consult the National Executive Committee of the party, then gathering at Bournemouth for the annual conference (it was the Whitsun weekend), and give a firm reply to both questions the next day. At no time were they given any say over who the leader of that coalition might be – that was an entirely private choice taken by just four Conservative politicians.

It was now virtually inevitable that Churchill would become Prime Minister the next day. In anticipation, he dined that evening with Sinclair, Eden and his two closest companions, Bracken and Linde-mann, and began allocating posts in the new Government. He was woken early on the morning of 10 May to be told that a German attack on the western front had started. During the day there were two meetings of the War Cabinet to consider what action was needed (Churchill wasted much of the time irrelevantly handing round a prototype of a new anti-aircraft fuse) and the Military Co-ordination Committee also met twice. But the eyes of the politicians were still on the political crisis. Chamberlain's first reaction that morning was that he should not resign while the German attack was underway. Many others took the same view and even Churchill's friend Sinclair issued a press statement saying that the Prime Minister should remain. Efforts continued to try and change Halifax's mind but to no avail. It was Kingsley Wood who told Chamberlain that the outbreak of real fighting meant that it was even more essential that he should go. The issue was resolved at the 4.30pm Cabinet meeting when a message was brought to Chamberlain saying that Labour refused to serve under him and he told his colleagues that he would resign immediately. During his audience with the King, the latter still pressed the claims of Halifax but eventually agreed that there was no alternative but to send for Churchill. Within the hour Churchill had been appointed Prime Minister.

It was a curious turn of events that had enabled him to finally achieve his ambition forty years after entering Parliament. Churchill had not been chosen by the people: he emerged as Prime Minister by a process that most resembled the 'high politics' of the nineteenth century that he so much admired. It was perhaps the crowning irony of his career that he should become Prime Minister because of the need to bring the Labour Party, which had so far only formed two minority governments, into a national coalition. One of the main motivating forces of his political life in the previous twenty years was his outright opposition to the claims of Labour and the trades unions, reflected in his often expressed belief that not only were they unfit to govern the country but that they were engaged in a campaign to subvert its political, economic and social institutions.

In constructing his new Government Churchill had to work within two constraints. First, the Conservative Party, which had still overwhelmingly supported Chamberlain in the vote two days earlier, was the largest party in the Commons and the ex-Prime Minister was still the party Leader. He could not afford to alienate this broad mass of support and so most of the Chamberlain administration, especially its senior members, continued in office. Second, he had to find posts for senior members of the Labour Party, although he was determined that they should not hold any of the key offices concerned with defence and foreign policy.

Churchill's first action was to secure Chamberlain's place in the new Government. He wrote to him immediately on his return from the Palace to say 'To a very large extent I am in your hands.'[63] He offered him the post of Lord President of the Council, and the effective deputy Premiership, together with Leader of the House of Commons. Luckily for Churchill, Chamberlain was magnanimous towards his successor (unlike Asquith in 1916) and agreed to serve. Churchill had great admiration for Chamberlain's abilities (he wrote to him in September 1939 after the Cabinet meeting that decided Britain's strategic priorities: 'I hope you will not think it inappropriate from one serving under you, if I say that in twenty years of Cabinets I have never heard a more commanding summing-up upon a great question'[64]) and left him to deal with large areas of policy, particularly on domestic questions. Lord Halifax was confirmed in post as Foreign Secretary. Of the other senior members of the Chamberlain Government, Simon moved from the Treasury to become Lord Chancellor and only Samuel Hoare was excluded from the Government. This was Churchill's revenge for their bitter conflict over the future of India, but Hoare was grateful to be sent to Madrid as Ambassador in order to escape from what he expected to be a Britain under Nazi rule.

On the evening of 10 May Churchill met Attlee and Greenwood, who had returned from the Labour Party conference at Bournemouth, to discuss the allocation of posts. Under pressure, he had to withdraw the offer of the leadership of the Commons from Chamberlain because they explained that Labour MPs would find him unacceptable, but Labour's eventual share was meagre – Attlee and Greenwood were given non-departmental posts (Greenwood's alcoholism meant he could not be entrusted with a real job), Morrison became Minister of Supply and Dalton went to Economic Warfare. The most important move was to bring in Ernest Bevin, the head of the Transport and General Workers Union, as Minister of Labour to oversee the mobilisation of the workforce.

Churchill was determined to combine his position as Prime Minister with effective control of defence planning and operations and to prevent anybody else developing an alternative power base as he had done under Chamberlain. It would also allow him scope to exercise what he believed were his considerable military abilities, rather like his hero Napoleon. He appointed himself Minister of Defence and carefully left the powers of this new post undefined. He had a small staff under Ismay, who acted as his link with the chiefs of staff, and he also chaired the new Defence Committee of the Cabinet. Over the next few months he was to increasingly monopolise the political direction of strategy and operations. The three service ministers were now excluded from the War Cabinet and reduced in status so that they were effectively little more than administrators of their services. (Only four months before he had vigorously argued with a journalist that they had to be members of the War Cabinet to ensure effective prosecution of the war, but he may have been influenced by the fact that he held one of the posts at the time.) A judicious political balance was struck by allocating one service to each of the parties in the new coalition – the Admiralty went to A. V. Alexander (Labour), the War Office to Anthony Eden (Conservative) and the Air Ministry to Sinclair (Liberal) and that political balance was to be retained for the rest of the war.

Some of Churchill's appointments acknowledged services rendered. Kingsley Wood was made Chancellor of the Exchequer as the price for switching his support from Chamberlain. Leo Amery, who had spoken against Chamberlain in the debate, was made Secretary of State for India, where Churchill thought his imperialist policies would coincide with his own. The same motivation was behind the appointment of Lord Lloyd, whom Churchill had defended in Egypt and worked with over India, as Colonial Secretary. Duff Cooper, the Munich rebel, was made Minister of Information at the expense of Lord Reith, the former Director-General of the BBC. Reith, seen as responsible for keeping Churchill off the radio in the 1930s, was relegated to Transport. Lord Beaverbrook was brought in to oversee aircraft production in a new ministry created out of part of the Air Ministry. Others had to be content with junior jobs. Churchill's old diehard ally over India, Sir Henry Page-Croft, became Junior Minister at the War Office. Harold Macmillan went to Supply, Robert Boothby to Agriculture and Harold Nicolson to Information.

Once installed in Downing Street, Churchill was able to find jobs for his personal entourage and members of his family. Lindemann became his scientific adviser and Bracken his Parliamentary Private Secretary and, despite strong opposition from the King, a Privy Councillor too. Desmond Morton was rewarded for giving Churchill top secret information in the pre-war period by becoming his main link with the intelligence agencies. General Spears, his link with the 'White' Russians in 1919–20, became his representative with the French Government, though his constant intrigues within French politics soon made him highly unpopular. Other military friends benefited too. The Earl of Cork and Orrery became Commander-in-Chief Shetlands after the Norwegian campaign collapsed and Admiral Keyes was brought back from retirement to become first Churchill's representative with the King of Belgium and then Director of Combined Operations, where his arrogance alienated nearly all his colleagues and his incompetence led to his fairly early dismissal. Churchill's friend in financial circles, Oliver Lyttleton, became his link with the Ministry of Supply. His son-in-law, Duncan Sandys, performed a similar role on Home Defence policy. Randolph turned up and helped remove Chamberlain's adviser, Horace Wilson, from No 10. Churchill was able to force his son on the party as an MP (for Preston from September 1940 until 1945) although he remained highly unpopular: it was his only time as an MP since he was never able to win an Election. Churchill's brother Jack became a constant member of the entourage, lived with him for most of the war and often accompanied him on visits. As one MP commented drily, the only member of Churchill's family not to find a role was Vic Oliver.

Although the administration was nominally a national coalition, it was in fact an overwhelmingly Conservative Government, consisting to a large part of members of Chamberlain's administration. Altogether there were fifty-two Conservative ministers, sixteen Labour and two Liberals: that proportion was to be maintained almost exactly throughout the war. With the exception of defence,

Churchill proved highly conservative in making changes in the way the Government was run. The senior civil service and military advisers were unchanged and the basic structure of Government, especially the network of committees within Whitehall to plan and co-ordinate the war effort, continued as before.

Churchill's political position was precarious. The overwhelming majority of Conservative MPs had supported Chamberlain in the vote of censure. He was not Leader of the Conservative Party and for many of its members he was no more than a disagreeable expedient imposed (like Lloyd George in 1916) by wartime politics. Most hoped that the war would soon be over and that Churchill would then be dropped, just like Lloyd George in 1922. On the day Churchill became Prime Minister, the rising young star of the Conservative Party remarked contemptuously: 'the good clean tradition of English politics . . . had been sold to the greatest adventurer in modern political history . . . a half-breed American'.[65] And the Secretary of the Conservative backbench 1922 Committee said privately on 13 May 'you must not underestimate the great reaction which has been caused among Conservative members, among whom you will find over three-quarters who are ready to put Chamberlain back'.[66] Certainly Neville Chamberlain still expected to resume the premiership once the war was over.

Churchill's position was made painfully clear when he arrived in the Commons for the first time on 13 May to tell MPs that his policy was: 'Victory at all costs, victory in spite of all terror, however long and hard the road may be, for without victory there is no survival.' He had nothing to offer them, he declared, but 'blood, toil, tears and sweat'. He was given a distinctly cool reception, as the MP 'Chips' Channon recorded:

> He [Churchill] went into the chamber and was greeted with some cheers but when, a moment later Neville entered with his usual shy retiring little manner, MPs lost their heads; they shouted; they cheered; they waved their Order Papers, and his reception was a regular ovation. The new PM spoke well, even dramatically . . . but he was not well received.[67]

It was not an encouraging Parliamentary debut as Britain's new wartime leader. Churchill's political fortune now depended on the course of the war. But far more was at stake than a political reputation. German success in Norway and its attack on the western front showed that victory was far from being a foregone conclusion. The allies had not won the first round of the war, nor had Hitler missed his best opportunity, as Churchill had claimed so optimistically only three months earlier. The Norway campaign, far from being the turning point of the war, as Churchill had forecast, had been an inglorious and largely irrelevant sideshow. Churchill's fitness to preside over the new national Government and over Britain's defence policy was about to be tested to the limit. The Norwegian fiasco was not an auspicious start.

1940 – Survival

For his first three days in power, while the German attack in the west developed, Churchill was entirely absorbed in the task of constructing the Government and allocating offices. Maurice Hankey, ex-Cabinet Secretary and Chancellor of the Duchy of Lancaster in the new Government, remarked on the curious priorities of Britain's new wartime leader: 'I found complete chaos this morning. No one was gripping the war in its crisis. The Dictator, instead of dictating, was engaged in a sordid wrangle with the politicians of the left about the secondary offices. NC [Chamberlain] was in a state of despair about it all.'[1] It was in these early days of his premiership that allied strategy was to be wrecked beyond recall, bringing about the worst disaster Britain and France had ever known. On emerging from the domestic political fray Churchill was immediately plunged into acrimonious discussions which threatened to tear apart the alliance against Germany. These negotiations took up nearly all his time during his first two months in office and he had to leave large areas of policy making to others.

Allied plans for a western-front battle were based on holding the Maginot line (which stretched, with varying degrees of effectiveness, from the Swiss to the Belgian border) and moving into Belgium in order to meet the German advance, which was expected to be on the lines of the Schlieffen plan adopted in 1914. The allies, who had far more troops than the Germans and heavily outnumbered them in tanks and artillery, though they were badly inferior in the air, would probably have countered such an unimaginative German attack very well. That was in fact the way Hitler intended to conduct the campaign had it been launched as he wanted during the autumn and winter of 1939–40 (the assault was postponed twenty-nine times). However in February 1940 he was convinced by a small group within the Army to keep holding forces only along the Maginot line, and to use about thirty divisions to move through Holland and Belgium, so stopping the main allied army from disengaging, while the bulk of the German Army, forty-five divisions, including seven Panzer divisions, moved through the Ardennes to cross the Meuse at Sedan and then turned towards the Channel, cutting the allied armies in two. It was a brilliant plan and it was brilliantly carried out.

By the time Churchill had settled the details of his administration on 14 May, the allies had advanced as planned into Belgium but the Germans were across the Meuse, had by chance encountered some third-rate French divisions stationed there and had started to open a huge gap in the French defences. He was first made aware of the impending disaster by a message from Paul Reynaud, the French Prime Minister, on 14 May. That evening there was also grim news from elsewhere. The American Ambassador, Joseph Kennedy, saw Churchill, Eden, Sinclair and Alexander and told them that Italy would soon enter the war against the allies. He reported afterwards: 'they are very low tonight although they are tough, and mean to fight'. He added that Churchill 'considers the chances of the Allies winning is [sic] slight with the entrance of Italy'.[2] And Churchill's first message as Prime Minister to President Roosevelt the next day was pessimistic: 'You may have a completely subjugated, Nazified Europe established with astonishing swiftness, and the weight may be more than we can bear.' By the end of that day (15 May) the Germans were forty miles beyond Sedan with the French disintegrating over a fifty-mile-wide front.

On the morning of 16 May Churchill was roused early to take a call from Reynaud in Paris. The scale of the disaster at Sedan was now clear to the French Government and they were expecting the German forces to advance directly on Paris where, given current progress and the lack of French reserves, they might arrive within a few days. Reynaud told Churchill bluntly 'we have lost the battle', but Churchill could not bring himself to believe what he heard – this was far worse than anything experienced in 1918 when the British collapsed – and he decided to fly to Paris that afternoon. The question he had to answer, and quickly, was what could, or should, Britain now do to help France. No Army reinforcements were available, but should Britain send additional fighter squadrons to try to eliminate the Luftwaffe's air supremacy and give time for the ground forces to re-establish a defensive front?

Since the autumn of 1939 the British had deployed six fighter squadrons in France, and the Cabinet had agreed that on the outbreak of full-scale fighting four more squadrons should join them. The first decision the Cabinet made (on 10 May) was that only two should go. On 13 May the Chief of the Air Staff advised the Cabinet that for home defence Britain needed sixty squadrons as a minimum but only had thirty-nine at present (these two figures were to change constantly in the next few weeks). Churchill took the view that home defence came first and declared 'it must not be thought that in any circumstances it would be possible to send large numbers of fighters to France'.[3] On the night the British first heard of the German breakthrough at Sedan (14 May), they rejected an urgent French request for ten extra squadrons. Churchill told his colleagues 'we should hesitate before we denuded still further the heart of the Empire'.[4] After Dowding (Commander-in-Chief Fighter Command) produced a highly misleading graph purporting to show he would have no aircraft left within a few weeks, that decision was reaffirmed the next day – 'no further fighter squadrons should for the present be sent to France'.[5]

Before flying to France on 16 May, Churchill held a Cabinet meeting to consider a renewed French request for ten fighter squadrons. The Chief of the Air Staff was now prepared to send four (despite his advice of three days earlier) and Churchill, despite his warnings over the previous days, wanted to send six. The Cabinet only agreed to send four immediately and make preparations to send two more, though the French were not to be told of this possibility. When Churchill arrived in Paris that afternoon, he found the French already burning Government papers. At a meeting of the Supreme War Council, the allied commander, General Gamelin, described the huge gap the Germans had created and explained that they could either move on Amiens and make for the Channel or go direct to Paris. Churchill asked where the strategic reserve was and Gamelin replied that 'no more' was left (not that he had 'none' as Churchill claimed in his memoirs).

Churchill and the rest of the British delegation had decided before they arrived that the French were beaten and that there was little that they could do to save them. He tactlessly told the meeting that Britain's position was very different from that of its ally: 'as long as the British could hold command of the air over England and could control the seas of the world, they were confident of the ultimate results, and it would always be possible to carry on'.[6] He refused to divert the RAF's bombing effort to the support of the allied armies but he did telephone London to back the French request for fighter squadrons. In a complete change of mind from that morning's meeting, he now argued for sending another six squadrons – i.e. the full ten the French had requested. His grounds for doing so were not that this action would save France but that a British refusal would look bad – 'It would not be good historically if their requests were denied and their ruin resulted.' At an emergency meeting his Cabinet colleagues would not agree to his request. As a concession, six extra squadrons would be available to operate over France (three in the morning, three in the afteroon) but they would remain based in Britain and so their effectiveness would be greatly reduced.[7]

This was the limit of British air assistance. On his return from Paris Churchill had already set his sights on home defence. He asked Chamberlain to co-ordinate work on evacuating the British Expeditionary Force (BEF) from the continent and its commander, Lord Gort, was told to start drawing up the necessary plans. Meanwhile the Cabinet continued to wrestle with their consciences and the air staff's elusive figurework. On 18 May the chiefs of staff, based on figures provided by Dowding (which were based on yet another different assessment of how many squadrons were needed for home defence), advised 'we have already reached the absolute limit of the air assistance we can afford to France'.[8] Two days later the Cabinet agreed (again) that no further aircraft should be sent to France (the previous day the RAF had already begun withdrawing units from the continent). The net result of their decisions on air assistance to France was that by the end of May the British had only half the number of squadrons in France that they had when fighting started on 10 May – and the number available for home defence had risen by over sixty per cent. The French had good reason to feel that they had been let down by their ally at the crucial moment.

Meanwhile the allies had been trying to put together a counterattack to contain the German penetration. The problem was that their command structure, designed to cope with the slow trench warfare of the 1914–18 war, was unable to devise a coherent response. Although the German High Command was worried by the speed at which the Panzer divisions were advancing (forty miles a day at times) and regularly called halts, the pace was still too fast to allow the allies to mount attacks from north and south to cut off the German forces. The situation was made worse by open disputes between the allies at every level and the French decision to replace Gamelin by the seventy-three-year-old Weygand. By the time the new French commander had flown home from the Levant, rested in Paris, travelled to the front and devised a new plan (virtually identical with the one Gamelin had drawn up before his dismissal), more time was lost. By 22 May, when the British and French Governments were discussing Weygand's plan, German units had already reached the Channel coast and split the allies into two forces unable to act together.

The BEF had started to retreat as soon as it reached its planned defensive positions in Belgium on 16 May. Although supposedly under French command, Gort refused to accept their orders to fight on the line of the River Senne (17 May) or to support the 1st French Army (19 May). By then, as ordered by Churchill on 17 May, he was already working on plans to evacuate the BEF. On 20 May he was ordered by London to try and fight his way through to the south, but the only result was a small-scale attack the next day around Arras by two territorial battalions and seventy-four tanks, although the move did cause some temporary difficulties for the Germans. On 22 May Churchill flew to Paris for a Supreme War Council meeting convened to discuss the joint counter-attack planned by Weygand. None of the participants knew that the British effort had come to nothing. Churchill agreed to the Weygand plan (for joint attacks from north and south to isolate German forces along the Channel) and on his return to London the next day the plan was sent to Gort, though altered in significant details. Churchill also telephoned Reynaud to tell him to order the counter-attack immediately. Yet later that same day, in a complete volte face, Gort's request to

441

withdraw was approved. As Ironside put it: 'We have sent complete discretion to Gort to move his army as he likes to try and save it.'[9]

The next morning (24 May) Churchill, abandoning the plan agreed in Paris two days earlier, told Reynaud that any counter-attack had to come from the south by the French thus reinforcing French fears that despite Churchill's assurances on 22 May the British had no intention of implementing the Weygand plan and were intent only on saving themselves. Their doubts were increased by events around Boulogne and Calais. On 22 May the British occupied Boulogne for twenty-four hours, then abandoned it and left the French to defend it for another thirty hours before it fell to the Germans. The French troops were unable to escape because the British on leaving had sunk a ship to block the harbour. When on 24 May Gort seemed set on abandoning Calais too, Churchill felt the speed of the British withdrawal was undignified and unjustified. (The British had done very little fighting so far – the BEF sustained only 500 casualties in the first eleven days of the campaign.) He commented sarcastically to Gort (in a passage omitted in his memoirs), 'of course if one side fights and the other does not, the war is apt to become somewhat unequal'. After French protests, in a message designed for public consumption, Churchill ordered the British commander at Calais to fight on and not surrender. Between 24 and 26 May the BEF rejected five appeals from the Belgian Army for a counter-attack to relieve German pressure. On the afternoon of 25 May Gort told Eden at the War Office that he was moving the BEF to the coast for evacuation (nearly 30,000 British troops had already gone). Eden agreed and told him 'It is obvious that you should not discuss the possibility of the move with the French or the Belgians.' That night the Defence Committee, with Churchill in the chair, issued formal orders for the final evacuation.

The next day (26 May) Reynaud flew to London for a meeting with Churchill, who, following Eden's advice to Gort, did not inform him of British plans to evacuate the BEF. The purpose of Reynaud's visit was to address the crucial question of whether the allies should somehow continue the war or whether they should consider negoti-ating peace terms. In his war memoirs Churchill wrote, 'Future generations may deem it noteworthy that the supreme question of whether we would fight on alone never found a place upon the War Cabinet agenda . . . we were much too busy to waste time upon such unreal, academic issues.'[10] That statement was untrue and designed to conceal the four occasions on which the Cabinet did discuss exactly this issue. It was hardly surprising that they did. May 1940 was the worst military disaster the allies had faced. They were totally unprepared for the scale of the German success. The British had built their strategy around the supposed strength of the French Army, which had after all survived every crisis in the previous war – the Marne, the 1917 mutinies and the 1918 spring offensive. It was, as Halifax put it in his diary, 'the one firm rock on which everybody had been willing to build for the last two years'.[11] As the western front collapsed after only a fortnight's fighting, the British Government, expecting to rescue no more than perhaps 50,000 troops from the continent, was in a state of panic. Plans were hastily drawn up to ship the Bank of England's gold to Canada, and the Canadian Government was warned to expect the arrival of the Royal Family shortly. On the morning of 26 May Churchill asked the chiefs of staff to consider whether Britain could fight on alone against Germany and Italy and whether they could 'hold out reasonable hopes of preventing serious invasion', with the aim, not of victory, but of achieving 'a prolongation of British resistance [which] might be very dangerous for Germany engaged in holding down the greater part of Europe'.[12]

At the War Cabinet meeting before Reynaud arrived, Churchill told his colleagues that he expected the French Premier to say that France wanted an armistice (such an eventuality had been openly discussed at the French Cabinet meeting the previous evening). Halifax indicated a willingness to see what was on offer, saying that 'we had to face the fact that it was not so much now a question of imposing complete defeat upon Germany but of safeguarding the independence of our own Empire and if possible that of France'. He had spoken to the Italian Ambassador the previous evening when the question of a peace conference had been raised and told him Britain would consider such ideas 'provided our liberty and independence were assured'. Churchill did not dissent and merely reformulated Halifax's statement by saying he opposed 'any negotiations that might lead to a derogation of our rights and power'.[13] Immediately after having lunch with Reynaud, Churchill met the Cabinet again briefly to tell them that the French felt that with little assistance coming from Britain and none from the United States they might not be able to continue the war much longer. There was no time for substantive discussion before he left to resume his talks with Reynaud.

The War Cabinet met again later in the afternoon to discuss a firm French proposal that Mussolini should be asked to find out what terms Hitler would suggest for peace. All the members were agreed that there was no point in trying to tempt Mussolini to remain neutral – it would not affect the campaign in France and anyway the allies would not be able to offer enough to make it worth his while. Instead Halifax and Chamberlain suggested that it might be worth playing on Mussolini's fears of a dominant Germany to see if some sort of European settlement was possible (this was the role Mussolini had played at Munich and the goal he had nearly achieved over Poland in September 1939). Churchill, Attlee and Greenwood did not agree. They clung to the belief that the German economy was stretched to breaking point and would collapse within a matter of months. Therefore, if Britain could hold out till the end of the year, that might be enough either for victory or to secure better terms than Hitler would offer in the immediate aftermath of military success. Churchill was opposed to any approach to Mussolini to ask for terms: 'we must not get entangled in a position of that kind before we had been involved in any serious fighting' (a very fair comment on the BEF's performance). In his view 'it was best to do nothing until we saw how much of the Army we could re-embark from France'.[14]

But that did not mean that Churchill refused to consider anything short of total victory. No one in the Government had ever contemplated enforcing a policy of unconditional surrender on Germany. In October 1939 Churchill had redrafted Chamberlain's reply to Hitler's opening peace offer: though negative, its wording did not, as he explained, 'close the door upon any genuine offer' from Germany.[15] During the discussion on the afternoon of 26 May Halifax asked the Prime Minister 'whether, if he was satisfied that matters vital to the independence of this country were unaffected, he would be prepared to discuss terms'. His reply was that 'he would be thankful to get out of our present difficulties on such terms, provided we retained the essentials and the elements of our vital strength even at the cost of some cession of territory'.[16] Neville Chamberlain recorded Churchill's response in less measured terms than the civil service minutes: 'if we could get out of this jam by giving up Malta and Gibraltar and some African colonies he would jump at it'.[17] No firm conclusions were reached that afternoon. In the evening Halifax, who had shown himself more anxious than any of the others to see whether reasonable terms might be available, circulated to his colleagues the text of a message designed to see whether it was possible to buy off Mussolini.

The War Cabinet met again the next afternoon (27 May) but with Sinclair present as well – in view of the gravity of the issues for discussion Churchill obviously felt it necessary to have all the parties in the coalition represented. There had been two developments overnight. President Roosevelt had agreed to a British request to approach Mussolini on the allies' behalf to find out what price he wanted for a settlement. The French had also asked for what the civil service minutes euphemistically called 'greater geographical precision' in the possible offer to Mussolini for a peace conference (i.e. a clear statement of what Britain was prepared to cede in the Mediterranean). Halifax was now isolated in arguing for finding out what the terms for peace might be before France collapsed. Churchill's position was that 'if Herr Hitler was prepared to make peace on the terms of the restoration of German colonies and the overlordship of Central Europe' (presumably including continued occupation of Czechoslovakia and western Poland and the handing back of East and South West Africa) that was something he was prepared to accept, but he rightly thought such an offer most unlikely.[18] At Chamberlain's suggestion, the War Cabinet agreed to wait and see what happened with Roosevelt's approach to the Italians. After the meeting Halifax was on the brink of resignation because he felt he could no longer work with the Prime Minister. But Churchill, whose political position was still very weak, could not afford to allow his Foreign Secretary to resign and during a long talk in the garden of No 10 persuaded him to stay on.

When the War Cabinet met again on 28 May in Churchill's room at the Commons, it was known that Roosevelt's approach to Mussolini had come to nothing. Halifax still felt it was best to see what terms Hitler might offer. All his colleagues objected to starting on that slippery slope which would almost inevitably lead to negotiations with Germany. Chamberlain thought it was best to save up any concessions such as Malta and Gibraltar so as, if necessary, to be in a position to give them to Hitler rather than Mussolini. Churchill's position was that Britain might, at some time in the future, have to seek peace but the terms would be no worse than those Hitler would grant in the aftermath of a stunning victory and they might be better if Britain were able to successfully counter a German attempt at invasion:

> we should get no worse terms if we went on fighting, even if we were beaten, than were open to us now ... A time might come when we felt that we had to put an end to the struggle, but the terms would not then be more mortal than those offered to us now.

Churchill therefore accepted Chamberlain's suggestion that the French should be given the bleak message that they were on their own although Britain would fight on for the moment in order to try and obtain better terms from Germany:

> We in this country felt that we had resources left to us of which we could make good use. If, as we believed, we could hold out, we should be able to obtain terms which would not affect our independence.[19]

That Churchill's policy was now far from the idea of total victory that he had announced to the House of Commons only a fortnight before was confirmed by the message he sent to all ministers on 29 May, urging them to keep up morale 'till we have broken the will of the enemy to bring all Europe under his domination'.[20]

Britain's chances of fighting on were immeasurably improved by the rescue of most of the BEF from Dunkirk, although the manner in which this was achieved further worsened relations with France. Churchill failed to tell Reynaud, when the latter was in London on 26 May, of the British decision to evacuate what they could of the BEF. A successful evacuation depended on maintaining a bridgehead and this depended on the French (and if possible the Belgians too) fighting on. The British were once again putting their own interests first, not those of the alliance. On 27 May Churchill told the Cabinet: 'It was clear that we could not allow the security of our Army to be compromised in order to save the First French Army.'[21] (By fighting on around Lille until 1 June that French Army made the British evacuation possible.) Two days later Churchill reinforced this message, telling his colleagues: 'British troops should on no account delay their withdrawal to conform with the French.'[22]

Full-scale British withdrawal began on 27 May, and by 29 May just over 55,000 troops had been rescued. That evening Churchill told Ironside that he thought there was 'very little chance of the whole BEF coming off ... very little more chance of getting any units off'.[23] He glumly told ministers they were facing: 'the greatest British military defeat for many centuries'.[24] In fact tough French resistance enabled the evacuation to continue for another six days. Captain Tennant, the senior naval officer at Dunkirk, recorded: 'The French staff at Dunkirk feel strongly that they are defending Dunkirk for us to evacuate, which is largely true' – indeed at this time the British were manhandling French troops off the boats. On 31 May Churchill again flew to Paris to discuss the situation. In a histrionic gesture he offered the French half the evacuation places. But this was not as generous as it appeared. By that stage over 135,000 British troops (about three-quarters of the BEF) had already been evacuated, compared with less than 25,000 French. By then relatively small numbers of British troops were left at Dunkirk (only another 47,000 were evacuated). Churchill also volunteered the British to act as the rearguard. But he never implemented his promise. Gort, the commander of the BEF, left Dunkirk later that day; his successor, General Alexander, was told that the safety of the BEF must be his prime consideration. No orders were issued to him that he should act as the rearguard. Throughout the evacuation the British also did what they had not done for the French Army – RAF fighters operated at full strength to counter Luftwaffe attacks.

By the beginning of June the French had lost a quarter of their Army; outnumbered two to one, they now faced a rapidly regrouping German Army along the line of the Somme. The British had rescued the overwhelming majority of the BEF (though not its equipment). Having written off the chances of French survival over two weeks earlier, continuing French resistance posed problems for the British over how to deal with their ally. At first Churchill seemed happy for them to drop out of the war – Sir Alexander Cadogan, head of the Foreign Office, reported on 26 May that Churchill 'seemed to think we might almost be better off if France *did* pull out and we could concentrate on defence here'.[25] By the beginning of June, however, he had swung back to a policy of trying to keep France fighting for as long as possible to buy time for Britain's defences to be improved. But there were strict limits on the help the Cabinet was prepared to give France. On 3 June they agreed not to send more than the six bomber and three fighter squadrons then operating in France. Churchill tried to reopen the question the next day, pointing out the poor level of British assistance, but his colleagues would not change the decision. Britain also had one infantry division in France (the French still had sixty-two divisions left). The Cabinet agreed to send one more division on 7 June. The British also opposed a French request for a unified air force command – they rejected it outright for fighters and accepted it for bombers only on condition the British were in charge.

On 5 June the second German offensive opened and within days the French line was shattered. On 8 June Churchill's message to the Defence Committee was that what mattered was saving Britain not France: 'we should recognise that whereas the present land battle was of great importance, it would not be decisive one way or the other for Great Britain ... If this country were defeated, the war would be lost for France no less than for ourselves.'[26] Two days later Paris was declared an open city and the Italians attempted to scramble on to the winning side by declaring war. On 11 June Churchill flew to Briare (just east of Orléans) for a two day meeting of the Supreme War Council. He had little to offer them apart from rhetoric, which they found unconvincing. He could offer the French no military support – in addition to the two British divisions already fighting, he promised one more but nothing else until 1941, and no extra aircraft. When he spoke of the spring 1918 crisis, Pétain, who had been recalled to the Government, rightly responded: 'In 1918 I gave you forty divisions to save the British Army, where are the forty British divisions that would be needed to save ourselves today?' Churchill then gave the French the bleak message that he did not regard the current battle as decisive – that was reserved for the German attack on Britain; if Britain could survive the next three or four months then 'we will win it all back for you'.[27]

On the morning of 12 June Churchill felt he had to agree to at least consider Reynaud's request for five extra fighter squadrons and he asked for further consultations before the French requested an armistice (which he realised was not far away). On his return to London he told the Cabinet that 'it was clear that France was near the end of organised resistance'.[28] He sent a message to the French Premier to say that the fighters he asked for would operate over France from British bases (in fact the front was now too far south for this to be possible). Late in the evening Reynaud telephoned to ask Churchill to go back to France – Weygand, supported by Pétain, had recommended an armistice and, unlike the discussion on 25 May, the French Cabinet were no longer prepared to rule it out. Once again Churchill flew out to France to a meeting with Reynaud, this time at the prefecture in Tours amongst the chaos of the collapse.

At what turned out to be the last Supreme War Council meeting, on 13 June, neither side was clear about what they wanted. Most of the important issues were not faced openly and what was said gave rise to chronic misunderstandings later. Reynaud explained the divisions within the French Cabinet and insisted that immediate American aid was the only way to keep France in the war. Churchill asked them to launch guerrilla warfare and move the Government to North Africa. Reynaud spoke of not abandoning France to Germany, which the British took as a request to pursue a separate armistice. Churchill told the French to wait for the result of Reynaud's appeal to Roosevelt and declared that Britain would not agree to a separate peace. But when, listening to the French case, he kept saying '*Je comprends*', they took this to mean that he understood why they would have to ask for an armistice. Since Churchill also told them there would be no recriminations if they did so, the French felt they had been given informal authority to go ahead. The French Cabinet had expected to meet Churchill after the War Council meeting, but Reynaud did not pass on the suggestion and so when Churchill left without seeing them, this added to the feeling that Britain was abandoning France.

On 14 June the British began withdrawing all their troops from France and the next day the French Cabinet, which had moved on to Bordeaux, decided, after Roosevelt had effectively rejected their appeal for help, to enquire what terms the Germans would offer. Reynaud asked for British agreement under a threat that a different government might bargain over the future of the fleet. On 16 June there was chaos in both London and Bordeaux: the British played their hand very badly and actually helped bring about the result they did not want in France. Reynaud hoped for an outright refusal from

Britain to accept a separate armistice (the two countries had agreed a policy of no separate peace at the end of March) so as to strengthen his hand in insisting the Government move to North Africa to continue the fight. But Churchill went back on his statement at Tours; he now told Reynaud he agreed to a Franco-German armistice, provided the French fleet sailed to British ports. This was the worst possible policy: it undermined Reynaud's position, it was bound to increase French suspicions that Britain was simply trying to pick up the pieces they wanted from the French collapse; and it removed the necessary protection of the fleet for the Government's move to North Africa.

Before Reynaud could put this before the French Cabinet, the British confused the picture further by coming up with a different proposal. For some days various people around Whitehall, together with the French Ambassador and the new Minister for War, Charles de Gaulle, had been considering the idea of an Anglo-French union as a way of strengthening Reynaud (both Frenchmen preferred this to Britain's demand to give up the fleet). Churchill was first told about the idea over lunch on the 16th and, in a rushed session, the War Cabinet agreed to tell Reynaud of the proposal for a union (still largely undefined) before the French Cabinet meeting. At that meeting Reynaud did not tell his colleagues about Britain's conditions for agreeing to an armistice and the idea of union was rejected as simply Britain's attempt to keep France fighting in her own interest. Britain's attempt to avoid a separate peace had failed. After further discussion Reynaud resigned, to be replaced by Pétain, who was prepared to ask for armistice terms. The same evening Churchill, accompanied by Attlee and Sinclair, was preparing to leave to meet Reynaud to discuss the union project, but had to turn round at Waterloo station when news of the change of Government reached London.

For the next two and a half weeks the future of the French fleet was to dominate British policy making and lead to open fighting between the ex-allies. During this period it was Churchill who continually pressed for the use of force. At the Briare conference on 11 June Churchill had asked Admiral Darlan, the Commander of the French Navy, not to surrender the fleet. Darlan indignantly rejected the idea and assured him the fleet would, if necessary, be scuttled. The day after Pétain asked for an armistice Churchill sent him a tough message about the consequences of surrendering the fleet to Germany, warning him, 'Such an act would scarify French names for a thousand years of history.' What Churchill and his colleagues did not know was that the Pétain Government had decided to reject any armistice that required the surrender of the fleet and that Hitler had been shrewd enough not to ask for it, guessing it would only increase French resistance. On 18 June Darlan informed Alexander, Pound and Lord Lloyd in Bordeaux that the fleet would not be surrendered and that instructions had been issued for it to sail to North Africa or scuttle itself if necessary. The armistice came into effect on 25 June. It divided France into two, in the north and centre a German-occupied zone and in the south a French administration led by Pétain, which controlled the Empire and the remaining military forces.

In his memoirs Churchill wrote, 'no French warship stirred or put itself beyond the reach of German power'. The statement was totally untrue. In accordance with Darlan's instructions, small ships were scuttled, harbour installations were destroyed and the large warships sailed for Africa or Toulon in the French-controlled zone. But Churchill and his colleagues were acutely concerned about the French fleet. With Italy now in the war, naval control of the Mediterranean was problematic and if the French fleet was made available to Germany and Italy then British naval supremacy might be difficult to maintain. Could they afford to rely on Pétain and Darlan to keep it out of hostile hands or should they take action to immobilise the fleet themselves? The terms of the armistice, which spoke (in the French version) of German 'contrôle' of the fleet, made them fear the worst. This was mistranslated as 'control', the British not realising the French word was much weaker and meant something nearer 'administrative verification'.

The issue had to be decided quickly – the Royal Navy had to be concentrated against the invasion threat. For Churchill the choice was clear. At the War Cabinet meeting on 22 June he told his colleagues 'in a matter so vital to the safety of the whole British Empire we could not afford to rely on the word of Admiral Darlan' and that if necessary 'we should have to fight and sink' the main units of the French fleet.[29] But at this stage he could not convince his colleagues to take such a drastic step. They were more conciliatory and were prepared to let the French ships then in Britain leave for the French colonies outside the Mediterranean; their main concern was over who controlled the ships, not sinking them. On 24 June the War Cabinet held three meetings on the future of the French fleet. At the second it was agreed that Churchill and Halifax would draft an ultimatum demanding that the fleet be scuttled – if not it would be sunk. However, just over four hours later when the Cabinet came to consider an Admiralty appreciation of such an operation, they realised the difficulties involved and decided to postpone a decision.

Over the next three days Churchill was gradually able to convince his colleagues of the need to use force. In this he was helped by the fact that no dissident French group seemed likely to start up effective resistance in North Africa and by growing fears that Darlan was merely a German puppet. (In fact he had just secured German agreement that the fleet should be stationed at Toulon in the French-controlled zone or in North Africa, well out of German reach.) On 27 June the Cabinet decided in principle to undertake an operation against the French ships at Mers-el-Kebir, near Oran; those at Casablanca and Dakar were thought to be secure from any German action and those in Britain and at Alexandria could be taken over very easily. After Churchill had put pressure on the chiefs of staff to disagree with the Admiralty and planning staff assessment that came down against the operation, formal approval for action on 3 July was given by the War Cabinet on 30 June. The chiefs of staff were prepared to accept the risk of France declaring war – they expected that to happen shortly anyway now that the British blockade of the continent had been extended to its former ally.

The French at Mers-el-Kebir were to be given four choices (all of which would breach the armistice conditions). They could sail to Britain and continue the war; or just leave the ships in Britain and the crews would be repatriated; they could sail to North America; or they could sink the ships. Churchill refused to give the French the option of demilitarising the ships (which would have achieved British aims); this course could only be accepted it if was offered by the French themselves and then only on very strict conditions. The French were to be given six hours to decide; after that, if none of the options were accepted, the ships were to be sunk. On 3 July the War Cabinet was in almost permanent session as tense negotiations between the British force commanded by Admiral Somerville and the French commander at Mers-el-Kebir were underway. The French procrastinated in order to bring up reinforcements – the British were intercepting these signals and ordered Somerville to hurry and take action that day. It seemed as though the French would accept an offer of demilitarisation but the Cabinet decided that 'we should not offer it now, as this would look like weakening'.[30]

Eventually when the talks failed the British fleet opened fire, but the operation at Mers-el-Kebir was, as the Admiralty planners had predicted, a failure. Somerville had been told that his main targets were the modern battleships *Dunquerque* and *Strasbourg* – the former escaped to Toulon and the latter, though damaged, was not put out of action; only an old battleship, *Bretagne*, was sunk. Nearly 1,300 French sailors were killed and 350 wounded. As Somerville admitted in his diary: 'Fear I've made a mess of this lousy operation', perhaps because, as he told his wife, 'The truth is my heart wasn't in it'.[31] Elsewhere action was more successful. In Britain about 200 French ships were taken over and at Alexandria the French ships were disarmed peacefully after Admiral Cunningham ignored a signal from Churchill ordering him to put to sea and be prepared to sink them instead. At Dakar the *Richelieu* was damaged but not put out of action. Although some of the French fleet was neutralised, in overall terms the British action was only partially successful. The French did not react very strongly – diplomatic relations, in abeyance since 23 June, were formally broken off and Gibraltar was subjected to a token bombing. (Whether the whole operation was really necessary is a difficult question – certainly when the Germans took over the unoccupied zone of France in November 1942 the French did scuttle seventy-seven ships at Toulon to stop them falling into enemy hands.) Churchill was caustic about the French response to the British ultimatum, saying they 'were now fighting with all their vigour for the first time since war broke out'.[32] That slur was typical of British reactions and totally unjustified by the casualty figures. During the battle for France the British lost 3,500 men killed; the French had 120,000 dead, 250,000 wounded and 1.5 million taken prisoner – a casualty rate higher than many stages of the slaughter at Verdun.

There seems little doubt that for Churchill personally the aim of the operation was less military than political and psychological, with an eye to public opinion both at home and abroad. Although Churchill was in tears in the Commons when he made a statement on the affair on 4 July, he had been primarily responsible for the resort to force against Britain's defeated ally. His aim was to demonstrate Britain's determination to fight on and also to cement his own political position. He told the Commons that day: 'The action we have already taken should be, in itself, sufficient to dispose once and for all of the lies and rumours . . . that we have the slightest intention of entering into negotiations . . . with the German and Italian Governments.' The operation was aimed particularly at American opinion – the British had informally consulted Roosevelt beforehand and obtained his approval (the Americans were also worried by what would happen if the French fleet fell into German hands). Until the attack Churchill's position as Prime Minister was insecure. He had presided over nothing but disaster and while Chamberlain remained leader of the Conservatives had no firm political base to fall back on. Some members of the Government, in particular Halifax and Butler at the Foreign Office, were more inclined towards seeking a compromise peace before the situation deteriorated even further. Conservative backbenchers were also cold or hostile towards him: throughout May and June his speeches in the Commons had been greeted with indifference at best. The action against the French and the speech in the Commons were designed to provide a show of determination and a rallying point. But his Parliamentary ovation only came after journalists told the Chief Whip, Margesson, that the hostility towards Churchill was causing great damage abroad and backbenchers were almost forced to their feet by the Whips to cheer the Prime Minister's statement.

For the first two months of his premiership Churchill had been almost totally engrossed in the problems caused by the collapse of Britain's only ally. Chamberlain and Attlee were left with a good deal of freedom on the domestic front. Yet as Britain's strategic position disintegrated the state of morale at home became increasingly important. A public already dismayed by the Norwegian fiasco had suffered a series of terrible shocks under his leadership. Within six weeks of the start of serious fighting Britain was isolated – Germany occupied Norway, Denmark, Holland, Belgium, Luxembourg and Czechoslovakia together with most of France and Poland. Moreover Germany was allied to Italy (not altogether an advantage), it had the benevolent neutrality of the Soviet Union and Spain, and the other European neutrals were quickly learning to adapt to the new balance of power. Britain had the support of the Empire, the moral backing of the governments-in-exile and the sympathy, though little else, of the United States. It was the worst position Britain had ever faced in its history. Churchill himself was privately far from optimistic about the future. Just after Dunkirk he wrote to Baldwin, 'We are going through vy hard times & I suspect worse to come: but I feel quite sure that better days will come! Though whether we shall live to see them is more doubtful.'[33] When he left the Briare conference to fly back to England, he fell into conversation with Ismay. He remarked that Britain would now be fighting alone and Ismay said that he was glad – 'we'll win the Battle of Britain'. Churchill replied morosely, 'You and I will be dead in three months time.'[34]

Among all the pressures of the crisis, Churchill had to decide how, and how often, he would address the nation. What is so striking about the speeches he made in 1940 is that most of them were addressed, in the first instance, to the House of Commons rather than the nation at large. (He broadcast only five times in the nine months after he became Prime Minister and he did not broadcast some of his most famous speeches at all – existing recordings were specially made long after the event.) Like many other members of the political and administrative élite in Britain he had little or no experience of the lives of ordinary citizens to draw on and was not convinced that they would withstand the strains of war. For him Parliament was the forum of the nation and his efforts were primarily directed there, not at communicating with the public. His first speech on taking office ('I have nothing to offer but blood, toil, tears and sweat') was only given in the House of Commons and was not broadcast. He did not give his first radio address to the nation, about the battle in France and the forthcoming Battle of Britain, until he had been in office for nine days. He did not broadcast again for a month, despite the great anxiety brought on by the débâcle of Dunkirk and the collapse of France. (His speech in the Commons on 4 June – 'We shall fight on the beaches' – was not broadcast; when it went out on the BBC World Service Churchill's words were read by an actor pretending to be Churchill.)

Although the French request for an armistice on 16 June came as a great shock to the public, Churchill decided not to broadcast for another three days. Under great pressure from the press, who were worried about the state of morale, he changed his mind and agreed to speak on 17 June. It was a perfunctory two minute address given in the middle of the day when few people were listening. The only encouragement he held out was: 'We are sure that in the end all will come right.' One of the editors who had asked for the broadcast commented that the speech was 'a few stumbling sentences to the effect that the situation was disastrous, but all right. Whether he was drunk or all-in from sheer fatigue, I don't know, but it was the poorest possible effort on an occasion when he should have produced the finest speech of his life.'[35] The next day he did produce perhaps the finest speech of his life. It was given to the Commons and he used the memorable phrase – that the period now facing the country would become known as 'their finest hour'. Churchill himself had no intention of broadcasting that speech to the country, but the Ministry of Information, worried over the state of morale, persuaded him, after a very long argument, to speak on the radio. Having nothing else available, he re-used his earlier speech. A disappointed junior minister, Harold Nicolson, described the reluctant performance:

> When we bullied him into speaking . . . he just sulked and read his House of Commons speech over again. Now, as delivered in the House of Commons, that speech was magnificent, especially the concluding sentences. But it sounded ghastly on the wireless. All the great vigour he put into it seemed to evaporate.[36]

Churchill's Private Secretary was also critical: 'It was too long and he sounded tired.'[37]

But Churchill was not going to make a practice of using the airwaves even during the most anxious period for the country. He spoke to the nation on 14 July in a specially prepared address. But his other famous speech about the Battle of Britain ('Never in the field of human conflict was so much owed by so many to so few') was given in the Commons on 20 August and not broadcast. This time he specifically rejected a Ministry of Information request to repeat it on the BBC and he also twice refused to give an address on the first anniversary of the war – 'I have rather decanted myself on this topic in H of C.'[38] During the most crucial period, when Britain faced the threat of invasion and the RAF fought the Luftwaffe in the skies over south-east England, Churchill did not speak to the country at all – after his speech on 14 July he was silent for almost two months until a broadcast on 11 September.

When he did speak Churchill emphasised his own rather idiosyncratic view of British history and the importance of traditional loyalties. It was a message that looked backwards – to the 'brave old days of the past'; that broadcast compared the present situation to those faced in 1588 (the Spanish Armada) and 1805 (Napoleon's invasion threat and Trafalgar). He had no interest in conjuring up a view of the future designed to appeal to a modern democracy fighting a totalitarian state in the twentieth century. Although the speeches and broadcasts contain fine rhetorical and inspirational phrases, they were couched in typically conservative Churchillian terms and reflected his preoccupations – an appeal to duty, the central importance of the empire, the qualities of the British 'race' and the continuity of Britain's institutions.

In Churchill's view the summer of 1940 was an opportunity for Britons to 'show the finest qualities of their race' (18 June); all depended on the 'whole life-strength of the British race' (14 July) and it would be an historic time for 'our famous island race' (11 September). Survival would be achieved 'if all do their duty' (4 June), 'let us therefore brace ourselves to our duty' (18 June). On 11 September he ordered 'every man and every woman will therefore prepare himself [sic] to do his duty.' The conflict was portrayed as part of the long story of the British Empire and Britain's institutions. He said that on the outcome of the Battle of Britain 'depends our own British life and the long continuity of our institutions and our Empire' (18 June). In the same speech he spoke of the British Empire lasting 'for a thousand years' (a direct comparison with Hitler's thousand year Reich). When London was bombed it was 'this mighty imperial city' (11 September).

This style was not something he developed in 1940. For instance in a broadcast in January 1935 Churchill produced one passage that could quite easily have been used in 1940 without any alteration:

> It will be settled by the spirit of the British nation, by the march of world events, and by the faithful discharge of their duty, by the men and women spread throughout the land, whose constant

thought is for the future of their country, and whose collective will power is unconquerable.

On that occasion he was talking about the need to oppose the new constitutional settlement in India.

Churchill's infrequent broadcasts and his conservative message were combined with a heavy handed and incompetent Government propaganda campaign, which included for example the highly ambiguous slogan 'Your courage, Your cheerfulness, Your resolution, will bring us victory'. Given the disastrous events on the continent it is hardly surprising that British morale remained low. On 18 May the Ministry of Information daily report assessed that 'public morale was at a low ebb'.[39] As France collapsed and the BEF retreated towards the Channel, they reported more gloom: 'Rumour during the last few days has tended to emphasise some aspect of our own feebleness and futility ... This kind of rumour is clearly unhealthy for it is an unconscious reflection of privately held opinion.'[40]

In retrospect Churchill's speeches have come to be seen as great morale boosting exercises that united everyone and brought the nation through one of the most difficult times in its history. Contemporary, but secret, Government accounts, drawn from material supplied by assessors across the country, paint a very different picture. Reports after the fall of France and the broadcast of 18 June ('Their Finest Hour'), give the impression that Churchill's words had made little impact on the public. The assessment for 24 June gave a clear message: 'There is no escaping the tenor of our reports: leadership is in jeopardy.'[41] A more detailed report concluded:

> There is great restlessness, great depression at the fall of France. Home morale is still being bungled. The appeals of the leadership are failing to register. The reasons are partly that persons responsible for morale and propaganda have no sympathy with the majority of the masses.[42]

By the beginning of July the Cabinet was worried by what it described as the 'growing mood of pessimism'. It issued instructions to stop 'defeatist talk'.[43] Two days later they were alarmed at publication of the exact casualty figures from the small German air raid on

Newcastle and for the future banned anything more detailed than the use of 'slight', 'considerable' or 'heavy' casualties, because they thought actual statistics would 'have a demoralising effect in this country'.[44] At the end of the month the Ministry of Information's intelligence reports suggested a widespread feeling in the provinces that Churchill was too old and played out and that he should therefore retire.

Earlier in July Churchill had decided to launch a campaign that implied a considerable lack of confidence in 'our famous island race'. On 5 July he instructed the Ministry of Information that 'a wide campaign should be immediately put in hand against the dangers of rumour'.[45] They advised against this approach, but Churchill insisted. The result was the 'Silent Column' campaign, with its pedestrian humour about 'Mr Secrecy Hush-Hush' and 'Miss Leaky Mouth' and its laboured advice, 'If you know anybody who makes a habit of causing worry and anxiety by passing on rumour and who says things persistently that might help the enemy – tell the police, but only as a last resort.' It was followed by a rash of prosecutions (on 11 June it had been made a criminal offence to make or report any statement likely to cause 'alarm and despondency') – one case led to a month in jail for a man who said Britain had no chance of winning the war. The Ministry of Information reports concluded that the campaign was widely hated and was giving rise to 'increasing suspicion and unneighbourliness' and was thought to be 'sinister'.[46] Within a fortnight of the campaign starting, Harold Nicolson, the Junior Minister of Information, wrote, 'There is no doubt that our anti-rumour campaign has been a ghastly failure.'[47] Churchill then disowned the campaign he had himself started when he announced in the Commons on 23 July that it was being abandoned. Churchill's tendency to misjudge popular feeling may owe much to the fact that public opinion just was not important in his view. He told one newspaper editor in February 1940: 'in time of war the machinery of government is so strong it can afford largely to ignore popular feeling'.[48]

Undoubtedly the major factor worrying the public from the end of May was the threat of invasion. It was worrying the Government too. The first assessment made as the German Army reached the Channel was very pessimistic about the outcome: 'should the enemy succeed in establishing a force, with its vehicles, firmly ashore, the army in the United Kingdom, which is very short of equipment, has not got the offensive power to drive it out.'[49] However within days it became clear that Hitler intended to defeat France before dealing with Britain and the rescue of nearly 200,000 soldiers of the BEF from Dunkirk meant there was at least a nucleus around which a new army could be constructed once new equipment, in the first instance rifles, had arrived from the United States. Continued French resistance meant that it was not until the end of June that the Germans were in a position to even contemplate the possibility of a cross-Channel invasion.

When they studied the problem it was immediately clear that they faced almost unsuperable difficulties. Although the German Army had 150 divisions on the continent, it had no way of launching them across the Channel. It lacked amphibious capability (it had never done anything more ambitious than a river crossing) and putting together a hastily improvised invasion force from river barges and tugs was the only course possible. They had a small airborne capability – about 2,000 men – and just enough aircraft to transport them. The German Navy was not capable of protecting an invasion force as it crossed the Channel. It had lost half its destroyers (ten ships) and forty per cent of its cruisers in Norway and only had operational one heavy cruiser, two light cruisers, six destroyers and a few torpedo boats. This was hopelessly inadequate to confront the Royal Navy.

From the beginning the German military planners acceped that they could not mount a cross-Channel invasion; all they could hope to do was land forces to take over a country that was either already defeated or on the brink of defeat. The very first paper written on 30 June by General Jodl conceded this limitation: 'A landing in England, therefore, should not have as its objective the military defeat of England ... but rather to give the *coup de grace* ... An invasion must nevertheless be prepared in all details as a last resort.' Hitler was extremely reluctant to risk his prestige on an invasion against a country he still hoped would reach a deal with him to divide up the world. Failing that, he felt he could afford to ignore it as a military threat while he turned on his real enemy, the Soviet Union. Not until 16 July did he issue instructions to start preparing for an invasion 'if necessary'. Forces were gradually put in place but no agreed plan was ready until the end of August. By the middle of

September the preparations were far from complete and Hitler drew back from risking everything on a problematic attack. Once again the facts of geography – the twenty mile width of the Channel – had confounded a continental power that did not have the capability to launch a seaborne invasion.

Churchill himself never believed that an invasion attempt was likely. In early June he told the chiefs of staff that Germany would want to defeat France first and that Britain therefore had time to continue with preparations. On 12 July he said much the same to a gathering of senior Army officers at Chequers. One of his private secretaries noted in his diary: 'personally he doubts whether invasion is a serious menace'.[50] Nevertheless, with no firm intelligence ruling out an invasion, contingency planning had to go ahead.

Four days after the start of the German attack in the west Eden, as Secretary of State for War, had called for the creation of 'Local Defence Volunteers' – small groups of lightly armed troops drawn from local residents not in the armed forces. In fact it was not an idea devised by the Churchill Government; the plans had been developed by the Chamberlain Government in the winter of 1939–40. At first these groups were hardly armed at all, and their military effectiveness was very limited even when they eventually were given arms. What they did provide was a sense of involvement and commitment for ordinary members of the public. And it was Churchill who insisted on changing their name from the War Office's bureaucratic choice to the much more evocative 'Home Guard'.

It was difficult was to devise a strategy to counter a German landing. Within a couple of weeks of taking office Churchill had removed his old friend General Ironside from the post of CIGS (for which he was unsuited and where he was unhappy) and placed him in charge of counter-invasion preparations. Although he had a nominal twenty-seven divisions available, there was only enough equipment for two of them and even they were so short of transport that they were virtually immobile. Ironside had little choice therefore but to adopt a system of static defences along the beaches to stop the Germans getting ashore. There were defence lines further back but they existed largely on maps rather than on the ground. At the end of June Churchill told the commander of the north Kent coast defences that if the Germans did get ashore he was not confident of holding any defence line. By mid-July he had lost confidence in

Ironside and replaced him with General Brooke, an appointment justified in public on the grounds that he had experience of the fighting in France. Brooke decided to alter the plans for countering invasion and leave only light forces along the coast, which would in theory contain any German invasion long enough for mobile reserves to be brought up.

By the end of August Brooke had about twenty-eight divisions available at varying levels of competence and equipment. He was reasonably confident about beating off an attack, but it was probably just as well that his confidence was never put to the test. British intelligence and photo-reconnaissance was meanwhile monitoring the gradual build-up of German forces in the Channel and North Sea ports and assessed that any attempt would be made soon before the weather deteriorated. On 7 September the chiefs of staff, without consulting Churchill, issued the codeword 'Cromwell' – the signal for increased alert – but within ten days signs of the German postponement of the invasion plans (finally agreed by Hitler on 17 September) were detected.

Churchill devoted his efforts to pushing and prodding at different parts of the defence planning machine to try and ensure that everything possible was done to prepare for invasion. Many of these interventions were useful – for example the requisitioning of buses in Brighton after he discovered that local troops were desperately short of transport. He often visited the likely invasion areas, particularly in the last week of June and the first three weeks of July – he went to Kent and Essex on 26 June, Brighton on 2 July, watched Canadian troops on 7 July, went to Dover on 11 July and Dorset and Hampshire six days later. It was six weeks before he paid another visit (Dover again) and his last trip was on 12 September to the most likely invasion area, Dungeness and the North Foreland.

The reason for his two visits to Dover was his less than helpful obsession with using a large fourteen-inch naval gun from the First World War to bombard France. It took a huge effort to make it operational at a time when counter-invasion preparations were at their height. The gun itself was little more than a gesture because it could not fire more than a hundred rounds. At the end of August Churchill was still keen to put more eighteen-inch howitzers and 9.2-inch guns at Dover to fire over the Channel. He also wanted the use of his favourite weapon – gas warfare – as a last-ditch defence.

On 30 May he told the Cabinet 'we should not hesitate to contaminate our beaches with gas'.[51] By the end of September, with the invasion scare over, he decided against the first use of the weapon. He instructed Ismay that stocks should be maintained: 'We should never begin but we must be able to reply.'[52]

The Government found it difficult to decide what to do about the civilian population in the likely invasion areas. It was also in two minds about whether to advise people to move as refugees in front of any German troops or stay put and co-operate with the invaders. In the end it settled for the latter policy. In June they decided to rely on voluntary evacuation, encouraged by compulsory closing of state schools. By mid-July about half the population had left the affected coastal areas. In early July Churchill decided he wanted a stronger policy. He issued instructions to Ismay: 'Only those who are trustworthy should be allowed to stay. All doubtful elements should be removed.'[53] Since he provided no guidance on how these 'doubtful elements' were to be identified, the instruction was ignored.

The Government's best hope of warding off any invasion was the Royal Air Force. An invasion could not be launched as long as the RAF was able to maintain supremacy in the skies over south-east England. The Germans fully appreciated this and knew that the air battle had to be won first. Yet in trying to defeat an enemy relying exclusively on air operations, they were attempting something that had never been accomplished before. They were moreover singularly ill-equipped and ill-directed to achieve this task. The Luftwaffe had been designed and equipped with aircraft suitable for the role of close support of the Army, not for conducting an independent air offensive. From the end of June such an attack had to be improvised. Partly through Goering's arrogance and misjudgement, they were unable to devise a coherent strategy for the conduct of the campaign. Objectives shifted so frequently that none were ever fully achieved and no sustained pressure was ever put on British defences.

The fact that Britain was in a position to wage a highly successful air defence campaign was almost entirely attributable to the pre-war policies of the Baldwin and Chamberlain Governments. By May 1940 there was very little the Churchill Government could do, or needed to do. The pre-war Governments had ensured that Britain was the first country in the world to deploy a fully integrated system of air defence based on radar detection of incoming aircraft and ground control of fighters sent to intercept. They had ensured the rapid development and deployment of a chain of radar warning stations and the integration of this information with a complex command and control system. In the development phase Churchill's contribution had been to pour scorn on radar when he was in opposition in the 1930s. Fortunately his views were ignored and his Government inherited a well-tested and fully operational system.

The Baldwin and Chamberlain Governments had also ensured the development of effective fighter aircraft – the Spitfire and Hurricane – which were in most respects equal to the best German machine, the Me109. They also ensured that these were produced in adequate numbers, together with the trained pilots to fly them and the infrastructure to support them. Fighter output increased steadily from the mid-1930s but in November 1938 the Cabinet overrode the views of the RAF and concentrated production efforts on fighters, building only enough bombers to keep production lines open. It was the decision taken in 1938 that ensured that in 1940 Fighter Command was adequately equipped to take on the Luftwaffe and the aircraft industry was able to compete with German production levels. By 1939 Britain was producing as many aircraft as Germany and by 1940 output was higher. When Churchill became Prime Minister he inherited a situation where fighter production targets set at the beginning of the year were already being comfortably exceeded and where output was planned to expand by almost forty per cent by July.

Churchill's old friend Beaverbrook headed the newly formed Ministry of Aircraft Production. After a major row in Cabinet, the new ministry also took over the Air Ministry's responsibility for issuing aircraft to squadrons from depots and repairing damaged machines. Beaverbrook worked by methods learnt in the newspaper trade rather than in Whitehall and the new department was characterised by improvisation, a sense of urgency and a lack of bureaucracy. The Cabinet agreed an overriding priority for fighter production in May and June (after that development of the heavy bombers was resumed). What this achieved was a short-term increase in production to about fifty per cent above previously planned levels by adaptation and improvisation at every level.

Churchill always gave all the credit to Beaverbrook but in reality aircraft could not be built out of thin air. If earlier Governments had not allocated the funds and built the factories and machine tools and trained the labour force, the basic resources would not have been available to adapt to intensified fighter production in the summer of 1940. When Fighter Command had to fight the Battle of Britain, it was able to maintain its front-line strength throughout the battle and have increased reserves. Indeed the main problem facing the RAF was what it described as a 'pilot shortage'. In fact, as Lindemann pointed out to Churchill, only thirty per cent of the RAF's trained pilots were in operational units: throughout the crisis the RAF had as many pilots sitting behind desks as it had in the whole of Bomber and Fighter Commands. Churchill regularly took up this issue with his old friend Sinclair, but was unable to secure any change in RAF practice despite the gravity of the situation.

For most of July the air battle was concentrated over the Channel and it was not until the first week of August that attacks over land (for a short while concentrated on the radar stations) began in earnest. The main German tactic was to launch large waves of bombers, escorted by fighters, in order to tempt the RAF into combat where they hoped to defeat them. It was singularly unsuccessful. On 15 August, the day of the heaviest fighting in the whole battle, German losses were over twice those of the RAF and the aircraft flying from Norway (mainly the badly outclassed ME110) were so heavily mauled that they took little further part in the campaign. After a pause, in the second phase from 24 August until 6 September, the Germans concentrated on attacking airfields in south-east England. This was the time of the heaviest RAF casualties and the nearest it came to losing the battle. Then on 7 September Goering switched tactics again. Based on hopelessly erroneous intelligence estimates of the RAF's strength, he decided to bomb London in order to force the British into what he thought would be the final battle. In fact the change of tactics took the pressure off the RAF. The Luftwaffe made one last throw on 15 September with two heavy attacks aimed at London, but with no diversions the RAF was able to concentrate its fighters and destroyed about sixty German aircraft (not the 183 publicly claimed). After this failure the Germans concentrated almost exclusively on night bombing of London.

During these crucial battles there was little Churchill could contribute personally except watch the weapons he had derided in the 1930s – radar, Spitfires and Hurricanes – defeating the Luftwaffe. He paid his first visit to Fighter Command headquarters during the battle on 3 August, and was there again when the Germans launched their first big attack on 15 August, and again the next day. Afterwards he paid visits to the headquarters of No 11 Group at Uxbridge, which was responsible for the south east of England and bore the brunt of the fighting. He was there on 31 August and 1 September, when heavy attacks on RAF stations at Biggin Hill and Kenley led to the withdrawal of some squadrons. He returned on 15 September to watch the defeat of the last major German daylight attack and victory in the Battle of Britain.

Before the end of September it was clear that the RAF had beaten the Luftwaffe and that Hitler was not in these circumstances prepared to risk an invasion. Britain had therefore survived and was free of the threat of invasion during the bad weather in the winter and early spring. Now the doubts, hesitations and difficulties of the early summer were forgotten. Britain had demonstrated that it was possible to resist successfully what had seemed until then an unstoppable German war machine. British morale, which had been low until well into the summer, improved and it was soon forgotten the mood had not always been one of heroic resolution and defiance. Churchill too lost the very real doubts about the future that had assailed him during the fall of France.

As the nation's leader, Churchill inevitably benefited from this change of mood. Newspapers and public opinion turned on the pre-war leadership as scapegoats for the failures of the BEF and for Britain's dreadful predicament. He was lucky that his repeated bids to join the Government after 1935 had been rejected. People recalled only his attacks on pre-war policies and his warning of the dangers facing Britain. The extent to which he had benefited from the policies of the pre-war Governments was overlooked. The exaggeration and inconsistency of his pre-war calls to arms were ignored. Summer 1940 was the period when Churchill was seen at his best: the task was simple – survival. Churchill's energy, determination and appetite for work could concentrate (usually to good effect) on this single task. Even so in large areas there was nothing he could do but hope that the preparations made by others and the efforts of those who, for example, built the aircraft and flew them would be adequate.

Like many politicians Churchill was an actor who grew into his adopted role of defiance and heroism. In the past he had practised his speeches, gestures and expressions in front of a mirror. His doctor, Lord Moran, was convinced that, as Britain's immediate survival became more certain, he carefully cultivated the famous 'bulldog' expression (found to perfection in the Cecil Beaton photograph taken in the Cabinet room) as his public persona. He added other traits too – the inevitable cigar, the hunched shoulders, the reintroduction of the lisp, the deliberate mispronunciation of certain words, in particular 'Nazi', and later the 'V-sign' (he ignored what the sign normally meant).

During the summer of 1940, as Churchill became the symbol of Britain's continued resistance, his political position steadily improved. Feeling in the Conservative Party against him became more muted, although it did not disappear. At the end of September 'Chips' Channon reported that 'feeling at the Carlton Club is running high against him'.[54] Throughout the summer Churchill defended the members of the pre-war Goverments still in his own administration against attacks in the press and refused to countenance any attempt to remove them from Government. Indeed he relied greatly on Chamberlain – he told him at the beginning of September, 'I am up and down. You are more steady. It is helpful to feel that my decisions are approved by your judgement.'[55]

Although keen to make changes in order to consolidate his political position Churchill was only able to move slowly though he did to bring Beaverbrook into the War Cabinet in August. That month Chamberlain had an operation for cancer. During his recuperation Churchill insisted that he should continue to receive key Cabinet papers and give his advice whenever possible. Chamberlain recognised however that his illness ended any chance he might have of replacing Churchill after the war was over. He wrote in early September of the need 'to adjust myself to the new life of a partially crippled man which is what I am. Any ideas of another Premiership after the war have gone. I know that it out of the question.'[56] In fact within a couple of weeks he realised that that he had not long to live and resigned from the Government.

Churchill took this opportunity to move the dour Sir John Anderson from the Home Office, where he was judged to have been a failure in coping with the Blitz on London, to take over Chamberlain's old post as Lord President. Anderson was replaced by Herbert Morrison, the boss of the Labour Party machine in the capital, who was thought to have the confidence of its citizens. Just how limited Churchill's power still was became clear when he tried to make Eden Foreign Secretary in place of Halifax. The move was opposed by Chamberlain, who remained party Leader, on the grounds that 'the change at the Foreign Office would be taken to mean a change of policy and a condemnation of my policy'.[57] Churchill did not feel strong enough to override Chamberlain's objections and Halifax was left in his post.

When Chamberlain died in November, Churchill seized the opportunity to become Conservative Leader. In May he had rejected Chamberlain's offer to resign the leadership saying that he preferred to remain a 'non-party' leader of the national coalition. In fact he realised that Chamberlain was still far too popular within the party to be supplanted. Clementine wanted him to keep that 'non-party' role even after Chamberlain's death. But he was much too shrewd a politician to follow such advice. He understood the nature of political power and he had Lloyd George's experience to remind him of what happened to a Prime Minister who did not have a strong party behind him. He was not prepared to undermine his position by allowing anybody else to become Leader while he remained as Prime Minister. To do so would, almost certainly, fatally damage his chances of staying in power once the war was over. He therefore exercised his right to become party Leader.

Churchill's position as national leader was now unassailable. He led the largest party in the coalition. He symbolised Britain's resistance to a German-dominated Europe. There was no alternative leader in sight. But Churchill badly needed this pre-eminent position. Behind the scenes Britain's strategic, economic and financial position in 1940 was desperate; the country was living through its 'Finest Hour' but also its collapse as a world power and the beginning of dependence on the United States for survival. It had been Churchill's lot to preside over the last rites for Britain's position as a great power.

20

1940 – Twilight of a Great Power

In 1940 Britain had just enough power to ensure its own survival in the short term. The problem that Churchill faced was a much more acute version of that his predecessors had had to deal with in the 1930s – too few resources to defend a far-flung Empire. In the Far East Japan was likely to be tempted to exploit Britain's weakness. In the Mediterranean and Near East Britain now faced war with Italy. In neither case could significant military resources be spared from home defence. Although Churchill had pledged his political life to the maintenance of the Empire, his first two years as Prime Minister were to witness the disintegration of British power across the globe.

One of the most important problems to be faced was in the Far East. In the autumn of 1939, before Australia would consent to the despatch of its only trained forces out of the country, it very sensibly asked for a reaffirmation of British policy for the defence of the Antipodean dominions. As head of the Admiralty it fell to Churchill to advise the Cabinet how to respond. Before the war Australia and New Zealand had been reassured that in the event of any threat the fleet would be sent to Singapore. At the 1937 Imperial Conference they were told that 'the very existence of the British Commonwealth of Nations as now constituted rests on our ability to send our fleet to the Far East'.[1] And that this was a higher priority than the Mediterranean: 'no anxiety or risks connected with our interests in the Mediterranean can be allowed to interfere with a despatch of a fleet to the Far East'.[2] In 1939 Churchill adopted a Machiavellian approach because he took the view, as he told his colleagues, that the most important point was to 'reassure the Dominions, so that they would consent to the despatch of their forces'.[3] The period allowed for the relief of Singapore had been extended to ninety days earlier in 1939, and he now proposed, by subtle drafting, to make the new guarantees 'more elastic' than those given in 1937 by the Baldwin Government.[4]

Churchill made clear the new naval priorities: 'there could be no question of moving powerful naval forces to the Far East on the mere threat of a Japanese attack';[5] and it was 'out of the question' to send seven battleships to Singapore if war did break out.[6] He thought that war with Japan would not involve an attack on Singapore (which would be a 'forlorn' undertaking[7]) or the white dominions. The most that Australia had to fear was a 'tip-and-run raid, to repel which land forces were not required'.[8] The new 'commitment' which Churchill was prepared to give in 1939 on sending part of the fleet to Singapore only applied as long as Italy remained neutral and would not come into effect until there was an 'invasion in force' of Australia.[9] It was enough to convince the Australians to send their troops out of the country.

The entry of Italy into the war in July 1940 and the need to concentrate naval forces in home waters to counter the invasion threat meant that in the summer and autumn of 1940 the Far Eastern Empire was virtually defenceless. Malaya and Singapore were 'defended' by three brigades and 88 obsolescent aircraft and the fleet in the Far East consisted of three modern and four ancient cruisers together with five old destroyers. The chiefs of staff advised the Cabinet that these forces were 'entirely inadequate' for war with Japan. All that Britain could hope to do was to limit Japanese conquests 'and in the last resort to retain a footing from which we could eventually retrieve the position when stronger forces become available'.[10] Indeed the chiefs of staff had advised in May that 'we must rely on the United States of America to safeguard our interests in the Far East'.[11] The only problem with this policy was that, as Halifax told the Cabinet, the United States was 'unlikely to use force in defence of British or French interests in the Far East'.[12]

On 13 June Australia and New Zealand were told that adequate naval reinforcements were unlikely to be sent to the Far East. In August, when the Cabinet reviewed the situation, the chiefs of staff advised that the most Britain could do would be to send 'one battle-cruiser and one aircraft carrier to the Indian Ocean to be based at Ceylon for the purpose of protecting our vital communications and those round the Cape to the Middle East'.[13] This was the abandonment of the policy that successive British governments had regarded as central to the defence of the Empire – the despatch of the fleet to Singapore. The resources were simply not available given the size of the threats elsewhere. It was a painful irony that Churchill, one of the last great imperialists in British politics, presided over the decision. But he was not prepared to own up to it. During the Cabinet discussion he agreed that they should not tell the dominions in detail of this revised policy. He suggested instead that he should send a telegram to the Prime Ministers of Australia and New Zealand couched in much more optimistic terms, but with the British commitment to defend them subject to even more pre-conditions than it had been in his revised 'assurances' of the autumn of 1939. The message sent on 11 August argued that Japan would not attack until Britain had been invaded by Germany and told the dominions that there would be no automatic reinforcement of the Far East from the Mediterranean 'even if Japan declares war until it is found to be vital to your safety'. The fleet would only be sent if Japan invaded Australia and New Zealand 'on a large scale' and its size would be sufficient to 'parry any invading force' or cut its links with Japan.[14] The Australian Government, made suspicious by the British habit of redefining the policy upon which the dominions based their security, was already beginning to look towards the United States. As the Prime Minister, Menzies, told the War Council, 'the United Kingdom might be defeated in the war, and a regrouping of the English-speaking peoples might arise'.[15]

To some extent Churchill always underestimated Japanese power because of his convictions about white superiority. In the 1920s he viewed any threat as remote for decades. Little more than a year before this reappraisal of the British position in the Far East he had reassured Chamberlain:

> Consider how vain is the menace that Japan will send a fleet and army to conquer Singapore . . . [it] will never commend itself to them until England has been decisively beaten . . . You may be sure that provided [Singapore] is fully armed, garrisoned and supplied,

there will be no attack in any period which our foresight can measure.[16]

Luckily for Australia, New Zealand and Britain, the Japanese were not, at this time, willing to launch an all-out attack on British interests. Instead they decided to take advantage of Britain's weakness to attain lesser objectives. Just after the French armistice they demanded the withdrawal of all British troops and warships from Japanese-controlled areas of China, the stoppage of all supplies from Hong Kong to the Chinese, and the closure of the Burma Road, the main supply route (especially for American material) to the nationalist Chinese under Chiang Kai-shek. What is interesting about the Cabinet debates on how to respond to these demands is that it was Churchill who wanted to 'appease' the Japanese by accepting their demands and Halifax and others who wished to resist.

On 29 June Halifax outlined the Japanese demands to the Cabinet and argued that closure of the Burma Road would be extremely serious for Chiang Kai-shek and have a bad effect on US opinion. He concluded 'there is little doubt that we cannot, in fact, accede to this demand'.[17] Others in Whitehall took a similar view. Sir Alexander Cadogan, head of the Foreign Office, wrote, 'I am convinced we must stand out against closing of Burma Road, even at risk of war. If we give way, Americans will give us up, with hopeless results, not only in Pacific but also on this side.[sic]'[18] Churchill's Private Secretary thought 'it is a moral defeat to sacrifice in one part of the world the principles we are defending in another'.[19] The chiefs of staff looked to a solution through diplomacy: 'if we are not in a position to stand fast on all Japanese demands, accepting the risk of war, we must go for a sufficiently wide settlement to satisfy the Japanese'.[20]

At the Cabinet on 5 July Halifax said 'we should lose less by standing up to Japanese blackmail than by relinquishing our principles'. The Ambassador in Tokyo advised that rejection of the Japanese demands would not lead to war, only to a much more difficult atmosphere. But Churchill was, once again, unwilling to stand up to the Japanese. Apparently unmoved by the serious implications for the nationalist forces under Chiang Kai-shek, he told his colleagues: 'he did not think that we ought to incur Japanese hostility for reasons mainly of prestige'. Yet on taking office he had told Chiang Kai-shek: 'Your cause, too, is that of democracy. Have no doubt, therefore, that we shall do all we can to help China to maintain her independence.'[21] Eventually the Cabinet agreed to Churchill's suggestion that they try and put the onus on the Americans – 'unless we received a clear assurance of American support, we should be compelled to bow to *force majeure*' – and agree to closure of the Burma Road.[22] Cadogan's view – 'it's hopeless to do as Winston suggested – try to put the US on the spot. They simply won't stand there' – proved to be correct.[23] They left the decision to the British and refused to accept responsibility.

On 10 July the Cabinet considered what to do after the Japanese had rejected British proposals to ration supplies delivered via the Burma Road and threatened 'deplorable effects' on relations unless it was closed. The Ambassador now thought war was possible if Britain stood out. They decided to close the road for three months because of the 'grave risk' of war if they refused and to use that time to try and reach an agreement with the Tokyo Government.[24] The next day the Cabinet agreed that 'no time ought to be lost in coming to terms with Japan' because of the danger of an anti-British Government taking power and declaring war.[25] A month later they agreed to withdraw all British troops from the garrisons in Shanghai, Tientsin and Peiping. In public they used the excuse that they were needed in Singapore – in fact the Cabinet had given in to more Japanese blackmail. At the beginning of October 1940, with British prestige now higher following the Battle of Britain, the Cabinet accepted Halifax's proposal that they should re-open the Burma Road when the three month closure period expired. There was by then less need to appease Japan and no hope of an agreement with them following their pact with Germany and Italy.

Nearer home the Cabinet had similarly to decide whether it was necessary to make political concessions as a result of Britain's weak position. The most immediate problem as France collapsed was the position of neutral Eire. On joining the War Cabinet Churchill wanted to try and regain the 'treaty ports' that had been returned to the Irish Government in 1938. He also refused to accept that Eire (still a dominion) could be neutral. In October 1939 he told Halifax that 'So far as "legality" counts, the question surely turns on whether "Eire is to be regarded as a neutral state" . . . Legally I believe they are at war but sulking.'[26] On 24 October he told the Cabinet that

Britain should 'challenge the constitutional position of Eire's neutrality. We should not admit that her neutrality was compatible with her position under the Crown . . . [and] insist on the use of the harbours.'[27] The Government's legal advice was that this view was completely fallacious and would have grave implications for all the other dominions that had declared war but by their own free choice. Churchill's position was in fact consistent with his opposition to the 1931 Statute of Westminster and his refusal to accept that the dominions could develop into fully self-governing states within the Commonwealth.

The weakness of Churchill's position in June 1940 is demonstrated by the fact that he had to accept that Neville Chamberlain and Malcolm MacDonald, who had negotiated the 1938 deal giving the treaty ports back to Eire, should attempt to reach another agreement with the Irish. (He regarded MacDonald as 'rat poison' because of his part in the 1938 negotiations.[28]) During the course of these negotiations Churchill was forced to accept some very unpalatable proposals. The first contacts with the Irish came in May, as the German Armies broke through allied defences in France, when they asked the British to supply arms. At first Churchill hoped to exploit the situation in order to regain the treaty ports with or without Irish consent. But in June, when serious talks began, he rapidly discovered that the British would have to make serious concessions if they wanted to obtain Irish support.

At the first meeting with the Irish Premier, De Valera, on 17 June, MacDonald set out the Churchillian position. Ireland should abandon its neutrality and accept the presence of British troops and British use of the ports. In return, they would be granted a joint defence council with the British. This one-sided offer was indignantly rejected – De Valera would only accept British troops following a German invasion and he also demanded an announcement of a united Ireland. MacDonald rejected the latter because 'a great majority of Ulstermen would object strongly'.[29] When the Cabinet considered the outcome at its meeting on 20 June, Chamberlain suggested, and Churchill accepted, that Britain might have to make a declaration in favour of a united Ireland and that the Northern Ireland Premier would have to be told that 'the interests of Northern Ireland could not be allowed to stand against the vital interests of the British Empire'.[30] Churchill was not happy with this policy, which implied the coercion of Ulster into a united Ireland, but he did not stop MacDonald returning immediately to Dublin to put the proposals to De Valera.

On 21 June MacDonald proposed a package involving a declaration of unity in principle, a belligerent Ulster, a neutral Eire and British use of Irish ports. De Valera countered by suggesting a united but neutral Ireland, though once the Constitution was settled Ireland might decide to join the allies. On 25 June Chamberlain proposed, and the War Cabinet (with Churchill in the chair) accepted, that Britain should now make a formal offer of union in return for Irish entry into the war. MacDonald spent the next two days in Dublin trying to overcome Irish suspicions (grounded in years of British duplicity over the Ulster question) and convince them that this time Britain was serious. He told the Irish, as he reported to Churchill, that it was:

> absolutely definite that if the plan were accepted as a whole, a united Ireland would come into actual being within a comparatively short period of time ... I repeated that the establishment of a united Ireland was an integral part of our plan, from which there would be no turning back.

He even suggested that no declaration of war by Eire would be necessary as long as Britain could use the ports and that although there would be no military coercion of Ulster (the one point on which Churchill and his colleagues were adamant): 'the United Kingdom Government would take full responsibility to the Eire government for seeing that our obligations under the plan were carried out in full'.[31]

It was not until 26 June that Chamberlain informed the Ulster Government of the plans for their future. He outlined the proposals put to Dublin and said that the Belfast Government would be able to 'make your own comments or objections as you may think fit'.[32] This was carefully worded so as not to allow Ulster to veto an agreement. Churchill saw this correspondence and raised no objection. Craigavon responded in brief but trenchant terms, demonstrating that Ulster's 'loyalty' did not extend to committing suicide at Britain's suggestion: 'Am profoundly shocked and disgusted by your letter making suggestions so far-reaching behind my back and without any pre-consultations with me. To such treachery to loyal Ulster I will never be a party.'[33] Chamberlain's reply reminded him that he would have the opportunity of 'making your views known' before a decision was taken and added a warning: 'Meanwhile please remember the serious nature of the situation which requires that every effort be made to meet it.'[34]

Churchill only escaped having to go back on his long-expressed views about Ulster and Ireland, dating back to the early 1920s, because the Irish Government did not in the end trust the British to carry out their pledges. They believed they were being asked to make all the immediate concessions in return for 'guarantees' about the future. On 5 July they formally rejected the British proposals for union. By the end of 1940 Churchill was able to edge his colleagues back towards a policy he found much more congenial. The search for concessions was transformed into a policy of escalating pressure once Britain's overall position improved after the Battle of Britain. On 12 November he ordered the War Office to start planning for an invasion of Eire to secure the ports, though he hoped the mere threat of force might be enough to cow the Irish into agreement. On 21 November the Cabinet decided to delay implementation of the Anglo-Irish Trade Agreement and the next month to start mild economic warfare against the dependent Irish economy. Churchill's only worry was that his colleagues would 'fall into the error of being too tender-footed in this policy'.[35] For the rest of the war he tried to put indirect pressure on the Irish to co-operate but without success.

Elsewhere around the globe the Churchill Government considered political concessions to try and buy support. Britain was highly dependent on imports of Argentine wheat and beef and in an attempt to secure continued supplies the Government considered seeking a settlement of the long-running dispute over the Falkland Islands. They discussed the possibility of conceding the Argentine claim to sovereignty in return for a fixed-period lease of the islands. The British papers on this episode are still closed, but it seems likely that a formal offer was not made to Argentina. The future of Gibraltar (a British possession since 1714) was also discussed. The Foreign Office and Hoare, the Ambassador in Madrid, suggested, as France collapsed, that Britain should offer to discuss the future of Gibraltar after the war in return for continued Spanish neutrality. The Cabinet twice discussed the idea in June but rejected it because the Spanish would not be so naive as to believe Britain would hand the colony over if they did win the war, and Spain could expect to gain it anyway if Britain were defeated. However in September Churchill did agree to partially lift the blockade of Spain in order to sustain her neutrality. Although Gibraltar was off the agenda, he thought Franco should be encouraged to take over French territory instead. He agreed the Spanish dictator should be told that Britain would be 'no obstacle to their Moroccan ambitions'. His justification for overriding French interests was ingenuous: 'the letters exchanged with de Gaulle do not commit us to any exact restoration of the territories of France'.[36]

Churchill's reference to De Gaulle reflects the tangled and difficult relationship he had throughout the war with the man who saw himself as the saviour of France. When the Pétain Government asked for an armistice, General Charles de Gaulle, then a relatively obscure junior minister, flew to Britain with Churchill's friend General Spears. On 18 June he broadcast to France saying that all was not lost and the war would continue. He mentioned the idea of 'resistance' although the speech was extremely unclear about exactly what policy De Gaulle advocated. The British Government immediately realised that the broadcast had been a mistake while they still hoped to influence the Bordeaux Government. De Gaulle was kept under strict control and not allowed to broadcast again until the armistice came into force, when he spoke of forming forces to continue the fight. On 23 June the Cabinet agreed to recognise the French National Committee for Liberation but not De Gaulle as its head. They still hoped to find someone more prestigious for that role. British representatives were sent to Morocco to try and rally some of the French politicians who had arrived there from Bordeaux, but the authorities loyal to Pétain stopped any contacts.

On 28 June, with no alternative in sight, the British did recognise De Gaulle as the 'leader of all Free Frenchmen' who rallied to the allied cause. The wording was carefully chosen to avoid recognising him as a government – the British could hardly have done less. Churchill kept relations with De Gaulle on a tight personal rein through his two friends Spears and Morton. Although in public De Gaulle was promoted in an attempt to demonstrate that Britain was not alone, in practice the British were much more cautious. They refused to let the tiny Free French units (De Gaulle commanded just 2,000 soldiers and a navy of similar size) fight on their own because they feared they might defect. On 7 August Churchill and De Gaulle exchanged letters. The British formally refused to recognise him as head of a government and rejected his request to guarantee restoration of the territorial integrity and independence of France. They would do no more than pledge the much more ambiguous 'restoration of the independence and greatness of France'. This gave scope to dispose of some French colonial possessions that the British might want themselves or want to use to bargain with others, for example Spain. In September the Governor of Indo-China, General Catroux, was brought to London. Churchill offered him the leadership of the Free French but he turned the offer down, preferring to serve under De Gaulle.

Perhaps the greatest disadvantage facing De Gaulle in the summer of 1940 was that he did not control any French territory. Pétain had removed the French Government from Bordeaux to Vichy, abolished the Third Republic, and set up a new authoritarian Government, which continued to control not just the unoccupied zone in southern France but all the French colonial empire. At this stage De Gaulle was totally dependent on the British. Clearly if he was to be taken seriously as a French leader it was essential for him to be in charge of part of the French colonial empire. On 3 August Churchill agreed a rather vague plan, drawn up by De Gaulle, Spears and Morton, to establish Free French control over some of the west African colonies. This was the start of yet another fiasco in which Churchill played the main role in forcing an operation through against military advice.

On 5 August the Cabinet agreed to the idea of a Free French expedition to west Africa (no firm objective was stated) with no British troops and only a Royal Navy escort. The next day Churchill and De Gaulle agreed that Dakar in Senegal should be the goal (it was a key base along the convoy route to the Cape and the French also held £60 million of Belgian and Polish gold there, which the governments-in-exile, and the British, badly needed). De Gaulle insisted that he could not start by attacking fellow Frenchmen and would only take over already friendly territory. Then on 7 August the chiefs of staff decided that the expedition had no reasonable prospect of success and that the local French authorities would not defect to De Gaulle. Moreover, as the expedition would be 'in a theatre which was not vital to the prosecution of the war', they only agreed to it going ahead on the basis that it did not involve Britain in a 'considerable military commitment'.[37] Churchill refused to accept this advice because it would have meant abandoning the whole expedition. He intended to deal with De Gaulle's scruples by making it a British assault. He called another meeting of the chiefs of staff at 11pm that night and took the chair himself. Despite the War Cabinet decision and the views of the chiefs of staff, he decided the expedition 'should have sufficient backing by British forces to ensure its success' and that 'de Gaulle should be used to import a French character to it'. The chiefs of staff were advised not to interfere in political decisions.[38] On 9 August the chiefs of staff duly produced the plan that Churchill wanted and it was agreed by the Cabinet four days later – the main assault would be by Royal Marines with the Free French in the background.

This plan lasted a mere six days. Then the planning staff reported that there were heavy defences at Dakar and advised that the expedition should land at Conakry and march 630 miles overland to Dakar. Again Churchill refused to accept this advice. He called another meeting of the chiefs of staff, this time with De Gaulle present, and he again took the chair. At this meeting he suddenly proposed a different and apparently self-contradictory approach. In the first instance De Gaulle should try to enter Dakar by negotiation. If this failed, British ships would open fire 'with restraint', but then, if there was opposition, they 'would use all means to break down resistance' because 'it was essential that by nightfall General de Gaulle should be master of Dakar'.[39] The next day he accepted that the operation need not be completed in a single day. On this basis preparations went ahead, although the chances of success must have looked slim. The forces sent were known to be inadequate to overcome anything more than token resistance from the Dakar garrison. There were also numerous leaks of information (mainly from the Free French) and bungled logistic planning meant that the ships had to sail past Dakar to Freetown where they were reloaded.

The assault was due to go ahead, after many delays, on 18 September. A week before this Vichy ships sailed through the Straits of Gibraltar (no specific instructions were issued from London to stop them) and, although not bound for Dakar, were thought to be a major threat. On 15 September Churchill suggested to the chiefs of staff that the Dakar operation should be cancelled and that forces should, as they had suggested a month earlier, now land at Conakry and march overland to Dakar. The chiefs of staff suggested instead that De Gaulle should go to Duala and there establish firm control over the colonies of Chad, the French Cameroons and Congo, which had meanwhile already defected to him at the end of August. Churchill agreed, and the next day the Cabinet duly endorsed cancellation of the Dakar expedition. Churchill conceded that 'a fiasco had undoubtedly occurred and it was to be hoped that it would not too much engage public attention'.[40] In fact the fiasco was only beginning.

The decision to cancel brought strong opposition from De Gaulle and Spears, who were with the expedition. Over three meetings on 17–18 September the Cabinet decided to reverse their earlier decision and reinstate the assault on Dakar. Churchill was now in favour of going ahead, stressing the need to score a morale boosting victory. Despite all the earlier doubts, he was now sanguine, telling General Smuts (Prime Minister of South Africa): 'I think the odds are heavily against any serious resistance.'[41] Two days later on 23 September the attack began. De Gaulle's emissaries to the garrison were either arrested or fired on and when the Free French troops tried to land they got lost in fog. Churchill's view was that 'having begun we must go through to the end' and that the attack should now stop at nothing.[42] The next day a British naval bombardment was ineffectual against strong gunfire from the French shore batteries. On 25 September one of the escorting British battleships, *HMS Resolution*, was torpedoed and that morning the Cabinet finally agreed to throw in their hand and abandon the the whole operation. De Gaulle went off to take control of Chad. The official British communiqué claimed, rather lamely, that 'serious warlike operations' had never been intended. Dakar was the first British attempt to mount an offensive operation since Norway. Once again Churchill's direction, in particular his habits of shifting objectives and overriding military advice, had produced an abject failure.

The episode also demonstrated De Gaulle's limited appeal to fellow Frenchmen and the ability of the Vichy forces to fight. Churchill had, at first, taken a strong line against the Vichy Government, calling for 'no excessive scruples to be shown' and even threatening to bomb the town if necessary.[43] By the autumn though the situation began to change, and Churchill's views swung right round. Continued British resistance encouraged Pétain not to commit himself to Germany (a decision made clear at his meeting with Hitler at Montoire on 24 October and later by the dismissal from the Government of Pierre Laval, the main advocate of full-scale collaboration). The Vichy Government had much to offer the British, who wanted to keep the Germans out of the French colonial Empire and the fleet (still largely intact after British attempts to sink it) securely in French hands. The British in return could offer to relax the blockade imposed on France and keep De Gaulle under control.

Throughout the autumn of 1940 a whole series of semi-official and unofficial contacts were made with the Vichy Government, which was still recognised by the United States and within the Empire by Canada and South Africa. Those involved ranged from Hoare, the Ambassador in Madrid, who kept in touch with the Vichy representatives there, to two French Canadians, Professor Louis Rougier and an ex-diplomat in Paris, Pierre Dupuy. By the end of October it was clear to Churchill that a deal with Vichy was possible. He agreed that Hoare could open informal discussions and on 25–26 October he met Rougier, who had come to London as an unofficial emissary from Pétain. Neither side wanted a formal agreement, but both were prepared for an informal understanding. Nevertheless Churchill personally annotated the notes that Rougier was to take back to Pétain. While discussions with Rougier were underway, Churchill vetoed an expedition by De Gaulle to Libreville to take control of the colony of Gabon. He wrote that he objected to De Gaulle 'skirmishing around as an independent potentate' and expressed reluctance to take part in any such operation 'until we knew more clearly how we stood with Vichy'.[44] Indeed he now saw the Free French as more of a liability than an asset: 'de Gaulle is definitely an embarrassment to us now in our dealings with Vichy'[45] and 'he and his movement may now become an obstacle to a very considerable hiving off of the French Empire to our side'.[46] De Gaulle went ahead on his own and added Gabon to his little empire on 10 November.

The contacts initiated through Rougier were continued by Dupuy, who saw Pétain four times during the discussions. An 'understanding' was reached before the end of 1940, but it was informal enough for Churchill to be able to deny after the war that he had reached an 'agreement'. Britain and Vichy agreed to maintain the status quo in the colonial Empire – Vichy would not attack a colony controlled by De Gaulle (thereby avoiding any necessity for the British to help him) and the British undertook to stop De Gaulle extending his sphere any further. Pétain also agreed not to seek a separate peace before Britain was defeated, not to grant Germany the use of naval bases and to resist any attempt by German forces to take control of the empire. In return the British agreed to call off their propaganda attacks on Vichy, relax the blockade and begin discussions on commercial matters. These exchanges were kept highly secret and a semblance of hostility maintained for public consumption as opinion at home would not have approved co-operation with collaborators.

Just before Christmas Dupuy reported to Churchill that Pétain and other Vichy leaders had spoken about possible co-operation in North Africa 'under this vital condition – that the present atmosphere of tension between Great Britain and France be maintained as a smoke screen, behind which contacts could be made and information exchanged'.[47] Churchill impetuously took this hint too far too fast and wanted to move straight to outright military assistance. Under pressure the chiefs of staff suggested offering the French six divisions in North Africa if they would restart the war there. The offer was sent to Pétain through the Americans but he burnt the paper given to him and indignantly refused to leave France. A similar offer made to General Weygand, who now headed the Government in North Africa, was also rejected.

For the British Government, moving closer to Vichy meant distancing themselves from De Gaulle and the Free French. De Gaulle, now that he controlled part of the Empire, was also determined to assert his independence from Britain, although he maintained his HQ in London and relied on British funding. From the start Churchill seems to have had little sympathy with or understanding of De Gaulle's methods. He rejected the declaration made by the Free French leader from Africa that the Vichy Government was invalid and that he was the legal government of France. Churchill would go no further than he had in June – De Gaulle was the military leader of the Free French and the British would only have dealings with him in respect of those parts of the French Empire he actually controlled (which they hoped to keep as small as possible). The autumn of 1940 marked the beginning of Churchill's often vicious disputes with De

Gaulle which were to last for the rest of the war, interspersed with only infrequent periods of harmony.

Although the Dakar operation was a complete failure, it did demonstrate, as Britain's rearmament continued after Dunkirk and once the anti-invasion forces had been rebuilt, that it was possible to mount limited operations outside Europe. At the same time as the plans to put De Gaulle into the French African colonies were being developed, the Cabinet was also considering how to reinforce British forces in the Middle East. This was the only area where the British Army could engage its opponents, even though they were the Italians and not the Germans. But the decision to deploy Britain's military strength here, and build a huge supply base in Egypt to support it, was to profoundly affect the whole strategy of the war. In the Middle East, in a command that stretched from Cyprus to Somaliland and from Iraq to the Libyan border, Britain had just two divisions, two brigade groups, an understrength armoured division, sixty-four field guns and a 500-man camel corps. The Italians were in the process of driving British forces out of Somaliland and advancing into the frontier regions of Kenya and were also threatening to invade Egypt from Libya. On 12 August Eden presented to the Cabinet's Defence Committee a War Office plan which involved sending reinforcements to Egypt – over 100,000 men and three regiments of tanks (a large part of the total available) as the prelude to an attack on the Italians in Libya. Churchill, demonstrating his usual impatience and need for a dramatic gesture, wanted to send the tanks through the Mediterranean, despite the high risk of Italian attacks. He was overruled by the rest of the Cabinet, who accepted the advice of the War Office and General Wavell, the Commander-in-Chief Middle East, that the need was not great enough to justify the risks. (Two months later Churchill himself was arguing for sending reinforcements via the Cape.) The Italians advanced sixty miles into Egypt, stopped, and took no further offensive action.

While British forces were being built up in Egypt, developments elsewhere began to cloud the strategic picture and provide the opportunity for Churchill to demonstrate, yet again, his inability to decide between conflicting objectives or sustain a steady policy. Overwhelming German power in the summer of 1940 led to the dismemberment of Rumania, Britain's only ally in south eastern Europe. Although the Chamberlain Government had extended to them the same guarantee as to Poland in March 1939, the Churchill Government could only offer 'sympathy' as first the Soviet Union took Bessarabia and Bukovina in June, then Hungary took Transylvania in August and Bulgaria seized the Dobruja in September. (Churchill publicly accepted the latter seizure – indeed in Cabinet a year earlier he had argued that Britain should pressurise its ally into giving up the area.) In what was left of Rumania a pro-German Government took power. At the end of October Italy tried to take a share of the spoils and invaded Greece (also guaranteed by the British in March 1939).

For Churchill the case for giving assistance to Greece was essentially political: 'if Greece was overwhelmed it would be said that in spite of our guarantees we had allowed one more small ally to be swallowed up'. That was certainly a strong argument, but the difficulty for the Government was, as Halifax told the same meeting of the Cabinet, 'to find a way of heartening the Greeks without disclosing our weakness in the Middle East'.[48] Luckily for the British, the Greeks did not ask for more than aircraft – they received two squadrons of Blenheims, although the Cabinet refused to send twelve obsolete Gladiator biplane fighters. Within a matter of days the Greeks were on the offensive and had driven the Italian Army back into Albania. Churchill was now tempted by bigger objectives than the western desert. Eden noted in his diary at the beginning of November: 'tirade from Winston. This includes such assertions that Athens was more important than both Khartoum and Kenya etc.'[49] This tirade was the beginning of a long conflict of objectives in the eastern Mediterranean that was to bedevil British policy for the rest of 1940 and the first months of 1941.

Churchill, keen to help Greece and build up what he hoped might be a Balkan front, kept up the pressure on Eden. The latter was now in Egypt, arguing against splitting forces between Egypt and Greece. To try and contain Churchill he disclosed details of Wavell's plans for an offensive against Italian forces. The message was sent in a personal cipher used by the two men and Churchill refused to disclose the plans to the War Cabinet. At first he seemed happy to support Wavell's plans. However within three weeks, on 22 November he was telling Wavell that the 'importance of getting Turkey in and perhaps Jugoslavia would far outweigh any Libyan operation'.[50] Then four days later he was speculating about what to do once

Wavell's attack had succeeded. As he saw it, the theatre of operations would shift from Cairo to Constantinople, the Navy would operate in the Black Sea, the Army would be deployed in Greece and Thrace as well as having four divisions on Spanish territory in North Africa and capturing the Azores and Cape Verde Islands (which belonged to neutral Portugal) and numerous Mediterranean islands.

Churchill was impatient for action in the desert. Eden recorded in his diary their clash of views at the Defence Committee meeting on 4 December: Churchill was 'very critical of army and generals "High time army did something" etc. I made it plain that I did not believe in fussing Wavell with questions. I knew his plan, he knew our view, he had best be left to get on with it. This did not suit W.'[51] The British attack began five days later, using just an Indian infantry division and an armoured division; a total of 36,000 men. Within seventy-two hours they had defeated two Italian corps and taken 38,000 prisoners. Churchill was still not satisfied. In a telephone call to Eden he 'complained that we were not pursuing enemy and had much to say about missed opportunities . . . this all symptomatic of his distrust of local leaders . . . which has not abated at all'.[52] Altogether in ten weeks' fighting British forces advanced 500 miles, destroyed ten Italian divisions, 400 tanks and 1,300 guns and took 130,000 prisoners for the loss of less than 500 men killed.

Churchill's criticisms of Wavell were typical of his behaviour once he became Prime Minister. He had always been arrogant and overbearing in his relations with other people, convinced that he was right and resentful of any criticism. His staff had always been expected to be subservient to his slighest whim. Now that he was head of the Government these tendencies were given much freer rein and more people were subjected to them. Meetings, especially those of the Defence Committee, were arranged to suit Churchill's convenience and methods; this meant they were usually held late at night and lasted into the early hours. For Churchill, who slept in the afternoon and rose late, this was no problem but for everybody else it was a major burden. Many of the meetings were little more than monologues from Churchill and often little was actually decided.

Within six weeks of his taking office adverse comments were being made about Churchill's behaviour and his treatment of others. On 22 June Clementine wrote to him to say that not only had she noticed a deterioration in his manner but that 'a devoted friend' had told her that his behaviour – in particular his 'rough, sarcastic and overbearing manner' and 'contemptuous' attitude at conferences – was having a serious impact on those around him.[53] Churchill's old habit of standing on his dignity did not disappear once he had achieved the highest office. Far from rising above petty issues or criticism, he reacted strongly. His friend and admirer, the Conservative MP Victor Cazalet, noted in early July after a talk with Halifax that 'We are disturbed somewhat about Winston. He is getting very arrogant and hates criticism of any kind.'[54] When Churchill saw a note from General Macready (Assistant Chief of the Imperial General Staff) criticising his writing for being unintelligible, he wrote to his ex-Private Secretary, P. J. Grigg, now Permanent Secretary at the War Office, demanding a written formal apology from Macready. Similarly when Oliver Lampson, the British representative in Egypt, criticised the idea of sending troops to Greece, Churchill insisted that Halifax send him a formal censure for wasting public money in criticising Government policy, saying: 'I expect to be protected from this kind of insolence.' At times his tone seems more appropriate to an eighteenth-century absolute monarch. When he saw a report from a naval officer detailing leaks about the Dakar operation he told the Admiralty: 'The writer is granted protection by me, & must not be proceeded against in any way.'[55]

As Prime Minister Churchill was determined to keep military decisions as much as possible in his hands and away from the War Cabinet. As during his two periods at the Admiralty, he failed to even attempt to draw a distinction between the role of politicians and the role of military staffs, between the task of determining overall strategy and policy and that of detailed planning and implementation. He got embroiled in both and never set any store by consistency or singleness of purpose. He seems to have been convinced of his own military genius and reluctant to allow the chiefs of staff to determine the details of operations. He preferred to trust his own instincts and this made him dislike the decision-making framework he inherited. On 24 August he issued an instruction that within three days the Joint Planning Committee of the chiefs of staff was to work directly to him. He was to have 'direct access to and control of' the joint planning staff and they were to 'work out plans in accordance with directions which I shall give'. These plans would merely go to the chiefs of staff 'for their observations'.[56] This virtually amounted to an attempt to set himself up as a political and military dictator. Not surprisingly it was strongly resisted and the chiefs of staff kept ultimate control, albeit subject to endless harangues, criticism and interference from Churchill.

The chiefs of staff also suffered from Churchill's habit of giving vent to strong prejudices about certain individuals. Pound (First Sea Lord and a fellow insomniac) he grudgingly respected. He did not like Newall, the Chief of Air Staff, but was content to leave him in office until his retirement due in October, when he was replaced by Portal. Many of Churchill's criticisms fell on the Army. Within a few weeks of appointing him, he was criticising the CIGS, General Dill. He told Eden in July that 'I do not think we are having the help from General Dill which we hoped for at the time of his appointment, and he strikes me as being very tired, disheartened and over-impressed with the might of Germany.'[57] Having turned against Dill, he spent much of the next eighteen months criticising him before at last he managed to manoeuvre him out of the job. From the start he disliked Wavell and tried to relieve him of his command. He told Eden in August, 'I do not feel in him that sense of mental vigour and resolve to overcome obstacles, which is indispensable to successful war.'[58] When Admiral North criticised the operation against the French fleet, Churchill demanded his removal, telling A. V. Alexander: 'It is evident that Admiral Dudley North has not got the root of the matter in him, and I should be very glad to see you replace him by a more resolute and clear-sighted officer.'[59] Churchill was not successful on this occasion but two months later North was made the scapegoat for the passage of Vichy ships to west Africa at the time of the Dakar operation. In November he tried to get Admiral Somerville at Alexandria relieved of his command without any enquiry because he broke off chasing Italian ships in order to protect a convoy. (Somerville had also opposed the action against the French.) He was exonerated by a subsequent enquiry.

Churchill also had his favourites, whom he tried to promote. One of these was his old friend Admiral Keyes, whom he had liked since the Dardanelles operation and their time together in opposition over the Government's Indian policy. He wanted to make him Chairman of the Chiefs of Staff Committee, but the objections were so strong that he had to be content with putting him in charge of combined operations, where his arrogance and support for impractical schemes made him many enemies. Churchill also wanted to appoint the sixty-seven-year-old Lord Trenchard (whom he had known when he was Air Minister in 1919–21) as Commander-in-Chief of Home Forces to be in charge of all counter-invasion preparations. He was most offended when Trenchard declined and suggested a younger, more vigorous man was what the country needed.

Although he was now dealing with an enormously grave situation, Churchill was, as in the past, inconsistent in his views and subject to frequent whims. But as had happened before, he did not always get his way. For one thing, the system beneath him simply could not have coped with implementing the frequent changes of course emanating from Downing Street. Although he issued numerous 'Action This Day' minutes, they were often ignored and the military and civilian planning machine went on grappling with the problems involved in dealing with highly complex warfare as best it could. For example, on 16 October Churchill called for the use of land mines in retaliation for their use by Germany: four days later he argued against. On 15 October he wrote that the *Tirpitz* and *Bismarck* were the greatest prize available to Bomber Command. Five days later he wanted them to concentrate on the accurate bombing of military objectives in Germany, with the second line squadrons dropping their bombs over the Ruhr 'with no special accuracy'.[60] On 27 July, after two minutes' conversation with Lindemann, he ordered the CIGS to scrap all the Mills bombs (grenades) the Army held and replace them with the model his scientific adviser favoured. The Army kept the Mills bomb throughout the war. Often he could not even decide about the simplest domestic arrangements. After September 1940 Churchill spent most of the war living at the 'No 10 Annexe' – a flat above the Cabinet War Rooms which had been built by the Chamberlain Government – but on 3 December he changed his mind eight times about whether he would dine in Downing Street or at the Annexe.

The brunt of Churchill's behaviour was borne by those closest to him – the War Cabinet, the chiefs of staff and, in particular, his private staff. Major Morton, Churchill's source of intelligence information in the 1930s and now his intelligence adviser and liaison officer with the Free French, was rapidly disillusioned by working with the Prime Minister. He reflected later that Churchill was simply not interested in other people and had an 'overwhelming desire to dominate'. In particular he 'heartily disliked any person whose personal character was such that he could not avoid, most unwillingly, feeling respect for that person'. As a result, 'his junior staff, with few, if any, exceptions, disliked him to the point of detestation. He treated them like "flunkeys", without apparent interest in them or humanity.'[61] Even one of Churchill's greatest admirers, his Assistant Private Secretary 'Jock' Colville, wrote that Churchill was:

> more than normally inconsiderate and demanding during the last months of 1940. He complained of delays when there were none; he changed carefully prepared plans at the last minute; he cancelled meetings and appointments without caring for anybody's convenience but his own; and he was continually insisting on personal amenities which gave much trouble to overworked people and were, in a small way, diversions from the war effort.[62]

Churchill's dislike of any criticism was also apparent in his relations with the media. His general attitude had not changed from that shown in a speech he made in 1915 to his constituents in Dundee. Then he said it was wrong for newspapers to be allowed 'to attack the responsible leaders of the nation' or to write anything 'calculated to spread doubts and want of confidence in them'. On the outbreak of war the Government established a formal system of news censorship – opinion was still free. It also controlled much of the output of the BBC – political statements, news bulletins and talks. None of this went far enough for Churchill. Within a week of taking office he wanted to take advantage of the creation of a national coalition to impose greater controls. He wrote to Duff Cooper, the Minister of Information: 'I should be glad to receive some proposals from you for establishing a more effective control over the BBC. Now that we have a Government representing the Opposition as well as the Majority, we should have a much freer hand in this respect.'[63] He was unsuccessful on that occasion but returned to the charge in Cabinet in early November. Lord Reith, an ex-Director-General of the BBC, summarised the discussion: 'The PM spoke most bitterly about the BBC – enemy within the gate; continually causing trouble; more harm than good. Something drastic must be done with them, he said. Duff Cooper . . . agreed – more control probably and they ought to be civil servants.'[64] Again the Government drew back from outright State control and sent in two 'advisers' instead (one for foreign, one for home news) but they were more than advisers – they were in fact given 'supreme direction' over what could be said.

In June the Cabinet rejected the idea of total censorship of the press (including opinion), not on the grounds that it was authoritarian but because it would be administratively too difficult and would also create a bad impression in the United States at a time when Britain was supposed to be fighting for democracy. Churchill's most violent attack on the concept of press freedom though came not at the time of crisis during the threat of invasion but in the autumn, as a reaction to increasing, but still mild, criticism of his government. In general he was more prepared to accept such criticism from men like Lord Camrose of the *Daily Telegraph* (a friend who had published his articles before the war – Churchill thought he was patriotic) than from newspapers whose political stance he did not like. When the liberal *News Chronicle* deprecated the Government's willingness to conciliate Franco, Churchill asked Sinclair to put on pressure, telling him, 'I really must ask you to exert your influence to prevent these reckless & mischievous articles being written.'[65]

Then the *Daily Mirror* criticised the October ministerial reshuffle. They wrote: 'The shifting or shunting of mediocrities or reputed successes appears to have been directed by no principle plain to the outsider, unless it be the principle that new blood must rarely be transfixed into an old body.' This mild criticism threw Churchill into a paroxysm of rage. He told the Cabinet on 9 October that 'a continuance of such articles could not be tolerated' and declared the *Daily Mirror* 'stood for something dangerous and sinister'.[66] Attlee as Labour leader was delegated to put pressure on the editor and, at Churchill's insistence, a secret police investigation was launched into who owned shares in the paper. It revealed no sinister influences, but Churchill never forgave Cecil King, the editor – in 1943 he put pressure on Ernest Bevin to ensure that he was called up into the armed forces. Bevin ignored the pressure.

The growing criticism of the Government in the autumn of 1940 reflected, in part, its inadequate response to the start of the 'Blitz'. On the outbreak of war both sides had agreed not to bomb civilians. Churchill fully supported that policy and in January 1940 commended in public the policy of using the RAF to drop leaflets over Germany. That restraint lasted until May 1940. Then the German bombing of Rotterdam, which they regarded as a legitimate military target, gave the British the excuse they had been looking for to launch a bomber offensive. The RAF was ordered to bomb economic targets in the Ruhr. Unfortunately they were in practice incapable of hitting specific targets – their navigation was so bad the Germans could not even work out which cities they were trying to hit, let alone which targets. Hitler however refrained from attacking civilian targets throughout the campaign in the west and in the early stages of the Battle of Britain – as late as 24 August he issued orders that London was not to be bombed. It was Churchill who was anxious to extend the bombing to capital cities. He was given his opportunity when a German bomber overshot its target and some bombs fell in a London suburb. On 25 August the RAF was ordered to bomb Berlin but few planes found the target and there were no casualties. Hitler ignored this pinprick. Churchill insisted that the raids continue, rejecting Leipzig as an alternative. On 29 August ten people were killed in Berlin and Hitler ordered plans to be drawn up for retaliatory raids but did not give the go-ahead until 4 September.

German raids on London began on 7 September and spread to the provinces in November. Many people reacted by leaving the cities if possible – within ten days half the population of Stepney had gone and by October about a quarter of the population of London had left the capital. Although the Government had been engaged in planning to cope with air raids since the mid-1930s, its actual response was grossly inadequate at every level – firewatching did not become effective until the Blitz was over in May 1941 and a national fire service with interoperable machines was not functioning until August 1941. Casualties were much lower than officially expected but the level of destruction was much higher. The Government was unable to bring adequate public services to those affected by bombing. People found themselves facing a multiplicity of uncoordinated authorities providing different forms of assistance, lack of information, inadequate transport, and appalling conditions in 'rest centres' – little food and the assistance that was provided was determined by the rigours of the poor law. Even the official historian was forced to record after the war:

> The same story for each of some thirty cities ... The same
> monotonous and insufficient food in the rest centres, the same

meagre provision of clothing, blankets and washing facilities, first aid, lavatories, furniture and information . . . the same inadequacy of unsupported public assistance officials and of casually organised volunteers, the same weak liaison with the police and civil defence controls . . . All these faults were constantly in evidence . . . as one city after another was bombed.[67]

Churchill, like other ministers, senior officials and members of the social élite, lived sheltered lives, far removed from such scenes of deprivation.

In Britain, as in other countries subjected to bombing (including Germany later in the war), morale did not 'crack'. Nevertheless it was far from the tough cheerfulness depicted by Government propaganda – most people tried to continue their lives as normally as possible and had no alternative but to make the best of circumstances. Official reports showed the strain people were living under after cities were bombed:

> Coventry: there was great depression, a widespread feeling of impotence and many open signs of hysteria.
> Bristol: much talk of having been let down by the Government, and of the possibility of a negotiated peace.
> Portsmouth: On all sides we hear looting and wanton destruction had reached alarming proportions. The police seem unable to exercise control . . . The effect on morale is bad and there is a general feeling of desperation.[68]

In the East End of London the King and Queen were booed when they paid a visit and Herbert Morrison, the Home Secretary, gave his opinion in May 1941: 'the people cannot stand this intensive bombing indefinitely, sooner or later the morale of other towns will go even as Plymouth's has gone'.[69]

Pre-war Governments had little confidence in the ability of ordinary people to withstand the pressures of total war. Churchill's Government was no different. The policy before 1939 had been to deny people access to the tube stations for use as deep shelters because they believed that once people had taken refuge there they would not come back to the surface and carry on their normal lives. When the bombing of London began in September 1940 the Government instructed London Transport to close the stations. It proved to be impossible to carry out the directive – people simply took them over. Although Churchill was happy to use a specially converted disused tube station (Down Street near Hyde Park Corner) as his own personal shelter, he objected to other people doing the same. His Private Secretary reported in mid-October that 'the PM is thinking on authoritarian lines about shelters and talks of forcibly preventing people from going into the underground'.[70] In practice he could not maintain this opposition. At the beginning of October the Government announced that deep shelters for 100,000 would be built (they were too late and were used instead as troop billets before D-Day) and that tube shelters would be properly organised with Government help – tickets, reserved places, bunks, chemical lavatories, lighting and canteens. By the time the Blitz on London ended in May 1941 reasonable conditions had finally been established.

During the Blitz Churchill showed a strange reluctance to encourage and inspire the nation. The explanation may lie in his view of war as essentially a matter of high policy and strategic decision-making. His broadcast on 11 September about the invasion threat was his last address to the nation for five months. Throughout the autumn and winter of 1940–1, as London was bombed night after night and provincial cities strove to cope with intermittent bombing, he had no message to give. He did find time to speak to Czechoslovakia and France in late September and October, and to Italy at the end of the year, but not to the British people. His visits to see for himself the scale of destruction were infrequent in the extreme. He went to the City and East End, together with Ismay and Sandys, on 8 September, the day after the first heavy air raid, and almost three weeks later took a boat trip along the Thames accompanied by Clementine. He did not visit the bombed areas of London again until a brief visit two months later, although he did send Clementine and his Private Secretary Jock Colville to his constituency, where their welcome was less than ecstatic – the latter reported one refugee saying, 'It is all very well for them (looking at us!) who have all they want; but we have lost everything.'[71] He did visit the House of Commons after the raid in May 1941 for a carefully staged photograph amidst the rubble.

Churchill made only a few visits to provincial cities. On 31 January 1941 he paid a brief visit to Southampton and Portsmouth in order to accompany Harry Hopkins, President Roosevelt's personal representative. In mid-April he made a trip to west Wales to visit the Aberporth weapons range. He made a short stop at Swansea on the way and on the way back stopped in Bristol to present honorary degrees at the University, where he was Chancellor. By chance he was in the city on the night of a heavy raid – the degree ceremony went ahead while clearing-up operations were still underway. His only other trip was to Plymouth on 1 May, but that was primarily to inspect Devonport dockyard and Churchill only spent about an hour looking at the devastation in one of the most badly bombed cities in the country.

Although the German raids on Britain were largely over after early May 1941, when the Luftwaffe was redeployed to the east for the attack on the Soviet Union, mass bombing had become central to British strategy in the summer of 1940. It was one of the few ways in which it seemed possible that Britain might still win the war. After the German conquest of most of western Europe, the British blockade was far less effective and the German economy had access to a much wider supply of raw materials and food. Britain had no forces left on the mainland of Europe and the Army, even when rebuilt after Dunkirk, would never be strong enough to invade the continent in the face of a vastly superior German Army – about four times the size of British forces. Churchill accepted that Britain would never be the equal of Germany militarily. He told Beaverbrook bluntly in July 1940 'we have no continental army which can defeat the German military power'.[72] At the end of the year he informed Roosevelt that Britain would not be able 'to match the immense armies of Germany in any theatre where their main power can be brought to bear'.[73]

It is not surprising, therefore, to find Churchill expressing a mixture of resolution and uncertainty at this time. He told the Chief of the Air Staff and other senior officers on 13 October that 'he was sure we were going to win the war, but he confessed he did not see clearly how it was to be achieved'.[74] During the second half of 1940 British military planners gradually evolved a threefold strategy which might hold out some hope of winning the war. The blockade was to be maintained, in the hope that intelligence assessments which suggested that the German economy was on the point of collapse because of the pressure of arms production and shortage of raw materials were correct. The second strand of the strategy was a widespread campaign of subversion across occupied Europe. A Special Operations Executive was set up to 'set Europe ablaze', as Churchill put it. The final strand was widespread bombing of Germany, in the hope of destroying the industrial base and the morale of the population to carry on the war. If all these elements worked, then it was hoped that a numerically inferior army might be able to re-enter the continent to deal the *coup de grace* or possibly occupy an already defeated country. It was a strategy determined by Britain's weak position and limited resources but Churchill was to cling to it even after the German attack on the Soviet Union and US entry into the war when it no longer bore any relation to the respective strength of the two sides.

For Churchill mass bombing of Germany became the central element of his strategy to win the war. He told Beaverbrook in July 1940 that the only way Hitler would be defeated was through 'an absolutely devastating, exterminating attack by very heavy bombers . . . without which I do not see a way through'.[75] At the beginning of September he told the Cabinet that the central element of Britain's arms production must be bombers 'so as to pulverise the entire industry and scientific structure' of Germany.[76] And again at the end of October he argued that although the bulk of the Army would be deployed in the Middle East the only way to defeat Germany was 'to bank on the pressure of the blockade accompanied by the remorseless bombing of Germany and Italy'.[77]

However in 1940 Britain was not in a position to launch heavy bombers to carry out sustained bombing. The implications of the other two elements in the strategy presented fewer problems – apart from their limited impact on the course of the war. Maintaining the blockade was relatively simple and cheap, but it was having little effect on the German economy, which was far from fully mobilised and could draw on the resources of the occupied countries and friendly neutrals. Propaganda was cheap but had little impact when Germany looked impregnable. Subversion was also inexpensive, though largely ineffective while few people on the continent were prepared to commit themselves to resistance. Since Britain lacked a large heavy bomber force, and creating one would take not just time but a huge proportion of Britain's resources. Decisions by Churchill's Government to create such a force determined the structure of a large part of the wartime economy and made it virtually impossible to change course later in the war.

Until heavy bombing of Germany could begin in 1942, Britain's ability to undertake any offensive operations against Germany would be very limited. Churchill grew restive under these limitations and was liable to get carried away on flights of fancy about what might be possible. At the end of August he told the Joint Planning Staff that during 1941 Britain would be deploying armoured forces of 120,000 men (he refused to accept Eden's advice that they would not be equipped by then). He anticipated using them for the capture of Oslo (having specifically rejected such an operation only three weeks earlier) and 'the invasion of Italy; the cutting off of the Cherbourg peninsula, a landing in the Low Countries followed by the seizure of the Ruhr'.[78] How this was to be achieved against a German Army of over 150 divisions he did not elaborate and these dreams were quietly buried in the Whitehall bureaucracy. By the end of the year he was more realistic – on 5 November he offered the House of Commons no policy or plans for 1941 apart from survival and fighting as best Britain could.

It became clear to Churchill during the summer and autumn of 1940 that whether or not Britain would be able to continue the war into 1941 would depend on decisions made by the United States. Without massive financial and economic help Britain would have to seek a compromise peace. Even before the outbreak of war the Chamberlain Government had accepted that a long war involving Germany, Italy and possibly Japan could not be sustained. In January 1939 the chiefs of staff had warned that such a war would create 'a position more serious than the Empire has ever faced before. The ultimate outcome ... might well depend upon the intervention of other Powers, in particular of the United States.'[79] The collapse of France in May 1940 brought this moment nearer. When Churchill asked the chiefs of staff about the chances of Britain continuing the war on its own, they advised him that it was possible, but only if one essential condition was fulfilled. That was that the United States:

> is willing to give us full economic and financial support, *without which we do not think we could continue the war with any chance of success*.[80] (Italics in original)

It was a grim message because there was little evidence at the time that the United States would be prepared to give such assistance. Nevertheless one of the strongest arguments Churchill used for fighting on in the summer of 1940 was that somehow the United States would save Britain.

It was therefore absolutely vital to develop good personal relations with President Roosevelt, who had been in office since 1933 and seemed likely to seek an unprecedented third term in the November 1940 elections. Both during the war and after Churchill was to make much of his personal relationship with President Roosevelt, which he liked to portray as one of great intimacy. He also suggests they were usually of one mind about what needed to be done to defeat Hitler. That was far from the case at any time during the war, and particularly untrue in 1940. Churchill's own knowledge of the United States was limited, despite two visits since 1929. His American friends and acquaintances were nearly all millionaires, he saw the country as an outpost of the Anglo-Saxon world and knew little of the isolationist mentality of the middle and far west and even less of the experience of the black and immigrant communities and the social tensions within the country. It was to be expected that he would dislike the social and economic reforms introduced in Roosevelt's 'New Deal'. He had expressed his opposition in numerous newspaper articles, with attacks on its pernicious effects including 'the extension of the activities of the Executive', the 'pillorying by irresponsible agitators' of business leaders and 'the erosion of American individualism'.[81] Roosevelt and his advisers were well aware of these views.

Roosevelt had met Churchill when he visited Europe at the end of the First World War and disliked him on sight. A more recent report from a close friend of Roosevelt's would not have improved matters. Under Secretary of State Sumner Welles had met Churchill in March 1940 when in Europe on a peace mission for the President. Welles found him reading the paper, smoking a large cigar and drinking whisky and commented, 'it was quite obvious that he had consumed a good many whiskeys before I arrived'. Churchill subjected his visitor to a two-hour monologue on how Britain would win the war 'in the course of which he became quite sober'.[82] These reports clearly had an effect in Washington; when Churchill became Prime Minister, Roosevelt observed to the Cabinet that 'he supposed

Churchill was the best man that England had, even if he was drunk half of his time'.[83]

On the outbreak of war Roosevelt had, however, taken the initiative in opening a direct correspondence with Churchill at the Admiralty. Before May 1940 they exchanged a dozen messages in total (only three were from Roosevelt). They were all about naval affairs and details of British operations and none contained anything of political or strategic importance. Churchill continued the correspondence when he became Prime Minister, but for months it was very one-sided. Between 15 May and 15 June he sent ten messages to the President and received three replies. The first of these rejected his wide ranging appeal of 15 May for American assistance, the second was a copy of a message sent to Reynaud and the third made it clear that the United States was not committed to the military support of the allies. For the next six weeks, until the end of July, one of the most anxious periods of all for Britain as it faced the threat of imminent invasion, there was no correspondence at all apart from a short message from Churchill telling Roosevelt about the appointment of the Duke of Windsor as Governor of the Bahamas which elicited no reply.

During the collapse of France there were no signs of mutual trust between Britain and the United States, indeed there was a great deal of mistrust, reflecting the fact that the United States was taking a clear-headed view about where its national interests lay and it was far from convinced that they involved supporting Britain. In May 1940 the United States was poorly armed – it had a moderate-sized Navy, an Army of just 200,000 men not equipped for serious warfare, and an Air Force of less than 2,000 largely obsolescent planes. The collapse of the allies transformed its strategic position. Realising it faced the possibility of a direct threat from Germany and probably Japan too, it embarked on a major rearmament programme. The aim was to build a navy that would dominate both the Atlantic and Pacific, an army of 2 million men by the end of 1941 (with equipment planned for one of 4 million) and production of 18,000 aircraft a year. Until these planned strengths were reached, the US Government had to decide whether to stand aside from Europe and concentrate solely on its own defence or whether to support Britain so as to keep Germany occupied, with the risk that any equipment that was sent would fall into German hands if Britain surrendered.

The first argument between the two countries was over the future of the Royal Navy if Britain was defeated. If Germany gained control of the British fleet then American security would be severely threatened. The arguments were essentially a replay of those between Britain and France, but with Churchill now adopting a position virtually identical with that of the French. On 17 May, as soon as he realised the impending scale of the allied defeat in France, Roosevelt suggested to the British Ambassador, Lord Lothian, that if the worst should happen the Navy should sail for Canada or the United States. Without any instructions from London, Lothian said that such action would depend on whether the Americans were in the war or not. Churchill promptly approved this line and on 20 May he told Roosevelt that if Britain were defeated then another government would almost certainly use the fleet as a way of trying to obtain better terms from Germany and the Americans could not count on it coming to North America. This mild blackmail, to increase the pressure on the United States to aid the allies and perhaps even enter the war, failed. On 24 May Roosevelt, in talks with the Canadians, told them Britain and France were finished and asked them to put pressure on Britain to sail the fleet across the Atlantic. The Canadians refused and told the British what had happened. The next day the Cabinet expressed its displeasure with Roosevelt who 'seemed to be taking the view that it would be nice of him to pick up the bits of the British Empire if this country was overrun'.[84]

With the fate of the Royal Navy if Britain were defeated still unresolved, the allies appealed in late May for any surplus US munitions that might be made available. Until mid-June the US Government (which could not legally sell arms direct to Britain and France) sold back to the contractors, who sold them to the allies, 250,000 rifles (mainly used to equip the Home Guard), 130 million rounds of ammunition and 80,000 machine guns. This was in line with the established US policy of trying to keep the allies fighting Germany in the hope first that they would defeat Hitler but increasingly after May in the hope of prolonging resistance for as long as possible to give time for American rearmament. Just how limited US help would be was made clear in mid-June. On 10 June Reynaud (without consulting Churchill) sent a message to Roosevelt emphasising the need for American entry into the war to help keep

France fighting. Roosevelt's reply on 13 June was, like his policy at the time, long on rhetoric (he was impressed by the likely French decision to fight on in North Africa) but short on action. That night, clutching at straws, the War Cabinet decided that Roosevelt was on the brink of entering the war, and Churchill himself expected a declaration within a fortnight. Their hopes were rudely shattered when, next day, Roosevelt sent a colder message and refused to allow his earlier reply to be published.

American opinion was still overwhelmingly opposed to involvement in Europe's quarrels and inclined to rely on their own resources for hemispheric defence. From the fall of France till early August that remained Roosevelt's policy, and even afterwards he only edged away from it very slowly. Privately he expected Britain and France to be defeated. He told a conference on national defence on 30 May that the situation was 'extremely serious for England and France. We are not saying so out loud because we do not want to intimate in this country that England and France have gone.'[85] At this juncture he therefore backed a policy of not selling any more arms to Britain because they would probably end up in German hands and therefore worsen the US position. He told Harold Ickes, the Secretary of the Interior, in early June that selling Britain equipment would only enrage Hitler and 'we cannot tell the turn the war will take, and there is no use endangering ourselves unless we can achieve some results for the allies'.[86] At the beginning of July he signed a Congressional Bill that severely restricted the possible supply of weapons. In future arms sales could only be made if the Chief of Staff of either the Army or Navy certified that the material was 'not essential for US defense'.

In his first letter to Roosevelt as Prime Minister, Churchill had, among a long list of requests, asked for the loan of forty or fifty old destroyers until new British construction arrived. (Before the war the Admiralty had insisted on giving priority to battleships rather than the less glamorous convoy escorts.) Roosevelt turned down the appeal on several grounds: it would need Congressional approval which was unlikely to be given, the ships were needed by the US and they could not be made available in time to help Britain. On the advice of both Lothian and the US Ambassador in Britain, Joseph Kennedy, Churchill dropped the subject until the end of July – by then Roosevelt had been renominated by the Democrats for a third

17 Churchill leaves No 10 Downing Street
for the House of Commons, 18 June 1940
(Brendan Bracken is behind Churchill)

18a Churchill
with the
commander of the
BEF, Lord Gort,
and his deputy
General Pownall

18b Churchill
inspecting coastal
defences 1940

19 Churchill during a visit to Dover, summer 1940

20a Churchill during his visit to Bristol, 1941

20b Churchill in the damaged House of Commons, May 1941

21a Churchill meets President Roosevelt
at the Newfoundland Conference August 1941

21b Churchill on his return from Newfoundland

22a Churchill with Roosevelt's close adviser Harry Hopkins.
(Brendan Bracken is behind them)

22b Churchill during his visit to the 8th Army in Egypt, 1942

23a Churchill at the British Embassy Cairo, 1942. From left to right: Back Row: Air Chief Marshal Tedder, General Brooke, Admiral Horwood, R.G. Casey. Front Row: Field Marshal Smuts, Churchill, General Auchinleck, Field Marshal Wavell

23b Casablanca Conference 1943. Left to right: General Giraud, President Roosevelt, General De Gaulle and Churchill

24a Churchill broadcasting from the White House, May 1943

24b Churchill inspects US troops in Britain before D-Day

term. When he did return to the request, it was linked to an offer of defence facilities for the US on British possessions in the western hemisphere. That idea had originally been raised by Lothian at the end of May, and was supported by the Foreign Office and the chiefs of staff, but opposed by the Colonial and Dominions Offices and Churchill himself. Britain's precarious position forced a reassessment. In mid-July Halifax put a paper to the Cabinet which for the first time accepted that Britain's future survival increasingly depended upon substantial assistance from the United States – or 'collaboration' as the Foreign Office preferred to call it: 'the future of our widely scattered Empire is likely to depend on the evolution of an effective and enduring collaboration between ourselves and the United States'.[87] The offer of bases was to be part of the process.

Also part of the process was giving the US access to virtually all of Britain's intelligence assets and technical secrets. In July Roosevelt's close adviser 'Colonel' Bill Donovan was shown Britain's codebreaking centre at Bletchley Park and by the end of August an exchange of intelligence information was underway. The question of giving them technical secrets was more difficult, because American industry might well use them to the long-term detriment of Britain's position. Churchill's initial reaction was to try and trade these secrets for US entry into the war. He told Ismay on 17 July, 'Are we going to throw all our secrets into the American lap, and see what they give us in exchange? If so I am against it . . . Generally speaking, I am not in a hurry to give our secrets until the United States is much nearer to the war than she is now.'[88] Within a matter of days his opposition had collapsed and he accepted the policy he had condemned – giving Britain's secrets in the hope that it would make the Americans more sympathetic. On 14 August Professor Tizard left for the United States, taking with him design details and in some cases samples of Britain's most secret inventions – microwave radar, the cavity magnetron, chemical warfare formulae, special explosives, jet engine design and miniaturised valves, as well as details of German magnetic mines.

Churchill reopened the question of the destroyers on 30 July, the day after the Cabinet agreed to offer the US commercial air facilities on three British possessions – Jamaica, Trinidad and British Guiana. In parallel Roosevelt and his Cabinet had decided that Britain really did need the destroyers but that the deal would not be acceptable to either Congress or the American public without military bases and a British commitment to sail the Royal Navy to North America in the event of defeat. Roosevelt told Lothian of these terms the next day and Churchill indignantly rejected giving any guarantees on the fleet – 'we must refuse any declaration as is suggested and confine the deal solely to the Colonial bases'.[89] The British decided to ask for ninety-six destroyers in return for facilities at three bases. On 13 August Roosevelt set out the US counter-proposals – fifty destroyers, a private assurance on the fleet and the right to build military bases on Newfoundland, Bermuda and five West Indian colonies on ninety-nine year leases, with the US also undertaking to defend these territories. The next day the Cabinet agreed to negotiate on this basis although they were unhappy about it and felt the US terms were very harsh. They realised however that, in the last resort, American help was so crucial that they could not reject the demands.

On 19 August the US demanded that the deal should be presented as a single entity. The British had been hoping it would appear as two separate gifts so as to help disguise the unequal nature of the agreement. On 21 August the Cabinet rejected this last US demand, saying 'a formal bargain on the lines proposed was out of the question'.[90] Four days later Churchill protested to Roosevelt that US demands amounted to seeking 'a blank cheque on the whole of our transatlantic possessions'.[91] At the end of August the United States laid out its final terms. There was to be an explicit bargain (only bases on Newfoundland and Bermuda could be a gift) and Britain was to make a public declaration that, if necessary, the fleet would sail to North America. The British gave in and the deal was signed on 2 September.

The treatment meted out by the US Government to Britain in its hour of need was a sharp reminder of the relative power of the two countries. Churchill and the Cabinet had been forced to give way on every point, even those they had explicitly rejected as unacceptable only a few weeks earlier. The Americans gave fifty not ninety-six ships and they were explicitly given in return for bases. Those bases were in seven colonies not three, and were not commercial facilities but military bases on very long leases. And they had obtained an explicit assurance that, in the worst circumstances, the fleet would sail to North America – the one commitment Churchill had rejected ever since he had become Prime Minister. Apart from additional protection for convoys, the main value of the deal to Britain was that it was an openly unneutral act by the United States and it could be presented as a sign of an American commitment to help Britain. This was not how the Roosevelt administration saw the deal; they were still hedging their bets about Britain's ability to survive. In return for ships of dubious military value, they had secured a huge increase in the ability of the US Navy to provide hemispheric defence and a series of bases they had long coveted, together with a commitment on the future of the British fleet.

In practice the US destroyers turned out to be of little immediate value. Only nine out of the fifty were in service by the end of 1940 and only thirty by May 1941. Many of them needed refits, especially to provide an anti-submarine capability, and the Navy lacked the trained crews to man them. The detailed negotiations over the sites to be leased by the Americans and the powers they were to exercise in British territory took until March 1941. Once again the British gave in on virtually every point in the hope that it would improve Anglo-American relations. As Churchill put it, 'We cannot afford to risk the major issue in order to maintain our pride and to preserve the dignity of a few small islands.'[92]

The 'major issue' to which Churchill referred was American financial assistance to enable Britain to continue the war. Immediately on becoming Prime Minister Churchill had sought assurances from the American President. In his message of 15 May he told Roosevelt: 'we shall go on paying dollars for as long as we can, but I should like to feel reasonably sure that when we can pay no more, you will give us the stuff all the same'.[93] Roosevelt ignored the request and made no mention of it in his reply. In mid-July a senior Treasury official, Sir Frederick Phillips, was sent to Washington to tell the Americans of the forthcoming problems. He told them that Britain would be able to go on selling its assets until mid-1941 but after that it would need massive credits. The Americans suggested that Britain could help by selling assets in South America (which the US would then be able to purchase cheaply). Phillips saw Roosevelt and the Treasury Secretary, Henry Morgenthau, but reported that the President 'said nothing which could be regarded as a commitment' and he advised that nothing could be done until after the Presidential Election in November at the earliest. According to Phillips, the US position was that they would not 'be willing to furnish us with credits on a large scale until they are satisfied that our existing resources are in fact exhausted or near exhaustion'.[94]

In May Churchill's arguments for fighting on were based on the expectation that extensive American help would be available to enable Britain to continue the war. Despite the lack of a firm US commitment the British had little alternative but to carry on and hope for the best. But during the summer of 1940 Britain's financial position declined more rapidly than the Government expected. As late as June the Treasury thought the gold and dollar reserves and the securities in the US that could be sold would see them through for about another year. The rapid deterioration was caused by three factors. First, armaments orders were greatly increased in the aftermath of Dunkirk – in total they were now nearly $10 billion, already far beyond Britain's total debts in the First World War. Second, the British took over all French orders placed in the United States. Third, Britain's own war production was becoming increasingly dependent on US raw materials – steel imports were worth just over £12 million in 1940 but by July 1940 orders for 1941 had already risen to over £100 million.

On 22 August the Cabinet discussed a paper from the Chancellor of the Exchequer forecasting Britain's imminent bankruptcy and inability to continue the war without massive American assistance. Its contents were so sensitive that all copies had to be returned at the end of the meeting. Kingsley Wood told his colleagues that Britain had only £310 million of assets left to pay for American arms and materials. The reserves were being depleted at about £80 million a month and this rate was set to increase. It was doubtful whether Britain had enough resources to last until the end of the year. 'We are faced with the immediate practical problem of holding out well into November in the case of a Democratic victory, or until after the 20th of January, when the new President takes office, in the case of a Republican victory.' Churchill and his colleagues had to face the unwelcome news that Britain's future depended upon the vagaries of American domestic politics – if Wendell Willkie, the Republican candidate, beat Roosevelt then any help would probably arrive too late to save Britain. Even if assistance was forthcoming in time, Britain would become dependent on the United States. Wood forecast that 'The United States will no doubt settle both the extent to which and the conditions under which we can enjoy the products of American industry and agriculture, and in that way may materially influence the character of the war.'⁹⁵

The paper made grim reading – it marked the effective end of Britain's status as an independent power. The Cabinet decided that there was little they could do except to continue to hope for the best. The Treasury advised that requisitioning all gold ornaments in the country, including wedding rings, might raise £20 million but Churchill wanted to keep this option in reserve for propaganda purposes – 'this was a measure to be adopted at a later stage, if we wished to make some striking gesture for the purpose of shaming the Americans'. He was also, if necessary, prepared to go even further in the event of a crisis that autumn: 'If the military position should unexpectedly deteriorate, we should have to pledge everything we had for the sake of victory, giving the United States, if necessary, a lien on any and every part of British industry.'⁹⁶

Britain's imminent penury was demonstrated again within a couple of weeks. Beaverbrook asked his colleagues to approve a huge programme of aircraft orders in the United States in order to provide the aircraft Britain's own industry could not produce. There were two alternatives – 1,250 aircraft a month at an eventual cost of £300 million a year (to be paid in dollars) or 3,000 aircraft a month at a cost of £800 million a year. The Treasury's advice was clear: 'There is no prospect of our having dollars to pay these sums, nor of our ever repaying those amounts, if lent to us by the U.S.A.'⁹⁷ When the Cabinet discussed the issue they accepted Beaverbrook's argument that they should go for the larger programme. Since Britain could afford neither option, Beaverbrook argued, the larger one would increase the direct interest American industry had in Britain continuing the war and it would demonstrate determination. At best it would simply increase the amount of assistance the Americans would have to provide, at worst Britain would default on an even bigger debt.

During its discussion the Cabinet concluded: 'It was now fairly widely appreciated in the United States that there was no prospect of our ever having dollars to repay the colossal sums for which we were becoming indebted to them . . . We had no knowledge of what conditions the United States were likely to attach to the credits which we assumed they were about to extend to us.'⁹⁸ Perhaps because of the lack of rapport at the top between Churchill and Roosevelt, it was certainly true that the two sides were not fully aware of each other's thinking during this period. The unfortunate implications of this from Britain's viewpoint were made clear later in September when Lothian reported from Washington: 'Public opinion here has not yet grasped that it will have to make far reaching decisions to finance and supply us and possibly still graver ones next Spring or Summer unless it is to take the responsibility of forcing us to make a compromise peace.'[99]

For the rest of September and October, while the assets dwindled the Government waited on the outcome of the American Election on 5 November. Roosevelt was re-elected with a popular majority of over 5 million votes and by 449:82 in the electoral college. Churchill had initially hoped for an American declaration of war during the fall of France and again once the bombing of British cities began but had been disappointed. Then he became convinced that Roosevelt was waiting until the Election was over before entering the war. He expressed this expectation in the notes he made for his speech to the Commons in secret session on 20 June: 'All depends on our resolute bearing and holding out until Election issues are settled there. If we can do so, I cannot doubt whole English-speaking world will be in line together [sic].' Just before the Election he told one of his private secretaries that Roosevelt would win a large majority and 'America would come into the war'.[100] His own forecast was US entry within a fortnight of the Election.

Churchill's wishful thinking was based on a profound misunderstanding of the state of American opinion, the nature of the Constitution and Roosevelt's own intentions. Although opinion polls showed Americans as sympathetic to Britain's plight and a majority in favour of giving Britain extensive aid, over eighty per cent did not want to enter the war. Even if he had wanted to, it was impossible for Roosevelt to ignore such a strong body of opinion. Although Churchill believed that Roosevelt, once re-elected, would have a majority in Congress which would follow whatever he wanted to do, Congressional opinion in fact remained highly cautious about involvement in what was still a European war. Roosevelt himself simply continued his old policy of carefully balancing US defence needs against the advantages for the United States of keeping Britain fighting during the rearmament process. Like many other Americans, he also took the British Empire at its face value and found it difficult to accept that it really was on the point of bankruptcy, as Churchill had hinted in his earlier message.

The aftermath of the Election was therefore a huge disappointment to Churchill and the rest of the Government. No change of policy was signalled and most of the senior members of the administration went on extended leave to recover from the rigours of the campaign. The British financial situation was now extremely serious: bankruptcy was only a matter of weeks away. At the beginning of December Churchill told the Cabinet that he had been 'rather chilled by the attitude of the United States since the election'.[101] He remarked bitterly to Halifax (who had finally been levered out of the Foreign Office and despatched to the Washington Embassy after the death of Lothian): 'we have not had anything from the US that we have not paid for and what we have had has not played an essential part in our resistance'.[102] By then Churchill had been persuaded by Lothian, who had returned to Britain in November, that the only solution was to spell out Britain's position to Roosevelt in all its starkness in an attempt to make him face up to the consequences of not helping Britain. The draft that Lothian submitted to Churchill was certainly blunt: 'it is only a question of weeks before the resources we have available with which to pay for our requirements and the munitions ordered from the United States are exhausted. Unless we get financial assistance from the United States on the largest scale, it is obvious that our capacity to carry on the war on the current basis must abruptly come to an end.'[103]

Churchill, with more than half an eye on history, decided that this was too strong for him to state personally. His redraft, agreed by numerous departments in Whitehall and cleared by the Cabinet, was rather less direct if equally bleak. It was a terrible catalogue of British weakness. Churchill told Roosevelt that Britain could not take on more than small elements of the German Army and, without US escorts for Atlantic convoys and provision of merchant shipping, supplies to Britain and the Middle East could not be maintained at adequate levels. Without US munitions, in particular aircraft, Britain could not adequately arm either itself or its allies. Then came a more guarded reference to Britain's imminent bankruptcy: 'last of all, I come to the question of Finance'. Churchill explained that British orders in the US 'many times exceed the total exchange resources remaining at the disposal of Great Britain. The moment fast approaches when we shall no longer be able to pay cash for shipping and other supplies.' He argued that it would not be right to strip Britain of all its remaining resources. Finally he left the fate of Britain 'with confidence to you and to your people'.[104]

In the First World War Britain had fought for more than two and a half years before its resources were depleted and it had to be rescued by the Americans. Now after just over a year of war, Churchill had to admit that it could not continue fighting for financial reasons. This time Britain, if it was to avoid a compromise peace with Germany, was looking to be rescued not by an ally but by a neutral state. Roosevelt never formally responded to Churchill's letter of 8 December, but it did achieve its purpose in convincing the President that a major policy initiative was required. He did not, however, consult Churchill about what form this would take. At a press conference on 17 December, using a vivid metaphor about lending a neighbour a hose to put out a fire rather than selling it to him, he first outlined the idea of 'Lend-Lease'. Again Britain was not consulted about how that concept would be developed and knew little about what the President had in mind until a Bill was published in January.

The changing nature of the Anglo-American relationship was made painfully clear in the next few months as Britain first tried to convince the Americans that it really was bankrupt and then tried to survive until US help arrived. Churchill sent the Treasury official, Sir Frederick Phillips, back to Washington to negotiate with the American administration. He went with a carefully prepared brief on Britain's requirements but found it was useless because the Americans simply laid down the terms on which help would be forthcoming. Their first requirement was that Britain had to be completely open about its finances. Phillips reported that Morgenthau (Treasury Secretary) had told him: 'Mr Churchill must put himself in Mr Roosevelt's hands with complete confidence; if he trusts him, he will not find him in any bargaining mood.' (That was true – the US Government was not prepared to bargain, only to lay down terms.) Phillips then added the rider, in a passage that encapsulated Britain's new dependence on the United States, 'it should be for them to allow us to keep our assets, not for us to withhold them'.[105]

The administration had to convince Congress that aid was essential. To do this Morgenthau demanded a full statement of Britain's financial plight and he also assured Congress that all British assets in the United States would be sold before help was forthcoming: 'Every dollar of property, real property or securities that any English citizen owns in the United States, they have agreed to sell during the next 12 months, in order to raise the money to pay for the orders they have already placed, they are going to sell – every dollar of it.' In March 1941, in order to convince Congress that this was happening, he demanded that an important British company be sold within a week to show good faith. The American Viscose Corporation, a subsidiary of Courtaulds and the largest British holding in the United States, was sold at half its market value to a group of American investors.

The Bill to provide lend-lease assistance made its slow way through Congress between January and March 1941 – it was numbered 1776 (the year of the declaration of independence) as a deliberate snub to the British and entitled 'An Act to promote the defense of the United States'. The British Government had to sit by helplessly as it passed through its legislative stages and Congress decided whether and how Britain was to be rescued. As its provisions were not retrospective, they would apply only to orders placed after it eventually became law. Although the Bill held out the prospect of large-scale assistance, it was not going to solve the most acute British problem of how to pay the instalments on its existing contracts. Churchill and the Government found increasingly that decisions were simply taken out of their hands during this waiting period. On 19 December the Americans stopped Britain from placing any new orders. Just before Christmas the US despatched a cruiser to Cape Town to take Britain's last £50 million of gold reserves in part payment of existing orders. Seriously affronted by this high-handed American action, Churchill wrote a letter to Roosevelt complaining, quite accurately, that the US action was like that of 'a sheriff collecting the last assets of a helpless debtor'.[106] But the Embassy in Washington persuaded him that it would be counter-productive to send it. A month later Morgenthau finally persuaded Roosevelt that Britain really did not have any money left and the President agreed to take over from Britain the funding of new armaments factories in the United States; the consequence was that Britain could only order US-designed equipment, not British items. At the end of January Morgenthau unilaterally rationed British orders to $35 million a week until lend-lease became law.

Britain only managed to survive until that time and avoid a politically disastrous default on its contracts by timely help from two small allies and from Canada. In October 1940 Benes, the Czechoslovak leader, generously lent £7.5 million, even though Britain did not recognise his government-in-exile as legitimate. In early 1941 Canada began selling British assets to pay for raw materials from the United States. By then Britain's gold and dollar reserves had fallen to just £3 million – it was on the edge of bankruptcy. It was saved from default on its US orders by the Belgian government-in-exile, which lent £60 million on condition that Britain repaid it after the war. It was enough to see Britain through until lend-lease became effective.

In public Churchill praised lend-lease as 'the most unsordid act' in the history of any nation. In private he was much more critical. Just after it became law he wrote to Kingsley Wood, asking whether Britain would get back the advances made earlier to set up factories in the United States (he obviously still did not appreciate that lend-lease was not retrospective) and added: 'As far as *I* can make out we are not only to be skinned, but flayed to the bone.'[107] Churchill and the rest of the Government also resented the fact that lend-lease goods were not free. Congress had insisted that there should be a 'consideration' in return for all the US help. What that should be was left to the President to decide and the issue was to cause considerable friction between the two Governments for the rest of the war. Lend-lease was essentially an extension of what the US had been doing throughout 1940 – trying to provide enough help to the allies to keep them fighting while it rearmed. The severity of Britain's plight at the end of 1940 meant that they had to go rather further and rather faster than they had anticipated. Churchill was belatedly realising it was not a change of course and did not bring nearer an American declaration of war. But it did drastically change the nature of the Anglo-American relationship. Britain was now utterly dependent on the United States to continue the war. As Churchill described it later in a moment of candour, Britain had become 'a client receiving help from a generous patron'.[108]

Although Churchill told the Americans during the passage of lend-lease 'give us the tools and we will finish the job', he knew that, apart from a sudden and unexpected collapse in Germany, there was little prospect of Britain accomplishing that task in the foreseeable future. Britain's military power was extremely limited – it could provide enough for an effective defence of its homeland, a little for operations in the Mediterranean against the weaker of its opponents, but virtually nothing against the potential threat from Japan in the Far East. It was on the defensive and only just able to ensure the delivery of enough food and raw materials to survive. Although the military planners had devised a scenario that envisaged victory, primarily through a massive bombing campaign, that offensive was still some way off. For Churchill, therefore, 1941 promised to be a bleak year: Britain would be forced to react to initiatives taken by its opponents, unable itself to take decisive action to win the war. The United States had done enough to avoid the necessity of a compromise peace. But it had not fulfilled his hopes of an early entry into the war. There was no alternative but to carry on although without US participation victory seemed impossibly distant.

21

1941 – The Grimmest Year

Churchill's first task in 1941 was to sell himself to the Americans. He was advised by some of Brendan Bracken's American friends that the Roosevelt administration regarded him with suspicion because of his known opposition to the New Deal and what they regarded as his generally reactionary tendencies. When Roosevelt decided that it was in America's national interest to keep Britain in the war by extending unlimited financial assistance, he felt he needed his own assessment of the situation in Britain and of its Prime Minister. He sent Harry Hopkins, his closest friend and adviser, to Britain. Churchill knew that he had to make a good impression on Hopkins and through him on Roosevelt.

No effort was spared to impress Hopkins, who was already favourably disposed to Britain because of his hatred of Nazi Germany. At their first meeting over lunch at 10 Downing Street on 10 January, Churchill suggested that he should meet Roosevelt as soon as possible and they tentatively agreed a date in April or May. During his visit Hopkins was allowed access to every part of the British Government and very little information was withheld from him. He spent several weekends with Churchill at Chequers or at the Prime Minister's other country residence, Ditchley Park (used when bombing of Chequers was a possibility), and was also invited to Blenheim. Brendan Bracken was given the job of more or less permanent escort and Churchill joined them for trips to Dover, Portsmouth, Southampton and finally to Glasgow. The visit lasted almost a month and proved a success. Hopkins returned convinced that Britain would fight on and that American assistance would not be wasted.

One of the most important papers Hopkins took back with him was a document prepared by Lindemann and agreed by the Cabinet. It spelled out in detail what Churchill had outlined to Roosevelt in his letter of 8 December – the growing crisis in Britain's supply lines. In the summer and autumn of 1940, even though there were only eight or nine German U-boats at sea, the British were losing about 300,000 tons of shipping a month. By the turn of the year a real crisis was emerging. With Europe and the Mediterranean largely closed to British shipping, goods had to come over longer distances than normal and this, together with slower turn-round times in ports affected by bombing and the blackout, reduced import capacity to 40 million tons. This was only two-thirds of pre-war levels and was considered to be Britain's minimum requirement for survival. Much of the reduced capacity had to be devoted to munitions and raw materials to make armaments. Food imports were cut by almost thirty per cent and other goods by nearly as much. In the winter of 1940–1, continuing losses and the inability of the British shipbuilding industry to build enough ships meant that even the 'minimum' figure of 40 million tons was not met. Altogether there was a shortfall of over ten per cent. Since food imports were already at an irreducible minimum, the message for the Americans in Lindemann's paper was clear – unless they could help, Britain's war making capacity was likely to decline.

Apart from American financial assistance relations between the two countries were also deepening on defence planning and foreign policy. Here too there was evidence that this relationship was going to be difficult and frequently one-sided. The first formal defence staff talks opened in Washington at the end of January (Churchill had opposed an early move in this direction in the summer of 1940). Although these closer contacts were symbolic of an increasing American interest in the outcome of the war, they also very clearly showed Britain's increasing dependence on the United States. In the autumn of 1940 American defence planners had agreed with Roosevelt a strategy to give coherence to their rearmament plans and an outline of operations if they did enter the war. The US decided that the defeat of Germany was the top priority and that if Japan entered the war a defensive posture should be adopted in the Pacific. They assessed that Britain could not defeat Germany on its own and would need American economic help and eventually US forces. This exercise was carried out without any consultation with the British: 'We cannot afford nor do we need to entrust our national future to British direction . . . Never absent from British minds are their post-war interests, commercial and military. We should likewise safeguard our own eventual interests.'[1] Churchill was, however, happy with the US emphasis on the defeat of Germany, saying in November 1940 that it was 'strategically sound and also most highly adapted to our interests'.[2]

The military talks reached agreement fairly easily over the priority to be given to the defeat of Germany (which was in the interests of both countries) and the immediate need to keep open the supply lines to Britain, but elsewhere there was little agreement. The United States did not accept the priority Britain gave to the Mediterranean and in the Pacific the Americans refused to send part of their fleet to Singapore to defend British interests. This strictly limited convergence of views was a constant factor throughout the war – a common interest in the security of Britain (which the US would need as a base to mount an invasion of the continent), and in the security of the Atlantic, but elsewhere a wide range of divergent interests. Although the United States, still neutral, was discussing a possible future strategy, there was still no American commitment to enter the war. The talks remained highly secret and the idea of joint operations entirely hypothetical.

Before the staff talks started, the Americans demanded that Britain should reveal all the secret treaties they had signed making commitments about the post-war settlement. The British had no choice but to comply. Indeed the Americans were increasingly making it clear that if they were keeping Britain in the war they were going to have the major say in the shaping of the post-war world. In his State of the Union address at the beginning of January Roosevelt set out his policy of the Four Freedoms – of speech and expression and of worship together with freedom from want and from fear. At the end of the month Hopkins told the British that Roosevelt 'regarded the post-war settlement so to speak as being his particular preserve'.[3]

While Hopkins was in London, he was reporting to Roosevelt on the only active military campaign Britain was fighting – that in North

Africa with the Italians – and on Britain's plans for operations in the Mediterranean. Immediately on his arrival he wrote that Churchill thought Greece was lost and that although he was 'prepared for a setback in Greece – the African campaign will proceed favourably'.[4] Just before Christmas Churchill had given Wavell instructions to concentrate on the African campaign: 'Your first objective now must be to maul the Italian Army and rip them off the African shore to the utmost possible extent'.[5] But the Cabinet, and in particular Churchill, were unable to stick with this strategy and instead, as earlier in the autumn, felt the need to help their ally Greece and were attracted by the prospect of establishing a Balkan front. The result was that they fell between two stools and produced a major setback in North Africa together with a dismal failure in Greece and the loss of the whole of the Balkans to Germany.

By early 1941 the British ability to break some German military codes began to affect strategic and tactical decisions. Britain had obtained a model of the German Enigma coding machine from the Poles just before the outbreak of war and further theoretical help from France before the armistice. Until well into 1941, however, only some of the Luftwaffe codes could be broken by the teams assembled at Bletchley Park and the information they provided was therefore sketchy and difficult to interpret. Codebreaking had played little part in the Battle of Britain, though the relative ease with which Italian communications could be broken had greatly helped in the December 1940 offensive in Egypt and Libya. From May 1940 Churchill took a close personal interest in this codebreaking effort and insisted that he should be shown translations of the actual German signals not a summary. He rightly insisted that this information should be kept within a very small circle; he allowed no-one in his private office to have access.

In the winter of 1940–1 Bletchley Park could offer little guidance about German strategic intentions. Until the end of 1940 Churchill thought that Spain was their next target and an attack on the Soviet Union, which had been in the planning stage since the summer of 1940, was still thought to be unlikely as late as March 1941. In early January 1941 Enigma seemed to show a likely German attack in the Balkans around the 20th. The Defence Committee agreed to offer further assistance to Greece. Wavell was despatched to Athens but the Greek Government, suspecting the British wanted to involve them in a conflict with Germany, refused any land forces as too provocative and asked only for some more modern aircraft. On 20 January Churchill told the Defence Committee 'it was hopeless for us to imagine that we could fight for Salonika'.[6] In fact the British interpretation of the Enigma decrypts was wrong – the Germans intended to first secure their position in Bulgaria by obtaining the right to move forces through the country, which they did early in March, and only then did they plan to attack Greece to rescue Mussolini from his self-created quagmire. Not until mid-February was this policy clear to the British.

The growing threat to Greece coincided with continued success in North Africa culminating in the capture of Benghazi on 7 February. The British were on the verge of driving the Italians out of North Africa before the Germans could intervene effectively. Churchill, believing Egypt was now secure, wanted to shift the emphasis in British strategy and go to the aid of Greece before the German attack, now expected in mid-March. He held to his opinion in the face of advice from Wavell that this would be a fatal mistake. In January Wavell told him that the German concentration against Greece was intended to relieve the pressure on the Italians by inducing Britain to disperse its forces and his message ended with a heartfelt plea: 'Nothing (*repeat* nothing) we can do from here is likely to be in time to stop German advance if really intended, it will lead to most dangerous dispersion of force . . . I am desperately anxious lest we play enemy's game and expose ourselves to defeat in detail.'[7] Churchill responded in his most arrogant vein and contrary to the instructions he had given in December: 'Destruction of Greece would eclipse victories you have gained in Libya and might affect decisively Turkish attitude, especially if we had shown ourselves callous of fate of allies. You must therefore conform your plans to larger interests at stake. We expect and require prompt and active compliance with our decisions for which we bear full responsibility.'[8]

At the Defence Committee meeting on 10 February Churchill reversed his view that there was no point in fighting for Salonika and said he 'did not think that it was necessarily impossible for the Greeks and ourselves to hold the Germans . . . if we could support them with air and mechanised forces, we might delay them long enough to encourage the Turks, and possibly the Yugoslavs, to join the battle'. The Committee agreed to immediately go over to the defensive in North Africa and 'shift the largest possible force from Egypt to the European continent'.[9] The next day, when Dill (CIGS) argued that Wavell did not have enough troops available, Churchill responded 'we should have to intervene with at least 4 divisions, rising to 6 or 10 in the summer'.[10] In fact all that could be found were three infantry divisions and an armoured brigade to help withstand what the British thought were twenty-three German divisions in Rumania (the actual figure was nine).

The Defence Committee agreed that Eden and Dill should travel to the Middle East. Churchill gave the two men sealed orders which, in a melodramatic touch, they were not allowed to open until they reached Gibraltar. When they read them they were told that they had two aims – to 'send speedy succour to Greece' and 'to make Jugoslavia and Turkey fight or do the best they could'. Then on a more grandiose and completely unrealistic scale the ultimate aim was described as 'to use the Balkan theatre as the stage on which to inflict a military defeat on the Germans when the will to resist of the German people was on the point of breaking down'.[11] If Churchill believed that after the stunning triumphs of 1940 the Germans were about to collapse then it was yet another example of the wishful thinking about the internal weaknesses in their enemy that had dominated British thinking since before the start of the war. On 21 February Eden and Dill held a conference with the Middle East commanders-in-chief in Cairo. The policy agreed by the Cabinet Defence Committee under Churchill's prompting was accepted – four divisions would be diverted to Greece. The moment he heard this news Churchill started to have doubts about the policy he had initiated. He gave Eden the remarkably unhelpful advice: 'Do not consider yourselves obligated to a Greek enterprise, if in your hearts it will be only another Norwegian fiasco. If no good plan can be made, please say so. But of course you know how valuable success would be.'[12]

On 22–23 February Eden and Dill held a secret meeting with the Greeks in Athens to try and resolve how to defend Greece – the end result was disastrous confusion. The Greeks wanted to defend their country as far to the east as possible starting at the Bulgarian border and not abandoning cities such as Salonika. The British, worried that the Germans might advance through Yugoslavia, thereby cutting off any forces deployed so far to the east, wanted a defensive line on the Aliakmon River. At the end of the talks each side thought the other had agreed to its position, although most of the blame can be laid on Eden for not insisting on a clear agreement about where the Greeks would base their main defences and for further confusing the issue by offering a mission to Yugoslavia.

When the War Cabinet met on 24 February Churchill ignored the negative views of the chiefs of staff. They felt that British support for Greece was 'unlikely to have a favourable effect on the war as a whole' and that Britain was 'undertaking a commitment of which we cannot foresee the extent'.[13] He based his strong support for moving forces to Greece on the views of Eden, Wavell and Dill (who were in fact only agreeing with the decisions of the Defence Committee a fortnight earlier). He was also partly influenced by Roosevelt's adviser 'Colonel' Bill Donovan, who strongly supported the idea of a Balkan front. He now tried to rationalise the division of effort and produced contradictory conclusions. Operations in Greece were the most important and holding Egypt was only of secondary importance but 'The enterprise in Greece was an advance position which we could try to hold, without jeopardising our main position [i.e. Egypt]'. Overall it was 'a risk we must undertake'.[14] On this ambivalent basis the plans for intervention in Greece continued.

Shortly after the German occupation of Bulgaria on 1 March Churchill began to have further doubts about the wisdom of sending troops to Greece. The British mission to Yugoslavia had failed to secure any co-operation as had the attempts to draw in Turkey. This failure was compounded when Eden, still in the Middle East, reported on 5 March that the Greeks had not prepared any defensive positions on the Aliakmon and had left troops against the Bulgarian border. After a Defence Committee meeting, which accepted an intelligence assessment that the Germans would attack any time after 22 March, Churchill sent Eden a telegram setting out the doubts in the Defence Committee and in the Australian and New Zealand Governments (who were providing most of the troops). He told the Foreign Secretary that the situation:

> makes it difficult for Cabinet to believe that we now have any power
> to avert the fate of Greece unless Turkey and/or Yugoslavia come
> in, which seems most improbable ... We must be careful not to
> urge Greece against her better judgement into a hopeless resistance

alone when we have only handfuls of troops which can reach the scene in time.[15]

But the situation Churchill described was no different from that a month earlier when he had so enthusiastically helped set up the intervention.

The Cabinet agreed to wait for the Foreign Secretary's reply before making a final decision. They discovered that Eden, despite his failure to reach an acceptable military agreement with the Greeks, had nevertheless given a firm commitment of British support. He also told the Cabinet that all the commanders in the Middle East still supported intervention, which glossed over their very real doubts. On this basis the Cabinet decided to go ahead. Churchill thought this was justified because 'Dill, Wavell, and other Commanders-in-Chief are convinced there is a reasonable fighting chance'. (He had no doubt forgotten that he had ordered Wavell to disperse his forces and told him that he would himself take full responsibility.) He told Eden, 'It must not be said, and on your showing it cannot be said that having so little to give that we dragged them [the Greeks] in by over persuasion'. Indeed Churchill thought British troops would get to the Aliakmon line in time to stop the German advance and would in any case be able to retreat to strong defensive positions. In the last resort 'It was our duty to go forward.'[16] After a month of inept and confused decision taking the British had ended up with the worst of every possible world. They had withdrawn forces from North Africa before the campaign was won, they had persuaded the Greeks to accept military intervention and then adopted a plan that was almost inevitably going to end in military disaster in the absence of a Balkan front with Yugoslavia and Turkey.

Churchill's hopes for a Balkan front were briefly revived in the last three weeks of March by events in Yugoslavia. Britain had been unable to offer Yugoslavia any military help because it controlled neither of the two possible supply routes – the Adriatic and through Salonika – although at the beginning of March they had tried to bribe the Government with the offer of Italian territory after the war (in direct contradiction of pledges given to Roosevelt). The Yugoslav Government was badly split between Serb and Croat factions and between the Prince Regent and the young King Peter. During March, under considerable German pressure, they moved towards a

German alliance, which was finally accepted on 25 March though with so many exclusions as to make it virtually worthless to the Germans. The British were in touch with some of the Serb faction which on 27 March carried out a coup and installed King Peter on the throne. Churchill was ecstatic. Without consulting the Cabinet, he sent Eden and Dill back to Cairo with orders to support the coup and construct a Balkan front which he thought would now consist of about seventy divisions. Within a day it was clear that the new Yugoslav Government, anxious about the Croats (who tended to be pro-German) and still hoping to maintain their neutrality, would not take part in British designs. They refused to allow Eden to travel to Belgrade and although Dill did so he achieved nothing.

Hitler had already decided to attack Yugoslavia and did so on 6 April, combined with an attack on Greece. Yugoslavia, which received no British help, was overrun in ten days and by then the campaign in Greece was already lost. British forces arrived at the 'Aliakmon line' to find no effective defences and withdrew shortly after making contact with German troops. Churchill was already blaming Eden for the fiasco and claiming he had never wanted to send forces to Greece. By 16 April Wavell stopped all further reinforcements and five days later withdrawal was ordered. It was completed on 27 April, by which time Greece had been overrun and the British and Commonwealth forces had lost 10,000 men killed, wounded and missing, and over 200 aircraft, 8,000 trucks and all tanks and stores.

Many of the troops were evacuated to Crete, which Britain had occupied in the autumn of 1940. Then Churchill had told the chiefs of staff that possession of the island, particularly the naval base at Suda Bay, had transformed the position in the eastern Mediterranean. In practice little was done to take advantage of holding Crete. The forces there had six different commanders in as many months, few defences were built and no plans were devised for the defence of the island. The day after the final evacuation from the mainland Churchill told Wavell that Crete 'must be stubbornly defended', though he also told the Cabinet he was 'somewhat doubtful of our ability to hold Crete against a prolonged attack'.[17] Nevertheless he now immersed himself in every detail of the defensive plans being belatedly drawn up, ranging from how many maps of the island were to be provided and the tactics to be employed – he thought it was best to allow the airfields to be captured and then counter-attack. By the middle of May he was more optimistic about the outcome and told Wavell: 'I should particularly welcome chance for our high-class troops to come to close grips with those people under conditions where enemy has not got his usual mechanical advantages and where we can surely re-inforce much easier than he can.'[18]

Churchill's hopes were to be rapidly dashed. The German airborne assault began on 20 May. Although the British forces outnumbered the Germans by over two-to-one (and thanks to Enigma intercepts had a good idea of the German plans), they were unable to withstand German air superiority (the British withdrew their fighters from the island the day before the attack) and the greater tactical skill of the German commanders. Within a week the British had withdrawn with the loss of 15,000 men (half the force) either killed or taken prisoner. Despite his earlier doubts about the defensibility of the island, Churchill nonetheless blamed Wavell for yet another ignominious defeat at the hands of the Germans. He told the chiefs of staff: 'I cannot feel that there was any real grip shown by Middle East H.Q. upon this operation . . . the general evidence of lack of drive and precision filled me with disquiet . . . It is evident that very far-reaching steps will have to be taken.'[19] The campaign in Greece and Crete had turned out as the commanders on the spot had predicted it would earlier in the year – the British forces were simply too weak to hold the German attack. Meanwhile the denuded units left in North Africa had had to meet a German offensive. They were driven back through Libya to the Egyptian frontier by the end of April, leaving Australian troops besieged in Tobruk. General Rommel, the Commander of the Afrika Corps, was only forced to stop because he ran out of fuel and supplies – his main base was in Tripoli over 1,000 miles away. Having stripped Wavell of his main force and sent them to Greece, Churchill then blamed him for failing to stop the Germans in Libya. He told his Private Secretary 'he thought Wavell etc had been very silly in North Africa and should have been prepared to meet an attack there'.[20]

The collapse of the British position in the Balkans and the eastern Mediterranean, the retreat in North Africa, combined with continuing high shipping losses (700,000 tons in April alone) and the prospect that Vichy France and Spain would fall further under German influence caused a decline in confidence in Washington as to whether Britain could continue the war. American public opinion remained as divided as it had been in 1940 – in April polls showed that two-thirds of the country wanted to help Britain but eighty-three per cent wanted to stay out of the war. Roosevelt too was still moving with great caution and restricted assistance to Britain to steps that could also been seen clearly as meeting US security concerns. The repair of British naval and merchant ships in American yards was allowed – this helped the British shipping shortage but also built up American capacity. US naval patrols were extended eastward to 26° West and included Greenland but they were not allowed to escort convoys and could do no more than report the position of any U-boats to British forces.

On 1 May Churchill received a discouraging message from Roosevelt, in which the American President refused the Prime Minister's request to put diplomatic pressure on Portugal, Turkey and the Vichy Government with the aim of bolstering them against German pressure. He was disconsolate: he thought the Americans were preparing themselves for a total collapse of the British position in the Mediterranean and told Eden he felt increasingly abandoned: 'there has been a considerable recession across the Atlantic, . . . quite unconsciously we are being left very much to our fate'.[21] The same day he spoke to his close advisers about the possibility of such a collapse in the Middle East and of having to make a compromise peace. He conjured up 'a world in which Hitler dominated all Europe, Asia and Africa and left the U.S. and ourselves no option but an unwilling peace'.[22] The reply Churchill wanted to send to Roosevelt read 'Naturally I am depressed by your message in spite of all the kindness it displays.' The Foreign Office advised against including that part but even so his message of 4 May was gloomy. In it he spoke of the possible loss of Egypt and the Middle East, of strong German influence on Turkey, Spain and France and the prospect of a long and extremely difficult oceanic war against the continent, with most of Africa and Asia dominated by Germany. For the first time since the collapse of France in June 1940 Churchill asked for an American declaration of war.

Roosevelt never directly responded to Churchill's appeal. Within days the possibility of a compromise peace was again being discussed. On 11 May Hitler's deputy, Rudolf Hess, flew to Britain to try and secure a settlement before Germany attacked the Soviet Union. The terms were the same as Hitler would have offered in 1940 – the continuance of the British Empire in return for accepting German domination of the continent. Britain was no longer in a position to accept such an offer even if it had been prepared to trust Hitler to stick to the terms. For a year it had fought on assuming at some point that the United States would join the war. Now it was bankrupt and dependent on US assistance. If it now accepted a compromise peace with Hitler, it would lose all American help in the form of munitions, raw materials and food. In these circumstances it would no longer have the power to defend the Empire, and even home defence, and the maintenance of adequate levels of food for the population and raw materials for industry, would be difficult. There was no alternative but to carry on and hope for US intervention before it was too late. What Churchill was prepared to do at this stage was to use his knowledge of the German terms as a form of blackmail to bring the United States into the war. Four days after Hess arrived, he spoke to Eden about the idea and it was the Foreign Secretary who dissuaded him from the attempt. The record of the meeting quoted Churchill as saying, 'The master key to American action would be the knowledge that the British Empire could at this time get out of the war intact, leaving the future struggle with a Germanized Europe to the United States. But this you did not want me to say.'[23] A week later he wanted to use a similar, though slightly more subtle, variant of the threat of a compromise peace, together with a stark reminder of Britain's inability to win the war on its own. In a message to be sent via Roosevelt to the defeated Republican presidential candidate Wendell Willkie. His draft contained the passage: 'I have never said that the British Empire cannot make its way out of this war without American belligerence, but no peace that is any use to you or which will liberate Europe can be obtained without American belligerence.'[24] Again Eden dissuaded him from sending it.

Later in May Roosevelt took two further cautious steps towards a more active policy. He agreed to transfer three battleships, four cruisers and fourteen destroyers to the Atlantic; the aim being to release British ships for the Far East (the Americans still refused to defend Singapore directly). In his speech to the nation on 27 May he declared a state of 'unlimited national emergency' and the next day told Halifax that the United States would take over the defence of Iceland from the British in late June and extend naval patrols into the area. But these were further instances of a careful balancing act that remained compatible with increasing the defences of the western hemisphere. It did not bring any nearer the American declaration of war that Churchill so desperately wanted.

Britain's inability to win the war without such a declaration was made abundantly clear with the results of the strategic review Churchill had initiated earlier in the year. Its conclusions made grim reading. The British Army would reach its maximum size of sixty divisions in the autumn of 1942 but Germany had 250. American armaments could not compensate for this inferiority, which meant: 'we cannot hope to defeat the existing German army in the field and so open the road to Germany and victory'.[25] The only hope was that the combined pressure of bombing and subversion would make an unopposed landing possible late in 1942. The problem was that these two options were competing for the same scarce resources: to arm 130,000 people in France, Czechoslovakia and Poland (assuming resistance on such a scale was even possible) would take a minimum of 8,000 RAF sorties; for the whole of Europe 12,000 sorties – the equivalent of all of Bomber Command's effort for six months. In practice bombing had an overwhelming priority, although Churchill and his colleagues were shortly to be made aware of the almost complete ineffectiveness of that effort.

Some of the immediate pressure on Britain's strategic position, together with the pressure on the Americans to help, was removed by the German attack on the Soviet Union on 22 June. Churchill had been receiving indications of a possible German attack from Ultra (as Enigma decrypts were known) from mid-March, but they seem to have made little impression on him. On 3 April he drafted a 'warning' to Stalin but for a variety of reasons, some of which he endorsed, it was not delivered until 22 April and then only in a general way. However the message was handled it was unlikely that it would have made much difference – Stalin was highly suspicious about any attempt by Britain to involve him in the war and determined to discount increasing evidence of a forthcoming German attack.

By mid-June the indications were unmistakable. Churchill shared the view of the chiefs of staff that the Soviet Union would succumb within a matter of weeks. The day before the attack he told his

Private Secretary 'a German attack on Russia is certain and Russia will assuredly be defeated'.[26] He saw the attack as giving a breathing space rather than heralding the creation of a grand alliance against Germany, and he told the Defence Committee that Britain must take 'every advantage such a conflict offered'.[27] In his broadcast to the nation on the evening of the attack he spoke of it as 'no more than a prelude to an attempted invasion of the British Isles' and three days later ordered counter-invasion preparations to be brought to full readiness by 1 September. Churchill's main hope was that the Soviets would last out for as long as possible. He sent a message to Stalin saying: 'we have only to go on fighting to beat the life out of these villains'.[28] In private he said 'as long as they go on, it does not matter so much where the front lies'.[29] (The Soviets had other ideas.)

For the British Government the pressing problem to be resolved was what, if any, assistance they should offer. A military mission was sent to Moscow but its aim was intelligence gathering and its head, General Mason-Macfarlane, was passionately anti-Soviet. His instructions were that the Soviets 'must save themselves just as we saved ourselves'.[30] The Soviet Government asked for 6,000 aircraft, 20,000 anti-aircraft guns, raw materials, food and 3 million pairs of boots. What they were offered was one Hurricane fighter and some 1,000lb bombs, and the British also volunteered to destroy all their oil wells at Baku in Azerbaijan to stop them falling into German hands (which demonstrated where the British thought the fighting would finish up). Later 200 ex-American Tomahawk fighters were included (only because the RAF was phasing them out as obsolescent) and boots (sold at a considerable profit). The first small convoy of supplies did not sail till August.

In July the Government accepted Stalin's request for an agreement on mutual assistance and no separate peace (Churchill told the Cabinet he would not rule out a separate peace by the Soviets) but they rejected his appeal on 19 July for the creation of a second front. The assistance agreement was silent on what was to prove one of the most contentious issues of the war – the location of the western boundary of the Soviet Union. In August 1940 Churchill and the Cabinet had given de facto recognition to the annexation of the three Baltic states by the Soviet Union. A more difficult problem was Poland, Britain's ally and the country for which she had gone to war, where, following the pact with Germany in August 1939, the Soviets had occupied the eastern half of the country. In a speech on 1 October 1939 Churchill had approved of this action, saying it was 'clearly necessary for the safety of Russia against Nazi menace'. Later comments in a broadcast on the day of the German attack reinforced this acceptance of Soviet aggression: 'the Russian people are defending their native soil. The Russian soldiers are standing on the threshold of their native land.' To many this implied that he accepted that the Soviet Union's borders were now in what was once Poland. Although Churchill appeared to be modifying his earlier rooted hostility to the expansion of the Soviet Union, his anti-Communism was not altered by Soviet entry into the war. In July he stopped the BBC from playing the Internationale in its regular programme of the national anthems of Britain's allies. At the beginning of September, alarmed at the growing sympathy for Soviet resistance to Germany, he ordered the Ministry of Information to 'consider what action was required to counter the present tendency of the British Public to forget the dangers of Communism in their enthusiasm over the resistance of Russia'.[31]

Although Churchill expected the Soviet Union to collapse in a matter of weeks, this view was based on a massive underestimation of Soviet capabilities and strength. They had an army the same size as the Germans deployed and a considerable superiority in tanks and aircraft (both numbers and quality). The Germans never had adequate forces and supplies for a broad front attack and therefore finished up shifting their concentration of effort from one area to another. Although they managed to surround large numbers of Soviet troops, they failed to secure a strategic victory or occupy Leningrad or Moscow. The Soviets were weak in tactics and strategy and this did indeed lead to massive losses during the first weeks of the campaign. But they held out and were able to mobilise 3 million men in the second half of 1941 and build 7,000 tanks and 5,000 aircraft while moving large parts of their industry to the east.

The continuing Soviet resistance, while it removed any likelihood of a German invasion of Britain, posed new difficulties for the Churchill Government. Public pressure meant that more had to be done to supply the first country to offer prolonged resistance to the German Army. At the end of August Churchill promised 200 more aircraft but again rejected pleas for a second front or any aggressive action in the west to try and divert German forces. This aid was later increased to 200 aircraft and 250 tanks a month, in the expectation that it would come, not from Britain's supplies from the United States, but from extra American production. In the middle of September he discovered that it was to come from the British allocation. From September supplies to the Soviet Union increased, but the amounts provided were still small compared with its own production and unlikely to have much impact on their ability to resist. Churchill continued to send messages to Stalin that were long on words but short on action. Eventually at the beginning of September he gave him the bleak message that they were on their own, saying he was 'convinced that there was no action which it was in our power to take which could affect events in Russia in the next two months'.[32]

The Soviet Union was facing 134 German divisions (ninety-eight per cent of its active strength) while the British fought two under-strength divisions in North Africa. Britain's army strength in Egypt increased from 80,000 in August 1940 to 600,000 a year later, yet Wavell's forces were still unable to mount an effective attack. Under pressure from Churchill, who was reading Ultra material but drawing the wrong conclusions about the effectiveness of Rommel's forces, Wavell launched Operation Battleaxe on 15 June 1941. Although the British had twice as many tanks as Rommel (they had been sent through the Mediterranean in a special convoy in April), they lost almost half of them on the first day through an unimaginative frontal assault. On 17 June Wavell reported the failure of the attack. Churchill had been trying to sack the Middle East Commander since April, but had met objections first from Dill and then from Amery when he proposed substituting the commander in India, General Auchinleck. Now, after yet another failure, Churchill was finally able to remove Wavell: he was to swap jobs with Auchinleck. One of the reasons Churchill was impressed by Auchinleck was that he had acted decisively to counter a pro-German coup in Iraq whereas Wavell had had to be ordered to carry out an attack into Syria to stop German use of Vichy French facilities.

That attack on Syria, to remove the Vichy administration that co-operated with the German attempt to support the anti-British coup in Iraq, led to an almost complete breakdown in relations with

General de Gaulle, whose Free French forces accompanied the British troops. Relations had been deteriorating for some time. After the series of disagreements with De Gaulle in the autumn of 1940, relations got off to a bad start in the new year when on 1 January the British arrested Admiral Muselier (the head of the Free French Navy) for betraying the Dakar operation to Vichy. Churchill insisted that the arrest be carried out without consulting De Gaulle; he even talked wildly of declaring war on Brazil, whose embassy had allegedly been used as a channel of communication. Within three days De Gaulle showed that the documents on which the British were relying were forgeries (produced by MI5 agents introduced into the Free French organisation). After a week Muselier was released and Churchill reluctantly apologised to De Gaulle. Then in March De Gaulle was refused assistance in order to take control of Djibouti and French Somaliland. Finally during the Syrian operation the Free French were kept in the background.

Churchill played a key role in the handling of the Syrian episode. He looked back to the Anglo-French quarrels twenty-five years earlier over the carving up of the Ottoman Empire and was determined to use the invasion as a way of ending French control of the country and eliminating a colonial rival. Before the attack he declared that the French mandate under the League of Nations had ended with the Vichy Government (a view that had no legal basis), that the British had not promised De Gaulle to restore the mandated territories to France (which was true) and that if the forces there did not declare for De Gaulle 'we should proclaim that the French mandate has lapsed [and establish] an independent Sovereign Arab State in Syria in permanent alliance with Turkey . . . and Great Britain'. Such a declaration would, he thought, 'gratify the Arab race and rally them to a strong Nationalist movement to expel all European masters, or would-be masters, from their country'.[33] It took Eden to point out that this was a peculiar policy for the British to adopt since they controlled even more Arab contries than the French. Churchill, however, insisted that a vague and highly ambiguous promise made by the Free French of 'independence' (on the model of Egypt under British control), designed to encourage a revolt against the Vichy authorities, should be maintained, although he envisaged Syria would be only semi-independent and come under British tutelage and influence like Iraq – 'our policy is to give the

Syrian Arabs independence ... the Arabs bulk far more largely in our minds than the Free French'.[34]

When Churchill overrode the Cabinet and allowed the Vichy authorities in Syria to surrender to the British rather than De Gaulle's forces and then allowed the Vichy forces to be repatriated to France, De Gaulle protested. Churchill sent instructions for the minister on the spot (Oliver Lyttleton) to 'let [De Gaulle] know where he gets off'.[35] When De Gaulle, in a towering rage, threatened to withdraw Free French forces from British command, the British in Cairo prepared to put him in jail. Churchill sent a telegram saying 'your attitude towards De Gaulle is strongly approved. [Do not] allow him to to upset or impede our policy in Syria.'[36] Eventually the commanders on the spot agreed on a joint occupation with the Free French. Nevertheless Churchill told the Commons on 9 September that France would not regain control of Syria: 'There is no question of France maintaining the same position which she exercised in Syria before the war ... There must be no question even in wartime of a mere substitution of Free French interests for Vichy French interests.' Virtually the first successful British military action of the war had therefore been to remove its major ally from control of one of its own colonies.

Relations between Britain (in particular Churchill) and De Gaulle remained extremely stormy. There was a huge difference in expectations between the two sides. De Gaulle was in a difficult situation trying to protect, as he saw it, the interests of France, even if they diverged from British interests, while remaining almost totally dependent on the British. For their part the British wanted to control him and expected him to be more subservient. In addition there was a clash of personalities between the two enormous egos of Churchill and De Gaulle. Churchill made virtually no allowances for De Gaulle's position and especially resented any show of independence. His personal, highly emotional reactions to De Gaulle tended to dictate policy towards the Free French, even though a cooler assessment (which Eden supported) suggested that De Gaulle was likely to be a powerful force in post-war France and therefore long-term British interests indicated a need to maintain good relations.

In the autumn of 1941 Churchill and the British Government hatched a plot to cramp De Gaulle's style and limit his freedom of manoeuvre. The trigger was Churchill's fury over reports of an interview De Gaulle had given in an American paper, in which he referred to Britain's relations with Vichy as equivalent to doing a deal with Hitler. Churchill wrote to Eden that if the interview was authentic then De Gaulle had 'clearly gone off his head. This would be very good riddance and will simplify our further course.'[37] He issued instructions that no one was to see De Gaulle or his staff, requests for assistance were to be turned down and no broadcasts were to be allowed. He wrote to De Gaulle, 'until I am in possession of any explanation you may do me the honour to offer, I am unable to judge whether any interview between us would serve any useful purpose'.[38]

Churchill did see De Gaulle on 12 September without having received an apology (though he refused to shake hands with him). After a bitter row over the newspaper interview and events in Syria, he revealed the real reason for the meeting – the British idea for a council for the Free French movement. De Gaulle was non-committal and the British went off to plot with other members of the movement to impose the idea on him. In private Churchill made clear British intentions: De Gaulle 'would remain as a War Lord in control of the military aspect of the movement, and in this capacity we could easily control him'. He was prepared to 'knock heads together' if necessary.[39]

The plot started to go wrong on 22 September when De Gaulle refused to accept an ultimatum from the British-inspired conspirators and said he would form a council without them and sack Muselier (who had planned to remove the Navy from De Gaulle's control). De Gaulle was persuaded to delay for twenty-four hours and Churchill put Eden in charge of a frantic British mediation effort, giving him full powers including 'the forcible restraint of individuals'.[40] Eventually Muselier was persuaded to apologise and De Gaulle was persuaded to set up a new council. But as he became its president with as much power as he had before the failed coup, the plot had totally backfired. Churchill commented wryly on the outcome: 'This is very unpleasant. Our intention was to compel De Gaulle to accept a suitable council. All we have done is to compel Muselier and Co to submit themselves to De Gaulle.' But he reasserted his determination to rein back the French leader: 'our weight in the immediate future must be thrown more heavily against de Gaulle than I had hoped would be necessary'.[41] Resorting to methods within his control, Churchill banned him from leaving the country but since De Gaulle did not ask to travel he did not discover the restriction.

De Gaulle's caustic comments about Britain's relations with the Vichy Government were not entirely without justification. The 'deal' unofficially agreed in the autumn of 1940 continued (hence Britain's refusal to help De Gaulle in the Horn of Africa). The blockade was not strictly enforced (only seven per cent of French ships passing through the Straits of Gibraltar were intercepted) and Churchill himself was prepared to go further in assisting Vichy. On 9 March he wrote 'I am becoming ready to ease up about letting food into Unoccupied France.'⁴² Three days later he proposed to Roosevelt that the President should broker a secret deal with Vichy. He envisaged much less stringent conditions than before – as long as Vichy kept to the armistice provisions food would be allowed into France and North Africa. The proposal got no further because the Americans wanted to keep dealings with Vichy in their own hands. Through the rest of 1941 Churchill was willing to go along with Roosevelt's pro-Vichy policy. He wrote in June: 'We must do what they tell us in these small ways. It is not a question of who is right or wrong.'⁴³

Although Churchill had replaced Wavell with Auchinleck because of the latter's forceful handling of the coup in Iraq compared with Wavell's reluctance to intervene in Vichy controlled Syria, he found him as stubborn as Wavell in refusing to mount an early offensive against Rommel. Immediately after the new commander took over in early July, he told London he was not prepared to attack until the operation in Syria was over and reinforcements had arrived. This provoked an exchange of telegrams, which continued for the rest of the month with increasing bitterness, as Churchill tried to bribe Auchinleck to attack in September with the promise of 150 new tanks. He refused to do more than try to relieve Tobruk in November and launch a new offensive early in 1942. Churchill summoned him to London. The new commander explained his reasons for delay to the Cabinet on 31 July and the next day there was a long meeting of the Defence Committee, at which Churchill finally gave way and accepted Auchinleck's judgement.

After the meeting Eden's Private Secretary reported 'A.E. very cross today after spending five hours in Defence Committee – completely wasting time while PM discoursed on strategy to Auchinleck. A.E. finds PM's views on strategy disastrous . . . PM very rude but General very calm and answered well. The meeting broke up in some confusion. PM grumbling and growling – purple in face and with streaming eyes. A.E. is really worried at the PM's management or lack of management – feels he is wearing out Chiefs of Staff to no purpose.'[44] These complaints were symptomatic of simmering discontent with Churchill's style – in particular his reluctance to listen to other people's views and his penchant for protracted meetings in which he would inflict long monologues on his colleagues but where little of substance would actually be decided. Sir Alexander Cadogan, the head of the Foreign Office, described in his diary meetings chaired by Churchill on 28 April: 'Cabinet at 5, till 7.30 Hopelessly rambling. Winston tired, I think. Bevin made some more than usually fatuous remarks, which annoyed the P.M. who immersed himself in papers and let the Cabinet rip for half hr. Hopeless waste of time! . . . Defence Cttee at 9.30 – till 12.30. More diffuse and useless than ever.'[45] Six weeks later he reported: '11.30 hastily summoned meeting with P.M. and C's of S, nominally to discuss Syria. Actually there was only desultory conversation about anything that came into the P.M.'s head.'[46]

In private Churchill's political colleagues reflected growing concern about his personal contribution to the war effort. Eden's Private Secretary reported on 22 July that 'A.E. says War Cabinet and after that Defence Committee spent 7 hours yesterday in so-called discussions – all of which could have been boiled down to one hour, the rest being interminable speeches by P.M. It is really a very serious situation. No decisions are taken nor proper plans thought out.'[47] A week later Eden described Defence Committee meetings as 'a monologue – any opposition treated as factious – policy and operations decided by impulse – no proper planning.'[48] Earlier he thought Churchill had 'a devastating effect on planning'.[49] Eden also objected to the Prime Minister's habit of wanting 'to take all the decisions and get all the credit'[50] and was 'fed up with P.M.'s monopolistic tendencies'.[51] An equally negative view of Churchill as wartime leader was voiced by Dill, the CIGS. He felt Churchill 'dealt far too much with detail and seemed often unable to appreciate or understand major issues' and complained 'a great part of the time of responsible ministers was taken up dealing with silly minutes from the PM'.[52] After dinner with Dill at the beginning of September

Lord Reith reported his sense of frustration: 'Scathing comment on Churchill's inevitable habit of putting the blame on the chiefs of staff whenever he could but of giving them no credit when things went right and contrary to his expectations. CIGS said he had never known subordinates treated as Churchill treats them.'[53]

Dill's latter complaint was widely shared. Both ministers and service chiefs did not expect to be treated as if they were at Churchill's beck and call and expected to fall in with his slightest whim. Events on Sunday 2 August provide a good example of how the Prime Minister behaved. Eden was at home in the country trying to have a short rest. He was summoned to Chequers for an emergency Defence Committee meeting, including the chiefs of staff and other ministers, set for 6pm. When they arrived, Churchill immediately went off to his bedroom to sleep and the meeting was postponed until after dinner. Then at dinner he decided he wanted to see his favourite film about Lady Hamilton yet again. But the film unit, assuming they were not required because of the meeting, had already left for London. His staff had to organise road blocks to try and stop the unit but without success. With nothing else to do, Churchill reluctantly decided to hold the meeting after all. It finally started at midnight and did not finish until 2am – but nothing was decided. This incident was symptomatic of Churchill's insensitive and high-handed treatment of his colleagues, military chiefs and civil servants, and his permanent readiness to indulge his own preferences at the expense of others. A few weeks after this incident one of Churchill's closest aides, Jock Colville, was warning his brother Jack and Desmond Morton of 'the offence which has been given to many people, including Ministers, by his treatment of them. Desmond goes so far as to say that the PM is losing many people's friendship.'[54]

After giving his reluctant assent to Auchinleck's date for an attack in the desert, Churchill's main preoccupation throughout August 1941 was his first meeting with Roosevelt, postponed from the spring because of the disasters in the Mediterranean theatre. It was due to take place on 9–12 August at Placentia Bay in Newfoundland, a site deliberately chosen by the Americans – it was one of the bases they had acquired from Britain in 1940. Churchill was still worried by the paucity of American assistance and felt that Roosevelt was 'slackening up' despite US occupation of Iceland on 7 July.[55] He was also unhappy about the way Roosevelt was becoming more dictatorial about war aims. As America was keeping Britain in the war, it clearly intended to dominate the peace settlement. On 14 July Churchill had received a peremptory message from Roosevelt telling him to make a public commitment that no pledges would be given about the post-war settlement on territory, population transfer and economic conditions. He did not reply but this merely made the American administration more determined to achieve its aims at the forthcoming conference.

Churchill began the long journey by train to Thurso and then by boat to Scapa Flow, where he boarded the *Prince of Wales*. There he was joined by Harry Hopkins who, despite Churchill's opposition, had been to Moscow. He brought with him a vast amount of caviare which Churchill consumed greedily, telling Cadogan: 'It was very good to have such caviare, even though it meant fighting with the Russians to get it.'[56] Although it was not yet the 'Glorious Twelfth', he had with him ninety grouse for Roosevelt and altogether he and his entourage drank £450 worth of wine during the trip (equivalent to almost £10,000 at today's prices). Churchill was undertaking the journey in an optimistic mood. He told the monarch before he left that he did not think 'our friend would have asked me to go so far for what must be a meeting of world-wide importance, unless he had in mind some further forward step'.[57] He was to be gravely disappointed.

The conference itself was an organisational shambles – there was no agenda and the discussion rambled somewhat aimlessly from one subject to another. The main benefit was the personal contact established between the staffs, in particular that between Dill and the US Army chief, General Marshall. The first meeting between the two leaders over lunch on 9 August got off to a bad start. Churchill insulted the President by remarking that it was good to meet him for the first time. He had forgotten their earlier meeting in 1918 and Roosevelt (as much an egoist as Churchill) did not forgive him for not remembering the budding political genius who was then US Junior Navy Minister. That evening after dinner Churchill gave one of his long lectures on the war but Roosevelt made no response to the implicit request for American entry that it contained and Churchill had to accept the President's unwillingness even to discuss the subject. On 10 August there were no formal meetings – in the morning there was a symbolic joint church service on the *Prince of*

Wales (which Churchill had carefully rehearsed during the voyage). After an excursion round the bay in the afternoon there was an informal dinner with the President in the evening. The next day there was a formal meeting in the morning and a dinner in the evening. On the last day Churchill and Roosevelt met briefly before a final lunch and the formal farewells at 3pm.

Much of the work of the conference was concentrated on the American proposal for a declaration of principles about the post-war world, designed to constrain British action. In order to obtain a symbolically important joint statement with the United States Churchill decided to reverse his earlier opposition to any declaration of war aims. There were however a number of difficulties, in particular over the proposed point four (no discrimination in post-war trade) which threatened (and was designed to threaten) the system of imperial preference. Churchill was able to use Roosevelt's anxiety to tie Britain to a common declaration to obtain a possible let-out. He argued that without it all the dominions would have to be consulted and so there would be no declaration. The commitment that all states should enjoy 'equal access to trade and raw materials' was therefore qualified by the phrase 'with due respect for their existing obligations'. Churchill consulted the Cabinet but then ignored their request for an even stronger addition to the text.

The resulting document, which was intended as little more than a press release, later became known as the 'Atlantic Charter' and was held to embody a set of principles to which allied nations could subscribe. The hurried drafting of these 'principles' at Newfoundland was to cause numerous problems among the allies later in the war when they came to make decisions on the post-war settlement. For example, point two, which stated that there would be 'no territorial changes that do not accord with the freely expressed wishes of the people concerned', was to be widely ignored. Churchill also had problems with point three – the right of all peoples to national sovereignty and self-government. That was initially drafted by him with a view to allaying American suspicions about secret British deals in Europe. However when the Americans suggested that these principles should also apply to the colonial empires, he indignantly rejected the idea of extending the principle of self-government to the British Empire. On his return he told Leo Amery it was not intended 'that the natives of Nigeria or East Africa could

535

by a majority vote choose the form of Government under which they live, or the Arabs by such a vote expel the Jews from Palestine'.[58]

The discussions held between the military staffs were unproductive. The American chiefs of staff were not well prepared and avoided a general discussion of strategy. They took away a British paper which sought to justify their Middle East strategy and the concept of defeating Germany through peripheral operations combined with the well-established triad of blockade, bombing and subversion. The British paper seems to have been counter-productive. After the conference the US military planners dismissed it as disjointed, 'groping for panaceas' and no more than an effort to get the US into the war as soon as possible so as to use American troops 'to protect the British Empire while they take care of the United Kingdom with our material help'.[59]

The outcome of the conference was a serious blow to Churchill, who had achieved very little positive apart from a declaration of general principles to which he had been opposed before the meeting. When he reported to the Cabinet on 19 August, aware that his colleagues were expecting a major step forward he tried to put an optimistic gloss on Roosevelt's silence over US entry into the war, by saying he thought the President 'was obviously determined that they should come in'. He also told them he expected the US would become more provocative in the Atlantic by attacking U-boats and escorting convoys west of 26°. (It very rapidly turned out that he had misunderstood Roosevelt, who had been talking entirely hypothetically and was not planning to take further measures.) He admitted to his colleagues that he had threatened Roosevelt with a compromise peace if the US did not declare war soon – 'he had thought it right to give the President a warning. He had told him that he would not answer for the consequences if Russia was compelled to sue for peace, and, say, by the spring of next year, hope died in Britain.'[60]

The Cabinet's depression was increased when Roosevelt reassured the American public on his return to Washington that no commitments had been made and the country was no nearer entering the war. Roosevelt's stance reflected the lack of enthusiasm for preparations for war – on the last day of the Newfoundland conference the House of Representatives had only approved continuation of the draft by a single vote. Churchill chaired another long Cabinet discussion on 25 August. Although they thought Roosevelt himself probably did want to enter the war, they had to recognise there was no hope of such action in the immediate future. It now seemed possible that the Soviet Union could survive till the winter but few ministers expected it to stay in the war far into 1942. British lend-lease supplies would continue to be diverted to the Soviet Union and China, but even with US assistance Britain would not be able to do more than hold on to its existing positions. The possibility of a very long drawn-out war stretched ahead with no hope of ultimate victory without US entry.

Anxious to keep up pressure on the Americans, on 28 August Churchill told Hopkins a 'wave of depression' was affecting the War Cabinet. He expressed the view that the Soviet Union might be forced out of the war and warned: 'If 1942 opens with Russia knocked out and Britain left again alone, all kinds of dangers may arise.' He thought that Germany would continue to be careful not to cause a naval incident with the Americans in the Atlantic and concluded with a rather forlorn plea: he would be grateful if Hopkins could give him 'any sort of hope'.[61] Two days later, at Chequers with Eden and Winant (the US Ambassador in London), he again gave vent to his belief that Britain could not win the war on its own to his increasing sense of desperation: 'we must have an American declaration of war'. If not the war would go on for another four or five years 'and civilisation and culture would be wiped out. If America came in, she could stop this. She alone could bring the war to and end.'[62] Hopkins faithfully relayed to Roosevelt the extent to which the British were relying on eventual US intervention, saying that Churchill and the Cabinet 'believed that ultimately we will get into the war on some basis or other and if they ever reached the conclusion that this was not to be the case, that there would be a very critical moment in the war and the British appeasers might have some influence on Churchill'.[63]

The Cabinet received a further blow to their morale at the beginning of September when they discovered that the main weapon on which Churchill was relying to win the war – the bomber – had turned out to be ineffective. A survey initiated by Lindemann in the summer of 1941 showed that the enormous effort devoted to bombing operations had been almost entirely nugatory. The RAF had been designed and developed around the doctrine of an independent air offensive designed to shatter the industry and morale of the enemy. The survey revealed that it sitll lacked the capacity to mount a major bombing campaign. The RAF had no effective bombsight and navigation systems remained primitive (unlike the German radio beams used during the Blitz). Just before the outbreak of war in a carefully planned training exercise forty per cent of the bombers involved could not find a designated 'target' in broad daylight in a friendly city with no fighter or anti-aircraft defences. Given this level of competence it is hardly surprising that night bombing was highly inaccurate. (Daylight bombing was ruled out as too dangerous.) By 1941 although two-thirds of crews thought they had found the target in fact only a fifth of the bombers got within five miles of the target and two-thirds of the bombs dropped fell on open ground or decoys. Over the key industrial area of the Ruhr accuracy was even worse – only one crew in ten got within five miles. On moonless nights accuracy was worse still – only one bomber in every fifteen was within five miles of the target.

As Prime Minister Churchill had insisted on giving priority to bomber production after July 1940 and to the strategy of bombing economic and industrial targets. The RAF insisted that their raids over Germany, which began in mid–May 1940, were hitting specific economic and industrial targets. Churchill clearly shared these hopes about what the RAF could and should do since he told Ismay in September 1940: 'It pays us better to concentrate upon limited high-class military objectives.'[64]

During the autumn of 1940 the RAF, Churchill, and other ministers came to accept that precise objectives were not realistic so that attacks on 'military and economic targets' were increasingly equated to bombing the cities that contained them, but they never liked to admit openly what was happening. Privately Churchill told Halifax in October 1940: 'even if Germany offered to stop bombing now, we should not consent to it. Bombing of military objectives, increasingly widely interpreted, seems at present our main road home.'[65] Later in the month he told the Chief of the Air Staff, against his strong opposition and that of Sinclair, that straightforward attacks on civilians were now the objective: 'we wish to place our fullest effort upon Italy, and that the morale of the Italian population may for the time being be considered a military objective'[66] – or what he described more euphemistically two days later as 'less precise objectives'.[67] Although Churchill issued no formal instructions, he endorsed a strategy under which bombing operations were now concentrated on German civilians as a primary aim. The directives given by the Air Ministry to Bomber Command in July and August 1941 set out the aim of destroying 'the morale of the civil population as a whole and of the industrial workers in particular' by concentrating on 'congested industrial towns where the psychological effect will be the greatest'.[68]

Characteristically Churchill made a number of interventions at intermittent intervals in the conduct of the bombing campaign during 1941. At the beginning of June he wanted no longer term bombing strategy, just a series of short-term objectives lasting for a month – the chiefs of staff dissented strongly. Later in the month his proposal to try and set the Black Forest on fire was rejected by the Air Ministry but he was more successful a month later when he asked for the Forest of Nieppe to be set on fire. His interventions made little difference to a campaign that already lacked focus and effectiveness – in 1941 the RAF lost more men in the operations than the number of Germans killed.

What is significant about the Cabinet discussions in September 1941 after Lindemann's damning report is that there was no consideration of diverting Britain's limited war effort towards a more effective use. The Government allowed the bomber offensive to continue, waiting for the new four-engined bombers to come into service in 1942 together with improved navigational systems, in the hope that bombing might still prove to be a way of winning the war. On 25 September the Chief of the Air Staff set out for Churchill the aims of the campaign: 'the weakest point in the German war machine is the morale of the civil population and in particular of the industrial workers. . . . [the] attack on morale is not a matter of pure killing . . . It is rather the general dislocation of industrial and social life arising from damage to industrial plant, dwelling houses, shops, utility and transportation services, from the resultant absenteeism and, in fact, from interference with all that goes to make up the general activity of a community . . . it is in the thickly populated towns that the moral effect of bombing will be chiefly felt.'[69] It is difficult to imagine a clearer statement of the policy of deliberate bombing of the German civil population. Churchill accepted that policy without demur.

What he did object to, not surprisingly in the light of the report on the ineffectiveness of the campaign so far, was the RAF's claim that if they had 4,000 bombers they could guarantee to demolish the morale of the German civil population in six months. (In the first place Britain could never have supported a front-line bomber force of 4,000 aircraft. By the end of the war it had reached 1,600 aircraft but that took up about a third of Britain's war effort.) Churchill did not like dubious arithmetical calculations being used to show how the war could be won. (The RAF's calculations were based on the collapse of British morale during the Blitz after a certain weight of bombs dropped.) In September 1941 he would only commit himself to the statement: 'The most we can say is that it will be a heavy and I trust seriously increasing annoyance.'[70] After a protest from the RAF about his doubts, Churchill hastened to reassure them: 'Everything is being done to create the Bombing force desired on the largest possible scale, and there is no intention of changing this policy.'[71] Nor was there any intention of changing the aims of the campaign. But the loss rate they sustained in the autumn and winter of 1941–2 – the equivalent of the whole of the RAF's front-line bomber force in just four months – led to a drastic scaling down of the offensive. By February 1942 the weight of bombs being dropped was a quarter of that in August 1941.

If the bomber offensive was failing to produce results there was better news from what Churchill had dubbed in March 1941 the 'Battle of the Atlantic'. After the disastrous shipping losses suffered in 1940, the situation improved slightly in early 1941 but deteriorated again from April as the U-boats adopted 'wolf-pack' tactics, concentrating on a single convoy. Losses mounted towards an unsustainable 500,000 tons a month. British equipment such as asdic (underwater detection of submarines) and depth charges were largely ineffective and the number of escorts available for the convoys was still inadequate. The worst deficiency though was in long-range patrol aircraft, which were the most effective way of keeping the U-boats submerged. There was a gap of over 300 miles in the centre of the Atlantic which could not be reached from Britain, Canada or Iceland except by the longer-range American Liberator aircraft. There was only one Liberator squadron operational, and its numbers were in decline as Churchill and his advisers gave Bomber Command top priority and used half the Liberators obtained from the United States to ferry VIPs across the Atlantic. The situation was saved by the success in breaking one of the German Navy's Enigma codes, thereby enabling the convoys to be re-routed away from the relatively small number of operational U-boats.

One of the other crucial factors tipping the balance against Germany in the Atlantic was the adoption by the United States of a more aggressive policy from September 1941. On 4 September the *USS Gear* was attacked by a U-boat off Iceland. In a broadcast on 11 September Roosevelt used the attack to justify a new policy of escorting all ships in the US defence zone west of 26°. Before the end of the month the Royal Navy had been able to withdraw from the western Atlantic and leave the United States to protect all convoys except troop ships. Congress also repealed the part of the Neutrality Acts that stopped the arming of US merchant ships and in addition allowed US ships to enter belligerent ports. But Roosevelt's policy remained cautious – he only allowed US ships to travel to Lisbon and not into British ports. Escorting ships in the western Atlantic could be presented as yet another extension of the policy of hemispheric defence. He refused to break diplomatic relations with Germany even after a US merchant ship was sunk. He realised there was no possibility of a declaration of war securing Congressional approval and was content to continue with the role the US had adopted for the last eighteen months – ensuring that sufficient supplies reached Britain to enable it to stay in the war.

The war situation in the autumn of 1941 was grim. In Britain just enough imports were getting through to keep the war economy going. The bomber campaign was having virtually no impact on the German war effort. The United States seemed little nearer joining the war. Churchill told Smuts in November that as far as the Americans were concerned he saw no way 'of helping lift this situation on to a higher plane ... in the meantime we must have patience and trust to the tide which is flowing our way and to events'.[72] Germany dominated most of the continent. On the eastern front the Soviets seemed on the point of collapse after German troops had overrun the west of the country and were fighting in the suburbs of Leningrad and Moscow. Under Soviet pressure, Churchill had reluctantly declared war on Finland, Hungary and Rumania, who had attacked the Soviet Union with the Germans in the summer but were not at war with Britain. Before doing so he wrote to the Finnish leader General Mannerheim explaining his reluctance and he told the Cabinet 'that in his view this declaration on Finland (and also on Hungary and Roumania) would not assist either our cause or that of the Russians. The sole justification for it was that it was necessary in order to satisfy the Russian government.'[73]

There was slightly better news from the desert when on 18 November Auchinleck launched his long awaited offensive. He had over twice as many tanks as the Germans but the attack was badly handled – 400 tanks were lost in the first six days. But by the end of the month Rommel had only thirty-four operational tanks and was also short of fuel. He began a steady retreat and the British followed along in his wake, retaking Benghazi just before Christmas. But a limited success against small German forces in the desert could not alter Britain's inability to defeat the mass of the German Army.

In this situation Churchill found it difficult to find a way foward that offered some hope of winning the war and he therefore wanted to keep his options open on the diplomatic front. In a paper for the Defence Committee in the autumn of 1941 he proposed that about half the Army would stay in Britain and some twenty-five divisions would eventually be deployed in the Middle East. That left six or seven as 'the maximum that can be conceived' as an expeditionary force. Any ideas of anything larger 'being launched by Great Britain against the western shores of the continent . . . have no foundation of reality on which to rest'. Britain could therefore only go on with the combination of blockade, bombing and subversion 'till the Nazi system breaks up'.[74] It was this inability to see a probable route to victory without US entry into the war that led Churchill not to insist on unconditional surrender by Germany and not to rule out a compromise peace if Hitler was overthrown by the Army. He told the Cabinet at the end of November 'it would be going too far to say that we should not negotiate with a Germany controlled by the Army. It was impossible to forecast what form of Government there might be at a time when their resistance weakened and they wished to negotiate.'[75]

By the autumn of 1941 one of the most crucial issues facing the Cabinet, and the one that was unexpectedly to transform this depressing situation, was the defence of the Far East. Questions about the defence of Singapore and the dominions did come up at intervals during the year, but Churchill consistently refused to regard developments in the Far East as a serious threat to British interests.

He continued to believe, as he had done for the previous fifteen years, that the Japanese would not dare to attack the white powers. He remained confident that little needed to be done to reinforce the area and that existing British and American naval deployments would be a sufficient deterrent, telling the Admiralty: 'The Japanese Navy is not likely to venture far from its home bases so long as a superior battle-fleet is maintained at Singapore or at Honolulu. The Japanese would never attempt a seige of Singapore with a hostile, superior American fleet in the Pacific.'[76] At the beginning of 1941, when he saw plans for a build-up to just over 300 aircraft in the Far East, he told the chiefs of staff: 'The political situation in the Far East does not seem to require, and the strength of our Air Force by no means warrants, the maintenance of such large forces in the Far East at this time.'[77] After a meeting with the Japanese Ambassador he wrote, 'I do not think Japan is likely to attack us unless she is sure we are going to be defeated.'[78]

At the staff talks with the Americans in Washington early in 1941 there was almost complete disagreement about the Pacific. The US would not accept responsibility for defending British interests and refused to send part of their Navy to Singapore. When the Australian Prime Minister, Robert Menzies, was in London in the spring, the old questions about reinforcing the Far East that had dogged British governments for twenty years reappeared. First he asked for extra aircraft to defend Australia. Beaverbrook told Churchill that he was producing 'more aircraft than the Air Ministry can use' – production was twice 1940 levels.[79] Churchill, however, thought it was 'most unwise to fritter away aircraft to Australia'.[80] He thought one unarmed Hurricane would be a suitable offer but was overriden by his colleagues.

Menzies also asked for reassurances over the despatch of the fleet to Singapore. Although the 'reassurances' Churchill had given in the autumn of 1939 and August 1940 had become progressively more elastic, he now insisted on adding another caveat, namely that existing 'commitments' to Australia and New Zealand 'did not mean that we would give up our great interests in the Middle East on account of a few raids by Japanese cruisers'.[81] The chiefs of staff therefore told Menzies it would be 'misleading to attempt to lay down possible strength in the Far East in advance ... It is vital to avoid being weak everywhere ... we should send a battle-cruiser and an aircraft carrier to the Indian Ocean [not Singapore]. Our ability to do more must be judged entirely on the situation at the time.'[82] At the end of April Churchill instructed the chiefs of staff not to 'make any further dispositions for the defence of Malaya and Singapore beyond those modest arrangements which are in progress'.[83]

Churchill and his colleagues had accepted in 1940 that Britain's position in the Far East depended on American support and that the Americans would therefore have to be allowed to take the lead in formulating policy in the region. But they found that the Americans showed little interest in developing a joint policy. At the beginning of February 1941 Churchill asked Roosevelt to agree a joint Anglo-US warning to Japan combined with an American guarantee of support if British territory was attacked. The President rejected the proposal. He was more interested in trying to reach an accommodation with the Japanese. In February the American administration began a series of nearly sixty meetings with the Japanese Ambassador, Admiral Nomura. Although the talks were of crucial importance to Britain, the Americans did not consult the British Government or even inform them of their intentions. The British only found out about the talks by accident in May when they were mentioned in some other documents. Even then their nature and content was not fully disclosed. American aims were wide ranging, especially over free trade and access to markets, and cut across what the Japanese saw as their national interests. The Japanese Government was divided over what to do but at the beginning of July decided to extend its influence southwards while trying to avoid war with the Americans. At the end of the month it occupied Vichy controlled southern Indochina (it had taken over the northern part in 1940).

The Americans reacted by freezing Japanese assets and although Roosevelt had intended to release some of them to allow the purchase of oil, in practice a total embargo resulted. Japan was completely dependent on imported oil and they were therefore faced with the option of either accepting US demands or going to war to try and obtain the necessary oil. The British Government decided it could not intervene with the Americans even though it opposed a complete embargo which it thought too provocative. It specifically rejected an Australian request to seek a US commitment to defend British territory before introducing an embargo and freezing of assets. Instead the Churchill Government followed the American line.

If Japan did react to the embargo with an attack to gain possession of some oilfields, the most likely target was the Dutch East Indies, still controlled by Britain's ally, the Dutch government-in-exile in London. Without a guarantee of American help, the British Government was not prepared to give a commitment to the Dutch that they would fight to defend their possessions in the Far East. But as the risk of a Japanese attack increased, Eden proposed to the Cabinet on 21 July that a secret undertaking to defend Dutch territory should be given (the Americans would be told too) and informed his colleagues that the dominions supported such a move. Churchill disagreed and vetoed the proposal. He told the Cabinet he was prepared to contemplate further Japanese aggression:

> As for a Japanese attack on Singapore, he did not believe anything of the sort was contemplated. It might well be that, even if Japan encroached on the Dutch East Indies, the right policy would be that we should not make an immediate declaration of war on Japan.[84]

A year earlier he had in fact pointed out to the Cabinet the serious dangers inherent in the policy of tolerating such encroachment:

> to his mind the central facet of the situation ... was that she [Japan] would be able to prepare strong positions facing Singapore, including a base for her fleet. If we did not fight, she would be able to prepare these positions in peace, and to use them against us at the moment which suited her best. [An attack on the Dutch East Indies] is an ever greater menace to our safety and interests than an attack on Hong Kong. [If Britain made its position clear] Japan might very well decide against attack.[85]

This time Churchill's second thoughts prevailed and no guarantee was given to the Dutch in the absence of any American guarantee to the British.

At the Newfoundland conference Churchill had tried again to obtain an Anglo-American front in the Far East. On the second day of the talks he suggested to Roosevelt that there should be joint declarations against further Japanese aggression and mutual guarantees of support. In particular the Americans were to state that any further Japanese moves in the south-west Pacific would mean war. He told the President that if this were not done, Japan would 'seize or destroy' all British merchant ships in the area giving an 'almost decisive' blow to his government.[86] Roosevelt rejected Churchill's plea two days later. All he obtained was a commitment to maintain the economic measures against Japan (which was American policy anyway). But Churchill thought he had succeeded in obtaining Roosevelt's agreement to issue a warning to Japan using a British-prepared draft. He told the Cabinet after the meeting that Roosevelt had 'on more than one occasion' agreed to use the British draft and he was 'confident that the President would not tone it down'.[87]

Churchill's confidence quickly proved to be misplaced. On his return from Newfoundland Roosevelt did arrange for a note to be sent to the Japanese but it was not a warning, only a mild statement of the American position, and it contained no mention of anything other than American interests. It was not shown to the British until six days after it was sent to the Japanese. The British were now committed to a policy of tough economic sanctions against Japan which might well lead to war but without any guarantee of American support. Churchill was happy with what other colleagues saw as an overexposed position, because he held strongly to his belief that an inferior race such as the Japanese would not dare to challenge the white powers. Describing them to newspaper editors as the 'Wops of the Pacific', he maintained: 'the Japs would shout and threaten but would not move'.[88]

Churchill was, therefore, still opposed to sending any significant reinforcements to the Far East – it was to receive no tanks before March 1942 at the earliest and none of the 336 modern aircraft the chiefs of staff judged to be the minimum necessary. The Army was also short of its planned strength by seventeen infantry battalions and two tank regiments. (What limited reinforcements were made available were sent to Hong Kong, which Churchill had described as an indefensible outpost.) Since 1937 the chiefs of staff had accepted that a successful Japanese invasion of Malaya would result in the fall of Singapore within two months and they believed that the main threat to the latter came not from the sea but from the land. They argued that it was essential for British forces to move quickly on any threat of war (particularly to secure the Kra isthmus in

Thailand) and to deploy effective forward air cover. Once Malaya was lost Singapore was indefensible – the naval base was on the north of the island next to the mainland and would be within artillery range even if no attempt at a landing was made. Churchill did not accept that military judgement. He thought there was no need to hold all of Malaya (such a policy 'cannot be entertained') because Singapore could be defended by a strong local garrison and what he called 'the general potentialities of seapower'.[89]

Even after the Japanese take-over of southern Indochina at the end of July 1941 the only reinforcements Churchill would consider were a few warships, which he thought would be adequate to show resolve. The Australian Government asked for five major warships to be sent to Singapore as a deterrent. This proposal was far too much for Churchill. He thought a force of one modern battleship, one older model and an aircraft carrier would be sufficient. They were to be based not at Singapore but would operate in the triangle Aden-Simonstown-Singapore, where he thought the force would 'exert a paralyzing effect upon Japanese naval action',[90] even though it was far inferior to the Japanese fleet. The First Sea Lord, Pound, opposed his ideas – 'I cannot recommend it'.[91] He wanted to keep all the most modern ships in the Atlantic and send a larger force to be based at Trincomalee in Ceylon early in the new year when extra ships would be available. Churchill responded by giving Pound a long lecture on naval strategy and argued that just one modern battleship could deter the whole of the Japanese fleet – 'This might indeed be a decisive deterrent.'[92] But he was himself uncertain about whether the British ships were merely a deterrent or would be expected to fight. At one point he argued that Japan would negotiate for another three months before talks collapsed (an accurate assessment), but what would happen then? Churchill did not force the issue to a conclusion at this point and no decisions were taken.

Meanwhile the Japanese Government was moving closer to a decision in favour of war. On 6 September they decided that preparations should be completed by October as the oil embargo started to bite. The British badly misread the Japanese position. At the end of September Eden asked the Cabinet to take a firmer line with Japan in an attempt to deter them from taking any action. The military in the Far East also advised that 'the last thing Japan wants at this juncture is a campaign in the south. Consequently she must now be susceptible to pressure . . . we would stress propaganda value of even one or two battleships at Singapore' and they thought it was time to demand Japanese withdrawal from Indochina.[93] The Americans, as before, were only giving the British very limited information about their continuing talks with Japan. Churchill accepted this position, telling the Cabinet 'we ought to regard the United States as having taken charge in the Far East. . . . We are prepared to support any action, however serious, which the United States may decide to take.'[94] On 2 October the Japanese were told that there could be no meeting between their Prime Minister (Konoye) and Roosevelt until they accepted the American position in the discussions, including withdrawal from China. The demand caused a crisis in Tokyo, resolved by the fall of the Konoye Government and its replacement by a military-dominated Government under General Tojo.

In London the change of Government was rightly taken as an ominous sign. Eden repeated his request for some firm action, preferably fleet movements. The day after Tojo's government took power the Defence Committee met to discuss what to do. Churchill stuck to his proposal made in August to send a small force of two battleships (one old, one modern) and an aircraft carrier. The Admiralty wanted a force of six or seven battleships operating under shore-based aircraft cover. Eden and Attlee supported Churchill but, in the absence of Pound, a decision was postponed. The discussion was resumed on 20 October. Churchill told the chiefs of staff 'he did not believe that the Japanese would go to war with the United States and ourselves'.[95] The force was therefore to be a deterrent. Pound preferred a stronger fleet of at least six battleships at Singapore which, even if they were not modern, would still make the Japanese split their forces, thereby making them more vulnerable to the US Navy. Churchill repeated his view that Japan would not go to war but if they did 'he did not foresee an attack in force on Malaya. He thought the main danger would be to our trade from Japanese battle-cruisers. The only thing which would induce caution in the Japanese would be the presence in Eastern Waters of a fast striking force.'[96] He kept pressing his ideas and eventually Pound suggested a compromise – one modern ship (*HMS Prince of Wales*) would go to Cape Town and a decision would be made later on whether or not it joined the older *HMS Repulse* already in the Indian

Ocean. In practice the compromise was never implemented and it was always assumed that *HMS Prince of Wales* would go to Singapore. (No papers survive to suggest why this happened.) During the discussion on 20 October no mention was made of an accompanying aircraft carrier. None in fact were available (the only possibility, *HMS Indomitable*, had just run aground in the West Indies) and Churchill was obviously content for the two battleships to operate without air support.

After this prolonged clash of wills between the Prime Minister and his military advisers, the decision finally reached on naval reinforcements for the Far East reflected above all Churchill's judgement that the Japanese would probably not attack, little force would be needed to deter them or defend Singapore if deterrence unexpectedly failed. The decision was a combination of ill-thought-out ideas. Sending a token force to an area dominated by the enemy was courting disaster. Two battleships could not act as a genuine deterrent to a numerically superior Japanese fleet that could choose the moment to attack and easily protect its lines of communication to the north of Singapore. Pound's arguments for sending a far larger force that would make the Japanese split their fleet were far more soundly based. The lack of air support was also a fatal error of judgement and reflected Churchill's persistent tendency to under-estimate the air threat to ships, which he had first demonstrated before the war. Yet he had at one stage argued it was possible to send a modern ship to the Far East because the main German threat in the Atlantic, the *Tirpitz*, could be sunk by British air power. He failed to apply the same logic to the Japanese.

Altogether Churchill demonstrated an arrogant and wilful under-estimating of the Japanese, at a time when others did see the dangers. When Admiral Phillips, the new Commander of the Far East Fleet, arrived at Cape Town, he saw Smuts and discussed the situation with him. The South African Premier immediately sent a telegram to Churchill saying he was unhappy with the naval dispositions and pointing out that the Japanese would have the opportunity to defeat the British and American fleets separately. He concluded: 'If Japanese are really nippy there is here opening for a first-class disaster.'[97] It then became clearer than ever that Churchill saw the whole operation as a bluff. He wanted Admiral Phillips to tow a dummy battleship from Cape Town to give the illusion that two modern ships were arriving and Australia to send public thanks for 'the formation of an Eastern battle fleet'.[98] No one else took such ideas seriously.

The Japanese were not influenced by the public despatch of *HMS Prince of Wales* to the Far East. In early November they secretly set 25 November as the date by which negotiations with the Americans must succeed (this was known by the Americans and British on 11 November). On 20 November Admiral Nomura suggested to the Americans a temporary agreement while talks continued for a further three months. The British and other interested countries were consulted on 22 November. Churchill's reaction was highly favourable: 'Our major interest is: no further encroachments and no war, as we have enough of the latter . . . I must say I should feel pleased if I read that an American-Japanese agreement had been made by which we were no worse off three months hence in the Far East than we are now.'[99] Eden and the Foreign Office were less favourably inclined and wanted to reject any deal. Churchill's reply to Roosevelt agreed with the continuation of talks and argued that the Japanese were unsure what to do next. Before Churchill's message arrived the Americans had decided to reject the Japanese proposal. This was a decision with very serious implications but the British were not consulted on the change of position and only saw a copy of the American proposals a week after they were given to the Japanese. Churchill's assessment of the Japanese was wrong. They had decided on war – the task force to attack Pearl Harbor put to sea on 26 November.

At the beginning of November Churchill told the Cabinet, 'Our policy in the Far East should be to persuade the United States to cover our weak position in the area. We should not run the risk of finding ourselves at war with Japan without American support.'[100] The problem was that despite eighteen months of effort the British still had no guarantee of American support and little agreement about a common policy. Although Churchill and the Government had made it clear that if Japan attacked the United States Britain would immediately declare war, Churchill was far from sure it would apply the other way round. On 1 December he told the Cabinet and chiefs of staff 'he did not share the view of the Australian Government that the outbreak of Anglo-Japanese hostilities would precipitate American entry into the war'.[101] Churchill however remained certain that Japan would not dare start a war. On 12 November he spoke in Cabinet about the futility of sending more forces to the Far East where they would be inactive for at least a year. On 3 December (just four days before the attack on Pearl Harbor) he told the Defence Committee that the prospect of Japan starting a war was 'a remote contingency'.[102]

President Roosevelt was expecting a Japanese attack, probably in Thailand or the Dutch East Indies. By the end of November he decided that the United States would have to fight in those circumstances and on 1 December told Halifax, in a vague way, of American intentions. Churchill remained suspicious about American intentions and he opposed any move to secure the Kra isthmus in Thailand, which was vital for the defence of Malaya, or any commitment to defend the Dutch East Indies, without a clear declaration of US support. That was finally forthcoming late on 3 December (Roosevelt was prepared to do in the Pacific what he was not willing to do in the Atlantic). The British immediately gave the Dutch the commitment they had sought for eighteen months and began to implement plans to secure the Kra isthmus.

The move came too late. On 7 December Japanese forces sank a large part of the American Pacific fleet at Pearl Harbor and launched an invasion of Malaya. One immediate problem was to decide what to do with the two British battleships at Singapore now that their supposed deterrent role had been overtaken by events. On 9 December Churchill and the Admiralty agreed that they should probably be sent to Hawaii to join up with the remains of the US fleet, leaving British possessions open to naval attack. A final decision was to be taken the next morning. By then it was too late. The commanders at Singapore decided to use the ships to disrupt the Japanese landings along the Malayan coast. But such an unbalanced force with no air cover was intensely vulnerable and both *HMS Prince of Wales* and *HMS Repulse* were sunk by Japanese torpedo bombers. Trying to distance himself from the tragedy he had largely created, Churchill blamed the Admiralty for letting the ships become involved in operations. He told the Cabinet on 12 December that the Admiralty had known what was happening 'but they had not intervened to stop the operation', with the clear implication that he would have done so.[103] The position in the Far East was now desperate. There was no effective defence for Singapore or the

Indian Ocean – no naval reinforcements were available, the troops in the area were at a third of the level thought necessary, they had no tanks, and there were only 180 obsolete aircraft.

The United States and Britain were now both involved in the war against Japan. But although immediately after the attack on Pearl Harbor Roosevelt successfully obtained a declaration of war against Japan, he made no effort to obtain one against Germany. This odd situation was only resolved when Hitler and Mussolini decided to stand by their Japanese ally and declare war on the United States on 12 December. At last all the terrible uncertainties of the previous eighteen months were over. Churchill and his colleagues realised that it was now virtually inevitable that Britain would be on the winning side in the war. But the entry of an enormously powerful ally brought new complications and questions about the future conduct of the war.

Despite its dependence on American economic and financial assistance, Britain had been free to make decisions about how to use its limited military power. Now the problems involved in the higher direction of the war were changing. Churchill had to adjust to the prospect of becoming a junior partner to the United States and had to find a way of exerting influence within the alliance. He had not at this stage managed to develop anything like a close personal relationship with Roosevelt. There were already indications of a divergence of interests between the two countries and signs of American lack of sympathy for Britain's imperial interests so dear to Churchill's heart. What would be the strategic priorities of the United States, how could it use its overwhelming economic strength to ensure victory and what role would Britain play in that process?

22

1942 – Strategy and Survival

Immediately after the attack on Pearl Harbor Churchill was concerned that unilateral American decisions might adversely affect Britain. He told the Cabinet 'there were already indications that the United States Naval authorities proposed to make certain redispositions of their Naval forces which would vitally effect us. There was also the risk that they would wish to retain . . . munitions of war which they had promised to allocate to us.'[1] Before the German declaration of war US ships were being diverted from the Atlantic, leaving the British and Canadians to cope as best they could, and lend-lease supplies were stopped for a few days. The British were worried that the whole strategy agreed with the Americans earlier in the year (Germany First) was collapsing now that the US faced actual war in the Pacific and no declared war in the Atlantic. To try and keep some control over the situation Churchill suggested to Roosevelt that he should immediately travel to Washington where they could together 'review the whole war plan in the light of reality and new facts, as well as the problems of production and distribution'.[2] Roosevelt was reluctant to see him for at least a month and only agreed to the visit after the German declaration of war.

Churchill left immediately on board *HMS Duke of York*, accompanied by Beaverbrook and the chiefs of staff. During an extremely rough crossing he spent most of the time in bed, producing three papers on future plans. His ideas were essentially a reworking of the strategy that had dominated British thinking for the last eighteen

553

months. Looking ahead to 1942, he saw the main effort taking place in North Africa with perhaps Vichy joining the allied side, and a continued bombing campaign. In the Pacific he envisaged the situation would be stabilised rapidly and contained without major losses and without involving major effort. Although privately he thought the most likely date for a continental invasion was 1944, he played up the chances of success in 1943 in an attempt to stop the Americans diverting forces to the Pacific. He thought Turkey would join the allies and, as he told the chiefs of staff, 'there is a good chance of our being able to make four or five simultaneous Anglo-American landings on the Continent in the summer of 1943' as German morale collapsed.[3] The missing element in his calculations were Soviet forces, who were still fighting about ninety-eight per cent of the German Army.

Churchill's visit was only superficially successful in establishing better relations with Roosevelt. He stayed at the White House, occasionally even listened to what the President had to say and took part in a number of effective demonstrations of Anglo-American unity – on Christmas Eve he lit the White House Christmas tree, on Christmas Day he joined Roosevelt and the chiefs of staff for dinner and he also made a well-received speech to Congress. Behind the scenes though the relationship was far from straightforward and Churchill was brought up against American determination to run the war as they wanted. Before the British could even submit their papers on future strategy, the Americans announced that they had decided to stick with the 'Germany First' policy, reflecting the classic military doctrine of concentrating efforts against the strongest opponent and leaving the two weaker powers (Italy and Japan) till later.

During the summer of 1941 the American military planners had been working out how this would be accomplished. They did not expect a bombing campaign to be sufficient and therefore planned to build an army of about 200 divisions for an invasion in July 1943. Until then a few peripheral operations would be possible but they 'must be so conducted as to facilitate the decisive employment of allied forces in Central Europe [which is] our principal theater of war'.[4] As early as September 1941 Roosevelt had contemplated using US troops first in North Africa against Vichy territory. On 21 December the talks agreed that this would be the 'foremost' area for any American expeditionary force.[5] But no definite plans were agreed. The Americans deleted the British idea of an invasion across the Mediterranean against Italy and Churchill's ideas for several simultaneous landings across Europe – everything was to be concentrated on a major invasion in 1943.

The United States would need time to mobilise, train and deploy a large army and for full industrial mobilisation to take place. For most of 1942 the British would be providing as big a part of the military effort in Europe and the Mediterranean as the Americans. During the discussions in Washington they sought to use this opportunity to gain as much control over the conduct of the war as possible. The chiefs of staff suggested to Churchill that he should propose a Combined Chiefs of Staff organisation. The Americans accepted the idea and other joint organisations were set up – a Combined Raw Materials Board and a Combined Shipping Adjustment Board to control Anglo-American production and resources and allocate them in the best possible way. This did give the British considerable scope for exercising influence but all these Boards were established in Washington and were dominated by the Americans. The Americans also offered a joint command with the British, Dutch and Australians in the south-west Pacific and even insisted on selecting a British overall commander (Wavell). This was a less generous offer than it seemed – the area was likely to be overrun by the Japanese and the Americans were quite happy for the British to bear the responsibility.

Churchill soon found that the Pacific war was to be directed from Washington by the Americans (the Combined Chiefs of Staff were to have virtually no say in US operations) and, worse still, the European war was not to be run from London as he hoped. The Americans insisted on keeping control in Washington, subject to discussions with the British. The naval spheres of influence agreed during the Christmas/New Year talks reflected this situation. He had to agree that the Royal Navy should be limited to the eastern Atlantic, the Arctic convoys to the Soviet Union, the Mediterranean and the Indian Ocean. The United States took responsibility for the western Atlantic and the whole of the Pacific, including such normally British-controlled areas as Australia and New Zealand. Churchill had also hoped that American entry into the war would mean the end of lend-lease and instead a free pooling of the two nations' resources, but the Americans never considered abandoning a programme which kept Britain in a dependent position.

Although the conference had agreed a structure for directing the war, it had not settled a way of carrying out the 'Germany First' strategy. Personal relations had proved far from happy in Washington. Roosevelt was quickly bored with Churchill's long monologues on the war and preferred the company of the more stimulating and flattering Beaverbrook. Churchill was jealous of his friend's success and even provoked one of his numerous resignations when he openly criticised him in front of the Americans. After the conference was over Roosevelt told his Cabinet 'the British were hard to work with ... they were high hat and selfish'.[6] On his return to London Churchill was condescending about the Americans and thought Britain would be able to instruct them in the ways of the world. He told the Cabinet 'there was little risk of the Americans abandoning the conventional principles of war. They were not above learning from us provided that we did not set out to teach them.'[7]

On 14 January Churchill left Washington for Bermuda (after fitting in a short break in Florida). He had intended to return on *HMS Duke of York* but decided instead to undertake the long flight home because of a rapidly deteriorating situation in the Far East and a developing domestic political crisis. Immediately after their assault on northern Malaya the Japanese had begun moving south down the west coast of the peninsula towards Singapore against feeble British resistance. Disagreement over deployment of reinforcements for the area continued. Churchill thought that the Navy should be concentrated in the Indian Ocean to protect the supply lane to the Middle East and not in the Far East, and that reinforcements from the Army should be sent to India and secondly to Singapore but not to Malaya. He was convinced, against all the military advice, that there was no need to defend Malaya and that Singapore was a fortress that could withstand a siege for probably six months. During the trip to Washington he had specifically ordered the chiefs of staff to plan on this basis.

Now that the threat which Australia and New Zealand had seen looming for several years had become concrete the dominions found that the British Government did not rush to the aid of the largely defenceless Empire in the Far East. Just after Christmas, Curtin, the Australian Prime Minister, asked for greater emphasis to be placed on the defence of the Far East and raised the possibility of an Australian-American alliance. Churchill (in Washington) took a strong line against a subordinate member of the Empire daring to take such a stand. He told Attlee, who was in charge of the Government in London (Eden was in Moscow), that there was to be 'a firm stand against this misbehaviour' and 'no weakness or pandering to them'.[8] Privately he was even more dismissive, telling his doctor Lord Moran that no more could be expected because 'the Australians came of bad stock'.[9] Curtin himself received a message from Churchill to say that the loss of Malaya had been inevitable and that the only important point was the defence of the 'Singapore fortress and its essential hinterland'.

From Bermuda he also instructed Wavell: 'the vital need is to prolong the defence of the Island to the last possible moment'.[10] On his return to London he received a telegram from Wavell pointing out what had been accepted by the chiefs of staff since 1937, namely that Singapore was not a fortress and could not be defended once Malaya was lost. He now faced a desperate situation as the base which symbolised British power in the Far East was on the verge of being conquered by the Japanese. Before this happened Churchill wanted some futile but heroic gestures. He told Wavell on 20 January that everything on Singapore Island was to be blown up and 'no question of surrender [is] to be entertained until after protracted fighting among the ruins of Singapore City'.[11] Indeed he told the chiefs of staff that Wavell, his staff and all senior officers were to die at their posts, but they refused to pass on the message.

Even before the attack on Singapore the Japanese had begun the invasion of Burma. Churchill was in two minds what to do – Burma was important because of the links to the nationalist Chinese yet Singapore was the great symbol. At the Defence Committee meeting on 21 January he declared 'taking the widest view, Burma was more important than Singapore', but it was in fact agreed to reinforce Singapore as the 'highest priority'.[12] As a result troops were poured into Singapore – the last reinforcements were sent on 30 January, but within a few days it was clear that the end could not be long postponed. Faced with defeat at the hands of an oriental nation Churchill returned to his demand for a truly apocalyptic end to the campaign among the troops and civilians on the island. He told Wavell to put aside 'any thought of saving the troops or saving the population. The battle must be fought to the bitter end at all costs.' Commanders and senior officers 'should die with their troops'. This must be done for the sake of honour – 'the whole reputation of our country and our race is involved'.[13] The commanders on the spot refused to carry out these orders and tried to save as many lives as possible from the débâcle. Five days after this message, 85,000 British troops surrendered to the Japanese – altogether the British lost 125,000 troops during the campaign against Japanese casualties of about 10,000. Churchill, acutely sensitive to the humiliation involved in defeat by an Asiatic country, told Roosevelt it was 'the greatest disaster in our history'.[14]

For eighteen months Churchill had presided over an almost unbroken series of British reverses and for many the collapse of Britain's position in the Far East was the last straw. Churchill appreciated that despite his position as the symbol of resistance established in 1940 it was not pre-ordained that he would remain as Prime Minister throughout the war. On his return from the United States he acted quickly to secure his position. He summoned the Chairman of the backbench 1922 Committee and in a rage told him that only he stood between the Conservative Party and extinction and that MPs had to support him. He demanded an immediate vote of confidence from the Commons (before Singapore fell). He secured it by 464 votes to one. But in the course of the debate on 27 January he was forced to make a frank admission of Britain's inability to defend its empire that encapsulated the dilemmas faced by the pre-war governments he had himself criticised for incompetence and unpreparedness. He told MPs:

> There has never been a moment, there never could have been a moment, when Great Britain or the British Empire, single-handed, could fight Germany and Italy, could wage the Battle of Britain, the Battle of the Atlantic and the Battle of the Middle East – and at the same time stand thoroughly prepared in Burma, the Malay Peninsula, and generally in the Far East.

Churchill too could find no solution to what was in fact an insoluble problem.

At this time Churchill was trying to avoid any reconstruction of the Cabinet, telling Eden 'I'd rather have a Cabinet of obedient mugwumps than awkward freaks.'[15] One 'awkward freak' was undoubtedly Stafford Cripps, who had just resigned as Ambassador in Moscow and returned to the country invested with the halo of Soviet resistance. His political popularity was soaring, although many within the Labour Party, in particular Attlee, were less enthusiastic about him after his opposition to party policy in the 1930s. Nevertheless Churchill felt that he had to offer Cripps a job. He did so but Cripps rejected it because it did not give him a place in the War Cabinet. A furious Churchill was described by one member of the Government as 'ramping around denouncing Cripps with every kind of imprecation'.[16]

The question of a Government reconstruction now became caught up in the future of Churchill's most difficult colleague, Beaverbrook. At the beginning of the year he had been made Minister of Supply and early in February the job was expanded to become Minister of Production. The problem was what powers the new ministry should have. Beaverbrook wanted total control over resources including manpower, which would have made him virtually supreme on the home front and powerful enough to challenge the Prime Minister himself. Churchill therefore backed Bevin, who refused to give up his powers over the direction of labour (the main way the economy was in practice controlled), and Alexander, who wanted to retain the Admiralty's responsibilities for shipbuilding. On 10 February Beaverbrook accepted a draft White Paper setting out limited powers for him but the political atmosphere remained tense.

The next day Churchill decided not to travel to the Middle East and India in order to be in the country for the inevitable crisis when Singapore fell. Despite the formal vote of confidence from the Commons the Cabinet was growing restive, increasingly discontented with Churchill's style and methods. Sir Alexander Cadogan reported: 'After last week's debate P.M. hectors more brutally a more subservient cabinet.'[17] The Secretary of State for India Leo Amery wrote, 'This is in essence a one-man government so far as the conduct of the war is concerned, subject to a certain amount of conversation in Cabinet.'[18] Eden thought Churchill was becoming 'more and more obstinate and losing grip'.[19] Hugh Dalton, the Minister of Economic Warfare, noted the unfortunate results: 'we just don't deserve to win the war. We are all fighting each other instead of the enemy, and with such zest.'[20]

After the fall of Singapore Churchill was under great pressure from colleagues and the press to make major changes in the way decisions were taken. There were calls for him to appoint a Minister for Defence and to create a small war cabinet of non-departmental ministers (similar to the system Lloyd George operated in the First World War) to give a clearer sense of direction to the war effort and strategy. His close friend Brendan Bracken wanted Eden to become Minister of Defence. This would have seriously weakened Churchill's position and he refused pointblank to entertain such a suggestion. His most obvious rival for the premiership was indeed Eden, but he was greatly helped to sustain his position and keep control of the political crisis by Eden's consistent refusal to conspire against him. He had promised Eden the succession to the Conservative leadership after the war and Eden, knowing there was still considerable opposition to him among Conservative backbenchers, was not prepared to try and overthrow Churchill. But while content to remain Foreign Secretary he did want to see changes in the way the Government was run, making for greater influence for himself and more control over the Prime Minister. He had in mind a War Cabinet of Churchill, himself, Attlee and Cripps and he wanted to be made Deputy Minister of Defence.

Churchill embarked on a reshuffle of the Government, hoping that a change of faces would avoid the necessity for far-reaching structural changes. He offered Cripps the leadership of the Commons (even though Eden wanted the job) and a place in the War Cabinet. Cripps accepted and by way of compensation for this move and the sacking of the official deputy leader of the party, the alcoholic Arthur Greenwood, Attlee was given the honorific title of Deputy Prime Minister. This alienated Beaverbrook, who wanted a much more pro-Soviet policy than Attlee would support. After turning down an offer of the embassy in Washington, the Minister of Production really did resign after a fortnight in the job. He was replaced by Oliver Lyttleton, a friend of Churchill's whose main experience had been in the City. To balance the removal of Greenwood, Kingsley Wood was dismissed from the War Cabinet although he remained at the Treasury. Some ex-members of the Chamberlain Government – Hankey and Margesson – were sacked. Churchill showed what he thought of the status of the service ministers by replacing Margesson at the War Office by its civil service head, P. J. Grigg, his former Private Secretary at the Treasury.

The reshuffle appeased some of the immediate demands for change after Singapore, but dissatisfaction persisted within the Government. Churchill himself seemed to have lost his way and his behaviour became even more erratic. The senior Conservative Lord Salisbury told Eden: 'If he is not careful Winston will be in his grave or in a lunatic asylum.'[21] The American lend-lease co-ordinator Averell Harriman (who was close to the Churchill entourage) told Roosevelt, 'Unfortunately Singapore shook the Prime Minister himself to such an extent that he has not been able to stand up to adversity with his old vigor.'[22] At the beginning of March Eden thought that 'for the last fortnight there has been no direction of the war. War Cabinet doesn't function – there hasn't been a meeting of the Defence Committee. There's no hand on the wheel. (Probably due to PM's health.)'[23] Ernest Bevin shared many of these views, telling a colleague 'he felt the present set-up could not last very long and that the P.M. in Cabinet now seemed to alternate between being a "beaten man", sitting collapsed in his chair and plaintively saying, "I suppose this is another of the concessions that I must make for the sake of national unity", and a violently aggressive, resentful, man'.[24] At the beginning of April Eden was again expressing dissatisfaction: 'There is no day to day direction of war except by Chiefs of Staff & Winston. I would not object to this if it gave results, but it doesn't.' He thought the real problem was that Churchill 'wants to move all the pieces himself'.[25] The public too were unhappy. In March an opinion poll recorded only thirty-five per cent of the population were satisfied with the Government's conduct of the war. On reflection Churchill regarded the Government changes as his weakest moment – 'a concession or rather submission to Press criticism and public opinion' and thought he had really been 'strong enough to spit in all their faces'.[26]

The series of military defeats did not end with the fall of Singapore. In the same week three German warships (*Scharnhorst*, *Prinz Eugen* and *Gneisenau*) sailed up the Channel from Brest to a safe German port without effective interference from the Royal Navy or the RAF. Rommel also counter-attacked in the desert: the British 1st Armoured Division disintegrated and the fall of Benghazi was accompanied by a huge loss of stores and a retreat towards the

Egyptian border. The Ministry of Information weekly intelligence report described the middle of February as 'the blackest week since Dunkirk'.[27] In the Far East too the Japanese advance continued through the Dutch East Indies, to New Guinea and also into Burma and towards India. Churchill warned the King, 'Burma, Ceylon, Calcutta and Madras in India and part of Australia may fall into enemy hands.'[28]

Despite these private worries about the fate of Australia he was still reluctant to send any help. At the end of January he had suspended his personal telegrams to the Australian Prime Minister 'in view of Mr Curtin's tone'.[29] On 19 February, after a Japanese air raid on Darwin in the Northern Territory, the Australian Government insisted that its troops on the way back from the Middle East should return home and not be diverted to Rangoon as Churchill wanted. He sent a threatening message to Curtin demanding a change in policy and diverted the convoy to Colombo. When the Australians stood firm, he responded that he had ignored their demands because he 'could not contemplate that [they] would refuse our request'.[30] After further arguments Churchill, with bad grace, gave in and the Australian troops were not sent to Rangoon where, in a replica of the Singapore disaster, they would have been immediately captured (the city was already in a state of anarchy and it surrendered to the Japanese on 27 February). The Japanese soon overran the rest of Burma and reached the Indian frontier. A small naval raid led to the withdrawal of the Royal Navy from Trincomalee in Ceylon and its evacuation to Mombasa in Kenya, thereby opening up the Indian Ocean to Japanese warships.

Churchill still remained unwilling to assist Australia. In the middle of March he promised that two divisions would be sent from the Middle East, but only if the Japanese invaded with a force of at least eight divisions (two more than they had used in the Malayan campaign). Not surprisingly the Australians turned to the Americans for their defence. In mid-March General MacArthur arrived in the country to set up his headquarters for the defence of the south-west Pacific. At the end of April Churchill asked Roosevelt to put pressure on MacArthur to stop asking for British reinforcements for Australia; he sent them instead to India, which he always regarded as a higher priority. In May he suddenly began to worry about the future and suggested arms should be sent because it was necessary to consider the 'permanent relationship with Australia and it seems very detrimental to the future of the Empire for us not to be represented in any way in their defence'.[31] But by then it was already too late. The Australians had begun to depend on the United States rather than Britain for their defence, a situation brought about by the British failure to come to their aid at the crucial moment despite all the earlier promises.

In the desert war the front had stabilised after the British retreat in January and by March Churchill was again urging Auchinleck to attack. He was writing a series of very rude telegrams addressed to the Middle East commander and the task of stopping some of the more extreme examples fell to the new CIGS, General Alan Brooke, who had replaced Dill at the turn of the year (Dill went to Washington to head the military mission there although Churchill originally intended to exile him as Governor of Bengal). On 7 March Churchill ordered Auchinleck to return to London, where he would obviously come under severe pressure to launch a new attack. Auchinleck refused because of the state of his army. Churchill wanted him sacked immediately but he and Brooke could not agree on who should succeed him. Eventually Churchill settled for a visit by Stafford Cripps on his way to India and Cripps accepted the commander's reasons for not attacking until mid-May. At the end of the month Brooke was able to reassure Auchinleck, 'We have now got the PM to accept your dates and arguments, but not in a very pleasant manner.'[32]

One of the reasons Churchill was pressing for an early attack, despite Ultra intelligence showing an imminent German offensive, was the need to try and gain control of the airfields along the North African coast to relieve the increasing pressure on Malta. Under heavy air attacks all warships had withdrawn to Alexandria, and although the island had little strategic value, it had become, like Verdun, a symbol of resistance. Churchill was adamant: 'We are absolutely bound to save Malta in one way or another.'[33] The price during 1942 was high – twenty supply ships sunk (mainly by air attacks) together with an aircraft carrier, three cruisers, nine destroyers and a huge amount of damage to other ships.

By the beginning of May Auchinleck wanted to postpone the agreed offensive for a month while preparations continued and forces were built up. After long discussions the chiefs of staff and the War Cabinet agreed on 10 May that Auchinleck should be ordered to attack on pain of being relieved if he refused. He accepted the order and also Churchill's suggestion that he should take personal command of the operation if necessary. The result was that when Rommel launched his offensive on 26 May British forces were not in defensive positions as Auchinleck had recommended earlier, but were preparing for their own operations and the 7th Armoured Division was quickly overrun. A British counter-attack on 5 June, launched even though Ultra showed the Germans were prepared for just such an attack, failed and on 11–12 June a major German thrust destroyed 260 British tanks and left British troops in danger of finding their retreat to Egypt cut off. At this stage Churchill wanted to hold Tobruk at all costs even though the commanders-in-chief in the Middle East and the chiefs of staff had decided in January that it was not a fortress and should not be left under siege as it had been in 1941. By 15 June the British had been forced out of the Gazala defences and most troops were retreating over the Egyptian border. Tobruk fell after a single day's fighting on 20 June. About 30,000 troops surrendered. Within five days Rommel was at the Mersa Matruh defences and with just sixty tanks and 2,500 infantry went on to inflict another defeat on two disorganised British corps. Auchinleck, who had taken personal command of the battle, fell back on the last line of defences before Alexandria at El Alamein. The Royal Navy left Alexandria and the chiefs of staff and the Cabinet discussed contingency plans for the fall of Egypt.

The worst-case situation foreseen by the chiefs of staff in the 1930s had finally arrived. Britain had indeed proved unable to defend its Empire against three enemies at the same time. In the Middle East it was hanging on to Egypt with its fingernails against a very minor part of the German Army. The Empire in the Far East had collapsed in less than six months under the Japanese assault. Their forces were now on the borders of India, which was itself in almost open revolt against British rule. The Navy had retreated to East Africa. In the absence of British help, the dominions of Australia and New Zealand had turned to the Americans. With American aid Britain had found enough military power to defend the British Isles and keep open the supply lanes. But its finances had collapsed and it was completely dependent on US assistance to stay in the war. Churchill, the die-hard imperialist and passionate believer in the greatness of Britain, had presided over the collapse of British power and the crumbling away of the British Empire. Given this dire situation, it is hardly surprising that he faced another political crisis at home.

The Government's popularity, which had recovered a little in the months after Singapore, slumped after the fall of Tobruk. The proportion of the country satisfied with the Government's handling of the war, after recovering in the weeks after the surrender of Singapore, fell again to just forty-one per cent. Churchill's personal rating too reached its lowest level, although at seventy-eight per cent it showed just how far the reputation he had established in 1940 was sustained. In by-elections, despite the truce between the major parties, the Government suffered a series of defeats. They lost three in March and April but the most sensational result was at Maldon in Essex, just after the fall of Tobruk, when the Conservative vote fell by twenty-two per cent and the normally safe seat was won by the radical Common Wealth Party. Political circles again started to contemplate the possibility of getting rid of Churchill. Within the Government Stafford Cripps was sounding opinion about his suitability to replace Churchill and at Westminster Beaverbrook was, as so often, deeply involved in political conspiracies; he approached Bevin who expressed doubts as to whether the Government could survive. But Eden kept firmly to his position of waiting in the wings – as he told a fellow MP, 'he would do nothing against Winston, now or ever'.[34] Even if he had wanted to make a move, the majority of Conservative backbenchers were not keen on seeing him as leader.

The first overt move against Churchill came with a formal vote of no confidence in the Government moved by the Conservative backbencher Sir John Wardlaw-Milne, chairman of the Select Committee on National Expenditure – something that was never done to Lloyd George in the First World War. After a competent opening to his speech, he ruined his case by suggesting that the King's brother, the Duke of Gloucester, should relieve Churchill of his military responsibilities and become the Commander-in-Chief of British Forces. The credibility of the Government's opponents was further undermined when another critic – Admiral Keyes (whom Churchill had finally sacked as Head of Combined Operations) – suggested that Churchill should be given dictatorial powers over all operations. With this sort of opposition and the official support of all the political parties, it is hardly surprising that the Government obtained 476 votes. What is more surprising is that twenty-five MPs were still prepared to vote against the Government (forty-two Conservatives had voted against Chamberlain in May 1940) and another twenty-seven abstained (about thirty-six had abstained in the earlier confidence vote). Many who did give their support did so only reluctantly. As one of them commented, 'never before have so many members entered a division lobby with so many reservations in their minds'.[35] Most felt that the Government had gained no more than a breathing space and that without military success it would not survive.

The British Empire was to be saved and victory finally achieved by the combined military and economic power of the United States and the Soviet Union. By 1942 the differences in potential were already apparent. The Soviet Union had mobilised its vastly superior manpower and its massive industrial resources capable of supporting a huge army and air force with high-class equipment. Throughout 1942 the Soviet Army was fighting ninety-eight per cent of the operational German Army – 178 divisions massed on the eastern front – while the British were fighting four in North Africa. By 1942 the British war effort was already near its peak in terms of the proportion of national output devoted to the war. At forty-seven per cent this was less than any of the other major combatants (fifty-four per cent in the United States and sixty-six per cent in the Soviet Union for example) and far smaller in absolute terms. Apart from heavy bombers the British relied heavily on the United States for military equipment. By the autumn of 1943 the United States supplied seventy-seven per cent of Britain's escort vessels, eighty-eight per cent of its landing craft, sixty-eight per cent of its light bombers, virtually all of its transort aircraft and self-propelled atrillery, sixty per cent of its tanks and 100 per cent of its heavy tank transporters and ten-ton trucks.

American arms production passed that of Britain in 1942 and by 1944, when it was making about sixty per cent of the allies' armaments, it was six times higher. A few statistics give an impression of what this level of output meant. In 1939 the United States built 2,100 military aircraft, in 1944 the figure was 96,300. Between 1941 and 1945 they constructed ten battleships, eighteen fleet carriers, 119 smaller carriers, forty-five cruisers, 358 destroyers and 504 escorts. In the same period Britain built just three major warships (a battleship and two aircraft carriers, all ordered before the war began). The strength of the American economy can be judged from the fact that despite this vast increase in military production, consumer expenditure also increased by twelve per cent during the war.

Allied success in the war was built upon a massive material superiority over the forces of Germany, Italy and Japan, which depended on much smaller economies. The allies together produced five times as much steel as Germany and forty-seven times as much oil. During the war the Axis countries produced 52,000 tanks compared with the allies' 227,000. It was the same picture in artillery (180,000 against 914,000) and in trucks (600,000 against 3 million). The allies produced over five times as many aircraft as the Axis powers. From 1942 the allies relied on the sheer weight of numbers, which could, and often did, successfully compensate for lack of tactical or strategic brilliance, to produce success on the battlefield. In a comment made at the end of 1943, Churchill encapsulated this way of fighting the war by attrition: 'it pays us anyhow to lose one aircraft for every German machine shot down'.[36]

The challenge facing Churchill and Roosevelt was how to use this superior power in the most effective way to achieve victory as quickly as possible. (Stalin was rarely consulted; the Soviet Union was left to fight the huge battles on the eastern front as almost a separate war.) Making, and keeping to, decisions about the type of war to be fought was vital. The war effort would involve decisions about the relative priorities to be given to the production of different types of weapons and equipment, the movement of hundreds of thousands of men around the globe, the use of vast quantities of shipping and the construction of huge bases and support facilities. Given the scale and complexity of these operations, it was not possible to change course rapidly. Once a strategy was decided, it had to be followed decisively otherwise chaos and waste would result and the war would be prolonged unnecessarily. Even though the allies had a stunning material superiority, this could be neutered by poor decision taking.

The vague, outline agreements over Anglo-American strategy made at Washington in January – Germany as the first priority and a possible landing in French North Africa – still needed to be built into a planned programme that would provide the framework for the build up of American forces and their deployment. In March the idea of an early attack on French North Africa (codenamed GYM-

NAST) was abandoned by Roosevelt and Churchill because the necessary forces and supplies could not be found. Meanwhile the US military were deciding on their preferred strategy. There was a split between the Navy that advocated primacy for the Pacific (where they would be dominant) and the Army and Air Force, which wanted priority for Europe. The US joint chiefs of staff were concerned that the dispersal of forces would lead to ineffective operations and that the Soviet Union would be defeated, making an Anglo-American invasion of the continent almost impossible. By the end of March they had agreed on the way forward. Although some diversion of effort to the Pacific was accepted to keep the Navy happy, they planned to concentrate their efforts on a build up of forces in Britain (codename BOLERO) for a cross-channel invasion (codename ROUNDUP) in the spring of 1943. This would involve thirty US and eighteen British divisions supported by nearly 6,000 aircraft. In 1942 activities would be limited while this force was assembled and trained but a five division attack on western Europe (probably in the Cotentin peninsula) was a possibility if the Germans showed signs of collapsing or the Soviets were on the point of defeat (codename SLEDGEHAMMER).

The plan was approved by Roosevelt as a way of winning the war on American terms. But it was also the best military option. An invasion of north-west Europe would open the shortest route to Germany (in particular the Ruhr) and enable existing British bases to be used to obtain air supremacy. The Atlantic route from the United States to Britain was also the shortest and there were adequate ports to cope with the influx of men and equipment. And this route would still have to be kept open and defended even if an invasion took place elsewhere. On 2 April Roosevelt told Churchill that Hopkins and General Marshall were flying to Britain to outline the plan. The Americans were convinced that the British Premier was in such a weak position politically that he would not, as Hopkins put it, 'dare do anything but go along with us'.[37] On 12 April Churchill informed the President that he and the chiefs of staff approved the American proposals. As he told the chiefs of staff, 'The conception underlying it accorded with the classic principles of war – namely concentration against the main enemy. One broad reservation must however be made – it was essential to carry on the defence of India and the Middle East.'[38] Since the Americans were not proposing that Britain should not defend either India or the Middle East, Churchill's reservation did not invalidate the plan. Indeed the presence of an increasing number of American troops in Britain would remove any lingering fears of an invasion and give the British scope to deploy more troops overseas.

Consideration of Anglo-American strategy then became entangled with Soviet political demands and their desire for a second front to make the Germans move some of their forces from the eastern front. At the end of 1941 Stalin insisted that the British should discuss war aims and the post-war settlement. Eden went to Moscow but he was told not to discuss these subjects. Churchill was opposed to any concessions because, as he told Attlee, the Soviets 'have got to go on fighting for their lives anyway' and they were dependent on British and American supplies (the latter point was not correct).[39] At his first meeting with Stalin, Eden was presented with a draft agreement providing for recognition of the 1941 frontiers of the Soviet Union (involving the incorporation of Latvia, Estonia and Lithuania together with the gains made in the war with Finland in 1939–40). Even more difficult for the British, his proposals entailed a major extension of the Soviet Union westward into the territory of Britain's ally Poland, effectively recognising the border agreed in the Nazi-Soviet pact of August 1939 and achieved a month later. Poland was to be compensated by being given East Prussia. Stalin made it clear to Eden that recognition of the 1941 frontiers was the main issue of the war as far as the Soviet Union was concerned.

Eden refused to embark on detailed discussions until he had consulted his colleagues. On his return he argued that Britain had little choice but to accept these demands in return for Soviet concessions on post-war policy. He felt the matter would be a *fait accompli* anyway: 'It must in any case be borne in mind that we shall not be able to affect the issue at the end of the war by anything we do or say or refuse to say.'[40] When he put this pragmatic view to Churchill, he was given a long lecture on morality in international affairs. Churchill, who in 1939 had welcomed the Soviet move into Poland, told him that the 1941 frontiers 'were acquired by acts of aggression in shameful collusion with Hitler. The transfer of the peoples of the Baltic states to Soviet Russia against their will would be contrary to all the principles for which we are fighting this war and would dishonour our cause. This also applies to Bessarabia and to Northern

Bukhovina and in a lesser degree to Finland.' Britain should stand by the Atlantic Charter and could make this stand because at the end of the war Britain and the United States 'will be the most powerfully armed and economic block the world has ever seen, and . . . the Soviet Union will need our aid for reconstruction'. Churchill impressed upon Eden that he and Britain adhered 'to the principles of freedom and democracy set forth in the Atlantic Charter and . . . these principles must become especially active whenever any question of transferring territory is raised . . . all questions of territorial frontiers must be left to the decision of the Peace Conference'.[41]

The Cabinet first discussed the issue on 6 February and was badly divided. Beaverbrook was strongly in favour of accepting Soviet demands, whereas Attlee equally strongly opposed them. Churchill, who wanted to put off all decisions until after the war, suggested a 'compromise' of consulting the United States; he knew that Roosevelt, with a large number of east European immigrants in the country, was firmly opposed to accepting Soviet demands. A month later Churchill made a complete volte face over everything in his lecture to Eden. He now wrote to Roosevelt, 'The increasing gravity of the war has led me to feel that the principles of the Atlantic Charter ought not to be constructed so as to deny Russia the frontiers she occupied when Germany attacked her.'[42] All the fine words about such action being 'contrary to all the principles for which we are fighting this war' and the 'dishonour' to our cause were forgotten. It was impossible to construct the principles of freedom and democracy set forth in the Atlantic Charter so as to make them compatible with the recognition of the 1941 Soviet frontiers.

Beaverbrook, who had just resigned from the Cabinet, was sent to Washington with Churchill's private approval to try to secure Roosevelt's agreement to these second thoughts. He failed and Roosevelt never formally responded. On 24 March the Cabinet agreed to go ahead and recognise the 1941 frontiers without American consent and on this basis Stalin allowed Molotov, the Soviet Foreign Minister, to travel to London. Before he arrived the Government came under pressure not to concede on the frontiers question. A revolt was brewing among Conservative backbenchers; Lord Simon, the Lord Chancellor, was threatening not to support the proposals in the House of Lords and Duff Cooper, the Minister of Information, was taking the same line. Churchill, recognising the weakness of his position after Singapore and the Government reconstruction in February, told Eden, 'I do not want to face a bunch of resignations.'[43] He now made another volte face and reverted to the line he had originally taken with Eden in January.

When the talks with Molotov started on 21 May the Government was in a difficult position. The Soviets wanted a settlement on the frontier question. They also wanted a commitment to a second front. Their winter counter-attack against the Germans had been only partially successful, mainly because it was not concentrated on one part of the front. With the summer campaigning season approaching they faced another onslaught from the full weight of the German Army. The British did not now want to commit themselves on either subject. Eden proposed instead a twenty year mutual assistance pact and an agreement on no separate peace but no frontier settlement. Molotov rejected this, but then Winant, the US Ambassador in London, intervened. He too wanted to avoid any frontier agreement but he hinted that when Molotov visited Washington after leaving London Roosevelt would agree to a second front. On this basis, much to the relief of the Government, Molotov accepted Eden's proposals.

In Washington, Roosevelt, who had tried in April to meet Stalin without Churchill but had been rejected by the Soviet leader, gave Molotov a fairly firm commitment on the second front without consulting the British. The communiqué issued after their talks stated: 'In the course of the conversations full understanding was reached with regard to the urgent tasks of creating a second front in Europe in 1942.' Roosevelt had achieved his aims – a non-territorial British-Soviet treaty that enabled him to keep the initiative in allied diplomacy and a pledge on a second front without consulting the more reluctant British. When Molotov returned to London the British Government could do nothing else but give him a similar commitment to the Americans. In practice they were rapidly losing what little enthusiasm they ever had for an attack on the continent in 1942. Churchill told the Cabinet on 11 June that all he intended with his commitment to the Soviets was 'a small hit and run operation'.[44]

Before Molotov returned from Washington the British had turned against one element of the American proposals they had accepted in April – SLEDGEHAMMER, the possible small-scale invasion of Europe in 1942. They were in a strong position since the majority of troops for the operation would be British. But since the Americans had never looked on SLEDGEHAMMER as anything more than a contingency plan to be implemented if Germany suddenly collapsed or if the attack on the Soviet Union succeeded, it is difficult to see why the British were so opposed to planning going ahead. The reasons were undoubtedly complex. First, there was a strong feeling that the Soviets might indeed collapse. Second, there were fears that SLEDGEHAMMER was likely to be ineffective given the level of German forces in France and would almost inevitably lead to either the capture or evacuation of the allied forces. Third, Churchill himself, given his weak political position and need for some military success, could not face another British military failure. He wanted an attack on northern Norway (codename JUPITER) but the chiefs of staff were even more strongly opposed to this idea than to SLEDGEHAMMER.

On 28 May Churchill informed Roosevelt of his doubts about SLEDGEHAMMER and raised the idea of JUPITER and a revival of GYMNAST (the invasion of French North Africa). (It was after receiving this message that Roosevelt gave Molotov the commitment on the second front.) In early June Lord Mountbatten (son of Prince Louis of Battenberg, who had resigned as First Sea Lord in the autumn of 1914), the Head of Combined Operations, was sent to Washington to explain British hesitations to Roosevelt. The President had already decided that he wanted to discuss the situation with Churchill and asked him to come to the United States. On 17 June Churchill, together with the chiefs of staff, crossed the Atlantic in a luxurious converted flying boat.

The recommendations that emerged from a meeting of the combined chiefs of staff on 19–20 June were clear. The build up of forces in Britain for the cross-channel invasion in 1943 (BOLERO) was the top priority. Nothing should be done in 1942 that would damage that plan and other operations should be envisaged only if there was a great emergency (the collapse of the Soviet Union) or a great opportunity (the collapse of Germany). If action was required in 1942, SLEDGEHAMMER or JUPITER were the preferred operations. They were agreed that 'GYMNAST should not be undertaken under the existing situation'.[45] However the politicians had other ideas. By the time of his visit Churchill knew that British forces were in full retreat in the desert (Tobruk fell on 20 June) and there was a major political crisis looming – after two years of almost unbroken military failure he desperately needed a political success. His favoured option was an invasion of French North Africa. This would encounter no German troops but it could, by threatening the supply lines of the German forces in Egypt, make them retreat, thereby ensuring that Britain at last won the desert war. Roosevelt too was facing Congressional elections in November, after nearly a year of war, and wanted American forces in action somewhere in the European or at least the Mediterranean theatre by then. There was also the need to do something in order to appease the Soviet Union after the promises that had just been given.

Churchill and Roosevelt met at the President's home at Hyde Park in upstate New York away from their chiefs of staff. It was Churchill who took the initiative, writing to Roosevelt on 20 June: 'Ought we not to be preparing within the general structure of "Bolero" some other operation by which we may gain position of advantage and also directly or indirectly to take some of the weight off Russia. It is in this setting and on this background that the operation "Gymnast" should be studied.'[46] The two men had a long discussion, which produced the first stage of an agreement that was to wreck the clear Anglo-American strategy agreed earlier in the year. They agreed to continue with BOLERO (the pre-invasion build-up in Britain) until the beginning of September but nullified that agreement by stating that it was essential for both countries to act offensively in 1942. If SLEDGEHAMMER seemed unlikely to take place then GYMNAST was their preferred option. This reversed the chiefs of staff view that no action was preferable to GYMNAST, and it meant, with SLEDGEHAMMER facing strong opposition, that the two politicians had virtually committed themselves to an invasion of French North Africa.

The military were left to pick up the pieces from the Washington meeting. The British chiefs of staff immediately advised Churchill that if French North Africa was invaded in 1942, a cross-channel invasion in 1943 would not be possible because of the large scale diversion of forces involved and the impossibility of bringing them back to Britain in time. Their fully worked-out advice spelled out the implications: 'It is fairly certain that we cannot carry out "Gymnast" and "Roundup" within twelve months of each other. A properly executed "Gymnast" in fact must be regarded as an *alternative* and not in *addition* to "Roundup".'[47] Churchill refused to accept this advice and told his advisers to conceal their conclusions from the Americans. It made no difference because the American joint chiefs of staff reached the identical conclusion on their own. They told Roosevelt that GYMNAST 'will definitely curtail if not make impossible the execution of "Bolero-Roundup" in the spring of 1943. We are strongly of the opinion that "Gymnast" would be both indecisive and a heavy drain on our resources, and that if we undertake it, we would nowhere be acting decisively against the enemy.'[48]

With justification, the American joint chiefs regarded the political decisions made at Washington in June 1942 as unscrambling the policy accepted since 1940 of 'Germany First'. General Marshall recommended to Roosevelt that if GYMNAST went ahead then the United States should 'assume a defensive attitude against Germany ... and use all available means in the Pacific'.[49] In fact limited diversions to the Pacific were already underway after the US Navy's success at the Battle of Midway. Roosevelt did not, however, accept the revised military advice, and he sent Marshall, together with the Navy chief Admiral King and Harry Hopkins, to London to reach final agreement with the British on the choice of operations. Their remit was that US forces had to be in action in 1942; to this end they were to investigate SLEDGEHAMMER but if that was not possible they were to accept GYMNAST. The British had already ruled out SLEDGEHAMMER, so Roosevelt was virtually instructing them to accept GYMNAST. Churchill clung to his view that GYMNAST did not rule out ROUNDUP in 1943 – both should proceed at full pace. On 20–22 July during long talks with the American delegation he insisted that SLEDGEHAMMER was not acceptable. On 22 July Roosevelt was told of the position and instructed his advisers to agree to an invasion of French North Africa in 1942 (now renamed TORCH).

By July 1942 the clear strategy agreed in April had been discarded. Britain and the United States were now committed to major action in a secondary theatre that would lead to a massive dispersal of effort and rule out a decisive campaign to defeat Germany in 1943. The implications of the decision taken by Roosevelt and Churchill for the future conduct of the war against Germany were spelled out by the combined chiefs of staff at the London conference: the invasion of

North Africa 'renders ROUNDUP in all probability impracticable of successful execution in 1943 and therefore we have definitely accepted a defensive, encircling line of action for the Continental European Theater, except as to air operations and blockade'.[50] Churchill, at the time and afterwards, would not accept that the decision he was taking did postpone an early invasion of the continent. At the London conference he had alarmed the American delegation by talking about an invasion of Sicily and Italy and, on the same day as the combined chiefs of staff gave their judgement on his decision, flatly contradicting the military advice, he told the Cabinet that Europe could be invaded from both south and north in 1943. This view was symptomatic of Churchill's refusal to accept the problems involved in waging a complex war and the fact that huge numbers of men and large amounts of equipment could not be shifted rapidly from one theatre to another. As had become evident in his earlier approach to military campaigns, for example Norway, he heartily disliked the discipline of making a strategy and sticking to it. As he told General Brooke, 'I do not want any of your long-term policies, they only cripple initiative.'[51] It was also another example of his faculty for reaching utterly contradictory positions. In April he had originally accepted the proposal to concentrate on a continental invasion in 1943 as being in accordance with the 'classic principles' of concentrating on the defeat of the main enemy. Now he had adopted a strategy that meant diffusion of effort and postponement by a year of the main US-UK operation to defeat Germany.

After July 1942 US production and planning was based on no cross-Channel invasion in 1943 and there was a large diversion of equipment to the Pacific and Mediterranean. Fifteen groups of US aircraft were diverted from Europe to the Pacific and half of the squadrons that were in Britain were eventually sent to North Africa. By the end of 1942 the level of US forces in the Pacific was twice that intended at the beginning of the year and equal to those facing Germany. Before the decisions taken in July the US planned to have 540,000 troops in Britain by the end of 1942 ready for a cross-Channel invasion; in practice after the diversions to TORCH and the Pacific they had less than 100,000.

Without the change of plan in mid-1942 there is little doubt that a successful invasion of north-west Europe could have been mounted in 1943 rather than in 1944. German war production was only beginning to increase (it reached its peak in 1944) and the Anglo-American forces would have faced both smaller German forces (forty-nine divisions rather than fifty-seven in 1944) and had a greater advantage in tank numbers. The standard of fortifications and obstacles along the French coast would have been lower – they were greatly improved by 1944. The British and Americans would have had air superiority in 1943 (a prolonged period of bombing Germany made little or no difference to output, and German aircraft production reached its peak in 1944). Had there been no diversion of forces to the Pacific after the abandonment of the 1943 invasion, many more landing craft would have been available in Britain. (In May 1944 the US had 31,000 landing craft in the Pacific as against only 2,500 used in the Normandy invasion. Already in 1943 there were enough landing craft to put ashore seven divisions on Sicily during the first wave, the same size force as used in Normandy.) The decisions taken in July 1942, largely under Churchill's influence and against clear warnings from both sets of chiefs of staff about the consequences, ensured that the Anglo-American war effort was not used in the most effective way and meant therefore that the war in Europe lasted longer than it need have done. The consequences, not just in terms of the greater human suffering but also for the post-war settlement, were profound.

While preparations were underway to divert forces to invade French North Africa, Churchill was growing more concerned about the position in Egypt. After the retreat from Tobruk at the end of June British forces fought a month long series of difficult and confused battles around El Alamein that finally stopped Rommel's advance, although their attempt to go over to the offensive in the third week of July (under pressure from Churchill) was a disaster – 23rd Armoured Brigade lost eighty-six of its ninety-seven tanks in a day. But Auchinleck, aided by an increasing flow of accurate Ultra intelligence giving Rommel's exact position, was able to devise a plan for the defence of Egypt. On 25 June Churchill told him 'you have my entire confidence and I share your responsibilities to the full'.[52] In fact he actually wanted to fly out to Egypt himself and change commanders. Brooke was able to dissuade him from this course in early July because the crucial battles for the defence of Egypt were underway. However Churchill remained unconvinced by the abilities of the military commanders. Cadogan reported an instance of his sarcastic disapproval at a Cabinet meeting on 7 July: 'Chiefs of Staff have no ideas and oppose everything. P.M. said, "We'd better put an advertisement in the paper, asking for ideas".'53 Once the initial battles were over and it was clear that Auchinleck had held Rommel, Churchill insisted on flying to Egypt.

The Prime Minister's party had to fly in an unheated US Liberator bomber (the only plane that had the necessary range) with just two shelves to sleep on. Churchill underwent pressure chamber tests before the flight and had a specially designed oxygen mask to enable him to smoke. But it was a tough journey for a sixty-seven-year-old. Churchill and Brooke arrived in Cairo on 3 August and the Prime Minister made it clear he was determined on a radical shake up in the Middle East command structure. He began by offering Auchinleck's job to Brooke, who declined. The TORCH invasion was set for the end of October (just before the Congressional elections) and Churchill was desperate to see a last solely British victory of the war before American power became overwhelming. He visited Auchinleck at his spartan headquarters in the desert (the commander insisted on no luxuries for himself that his troops did not share) and did not appreciate the austerity. He did, however, enjoy the lunch laid on by the RAF who, knowing his proclivities, had taken the trouble to fly up large quantities of food from Cairo.

The next day (6 August) Churchill had long discussions with Brooke over the command. He wanted to cut the Middle East command in half along the line of the Suez Canal and give the eastern part to Auchinleck. (A year earlier when he wanted to get rid of Wavell Churchill had rejected such a division as militarily unsound.) Brooke was to command the western half. The CIGS again rejected the offer and it was agreed that General Alexander should command in the west with General Gott taking charge of the 8th Army and General Montgomery commanding British forces in TORCH. Churchill overrode War Cabinet objections to the plan but had to change course when Gott was killed in an air crash; Montgomery was shifted to the 8th Army. Auchinleck was finally told of his demotion on 8 August.

The other reason for Churchill's visit was his decision to travel to Moscow via Cairo to have a meeting with Stalin. Relations with the Soviet Union were still strained. The Soviets were fighting 178 German divisions and the German offensive, which had opened at the end of June, and was concentrated on the southern part of the front, appeared to be meeting with huge success as they thrust towards the Caucasus and Stalingrad. During the summer Stalin began to suspect that the 'promise' he had been given about the second front was worthless. The Soviets had been given no indication of Anglo-American plans and there was no attempt to reach a joint strategy. The other cause of contention was the Arctic convoys that took supplies to the Soviet Union. Bad misjudgements at the Admiralty resulted in the loss of twenty-three out of the thirty-four ships on the convoy that sailed on 3 June (PQ 17), and the decision by Churchill to abandon the convoys during the months of perpetual daylight meant that nothing would sail before the winter ice made the journey impossible anyway. Mounting Soviet frustration resulted in a vicious telegram from Stalin to Churchill in the last week of July, claiming that the Soviet Union was being abandoned and Britain and the United States were failing to make the necessary effort to fight the Germans. Under pressure Churchill reinstated the September convoy and on 28 July the Ambassador in Moscow, Sir Archibald Clark Kerr, suggested that Churchill should travel to Moscow to try to repair relations.

Churchill arrived in Moscow from Cairo on 12 August, though the rest of his entourage was delayed in Teheran with a defective aircraft. He stayed at Stalin's own dacha and that evening had a three-and-a-half-hour meeting with him at the Kremlin. (He finally shook hands with 'the hairy baboon'.) Churchill told the Soviet leader that there would be no second front that year though there would be an invasion of North Africa and continuous bombing of Germany. Then, despite the clear military advice that an invasion of north-west Europe would not be possible in 1943, he spoke about 'a very great operation' planned for the next year involving up to forty-eight divisions, half of them armoured.[54] By the end of his first, relatively friendly meeting with Stalin, Churchill was convinced that he had persuaded him that the Anglo-American plans were the only ones possible.

The next day he was subjected to the usual Soviet tactics at such meetings (Eden had found the same nine months earlier) – the Soviet representatives now became much tougher. Churchill met Molotov on the morning of 13 August in a less friendly atmosphere and little progress was made. Then he received a note from Stalin complaining that Britain and the United States were going back on the promises made earlier in the year ('the urgent tasks of creating a second front in Europe in 1942'). That evening he had a second meeting with Stalin, which he described as 'a most unpleasant discussion', not helped by very poor translation.[55] Stalin said that neither TORCH nor the level of supplies was adequate, and claimed that Britain was frightened of Germany and not doing its fair share of the fighting. In a rage Churchill told Stalin that he and Roosevelt had made up their minds and were not open to Soviet pressure. The meeting broke up with the arguments unresolved at 1am.

Churchill, still in a foul temper, spent the morning of 14 August at the dacha. Clark Kerr wrote in his diary: 'at Luncheon the P.M. was at his bloody worst and his worst is really bloody'.[56] He slept in the afternoon and then to the disgust of the Soviet leaders turned up to a formal dinner at the Kremlin wearing one of his one-piece 'siren suits' that resembled overalls. Throughout the dinner the British were rude to their hosts. Their condescending attitude is well encapsulated in the diary of Ian Jacob, the military head of the Cabinet Secretariat, who described his reaction to the Soviet leader: 'it was extraordinary to see this little peasant, who would not have looked at all out of place in a country lane with a pickaxe over his shoulder, calmly sitting down to a banquet in these magnificent halls'.[57] At 1.30 Churchill stormed out of the Kremlin, refusing Stalin's suggestion to watch a film. He was determined to leave the next day without seeing the Soviet leader again. He felt Stalin's refusal to go along with Anglo-American decisions (which left the Soviet Union doing all the real fighting for at least another year) as a personal insult: 'Did he not realise who he was speaking to? The representative of the most powerful empire the world has ever seen?'[58]

The next morning Churchill was convinced Stalin was deliberately trying to make the visit a failure in order to bring down his government. Clark Kerr finally persuaded him not to leave. At lunch Churchill defended government by the aristocracy and denounced the 'pedlars of Brummagum and the filthy iron works from which the Baldwins had made their money'.[59] When he went to see Stalin at 7pm, he found the Soviet leader decidedly grumpy after the British behaviour the previous evening. Eventually the mood mellowed and the two leaders settled down to a gargantuan banquet of suckling pigs, chickens, beef, mutton, fish and a range of desserts and fruit. Nothing more was decided but the atmosphere was better. Churchill returned to the dacha at 3am, undressed in front of his entourage and told his doctor, 'I was taken into the family, we ended friends.'[60] Clark Kerr's powers of persuasion had avoided a major breach in relations. The Soviet leadership remained unhappy about Anglo-American strategy but they knew their ability to influence it was very limited and meanwhile they had to go on fighting the overwhelming mass of the German Army and Air Force. It is difficult to see how the visit substantially improved relations, although personal contacts had been opened. Churchill was certainly over-optimistic if he felt he had become Stalin's friend. But he came away with a reasonably favourable impression of Stalin. He told the Cabinet on his return he had 'formed the highest opinion of his sagacity'.[61]

Throughout 1942 there were still difficult issues of priority to be decided about the bomber offensive and the Battle of the Atlantic, where problems were mounting. Between January and June U-boats sank over 3 million tons of shipping in the Atlantic, much of it off the eastern coast of the United States and in the Caribbean, where the Americans were very slow to introduce a convoy system. Then the U-boats exploited two major gaps in allied air cover near Greenland and the Azores. The addition of a fourth wheel to their Enigma machines made codebreaking much more difficult (the allies had to rely mainly on direction finding) and the Germans were reading about eighty per cent of allied convoy signal traffic. Altogether in 1942 Britain and the United States lost 7.8 million tons of merchant shipping, slightly more than they were able to build.

Churchill was still not prepared to give this battle a higher priority than the bombing campaign. He issued instructions that Bomber Command was to have priority for the new centimetric radar sets rather than Coastal Command which was responsible for anti-submarine operations. In June the latter's aircraft were diverted to the 1,000-bomber raid on Cologne (carried out partly for publicity reasons). Churchill intervened personally with the Admiralty: 'it will be necessary that Coastal Command should participate, and I must ask definitely for compliance with this request'.[62] He also refused to increase Coastal Command's resources (they needed about forty very long-range Liberators to close the air gaps). In July he told the

Admiralty that Coastal Command was highly inefficient and until that was put right 'there can be no case for transferring additional squadrons from Bomber to Coastal Command'.[63] He also objected to diverting bombers to patrols over the U-boat transit routes. He told Admiral Pound in August that such operations did not justify 'inroads on our Bomber resources'[64] and that 'You must not trench so heavily on the reserves of the RAF'.[65] In September he transferred two squadrons from Coastal to Bomber Command.

Because of the high level of sinkings a major supply crisis arrived that winter. In January 1943 British imports were down to half the level of January 1940 and half of the British consumption of raw materials came from stockpiles. Nevertheless Churchill continued to give priority to bombing. In October 1942 during a review of policy for the conduct of the war he described the U-boat attacks as 'the greatest danger to the United Nations, and particularly to our Island'. But any extra aircraft were to come from the United States and not be provided at the expense of the bombing campaign. He concluded: 'At present, in spite of U-boat losses, the Bomber offensive should have first place in our effort.'[66]

Churchill's determination to keep up the bomber offensive might have been justified if it had been producing more tangible results – in fact throughout 1942 the campaign was hardly more successful than in 1941. Even after the introduction of 'Gee', which provided a navigation aid to inland areas, less than a third of the bombers were attacking the target, let alone hitting it. In May a study showed that less than a quarter of the bombs dropped on an urban target fell within five miles and only a third even hit the urban area. Because of these limitations the RAF were following a policy of bombing German cities. When a new directive was issued in February 1942 the Chief of the Air Staff commented, 'it is clear that the aiming points are to be the built-up areas, not, for instance, the dockyards or aircraft factories'.[67] In October the Air Ministry instructions attempted to draw an important distinction. In occupied allied territory bombing was 'confined to military objectives' and the 'intentional bombardment of civilian populations, as such, is forbidden'. However 'the foregoing rules do not . . . apply to our conduct of air warfare against German, Italian and Japanese territory'.[68] In public the Government lied about its policy. For example, the

Secretary of State for Air, Sinclair, told the Commons in March 1943, 'The targets of Bomber Command are always military.'

The limited results to be gained from the campaign were clearly pointed out at the time. In April 1942, after a row between Lindemann and Tizard about what could be expected from bombing, the Cabinet appointed an enquiry under Justice Singleton to advise on what might be expected over the next eighteen months. His conclusions were: 'I do not think it [the bomber offensive] ought to be regarded *as of itself* sufficient to win the war or to produce decisive results; the area is too vast for the effort we can put forth.'[69] Within two months of the report Churchill upheld the opposite view, telling the Cabinet:

> it would be a mistake to cast aside our original thought . . . that the severe, ruthless bombing of Germany on an ever-increasing scale will not only cripple her war effort, including U-boat and aircraft production, but will also create conditions intolerable to the mass of the German population.[70]

Although he approved the large-scale bombing of German civilians he did not think that such bombing would 'produce decisive results in the next twelve months'.[71]

After his visit to Moscow he felt that bombing German cities was probably the only way of demonstrating to the Soviet Union that Britain was attacking Germany. He wanted to see an expansion of almost sixty per cent in the bomber force, from thirty-two squadrons to fifty, by the end of the year (including taking two from Coastal Command and retaining half the bombers due to go to the Middle East) and he called for a greater use of incendiary bombs to attack city centres. The Chief of the Air Staff briefed him on the implications: 'Apart from its major purpose, I think it will have the effect of spreading alarm and despondency over a much larger proportion of the German people.' Churchill wrote in the margin 'Good'.[72]

The decision to invade French North Africa raised acute problems for the British and Americans about how to deal with De Gaulle, the Free French and the Vichy Government, which still controlled Morocco, Algeria and Tunisia. Churchill's relations with De Gaulle during 1942 were, like the previous year, marked by acrimonious rows interspersed with shorter periods of calm. During a row in January over the Free French occupation of the Vichy-controlled colony of St Pierre et Miquelon off Newfoundland, Churchill wrote of 'the hope, which has since proved false, that de Gaulle would be able to rally an impressive number of Frenchmen'.[73] Privately he spoke to Eden of De Gaulle's 'want of faith for the cause of the United Nations' and the need, once again, to raise the question of his personal power.[74] To the American Chargé d'Affaires in London he spoke of De Gaulle as 'the real problem' in the Free French movement and said he was 'quite disappointed in him'.[75]

De Gaulle was pressing for an operation to take control of the important Vichy French colony of Madagascar. Ignoring the Free French, the British mounted their own attack (because of American sensitivities) at the beginning of May 1942; the aim of intervention was to avoid any collaboration between Vichy and the Japanese who were operating in the Indian Ocean. But the invasion did not go well. After heavy Vichy resistance the British only gained control of the key port of Diego Suarez. They did not attempt to take over the rest of the island and instead did a deal with the Vichy authorities. Churchill was personally keen on this deal, telling Eden later that the Governor, Armand Annet, was 'quite a good chap: Clemmie met him on a train somewhere once'.[76] De Gaulle was, naturally, outraged and talked of removing the Free French movement to the Soviet Union. Churchill had forestalled any such move by imposing another travel ban on him. He told Eden, who opposed the ban: 'I think it would be most dangerous to let this man begin again his campaign of Anglophobia ... which he is now more than ever attracted to.'[77] And again six weeks later: 'There is nothing hostile to England this man may not do once he gets off the chain.'[78]

Relations between the two men temporarily improved in early June after the strong fight put up by Free French forces in the desert campaign and at the end of July Churchill lifted the travel ban and allowed De Gaulle to visit a number of French colonies. But almost immediately there was another row over British policy in Syria (supporting the Arabs against the French) and more ill feeling over some of De Gaulle's comments during his tour. Churchill refused to allow him to visit Madagascar, telling Eden: 'I think it a great mistake to let de Gaulle into Madagascar, which he will only use as another field for anti-British activities' and said that he was determined to deal with his 'recent misbehaviour'.[79]

He did so at a meeting with De Gaulle on 30 September, which began with a long row over Syria and then moved on to differences over Madagascar. When De Gaulle protested that British actions called into question the collaboration between France and Britain, Churchill corrected him, saying: 'between General de Gaulle and England ... General de Gaulle was not France, but Fighting France'. After that deliberately belittling remark the atmosphere deteriorated. In a long harangue Churchill berated the Free French leader:

> There were other parts and aspects of France which might become more prominent ... General de Gaulle was his own worst enemy. [He] had hoped to work with him ... great difficulty lay in working with General de Gaulle ... he could not regard him as a comrade or a friend ... The General stood in the way of closer association ... Things could not go on as they were ... the General ... had lost a great deal ... he had made great mistakes ... he had not helped us at all. Instead of waging war with Germany, he had waged war with England. This was a great mistake. He had not shown the slightest desire to assist us, and he himself had been the main obstacle to effective collaboration with Britain and America.[80]

The meeting broke up in great acrimony. Afterwards Churchill decided that relations with De Gaulle were suspended; all Free French communications were cut and intelligence co-operation was banned. This was a deliberate policy on Churchill's part – he was preparing the way to cast aside the Free French and do a deal with the Vichy authorities in French North Africa when the Anglo-American forces invaded. In this he was following American policy.

When the United States joined the war they did not break off relations with Pétain's Government. Soon after American entry Churchill wanted to make another effort to reach an agreement with the Vichy Government – on terms which fell well short of their rejoining the war. He told the Cabinet on 12 December 1941 'the time might shortly come when we should say to the Vichy French Government that if they would stand with us in maintaining the independence and integrity of North Africa, we would do our best to restore their Empire. But if they failed us at this point we should have nothing more to do with them.'[81] At the same time Admiral Darlan made secret approaches to enquire whether the British would refuse to do a deal with him because of his past record. Churchill responded that if he sailed the French fleet to North Africa he would have 'an honourable place in the Allied ranks'.[82]

That remark typified Churchill's general views about Vichy, which were at variance with the Government's public line of distaste for the collaborators and support for the Free French. Throughout 1942 he was far more sympathetic towards Vichy than Eden and was quite happy to envisage coming to an agreement. He strongly supported the retention of Canadian and South African representatives in Vichy against the advice of the Foreign Office and despite the reluctance of the two governments concerned. When Pierre Laval, the arch pro-German, gained power in April 1942, the two dominion Governments broke relations and the United States withdrew its Ambassador while retaining the rest of its mission. During a major row with Eden in June Churchill was still prepared to defend Vichy against claims that it was a collaborationist government. He advanced the extraordinary argument that it had not 'done anything more than was absolutely necessary to stave off' full German occupation. He went on, 'we ought not to forget that it is the only government which may perhaps give us what we want from France, namely the Toulon fleet and the entry into the French North African provinces'. He thought the chances of this were 'not ... entirely negligible' and he still expected them to come over to the allied side.[83] This provoked a strong response from the Foreign Secretary but Churchill replied that he had 'a certain instinct' about France on which he relied and felt that Eden was not sympathetic enough to the Vichy dilemma. He concluded, 'There is much more in British policy towards France than abusing Pétain and backing de Gaulle' and forced Eden to withdraw a pro-De Gaulle paper before it was considered by the Cabinet.[84]

The scenario for Operation TORCH was for American and British troops (primarily the former) to land in French North Africa and take over the French colonies still under Vichy control. Britain had been obliged to concede the initiative to the United States over both the military aspects (where to land) and the political aspects (how to handle the Vichy regime). The British argued for landings as far east as possible in Tunisia as a way of moving on to Tripoli in the Italian colony of Libya and cutting supplies to Rommel's forces inside Egypt. Roosevelt wanted the easier option of landing far to the west at Casablanca and Oran. Only reluctantly did the Americans agree to an extra landing near Algiers. On the political front the Americans used their contacts with Vichy, notably Roosevelt's emissary Robert Murphy (who was particularly sympathetic to right-wing groups), to work out a deal with various elements in North Africa to ease the path of the invasion by minimising the risk of Vichy resistance.

The British were fully aware of American activities and Churchill was given detailed reports from the American agents sent to various Vichy officials on the chances of securing Vichy co-operation. One of the main aims of TORCH for the British was to bring over Vichy to the allied side, leave them in control of French affairs and provide an excuse for finally getting rid of De Gaulle altogether. Churchill's brief for his meeting with De Gaulle on 30 September stated:

> It is agreed between us and the Americans that de Gaulle will not participate in 'Torch' and will have no share in the administration of the territory ... If the French in North Africa join the war against the Axis, the importance of de Gaulle will diminish and he may coalesce with the larger body of dissident Frenchmen in North Africa. We should encourage this.[85]

The Americans were particularly keen to work with Admiral Darlan, the Commander of the French Navy and a minister in the Vichy Government, whom Churchill had refused to trust in 1940. The United States was also relying on General Giraud, whom they had smuggled out of France, to take overall command in French North Africa. He was installed alongside General Eisenhower, the Allied Commander-in-Chief, at Gibraltar. On 17 October (three weeks before the invasion) there was a meeting at No 10 to discuss the role Vichy would play during the landings. (Churchill omits all reference to this meeting in his memoirs.) The British and Americans agreed that Darlan should be brought into their planning (as deputy to Giraud, who had the support of most of those in North Africa working with the Americans) and that he could, if necessary, play a prominent role after the operation. The Free French and De Gaulle were totally excluded from the planning and from the post-invasion scenario.

The landings in French North Africa took place on 8 November. There was some resistance from Vichy forces at first but Darlan, who had gone to North Africa three days before, was able to organise the surrender of Algiers and issue orders for a general ceasefire. Giraud remained ineffectually at Gibraltar. Darlan's actions made the military side of the operation go smoothly but within days he was de facto head of the French Government in North Africa with the consent of Vichy. The allies, as their troops gradually took control of French North Africa, found themselves actively working with him and other Vichy officials who stayed in power even though many pro-allied Frenchmen remained in jail.

Operation TORCH was injected into Anglo-American planning for no other reason than to provide a demonstration of military capability and to allow hard-pressed leaders to notch up a victory. But it was a curious victory. The first Anglo-American military action of the war in Europe and the Mediterranean had been, not to attack Germany or Italy, but to invade the territory of an ex-ally, of a Government which the United States still recognised as the legitimate Government of France. Not only that, they had then done a deal to keep in power men whom most of the public despised as collaborators.

Within days Churchill faced a storm of opposition: protests came from Parliament, the press, the Labour Party, other governments-in-exile, De Gaulle and the Soviet Union. If this was allied policy, what would happen, they asked, when other countries were liberated? Faced with this hostile reception Churchill suffered from a bout of selective amnesia about his acceptance of the idea of dealing with Vichy, discarding De Gaulle and the meeting on 17 October at which he had approved bringing Darlan into the operation. He started blaming the Americans in public. In private he went along with their decisions. On 22 November Eisenhower signed a full-scale deal with Darlan, which recognised him as 'High Commissioner'. Churchill tried to pretend that this did not equate with diplomatic recognition, but Eden was worried: 'I cannot get W to see the damage Darlan may do the Allied cause if we don't watch it'.[86] Churchill consoled himself with the thought that 'D had done more for us than de G'.[87]

Churchill may not have anticipated the extent of public hostility, but he knew enough of De Gaulle to expect outrage. He gave the general lunch on the day of the invasion and tried to lay the blame on the United States. He said that De Gaulle and the National Committee were the only body recognised by Britain (which was technically true) but then expressed his hope for French unity, which would have suggested to De Gaulle that he was expected to compromise and accept a lesser position in the future. At another meeting a week later, as protests mounted, he tried to reassure De Gaulle that the arrangements with Darlan were only temporary. Meanwhile he told Roosevelt that De Gaulle should get 'a fair deal' but not control of French forces.[88] He also expressed the hope that Darlan would only be a 'temporary expedient'.[89] Luckily for the allies that was what he turned out to be.

Darlan was assassinated on Christmas Eve by people believed to be royalist supporters of the Comte de Paris. The assassins were executed within two days and Darlan was replaced by the allies' favoured candidate, Giraud. It was all very convenient for the British and the Americans that Darlan was disposed of once his immediate usefulness was over. Who was behind the plot has never been discovered, though Cadogan, the head of the Foreign Office (with responsibility for the Secret Intelligence Service), wrote in his diary six weeks before the shooting, 'we shall do no good till we've killed Darlan'.[90] Churchill ended the year with another violent denunciation of De Gaulle in a secret session of the Commons held to debate allied policy in North Africa. Once again Churchill implied the problems were all the fault of the Americans. He rehearsed all the complaints of the previous two years and said of De Gaulle: 'We have never recognised him as representing France ... We have never agreed that he and those associated with him, because they were right and brave at the moment of French surrender, have a monopoly on the future of France.'

Churchill was in a strong position to resist criticisms of the policy adopted in French North Africa because at last he had had a military success. In retrospect he always regarded the early autumn of 1942, the period before TORCH and the final battle of El Alamein, as his most difficult time politically. The criticisms voiced at the time of the fall of Singapore and later Tobruk had only been temporarily silenced by the vote of confidence in the summer. Only half the country was satisfied with the conduct of the war and it seemed likely that Churchill might not survive another military reverse. Certainly Stafford Cripps was busy establishing his position as the man most likely to take advantage of such a situation. Cripps put forward numerous schemes for the reform of the Government and was on the verge of resignation. Aware of the threat to his future, Churchill was described as being 'in a great state of anger, rolling out threats and invectives against C and declaring it was a conspiracy'.[91] Eventually Cripps was persuaded by Attlee to withhold his resignation until after TORCH and Montgomery's attack. If these failed, he would be in a strong position to exploit the likely wave of discontent against Churchill's direction of the war.

A great deal was therefore riding on the British attack on Rommel, fixed for just before the landings in Algeria and Morocco – the last chance for a purely British offensive. For the attack at El Alamein, the British were able to benefit from the long build-up of men and equipment. They had 220,000 men against 96,000 (only half of whom were German), a superiority of 4:1 in tanks and artillery (and a reserve of 1,200 tanks against the Germans' twenty-two) as well as air superiority. The plan drawn up by Montgomery to use this overwhelming strength was a crude frontal assault that showed none of Rommel's flair and subtlety. The result was that the seriously misnamed 'Operation Lightfoot' turned into a slogging match in which British casualties were, proportionately, as high as on the Somme. In the battle which began on 23 October the British lost six times more men killed and wounded than the Germans and Italians and over 600 tanks compared with the enemy's 180. For days Montgomery was stuck, unable to batter his way through, causing Churchill to shout at Brooke, 'Haven't we got a single general who can even win one battle?'[92]

Eventually, just before TORCH, British forces managed to break through. Rommel was reduced to an average tank strength of twenty (by the beginning of December he had only twelve operational), his ammunition and fuel were running low, most of his anti-tank weapons were lost and he had little air cover. He began a steady retreat westwards. It was at this point that Montgomery demonstrated a complete lack of imagination and tactical skill. Although

Ultra gave him a virtually complete picture of Rommel's overwhelm-ing weakness, he was unable to inflict a decisive defeat on a hopelessly outclassed opponent. His 'pursuit' of Rommel was con-ducted with excessive caution: he regularly stopped the British advance and sacked commanders who went too far too fast. Never-theless the British victory at El Alamein was greeted with relief and rejoicing after two and a half years of bad news. In terms of military importance, the achievement was dwarfed by the success of the massive Soviet counter-attack at Stalingrad, which began on 19 November and soon resulted in the German 6th Army being surrounded – a clear sign that the tide of war was at last turning in favour of the allies. With military success Churchill was no longer under political threat and his leadership was not to be in question for the rest of the war. He now felt secure enough to demote Cripps from the War Cabinet to Minister of Aircraft Production on 23 November and at the same time Eden took on the time-consuming job of being Leader of the Commons as well as Foreign Secretary. Nevertheless the weakness of the Prime Minister's position during 1942 had been very real. One Labour minister, Chuter-Ede, com-mented in his diary at the end of the year: 'Had anyone seen an alternative to Churchill the Government would have fallen.'[93]

Although Churchill's political position was now assured and British forces had at last achieved a significant victory, Anglo-American strategy lay in ruins. The simple and achievable plan agreed in April – concentrating forces for a decisive cross-Channel invasion in 1943 – had been abandoned. As many US forces were being despatched to the Pacific as to the European and Mediter-ranean theatre – the Americans had less than half the troops in the area planned under the BOLERO build up operation. The effect of TORCH was to trigger a major reinforcement of forces by both sides in the Mediterranean. Although Rommel was retreating west-ward along the coast and Anglo-American forces (mainly the latter) had secured Algeria and Morocco, the Germans had begun to pour troops into Tunisia (which the allied forces had failed to seize) and a long battle to dislodge them now had to be faced. Altogether 400,000 British and American troops moved from Britain (where they could have been used for an invasion) to North Africa. By early 1943 the number of US troops in Britain had fallen to about 50,000 compared with 388,000 deployed in the Mediterranean. Having overridden their military advisers in July and decided on the landings in French North Africa, Churchill and Roosevelt now had to embark on the task of devising another strategy to win the war.

1943–45 – Decline

Churchill was brought up against the consequences of the decision to invade French North Africa even before the landings took place. Despite the clear advice given by both sets of chiefs of staff less than three months before, he sent a message to Roosevelt expressing surprise that a cross-Channel invasion would not be possible in 1943. After talks with the chiefs of staff he wrote: 'I gained the impression . . . that "Roundup" was not only delayed or impinged upon by "Torch" but was to be regarded as definitely off for 1943.' Unfortunately during his visit in August he had given Stalin the clear impression that there would be an invasion and he now feared 'the most grave consequences'. His message ended with what amounted to a plea for some form of military initiative to placate the Soviet Union, which he termed 'my most perishing anxiety . . . and I do not see how we can reconcile it with our consciences or with our interests to have no more PQ's [convoys] till 1943, no offer to make joint plans for JUPITER [the invasion of north Norway], and no signs of a spring or even autumn offensive in Europe.'[1]

Churchill was again demonstrating his obstinate refusal to accept that the decision to go for operation TORCH necessarily ruled out other options. Comments he made to the chiefs of staff at this time about his own preferred way of conducting the war again reflect his dislike of any long-term strategic plan and his preference for backing his personal instinct without attempting to assess the wider or longer-term implications:

In settling what to do in a vast war situation like this it may sometimes be found better to take a particular major operation to which one is committed and follow that through vigorously to the end, making other things subordinate to it, rather than assemble all the data from the world scene in a baffling way.[2]

Such an approach was a recipe for disaster through dispersal of effort and concentration on endless sideshows.

It also became clear after TORCH that American entry into the war had not radically altered the strategy advocated by the British chiefs of staff. Immediately after the North African landings they recommended that there should be no invasion of north-west Europe until the bombing campaign and operations in the Mediterranean had weakened Germany. Despite all the extra military power now available from the United States and increasing Soviet success in the east, the chiefs of staff clung tenaciously to the old British strategy, adopted in 1940 when it was not possible to create an army capable of defeating Germany, that the invasion should be no more than a means of finishing off an already beaten enemy. They envisaged that allied forces would 're-enter the Continent at the psychological moment . . . when there was a definite crack in German morale'.[3] An American staff report to Marshall (US Army Chief of Staff) concluded that the British had cooled on ROUNDUP 'except as a final stroke against a tottering opponent'.[4] It is likely that the unstated British assumption was that now that the survival of the Soviet Union was assured they should be allowed to go on bearing the weight of the war, the task of defeating the massive German Army and the heavy casualties that would involve. Eden's Private Secretary commented: 'The Chiefs of Staff . . . wish to do nothing till 1944 except carry out a few raids and give arms to Russia to carry on the fight. The Russian Army having played the allotted role of killing Germans, our Chiefs of Staff think by 1944 they could stage a general onslaught on the exhausted animal.'[5]

Churchill's strategic views fluctuated wildly at this time between an invasion of north-west Europe in 1943 (which was no longer feasible) and operations in the Mediterranean. He wrote to Roosevelt on 17 November arguing that after Axis troops had been expelled from North Africa, British and American forces should move on to invade Sicily and Sardinia (he had derided both operations at a meeting with the chiefs of staff only eight days earlier), with the possibility of going on to mainland Italy, combined with an attempt to bring Turkey into the war. The next day he changed his mind. He told the chiefs of staff that all Mediterranean operations should be closed down and everything concentrated on a cross-Channel invasion in August 1943. On 3 December he set out a slightly modified version of this plan for the chiefs of staff – after the capture of Sardinia in June a cross-Channel invasion would be launched in August or September. When at a conference later that day the chiefs of staff explained once again the implications of the TORCH decision and how it ruled out an invasion in 1943, Churchill yet again refused to accept the unpalatable conclusion saying he had 'never accepted that idea, he had always held to the idea of a great offensive in 1943'.[6]

By the middle of December Churchill had come to accept the arguments of the chiefs of staff that Anglo-American strategy in 1943 would, *faute de mieux*, have to be an exploitation of opportunities in the Mediterranean. At first he thought both Sicily and Sardinia should be invaded in March but by the end of the month he thought Sicily was the only worthwhile operation and it would be worth waiting until May to carry it out. Britain was now committed to a Mediterranean strategy for 1943 and it was this position that Churchill took with him for a meeting with Roosevelt at Anfa near Casablanca in Morocco. Stalin was invited to attend but felt he could not leave the country as the battle of Stalingrad reached its climax. Churchill wanted Eden to accompany him but Roosevelt wanted to exclude his Secretary of State, Cordell Hull, and so Eden stayed in London.

The British military went to the conference well prepared and united, whereas the American chiefs of staff did not have an agreed position to put forward and found themselves at a disadvantage. The conference had to face the fact that allied forces had failed to capture Tunis in December and a major build up of troops would be needed before a spring offensive against the Germans. It would therefore be some months before operations in North Africa were completed. There would then be a surplus of troops deployed in the Mediterranean, and the British argued that rather than let them lie idle they should be used to capture Sicily. They thought it was possible that Germany might collapse in 1943 (mainly through Soviet efforts) and the US-UK contribution need be slight until 'there were definite signs that Germany was weakening'.[7] The US Navy wanted a third of the total Anglo-American war effort to be devoted to the Pacific and for the British to mount a major offensive in Burma. At one point they threatened that if Britain would not agree to a Burma campaign then 'that would necessitate the United States regretfully withdrawing from the commitments in the European theater'.[8] The British guessed it was just a bluff.

Eventually the combined chiefs of staff were able to make a report to Churchill and Roosevelt on 18 January. Three of their main recommendations were continuations of current policy – defeat of the U-boat threat, the continuation of supply convoys to the Soviet Union and a combined bomber offensive against Germany. The Anglo-American differences on future strategy were only papered over. The combined chiefs agreed that the invasion of Sicily (codename HUSKY) should go ahead in the summer. But they also decided that BOLERO (the build-up in the UK for a cross-Channel invasion) should continue (as the lowest priority), with the possibility of some sort of cross-Channel attack not ruled out – Churchill favoured reinstating a SLEDGEHAMMER type operation (a limited attack in exceptional circumstances) and secured the appointment of a commander to begin planning. There was some talk of a full-scale invasion in August but Marshall said that if HUSKY went ahead then such an operation would be 'difficult if not impossible'.[9] HUSKY would also require the suspension of the supply convoys to the Soviet Union during the build-up phase but Stalin was not told of this decision, only of the bomber offensive and the build-up of forces in Britain. Churchill and Roosevelt accepted the plan drawn up by the combined chiefs of staff and planning began for the operations involved.

Britain and the United States were committed to a piecemeal strategy. The invasion of French North Africa had become a much bigger operation than expected and would take far longer than planned to complete. The invasion of Sicily had been agreed as a next step but there was no consensus about longer-term strategy – should there be an invasion of Italy or even other operations in the Mediterranean? Just when would that theatre be run down to enable a cross-Channel invasion to take place? Having allowed themselves in the summer of 1942 to be sidetracked from a concentration of force against the main enemy, Britain and the United States now found themselves being drawn into continuing operations in a secondary theatre. The logic of events meant that having taken the TORCH decision they were forced into a Mediterranean strategy if they wanted to undertake offensive operations in 1943.

The main public outcome of the Casablanca conference was the adoption of a policy of unconditional surrender. Churchill had flatly opposed this idea; he had always envisaged that the war would end with armistice negotiations as in 1918 and he did not rule out coming to a deal with the German military once Hitler had been overthrown. However Roosevelt, acutely conscious of the dismay caused by the deal with Darlan and the need to reassure the Soviet Union that its allies would not negotiate with Germany behind its back, decided a clear statement of policy was needed. Churchill later claimed that Roosevelt thought the idea up off the cuff and that he had not been consulted. That was not the case. The President discussed the proposal with the joint chiefs of staff before leaving Washington and raised it with Churchill in the early stages of the conference. Churchill had time to consult the Cabinet and tried to get them to demand a specific exclusion of Italy but they refused. At Casablanca he objected to any mention of unconditional surrender in the final joint communiqué. He was outmanoeuvred by Roosevelt, who announced it at the final press conference, leaving Churchill no alternative but to acquiesce. It was a sign of the increasingly powerful US influence over policy.

Another problem at the conference was the handling of relations with the French. After Darlan's murder the Americans' favoured candidate, Giraud, was now in charge in North Africa but running what was virtually a Vichy administration. Just before leaving for the conference Churchill had been unable to stop release of a press communiqué from De Gaulle expressing willingness to work with Giraud. The communiqué started a strong press campaign in Britain in favour of De Gaulle and even the Americans were coming round to the view that the man who had led Free France for two and a half years could not be ignored altogether. They favoured setting up some sort of joint committee involving the two men. Roosevelt, who was in a light-hearted mood throughout the conference, told Churchill, 'We'll call Giraud the bridegroom, and I'll produce him from Algiers, and you get the bride, De Gaulle, down from London, and we'll have a shotgun wedding.'[10]

Giraud was summoned and on 16 January Churchill duly ordered De Gaulle to travel from London. Eden saw the French leader, who refused to accept the summons. Churchill received the message conveying the refusal while he was with Roosevelt and the President, enjoying Churchill's discomfiture, teased him about his inability to keep De Gaulle under control. An infuriated Churchill sent off a blistering message to London to the effect that if De Gaulle did not attend he would cut off all support and remove De Gaulle from the leadership of the Free French. The Cabinet refused to pass on the message – they thought it was not sensible politics to risk a breach with De Gaulle because he had too much popular support. Having built up De Gaulle as the leader of the Free French, the British could not suddenly dispose of him. Eventually De Gaulle was persuaded. On his arrival in Morocco on 22 January he was immediately alienated by the way the United States had taken over what was in fact French territory and established a massive armed camp around the conference.

De Gaulle's first meeting with Giraud was unproductive. He then saw Churchill who told him (in his own idea of French): 'Si vous m'obstaclerez, je vous liquiderai!'[11] He also informed De Gaulle that he was to be under Giraud and the rest of the Algiers group. The general simply refused to co-operate on those terms and did so again that evening when he saw Roosevelt. The next day (23 January) De Gaulle had another unproductive meeting with Giraud as the two men fenced for supremacy, and Roosevelt meanwhile worked on a communiqué stating that a joint committee had been set up but not saying who was in control. By the time of their second meeting (an event omitted from his memoirs) Churchill was in a towering rage and hurled abuse at De Gaulle. The latter described it as 'extremely bitter ... the roughest of all our wartime encounters' (which was saying something). When Churchill threatened to denounce De Gaulle in public, the French leader replied he was 'free to dishonour himself'.[12] The meeting ended in deadlock. Roosevelt then had a futher meeting with De Gaulle and ignored Churchill when he stormed in to resume abusing the Free French leader. It was the President who in the end was able to persuade Giraud and De Gaulle to shake hands in a symbolic gesture of reconciliation in front of the press cameras. The two Frenchmen then produced a communiqué which envisaged permanent liaison but resolved none of the important issues about who was to be supreme.

At the end of the Casablanca conference Churchill insisted that Roosevelt accompany him on a trip into the mountains to Marrakech, where he had stayed before the war. After the President left, he painted his only picture of the war period – a view of the Atlas mountains. He had also decided to fly on to Turkey to see President Inonu and persuade him to join the war. The War Cabinet opposed the trip, believing that it would be a waste of time. But Churchill insisted and flew to Turkey in a specially converted bomber. The War Cabinet's judgement was proved correct – the visit was fruitless. Churchill returned via Tripoli (for a visit to the 8th Army) and Algiers (for a visit to Eisenhower's headquarters). A week after his return to Britain he developed a cold, which turned into pneumonia. He did no work at all for a week and then spent a long time convalescing at Chequers.

Churchill left Casablanca still furious with De Gaulle. In Cairo he had a conversation with his old friend Louis Spears (now British representative in Syria). Spears remarked that his fundamental feelings towards France had not changed; Churchill replied that 'his had, that he found them either defeatist or arrogant and de Gaulle was the worst of the lot'.[13] On his return to London he was threatening, yet again, to break with De Gaulle. Eden and the King tried to talk him out of it but he told Massigli (De Gaulle's Commissioner for Foreign Affairs) that although he 'recognised an obligation to General de Gaulle . . . He was . . . no longer prepared to deal with de Gaulle personally so long as he claimed or acted as though he possessed supreme authority over the free French movement'.[14] (Churchill was ignoring the fact that he had recognised De Gaulle as leader of the Free French in 1940.) Once more he refused to allow De Gaulle to travel and the Foreign Office were instructed to prepare publicity material for a complete break with him.

The more immediate problem Churchill had to face once he was back at work in London was the uncertainty about future strategy that remained after Casablanca. Within a fortnight of his return, before the chiefs of staff had even worked out the full implications of the invasion of Sicily, he called for a re-examination of the

JUPITER plan for an attack on north Norway and for a reduction in the number of staff involved in planning the cross-Channel invasion. The crucial decisions about British preferences for future operations were made at a conference on 13 April. The chiefs of staff ruled out any cross-Channel attack in 1943. Once again Churchill tried at this meeting to claim, in the face of all the facts, that he had not been told this was the likely outcome of an invasion of Sicily: 'He had not realised hitherto and it had certainly not been made clear at Casablanca that the mounting of "Husky" would entail this sacrifice.'[15] Nevertheless he accepted that the BOLERO build-up should be further slowed down and that after Sicily British and American forces should invade the mainland of Italy. (At Casablanca Churchill had instructed the chiefs of staff to tell the Americans that there would be no invasion of Italy after Sicily.) Having been diverted from their primary objective, the British were now proposing an even bigger diversion – the only argument in favour was that there was nothing else that could be done for the rest of 1943.

In early May Churchill and the chiefs of staff left on the *Queen Mary* for a conference in Washington to discuss future operations. In a long series of discussions during the voyage they agreed to stick with their advocacy of an Italian invasion even though it might affect the build up for a 1944 invasion. Churchill and the Joint Intelligence Committee thought that Italy would collapse quickly and allied forces would therefore be able to reach the Alps easily. The invasion was not, as Churchill claimed later in his memoirs, an attempt to tie down German forces; that is what happened, not what was intended. For Churchill the action in the secondary theatre was now becoming the primary objective. He in theory accepted the 'Germany First' strategy but said 'the greatest step which we could take in 1943 towards this end would be the elimination of Italy'.[16]

Although the British regarded Casablanca as a great success, the Americans saw it as a major failure. They were determined to learn lessons from it: in future they would devise a coherent strategy of their own and then impose it on the British through their greater weight within the alliance. They were convinced that the British approach was above all political and aimed at maintaining its long-term influence in the Mediterranean. At this time there were thirty-eight divisions in the Mediterranean (nine American, twenty-nine British) and sixty-one US divisions still at home. In Britain there were two American divisions and thirty British (only nineteen of them combat units). This was the exact opposite of the plans agreed in 1942 to defeat Germany as quickly as possible. Anglo-American forces were not concentrated for an assault on Germany. Marshall in particular was worried that if this went on then there would be no invasion in 1944 either. At the beginning of May Roosevelt accepted the plans drawn up by the joint chiefs of staff to achieve US aims. Operations in the Mediterranean were in future to be strictly subordinated to ROUNDUP, and thirty-six combat divisions would move to Britain for an invasion in the spring of 1944. In particular six divisions were to be transferred from the Mediterranean to Britain in the autumn of 1943.

The May 1943 Washington conference (codename TRIDENT) lasted for a fortnight. American worries about Britain's long-term strategy and its committment to a cross-Channel invasion were confirmed at the start. Brooke, speaking for the chiefs of staff, said 'only by attacking in the Mediterranean could we achieve immediate results and that this was more valuable than building up for a 1944 ROUNDUP which might not even then be possible . . . The British Chiefs of Staff believed that the possibilities of ROUNDUP were dependent on the success or failure of the Russians on the Eastern Front. Allied cross-Channel operations could only form a very small part of the whole continental land war.'[17] Brooke spoke of no invasion until 1945 or possibly 1946. Churchill argued for an Italian campaign to isolate Germany, bring in Turkey (his perpetual illusion of the war) and open up the Dardanelles, and he compared these operations to the attack on Bulgaria in 1918 that had started the collapse of the Central Powers. After six days of talks there was almost complete deadlock between the two sides.

A series of informal discussions between the combined chiefs of staff followed, which resulted in a compromise set of proposals with the British having had to yield most ground. The invasion of north west Europe was to go ahead in May 1944, though scaled down by almost twenty per cent to twenty-nine divisions. Meanwhile operations in the Mediterranean for the rest of 1943 would aim to knock Italy out of the war (no invasion of the mainland was agreed) but at the beginning of November seven divisions would be withdrawn to Britain to take part in the 1944 invasion. (This figure was the maximum that the available shipping could move and shows vividly the problems caused by the diversion to the Mediterranean.) The only problem with this carefully worked-out compromise was that Churchill refused to accept it. He wanted an invasion of Italy and possibly the Balkans. (He told Smuts that he wanted Rome as the object of the 1943 campaign and intended to insist on it because Britain had the largest forces in the Mediterranean.) After long arguments with Roosevelt he reluctantly accepted the combined chiefs of staff plan, but promptly decided to fly to Algiers to try and persuade Eisenhower (the allied commander in the Mediterranean) to invade Italy. At this point Brooke wrote in his diary, 'There are times when he drives me to desperation.'[18]

From 29 May until 3 June Churchill was in Algiers putting intense pressure on Eisenhower and Marshall (who had flown from Washington with him) for an Italian invasion. In a series of long monologues he tried to wear them down and offered every possible incentive. British food rations would be drastically cut to provide the necessary shipping and he was prepared to move eight extra British divisions to the Mediterranean (claiming, despite the fact that not enough shipping was available, that they could be back in Britain before May 1944). There were two reasons behind Churchill's insistent pressure for an Italian campaign. First, operations in the Mediterranean would give the preponderant influence to the British because they had larger forces there than the Americans. Second, he thought the Italians would collapse quickly (which turned out to be correct) and Germany could not intervene quickly enough to stop Anglo-American forces getting to the Alps and possibly beyond (a view which turned out to be hopelessly optimistic). Churchill though was unable to persuade Eisenhower to make a decision until after the invasion of Sicily and returned to London empty handed.

During his trip to Washington and Algiers Churchill made another effort to remove De Gaulle from any influence over French affairs. Yet De Gaulle's position was becoming steadily stronger – the man who had made the right long-term decision in 1940 was beginning to reap the benefits. The main leader of the resistance (now at last beginning to form in France as the National Council of the Resistance), Jean Moulin, looked to him as leader, military support was growing and negotiations were already underway in Algiers between Giraud and De Gaulle's deputy Catroux. From Washington on 21 May Churchill sent a telegram to Eden and Attlee in London setting out a long list of complaints and leading up to the stark request 'I ask my colleagues to consider urgently whether we should not now eliminate de Gaulle as a political force'. If Churchill had his way, the French National Committee would be told that they would receive no more money and no help until De Gaulle went. He described De Gaulle as 'this vain and even malignant man . . . He hates England and has left a trail of Anglophobia behind him everywhere.' He then went on to smear his character: 'He has never fought since he left France and even took pains to have his wife brought out safely beforehand.' The first allegation was obviously untrue and Churchill also knew that the second was equally untrue (Mme de Gaulle left France after her husband). He concluded his message: 'When we consider the absolutely vital interest we have in preserving good relations with the United States, it seems to me most questionable that we should allow this marplot and mischief-maker to continue the harm he is doing.'[19] The Cabinet met on 23 May, knowing that Giraud had asked De Gaulle to travel to Algiers and a deal between the two men was imminent. They recognised that Britain did not have the power to 'eliminate' De Gaulle politically and any attempt to do so would probably only strengthen his position. They refused to act. Eden's Private Secretary wrote, 'A.E. and even Attlee are fed up at this lecturing and hectoring from across the Atlantic.'[20]

Another motive behind Churchill's trip to Algiers was his desire to be present when De Gaulle and Giraud met. At a meeting with Macmillan and Murphy (the Anglo-American political advisers in North Africa), Churchill 'arraigned de Gaulle more vehemently and vituperatively than at Anfa [Casablanca], saying that de Gaulle is anti-British and anti-American and that we could count on de Gaulle to play the fool . . . in his opinion de Gaulle is fully capable of a putsch. He said he had no illusions about de Gaulle's thirst for personal power.' Churchill planned to cancel all the 1940 agreements with the Free French and make new ones with the group in Algiers and 'whatever financial, lend-lease and political arrangements we may see fit', and De Gaulle was not to be allowed to broadcast over the BBC.[21] He had also arranged for Alexis Leger (the ex-head of the Quai d'Orsay) and his old friend General Georges, both of whom were strongly anti-De Gaulle, to be brought out of occupied France to Algiers to add their weight to the opposition to De Gaulle.

Eden, who had flown out to Algiers, dismissed Georges as 'a reactionary old defeatist'.[22]

De Gaulle and Giraud met on 30 May and within three days had agreed to be co-presidents of a new French Committee of National Liberation (FCNL) which would exercise French sovereignty and direct the war effort. All the ex-Vichy appointees were to go. On 6 June the FCNL lunched with Churchill, who afterwards told Roosevelt that De Gaulle was now well under control, Georges was extremely useful in the new organisation and all the 1940 agreements with De Gaulle as leader of the Free French were void. He returned to London determined to take steps to reduce De Gaulle's influence as much as possible. Eden's Private Secretary reported that he was 'wild over de G's activity in N. Africa . . . he would do anything now to blacken de G'.[23] On his return to London Churchill issued secret instructions to the press that De Gaulle's role was to be played down and told them, 'He has undoubtedly Fascist and dictatorial tendencies.'[24] One thing he was determined to do was ensure that De Gaulle did not control the resistance groups in France. Shortly after his return from Algiers he wrote to Lord Selborne, who was in political charge of SOE: 'We must be careful that the direction of the French Resistance movement does not fall into the control of de Gaulle and his satellites . . . Let me have your proposals . . . for carrying on the underground work without admitting de Gaulle or his agents to any effective share in it, and without letting any sums of money get into their hands.'[25] Such a proposal would have been impossible to implement because De Gaulle's standing with the resistance groups in France was too high. Lord Selborne raised so many objections that Churchill eventually had to drop the idea.

While these discussions on future strategy and relations with the French were underway, Anglo-American forces finally forced the surrender of the German and Italian forces in North Africa. Montgomery still moved at a ponderous pace even though he had ten times as many tanks as the Germans and the attack on the Mareth line was another unimaginative frontal assault by the infantry. After the fall of Tunis the Germans finally surrendered on 13 May, six months after the TORCH landings, by which time they had only sixty operational tanks left compared with the allies' 1,400. The long battle had failed to take the pressure off the Soviet Union: in the four months after November 1942 the Germans moved seventeen divisions from western Europe to the eastern front. After the surrender there was a two-month pause before the invasion of Sicily in the second week of July. Because no decision had been taken to invade the mainland of Italy, the campaign in Sicily lacked a strategic focus and the Anglo-American forces simply moved across the island as the low-quality German and Italian troops withdrew. There was little attempt to cut off their retreat and most of the German troops escaped (the allies suffered more casualties than their opponents despite outnumbering them 4:1 and having air supremacy). This attack convinced the German High Command that there would be no cross-Channel invasion that year and therefore it too did nothing to relieve the pressure on the Soviet Union. The scale of the fighting on the eastern front was far beyond anything the British or Americans ever encountered – in the huge tank battles around Kursk that summer the Soviets lost 2,000 tanks in a week but destroyed seventeen Panzer divisions.

It was not until 18 July, a week after the start of the Sicily operation, that Eisenhower finally decided to invade the Italian mainland, and it was another month before a plan was devised. Churchill still envisaged the Italian campaign as a large-scale operation, possibly involving the Balkans too. On 19 July he set out his views for the chiefs of staff. He now ruled out a cross-Channel invasion in 1944 – 'the forces available in the United Kingdom will not be equal to the task of landing and maintaining themselves on land'. In his view 'the right strategy for 1944' was an attack in Italy then a move either westwards into southern France or north east to Vienna 'and meanwhile to procure the expulsion of the enemy from the Balkans and Greece'. JUPITER (the invasion of northern Norway) was to be revived as 'a preferable alternative' to a cross-Channel attack and 'in all probability the only one which will be open in the west'.[26] (The Norwegian operation had been rejected as impracticable by the chiefs of staff as long ago as October 1941.) Churchill in fact favoured virtually every possible operation except the most direct route to the heart of Germany. He was now proposing dispersal of the Anglo-American effort on a truly grand scale. His ideas also paid little attention to military reality. The topography of Italy overwhelmingly favoured the defender, as the Germans were to show during their brilliant long defensive action until May 1945, and it was physically impossible to move rapidly from Calabria to

Lombardy. From there it was even more difficult to move through the narrow mountain passes into Austria. Nevertheless Churchill insisted on putting a formal request to the Americans to revoke the agreement made at Washington in May and stop the recall of troops from the Mediterranean. When the Americans refused, the British stopped the recall unilaterally. The fall of Mussolini on 25 July and his replacement by a military Government only encouraged Churchill in his delusions about an Italian campaign.

The US Secretary of War, Henry Stimson, was in London during the latter half of July assessing British attitudes. On his return he wrote a crucial report for Roosevelt. He told the President that as far as the invasion of north-west Europe was concerned 'Though they have rendered lip service to the operation, their hearts are not in it.' He went on to explain 'the British theory (which cropped out [sic] again and again in unguarded sentences . . .) is that Germany can be beaten by a series of attritions in northern Italy, in the eastern Mediterranean, in Greece, in the Balkans, in Rumania and other satellite countries, and that the only fighting which needs to be done will be done by Russia'. He concluded, 'the time has come for you to decide that your government must assume the responsibility of leadership in this great final movement of the European war'.[27] The US joint chiefs of staff were by now equally determined not to be dragged into any more of Churchill's sideshows and were seriously worried by the dangers they posed: 'The allocation of additional forces to the Mediterranean is uneconomical and assists Germany to create a strategic stalemate in Europe', and such a strategy, if adopted, would 'imperil the final victory'.[28]

Roosevelt held a meeting with the joint chiefs of staff and his other advisers on 10 August. Stimson told the meeting 'the Prime Minister was rather apathetic and somewhat apprehensive with regard to BOLERO'. The President accepted the view of his military advisers that an invasion of north-west Europe (now code-named OVERLORD) was the only possible route to victory. There was to be no Balkan campaign and the campaign in Italy was to be conducted within the current troop allocations (in other words the seven divisions would be withdrawn). Roosevelt also accepted that if a cross-Channel attack was to be carried out, it would have to be under American leadership: 'he was anxious to have American preponderance in the OVERLORD operation, starting from the first day of the assault' so that he would have 'the basis for insisting upon an American commander'.[29] After clarifying his own objectives, Roosevelt proposed another Anglo-American strategy meeting to be held in Quebec.

Churchill crossed the Atlantic on the *Queen Mary* for the meeting, which lasted for ten days from 14 August. At the beginning of the conference there was again a clear split between the two countries. The Americans wanted overriding priority to be given to OVER-LORD, withdrawal of the seven divisions from the Mediterranean and a limited Italian campaign. (Peace feelers from the new Italian Government had already been received.) The British wanted no withdrawal of the seven divisions, a conquest of the whole of Italy and no absolute priority for OVERLORD. Brooke specifically criticised the paper by the US joint chiefs of staff, saying that the idea that 'when there is a shortage of resources, OVERLORD will have an overriding priority, was too binding'.[30] Churchill spent some time at Hyde Park, Roosevelt's country home in New York State, where he found that the President was solidly behind his military advisers. He realised that he would have to give ground and the British chiefs of staff were told to reach a compromise with the Americans – in fact they had little choice but to accept their position. The joint report to Churchill and Roosevelt recommended that OVERLORD should have absolute priority, the Italian campaign should not go further north than Rome, the seven divisions should be withdrawn and the British would abandon their unilateral veto on the movement of troops and equipment for OVERLORD.

At two meetings with Roosevelt on 19 and 23 August Churchill still tried to modify the American position and did not accept the joint chiefs of staff recommendations. On the Italian campaign he said he 'wanted it definitely understood that he was not committed to an advance in Northern Italy beyond the Ancona-Pisa line' (i.e. he wanted to go some way north of Rome).[31] On OVERLORD, although he accepted the priority that the Americans wanted, he tried to introduce new conditions that would make the operation extremely unlikely. He argued it should only be carried out if the Germans had less than twelve divisions in Italy and France or if they could only reinforce with less than fifteen divisions in the two months after the landing. Roosevelt would not accept such conditions, but Churchill successfully insisted that examination of JUPITER as an alternative should also continue. The question of the commander for OVERLORD also had to be settled. Churchill had already promised the post to Brooke but once he knew that Roosevelt was set on having an American commander, he suggested Marshall should be appointed. Brooke was deeply hurt by his attitude: 'He offered no sympathy, no regrets at having to change his mind, and dealt with the matter as if it were one of minor importance.'[32] After the conference Churchill spent some time fishing at La Cabane deep in the Canadian countryside, then travelled to Washington for five days, gave a speech at Harvard University and returned to Washington and Hyde Park before finally sailing to Britain on *HMS Renown* after a month's stay altogether in the United States and Canada.

Another vexed question considered at the Quebec conference was, once again, relations with the French and in particular De Gaulle. Within days of the establishment of the FCNL at Algiers at the beginning of June, De Gaulle and his supporters had rapidly gained control of the movement at the expense of Giraud. Although Roosevelt and Churchill had instructed Eisenhower to intervene to stop De Gaulle controlling French forces in North Africa, the move was unsuccessful. Until the middle of July Churchill bowed to the strong pressure from Eden and Macmillan not to break with De Gaulle: they realised that his influence could not be reduced by Britain and the United States and any attempt to do so would only alienate the man who was almost inevitably going to be ruling France on its liberation and in the immediate post-war world. Eden was also trying to secure recognition of the FCNL as the body directing the French war effort. Churchill opposed this and his draft paper for the Cabinet was another outspoken attack on De Gaulle: 'I have . . . for some time past regarded him as a personage whose arrival at the summit of French affairs would be contrary to the interests of Great Britain. . . . He is animated by dictatorial instincts and consumed by personal ambition. He shows many of the signs of a budding Fuhrer.'[33]

Churchill gave in on 19 July and sent a message to Roosevelt suggesting he should do the same. In his memoirs he left out the final paragraph, which said he would rather have De Gaulle on the FCNL 'than strutting about as a combination of Joan of Arc and Clemenceau . . . I am no more enamoured of him than you are.'[34] Roosevelt refused American recognition and Churchill continued to waver. Eventually at Quebec, after long discussions between Eden and Hull and Churchill and Roosevelt, they agreed a limited form of recognition. The British announced the decision on 27 August – the FCNL was recognised as the body administering those overseas territories that accepted its authority and was responsible for the French war effort. The wording was virtually as restrictive as the 1940 agreements with the Free French; it was the minimum possible concession in the circumstances. Only the Soviet Union was more fulsome. By November 1943 De Gaulle was in sole charge of the FCNL, which controlled virtually the whole of the French overseas empire and directed the efforts of the 400,000 Free French forces (equipped by the United States).

While Churchill was in North America and after the first Anglo-American landings on the Italian mainland, the Italian Government under General Badoglio surrendered. In a confused situation the Germans moved far faster than the allies and secured control of most of Italy – Churchill's hope of a quick and easy campaign was over. The allies were stuck in southern Italy, forced to move in difficult country against a determined opponent. The surrender also opened the question of the future control of what remained of the Italian Empire in the Mediterranean – essentially the Dodecanese Islands. Churchill beame obsessed with gaining control of this group of small islands, which were strategically irrelevant. As early as February 1943 he had proposed an attack on them as one of the major operations for the year. At the beginning of August he told the chiefs of staff, 'Here is a business of great consequence to be thrust forward by any means . . . I hope the staffs will be able to stimulate action which may gain immense prizes at little cost, though not at little risk.'[35] The commander in the eastern Mediterranean, General Wilson, replied that he lacked the necessary resources to do more than mount raids on the islands. Churchill refused to accept such advice and instructed him: 'This is the time to play high. Improvise and dare.'[36]

In the middle of September the British captured Cos, Leros and Samos but the Germans, again acting with greater speed, secured the only important island, Rhodes. In 1941, when the chiefs of staff had been planning to take these outlying islands before assaulting Rhodes, Churchill had rejected the idea saying, 'I do not think it would be wise to attack these smaller islands. They are no use in themselves.'[37] Now he envisaged them as the focal point for a large-scale campaign aimed at capturing Rhodes, even after German forces went on to capture Cos with its vital airfield which gave them air supremacy in the area. He now identified operations in the Dodecanese as a higher priority than OVERLORD or even the Italian campaign. He wanted to withdraw one division from Italy and firmly told the chiefs of staff that 'a cardinal strategic decision was now at issue'.[38] The chiefs of staff had already told him that any withdrawal would give the Germans a good opportunity to counter-attack in Italy. He then contacted Roosevelt and tried to get him to order Eisenhower to release forces from Italy, but the President refused. Churchill then decided to fly out to Tunis to argue with Eisenhower in person. Roosevelt refused to agree to the meeting and also rejected the idea that the combined chiefs of staff should discuss the matter. Meanwhile Brooke was plunged into despair, saying of Churchill's obsession with the Dodecanese, 'he has magnified its importance so that he can no longer see anything else . . . He refused to listen to any arguments or to see any dangers.'[39] But against total opposition from every quarter Churchill could not impose his will. In November the Germans captured Leros and British troops were withdrawn from the remaining islands.

By the middle of October Churchill decided to try to undo the agreements reached at Quebec in August and stop the invasion of north-west Europe. On 19 October there was a major meeting between Churchill, the chiefs of staff, most of the War Cabinet and his trusted colleague General Smuts, the South African Prime Minister. (This is another meeting left out of his memoirs altogether.) He argued strongly that the Italian campaign should take precedence over OVERLORD and maintained that the latter operation was not only strategically wrong but would probably fail. As on earlier occasions his case was based on a strong preference for any sort of action in the short term even at the expense of ultimate aims: 'It was strategically unsound to miss present opportunities for the sake of an operation which could not take place for another seven months, and which might, in fact, have to be postponed to an even later date.' OVERLORD he argued would simply equalise forces between Italy and north-west Europe and allow the Germans to defeat both. The allies would get ashore in France but Germany would concentrate overwhelming strength and 'inflict on us a military disaster greater than that of Dunkirk'. His alternative plan was to reinforce Italy 'to the full', 'enter the Balkans' and expand the bombing campaign. US troops would continue to arrive in Britain but, in line with the strategy which he had favoured since the summer of 1940 when no better option was available, a cross-Channel invasion would only be 'taking advantage of the softening in the enemy's resistance due to our operations in other theatres'. When the chiefs of staff pointed out that if his ideas were adopted the United States would concentrate its forces in the Pacific, he was quite happy to accept such an outcome:

> He ... felt so strongly that our strategy, as at present agreed, was wrong ... that he was prepared to reopen the matter with the Americans. If, as a result, the latter wished to transfer the bulk of their forces to the Pacific, he would be prepared to accept this providing they would leave the forces already in this country and would build-up their Air Force for operations against Germany.[40]

Perhaps he was nurturing a dream that in this way the British would still be able to conclude the European war virtually on their own and without too much overt American help.

The next day Churchill asked Roosevelt for a special meeting at Casablanca to discuss strategy for 1944 before they went on to their first joint meeting with Stalin due to be held in Teheran at the end of November. On 26 October he told Eden he was determined to concentrate on the Mediterranean regardless of its effect on OVER-LORD. The same day he told Moran: 'I will not allow the great and fruitful campaign in Italy to be cast away and end in a frightful disaster, for the sake of crossing the Channel in May.'[41] In fact the campaign was already in stalemate – allied forces were nowhere near their original objective of Rome and the British chiefs of staff had accepted that progress could only be made by using large numbers of landing craft (which were in very short supply) to stage a series of landings along the coast, circumventing the difficulty of advancing up the mainland and forcing the Germans to withdraw.

Roosevelt did eventually agree to see Churchill at Cairo before they flew to Teheran but took care to ensure that he did not meet him alone when he might be forced to discuss strategy. He successfully insisted that most of the discussion concentrated on the Far East and brought Chiang Kai-shek to the meeting, much to Churchill's disgust. Churchill told the chiefs of staff that a fixed date for OVERLORD would 'continue to wreck and ruin the Mediterranean campaign'.[42] He was also worried that the Americans (under Roosevelt's instructions issued in early August) had ensured they would have a majority, though small, of the troops to be involved on D-Day – they would within a few weeks of the landing have overwhelming preponderance because the British had virtually no reserves to increase their front-line strength. Churchill told Brooke in early November, 'it seems to me a great pity that we cannot make our quota equal or, if possible, one better . . . In this way we shall maintain our right to be effectively consulted in operations which are of such capital consequence. For the above purpose I would run considerable risks with what is left in the island.' He wanted to mobilise the Home Guard to release more regular troops and was prepared to accept 'the resulting decline in the factory munition output'. These actions also 'might enable us to secure any necessary retardation of D-Day'.[43] Brooke told him that what he wanted was not possible. It was another reason why Churchill turned against OVERLORD.

At Cairo Churchill tried to put OVERLORD into a Mediterranean framework. For him the order of priorities was to recapture the Dodecanese, reach Rome and bring Turkey into the war. OVERLORD should therefore be delayed, no overall commander should be appointed and resources should be brought back from the Pacific to help Mediterranean operations. He was also seeking to secure British control in the Mediterranean to offset US command of OVERLORD. He suggested such a split on 25 November, telling Roosevelt:

> Such Commands would also correspond with the outlook of the two Governments, the Americans regarding OVERLORD of overwhelming importance, while the British believe that the greatest and most immediate results can be obtained in the Mediterranean and that OVERLORD is a knock-out blow, the timing of which must be settled in relation to the condition and dispositions of the enemy.[44]

After great confusion and protracted rows the British and Americans were unable to resolve their differences before the Teheran meeting;

they drifted into a position where they would put the alternatives to Stalin and allow him to choose. Each side expected him to support their case. At the very first meeting at Teheran Churchill found himself isolated – Stalin, no doubt worried that the long-promised second front would be postponed yet again, plumped for OVER-LORD immediately and asked for a commander to be appointed. He refused to accept Churchill's vehement arguments in favour of every possible Mediterranean operation and, not surprisingly, was supported by Roosevelt. Eventually it was Harry Hopkins who persuaded Churchill to yield.

Churchill and Roosevelt returned to Cairo in order to implement what had been agreed at their meeting with Stalin. They were joined by the Turkish leader Inonu. Both countries had approached him – the Americans had succeeded where Randolph Churchill's mission had failed. Despite Churchill's best endeavours, Inonu refused to fix a date for Turkish entry into the war and the Americans encouraged him not to do so in order to stop any more pressure from Churchill to continue operations in the eastern Mediterranean. On 4 December Roosevelt decided to appoint Eisenhower rather than Marshall as commander of OVERLORD. The next day he told Stalin but did not inform Churchill until 6 December. Final military agreement was reached on that date – OVERLORD and a small invasion of southern France (codename ANVIL) were to have priority; forces in Italy were to advance to around Pisa but operations in the Aegean were deemed no more than desirable and were not to be at the expense of either OVERLORD or ANVIL. It was a defeat for Churchill. The Americans, after numerous battles throughout 1943 and with Stalin's help, had finally forced him to go along with their strategic policy. It was a clear example of a trend that had been apparent throughout the year: Britain's and Churchill's ability to influence Anglo-American strategy declined as American economic and military power expanded.

Churchill was not a good loser. He remained deeply unhappy about OVERLORD, now describing it as a diversion to help the Soviets. He told Cadogan six weeks before D-Day, 'This battle has been *forced upon us* by the Russians and the United States military authorities.'[45] He made one more unavailing effort to stop OVER-LORD just before Easter 1944. He proposed a meeting with Roosevelt in Bermuda and drafted a message that was never sent:

'What is the latest date on which a decision can be taken as to whether "Overlord" is or is not to be launched on the prescribed date? . . . if 20 to 25 mobile German divisions are already in France on the date in question, what are we going to do?'[46] Roosevelt was unwell but the Americans also guessed what Churchill wanted and rejected the meeting. On the eve of D-Day Churchill was still convinced that OVERLORD would not succeed. He told a meeting of Dominion prime ministers that after its failure 'we must set our teeth and prepare for a longer war, or else reduce the severity of the terms which we were prepared to offer to the enemy. He was in no doubt which course we should adopt.'[47] As so often, Churchill was overlooking or seriously underestimating the effect of the Soviet military effort: the Soviet Union was already defeating about seventy per cent of the German Army and the eastern front was on the point of collapse.

In his memoirs Churchill gives the impression that he always favoured an invasion of northern France and was only worried about its timing and the casualty rate. Yet it is clear from all the contemporary papers (rather than the ones Churchill himself was prepared to print) that this was not the case. He preferred a Mediterranean strategy (and at times any possible minor operation) to a direct assault on Germany. Certainly there is no record of him raising the matter of possible casualties – on the contrary he frequently expected or even on occasion demanded a high level of casualties (as before the fall of Singapore). For his perennial favourite JUPITER he thought a thirty per cent casualty rate was acceptable. In his memoirs Churchill also seeks to present his espousal of a Mediterranean strategy as an attempt to enter central Europe before the Soviet Union – yet his arguments for it in 1943 were expressed in military rather than political terms. Other reasons or motives for his preferred strategy do not feature in his memoirs, yet were arguably far more influential with him at the time. To a large extent he was continuing with the old policy adopted in 1940 of only invading once Germany had collapsed. Also he wanted to keep operations confined to an area where Britain would have more influence over strategy than in an American-dominated invasion of north-west Europe, hence his lack of anxiety about the United States pulling out altogether and concentrating on the Pacific. In addition, after the long record of British military failure – France in 1940,

Greece in 1941, Singapore and the Far East in 1942 and Tobruk in 1942 – together with the generally inept Anglo-American performance in North Africa and Italy despite the amount of Ultra intelligence available, Churchill had little confidence in the capabilities of the allied armies. He told Attlee that long reflection had convinced him 'It certainly will be several years before British and American land forces will be capable of beating the Germans on even terms in the open field.'[48]

Looking ahead, Churchill still pinned his hopes on the bombing campaign breaking German morale and destroying its industrial base, thereby rendering an opposed invasion unnecessary. At Casablanca he and Roosevelt had agreed that the aim of the combined bomber offensive (the British were to attack area targets and the Americans precision targets – neither thought much of the other's policy) was 'the undermining of the morale of the German people to a point where their capacity for armed resistance is fatally weakened'.[49] It was during 1943 that the long preparations since the mid-1930s began to pay dividends. Heavy four-engined bombers were being produced in quantity, the weight of bombs dropped rose dramatically and technological improvements and new techniques such as using pathfinder squadrons increased accuracy considerably. Despite this extra accuracy, Bomber Command under Harris insisted on continuing with the policy of area bombing of German cities, convinced that this was the way to destroy German morale. At the beginning of November 1943 Harris erroneously told Churchill that nineteen German cities were completely destroyed, nineteen seriously damaged, the Ruhr was virtually destroyed and Germany was on the point of collapse. He thought another 15,000 sorties, aimed primarily at Berlin, would win the war by April 1944. It is likely that these views also influenced Churchill in maintaining his opposition to OVERLORD.

Churchill fully endorsed the bombing strategy and was content to let Harris continue with his campaign with little interference. Indeed he actively promoted the idea of primarily attacking the civilian population. In his paper on the aims of the Italian campaign he set out his view of what the bomber offensive should seek to do: 'All the industrial centres should be attacked in an intense fashion, every effort being made to render them uninhabitable and to terrorise and paralyse the population.'[50] Yet in strategic terms the bomber offensive, on which Churchill placed so much weight, was a failure. It did not reduce German munitions output. In fact as the weight of allied bombing increased so did production – between 1942 and 1944 German munitions output trebled (tank production rose five-fold) and aircraft production doubled to 40,000 in 1944 (fifty per cent higher than the British level). The official survey after the war found that Germany lost just under four per cent of its productive capacity to the bomber offensive that cost the RAF over 50,000 dead and the loss of 8,000 aircraft. What the bomber offensive did achieve was a huge civilian death toll. In total 590,000 German civilians were killed (nearly fifteen times British civilian casualties), 800,000 were seriously injured and 7,500,000 were made homeless. What allied bombing could achieve was demonstrated at Hamburg in August 1943 – the heavy use of incendiaries in the centre of the city produced a firestorm with temperatures of 1,000°C and winds of 150 mph. 50,000 people were killed and sixty per cent of the houses in the city were destroyed. Churchill said after the war 'we should never allow ourselves to apologize for what we did to Germany'.[51]

Although Churchill consistently favoured the bomber offensive against the needs of the Battle of the Atlantic, that particular battle was won in 1943. By early 1943 the Germans could deploy about twenty U-boats against each convoy: they operated in multiple patrol lines and were aided by plentiful intelligence about convoy routes and times. When over 540,000 tons of shipping was sunk in March, Churchill gloomily told the Cabinet that the Royal Navy's resources 'were stretched to the uttermost, and the strength of the escorts to our Atlantic convoys was inadequate to meet the enemy's concentration of U-boats'.[52] Yet by the end of May Admiral Donitz, the German commander, admitted privately that he had lost the battle. Allied victory was achieved through a series of improvements – better Ultra intelligence, more escorts and escort carriers as US production came on stream, better quality radar (Churchill had insisted that all the early production should go to Bomber Command), more direction-finding equipment on ships and, perhaps most important of all, very long-range aircraft to cover the remaining gaps that allowed the U-boats to operate almost unhindered. Only some twenty-four aircraft were needed but throughout 1942 Churchill had given Bomber Command priority. US merchant ship production would probably have tilted the balance in the allies' favour anyway – by 1943 they were building nearly 2,000 ships a year compared with 105 in 1941.

During 1943, and particularly at the Cairo conference in November, Churchill found that Far Eastern questions were coming increasingly to the fore. The British held the Japanese attack on the borders of India in 1942 but apart from the indecisive Arakan offensive which ended in February 1943 and Chindit operations behind the Japanese lines, there was little activity. The Americans meanwhile were conducting a largely separate war across the Pacific: although they were willing to tell the British what they were doing, they were not prepared to consult about operations and orders were issued direct from the US joint chiefs of staff and not through the combined chiefs of staff. The British had few spare resources to mount an active campaign and were unclear about priorities.

At first Churchill thought it would be best to by-pass Burma altogether. He told the Cabinet in April 1943 'it could not be said that the conquest of Burma was an essential step in the defeat of Japan. Nor would the occupation of North Burma mean immediate traffic on the Burma Road . . . Everything pointed to an alternative line of action.'[53] At the Washington conference in May he stuck to this view and told the Americans the best idea was to 'by-pass Burma and its swamps and jungles and strike out eastward across the sea'.[54] Three months later though, during the preparations for the Quebec conference, he thought 'we ought to make a strong new feature of the offensive from Assam into Upper Burma . . . to help re-open the Burma Road'.[55] At the Quebec conference Churchill changed his mind again. He reverted to his idea of an amphibious assault, probably on Sumatra, which he compared, ominously, 'in its promise of decisive consequences with the Dardanelles operation of 1915'. The chiefs of staff wanted from the politicians a clear choice between a Burma–China axis of attack and one through Malaya and south China. Churchill, once again revealing his reluctance to make any long-term plans, refused to make a firm decision in case 'the dead hand of a long-term plan paralysed action in the near future'.[56]

As he had been in the Middle East, Churchill was also worried about the commanders in the area. He told Stimson he was 'thoroughly dissatisfied with the way his commanders had acted' and much of the discussion at Quebec was about the arrangements to be made for this theatre.[57] He rejected Auchinleck as a possibility and also turned down Leo Amery's suggestion that Lord Mountbatten should command the new organisation being set up separate from the Government of India, called South East Asia Command (SEAC). The British chiefs of staff wanted an arrangement whereby they issued instructions direct to SEAC, just as the US did to its commanders in the Pacific such as MacArthur. The US authorities successfully insisted that general strategy was to be set by the combined chiefs of staff (as it was for Eisenhower in North Africa and the Mediterranean) with the British only dealing with specific operations within that framework. It was another sign of declining British influence over the war. Churchill suggested Air Marshal Sir Sholto Douglas as commander of SEAC but Roosevelt rejected him and Churchill in turn rejected the President's choice of either Air Marshal Tedder or Admiral Cunningham. Eventually they compromised on Mountbatten.

Strategy was finally decided at Cairo. Before the meeting Churchill had unwisely promised Chiang Kai-shek a major concentration of the British fleet in the Bay of Bengal (the eastern fleet was actually declining in numbers) and a 'considerable amphibious operation'.[58] Yet when Roosevelt offered such an operation (BUCCANEER) for the capture of the Andaman Islands, the British objected violently because they preferred to use the landing craft for operations in the Mediterranean. Harmony was only restored at the second Cairo conference (after Teheran), when it was agreed to abandon BUCCANEER. The combined chiefs of staff finally agreed that the India/Burma theatre was to be secondary and efforts were to be concentrated on a two-pronged attack in the Pacific. The first would be through the central Pacific, the second via New Guinea, the Dutch East Indies and the Philippines. These widely separate thrusts entailed a wasteful spreading of effort but they were adopted because they gave both the US Navy and Army a major sphere of activity.

Throughout the first Cairo conference and at Teheran Churchill had been affected by throat problems and intermittent loss of his voice. By the time he arrived back at Cairo on 2 December he was close to total physical collapse. He staggered through that conference but after arriving at Tunis on 11 December, he was taken seriously ill. Within two days pneumonia was diagnosed together with heart fibrillations. His doctor put him on digitalis and new antibiotic drugs specially flown in from Egypt. Clementine flew out from Britain to be with him but told Moran: 'Oh yes, he's very glad I've come, but in five minutes he'll forget I'm here.'[59] The worst of the attack was over in four days but Churchill spent another ten days in Tunis before flying to Marrakech to continue his recuperation. It was his first serious illness during the war (he had suffered a mild heart attack when opening a window at the White House during his visit in December 1941) and he never fully recovered from it.

Soon after his return his close advisers began to notice a deterioration in his performance as Prime Minister. Brooke noted in March 1944: 'We found him in a desperately tired mood. I am afraid he is losing ground rapidly. He seems quite incapable of concentrating for a few minutes on end and keeps wandering continuously. He kept yawning and said he was feeling desperately tired.'[60] A month later at the Dominion Prime Ministers' Conference Brooke again saw evidence of debility: 'he looks very old and tired, and in my opinion is failing fast'.[61] Six days later Churchill himself admitted that he was 'beginning to fail'.[62] There were still flashes of a better mood – 'P.M. in great form and full of chaff and leg-pulling' – but they were few and far between and most of his colleagues were still expressing exasperation at his way of conducting business.[63]

On the day of his return from convalescence in Marrakech Brooke noted in his diary a further example of Churchill's methods:

> The P.M. is starting off in his usual style. We had a Staff meeting with him at 5.30pm for two hours and a Defence Committee from 10.30pm for another two hours. And we accomplished nothing. In all his plans he lives from hand to mouth; he can never grasp a whole plan either in its width (i.e. all its fronts) or its depth (long-term projects).[64]

His tendency to hold long meetings at which he held forth at length and at which little if anything was decided had always infuriated his colleagues but this habit became steadily worse during the war, especially as more and more of the key decisions were taken out of British hands. It was as if Churchill was trying to convince himself he was still at the centre of affairs. Cadogan described one such meeting in July 1943: 'Defence Committee 10.30. About Azores: but that point was settled in 3½ minutes. Rest of the time, till midnight, taken up with rambling gossip.'[65] In September 1943 Brooke noted: 'Cabinet at 5.30pm which lasted till 7.45pm. We then had a C.O.S meeting from 9pm to 10.30pm to prepare for a meeting with P.M. which lasted from 10.30 to 1 am. We did practically nothing, or at any rate nothing that could not have been finished in an hour.'[66]

Admiral Cunningham, the new First Sea Lord, wrote in April 1944, 'Never has the PM been so discursive and wasted so much time.'[67] Later that month Cadogan wrote: 'P.M., I fear, is breaking down. He rambles without pause, and we got nowhere ... N. Chamberlain would have settled it in 6 minutes ... I really am fussed about the P.M. He is *not* the man he was 12 months ago.'[68] Six weeks later he noted: '5.30 Cabinet, as usual put off till 6.30 as there was nothing on agenda. Usual result that we rambled incoherently till 8.45.' It was the second time it had happened in ten days and Cadogan added, 'Of course *he* can stroll over to the Annexe at 9 or 10 and at a nod a dozen Marines spring to attention and produce dinner – *and* old brandy. I wonder has he the least idea of the difficulties of life for the ordinary British subject?'[69] Later in the summer Cadogan described Churchill as 'evidently ageing' and noted 'the rambling talk is *frightful* ... It's terrible that we have a P.M. who simply can't *conduct business*. It's all hot air.'[70]

Much of the 'hot air' was abuse of his colleagues and advisers. In February Brooke reported: 'Usual briefing for the Cabinet at 6pm where Winston was in an impossible mood with nothing but abuse about everything the Army was doing. Every commander from "Jumbo" Wilson [Commander-in-Chief Mediterranean] to last Company commander was useless, the Americans hopeless, etc., etc.'[71] Loss of direct influence over much of the decision making seems to have induced in him a growing distrust of everyone else's motives. At the chiefs of staff meeting on 8 September 1944 Cunningham described him as 'in his worst mood. Accusing the CoS of ganging up against him and keeping papers from him and so on ... The worst of it is his feeling against the Americans whom he accuses of doing the most awful things against the British.'[72]

Perhaps the worst meeting of all was of the Defence Committee on 6 July, which lasted from 10pm to 2am. Three separate records exist. Cunningham described Churchill as 'in no fit state to discuss anything – too tired and too much alcohol ... he was in a terrible mood. Rude and sarcastic.'[73] Eden wrote in his diary:

> After dinner a really ghastly Defence Ctte nominally on Far Eastern strategy. W hadn't read the paper and was perhaps rather tight. Anyway we opened with a reference from W to American criticism of Monty for over-caution which W appeared to endorse. This brought an explosion from CIGS. 'If you would keep your confidence in your generals for even a few days I think we should do better ... I have listened to you for two days on end undermining Cabinet's confidence in Alexander until I felt I could stand no more' ... W protested vehemently. He was clearly deeply hurt on his most sensitive spot, his knowledge of strategy & his relations with his generals.[74]

The meeting went on to discuss the paper and all the other politicians present backed the chiefs of staff against Churchill. Brooke described the conclusion: 'This infuriated him more than ever and he became ruder and ruder. He finished by falling out with Attlee and having a real row concerning the future of India.'[75]

During the early months of 1944, as Eisenhower and his staff developed the details of the OVERLORD plan and huge numbers of American troops poured into Britain, Churchill was concerned with two particular problems associated with the operation. First he had to pass control of Bomber Command to Eisenhower so that it could be used to support the operation in the period immediately before and after the landing set for the end of May in Normandy. He was worried that heavy bombing of France would turn the population against the allies, but could not prevail against strong military views. (Over 50,000 French civilians were killed by allied bombing, roughly the same as the number of British civilians killed by German bombing.) An even more difficult problem, almost inevitably, was relations with De Gaulle (now operating from Algiers) and the FCNL as parts of France were liberated. Were the British and Americans to set up a military Government (which was what Roosevelt wanted), deal with the local Vichy authorities or allow the FCNL to control the liberated areas? In January Churchill told Eden that De Gaulle and the FCNL should not take over the liberated areas of France: 'We have no guarantee at present that ... he and his vindictive crowd will not try to peg out their claims to be the sole judge for the time being of the conduct of all Frenchmen and the sole monopolists of official power. This is what the President dreads, and so do I.'[76] In early April, after failing to persuade Roosevelt to invite De Gaulle to the United States, Churchill agreed with the President that the FCNL and De Gaulle should be excluded from all aspects of the OVERLORD operation designed to liberate their country.

On 26 May the FCNL, suspecting an invasion was imminent, declared itself the 'Provisional Government of the French Republic'. Shortly after this Eden persuaded Churchill to invite De Gaulle to Britain so that he would be under control when he finally found out how he had been kept out of Anglo-American planning for the invasion of France. De Gaulle arrived in Britain on 4 June and went to Churchill's train in southern England. Because the King and the military commanders had refused to allow him to accompany the invasion force, Churchill had decided to spend the time around the invasion on a train in Hampshire. Here communications were primitive and so were living conditions (for everybody else), but it helped make him feel he was part of the operation and living in field conditions. De Gaulle was told about the operation and the date (now set for 6 June) and agreed to make a broadcast to France. But he was, not surprisingly, annoyed at the way he had been treated. He refused to accept any invitation to visit Roosevelt and objected to the sudden Anglo-American interest in the administration of France after they had rejected his repeated requests for talks earlier in the year. Quite openly Churchill told De Gaulle that he would always side with Roosevelt and the United States against him – Eden and Bevin who were present publicly dissented, telling the French leader they did not agree with the Prime Minister.

De Gaulle moved on to a meeting with Eisenhower and promptly rejected his proclamation confirming the existing Vichy administration and offering the French people a choice of Government once liberation was complete. He also refused to broadcast after Eisenhower because this would tacitly endorse his position. Anglo-French relations were once again in a terrible state. By the evening of 5 June, as the invasion force sailed from British ports, Churchill was in a furious rage. At the last moment De Gaulle had withdrawn his liaison officers from the invasion units. At 1am when Churchill was almost speechless with rage, De Gaulle's Ambassador left because of all the insults hurled at him and Churchill issued an order that De Gaulle should be expelled to Algiers. That order was rescinded at 6am and De Gaulle did finally broadcast. Cadogan commented wryly: 'We endured the usual passionate anti-de G harangue from P.M. On this subject, we get away from politics and diplomacy and even common sense. It's a girls school. Roosevelt, P.M and – it must be admitted de G – all behave like girls approaching the age of puberty.'[77]

The 'girls school' continued the next day. By midnight on the evening of D-Day Churchill gave vent to another violent outburst because Eden, Attlee and Bevin all wanted to open talks with De Gaulle about the administration of France. Eden wrote in his diary:

> I was accused of trying to break up the government, of stirring up the press on the issue. He said that nothing would induce him to give way, that de Gaulle must go. There would be a Cabinet tomorrow. House of Commons would back him against de Gaulle and me and any of the Cabinet who sided with me, etc. FDR and he would fight the world.[78]

At the Cabinet on 7 June there was another long row with Eden but Churchill gave way and agreed to ask Roosevelt to allow talks on recognition to start. However he remained bitter about De Gaulle, telling Eden, 'Remember that there is not a scrap of generosity about this man, who only wishes to pose as a saviour of France in this operation without a single French soldier at his back.'[79] Cadogan commented on the paradoxical way the politicians had behaved during the most crucial Anglo-American operation of the war: 'of these critical 72 hours, I suppose about 40 have been occupied by all the High-Ups wrangling about purely imaginary and manufactured grievances against de Gaulle.'[80]

Even after the process of liberating French territory was underway, Churchill tried to thwart De Gaulle: by opposing his first visit to France on 14 June and trying to stop him making a speech when he did go. The rest of the Cabinet refused to agree. De Gaulle set up his own administration in the liberated area of northern Normandy around Bayeux and, against strong British advice, was formally recognised by the other governments-in-exile. After this visit De

Gaulle wrote a long, magnanimous letter to Churchill praising his role in the liberation of France. Churchill sent a cold reply; Duff Cooper (acting as British representative with De Gaulle and present when the reply was drafted) told Eden: 'The Prime Minister says he will denounce him as the mortal foe of England.'[81] At the beginning of July De Gaulle finally did visit Roosevelt and within a week, without consulting Britain, the United States recognised the FCNL as the *de facto* civil administration in France. Churchill had no choice but to go along with the Americans. In October he and Roosevelt agreed that they had no alternative but to recognise De Gaulle and the FCNL as the provisional Government of France – by then they had already established themselves in Paris as the effective Government. Yet Churchill, harbouring his distrust of De Gaulle personally, made a remarkable statement to his doctor on the return voyage from the Quebec conference: 'I must not let de Gaulle come between me and the French nation.'[82]

Churchill's fears about the OVERLORD invasion proved groundless. The American and British forces had overwhelming superiority. They had total supremacy at sea, 12,800 aircraft against 500, and a 5:1 superiority in tanks. They were fighting less than a third of the available German combat units and most of these were in a poor state. The eight Panzer divisions committed to the battle of Normandy had just seventeen replacement tanks between them and the infantry and static units were even weaker. Once again the allies showed poor tactical skill and an inability to surround and completely defeat their far weaker opponent. In the end they were reduced to their usual tactic of frontal assaults, losing large amounts of equipment but overwhelming the Germans by sheer firepower. The OVERLORD plan broke down on the first day, when the British failed to capture Caen,and the battle for Normandy was not finally won till August after some of Montgomery's usual ponderous moves and a failure by the Americans to advance quickly enough to surround the Germans at Falaise. The Germans retreated eastward, followed by the allied forces, which were unable to stop them reaching the Siegfried line despite their battered condition – for much of the time 2nd Panzer Division was operating with three tanks. The allies ran out of fuel and Montgomery failed to clear the area around Antwerp, which would have enabled the port to be opened. After a disastrous failure at Arnhem, the allies, after liberating France and Belgium, settled down for the winter of 1944–5 on the borders of Germany.

The Americans were by now dominating operations and strategy – they had fifty-five divisions deployed to Britain's thirteen. This preponderance meant that they were no longer prepared to accept British strategic advice, a situation demonstrated in the long arguments over the invasion of southern France (codename ANVIL), which it had been agreed at Cairo should be launched at the same time as OVERLORD. The first problems arose at the end of 1943 when the British, realising that the Italian campaign was hopelessly bogged down, advocated an amphibious landing at Anzio, which they claimed would open the road to Rome. Churchill thought that this landing should have priority over ANVIL (they needed the same landing craft) because the Anzio assault would decide 'the success or ruin of our Italian campaign'.[83] Roosevelt approved the operation but Churchill remained worried about whether the British would get enough credit with an American general in command. As so often, he was wildly optimistic about the likely outcome of the landing. He expected it to force the Germans back to the Alps and the allies could then 'turn left into France or . . . pursue the Germans towards Vienna, or turn right towards the Balkans'.[84] Operations on the ground across the difficult terrain of Italy against a determined enemy were never that simple. Within six days of the Anzio landings on 21 January the allied forces were on the brink of disaster as the Germans quickly brought up reinforcements. Churchill blamed the Americans for the failure. Allied forces could not break out of the bridgehead until the third week of May and Rome did not fall until 4 June.

Churchill was opposed to ANVIL, an American operation, from the start. At first he wanted a landing at Bordeaux instead of on the Mediterranean coast. He told the chiefs of staff in February 1944, 'Such a force let loose in the south and centre of France would instantly arouse widespread revolt and would be of measureless assistance to the main battle.'[85] But as the chiefs of staff pointed out, the same arguments could be applied to ANVIL and Bordeaux was a much more difficult operation because of the need to operate in the heavily defended Gironde estuary. By the end of March the US joint chiefs of staff admitted that because of the pressure at Anzio ANVIL would have to be postponed until after OVERLORD. It now made little strategic sense but the Americans were determined to go ahead, largely because it was their operation and they were also determined to stop British attempts to build up the Italian campaign. They were prepared to find more landing craft to carry out ANVIL but not for British operations in Italy.

Churchill was right to oppose a postponed ANVIL as making no military sense. But neither did his alternatives. At first (on the day before D-Day) he wanted a twelve- to fourteen-division assault on the French Atlantic coast from Bordeaux to St Nazaire with six divisions withdrawn from Italy. It was to be mounted, he decided, within a few weeks (which only demonstrated his persistent failure to grasp the logistics of modern warfare). The chiefs of staff convinced him not to send the idea to Roosevelt and to stick with the mainly British Italian campaign. He then decided that it would be relatively simple to advance into northern Italy (although allied forces had taken nearly a year to get from southern Italy to Rome), capture Trieste, advance through the Alps (along the misnamed Ljubljana gap) to Prague and Vienna, thereby gaining a largely British success in the war. His idea was to stop any withdrawal of units from Italy for ANVIL and adopt this plan instead. The military planners pointed out the almost insuperable problems involved in such an operation. On 21 June the joint planning staff reported that 'the combination of weather, terrain and lack of roads would combine to limit drastically our rate of advance', it would be very difficult to support forces north and east of the mountains and any assault on Trieste 'presents very considerable difficulties'.[86] As Brooke pointed out to Churchill, 'the country in Istria was well adapted for defence and we must beware lest the Germans should succeed in containing us there with smaller forces than were deployed against them'.[87]

As usual Churchill was unwilling to accept counter-arguments. Brooke described the meeting called to discuss the proposed operation into the Alps:

> We had a long evening of it listening to Winston's strategic arguments . . . I pointed out that, even on Alex's optimistic reckoning, the advance beyond the Pisa-Rimini line would not start till after September; namely we should embark on a campaign through the Alps in winter. It was hard to make him realise that, if we took the season of the year and the topography of the country in league

against us, we should have three enemies instead of one. We were kept up till close on 1am and accomplished nothing.[88]

In fact it was the Americans who vetoed the operation. Eisenhower told Churchill bluntly on 23 June: 'France is the decisive theatre. The decision was taken long ago by the Combined Chiefs of Staff. In my view, the resources of Great Britain and the US will not permit us to maintain two major theatres in the European war, each with decisive missions.'[89] On 24 June the US joint chiefs of staff issued instructions to the chiefs of staff and the British commander in the Mediterranean, General Wilson, to release forces for ANVIL. On Churchill's instructions the chiefs of staff replied that such a decision was 'unacceptable to us'.[90] The joint chiefs of staff simply replied that they were not prepared to discuss the matter further. Churchill protested to Roosevelt on 1 July but got nowhere. The invasion of southern France was set for 15 August.

On 3 July the US Ambassador in London told Roosevelt 'how deeply the Prime Minister has felt the differences' and he had 'never seen him so badly shaken'.[91] In mid-July Churchill decided he could no longer tolerate the way Britain had been ignored over ANVIL and drafted a message to Roosevelt:

> This obviously cannot continue, and, with the very greatest respect, I must request a further and formal discussion upon the matter . . . We are entitled to press for better and more equal treatment. We have as many troops and forces engaged on the whole in Europe, including both theatres, as you have yet brought into action.

He argued for a 'reasonable and equal relationship. Otherwise it would be necessary, in particular, to devise some other machinery for conducting the war.' He went on to threaten that he would break up the combined chiefs of staff structure and joint commands in the field.[92] He showed the message to Eden who persuaded him that sending it would do no good. Although he made more attempts to switch the assault (this time to Brittany), including telling the chiefs of staff that Eisenhower had argued for such an operation when he had not. He finally gave in six days before the landing, which went ahead almost unopposed. The Italian campaign continued in stalemate for the rest of the war, with only a slow allied advance northwards.

Shortly after the allied landings in Normandy the Germans launched their new 'secret weapon' against Britain – the pilotless flying bomb (V-1), followed later by rocket attacks (V-2). Churchill was determined to retaliate and turned to an old favourite among weapons – chemical warfare. Although prepared as a last resort to use gas to defend the beaches during any invasion in 1940, he had opposed the offensive use of poison gas because the chiefs of staff advised that Germany was capable of dropping three or four times more bombs than Britain. He told Ismay at the end of September 1940: 'I am deeply anxious that gas warfare should not be adopted at the present time.'[93] In early 1941 it was decided not to use gas even if the Italians did so during the Abyssinian campaign and to censor any news about such attacks. However in 1943 the Cabinet agreed that if the Germans used gas against the Soviet Union then Britain would retaliate and a public warning was issued. Churchill told Ismay, 'We shall retaliate by drenching the German cities with gas on the largest possible scale.'[94]

For some time the British found it very difficult to devise counter-measures to the V-1 attacks. Churchill told the House of Commons on 6 July that the attack was 'essentially indiscriminate in its nature, purpose and effect'. (Though how it differed in these respects from the far larger Anglo-American bombing of Germany is difficult to see.) The day before, the chiefs of staff had rejected the idea of retaliating with gas because it would divert the bombers from their primary tasks. Churchill was however keen to act now that the British had built far larger stocks of poison gas than Germany. He wrote to Ismay on 6 July: 'It is absurd to consider morality on this topic when everybody used it in the last war without a nod of complaint from the moralists or the Church ... It is simply a question of fashion changing as she does between long and short skirts for women.' He wanted 'a cold-blooded calculation made as to how it would pay us to use poison gas' which he thought might be 'unpleasant' but no worse than high explosive and 'nearly everyone recovers ... One really must not be bound by silly conventions of the mind.' He described himself, if the V-1 and V-2 attacks continued, as 'prepared to do *anything* that would hit the enemy in a murderous place'. His message to the chiefs of staff was 'I may certainly have to ask you to support me in using poison gas. We could drench the cities of the Ruhr and many other cities in Germany in such a way that most of the population would be requiring constant medical attention. . . . if we do it, let us do it one hundred per cent. In the meanwhile, I want the matter studied in cold blood by sensible people and not by that particular set of psalm-singing uniformed defeatists which one runs across now here now there.'[95]

The chiefs of staff agreed, unenthusiastically, to look at the question. While this work was continuing Churchill reminded them that 'he was prepared, after consultation with the United States and the USSR, to threaten the enemy with large scale gas attacks in retaliation, should such a course appear profitable'.[96] On 25 July he demanded the chiefs of staff produce their report within three days. When they did so, they advised that gas warfare was possible and that Britain could drop more than Germany but they doubted whether it would cause many difficulties to the German authorities in controlling the country. They did, however, anticipate problems at home: 'the same cannot be said for our own people, who are in no such inarticulate condition'.[97] After reading the chiefs of staff assessment Churchill concluded gloomily, 'I am not at all convinced by this negative report. But clearly I cannot make head against the parsons and the warriors at the same time.'[sic][98] Churchill was not only prepared to escalate warfare against civilians by using chemical weapons, he was also ready to use bacteriological warfare against Germany by dropping anthrax bombs. In March 1944 he approved an order for 500,000 such bombs, which were to be dropped 'well behind the lines, to render towns uninhabitable and indeed dangerous to enter without a respirator'. These were US made bombs, but he also wanted British production. He told the minister responsible for the programme, 'I think we should be in a position to make and fill these bombs here . . . on a considerable scale.'[99]

Because of the decline in Britain's influence within the Anglo-American alliance and the fact that most of the key strategic decisions had been taken, Churchill found that in 1944 he had increasingly less influence over military affairs. He compensated for this with a series of visits to the front. Although he was unable to watch the D-Day landings, he went to Normandy on 12 June, together with Brooke and Smuts, for a brief visit to Montgomery and British troops in the bridgehead. Six weeks later he went to Cherbourg to see American troops and then travelled by boat to spend two days in the British area. On 7 August he went again, this time by plane, for a very short visit that was highly inconvenient for all of his hosts. Three days later he departed to the Mediterranean for almost three weeks. He took a trip to watch the landings in the south of France but was so far away he could see little. In Italy he visited Monte Cassino, scene of a vicious battle, visited the slow-moving front, went back to Rome and then back to the front again. Again this travelling took a toll on his health. When he returned to Britain he developed a high temperature and pneumonia was diagnosed. Treatment with antibiotics soon cured the problem.

Perhaps Churchill's most emotional visit was to Paris in November – his first since May 1940. He arrived on 10 November and was immediately won over by the treatment he received from the French, relishing especially use of the gold bath which had been reserved for Goering. On armistice day he went to the Arc de Triomphe, walked down the Champs Elysées with De Gaulle, laid a wreath on the tomb of Clemenceau, and visited the Invalides, where he saw Foch's grave and the tomb of his hero Napoleon. After lunch he had a surprisingly amicable discussion with De Gaulle, now head of the French Government, and the next day received the freedom of the city of Paris. For a while, even though Churchill rejected De Gaulle's suggestion of Anglo-French domination of Europe with both the US and USSR excluded, relations were warmer. But within a few weeks Churchill had returned to his old habit of abusing De Gaulle. He wrote to Eden: 'I cannot think of anything more unpleasant and impossible than having this menacing and hostile man in our midst, always trying to make a reputation in France by claiming a position far above what France occupies, and making faces at the Allies who are doing the work.'[100]

Churchill's other major trip that autumn was once again to Ottawa for the last Anglo-American conference of the war. He sailed on 5 September on board the *Queen Mary*. His vast entourage took up most of the boat. He was accompanied by Clementine and Mary, his doctor Lord Moran (with his son) and a team of supporting nurses and doctors, forty-two clerks, thirty cipher staff, thirty-six Royal Marine guards, the chiefs of staff and their advisers plus a number of other ministers. At a time when food rationing was at its height in Britain, his Private Secretary, Jock Colville, described the meals 'en famille', which he often shared, as 'gargantuan in scale and epicurean in quality'.[101] On one evening his dinner with Moran and Lord

Cherwell (as Lindemann had become) consisted of oysters, consommé, turbot, turkey, melon, stilton, fruit and petits fours, all washed down with large quantities of champagne and vintage 1870 brandy. Once in Quebec the meeting itself, which lasted for six days, was marred by many factors. Churchill, who had been unwell for part of the voyage, was in a particularly bad mood. He drove Eden almost to the point of resignation and Ismay, his military assistant since 1940, did resign, only to withdraw it later. Roosevelt was showing the first signs of the steep physical decline that was to lead to his death within six months and his close adviser Harry Hopkins was also ill.

The combined chiefs of staff organisation had little to settle now that allied forces were approaching Germany. Churchill though was still pressing for operations in secondary theatres rather than a direct assault on Germany and Japan. The first meeting the combined chiefs of staff held with Churchill and Roosevelt consisted according to Brooke 'of a long statement by the P.M. giving his views on how the war should be run. According to him we had two main objectives, first an advance on Vienna, secondly the capture of Singapore!'[102] Churchill's stated aim in reaching Vienna was to counter 'the consequent dangerous spread of Russian influence in this area'.[103] He told Wilson, the British commander in the Mediterranean, that the Americans had agreed to 'our pushing on to Vienna, if the war lasts long enough'.[104] Wilson did not, however, expect to advance into Istria until winter and any advance towards the Alps and Ljubljana would have to wait until the spring and so there was little chance of British forces reaching Vienna ahead of the advancing Soviet troops. By the end of the conference Churchill was manifestly unhappy with Britain's subservient position. He complained about operations in north-west Europe being under American command, that Italy was a dead-end and forces in Burma were only being used to keep open the road to China and so were contributing little to the war effort.

Most of the discussions at Quebec though were not about military affairs; they revolved round Britain's parlous economic situation and its need for American assistance, which had become steadily greater throughout the war. From early 1941 Britain was dependent on lend-lease supplies and in total during the war they amounted to $27 billion. But these goods were not 'free'. In September 1941 the

Government had to accept severe restrictions on Britain's exports –
no lend-lease goods nor goods similar to them if they were in
competition with American goods could be exported and even
materials bought in the United States could not be exported if they
were in short supply in the US. British commercial exports were to
be kept at very low levels. This not only gave the US control over
Britain's exports but also the opportunity to take over lucrative export
markets, particularly in Latin America.

During 1941 the US Government also decided what the 'consideration' (required by Congress) was to be for those lend-lease
goods not returnable at the end of the war. They demanded the end
of Britain's system of imperial preference and the dismantling of the
sterling area once the war was over, moves which would greatly
increase American economic power and influence. Acrimonious
negotiations continued throughout 1941, including an unproductive
exchange between the two leaders at the Newfoundland conference
in August. The British procrastinated in the hope that when the US
joined the war they would drop these demands. Churchill was
therefore extremely disappointed to find in early 1942 that not only
were lend-lease and its conditions to continue as before but that a
'consideration' was still required. He was caught between the
American demands and Conservative Party opinion reluctant to
abandon imperial preference. Eventually in February 1942 a compromise was agreed – the British had to agree to post-war talks to
establish open trade but were not committed to abolish imperial
preference.

Throughout the war the United States kept the British economy
and finances under close control. During 1942, as American forces
were stationed in Britain and other parts of the sterling area, Britain's
dollar reserves, which had been exhausted at the end of 1940, started
to rise again. Roosevelt was determined that Britain should not
benefit from this. He wanted to keep Britain's dollar reserves at a
level sufficient to stop them opting for an enclosed trading system at
the end of the war but not so high that they could afford to ignore
US demands. On 1 January 1943 he therefore decided, without
informing Churchill, that 'the United Kingdom's gold and dollar
balances should not be permitted to be less than about $600 million
nor above about $1 billion' (between £150 million and £250
million).[105] The US Government was able to achieve this by taking

goods (such as tobacco for civilian consumption) out of lend-lease and forcing the British to pay for them and requiring more goods to be given free under 'reverse lend-lease' rather than the US buying them. In early 1944, as the build-up for OVERLORD reached its peak, the number of goods taken out of lend-lease increased and on 22 February Roosevelt virtually ordered Churchill to reduce British reserves to the $1 billion level. This was the first time he had disclosed the figure to which the US Government was working. Sir John Anderson, the Chancellor of the Exchequer, advised Churchill that if this demand was accepted 'we should have lost our financial independence, in any case precarious, as soon as lend-lease comes to an end, and would emerge from the war, victorious indeed, but quite helpless financially'.[106] Churchill protested to Roosevelt but American policy was not changed.

Churchill was becoming increasingly aware of the implications of Britain's dependence on the United States. He told the Cabinet in July 1944 'if we accepted the financial help of the United States we might also be parting with political authority and control. Finance was interwoven with the power and sovereignty of the state'.[107] But it was not a question of 'if' Britain accepted US help, the undermining process had been underway since the end of 1940 and was to get worse as victory approached. Earlier in the month Anderson told his colleagues that Britain would be the world's largest debtor by the end of the war, with liabilities of over £3 billion and also with a balance of payments deficit of at least £1 billion a year. Even though exports would increase in peace, Britain would need about $1–2 billion in continued lend-lease together with an interest-free loan of about $2 billion. If this was not forthcoming then Britain would have to 'borrow all we can from the United States on any terms available'.[108] Anderson had earlier explained to his colleagues just how dependent Britain was on the United States: 'It would be impossible to maintain sterling without some assistance from the United States . . . if we antagonised the United States, the generous assistance we needed from that country would not be made available.'[109] Cherwell had given Churchill a similar message: 'without either lend-lease or a loan from the U.S.A. immediately after the war, we shall be completely at the mercy of our overseas suppliers and our economic position and standard of life will be affected for a generation'.[110]

At Quebec Churchill tried to negotiate continued American

assistance for Britain. To sustain the war against Japan after Germany was defeated, Britain would need, he told Roosevelt, a minimum of $7 billion for the first year alone. The President found this argument unpersuasive – the US joint chiefs of staff wanted to keep the Pacific war an entirely American affair anyway. Eventually Churchill had to ask, 'What do you want me to do? Get on my hind legs and beg like Fala [Roosevelt's dog]?'[111] Before obtaining a promise of continued American help, he was forced to accept a US plan, drawn up by the Secretary of the Treasury Henry Morgenthau, for the dismemberment of Germany and the destruction of most of its industrial base. Then Roosevelt was prepared to agree to lend-lease arrangements to provide $3.5 billion of military help and $3 billion of civilian materials after the war. Churchill believed he had obtained what was needed for Britain's immediate post-war situation. But within two months Roosevelt had decided against a formal deal and reneged on his discussions with Churchill at Quebec – he wanted to keep Britain in a dependent position. Churchill had no power to change the President's mind. When the war ended lend-lease was cancelled within a few days, leaving Britain desperately exposed and dependent on negotiating an American loan.

The Quebec conference had also highlighted divergences over operations in the Far East. Roosevelt told Morgenthau privately he knew why the British wanted to join the war in the Pacific. 'All they want is Singapore back.'[112] Britain had been deliberately excluded from the American war in the Pacific and its efforts in the war against Japan were always marginal. Churchill told the dominion prime ministers in May 1944, 'We must regard ourselves as junior partners in the war against Japan.'[113] But by 1944 in Burma British forces had acquired immense superiority over the Japanese (the Japanese always regarded this campaign as a sideshow) – during the Imphal-Kohima battle the British had air supremacy and just over six divisions ranged against a solitary Japanese division. The 'British' contribution though was small – sixty per cent of the troops were Indian or Gurkhas, twelve per cent were African and the same proportion British. (Churchill had little time for the Indian Army's role, describing it as 'a gigantic system of outdoor relief'.[114])

Although the British role was minor this did not mean that there were not bitter rows between Churchill and the chiefs of staff over the strategy to be adopted in the Far East. Indeed in 1944 it was this subject that brought his military advisers to the brink of resignation over his conduct. The problems began in January when Churchill rejected the strategy he had agreed with Roosevelt at Cairo only six weeks earlier – no amphibious operation in the Bay of Bengal and concentration on opening the route to China. He told the Defence Committee 'it was the first he had heard of these proposals' and 'he was dismayed at the thought that a large British army and air force would stand inactive in India during the whole of 1944'.[115] (The latter comment was a travesty of the proposed strategy.) As the Americans suspected, Churchill was indeed desperate to regain Singapore and to do so he wanted to mount a large amphibious operation from India aimed at that general area (either Rangoon or Sumatra first). His main worry was loss of British influence after the war: 'If the Japanese should withdraw from our Malayan possessions or make peace as a result of the main American thrust, the United States Government would ... feel with conviction "We have won this victory and liberated these places, and we must have the dominating say in their future and derive full profit from their produce especially oil."'[116]

The chiefs of staff disagreed with Churchill's proposals. They argued that because of social and political discontent India was incapable of supporting such a major operation and that the best strategy for Britain would be to help the main American thrust in the Pacific. To try and get his way Churchill persuaded Roosevelt to agree that British naval assistance was not needed in the Pacific in 1944 – allowing him to argue that naval forces could be used in the Bay of Bengal. At first he gained some support in the Cabinet, but once the opposition of the chiefs of staff became clear, this melted away. On 20 March he produced a series of 'rulings' for the chiefs of staff – Britain's interests were to fight in the Bay of Bengal, the fleet should be based at Ceylon and amphibious operations should be aimed at Singapore. The next day, with D-Day only ten weeks away, the chiefs of staff agreed between themselves to resign rather than accept these rulings. Brooke believed that the crisis might well 'lead to the resignation of the Chiefs of Staff Committee ... [since] Winston overrides our opinions and advice' and he told Dill in Washington 'I have just about reached the end of my tether'.[117] The threatened crisis did not come to a head – Churchill discovered that the Americans also opposed his proposals and the amphibious operation could not be carried out unless they released the necessary landing craft.

Changing tack, Churchill briefly showed interest in a chiefs of staff proposal for a campaign from Darwin northwards through Celebes and Borneo towards Singapore. As Brooke noted, 'This might give us the chance of running an entirely British Imperial campaign instead of furnishing reinforcements for American operations.'[118] Churchill too was determined that such an operation would not fall under US command. But the different political and military ways of approaching the situation were not reconciled and by April 1944 strategic planning for the Far East was in deadlock. Churchill would not accept the advice of the chiefs of staff and they would not accept his proposals. Even Churchill's ardent admirer Ismay wrote in May, 'I believe that the waffling that there has been for nearly nine months over the basic questions of strategy in the Far East will be one of the black spots in the record of British Higher Direction of War.'[119] Still the arguments went on. On 8 August there were three meetings between Churchill and the chiefs of staff lasting over seven hours in all but nothing was decided. For Churchill the overriding aim of the Far Eastern campaign should be to restore British prestige in the region. He told the chiefs of staff and other ministers: 'The British contribution to the recapture of our Empire in the Far East was minute. The shame of our disaster at Singapore could . . . only be wiped out by our recapture of that fortress.'[120]

Churchill maintained this position at the Quebec conference. He told the chiefs of staff that Singapore was 'the supreme objective in the whole of the Indian and Far Eastern theatres . . . the only prize that will restore British prestige in this region'.[121] And he told the Americans 'a grievous and shameful blow to British prestige must be avenged in battle'.[122] He asked Roosevelt for a 'fair share' in the war against Japan but admitted that Britain would be dependent on US assistance to carry it out. Eventually he abandoned the ideas he had clung to doggedly for months and accepted the chiefs of staff view that it would be best for Britain to have a minor role in the main American thrust against Japan and continue with operations in Burma, reluctantly abandoning his hope of recapturing Singapore. At Quebec he finally agreed that the main effort by the Royal Navy was to be in the Pacific, though its contribution was, in relation to the United States, very small – four carriers (US seventy-nine), two battleships (US twenty-three), three cruisers (US forty-five) and ten destroyers (US 296). In their plans for the final assault on Japan the US joint chiefs of staff refused to accept more than three imperial divisions (one each from Britain, Australia and Canada) and they were to be equipped with US weapons and be no more than a reserve corps within a US army. By 1945 the campaign in Burma was to have some success (the Japanese had only 20,000 men facing 260,000 and sixty-six aircraft against 4,600), but Malaya and Singapore were not recovered until after the Japanese surrender.

The long, unproductive rows between Churchill and the chiefs of staff over Far Eastern strategy were yet another manifestation of the simmering discontent provoked by Churchill's way of directing the war, in particular his inability to accept advice and his failure to be decisive. But towards the end of the war there were also increasing signs that his physical and mental state was declining. His Private Secretary, John Martin, told Lord Moran in January 1945 'his work has deteriorated a lot in the last few months ... he has become very wordy, irritating his colleagues in the Cabinet by his verbosity'.[123] Eden noted at the same time in his diary: 'W rambles so that everything takes many times longer to decide than is necessary.'[124] The Canadian Prime Minister Mackenzie King thought:

> Churchill was very domineering; he cowed his colleagues. I have seen him actually cruel to Mr Attlee. He had a way of shifting discussion when it was critical and when it did not agree with his views. Then the emotional stuff was brought out, there were tears in his eyes and he carried his colleagues with him ... This overbearing attitude ... prevented other members of the Cabinet giving of their best.[125]

In February 1945 Sir Alexander Cadogan wrote in his diary after a one-and-a-half-hour discussion in the Cabinet about manpower policy:

> The P.M. cannot say 'Yes' or 'No'. Instead, he makes long speech, of which, 5 mins later, he produces a slightly differently worded version. Why all the Cabinet aren't mad, I can't think ... *How* have we conducted this war with the P.M. spending *hours* of his own

and other people's time simply drivelling, welcoming every red herring so as only to have the pleasure of more irrelevant, redundant talk.[126]

In the past the complaints had largely been confined to diaries or talks with other people. But on 19 January 1945 the Labour Leader Clement Attlee (the only man apart from the Prime Minister to serve in the War Cabinet continuously since May 1940) felt sufficiently strongly to address Churchill himself. In what was probably the longest letter of his entire life he set out a series of complaints about the inefficient way the Government was run and Churchill's own behaviour. He began: 'I have for some time had it in mind to write to you on the method or rather lack of method of dealing with matters requiring Cabinet decisions ... I consider the present position inimical to the successful performance of the tasks imposed upon us as a Government and injurious to the war effort.' He explained that a lot of effort was devoted in Cabinet committees to subordinating party interests to the best interests of the country. However when papers came before Cabinet:

> it is very exceptional for you to have read them. More and more often you have not read even the note prepared for your guidance. Often half an hour or more is wasted in explaining what could have been grasped by two or three minutes reading of the document. Not infrequently a phrase catches your eye which gives rise to a disquisition on an interesting point only slightly connected with the subject matter. The result is long delays and unnecessarily long Cabinets imposed on Ministers who have already done a full day's work and will have more to deal with before they get to bed.

Too often, Attlee continued, Churchill referred subjects to Bracken and Beaverbrook, who were not members of the Cabinet and who knew nothing of the subject. He concluded:

> I do not think that you can complain of any lack of loyalty on my part, but I think that your Cabinet colleagues have the right to ask that in matters to which you cannot give your personal attention you should put confidence in them. . . . I would ask you to put yourself in the position of your colleagues and ask yourself whether

637

in the days when you were a Minister you would have been as patient as we have been.[127]

Churchill was furious, and even more so after he had spoken to Bracken, Beaverbrook and Clementine, who all agreed with Attlee's complaints. At first he was going to send a violently worded reply but eventually sent a thirteen-word brush-off. In private he called it 'a socialist conspiracy', and 'harped on nothing but the inadequate representation of the Tories in the Cabinet'.[128] He did not change his behaviour or method of working. Others started to feel the strain was too much. Two months later Brooke, the Chairman of the Chiefs of Staff, wrote, 'I feel that I can't stick another moment with him and would give almost anything never to see him again.'[129] Even Eden reflected sadly, 'fond as I am of Winston, I do not feel I have the strength to undertake life & work with him again; it is too much of a strain & struggle'.[130]

Churchill also alienated his colleagues by two other traits – the time wasted following up his enthusiasm for odd ideas and his attitude towards British casualties. Perhaps the oddest idea he ever supported was Project Habbakuk. He heard of this through Lindemann and was immediately attracted to the proposal to construct airfields from the Arctic ice cap by cutting out frozen blocks five thousand feet long, two thousand feet wide and one hundred feet high. They would be increased in depth by pumping over sea water until it froze, leaving passages in the ice for oil fuel storage and electrical equipment. These floating islands would then be towed south into the Atlantic. Churchill told Ismay in December 1942, 'I attach the greatest importance to the prompt examination of these ideas.' Even before they were examined he wanted an order placed with the 'highest priority'.[131] The floating ice airfields sank without trace.

More worrying for his colleagues was Churchill's attitude throughout the war to British casualties. His demand in February 1942 for a high death toll in Singapore before any surrender was no aberration. Almost a year earlier, during Rommel's first attack in the western desert, he had ordered: 'No surrenders by officers and men will be considered tolerable unless at least 50 per cent casualties are sustained.'[132] That same month he was convinced that blocking the port of Tripoli would stop all Rommel's supplies (in fact there were

638

plenty of alternatives available) and wanted *HMS Barham* and a cruiser to be sunk in the harbour as blockships. Even with reduced crews hundreds of British sailors would have died and Admiral Cunningham refused to carry out the operation. Churchill told him, 'The effectual blocking of Tripoli would be well worth a battleship upon the active list.'[133] Cunningham still refused to sacrifice his men and ships on such a vain operation. In January 1942 Churchill wrote to Ismay that an attack by Bomber Command on the *Tirpitz* at Trondheim was essential: 'The whole strategy of the war turns at this point on this ship.' That was a ridiculous over-emphasis but Churchill added, 'The loss of 100 bombers could be accepted if TIRPITZ were destroyed.'[134] The Chief of the Air Staff told him that such an attack was totally impracticable and he was not prepared to risk so many planes and their highly trained crews. At times Churchill even complained that British casualties were not high enough. For instance, in July 1943 he wrote to the Admiralty to draw their attention to 'a rather pregnant fact' – the Fleet Air Arm had only had thirty men killed out of a strength of 45,000 between February and April 1943. The Admiralty refused to reply to his letter.[135]

As the war drew to a close he took an equally severe attitude towards British civilian casualties. As the allies liberated France no attempt was made to take control of the Channel Islands, which had been occupied by German forces in 1940. The islands were extremely short of food and the German authorities offered to allow Britain to send in relief ships. Churchill insisted the offer be rejected: 'I am entirely opposed to our sending any rations to the Channel Islands ostensibly for the civil population but in fact enabling the German garrison to prolong their resistance.'[136] On 6 November he again rejected the advice of the chiefs of staff that the German offer should be accepted but he was overruled in Cabinet next day. In April 1945 the US joint chiefs of staff wanted to launch waves of pilotless old bombers loaded with 20,000 lbs of high explosive against German cities. The British chiefs of staff, worried about the risk of retaliation against Britain when the civilian population thought German bombing was over, advised Churchill to reject the proposal. He turned down their advice and went along with the Americans, saying 'we will not dissent' and 'We shall make no complaint if misfortune comes to us in consequence'.[137]

By this time such a bombing campaign was unlikely to add significantly to the impact the RAF and the USAAF had already achieved. Once the diversion of the bombing effort to support OVERLORD was ended, the RAF resumed its area bombing of German cities. In the last quarter of 1944 more bombs were dropped on Germany than in the whole of 1943. As German fighter defences collapsed, Anglo-American loss rates fell and accuracy improved. In July 1944 the chiefs of staff first considered 'Operation Thunderclap', a major increase in terror bombing. This was a plan to attack a city with a population of around 300,000 and inflict casualties of about 220,000, of which half would be deaths. It was thought that 'such an attack ... cannot help but have a shattering effect on political and civilian morale all over Germany'.[138] In the autumn of 1944 Churchill inspired Harris to write a letter to him about the need to bomb Germany thoroughly and responded: 'every effort should be made to crack it on to Germany now and every airplane that can be spared from the battlefield should be at them'.[139]

At the end of January 1945, just before he left for the Yalta conference, Churchill spoke to Sinclair, the Secretary of State for Air, and asked for attacks on the civilian population in large cities rather than on the German Army. He wrote after the meeting: 'I did not ask you last night about plans for harrying the German retreat from Breslau. On the contrary, I asked whether Berlin, and no doubt other large cities in East Germany, should not be considered especially attractive targets.'[140] Churchill's request brought 'Thunderclap' into operation – the attack on Dresden on 13–15 February. The total death toll in the city, which was crowded with refugees, will never be known but the best estimate is at least 100,000 people. Six weeks later Churchill, who until then had taken the view that bombing German civilians was one of the best ways of winning the war, suddenly decided he wanted a review of 'the question of bombing German cities simply for the sake of increasing the terror, though under other pretexts'. He now urged a concentration on military targets, not on moral grounds, but simply because of the growing problem the allies were facing in running a devastated Germany. He wrote a minute, with more than half an eye on history, which raised questions about the operation he had helped initiate: 'The destruction of Dresden remains a serious query against the conduct of Allied bombing.'[141] Not surprisingly the Chief of the Air

Staff, incensed by Churchill's suddenly discovered aversion to area bombing, forced him to withdraw the last remark and rewrote the minute himself.

By the spring of 1945 Germany was on the point of collapse. In the west allied armies under Eisenhower crossed the Rhine in late March (Churchill watched the operation with Montgomery). Although they were some 300 miles from Berlin and with the Elbe still to cross, whereas Soviet armies were only thirty miles away across the Oder, Churchill badly wanted American and British troops to get to Berlin first. He felt that if Soviet troops entered Berlin it would over-emphasise their contribution to the final victory. Eisenhower was more concerned to ensure the rout of German forces and no longer had any confidence in Montgomery's continual boasting about how quickly he could advance, when all the evidence of the last two and a half years showed he never achieved it in practice. Eisenhower withdrew troops from Montgomery and concentrated on reaching Leipzig and the south. He agreed with the Soviet commanders that the Elbe would mark the line along which the two armies would meet.

As the Soviet armies fought their way through the streets of Berlin, Hitler committed suicide and by early May his successor, Admiral Donitz, was ready to surrender. Churchill was aware of these indications on 4 May and two days later Eisenhower conducted the formal negotiations at his headquarters at Rheims. The end of the war in Europe was to be midnight on 8 May. That day Churchill lunched with the King, an announcement of the surrender was made at 3pm and afterwards he spoke to the Commons before MPs went to St Margaret's church for a service of thanksgiving. Afterwards Churchill went to Buckingham Palace with the War Cabinet and the chiefs of staff. Later, after a private dinner, he addressed the cheering crowds in Whitehall.

It was perhaps fitting, despite Churchill's objections, that Soviet forces entered the German capital because they had been overwhelmingly responsible for destroying the might of the German Army. Of the roughly thirteen and a half million German casualties and prisoners during the war, ten million occurred on the eastern front. The Soviet Union never fought less than two-thirds of the German combat units and for most of the war it faced over ninety per cent. Soviet casualties during the war were twenty times greater than the combined total of American and British casualties. Yet Churchill could never bring himself to acknowledge this effort. In July 1944 he told the Cabinet 'we had held the enemy at bay for a year and a half single-handed', i.e. until American entry in December 1941.[142] This conveniently overlooked the fact that the Soviet Union had joined the war in June 1941. In his victory broadcast to the nation on 13 May (which contained a biting attack on his old enemy the Irish Government) he would not say more than the Soviet Union had held 'many more troops on their front than we could'. In his memoirs he virtually ignored their efforts.

The war had been won by the combined weight of the economic and military power of the United States and the Soviet Union. When that power had been applied, the influence of Britain and Churchill over the war had been dramatically curtailed. In May 1945 Britain was on the winning side but it was dependent on the United States for its economic and financial survival. Its resistance earlier in the war was essential in order to provide the base from which the American-dominated armies could invade the continent once the Soviet Union had begun to destroy the German military machine. Hitler and the evil state he had created lay in ruins and the nations of Europe had been liberated. But that was not, for Churchill, the reason for such efforts and sacrifices. In February 1945 General Alexander said to him that the war had been fought 'to secure liberty and a decent existence for the peoples of Europe'. Churchill replied, 'Not a bit of it: we are fighting to secure the proper respect for the British people.'[143]

Creating the Post-War World

Until the end of 1942 when the Battle of Stalingrad, the invasion of French North Africa and the Battle of El Alamein showed that the tide of war was turning in favour of the allies, neither Churchill nor the Government spent much time discussing post-war issues. However during the last two years of the war these became increasingly important and at the meetings between the allied leaders at Teheran, Yalta and Potsdam they dominated the agenda. The problems were not just the fate of Germany and Italy but also the future of the liberated countries, national borders in Eastern Europe, huge population transfers, Britain's future relations with the United States and the Soviet Union, and the role and powers of any world organisation to replace the virtually defunct League of Nations. Throughout this complex process Churchill demonstrated a curious mix of attitudes – unwilling to even discuss some subjects during the war, reluctant to develop a clear policy on others, he displayed an old-fashioned, romantic view (particularly of monarchs) but also a ruthless *realpolitik* about the fate of millions of people.

To prepare for allied discussions the British Government had to decide on its priorities for the post-war world. At times Churchill's views could be so vague as to make them impossible to use as the basis for planning. On one occasion when the Foreign Office asked for guidance he told them 'the most intense effort will be made by the leading powers to prolong their honourable association, and by sacrifice and self-restraint win for themselves a glorious name in human annals'.[1] His fundamental idea was, however, that there should be a major redrawing of European boundaries, affecting not just the defeated but also the victors and even the neutrals. He had developed these views before the war under the influence of the eccentric Count Richard Coudenhove Kalergi, the President of the Pan-European Union, who regularly sent him his latest ideas for a United States of Europe. As early as the summer of 1940 Churchill was outlining these ideas to the Cabinet. As far as he was concerned there were only five great European nations that should remain independent – England [sic], France, Italy, Spain and Prussia. The rest should be grouped into four confederations. The Northern would be centred on The Hague, Mitteleuropa on either Prague or Warsaw, the Danubian (consisting of Bavaria, Württemberg, Austria and Hungary) on Vienna and the Balkan under the leadership of Turkey centred on Constantinople [sic]. These nine powers would form a Council of Europe, which would control an internationalised air force and individual countries would only be allowed a militia. For Churchill the key was the Danubian confederation and the dismemberment of Germany: 'The separation of the Austrians and Southern Germans from the Prussians is essential to the harmonious reconstitution of Europe.'[2] He allotted Britain a distinctive (if somewhat vague) role in this new structure: 'the English speaking world would be apart from this, but closely connected with it' – controlling the oceans of the world through the equal-sized navies of Britain and the United States.[3]

Churchill never thought through the practical obstacles inherent in this scheme. He did not consider the potential for national and ethnic conflict that these confederations would contain (for example why should the Balkan Christian countries consent to be under the leadership of a Muslim Turkey?). Nor did he work out how these arrangements might be implemented – were the states involved to be given a free choice or were they to be coerced? Nevertheless he stuck doggedly to the idea of confederations. He told the Cabinet in November 1942 that the only way to run Europe was for Britain and the Soviet Union to keep out and for a Grand Council of Prussia, Italy, Spain and a Scandinavian confederation to be formed (France was notably missing from this arrangement). In early 1943 he put some of these ideas to Roosevelt, suggesting that the future world organisation should only have places for the confederations, thereby eliminating the influence of the small powers, and that there should be a series of regional councils under the world organisation (excluding Asia and Africa which would still be European colonies).

In May 1943 during a lunch at the White House he expounded his ideas more fully: 'there ought to be three regional organisations and one supreme. He visioned [sic] the USA, British Empire and Russia really running the show. The USA would have membership in the American and Pacific region. Britain in all three. The USA might or might not have membership in the European.'⁴ The idea that Britain would be the only true world power after the war was a major misreading of the international situation and the Foreign Office had already warned him that the United States would not accept these ideas since they were unwilling to become involved in a series of regional councils. Roosevelt formally rejected his proposals at the Quebec conference in August 1943 and the Soviet Union did the same at the Moscow meeting of foreign ministers that autumn. Churchill thereupon lost interest in the whole subject. He continually obstructed work within the Government in preparing the structure of the future United Nations, arguing that it should all be settled between the end of the war in Europe and the defeat of Japan. Nevertheless planning went ahead and at the Dumbarton Oaks conference in August 1944 general agreement was reached over the future world organisation, including in particular a General Assembly and a Security Council where the victors would be able to exercise a veto. Churchill still objected, telling Eden: 'All these attempts to settle the world while we are still struggling with the enemy seem to me most injurious.'⁵ The main issue left to be resolved at this stage was the nature of the veto. The Soviet Union, fearing it would be outnumbered, wanted an absolute veto even over discussion of an issue, which would have rendered the UN virtually useless as a body. Churchill supported this position, telling Eden, 'I must warn you that as far as I can see the Foreign Office view now differs fundamentally from mine ... I am in entire agreement with the Russians.'⁶ After losing the argument in Cabinet in January 1945, he finally gave in and accepted Roosevelt's compromise proposal for a veto only over Security Council resolutions.

Although Churchill had been unable to secure any support for his idea of confederations in Europe, he still hoped to achieve one of his other great ambitions – the restoration of the Hapsburg monarchy.

He had lived through the collapse of both the Hapsburg empire and the German monarchy in the last days of the First World War as a result of revolution and the pressure of national aspirations. Now, rewriting history, he argued that it was the allies who had deliberately destroyed both monarchies with terrible consequences. He regularly saw Otto Hapsburg (the claimant to the Hapsburg throne) and always encouraged him, against Foreign Office advice. He gave Eden one of his lectures on the subject in September 1943:

> Please try to have a little confidence in my insight into Europe gathered over so many years ... One of the great mistakes made after the last war was the destruction by ignorant hands of the Austro-Hungarian Empire ... I really see no reason ... why we, the leading monarchical country, should seem to be more allergic to royalty than the Republic of the United States ... Wilson and Lloyd George thought they were ensuring peace as well as gratifying their raw prejudices in driving out monarchy. However if the Wittelsbachs had been substituted in Germany for the Hohenzollerns there would have been no Hitler and no war.[7]

Churchill tried unsuccessfully to get Otto Hapsburg as the replacement for Admiral Horthy, the ruler of Hungary, and also wanted to stop the Austrians having a free say over their future in order to secure a Hapsburg restoration. He pressed these claims against the consistent opposition of both the chiefs of staff and the Foreign Office, and clung to his belief that the war had been caused by the destruction of monarchy by Britain and the United States in 1918. As the war in Europe ended he once again told Eden (in a travesty of the historical facts): 'This war would never have come if, under American and modernising pressure, we had not driven the Hapsburgs out of Austria and Hungary and the Hohenzollerns out of Germany.'[8]

The other fixed point in Churchill's view of the post-war world was the relationship with the United States. Since the early summer of 1940 the Government had accepted that, in the words of a Foreign Office paper for the Cabinet in July: 'the future of our widely scattered Empire is likely to depend on the evolution of an effective and enduring collaboration between ourselves and the United States'.[9] But that collaboration had become increasingly unequal, given Britain's dependence on American economic and financial assistance to continue the war and the disparity in their military efforts. Churchill saw a close-knit relationship as central to Britain's future whereas colleagues such as Attlee, Eden, Halifax and Beaverbrook, although they accepted the need for an alliance with the United States to help preserve Britain's position, felt that it should not be exclusive and that Britain would need other partners in the post-war world, in particular France. Churchill also badly misjudged the way that the American administration and public saw Britain – they did not share his conviction that there was a 'special relationship' between the two countries.

In May 1943 at a White House lunch, Churchill urged that after the war the combined chiefs of staff organisation should continue, Britain and the United States should have a common foreign policy, common citizenship, free movement of peoples and full access by the United States to all British military bases around the world. Roosevelt never accepted this vision and told Churchill the next day he was 'a little anxious lest other countries should think that Britain and U.S. were trying to boss the world'.[10] The US was prepared for a close relationship with Britain in so far as it helped American national interests (for example use of British bases) but they were not prepared to limit their national power by, for example, continuing the combined chiefs of staff into peacetime. Churchill though was insistent. When he spoke at Harvard University in September 1943, he again put the case for a common citizenship and a continuation of the combined chiefs of staff after the war, but the Roosevelt administration made no sympathetic response. Later that month he told Eden and Attlee that nothing should be done in planning the post-war world to prejudice 'the natural Anglo-American special relationship'.[11]

Six months later he told Richard Law, the Junior Minister at the Foreign Office:

> It is my deepest conviction that unless Britain and the United States are joined in a special relationship, including Combined Staff organization and a wide measure of reciprocity in the use of bases – all within the ambit of a world organization – another destructive war will come to pass.[12]

But Britain's parlous economic situation, and its inevitable dependence on the United States both financially and militarily in the post-war world, meant that the relationship could never be realised in anything like the way that he wanted. The Americans were much too conscious of their position as by far the strongest power in the world. Roosevelt even said at one stage, 'We will have more trouble with Great Britain after the war than we are having with Germany now.'[13]

The real nature of the relationship between Britain and the United States was demonstrated very clearly in the development of the atomic bomb, which both powers saw as of primary importance for the distribution of power in the post-war world. Churchill discovered that his relationship with Roosevelt counted for little; the President often did not carry out what he had promised Churchill he would do and did just enough to ensure that Britain remained a loyal but dependent ally. Both countries had begun theoretical work on an atomic bomb in 1939 but it was British-based scientists who made a series of vital breakthroughs in the winter of 1940–1. Only Churchill and a small group of ministers and senior military figures were aware of this work. In the summer of 1941 crucial scientific information was given to the Americans and it convinced them that it was possible to make a bomb within two to three years given enough scientific and industrial resources.

The US decided to go ahead on 9 October 1941 and two days later Roosevelt offered Churchill a joint programme of research. After much discussion Churchill and his colleagues rejected the offer fearing the United States might be too dominant in the post-war world if the British helped them make the A-bomb. It was a bad miscalculation. Six months later they found out that the US was far ahead of the UK and they tried, belatedly, to construct a joint project. It was too late. In June 1942 Churchill and Roosevelt discussed the programme during their talks at Hyde Park, and although nothing was put on paper, Churchill thought he had obtained the President's agreement to full co-operation and sharing of results. In fact he had not. By the autumn of 1942 the US was ready to move into the development phase and Roosevelt accepted his advisers' views that Britain had no right to information on development and production since they were now contributing so little to the project. Roosevelt told his advisers to open talks and that the British were to be given no information on bomb design. The US decided it did not matter if the British decided as a consequence not to participate in the research programme any longer.

On 13 January 1943 the British were told formally that they would only be given information if it would be of use during the war (a concession, though little information would be forthcoming since they had no project of their own). Churchill spoke to Harry Hopkins (who was Roosevelt's main adviser on the project) at Casablanca and at the end of February sent a formal protest. Hopkins did not accept Churchill's interpretation of what had taken place at Hyde Park in June 1942. He did not reply to another letter on 20 March nor one at the beginning of April in which Churchill said, 'That we should each work separately would be a sombre decision'.[14] But the US administration had thought through the implications of the decision to exclude Britain from this work. US officials told Roosevelt that it was 'a major decision ... of national security and post-war significance'.[15]

Spurned by the Americans, Churchill was now determined to build a British atomic bomb. On 15 April he told Cherwell, who was his main adviser, 'In my view we cannot afford to wait.'[16] Unfortunately Britain had no choice in the matter because the US had secured all the available uranium supplies and heavy water production in Canada. At the end of May Cherwell told the Americans that Britain would make its own bomb after the war and Churchill told Sir John Anderson, who was overseeing the project within Whitehall: 'We cannot afford after the war to face the future without this weapon and rely entirely on America, should Russia or some other Power develop it.'[17] Indeed he told the two Americans in charge of the project when they were in London in July 1943: 'It would never do to have Germany or Russia win the race for something which might be used for international blackmail.'[18] (Exactly how Churchill proposed to use the atomic bomb for his own version of international blackmail after the war will become clear later.) His idea was that British scientists working in the US should get as much information as possible and to do this 'it may be tactically necessary to make use of the pretext of wartime collaboration'.[19]

Churchill held further talks with Roosevelt about the atomic bomb during the Washington conference in May 1943 but could obtain no more than an oral understanding about future collaboration. Roosevelt was not prepared to sign anything until Churchill accepted American strategy for the conduct of the war and in particular a cross-Channel invasion in the spring of 1944. When Churchill finally appeared to do so at the Quebec conference in September 1943, Roosevelt did enter into a written agreement, but it was one which put Britain in a subordinate position. Clearly Roosevelt was not prepared to damage the wartime alliance by denying all access to atomic information and he also saw Britain as a dependable and subordinate ally after the war who could be trusted with the bomb because it would follow American leadership. Although Churchill was able to secure the promise of a joint decision over the use of the atomic bomb and the flow of scientific information was resumed, that information was controlled by a committee over which the US had an effective veto. However, with the development of atomic energy after the war now a possibility, the agreement also recognised 'the heavy burden of production falling upon the United States' and Churchill had to concede that 'post-war advantages of an industrial or commercial character' would be settled after the war. The agreement stated, 'The Prime Minister expressly disclaims any interest in these industrial and commercial aspects beyond what may be considered by the President of the United States to be fair and just.'[20]

Churchill was determined that the new weapon should be used to give the United States and later Britain as much diplomatic and strategic leverage as possible. When both Cherwell and Anderson suggested that the Soviet Union should be told of the existence of the project (though not any technical details) and invited to collaborate on international control, Churchill minuted 'on no account . . . I do not agree'.[21] During the Quebec conference in September 1944 he signed another apparently more promising deal with Roosevelt during a stay at Hyde Park. They rejected any idea of international control, agreed on the possible use of the bomb against Japan (it was already clear it would not be ready for use against Germany), and co-operation after the war, which could only be terminated by joint agreement. Although Churchill thought he had secured what he wanted, there must be doubts about whether Roosevelt ever intended to carry out the agreement – it was never shown to those in charge of the US programme and it only gathered dust in an obscure file. The Americans never acted on the agreement.

Churchill stuck to his policy of trying to keep information about the atomic bomb exclusively Anglo-American. (He did not know that the Soviet Union had already begun work on its own weapon.) He saw it as a weapon to be used, or its use threatened, against the Soviet Union and possibly France. He told Eden in March 1945: 'In all the circumstances our policy should be to keep the matter so far as we can control it in American and British hands and leave the French and the Russians to do what they can ... Even six months will make a difference should it come to a show-down with Russia, or indeed with de Gaulle.'[22] He specifically rejected any idea of telling France about the bomb, fearing that De Gaulle might use it against Britain: 'One thing I am sure that there is nothing that De Gaulle would like better than to have plenty of TA [codename for the atomic bomb] to punish Britain.'[23]

The atomic bomb was still a weapon of the future and could not influence the making of the post-war settlement that was taking up more and more of Churchill's time in the last years of the war. One of the most difficult issues he had to deal with was the future of Poland, the country for which Britain had gone to war. The problem was that the Soviet Union had invaded and annexed the eastern half of the country in collusion with Germany in September 1939. The Soviet Government made it clear that its main aim in the war was to ensure its post-war boundaries were the same as those when the Germans invaded in 1941 (including the annexation of the three Baltic states). However Poland's pre-war eastern boundary was, because of its victory over Soviet forces in 1920, to the east of the 'Curzon line' which had been recognised by the allies at Versailles. If its post-war boundary reverted to the Curzon line (which was roughly the 1941 line), about twenty per cent of Polish territory in 1939 and five million people would be annexed by the Soviet Union. Even if Poland were compensated by allowing it to move westwards into parts of what had been Germany, the Polish government-in-exile was not prepared to agree to the dismemberment of their country. The British and Churchill were caught in an uncomfortable position between the demands of their two allies.

Before Soviet entry into the war Churchill was firm about the future of Poland: 'When we have abolished Germany we will certainly establish Poland and make them a permanent thing in Europe.'[24] When Germany invaded the Soviet Union in June 1941, the Polish government-in-exile in London reluctantly re-established relations with the Soviet Union, though nothing was settled on the crucial border question. Before they took this action, they very naturally sought an assurance from the British about their borders. On 24 July Churchill and the Cabinet agreed to a statement that 'His Majesty's Government did not recognise territorial changes affecting Poland made since August 1939'.[25] This was a clear declaration that they stood by the 1920 boundary. When the Soviets formally raised the borders question with Eden in Moscow in December 1941 and demanded recognition of the incorporation of the Baltic states and eastern Poland, Churchill was absolutely clear in his views. He told the Australian Prime Minister Curtin: 'the forcible transfer of large populations against their will into the Communist sphere' would be against the Atlantic Charter and 'by attempting it we should only vitiate the fundamental principles of freedom which are the main impulse of our Cause'.[26]

In a similar vein he lectured Eden that these territories had been 'acquired by acts of aggression in shameful collusion with Hitler', that the transfer of populations would be 'contrary to all the principles for which we are fighting this war' and that these principles, enshrined in the Atlantic Charter, 'must become especially active whenever any question of transferring territory is raised'.[27] Although within a couple of months Churchill had changed his mind and supported Soviet demands, he then changed it again under pressure from within the Government and from Conservative MPs. The Soviet demand was explicitly excluded from the Anglo-Soviet treaty agreed in May 1942, and Churchill told Stalin at this point: 'we cannot go back on our previous undertakings to Poland'.[28] Eden gave the Poles an assurance that Britain would not conclude any agreement affecting or compromising Polish territory. There the Polish question rested until April 1943.

On 13 April 1943 the German Government announced that it had found a mass grave of Polish officers and civilians (about 5,000 bodies) at Katyn. They claimed the murders had been carried out in 1940 when the area was under Soviet control. (That claim was correct – the killings were carried out on the direct orders of Stalin and the Politburo.) The Polish Government called for an investigation by the International Committee of the Red Cross, and so did the Germans. The Soviets (who claimed the Germans had carried out the killings when they controlled the area in 1941) accused the Poles of acting in collusion with the Germans and broke off relations with the London Government. Churchill had little time for the Polish Government, apart from its leader General Sikorski, describing their activities, ten days before the announcement of Katyn, as 'the usual fissiparous and subversive agitation'.[29] He told Stalin that he agreed there should be no Red Cross investigation since it would be 'a fraud and its conclusions reached by terrorism'.[30]

The day after he sent that message to Stalin, Churchill, Eden and a few other senior members of the Government saw a despatch from the British Ambassador to the Polish government-in-exile containing substantial evidence that made it virtually certain that it was the Soviets who had carried out the killings. Churchill sent a copy of the report to Roosevelt and told Eden on 28 April 'there is no use prowling round the three-year-old graves of Smolensk'.[31] (His use of the phrase 'three-year-old' shows that he did privately believe the killings had been carried out by the Soviets in 1940.) But he feared that to say this to the Soviet Government or in public would badly damage Anglo-Soviet relations. It was therefore decided to reduce potential embarrassment by repressing the Poles instead. Three days after he received the report that pointed the finger of guilt at the Soviets, Churchill and the Cabinet agreed to keep the Poles under control and to rigorously censor their press in Britain to stop it discussing Polish–Soviet relations. He afterwards reassured Stalin, 'The cabinet here is determined to have proper discipline in the Polish press in Great Britain' about what he termed this 'atrocious Nazi propaganda'.[32] In addition, worried by the possibility that the Soviets might establish their own puppet Polish Government, he wanted to put pressure on Sikorski to sack his main anti-Soviet ministers. He informed Eden: 'My feeling increasingly is that we must not be too tender with these unwise people. I trust you will be successful in inducing Sikorski to reconstruct his government.'[33]

Before any real progress could be made in that direction Sikorski was killed in an air crash when taking off from Gibraltar on 4 July. He was replaced by the much more anti-Soviet Mikolajczyk. The problem of the Polish borders now had to be resolved in a far more difficult atmosphere and as Soviet forces were beginning to force the Germans back towards the old 1939 frontier line. Churchill hoped that, because an Anglo-Soviet deal was politically difficult due to opposition in Britain, the Polish Government would resolve the problem he faced. He told Eden in October 1943: 'I think we should do everything in our power to persuade the Poles to agree with the Russians about their eastern frontier, in return for gains in East Prussia and Silesia.'[34] That was a forlorn hope.

The future of Poland was one of the main items discussed at the first meeting between Stalin, Roosevelt and Churchill at Teheran between 28 November and 1 December (the other was the final overruling of Churchill's strategic preferences and the decision to go for OVERLORD in May 1944). Attempts to hold a meeting between the three leaders in 1942 had failed for a variety of reasons, then on two occasions, in May and June 1943, Roosevelt had suggested to Stalin they should meet without Churchill and had rejected Iceland as a possible venue because it would be difficult not to invite him there. When Churchill found out about these moves, Roosevelt simply lied and denied he had ever suggested the idea. Eventually after long negotiations they settled on a tripartite meeting in Teheran (although Roosevelt was still determined not to hold any detailed Anglo-American discussions before the conference and he ensured that his meetings with Churchill beforehand at Cairo were either informal social affairs where no business was discussed, such as a Thanksgiving dinner, or else included Chiang Kai-shek as well). The Teheran meeting was the first tangible demonstration of Britain's junior status in the alliance and the changing nature of international politics. The Americans were keen to deal with the Soviets bi-laterally as befitted the two powers who would inevitably be the strongest in the post-war world. Churchill was marginalised and became more so later in the war.

The meeting at Teheran was an organisational shambles. Despite Stalin's pleas there was no agenda – Roosevelt wanted to keep it informal and Churchill had merely suggested they should cover 'the whole field of the war'.[35] The US delegation stayed with the Soviets at their embassy to avoid travelling across the city every day – they did not want to stay at the adjacent British Ambassador's residence. Churchill arrived with a large delegation including his son Randolph and his daughter Sarah. He was in a poor state, suffering from the early signs of the pneumonia that was to strike ten days later. Brooke wrote of the first morning: 'it was evident we were heading for chaos. P.M. has a throat and has practically lost his voice. He is not fit and consequently not in the best of moods.'[36]

Churchill was even more upset when he discovered that Roosevelt had held an informal meeting with Stalin before the first formal plenary. If he had known that Roosevelt had tried to draw Stalin into an alliance on colonial and Indian questions against Churchill he would have been livid. The first plenary, held at very short notice on the afternoon of 28 November, consisted mainly of long rambling speeches by the three leaders about the progress of the war. Churchill was in a very bad mood by the end because it was already clear that his ideas on strategy were going to be rejected. That evening, after a dismal dinner hosted by Roosevelt, Churchill took Stalin on one side and told him that after the war 'The three Powers should guide the future of the world.' He then took the initiative on the Polish question and using three matchsticks showed how to move both the Soviet Union and Poland westward at the expense of Germany and suggested 'the three heads might see if some sort of policy might be pressed on the Poles'.[37] Stalin was cautious and non-committal.

The next day was another bad one for Churchill. Roosevelt refused to have a private lunch with him and held another bilateral with Stalin before the afternoon plenary to discuss post-war issues. Half an hour before the plenary Churchill presented Stalin with the 'Sword of Stalingrad', a gift from King George VI to the people of Stalingrad to commemorate the historic victory. The second plenary was dominated by military discussions, during which Stalin bluntly asked Churchill whether he really believed in OVERLORD. Churchill was furious by the end of the meeting, and his bad mood carried over into the evening, when Stalin hosted a lavish buffet with endless toasts. That evening Stalin raised the question of what to do with German war criminals – the Moscow declaration agreed at the beginning of November stated that the major criminals would be dealt with by the allies jointly and others would be sent to the country where the crimes had been committed. When the British Cabinet had discussed the issue on 10 November, Churchill had proposed his own solution: he wanted a list of about 100 major criminals drawn up and those on the list declared outlaws. When captured, they would be formally identified by the senior officer in charge, then 'the said officer will have the outlaw or outlaws shot to death within six hours and without reference to higher authority'.[38] The Cabinet decided not to support his proposal and set up a committee to consider alternatives. At the buffet, when Stalin jokingly mentioned shooting 50,000 German officers at the end of the war, Churchill refused to see it as a joke, or to enter into the spirit of Roosevelt's 'compromise' suggestion of only 49,000 shootings, and stormed out of the gathering. Stalin brought him back. (Four months later Churchill admitted Stalin had been joking. Not that his own views changed – in March 1944 he told the Cabinet the 'summary execution of the persons on the list of the most prominent war criminals was the best solution'.[39])

Churchill's sixty-ninth birthday on 30 November was marked by his surrender over the invasion of north-west Europe in May 1944. During lunch with Roosevelt and Stalin he suggested that the Soviet Union should have access to warm water ports and said he wanted to see the Soviet Navy and merchant fleet in all the oceans of the world. He also expressed support for a revision of the Montreux convention that banned the passage of warships through the Straits from the Black Sea to the Mediterranean. The third plenary that afternoon settled little, with discussion centred mainly on the uninformative communiqué to be issued after the talks. That evening Churchill gave a birthday dinner for thirty-four people featuring salmon trout, soup, turkey, ice cream (most of which ended up over the head of Stalin's interpreter Pavlov when one of the waiters tripped) and cheese soufflé. Roosevelt gave Churchill a cheap porcelain bowl one of his staff had bought in the Teheran bazaar that afternoon. There was much cordiality and fine speeches accompanied the toasts but nothing was decided.

The last day of the conference, 1 December, was characterised by hurried discussion of a number of post-war issues. Roosevelt was the host for lunch, during which he made fun of Churchill in order to try and establish a rapport with Stalin. On a wide range of topics it was agreed there was no need to settle anything finally. That afternoon Roosevelt held his third private meeting with Stalin. He explained his political difficulties over Poland (there were about seven million Polish votes at stake in the 1944 elections) but he supported a move of Polish borders westwards as far as the Oder

River to compensate for Soviet gains in the east. But when he asked for a plebiscite on the incorporation of the Baltic states into the Soviet Union, Stalin effectively rejected the request.

The final plenary began at 6pm. On Poland Churchill suggested that the country should be moved westwards and said that he was prepared to put almost anything reasonable to them; if they did not accept he would wash his hands of them and he pledged that on the Polish borders he would not 'oppose the Soviet government under any condition at the peace table'.[40] Stalin teased him: 'I can't understand you at all; in 1919 you were so keen to fight and now you don't seem to be at all. What happened? Is it advancing age?'[41] By the end of the meeting there was a general, but informal, agreement that the 1941 Soviet borders should be accepted, that the eastern border of Poland should follow roughly the Curzon line (except that Lvov, which was to the west of it, should go to the Soviets), with a slight compensation for Poland in the north and that the German city of Konigsberg should go to the Soviet Union. In the west the Oder River should form the new Polish border. Roosevelt suggested the transfer of millions of Germans and Poles to coincide with the new borders. Churchill said that he liked the general arrangement and he would advise the Poles to accept. With that, and general agreement to divide Germany after the war, the meeting ended.

The Teheran conference was important because the three leaders had met for the first time, reached general agreement on military strategy and made a start on the post-war settlement. But the latter involved making major concessions to the Soviet Union and abandoning the fine words in the Atlantic Charter about self-determination and the right of the people to choose their government. On the Baltic states Churchill and Roosevelt had effectively conceded their incorporation into the Soviet Union. On Poland Churchill accepted Soviet demands on the border question and his handling of the issue was so off-hand that he gave Stalin the impression that the British were not particularly bothered about the fate of their ally.

At Teheran Churchill had willingly taken on the task of forcing Britain's ally to accept the dismemberment of their country and the forcible transfer of millions of people. With Churchill ill in Morocco, it was Eden who broke the news to the Poles of Britain's position that they should accept the Curzon line as their eastern boundary. He carefully did not tell them that the three powers at Teheran had effectively already settled the border question between themselves. On Churchill's return the Polish leader Mikolajczyk informed him that with four million Poles living east of the Curzon line he could not accept it as Poland's eastern border. Churchill and Eden discussed how to handle the government-in-exile and public opinion. Churchill remarked: 'I rather contemplate telling the world that we declared war for Poland and that the Polish nation shall have a proper land to live in, but we have never undertaken to defend existing Polish frontiers.' (That was not true – the pledges given by the Cabinet in July 1941 did not recognise the transfer of parts of Poland to the Soviet Union.) He continued that the Soviet Union had the right to 'inexpungeable security of her western borders' and that the Poles 'must be very silly if they imagine we are going to begin a new war with Russia for the sake of the Polish eastern border'.[42]

On 25 January 1944 he told the Cabinet that the Soviet Union would have effective power in Poland and that whatever the outcome Britain was bound to be charged with violating the Atlantic Charter; that Britain was in an impossible position and could not win. On 4 February the Cabinet agreed to cut off paper supplies to many Polish newspapers to try and stop anti-Soviet articles and accepted Stalin's request for the removal of the main anti-Soviet ministers. On 6 February Churchill again saw the Polish leaders at Chequers. He told them bluntly there was no point in their thinking about negotiating frontiers; the Curzon line was 'the best that the Poles could expect and all that he would ask the British people to demand on their behalf'. He added that the Soviets were also to have Lvov, an agreeent with the Soviet Government would be made without Polish consent if necessary and that the Soviets had a 'moral right' to the territory.[43] He then suggested to Eden 'we should make an agreement with Russia about the Poles, assuring them of our support if reasonable terms are offered & observed' (i.e. the Curzon line).[44] Again he told Eden that the Soviet demands on Britain's ally 'are in my opinion no more than what is right and just for Russia'.[45] After another unproductive meeting with Mikolajczyk, Churchill announced publicly Britain's acceptance of the Curzon line.

It is perhaps not surprising that about this time Churchill was acutely sensitive over accusations in the press and Parliament that he was carrying out a second 'Munich' in redrawing the boundary of Poland in conjunction with Stalin and without the consent of the Polish Government. In fact in many ways the action Churchill took was worse than the Munich agreement. Then Britain had not been allied with Czechoslovakia, the territory ceded to Germany did have a majority German population and a referendum was held in other areas. On Poland, Britain was dealing with an ally for whom she had gone to war and the British Government had explicitly recognised the 1939 borders as late as July 1941. The territory given to the Soviet Union, without a referendum, was not ethnically Russian or Ukrainian and the territory given to Poland as compensation was ethnically German and had been for centuries. There was no possible way such action could be squared with the Atlantic Charter Churchill had endorsed in August 1941. The only argument he could put forward was the necessity of agreeing with Britain's stronger ally, the Soviet Union.

In February 1944 the Soviets published the results of their 'investigation' into Katyn, which purported to show the massacre was carried out by the Germans. Churchill sought to play down the significance of the issue, telling Eden, 'This is not one of those matters where absolute certainty is either urgent or desirable.'[46] In May he again urged pragmatism upon the Polish government-in-exile, pointing out that they had to come to a deal with the Soviet Union: 'it was perfectly useless for any Pole to suppose that their country could possibly exist as a powerful and independent state unless it were on friendly terms with Russia'.[47] They still refused to do so and in July Churchill was told by Stalin that the Soviet Union would use the 'Lublin Committee of National Liberation' (a puppet organisation dominated by Communists) to govern the liberated areas of Poland as Soviet troops moved westwards. He in turn informed the Cabinet that the Lublin Committee was composed of genuine Polish patriots and he hoped the London Poles would fuse with them.

By late July 1944 Soviet forces were nearing Warsaw and the Polish Home Army, owing nominal allegiance to the London government, launched a full-scale uprising in the city at the beginning of August. The resistance groups were soon under heavy German pressure in fierce house to house fighting. At first, Churchill refused a meeting with the Polish government-in-exile and the RAF made only limited supply drops. As the fighting continued, he became more moved by the plight of the Polish resistance and on 22 August made a joint appeal with Roosevelt to Stalin for the Soviet Army to give help and allow British and American planes to fly from their air bases. Stalin refused on both counts. Not until 10 September did the Soviet Government agree to make its own relief flights. The RAF now decided that flights to Warsaw were too risky, although the USAAF did continue until near the end of the fighting at the beginning of October. The Soviet Army was accused of deliberately waiting in front of Warsaw while the uprising was crushed and one of the main forces opposing Soviet power in liberated Poland destroyed, but Churchill was personally convinced this was not the case. Immediately after the failed uprising, he made another attempt at forcing the London Poles to yield – he wanted Mikolajczyk removed but had to settle for the dismissal of a few of the more anti-Soviet ministers.

Churchill now hoped to settle the Polish question and other postwar issues during a visit to Moscow in early October. He was accompanied by Eden and Brooke, and Roosevelt had insisted that Harriman should join the party to keep an eye on Churchill's negotiations with Stalin. Since the Teheran conference nine months earlier Soviet armies had advanced across much of Eastern Europe, 'liberating' Rumania and Bulgaria together with parts of Yugoslavia, moving into eastern Poland and then approaching Hungary. Yet Churchill relished the opportunity to deal directly with Stalin. His views about the role the Soviet Union would play after the war were highly unstable around this time, and could vary almost from day to day. For example, on 5 May 1944 he told the meeting of Commonwealth Prime Ministers he 'refused to consider the possibility of a confrontation between Russia and the English-speaking peoples'.[48] Three days later he wrote to Eden: 'I fear that a great evil may come upon the world. This time at any rate we and the Americans will be heavily armed. The Russians are drunk with victory and there is no length they may not go.'[49] Of one thing, however, Churchill was firmly convinced – he knew how to handle Stalin.

Rather like Chamberlain in his relations with Hitler, he took the view that Stalin was personally moderate and willing to settle even though behind him he had the extremists. He told Eden there were two forces in the Soviet Union: '(a) Stalin himself, personally cordial to me, (b) Stalin in Council, a grim thing behind him, which we and he have to reckon with.'[50] But he was optimistic that the Soviet Union was changing for the better. Again he told Eden of 'the deep-seated changes which have taken place in the character of the Russian state and government, the new confidence which has grown in our hearts towards Stalin – these have all had their effect'.[51] During his visit in August 1942 he told Air Marshal Tedder that Stalin was 'just a peasant' and he knew exactly how to handle him.[52] Churchill was fascinated by Stalin – there was in some ways a meeting of minds between the two men who both understood power and how to use it and who enjoyed deciding the destinies of millions of people. (Churchill's relationship with Roosevelt was very different because they had little in common apart from running the war – Roosevelt's interest in social reform was a closed book to Churchill.) At the end of May he criticised Clark Kerr, the Ambassador in Moscow, for his attitude over Rumania: 'he cringes before Molotov and thinks we cannot pursue the matter further. Believe me, this is not the way to get on with the Russians. It is a terrible mistake to quit this kind of battlefield unsatisfied.'[53] He now had the opportunity to demonstrate his way of dealing with Stalin.

Churchill made his position clear at the very first meeting with Stalin, held in the Kremlin at 10pm on the night of 9 October, in the course of a discussion steeped in *realpolitik* and self-interest. By now he was not just shaking the hand of the 'hairy baboon' but embracing the animal. He suggested that if Stalin supported Britain against the Americans in getting back the empire in the Far East then Britain would, subject to certain agreements, support the Soviet Union in Eastern Europe. He again offered Stalin a revision of the Montreux convention, which stopped Soviet warships passing into the Mediterranean, saying he thought it was 'inadmissable' and 'obsolete' and the Soviet Union had a 'moral claim' to revision. But he balanced this concession by remarking that over the future of Greece Britain must have the lead and that 'Britain must be the leading Mediterranean power'. On Bulgaria Stalin suggested that Britain ought not to be very interested in the fate of the country and did not press Churchill on the future of Italy. (Churchill merely commented he 'did not think much of them as a people'.)[54]

The outlines of a deal were already apparent when Churchill passed Stalin what he described as 'a naughty document'. In a passage only recorded in the Ambassador's diary, not the official record, Churchill showed how far he was prepared to go to reach a bilateral understanding: 'Marshal Stalin was a realist. He himself was not sentimental while Mr Eden was a bad man. He had not consulted his Cabinet or Parliament.'[55] The document Churchill handed over proposed a division of Eastern Europe into spheres of interest. It contained figures intended to show the extent of future influence in five countries. Churchill suggested: Rumania: ninety per cent Soviet Union, Greece: ninety per cent Britain, Bulgaria: seventy-five per cent Soviet Union, Yugoslavia and Hungary: fifty per cent each. After Stalin's interpreter Pavlov had written in the names of the countries in Cyrillic script, Stalin, using a thick blue pencil, changed Bulgaria to ninety per cent Soviet Union and ticked the document. Churchill suggested burning the piece of paper, but Stalin suggested Churchill should keep it. Realising that some of the discussion would probably leak to the Americans, Churchill suggested it was 'better to express these things in diplomatic terms and not use the phrase "dividing into spheres of influence", because the Americans might be shocked'.[56]

The discussion then moved on to Poland. Churchill callously expressed satisfaction that the leader of the Warsaw uprising, General Bor, had surrendered and 'the Germans were looking after him'. The Home Army, he said, was now led by 'some colourless man. He could not remember his name.'[57] They then discussed what would happen to the Germans who lived in the area up to the Oder that the allies had decided should become Polish. (The British Government had already agreed with the Czech government-in-exile that the roughly three million ethnic Germans in the Sudetenland should be expelled.) Making the Curzon line the eastern border of Poland involved resettling one and a half million Polish refugees, and giving Poland a border on the Oder meant moving another five million Germans. He told Stalin: 'the population might be moved from Silesia and east Prussia to Germany. If seven million had been killed in the war there would be plenty of room for them.'[58] The two leaders agreed on these forced population movements (again completely at variance with Churchill's adherence to the Atlantic Charter). It became clear later that Churchill saw this policy as part of a collective German atonement when he told the House of

Commons on 5 December that 'a clean sweep will be made' and he was 'not alarmed' at the prospect.

Churchill's immediate objectives had been agreed at the first meeting with Stalin but it left him with the difficult problem of what to tell the Americans. Roosevelt had told them both just before the meeting 'in this global war there is literally no question, political or military, in which the United States is not interested'.[59] After Harriman began to work out the main thrust of what the two men had agreed on the night of 9 October, Churchill did draft a letter to Stalin saying that the deal might be 'considered crude, and even callous' but decided against sending it (and another he had written suggesting that the Communist and capitalist systems were growing closer together).[60] In the end Churchill left things as they were and later developments showed that both men were willing to abide by the spirit of their understanding.

Churchill had earlier persuaded Stalin to invite Mikolajczyk to Moscow, where, as Churchill put it to Stalin, the London Poles should 'be forced to settle'.[61] At a meeting on 13 October Mikolajczyk told the two leaders he was willing to include a few Communists in his Government and make an alliance with the Soviet Union but he would not accept either the Lublin Poles or the Curzon line. Churchill said he supported Stalin on the border question and the meeting broke up without agreement. Later in the day he also met the Lublin Committee and simply appealed for a compromise with the London Poles. Afterwards he put more pressure on Mikolajczyk by disclosing for the first time that all three powers had agreed at Teheran on the Curzon line.

The next day Churchill and Eden saw Mikolajczyk, and the Prime Minister tried to force the Polish leader to fall in with what had been agreed about his country. He told him this was his last chance to compromise and Mikolajczyk replied, quite correctly, that since the great powers had already made their decision he was only being offered a *fait accompli*. At this Churchill lost his temper and kept repeating, 'You hate the Russians.' He then launched into a tirade: 'You are absolutely crazy ... unless you accept the frontier you are out of business forever ... We will be sick and tired of you if you go on arguing ... You are callous people who want to wreck Europe. I shall leave you to your own troubles ... You have only your own miserable selfish interest in mind ... In this war what is your contribution to the Allied effort? What did you throw into the common pool?'[62] (He was forgetting the Polish fighter pilots who provided the most successful squadron in the Battle of Britain, the Polish Army that was still fighting in Italy, the terrible sufferings of the population during five years of German occupation and the Warsaw uprising just recently brutally suppressed.) He finished by telling Mikolajczyk that he ought to be locked up in a lunatic asylum and stormed out of the meeting.

A further meeting on 15 October was little better. Mikolajczyk partially accepted the Curzon line but asked for Lvov to stay in Poland. Churchill refused, saying, 'I will have nothing more to do with you ... I don't care where you go ... You only deserve to be in your Pripet marshes.'[63] He also said that the Lublin Poles would become the Government, a clear threat that in the not too distant future Britain would recognise them rather than the London Poles as the legitimate Government of Poland. As a gesture he did later suggest to Stalin that there should be a 'demarcation line' instead of a border (Lvov would still go to the Soviet Union), but Stalin, knowing Churchill's consistent position on the issue for the last year, rejected the idea. Mikolajczyk tried to obtain Roosevelt's support (the President had been ambiguous but encouraging before the November election) but failed to do so. Despite Churchill's dramatic and hectoring performance the visit ended without Mikolajczyk's consent to the radical restructuring of his country. Back in London on 24 November he resigned as Premier of the Polish government-in-exile. Britain technically still recognised this Government, but Churchill told the Cabinet he would 'adopt an attitude of complete detachment and frigidity and leave them to look after their own affairs'.[64] Just before Christmas Roosevelt told Stalin he too accepted the agreement Churchill had reached with him in Moscow on population transfers and the revised borders. Britain and the United States had done a deal with the Soviet Union against the wishes of the legitimate Polish Government. At the end of the year the Lublin Committee declared itself the provisional Government of Poland and was quickly recognised by the Soviet Union.

The trip to Moscow put Churchill in a highly optimistic mood about his relations with Stalin and the role the Soviet Union would play after the war. After four days in Moscow he wrote to Clementine, 'I have had very nice talks with the old Bear. I like him the more I see him. *Now* they respect us & I am sure they wish to work with us.'[65] At the end of the visit he wrote to Attlee: 'We have talked with an ease, freedom and a *beau geste* never before attained between our two countries. Stalin has made several expressions of personal regard which I feel were all sincere.'[66] This mood lasted long after his return from Moscow. At the end of November he objected to the chiefs of staff view that it would be necessary to build a western bloc to stop further Soviet expansion after the war. He told the Cabinet the Soviets were 'ready and anxious' to co-operate and 'No immediate threat of war lay ahead of us once the present war was over and we should be careful of assuming commitments consequent on the formation of a Western bloc that might impose a very heavy military burden upon us.'[67] He had other objections to a Western bloc: he told Eden: 'The Belgians are extremely weak and their behaviour before the war was shocking. The Dutch are entirely selfish and fought only when they were attacked and then for a few hours. Denmark is helpless and defenceless and Norway practically so.' It was therefore not possible to defend the continent and in his view Britain should adopt an isolationist policy after the war.[68]

Churchill was determined to carry out the spheres of influence agreement he had reached with Stalin. In early January 1945 news reached Britain that Soviet forces in Rumania were deporting the German minority in the country. The Foreign Office wanted to protest – Churchill did not: 'why are we making a fuss about the Russian deportations in Rumania of Saxons and others? It is understood that the Russians were to work their will in this sphere. Anyhow we cannot prevent them.'[69] A day later it was discovered that Rumanian citizens were being sent to the Soviet Union to carry out forced labour. Again Churchill was not prepared to interfere: 'I cannot see the Russians are wrong in making 100 or 150 thousand of these people work their passage. Also we must bear in mind what we promised about leaving Roumania's fate to a large extent in Russian hands. I cannot myself consider that it is wrong of the Russians to take Roumanians of any origin they like to work in the Russian coal-fields.'[70]

The question of restoring or establishing new Governments had to be faced not just in the areas controlled by the Soviet Union.

Britain and the United States had to cope with the issue elsewhere. In France, after many arguments, De Gaulle was in control and in Belgium and Holland the allies were able to ensure that sympathetic governments took over. The first major problem arose in Italy. On 25 July 1943 the Fascist Grand Council voted to remove Mussolini but he was replaced by General Badoglio, who was sympathetic to Fascism, and the ageing and infirm King Victor Emmanuel III, who had supported Mussolini, remained on the throne. Churchill immediately sent a message to Roosevelt suggesting that they should support Badoglio and the monarchy. Despite Roosevelt's known worries over supporting ex-Fascists and the public discontent only eight months earlier over the deal with Darlan in Algiers, Churchill was prepared to argue with the President that there would be no problems in backing Badoglio.

On 3 August the new Italian Government asked for an armistice but did nothing to stop the Germans rapidly tripling the size of their forces in the country to twenty divisions and disarming sixty-one Italian divisions. On 5 August Churchill produced further arguments to persuade Roosevelt to support Badoglio. Without any evidence to back his assertion he declared: 'Fascism in Italy is extinct. Every vestige has been swept away.' Using information from a Fascist sympathiser he also warned of the Communist threat:

> Italy turned Red overnight. In Turin and Milan there were Communist demonstrations which had to be put down by armed force. Twenty years of Fascism had obliterated the middle class. There is nothing between the King, with the Patriots who have rallied round him, who have complete control, and rampant Bolshevism.[71]

Churchill's old sympathy for Fascism in Italy, his fear of social revolution and his devotion to monarchy, all pointed in the same direction – support for Badoglio and the King as the only possible Italian Government.

Both Churchill and Roosevelt were however united in their determination to exclude the Soviet Union from any part of the administration of defeated Italy. They drew up their own surrender terms (despite the fact that Italy had declared war on the Soviet Union and had units still fighting on the eastern front), which came into effect at the end of August. This was to be an unfortunate precedent for the Soviet Union to exclude the western allies from the countries that Soviet forces liberated. Almost immediately though differences arose over which Italian politicians should be supported. Roosevelt backed the more liberal republican Count Sforza and allowed him to travel from exile in the United States to the liberated areas in the south of Italy. Churchill, who had a strong personal dislike of Sforza, called him 'a useless gaga conceited politician'[72] and argued 'It is quite evident to me that the old fool wants to be king himself, hence his republicanism.'[73] (Sforza was actually only a year older than Churchill.)

For a while Churchill and Roosevelt were able to agree to differ on the basis that nothing should be done until Rome was liberated. The Allied Commander, Eisenhower, went along with keeping Badoglio for the moment as the easiest way of ensuring the security of allied communications in Italy. Once Eisenhower left to command OVERLORD and was replaced by a British commander, Wilson, Churchill tried to cut out the Americans by setting up a special communications channel via British intelligence so that he could have closer control over political affairs in Italy. When Wilson reported through the normal allied communications channels that the King would abdicate in favour of his son when Rome was liberated, Roosevelt asked Churchill to support 'liberal political groups'. He refused, denouncing what he called 'the ambitious wind-bags now agitating behind our front'.[74]

Rome finally fell on 4 June 1944 and Victor Emmanuel abdicated in favour of his son Umberto. All the political parties refused to serve under Badoglio and a new administration was formed under a former Prime Minister, Ivanoe Bonomi. Churchill expressed disgust: 'I am surprised and shocked about Badoglio being replaced by this wretched old Bonomi. We have lost the only competent Italian with whom we could deal.' To Roosevelt he described the new Government as 'this group of aged and hungry politicians' and claimed that he had always wanted to wait until the north was liberated before making any changes (in Cabinet on 22 February he had agreed the changes should be made after the fall of Rome).[75] At this juncture Attlee led a Cabinet revolt over Churchill's failure to consult his colleagues before sending the messages to Roosevelt and the general view in Cabinet was that there was little alternative but to accept the new Government. Churchill reluctantly agreed, but when he found out that the administration in Rome had taken an oath of allegiance to the nation but not to King Umberto he wrote to Eden: 'This is very unpleasant, and shows the class of people we now have to deal with.'[76]

Churchill's view of the Italian Government became slightly warmer after his visit to the country in August 1944 and the next month he agreed to Roosevelt's proposal (made with the Presidential Election in mind) of a declaration promising increasing responsibility to the Italian Government as the allied Military Government reduced its powers. However in November Churchill insisted on pressure being applied to try to stop Sforza becoming Foreign Minister and Deputy Prime Minister. The US Government issued a public statement that they did not support British interference. Although Churchill sent a message saying 'I am much hurt over a public rebuke to H.M.G.',[77] Roosevelt refused to give way and complained (with justification) that he had not been consulted over the action taken against Sforza. Churchill's opposition to Sforza continued. In June 1945, when it seemed likely that he would become Prime Minister, he wrote: 'It is no part of our policy to interfere in the turmoil of Italian politics [sic] . . . If the foolish and crooked old man becomes prime minister, I shall have the pleasure of having as little to do with him as possible.'[78]

Churchill faced more complex problems across the Adriatic in Yugoslavia and here Britain had far less influence over events. After the German invasion of June 1941 the Belgrade Government fled into exile (eventually finishing up in London and Cairo) and resistance in the country was split between Mihajlovic and his Serbian groups, which at least nominally accepted the authority of King Peter and the government-in-exile, and Tito and his Communist partisans. Until well into 1943 the British, even though they could provide little material support, backed Mihajlovic but they had increasing evidence that he was doing little, if any, fighting against the Germans, spending most of his time instead attacking Tito, who was successfully pinning down large numbers of German troops (more than the British and Americans were in Italy). Churchill had little time for the government-in-exile, describing it as 'the feeble trash that has been flung out of Yugoslavia'.[79] But he was keen to try and ensure King Peter was restored to the throne and was largely instrumental in insisting on an unrealistic policy of trying to unite all the Yugoslavian factions under the King.

That policy could not survive the increasing evidence of Mihajlovic's collaboration and at the beginning of December 1943 Churchill warned the King that he would soon be required to dismiss the Serb leader, who was technically Minister of War in the Government. Mihajlovic was to be set a test operation to carry out (largely to protect the fact that most of the information about his collaboration came from Enigma intercepts) and if he failed he was to go. When he failed the test, Churchill approved a policy of switching British support to Tito and his Communist partisans, but he still hoped to keep the King as ruler of Yugoslavia. He told Eden in early 1944: 'My unchanging object is to get Tito to let the King come out and share luck with him, and thus unite Yugoslavia and bring in the old Serbian core. I believe the dismissal of Mihailovic is an essential preliminary.'[80] However Tito consistently refused to allow the King back into the country and would not even send an emissary to discuss matters with the King unless the whole government-in-exile was sacked and the partisans recognised in their place. Churchill wanted to accept Tito's pre-conditions, telling Eden: 'You know how strongly I am attached to the monarchical principle and how much I would like to see this boy restored to his throne. Here is the only hope.'[81]

In April 1944 Churchill and Eden finally forced a reluctant King Peter to recall the exiled politician, Subasic, from the United States in the hope that he would be more acceptable to Tito and at the end of May the existing government-in-exile was sacked and replaced by one under Subasic. By then Churchill and his advisers had accepted that the best they were going to achieve at the end of the war was a Yugoslavia under Tito as independent as possible from the Soviet Union. In June 1944, after a German attack, Tito and his headquarters had to be evacuated to the Adriatic island of Vis, which was under British control. There he reached agreement with Subasic on the mutual recognition of the government abroad and the partisan army and administration in Yugoslavia, with Tito as Commander-in-Chief. Subasic accepted a federal post-war structure and a 'progressive and democratic' Government. The King would not be allowed to return and the future of the monarchy would be settled after the war. In practice this deal recognised that effective power belonged to Tito and the Communist partisans, yet Churchill was pleased with the outcome, telling Eden: 'It looks to me splendid.'[82]

By the time Churchill and the Government had finally accepted Tito's effective control of post-war Yugoslavia, they had to deal with an equally difficult situation in neighbouring Greece. The Greek Government under King George II had fled into exile in 1941 after the German occupation but the King was tarnished within Greek politics because of his association with the pre-war Metaxas dictatorship (the King had only returned to the throne in 1935 through a rigged plebiscite) and virtually all Greek politicians and resistance movements were opposed to his return. As in Yugoslavia the resistance was divided into two factions (though without the underlying ethnic conflict) – EAM/ELAS, which was by far the largest and most popular and although nominally a popular front was in practice Communist-dominated, and the moderate EDES. In March 1943 Churchill sent a directive to Cairo on the policy to be adopted towards Greece, which attempted to have it both ways. It was British policy, he informed them, to strengthen the existing monarchical government but the Special Operations Executive, responsible for fomenting resistance, could aid any of the resistance groups. Privately Churchill was fully determined to restore the monarchy and the old social and political order of pre-war Greece. He also tended to treat Greece as a British protectorate, almost part of the Empire and a country where it was possible for the British to impose their wishes. He told Eden in June 1943: 'Why should his Kingship be called into question at this stage? he should go back as he left as King and General.'[83] In November he opposed Eden's idea of a post-war regency as the only way of saving the long-term position of the monarchy.

By the winter of 1943–4 there was a crisis both within Greece and within the government-in-exile. The King's offer of free elections to a constituent assembly within six months of liberation was rejected by all the parties, who demanded he stay out of the country until elections were held. Within Greece EAM/ELAS demanded control of the Interior, Justice and Defence Ministries (which were to be located in 'liberated' Greece) and when the government-in-exile rejected that request the Communist guerrillas opened a civil war against the moderate EDES groups. Churchill reversed his directive of March 1943: 'There seems to be no limit to the baseness and treachery of ELAS and we ought not to touch them with a barge pole.'[84] Under Soviet pressure ELAS agreed to a truce in February 1944 but the government-in-exile was still badly divided and Churchill still opposed to any move to oust the King. At the end of March 1944 the Greek forces in Egypt mutinied against the King and his government. British troops surrounded the mutineers and Churchill wanted tough action, signalling to Cairo, 'We cannot tolerate political revolutions carried out by foreign military formations.'[85] He wanted the existing Government to continue but eventually had to accept a new administration under Papandreou after the mutiny was suppressed. In May 1944 Papandreou obtained agreement from all the Greek parties in exile except the monarchists to form a Government of national unity, which then accepted the idea of a plebiscite on the monarchy after liberation, although no decision was taken about when the King could return to Greece.

As Soviet forces swept through the Balkans, it was clear that the Germans would soon have to evacuate Greece and the British prepared to send troops into the country to back Papandreou's Government on its return. On 9 August the Cabinet agreed to send 10,000 troops, all that could be spared from Italy and just enough, it was hoped, to control Athens. A week later Churchill wrote to Roosevelt to get his approval for the move, since it could only be carried out using US transport aircraft. The King still wanted to return before a plebiscite on the monarchy, and Churchill supported his position and rejected the idea of a regency as he had done since it was first raised in November 1943. The Cabinet, however, agreed there was 'no question of our forcing any particular form of government on the Greeks ... nor were we in any way committed as regards the position of the King'.[86]

When Churchill met Papandreou in Rome later in August he said the King had earned Britain's 'friendly and chivalrous feelings' by his conduct in 1940–1 but the matter was for the Greeks to decide – 'so long as the matter was settled by a fair plebiscite H.M. Government were politically indifferent to the question'.[87] At the end of September he appeared to agree with Eden that the King could not return (it was 'impossible even to consider') and accepted that until Papandreou and the Government were established 'the

671

King must keep out of the way'.[88] He told King George II of this view in early October but at the same time promised to push for his return and told Eden afterwards 'as he knows I am his friend and working constantly for his return if that can be done in accordance with the wishes of his people.'[89] Four days later at Caserta in Italy he gave Papandreou a lecture on the merits of constitutional monarchy but the Greek Premier continued to oppose the return of the King before a plebiscite was held.

The British had already secured agreement among the various factions of the Greek resistance to establish zones of control as the Germans evacuated the country – the British were to occupy Athens. The Germans finally left the Greek capital on 14 October and within twenty-four hours British troops had arrived, followed three days later by Papandreou and the Government. The country was left in a state of economic and political chaos, with the Communist EAM/ELAS forces controlling most of the country outside Athens, Patras and Salonika – they could have taken Athens if they had wanted but stuck by the agreement. The British brought the Greek Army back from Egypt purged of all but its royalist elements, and amalgamated it with the ex-German-controlled 'security battalions', which until a month earlier had been fighting the partisans. By early November Churchill expected civil war to break out. He told Eden, 'I fully expect a clash with EAM and we must not shrink from it, provided the ground is well chosen.'[90] He was therefore upset when Papandreou reached an agreement with ELAS on 20 November to disband their forces. He wanted to send a message that Papandreou was to take on ELAS or the British would pull out.

Clashes between the Government and ELAS began on 4 December in the wake of complex negotiations over demobilising the partisan groups, a series of demonstrations against the Government and the threat of a general strike. Churchill was determined to use the opportunity for British troops to crush the Communist groups with the support of the Greek Government. When it seemed likely that Papandreou might resign rather than fight and be replaced by an all-party government, Churchill telegraphed to the British representative in Athens: 'you must force Papandreou to stand to his duty . . . should he resign, he should be locked up till he comes to his senses'.[91] His instructions to General Scobie, the Commander of British Forces in Athens, were: 'Do not . . . hesitate to act as if you were in a conquered city where a local rebellion was in progress . . . We have to hold and dominate Athens. It would be a great thing for you to succeed in this without bloodshed if possible, but also with bloodshed if necessary.'[92] The Cabinet's decision taken in August that there was 'no question of our forcing any particular form of government on the Greeks' had clearly been abandoned. EAM offered a settlement based on general demobilisation and a regency but Churchill told the British representative in Athens that it was more important to defeat EAM than to end the fighting.

Churchill expected the situation to be resolved quickly and with little fuss. In fact it took weeks for British troops just to gain control of Athens (a further 75,000 men were brought in from Italy). The sight of British troops turning on partisans who only months earlier had been fighting the Germans brought an upsurge of dissent within Britain and failed to gain support in the United States. On 12 December Roosevelt publicly refused to support the British action and called for a regency and no return of the King. The Soviet Union said nothing – they had already agreed Greece was in the British sphere of influence and they saw British actions as a convenient precedent for any similar actions they might want to take in Eastern Europe.

By 10 December the British representatives in Athens concluded that control could only be extended into the country very slowly and for this process to be effective it was essential to make clear that the King would not return by appointing a regent – the favoured candidate was Archbishop Damaskinos. Papandreou was prepared to accept this arrangement but the King refused to stand down. While most of the British Cabinet agreed that a regency was the only possible solution, Churchill did not. He decided that the Archbishop was too favourable to the Communist partisans and he did not like removing the King. He told Roosevelt on 14 December: 'I know nothing to the credit of the Archbishop'[93] and later asserted Damaskinos would form a dictatorship in alliance with EAM/ELAS. His position was that 'it would be a very serious thing to overthrow a constitutional sovereign . . . I do not like setting up dictators as a result of using British troops.'[94] Three long Cabinet meetings on the subject, on 16, 18 and 21 December, could reach no agreement because of Churchill's refusal to accept a regency despite all the evidence that this was what everybody on the ground in Athens thought was the best solution. He told his colleagues, 'I won't install a Dictator – a Dictator of the Left.'[95]

On Christmas Eve Churchill decided to fly to Athens himself although it was not clear what he expected to achieve or even what he planned to do. When he arrived on Christmas Day he found the city still in the middle of a civil war but accepted the proposal by General Scobie and Harold Macmillan, who were in charge of British policy, that he should chair a meeting of Greek groups. When Churchill met Archbishop Damaskinos for the first time he described him as 'a magnificent figure'.[96] He then opened a conference of the Greek political parties, told them it was up to them to settle their differences and withdrew. While the talks continued, Churchill lectured the US Ambassador on the need to support British policy and decided that a regency under the Archbishop was 'the only course open'.[97] He accepted the Archbishop's suggestion that there should be a government without any Communist participation. On 29 December he flew back to London, saw the King that evening and demanded he appoint Archbishop Damaskinos as Regent pending a plebiscite. When the King refused, Churchill told him that Britain would recognise the regent anyway and the King gave in. Churchill therefore finished up accepting the policy and the man he had so vehemently opposed. His trip to Athens, apart from giving him the excitement he always craved, served no purpose other than to convince him that the solution which the Greeks, the Americans, the British on the spot and the rest of the Cabinet had advocated for the previous three weeks was right after all.

The appointment of Damaskinos had no effect on the civil war, but the British troops did finally drive the Communist forces out of Athens. The regent created a new government under General Plastiras, which drifted to the far right and began a campaign of counter-terror. When the British Ambassador suggested he should talk to the new government about measures of greater social justice in order to combat Communism, Churchill refused permission, telling him, 'I do not think that we ought to make ourselves responsible for teaching the Greeks how to frame a programme of "social justice".'[98] Privately he told Clementine that opposition to his Greek policy only came from degenerate circles. The Plastiras Government left collaborationists in charge in many areas, a policy Churchill strongly supported, as he told Eden: 'It seems to me that the collaborators in Greece in many cases did the best they could to shelter the Greek population from German oppression ... The Communists are the main foe ... There should be no question of increasing the severities against the collaborationists in order to win Communist approval.'[99] When it was clear that the strongly royalist government under the regent would be able to manipulate a plebiscite in favour of a return of the King, Churchill directed it should be held before the Election of a constituent assembly. The royalists won the General Election in April 1946 and the British eventually withdrew in 1947 leaving Greece in a state of civil war.

Although until the end of the war none of the allies were in a position to implement any decisions about the nature of post-war Germany, a considerable amount of effort had been devoted to the subject by the end of 1944. Churchill's general attitude to the Germans was harsh. As early as September 1940 his Private Secretary reported that he was 'becoming less and less benevolent towards the Germans ... and talks about castrating the lot. He says there will be no nonsense about a "just peace".'[100] By 1943 his method for reducing the German population had become marginally more humane. He told the Cabinet 'we should have to consider, after the war, segregating 3 or 4 million German males for some years, to arrive at a balance of population with France'.[101] When Churchill met Stalin in Moscow in October 1944 he told him 'he was all for hard terms ... The problem was how to prevent Germany getting on her feet in the lifetime of our grandchildren.'[102]

By the time of this visit Churchill had enthusiastically endorsed the Morgenthau plan, devised by the US Treasury Secretary and designed to turn Germany into a 'pastoral' economy by dismantling the industrial base and taking reparations not in cash, as happened after the First World War, but in kind, as had been agreed at the Moscow meeting of foreign ministers in October 1943. Roosevelt put the plan forward during the Quebec conference in September 1944. Germany was to be dismembered – East Prussia would be split between Poland and the Soviet Union and the Saar, the Rhineland, Schleswig-Holstein and the Kiel Canal were to be separated from the rest of Germany, which was to be divided into two separate states. Reparations would come from dismantling German industry and from forced labour. At first Churchill felt this plan went too far, telling Roosevelt over dinner on 13 September:

'I'm all for disarming Germany but we ought not to prevent her living decently . . . the English people will not stand for the policy you are advocating.'[103] Eden also strongly opposed the US ideas which he felt would leave Britain to deal with a power vacuum in the middle of Europe.

However Churchill found that Roosevelt was making his willingness to provide Britain with the financial and economic assistance required for the war against Japan and immediate peacetime needs contingent on acceptance of the Morgenthau plan. This left him with no choice but to agree. Within two days he was saying of the Morgenthau plan 'Why shouldn't it work?'[104] In a message to Attlee in London he expounded the case for the Morgenthau plan at some length: 'the Ruhr and Saar steel industries shall be completely dismantled', much would go to the Soviet Union and international control 'would keep these potential centres of rearmament completely out of action for many years to come'. The consequence would be 'to emphasise the pastoral character of German life'. Britain would be able to replace the output of the Ruhr and Saar from its own industries and benefit by £300–£400 million a year. He concluded, 'I was at first taken aback at this but I consider that the disarmament argument is decisive and the beneficial consequences to us flow naturally.'[105]

Churchill was still advocating this scheme when he visited Stalin a month later. Stalin accepted the idea of detaching the Ruhr, the Saar and the Rhineland and also endorsed Churchill's favourite proposal – a Bavarian/Austrian confederation – although he opposed Hungary joining this grouping. Churchill explained to Stalin the plan's rationale: the Soviet Union, Belgium, Holland and France would take away 'all the machinery and machine tools [they] needed' to repair the damage the Germans had done. 'It was only fair . . . This was the policy which Mr Morgenthau had laid before the President – to put the Ruhr and Saar out of action.'[106] Shortly after this visit Roosevelt abandoned the Morgenthau plan because of hostility to it in the United States after details were leaked.

This meant that by the end of 1944 the three major allies had not agreed on how to treat Germany in the post-war period. All they had decided was the division of the country into zones of occupation with the British in the north-west, the Americans in the south, the Soviets in the north-east and Berlin shared between them. Churchill took little interest in the details of this work, which was undertaken by the combined chiefs of staff and settled in the European Advisory Commission during 1944. There was no dispute over where the Soviet zone was to be – the only difficulty was between the United States and Britain. Initially Roosevelt was determined to take the north-west area but the difficulty of swapping over the allied armies after the Normandy invasion finally convinced him it was impossible and at Quebec in September 1944 he and Churchill agreed that the Americans would be in the south but could use British controlled ports in the north-west to avoid having their supply lines coming through France. They were keen to have the zonal division settled before any allied armies reached Germany because they expected (due to the delay in mounting the cross-Channel invasion) not to reach Germany before the Soviet Union.

Although the invasion of the other main belligerent, Japan, still seemed some way away, the allies were also beginning to turn their minds to a Far Eastern settlement. For Churchill, the war in the Far East was a racial war – its only purpose was to reconstitute the European empires that the Japanese had virtually destroyed. His main worry in 1942, during the initial Japanese successes, was that the Chinese would ally with them in a 'Pan-Asiatic movement all over the Far East, including all the brown and yellow races'.[107] When Britain's ally Chiang Kai-shek visited India, his main concern was the spread of a 'Pan-Asian malaise through all the bazaars of India'.[108] He was therefore relieved later in 1942, as he told the Pacific War Council in London, to hear 'the natives were looking to Europeans for their future and were not making common cause with their fellow Asiatics. This augured well.'[109] Nevertheless in 1944 he wanted to create a European-dominated Council of Asia 'to prevent trouble arising with the yellow races'.[110] And he assured the Dutch Prime Minister 'he was going to stand up for the Dutch Empire after the war'.[111] Indeed he even envisaged a further expansion of the European empires. Unlike the United States and China, he refused to agree to a public declaration on the post-war independence and territorial integrity of Siam and also refused to allow the Foreign Office to reassure the Siamese privately. The reason was that, despite the Atlantic Charter, 'it might be found necessary after the war to consider some sort of Protectorate over the Kra Peninsula area . . . in the interests of the future security of Singapore'.[112]

677

One of the most important elements in policy-making on the future of the Far East was the role of China, by far the biggest country in the region. It was partly occupied by Japan, with a weak nationalist Government under Chiang Kai-shek, and it faced the prospect of civil war between the Nationalists and the Communists after Japan was defeated. Britain and the United States had long contended for supremacy in China but after Pearl Harbor the British increasingly recognised US predominance. The American administration, and particularly Roosevelt, were determined to treat China as one of the four great powers, partly because they believed it would revive after the war but partly because they expected it to be under American influence. Churchill would have none of that. He annoyed Roosevelt by the slighting way he referred to them as 'little yellow men',[113] 'pigtails' and 'chinks'.[114] Lord Moran summed up the difference in attitude of the two men: 'To the President China means four hundred million people who are going to count in the world of tomorrow, but Winston thinks only of the colour of their skin.'[115]

In early 1943 the United States forced Britain to sign agreements with China abolishing extra-territoriality as a signal of China's equal status with the other powers. Churchill though was far from convinced about the future status of the country. He told Eden: 'It is an affectation to pretend that China is a power in any way comparable to the other three . . . China might fall again into a state of great confusion and possibly civil war.'[116] And he also believed that they were no more than a dependency of the Americans – 'a faggot vote on the side of the United States in any attempt to liquidate the British Overseas Empire'.[117] Nevertheless Churchill felt constrained to follow Roosevelt's policy although, as he explained to Eden, he thought it 'an absolute farce. I have told the President I would be reasonably polite about this American obsession, but I cannot agree that we should take a positive attitude on the matter.'[118]

By the end of 1944 the post-war world was already beginning to take shape. The Americans and British had liberated large parts of western Europe, Italy and Greece and ensured that sympathetic regimes were in control. In Eastern Europe the Soviet Union had liberated Rumania, Bulgaria and Poland and established regimes they regarded as sympathetic to their aims. Communist control of Hungary seemed likely, although Yugoslavia remained slightly more independent. The United States and Britain had effectively conceded Soviet control of Rumania and Bulgaria. As for Poland, the allies were united in agreeing on a major redrawing of the country's boundaries that would recognise the Soviet gains made in 1939 in collusion with Hitler. (They also accepted the conquest of the three Baltic states by the Soviet Union.) As in so many wars, the military position largely determined the post-war settlement. The remaining major problems for the allies to solve centred on the future of Germany – its possible division and the level of reparations – and the government of Poland, which was not covered by Churchill's 'spheres of influence' agreement with Stalin and where the Lublin Committee was in control but Britain and the United States still hoped to obtain a face-saving formula that would produce some involvement for the London Poles.

Arrangements for the second summit between the three wartime leaders were agreed between Roosevelt and Stalin as befitted the two strongest nations who would determine the post-war settlement. Only after they had decided on Yalta in the Crimea and a date in early February 1945 was Churchill invited to attend. He met Roosevelt briefly at Malta beforehand but they discussed little of significance. They and their staffs (700 altogether) then flew on twenty-five aircraft to Saki airport. Churchill arrived early on 3 February. He drove across the devastated Crimea to Yalta, where a series of villas and palaces had been lavishly refitted by the Soviet authorities. His quarters were in the Vorontzov Palace, ten miles from the Livadia Palace where Roosevelt was staying and where the main meetings were held. He had three rooms in the Vorontzov overlooking the sea and one of the two bathrooms. The delegation had to face some eccentric breakfasts of caviare and mince pies until they taught the staff to cook omelettes. Churchill drank 'buckets of Caucasian champagne'.[119]

The conference itself was affected by the mental or physical state of the three leaders. Roosevelt was in steep physical decline and Moran was convinced he had only a few months left to live. Churchill was disappointed to find him taking little interest in the proceedings and Eden noted in his diary that he 'gives the impression of fading powers ... Impossible to get even near business.'[120] Churchill himself was described by Moran as being 'in a vile mood throughout the Conference, irritable and bad tempered'.[121] A robustly healthy

Stalin dominated the proceedings and was very much in control of the discussions. Cadogan thought that Stalin 'shows up very impressively against the background of the other two ageing statesmen . . . the President flapped about and the P.M. boomed'.[122]

The conference centred around the future of Poland. At the plenary on 6 February, agreement about the eastern border was quickly reached. On the future Government Churchill said that it must be friendly to the Soviet Union so that they would have secure lines of communication. He also declared that although he had no dealings with the London Poles, he thought a few of them were acceptable. This was hardly a strong opening position and Stalin prevaricated on Roosevelt's suggestion of forming a new Government. The next day, after Roosevelt had written to Stalin suggesting all the Polish representatives should come to Yalta and Stalin had responded that he did not know where the Lublin Poles were, the Soviets put forward their own proposals that formed the basis of the eventual settlement. They suggested an enlarged Lublin Government including some London Poles, and Elections supervised by an allied commission to be based in Moscow and they endorsed the Lublin Government's demand for their western border to be along the line of the Oder and western Neisse Rivers, which would involve the deportation of an additional 4 million Germans.

On 8 February Roosevelt's plan (which Churchill endorsed) for a completely new provisional Government followed by Elections and no agreement to the Oder-Neisse line was rejected by Stalin. Churchill then tried to toughen his position by saying he would not abandon the government-in-exile and that there should be no recognition of the Lublin Government until after free Elections. Stalin rejected these demands and reminded Churchill and Roosevelt of their actions in France and Greece which paralleled Soviet moves in Poland. At the 9 February plenary Churchill was left isolated after the Americans in effect accepted the Soviet position. After a recess he agreed to the expansion of the Lublin Government (finally abandoning the London Poles) and discussion moved on to the mechanics of the free Elections. Churchill made the mistake of comparing Poland to Egypt but could not answer Stalin's question about the comparative literacy rates in the two countries. He then undermined all his arguments by claiming, 'I do not care much about Poles myself.'[123]

Under pressure from the Cabinet in London, which did not like Churchill's acceptance of the Soviet and American position, Eden tried to reopen the question of constructing an entirely new Polish Government but was unsuccessful. The United States then conceded that monitoring of the elections could be carried out by allied staffs in Moscow. But Stalin insisted that the Lublin Government would set the rules under which they operated. If the allied mission was to be based in Poland then they would have to recognise the Lublin Government. Churchill tried to get an agreement on frontiers but the three powers could only agree on the eastern border. In the west Churchill said he could not accept the western Neisse as the border, only the Oder. In the end Roosevelt's suggestion of consulting the Polish Government was accepted as a way of postponing the issue. On Poland therefore Britain and the United States had achieved little – a slight widening of the Lublin Government and Elections which would be under the supervision of the Lublin Poles with only minimal outside monitoring. Only the eastern border was settled (as it effectively had been since Teheran). Churchill and Roosevelt had almost no cards in their hand; they had to accept the power of the Soviets and the Lublin Poles to determine matters on the ground – the best they could achieve was a formula which they hoped might save some face even though they must have expected the Communists to rig the 'free' elections.

On Germany the Soviet Union took a tough line over dismemberment and the need for reparations, both issues on which, not surprisingly after the Morgenthau plan and Churchill's visit in October 1944, they thought they were advocating agreed allied policy. They were taken aback therefore to find Churchill retreating on dismemberment, which he had advocated throughout the war. As on Poland he was forced back into line by agreement between Roosevelt and Stalin. Churchill was also obstructive over reparations – he did not want to set a specific figure and seemed to imply that Soviet sufferings (nearly 30 million dead and enormous damage to the infrastructure of the western part of the country) had not been that great and many other countries had claims to be met. To Stalin, Britain seemed more interested in German recovery than the needs of the Soviet Union. Roosevelt was more sympathetic to the Soviet position and eventually Churchill was forced to accept a Soviet-American compromise. Germany would pay reparations in kind for an unspecified period (Britain wanted five years, the other two ten years). The Soviet Union and the US proposed a total figure of $20 billion, with half going to the Soviet Union. Britain refused to endorse this and the matter was remitted to the reparations commission, which was to be set up in Moscow.

For the Americans one of their main aims was to reach agreement on a new United Nations organisation which had been agreed in outline between the allies in the autumn of 1944. The main area of disagreement was eliminated when Stalin accepted Roosevelt's suggestion on the veto: all five permanent members of the Security Council were to have a veto on resolutions but not debates. Churchill backed Stalin's demand for some of the constituent republics of the Soviet Union to be given seats in the General Assembly, because he wanted to protect the position of the Dominions (eventually Ukraine and Belorussia were admitted). Another question to be resolved was the timing of the conference to establish the UN, which the Americans wanted to hold in March. Churchill wanted to wait until the war was over. His contributions on this subject were often far from helpful, even for his own side, as Cadogan recorded:

> The P.M. got rather off the rails. Silly old man – without a word of warning to Anthony or me, he plunged into a long harangue about World Organisation, knowing nothing whatever of what he was talking about and making complete nonsense of the whole thing. The worst of it was that what he said was completely contrary to the line already agreed with the Americans.[124]

Eventually Churchill accepted a meeting at the end of April.

The rest of the conference was devoted to a declaration on liberated Europe, agreement on the exchange of prisoners of war, the inclusion of France in the Allied Control Commission for Germany and the creation of her own zone from the area allocated to Britain and the US, largely at Britain's insistence. On the Far East Churchill's lack of influence was made painfully apparent. Roosevelt and Stalin settled between them the terms on which the Soviet Union would enter the war against Japan (recovery of the Czarist territories lost in the 1904–5 war plus the Kurile islands and South Sakhalin island) and agreed on the military co-operation necessary. Churchill was shown the resulting document on the last day of the conference and had no alternative but to accept it.

The conference dispersed rapidly after the final session on 11 February and the British delegation headed for the liner *Franconia*; it had been a troop ship but 5,000 people had worked on it for a week to convert it back to its luxurious pre-war standards to accommodate Churchill. Once on board rows broke out. To everyone's annoyance Churchill insisted that all the heating on the boat was turned off after his state room became slightly too warm. Then Eden wanted to go to Athens on his own but Churchill refused, not wishing to give him any of the limelight. As Cadogan noted sourly in his diary, it was 'rather like travelling about with Melba and Tetrazzini in one company'.[125] Eventually the whole party went to Athens and on to Alexandria, where Churchill had meetings with the Emperor of Ethiopia, the King of Egypt, the President of Syria and King Saud of Saudi Arabia (he even managed not to smoke or drink in the latter's presence).

On his return to London Cadogan reported 'The P.M. and Anthony are well satisfied – if not more' with the results of Yalta.[126] Churchill told the Cabinet Stalin 'meant well to the world and Poland'[127] and later remarked, 'Poor Neville Chamberlain believed he could trust Hitler. He was wrong. But I don't think I'm wrong about Stalin.'[128] In the period after Yalta Churchill once again showed himself determined to stick with the deal over spheres of influence that he had made in Moscow. At the end of February 1945 the Soviets engineered a coup in Rumania which installed a Communist Government. The Foreign Office wanted to criticise Soviet actions but Churchill stopped them, saying 'we really have no justification for intervening in this extraordinarily vigorous manner for our late Rumanian enemies thus compromising our position in Poland and jarring Russian acquiescence in our long fight for Athens', and adding later 'we, for considerations well known to you, accepted in a special degree the predominance of Russia in this theatre'.[129] He took the same line over Bulgaria and refused to protest when Soviet forces took fifteen Polish leaders as prisoners to Moscow, and did not change his stance even when they were given prison sentences.

Others in Britain were less sanguine about Soviet intentions, and Churchill came under pressure in Parliament over the deal he had reached at Yalta on Poland – twenty-five MPs voted against the agreement on the Curzon line as the eastern border and thirty abstained in a vote at the end of February. When he wrote to Roosevelt in the first week of March he was painfully aware that the October 1944 deal and British actions in Greece made it very difficult to criticise the Soviet Union over its actions in Eastern Europe. He argued against complaining to Moscow about the coup in Rumania: 'This again would lead to comparisons between the aims of his action and those of ours. On this neither side would convince the other. Having regard to my personal relations with Stalin, I am sure it would be a mistake for me at this stage to embark on the argument.' He was prepared to admit privately to Roosevelt that the settlement over Poland reached at Yalta might not turn out as the public expected and he told the President: 'if we do not get things right now, it will soon be seen by the world that you and I by putting our signatures to the Crimea settlement have under-written a fraudulent prospectus'.[130] In his next message to Roosevelt he said that what he wanted on Poland was a 'process of consultations among Poles to form a new government'.[131] That was in fact taking place but the problem from Churchill's point of view was that the Communist controlled Lublin dominated the negotiations and seemed certain to run post-war Poland.

The Soviet Union, as a major military power, was able to impose its will in eastern Europe and Britain was a minor military power unable to significantly affect the process. The expansion of Soviet power westwards posed difficult problems for the British as they considered how to adapt to the post-war world. The Foreign Office felt that although the Soviets were being tough they were simply securing control in an area vital for their security whereas the chiefs of staff believed this expansion posed a threat to western Europe. Churchill acknowledged the dilemma to Commonwealth leaders in early April 1945: 'It was by no means clear that we could count on Russia as a beneficent influence in Europe, or as a willing partner in maintaining the peace of the world. Yet, at the end of the war, Russia would be left in a position of preponderant power and influence throughout the whole of Europe.'[132]

Churchill fluctuated between optimism and pessimism, between pragmatism and the desire to restrain Soviet actions. When Clementine travelled to the Soviet Union as head of the British Red Cross

Assistance Committee, he told her to tell Stalin that he thought their personal relations were still very good and of his 'cordial feelings and ... resolve and confidence that a complete understanding between the English-speaking world and Russia will be achieved and maintained'.[133] Yet his sense of frustration was well illustrated in a conversation over lunch with the Soviet Ambassador Gusev ten days after the defeat of Germany. Foreshadowing a later famous phrase, he told Gusev the Soviets were 'dropping an iron screen across Europe from Lubeck to Trieste behind which we had no knowledge of what was happening. All we knew was that puppet governments were being set up about which we were not consulted ... [Britain objected] to being treated as if they were of no account in the after-war world. They felt that they still counted for something and they refused to be pushed about.'[134] He told Eden ten days later 'we shall have to raise the great question of police government versus free government, it always being understood that the intermediate states must not pursue a hostile policy to Russia'.[135] But he offered no suggestions as to how and when the question might be raised or how to reconcile 'free government' with Soviet perceived security needs. In the end though Churchill conceded that Britain could not determine the course of events in Eastern Europe. He wrote in June 1945: 'It is beyond the power of this country to prevent all sorts of things crashing at the present time. The responsibility lies with the U.S. and my desire is to give them all the support in our power. If they do not feel able to do anything, then we must let matters take their course.'[136]

By the time Churchill wrote that minute he had also had to accept American policy over the zonal agreement in Germany. When the fighting finally finished in May, the British and American Armies were slightly to the east of their zonal boundaries and the Soviets controlled all of Berlin and most of Austria. Churchill now wanted to tear up the carefully constructed wartime agreement on control of Germany and to refuse to withdraw the Anglo-American armies until there was a general settlement with the Soviet Union. A confrontation with the Soviet Union was not a realistic option, given the pressing need to demobilise forces, and if Churchill's proposals had been carried out they would have left Berlin and Austria under Soviet control. It is difficult to see why Churchill felt it necessary to alienate the Soviet Union over a relatively small stretch of territory in the middle of Germany. At the beginning of June he warned Eden: 'If the Russian frontier advances to Eisenach we shall rue the day, and so will the Americans, and you may live to see the evil consequences.'[137] Nevertheless a fortnight later he accepted US proposals for Anglo-American troop withdrawals at the same time as the Soviets withdrew from what was to become the British zone in Austria, the creation of an Allied Control Commission in Berlin, the setting up of three zones for the western allies in Berlin together with an access agreement and the ending of the joint wartime command arrangements.

Once this agreement had been implemented the plans for the next three-power summit at Potsdam near Berlin could be finalised. Churchill left Britain on 7 July, immediately after voting took place in the General Election (the votes would not be counted for three weeks to allow time to collect service votes). Accompanied by Clementine, Mary, Lord Moran, Jock Colville and two secretaries he travelled first to Château de Bordaberry near Hendaye in south-west France, which had been lent by a French-Canadian, Brigadier Brutinel. There he took up painting again. He stayed for a week, on one occasion rudely walking out of a special demonstration of Basque games and dancing put on for him, and arrived in Berlin on 15 July. The next day he met President Truman for the first time (Roosevelt had died on 12 April and Churchill had decided not to attend his funeral despite their wartime association and Truman's express desire to meet him). In the afternoon he toured a ruined Berlin, including the Chancellery and Hitler's bunker.

The Potsdam conference got underway on 17 July. It was the last of the three-power conferences and even more than at Teheran and Yalta the British were relegated to the sidelines, with the key discussions taking place between the Americans and the Soviets. Once again Churchill's performance left much to be desired. The Cabinet Secretary, Sir Edward Bridges, and Churchill's Private Secretary, Rowan, told Lord Moran, 'The P.M. is not mastering his brief. He is too tired to prepare anything; he just deals with things as they come up.'[138] Cadogan noted 'The P.M., since he left London, has refused to do any work or read anything ... he butts in on every occasion and talks the most irrelevant rubbish, and risks giving away our case at every point.'[139] After the first plenary meeting Cadogan commented, 'He is again under Stalin's spell. He kept repeating "I like that man".'[140] This first plenary was chaired by the American President in a brisk manner quite unlike Roosevelt's rambling style. Truman wrote to his mother afterwards, 'It is hard as presiding over the Senate. Churchill talks all the time and Stalin just grunts but you know what he means.'[141] The meeting was largely devoted to deciding what topics needed to be discussed – both Truman and Stalin made numerous suggestions, Churchill none. Eden described the meeting in his diary: 'W was very bad. He had read no brief & was confused and woolly & verbose about the new Council of Foreign Ministers. We had an anti-Chinese tirade from him. Americans not a little exasperated ... Alec [Cadogan] & I & Bob [Dixon] have never seen W worse.'[142]

Churchill had lunch alone with Truman on 18 July, when they discussed what to tell Stalin about the atomic bomb (Churchill had learnt of the successful trial in New Mexico from the Americans the previous day). He agreed with Truman's suggestion that the President should do it casually and without going into any detail. Churchill also pleaded for American sympathy over Britain's financial position. Truman promised no more than that he would look into the subject and in return asked for American use of British bases, which Churchill immediately agreed to. The second plenary that afternoon at 4pm consisted largely of a long rambling monologue from Churchill about Poland, in which he conceded there had been 'great improvements' in the country in the last two months but then went on to raise such detailed questions as the disposal of the Ambassador's residence in London and severance pay for the staff.[143] Truman was not interested in pursuing such matters and brought the meeting to a close. Cadogan noted that the meeting 'went so efficiently that we got through our agenda by about 6 – much to the P.M.'s annoyance, as he wanted to go on talking at random and was most disappointed – just like a child with its toy taken away from it'.[144] That evening Churchill dined with Stalin at the latter's residence and again offered to revise the Montreux convention and welcomed the Soviets as a major naval power throughout the world. The meeting left Churchill convinced that Stalin was trying to be co-operative.

Over the next six days the conference edged around a number of issues and settled some – Konigsberg was allotted to the Soviet Union, Spain was not to be invited to join the United Nations (Churchill was strongly opposed to breaking off relations with

Franco's regime) and a third of the German fleet was allotted to each of the main allied powers. The most difficult issue was still the western border of Poland: in practice the Soviets were already allowing the Poles to administer the territory up to the Oder-Neisse line. Stalin was insistent that this should be recognised as the new border. Truman rejected the demand, but was moving towards acceptance in return for an effective economic division of Germany (which implied a political division), with each ally taking reparations from its own zone and with a specified amount from the Ruhr to go to the Soviets. Churchill remained opposed.

The formal proceedings were interspersed with competitive dining and dubious forms of entertainment laid on by the three delegations. On 19 July Truman gave a copious dinner for Stalin and Churchill accompanied by music. On the 21st Stalin gave a lavish banquet followed by music; Churchill hated the music and he sulked throughout the evening. On the 23rd it was Churchill's turn. When he saw the menu he demanded that cold ham be added. This had to be flown out from England by a special RAF flight, but unfortunately nobody ate any. He also insisted on an RAF band playing through-out, but it went through its repertoire so loudly that it made Stalin furious. Churchill and Attlee (who was part of the delegation in case Labour won the Election) also took the salute at the British victory parade in Berlin on 21 July, when the largest cheers were reserved for Attlee.

On 25 July the plenary session was held in the morning in order to allow time for Churchill and Attlee to fly back to Britain for the declaration of the General Election results the next day. There was only desultory conversation at the meeting and the conference then went into recess to await the return of the British delegation. Virtually everyone at Potsdam expected Churchill to reappear, but this turned out to be his last contribution to discussions with the United States and the Soviet Union about the shaping of the post-war world. His unexpected defeat in the 1945 Election was almost entirely the consequence of the electorate's views about domestic policy, a subject which throughout the war Churchill had regarded as of little importance.

Towards a New World?

The stresses and strains caused by global conflict and the need to mobilise British society for total war posed severe challenges to existing power structures both at home and abroad. Domestically as the war went on there was a rising demand for a decisive break with the past; in particular people wanted to see changes from the policies that in the 1930s had failed to solve the evils of mass unemployment and poverty, and they expected some sort of a reward for the sacrifices entailed by the war. Abroad the stresses were felt particularly strongly in the Empire. There Churchill's lifelong determination to preserve the imperial inheritance was challenged by two forces. First, the rapid collapse of British power in the Far East meant that not only was British prestige badly shaken but control would have to be reasserted over large tracts of territory after the war. Second, the increasing involvement of the United States in every aspect of the conflict meant that their views, and particularly Roosevelt's, about decolonisation could not be ignored, especially given Britain's dependence on the Americans in so many other spheres.

Churchill's views on the integrity of the Empire and its central role in Britain's greatness did not change during the war. In a speech in November 1942 he declared: 'We mean to hold our own. I have not become the King's First Minister in order to preside over the liquidation of the British Empire.' In April 1945 he told the US Ambassador to China, 'Never would we yield an inch of the territory that was under the British flag.'¹ Similarly he was not prepared to contemplate any constitutional change within the Empire. During a weekend at Chequers, the Governor of Burma, Sir Reginald Dorman-Smith, raised the possibility of self-government for some colonies but he found that Churchill would not listen. The Prime Minister's response was to say, 'What those people need is the sjambok' and to order the Governor to leave Chequers immediately.² In order to strengthen opposition to change he insisted on appointing men of similar views to his own as Colonial Secretary – for example Lord Lloyd in 1940 and Oliver Stanley, who held the post from November 1942 until the end of the war.

The first time Churchill faced American pressure on colonial issues was at the Newfoundland conference in August 1941. One clause of the Atlantic Charter spoke of the restoration of 'sovereign rights and self-government'. Roosevelt intended this to apply to the colonial empires, whereas Churchill's interpretation was that it would only apply to countries under German rule. The Cabinet endorsed Churchill's interpretation and agreed that he should make a statement in Parliament to this effect. On 9 September he took the line that this part of the Charter was 'primarily' concerned with 'the restoration of the sovereignty, self-government and national life of the States and nations of Europe now under Nazi yoke'. He referred to developments within the Empire as 'a separate problem', though he left open, because of conflicts within the coalition, what form those developments should take. When Attlee later told a group of students that the Charter did apply to all peoples, Churchill expressed astonishment and told the Labour leader he was sure he had not meant to imply 'that the natives of Nigeria or East Africa could by a majority vote choose the form of government under which they live'.³ He did not bother to disguise his views from the Americans. For instance he told Charles Taussig, Roosevelt's adviser on colonial issues, 'We will not let the Hottentots by popular vote throw the white people into the sea.'⁴

Churchill found however that it was not so easy to dismiss American aspirations. Looking ahead to the post-war world, the US concentrated its efforts on ensuring the United Nations Charter contained the provisions they wanted. The UN was to take over from the old League of Nations the mandated territories created after the First World War, and the Americans wanted much stronger supervision by the UN and acceptance of their eventual right to self-determination. Whatever the technical legal position, Churchill regarded the British mandated territories simply as another part of the Empire and therefore solely Britain's responsibility. He was worried by the way discussions about the establishment of the UN were going during the winter of 1944–5. At the end of 1944 he wrote that if the US wanted to take over the islands in the Pacific held by Japan on mandates, that was acceptable but there were to be no 'declarations affecting British sovereignty in any of the Dominions or Colonies' (which also demonstrates once again the essentially subordinate position he thought the Dominions held). He went on: '"Hands off the British Empire" is our maxim and it must not be weakened or smirched to please sob-stuff merchants at home or foreigners of any hue.'[5] At the same time he was worried that as a result of external pressure Britain was 'being jockeyed out or edged near the abyss'.[6]

Roosevelt was determined to raise colonial issues at the Yalta conference in February 1945. He put three propositions to Stalin: Hong Kong should be given to China rather than restored to Britain, Korea should be a trusteeship with Britain excluded and Indochina should be made independent rather than restored to France. (Churchill had been working hard to ensure that France did regain Indochina.) Stalin was sympathetic but cautious, partly because of the deal he had done with Churchill over the Far East and Eastern Europe during their meeting in October 1944. At the 9 February plenary session Roosevelt merely suggested that trusteeship should be discussed at the forthcoming conference setting up the UN. Churchill flew into a rage and shouted: 'I will not have one scrap of the British territory flung into that area . . . I will have no suggestion that the British Empire is to be put into the dock and examined by everybody to see whether it is up to their standard.'[7] Changing his analogy he declared he would not 'consent to forty or fifty nations thrusting interfering fingers into the life's existence of the British Empire'.[8]

After Roosevelt reassured him that his ideas only referred to 'ex-enemy possesions', Churchill accepted the US proposal. If he had read the US document he would have realised that the 'ex-enemy possessions' were in fact the post-First World War mandates, as Eden and Stanley appreciated. Churchill had therefore conceded

UN 'interference' in areas that he regarded as an integral part of the Empire. At the San Francisco conference Britain had to accept the principle of free trade in the trusteeship territories (as the mandates became), regular reports to the General Assembly, inspections and the right of the native peoples to petition the UN Trusteeship Council. Chapter XI of the UN Charter also committed the colonial powers 'to develop self-government and to take due account of the political aspirations of the peoples'. Although falling short of a commitment to granting independence, it went further than the British Government wanted.

As in the past the issue that was closest to Churchill's heart was the future of India. The scheme to create a federation that he had opposed so strongly during the early 1930s had by 1939 hardly got off the ground, as the Conservatives who devised it expected. Virtually all the princes had refused to join though eight provinces did have Congress controlled administrations. In September 1939 the Viceroy's declaration of war, made without consulting any Indians, as he was legally entitled to do, led to widespread discontent. As a palliative measure, Linlithgow, Viceroy since the mid-1930s, suggested adding some Congress Party members to the executive committee that advised him. Although Chamberlain and the rest of the Cabinet were prepared to agree, Churchill was not. He spoke of starting down the 'slippery slope of concessions' and 'yielding to the pressures of parties who were, after all, only exploiting the dangers with which Britain was faced', and he suggested backing the Viceroy in 'a policy of firm administration' if Congress resigned from its provincial governments.[9] In a minority of one Churchill successfully insisted on four conditions. As a result Linlithgow's suggestion was accepted – but the Cabinet agreed that the supreme power of the Viceroy would remain intact, Britain would be free to deploy troops as it liked in India, there would be no constitutional legislation during the war and no promises would be made about what might happen at the end of the war. A fortnight later the Cabinet agreed to reject the Congress demand for India to draw up its own constitution at the end of the war. The Congress Party therefore resigned from all provincial governments it controlled and British governors resumed full powers, much to Churchill's relief.

In February 1940 the Secretary of State for India, Lord Zetland, presented the Cabinet with a scheme worked out in conjunction with

25a Churchill during one of his visits to the Normandy bridgehead 1944
(General Montgomery on the left)

25b Churchill with De Gaulle at the Armistice Day parade in Paris, November 1944
(Sir Alexander Cadogan is behind Churchill's right shoulder)

26a Churchill picnics with Generals Brooke (centre) and Montgomery (right) on the banks of the Rhine, March 1945

26b Churchill with the crowds in Whitehall, V-E Day

27a Churchill in the Cabinet Room at No 10 Downing Street
before his broadcast on V-E Day

27b Churchill tours the ruins of Berlin
before the Potsdam conference, July 1945
(To Churchill's right his daughter Mary and Anthony Eden)

28a Churchill leaves No 10 Downing Street
on the day of his retirement – 5 April 1955

28b Churchill after his horse 'Colonist II' had won
the Lowther Stakes at Newmarket

29a Sarah Churchill

29b Randolph Churchill
unsuccessfully campaigning
at Devonport

30a Churchill with President Eisenhower in London, 1959.
(Field Marshal Montgomery behind)

30b Churchill with ex-President Truman at Chartwell.
(Left to right: Mary Soames, Sarah, Mrs Truman, Churchill,
Truman, Clementine, Lord Beaverbrook, Christopher Soames)

31 The Bleak Years

32 The State Funeral
30 January 1965

a above: from left to right: Earl Attlee, Lord Avon, Field Marshal Lord Slim, Marshal of the RAF, Lord Portal, Lord Bridges, Lord Normanbrook, Sir Robert Menzies, Harold Macmillan

b below: Churchill's coffin is carried down the steps of St Paul's Cathedral, Clementine and Randolph Churchill immediately behind

Linlithgow; it included a promise of dominion status and the right to frame a constitution after the war but with very strict safeguards for Britain's position. Churchill led the opposition. He told his colleagues he welcomed 'the Hindu/Muslim feud' as 'a bulwark of British rule in India'. If it were ended he feared it would lead to 'the united communities joining in showing us the door'.[10] (This was his position in the 1930s too.) This time his colleagues agreed with Churchill's doubts. Linlithgow was authorised to open discussions with Ghandi but only on terms that ensured their failure. Churchill was still concerned that the Government might be pushed too far. He wrote to Chamberlain: 'The policy of running after Ghandi and the Congress, which the Viceroy conceives it his duty to pursue, is steadily wearing down every pillar of British authority. The Secretary of State ought to send him clear instructions defining and correcting his course during the war.'[11]

When he became Prime Minister Churchill did not find it easy to impose the policy he wanted against the views of his colleagues and the Viceroy. The new Secretary of State, Leo Amery, though a staunch imperialist, was acutely aware of the problems of controlling India without any statement about its status after the war. In mid-July 1940 he proposed making a declaration setting out India's right to frame a constitution after the war and acceptance of dominion status. Churchill, backed by an old friend from his Indian campaign ten years earlier, Lord Lloyd, was totally opposed to Amery's plan. To stop it he first persuaded the Viceroy to withdraw his support and then accused Amery of misleading the Cabinet about the Viceroy's views. Churchill personally redrafted the declaration and forced it through the Cabinet on 30 July. The Government rejected India's right to a constituent assembly to devise a constitution, the goal of dominion status was held out but no time limit was set and all the steps towards that goal were to be controlled by Britain. In addition the role of minorities was emphasised in a way that would make it almost impossible to achieve a united India. The Cabinet expected Congress to react by starting a campaign of mass civil disobedience but they did not do so at this stage. However it was simply not possible to resist all constitutional change. A year later Churchill was forced by his colleagues, after successful lobbying from Amery, to agree to the creation of an advisory National Defence

Council (originally promised in 1939) and the addition of more Indians to the Viceroy's Council.

War with Japan, and the rapid disintegration of the Empire in the Far East, produced a real crisis in India. The sight of British power collapsing before an oriental nation, which so appalled Churchill, opened up the prospect of ending British rule to an increasing number of Indians. At first Churchill opposed reaching any agreement with the detested Congress Party. In a letter to Attlee written in early January 1942 he expressed his views about India's contribution to the war: 'The Indian troops are fighting splendidly, but it must be remembered that their allegiance is to the King Emperor, and that the rule of Congress and the Hindoo Priesthood machine would never be tolerated by a fighting race.'[12] (Privately he blamed the loss of Malaya on the fact that the Japanese faced only two white battalions, the rest being Indian soldiers.) As the situation in Malaya and then Burma continued to deteriorate, Attlee pressed the Cabinet for some political action to save India for the Empire, although both Amery and the Viceroy were unwilling to make a move. To pre-empt discussion of any fundamental change, Churchill put forward his own plan for an expanded advisory National Defence Council of 100 members (largely appointed from the princes and provinces) which would discuss the war effort and also draw up a constitution after the war. The plan was deliberately designed to exclude Congress, ensure that there was no Indian unity and allow Britain to effectively control the process of drawing up the constitution. Linlithgow quickly demolished Churchill's plan as unsaleable.

A combination of events (the fall of Singapore, the approach of the Japanese Army to the borders of India and Churchill's political weakness evident in the Cabinet reshuffle in mid-February that elevated Attlee to the role of Deputy Prime Minister and brought Stafford Cripps into the War Cabinet) significantly tilted the balance against Churchill's chances of stopping or crippling Indian constitutional change. He had to adopt more subtle methods to prevent progress. In March 1942 Attlee, who now chaired the Cabinet Committee on India, developed a scheme for a new constitution aimed at stopping an open revolt in the country. At the same time, Roosevelt, concerned at the implications for allied strategy of the loss of India, was also pressing Churchill to make some substantial advance and sent his own representative, Colonel Louis Johnson, to India to act as a mediator between the two sides.

The Government was badly divided over how to handle Attlee's proposals, with Churchill pressing the need to consult all ministers of Cabinet rank (where the Conservatives had an overwhelming majority), rather than just the War Cabinet. Eventually the conflicts were put on one side when Cripps suggested he should go to India to try to negotiate a settlement. Churchill's political position was so weak at this time that not only did he have to agree to the mission, he also had to accept a declaration drawn up by the Cabinet committee, to be used as the basis for the talks that ran counter to everything he believed about the future of India. There was a guarantee of the right of India after the war to devise its own constitution and move to either dominion status or independence, and dissenting provinces (i.e. the Muslim provinces) could be given independence separately.

Churchill sought to undermine the Cripps mission from the start for both personal and political reasons. He wanted to protect his own political position from any further rise in Cripps' increasing popularity and to stop any immediate Indian constitutional advance or guarantees about the future, thereby giving more room to change direction after the war. His first move was to seek to minimise the scope of the mission by speaking in Parliament of Cripps as only seeking Indian 'assent' to the proposals (i.e. there would be no negotiations) and by describing the aim as being to promote the 'concentration of all Indian thought upon the defence of the native soil'. Privately he told Linlithgow that the Cabinet declaration was 'our utmost limit' when in fact the Cabinet had agreed that Cripps could negotiate on how to widen the Executive Council immediately and bring in more Indian members.[13] On his arrival in India Cripps made the purpose of the visit clear at a press conference – the administration, apart from defence affairs, was to be Indianised – and he was not disowned by either the British Government or the Viceroy. Congress however pressed for some Indian involvement with defence and the way in which this should be organised became the most difficult part of the talks. The Cabinet agreed to Cripps' suggestion that he should discuss defence on the basis that the British would retain ultimate responsibility and the Indian Government would organise the 'military, moral and material resources of India'.[14]

At the beginning of April Cripps asked for authority to go beyond this remit. His appeal was accepted, but Churchill, who with Cripps temporarily absent from the War Cabinet had more support, persuaded his colleagues to agree to him sending a message to Cripps. This stated that the declaration had 'made our position plain to the world and . . . won general approval. We all reached agreement on it before you started and it represents our final position.'[15] (This was misleading – the Cabinet had agreed to go beyond it some weeks earlier.) There is a hint in this message that to some Conservatives the whole point of the declaration on the future of India was to convince the rest of the world, particularly the Americans, that Britain had made an offer, even if it proved unacceptable. Churchill now also went behind Cripps' back and invited Linlithgow to send his own views about what Cripps was doing: 'Of course telegraph personal to me or Secretary of State exactly what you think. It is my responsibility to decide to whom it is to be shown after I have read it.'[16] He was clearly preparing to use the opinions of an official to undermine the work of his Cabinet colleague.

As a result of this manoeuvre Churchill knew by early April that Linlithgow and Wavell (the Commander-in-Chief) only wanted a largely powerless Minister for Defence Co-ordination and that Linlithgow objected violently to what he thought of as an 'Indian Cabinet' from whom he would have to accept directions. Churchill waited until Cripps suggested giving responsibility for defence to an Indian minister subject to directions from the British Commander-in-Chief (thereby keeping real control with the British). Cripps did not suggest any change in the Viceroy's powers over his 'Cabinet', only that he should try to give the Indian ministers the illusion that they were being treated like a real Cabinet. His proposals were accepted by the Cabinet Committee on India. By 9 April Congress was on the verge of agreeing to his proposals on defence – the only remaining obstacle to their acceptance of the declaration as a whole. Churchill moved with speed and political duplicity to abort the talks at the critical moment. Having already sent a message to Cripps to stop him reaching an immediate agreement with Congress, he insisted that the War Cabinet consider Cripps' proposals. He saw Harry Hopkins, who was trying to contain the developing Anglo-American rift over the future of India, at 10.30 that morning. Hopkins accidentally gave him the impression that Roosevelt's personal representative in India, Colonel Louis Johnson, with whom Cripps had agreed his formula, did not have the President's full confidence. (When Roosevelt realised what Hopkins had done, he sent a message repudiating the suggestion but by then it was too late.) Churchill had found another weapon to use against Cripps.

Immediately after his discussion with Hopkins, Churchill personally drafted another telegram to Cripps containing two misleading statements: Johnson was not Roosevelt's representative and the American President was opposed to US mediation. When the Cabinet met at 11.00, Churchill read out his message to Cripps but did it in such a way as to give the impression that Cripps was involving Johnson and the Americans in British policy making and using Johnson to by-pass Linlithgow and Wavell. He went on to state that what he described as the 'Cripps-Johnson' formula on defence could not be accepted because it derogated from the powers of the Viceroy and Commander-in-Chief. Churchill, without referring directly to his private communications with the Viceroy, also hinted that Linlithgow and Wavell did not support the Cripps plan. On the basis of this slanted and misleading information he got the Cabinet to agree a message repudiating the Cripps proposals as agreed by the India Committee – 'It is essential to bring the whole matter back to Cabinet's plan which you went out to urge, with only such amplifications as are agreed to be put forward.'[17] This message removed the Government's support for Cripps at the crucial moment.

The next day the Cabinet's India Committee accepted the Cripps defence formula subject to Linlithgow's and Wavell's agreement. While the committee was meeting Churchill received another private message from Linlithgow in which he made clear his refusal to work with Indian ministers as a Cabinet and demanded retention of his old powers. Churchill promptly summoned the India Committee and took over the discussions. He harangued them until they backed Linlithgow against Cripps and agreed to the despatch of a message of support to the Viceroy saying 'there can be no question of any convention limiting in any way your powers under the existing constitution'.[18] He also sent a message to Cripps: 'It was certainly agreed between us all that there were not to be negotiations' on what he described as 'our great offer'.[19] The Cripps mission was at an end. Churchill, by backing an intransigent Viceroy against a member of his own Cabinet and by misrepresenting the proposals on the table, had ensured that it was aborted. On 11 April Roosevelt sent a stiff message asking for one more effort and blaming the failure on London. Churchill refused to put the message before the Cabinet and in his reply did his utmost to ensure that there was no further American involvement. He warned the President that there would be grave damage to relations if Britain had to conform to American views on an imperial matter and made the rather empty threat that if the Americans continued in this way 'I should personally make no objection at all to retiring into private life'.[20]

The failure of the Cripps mission in April 1942 inevitably moved Congress towards a 'Quit India' policy supported by mass non-co-operation just as Japanese armies were poised to invade. But the pressures that had led to the Cripps proposals could not be ignored for long, despite Churchill's desire to postpone as long as possible any consideration of India's post-war future. Amery secured Cabinet agreement at the end of July to a major revision of the Cripps offer – it envisaged India moving to dominion status but as a medley of small states not as a united country and with the Viceroy retaining wide 'federal' powers and Britain keeping control over defence policy. Churchill tried to remove the right to leave the Commonwealth but was overridden by his colleagues. This new proposal, the exact opposite of the Congress policy of a united India obtaining full independence, showed the same British determination as in the 1930s to divide India so as to retain as much control as possible. In parallel with this offer, the War Cabinet agreed to arrest the leadership of Congress, seize its funds and declare it illegal. This move was made in early August to the accompaniment of widespread civil disobedience which could only be contained by fifty-seven battalions of British troops.

Churchill believed he had secured the outcome he wanted. His basic aims had never changed. He told a leading Indian, Sir A. R. Mundaliar, on 9 September, the day before he was to speak about India in Parliament: 'for the last 25 years the Conservative Party has gone on the wrong tracks ... it has given way perpetually until the present state of affairs has come about. It is all wrong, thoroughly wrong. ... That will be my statement on India tomorrow. No apology, no quitting, no idea of weakening or scuttling.'[21] In mid-November, when Cripps suggested in Cabinet inviting Indian moderates to London to discuss Hindu-Muslim unity, Churchill responded with a 'terrific tirade against the whole conception of Indian self-government'.[22] As Amery reported to Linlithgow, Churchill was worried about the increasing size of the Indian Army and the possibility of another 'mutiny': 'Winston at the moment has got one of his fits of panic and talks about a drastic reduction of any army that might shoot us in the back.'[23] Amery also told Wavell that Churchill 'has got a curious complex about India and is always loth to hear good of it and is apt to believe the worst. He has, at heart, his cavalry subaltern's idea of India.'[24]

By this time (mid-1943) Churchill had with great reluctance settled on Wavell as the replacement for Linlithgow; he expected the new Viceroy to do little about the future of India for the rest of the war. Wavell himself distrusted Churchill's judgement, commenting that he 'hates India and everything to do with it' and that he knew 'as much about the Indian problem as George III did of the American colonies'.[25] Churchill remained worried that 'the "softy" English people at home' would let India slide into chaos,[26] and preferred to take much of his advice about India from Cherwell, a confirmed racist. For example, he accepted Cherwell's advice not to send relief supplies during the terrible Bengal famine of 1943–4 when three million people died. Wavell thought he 'seemed to regard sending food to India as an "appeasement" of Congress'[27] and Amery judged his attitude 'Hitler-like'.[28] Ghandi was for Churchill Britain's 'bitter enemy'[29] and he was convinced that during Gandhi's hunger strike in 1943 he was taking glucose with his water and only reluctantly accepted the Viceroy's statement that this was not the case. When Wavell suggested in October 1943, with the support of the Cabinet's India Committee, that there might be a limited attempt to reopen negotiations on some parts of the aborted Cripps plan, Churchill told the Viceroy 'only over his dead body would any approach to Ghandi take place'.[30]

Wavell raised this idea again in October 1944. Churchill ignored it for a month and then said nothing could be done until after the war. But Amery and Attlee insisted this policy of total negativity could not be accepted and there must be some discussion of options for the future. Overruled in Cabinet, Churchill finally accepted at the end of May 1945 the suggestion that Wavell should summon Indian political and religious leaders and ask them to suggest names of people he could appoint to his Executive Council. He insisted that even on this very limited scheme that involved no constitutional advance there could be no negotiations – the Indians could only accept or reject it. He himself only accepted the idea because, as he told Wavell, 'the India Committee had all told him it was bound to fail'.[31] Churchill viewed with equal distaste looking ahead to the future of Burma. In December 1944 he wrote to the Chief Whip to object to pressure from Conservative backbenchers to consider Burma's future, telling him: 'I see that the policy which has brought us to the present miserable pass in India is still thriving in some quarters, and that we are being urged to take steps in miniature in Burma which will afterwards bring the destruction of our Indian Empire.'[32] During this period there are further examples of Churchill's loathing of Indians generally and Hindus in particular – he referred to them as 'baboos', saying they were 'gross, dirty and corrupt'.[33] Towards the end of the war he told Jock Colville 'the Hindus were a foul race "protected by their mere pullulation from the doom that is their due"' and he expressed a wish that 'Bert Harris could send some of his surplus bombers to destroy them'.[34]

Churchill found it even more difficult than over India to impose his views on the future of another part of the Empire, Palestine, where before the war he had vigorously espoused the Zionist cause. The overwhelming majority of ministers though continued to back the 1939 White Paper with its plan for strictly limited Jewish immigration and its rejection of a purely Jewish state. Churchill himself continued to express scorn for the Arabs, telling the Cabinet that with few exceptions they 'have been virtually of no use to us in the present war ... They have created no new claims on us should we be victorious.'[35] He stuck to his aim of creating a Jewish state of three to four million people and was impervious to any argument about the injustice of this policy, as General Spears found when he tried to raise it in June 1943: 'He said he had formed an opinion which nothing would change. He intended to see to it that there was a Jewish state. He told me not to argue with him as this would merely make him angry and would change nothing.'[36]

However Churchill found that the rest of the Cabinet would not accept this policy and he was forced to give way. At the beginning of July 1943 during a discussion on the future of Palestine the Cabinet agreed to continuing immigration but only up to the limit set in the

1939 White Paper and they began to look favourably on the partition of the territory after the war to form a small Jewish state, a small Arab state attached to Syria and a British mandatory area. In December 1943 Churchill, who had strongly opposed this policy before the war, reluctantly accepted the recommendations of a Cabinet committee in favour of the scheme, although the Cabinet agreed nothing was to be said publicly before the end of the war. He continued to meet the Zionist leader Weizmann privately and encouraged him to campaign against British policy when he was in the United States. He also refused to take measures against the growing Jewish underground movement or its store of weapons and rejected a policy of random searches of Jewish settlers.

However when Jewish terrorists started a campaign of murders to try and force the British to concede a Jewish state, Churchill began to have second thoughts. He told the Defence Committee in April 1944 it might be advisable 'to tell Dr Weizmann that if such murders continued and the campaign of abuse of the British in the American papers did not stop we might well lose interest in Jewish welfare'.[37] When his friend Lord Moyne was assassinated in Cairo at the beginning of November 1944, his views became even stronger. In Parliament he spoke of Zionism producing 'a new set of gangsters worthy of Nazi Germany' and he felt that such actions would make 'many like myself . . . reconsider the position we have maintained so consistently and so long in the past'. Churchill immediately stopped any further Cabinet discussion on the future of Palestine and no decision was taken on the difficult question of further immigration. By the time he lost power in July 1945 nothing substantive had been decided.

Questions about the future of the Empire were of vital importance to Churchill, but most people in the country were more concerned about the domestic post-war situation. They had faced years of the problems and difficulties entailed in total war; they had suffered from conscription, bereavement, direction of labour, evacuation, disruption of family life, rationing and the often grinding tedium of a long war. Increasingly the public mood reflected anxiety about a return to the mass unemployment and poverty of the 1930s and a feeling that the war should be followed by a fairer society when it was over. Unfortunately Churchill was unable to sympathise with these concerns and respond to this growing mood. After the First

World War he had rejected the new world coming into being and had, quite consciously, become more reactionary. In the 1930s he had had virtually nothing to say about mass unemployment. When he became Prime Minister he was, as in the past, only interested in strategy and diplomacy and simply did not want to discuss anything about the future of Britain until the war was over. This sense of being dedicated to higher things was reinforced by his inveterate hostility to social or economic reform.

Churchill's first reaction was to keep a tight control over discussion of public affairs. The Government was in any case largely shielded from day-to-day Parliamentary criticism – there was no formal opposition and the Commons only met on two or three days a week for a short time. During 1940 the Government had established strict control over the media and Churchill, who disliked even the mildest criticism, had taken measures to extend that control. In June 1941 he laid down a new policy – 'the Ministry of Information will take full day-to-day editorial control of the BBC and will be responsible for both initiative and censorship'. Ministers had to observe strict limits and the public were to be treated in a generally dismissive way. Only members of the War Cabinet 'are free to make speeches expounding the policy of the War Cabinet. . . . the making of speeches by many different Ministers in time of war is to be deprecated . . . Ministers not of Cabinet rank ought not to discuss the general policy of the war except for exhortations to zeal and the happy restatement of the accepted commonplaces.'[38]

In particular Churchill was determined to control opinion in the armed forces. Later in 1941 he learnt about the existence of the Army Bureau of Current Affairs (ABCA), an organisation designed to encourage discussion of public affairs and help soldiers under-stand the war they were being asked to fight. The idea of an informed Army was exactly the sort of thing Churchill strongly opposed. In a letter to Margesson, Secretary of State for War, he confessed to 'some anxiety' about ABCA and wondered whether it would weaken the 'highly tempered discipline' required in the Army, and he added, 'Will not such discussions only provide opportunities for the professional grouser and agitator with a glib tongue?' He ordered all work on the scheme to stop.[39] When Margesson replied that the whole of the Army Board supported the scheme, he was not impressed and consulted Brendan Bracken, who came down against

ABCA. Churchill therefore told Margesson: 'I do not approve of this system of encouraging political discussion in the Army among soldiers . . . Discussions in which no controversy is desired are a farce. There cannot be controversy without prejudice to discipline. The only sound principle is "no politics in the Army". I hope you will wind up this business as quickly and as decently as possible and set the persons concerned in it to useful work.'[40]

Churchill's instructions were ignored and the scheme continued to flourish. His opposition broke out again in April 1943 when he saw an ABCA poster about pre-war society which he described as a 'disgraceful libel on the conditions prevailing in Great Britain before the war'.[41] In fact his outburst only exposed his own ignorance of the reality of life for many of Britain's citizens in the 1930s – the Secretary of State for War told him the poster was highly accurate and based on conditions in the Finsbury Health Centre and adjacent flats in central London. Nevertheless Churchill insisted on a ministerial investigation of ABCA and he was no doubt disappointed to find it concluded that ABCA was 'a most successful experiment'. He had to tolerate its continued existence but he ordered 'no man fit to fight should be drawn into this organisation'.[42] As late as April 1945 he intervened to veto the distribution to troops in the Far East of a booklet about the Government's social policy.

Churchill also disliked any modern approach to the better understanding and management of a mass army. When he discovered that a ministerial committee was reviewing the work of psychologists in the armed forces, he set out his objections:

> I am sure it would be sensible to restrict as much as possible the work of these gentlemen, who are capable of doing an immense amount of harm with what may easily degenerate into charlatanry. The tightest hand should be kept over them . . . it is very wrong to disturb large numbers of healthy, normal men and women by asking the kind of odd questions in which psychiatrists specialise. There are quite enough hangers-on and camp followers already.[43]

In March 1943 Churchill was told by Lord Horder that the Adjutant-General, General Sir Ronald Adam, had, when Commander-in-Chief Northern Command, employed psychologists to examine the attitudes of Army recruits. This drove Churchill to send a 'Personal, Private and Most Secret' minute to the Secretary of State for War in what was obviously a long-running feud with Adam. He declared 'anything more subversive to morale could hardly be imagined. Generally speaking I am informed that the Adjutant-General has an altogether abnormal fad for this questionable process . . . I have already drawn your attention to the disadvantage of having an artillery officer, who cannot possibly understand the ordinary feelings of battalion officers, in the position of Adjutant-General. Some other employment could no doubt be found for Sir Ronald Adam.'[44] Churchill was told that the allegations were untrue and he had to drop the matter.

Although feeling free to indulge his own private criticism of military officers and practices, Churchill was determined to repress anything which he thought was critical of the armed forces. In September 1942 he heard about the film *Colonel Blimp*, then in production. No-one in Whitehall had actually seen the film but the panic-stricken War Office argued it was of 'the utmost importance to get [it] stopped' because 'it focuses attention on an imaginary type of Army officer which has become an object of ridicule to the general public'. (The film is in fact quite a touching portrait of an Army officer in the first forty years of the century.) However, when the War Office advised him that the Ministry of Information did not have powers to stop the making of the film, Churchill instructed Bracken: 'Pray propose to me the measures necessary to stop this foolish production before it gets any further. I am not prepared to allow propaganda detrimental to the morale of the Army, and I am sure the Cabinet will take all necessary action. Who are the people behind it?'[45]

Bracken told the Prime Minister the Government would have to take general powers to suppress any film on any grounds the Government chose. Churchill replied 'we should act not on the grounds of "expressing harmful or misguided opinions" [as Bracken had suggested in this case] but on the perfectly precise point of "undermining the discipline of the Army"'. He ordered that the subject was to go to Cabinet 'when I have no doubt any special authority you may require will be given you'.[46] He ignored Bracken's suggestion that they should discreetly approach Rank, who were financing the film. Despite Churchill's instructions, Bracken did this anyway and the producers agreed to pre-censorship by the Ministry of Information and the War Office.

In May 1943 Bracken reported that the film was now acceptable and the War Cabinet agreed to its distribution. Churchill however issued special instructions that it was not to be exported. Bracken felt it should be allowed to go, but, as Churchill insisted otherwise, they promised to 'try to find means of continuing our illegal ban'.[47] Unfortunately for Churchill a fortnight later Rank officially asked for export permission. Bracken reported that the film was 'so boring I cannot believe that it will do any harm abroad to anyone except the Company which made it'. Churchill, who had not seen the film, remained adamant: 'I do not agree with this surrender ... If necessary we must take more powers.'[48] At the beginning of August Bracken reported that the Government's ban was only making the film more popular but by now Churchill was reduced to not replying to Bracken; when his Private Office reminded him about the letter, he wrote, 'I am obstructing. Leave it.'[49] He eventually abandoned his opposition a month later.

Churchill also took a close personal interest in trying to minimise the impact of the presence of the United States Army in Britain, in particular the influx of what were called at the time 'coloured' troops, which the American authorities still kept in rigidly segregated units. In April 1942 the chiefs of staff, with Churchill's knowledge, told their US counterparts that they did not want any coloured troops sent to Britain. The Americans refused to accede to their request and three months later Churchill himself appealed, again without success, to Harry Hopkins to prevent any more 'coloured' troops arriving – there were then about 12,000 in Britain. In general these troops were treated better by British citizens than the US authorities liked and this tended to alienate white US troops. In October 1942 the War Cabinet agreed a policy of double standards – there was to be no formal segregation in Britain, but British troops were to be educated about US policies and were to be encouraged to avoid contact with black troops. In addition it was agreed that 'it was desirable that the people of this country should avoid becoming too friendly with coloured American troops'.[50] At this meeting when Lord Cranborne, the Colonial Secretary, raised the question of one of his 'coloured' staff who had been excluded from his normal lunchtime restaurant by white US troops, Churchill replied: 'That's all right. If he takes a banjo with him they'll think he's one of the band.'[51]

A year later Churchill met his close relation, the Duke of Marlborough, who was acting as a liaison officer with the American forces. He asked him a series of questions about the number of black soldiers as a percentage of the total, the number of illegitimate children they had fathered on white women and the number of cases of murder, attempted murder and 'carnal knowledge' with which they were charged. The Duke of Marlborough took the view that there was 'a serious subversive element' stemming from these offences and in areas where black troops were quartered he detected the feeling that 'it is unwise to go out into the roads and country lanes after dark'. Churchill showed the figures produced by the Duke of Marlborough to Clementine and wrote to the Secretary of State for War about them, telling him: 'I consider the matter serious' and that these reports were causing him 'anxiety'. He demanded a full set of statistics on 'the number of cases of mutiny, violence, rape, illegitimate children' among black soldiers and a report of what was being done to stop it.[52] Sir James Grigg replied that British people were often supporting black troops against white US soldiers and that the manner in which some British women associated with black men was 'of a far more mundane and vicious nature which calls for measures more stringent than education'.[53] Churchill subsequently passed on more complaints from his relation, including one of marijuana smoking by black troops which 'if given to women may excite their sexual desires'.[54] Grigg then sent another long report which concluded: 'the trouble is due to the natural propensities of the coloured man'.[55] Churchill took no more action and was no doubt relieved once American troops began to move out of Britain to the continent after the Normandy invasion.

Churchill found time to dabble in peripheral domestic issues like these, but he was never willing to shift his attention for long to economic and social affairs. During the first three years of the war little was done about post-war planning because the energies of virtually every minister and all departments were concentrated on the war effort. This state of affairs fitted easily with Churchill's own conception that fighting the war should dominate all other factors. As Halifax commented to Eden at the beginning of 1942, Churchill was always 'pretty bored with anything except the actual war'.[56]

Overall responsibility for 'reconstruction' policy (as this area was called in Whitehall) was allocated to a committee under Arthur Greenwood in January 1941 (which gave a good insight into Churchill's views of its importance). The committee met only four times during its first year and effectively nothing had been achieved by the end of 1942, long after Greenwood had resigned. There was certainly no sense of urgency coming from the Prime Minister. He told Jock Colville in August 1940, 'the Tory party was the strength of the country: few things need to be changed quickly and drastically'.[57]

However after 1942 it was clear that the allies were going to win the war and unlike Lloyd George's coalition, Churchill's Government had a considerable period in which to plan post-war policy. The problem was that unlike Lloyd George's Government it was fundamentally divided on party lines about what social and economic policy to adopt after the war. Although many Conservatives were far more liberal than Churchill, they too were opposed to Labour's ideas for an interventionist industrial policy, greater state control and higher welfare benefits. They wanted a return to the free market as quickly as possible and the emphasis placed on industry and exports rather than social measures. This meant that it was extremely difficult for the Government to agree on any firm policies and usually decisions were put off.

The first serious problem was raised by the Beveridge Report about the post-war welfare system, published on 1 December 1942, just as the tide of the war began to turn. It was a rather uninspiring document that recommended administrative tidying up by unifying the existing insurance schemes and making them universally applicable, although they would still be funded by contributions. Beveridge's proposals were only mildly redistributive – for example State pensions were only to rise to subsistence levels over a twenty-year period. Where the report was politically radical, and where it caught the public attention, was in its assumptions (adopted to keep down costs) of a national health service and full employment. Despite its limitations it was widely seen as the appropriate reward for wartime sacrifices. Churchill was not impressed. He dismissed Beveridge as 'an awful windbag and a dreamer' and insisted that a committee of Conservative MPs study the the report.[58] They accepted the idea of children's allowances (which would also go to the middle and upper classes) and universal contributions to pensions but wanted to restrict unemployment benefits. They thought these should be set well below wage rates and made payable for six months only; once this period was completed the unemployed would be subject to State direction of labour. They wanted compulsory medical insurance to be confined to the low-paid so that private medical practice could survive and thought that the Government's priorities after the war should be defence spending, reduction of the national debt and lower taxes, not social security.

Before the Cabinet discussed the Beveridge Report Churchill set out his own views. No commitments should be made until after the war apart from on children's allowances. He explained his reasoning to his colleagues: 'Ministers should, in my view, be careful not to raise false hopes as was done last time by speeches about "Homes and Heroes" . . . It is for this reason of not wishing to deceive the people by false hopes and airy visions of Utopia and Eldorado that I have refrained so far from making promises about the future.' The Cabinet agreed to welcome the Beveridge Report in principle, but Churchill insisted there was to be no legislation during the war and as for the post-war period it was 'impossible at this stage to establish any order of priority or to enter into definite commitments'.[59] In the House of Commons debate on the report on 18 February, 121 MPs voted against the Government and in favour of immediate implementation – it was the largest of all the revolts against the wartime coalition.

Conservative members of the Government were worried that the public were unhappy about the Government's ultra-cautious approach and they persuaded Churchill to make a radio broadcast to tell the nation what it could expect in the post-war world. It was an opportunity for him to exercise his powers of oratory and provide the nation with another kind of vision beyond the blood, toil, tears and sweat of the wartime effort. Churchill signally failed to rise to the challenge. His speech all too clearly reflected his own distaste for domestic policy and Beveridge's ideas. He avoided making any reference to the report and gave only a series of general reassurances about the future. He spoke of a four-year plan but supplied no details about what would be in that plan. During the war he promised no more than 'preliminary legislative preparation'. (A few days later he privately conceded that there would be little legislation to prepare for.) His real message and 'earnest advice' to the public was that they should forget about what might happen after the war and concentrate 'even more zealously upon the war effort, and if possible not to take your eye off the ball even for a moment'. The speech was symptomatic of Churchill's growing lack of interest in public opinion and reluctance to broadcast to the nation at all about the war or the policy of the Government on any issue. This was the only broadcast he gave in the whole of 1943 – it was the first since May 1942 and the next was not until March 1944 (about the threat of the V-weapons), which was the only one that year too. By the time the war was ending in Europe in April 1945 Churchill had spoken to the nation just twice in three years.

Although Churchill tried to turn people away from thinking about the post-war world he did have his own personal set of priorities. He was not however prepared to make them public at this stage, probably because he guessed they would not be popular. He told his closest advisers at this time that the main post-war political issues would be India, the colonies, Britain's solvency and air power. It was typical of Churchill's narrow approach to politics that no social issues figured in the list and the order reflected the same misjudgement of the importance of India which he had displayed in the 1930s. Although head of a coalition Government pledged to maintain national unity, Churchill was determined to keep reconstruction policy in Conservative hands. In February 1942 when the Cabinet agreed that draconian planning powers should be given to the Minister of Works, Churchill sacked Lord Reith from the job within ten days and replaced him with Lord Portal, one of his millionaire friends and a man who had been very close to Oswald Mosley throughout the 1930s. Such an appointment was to ensure that these powers were not used against the interests of property owners. In December 1942 he appointed an old-style Conservative, W. S. Morrison, as Minister of Town and Country Planning with the brief not to implement the Uthwatt Report which had recommended the nationalisation of all development land. Morrison carried out his unwritten instructions in the 1944 White Paper on planning. When reform of the health service became a live issue after the Beveridge Report, the National Liberal Minister of Health, Ernest Brown, was quickly replaced by a Conservative, Henry Willink. R. A. Butler was moved to the Board of Education to oversee a very conservative reform of the education system, with its emphasis on traditional religious values, no reform of public schools, no date for the raising of the school leaving age to sixteen and continued fee paying even in schools that received a direct Government grant. (When an amendment giving equal pay for women teachers was passed by the Commons, Churchill went to the House the next day and successfully demanded its removal as an issue of confidence.) The Government had in fact only agreed to legislate on education because it could agree about little else. After he gained approval for his proposals Butler noted in his diary that the Government 'have been prompted to come the way of education because it has been very difficult to obtain agreement between the parties on any matters which involve property or the pocket'.[60] (Churchill had orginally been opposed to any legislation in this area too.)

On health the White Paper that emerged in early 1944 was the result of a compromise between the two parties but it built on the fact that the Ministry of Health had actually run a national service during the war and that all those involved in operating the existing rather chaotic system recognised there needed to be changes. Although the Ministry of Health would be generally responsible for a national health service, health care would be delivered through local boards supervising local-authority-controlled hospitals and the voluntary hospitals, which were to remain independent. Only a few general practitioners would receive a salary; most would remain independent and doctors were allowed to retain their private practices. The Conservatives had persuaded Labour to accept that doctors should not be salaried State employees but in return had had to concede universal coverage and no 'hotel' charges for patients in hospital. The coalition's White Paper was a long way from the National Health Service introduced by the Labour Government after the war, but it went too far in Churchill's opinion.

Churchill wanted to destroy the carefully crafted compromise between the two parties. Although he had not read the draft White Paper – he told his colleagues he did not have time to 'pass such a vast scheme of social change through [his] mind, under present conditions' – he thought 'The Chancellor of the Exchequer seems very easy about great additions to the annual Budget.'[61] He told Attlee that he wanted to re-open the whole scheme and start again. The Labour leader told him that if he did then the Labour Party would press for a full-time salaried service and other measures equally repugnant to the Conservatives. Churchill let the White Paper go ahead but it received a cool welcome because of its limited nature. Churchill also did not read the draft White Paper on the sensitive issue of unemployment when it came to the Cabinet in May 1944. The paper's proposals reflected the highly cautious nature of the Chancellor, Sir John Anderson. It did not advocate full employment as a goal – rather a 'high and stable' level of employment that would leave about eight per cent of the working population out of a job. It was not a great policy departure – it specifically ruled out allowing a budget deficit in a recession in order to stimulate demand and had little to say about industrial policy. Labour would have preferred a policy of more physical controls over the economy (as was the case during the war), and once again the White Paper when published made little impact.

At this time the Cabinet also had to consider the draft White Paper on the Beveridge scheme. Churchill had earlier tried to block an increase in supplementary payments to the poorest pensioners, saying 'this does not look good'.[62] He continued his opposition even though the Chancellor of the Exchequer was prepared to find the money, and the scheme was eventually agreed by the Cabinet in his absence. On Beveridge Churchill told the Chancellor: 'If you do not resist the rapid growth of our national burdens, it is difficult, while I and other Ministers are involved in the conduct of the war, to fill the gap.' He thought that the rest of 1944 was 'very unsuited for final decisions in these matters'.[63] The White Paper, which was non-committal, went ahead anyway even after Churchill complained to the Cabinet about 'the many charges accumulating against our future solvency' and his deliberate procrastination over the publication date for more than two months.

Churchill was also determined to block another reform wanted by the Labour Party and the trades unions – changes to the Trade Disputes Act. This was a law that as Chancellor of the Exchequer he had strongly advocated after the 1926 general strike. The coalition established in May 1940 was intended to create a sense of national unity and bringing Ernest Bevin, the leader of the Transport Workers Union, into the Government as Minister of Labour. It was one of the most important symbols of that new era. The trades unions felt that the clauses that restricted their industrial activities (not those outlawing a general strike and restricting picketing) were particularly objectionable and should be repealed as a recognition of their new status in British society. Churchill did not agree and he wanted to retain these provisions. When various trades union leaders first raised the subject in August 1940 he vetoed any action, saying, 'I see no hurry. Anyway this legislation could not be passed in wartime.'[64]

The trades unions took up the subject again in April 1941 and for a year the coalition was divided on party lines over what to do. Churchill asked Bevin and Kingsley Wood to see if they could reach a compromise but they failed, as did other efforts. Conservative backbenchers were strongly opposed to any changes that might benefit the trades unions and Churchill was happy to use them as an excuse for taking no action. He turned round the argument about national unity and in a letter of 2 September 1942 asked 'as strongly as possible' for the trades unions not to be divisive and press the matter 'at this critical period in the war'.[65] That was yet another convenient pretext for inaction, as became clear when the subject came up again in 1944 and early 1945, by which time victory was assured. Churchill resorted to the tactic of simply refusing for over a year to meet a TUC delegation to discuss the issue.

As post-war reconstruction climbed higher up the political agenda, despite Churchill's best efforts to remove it, he continued to ensure that Conservatives within the coalition dominated policy making. On 26 June 1943 the three senior Labour ministers in the Government (Attlee, Morrison and Bevin) put a paper to the Cabinet on 'The Need for Decisions' about post-war policy on finance, land use, planning, transport and electricity supply among other subjects. Churchill did not accept their case for early consideration of the paper, which was not discussed until the middle of October. Then at the Cabinet discussion he introduced a new argument why no decisions should be taken – Labour was not committed to staying in the coalition after the war therefore there should be no legislation during the war. Nevertheless he reluctantly agreed to set up a Ministry of Reconstruction but it was not to be an executive ministry; it would merely co-ordinate the efforts of others. He chose as its head Lord Woolton, a businessman who was nominally independent but in practice a strong believer in free enterprise (and who later became Chairman of the Conservative Party). The Cabinet also set up a Reconstruction Committee under Woolton's chairmanship, which meant removing the subject from Attlee and giving it to a committee with a strong Conservative bias in practice – they had four members to Labour's four but in addition to Woolton there was also Sir John Anderson, another nominally non-party man but in practice of strong Conservative views. When Attlee complained about the committee's composition, Churchill objected in his turn, complaining, rather disingenuously, 'I feel very much the domination of these Committees by the force and power of your representatives, when those members who come out of the Conservative quota are largely non-Party or have little political experience or party views.'[66]

The consequence of this party conflict within the coalition and Churchill's unwillingness to consider proposals that might involve social and economic changes was that by the end of 1944 the coalition had achieved very little in reconstruction policy. There was no official policy on the future of national insurance or on a system of social security, little on economic policy and the management of the economy, little on planning policy, and the idea of establishing a national health service, cautiously put forward in the 1944 White Paper, was slowly disintegrating as the minister Henry Willink made further concessions to the various powerful lobbies involved. As the end of the war approached and with it the almost inevitable end of the coalition, there was even less pressure to produce an agreed policy. Churchill acted in early 1945 to ensure that various proposals working their way up through the Whitehall machine would not come to fruition. In February he issued instructions that no controversial legislation was to go forward unless it had been agreed by the full Cabinet – he still distrusted the network of Cabinet committees that would normally have agreed such proposals because he suspected they were dominated by the Labour Party. The result was that legislation dried up altogether. Despite the fact that so little had been agreed, he continued to object to what he called the 'rapid growth of our national burdens' in terms of post-war commitments.[67]

Churchill had failed to judge the public mood. From February 1943, after the Government's failure to promise to implement the Beveridge Report, there was evidence of a growing public anxiety, identified in the Ministry of Information's surveys, about the future. In June 1944 they found 'the Government is variously accused of slowness, vagueness and making promises which are either beyond its intentions or its powers'.[68] Four months later they reported 'widespread apprehension . . . people dread and expect mass unemployment'.[69] Many people feared a repetition of the broken promises after the First World War. Churchill's own standing started to suffer. Although he remained highly popular as a war leader, there were growing doubts about his suitability to lead the country in the post-war period – hardly surprising given the fact that he refused to provide any leadership on these issues. As early as November 1942 Mass Observation conducted a survey which found that the majority of people thought Churchill should not be Prime Minister after the war. By February 1944 this figure had risen to over sixty per cent. Churchill's American publisher, Walter Graebner, detected latent discontent as early as 1941 when he wrote:

> very few will criticize Churchill openly except in the House of Commons. It is so much in vogue to say that Churchill is a great man and a great leader that criticism by the masses is almost unknown. However, if one hints that perhaps Churchill isn't all that he's supposed to be, a great many people respond immediately and will begin to tell all kinds of things that they dislike about him.[70]

The Conservative Party too was rapidly losing popularity. When Gallup resumed taking opinion polls in the summer of 1943, it found that the large Conservative lead that had been apparent in 1939 had gone. The Labour Party was ahead by about twelve per cent, and that lead was maintained, and even increased, throughout the rest of the war. In 1942 there had been a series of defeats at by-elections when Conservative candidates lost to independents and then to the newly formed Common Wealth Party, which was more radical than Labour. After 1943 the Conservatives were defeated on four occasions by Common Wealth or independent socialist candidates in what were normally regarded as safe seats. The most spectacular loss was West Derbyshire in February 1944, which was virtually a family seat of the Dukes of Devonshire but on this occasion it voted heavily against the Duke's son, the Marquess of Hartingdon. This result caused 'a pall of the blackest gloom' to fall on Churchill and he decided it was time to try and revitalise the Conservative Party machine.[71] By late 1944 Churchill privately suspected that he was losing his appeal: 'I have a strong feeling that my work is done. I have no message. I had a message. Now I can only say "fight the damned Socialists". I do not believe in this brave new world.'[72]

At the end of 1940 Churchill told Jock Colville: 'He did not wish to lead a party struggle or a class struggle against the Labour leaders who were now serving him so well ... he was determined not to prolong his career into the period of reconstruction.'[73] That mood did not last long, however, and his own deep-rooted opposition to Labour policies and his delight in power meant that he was determined to lead the Conservatives after the war and to remain Prime Minister. Time and time again Churchill's remarks show that he saw his role as that of a party leader and in the interests of his party he sought to minimise the Labour Party's contribution to the war effort. In a speech as early as March 1942 he urged the Conservative Party to claim the credit for the events of 1940 – they should establish their position as 'the main part of the rock on which the salvation of Britain was founded'. Even before the war in Europe was over he was attacking the Labour Party at the Conservative Party conference in March 1945. He claimed that any controls over the economy were 'designed to favour the accomplishment of totalitarian systems', that nationalisation would destroy 'the whole of our existing system of society' and establish 'another system ... borrowed from foreign lands and alien minds'. It was a foretaste of the message he was to put across during the election campaign. The only Labour politician Churchill showed any respect for was Ernest Bevin. He disliked Attlee and refused to have him as a member of the Other Club. Herbert Morrison he described as 'a loathsome creature with a warped mind; he was a "conchy" in the last war'.[74]

By late 1944 it was clear that the coalition would break up at the end of the war; the only question was when, and both parties were manoeuvring to ensure maximum advantage. At a time when little attention was paid to opinion polls, many in the Labour Party thought that Churchill, as the war leader, would, like Lloyd George before him, sweep to victory and they therefore wanted to postpone the contest for as long as possible to allow his popularity to wane. Churchill, equally aware of the situation, wanted an early contest – he told Randolph in November 1944 that the Election would be held within two months of the end of the war against Germany. His other aim was to try and put the blame on Labour for breaking up the coalition, hence his vague call in March 1945 for some form of continued national Government. Meanwhile all that the coalition Cabinet could agree on was that there should be no hasty Election as in 1918.

A week before VE day Churchill was already discussing party propaganda for the Election campaign and immediately after the victory celebrations were over he agreed in consultation with party organisers that June was the best possible date for an Election from the Conservatives' point of view. On 18 May he offered Attlee either an immediate General Election or a referendum on prolonging the existing Parliament until the end of the Japanese war. Among the Labour leadership Attlee, Bevin and Dalton seemed to favour continuing the coalition at least until October when a new electoral register would be completed, which they thought would favour Labour. However, on 20 May Labour's National Executive Committee rejected the idea and even before that decision Churchill was talking in terms of an immediate Election. The following day the Labour Party conference at Blackpool voted against the coalition and on 23 May the Government, which had been formed just over five years earlier, resigned.

Churchill, as leader of the largest party in the existing House of Commons, headed a caretaker government until the Election. It was drawn, with few exceptions, from the ranks of the Conservative Party or Churchill's friends. His provisional administration was a good guide to the composition of a post-war Government if Churchill won the Election. Many ministers kept their wartime jobs – Eden stayed at the Foreign Office, Amery at the India Office, and Grigg at the War Office; Stanley remained in charge of colonial policy and Lord Cranborne kept the Dominions Office. Even the old appeaser, Lord Simon, stayed on as Lord Chancellor. Economic policy was again entrusted to the cautious Anderson as Chancellor, with Oliver Lyttleton at the Board of Trade. Lord Woolton remained in charge of reconstruction policy. Churchill's two close personal friends were also included in the Cabinet – Beaverbrook as Lord Privy Seal and Brendan Bracken at the Admiralty. Churchill's old ally, Harold Macmillan, was brought in as Secretary of State for Air. Hore-Belisha, nominally a National Liberal, took over at National Insurance to deal with the report of a fellow Liberal, Beveridge.

The Government had little time to settle policy but in any case Churchill still showed no inclination to make progress on social or economic issues or start work on implementing the promises made during the war. Within six days of taking office it announced that the coal industry, under State control during the war, would be run by private enterprise and the same voluntary arrangements for planning and rationalisation as existed before the war. Since the publication of the White Paper on the health service in February 1944, the Minister of Health, Winnik, had been engaged in negotiations with the various health lobbies and had made a series of concessions. The voluntary hospitals were to be given more power over local administration, general practitioners were to have more freedom and central administration was to be weakened. In early June the Cabinet discussed new proposals that greatly weakened the wartime scheme. Churchill rejected advice to publish them. Fearing a public outcry, he ordered that nothing should be done until after the Election. He also wanted the Beveridge insurance scheme dismantled: his instructions to Hore-Belisha were that it needed revising and 'purging of its present traces of socialism'.[75] These plans still failed to engage Churchill's interest: he was generally unhappy and ill at ease with the world of peacetime politics, telling Lord Moran six weeks after VE Day: 'I feel very lonely without a war.'[76]

Much of Churchill's time was devoted to the Election campaign. He was optimistic about the outcome, convinced that he would be rewarded for his wartime leadership: 'The desire for a new world is nothing like universal; the gratitude is.'[77] The Conservative campaign revolved around Churchill. The manifesto was called 'Mr Churchill's declaration of policy to the electors' and they were asked, in the words of one poster, to 'Help him finish the job'. The declaration of policy was Churchillian in its priorities. It began, 'Britain is still at war, and must not turn aside from the vast further efforts still needed to bring Japan to the same end as Germany.' Even then 'that will not be the end of our task', Britain had the opportunity 'to play our part' in the 'wise and helpful guidance of the world'. For Churchill, as he made clear in a speech on 13 June, the political priorities were the war against Japan, demobilisation, exports and what he described as a four-year plan for 'food, work and homes'. Still fighting on essentially the economic policy of the 1930s, he made no commitments on employment. The voters, according to opinion polls, were signalling a different set of priorities: housing, jobs, social security and nationalisation. The Prime Minister's almost complete inability to understand life in modern Britain was reflected in his choice of phrase to guide the electors – they should 'make sure that the cottage home to which the warrior will return is blessed with modest but solid prosperity'.

Churchill's main theme of the campaign, however, was a violent dununciation of the Labour Party: it recalled his extremist language of the 1920s and made no allowance for the fact that Labour members had served in his Coalition Government for five years. The attack was launched in his first broadcast on 4 June, into which he had put a great deal of effort, ignoring Clementine's advice that it would alienate the public. He started: 'I declare to you, from the bottom of my heart, that no socialist system can be established without a political police. . . . No Socialist Government . . . could afford to allow free, sharp, or violently-worded expressions of public discontent. They would have to fall back on some form of Gestapo, no doubt very humanely directed at first.' Later he said 'A Socialist policy is abhorrent to British ideas of freedom . . . Socialism is inseparably woven with totalitarianism and the abject worship of the state.' And he went on to denounce socialism as an attack 'upon the right of an ordinary man or woman to breathe freely without having a harsh, clumsy, tyrannical hand clapped across their mouth and nostrils'.

This speech, given just as the allies were discovering the full horror of what the Gestapo and the Nazi state had done, drew storms of protest, even from within the Conservative Party, many members of which felt that it was not only untrue but counter-productive. However Churchill was not at all worried by the consequences of what he said – this was what he firmly believed about the Labour Party. Despite advice to drop this line of attack, he was determined to return to it in each of his broadcasts. In his next political broadcast he attacked 'in the most severe terms the Socialist effort to drag their long-term fads and wavy utopias across the path of need and duty' and then repeated the themes of his earlier address. For good measure he added that the Labour Party, in particular people like Morrison and Cripps, would reduce Parliament, refuse to tolerate any opposition and not allow any other party to take office again – 'a political police would be required to enforce an absolute and permanent system upon the nation'. He repeated the message in his third broadcast on 20 June, declaring that a

Labour Government would 'plan for all our lives and tell us exactly where we are to go and what we are to do, and any resistance to their commands will be punished'. Recalling how his warnings in the 1930s had been ignored, this time he warned that his opponents would inevitably set up a permanent dictatorship – a Labour Government 'could not allow itself to be challenged or defeated at any time in any form of Parliament they might allow'.

After this broadcast Churchill went on a four-day Election tour to Manchester, Leeds and Scotland by special train but otherwise did very little active campaigning. Just before polling he did tour London but it was a failure – stones were thrown at him in Ladbroke Grove and he was booed by a crowd of over 20,000 at Walthamstow Stadium. In his last broadcast on 30 June he once again attacked the Labour Party in his usual uncompromising terms and attempted to turn the Election into a personal vote of confidence. He warned the electorate: 'Beware that you are not deceived about the workings of our political system at this Election. There is no truth in the stories now being put about that you can vote for my political opponents at this election, whether they be Labour or Liberal, without at the same time voting for my dismissal from power.' The peroration was, as could have been expected, all about Britain's place in the world. The British people needed to avoid 'by our folly fall[ing] to the rank of a secondary power'. His final message to the people was that in the post-war world they should 'march in the vanguard of the United Nations in majestic enjoyment of our fame and power'.

Churchill then left for a short holiday and the Potsdam conference. He returned on the evening of 25 July to await the declaration of results the next day. The consensus among politicians and comment-ators was that Churchill and the Conservatives would win an easy victory and even most of the Labour leadership only hoped to keep the size of the majority as low as possible. Churchill watched the results come in on the morning of 26 July, ensconced in the wartime Map Room, which had been specially adapted by his staff to show the changing state of the parties across the country. It was hardly needed. The very first result from Salford South showed a Labour gain and within an hour it was clear that Labour was likely to win a landslide victory. By lunchtime they had already gained 106 seats and the result was a foregone conclusion. By 7pm Churchill had been to Buckingham Palace and was no longer Prime Minister.

The outcome was a humiliating defeat for Churchill and the Conservative Party. Labour won nearly forty-eight per cent of the votes, a lead of eight per cent over the Conservatives. In total they gained 227 seats and the Conservatives lost 193 on a swing of twelve per cent to Labour. In the new House of Commons they would have 393 MPs to the Conservatives' 213 and an overall majority of 146. Churchill could take little comfort about his popularity from the result in his own constituency where he was not opposed by any of the major parties. Nevertheless the strength of feeling against Churchill was sufficient to give his solitary opponent (an eccentric independent who advocated working one day a week) over 10,000 votes.

Despite the fact that Churchill had been so confident about the public's gratitude, he had led the Conservatives to their greatest ever defeat under universal suffrage, and the Labour Party, which he hated so much, and abused so vehemently, became a majority Government for the first time in its history. Not only that, Churchill was the only wartime leader to be rejected by the British electorate in the subsequent Election. He himself had become an MP in 1900 as Lord Salisbury led the Conservatives to a sweeping victory after the Boer War. Lloyd George had achieved an even bigger success in 1918. But in 1945 Churchill was unable to judge the mood of the nation. After May 1940 he had come to symbolise the nation's resistance and been readily endorsed as a wartime leader. In 1945 Churchill remained true to his limited view of politics at a time when his chosen themes of duty, British prestige and the totalitarian nature of the Labour Party were at variance with popular aspirations. His inability to provide an inspiring message to the nation in the last years of the war, demonstrated by his lack of broadcasts, only increased popular perceptions that he was not the man to win the peace.

His role as popular wartime Prime Minister had enabled him to impose his often idiosyncratic, deeply held views on his party and the manifesto. They staked everything on his appeal to the voters. His autocratic temperament and hypersensitivity to personal criticism led him to reject advice or warnings. Yet Churchill would not accept responsibility for his defeat. Writing to Duff Cooper afterwards, he distributed blame widely among various elements in British society:

> there are some unpleasant features in this election which indicate
> the rise of bad elements. Conscientious objectors were preferred to

candidates of real military achievement and service. All the Members of Parliament who had done most to hamper and obstruct the war were returned by enormously increased majorities. None of the values of the years before were preserved. . . . The soldiers voted with mirthful irresponsibility . . . Also, there is the latent antagonism of the rank and file for the officer class.[78]

Part 4

THE NATIONAL MONUMENT

1945–1965

26

Opposition

Overwhelming rejection in the 1945 Election was a shattering blow to Churchill's morale and his highly developed sense of self-esteem. He had expected to be returning immediately to Potsdam but now had to watch Attlee and Bevin undertake the task. Suddenly he was left not just with no war to run, a deprivation he had already complained about in June, but with no role in the direction of peacetime policy. The supply of official papers and succession of meetings on which he relied to ward off his depression and fill up his days came to an abrupt end. He resented what he saw as the ingratitude of the British people. He was subject to what Moran described as 'constant outbursts of childish petulance' and had to be prescribed a course of sleeping pills.[1] Bereft of the only role he really wanted and felt he deserved, he seems to have been reluctant to rally his defeated party as he took on a new role – Leader of the Opposition at the age of seventy. Speaking to the Conservative backbench 1922 Committee just after the opening of Parliament in mid-August he was described as 'totally unprepared, indifferent and deaf and [he] failed to stir the crowded audience'.[2]

Domestically too he faced the need for major readjustment. As is customary for outgoing Prime Ministers he spent the week-end after the election at Chequers. After a short stay in Claridges, he moved into Duncan Sandys' flat in Westminster Gardens while Chartwell was reopened after its wartime closure. Throughout the war he had seen little of Clementine; they normally only met at occasional meals with guests present. Between January and September 1944 for example they dined alone on just four occasions. Now they were thrust together in what rapidly proved to be difficult circumstances for them both. In addition to the mental anguish inflicted by the political reversal, they were brought up against material problems – they had to exist on the same rations as the rest of the population (something which Churchill had not experienced during the war) and for some time without any servants. Within a month Clementine asked Mary to return home as soon as possible: 'in our misery we seem, instead of clinging to each other to be always having scenes. I'm sure it's all my fault, but I'm finding life more than I can bear. He is so unhappy & that makes him very difficult.'[3]

In early September Clementine was left behind while Sarah and Lord Moran accompanied Churchill on a holiday on Lake Como at a millionaire's luxury villa which had been requisitioned by the Army and made available to Churchill, complete with staff and free food and drink, by General Alexander. There Churchill took up painting again and began the slow, and never fully completed, process of adjustment to loss of office. They lived well, consuming ninety-six bottles of champagne in just over a fortnight. In addition Churchill drank about six or seven whiskys and soda and three brandys a day. On 19 September he left for Genoa and then Monte Carlo where, defying Clementine's instructions, he gambled at the Casino. He lost £7,000 (about £140,000 at current prices) but the management wrote it off. He then went on to stay at a villa near Antibes, which had been commandeered by Eisenhower, paid another visit to Monte Carlo and eventually arrived in London during the first week of October. There he moved into 28 Hyde Park Gate, which Clementine had found as a home for what she hoped would be Churchill's immediate retirement from politics. They quickly found that the house was not big enough to accommodate the four secretaries they now employed and so they bought the adjoining house (No 27).

Churchill's finances had been transformed during the war – exactly how is not known, although one helpful development was that the Inland Revenue secretly wrote off all his outstanding taxes. By early 1946 he had £120,000 in the bank (equivalent to over £2 million today) and he did not draw a pension as a former Prime Minister or a salary as Leader of the Opposition. Chartwell, which was slowly being brought back to its pre-war state through the work of German prisoners-of-war, was bought by a group of rich admirers organised by Churchill's close friend, the newspaper publisher Lord Camrose. They paid him almost £44,000 (twice its pre-war value), and gave it to the National Trust, on condition that Churchill could live there for life in return for a nominal rent. This money helped him to buy two farms adjoining Chartwell, a market garden slightly further away and then another ninety-acre farm in the area. Altogether he now owned about 500 acres and employed his son-in-law Christopher Soames, who had just married Mary, as farm manager. It was under Soames' influence that Churchill began horse racing (using Lord Randolph's colours) at a cost of about £9,000 a year (almost £200,000 at current prices). He became an enthusiastic owner and in particular enjoyed backing his own hores, winning over £7,000 between 1949 and 1951. He also made £5,000 from *Time-Life* for the reproduction of a few of his paintings and £12,500 for a book of his secret session speeches during the war.

Churchill's most important literary project, which was to take up a large part of his time during the next six years, was his memoirs of the Second World War. Its particular importance to him was that he saw it as an opportunity to present his case and establish his version of events by publishing the first inside account of the war. During the war he had had a special collection of his minutes and telegrams made every month and he began studying this material on his way to Lake Como in September 1945. He had already begun thinking about the commercial side but no firm decisions were taken until early 1946. Then he discussed possible deals with Emery Reves (his pre-war agent for foreign rights) and Henry Luce of *Time-Life*, who looked after the American negotiations. Lord Camrose master-minded the British and Commonwealth aspects. Nothing was signed until Churchill's legal advisers had set up the Chartwell Trust, into which all his literary earnings were to be paid as a way of avoiding tax. The trust paid Churchill a tax-free annual sum of about £20,000 (£400,000 at current prices) and provided for his children and their descendants after he died. Once the trust was established the complex memoir deal was concluded. Just over £250,000 was paid for the British, Commonwealth and foreign rights. Houghton Mifflin paid $250,000 for the US book rights and publication in the US before Britain and Luce paid $1.5 million for the US serial rights. In total the deal was worth about £600,000 and another £50,000 was added when the project was expanded from four volumes to six. At current prices about £13 million was paid into the trust for the memoirs. (Lloyd George donated his earnings from his memoirs of his time as Prime Minister in the First World War to charity.)

In May 1946 Churchill wrote to Attlee to let him know that he wanted to publish a vast number of official documents in his memoirs. His formal request, made in September, was approved by the Cabinet in October. Churchill was given the unprecedented right to publish official papers within eighteen months of the end of the war. He was able to select those that supported the story he wanted to tell and quote from them extensively. The new Secretary to the Cabinet, Norman Brook, who had been the Deputy Secretary to the War Cabinet, was closely involved in the process and regularly visited Chartwell to read a large number of passages even before they were submitted for formal approval.

Following the method he had used before to write the biography of Marlborough, Churchill put together a large team to do the basic work. Bill Deakin, who had helped on *A History of the English Speaking Peoples* before the war, was the chief assistant and also in charge of political and diplomatic aspects. General Ismay together with General Pownall worked on the military side, and Commodore Allen oversaw the naval aspects. Later they were joined by Denis Kelly, Churchill's archivist, who soon became a major contributor. Churchill chose to construct the books in his normal way – extensive quotations from original documents linked together by his commentaries. His assistants would first produce the basic structure and he would then cut out any parts of the official documents he did not like and dictate the linking passages to a secretary.

The first volume covering the pre-war years and the war until May 1940 was ready by early 1948. *Life* began serialisation in May before publication in the United States in June. Some of the passages on Britain's ally, Poland – 'squalid and shameful in triumph', 'too often led by the vilest of the vile' and 'two Polands: one struggling to proclaim the truth and the other grovelling in villainy' – produced such a storm of protest that they were removed from the British edition published later in 1948. Further volumes appeared in a steady stream over the next five years. After 1951 and his return to power, Churchill took less interest in the work, which by then had reached the last volume, and this was largely written by 'the syndicate', as his helpers had become known. These volumes had an immediate impact – and helped form many people's views on why the war had happened and the way in which it had been fought. Churchill was a skilled enough writer to select his evidence and present his case in an adroit way. He portrayed himself as the animator of the whole British Government and by implication as the man who had taken every key decision and been right on virtually every issue. His reputation as a war leader was naturally high in the late 1940s and his memoirs helped to entrench him as a national monument – the man who, almost single-handed, had guided Britain and the allies to victory. The full story of the war and other people's views took much longer to emerge.

Although now immensely rich himself, Churchill was still prepared to accept gifts from wealthy friends. Beaverbrook paid for the installation of a lift at Chartwell and his cigars and most of his brandy were supplied by a rich Cuban, Antonio Giraudier, and whisky by Lewis Rosentiel, the head of the largest distillers in the United States. But the most substantial gifts came from *Time-Life*. Churchill claimed that he needed to travel abroad in order to write but in the severe post-war economic crisis foreign currency was not available for holidays. He therefore persuaded *Time-Life* to agree to pay for foreign travel in addition to the substantial advance they had already made on the memoirs.

In the winter of 1947–8 he spent six weeks at Marrakech at their expense, accompanied by Sarah, two secretaries, a valet, a detective, Deakin and at various times guests such as Moran and Cherwell. The total cost was about £2,800 or over £55,000 at today's prices and Silver City Airways provided free air travel. In August *Time-Life* paid for a family holiday spent at the Hotel du Roy Rene at Aix-en-Provence (Churchill was accompanied by Clementine, Mary and Christopher Soames, secretaries, a valet and a detective) at a cost of nearly £1,800 (£35,000 at current prices). In the winter of 1948–9 he spent a fortnight in Monte Carlo, and in the summer a week in Italy cost *Time-Life* another £1,700. The winter of 1950–1 was again spent at the Hotel de la Mamounia at Marrakech in the company of Powell, Kelly, two secretaries, a detective, a valet and Cherwell and his valet. Later they were joined by Clementine, Diana Churchill and Bill Deakin with his wife. By now *Time-Life* felt that Churchill was abusing their hospitality: instead of funding literary retreats they had picked up the bill for holidays and lavish dinners for himself and a large entourage of family and friends at a cost amounting to a total of nearly $70,000 or £300,000 at today's prices. When he asked for more money to go to Annecy in August 1951 they agreed to provide the foreign currency (still unobtainable in Britain) but deducted it from their extra advance for the sixth volume. This time Churchill was accompanied by two secretaries and Christopher Soames and he spent $5,000 in a week. In November 1953 Churchill wrote to *Time-Life* asking for more money for the serialisation of volume six in addition to what they had already spent on his visits abroad.

Churchill imposed a regular pattern on his guests during these visits. There were frequent outings to the countryside involving a convoy of a police escort, Churchill's car, four or five cars for his guests and a van loaded with food, tables, chairs and painting equipment. Churchill would choose the site and the first task was to set up his easel and paints – his valet had to squeeze the paint from the tubes for him while someone else poured his whisky and soda. He would hold forth to them over a lavish lunch accompanied by champagne, port and brandy. Painting in the open air was not an occasion for solitary communion with nature in Churchill's case. He wanted to be surrounded by servants who responded to his every whim and by acoltyes who hung on every word of his long monologues. Lord Moran commented on the way he absorbed flattery as his due: 'wherever he goes people say acceptable things, selecting what they think will be most gratifying to him'.[4] Everywhere he went he travelled in grand style – on his trip to Annecy and Venice in 1951 he had fifty-five suitcases and trunks and sixty-five other pieces of baggage. He was also well aware of his own status and determined to trade on it. During that trip when he wanted to leave Annecy by a train that only stopped in Geneva, he instructed his secretary, 'Kindly remember I am Winston Churchill. Tell the station master to stop the train.' The train was stopped.[5]

Churchill was now in his seventies and his health deteriorated further. In June 1947 he had a successful operation for a hernia, for which he had been wearing a truss since August 1945. He was becoming increasingly deaf and finding it difficult to understand others but he refused to wear a hearing aid. For example, at the English Speaking Union dinner in July 1951 he heard virtually nothing of Eisenhower's address and had to ask for the text afterwards. The most serious problem though was the mild stroke he suffered on his right side in August 1949 while staying at Beaverbrook's villa, La Capponcina, near Monte Carlo. Moran was summoned and announced that Churchill had a 'chill', a fiction that was kept up on his return to England at the end of the month. He cancelled a painting holiday in Switzerland but was soon back at work on his memoirs.

Despite his age and state of health Churchill was determined to remain as Conservative leader and he wanted to become Prime Minister again. In the immediate aftermath of the 1945 Election he took little interest in British domestic politics and was rarely in the House of Commons. By early November 1945 the neglect was so apparent that at a meeting of the backbench 1922 Committee Churchill and Eden had to promise that they would provide a more effective opposition and actually be present in the chamber during important debates. Churchill's response was to launch an attack on the Labour Government at a meeting of the Conservative Central Council on 28 November and in the first week of December he put down a censure motion on the Government. In the debate he was trounced by Attlee, who berated him for refusing to accept the decision of the electorate and showed that the demobilisation plan Churchill was criticising was one he had agreed when in office. Soon after this episode the opposition was in disarray over the $3.75 billion loan the Labour Government had negotiated with the United States. Churchill gave one of his weakest ever speeches and advised his party to abstain: some did but seventy-one MPs voted against and eight even voted in favour. However Churchill was not prepared to let the task of leading the opposition tie him to London for long. Early in the New Year he left for a two-month holiday in Florida as the guest of Colonel Frank Clarke, his host after the 1943 Quebec conference.

During his holiday Churchill intended to make only one public appearance – to give a lecture at the obscure Westminster College at Fulton in Missouri, President Truman's home state. The invitation had been extended, with Truman's endorsement, in October 1945 and Churchill had accepted it after consulting Attlee, who had sounded out Lord Halifax, the British Ambassador in Washington. He had hoped to address Congress but Halifax, not surprisingly, had been unable to persuade the Truman administration to organise such a prestigious event for a leader of the opposition. On 10

February he travelled from Florida to Washington for a meeting with the President to discuss the content of the speech he was to give, in Truman's presence, in just over three weeks' time. It was to have two themes – a call for a close, worldwide Anglo-American alliance and the importance of opposition to the aims of the Soviet Union. Having first obtained Truman's general agreement, he showed an early version to the Secretary of State, Byrnes, on 17 February and two weeks later a revised version. Truman himself read the final text as they travelled together on the train to Missouri. Churchill, however, deliberately misled the British Government about the content of his lecture. On 21 February he told Attlee that it would be like his speech at Harvard University in 1943, when he had called for a continuing Anglo-American alliance. He did not tell him about the strongly anti-Soviet parts of the speech.

Churchill's speech came at a crucial period in the immediate post-war period as the United States and the Soviet Union sought to assess each other's intentions. After Potsdam relations had become more difficult as the US tried to use its military and economic power to secure a more favourable post-war settlement and the Soviet Union, feeling itself increasingly isolated and threatened, tightened control in its own sphere of influence. But by early 1946 it was not pre-ordained that there would be a Cold War and both countries were uncertain about how tough a line to take on the various issues that needed to be resolved around the world from Iran to Eastern Europe and the future of Germany. Truman was, therefore, happy to let Churchill make a hard-line speech – it would convey a clear message to the Soviet Union but also enable him to judge American reaction without being committed to Churchill's position.

In preparing his Fulton address Churchill was not so much looking ahead to a new post-war scenario as recycling anti-Soviet rhetoric of the 1920s and early 1930s. During his trip to the United States in 1931 he had declared in virtually every speech that 'The two great opposing forces of the future . . . would be the English speaking peoples and communism.' But in the intervening period, both in and out of office his actions and rhetoric had not been consistent with these views. In the late 1930s he had publicly called for an alliance with the Soviet Union. Not until much later did the first information emerge about his private diplomacy during the war – only eighteen months before the Fulton speech he had suggested and concluded a deal with Stalin on the division of Eastern Europe into spheres of influence that recognised the Soviet Union's predominant position in most of the region. At Yalta too he had conceded effective Soviet control of Poland. Now he was to attack the consequences of what he had agreed during the war.

Churchill was, however, keeping faith with one of his life-long concerns – Britain's place in the world. He was conscious of Britain's financial and economic weakness at the end of the war and the fact that much of the Empire had only been recovered with American help. The Fulton speech was an attempt to find a way of preserving Britain's world position as its economic and financial power declined and it became more dependent upon the United States. By insisting on the worldwide Soviet threat he hoped to encourage a long-term alliance between Britain and the United States which would ensure that the Americans would have a direct interest in the continuation of the British Empire as an anti-Communist bulwark which would provide them with military bases and political support around the globe. The corollary was that the United States would defend the empire, something that was increasingly beyond Britain's means.

Churchill gave his speech at Fulton on 5 March. He described an 'iron curtain' falling across the centre of Europe from the Baltic to Trieste. (The use of that phrase was not new – it was a popular way of describing the isolation of the Soviet Union in the 1920s and he himself had used it in telegrams to Truman in May and June 1945 and in a speech in the Commons in August. So too had Goebbels in February 1945 when he warned of the threat of a Soviet victory.) Beyond the 'iron curtain' he warned of a threat to Turkey and Iran and the possible Communist domination of Germany. He spoke of France's large Communist Party and suggested 'the future of Italy hangs in the balance'. According to Churchill, the real danger lay in a vast Communist plot to subvert western Europe. Everywhere, he warned, 'Communist fifth columns are established and work in complete unity and absolute obedience to the directions they receive from the Communist centre.' All of this posed a threat to 'Christian civilization'. Rejecting outright any policy of accommodation with the Soviet Union, he embarked on a theme that was to be a vital part of his message for many years and a central feature of his memoirs – he alone had consistently warned about the danger from Germany in the 1930s and had been right then but had been ignored; therefore

733

he was right now when he warned of the danger from the Soviet Union and must be listened to this time. He told the audience at Fulton that he had seen the war coming and 'cried aloud to my fellow countrymen and to the world, but no one paid any attention'.

Churchill then described how to meet the worldwide Soviet threat. There must be a 'special relationship' between the British Commonwealth and Empire and the United States. There should be 'joint use of all naval and air force bases in the possession of either country all over the world' and joint military planning (a re-creation of the combined chiefs of staff). The United States would of course have 'primacy in power' but Britain could offer its worldwide facilities. Churchill was quite open that his idea was for a joint Anglo-American domination of the world. By the end of the twentieth century he envisaged seventy or eighty million Britons 'spread about the world and united in defence of our tradition, our way of life'. (The white dominions were intended to be subordinate to Britain – the rest of the Empire was obviously not given any say.) He argued that this white Empire added to the power of the United States would produce 'no quivering, precarious balance of power to offer temptation to ambition or adventure. On the contrary, there will be an overwhelming assurance of security.' For a minimum of fifty years the Americans were to prop up the British Empire, rule the world and ensure that Communism was not a threat.

Reaction to Churchill's speech was mixed. In Britain the Government refused to endorse his views and said it was merely a 'private statement'. *The Times*, speaking of relations between the western democracies and the Soviet Union, declared it was 'an assumption of despair to hold that they are doomed to a fatal contest'. In the United States there was little support for the idea of an Anglo-American alliance (opinion polls showed only eighteen per cent agreed with the idea) but much more for the anti-Soviet parts of the speech. Nevertheless Truman virtually disowned the speech, saying he had not seen it beforehand (which was untrue). Churchill too felt he had to backtrack on some of his proposals. In a speech in New York on 15 March he claimed, 'I have never asked for an Anglo-American military alliance or a treaty.' The speech naturally increased Stalin's existing suspicions that he was faced with an Anglo-American alliance. But he remained conciliatory – Soviet forces withdrew from Mukden in Manchuria and the Danish island of Borkholm in the Baltic and he also accepted a settlement in Iran once the Americans backed the British.

Churchill himself was convinced that there would be war with the Soviet Union within a few years. In May 1946 he told Mackenzie King, the Canadian Prime Minister, that within eight years (when the Soviets had developed their own atomic bomb) there would be 'The greatest war – the most terrible war which may mean the end of our civilization'. But he still retained his admiration for Stalin, stating 'he would trust him further than any other Russian leader. He felt Stalin's word could be relied on. He was the one man in Russia to-day who could save a situation and might save it.'[6] In public Churchill asserted that the Soviets had roughly 200 combat-ready divisions in Eastern Europe poised to attack the West. In fact the Soviet Army was being rapidly demobilised; they were even ripping up many of the railway lines in eastern Germany they would require for mounting an invasion and were taking them to the Soviet Union as reparations. British intelligence estimates, which Churchill was later shown privately by Attlee in the autumn of 1946, suggested a Soviet total of about 100 divisions, most of which were far from combat-ready.

As the Fulton address made clear, Churchill had convinced himself that by virtue of his prophecies in the 1930s he was a reliable forecaster of world events in the 1940s. As he was now predicting that war with the Soviet Union was inevitable, he believed there should be a pre-emptive nuclear strike before the Soviet Union developed its own weapon. He was not prepared to publicly advocate this course but he privately began to develop his idea of nuclear diplomacy directed against the Soviet Union. He told Lord Moran in August 1946:

> We ought not to wait until Russia is ready. I believe it will be eight years before she has these bombs [in fact it was less than three] . . . America knows that 52% of Russia's motor industry is in Moscow and could be wiped out by a single bomb. It might mean wiping out three million people, but they would think nothing of that.[7]

The next year as the Cold War deepened he again spoke privately of an immediate nuclear attack on the Soviet Union if they did not accept the West's terms for their withdrawal from Eastern Europe.

(This was exactly the nuclear blackmail he had feared if the Soviets obtained the bomb first.) He told Mackenzie King in November 1947 that the war of nerves had gone on long enough and if a 'stand is not taken within the next few weeks, within five years or a much shorter time, there would be another world war in which we shall all be finished'. Therefore there should be an attack before the Soviets could retaliate with nuclear weapons. They should be given the West's terms and told, 'If you do not agree to that here and now, within so many days, we will attack Moscow and your other cities and destroy them with atomic bombs from the air.'[8]

Six months later he tried to interest the Americans in the same policy. He spoke to Lew Douglas, the US Ambassador in London, and told him 'now is the time, promptly, to tell the Soviets that if they do not retire from Berlin and abandon Eastern Germany, withdrawing to the Polish frontier, we will raze their cities'.[9] In July he wrote to Eisenhower that the time had come for a 'settlement' with the Soviet Union. Now they were to be forced to give up the whole of Eastern Europe and retire within their borders. He argued 'the moment for this settlement should be chosen when they will realise that the United States and its Allies possess overwhelming force'.[10] Churchill outlined the same ideas to Eden but admitted 'None of this argument is fit for public use', indeed he does not seem to have considered what role Western public opinion would play in all these schemes to threaten a nuclear war.[11] The furthest he would go was at the Conservative Party conference at Llandudno in October 1948, when he called for a 'settlement' with the Soviet Union on Western terms but did not make clear what that entailed. The development of the first Soviet atomic weapon in 1949 cooled Churchill's ardour. Nevertheless he still thought there would have to be an ultimatum to the Soviet Union and the threat of war. He told guests at the British Embassy in Paris in September 1951 that the United States would not stay long in Europe but 'in two or three years [they] would insist on having a show-down, and Russia would then have to withdraw from her present forward positions in Poland and Czechoslovakia, or there would be war'.[12] Once in power Churchill took a very different view of the situation.

As part of the response to what was being widely seen as an increasing Soviet threat Churchill advocated a European union, as did many other prominent European statesmen in the aftermath of the second destructive war on the continent within thirty years. Churchill had for long been under the influence of Count Coudenhove-Kalergi and his Pan-European Union and during the war he had advocated a series of regional groupings (including Europe) within the new United Nations though this had been rejected by the Americans among others. But when Churchill talked about Europe, he had continental Europe in mind. Britain was not to be part of this European Union. As early as February 1930 in an article in the *Saturday Evening Post* (which he recycled in the *News of the World* in May 1938) he wrote:

> We see nothing but good and hope in a richer, freer, more contented European commonality. But we have our own dream and our own task. We are with Europe, but not of it. We are linked but not compromised. We are interested and associated but not absorbed.

In parallel, he argued, there needed to be a 'proportionate growth of solidarity throughout the British Empire' and 'a deepening self-knowledge and mutual recognition among the English-speaking peoples'. Britain would only 'watch and aid' the process of European union.

Churchill made his first post-war appeal for European union in a speech in Zurich on 19 September 1946. Wartime experience of alliance with other European nations had not changed his views about Britain's benevolent aloofness. Neither was there any sign of his developing any more practical vision of an institutional framework that would underpin and organise the 'groupings' he advocated. The scheme he outlined very vaguely was based on a division of Europe into west and east, with a union of western states forming a bulwark against Communism. He favoured a partnership between France and Germany as part of 'a regional structure called, it may be, the United States of Europe'. This regional organisation would be within the UN framework because this 'larger synthesis will only survive if it is founded upon coherent natural groupings. There is already a natural grouping in the Western hemisphere. We British have our own Commonwealth of Nations . . . And why should there not be a European group . . .?' Britain, along with the United States and possibly the Soviet Union, would be one of the 'friends and sponsors of the new Europe'. Nowhere in the speech did he suggest that Britain would be part of this new European entity. Indeed, to the extent that a more unified and stronger Europe would be able to stand up to the Soviet Union, it would lessen the need for any British intervention on the continent and allow her to concentrate on the Empire and the relationship with the United States.

In April 1947, at a rally in the Albert Hall entitled 'Let Europe Arise', Churchill, though favouring European unity, made his own priority absolutely clear: 'we shall allow no wedge to be driven between Great Britain and the United States of America'. At the party conference that year at Brighton in October he suggested that Britain should be 'the vital link' between the United States, the Commonwealth and a European union. In May 1948 he attended the Hague Congress on European Union – a meeting of largely unelected delegates, many in opposition and some not in politics at all. Apart from Churchill the other senior figures were Spaak, Bidault, Schuman, Blum, Reynaud and Monnet. Much of Churchill's speech was taken up by the need for unity in the face of the Communist threat. His one proposal was for a European Assembly to 'enable the voice of a United Europe to be heard'. But he did not spell out what powers it would have apart from debate and propaganda or how it would be linked to the Governments of Europe. The Congress went further and called for European economic and political union, together with a European Parliament and a Court of Human Rights.

At this point the British Government, which had been positive about the idea of European co-operation in the immediate post-war period, became sceptical once it became clear that the aim was to establish supranational institutions. The Labour Government insisted on watering down the Hague proposals into the Council of Europe, controlled by ministers from national governments, and a virtually powerless Assembly that was not allowed to discuss economics or defence and had only consultative powers on other subjects. The British delegation to the Council was not elected but appointed by the Government. Churchill led the Conservative members to the first meeting of the Assembly in Strasbourg in August 1949 but arrived two days after the opening and left immediately after his own speech.

While the rest of western Europe was moving towards a form of union that went further than just co-operation between governments, Britain was on the sidelines. Like the Government, Churchill rejected any idea of Britain participating in European supranational institutions. Much of his pro-Europe rhetoric was carefully chosen, designed mainly to embarrass the Labour Government rather than advance the cause of European unity. In November 1949 in the House of Commons he accepted the Government's view that Britain could not join a European economic system if the Commonwealth were excluded and took the unrealistic position that the Common-wealth should be part of any European trading bloc. Although he urged the Government to take part in the talks on the Schuman plan for a European coal and steel community (which would have supranational institutions), he did so only because he wanted Britain to wreck the plan. Without the removal of the offending suprana-tional parts of the proposed treaty he thought Britain should not join. In office Churchill was to take no interest in advancing the cause of European union or promoting Britain's role within it.

At one with the Labour Government over its policy on Europe, Churchill also found it difficult to articulate a clear alternative to their policy in one of the most complex issues it had to face – the future of India. Although he had been forced under political pressure to agree to the Cripps offer in 1942 and had subsequently done his best to sabotage it, in public he was still committed to it, however much he disliked any move towards Indian independence. In practice by 1945 the policy that Churchill would have preferred – no concessions – was no longer practicable. The British did not have the power to rule India in the face of a widespread demand for independence and the only questions remaining were about the terms on which independence would be granted, in particular whether unity would be maintained or whether the Muslim provinces would be given the right to secede. In these circumstances Churchill personally favoured a highly fragmented India becoming a multitude of subordinate Dominions with a long-term British presence backed by an army, but it was difficult to advocate such a policy openly. The result was a policy of opposition to the Government but no coherent statement of an alternative.

The Government too lacked a clear policy in 1945. Under pressure from Wavell (the Viceroy), they first dropped the Cripps plan and then, lacking an alternative, sent a Cabinet mission which eventually advocated a complex three-tier Indian union. The plan collapsed because of Congress opposition, taking with it the last chance of independence for a united India. In the House of Commons debate on 1 August 1946 after the failure of the Cabinet mission, Churchill spoke of 'the mighty Empire and Continent of India with all the work we have done in the last 200 years' and accused the Government of placing the independence of India 'in hostile and feeble hands, heedless of the dark carnage and confusion which will follow'. He thought the Government was 'ready to leave the 400 million Indians to fall into all the horrors of sanguinary civil war'.

In early September an interim Government (with some representation for minorities) was established in Delhi with Nehru as Prime Minister but the Muslim League refused to take part in the constituent assembly which was to devise a Constitution for India. British authority was collapsing rapidly and the Government was only just in charge of the process of independence. Churchill made it clear that he favoured the break-up of India. In early December he saw Jinnah in London and assured him that if Pakistan were created, as the Muslim League wanted, then it could not be expelled from the Commonwealth. He also set up a highly secret method of communication with Jinnah, giving him a safe address to use in India and proposing to send him letters under the name of 'Gilliatt', his secretary. In Parliament he spoke against any ideas of negotiation between the parties in India and in favour of partition.

Speaking in the Commons on 20 December 1946, Churchill objected strongly to the fact that India was not to be given dominion status as an intermediate step towards full independence. He was still under the illusion that if this stage were retained it would provide 'an opportunity for the friends of this country who desire that we should stay to rally'. Early in 1947, as British control weakened still further and the inability of the Indians to agree on a Constitution for a unified India became ever more apparent, Attlee persuaded Lord Mountbatten to become Viceroy with a timetable for independence by June 1948. On 6 March 1947 Churchill, speaking in the Commons, continued with the anti-Congress campaign that had been one of the hallmarks of his policy in the 1930s. He told MPs it had been 'a critical mistake' to involve 'the leader of the caste Hindus, Mr Nehru' to head the interim Government. The result was 'a complete disaster'. It was now time to involve the United Nations. But he sadly acknowledged that India, which he had always seen as the centrepiece of the British Empire and which he had wanted to preserve in its ninteeenth-century state, would soon be independent: 'It is with deep grief that I watch the clattering down of the British Empire . . . Many have defended Britain against her foes. None can defend her against herself.'

In fact, as the Labour Government was discovering, it was impossible to hold India any longer, whatever Britain might want to do. In May Mountbatten and the Government decided not to address all the complex questions independence would raise, but to clear out as quickly as possible, handing over power to two separate states. Churchill and the Conservatives hoped for a weak and divided India still dependent on Britain. They wanted as many as possible of the 562 princely states to opt out of India and be recognised as separate Dominions by Britain. The Labour Government however left the princes to make the best deal they could with the new Government in Delhi. On 10 July 1947, on the occasion of the second reading of the Government of India Bill granting independence to India and Pakistan, Churchill refused to be in the Commons and left the job of opposition to Harold Macmillan. The two countries became independent a month later. For another year Churchill tried to secure at least Kashmir and Hyderabad as separate dominions but failed.

India was the one of the few political issues Churchill cared about deeply. He passionately wanted India to continue to be ruled as it had been in the nineteenth century without any advance towards self-government let alone independence. He had always seen it as the keystone of the British Empire he wanted to uphold and preserve for centuries. For the rest of his life he remained bitter and resentful about the granting of independence, convinced that the Indians would be unable to govern themselves. He told his constituents at the end of September 1947 that there would be a vast slaughter in India for years to come and 'there will come a retrogression of civilization throughout these enormous regions, constituting one of the most melancholy tragedies Asia has ever known'. Attlee's decision to consult him in December 1948 about the possibility of allowing India into the Commonwealth but without subordination to the Crown provoked a vengeful outburst against independent India.

He 'at once went off the deep end with his usual attitude on Indian matters and suggested that India should now be a foreign power; if we wanted anything from them we should make a treaty, and poured scorn on any suggestion of an association'.[14]

Churchill also, as so often in his political views, took it as a personal matter. He refused to shake hands with Mountbatten for years and told him, 'What you did in India is as though you had struck me across the face with a riding whip.'[15] Six years later at the Bermuda conference with Eisenhower he was still deeply upset over giving independence to India. In front of the US President, the French Prime Minister and all their advisers he lamented the passing of the British Raj:

> This was a colossal disaster which he had lived to see . . . many of those around the table would realize what a great misfortune it was when Great Britain cast away her duties in India. . . . He felt it was a great mistake to suppose that the ancient powers of Europe had not made a contribution to the progress of these races in Asia and that all they had done was obsolete and that it was good that it had passed away . . . Dark days lie ahead in Asia as a result of those who thought they could do without the guidance and aid of the European nations to whom they owed so much.[16]

There was, however, one part of the Empire that Churchill thought should be given up, and that was Palestine. Here he saw Britain's duty in an altogether different light. On 1 August 1946 he announced in the Commons 'it is our duty . . . to offer to lay down the mandate'. What would happen after that he did not spell out. On one thing though Churchill was clear. Despite the existence of at least 100,000 displaced Jewish refugees and survivors of the death camps in Europe, he told the Commons that 'No one can imagine that there is room in Palestine for the great masses of Jews who wish to leave Europe, or that they could be absorbed in any period which it is now useful to contemplate.' At the time when the case for some Jewish immigration into Palestine was at its strongest, Churchill was beginning to lose his enthusiasm.

Nevertheless Churchill continued to support the Jewish settlers and organisations against the Arabs, as the campaign of Jewish terrorism increased and Britain prepared to abandon the mandate without handing over to any coherent government. In the early 1920s when he was Colonial Secretary, he had approved of the use of reprisals against Arab villages if they resisted the influx of Jewish settlers. In the 1940s he took the opposite line. Speaking in the Commons on 31 January 1947, he condemned the use of reprisals against Jews and said 'every effort should be made to avoid getting into warfare with terrorists'. He spoke of the 'fortitude' of a Jew who attacked a police station and killed an Arab policeman. He did not condemn the actions of the Jewish terrorist organisations – Irgun and Lehi.

Out of the chaos of the mandate the new state of Israel was formed and was immediately at war with its Arab neighbours as it tried to establish its borders beyond the UN-agreed positions and started the mass expulsion of Arabs. Churchill wanted immediate recognition of the new state and even refused to condemn Israeli attacks on the RAF. In January 1949 Israeli forces shot down five RAF reconnaissance planes over Sinai, which were monitoring Israeli withdrawal behind the ceasefire line, and dragged part of the wreckage over the line to make it look as if the planes had been intruding into Israeli airspace. Two of the pilots were killed. Churchill blamed the British Government for sending the planes into the area. That same month he looked back on the imperial venture in Palestine. It was part of Britain's imperial record, which, unusually for him, he had no desire to defend. He told the Commons it had led to a 'vast waste of money, to the repeated loss of British lives, to humiliation of every kind'.

While he was Leader of the Opposition Churchill was, as in the past, largely preoccupied with foreign and imperial policy. In this area there was less difference between the parties than on other issues. He supported the strong anti-Communist line the Labour Government was taking, including the development of a western European alliance, support for the United States and the Marshall aid plan, and in 1949 the signing of the North Atlantic Treaty and the creation of NATO. The greatest political issues though were in the domestic field as the Labour Government struggled to cope with the post-war inheritance of debilitated finances and weak exports and the problems of demobilisation. These were the problems that had been predicted in the deeply pessimistic papers Churchill had seen in the last months of the coalition. He had hoped to cope with them through massive American assistance in the form of continued lend-lease but this had not been forthcoming. The Government dealt with these problems and at the same time embarked on a series of major economic and social reforms. It nationalised a range of industries – the Bank of England, coal, railways, electricity, gas and eventually iron and steel – and created a comprehensive system of social security and a National Health Service that was paid for out of taxation and free to those in need.

Churchill, as earlier in his life and during the 1945 Election, continued to predict the most dire consequences for Britain under a Labour Government. In October 1945 he told Mackenzie King 'he feared conditions were going to be pretty serious in England [sic] as a consequence of the policy of destroying the rich to equalise incomes of all'.[17] A month later when he spoke at a meeting of the Central Council of the Conservative Party he claimed that there would soon be a contest of 'The People versus the Socialists' which would involve 'the ancient glorious, British people, who carried our name so high and our aims so far in this formidable world' against 'the Socialist doctrinaires with all their pervasive propaganda, with all their bitter class hatred, with all their love of tyrannising'.

The end of 1945 probably marked the low point of Conservative fortunes after the July Election defeat, and in early 1946 they began to offer a more effective opposition. This was achieved largely under Eden's leadership as Churchill was away in the United States for nearly three months. Nevertheless the Conservatives found it difficult to oppose popular measures such as the creation of a social security system and the nationalisation of industries that had clearly failed in private ownership – coal and railways for example. Churchill concentrated his fire on the withdrawal of troops in Egypt to the Canal Zone (even though they remained in far greater numbers than allowed under the 1936 Treaty), the announcement of the intention to nationalise the iron and steel industry and the decision to introduce bread rationing, something that had not been necessary during the war. The Conservatives also attacked the setting up of the NHS. Labour's scheme was on a very different basis from the plan the Churchill Government had contemplated just before the 1945 Election but had not had the courage to announce. Now all hospitals were to be nationalised and centralised control was to be established through the Ministry of Health, although doctors were not to become State employees. On the second reading of the Bill on 2 May 1946, Churchill and the opposition twice voted against creation of the NHS.

1947 was politically a much easier year for the Conservatives as the Labour Government suffered major setbacks. One of the most dreadful winters in living memory and a severe fuel crisis were followed by a major currency crisis when sterling was made convertible (as the Americans had insisted when their massive loan was accepted). Within weeks Britain's exchange reserves were exhausted and sterling convertibility had to be abandoned. By the autumn the Conservatives were ahead in the opinion polls. Throughout the year Churchill kept up his fierce rhetorical onslaughts on the people with whom he had shared Government for five years and whom he now dismissed as unworthy to hold power in their own right. The only domestic issue on which he did support them was the retention of conscription in peacetime. In the Commons on 12 March he spoke of the Government 'mouthing slogans of envy, hatred and malice' and said it had 'spread class warfare throughout the land and all sections of society'. Speaking at Ayr in May Churchill bitterly regretted that Britain, having 'rendered services for which the whole world should be grateful', had then been laid low by 'a narrow, bigoted, incapable Socialist faction'. According to him a 'misguided electorate' had in 'an unthinking moment' in 1945 voted them into power. In October at the party conference he accused the Labour Government of 'having promised to abolish poverty and only abolished wealth, of having vaunted their new world and only wrecked the old'. Six weeks later in private he spoke of the Government's 'insatiable lust for power' which was 'only equalled by their incurable impotence in exercising it'.[18] He refused to accept the popular verdict in 1945, describing the House of Commons as 'the most unrepresentative and irresponsible . . . that ever sat at Westminster'.

By 1947 Churchill was increasingly concentrating his efforts on writing his memoirs and only spent about three days a week in London, even during the Parliamentary session. The rest of the time he was at Chartwell. His appearances in the House of Commons to head the opposition were therefore rather limited. Not surprisingly his leadership began to come in for criticism but he had no intention of making way for a younger or more active man. At one time he had discussed not continuing in politics after the war. In the autumn of

1940 he told Eden that he would 'not make Lloyd George's mistake of carrying on after the war' and he, Eden, must have the succession.[19] But Churchill's whole life had been built around politics and at the end of the war he was not prepared to retire. The terrible shock of rejection by the people in July 1945 only made him more determined to go on and seek a reversal of that verdict. He was convinced that as the successful wartime leader the Conservative Party would not dare force him out. He summed up his position with regard to the Conservative Party for Lord Moran's benefit during the Potsdam conference: 'I can deal with them. I am indispensable to them.'[20]

By 1945 Eden was recognised as the natural successor to Churchill when the latter chose to retire. Churchill himself was very happy with that arrangement, because he knew that Eden would not stab him in the back or plot against him and would wait, whatever the provocation, until he chose to go. For the next ten years Churchill continually hinted at his forthcoming retirement and periodically dates would be discussed, but he never showed the slightest inclination actually to depart. On his return from the United States in March 1946 he suggested that Eden should play a more prominent role in the House of Commons but that was largely because he did not want to be there too often himself. He told Eden this would help him establish his position over the next year or two but added: 'All my most intimate friends recommend retirement and I will fight the lot till the bitter end and challenge them to sack me.'[21]

In 1947 discontent with Churchill's leadership within the Conservative Party was such that a group of senior party members – Lord Woolton (the Party Chairman), R. A. Butler, Oliver Stanley and Lord Salisbury (but significantly not Eden) – met at Harry Crookshank's house to discuss Churchill's retirement. The Chief Whip, James Stuart, drew the short straw and was sent to tell him their advice. The result was a flat refusal to accept their views and resign. He judged that they would not have the nerve to lead an open revolt because it would be seen as too damaging to defy him publicly: secure in his status as the symbol of victory in the war, he stayed put and showed no sign of mending his ways. Two years later Clementine told him 'you do only just as much as will keep you in Power'.[22] Attitudes to Churchill at this time reveal a striking parallel with the ambiguity of his wartime position: reluctance to do other than praise him in public co-existed with major reservations in private. The public sycophancy masked considerable lack of enthusiasm for Churchill. In August 1949 a confidential poll carried out by the Conservative Party showed that Churchill added nothing to the Conservative vote whereas Eden as leader would be likely to increase their standing because he would attract more floating voters. Later in September 1951, just before the General Election, a Gallup poll found that even a majority of Conservative voters would prefer Eden as leader.

Not only did Churchill take a minimal interest in leading the party in Parliament, he took only a minor role in the changes made to party organisation and in policy formulation during the period of opposition. Originally he wanted his protégé Harold Macmillan to be Chairman of the party, but he had to settle for the more senior Lord Woolton, who was appointed in July 1946. Although given a free hand, the new Chairman made no radical changes. A drive to increase membership only restored it to pre-war levels. The practice of 'selling' a Parliamentary seat to the candidate who put up the largest contribution to party funds was abolished, but it had been dying out since the 1920s. The mass party in the country was given a little more influence, but it was within existing structures and policy making remained the preserve of the leadership and the party conference was no more influential than it had been before the war. The research department was re-established after its wartime demise, and the Young Conservative organisation was developed.

In policy too there was no fundamentally new departure. Churchill did not favour a firm statement of policy or working out detailed proposals in opposition. Addressing the Scottish party in 1946, he would say no more than policy could be 'added to from time to time as circumstances change'. His own idea of a declaration of Conservative policy was essentially a collection of resounding platitudes – they stood for 'Liberty with security; stability combined with progress; the maintenance of religion, the Crown and Parliamentary Government'. Later in the year he went so far as to say that he favoured 'the native energies, genius and continuance of our race'. In a broadcast on 16 August 1947 he asked rhetorically what he would do if he were returned to power. He reassured his listeners that he would gather a Cabinet of great ability and then 'I would give you promptly and in good time the decisions which are necessary'.

Others in the party felt that they needed to go into a little more detail than this.

The first area to be addressed was industrial policy which led to the publication of the Industrial Charter in May 1947. Although often hailed as a radical departure in Conservative policy, it was in fact little more than a restatement of existing ideas, designed mainly to attract publicity. It accepted nationalisation of the Bank of England and the coal and rail industries (largely because no part of private enterprise wanted to buy them back and operate them). In itself this was not a new departure – before the war the Conservatives had set up State bodies to run air services and distribute electricity. Other nationalised industries were to be de-nationalised, and the Charter went on to set out standard Conservative themes such as the importance of private enterprise, tax cuts, wages pegged to productivity (how was not specified), abolition of the closed shop and a return to contracting-in for the payment of the trades union political levy. It is unlikely that Churchill ever read the Industrial Charter before its ratification by the party conference in October 1947. After it had been duly agreed he asked Reginald Maudling, the young researcher helping to draft his conference speech, to include a few references. When he read them Churchill exclaimed, 'But I don't agree with a word of this'. Two months after the conference Churchill explained his personal view of Britain's future at a party rally in Manchester. He thought that a quarter of Britain's population (over twelve million people) would 'have to disappear in one way or another'. He did not believe that many could emigrate and therefore a large number would die of poverty or malnutrition. It was a grim view of the future, the ability of industry to win markets and provide jobs and the Government's willingness to support the population.

The final statement of Conservative policy came in July 1949 in 'The Right Road for Britain' produced by a committee under Eden's chairmanship. Some of the ideas of the Industrial Charter, such as an economic plan and anti-monopoly policy, had already disappeared. Some aspects of Labour policy, in particular social security, were accepted because it was felt they were too popular to oppose. In other areas traditional Conservative policies were re-asserted. Housing was to concentrate on property-owning and rent control would only remain while there was a severe housing shortage. There was to be reform of the House of Lords (Churchill had strongly opposed the 1949 Parliament Act which reduced the Lords' powers of delay to one year) and university seats were to be restored in the Commons. Before its publication Churchill did look at this document in detail and he wrote the foreword, putting in passages about Lord Randolph and liberalism.

When the document was published, the Conservatives seemed to be in a strong position. Labour was behind in the opinion polls; within a couple of months the devaluation of the pound added to its unpopularity. Immediately afterwards the Conservative lead surged to over eleven per cent, but by early 1950 it had fallen back to about 2 per cent. Churchill had been unable or unwilling to develop a clear and coherent alternative to Labour's policies and his strategy was to hope that increasing Government unpopularity would be enough to ensure the Conservatives won the next Election. During the life of the Labour Government the Conservatives did not win a single by-election. With an Election due by the summer of 1951 at the latest, Attlee decided to go for a winter poll on 23 February. Churchill, who was on holiday in Madeira when the Election was announced on 10 January, returned immediately by flying boat to Southampton.

The first task was to prepare the Election manifesto. The problem in doing this was Churchill's habitual reluctance to spell out policy. As Butler commented, 'He has been so passionately keen to resume power that he has not wanted to tie himself to any statement which might make that objective more distant.'[23] The manifesto, entitled 'This is the Road', emerged as even less radical than 'The Right Road for Britain'. In private the Conservatives were already looking at major changes to the free health service – they were considering charges for hospital stays, appliances and prescriptions, but the manifesto said nothing of this. The maintenance of full employment was cited as the main aim. The iron and steel industry would be denationalised, road transport would be returned as far as possible to the previous owners but other nationalised industries, in particular rail and coal, were only to be decentralised as much as possible. Rationing and direction of labour would be abolished. The principle to be applied to the social services was 'Britain can only enjoy the social services for which she is prepared to work'. In general Britain under the Conservatives was to be a place of 'hard work, thrift, honesty and neighbourliness'. In a very Churchillian passage, the past was to be 'restored' not attacked as under Labour.

749

The campaign got underway at the beginning of February. The Churchill factor was given much less prominence than in 1945. Then nearly every Conservative candidate had referred to him in their Election address; now half had no reference at all and only just over ten per cent contained a letter of endorsement from the Leader. Churchill gave two of their five party political broadcasts. (In 1949 he had wanted to revive his 'Gestapo' speech of 1945 but he was talked out of it by Conservative Party officials.) His speeches contained his usual quota of vehement attacks on the Labour Party. Their policy was characterised as 'wild extravagance', 'class hatred', a 'muddle and mismanagement' and he argued that they wanted to create a monster State monopoly with 'a levelling down of British society to a degree not hitherto presented by any responsible person'. He also introduced foreign affairs into the campaign. In a speech at Edinburgh on 15 February, he accused the Labour Government of 'extraordinary administrative lapses' in not having British nuclear weapons operational (in fact it was the highest priority item in the Government's programme and work was nearing completion). He called for 'a parley at the summit' with the Soviet Union, a theme that was to become the cornerstone of his ambitions for the next five years. In his last broadcast he also condemned 'the utter failure of Socialist governments to make any effective resistance to Communist aggression and permeation' despite the Labour Government's huge efforts to build a western defence system.

When the results were declared, the Conservatives had done well but not well enough. On a swing of just over three per cent they had a net gain of eighty-five seats, giving them a total of 298 compared with Labour's 315. As the Liberals had nine MPs, the Labour Government was returned with an overall majority of six but a majority over the Conservatives of seventeen. In terms of the popular vote the Conservatives were still nearly three per cent behind Labour. For the second time Churchill had been rejected by the British electorate. But the narrowness of Labour's victory provided a new safeguard against any immediate change of leadership. If Labour had been returned with a majority sufficient for a full Parliament, it is certain that Churchill would have had to retire without ever gaining the rehabilitation he so desperately wanted after his 1945 humiliation. As it was, Labour seemed likely to call another Election within a short period and there was therefore no question of Churchill being asked to stand down.

Once again thrust reluctantly into the role of Leader of the Opposition, Churchill found it difficult to exploit Labour's small majority. Amendments were put down on the King's Speech but the Government had comfortable majorities of fourteen and twenty-five and it also survived a vote on its rejection of the Schuman plan for a European coal and steel community, where the Liberals supported the Conservatives. Even on the most controversial issue – iron and steel nationalisation – the Government was able to obtain its majority of six. Until the autumn Labour was also consistently ahead in the opinion polls which meant that Churchill had no incentive to bring down the Government. In June on the outbreak of the Korean War he supported the Government's decision to send British troops to fight as part of the nominally United Nations forces.

The atmosphere changed at the end of 1950: the Conservatives took a big lead in the opinion polls as the economic crisis caused by the Korean War and a mounting rearmament programme became more acute. On 14 December Churchill linked the nationalisation of iron and steel with the Communist attack in Korea and said 'we cannot in these circumstances feel confidence in the loyalty of the Government to the people of this country'. More active opposition continued early in 1951 as the Conservatives tried to force an Election while they were ahead in the polls. They put down four censure motions in a fortnight on coal supplies, iron and steel nationalisation, meat supplies and defence but lost them all. In March they started a campaign of attrition using procedural devices to ensure long sittings in an attempt to wear out the Government but they gave up after only four days. Churchill himself took part in two all-night sittings in June in an attempt to demonstrate that he was still fit enough to take over the Government at the age of seventy-six.

The Conservative opposition was much less active during the summer but by then the Government was in deep trouble. Many of the senior ministers were worn out after ten gruelling years in office, Bevin and Cripps were dying, Morrison was proving a poor Foreign Secretary and others were divided over the scale and pace of the post-Korea rearmament programme. The new Chancellor of the Exchequer (Hugh Gaitskell) proposed to introduce charges for some

items within the health service. Eventually Nye Bevan, the creator of
the National Health Service, and Harold Wilson, the President of
the Board of Trade, resigned. The Government had survived far
longer than expected after the 1950 Election but now seemed to lose
its nerve. Attlee, with bad political judgement, called an Election in
September for 25 October even though Labour was behind in the
polls.

Churchill embarked on what was certain to be his last General
Election campaign as Leader. The Conservative manifesto published
at the end of September was, like that of 1945, a personal statement.
It was, as might have been expected, strong on rhetoric and lacking
in precision. Its limited policy content was less radical than in 1950.
Its declared aim was to put Britain back in what Churchill described
as its 'pre-eminent position' of 1945 that had been wasted, he
believed, by Labour's nationalisation and extravagance. In foreign
affairs the Empire was to come first and imperial preference would
be maintained. Iron and steel were to be denationalised, together
with parts of the road transport industry. The main departure was
inclusion of a target of building 300,000 homes a year. (This had
been adopted by the party conference against the wishes of the
leadership.) There was to be an excess profits tax on the rearmament
programme (something Churchill had supported since the early
1920s) but nothing was said about how to deal with the economic
crisis. There was a pledge not to cut food subsidies. The House of
Lords was to be reformed and university constituencies restored.
The final message was the need to preserve the British way of life
against socialism.

Churchill's contribution to the actual campaign was even less than
in 1950. His one party political broadcast came at the beginning of
the campaign. His treatment of domestic issues was markedly
moderate in tone, reflecting the extent of his determination not to
alienate potential floating voters. He stressed the similarities between
Labour and Conservative policies in an attempt to reassure people
that they could vote Conservative without losing all the advances
made by Labour in the previous six years. On foreign policy he
stressed the need for rearmament and the importance of making no
concessions over the British role in Egypt and taking firm action over
the nationalisation of British oil interests in Persia. Apart from the
broadcast he made two speeches in his constituency and just five

outside – including one for Randolph, who was to fail yet again to become an MP, and one for an old friend, Violet Bonham-Carter, who was standing as a Liberal in Colne Valley. (This was part of his efforts to forge a link with the Liberals, although the party machine had rejected his ideas for an electoral pact.) Some of his speeches brought out old themes. On 6 October, speaking about the situation in Persia, he described 'the great decline of British prestige and authority in the Middle East following inevitably the loss of our military power in India'. Three days later he launched an attack on Nye Bevan – 'a vote for Bevanite Socialism is in fact, whatever its intention, a vote which increases the hazard of world catastrophe'.

At the start of the campaign the Conservatives had been in the lead in the opinion polls by over nine per cent but by the end the two parties were neck and neck. When the results were declared, it was clear that the British people had rejected Churchill's leadership for the third time. Labour gained over 230,000 more votes than the Conservatives. Yet the electoral system ensured the Conservatives won more seats – 321 to Labour's 295 – and Churchill became Prime Minister again with an overall majority of seventeen. There was a small swing of support of about one per cent to the Conservatives but the reason they won a Parliamentary majority was a collapse in the Liberal vote. In the 1950 Election the Liberal Party had put up 475 candidates but in a débâcle lost 319 deposits. In 1951 they put up just 109 candidates and won six seats. The slump in the Liberal vote from nine per cent to two and a half per cent was enough to let the Conservatives win. Churchill had achieved one of his last ambitions – to reverse the verdict of 1945 – but he had once again failed to win popular endorsement.

Return to Power

On his return as Prime Minister in 1951 Churchill showed an almost pathetic determination to re-create the world he had known in Whitehall during the Second World War. Once again he became both Prime Minister and Minister of Defence. He wanted his principal Private Secretary, David Pitblado, replaced by his wartime predecessor, Leslie Rowan, but Rowan was now too senior for the job. So he turned once again to Jock Colville. As Colville refused to oust Pitblado, Churchill ended up with two senior Private Secretaries, although Colville was always the favourite because the family liked him. Another face new to Churchill was Sir Kenneth McLean, Chief Staff Officer to the Minister of Defence and he was promptly replaced by Sir Ian Jacob, who had been Military Assistant to the War Cabinet. Churchill also stopped Sir Thomas Padmore becoming Secretary to the Cabinet, insisting that Norman Brook, who had been Bridges' deputy during the war, must stay on.

The same determination was also reflected in his Cabinet. Eden, as always, became Foreign Secretary, though he refused to take on the role of Leader of the House of Commons again as he had during the latter half of the war, and that job went to Harry Crookshank, whom Churchill disliked. Butler became Chancellor of the Exchequer only because Oliver Lyttleton, Churchill's friend from the war and his first choice for the job, was thought to be too close to certain firms in the City of London. Lyttleton went to the Colonial Office instead. Harold Macmillan was made Minister of Housing, with responsibility for building 300,000 homes a year. Ismay became Commonwealth Relations Secretary, but was a disaster and moved on to become Secretary-General of NATO after just five months. Lord Swinton was made Minister of Materials but not given a place in the Cabinet. Cherwell became Paymaster-General (and was given No 11 Downing Street in preference to Butler). He re-created a statistical section and acted as the Prime Minister's personal adviser on all scientific matters, in particular atomic weapons and energy policy. Churchill also introduced the idea of 'overlords' to co-ordinate several departments and so reduce the size of the Cabinet. Lord Woolton took on Food and Agriculture but to little effect. Lord Leathers, Churchill's close friend and previously Minister of War Transport, was another unsuccessful overlord of Transport and Fuel and Power. The concept of 'overlords' had to be abandoned fairly rapidly. Sir John Anderson (Home Secretary and Chancellor of the Exchequer in the wartime coalition) was offered the post of Chancellor of the Duchy of Lancaster to co-ordinate supply and raw materials but refused because he thought the offer an insult and he wanted to retain lucrative outside directorships. Churchill offered Clement Davies, the leader of the Liberals, the post of Education Secretary – given Churchill's views on the importance of education it was a poor offer. After consulting his Parliamentary party, Davies declined and the Liberals maintained their independence.

As usual Churchill brought into Government other friends and relations. His son-in-law Duncan Sandys was appointed Minister of Supply (Clementine talked him out of making him Secretary of State for War as too blatant a piece of nepotism). The War Office went instead to one of Churchill's wartime assistants on defence, Anthony Head. His other son-in-law, Christopher Soames, was made his unofficial Parliamentary Private Secretary – he did not dare make it official for almost eighteen months. Brendan Bracken was offered the Colonial Office but was too ill to accept and received a peerage instead. (Churchill was also able to make his old friend Louis Spears a baronet.) Lord de L'Isle was made Secretary of State for Air; he had won a VC in the war – in Churchill's mind military decorations were always a prime qualification for public office. He offered the Ministry of Defence to Lord Portal, his wartime Chief of the Air Staff, who declined. After a few months it was accepted by Lord Alexander, always Churchill's favourite commander during the war.

The new Cabinet was small – only sixteen members – and by early 1952 over forty per cent of them were peers. It was also predominantly elderly – only Peter Thornycroft, President of the Board of Trade at the age of forty-two, was from the rising generation. There was only one woman minister, Florence Horsburgh at Education, but she was left out of the Cabinet (only the third time since 1919 the Minister of Education was not a member).

Even before he took office one of the main worries for Churchill's ministers and close confidants was whether he was fit to be Prime Minister. The general view, confirmed within the first months of the new Government, was that he was not. Just after becoming Prime Minister he had celebrated his seventy-seventh birthday and there were numerous signs of a decline in his powers. He was increasingly deaf (and still very reluctant to use a hearing aid) and had difficulty concentrating on an issue as well as a tendency to reminisce at the slightest opportunity. At Cabinet meetings he was a poor chairman and indulged to the full his tendency to ramble on at inordinate length. The huge appetite for work and intervention in the affairs of every department that had characterised his approach to office had faded. He spent much of his time reading newspapers, playing cards, eating and drinking. He had better intervals, but they became few and far between.

He had already suffered one stroke in 1949 and just before the 1951 Election Churchill's doctor Lord Moran wrote in his diary, 'if he wins this election and goes back to No 10 I doubt whether he is up to the job'.[1] Within three months of becoming Prime Minister he suffered another mild stroke, which for a while left him unable to speak coherently. Moran advised him to cut back even further on his workload. Colville told Moran at this time: 'I hate to be disloyal, but the PM is not doing his work', and Lord Salisbury remarked, 'in Cabinet he will talk about something for two and a half hours without once coming to the point'.[2] Even Macmillan, a devoted admirer, writing in his diary in early June 1952, noted the lack of any 'real directing hand or inspiration' in Cabinet and concluded: 'if he stays – without a policy – he will drift to an inglorious decline. I try to tell him this . . . but it is not easy to move him.'[3] On the same day Eden wrote in his diary, 'I didn't think W looked well, & he is doing very little work.'[4] A month after taking office Churchill met Eisenhower, who wrote in his diary, 'He simply will not think in terms of today, but rather only those of the war years ... My regretful opinion is that the Prime Minister no longer absorbs new ideas.'[5]

But British Prime Ministers are served by a strong machine which can process the business of State even with a relatively inactive incumbent. Churchill was moreover surrounded by flattering courtiers such as Colville and Soames, who set out to boost his morale and convince him that his performance was just as good as during the war – and listened patiently to his endless reminiscences. By May 1952 even Colville was forced to admit 'his periods of lowness grow more frequent and his concentration less good. The bright and sparkling intervals still come, and they are unequalled, but age is beginning to show.'[6] Six months later others were more forthright. Crookshank described him as 'terribly drooling ... fast losing his grip'.[7] The outgoing American Ambassador, Walter Gifford, told Eisenhower, who had just become President, that Churchill 'is really stretching, if he has not outlived his usefulness'.[8] The President himself thought 'he is quite definitely showing the effects of the passing years'.[9] A habit that Churchill clung to was his heavy drinking. In May 1953 while Eden was away ill he took over control of the Foreign Office and invited one of the Deputy Secretaries there, Sir Pierson Dixon, to lunch at No 10. Dixon noted: 'The lunch lasted for $3\frac{3}{4}$ hours. A varied and noble procession of wines with which I could not keep pace – champagne, port, brandy, cointreau: W drank a great deal of all, and ended up with two glasses of whisky and soda.'[10]

As Prime Minister Churchill simply ignored vast areas of Government activity. He took little or no interest in economic, financial or domestic policy of any sort. His office files reveal an almost complete vacuum in these areas and what few interventions he made were usually random, brought about by some item he had read in the newspaper rather than as part of the policy debate within Government. (They include such subjects as horror comics and flying saucers.) The Government faced a severe economic crisis when it took office, but Churchill found it difficult to understand the complexities of modern financial policy making. He took some part in discussions in early 1952 on the possible floating of the pound but the background to the 1952 budget was too difficult for him and after that he took little further part in economic policy. The Government's early economic policy was to double interest rates, cut the foreign travel allowance in half and, contrary to their pledge in the Election manifesto, cut food subsidies by forty per cent. The meat ration was reduced to less than its wartime value. Prescription and dental charges were introduced and education expenditure cut by five per cent despite the rapidly rising number of pupils. But from the second half of 1952 the long post-Korean War boom in the world economy eased British problems and for the next three years the Government was able to adopt a generally expansionist and tax cutting policy.

Churchill took little interest in the subject of denationalisation (in 1953 he didn't even know whether the electricity industry was State-owned or not) apart from trying to increase the number of private lorries. Despite the pledges in the manifesto, the iron and steel industry was only partially denationalised because few private companies wanted to become involved. Controls and rationing were slowly ended as world trade expanded. On labour relations Churchill, who was well aware of his small Parliamentary majority and lack of a convincing mandate, wanted to avoid any major disputes. He instructed Walter Monckton as Minister of Labour to follow a generally conciliatory policy. This was possible because the trades union leadership was still moderate and influenced by the wartime experience of co-operation with the Government. Churchill though was worried by some of the actions of the trades unions, especially if they tried to make their strikes effective. He told the Cabinet in September 1953 that he welcomed a committee of enquiry into a strike by the electricians because 'he thought it important that there should be a full public exposure of the new and sinister techniques adopted by this Union in calling out on strike selected workers in undertakings of special importance to the national economy'.[11]

Churchill took even less of an interest in the social field apart from supporting Macmillan in achieving the 300,000-homes target. On education no extra money was provided to cope with a large increase in the school population caused by the immediate post-war 'bulge' in births – the number of schools built fell by twenty per cent as school numbers rose by twenty per cent, and class sizes increased rapidly. His main concern was to lower the school leaving age from fifteen. Within a month of taking office he had raised the subject and in June 1952 did so again when he spotted an article in *The Scotsman* reporting conference speeches advocating that the school leaving age should be fourteen and children should be taught practical and mechanical skills outside school. He told the Minister of Education: 'as you know, the speakers fully represent my view'.[12] On both occasions his views were ignored: he was reminded that it had been the policy of all Governments since 1926 that the school leaving age should be fifteen and his own Government in 1944 had set itself the target of raising it to sixteen.

One issue he felt strongly about in education was the proposal for simplified spelling. When a Private Member's Bill on the subject was published in February 1953, he told the Chief Whip that every step in his power was to be taken to see that the Bill did not proceed. He declared himself willing to see personally any MP opposing it and he wanted to see a list of Conservative MPs prepared to support it. He lamented gloomily: 'The days are coming when it will be considered unsocial and anti-democratic and even snobbish to brush teeth or have clean finger-nails.'[13] He also intervened to help out his friends in the Jockey Club, who were seeking to defer military service for apprentices. He told the Minister of Labour to follow it up 'as I think endless harm, though on a small scale, is being done'.[14]

Churchill remained convinced that the BBC was being subverted by Communists. From the opposition benches he had written to the Government in February 1948 to protest at 'the undue prominence given by the BBC to Communist and neo-Communist speakers'. Two months later he told Herbert Morrison 'His fear was that a nest of Communist sympathisers within the BBC were seeking to organise the propagation of these views.'[15] On his return to power he told Moran the BBC was 'honeycombed with Socialists – probably with Communists'.[16] In May 1953 he wrote to Sir Ian Jacob, who was Director-General of the BBC, to complain that they were using too many prospective Labour Parliamentary candidates as a way of deliberately getting round the formal equal allocation of time to the two main parties. Jacob refused to start monitoring the time given.[17] Later Churchill wrote again complaining that slightly too much time had been given to Labour speakers at the European Assembly meeting in September 1954.

One domestic subject that did rouse Churchill's interest was the level of 'coloured' immigration which had begun on a considerable scale in the late 1940s. At the end of November 1952 he asked for details of the number of coloured people already in Britain, and where they lived and also the number of coloured students. Two days later in Cabinet he specifically asked whether the Post Office were employing many coloured workers, pointing out that if they were, there was 'some risk that difficult social problems would be created'.[18] A fortnight later he was told that the Post Office employed about five hundred coloured workers. He thought the number was 'considerable' and demanded another discussion in Cabinet.[19] On 18 December, under Churchill's influence, the Cabinet set up an enquiry to look at the possibility of preventing any increase in the number of coloured immigrants coming to Britain to seek work and the scope for restricting the number entering the civil service. The various reports took a year to compile. When they were ready in February 1954, Churchill told the Cabinet the 'continuing increase in the number of coloured people coming to this country and their presence here would sooner or later come to be resented by large sections of the British people'.[20] He agreed it was too soon to take action but preparatory work was put in hand to draft deportation powers and severe entry restrictions. There were more discussions in the autumn of 1954, but the Cabinet again felt the time was not yet ripe for action.

Churchill's interest in colonial affairs, although less energetic than before, took the same path as in the past. The policy of the Conservative Government was not to continue in the direction taken by the Labour Government, which had led to India, Pakistan, Ceylon and Israel becoming independent states. Under Churchill no colony was to be granted independence and the objective was to consolidate the Empire and if possible extend white control. In this the Government was following the policy agreed while in opposition. The 1949 statement on imperial policy said that power should not be handed over to 'a small and clamourous political group' out of touch with the masses, the position of minorities (i.e. the whites) needed to be protected, tribal government was important, 'progress must be gradual', some strategic colonies would never become independent and white settlement was to be encouraged in climatically suitable colonies and would come before the rights of 'native peoples' – a reversal of the 1923 declaration that in Kenya native rights came first (something Churchill had always opposed in that colony). On taking power Churchill abolished the Cabinet Committee on Colonial Development and supported Lyttleton's ultra-cautious views. In July 1954 Eisenhower unwisely suggested to him that his political swansong should be a declaration in favour of self-determination and a twenty-five-year deadline for the end of all colonies. Churchill told him, in something of an understatement, 'I am a bit sceptical about universal suffrage for hottentots.'[21]

Internal security in the colonies became of paramount importance. The Communist guerrilla campaign in Malaya was finally defeated, troops were brought into Kenya to deal with the Mau-Mau rebellion and the African leader Jomo Kenyatta was exiled. When two Labour MPs went to Kenya to study conditions there, Churchill sent a secret message to Lyttleton, who was also in the colony at the time, saying 'If you deem the presence of 2 Socialist MPs a danger to Kenya the Governor is of course free to send them home ... You have full freedom to decide.'[22] Lyttleton reassured Churchill that the powers were not likely to be needed – one of the MPs had arrived not wearing a tie and therefore carried little weight. In British Guiana troops were sent in and the constitution suspended when the left-wing leader Cheddi Jagan won the Election. These security actions gave the Government increasing confidence that the Empire could largely be maintained, and white control was indeed extended in parts of Africa. The Central African Federation was established giving effective power to the white minorities in Southern and Northern Rhodesia with the ultimate aim of granting dominion status under white control. Lyttleton also considered a similar scheme for a federation in east Africa that would be controlled by the whites of Kenya.

There was one colony where the Conservatives were left to implement, extremely unwillingly, the policies they inherited. That was Gold Coast, where in 1948–9 decisions had been taken to move towards responsible Government under black politicians. On 12 February 1952 Lyttleton told the Cabinet he would reluctantly have to go ahead with the appointment of Kwame Nkrumah as Prime Minister of Gold Coast. Churchill's first reaction was to write a letter of explanation to the apartheid Government in South Africa, as he thought they would feel threatened by the first black administration in a British colony: 'I hope you recognise that the decisions taken about the Gold Coast are the consequences of what was done before we became responsible.'[23] He was talked out of sending the message. Worried by the thought that if the Governor were absent,

Nkrumah might actually chair the Cabinet, Churchill issued instructions that the Deputy Governor was never to be out of the country in the Governor's absence. In May 1953 the Cabinet agreed to open negotiations to transfer control of the ministries of finance and justice in the Gold Coast to African control only because Lyttleton thought such action was 'inescapable'. Churchill said he would give him support in 'resisting any pressure' for more concessions. In particular, if the Africans wanted responsibility for external affairs or defence, then they would have to leave the Commonwealth.[24]

The status of the Crown and the Commonwealth gave Churchill and the Cabinet considerable cause for concern. In February 1952, after the death of George VI, the Cabinet agreed a revised wording for the proclamation declaring the accession of the new sovereign. In particular, the phrase 'Imperial Crown' was deleted, since, following the end of the Indian Empire, it was no longer thought to be appropriate. Churchill opposed this move as both unnecessary and mistaken. He refused to accept Norman Brook's advice that 'We cannot restore the Empire of the 19th Century by talking as though it still existed' and demanded an investigation of every previous accession proclamation and historical usage of the term 'Imperial Crown'. A long Cabinet paper was prepared as a result but never discussed because Churchill lost interest. A more concrete problem was the status of the Commonwealth now that non-white states had become independent and been included in what had been until then a white men's club. Ministers were keen on the idea of a two-tier Commonwealth, with only the white dominions in the top rank, but officials talked them out of it. Eventually, in Churchill's last months as Prime Minister, the Cabinet agreed that:

> They greatly regretted the course of Commonwealth development which was envisaged ... The admission of three Asiatic countries to Commonwealth membership [India, Pakistan and Ceylon] had altered the character of the Commonwealth, and there was great danger that the Commonwealth relationship would be further diluted if full membership had to be conceded to the Gold Coast and other countries ... It was unfortunate that the policy of assisting dependent peoples to attain self-government had been carried forward so fast and so far.[25]

At this time the Churchill Cabinet also discussed the future development of the Empire. They accepted the view that some colonies – Malta, Aden, Somaliland and Cyprus – would never gain their independence because Britain would need them in perpetuity as strategic bases. Cyprus was to be the new British base in the Middle East and the Cabinet agreed 'we can contemplate no change in the sovereignty of Cyprus ... a containment of the Enosis movement is overdue, and ... this calls for the dispelling of the notion that Her Majesty's Government may allow self-determination for Cyprus.'[26] (That policy was to lead to an ultimately futile military campaign.) Elsewhere they still hoped to create a white-dominated dominion in east Africa and looking ahead over the next twenty years they thought that only the Gold Coast, Nigeria, Malaya, a West Indian Federation and the white-dominated Central African Federation would become independent. For the majority of British colonies the prospect of self-government and independence was considered even more remote, if indeed they ever reached that stage. The Churchill Cabinet badly misread the situation. Within a decade, and before Churchill died, the last attempt to create a white dominion in central Africa had collapsed and virtually every colony was either independent or far advanced along the road to independence.

Churchill largely devoted what little energy he had for Government business to defence and foreign affairs. On defence the British strategic position was in a strange transitional state that temporarily masked its fundamental weaknesses. Thanks to American help, the bulk of the Empire had been reassembled after the war. The defeat of Germany, Japan and Italy meant that the external threat to the Empire was reduced. The United States was prepared to meet what they saw as worldwide Communist subversion and their guarantee to western Europe under NATO reduced Britain's defence burdens in that area and allowed it to concentrate more of its limited resources on extra-European concerns, in particular the maintenance of its position in the Middle East. But, as in the Second World War, Britain remained heavily dependent on US aid, not just Marshall aid for the economy but also military assistance (for which Britain had to account in detail to Congress each year before the next year's provision was forthcoming). The Cabinet committee on the subject did not relish the situation and noted tetchily: 'U.K. dependence on

U.S. economic aid is not in the longer term compatible with our position as a great power with worldwide responsibilities. Nor is it conducive to cordial relations with the United States.'27

The Churchill Government, like its Labour predecessor, was clinging on to the conviction that Britain was still a great power. The problem was paying for the armed forces needed to maintain its world role from a weakened economy and with insufficient reserves to sustain the currency. They inherited a massive rearmament programme agreed by the Attlee Government in the wake of the Korean War. Estimated to cost £4.7 billion (over £80 billion at current prices), it quickly proved far beyond Britain's capabilities. One of Churchill's first actions was to cut back the programme. Even so the new programme (which took up ten per cent of the nation's wealth) envisaged military manpower at 900,000 (nearly three times that of the 1930s), continuing peacetime conscription and a vast array of worldwide commitments. Butler, the Chancellor of the Exchequer, sought to persuade his colleagues that they had only made the minimum necessary cuts: 'We were all agreed when we took office that the defence programme which we inherited was beyond the nation's means ... We are attempting to do too much ... Anything more than the current level of expenditure means moving towards a war economy with radical revision of our social and economic policies.'28

Even at this historically high level of expenditure the British had to cut back on their defence aims. In 1950 Churchill told Attlee that NATO needed at least 70–100 divisions in Europe to deter the Soviets. At their Lisbon conference in early 1952 NATO members agreed to provide large conventional forces, but soon afterwards the Churchill Government had to renege on its commitments. Under the Lisbon agreement Britain was supposed to provide nine divisions on the continent by 1954 yet it only had eleven to cover the whole world. It never reached even half the NATO target. Churchill, living in the past, insisted on re-creating the Home Guard, but few volunteers came forward and the scheme was a failure. As for civil defence generally he wanted to cut back expenditure. He told the Defence Committee in May 1952, 'although it would be wise to do enough to create an impression of activity in civil defence, care must be taken to avoid spending large sums of money on measures which would pay no dividend'.29

One area which was expected to transform strategy was the development of nuclear weapons. Above all it was hoped that possession of the A-bomb would reduce the need for costly conventional forces. Although Churchill had criticised the Labour Government for slow progress in the construction of Britain's own nuclear weapon, he found, once back at No 10, that the programme was on the point of completion. Now he wanted to radically change the policy: Britain should not manufacture its own weapons, as he was convinced that he could re-establish the agreements he had made with Roosevelt during the war. In doing so he ignored the fact that under the 1946 McMahon Act the US was prohibited from exchanging information with other countries, let alone supplying them with actual weapons. In November 1951 he told Cherwell of his idea (essentially another attempted reconstruction of his wartime world) which involved incurring all the expense of developing the new technology without actually going into the production stage:

> I have never wished since our decision during the war that England [sic] should start the manufacture of atomic bombs. Research however must be energetically pursued. We should have the art rather than the article. A large sum of money will have to be provided for this. There is however no point in our going into bulk production even if we were able to. When we go to Washington in January we can, I have no doubt, arrange to be allocated a reasonable share of what they have made so largely on our initiative and substantial scientific contribution.[30]

Later he told Cherwell: 'I am sure when we produce the treaty we made in the war and demand that it shall be published we shall get very decent treatment from Truman.'[31]

Churchill left for the United States on board the *Queen Mary* in a sanguine mood: he expected his meeting with Truman to be like one of his wartime visits to Roosevelt. He did little preparatory work and confided to his doctor: 'I am not so good mentally as I used to be.'[32] His visit to North America lasted for just over a fortnight, taking in Ottawa and an address to Congress as well as discussions with Truman, mainly on defence matters. There was a heated dispute over the American intention to appoint a US admiral as NATO commander in the Atlantic. Churchill wanted the Royal Navy to have the post: for him it was a way of underlining Britain's continued world role and of retaining control over its own immediate sea lanes. He only gave way after long arguments. The appointment of an American admiral was symbolic of the major decline in British naval power that had taken place in Churchill's lifetime from being the largest fleet in the world to it now no longer being responsible for the defence of the waters around Britain. The talks on nuclear matters were equally unproductive from Churchill's point of view. He gained no access to US nuclear information and no agreement to the transfer of the weapons themselves. Neither did he gain the right of joint decision over American use of their nuclear weapons as he seems to have thought possible. He at last began to realise what the restrictions of the McMahon Act really meant – his wartime agreements were no longer valid (and they had been far more restricted during the war than he appreciated). Churchill also raised the question of British control over US nuclear-armed bombers using British bases. The British were worried that, since the USA was still beyond the reach of Soviet bombers, they might suffer nuclear retaliation without having any say in when or how these bombers were used. Attlee had earlier reached an understanding with Truman on the use of these bases. Churchill gained no extra guarantees, just a reaffirmation of the Attlee understanding. He was given some information about the US bombing plan for nuclear weapons on a 'personal basis', as were the chiefs of staff, but it was of little value.

Churchill's trip to see Truman was a major disappointment. He failed to establish a good rapport with the President. Truman, bored by his long monologues, sought to cut them off as quickly as he could. The real problem for Churchill was that he found it difficult to accept the changed nature of the Anglo-American relationship. The United States was now even more dominant than in the latter stages of the war and the Truman administration was simply not prepared to accept the relationship between equals that Churchill wanted to see. Others in the party had a clearer understanding of the situation. Eden's Private Secretary wrote in his diary: 'It was impossible not to be conscious that we are playing second fiddle.'[33] Despite the inauspicious visit, the Churchill Government still hoped to use the Americans to prop up its own position. In June 1952 Eden circulated a paper to the Cabinet on 'Britain's Overseas Obligations'.

It accepted that these obligations went far beyond Britain's resources and warned they could not be reduced without Britain 'sink[ing] to the level of a second-class power'. To try and resolve the dilemma Eden suggested the creation of international defence organisations. 'Our aim should be to persuade the United States to assume the real burdens in such organisations while retaining for ourselves as much political control – and hence prestige and world influence – as we can.'[34]

For the next year the Anglo-American relationship remained cool. However the Election of Eisenhower (the wartime allied military commander) in November 1952 raised Churchill's hopes. He was determined to get together with the new President even before he took office and almost exactly a year after his visit to Truman sailed again on the *Queen Mary* for the United States. There he met Eisenhower and his new Secretary of State John Foster Dulles, whom he disliked on sight, as well as the new American Ambassador to London, Winthrop Aldrich. Churchill made a major effort to insist on Britain's special relationship with the United States. He told Eisenhower that he abhorred the idea that Britain, with its Commonwealth, 'was just one among other foreign nations'. In his view 'The English-speaking world was the hope. We had 80 million whites, which added to their population, was the foundation of all effective policy.'[35]

In his diary Eisenhower recorded his reaction to these ideas. He registered the point that in Churchill's view 'Britain and the British Commonwealth [were] not to be treated just as other nations would be treated by the United States' and he felt: 'Winston is trying to relive the days of World War II'. He thought Churchill 'had developed an almost childlike faith that all of the answers are to be found merely in British-American partnership'. Eisenhower's own view was that even in the war the United States and Britain had not been able 'to direct world affairs from some rather Olympian platform' and that they certainly could not do so now.[36] While he was happy to try and reach general agreement with Britain over issues, he was not prepared for a 'special relationship'. As far as Churchill personally was concerned, he thought, despite personal affection for him, that he should retire and he was saddened and embarrassed by his condition. He agreed to correspond direct with Churchill but their letters, exchanged about once a fortnight, had no great effect because Eisenhower did not believe in personal diplomacy and preferred to work through normal diplomatic channels.

Churchill's bid to re-open the nuclear issue was equally unsuccessful. During his December visit he gave Eisenhower copies of the two wartime agreements (Quebec 1943 and Hyde Park 1944) and hoped that the successful first British nuclear test at Monte Bello in October 1952 would make the United States more willing to exchange information. But the Americans were not impressed: they regarded the British programme as largely a propaganda exercise designed to try and get more information out of them. Given US legislation it was inevitable that Churchill obtained no more information and no agreement that Britain could be given US nuclear weapons. Neither did he obtain any further clarification over American use of their air bases in Britain. He made another appeal later in a letter to the President: 'I am sure you will not overlook the fact that by the Anglo-American base in East Anglia we have made ourselves for the next year or two the nearest, and perhaps the only bull's eye of the target.'[37] But Britain did not gain any greater access to US war plans.

On his return to Britain in February 1953 he wrote to Eisenhower a rather ambivalently worded letter that neatly encapsulated the real power relationship between the two countries. He hoped that 'where joint action affecting our common destiny is desired, you will let us know beforehand so that we can give our opinion'.[38] Churchill's aspirations never changed despite rebuffs from Washington. Dulles reported to Eisenhower a conversation he had with Churchill in April 1954: 'The Prime Minister followed his usual line. He said only the English-speaking peoples counted, that together they could rule the world.'[39]

It was the belief in a special relationship with the United States and also the Commonwealth links that determined the Government's policy towards Europe. In opposition Churchill had often criticised the Labour Government's unwillingness to take the lead in Europe and to join European organisations. In Government he was to be equally, if not more, cautious. Immediately on taking office the Cabinet had to decide what line to take on the emerging European Coal and Steel Community. In opposition Churchill had argued that Britain should take part in the talks and resist any supranational institutions (which were the *raison d'être* of the whole plan). The

Cabinet now agreed that Britain could not join the new community and that no more than an encouraging speech about unity should be made. A week later Churchill circulated his own paper to his colleagues on 'United Europe'. He recalled his 1946 speech in Europe but in private he spelled out what he had not made explicit in public: 'I have never thought that Britain . . . should become an integral part of a European Federation.'[40]

The same attitude was apparent on the plan for the creation of a European Army. In August 1950 at the Council of Europe in Strasbourg Churchill had called for the creation of a European Army as a counterweight to the Soviets. It was to be under a unified command and Britain would play 'a worthy and honourable part'. Typically Churchill had not worked out a detailed plan, but he seemed to envisage a single command structure for an army not integrated below divisional level. For the French, who initially took up the basic idea with some enthusiasm, such a scheme might allow German rearmament as a boost to European defences while at the same time ensuring that the German Army would not be able to operate independently. The scheme they worked out (the Pleven Plan for a European Defence Community) was very different from Churchill's: it depended on close integration of the European armies. As Prime Minister Churchill rejected the Pleven plan, convinced that Britain was still a world power and telling the House of Commons on 6 December 1951: 'we do not propose to merge in the European army'. During his visit to Truman in early 1952 he told Moran: 'I have been doubtful about a European army only because I was concerned with its fighting power. It will not fight if you remove all traces of nationalism. I love France and Belgium, but we cannot be reduced to that level.'[41]

The Churchill Government therefore stood aloof from the moves towards European integration which began with the establishment of the European Coal and Steel Community in August 1952. The British merely sent an observer to its headquarters in Luxembourg. Their main contribution was the so-called 'Eden plan', set out in March 1952, which sought to put both the Coal and Steel Community and the proposed Defence Community under the weak co-operative structure of the Council of Europe. The other European powers saw through the British proposals as a bid to enfeeble both organisations and counter their supranational characteristics and rejected them. Sometimes even discussions in the Assembly of the Council could go too far for Britain. In May 1952 the Cabinet rejected out of hand a resolution of the Assembly for closer economic union between Europe and the Commonwealth. Churchill commented that although the Commonwealth was welcome to show interest in the work of the Council of Europe, 'he would certainly deprecate any project for economic association between Europe and the sterling Commonwealth'.[42]

From 1951 the Government had to deal with a series of foreign policy issues affecting British interests across the globe. During the war Churchill had resented the fact that Britain's influence over operations in the Pacific was minimal. On his return to office he found that Britain was being given almost no say in formulating Far Eastern policy. Privately he did not share the American obsession about the threat posed by Communist China. He wrote in August 1952: 'I do not regard Communist China as a formidable adversary ... I doubt whether [it] is going to be the monster some people imagine.' Nevertheless he thought Britain must keep in step with the United States, and added, 'Do not let us be too hard on the Americans in this part of the world.'[43]

On regaining power in November 1951 he discovered that the British Government, despite having troops deployed as part of the UN force in Korea, had no idea how the United States was handling the armistice negotiations underway at Panmunjon. When the US told Britain that they wanted to take action outside Korea, including a blockade of Soviet ports, if the ceasefire broke down, both Churchill and Eden objected in the strongest terms, but the United States refused to accept the British position and Churchill had to give in. In July 1953, as the armistice negotiations reached a critical point, the Americans came up against major problems in forcing the South Korean leader Syngman Rhee to accept the provisions. Churchill thought the Americans might as well wash their hands of Korea: 'Myself, I think the United States are so powerful that they can afford to be indifferent to a local Communist success.' (This was a severe misreading of the American mood in the McCarthy period.) He concluded 'I would vote for Rhee going to hell and taking Korea with him and would talk to Russia directly on a heavily armed basis.'[44]

British advice was also ignored in the next crisis in the Far East –

the Chinese shelling of the Nationalist-held islands of Quemoy and Matsu in early 1955. Churchill strongly supported the Foreign Office line that the Nationalists should be kept under control (unlike the US, Britain did not recognise the Nationalists) and their forces should be withdrawn from these small, outlying islands and concentrated on Formosa. At the end of January Churchill urged the US President to do just this and 'draw a clear, clean line about Formosa'.[45] Eisenhower rejected Churchill's plea and the British became worried about being dragged into a war with China and possibly the Soviet Union. Churchill vetoed Eden's idea of a visit to Peking to mediate. Almost the last letter he received from Eisenhower before his retirement was one complaining bitterly about the 'mutually antagonistic' attitude of the two countries in the Far East (similar complaints were made throughout the war) and accusing the British of regarding 'Communistic aggression as of little significance to the future of the free world'.[46]

Anglo-American relations were slightly more harmonious in Persia, but the consequence was a marked decline in British influence. In May 1951 the Government of Persia, led by the nationalist Mossadeq, had nationalised the Anglo-Iranian Oil Company (which Churchill had helped to establish before the First World War). It was Britain's largest single overseas asset. The company employed 4,500 British staff at the terminal at Abadan and produced more oil than all the Arab states combined, amounting to almost twenty per cent of the world's production. At the time Churchill, as Leader of the Opposition, was consulted by Attlee and he told the Prime Minister 'he had never thought that the Persian oil fields could be held by force' but 'Abadan Island was quite another matter'.[47] When Mossadeq expelled the British technicians, Churchill publicly condemned this 'scuttle' and implied that he favoured the use of force. However the Government was under strong pressure from the Americans not to do so and they took the case to the International Court instead. Meanwhile Persian oil exports were boycotted and the country soon found itself in a financial crisis.

The Persian problem was discussed when Churchill was in Washington in January 1952. The Churchill Government was content to see Persia slip into chaos as a lesson to others who might try to nationalise British assets but, subjected in their turn to American pressure, like the Attlee Government, they felt they could not use force. The Americans wanted the oil to flow again (they were reluctantly supporting the British boycott) and were more worried about creeping radical influence through the Tudeh Party, which they feared might overthrow Mossadeq. Nothing was settled for the remainder of the year. The new Eisenhower administration appeared more sympathetic to the British position and were prepared to try and overthrow Mossadeq. A joint intelligence operation was agreed but it was largely run by the CIA. Persian Army officers were heavily bribed to provoke anti-Government demonstrations and once the Shah had fled in August 1953 they mounted a coup to restore him to power. With the Shah in power a new oil agreement was negotiated, under which the British lost their monopoly position and were able to keep only a minority stake in oil exports, with the Americans taking the major share. Eventually in October 1954 the British Government accepted compensation for the naitonalisation of their assets totalling £25 million spread over ten years. It was a very poor deal but they felt they had no alternative but to accept because the US was not prepared to support the oil boycott any longer.

After Indian independence the Middle East was seen, both by the Labour Government and by Churchill's, as central to Britain's claim to be a world power. From 1948 the Government was looking for some sort of regional defence pact that would legitimise their military presence, ease their financial burden and involve the United States. The Attlee Government wanted to involve Britain, France, the US and Turkey in the pact but the idea found little favour even with normally compliant Arab regimes because it gave them little role and seemed simply designed to legitimise external influences across the region. The Americans too showed no enthusiasm. Nevertheless the Churchill Government continued Labour's policy of trying to involve the United States in such a pact. Eden told the Cabinet in June 1952:

> It is clearly beyond the resources of the U.K. to continue to assume the responsibility alone for the security of the Middle East. Our aim should be to make the whole of this area and, in particular, the Canal Zone, an international responsibility ... The U.S. have refused to enter into any precise commitments in the Middle East

or to allocate forces, and it should be the constant policy of HMG to persuade them to do so.[48]

Until July 1953, when the Eisenhower administration finally vetoed the idea, the attempt to put together a Middle East pact greatly influenced relations with Egypt, the centre of British influence in the region and a country where Churchill had strong views about the aims of British policy.

Under the 1936 Treaty, which Eden had negotiated, Britain retained substantial control over a nominally independent Egypt. British troops were supposed to withdraw to the Canal Zone (something Churchill always opposed) but during the war the country became a huge military base. In 1946 the Labour Government did withdraw troops to the Canal Zone but retained far more troops than allowed under the 1936 Treaty. The British base there covered over 200 square miles, contained 600,000 tons of stores and employed 75,000 workers but its precise function was difficult to define. The 1936 Treaty was due to expire in 1956 but the Egyptians abrogated it just as Churchill took office.

Churchill, who had strongly opposed all manifestations of Egyptian nationalism since the 1920s, wanted to be tough with them. Using Labour Government plans a major reinforcement of the Canal Zone was carried out. Soon nearly 80,000 British troops were tied up in static defence duties. The Egyptian labour force went on strike and workers had to be imported from Cyprus and Mauritius. Churchill gave vent to his usual contempt for Egyptians when in the middle of December 1951 he told Eden to tell them 'that if we have any more of their cheek we will set the Jews on them and drive them into the gutter, from which they should never have emerged'.[49]

On 25 January 1952 the British Army ordered the surrender of the police barracks at Ismailia, where about 100 regular police were reinforced by over 700 armed auxiliaries. On the direct orders of the Egyptian Ministry of the Interior they refused, fought for the whole day and only surrendered after forty-six of them had been killed. The result was that next day mobs in Cairo attacked and burnt down British- and foreign-owned property, killing twenty people including eleven Britons. Churchill, neglecting the provocation of the British attack on the Egyptian police, was confirmed in his view of the Egyptians. He wrote to Eden: 'The horrible behaviour of the mob puts them even lower than the most degraded savages now known. Unless the Egyptian Government can purge themselves . . . I doubt whether any relationship is possible with them. They cannot be classed as a civilised power until they have purged themselves.'[50] A fortnight later he added that Eden should not be intimidated and 'make what looks like a surrender to violence and evacuation of forces by threats and atrocities'.[51]

Churchill though was unable to stop the Cabinet agreeing to open negotiations with the Egyptians. The British were coming under pressure from the United States to compromise (Truman had refused Britain's request to send US troops to the Canal Zone and make it an international base) but Churchill was insisting that the base should be handed over not to the Egyptians but to some new defence pact organisation which did not exist. The negotiations with Egypt quickly broke down over their claim to the Sudan (which it administered jointly with Britain) and their refusal to accept its independence. The situation was changed by the revolution in late July 1952 which overthrew the Egptian monarchy and replaced it with a military Government. The first impressions of the new regime in London were favourable. Churchill minuted 'I am not opposed to a policy of giving Neguib a good chance provided he shows himself to be a friend' and a week later at the end of August noted, 'The more I read the news from Egypt the more I like the Neguib programme. We ought to help Neguib and Co all we can unless they turn spiteful.' What Churchill meant by 'spiteful' was made clear when he wrote: 'I am quite sure that we could not agree to be kicked out of Egypt by Nahas, Farouk or Neguib and leave our base, worth £500 millions, to be despoiled or put in their care.'[52]

Eden felt that the best way to start was with talks on Sudan, and by early 1953 he had secured an agreement which endorsed the idea of unity but in practice allowed Sudan the final say over whether it wanted to join Egypt when it became independent. When Churchill returned to London after his visit to see the newly-elected Eisenhower followed by a holiday in Jamaica, he was furious about the deal. He spoke of 'appeasement' and commented caustically 'he never knew before that Munich was situated on the Nile'. And he told Colville he 'positively desired the talks on the Sudan to fail, just as he positively hoped we should not succeed in getting into conversations with the Egyptians on defence which might lead to our abandonment of the Canal Zone'.[53] The next day at a ministerial meeting Churchill urged a break with Egypt over Sudan and a simple refusal to quit Egypt before the expiry of the treaty in 1956. He later told his staff that if Eden resigned over the issue, 'I will accept it and take the Foreign Office myself.'[54] He wanted to send troops and aircraft to the Sudan to ensure British control was maintained. But he could not get the Cabinet to agree. Ten days later on 11 February he told them that Eden's agreement 'represented an enormous surrender of our responsibilities in the Sudan and a serious blow to British prestige throughout the Middle East'.[55] He also doubted whether the Conservative Party would support it. The agreement was signed the next day and Eden carried the party with him.

What Churchill saw as surrender over Sudan only increased his determination to oppose Egyptian nationalism to the utmost and refuse any concessions over the Canal Zone. At the Defence Committee on the day he lost the battle in Cabinet over the future of Sudan, he ordered the chiefs of staff to draw up plans to take on the Egyptians. 'The least sign of military activity, whether by the Egyptian Army or by guerrilla forces against us, would be sufficient justification for rounding up and disarming that part of the Egyptian Army which was located in the Sinai Peninsula.'[56] Five days later Eden told the Cabinet that a deal was essential: Britain was in breach of the 1936 Treaty, it could not afford to maintain the canal base and it could not reoccupy Egypt. Churchill disagreed: 'This military dictator is under the impression that he has only to kick to make us run. I would like him to kick us and show him that we did not run.' Only by showing 'that we have imposed our will upon Neguib' did he think it would be possible to sell any deal to the party.[57] Again Churchill was unable to stop the Cabinet agreeing that talks with Egypt should be opened. On 18 February 1953 he frightened the Americans with a message to Eisenhower saying that British forces were ready to enter Cairo and Alexandria 'in order to prevent a massacre of white people'. He went on, 'Our forces are in ample strength to resist any attacks ... Nearly half the effective Egptian Army, about 15,000 men, stands on the eastern side of the Canal watching Israel. They could easily be forced to surrender, perhaps, indeed, merely by cutting off supplies.'[58]

Churchill wanted to bring the Americans into the talks with the

Egyptians but they refused and indeed were edging towards a willingness to arbitrate between the two sides. Churchill thought this development was ominous and therefore decided to show the United States that Britain could get tough. He told Eisenhower at the end of March: 'I have reached my limit. We are neither unable nor afraid to deal with Neguib ourselves.'[59] Then fate gave Churchill the opportunity to impose his views. Eden was taken ill and underwent the first of three operations for gall bladder problems (the first two were botched and a third in the United States was needed to repair the damage). Churchill immediately assumed control of negotiations with Egypt when he took over the Foreign Office. He insisted that the attitude the British negotiators should adopt was that it was the Egyptians who wanted the talks not the British. The day before they started he instructed the chiefs of staff to draw up contingency plans to reinforce Egypt. The first round of talks predictably ended in failure.

In the latter part of May Churchill, still acting Foreign Secretary, personally briefed Robin Hankey (the son of Maurice Hankey) who was leaving for Cairo to become acting Ambassador. He told Hankey that he wanted a minimum twenty-year treaty for British forces to stay in Egypt in some form and 'If H M Embassy did nothing for six months except avoiding giving things away, he would be very happy.' Hankey was advised to be 'a patient sulky pig' and Churchill also made it clear that 'he was not afraid of physical trouble. Although we should not of course say so, he would in some ways welcome it. It would do the Egyptians no sort of good. The Egyptians would come round all right when they found how determined we were.'[60] (Churchill was to be disappointed in Hankey who found he got on well with one increasingly important member of the military government, Gamel Nasser.) This piece of diplomatic advice was the Prime Minister's last contribution on Egyptian affairs for some months.

One of Churchill's main foreign policy preoccupations when he returned to power was the idea of a summit meeting with the Soviet Union and the United States. It was to be a revival of the wartime meetings and a reaffirmation of Britain's role as a world power. Such a meeting would also, Churchill believed, enhance his historical reputation and complement his role as a war leader. Once the Soviet Union had produced its own nuclear weapons he dropped his ideas for a pre-emptive strike and began to advocate talks. (In 1946 he had rejected the idea of holding talks with Stalin on the grounds that it would be like 'going to see Hitler just before the war'.[61]) But in his Election broadcast and one of his speeches during the 1951 campaign and again on taking office he advocated high level talks with Stalin. Then during his visit to Truman in January 1952 he found the Americans totally opposed to the idea and he accepted there should be no movement until the Soviets became more conciliatory. In June 1952 he told his Private Secretary that there might be more chance if Eisenhower became President and that the best opportunity would be under Stalin rather than his successors, who were likely to be worse. When he met Eisenhower in January 1953 he found that the new President favoured a meeting alone with Stalin. Alarmed at the prospect of such an obvious affront to Britain's prestige, he managed to talk the President out of the idea.

When Stalin died on 5 March 1953 Churchill reversed his earlier view and declared that this was the right moment to arrange talks. Less than a week later he suggested this policy to Eisenhower, who proved very cautious. To Eden Churchill suggested writing to Molotov, the Soviet Foreign Minister, to propose a meeting in Vienna. Eden persuaded him to wait and see how the new leadership acted. On 16 April Eisenhower sent Churchill an advance copy of his 'Chance for Peace' speech that held out the hope of talks. This only increased his worry about a bi-lateral American-Soviet summit and he wrote to Eisenhower suggesting a three-power meeting. (He strongly opposed the French being involved.) The American administration remained non-committal. On 4 May he suggested he might make a solo visit to Moscow. Eisenhower immediately raised the threat of a cut-off of US aid and trade restrictions if Britain acted alone. He warned him on 5 May that the effect on Congress 'which is this week taking up consideration of our Mutual Defense Program and extension of our Reciprocal Trade Act would be unpredictable'.[62] Churchill backed down – the episode illustrated only too clearly the conclusion reached by the Cabinet's Mutual Aid Committee a few months earlier: 'no nation can fully maintain its independence if it is receiving subsidies'.[63]

With Eden away ill Churchill tried a different approach. Through Colville and Soames in his Private Office he opened secret talks with the Soviet Embassy in London to explore possibilities, and in a speech in the Commons on 11 May he openly called for a summit meeting. Churchill's initiative caused an immense amount of trouble within both the British Government and the western alliance. His speech was made despite a specific Cabinet agreement on 28 April that there should be no public statements about the idea of a summit. Within an alliance that had been created less than four years earlier on a specific platform of resistance to Communism and greater defence effort (both causes Churchill strongly espoused), this unexpected call to change tack was also highly controversial. Churchill found that it was not easy to change the stance and modify the rhetoric of an alliance just to fit in with his new enthusiasm for dialogue. In the United States, still under the influence of the anti-Communist crusade and where in the recent Election Dulles had called for the liberation of Eastern Europe, Eisenhower was not ready to move away from confrontation and he privately urged Churchill to be more cautious. The French were greatly alarmed at the effect the speech might have on the plans for a European Defence Community and their desire to contain West German rearmament. They also resented Churchill's attempt to exclude them from the summit (Eisenhower was prepared to insist that they should attend any future meeting). Adenauer and the West German Government were alarmed that a deal might be reached over their heads for a reunited and neutral Germany (something that Churchill was quite ready to contemplate).

On 20 May the French Prime Minister, Réné Mayer, suggested to Eisenhower a three-power western summit. The President's preferred venue was Maine but Churchill persuaded them to meet on British territory in Bermuda. Although publicly the idea of the meeting became associated with Churchill, it was in fact a French initiative designed to contain him. Despite one of the frequent political crises that plagued the Fourth Republic, plans went ahead for a meeting on 8 July. Churchill insisted on dealing with all the details, including arrangements for the honour guard that would greet Eisenhower. The President made it clear beforehand that a summit would not automatically follow from the Bermuda meeting and privately used Churchill's old friend Bernard Baruch to pass on the message that he was worried about western unity and the need to continue with rearmament. Churchill was still determined to secure a summit meeting which he believed would be the crowning achievement of his political career. On 2 June he sent a message to

Molotov saying that 'bridges' not 'barriers' should be built between East and West.[64]

It is very doubtful whether Churchill's initiative would have got off the ground. The Americans were strongly opposed to it and the Soviets were clearly unwilling to make major concessions, except perhaps on a united but neutral Germany, which was unacceptable to the rest of the relatively new and fragile western alliance. The strongly bi-polar world of the early 1950s could not be unscrambled simply by Churchill's desire to recreate the personal diplomacy of the wartime period. But the initiative was not put to the test in the summer of 1953. In late June Churchill suffered a major stroke.

Resignation

Churchill suffered his second stroke on the evening of 23 June 1953 during a dinner for the Italian Prime Minister. He was unable to walk and his speech was indistinct (many present simply thought he was drunk). His son-in-law Christopher Soames told Butler that the Prime Minister was 'tired' – the first in a whole series of deceptions. The next day he insisted on chairing a Cabinet meeting but his mouth drooped and he could not use his left arm. His colleagues guessed something was wrong because he was unnaturally quiet. On 25 June the effects of the stroke worsened. He was unable to chair the Cabinet and was hurried away to Chartwell. By that evening most of his left side was paralysed. The next day, as he continued to deteriorate, the Bermuda meeting was cancelled. On 27 June Jane Portal, Butler's niece who worked at No 10, reported: 'He is definitely weaker physically and fell down today. In fact he cannot really walk at all and his swallowing is bad.'[1] At this stage he needed two people to help him walk.

It was clearly necessary to say something to the public about Churchill's condition because his absence was bound to be noticed shortly. Lord Moran, in consultation with an eminent physician, drafted a statement saying:

> The Prime Minister has had no respite for a long time from his very arduous duties and there has developed a disturbance of the cerebral circulation which has resulted in attacks of giddiness. We

have therefore advised him to abandon his journey to Bermuda and to have a month's rest. Sir Winston Churchill had a similar though less serious attack in August 1949 when staying at Cap d'Ail.

It was so reticent as to be deliberately misleading. Even so it was too near the bone for Churchill's immediate entourage. They turned the doctor's statement into the mendacious announcement made to the public:

> The Prime Minister has had no respite for a long time from his very arduous duties and is in need of a complete rest. We have therefore advised him to abandon his journey to Bermuda and lighten his duties for at least a month.

This completely ignored the central fact of his medical condition and also sought to give the impression he was still at work as Prime Minister.

The reason for the deliberate concealment of Churchill's state was his political position. His closest advisers, in particular Colville and Soames, felt that any announcement of a stroke would make his retirement inevitable. Senior members of the Cabinet went along with the concealment because Eden, his acknowledged successor, was still in Boston recovering from his third gall bladder operation and unable to take over. If Eden had been fit, there is little doubt that Churchill would have had to resign. As it was, leadership of the Government was split between Salisbury, Butler and Crookshank.

By the time of his stroke Churchill's leadership was being questioned among his senior colleagues, many of whom thought his retirement was long overdue. On his return to office he had hinted that he would only stay a year. Eden hoped for a quick succession to pre-empt younger rivals, in particular Butler. In April 1952 Churchill had mentioned to Eden that he would go soon and other members of the Cabinet were discussing his forthcoming peerage. By the middle of June, with no sign of his imminent departure, the Chief Whip, Buchan-Hepburn, was deputed to see him and pass on the opinion of some senior members of the Cabinet that he should now retire. Churchill was unreceptive and started making it clear that he intended to stay until after the Coronation in the summer of 1953. Lord Salisbury thought there should be an open confrontation to make Churchill give way to Eden, but other members of the Cabinet were unwilling to force the issue. In December 1952 Eden again pressed him for a date but he remained vague. On holiday in Jamaica in January 1953, Churchill told Colville, 'I think Anthony should have it, but I have not decided when.'[2]

Churchill, just as he had done since 1945, was prepared to exploit his status and dare his colleagues to face the public ignominy of forcing him out before he was ready to go. They in turn were becoming acutely aware of two problems for the Government and the Conservative Party. Churchill was still invested in popular perception with the halo of his wartime leadership. But his actual performance as Prime Minister and party leader was proving a liability rather than an asset. The trend that opinion polls had detected in the late 1940s was still apparent – Churchill did not add to the Conservative vote. Within six months of his taking office, only half the country was satisfied with his performance as Prime Minister and that percentage was dropping steadily. Many Cabinet colleagues shared that view. In January 1953 Crookshank told Eden: 'He was convinced that W was an increasing liability to us, that if he had not been leading us at the General Election we should have had another sixty seats.'[3] But these pressures did not lead to a decisive move against him within the party and events conspired against such action. Stalin's death in early March 1953 made Churchill even keener to stay on and secure a summit and Eden's illness at the end of the month ended any immediate pressure.

Churchill was aware that his hold on power was increasingly tenuous. But he was determined to stay on as Prime Minister. He was never particularly sensitive to others' views and feelings. His life for over fifty years had been taken up with politics and he could not face the end of his career and the emptiness that would follow. His personal staff accepted this selfish view (it also helped preserve their own positions) and Churchill's doctors, in particular Lord Moran, fearing his mental deterioration if he stopped working, felt he should stay in office. When his own interests were at stake, Churchill could be incredibly stubborn and he was simply not prepared to make way for Eden. As Lord Salisbury remarked in July 1953: 'The fact is that the PM is much tougher than Anthony. He very soon brings Anthony to the point beyond which he knows he will not go and then he has won the day.'[4] Nevertheless after his second stroke Churchill only had a few months to prove he was capable of giving at least the appearance of doing the job.

By the end of June 1953 Churchill's medical condition had stabilised and a slow recovery began but he was still confined to bed or a wheelchair. For a month he did no work at all. Papers were sent to Chartwell but decisions were taken by Soames or Colville in Churchill's name and the Prime Minister's true condition was disguised from almost everybody except Eisenhower and the Queen. Churchill left Chartwell for Chequers at the end of July and did a little intermittent work but spent most of his time reading novels (including *Jane Eyre*, *Wuthering Heights* and Trollope), most of which he had never read before. He chaired one Cabinet meeting on 18 August but took almost no part in the discussion; he simply wanted to show he was still in charge. His immediate aim was to be fit enough to address the party conference at Margate in October. In the longer term, he still hoped to go on until the summer of 1954, when the Queen's tour of Australia and New Zealand would be completed. Most of the Cabinet thought he should go in the autumn once Eden, who was now back in Britain, was fully recovered from his operations. But even now they were not prepared to force the issue.

By September Churchill was able to chair a few Cabinet meetings, go to Doncaster races with the Queen and stay at Balmoral. He found the visit so exhausting that it made him depressed about his state and caused him to wonder whether he would be able to continue. In the second half of the month he spent a fortnight at Beaverbrook's villa at Cap d'Ail with Mary and Christopher Soames. At the beginning of October he told Eden he would see how he got on at Margate and during the first Parliamentary occasions and then decide. By the end of the month he had successfully made the Leader's speech at the conference and answered questions in Parliament. He was determined to go on. But his ability to do so now depended on drugs. Since the last years of the war Churchill had needed barbiturates to sleep; now Moran gave him stimulants to get him through every important occasion.

Churchill's first concern that autumn was to resurrect the Bermuda meeting. He found that in his absence western leaders had taken the opportunity to agree a tough negotiating stance with the Soviet Union. No summit was to be held until after ratification of the European Defence Community and elections in West Germany, which it was expected would strengthen Adenauer's position. Talks would be held on a four-power basis (including France) at Foreign Secretary level first and the West's position would be to support a reunited Germany able to join NATO, a condition which would ensure their failure. Throughout the autumn Churchill suggested numerous ideas for seeing the Soviets, all of which were rejected by either Eden or Eisenhower or both. The American President refused to meet Churchill alone and insisted on the French and the Secretary-General of NATO being present. Left with no alternative, Churchill suggested a meeting in Bermuda. He had not wanted the French to attend and sent a calculatedly insulting message of welcome to the French Premier Laniel, saying, 'I am glad to hear from various sources that you are coming to our meeting in Bermuda.' The British Ambassador in Paris refused to deliver it.

On 26 November, ten days before the Bermuda meeting, the Soviets accepted a four-power meeting at Foreign Secretary level in Berlin. Little was expected of that meeting but it gave the Bermuda conference something to discuss. The Foreign Office brief for Bermuda argued for fully incorporating West Germany into the western system and pointed out that since the death of Stalin the Soviets had made no more than 'certain gestures which cost them little'.[5] Churchill was so annoyed by this line that he refused to allow the brief to be circulated to the Cabinet. In fact he refused to read the briefing papers for the meeting on the long flight via Gander, and instead spent his time reading C. S. Forester's novel *Death to the French*, which only reinforced his anti-French views.

The Bermuda conference, spread over four days from 4 December, was a shambles. There was no agenda, Laniel was ill and anyway not on speaking terms with his Foreign Minister Bidault, who was left to undertake all the talks. Churchill was reluctant to talk to the French and left that disagreeable task to Eden while concentrating on relations with Eisenhower. Churchill was in a difficult mood, deliberately arriving late for every plenary session so he could make a grand entrance on his own. Despite his deafness he refused to use a hearing aid. Eden wrote to his wife: 'W hears nothing at the conferences, which doesn't reduce my problems.'[6] Eden's Private Secretary noted other problems for the British delegation in his diary: 'He hardly listens to argument and constantly reverts to wartime and post-war analogies. I was . . . shocked how old, weary and inconsequent he seemed.'[7]

On the first day the three Foreign Ministers accepted the Soviet proposal for a four-power meeting in Berlin and at the same time endorsed Dulles' view that it should be held quickly so that its failure would be obvious and the West could then get on with the job of consolidating its bloc. At the first plenary session Churchill did not press for a summit, as he knew his colleagues would not agree, merely for the opening of contacts. But even this idea produced a storm of opposition. Bidault was very anti-Soviet and Eisenhower likened them to a 'whore' who needed to be beaten 'into the back streets'. When Churchill, in jest, talked about invading the Soviet Union, Eisenhower actually agreed the idea should be studied. Churchill's main contribution was to suggest a 'Locarno'-type agreement for the mutual recognition of existing frontiers – which included the Oder-Neisse line for the western border of Poland (which he claimed in his memoirs he would never have accepted even *de facto* at Potsdam).

The communiqué, when it was finally agreed, was hardline. It said 'if the danger of aggression now appears less imminent we attribute this to the mounting strength of the free world and the firmness of its policies'. The western position for the Berlin talks with the Soviets guaranteed their failure. Churchill complained to Eden that there was 'nothing in this communiqué which shows the slightest desire for the success of the conference or for an easement in relations with Russia. We are going to gang up on them.'[8] He was again finding that the western anti-Communist bloc which he had wanted in the 1940s was not easily going to change direction. The Bermuda conference was generally seen as a failure. It settled nothing on the Soviet proposal for a four-power conference that could not have been agreed through normal diplomatic discussions. The Anglo-American bilateral exchanges were hardly more productive. Eisenhower, worried by Churchill's state of health and determined not to imply there was any 'special relationship', did not tell Churchill that the US had made an H-bomb. Churchill initially agreed with Eisenhower's suggestion that nuclear weapons should be seen 'as a proper part of a conventional armament'.[9] However the rest of the British delegation, especially Eden, understood the sensitive problems this raised for European states (fearful they would in any war rapidly become a nuclear battlefield) and forced Churchill to withdraw his consent to the idea. Churchill was consulted over Eisenhower's 'Atoms for Peace' speech to the UN on 8 December that in public immediately overshadowed the Bermuda meeting. At the end of the meeting Churchill wanted to stay on for an extra day's holiday. When Eden complained that this meant he would have to cancel a number of engagements in London, Churchill's response was, 'To hell with his engagements. He's not running this show.'[10]

By the end of 1953 Churchill's colleagues were seriously concerned about his performance and the problems it was causing for the Government. On 13 December Macmillan met Lord Woolton and another senior colleague David Eccles to discuss the situation. Their conclusion was 'we shall drift on to disaster ... unless Churchill goes'.[11] Just after Christmas there was a secret meeting between Eden, Macmillan and Butler at the Chancellor's house. They were all worried about Churchill's lack of interest in public affairs and his slowness in Cabinet. Macmillan, as the one who was not an immediate rival to Churchill and also one of his closest political friends, was given the difficult task of telling him it was time for him to go. Churchill would only say that he would go before the next Election (that could be held as late as the autumn of 1956) but nothing more concrete.

Ever since 1951 Churchill had not bothered with large areas of Government activity, but now he was reduced to no more than dabbling in a few issues. At the end of October 1953 even Christopher Soames was prepared to admit to Lord Moran, 'he has no zest for work. He does not want to be bothered with anything.'[12] But Churchill did not admit the change in him was so drastic. Early in 1954 he told his doctor: 'I am less keen than I was on the political scene. I don't know where I am ... I told Woolton that I had been reading *The Dynasts* for hours on end. He wondered how I found the time. I explained that I didn't bother about other things as much as I used to do.'[13]

One of the few issues that Churchill did concern himself with after his stroke was negotiations with Egypt. In his absence from office the talks had made considerable progress. By October 1953 the outlines of an agreement were clear. British troops would evacuate Egypt by early 1956 and the stores and workshops at the Canal Zone base would be kept operational by British civilian technicians. Britain would have the right of re-entry into Egypt if the country (or some neighbouring countries) were attacked. Only two major issues remained to be resolved – whether the British technicians could wear uniforms and whether Turkey (a NATO member) would be one of the countries which if attacked would allow British troops to re-enter Egypt. For Churchill this new agreement would mark the conclusion of eighty years of history – it would end the British occupation that he had seen at first hand in the 1890s and had fought to preserve ever since.

Churchill realised that he could not unscramble everything that had been done in his absence. Instead he wanted to stand firm on the remaining issues and hope that this would lead to a total breakdown in the talks and thus ensure continuing British occupation. He insisted that the wearing of uniforms by the technicians was 'a matter of cardinal importance to us' – it was for the Egyptians too because of its symbolic value.[14] He tried once again to persuade the Americans to run the Canal base as a joint international effort. When Eisenhower refused, Churchill told him his actions could cause 'a deep and serious setback' to Anglo-American relations.[15] He was more successful in convincing the President to withhold American economic aid until Egypt came to an agreement. He did so by warning of dissent on the Conservative backbenches. The danger was, he told Eisenhower, 'that the offended Conservatives might add their voices to that section of the Socialist party who criticize the United States' and that the 'increasingly angered section' of the Conservatives might 'cancel our modest majority'.[16] What Churchill did not tell the President was that he was working secretly to try and achieve exactly that end. He was encouraging the 'Suez group', which opposed Government policy, to continue with their opposition and wrote them supportive letters whenever they attacked Eden.

At the end of 1953 Churchill told Eisenhower that Britain would act 'in accordance with what we think are our long-term interests'.[17] This he interpreted as meaning no agreement with Egypt. He wanted to try and force the Egyptians to break off the talks and possibly even to attack the British. He said 'It has been my constant fear – that the Egyptians might accept. If they attack us, that would be war, and you can do a lot of things then.'[18] But he was under pressure to be more conciliatory. The Treasury wanted more defence cuts and the canal base cost £56 million a year (about £800 million at today's prices) to maintain. The chiefs of staff wanted an agreement as the prelude to re-deployment elsewhere in the Middle East. Churchill reluctantly accepted that argument but insisted to Eden 'we are not animated by fear or weakness, but only by the need of making a better redeployment of our forces, and . . . in any case we are not going to be in any hurry'.[19]

Churchill thought he had his last chance to torpedo an agreement early in 1954. At the end of February it seemed as though Nasser would become the most important figure in Egypt's military leadership. Churchill was pleased at the prospect. He thought Nasser was 'much worse. That's the point. Perhaps he will bring it to a head. I have been afraid they might agree.'[20] At the beginning of March, following riots in Khartoum, he wanted to occupy the city immediately, saying 'You will never have such an opportunity again', but his orders to do so were stopped by Eden.[21] A fortnight later he was still arguing for sending the Army into the Sudan, keeping 10,000 troops in the Canal Zone and ending the Anglo-Egyptian negotiations. In practice Churchill's views were regarded as little more than an irritant within the Government, where there was a general consensus on the need for an agreement with Egypt. In June Eden put a paper to the Cabinet on the British position for the last round of negotiations. Nasser had made major concessions and accepted a seven-year agreement giving Britain the right to reactivate the base if Turkey or any Arab state were attacked (other than by Israel). In return Britain was prepared to agree to the technicians in the Canal base not wearing uniform. Churchill, who had consistently fought any concession to Egypt since the early 1920s, reluctantly accepted an agreement but for him it was a wrench to give up another part of the Empire and he spoke of 'the political disadvantages of abandoning the position which we had held in Egypt since 1882'.[22]

In 1954 Churchill presided reluctantly over another diminution of the imperial world he had known – the return of the Royal Navy's base at Simonstown to the apartheid Government of South Africa. When it was first suggested by the Commonwealth Relations Office in late 1951, he was instrumental in securing the rejection of the idea in the Defence Committee. He told his colleagues that the base was 'an essential link in Imperial communications', that he would resist any South African pressure and that before anything could be agreed there would have to be 'an unqualified assurance that facilities would be available to us in both peace and war'.[23] The next year, when the Admiralty suggested closing the base to save money, Churchill, still obsessed with imperial defence, wrote: 'it would be more reasonable to shut down Portsmouth'.[24]

The matter hung fire until the visit to Britain in August 1954 of the South African Defence Minister, when assurances were given on all the points that concerned the British, including the exemption of the base from the apartheid laws. Churchill fought unavailingly against the deal. He argued world conditions had worsened since 1951 and there was no case for giving South Africa control over the base: 'To weaken our rights over Simonstown as settled in Treaty by me and Smuts in 1921 and in 1930 is a very serious step. To do so at the same time as we are giving up the Suez Canal in fact is cutting off the remaining link between Britain and Australia and New Zealand.'[25] He told the Cabinet he 'would find it hard to reconcile himself to its surrender'[26] and 'he was reluctant to contemplate any transaction which would be represented as yet another surrender of the rights and responsibilities of the United Kingdom'.[27] But, as so often in the past, he had to give way and accept another manifestation of the decline of British power.

In the summer of 1954 the Cabinet made an effort to reassert Britain's position as a great power by deciding to produce the H-bomb. The theoretical physics behind this weapon, with a destructive potential far greater than the A-bomb developed during the war, had been known for some years but the effort required seemed too much for Britain. Cherwell told Churchill in late 1952 that the H-bomb was 'quite beyond our means'.[28] In fact Britain was only capable of manufacturing a tiny number of A-bombs – the first operational bomb was not delivered until December 1953 and in the middle of 1954 the stockpile was about four weapons. By then both the US and the USSR had exploded test H-bombs, though this fact was not announced by the Americans until March 1954. At the Bermuda conference before this announcement Churchill had told Eisenhower that Britain would not work on the H-bomb.

Just six weeks after the American announcement the Cabinet Committee on Atomic Energy, chaired by Churchill, agreed to purchase certain key materials such as thorium and build a heavy-water plant, both needed for H-bomb production. On 16 June the Defence Committee, again with the Prime Minister in the chair, agreed that Britain should manufacture H-bombs. Churchill then raised the question informally at the Cabinet on 7 July and told his colleagues 'we could not expect to maintain our influence as a World Power unless we possessed the most up-to-date nuclear weapons'.[29] Many of his colleagues were surprised that Britain was considering production without the Cabinet having been consulted. They asked for time to think about the issues. A full discussion was held the next day when some members of the Cabinet argued Britain could not fight the Soviet Union without the United States and therefore reliance should be placed on US nuclear weapons. Others thought 'unless we possessed thermo-nuclear weapons, we should lose our influence and standing in world affairs'.[30] The final decision was made on 26 July – Britain would make a last effort to survive as a world power, as the minutes recorded: 'The Cabinet agreed that in order to preserve our position as a leading military Power and to maintain our influence in world affairs it was necessary we should possess a stock of the most up-to-date thermo-nuclear weapons.'[31]

The other major defence issue in the summer of 1954 was brought about by the failure of France to ratify the treaty establishing the European Defence Community (EDC) and the need to devise some other mechanism for the defence of western Europe which would also resolve the question of West Germany's future. Churchill was not convinced about the case for the rearmament of West Germany or its integration into the western defence and economic system. On many occasions he was attracted by the idea of the reunification and neutralisation of Germany. Such a solution was anathema to the West German Government and in particular its leader Adenauer. Both the Americans and the Foreign Office supported Adenauer's position – Churchill did not.

Churchill's strongest interest in the idea of German reunification came during the summer of 1953. Yet when the Soviet Army put down demonstrations against Communist rule in East Germany and East Berlin in June 1953, he appeared to accept their right to enforce control in their zone and objected to the strong protest issued by the Foreign Office. He wrote: 'Is it suggested that the Soviets should have allowed the Eastern Zone to fall into anarchy and riot? I had the impression that they acted with considerable restraint in the face of mounting disorder.'[32] It was Churchill's plans for a summit meeting with the Soviet Union that raised Adenauer's fears that he would do a deal on the future of Germany over the heads of the West German Government. Facing elections in the autumn, the West German leader moved to secure his position. He went to Washington and obtained American support and then persuaded the Bundestag to pass a resolution that a united Germany would have to belong to NATO and that it would not recognise the Oder-Neisse line. When Churchill learnt of this he was annoyed that the Germans might be trying to decide their own future and wrote: 'But *we* won the War did we not? Unconditional surrender . . .'[33]

In an undated memorandum written around this time, Churchill set out his vision of the future of Germany. He was not worried by the prospect of a united country of 70 million rather than 50 million people and he did not believe the Communists would rule a united Germany. He expected the EDC to fail and following that German unification to become a possibility. He wanted the western powers to offer unity before the Soviets did. Churchill was clearly edging towards the 'Austrian solution' for Germany – a reunified but neutral state. This went against the whole drift of western policy at this time, which was to harden the divisions of Europe and incorporate West Germany into existing defence and economic structures.

When the EDC finally collapsed in August 1954 Churchill was unable to influence the final outcome. Now he dropped the idea of German reunification and wanted instead to abandon the French and organise an Anglo-American-German alliance. He thought the French were a disgrace – 'We picked them out of the gutter and now they think of nothing but themselves all the time.'[34] It was Eden who through some astute diplomacy was able to set up a series of interlocking agreements which incorporated Germany into NATO, accepted their voluntary renunciation of certain types of weapons, assuaged France through the creation of the Western European Union and the stationing of British forces in Germany (ostensibly against the Soviet threat but also as a way of reassuring the French about any future German aggression). Churchill played little part in Eden's diplomatic triumph. He also had a minimal role in Eden's other diplomatic success – the Geneva conference on Indochina that extricated the French from a calamitous war, divided Indochina, neutralised the states of Laos and Cambodia and stopped the United States from intervening. The agreement did not provide a long-term solution but at the time it was regarded as a major achievement.

During 1954 what little energy Churchill had for politics was concentrated on a last despairing effort to achieve a summit. After the Bermuda conference the four-power meeting of Foreign Secretaries went ahead in Berlin for three weeks from the end of January 1954. Predictably it ended in deadlock. In the middle of the meeting both Churchill and Eden were alarmed by a dramatically worded message from Eisenhower talking of 'atheistic materialism in complete domination of all human life' and taking strength from God to 'sharpen the sword for the struggle that cannot possibly be escaped'.[35] This only encouraged Churchill to try to set up a summit meeting. Through Soames he opened discreet communications with the Soviet Embassy in London and obtained assurances that the leadership would be prepared to meet him. On 22 April he proposed to Eisenhower that he should come to Washington for a series of discussions on various issues. Eisenhower was unenthusiastic about the prospect but reluctantly agreed. Churchill did not tell the Cabinet about the meeting until early June when all the arrangements were complete. They insisted that Eden must accompany him.

Churchill was in the American capital from 25 to 29 June. Much of the time he spent reminiscing at length. On 25 June at lunch with Eisenhower, who was once again embarrassed by his guest's condition and the need to keep shouting at him, Churchill dwelt on the Hapsburg and Ottoman Empires, the Kerensky Goverment in Russia, the Boer War and the Second World War. Later that afternoon there was 'a prolonged and rather emotional discussion' about Egypt, with Churchill speaking of 50,000 British graves in the country.[36] His rhetoric failed to persuade the Americans to help Britain maintain its position in Egypt. The main topic of discussion was a possible summit. Churchill was still keen to talk to the Soviets before the western alliance had solidified with the incorporation of West Germany either through the EDC or some other mechanism. He was still attracted by the idea of a unified and neutralised Germany. He began by proposing that he and Eden should go to Moscow in July, with the possibility of a further meeting in London. Eisenhower refused to accept such an idea or any meeting on Soviet-controlled territory. He wanted the first moves (if there were to be any) made through diplomatic channels, with France included (always anathema with Churchill because it went against his attempt to equate Britain's status with that of the US and USSR). Additionally Eisenhower wanted any meeting to discuss only European affairs (further demoting Britain's position) and for any meeting to be prepared by Eden and Dulles first. (The latter was even less enthusiastic about summitry than the President.)

On 26 June Churchill shifted his position and proposed a meeting in London of the main western European powers, with Eisenhower present at the start, as a first step towards a summit. He told the President, 'I swear to you that I will not compromise you in the slightest.'[37] But the next day he told Dulles he was still thinking of going to Stockholm to meet the Soviets as a preliminary to a three-power meeting. Dulles was strongly against this. By the time Churchill left Washington for Ottawa no clear decision had been reached, but he can have been left in no doubt about the strength of American opposition to any meeting with the Soviet leadership either bilaterally or in a three-power format and about the fact that Eisenhower expected to be consulted before any move was made.

During the return journey to Britain on the *Queen Elizabeth*, Churchill seized the opportunity to practise the political cunning he had acquired over fifty years; his aim was to present both the rest of his Cabinet and the American administration with a *fait accompli*. His actions were to nearly break up the Government. On 2 June he and Eden had a long row over whether a message should be sent to Molotov suggesting a meeting. Eden opposed the idea – he believed such a meeting would almost certainly be unproductive and its main consequence would be disruption of the western alliance. Churchill put forward what he described as a 'compromise'. If he could send the message and arrange to go to Moscow in August, he would retire in September. Eden agreed on condition that the Cabinet was consulted first. But Churchill knew the Cabinet would not agree because the Americans were opposed to the idea. Over a weekend he sent Butler, who was temporarily in charge of the Government in Churchill's and Eden's absence, the draft of a message intended for the Soviet leadership. He very carefully did not ask Butler to obtain Cabinet approval. Before Butler could send a reply, Churchill followed up with another telegram asking whether the message to Molotov had been sent on yet. Butler then allowed the message to be despatched. Churchill's hope was that once the Soviets had accepted a meeting it would be difficult for his colleagues and the Americans to reject it.

When the Cabinet met on 7 July there was uproar. (The record of the discussion is regarded as so sensitive that it is still not available to the public after nearly forty years.) It is clear, however, that there was a chorus of complaints and probably threats of resignation led by Eden, Salisbury and Crookshank prompted by Churchill's high-handed attempt to bounce the Cabinet. Outside the Cabinet the two Junior Ministers at the Foreign Office, Selwyn Lloyd and Anthony Nutting, were on the point of resignation over the failure to consult the Americans. Eden and Butler were strongly criticised as weak in letting themselves be manipulated by Churchill. Eisenhower, who had discovered what was happening, sent a message of protest, complaining that he had expected to be consulted. Churchill was forced by the Cabinet to do what he not done before: consult the President. Later that day Molotov replied, accepting a meeting in principle, but by this stage there was no longer any prospect of imposing a *fait accompli*. After another major row in the Cabinet the following day Churchill continued his retreat, realising that unless he did so he would face a number of resignations and probably the end of his career in the worst possible circumstances. In further correspondence with Eisenhower, he agreed not to go to Moscow and to ask for a Soviet gesture before any meeting – probably agreement to an Austrian peace treaty. On this basis the Cabinet eventually agreed to wait and see how matters developed.

On 20 July Eden secured agreement on Indochina at the Geneva conference and this inspired Churchill to try once again for a summit. On 23 July there was another furious argument in Cabinet: Salisbury was threatening to resign while Churchill was saying he would appeal to the country over the heads of his colleagues. The Cabinet refused to allow him to send any more 'personal' messages to Moscow. The next day the argument was defused by the arrival of a Soviet note suggesting a European collective security treaty. This was such an obvious attempt to disrupt the western alliance that Churchill accepted that any idea of an initiative was dead and he withdrew his proposal for a summit meeting. But he reverted to it again in August after he felt he had been upstaged by Attlee, who visited Moscow on his way to Peking. But at the end of the month, after the French rejected the EDC, he accepted that nothing could be done on a summit until a new defence structure was firmly agreed. That process was likely to take months, and when it was complete the Federal Republic would be part of the western alliance and any chance of a summit agreement much reduced. It was also unclear whether Churchill would be able to cling on to office that long.

Although Churchill could rouse himself into periodic bursts of activity for the few issues that meant a great deal to him, it was becoming increasingly apparent to others that he simply was not up to the job. Early in March 1954 one of Churchill's secretaries thought he was 'getting senile and failing more and more each day' yet she recognised 'It is impossible for him to resign, because he can no longer write, dreads solitude and oblivion, fears rest.'[38] That month Crookshank described him as 'ga-ga'[39] and Eden too used the same expression, saying, 'This simply cannot go on; he is gaga; he cannot finish his sentences' and adding he was 'taking nothing in'.[40] In March Churchill told Eden that he would go in May or possibly the end of the summer but, like all his other promises to retire, it was soon forgotten once he faced up to the reality of losing power. In early April he made a very poor speech in the Commons attacking Attlee and the 1945–51 Labour Government for going back on the Quebec agreement on the atomic bomb. To most MPs this speech seemed to be living in the past. An opinion poll that month showed that less than half the country were satisfied with his performance as Prime Minister.

None of this influenced Churchill; he was determined to stay in office. On 13 April he called a meeting of senior colleagues to discuss possible Election dates (the party wanted to go to the country soon and secure a bigger majority before the economic boom collapsed). Even Churchill seemed to accept that he could not lead the party into the next Election, but he told them he firmly intended to have a fourth year in office before then (which implied he would stay on into 1955) and recalled the fact that Gladstone was still Prime Minister at the age of eighty-two (which suggested retirement in late 1956 or even 1957). Ten days later he dropped one of his hints that he might retire in the summer if he were not pressurised, but when Eden wrote to him in early June suggesting a hand-over at the end of the month, Churchill argued he could not go now because of the talks with Eisenhower about a possible summit and mentioned

September as a possibility. When his plans for a meeting with the Soviet leaders failed to win the support of either the Cabinet or the Americans, he refused to fulfil his part of the agreement he had made with Eden on board the *Queen Elizabeth* (to retire if Eden went along with the initiative).

By this stage even Churchill's main supporters thought he should go. On 18 June Macmillan, who had been close to him since the 1920s, wrote and told him he should go before the summer recess. Churchill merely replied that he was aware of his views. A month later Macmillan saw Clementine and both were convinced that Churchill must now retire. Churchill immediately summoned Macmillan to No 10 and told him that he intended to continue as Prime Minister and that the party was welcome to try and force him out – he guessed they would not dare and they didn't. Macmillan, in despair, wrote in his dairy:

> All of us, who have really loved as well as admired him, are being slowly driven into something like hatred. Yet we know that illness has enormously altered and worsened his character. He was always an egoist, but a magnanimous one. Now he has become almost a monomaniac ... It breaks my heart to see the lion-hearted Churchill begin to sink into a sort of Petain.[41]

After the failure of his last attempt to secure a summit Churchill did even less work – by now the Government was virtually operating without a Prime Minister apart from his taking the chair at Cabinet meetings. He spent most of his time playing cards with Colville and Soames, reading the newspapers or sleeping. He was reluctant to read official documents or sign papers. He was still drinking prodigiously – even while shaving in the morning, and before lunch he would drink the champagne. The American Ambassador reported to Washington in June 'he has good days and bad days but the former are becoming rarer'.[42] And Moran wrote in August of 'Winston's advancing decrepitude. The fact is he is in poor shape.'[43]

Yet despite his increasingly apparent inability to carry out the tasks of the Prime Minister, in August 1954 he began to talk of leading the party into the next Election. As an accomplished politician, he began to involve Butler in discussions about his future, since Butler had an interest in Churchill staying on and the succession skipping over Eden. Churchill held talks with his Chancellor and Lord Woolton in mid-August. He now put forward the argument that if there was to be an early Election, there would not be time for a new leader to establish himself and he should therefore lead the Conservatives at that Election, perhaps in the spring of 1955. Butler supported this line. Soon afterwards Macmillan lunched with Churchill at Chartwell and again tried to persuade him to retire but again his advice was rejected. (Macmillan wanted Eden to succeed to give himself more time to become established as the main rival to Butler.) Churchill then wrote to Eden (a letter vetted by Butler) telling him he would not resign and offering him a move to home affairs. At a meeting with Churchill on 27 August, Eden declined to move from the Foreign Office but, as always, accepted Churchill's decision.

At the party conference at Blackpool in early October Churchill gave no sign of any intention to retire. He told Moran, 'I think I can harangue the bastards for fifty minutes.'[44] But Moran's drugs could not produce an adequate performance. The speech, badly delivered and full of mistakes and mispronunciations, left a poor impression even on a docile audience. Soames' reaction was to advise him to go before he damaged his reputation. Churchill's next move was to reshuffle the Government, promoting Macmillan to the Ministry of Defence and bringing his son-in-law, Duncan Sandys, into the Cabinet. Even chairing Cabinet meetings now seemed beyond his failing powers – in December he took charge of just two of the seven meetings and his own contributions were embarrassingly irrelevant. In public too he gave another disastrous performance, in a speech in his constituency on 23 November. He made the astonishing claim that at the end of the war he had instructed Montgomery to store German Army weapons and be ready to use the defeated Wehrmacht against the Soviet Union. He said later he thought the telegram was in his memoirs (it wasn't) and no trace of such a message could be found. Churchill finished up apologising to the Commons for what he had said.

Churchill was eighty at the end of November 1954 – the first time since Gladstone that a British Prime Minister had reached that age in office. He expressed concern about the purposes of a commemorative fund that was being organised by several national newspapers. Although he was now very wealthy, he wanted the money for his own use and objected to it being used to establish a charity. He told Moran, 'If it's for me, so that I can do what I want with it, I would like it very much. But I don't want them to raise a sum for charity just to bring some coloured gentleman from Jamaica to complete his education. I'd rather they did nothing.'[45] To mark the occasion Parliament had commissioned a portrait by Sir Graham Sutherland. During the sittings at Chequers in August and September Clementine wrote to her daughter Mary Soames: 'no one has seen the beginnings of the portrait except Papa & he is much struck by the power of his drawing'.[46] However when the work was complete Churchill objected strongly – he told Moran it was 'Filthy. I think it is malignant.'[47] After the official ceremony the portrait was hidden away and within about eighteen months destroyed by Clementine. (This was not the first portrait of Churchill she had destroyed. She did the same to one by Sickert in 1927 and also to one by Churchill's friend, Paul Maze, which President Roosevelt had at his home.) Nothing was said in public about the fate of the painting until after Clementine's death.

The mounting feeling within the Government over Churchill's failure to retire reached a climax three weeks after the public well-wishing and congratulations of the eightieth birthday celebrations. After the Cabinet on 15 December Eden, Woolton and Salisbury discussed the pressing need to finally settle Churchill's retirement date. On 21 December Churchill told Eden that he thought of going on until the summer of 1955, possibly after a spring Election. Eden, fortified by his colleagues, got him to agree to a wider discussion of the position at the next day's Cabinet meeting. The discussion was ostensibly about Election dates but in practice about Churchill's retirement. Churchill stuck to his latest idea of retirement in June or July 1955. Eden said that was not long enough before an autumn election to give him time to establish himself. Rounding on his colleagues, Churchill accused them of wanting him out of office. No-one denied the accusation. He then threatened to resign and tell the country he had been forced out or alternatively they could all resign and he would call an Election but make it clear he had not wanted it. In the face of Churchill's obduracy there was little that the Cabinet could do. Eden recorded in his diary that the rest of Cabinet were fed up with Churchill pursuing 'a course of such utter selfishness' and that they were 'unanimous about drawling Cabinets, the failure to take decisions, the general atmosphere of *aprés moi le déluge*'.[48]

Nevertheless by early in the new year Churchill seemed at last to realise he could not maintain his position against the strength of feeling within the party. Two factors were concentrating their minds and increasing their pressure on Churchill: they were desperate to hold an Election in the spring or early summer before the economy ran into trouble and Churchill's mental and physical condition continued to deteriorate. On 7 January 1955 he talked to Macmillan about going by Easter, and Macmillan made no attempt to dissuade him. Early in February he also told Eden he would go by Easter and at the end of the month he told Macmillan he would depart on 5 April. Not surprisingly Macmillan did not believe him, but Churchill had in fact finally given in and had actually made arrangements for the Queen to dine at No 10 on the evening before he planned to resign. Early in March some members of the Cabinet were told of the date for the retirement.

Yet in the second week of March, only days before the agreed date, Churchill drew back. Eisenhower had just proposed visiting Europe for the tenth anniversary of VE Day in May, combining it with celebrations for the ratification of the Western European Union and a four-power meeting with the Soviets at Foreign Minister level. Churchill, grasping at straws, decided that this move opened the way to a summit and he told Eden on 13 March that he was withdrawing his offer to retire. At the Cabinet on 14 March he made it clear he wanted to continue. Eden blurted out, 'I have been Foreign Secretary for 10 years. Am I not to be trusted?' Churchill told him bluntly he could resign if he liked. Macmillan commented afterwards that it was 'the most dramatic, but harrowing discussion at which I have ever been present'.[49] The senior members of the Cabinet (Salisbury, Butler, Crookshank, Woolton and Macmillan) decided that Churchill could not be allowed to change his mind again. The US Ambassador was informed of the Government's plans to hold a General Election immediately after Churchill's retirement in early April and asked him to persuade Eisenhower to postpone his visit. Eisenhower, fully alert to the need for Churchill to go, co-operated by putting off his visit. He told Dulles they could not 'let that man act indecisively again'.[50]

Eisenhower's postponement of his visit and confirmation of his continuing opposition to any immediate summit put paid to that particular bid by Churchill to prolong his premiership. On 17 March he confirmed his intention to go on 5 April. The rapidly approaching end of his public life plunged him into a state of complete apathy. He did nothing – one of his secretaries reported, 'He has given up reading the newspaper and sits about staring into space.'[51] He began to hate Eden for, as he saw it, driving him from office. On 28 March he glimpsed another opportunity to postpone the dreaded moment. With the budget due, two national strikes in progress (newspapers and docks) and a favourable reference by Marshal Bulganin to a possible summit, he told Colville 'He could not possibly go at such a moment just to satisfy Anthony's personal hunger for power.'[52] The next day he sent Butler to Eden to tell him that the timetable for the hand-over had to be changed. He threatened to call a party meeting and demand a vote of confidence (he had made a similar threat during the crisis in the middle of the month) and he mentioned to the Queen that he might postpone his retirement. On 30 March at the Cabinet he tried to discuss possible Election dates as though he would be in charge. However, the Cabinet were united in refusing to discuss these ideas and by that evening he had reluctantly and bitterly come to accept the inevitable. On 31 March he confirmed to the Queen that he would indeed go. On 1 April, at a party at No 10 for Clementine's seventieth birthday, he told Moran, 'I don't want to go, but Anthony wants it so much.'[53]

Churchill began to make preparations. He undertook a television test for a resignation speech but the results were so bad that he abandoned the project. He drafted a last letter to Eisenhower which reverted to his life-long theme of the Labour Party's unsuitability to hold power. He wanted to tell the President:

> It will in many ways be a disaster to most of the causes with which we are both concerned if the Socialist Party in its present feebleness and disarray should again obtain what might be a long lease of power in Britain. I do not feel sure that our national vitality and wisdom would survive the event and the impression it would make on the world.[54]

The letter was not sent. On 3 April he held a farewell dinner for the Cabinet. The next evening he gave a dinner at No 10 for the Queen and the Duke of Edinburgh. Among those present were Clement Attlee and Neville Chamberlain's widow; Randolph, as so often, was drunk. Churchill was still feeling bitter. He told Moran, 'Things are not very friendly – it is difficult to be friendly at the top. There is a clash of interests.'[55] He was also ungracious about his successor's abilities, saying, 'I don't believe Anthony can do it.'[56]

Churchill's last day in power was 5 April 1955. At noon he chaired his last Cabinet meeting, a purely formal affair. Then he went to Buckingham Palace to resign where another formality was played out. Before this last meeting with the Queen Colville had suggested that a Dukedom should be created for Churchill. The Palace opposed making Churchill a Duke and were only prepared for the Queen to make the offer if they knew beforehand that it would be declined. Colville had then taken discreet soundings and felt confident Churchill would not accept a hereditary peerage so as not to damage the political prospects of his grandson (Randolph's son, Winston). The Queen duly made the offer and Churchill duly declined. He had felt strongly tempted to accept and go to the House of Lords. What he decided to do was to stay a member of the House of Commons for a short while and he was hopeful that the Queen would renew the offer later. On his return from the Palace to No 10 Churchill held a party for his staff and then left for Chartwell. His political career that had spanned more than fifty-five years was over.

29

The Bleak Years

For the whole of his adult life Churchill had played the game of politics and filled as much of his time as possible with activity in order to try and stave off the depressions to which he had been subject since the mid-1890s. Now he had to face a future without this mental crutch. His dread of boredom and depression had been one of the major reasons why he had clung to power far beyond the point where he could make a reasonable contribution as Prime Minister. It was also the reason why Lord Moran, who feared the effect of retirement on his patient, had encouraged him to stay in office. Churchill, who always claimed he had no fear of death, only of incapacity, wanted to die quickly once he renounced power and political stimulus. He told Moran in December 1954 as he began to face the terrible reality of retirement, 'I shall die quickly once I retire. There would be no purpose in living when there is nothing to do.'[1] But his strong constitution, which had coped with years of high alcohol intake and a generally unhealthy lifestyle, refused to let him die.

Churchill's first resort was to go abroad. As was his usual custom, he got together a party to accompany him and headed for the Mediterranean. Within a week of his resignation he flew to Sicily with Clementine, Cherwell and Colville for a holiday at the Hotel Villa Politi outside Syracuse. It was not a success – the late-spring weather was bad – he managed only a little painting and spent about eight hours a day playing cards. He returned to Britain for the

Election which Eden had called almost immediately on taking office, once an imprudent tax-cutting budget had been introduced. Churchill offered to make a party political broadcast but when Eden, naturally determined to be his own man after fifteen years in the understudy role, declined, he was confined to making a few speeches in his own constituency and for Christopher Soames in Bedford. Eden led the Conservatives to an increased majority over Labour and his predecessor returned to sit on the backbenches.

Churchill had no interest in carving out a new role for himself as an elder statesman on the backbenches. Although he remained an MP for nine and a half years after his resignation as Prime Minister, he refused to make a single speech and only rarely went to the House of Commons. At first he turned to finishing the work on his *History of the English Speaking Peoples*. The great bulk of the manuscript had been completed in 1939 and then put aside. Churchill did not return to it until 1953 when work on the war memoirs was complete. He brought in Alan Hodge, editor of *History Today* (which was owned by Brendan Bracken), and he in turn recruited a group of young historians. Hodge decided to restructure the work and abolish the framework Churchill had adopted based on the reigns of kings. New material was provided by noted historians such as Jack Plumb, Joel Hurstfield and Alan Bullock.

Churchill's personal contribution was mainly made after the 1955 Election, when he worked for a short while each day, polishing drafts prepared by his assistants. He made a few suggestions of his own but as his main researcher for the war memoirs, Bill Deakin (who did some work on this project too), told Moran, 'he hasn't any longer the energy to handle great masses of material'. His assessment was that Churchill's contributions were 'frankly not of much value'.[2] The work was finished in early 1957 and the four-volume history was published between April 1956 and March 1958. It sold because of Churchill's name rather than its historical value. Although a large number of historians had been used to assemble and check the facts, the interpretation remained Churchill's, as written in the 1930s and already decades out of date even when he wrote it. The work is mainly of interest for what it confirms about his lifelong view of the significant factors in history. He lays particular emphasis on the role of wars as positive factors. The books contain little about underlying social and economic forces and virtually nothing about the lives of ordinary people or developments in culture and science. Churchill also projects quintessentially nineteenth-century ideas that the most important factors in English history (Scotland, Wales and Ireland are virtually ignored) were the struggle between the Crown and Parliament and the triumph of the landowners in the late seventeenth century.

Writing was one way of filling the huge void in his life left by the loss of office. Certainly at this stage he no longer needed to write to earn money. Churchill and his family were now immensely rich from his literary sales and the income from the charitable trust he had established in the 1940s. The Churchill name continued to guarantee large advances. When Churchill's publishers brought out a one-volume abridgement of his war memoirs in February 1959 (with the work undertaken by his archivist, Denis Kelly), his foreign literary agent Emery Reves paid £20,000 (over £250,000 at current prices) for a 10,000-word epilogue on the post-1945 period, which was written jointly by Hodge, Kelly and his Private Secretary Montague-Brown. He also made money from the film rights to *My Early Life*. They had been bought by Warner Brothers during the war for £7,500 but they generously returned them in the 1950s. In 1960 they were bought by Columbia for £100,000 (over £1 million today) plus a percentage of the takings. Churchill's literary activities had been recognised in October 1953 with the award of the Nobel Prize. He was pleased with the money – £12,000 tax-free – but did not bother to go to Stockholm for the ceremony, sending Clementine and Mary Soames instead.

Churchill no longer had financial worries but he had to face declining health, incapacity, boredom, terrible mental suffering and long bouts of acute depression. The first signs of Churchill's depressed state were apparent within a few weeks of the 1955 Election as the reality of his new life began to sink in. He hardly spoke at meals and told Moran at various times 'I'm finished. I'm only waiting', 'Life for me is over. The sooner the better' and 'I am only waiting about for death'.[3] On 1 June he suffered an arterial spasm, which left him with poor co-ordination in his hands and difficulty in walking. The effects passed off and a week later he was able to go to the House of Commons to sign his name on the roll of the new Parliament. On 22 June he made a short speech at the Guildhall in the City of London to mark the unveiling of his statue.

But in July Moran found it difficult to understand what Churchill was saying. He was incoherent and unable to finish his sentences and he now relied on Moran's drugs to get him through even minor social events, such as receiving visitors for lunch. In mid-September he left for a two-month stay at Beaverbrook's villa in the south of France. He was joined by Clementine and the Soames family but after mid-October he stayed on without them, doing a little painting and occasional work on *The History of the English Speaking Peoples*. He even undertook a desultory search for his own villa in the area.

After his return to Britain in mid-November 1955 his mental condition continued to deteriorate – on 13 December he told Moran, 'I keep losing my memory. I could not remember Anthony's name today.'[4] Early in the new year he returned to the south of France to stay with his literary agent Emery Reves and his mistress, the ex-model Wendy Russell, whom he was shortly to marry. Reves, whom Churchill had helped to make wealthy, owned a villa, La Pausa, built in the 1920s by Churchill's old friend the Duke of Westminster for his mistress, Coco Chanel. He stayed for six weeks surrounded by the cosseting and flattery he loved. (Knowing Churchill's love of fine food his host had specially engaged an eminent chef for the visit.) He spent most of his time in bed, but managed to do some painting. Again he looked at possible villas, but decided there was little point in incurring the expense of buying if he could come as a guest.

During 1956 Churchill settled into a pattern that was to last through most of the last decade of his life. With little to do and still having to cope with his fits of depression, he sought to distract himself by frequent changes of scene. He made four visits to La Pausa in 1956, nearly always on his own – Clementine disliked both Reves and his wife and would not stay for more than a few days. As in the past she took separate holidays – including a cruise to Ceylon with her cousin in early February 1956, when she refused to stop off at La Pausa on the return journey even though the boat called at Marseilles. In 1957 he spent much of the first half of the year with Reves and another three weeks at La Pausa in the autumn. He was there for most of the first three months of 1958 and again in the autumn and for another month at the beginning of 1959. He did take some holidays with Clementine – five weeks at Marrakech in the winter of 1958–9, where he painted his last two pictures at one of his favourite resorts. They were also together in September 1958 to celebrate their golden wedding at Beaverbrook's villa at Cap d'Ail joined by Randolph and his daughter Arabella. But for much of the time they were, as in the past, apart. Clementine spent most of the summer of 1956 in St Moritz, at first to avoid going to La Pausa, but she did not return home even when Churchill went back to Chartwell.

Churchill also made a few other trips. In early May 1956 he travelled to Germany. He visited Aachen, where he was greeted by lukewarm crowds, to receive the Charlemagne Prize for his advocacy of a united Europe. Afterwards he went on to pay a short visit to British troops. In November 1958 he visited Paris on his way home from La Pausa where his old sparring partner General de Gaulle, recently returned to power, invested him with the Croix de la Libération. A few months later he went to the United States, where he stayed with Eisenhower for three days at the White House. The visit was purely informal but even so Moran had to prescribe massive doses of stimulants to get him through.

Churchill found it difficult to fall back on his family for support. His relationship with Clementine was still far from good. Although she was more reconciled to life at Chartwell, she was herself in poor health after a major internal operation followed by neuritis. She also suffered several attacks of acute lethargy and found it very difficult to cope with her husband's depressed state. Churchill had been much affected by the death of his brother Jack in 1947 ('Goonie' had died of cancer during the war), and three of his children had plenty of problems and unhappiness in their own lives.

Randolph's wartime marriage (undertaken largely to provide an heir for the family) ended in divorce and although he remarried in 1948 that too ended in acrimony and divorce. Randolph's desire for a political career was frustrated by his failure to win a seat in the Commons and he had gained a reputation as a difficult, rude, hard-drinking journalist. His scorn was directed especially at Anthony Eden, who he felt had replaced him in his father's affections. Churchill's relationship with Randolph remained bad; they could rarely meet without quarrelling, although increasingly their disagreements were started by Churchill himself. He did, however, appoint Randolph, who still hero-worshipped his father, as his official biographer. Sarah's marriage to Vic Oliver, which Churchill had always opposed, ended in divorce in 1944. She had an affair with Gil Winant, the American Ambassador in London during the war, who committed suicide when she refused to join him in America in 1947. By then it was clear she would never be a successful actress. She married for a second time in 1949, to photographer Anthony Beauchamp, who was disliked by both Churchill and Clementine for being common. That marriage too was a failure. After long periods of separation they were divorced in 1955 and Beauchamp committed suicide in 1957. Sarah turned to drink and her frequent arrests were well publicised; she even spent a short spell in Holloway prison. Her father paid for her to be 'dried out' in a Zurich clinic but the treatment failed. She was married for a third time in 1962, to Baron Audley (another alcoholic), and went to live in southern Spain. But Audley died of a massive heart attack within little more than a year.

Diana, married to her second husband, Duncan Sandys, since the mid-1930s, devoted her life to his political career (he lost his seat in 1945, became an MP again in 1950 and joined the Government in 1951). But the marriage began to disintegrate through a combination of Sandys' workaholic tendencies and numerous affairs. Diana's relations with Clementine had always been bad and by the early 1950s they had broken down completely. In 1953 Diana suffered a major mental breakdown, and underwent a series of unsuccessful treatments in various clinics. In 1956 she and Sandys formally separated and in 1960 they were divorced. Sandys remarried, but in October 1963 Diana committed suicide. The only member of Churchill's immediate family to have a happy life and successful marriage was Mary, who was devoted to her large family and Christopher Soames' career as he rose steadily through the Government ranks.

During the first eighteen months after his resignation Churchill did maintain a slight interest in politics. He was particularly upset in early 1956 when the House of Commons voted against the death penalty. He even thought of speaking in the House where he intended to warn 'the country is going soft' and he expressed concern at 'the unmasculinity of the island'.[5] As might be expected, he was outraged by the Egyptian nationalisation of the Suez Canal at the end of July 1956. He described Nasser as a 'malicious swine' and believed that Britain could deal with him without any help – 'we don't need the Americans for this'.[6] That was exactly the mistake that Eden also made, and the Anglo-French operation in collusion with Israel ended ignominiously in early November. Within weeks Eden resigned, ostensibly over his health, which had never been strong since his operations in 1953. Churchill was one of those consulted by the Queen about the succession and he recommended his old protégé Macmillan. Churchill's support was not decisive; an overwhelming majority of the Cabinet favoured Macmillan over Butler.

With little to occupy his time Churchill turned in on himself as his fits of depression worsened. His long years of hectic political activity had allowed little time for reflection but now he thought about his political life and concluded that it had been a failure. Everything he really believed in had disintegrated. As an aristocrat he regretted the passing of the social world he had enjoyed and the privileged position he had known in his youth. He told Moran: 'I'm glad I've not to live my life over again. There is a dreadful degradation of standards.'[7] The main aim of his political life – 'to improve the British breed' – had come to nothing. The one cause which moved Churchill throughout his life was the preservation of the British Empire in the state in which he had first encountered it in the 1890s. Then he had written to his brother of 'this great Empire of ours – to the maintenance of which I shall devote my life'.[8] For decades he had fought against constitutional changes in India or alterations to the British position in Egypt. He had opposed granting any greater independence to the white dominions and objected to self-government for non-white peoples. Yet he had had to watch all that he held dear pass away. India had become independent, Britain had withdrawn from Egypt, the dominions had loosened their ties with Britain (Australia and New Zealand came to depend on the United States for their defence and South Africa left the Commonwealth altogether), and the colonies of Africa and Asia were moving rapidly towards independence. He remained a convinced white supremacist, and the last political remark he was heard to make was in 1960 when he criticised Macmillan for his 'Wind of Change' speech to the South African Parliament in Cape Town. He thought Macmillan 'ought not to have gone to Africa, encouraging the black men'.[9]

Another consuming passion of his political life had been the greatness of Britain (or England as he normally called it). Yet his career had spanned the period of Britain's decline from world power to small European state and he had spent much of his time dealing with the problems arising from Britain's inability to sustain the great-power status he had known in his youth. He experienced at first hand the decline of British naval supremacy in the years before the First World War, the financial collapse of 1940 and Britain's dependence on, and increasing subservience to, the United States during the Second World War and beyond. At the end of his life Churchill concluded gloomily, 'I am afraid we are going downhill.'[10] Increasingly he came to view the Second World War, the period when he had seemed to score his greatest personal triumph, as a failure too. He mused for hours at a time on where it had gone wrong: he saw that one evil state had been destroyed but at vast cost and replaced by another almost as bad, with which Britain had been allied. He had been the great anti-Bolshevik but had finished up making agreements for their domination of half Europe. At the end of the war two world superpowers had displaced Britain and the world now lived in fear of an even more terrible war. Churchill therefore made a conscious decision not to bring his *History of the English Speaking Peoples* into the twentieth century. It would have been too painful to record the decline of Britain, two wars that at best were only partial successes and the replacement of Britain by the United States as the most powerful English-speaking state. He told Moran: 'I could not write about the woe and ruin of the terrible twentieth century ... We answered all the tests. But it was useless.'[11]

A similar sense of failure pervaded Churchill when he looked at domestic politics. The political system he knew in his youth was dominated by an élite which, although divided on some issues such as Ireland and free trade, was united in wanting to preserve the existing social and economic order. He had consistently opposed the principle of full democracy but had had to accept what he saw as a major degradation of the political system. One of his heartfelt concerns throughout his life had been to block the rise of the Labour Party and the trades unions with their demands for social and economic reforms. Despite his sustained attacks on all they stood for, they had become one of the major political parties and, worse still, he had himself, in order to secure power, had to accept them in Government in 1940, and had then been humiliated by the Labour Election victory in 1945.

From 1957 Churchill, now eighty-two, suffered increasing incapacity. Moran diagnosed cerebral arteriosclerosis, which slowly reduced brain functions. He had one male and two female nurses in constant attendance. He was unable to fight off bouts of deep depression and spent long hours not reading, seldom speaking, slumped in a state of total apathy. The type of life in old age that he had always feared was upon him. When he did manage to rouse himself he would paint, play cards or read a few novels. He was also dogged with other illnesses. In mid-February 1958 he developed bronchial pneumonia. Moran flew out and stayed with him at La Pausa for three weeks, prescribing a course of antibiotics. Then at the end of March he suffered an attack of obstructive jaundice. Although well enough to return to England in early April, he developed jaundice again. Another source of sadness was the loss of old companions. In July 1958 he visited Brendan Bracken in Westminster Hospital where he was dying of cancer – his other close friend Lindemann, 'The Prof', had died the previous year. One of his last companions from the past, Lord Beaverbrook, was still alive, and they were now quietly friendly after their tempestuous relationship over many decades.

Churchill suffered a slight stroke in April 1959 and his circulation was beginning to fail. He developed gangrene in one finger, part of which eventually fell off. He insisted on speaking in his constituency on 20 April. Although his speech was barely audible, he was readopted as a Conservative candidate because no one had the heart to oppose his determination to remain an MP, his last link with political life. He made a few speeches in the 1959 Election campaign, all of which were written for him by his secretary. The Conservatives under Harold Macmillan won with an increased majority, although Churchill's own majority at Woodford fell. On 17 October he planted an oak tree to mark the foundation of Churchill College, Cambridge, which had been endowed in his honour. He attended the Commons on 30 November, his eighty-fifth birthday.

Clementine described him at this time as 'profoundly depressed'.[12] He hated the life to which he was reduced, telling Moran that though he felt well at times 'I hope I don't go on feeling very well. I don't want to waste time reading novels and playing cards.'[13] When he returned to the south of France in early 1960, he did not stay with his usual hosts, Emery Reves and his wife, who had devotedly looked after him for long spells during the previous five years. He went instead to the Hôtel de Paris in Monte Carlo as the guest of the millionaire Greek shipping magnate Aristotle Onassis. The two men had been introduced through Randolph in January 1956 and Onassis had determinedly cultivated Churchill's acquaintance as a way to social and business respectability. (Reves was deeply insulted and although Churchill tried to invite himself to La Pausa again, he always refused.) Churchill had taken his first cruise on Onassis' yacht *Christina* in September 1958; it was the first of eight to various parts of the Mediterranean and the West Indies. His main occupations were playing cards (Onassis always allowed him to win) and watching films while being entertained in great luxury.

On 15 November 1960 Churchill fell and broke a bone in his back and later that month suffered another mild stroke. By the end of the year his mental condition had declined greatly, so much so that Lord Moran, although he remained Churchill's doctor for another four years, closed his detailed personal account of his relationship with Churchill at this juncture. The reason he gave was that the rest of Churchill's life had no historical interest as he lived on as an invalid with his intellectual faculties badly impaired. The last four years were indeed a torment for Churchill. His strong constitution kept him alive but seriously incapacitated. Yet his search for constant changes of scene and the hospitality of others continued. In March 1961 he went on another cruise with Onassis in the West Indies and he stopped at New York, where he saw his old friend Bernard Baruch for the last time. He spent most of that summer at Monte Carlo as Onassis' guest. Macmillan was being kept in touch with the state of Churchill's failing health as arrangements for his funeral needed to be made. In July 1961 he heard from Montague-Brown: 'Sir Winston's condition had deteriorated quite seriously in the last three months; it was not that there was anything specifically wrong with him but just that he was getting more depressed and speechless. This made him restless and explained his constant changes of abode.'[14]

In the autumn of 1961 Churchill was strong enough to attend the State opening of Parliament but not to lay the foundation stone at Churchill College. He spent his eighty-seventh birthday with Beaverbrook and then returned to Monte Carlo without Clementine. He was back at Chartwell for Christmas but was very low. On 28

June 1962, during his second visit to Monte Carlo that year, he slipped and broke his hip. He told Montague-Brown 'I want to die in England' and was flown back by RAF Comet to have his hip pinned at the Middlesex Hospital. He stayed in hospital for three weeks and then moved to his London home at Hyde Park Gate, which was modified so that he could live and sleep on the ground floor and use the lift to the lower ground floor, where he could dine and also see the garden.

The effect of the operation was to further restrict Churchill's mobility and intensify his boredom. His main activity now was playing bezique, his favourite card game, with Clementine, her cousin Sylvia Henley or the Marchioness of Cholmondeley. On 1 November he managed to dine at the Other Club, where Onassis was now a member. A few weeks later when his old Parliamentary Private Secretary Lord Boothby (whose career Churchill had broken in 1940) dined with him, he found that Churchill could not even talk about the Second World War and could remember little about his life. In 1963 the long, sad decline continued, and the receipt of more honours commemorating his earlier life failed to rouse him from his state of lethargy. On 8 April he was made a citizen of the United States. He had to face the fact that he would finally have to step down as an MP since he was unable to carry out any of the normal functions expected of a member. The local constituency association was reluctant to press him, but in early 1963 decided they would have to have a new candidate for the next general election. Churchill was at first reluctant to give way and so cut his last tenuous ties with political life but finally accepted the inevitable in early May.

The approaching end of his time as an MP plunged Churchill into acute depression. In June 1963 he was just fit enough to take his last cruise with Onassis from Monte Carlo. In August he suffered another mild stroke. This left him almost entirely confined to bed, unable to read, just lying doing nothing hour after hour, day after day. In the autumn he rallied and was able to meet a few friends over dinner. The slight recovery continued in the first months of 1964 and he attended the House of Commons a few times, though in a wheelchair. He could understand little of what was going on and did not even recognise the new Prime Minister, Sir Alec Douglas-Home, who had been Chamberlain's Parliamentary Private Secretary and a member of Churchill's own Government after 1951.

On 9 June his longest-surviving friend, and probably his closest companion during his retirement, Lord Beaverbrook, died. On 27 July he went to the House of Commons for the last time. The next day the three party leaders called at Hyde Park Gate to present a Vote of Thanks from the House for Churchill's work. (It had been agreed that his condition did not allow the ceremony to take place in the Chamber.) It marked the end of a long Parliamentary career which stretched back, with a two-year break in the early 1920s, to 1900.

The House of Commons was paying tribute to the shell of a man. Even reading was now beyond him and he would sit or lie in bed listening to Gilbert and Sullivan or military band music and looking at picture books. At other times he just lay staring into space, his memory largely gone, almost totally deaf, waiting for death. In October 1964 he left his beloved Chartwell for the last time and returned to Hyde Park Gate. On 30 November, his ninetieth birthday, there was a family party and he was taken, uncomprehending, on to the balcony to wave at the crowd gathered in the street. On 10 December he went with Bill Deakin to the Other Club for the last time. He hardly spoke but seemed happy just to be present. Churchill's long suffering was now nearly over. His last recorded words were 'I'm so bored with it all'. On 10 January 1965 he suffered a massive stroke. For fourteen days he lay in a coma. The end finally came just after 8am on 24 January.

Arrangements for Churchill's funeral had been made some years before. After a visit to Blenheim in September 1958 he had decided to remain true to his aristocratic roots and be buried in Bladon churchyard just a few miles from where he was born. He also knew that he was to be given a State funeral. The arrangements were worked out by a small committee which included his Private Secretary, Montague-Brown. Churchill's main request was that there should be plenty of military bands in the procession. On 27 January his coffin was taken from Hyde Park Gate to lie in state in Westminster Hall. During the next three days 300,000 people filed past to pay their last respects. On the third evening the guard was mounted by the three party leaders and the Speaker of the House of Commons. Parliament was adjourned not for the customary one day on the death of a Prime Minister but for a week until after the funeral.

The State funeral took place on Saturday 30 January. It was a carefully stage-managed performance that Churchill would have appreciated, even if it included a church service. At 9.45 Big Ben was silenced and the coffin was placed on a gun carriage to be drawn slowly through the streets of London to St Paul's Cathedral. The coffin was followed by members of the family and escorted by military bands. Over 3,000 people were in the Cathedral for the service. They included the Queen and members of the Royal Family, five other monarchs, fifteen heads of state (including Churchill's old *bête noire* De Gaulle) and Vice President Humphrey of the United States (President Johnson did not attend because of Churchill's failure to attend Roosevelt's funeral). Also present were ex-President Eisenhower, the ex-Premier of Israel Ben Gurion and Churchill's colleague from the dark days of the fall of France, Paul Reynaud. Many of the surviving members of Churchill's wartime administration were also present. The pall bearers included a grey-faced, ill Anthony Eden and an aged, infirm Clement Attlee.

After the service the superbly organised procession made its way through the City to Tower Pier. From there the coffin was taken by Port of London Authority launch to Festival Pier on the South Bank and finally to Waterloo Station. It was then placed on a special train hauled by the ex-Southern Railway 'Battle of Britain' class *Winston Churchill* for the journey to Long Handborough station. Churchill was finally laid to rest next to the graves of his father, mother and brother in Bladon churchyard.

Notes

Abbreviations

WSC   Official biography. Main volumes
CV   Official biography. Companion volumes

Public Record Office Papers
ADM   Admiralty
AIR   Air Ministry
CAB   Cabinet Office
CO   Colonial Office
DEFE   Ministry of Defence
FO   Foreign Office
HO   Home Office
INF   Ministry of Information
LAB   Ministry of Labour
PREM   Prime Minister's Office
T   Treasury
WO   War Office

Chapter 1: Introduction

1. Moran, *Winston Churchill: The Struggle for Survival*, p. xvi
2. N. Chamberlain Papers, NC 18/1/1121, 17.9.39
3. Foster, *Lord Randolph Churchill*, p. 2
4. Ibid, p. 1

Chapter 2: Youth

1. Churchill & Mitchell, *Jennie, Lady Randolph Churchill*, p. 126
2. WSC Vol 1, p. 104
3. CV Vol 1, p 424, 29.10.93
4. *Ibid*, p. 87, 24.2.84
5. *Ibid*, p. 113, 20.10.85
6. WSC Vol 1, p. 83 10.11.86
7. Foster, *op cit*, pp. 311–2
8. CV, Vol 1, pp. 168–9
9. WSC Vol 1, p. 125, 2.7.89
10. CV Vol 1, p. 191
11. WSC Vol 1, p. 143, June 1889
12. *Ibid*, p. 144
13. CV, Vol 1, pp. 390–1
14. Balsam, *The Glitter and the Gold*, p. 72

Chapter 3: Ambition

1. CV, Vol 1, p. 583, 16.8.95
2. *Ibid*, pp. 701–2, 12.11.96
3. *Ibid*, pp. 675–6, 4.8.96
4. *Ibid*, pp. 681–2, September 1896
5. WSC Vol 1, p. 324, 11.12.96
6. CV, Vol 1, p. 839, 22.12.97
7. *Ibid*, p. 928, 10.5.98
8. *Ibid*, p. 993, 4.12.98
9. WSC Vol 1, p. 441, 11.1.99
10. CV, Vol 1, pp. 675–6, 4.8.96
11. *Ibid*, pp. 696–9, 4.11.96
12. *Ibid*, p. 969, 24.8.98
13. *Ibid*, p. 907, 31.3.98
14. Moran, *op cit*, p. 122
15. *Ibid*, p. 525
16. CV, Vol 1, p. 893, 20.3.98
17. Sir Algernon West *Diaries*, p. 232
18. CV, Vol 1, p. 1151, 21.2.00
19. *Ibid*, pp. 767–8
20. CAB 131/13, 28.10.53
21. CV, Vol 1, p. 765
22. WSC Vol 1, p. 268–9
23. Moran, *op cit*, p. 690
24. CV, Vol 1, p. 828, 17.11.97
25. *Ibid*, pp. 835–6, 2.12.97

26. *Ibid*, p. 784, 5.9.97
27. *Ibid*, pp. 780–2, 29.8.97
28. *Ibid*, pp. 835–6, 2.12.97
29. *Ibid*, p. 793, 19.9.97
30. *Ibid*, p. 811, 25.10.97
31. *Ibid*, p. 814, 2.11.97
32. *Ibid*, p. 811
33. *Ibid*, p. 717, December 1896
34. *Ibid*, p. 855, 6.1.98
35. *Ibid*, pp. 864–5, 26.1.98
36. *Ibid*, p. 997, 29.12.98
37. *Ibid*, p. 963, 10.8.98
38. *Ibid*, p. 979, 16.9.98
39. *Ibid*, p. 863, 26.1.98
40. *Ibid*, p. 933, 16.5.98
41. *Ibid*, pp. 1076–7
42. Aylmer Haldane *Diary*
43. *Morning Post*, 12.4.00
44. CV, Vol 1, p. 869, 28.1.98

Chapter 4: Changing Sides

1. *My Early Life*, p. 372
2. CV, Vol 1, pp. 699–700
3. *My African Journey*, p. 125
4. WSC Vol 1, p. 315
5. Dilke Papers
6. B. Webb, *Our Partnership*, pp. 269–70
7. Quoted in T. Morgan, *Winston Churchill*, p. 184
8. CV, Vol 2, p. 679, 19.9.07
9. CV, Vol 1, p. 766
10. *Ibid*, p. 315
11. CV, Vol 2, p. 168, 10.10.02
12. *Ibid*, p. 122
13. *Ibid*, pp. 174–5
14. *Ibid*, pp. 183–4, 25.5.03
15. *Ibid*, p. 185, 29.5.03
16. *Ibid*, pp. 212–3, 14.7.03
17. *Ibid*, pp. 242–4
18. Campbell Bannerman to Gladstone, 3.12.03, quoted in Sykes, *Tariff Reform in British Politics*, p. 74
19. *Ibid*, p. 71, Campbell Bannerman to Harcourt, 7.12.03
20. *Ibid*, p. 75, Campbell Bannerman to Gladstone, 26.12.03
21. WSC Vol 2, pp. 72–4, 12.10.03

22. CV, Vol 2, p. 104, 23.12.01
23. *Ibid*, p. 346, 2.6.04
24. Quoted in James, *Rosebery*, p. 461

Chapter 5: Junior Minister

1. WSC Vol 2, p. 207, Elgin to Crewe, 7.5.08
2. Quoted in Hassall, *Edward Marsh*, p. 142
3. CO 291/98/12925, 17.4.06
4. Quoted in Hyam, *Elgin and Churchill at the Colonial Office*, p. 99
5. CO 879/106, African (S) 804, 2.1.06
6. *Ibid*
7. CO 879/106, African (S) 817, 30.1.06
8. CO 879/106, African (S) 815, 25.1.06
9. CAB 37/82/16
10. CO 879/106, African (S) 834, 15.3.06
11. CO 879/106, African (S) 804, 2.1.06
12. CV, Vol 2, p. 563, WSC to King, 15.8.06
13. Quoted in Thorne, *Allies of a Kind*, p. xxiii
14. CV, Vol 1, p. 1216, WSC to JC, 16.11.00
15. House of Commons, 28.2.06
16. African (S) 804, *op cit*
17. CO 446/52/5712, 24.2.06
18. CO 54/696/45379, 31.1.06
19. Elgin Papers, quoted in Hyam, *op cit*, p. 227
20. CO 54/705/36699, 18.11.06
21. CO 179/243/21853, 27.6.07
22. House of Commons, 14.6.06
23. Wilson, C. B.: *A Life of Sir Henry Campbell-Bannerman*, p. 499
24. WSC to Campbell-Bannerman, 19.5.06, *ibid*, p. 583
25. Elgin to WSC, 4.1.07, CV, Vol 2, p. 609
26. *Ibid*, p. 699, 15.11.07
27. *My African Journey*, pp. 87, 37–8
28. *Ibid*, pp. 41–3
29. *Ibid*, p. 51
30. *Ibid*, p. 55
31. Hyam, *op cit*, p. 498, 3.4.07
32. *Ibid*, p. 502, 27.12.07
33. *Ibid*, 19.2.08, 12.3.08, 30.4.08
34. Asquith Papers, 10/222, 5.1.07
35. Wilson, *op cit*, p. 590
36. *Ibid*, pp. 590–1, 1.1.07
37. CV, Vol 2, pp. 754–6
38. Esher Journals, 9.3.08

Chapter 6: Cabinet

1. WSC to CC, 27.4.08, CV, Vol 2, p. 789
2. See for example CV, Vol 2, p. 408
3. Colville, *Fringes of Power*, 21.12.40, p. 322
4. WSC to CC, 12.9.18, CV, Vol 4, pp. 394–5
5. Moran, *op cit*, p. 103
6. Quoted in Campbell, *F. E. Smith*, p. 834
7. WSC, Vol 2, p. 113
8. Riddell Diaries, 21.3.13, p. 58
9. WSC to Asquith, 29.12.08, CV, Vol 2, pp. 862–4
10. WSC to Asquith, 13.3.08, *ibid*, pp. 755–6
11. WSC to Lloyd George, 20.6.09, *ibid*, pp. 895–8
12. Quoted in Masterman, *Charles Masterman*, p. 97
13. CV, Vol 2, pp. 879–81
14. WSC to Gladstone, 8.7.08, *Ibid*, pp. 825–6
15. Quoted in Addison, *The Road to 1945*, p. 212
16. Quoted in Freeden, *The New Liberalism*, pp. 184–5
17. Quoted in Harris, *Unemployment and Politics*, p. 285
18. LAB 2/211/LE 500, 18.8.09
19. *Ibid*
20. Quoted in Murray, *Master and Brother*, p. 88
21. CAB 37/96/159
22. WSC to Beveridge, 6.6.09, Harris, *op cit*, p. 310
23. CAB 37/99/69
24. Harris, *op cit*, p. 310
25. Pease Diary, 19.7.09
26. Asquith Papers, 5.f.134
27. CAB 27/113, 6.5.21
28. Haldane Papers, MS 5909 fi
29. WSC to Asquithy, 10.11.09, CV, Vol 2, p. 919
30. *Ibid*, pp. 965–71
31. Murray, *op cit*, p. 47
32. WSC to Lloyd George, 6.10.10, CV, Vol 2, pp. 1024–5
33. Masterman, *op cit*, p. 131
34. Asquith to WSC, 1.2.10, CV, Vol 2, pp. 1132–3
35. WSC, Vol 2, p. 247
36. Runciman to Trevelyan, 4.1.14, quoted in Hazelhurst, *Politicians at War*, p. 253
37. Quoted in Lord Riddell, *More Pages from My Diary*, p. 181
38. Wilson, *The Political Diaries of C. P. Scott 1911–1928* (Scott Diary), p. 64
39. David, *Inside Asquith's Cabinet: From the Diaries of Charles Hobhouse* (Hobhouse Diary), 27.7.08, p. 73
40. *Ibid*, 13.8.12 p. 121

41. Asquith Papers, Box XLVI, F183
42. Hobhouse, *op cit*, 24.6.13, p. 140
43. Harcourt Papers, 29.2.12
44. Pease Diary, 21.5.12
45. HO/45/10660/213025
46. CV, Vol 2, p. xxvii, 19.1.99
47. Cd 4202
48. CAB 37/108/189
49. Asquith Papers, MS 12, f 224–8
50. HO 144/1098/197900
51. HO 144/1088/194663
52. HO 144/1098/197900
53. HO 144/1042/183256
54. Quoted in Rowland, *The Last Liberal Governments*, Vol pp. 355–7
55. HO 144/1042/183256
56. HO 144/1107/200655
57. HO 45/10631/200605
58. HO 45/10633/201432
59. HO 144/1106/200455
60. HO 144/1148/210238
61. HO 144/1107/200655
62. HO 144/1087/194175
63. HO 144/1087/194478
64. HO 144/938/A59031
65. HO 144/1144/209195
66. HO 144/1018/152273
67. HO 144/1134/207057
68. HO 144/1102/199183
69. HO 45/10643/207426
70. CV, Vol 2, pp. 1244–5
71. House of Commons, 18.9.11
72. HO 45/10629/199699
73. CAB 17/91

Chapter 7: Admiralty

1. WSC to Asquith, 14.3.08, CV, Vol 2, pp. 754–5
2. WSC to F. Guest, 3.11.17, CV, Vol 4, p. 187
3. Esher Journals 8.7.08
4. Knollys to Esher, 10.2.09, Esher MSS
5. WSC to Grey, 16.2.09, CV, Vol 2, p. 955
6. *Ibid*, pp. 939–42
7. WSC to Asquith, 3.2.09, *Ibid*, pp. 942–3
8. C. P. Scott Diaries, 22.7.11, pp. 48–9

9. Asquith to Haldane, 31.8.11, Haldane Papers, MSS 5909
10. WSC to Lloyd George, 14.9.11, Lloyd George Papers, C/3/15/12
11. Fisher to WSC, 10.11.11, CV, Vol 2, p. 1328
12. Quoted in Marder, *Dreadnought to Scapa Flow*, Vol 1. p. 261
13. WSC to Admiral Limpus, 10.12.13, WSC, Vol 2, pp. 645–6
14. CV, Vol 2, pp. 1632–3
15. Hobhouse, *op cit*, 27.11.12, p. 124
16. CAB 41/34, 11.7.13
17. WSC to Haldane, 6.5.12, Haldane MSS 5909
18. CAB 37/111/76, 15.6.12
19. Fisher to his son, 5.7.12, quoted in *Fear God*, Vol II, pp. 470–1
20. Hobhouse, *op cit*, 5.7.12 & 10.7.12, pp. 116–8
21. CV, Vol 2, pp. 1638–9, 23.8.12
22. WSC to Grey, 31.1.12, *ibid* pp. 1503–5
23. Paper, 23.8.12, *op cit*
24. Hobhouse, *op cit*, 16.12.13, p. 154
25. CAB 37/116/48, 10.1.14
26. CV, Vol 2, pp. 1842–3, 5.1.14
27. Scott, *op cit*, 15.1.14, p. 73
28. CV, Vol 2, p. 1847, 14.1.14
29. Memo 19.7.10, CV, Vol 2, p. 1447
30. H. N. Brailsford to WSC, 12.7.10, *Ibid*, p. 1441
31. WSC to Brailsford, 13.7.10, *Ibid*, p. 1442
32. WSC to Lloyd George, 16.12.11, Lloyd George Papers C/3/15/12
33. WSC to Elibank, 18.12.11, Elibank Papers, 2B
34. WSC to Asquith, 21.12.11, CV, Vol 2, pp. 1475–6
35. Scott, *op cit*, 23.1.12, p. 59
36. CAB 37/114/4, 7.1.13
37. Riddell Diary, 31.3.12
38. WSC to Balfour, 2.2.04, CV, Vol 2, p. 310
39. *Ibid*, p. 337
40. Quoted in Beckett and Jeffrey, *The Royal Navy and the Curragh Incident*, p. 56
41. Asquith to Venetia Stanley, 23.3.14, p. 59
42. Hobhouse, *op cit*, 20.5.15, p. 246

Chapter 8: War

1. Asquith to Venetia Stanley, 24.7.14, p. 121
2. WSC to CC, 28.7.14, WSC, Vol 2, pp. 710–11
3. Asquith to Venetia Stanley, 28.7.14, pp. 129–30
4. CAB 37/120/95, 30.7.14
5. Masterman, *op cit*, p. 265
6. Asquith to Venetia Stanley, 1.8.14, pp. 139–40

7. Margot Asquith Diary, 8.5.15
8. Asquith to Venetia Stanley, 4.8.14, pp. 149–51
9. WSC to Fisher, 1.1.14, Fisher Papers 763
10. Asquith to Venetia Stanley, 9.8.14, p. 161
11. *Ibid*, 1.10.14, p. 258
12. WSC to Beaverbrook, CV Vol 5–II, pp. 970–1
13. WSC to Kitchener, 5.10.14, CV Vol 3, p. 167
14. Asquith to Venetia Stanley, 8.10.14, p. 268
15. *Ibid*, 13.10.14, p. 275
16. Frances Stevenson Diary, 23.10.14, p. 6
17. Richmond Diary, 4.10.14, quoted in Marder, *Portrait of an Admiral*, pp. 111–2
18. Beatty to his wife, 18.10.14, Beatty MSS
19. Quoted in Blake, *The Unknown Prime Minister*, pp. 234–5
20. Asquith to Venetia Stanley, 11.8.14, p. 165
21. *Ibid*, 7.10.14, p. 266
22. *Ibid*, 29.10.14, p. 291
23. Beatty to his wife, 4.12.14, Beatty Papers
24. Asquith to King, 4.11.14, Asquith Papers
25. Asquith to Venetia Stanley, 4.11.14, p. 309
26. Frances Stevenson Diary, 5.11.14, p. 10
27. WSC to Beatty, 22.11.14, Beatty Papers
28. Beatty to Keyes, 10.2.15, quoted in Marder, *The War Years to the Eve of Jutland*, p. 167
29. ADM 116/1351, 22.10.14 and 23.12.14
30. Richmond Diary, 24.10.14, quoted in Marder, *op cit*, p. 50
31. Hobhouse Diary, 21.8.14, p. 183
32. Balfour to Hankey, 5.12.14, Hankey Papers
33. Memo 1.8.14, CV Vol 2, p. 1997

Chapter 9: Disaster at the Dardanelles

1. CAB 2/2/2, CID 96th Meeting, 28.2.07
2. ADM 137/96, 30.10.14
3. Asquith to Venetia Stanley, 5.12.14, p. 327
4. Letter of 6.1.15 quoted in Hazlehurst, *Politicians at War*, p. 188
5. Asquith to Venetia Stanley, 30.12.14, pp. 345–6
6. CV, Vol 3, p. 347
7. Kitchener to WSC, 2.1.15, *Ibid*, pp. 360–1
8. Stevenson Diary, 8.4.15, p. 41
9. CAB 37/105/27, 15.3.11
10. WSC to Fisher, 23.12.14, Fisher Papers
11. WSC to French, 11.1.15, CV, Vol 3, pp. 401–2
12. CAB 22/1, 13.1.15

13. WSC to Fisher and Oliver, 23.1.15, CV, Vol 3, p. 444
14. Richmond Diary, 19.1.15, quoted in Marder, *Portrait of an Admiral*, pp. 137–8
15. Fisher to Jellicoe, 19.1.15, *Fear God and Dread Nought*, Vol 3, p. 133
16. Asquith to Venetia Stanley, 20.1.15, pp. 387–8
17. Fisher to Jellicoe, 21.1.15, *Fear God and Dread Nought*, Vol 3, p. 142
18. Fisher to WSC, 25.1.15, CV, Vol 3, p. 460
19. WSC to Kitchener, 20.1.15, Kitchener Papers 30/57/72
20. Richmond Diary, Marder, *op cit*, p. 212
21. Hankey to Balfour, 10.12.15, Balfour Papers
22. CAB 22/1, 26.2.15
23. Aubert to Augagneur, 7.2.15, quoted in Cassar, *French and the Dardanelles*, pp. 67–8
24. CAB 19/33 Q 5415
25. Hobhouse Diary, 16.2.15, p. 222
26. WSC to Kitchener, 18.2.15, CV, Vol 3, pp. 518
27. WSC to Grey and Kitchener, 18.2.15, Kitchener Papers 30/57/39
28. CAB 22/1, 19.2.15
29. CV, Vol 3, p. 550
30. Fisher to Lloyd George, 23.2.15, Lloyd George Papers E/2/15/4
31. CAB 22/1, 26.2.15
32. Asquith to Venetia Stanley, 26.2.15, pp. 449–50
33. WSC to Kitchener, 4.3.15, CV, Vol 3, pp. 628–9
34. WSC to Jellicoe, 9.3.15, Jellicoe Papers
35. CAB 22/1, 10.3.15
36. Quoted in Marder, *To the Eve of Jutland*, p. 241
37. CAB 42/2, 16.3.15
38. Asquith to Venetia Stanley, 18.3.15, pp. 487–8
39. French Diary, 29.3.15
40. Esher Diary, 20.3.15
41. Asquith to Venetia Stanley, 21.3.15, pp. 497–8
42. Fisher to WSC, 5.4.15, CV, Vol 3, p. 770
43. CAB 22/1, 6.4.15
44. Asquith to Venetia Stanley, 4.2.15, p. 415
45. Stevenson Diary, 8.4.15, p. 41
46. Hobhouse Diary, 23.3.15, p. 231
47. Asquith to Venetia Stanley, 7.3.15, p. 464
48. Margot Asquith Diary, 19.2.15
49. Asquith to Venetia Stanley, 25.3.15, p. 508
50. Quoted in French, *British Strategy and War Aims*, p. 2
51. Pound and Harmsworth, *Northcliffe*, p. 475
52. Fisher to Hankey, 12.5.15, Roskill, Vol I, p. 173
53. Fisher to Hankey, 14.5.15, *Ibid*, pp. 173–4
54. Fisher to WSC, 16.5.15, *Fear God and Dread Nought*, Vol 3, p. 231

55. Stevenson Diary, 15.5.15, p. 44
56. Fisher to Bonar Law, 17.5.15, *Fear God and Dread Nought*, Vol 3, pp. 230–4
57. Asquith to Balfour, 20.5.15, Balfour MSS 49692
58. Jellicoe to Hamilton, 19.5.15, Hamilton MSS
59. Quoted in Koss, *Haldane*, p. 207
60. *Ibid*, p. 208
61. Pringle to Asquith, 20.5.15, Asquith Papers
62. Emott to Asquith, 20.5.15, *Ibid*
63. Beauchamp to Harcourt, 21.5.15, Harcourt Papers Box 28
64. Lord Riddell's War Diaries, p. 89
65. WSC to Asquith, 21.5.15, CV, Vol 3, p. 922
66. WSC to Asquith, 21.5.15, *Ibid*, p. 924
67. Stevenson Diary, 24.5.15, p. 53

Chapter 10: The Wilderness

1. WSC to Runciman, 30.12.07, CV, Vol 2, p. 734
2. WSC to Sinclair, 9.6.15, CV, Vol 4, pp. 5–6
3. WSC to Lord Roberts, 23.1.12, CV, Vol 2, pp. 1499–1500
4. Asquith to Venetia Stanley, 26.8.14, p. 198
   Pease Diary, 25.8.14, Gainsford MSS
   Emott Diary, 25.814, Emott MSS
5. Hankey Diary, 22.9.14
6. Wilson Diary, 2.12.15
7. WSC to CC, 15.12.15, CV Vol 3, p. 1330–1
8. WSC to CC, 20.12.15, *Ibid*, pp. 1339–40
9. WSC to CC, 18.12.15, *Ibid*, pp. 1333–4
10. WSC to CC, 6.1.16, *Ibid*, pp. 1358–9
11. WSC to Balfour, 9.7.15, *Ibid*, pp. 1083–4
12. WSC to CC, 13.3.16, *Ibid*, pp. 1452–6
13. WSC to CC, 2.5.16, *Ibid*, p. 1498
14. Derby to Lloyd George, 19.8.16, Lloyd George Papers
15. CV, Vol 3, pp. 1553–7
16. Scott Diaries, 20.11.16
17. WSC to Sinclair, 10.12.16, CV, Vol 4, pp. 35–6
18. Curzon to Lloyd George, 8.6.17, Lloyd George Papers

Chapter 11: The Fringes of Power

1. Hankey Diary, 22.7.17, Roskill, Vol 1, p. 415
2. WSC to Lloyd George (not sent) April 1918, CV, Vol 4, pp. 302–3
3. WSC to Lloyd George, 4.5.18, *ibid*, pp. 309–10
4. WSC to Loucheur, 6.4.18, *ibid*, pp. 300–1

5. CV, Vol 3, pp. 640–1
6. CAB 23/8, 16.10.18
7. Quoted in Burke, *Sinews of War*, p. 81
8. FO 371/3120, 23.7.17
9. CV, Vol 4, pp. 395–6
10. WSC to Lloyd George, 26.12.18, *Ibid*, pp. 443–7

Chapter 12: 'The Only Remaining Specimen of a Real Tory'

1. *The Times*, 30.1.19
2. CAB 23/25, 30.5.21 and CAB 23/26, 23.7.21
3. WSC, Vol 4, p. 207
4. CAB 23/9 WC 523, 31.1.19
5. Riddell Diary, 22.7.19
6. Haig Diary, 27.9.19
7. CAB 27/73, 15.1.20
8. Wilson Diary, 15.1.20
9. Jones Diary, 15.1.20, Vol 1, p. 98
10. CV, Vol 5–1, pp. 577–87
11. *The Times*, 14.2.20 (speech in Dundee), press statement 9.1.22, CV, Vol 4, pp. 1719–21
12. House of Commons, 23.1.22
13. *Daily Chronicle*, 6.1.22
14. Stevenson Diary, 17.1.20, p. 197
15. Kerr to Lloyd George, 15.2.19, Lloyd George Papers
16. *Evening News*, 28.7.20
17. *The Aftermath*, p. 263
18. *Weekly Dispatch*, 22.6.19
19. WSC to Curzon, 24.12.21, Curzon Papers
20. *Sunday Herald*, 8.2.20
21. CAB 23/42, 23.12.18
22. CAB 23/9, 12.2.19
23. Kerr to Lloyd George, 15.2.19, Lloyd George Papers
24. WSC to Lloyd George, 27.2.19, CV, Vol 4, pp. 555–6
25. FO 608/177, 16.2.19
26. WSC to Wilson, 30.4.19, CV, Vol 4, p. 631
27. Eyre Crowe to Curzon, 28.12.21, Curzon Papers
28. Lloyd George to WSC, 15.10.19, Lloyd George Papers
29. CAB 23/11, 29.7.19
30. CV, Vol 4, pp. 975–8, 15.12.19
31. CAB 23/14, 10.11.18
32. CAB 23/9, 10.1.19
33. CV, Vol 4, p. 606, 4.4.19
34. WO 32/5749

35. House of Commons, 29.5.19
36. WO 106/1170
37. CAB 23/15, 11.6.19
38. CAB 23/12, 25.9.19
39. Lloyd George to WSC 22.9.19, Lloyd George Papers
40. CAB 24/14, 16.8.20
41. Wilson Diary, 15.1.20
42. *Ibid*, 27.5.20
43. *Ibid*, 18.8.20
44. Paper by WSC, 25.8.20, JCC Davidson Papers
45. Wilson Diary, 24.8.20
46. WSC to Lloyd George, 26.8.20, Lloyd George Papers
47. CAB 23/23, 18.11.20
48. Chamberlain to Lloyd George, 21.3.22, Lloyd George Papers
49. Lloyd George to Horne, 22.3.22 and to Chamberlain, 22.3.22, *Ibid*
50. CAB 23/29, 28.3.22
51. CAB 23/9, 4.2.19
52. *Daily Telegraph*, 5.11.20 (speech of 4.11.20)
53. Jones Diary, Vol 3, pp. 19–20, 31.5.20
54. Wilson Diary, 23.9.20
55. *Ibid*, 30.8.20
56. *The Aftermath*, p. 287
57. CAB 23/23, 10.11.20
58. Wilson Diary, 16.11.20
59. *Ibid*, 30.11.20
60. *Ibid*, 23.1.21

Chapter 13: The Imperial Scene

1. CAB 24/111, CP 1803, 24.8.20
2. Speech in Dundee, 11.11.22
3. CAB 24/111, 24.8.20
4. WSC to Curzon, 13.6.21 Curzon Papers
5. Lloyd George Papers
6. Wilson Diary, 12.2.22
7. To Curzon, Cabinet 7.2.21, Curzon Papers
8. FO 371/6342, 14.3.21
9. FO 371/6343, 17.3.21
10. CO 730/3, 9.7.22
11. CO 730/16, 24.11.21
12. CV, Vol 5–III, p. 616, 12.3.37
13. Jeffries, *Palestine the Reality*, p. 73
14. CAB 24/127, CP 3213, 11.8.21
15. CV, Vol 4, pp. 1610–8

16. CO 733/3, 2.6.21
17. CV, Vol 5–III, p. 617
18. CAB 24/127 CP 3213, 11.8.21
19. CAB 24/106
20. WSC to CC, 15.9.18, CV, Vol 4, p. 396
21. WO 32/5191, 12.5.19
22. WSC to Trenchard, 29.8.20, CV, Vol 4, p. 1190
23. WO 32/5185, 22.5.19
24. *Ibid*
25. CO 730/7, 16.12.21
26. CO 593/257, 18.3.21
27. CO 537/782, 20.8.21
28. CO 533/276, 6.4.22
29. WSC to Montagu, 8.10.21 Not quoted in full in CV, Vol 4, p. 1644. See Montagu Papers
30. Montagu to WSC, 12.10.21, Montagu Papers
31. Jones Diary, 27.4.21, Vol 3, p. 56
32. *Ibid*, 2.6.21, p. 73
33. *Ibid*, 7.9.21, pp. 107–9
34. Beaverbrook to Rothermere, 12.2.25, Beaverbrook Papers
35. Jones Diary, 16.5.22, Vol 3, p. 201
36. CV, Vol 2, p. 1397, 14.9.12
37. CAB 16/42, 1.6.22
38. Jones Diary, 8.6.22, Vol 3, p. 212
39. CAB 43/2, 31.7.22
40. WSC to CC, 27.3.20, CV, Vol 4, pp. 1057–9
41. Fisher Diary, 23.9.19
42. Stevenson Diary, 20.1.20
43. Wilson Diary, 19.2.21
44. Chamberlain to Curzon, 23.7.21, Curzon Papers
45. Northcliffe Papers, 30.5.21
46. Stevenson Diary, 21.5.21, p. 219
47. C. P. Scott Diary, p. 416
48. Beaverbrook to Lloyd George, 13.3.22, Lloyd George Papers
49. CAB 23/39, 7.9.22
50. Hankey Diary, 27.9.22
51. CAB 23/31, 1.10.22
52. Hankey Diary, 17.10.22
53. WSC to Balfour, 12.9.22, CV, Vol 4, pp. 1984–5

Chapter 14: Changing Sides – Again

1. Riddell Diary, 30.5.23
2. WSC to V. Bonham-Carter, 8.1.24, CV, Vol 5–I, p. 94

3. Chamberlain to Birkenhead, 26.2.24, Austen Chamberlain Papers
4. A. Chamberlain to his sister, 4.11.24, *Ibid*
5. Jones Diary, 4.11.24, p. 299
6. N. Chamberlain to his sister, 5.11.24, N. Chamberlain Papers
7. Jones Diary, 8.11.24, p. 303
8. Davidson to Baldwin, 6.11.24, Baldwin Papers
9. Jones Diary, 8.11.24, *op cit*
10. *New Republic*, 28.3.29
11. WSC to CC, 17.4.24, CV, Vol 5–I, p. 197
12. Hoare to Beaverbrook, 13.2.26, Beaverbrook Papers

Chapter 15: The Summit?

1. WSC to Baldwin, 12.12.24, Austen Chamberlain Papers
2. T 172/1499B, 25.1.25
3. *Ibid*, 22.2. 25
4. WSC to Grigg and Hopkins, 2.7.28 & 22.7.28, CV, Vol 5–I, pp. 1307–10
5. WSC to Salisbury, 9.12.24, Ibid, p. 297
6. *Ibid*, p. 1128 (Dec 27)
7. N. Chamberlain Diary, 1.11.25
8. CV Vol 5–1, pp. 1456–7
9. WSC to Grigg, 2.7.28, *Ibid*, p. 1306
10. CAB 23/49, 26.11.24
11. T 172/1452, late Nov 24
12. Chamberlain Diary, 26.11.24
13. CAB 27/276, 9.4.25
14. Dilks *Neville Chamberlain*, p. 428
15. T 171/247, 4.3.25
16. Jones Diary, 17.5.25, p. 316
17. WSC to Steel-Maitland, 19.9.25, Baldwin Papers
18. WSC to Baldwin, 20.9.25, *Ibid*
19. CAB 24/175, CP (487)25, 24.11.25
20. WSC to Baldwin, 20.12.25, Baldwin Papers
21. Minute 30.11.27, CV, Vol5–I, pp. 1119–20
22. WSC to Joynson-Hicks, 19.12.27, *Ibid*, pp. 1142–4
23. WSC to Joynson-Hicks, 21.12.27, *Ibid*, p. 1146
24. Middlemas and Barnes *Baldwin*, p. 387
25. Chamberlain to his wife, 1.5.26, N. Chamberlain Papers
26. CAB 27/323, 7.5.26
27. British Gazette, 8.5.26
28. James(ed) *J.C.C. Davidson*, p. 238
29. *Ibid*, p. 239
30. *Ibid*, p. 245

31. Davidson to Baldwin, undated (probably 5.2.26), *Ibid*, pp. 244–5
32. *Ibid*, pp. 242–3
33. Jones, Diary, 7.5.26, p. 41.
34. Chamberlain to his wife, 9.5.26, N. Chamberlain Papers
35. CAB 24/181, CP 368(26), 2.11.26
36. CAB 24/184, CP 44(27), 9.2.27
37. CAB 24/181, CP 365(26). 30.10.26
38. WSC to Baldwin, 10.1.27, Baldwin Papers
39. WSC to Baldwin, 13.12.24, *Ibid*
40. WSC to Keyes, 22.3.25, Keyes Papers
41. CAB 2/5, 5.7.28
42. CAB 24/172, CP 118(25), 24.2.25
43. CAB 2/5, 13.2.25
44. CAB 24/172, CP 118(25), 24.2.25
45. WSC to CC, 7.11.28, CV, Vol5–I, p. 1370
46. *Ibid*, p. 1342
47. WSC to CC, 14.11.28, *Ibid*, p. 1378
48. CAB 24/187, CP 189(27), 29.6.27
49. WSC to Baldwin, 7.1.28, Baldwin Papers
50. N. Chamberlain Diary, 29.4.28
51. Scott Diaries, 30.6.25, p. 481
52. WSC to Mond, 29.1.26, Melchett Papers
53. N. Chamberlain Diary, 1.11.25
54. Davidson, *op cit*., p. 202
55. Chamberlain to Irwin, 15.8.26, Halifax Papers
56. Chamberlain to Irwin, 12.8.28, Dilks, *op. cit*., p. 581
57. Beaverbrook to Amery, 12.11.28, Beaverbrook Papers
58. CAB 24/202, CP (53)29, 25.2.29
59. WSC to Baldwin, 7.1.29, Baldwin Papers
60. WSC to Baldwin, 29.6.29, *Ibid*

Chapter 16: Backbencher – the DieHard

1. Ashley, *Churchill as Historian*, p. 18
2. Colville, *op cit*, 22.10.40, p. 273
3. WSC to CC, 8.8.29, CV, Vol 5–II, p. 39
4. WSC to CC, 12.11.28, CV, Vol 5–I, p. 1375
5. WSC to Baldwin, 24.9.30, Baldwin Papers
6. WSC to Linlithgow, 3.11.37, CV, Vol 5–III, p. 827–8
7. Evidence to Peel Commission, 12. 3. 37, *Ibid*, p. 615
8. *Colliers*, 17.12.32
9. *Daily Mail*, 6.2.36
10. WSC to Beaverbrook, 23.9.30, CV, Vol 5–II, pp. 185–6
11. House of Commons, 20.11.31

12. CAB 24/169, CP 555(24), 30.12.24
13. WSC to CC, 8.8.29, CV, Vol 5–II, p. 39
14. WSC to Lord Camrose, 22.7.29, *ibid*, p. 27
15. WSC to JC, 6.4.97, CV, Vol 1, p. 751
16. House of Commons, 27.6.32, *My Early Life*, p. 118, House of Commons, 11.2.35
17. Pimlott, *The Second War Diary of Hugh Dalton 1939–45* (Dalton Diary), 18.12.40, p. 125
18. CAB 23/39, 5.2.22
19. WSC to Lady Lytton, 12.9.22, CV, Vol 4, pp. 1985–6
20. *Daily Mail*, 16.11.29
21. WSC to Irwin, 1.1.30, Halifax Papers
22. Paper, 12.12.30, Templewood Papers
23. House of Commons, 26.1.31
24. WSC to Boothby, 6.2.32, CV, Vol 5–11, pp. 399–400
25. CAB 23/75, 10.3.33
26. Davidson, *op cit*, p. 385
27. WSC to Linlithgow, 7.5.33, CV, Vol5–II, pp. 595–6
28. Hoare to Willingdon, 6.4.33, Hoare Papers
29. WSC to CC, 6.1.27, CV, Vol 5–I, pp. 907–8
30. *My Early Life*, p. 373
31. WSC to Randolph Churchill, 8.1.31, CV, Vol 5–11, p. 243
32. WSC to Abe Bailey, 31.10.35, *ibid*, p. 1308
33. *Evening Standard*, 24.1.34
34. Bridge *Holding India to the Empire*, p. 109
35. Hoare to Willingdon, 3.11.33, Hoare Papers
36. Charnley *Lord Lloyd*, p. 193

Chapter 17: Backbencher – The Uncertain Call

1. WSC to Linlithgow, 2.5.33, CV, Vol 5–11, p. 591
2. *The Times*, 9.11.34
3. *Ibid*, 28.2.33
4. *Daily Mail*, 26.5.32
5. *The Times*, 25.2.33
6. WSC to Editor, *News of the World*, 5.6.38, CV, Vol 5–III, pp. 1054–5
7. PREM 1/193, 29.7.36
8. PREM 1/237, 12.3.38
9. PREM 1/253, 9.6.38
10. CAB 2/5, 13.2.25
11. *Ibid*, 4.12.24
12. House of Commons, 13.7.34
13. Speech of 17.2.33 & *Sunday Chronicle*, 26.5.35
14. WSC to Lord Cranborne, 8.4.36, CV, Vol 5–III, pp. 92–3

15. WSC to Vansittart, 28.9.35, CV, Vol 5–II, pp. 1270–2
16. WSC to Austen Chamberlain, 1.10.35, *Ibid*, p. 1279
17. R. A. Butler Diary, 20–21.7.35
18. WSC to CC, 8.1.36, CV, Vol 5–III, pp. 5–11
19. CAB 21/435, 19.4.36
20. *News of the World*, 10.10.37
21. Speech of 11.7.35
22. WSC to Violet Bonham-Carter, 25.5.36, CV, Vol 5–III, pp. 171–3
23. Middlemas and Barnes *Baldwin*, p. 999
24. Zetland to Linlithgow, 27.11.36, Zetland Papers
25. Nicolson Diary, 8.12.36
26. WSC to CC, 21.2.36, CV, Vol 5–III pp. 52–3
27. CV Vol 5–I p. 894
28. CV Vol 5–II p. 369
29. *Ibid*, pp. 1085–7
30. CV Vol–III p. 912
31. Pearson *Citadel of the Heart*, p. 234
32. WSC to Lord Davies, 16.1.37, CV, Vol 5–III, p. 540
33. *The Gathering Storm*, p. 214
34. Packenham-Walsh Diary, 17.10.37, CV, Vol 5–III, pp. 799–800
35. *Step by Step*, p. 50
36. CAB 4/24, 21.11.35, DRC Third Report
37. CAB 4/26, 12.11.37
38. WSC Vol. 5, p. 956
39. *Evening Standard*, 15.10.37
40. House of Commons, 21.12.37
41. CAB 53/37, COS 698, 28.3.38
42. WSC to Reynaud, 10.10.38, CV, Vol 5–III, pp. 1208–9
43. WSC to Minney, 12.11.38, *ibid*, p. 1273
44. WSC to CC, 8.1.39, *ibid*, pp. 1342–4

Chapter 18: The Road to Power

1. *News of the World*, 24.4.38
2. *Colliers*, 14.1.39
3. *Daily Telegraph*, 4.5.39
4. House of Commons, 19.5.39
5. *News of the World*, 4.6.39
6. CAB 66/1, WP(39)15, 8.9.39
7. Paper 23.8.39, CV, Vol 5–III, pp. 1593–6
8. CAB 65/3, WM 20(39), 19.9.39
9. Speech 27.1.40, *Times* 29.1.40
10. Marder *Dardanelles to Oran*, p. 109
11. ADM 1/10818, 14.10.39

12. Marder, *op.cit.*, p. 124
13. ADM 205/2, 28.10.39
14. Marder, *op.cit.*, p. 130
15. ADM 199/299, 3.12.39
16. ADM 199/1928, 12.9.39
17. *Ibid*, 10.1.40
18. CAB 65/2, WM(85)39, 16.10.39
19. ADM 199/1928, 5.12.39
20. *Ibid*, 11.12.39
21. CAB 66/4, WP(39)162, 16.12.39
22. CAB 83/1, 20.12.39
23. WSC to Chamberlain, 25.12.39, Chamberlain Papers
24. CAB 65/11, WM(8)40, 10.1.40
25. CAB 65/5, WM(50)40, 23.2.40
26. CAB 65/12, WM(66)40, 14.3.40
27. FO 800/328, 14.3.40
28. CAB 99/3, SWC No 6, 28.3.40
29. CAB 65/5, WM(76)40, 27.3.40
30. CAB 65/6, WM(82)40, 5.4.40
31. CAB 127/50, 26.5.46
32. Templewood Diary, 8.4.40
33. CAB 65/6, WM(85)40, 9.4.40
34. CAB 65/6, WM(86)40, 9.4.40
35. CAB 99/3, 9.4.40
36. ADM 116/4471, 10.4.40
37. Nicolson Diary, 11.4.40, p. 70
38. CAB 83/3, 11.4.40
39. Ironside Diary, p. 253
40. CAB 65/12, WM(89)40, 12.4.40
41. *Ibid*, WM(90)40, 12.4.40
42. *Ibid*, WM(91)40, 13.4.40
43. Ironside Diary, p. 263
44. *Ibid*, p. 260
45. PREM 1/404, 16.4.40
46. Roskill Papers, 4/76
47. Ironside Diary, p. 272
48. CAB 65/6 WM(99)40, 21.4.40
49. Ironside Diary, p. 278
50. CAB 65/6 WM(105)40, 27.4.40, Ironside Diary, p. 287
51. Ironside Diary, p. 287
52. *Ibid*, p. 285
53. *Ibid*, p. 288
54. Colville *op.cit.*, 25.4.40
55. Channon Diary, 25.4.40, p. 242, & Nicolson Diary, 30.4.40, p. 74

56. Channon, *ibid*
57. *Ibid*, p. 244
58. Cecil King Diary, 3.5.40
59. Ironside Diary, 4.5.40, p. 294
60. Chamberlain to his sister, 17.9.39, Chamberlain Papers
61. Cadogan Diary, 9.5.40, p. 277
62. Halifax Diary, 9.5.40
63. WSC to Chamberlain, 10.5.40, Chamberlain Papers
64. WSC to Chamberlain, 16.9.39, *Ibid*
65. Colville, *op.cit.*, p. 122
66. R. A. Butler Diary, 13.5.40
67. Channon Diary, 13.5.40, p. 252

Chapter 19: 1940 – Survival

1. Hankey to Hoare, 12.5.40, Hoare Papers
2. Kennedy to State Dept, 15.5.40, FDR Library, PSF Box 26
3. CAB 65/13, WM(120)40, 13.5.40
4. CAB 65/7, WM(122)40, 14.5.40
5. CAB 65/13, WM(123)40, 15.5.40
6. CAB 99/3, SWC No 11, 16.5.40
7. CAB 65/7, WM(125)40, 16.5.40
8. CAB 66/7, WP(40)159, 18.5.40
9. Ironside Diary, 23.5.40, p. 331
10. *Their Finest Hour*, p. 157
11. Halifax Diary, 2.5.40
12. CAB 65/13, WM(139)40, 26.5.40
13. *Ibid*
14. CAB 65/13, WM(140)40, 26.5.40
15. PREM 1/395, 9.10.39
16. CAB 65/13, WM(142)40, 27.5.40
17. Chamberlain Diary, 26.5.40
18. CAB 65/13, WM(142)40, 27.5.40
19. *Ibid*, WM(145)40, 28.5.40
20. PREM 4/68/9, 29.5.40
21. CAB 65/13, WM(141)40, 27.5.40
22. *Ibid*, WM(146)40, 29.5.40
23. Ironside Diary, 29.5.40, pp. 344–5
24. Dalton Diary, 28.5.40, p. 27
25. Cadogan Diary, 26.5.40, p. 290
26. CAB 69/1, 8.6.40
27. CAB 99/3, 11.6.40
28. CAB 65/7, WM(163)40, 12.6.40
29. CAB 65/13, WM(176)40, 22.6.40

30. CAB 65/14, WM(192)40, 3.7.40
31. Quoted Marder, *op.cit.*, p. 267
32. Colville Diary, 3.7.40, pp. 183–4
33. WSC to Baldwin, 4.6.40, Baldwin papers
34. Record of Ismay-Sherwood conversation July 46, Sherwood Papers, f1891
35. Cecil King Diary, 18.6.40, p. 55
36. Nicolson Diary, 19.6.40, p. 97
37. Colville Diary, 18.6.40, p. 168
38. PREM 4/101/2, 25.8.40
39. INF 1/264, 18.5.40
40. *Ibid*, 24.5.40
41. *Ibid*, 24.6.40
42. *Ibid*, 30.6.40
43. CAB 65/8, WM(189)40, 1.7.40
44. *Ibid*, WM(192)40, 3.7.40
45. INF 1/849, 5.7.40
46. INF 1/264, 16.7.40 & 22.7.40
47. Nicolson Diary, 21.7.40
48. Cecil King Diary, 8.2.40, p. 22
49. CAB 66/7, WP(40)168, 25.5.40
50. Colville Diary, 12.7.40, p. 192
51. CAB 65/7, WM(148)40, 30.5.40
52. PREM 3/88/3, 28.9.40
53. PREM 3/222/3, 5.7.40
54. Channon Diary, 26.9.40, p. 268
55. Chamberlain Diary, 9.9.40
56. *Ibid*
57. *Ibid*, 30.9.40

Chapter 20: 1940 – Twilight of a Great Power

1. CAB 132/28, 24.5.37
2. CAB 51/31, 31.5.37
3. CAB 65/2, WM(89)39, 20.11.39
4. *Ibid*, WM(92)39, 23.11.39
5. CAB 99/1, 20.11.39
6. CAB 65/2, WM(92)39, 23.11.39
7. CAB 66/3, WP(39)135, 17.11.39
8. CAB 65/2, WM(68)39, 2.11.39
9. *Ibid*, WM(89)39, 20.11.39
10. CAB 80/16, COS(40)592, 15.8.40
11. CAB 66/7, WP(40)168, 25.5.40
12. CAB 66/9, WP(40)234, 29.6.40

13. CAB 66/10, WP(40)308, 6.8.40
14. PREM 4/438/1, 11.8.40
15. Thorne *Allies of a Kind*, p. 72
16. PREM 1/345, 25.3.39
17. CAB 66/9, WP(40)234, 29.6.40
18. Cadogan Diary, 4.7.40, p. 310
19. Colville Diary, 25.6.40, p. 200
20. CAB 66/9, WP(40)249, 4.7.40
21. PREM 4/42/8, 20.5.40
22. CAB 65/8, WM(194)40, 5.7.40
23. Cadogan Diary, 5.7.40, p. 311
24. CAB 65/8, WM(199)40, 10.7.40
25. *Ibid*, WM(200)40, 11.7.40
26. FO 800/310, 20.10.39
27. CAB 65/1, WM(58)39, 24.10.39
28. Cadogan Diary, p. 341
29. PREM 3/131/1, 17.6.40
30. CAB 65/7, WM(173)40, 20.6.40
31. PREM 3/131/1, 27.6.40
32. PREM 3/131/2, 26.6.40
33. *Ibid*, 27.6.40
34. *Ibid*
35. PREM 3/128/22, 17.2.41
36. PREM 4/21/1, 29.9.40
37. CAB 79/6, 7.8.40 252nd Meeting, 3.30pm
38. *Ibid*, 7.8.40, 253rd Meeting, 11pm
39. *Ibid*, 20.8.40
40. CAB 65/15, WM(250)40, 16.9.40
41. PREM 3/276, 21.9.40
42. *Ibid*, 23.9.40
43. CAB 121/1454, 7.8.40
44. FO 371/24335 & FO 371/24302, 31.10.40
45. Colville Diary, 1.11.40, p. 283
46. PREM 3/178/5, 8.11.40
47. FO 371/28234, 21.12.40
48. CAB 65/13, WM(282)40, 4.11.40
49. Eden Diary 2.11.40
50. PREM 3/288/1, 22.11.40
51. Avon, *The Reckoning*, p. 178
52. *Ibid*, p. 181
53. WSC Vol 6 pp 587-8
54. James, *Victor Cazalet*, p. 231
55. ADM 199/1931, 29.8.40
56. PREM 3/119/10, 24/31.8.40

57. Colville Diary, 10.7.40, p. 188
58. *Ibid*, 13.8.40, p. 122
59. ADM 1/19177, 20.7.40
60. PREM 3/314/2, 20.10.40
61. Thompson, *Churchill and Morton*, pp 71 & 174
62. Colville Diary, pp. 280–1
63. INF 1/869, 17.5.40
64. Reith Diary, 6.11.40, p. 270
65. PREM 4/66/2, 5.10.40
66. CAB 65/13, WM(268)40, 9.10.40
67. Titmuss, *Social Policy* p. 309
68. INF 1/292, Coventry 19.11.40, Bristol 4–11.12.40, Portsmouth May 41
69. Nicolson Diary, 7.5.41, p. 164
70. Colville Diary, 12.10.40, p. 264
71. *Ibid*, 4.10.40, p. 257
72. *Ibid*, 8.7.40, pp. 186–7
73. CAB 66/13, WP(40)466, 8.12.40
74. Colville Diary, 13.10.40, p. 255
75. *Ibid*, 8.7.40, pp. 186–7
76. CAB 66/11, WP(40)352, 3.9.40
77. CAB 69/1, 30.10.40
78. Colville Diary, 30.8.40, p. 233
79. CAB 24/282, 15.1.39
80. CAB 66/7, WP(40)168, 25.5.40
81. *Colliers*, 22.8.35, *Daily Mail*, 24.4.35 & 22.8.35
82. FDR Library, PSF Box 9, 12.3.40
83. Harold Ickes Diary, 12.5.40
84. CAB 65/7, WM(129)40, 25.5.40
85. Complete Presidential Press Conferences of Franklin D. Roosevelt Vol 15, pp. 412–3
86. Ickes Diary, 4.6.40
87. CAB 66/10, WP(40)276, 18.7.40
88. PREM 3/475/1, 17.7.40
89. FO 371/24241, 7.8.40
90. CAB 65/8, WM(231)40, 21. 8. 40
91. PREM 3/468, 25.8.40
92. Colville Diary, 5.3.41, p. 317
93. PREM 3/468, 15.5.40
94. FO 371/25209, 17.7.40 & 2.8.40
95. CAB 66/11, WP(40)324, 21.8.40
96. CAB 65/14, WM(232)40, 22.8.40
97. CAB 66/11, WP(40)355, 4.9.40
98. CAB 65/15, WM(244)40, 6.9.40
99. FO 371/24246, 21.9.40

100. Colville Diary, 1.11.40, p. 283
101. CAB 65/10, WM(299)40, 2.12.40
102. PREM 4/25/8, 20.12.40
103. PREM 3/486/1, 12.11.40
104. CAB 66/13, WP(40)466, 8.12.40
105. FO 371/25209, 10.12.40
106. PREM 4/17/1, 28.12.40
107. PREM 4/17/2, 20.3.41
108. PREM 4/17/3, 5.2.42

Chapter 21: 1941 – The Grimmest Year

1. Stoler *Politics of the Second Front*, pp. 6–7
2. PREM 3/489/4, 22.11.40
3. FO 371/28899, 27.1.40
4. Hopkins Diary, 10.1.41
5. PREM 3/309/1, 17.12.40
6. CAB 69/2, 20.1.41
7. CAB 105/1
8. *Ibid*
9. CAB 69/2, 10.2.41
10. *Ibid*, 11.2.41
11. FO 371/33145, 15.2.41
12. PREM 3/294/1, 22.2.41
13. CAB 80/57, 24.2.41
14. CAB 65/21, WM(20)41, 24.2.41
15. CAB 69/2, 5.3.41
16. CAB 65/22, WM(26)41, 7.3.41
17. CAB 65/22, WM(41)41, 28.4.41
18. PREM 3/109, 14.5.41
19. *Ibid*, 14.6.41
20. Colville Diary, 7.4.41, p. 372
21. PREM 3/469, 2.5.41
22. Colville Diary, 2.5.41, p. 382
23. PREM 3/476/10, 15.5.41
24. FO 954/29, 21.5.41
25. CAB 79.12, JP(41)444, 16.6.41
26. Colville Diary, 21.6.41, p. 404
27. CAB 69/2, 17.6.41
28. PREM 3/401/1, 7.7.41
29. PREM 3/395/16, 10.7.41
30. CAB 79/12, COS(41)244, 14.7.41
31. INF 1/849, 4.9.41
32. FO 954/24, 4.9.41

33. PREM 3/422/1, 19.5.41
34. FO 371/27298, 7.7.41
35. PREM 3/422/8, 22.7.41
36. PREM 3/422/6, 24.7.41
37. PREM 3/120/5, 27.8.41
38. *Ibid*, 2.9.41
39. FO 371/28545, 19.9.41
40. PREM 4/120/4, 23.9.41
41. *Ibid*, 26.9.41
42. PREM 3/74/6, 9.3.41
43. FO 371/28477, 5.6.41
44. Harvey Diary, 1.8.41, p. 26
45. Cadogan Diary, 28.4.41, p. 374
46. *Ibid*, 4.6.41, p. 386
47. Harvey Diary, 22.7.41, p. 22
48. *Ibid*, 3.8.41, p. 26
49. *Ibid*, 25.6.41, p. 15
50. *Ibid*, 9.7.41, p. 17
51. *Ibid*, 10.7.41, p. 18
52. Reith Diary, 31.1.41, pp. 274–5
53. *Ibid*, 2.9.41, p. 280
54. Colville Diary, 18.8.41, p. 428
55. Harvey Diary, 25.6.41 & 6.7.41, pp. 25–6
56. Cadogan Diary, 6.8.41, p. 423
57. PREM 3/485/6, 3.8.41
58. PREM 4/43A/3, 17.8.41
59. US National Archives, MM WPD 4402–64
60. CAB 65/19, WM(84)41, 19.8.41
61. PREM 3/224/2, 28.8.41
62. Colville Diary, 30.8.41, p. 434
63. Hopkins to Roosevelt, 2.9.41, Hopkins Papers Box 308
64. CAB 120/300, 19.9.40
65. *Ibid*, Oct 40
66. *Ibid*, 31.10.40
67. *Ibid*, 2.11.40
68. Webster and Frankland *The Strategic Air Offensive Against Germany*, Vol 4, p. 138
69. CAB 120/300, 25.9.41
70. *Ibid*, 27.9.41
71. *Ibid*, 7.10.41
72. PREM 3/476/3, 8.11.41
73. CAB 65/24, WM(123)41, 3.12.41
74. CAB 69/3, 22.9.41
75. CAB 65/24, WM(120)41, 27.11.41

76. CAB 84/24, 22.11.40
77. CAB 79/8, COS(30)41, 25.1.41
78. Marder *Old Friends, New Enemies*, p. 188
79. Beaverbrook to WSC, 5.4.41, Beaverbrook papers D416
80. CAB 69/2, 9.4.41
81. *Ibid*
82. CAB 80/27, 11.4.41
83. PREM 3/156/6, 28.4.41
84. CAB 65/23, WM(72)41, 21.7.41
85. CAB 65/14, WM(214)40, 29.7.40
86. FRUS 1941, Vol 1, pp. 354–6
87. CAB 66/18, WP(41)202, 18.8.41
88. Cecil King Diary, 23.8.41, p. 140
89. WSC to Ismay, 10.9.40, Ismay Papers
90. ADM 199/1934, 25.8.41
91. ADM 205/10, 28.8.41
92. *Ibid*, 29.8.41
93. CAB 84/35, 7.10.41
94. CAB 63/23, WM(103)41, 16.10.41 & WM(104)41, 20.10.41
95. CAB 79/24, 20.10.41
96. CAB 69/8, 20.10.41
97. PREM 3/163/3, 18.11.41
98. ADM 205/101, 1.11.41 & 3.11.41
99. PREM 3/156/6, 23.11.41
100. CAB 65/24, WM(108)41, 3.11.41
101. CAB 79/6, 1.12.41
102. CAB 69/2, 3.12.41
103. CAB 65/20, WM(127)41, 12.12.41

Chapter 22: 1942 – Strategy and Survival

1. CAB 65/20, WM(125(41), 8.12.41
2. PREM 3/469, 9.12.41
3. PREM 3/499/2, 21.12.41
4. MM WPD 4494–21
5. FRUS, Conferences at Washington 1941–2 & Casablanca pp. 56–8
6. FDR Library, Wickard Diary, 23.1.42
7. CAB 65/25, WM(8)42, 17.1.42
8. Day, *The Great Betrayal*, p. 229
9. Moran, 9.1.42, p. 21
10. Ismay Papers VI/2, 14.1.42
11. *Ibid*, 20.1.42
12. CAB 69/4, 21.1.42
13. Ismay Papers VI/2, 10.2.42

14. CAB 69/4
15. Harvey Diary, 20.1.42, p. 87
16. Dalton Diary, 4–5.2.42, pp. 360–2
17. Cadogan Diary, 2.2.42, p. 430
18. Amery to Linlithgow, 13.1.42, Linlithgow Papers
19. Harvey Diary, 12.2.42, p. 94
20. Dalton Diary, 6.2.42, p. 362
21. FO 954/4, 20.2.41
22. FDR Papers, PSF Box 50, 7.3.42
23. Cadogan Diary, 2.3.42, p. 438
24. Dalton Diary, 5.3.42, p. 390
25. Eden Diary, 7.4.42
26. WSC to Ismay, 12.7.49, Ismay Papers, II/2/165
27. INF 1/292, 19.2.42
28. WSC Vol 7, pp. 66–7
29. PREM 4/50/7, 30.1.42
30. WSC to Curtin, 22.2.42, Quoted Day, *op. cit.*, p. 270
31. PREM 3/151/4, 17.5.42
32. Parkinson, *Auk*, p. 166
33. ADM 205/14, 16.6.42
34. Harvey Diary, 13.8.42, p. 149
35. Cuthbert Hedlam Diary, Quoted Jeffrys, *Politics in the Second World War*, p. 100
36. PREM 3/136/8, 1.12.43
37. Stoler, *op. cit.*, p. 41
38. CAB 79/56, 14.4.42
39. PREM 3/399, 20.12.41
40. FO 371/32874, Jan 42
41. PREM 3/399/7, 8.1.42
42. PREM 3/470, 7.3.42
43. PREM 3/399/8, 13.5.42
44. CAB 65/30, WM(73)42, 11.6.42
45. CCS 28th Meeting, 20.6.42
46. CAB 99/20, 20.6.42
47. CAB 80/33, JP(42)670, 14.7.42
48. Howard, *Grand Strategy*, p. xx
49. MM OPD 381 Gen (Sec II)73, 10.7.42
50. CCS 94, 24.7.42
51. Bryant, *Turn of the Tide*, p. 138
52. CAB 120/34, 25.6.42
53. Cadogan Diary, 7.7.42, p. 461
54. PREM 3/76A/12, 12.8.42
55. PREM 3/76A/9, 13.8.42
56. FO 800/300, 14.8.42

57. Jacob Diary, 14.8.42
58. Moran, 14.8.42, p. 62
59. FO 800/300, 15.8.42
60. Moran, 15.8.42, p. 64
61. CAB 65/31, WM(118)42, 25.8.42
62. CAB 120/300, 15.6.42
63. ADM 205/24, 14.7.42
64. *Ibid*, 24.8.42
65. PREM 3/97/1, 13.8.42
66. CAB 66/30, WP(42)483, 24.10.42
67. Hastings, *Bomber Command*, p. 134
68. *Ibid*, p. 170
69. Webster & Frankland, Vol 1, p. 479
70. CAB 66/26, WP(42)311, 21.7.42
71. CAB 120/300, 13.9.42
72. AIR 8/424 – 601/1, 18.9.42 & 22.9.42
73. FO 371/31873, 22.1.42
74. PREM 3/120/10, 16.1.42
75. State Dept 740.0011 EW/39/20906, 9.4.42
76. Cadogan Diary, 19.9.42, p. 478
77. PREM 3/120/7, 11.4.42
78. *Ibid*, 30.5.42
79. PREM 3/265/11, 22.9.42
80. PREM 3/120/6, 30.9.42
81. CAB 65/20 WM(127)41, 12.12.41
82. PREM 3/186A/7, Dec 41
83. CAB 66/25, WP(42)239, 5.6.42
84. PREM 3/186A/7, 14.6.42
85. PREM 3/120/6, 22.9.42
86. Eden Diary, 20.11.42
87. Harvey Diary, 26.11.42, pp. 192–3
88. PREM 3/442/9, 11.11.42
89. *Ibid*, 17.11.42
90. Cadogan Diary, 14.11.42, pp. 492–3
91. Harvey Diary, 2.10.42, p. 165
92. Moran, p. 76
93. Chuter Ede Diary, 31.12.42

Chapter 23: 1943–45 – Decline

1. FDR Papers, MRF Box 2, 22.9.42
2. CAB 79/58, COS(42)392, 15.11.42
3. CAB 80/65, 30.10.42
4. MM OPD Exec 5 Item 5 Tab 11/11, 11.11.42

5. Harvey Diary, 14.11.42, p. 183
6. CAB 79/58, 3.12.42
7. CAB 80/67, CCS 14–16.1.43
8. FRUS Conferences at Washington & Casablanca pp. 601–4 & 614–22
9. *Ibid*, p. 631
10. S. Rosenman: Public Papers and Addresses of F. D. Roosevelt, 1943, p. 83
11. C. de Gaulle, *L'Unite*, p. 79
12. *Ibid*, pp. 84–5
13. Spears Papers, 2.2.43
14. FO 371/36064, 10.2.43
15. CAB 79/60, 13.4.43
16. CAB 99/22, 10.5.43
17. FRUS Conferences at Washington and Quebec 1943, pp. 46–53
18. Bryant, Vol 1, p. 626
19. FO 371/36047. 21.5.43
20. Harvey Diary, 25.5.43, p. 261
21. FDR Library MR/Special File, FNC/Sect 1, 30.5.43 (Version in FRUS 1943 is censored)
22. Avon *The Reckoning* p. 388
23. Harvey Diary, 14.6.43, p. 266
24. PREM 3/121/1, 12.6.43
25. PREM 3/184/6, 19.6.43
26. PREM 3/333/19, 19.7.43
27. FRUS Conferences at Washington and Quebec 1943, pp. 496–8
28. Ibid, p. 470
29. Ibid, pp. 498–503
30. Ibid, p. 865
31. Ibid, p. 897
32. Bryant, Vol 1, p. 707
33. PREM 3/181/8, 14.7.43
34. PREM 3/181/2, 21.7.43
35. PREM 3/3, 2.8.43
36. Ibid, 9.9.43
37. PREM 3/124/2, 13.1.41
38. CAB 79/65, 7.10.43
39. Bryant Vol 2, p. 51
40. CAB 79/66, 19.10.43
41. Moran, 26.10.43, p. 122
42. CAB 80/77, 20.11.43
43. PREM 3/342/5, 6.11.43
44. FRUS Conferences at Cairo and Teheran 1943, pp. 407–8
45. PREM 3/197/2, 19.4.44
46. PREM 3/367, 18.3.44
47. CAB 99/28, 3.5.44

48. PREM 3/499/9, 29.7.42
49. Webster & Frankland Vol 4, p. 153
50. CAB 80/70, COS(42)392, 15.11.42
51. Hastings, *Bomber Command*, p. 107
52. CAB 65/37, WM(42)43, 18.3.43
53. CAB 65/34, WM(52)43, 29.4.43
54. CAB 99/22, 12.5.43
55. PREM 3/147/3, 7.8.43
56. CAB 99/23, 19.8.43
57. FRUS Conferences at Washington and Quebec 1943, p. 172
58. PREM 3/147/10, 2.10.43
59. Moran, 15.12.43, p. 152
60. Bryant Vol 2, p. 175
61. *Ibid*, p. 185
62. *Ibid*, p. 187
63. *Ibid*, p. 142
64. *Ibid*, p. 137
65. Cadogan Diary, 8.7.43, pp. 541–2
66. Bryant Vol 2, p. 43
67. Cunningham Diary, 2.4.44
68. Cadogan Diary, 19.4.44, p. 621
69. *Ibid*, 30.5.44, pp. 630–1
70. *Ibid*, 17.7.44 & 3.8.44, p. 647 & 653
71. Bryant Vol 2, p. 159
72. Cunningham Diary 8.9.44
73. *Ibid*, 6.7.44
74. Eden Diary, 6.7.44
75. Bryant Vol 2, p. 230
76. PREM 3/177/6, 26.1.44
77. Cadogan Diary, 5.6.44, pp. 634–5
78. Eden Diary, 6.6.44
79. FO 371/41994, 13.6.44
80. Cadogan Diary, 7.6.44, p. 635
81. FO 954/9, 16.6.44
82. Moran, 22.9.44, p. 185
83. CAB 120/122, 26.12.43
84. CAB 79/69, 19.1.44
85. CAB 119/3, 2.2.4
86. CAB 79/76, 21.6.44 (JPS 170(44))
87. *Ibid*, 21.6.44 (COS(203)44)
88. Bryant Vol 2, p. 223
89. CAB 122/1246, 23.6.44
90. *Ibid*, 26.6.44
91. FDR Papers MR Box 11, 3.7.44

92. FO 954/17, 17.7.44
93. PREM 3/88/3, 28.9.40
94. *Ibid*, 27.2.43
95. CAB 120/775, 6.7.44
96. CAB 98/36, 18.7.44
97. CAB 120/775, 28.7.44
98. *Ibid*, 29.7.44
99. PREM 3/65, Minutes of 25.2.44, 21.5.44 & 8.3.44
100. FO 954/9, 19.1.45
101. Colville Diary, 6.9.44, p. 509
102. Bryant Vol 2, p. 273
103. CAB 120/144, 13.9.44
104. CAB 120/156, 13.9.44
105. Quoted Kolko, *The Politics of War*, p. 283
106. FO 371/40881, 24.2.44
107. CAB 65/43, WM(93)44, 18.7.44
108. CAB 66/52, WP(44)360, 14.7.44
109. CAB 65/40, WM(61)44, 14.4.44
110. Cherwell to WSC, 17.3.44, Cherwell Papers
111. FRUS The Conference at Quebec 1944, p. 348
112. Morgenthau Diaries, 15.9.44
113. PREM 4/42/5, 3.5.44
114. Dalton Diary, 4.8.44, p. 373
115. CAB 69/6, 19.1.44
116. PREM 3/160/7, 29.2.44
117. Bryant Vol 2, p. 161–6, 170
118. *Ibid*, p. 182
119. Ismay to Pownall, 27.5.44, Ismay Papers
120. CAB 79/77, 6.7.44
121. PREM 3/160/6, 12.9.44
122. FRUS The Conference at Quebec 1944, p. 267
123. Moran, 30.1.45, p. 216
124. Eden Diary, 12.1.45
125. Moran, p. 308
126. Cadogan Diary, 22.2.45, pp. 719–20
127. Attlee to WSC, 19.1.45, Attlee Papers
128. Colville Diary, 20.1.45, p. 554
129. Bryant Vol 2, p. 481
130. Eden Diary, 31.8.45
131. CAB 120/840, 7.12.42 & 21.3.43
132. PREM 3/156/6, 28.4.41
133. C. Barett, *Engage the Enemy More Closely*, p. 366
134. CAB 120/300, 25.1.42
135. ADM 205/56, 23.7.43

136. PREM 3/87, 27.9.44
137. PREM 3/473, 14.4.45
138. Quoted Hastings, *op. cit.*, p. 301
139. CAB 120/301, 1.10.44
140. *Ibid*, 26.1.45
141. PREM 3/12, 28.3.45
142. CAB 65/43, WM(93)44, 18.7.44
143. Cadogan Diary, 13.2.45

Chapter 24: Creating the Post-War World

1. PREM 4/30/2, 10.2.42
2. PREM 4/33/3, 13.12.42
3. Colville Diary, 13.12.40, pp. 312–3
4. Blum, *The Diary of Henry Wallace*, p. 202, 22.5.43
5. PREM 4/30/10, 6.12.44
6. *Ibid*
7. PREM 4/33/5, 5.9.43
8. *Ibid*, 8.4.45
9. CAB 66/10, WP(40)276, 18.7.40
10. CAB 66/39, WP(43)233, 28.5.43
11. FO 954/22, 24.9.43
12. PREM 4/27/10, 16.2.44
13. Kimball Vol 3, p. 535
14. FDR Library, Harry Hopkins A-bomb folder, 1.4.43
15. *Ibid*, 23.3.43
16. PREM 3/139/8A, 15.4.43
17. *Ibid*, 21.7.43
18. Sherwin, *A World Destroyed*, p. 83
19. PREM 3/139/8A, 21.7.43
20. Gowing, *Britain and Atomic Energy*, Appendix 4
21. PREM 3/139/2, 21.3.44
22. PREM 3/139/6, 25.3.45
23. *Ibid*
24. Colville Diary, 21.9.40, p. 245
25. CAB 65/19, WM(74)41, 24.7.41
26. PREM 3/399/6, 25.12.41
27. PREM 3/399/7, 8.1.42
28. PREM 3/399/6, 23.5.42
29. PREM 3/354/8, 3.4.43
30. *Ibid*, 23.4.43
31. *Ibid*, 28.4.43
32. *Ibid*, 27.4.43
33. *Ibid*, 10.5.43

34. PREM 3/355/4, 6.10.43
35. Mayle, p. 60
36. Bryant Vol 2, p. 88
37. PREM 3/136/8, 28.11.43
38. FO 371/34378, 9.11.43
39. CAB 65/41, WM(34)44, 13.3.44
40. FRUS Conferences at Cairo and Teheran 1943, p. 599
41. Cadogan Diary, 1.12.43, p. 581
42. PREM 3/355/7, 7.1.44
43. FO 954/20, 6.2.44
44. FO 371/39422, 9.2.44
45. PREM 3/355/8, 15.2.44
46. PREM 3/353, 26.2.44
47. FO 371/39402, 31.5.44
48. PREM 4/42/5, 5.5.44
49. FO 954/20, 8.5.44
50. FO 954/26, 18.3.43
51. PREM 3/399/6, 16.1.44
52. Lord Tedder, *With Prejudice*, p. 330
53. FO 371/44001, 28.5.44
54. PREM 3/434/4, 9.10.44
55. FO 800/302, 9.10.44
56. PREM 3/434/4, 9.10.44
57. *Ibid*
58. *Ibid*
59. FRUS The Conferences at Malta and Yalta, pp. 6–7
60. PREM 3/66/7, 11.10.44
61. PREM 3/343/5, 13.10.44
62. Quoted de Zayas, *Nemesis at Potsdam*, pp. 47–8
63. Harvey Diary, 15.10.44, pp. 361–2
64. CAB 65/48, WM(157)44, 27.11.44
65. Soames, *Clementine Churchill*, p. 361
66. PREM 3/397/3, 18.10.44
67. CAB 65/48, WM(157)44, 27.11.44
68. CAB 21/1614, 25.11.44
69. FO 954/23, 18.1.45
70. *Ibid*, 19.1.45
71. PREM 3/472, 5.8.43
72. PREM 3/242/8, 21.10.43
73. PREM 3/243/5, 25.10.43
74. PREM 3/472, 13.3.44
75. PREM 3/243/12, 10.6.44
76. *Ibid*, 25.6.44
77. PREM 3/472, 6.12.44

78. FO 954/14, 16.6.45
79. FO 371/37625, 11.7.43
80. PREM 3/511/2, 6.1.44
81. FO 371/44247, 16.2.44
82. PREM 3/512/5, 19.6.44
83. FO 371/37203, 15.6.43
84. PREM 3/211/9, 6.2.44
85. PREM 3/211/11, 8.4.44
86. CAB 65/43, WM(103) 44 & CAB 66/53, WP(44)433, 9.8.44
87. FO 371/43778, 21.8.44
88. FO 371/43777, 29.9.44
89. PREM 3/212/9, 4.10.44
90. FO 371/43695, 7.11.44
91. FO 371/43736, 5.12.44
92. *Ibid*
93. FO 954/11, 14.12.44
94. PREM 3/212/13, 24.12.44
95. Cadogan Diary, 21.12.44, p. 689
96. FO 800/414/54, 26.12.44
97. FO 954/11, 27.12.44
98. FO 371/48245, 7.1.45
99. FO 371/48267, 22.4.45
100. Colville Diary, 20.9.40, p. 245
101. Cadogan Diary, 19.7.43, p. 545
102. PREM 3/434/4, 9.10.44
103. Moran, 13.9.44, p. 177
104. *Ibid*, 15.9.44, p. 178
105. CAB 120/153, 15.9.44
106. PREM 3/343/4, 17.10.44
107. Sherwood, *White House Papers of Harry Hopkins*, Vol 1, p. 478
108. PREM 4/45/3, 3.2.42
109. CAB 99/26, 21.10.42
110. PREM 4/42/5, 9.5.44
111. PREM 3/326, 11.2.44
112. FO 371/31866, 20.5.42
113. Moran, p. 559
114. Sir F. Eggleston Diary, 14.11.44, Louis, *Imperialism at Bay*, p. 7 & p. 424
115. Moran, 24.11.43, p. 131
116. PREM 4/30/5, 8.10.43
117. PREM 4/100/7, 21.10.42
118. PREM 4/30/11, 23.8.44
119. Cadogan Diary, 9.2.45, p. 707
120. James, *Anthony Eden*, p. 289
121. Moran, 11.2.45, p. 231

122. Cadogan Diary, 8.2.45 & 11.2.45, pp. 706–9
123. FRUS Conferences at Malta and Yalta, p. 853
124. Cadogan Diary, 8.2.45, p. 706
125. *Ibid*, 13.2.45, p. 710
126. *Ibid*, 20.2.45, p. 717
127. CAB 65/49, WM(13)45, 12.2.45
128. Dalton Diary, 23.2.45
129. FO 954/23, 5.3.45 & 13.3.45
130. PREM 3/472, 8.3.45
131. *Ibid*, 13.3.45
132. CAB 65/52, WM(39)45, 3.4.45
133. FO 954/26, 25.3.45
134. PREM 3/396/12, 18.5.45
135. FO 371/48192, 29.5.45
136. FO 371/48193, 17.6.45
137. FO 371/50776, 1.6.45
138. Moran, 22.7.45, p. 279
139. Cadogan Diary, 18.7.45, p. 765
140. *Ibid*, 17.7.45, p. 764
141. Mee, *Meeting at Potsdam*, p. 96
142. Eden Diary, 17.7.45
143. CAB 99/38, 18.7.45
144. Cadogan Diary, 18.7.45, p. 766

Chapter 25: Towards a New World?

1. FO 371/46325, 11.4.45
2. Thorne, *Allies of a Kind*, p. 60
3. PREM 4/43A/3, 17.8.43
4. Louis, *Imperialism at Bay*, p. 181
5. PREM 4/31/4, 31.12.44
6. *Ibid*, 10.1.45
7. Byrnes, *Speaking Frankly*, p. x
8. FRUS Conferences at Malta and Yalta, p. 844
9. CAB 65/2 WM(94)39, 25.10.39
10. CAB 65/5, WM(22)40, 2.2.40
11. PREM 1/414, 20.2.40
12. Transfer of Power Vol 1: Cripps Mission (CM) Doc 6, 7.1.42
13. CM 294, 11.3.42
14. CM 430/431, 29.3.42
15. CM 502, 2.4.42
16. CM 522, 4.4.42
17. CM 567, 9.4.42
18. CM 581, 10.4.42

19. CM 582, 10.4.42
20. PREM 4/48/9, 12.4.42
21. Transfer of Power Vol 3 Doc 2, 9.9.42
22. *Ibid*, 178, 12.11.42
23. Amery to Linlithgow, 21.6.43, Linlithgow Papers
24. Wavell Journal, 24.6.43
25. *Ibid*, 27.6.43
26. Moran, p. 31
27. Wavell Journal, 10.3.44
28. Dalton Diary, 3.8.44
29. CAB 65/43, WM(100)44, 3.8.44
30. Wavell Journal, 8.10.43
31. *Ibid*, 31.5.45
32. PREM 4/50/3, 3.12.44
33. Butler, *Art of the Possible*, p. 111
34. Colville Diary, 23.2.45, p. 563
35. CAB 66/36, WP(43)178, 28.4.43
36. Spears Papers, 27.6.43
37. CAB 69/9, 19.4.44
38. CAB 66/17, WP(41)142, 26.6.41
39. PREM 4/6/2, 6.10.41
40. *Ibid*, 17.10.41
41. *Ibid*, 17.4.43
42. *Ibid*, 30.7.43 & 2.8.43
43. PREM 4/15/2, 19.12.42
44. *Ibid*, 13.3.43
45. PREM 4/14/15, 8.9.42 & 10.9.42
46. *Ibid*, 17.9.42
47. *Ibid*, 9.7.43
48. *Ibid*, 23.7.43 & 25.7.43
49. *Ibid*, 15.8.43
50. CAB 65/28, WM(140)42, 13.10.42
51. Cadogan Diary, 13.10.42, p. 483
52. PREM 4/26/9, 20.10.43
53. *Ibid*, 21.10.43
54. *Ibid*, 18.11.43
55. *Ibid*, 2.12.43
56. FO 954/29A, 5.1.42
57. Colville Diary, 10.8.40, p. 216
58. Harvie-Watt, *Most of My Life*, p. 117
59. CAB 65/33, WM(18)43, 15.2.43
60. Butler Diary, 9.9.43
61. PREM 4/36/3, 10.2.44
62. PREM 4/89/3, 15.11.43

63. PREM 4/89/4, 25.6.44
64. PREM 4/82/1, 15.8.40
65. *Ibid*, 2.9.42
66. PREM 4/88/1, 20.11.44
67. PREM 4/89/5, 27.6.44
68. INF 1/292, 22.6.44
69. *Ibid*, 20.10.44
70. Calder *People's War*, p. 280
71. Colville Diary, 18.2.44, p. 474
72. Moran, 20.9.44, p. 205
73. Colville Diary, 12.12.40, p. 310
74. Moran, 8.7.45, p. 258
75. Minney, *Private Papers of Hore-Belisha*, p. 229
76. Moran, 22.6.45, p. 254
77. *Ibid*, 20.5.45, p. 251
78. WSC to Duff Cooper, 17.9.45, WSC Vol 8, p. 148

Chapter 26: Opposition

1. Moran, p. 299.
2. Channon Diary, 21.8.45, p. 412
3. Soames, *Clementine Churchill*, p. 391
4. Moran, p. 256
5. WSC, Vol 8, p. 631
6. The Mackenzie King Record Vol 3, p. 236
7. Moran, 8.8.46, p. 315
8. The Mackenzie King Record Vol 4, pp. 112–3
9. FRUS 1948 Vol 3, 17.4.48, pp. 90–1
10. WSC Vol 8, p. 422
11. *Ibid*, p. 435
12. *Ibid*, p. 635
13. *Saturday Evening Post*, 15.2.30 (*News of the World*, 29.5.38)
14. CAB 128/15, 16.12.48
15. Roskill *Churchill and the Admirals*, p. 281
16. Eisenhower Papers, Bermuda Conference, 5th plenary session, 7.12.53, 5.30pm
17. The Mackenzie King Record Vol 3, p. 83
18. Colville Diary, 30.11.47, pp. 620–1
19. Avon, *The Reckoning*, p. 145
20. Moran, 22.7.45, p. 279
21. Carlton, *Anthony Eden*, pp. 266–7
22. CC to WSC, 5.3.49, WSC Vol 8, p. 462
23. Ramsden *Making of Conservative Party Policy*, p. 146

Chapter 27: Return to Power

1. Moran, p. 339
2. *Ibid*, 22.2.52, p. 375
3. *Macmillan Diary*, Vol 1, 4.6.52, Horne, p. 352
4. Eden Diary, 4.6.52
5. Eisenhower Diary, 21.12.51
6. Colville Diary, 16.5.52, p. 647
7. Crookshank Diary, 26.2.53
8. Eisenhower Diary, 13.2.53
9. *Ibid*, 5.1.53
10. Dixon Diary, 5.5.53, Carlton, *Anthony Eden*, p. 328
11. CAB 128/26, CC(53)51, 8.9.53
12. PREM 11/84, 16.6.52
13. PREM 11/507, 28.2.52
14. PREM 11/477, 30.5.53
15. WSC Vol 8, p. 403
16. Moran, p. 390
17. PREM 11/336
18. PREM 11/824, CC(52)100, 25.11.52
19. *Ibid*, 15.12.52
20. *Ibid*, CC(54)10, 3.2.54
21. PREM 11/1074, 8.8.54
22. PREM 11/190, 30.10.52
23. PREM 11/1367, 12.2.52
24. CAB 128/26, CC(53)34, 27.5.53
25. CAB 128/27, CC(54)83, 7.12.54
26. CAB 129/69, C(54)245, 28.7.54
27. CAB 134/762, 12.8.52
28. CAB 129/55, C(52)320, 3.10.52
29. CAB 131/12, 14.5.52
30. CAB 21./2281B, 15.11.51
31. Gowing, *Independence and Deterrence*, p. 410
32. Moran, 1.1.52, p. 352
33. Shuckburgh *Descent to Suez*, p. 32
34. CAB 129/52, C(52)282, 12.6.52
35. PREM 11/392, 10.1.53
36. Eisenhower Diary, 5/6.1.53
37. Eisenhower Library, WFIS Box 17, 21.6.54
38. *Ibid*, Box 16, 7.2.53
39. *Ibid*, J. F. Dulles, White House Memos Box 1, 12.4.54
40. CAB 129/48, C(51)32, 29.11.51
41. Moran, 10.1.52, p. 362
42. CAB 128/25, CC(52)53, 15.5.52

43. PREM 11/301, 26.8.52
44. FO 371/105508, 2.7.53
45. FO 371/115029, 29.1.55
46. *Ibid*, 29.3.55
47. FO 371/91555, 27.6.51
48. CAB 129/52, C(52)292, 18.6.52
49. Shuckburgh Diary, 16.12.51, p. 29
50. PREM 11/91, 30.1.52
51. *Ibid*, 15.2.52
52. PREM 11/392, 19/26.8.52
53. Shuckburgh Diary, 29.1.53, p. 75
54. *Ibid*, 31.1.53, p. 76
55. CAB 128/26, CC(53)9, 11.2.53
56. CAB 131/13, 11.2.53
57. PREM 11/392, 16.2.53
58. PREM 11/1074, 18.2.53
59. PREM 11/486, 26.3.53
60. FO 371/102765, 22.5.53
61. Halifax Diary, 18.3.46
62. Eisenhower Library, WFIS Box 16, 5.5.53
63. CAB 134/1012, 4.6.52
64. PREM 11/406, 2.6.53

Chapter 28: Resignation

1. Butler Papers G 26, 27.6.53
2. Shuckburgh Diary, 16.1.53, p. 74
3. Eden Diary, 23.1.53
4. Shuckburgh Diary, 28.7.53, p. 93
5. PREM 11/418, 19.11.53
6. James, *Eden*, p. 375
7. Shuckburgh Diary, 3.12.53, p. 112
8. PREM 11/418, 7.12.53
9. Eisenhower Library, Meeting Churchill, Cherwell, Eisenhower, Strauss, 12.45pm, 5.12.53
10. Moran, p. 508
11. Macmillan Diary 13.12.53, Horne Vol 1, p. 352
12. Moran, 27.10.53, pp. 486–7
13. *Ibid*, 21.1.54, p. 521
14. FO 371/102860, 20.9.53
15. PREM 11/484, 6.12.53
16. PREM 11/699, 19.12.53
17. PREM 11/484, 28.12.53
18. Shuckburgh Diary, 17.12.53, p. 121

19. FO 800/827/61, 14.12.53
20. Shuckburgh Diary, 25.2.54, p. 136
21. *Ibid*, 2.3.54, p. 138
22. CAB 128/27, CC(54)43, 22.6.54
23. DEFE 7/177, 12.3.52
24. ADM 116/6050, 11.4.53
25. ADM 116/5979, 10.8.54
26. CAB 128/27, CC(54)59, 8.9.54
27. *Ibid*, CC(54)58, 2.9.54
28. Gowing *Independence and Deterrence*, p. 439
29. CAB 128/27, CC(54)47, 7.7.54
30. *Ibid*, CC(54)48, 8.7.54
31. *Ibid*, CC(54)51, 26.7.54
32. FO 371/103842, 17.6.53
33. *Ibid*, 8.6.53
34. Moran, 4.7.54, p. 574
35. PREM 11/1074, 9.2.54
36. Eisenhower Library, Record of Meeting 3pm–5pm, 25.6.54
37. *Ibid*, Memo 'Saturday June 26 1954
38. Shuckburgh Diary, 4.3.54, p. 141
39. Crookshank Diary, 22.3.54
40. Shuckburgh Diary, 31.3.54 & 8.4.54, p. 157 & p. 161
41. Macmillan Diary, 31.7.54, Horne Vol 1, p. 353
42. FRUS 1952–54 Vol 6, p. 1066
43. Moran, 29.8.54, p. 595
44. *Ibid*, 9.10.54, p. 602
45. *Ibid*, 26.10.54, p. 607
46. Soames *Clementine Churchill*, p. 445
47. Moran, 3.12.54, p. 620
48. Eden Diary, 22.12.54
49. Macmillan Diary, 14.3.55, Horne Vol 1, p. 354
50. Eisenhower Library, Eisenhower to Dulles, 15.3.55
51. Moran, 21.3.55, p. 640
52. Colville Diary, 29.3.55, pp. 704–7
53. Moran, 1.4.55, p. 643
54. WSC Vol 8, p. 1118
55. Moran, 4.4.55, p. 644
56. Colville Diary, 4.4.55, pp. 707–9

Chapter 29: The Bleak Years

1. Moran, 16.12.54, p. 623
2. *Ibid*, 9.8.55, p. 683
3. *Ibid*, 19.5.55, 20.6.55 & 28.12.55, pp. 657, 670 & 688

4. *Ibid*, 13.12.55, p. 687
5. *Ibid*, 18.2.56, pp. 690–1
6. *Ibid*, 1.8.56, p. 702
7. *Ibid*, 5.2.50, p. 337
8. CV Vol 1, 2.12.97, pp. 835–6
9. Moran, 17.3.60, pp. 768–9
10. *Ibid*, 16.9.56, pp. 705–6
11. *Ibid*, 19.6.56, p. 699
12. *Ibid*, 15.4.59, p. 749
13. *Ibid*, 30.11.59, p. 762
14. PREM 11/3330, 4.7.61

Bibliography

Primary Sources

Official Papers
Public Record Office, Kew:
Admiralty (ADM)
Air Ministry (AIR)
Cabinet Office (CAB)
Colonial Office (CO)
Ministry of Defence (DEFE)
Foreign Office (FO)
Home Office (HO)
Ministry of Information (INF)
Ministry of Labour (LAB)
Prime Minister's Office (PREM)
Treasury (T)
War Office (WO)

United States
US National Archives, Washington
Roosevelt Papers, New York
Eisenhower Papers, Kansas

Private Papers

Asquith Papers	Bodleian Library, Oxford
Attlee Papers	Churchill College, Cambridge
Baldwin Papers	Cambridge University Library
Balfour Papers	British Library
Beaverbrook Papers	House of Lords Record Office

Butler Papers	Trinity College, Cambridge
Austen Chamberlain Papers	University of Birmingham Library
Neville Chamberlain Papers	University of Birmingham Library
Cherwell Papers	Nuffield College, Oxford
Crookshank Papers	Bodleian Library, Oxford
Cunningham Papers	British Library
Curzon Papers	India Office Library
Eden Papers	University of Birmingham Library
Esher Papers	Churchill College, Cambridge
Gainsford Papers	Nuffield College, Oxford
Haldane Papers	National Library of Scotland
Aylmer Haldane Papers	National Library of Scotland
Halifax Papers	Record Office, York & India Office
Hamilton Papers	National Maritime Museum
Hankey Papers	Churchill College, Cambridge
Harcourt Papers	Bodleian Library, Oxford
Hoare Papers	India Office & Cambridge
Ismay Papers	King's College, London
Jellicoe Papers	British Library
Lloyd George Papers	House of Lords Record Office
Montagu Papers	Trinity College, Cambridge
Runciman Papers	University of Newcastle Library
Trevelyan Papers	University of Newcastle Library
Wilson Papers	Imperial War Museum

Secondary Sources
(All books are published in London unless specifically mentioned)

Works by Winston Churchill
Woods, F. (ed), *Bibliography of the Works of Sir Winston Churchill* (1969)
James, R. R. (ed), *Winston S. Churchill: His Complete Speeches 1897–1963* (8
Vols) (1974)

Official Biography
Churchill, R., *Vol 1: Youth 1874–1900* (1966)
       Vol 2: Young Statesman 1901–1914 (1967)
Gilbert, M., *Vol 3: 1914–1916* (1971)
       Vol 4: 1916–1922 (1975)
       Vol 5: 1922–1939 (1976)
       Vol 6: Finest Hour: 1939–1941 (1983)
       Vol 7: Road to Victory: 1941–1945 (1986)
       Vol 8: 'Never Despair': 1945–1965 (1988)

Official Biography: Companion Volumes
Churchill, R., *Vol 1: Part 1: 1874–1896* (1967)
     Part 2: 1896–1900 (1967)
    Vol 2: Part 1: 1901–1907 (1969)
     Part 2: 1907–1911 (1969)
     Part 3: 1911–1914 (1969)
Gilbert, M., *Vol 3: Part 1: 1914–1915* (1972)
     Part 2: 1915–1916 (1972)
    Vol 4: Part 1: 1917–1919 (1977)
     Part 2: 1919–1921 (1977)
     Part 3: 1921–1922 (1977)
    Vol 5: Part 1: The Exchequer Years 1922–1929 (1979)
     Part 2: The Wilderness Years 1929–1935 (1981)
     Part 3: The Coming of War 1936–1939 (1982)

Works about Winston Churchill and the Churchill family
Addison, P., *The Political Beliefs of Winston Churchill* (TRHS 1980 pp. 23–47)
Addison, P., *Churchill on the Home Front* (1992)
Ashley, M., *Churchill as Historian* (1968)
Blake, R. & Louis, W. R. (eds), *Churchill* (Oxford 1993)
Broad, L., *Winston Churchill: The Years of Preparation* (1963)
Broad, L., *Winston Churchill: The Years of Achievement* (1963)
Callaghan, R., *Churchill: Retreat from Empire* (Wilmington 1984)
Charmley, J., *Churchill: The End of Glory* (1993)
Eade, C. (ed), *Churchill By His Contemporaries* (1953)
Churchill, P. & Mitchell, J., *Jennie, Lady Randolph Churchill: A Portrait with Letters* (1974)
Cornwallis-West, J., *The Reminiscences of Lady Randolph Churchill* (1908)
Foster, R., *Lord Randolph Churchill: A Political Life* (Oxford 1981)
Hough, R., *Winston and Clementine: The Triumph of the Churchill's* (1990)
Irving, D., *Churchill's War: Vol 1: The Struggle for Power* (Bullsbrook W. A. 1987)
James, R. R., *Churchill: A Study in Failure 1900–1939* (1970)
Lewin, R., *Churchill as Warlord* (1973)
Manchester, W., *The Last Lion: Winston Spencer Churchill, Visions of Glory 1874–1932* (1983)
Manchester, W., *The Caged Lion: Winston Spencer Churchill 1932–1940* (1988)
Martin, R., *Lady Randolph Churchill* (1972)
de Mendelssohn, P., *The Age of Churchill: Heritage and Adventure 1874–1911* (1961)
Moran, Lord, *Winston Churchill: The Struggle for Survival 1940–1965* (1966)
Morgan, T., *Churchill: Young Man in a Hurry 1874–1915* (New York 1982)
Pearson, J., *Citadel of the Heart: Winston and the Churchill Dynasty* (1991)
Pelling, H., *Winston Churchill* (1974)

Prior, R., *Churchill's 'World Crisis' as History* (1983)
Roberts, B., *Randolph: A Study of Churchill's Son* (1984)
Roskill, S., *Churchill and the Admirals* (1977)
Soames, M., *Clementine Churchill* (1979)
Taylor, A. (ed), *Churchill: Four Faces and the Man* (1968)
Thompson, R., *Churchill and Morton* (1976)
Wheeler-Bennett, J. (ed), *Action This Day: Working With Churchill* (1968)

Biographies, Autobiographies and Diaries
Avon, Earl of, *The Reckoning* (1965)
Birkenhead, Earl of, *The Prof in Two Worlds* (1961)
Birkenhead, Earl of, *Halifax* (1965)
Brock, M. & E. (eds), *H. H. Asquith: Letters to Venetia Stanley* (Oxford, 1982)
Bryant, A., *The Turn of the Tide* (1957)
Bryant, A., *Triumph in the West* (1959)
Bullock, A., *The Life and Times of Ernest Bevin Vol. 2: Minister of Labour 1940–45* (1967)
Campbell, J., *F. E. Smith: First Earl of Birkenhead* (1983)
Carlton, D., *Anthony Eden* (1981)
Charmley, J., *Lord Lloyd and the Decline of the British Empire* (1987)
Charmley, J., *Duff Cooper* (1986)
Colville, J., *The Fringes of Power: Downing Street Diaries 1939–1955* (1985)
Connell, J., *Auchinleck* (1957)
Cross, J., *Sir Samuel Hoare: A Political Biography* (1977)
David, E., *Inside Asquith's Cabinet: From the Diaries of Charles Hobhouse* (1977)
Dilks, D. (ed), *The Diaries of Sir Alexander Cadogan 1938–45* (1971)
Dilks, D., *Neville Chamberlain Vol. 1: Pioneering and Reform 1869–1929* (Cambridge 1984)
Donoughue, B. & Jones, C., *Herbert Morrison* (1973)
Dutton, D., *Austen Chamberlain: Gentleman in Politics* (Bolton, 1985)
Harris, J., *William Beveridge* (Oxford, 1977)
Harris, K., *Attlee* (1982)
Harvey, J. (ed), *The War Diaries of Oliver Harvey* (1978)
Hassall, C., *Edward Marsh: Patron of the Arts* (1959)
Hicks-Beach, Lady V., *Life of Sir Michael Hicks Beach* (1932)
Horne, A., *Macmillan Vol. 1: 1894–1956* (1986)
Howard, A., *RAB: The Life of R A Butler* (1987)
James, R. R., *Rosebery* (1963)
James, R. R., *Memoirs of a Conservative: J C C Davidson's Memoirs and Papers 1910–37* (1969)
James, R. R., *Chips: The Diaries of Sir Henry Channon* (1967)
James, R. R., *Anthony Eden* (1986)
Jay, R., *Joseph Chamberlain: A Political Study* (Oxford, 1981)
Jenkins, R., *Asquith* (1964)

King, C., *With Malice Towards None – A War Diary* (1970)

Koss, S., *Lord Haldane: Scapegoat for Liberalism* (New York 1969)

Koss, S., *Asquith* (1976)

Mackay, R., *Fisher of Kilverstone* (Oxford, 1973)

Maclead, R. & Kelly, D., *The Ironside Diaries 1937–1940* (1962)

Middlemas, K. & Barnes, J., *Baldwin* (1969)

Middlemas, K., *Thomas Jones: Whitehall Diary* (3 Vols) (1969–71)

Minney, R., *The Private Papers of Hore-Belisha* (1960)

Nicolson, N., *Harold Nicolson: Diaries and Letters 1939–45* (1967)

Parkinson, R., *The Auk; Auchinleck, Victor at Alamein* (1977)

Pickersgill, J. & Forster, D. (eds), *The Mackenzie King Record Vols. 3 & 4* (1970)

Pimlott, B., *The Second World War Diary of Hugh Dalton 1939–45* (1986)

Roskill, S., *Hankey: Man of Secrets Vol. 1: 1877–1918* (1970)

Roskill, S., *Hankey: Man of Secrets Vol. 2: 1919–1931* (1972)

Shuckburgh, E., *Descent to Suez: Diaries 1951–56* (1986)

Stuart, C. (ed), *The Reith Diaries* (1975)

Taylor, A., *Lloyd George: A Diary by Frances Stevenson* (1971)

Taylor, A., *Beaverbrook* (1972)

Taylor, A., *Off the Record: Political Interviews 1933–1943, W. P. Crozier* (1973)

Wilson, J., *C. B: A Life of Sir Henry Campbell-Bannerman* (1973)

Wilson, T., *The Political Diaries of C. P. Scott 1911–1928* (1970)

Zebel, S., *Balfour: A Political Biography* (Cambridge, 1973)

Other Books and Articles
(Journal Abbreviations – AHR – American Historical Review, BIHR – Bulletin of the Institute of Historial Research, DH – Diplomatic History, EHR – English Historical Review, HJ – Historical Journal, JBS – Journal of British Studies, JCH – Journal of Contemporary History, JICH – Journal of Imperial and Commonwealth History, JMH – Journal of Modern History, JSS – Journal of Strategic Studies, P & P – Past and Present, SJH – Scandinavian Journal of History, TRHS – Transactions of the Royal Historical Society.)

Part I – 1874–1915

Andrew, C., *Secret Service: The Making of the British Intelligence Community* (1985)

Arnot, R., *South Wales Miners: A History of the South Wales Miners Federation 1898–1914* (1967)

Beckett, I. & Jeffrey, K., *The Royal Navy and the Curragh Incident* (BIHR Vol 62 1989 pp. 54–69)

Bernstein, G., *Liberalism and Liberal Politics in Edwardian England* (1986)

Blewitt, N., *The Peers, The Parties and The People: The General Elections of 1910* (1972)

Brock, M., *Britain Enters the War*, in Evans, R. & von Standmann, H., *The Coming of the First World War* (Oxford 1988)

Bruce, M., *The Coming of the Welfare State* (1968)

Callaghan, R., *What About the Dardanelles?* (AHR Vol 78 No 3 1973 pp. 641–8)

Carew, A., *The Lower Deck of the Royal Navy 1900–39* (Manchester 1981)

Cassar, G., *The French and the Dardanelles: A Study of Failure in the Conduct of War* (1971)

Coogan, J. & Coogan, P., *The British Cabinet and the Anglo-French Staff Talks, 1905–1914: Who Knew What and When did he Know it?* (JBS Vol 24 1985 pp. 110–131)

Dangerfield, G., *The Strange Death of Liberal England* (1935)

d'Ombrain, N., *War Machinery and High Policy: Defence Administration in Peacetime Britain 1902–1914* (Oxford 1973)

Emy, H., *Liberals, Radicals and Social Politics 1892–1914* (Cambridge 1973)

Fraser, D., *The Evolution of the British Welfare State* (1973)

Freeden, M., *The New Liberalism: An Ideology of Social Reform* (Oxford 1978)

French, D., *The Origins of the Dardanelles Campaign Reconsidered* (History Vol 68 1983 pp. 210–224)

French, D., *British Economic and Strategic Planning 1905–1915* (1982)

French, D., *British Strategy and War Aims 1914–16* (1986)

Gilbert, B. *The Evolution of National Insurance in England: The Origins of the Welfare State* (1966)

Gollin, A., *Balfour's Burden* (1965)

Haggie, P., *The Royal Navy and War Planning in the Fisher Era* (JCH No 8 1971)

Halpern, P., *The Mediterranean Naval Situation 1908–1914* (Cambridge (Mass) 1971)

Harris, J., *Unemployment and Politics: A Study of English Social Policy 1886–1914* (Oxford 1972)

Hazlehurst, C., *Politicians at War July 1914–May 1915: A Prelude to the Triumph of Lloyd George* (1971)

Hinsley, F., *British Foreign Policy under Sir Edward Grey* (Cambridge 1977)

Hyam, R., *Elgin and Churchill at the Colonial Office 1905–1908: The Watershed of the Empire-Commonwealth* (1968)

Hyam, R., *'The Myth of the Magnanimous Gesture': the Liberal Government, Smuts and Conciliation in 1906*, in Hyam, R. & Martin, G. (eds), *Reappraisals in British Imperial History* (1975)

Jack, M., *The Purchase of the British Government's Shares in the British Petroleum Company 1912–1914* (P & P No 39 1968)

Jalland, P., *The Liberals and Ireland: The Ulster Question in British Politics to 1914* (Brighton 1980)

James, R. R., *Gallipoli* (1965)

Jenkins, R., *Mr Balfour's Poodle* (1954)

Kennedy, P., *The Rise of Anglo-German Antagonism 1860–1914* (1980)

Koss, S., *The Destruction of Britain's Last Liberal Government* (JMH June 1968)

Langhorne, R., *The Naval Question in Anglo-German Relations 1912–14* (HJ Vol 14 1971 pp. 359–370)

Le May, G., *British Supremacy in South Africa 1899–1907* (Oxford 1965)

Marder, A., *From the Dreadnought to Scapa Flow: The Royal Navy in the Fisher Era, 1904–1919*
Vol 1: The Road to War 1904–1914 (Oxford 1961)
Vol 2: The War Years to the Eve of Jutland (Oxford 1965)

Morgan, D., *Suffragists and Liberals: The Politics of Women's Suffrage in England* (Oxford 1975)

Murray, B., *The People's Budget 1909–10: Lloyd George and Liberal Politics* (Oxford 1980)

Palmer, A., *The History of the D-Notice Committee* in Andrew, C. & Dilks, D., *The Missing Dimension: Governments and Intelligence Communities in the Twentieth Century* (1984)

Pugh, M., *Asquith, Bonar Law and the First Coalition* (HJ Vol 17 No 4 1974 pp. 813–836)

Quinault, R., *Lord Randolph Churchill and Tory Democracy 1880–1885* (HJ Vol 22 1979 pp. 141–65)

Rempel, R., *Unionists Divided: Arthur Balfour, Joseph Chamberlain and the Unionist Free Traders* (Newton Abbot 1972)

Rowland, P., *The Last Liberal Governments:*
The Promised Land 1905–1910 (1968)
Unfinished Business 1911–1914 (1971)

Russell, A., *Liberal Landslide: The General Election of 1906* (Newton Abbot 1973)

Satre, L., *St John Broderick & Army Reform 1901–1903* (JBS Vol 15 1975–6 pp. 117–139)

Scally, R., *The Origins of the Lloyd George Coalition: The Politics of Social Imperialism 1900–1918* (Princeton 1975)

Searle, G., *The Quest for National Efficiency: A Study in British Politics and Political Thought* (Oxford 1971)

Smith, D., *Tonypandy 1910: Definitions of Community* (P & P No 87 1980 pp. 158–184)

Sykes, A., *Tariff Reform in British Politics 1903–1913* (Oxford 1979)

Thompson, L., *The Unification of South Africa 1902–1910* (Oxford 1960)

Weinroth, H., *Left-Wing Opposition to Naval Armaments in Britain before 1914* (JCH Vol 6 No 4 1971 pp. 93–120)

Wiemann, F., *Lloyd George and the Struggle for the Navy Estimates of 1914* in Taylor, A., *Lloyd George: Twelve Essays* (1971)

Williamson, S., *The Politics of Grand Strategy: Britain and France Prepare for War 1904–1914* (Cambridge (Mass) 1969)

Wilson, K., *The War Office, Churchill and the Belgian Option: August to December 1911* (BIHR Vol 50 1977 pp. 218–228)

Wilson, K., *The Policy of the Entente: Essays on the Determinants of British Foreign Policy 1904–1914* (Cambridge 1985)

Part II: 1915–1938

Adams, R., *Arms and the Wizard: Lloyd George and the Ministry of Munitions 1915–16* (1978)

Bridge, C., *Churchill, Hoare, Derby and the Committee of Privileges, April to June 1934* (HJ Vol 22 1979 pp. 215–227)

Bridge, C., *Holding India to the Empire: The British Conservative Party and the 1935 Constitution* (New York 1986)

Brown, K., *Essays in Anti-Labour History: Responses to the Rise of Labour in Britain* (1974)

Burk, K., *Britain, America and the Sinews of War 1914–18* (1985)

Canning, P., *British Policy Towards Ireland 1921–1941* (Oxford 1985)

Cook, C., *The Age of Alignment: Electoral Politics in Britain 1922–29* (1975)

Cowling, M., *The Impact of Labour 1920–1924: The Beginning of Modern British Politics* (Cambridge 1971)

Cowling, M., *The Impact of Hitler: British Politics and British Policy 1933–1940* (Cambridge 1975)

Cox, J., *A Splendid Training Ground: The Importance to the Royal Air Force of its role in Iraq 1919–32* (JICH Vol 13 1985 pp. 157–184)

Curran, J., *The Birth of the Irish Free State* (Alabama 1980)

Darwin, J., *Britain, Egypt and the Middle East: Imperial Policy in the Aftermath of War 1918–1922* (1981)

Darwin, J., *Imperialism in Decline? Tendencies in British Imperial Policy Between the Wars* (HJ Vol 23 No 3 1980 pp. 657–679)

Darwin, J., *The Chanak Crisis and the British Cabinet* (History Vol 65 1980 pp. 32–48)

Deacon, A., *Concession and Coercion: The Politics of Unemployment Insurance in the Twenties* in Briggs, A. & Saville, J., *Essays in Labour History 1918–1939* (1977)

Draper, A., *Amritsar* (1981)

Ferris, J., *The Evolution of British Strategic Policy 1919–26* (1989)

Gibbs, N., *Grand Strategy Vol 1: Rearmament Policy* (1976)

Gilbert, G., *British Social Policy 1914–1939* (1970)

Harris, J., *The 'Sandys Storm': The Politics of British Air Defence in 1938* (BIHR Vol 62 1989 pp. 318–336)

Jeffery, K. & Hennessy, P., *States of Emergency: British Governments and Strikebreaking since 1919* (1983)

Jeffery, K., *The British Army and the Crisis of Empire 1918–1922* (Manchester 1984)

Kinnear, M., *The Fall of Lloyd George: The Political Crisis of 1922* (1973)

Klieman, A., *Foundations of British Policy in the Arab World: The Cairo Conference of 1921* (Baltimore 1970)

McCormack, R., *Missed Opportunities: Winston Churchill, the Air Ministry and Africa 1919–21* (International History Review Vol XI No 2 1989 pp. 205–28)

Middlemas, K., *Politics in Industrial Society: The Experience of the British System since 1911* (1979)

Ministry of Munitions, *History of the Ministry of Munitions* (12 Vols) (1921)

Moggridge, D., *British Monetary Policy 1924–1931: The Norman Conquest of $4.86* (Cambridge 1972)

Moore, R., *The Crisis of Indian Unity* (Oxford 1974)

Morgan, K., *Consensus and Disunity: The Lloyd George Coalition Government 1918–1922* (Oxford 1979)

Overy, R., *The German pre-War Aircraft Production Plans: November 1936–April 1939* (EHR Vol XC 1975 pp. 778–797)

Phillips, G., *The General Strike: The Politics of Industrial Conflict* (1976)

Pollard, S., *The Gold Standard and Employment Policies Between the Wars* (1970)

Ramsden, J., *A History of the Conservative Party: The Age of Balfour and Baldwin 1902–1940* (1978)

Rasmussen, J., *Government and Intra-Party Opposition: Dissent within the Conservative Parliamentary Party in the 1930s* (Political Studies Vol XIX No 2 1977 pp. 171–183)

Rock, W., *Appeasement on Trial: British Foreign Policy and its Critics 1938–9* (New York 1966)

Roskill, S., *Naval Policy Between the Wars, Vol 1: The Period of Anglo-American Antagonism 1919–1929* (1968)

Silverlight, J., *The Victor's Dilemma: Allied Intervention in the Russian Civil War* (1970)

Sluglett, P., *Britain in Iraq 1914–1932* (1976)

Spears, E., *Gas and the North West Frontier* (JSS Vol 6 No 4 1983 pp. 94–112)

Spier, E., *Focus: A Footnote to the History of the Thirties* (1963)

Thompson, N., *The Anti-Appeasers: Conservative Opposition to Appeasement in the 1930s* (Oxford 1971)

Townshend, C., *The British Campaign in Ireland 1919–1921: The development of political and military policies* (Oxford 1975)

Ullman, R., *Britain and the Russian Civil War, November 1918–February 1920* (Princeton 1968)

Ullman, R., *The Anglo-Soviet Accord* (Priceton 1972)

Wark, W., *British Intelligence on the German Air Force and Aircraft Industry 1933–1939* (HJ Vol 25 No 3 1982 pp. 627–648)

Wark, W., *British Military and Economic Intelligence: Assessments of Nazi Germany before the Second World War* in Dilks, D. & Andrew, C., *The Missing Dimension: Governments and Intelligence Communities in the Twentieth century* (1984)

Williamson, P., *'Safety First': Baldwin, the Conservative Party, and the 1929 General Election* (HJ Vol 25 No 2 1982 pp. 385–409)

Wilson, T., *The Downfall of the Liberal Party 1914–1935* (1966)

Wrigley, C., *The Ministry of Munitions: An Innovatory Department* in Burk, K., *War and the State: The Transformation of British Government, 1914–1918* (1982)

Part III: 1939–1945

Addison, P., *The Road to 1945: British Politics and the Second World War* (1975)

Alexander, G., *Prelude to the Truman Doctrine: British Policy in Greece 1944–47* (Oxford 1982)

Auty, P. & Clogg, R. (eds), *British Policy Towards Wartime Resistance in Yugoslavia and Greece* (1975)

Balfour, M., *Propaganda in War 1939–45: Organisations, Policies and Publics in Britain and Germany* (1979)

Barker, E., *British Policy in South-East Europe in the Second World War* (1976)

Barker, E., *Churchill and Eden at War* (1978)

Barnett, C., *The Desert Generals* (2nd edition 1983)

Barnett, C., *Engage the Enemy More Closely: The Royal Navy in the Second World War* (1991)

Beaumont, R., *The Bomber Offensive as a Second Front* (JCH Vol 22 No 1 1987 pp. 3–19

Bedarida, F., *France, Britain and the Nordic Countries 1939–40* (SJH Vol 2 1977 pp. 7–27)

Bell, P., *A Certain Eventuality: Britain and the Fall of France* (1974)

Bell, P., *Censorship, Propaganda and Public Opinion: The Case of the Katyn Graves 1943* (TRHS Vol 39 1989 pp. 53–83)

Bell, P., *John Bull and the Bear: British Public Opinion, Foreign Policy and the Soviet Union 1941–45* (1990)

Ben-Moshe, T., *Winston Churchill and the 'Second Front': A Reappraisal* (JMH Vol 62 No 3 1990 pp. 503–537)

Bennett, R., *Ultra and Mediterranean Strategy 1941–45* (1989)

Calder, A., *The People's War: Britain 1939–45* (1971)

Callaghan, R., *The Worst Disaster: The Fall of Singapore* (Newark (NJ) 1977)

Clemens, D., *Yalta* (New York 1970)

Cohen, M., *The British White Paper on Palestine, May 1939: Part II; The Testing of a Policy 1942–45* (HJ Vol 19 1976 pp. 727–758)

Cruickshank, C., *Greece 1940–41* (1976)

Dallek, R., *Franklin D. Roosevelt and American Foreign Policy* (New York 1979)

Danchev, A., *Very Special Relationship: Field Marshal Sir John Dill and the Anglo-American Alliance 1941–44* (London 1986)

Danchev, A., *The Central Direction of War 1940–41* in Sweetman, J. (ed), *Sword and Mace: Twentieth Century Civil-Military Relations in Britain* (1986)

Danchev, A., *'Dilly-Dally', or Having the Last Word: Field Marshal Sir John Dill and Prime Minister Winston Churchill* (JCH Vol 22 No 1 1987 pp. 21–44)

Day, D., *The Great Betrayal: Britain, Australia and the Onset of the Pacific War* (North Ryde, NSW, 1988)

Dilks, D., *Great Britain and Scandinavia in the 'Phoney War'* (SJH Vol 2 1977 pp. 29–51)

Dilks, D., *The Twilight War and the Fall of France: Chamberlain and Churchill in 1940* (TRHS Vol 28 1978 pp. 61–86)

Dobson, A., *US Wartime Aid to Britain 1940–1946* (1986)

Dunn, W., *Second Front Now – 1943* (Alabama 1980)

Ellis, J., *Brute Force: Allied Strategy and Tactics in the Second World War* (1990)

Fisk, R., *In Time of War: Ireland, Ulster and the Price of Neutrality* (1983)

Funk, A., *The Politics of Torch: The Allied Landings and the Algiers Putsch 1942* (Lawrence (Kan) 1974)

Gates, E., *The End of the Affair: The Collapse of the Anglo-French Alliance 1939–1940* (1981)

Gaunson, A., *The Anglo-French Clash in Lebanon and Syria 1940–45* (1987)

Glover, M., *Invasion Scare* (1990)

Gorodetsky, G., *Churchill's Warning to Stalin: A Reappraisal* (HJ Vol 29 1986 pp. 979–990)

Gowing, M., *Britain and Atomic Energy* (1964)

Grace, R., *Whitehall and the Ghost of Appeasement: November 1941* (DH Vol 3 1979 pp. 173–191)

Grigg, J., *1943 – The Victory That Never Was* (1980)

Haggie, P., *Britannia at Bay: The Defence of the British Empire against Japan 1931–1941* (Oxford 1981)

Harrison, M., *Resource Mobilization for World War II: the USA, UK, USSR and Germany 1938–45* (Economic History Review Vol 41 1988 pp. 171–192)

Hastings, M., *Bomber Command* (1979)

Heinrichs, W., *President Franklin D. Roosevelt's Intervention in the Battle of the Atlantic, 1941* (DH Vol 10 No 4 1986 pp. 311–332)

Heinrichs, W., *Threshold of War: Franklin D. Roosevelt and American Entry into World War II* (Oxford 1988)

Hinsley, F., *British Intelligence in the Second World War: Its Influence on Strategy and Operations. 3 Vols* (London 1979–84)

Hoffman, P., *The Question of Western Allied Co-operation with the German Anti-Nazi Conspiracy 1938–44* (HJ Vol 34 1991 pp. 437–464)

Honigsbaum, F., *Health, Happiness and Security: The Creation of the National Health Service* (1989)

Howard, M., *The Mediterranean Strategy in the Second World War* (1968)

Howard, M., *Grand Strategy Vol 4: August 1942–September 1943* (1972)

Hughes, E., *Winston Churchill and the Formation of the United Nations Organisation* (JCH Vol 9 No 4 1974 pp. 177–194)

Jeffrys K., *British Politics and Social Policy during the Second World War* (HJ Vol 30 1987 pp. 123–144)

865

Jeffrys, K., *The Churchill Coalition and Wartime Politics, 1940–45* (Manchester 1991)

Keegan, J. (ed), *Churchill's Generals* (1991)

Kersaudy, F., *Churchill and De Gaulle* (1981)

Kersaudy, F., *Norway 1940* (1990)

Kettenacker, L., *The Anglo-Soviet Alliance and the Problem of Germany 1941–45* (JCH Vol 17 1982) pp. 435–58)

Kimball, W., *Churchill and Roosevelt: The Complete Correspondence* 3 Vols (Princeton 1984)

Kimball, W., *Naked Reverse Right: Roosevelt, Churchill and Eastern Europe from TOLSTOY to Yalta – and a little beyond* (DH Vol 9 No 1 1985 pp. 1–24)

King, F., *The New Internationalism: Allied Policy and the European Peace 1939–45* (Newton Abbot 1973)

Kitchen, M., *British Policy Towards the Soviet Union During the Second World War* (1986)

Kitchen, M., *Winston Churchill and the Soviet Union during the Second World War* (HJ Vol 30 1987 pp. 415–436)

Koch, H., *The Strategic Air Offensive against Germany: The Early Phase May–September 1940* (HJ Vol 34 1991 pp. 117–141)

Kochavi, A., *The Moscow Declaration, the Kharkov Trial, and the Question of a Policy on Major War Criminals in the Second World War* (History Vol 76 1991 pp. 401–417)

Lacquer, W. (ed), *The Second World War: Essays in Military and Political History* (1982)

La Feber, W., *Roosevelt, Churchill and Indochina 1942–45* (AHR Vol 80 1975 pp. 1277–1295)

Langer, J., *The Harriman-Beaverbrook Mission and the debate over Unconditional Aid for the Soviet Union 1941* (JCH Vol 14 1979 pp. 463–82)

Langhorne, R. (ed), *Diplomacy and Intelligence during the Second World War* (Cambridge 1985)

Larrabee, E., *Commander-in-Chief: Franklin D. Roosevelt, His Lieutenants and their War* (New York 1987)

Lawlor, S., *Greece, March 1941: The Politics of British Military Intervention* (HJ Vol 25 1982 pp. 933–46)

Lee, J., *The Churchill Coalition 1940–45* (1980)

Leutze, M., *The Secret of the Churchill–Roosevelt Correspondence September 1939–May 1940* (JCH Vol 10 1975 pp. 465–491)

Leutze, J., *Bargaining for Supremacy: Anglo–American Naval Relations 1937–1941* (Chapel Hill (NC) 1977)

Louis, W., *Imperialism at Bay 1941–45: The United States and the Decolonization of the British Empire* (Oxford 1977)

Lowe, P., *Great Britain and the Coming of the Pacific War 1939–41* (TRHS Vol 24 1974 pp. 43–62)

McCallum, R & Readman, A., *The British General Election of 1945* (1947)

McLaine, I., *Ministry of Morale: Home Front Morale and the Ministry of Information in World War II* (1979)

Mansergh, N. & Lumby, E. (eds), *The Transfer of Power 1942–47 Vol 1: The Cripps Mission* (1970)

Marder, A., *Old Friends, New Enemies: The Royal Navy and the Imperial Japanese Navy. Strategic Illusions 1936–41* (Oxford 1981)

Mastny, V., *Russia's Road to the Cold War* (New York 1979)

Mayle, P., *Eureka Summit: Agreement in Principle and the Big Three at Teheran 1943* (Newark (NJ) 1987)

Mee, C., *Meeting at Potsdam* (New York 1975)

Milward, A., *War, Economy and Society 1939–45* (1977)

Moore, R., *Churchill, Cripps and India 1939–1945* (Oxford 1979)

Overy, R., *The Air War 1939–1945* (1980)

Papastrakis, P., *British Policy Towards Greece during the Second World War 1941–44* (1984)

Parker, R., *Britain, France and Scandinavia 1939–40* (History Vol 61 1976 pp. 369–387)

Pater, J., *The Making of the National Health Service* (1981)

Pelling, H., *The 1945 General Election Reconsidered* (HJ Vol 23 No 2 1980 pp. 399–414)

Ponting, C., *1940: Myth and Reality* (1990)

Rasmussen, J., *Party Discipline in Wartime: The Downfall of the Chamberlain Government* (Journal of Politics Vol 32 1970 pp. 379–406)

Reynolds, D., *The Creation of the Anglo-American Alliance 1937–41: A Study in Competitive Co-operation* (1981)

Reynolds, D., *The Churchill Government and the Black American Troops in Britain during World War II* (TRHS Vol 35 1985 pp. 113–133)

Reynolds, D., *Roosevelt, Churchill and the Wartime Anglo-American Alliance 1939–45: Towards a New Synthesis* in Louis, M. and Bull, H. (eds), *The Special Relationship: Anglo-American Relations since 1945* (Oxford 1945)

Resis, A., *The Churchill-Stalin Secret 'Percentages' Agreement on the Balkans. Moscow, October 1944* (AHR Vol 83 1978 pp. 368–387)

Rubin, B., *Anglo-American Relations in Saudi Arabia 1941–45* (JCH Vol 14 1979 pp. 253–267)

Sainsbury, K., *The Turning Point: Roosevelt, Stalin, Churchill and Chiang Kai-Shek 1943. The Moscow, Cairo and Teheran Conferences* (Oxford 1985)

Sainsbury, K., *British Policy and German Unity at the end of the Second World War* (EHR Vol 94 1979 pp. 786–804)

Salmon, P., *Churchill, the Admiralty and the Narvik Traffic, September–November 1939* (SJH Vol 2 1977 pp. 29–51)

Sfikas, T., *'The People at the Top can do these things, which others can't do': Winston Churchill and the Greeks, 1940–45* (JCH Vol 26 1991 pp. 307–322)

Sharp, T., *The Wartime Alliance and the Zonal Division of Germany* (Oxford 1975)

Sherwin, M., *The Atomic Bomb and the origins of the Cold War: US Atomic Energy Policy and Diplomacy 1941–45* (AHR Vol 78 1973 pp. 945–968)

Sherwin, M., *A World Destroyed: The Atomic Bomb and the Grand Alliance* (New York 1975)

Shlaim, A., *Prelude to Downfall: The British Offer of Union to France, June 1940* (JCH Vol 9 No 3 1974 pp. 27–63)

Siracusa, J., *The Meaning of TOLSTOY: Churchill, Stalin and the Balkans Moscow, October 1944* (DH Vol 3 1979 pp. 443–463)

Smith, A., *Churchill's German Army: Wartime Strategy and Cold War Politics 1943–47* (Beverley Hills (CA) 1977)

Stafford, D., *Britain and European Resistance 1940–45* (1980)

Stammers, N., *Civil Liberties in Britain during the Second World War* (1983)

Stoler, M., *The Politics of the Second Front: American Military Planning and Diplomacy in Coalition Warfare 1941–43* (Westport (Conn) 1977)

Thomas, R., *Britain and Vichy: The Dilemma of Anglo-French Relations 1940–1942* (1979)

Thorne, C., *Allies of a Kind: The United States, Britain and the War against Japan 1941–45* (1978)

Thorne, C., *Border Crossings: Studies in International History* (Oxford 1988)

Tsakaloyannis, P., *The Moscow Puzzle* (JCH Vol 21 1986 pp. 37–55)

Tuttle, D., *Harry L. Hopkins and Anglo-American-Soviet Relations 1941–45* (New York 1983)

US State Department, *Foreign Relations of the United States:*
The Conferences at Washington and Casablanca 1942–43 (Washington DC 1967)
The Conferences at Washington and Quebec 1943 (Washington DC 1970)
The Conferences at Cairo and Teheran 1943 (Washington DC 1961)
The Conferences at Malta and Yalta 1945 (Washington DC 1955)
The Conference of Berlin 1945 (Washington DC 1960)

Van Creveld, M., *Prelude to Disaster: The British Decision to Aid Greece 1940–41* (JCH Vol 9 No 3 1974 pp. 65–92)

Van der Vat, D., *The Atlantic Campaign: The Great Struggle at Sea 1914–45* (1988)

Villa, B., *The Atomic Bomb and the Normandy Invasion* (Perspectives in American History Vol 11 1977–8 pp. 463–502)

Wasserstein, B., *Britain and the Jews of Europe 1939–45* (Oxford 1979)

Wilson, T., *The First Summit: Roosevelt and Churchill at Placentia Bay 1941* (Boston (Mass) 1969)

de Zayas, G., *Nemesis at Potsdam: The Anglo-Americans and the Expulsion of the Germans* (1977)

Part IV: 1945–1965

Baines, M., *A United Anti-Socialist Party? Liberal-Conservative Relations 1945–55* (Contemporary Record Vol 4 February 1991)

Boyle, P., *The Churchill-Eisenhower Correspondence 1953–55* (Chapel Hill (NC) 1990)

Butler, D., *The British General Election of 1951* (1952)

Darwin, J., *British Decolonization since 1945: A Pattern or a Puzzle?* (JICH Vol 12 1984 pp. 187–209)

Devereux, D., *Britain and the Failure of Collective Defence in the Middle East 1948–53* in Deighton, A. (ed), *Britain and the First Cold War* (1990)

Dockrill, M. & Young, J., *British Foreign Policy 1945–56* (1989)

Fish, M., *After Stalin's Death: The Anglo-American debate over a New Cold War* (DH Vol 10 No 4 1986 pp. 333–355)

Gaddis, J., *The Long Peace: Inquiries into the History of the Cold War* (Oxford 1987)

Glees, A., *Churchill's Last Gambit* (*Encounter* No 374 April 1985 pp. 27–35)

Goldsworthy, D., *Colonial Issues in British Politics 1945–61* (Oxford 1971)

Goldsworthy, D., *Keeping Change Within Bounds: Aspects of Colonial Policy during the Churchill and Eden Governments 1951–7* (JICH Vol 18 1990 pp 81–108)

Gowing, M., *Independence and Deterrence: Britain and Atomic Energy 1945–1952 Vol 1: Policy Making* (1974)

Harbutt, F., *The Iron Curtain: Churchill, America and the Origins of the Cold War* (Oxford 1986)

Hoffman, J., *The Conservative Party in Opposition 1945–51* (1964)

Holland, R., *The Imperial Factor in British Strategies from Attlee to Macmillan 1945–63* (JICH Vol 12 1984 pp. 165–186)

Louis, W., *The British Empire in the Middle East 1945–51: Arab Nationalism, the United States and PostWar Imperialism* (Oxford 1984)

Louis, W., *The Tragedy of the Anglo-Egyptian Settlement of 1954* in Louis, W. & Owen, R. (eds), *Suez 1956: The Crisis and its Consequences* (Oxford 1989)

Middlemas, K., *Power, Competition and the State Vol 1: Britain in Search of Balance 1940–61* (1986)

Moore, R., *Escape from Empire: The Attlee Government and the Indian Problem* (Oxford 1983)

Morgan, K., *Labour in Power 1945–51* (Oxford 1984)

Nicolas, H., *The British General Election of 1950* (1951)

Ramsden, J., *The Making of Conservative Party Policy: The Conservative Research Department since 1929* (1980)

Ramsden, J., *'A Party for Owners or a Party for Earners?' How far did the British Conservative Party really change after 1945?* (TRHS Vol 37 1987 pp. 49–63)

Ryan, H., *A New Look at Churchill's 'Iron Curtain' Speech* (HJ Vol 22 1979 pp. 895–920)

Seldon, A., *Churchill's Indian Summer: The Conservative Government 1951–55* (1981)

Yergin, D., *Shattered Peace: The Origins of the Cold War* (1990)

Young, J., *Britain, France and the Unity of Europe 1945–51* (Leicester 1984)

Young, J., *Churchill's 'No' to Europe: the 'Rejection' of European Union by Churchill's Post-War Government 1951–52* (HJ Vol 28 1985 pp. 923–937)

Young, J., *Churchill, the Russians and the Western Alliance: the three-power conference at Bermuda, December 1953* (EHR Vol 101 1987 pp. 889–912)

Young, J., *Churchill's bid for peace with Moscow, 1954* (History Vol 73 1988 pp. 425–448)

Young, J. (ed) *The Foreign Policy of Churchill's Peacetime Administration 1951–1955* (Leicester 1988)

APPENDIX

Outline Biographies of Major Political Figures Mentioned in the Book

ADDISON Christopher; Liberal MP 1910, junior minister 1914–16, Minister of Munitions 1916–7, Minister of Reconstruction 1917–19, President Local Government Board 1919–21, later member of Labour Party and Labour governments.

ALEXANDER Albert; Labour MP 1922–31, 1935–50. Junior minister 1924 Government. First Lord of the Admiralty 1929–31, 1940–5, 1945–6, Minister of Defence 1946–50, Chancellor of the Duchy of Lancaster 1950–1.

AMERY Leo; Journalist, Conservative MP 1911, junior minister at Colonial Office and Admiralty in Lloyd George administration, First Lord of the Admiralty 1922–24, Colonial Secretary 1924–9, Secretary of State for India 1940–5.

ANDERSON John; civil servant, head of administration in Ireland after First World War, Permanent Secretary at Home Office 1923–32, Governor of Bengal 1932–7. Independent MP 1938. Lord Privy Seal 1938–9, Home Secretary 1939–40, joined War Cabinet as Lord President in October 1940, Chancellor of the Exchequer 1943–5.

ASQUITH Herbert Henry; Liberal MP from 1886, Home Secretary 1892–5, Chancellor of the Exchequer 1905–8, Prime Minister 1908–16. Remained leader of the Liberal Party until 1926.

ATTLEE Clement; Junior minister in Labour governments of 1920s, Labour Party leader 1935–55, led Labour Party in Churchill coalition 1940–5, Prime Minister 1945–51.

BALFOUR Arthur James; succeeded his uncle, Lord Salisbury, as Prime Minister 1902–5 and leader of the Conservative Party 1902–11. Associated with Lord Randolph Churchill in early 1880s. Number of government posts, including Chief Secretary for Ireland and Leader of the House before 1902. First Lord of the Admiralty 1915–16, Foreign Secretary 1916–19, Lord President of the Council 1919–22 & 1924–9.

BEAVERBROOK Max (Aitken); Canadian newspaper owner, Conservative MP 1910. Chancellor of the Duchy of Lancaster 1916–8, Minister of Information 1918. Minister for Aircraft Production 1940–1, Minister of State and Minister of Supply 1941–2, briefly Minister of Production 1942. Lord Privy Seal 1943–5.

BEVIN Ernest; from 1922 Secretary of TWU. Minister of Labour 1940–5, Foreign Secretary 1945–50.

BIRKENHEAD, Frederick Edwin (FE); Conservative MP 1906, Solicitor-General 1915, Attorney-General 1915–9, Lord Chancellor 1919–22, Secretary of State for India 1924–8.

BRACKEN Brendan; Publisher and owner of numerous financial papers. Friend of Churchill from 1923, Conservative MP 1929. Parliamentary Private Secretary to Churchill at Admiralty and as Prime Minister 1939–41. Minister of Information 1941–5. First Lord of the Admiralty in 1945 caretaker government.

BUTLER Richard Austen; Conservative MP 1929, junior minister 1932–42, Board of Education 1942–5, head of Conservative Research Department 1945–51, Chancellor of the Exchequer 1951–5, later Home Secretary and Foreign Secretary.

CAMPBELL-BANNERMAN Henry; Liberal MP 1868, junior minister in governments of 1880s & 1890s. Leader of Liberal Party after 1899, Prime Minister 1905–8.

CARSON Edward; Conservative MP 1892, Solicitor-General 1900–5, leader of Ulster Unionists after 1910, Attorney-General 1915–6, First Lord of Admiralty 1916–7, member of War Cabinet until 1918.

CAVE George, Conservative MP 1906, Solicitor-General 1915–16, Home Secretary 1916–9, Lord Chancellor 1924–9.

CHAMBERLAIN Austen; son of Joseph, junior minister 1900–3, Chancellor of the Exchequer 1903–5, Secretary of State for India 1915–7 & 1918–9,

Chancellor of the Exchequer 1919–21, leader of Conservative Party 1921–2, Foreign Secretary 1924–9, First Lord of the Admiralty 1931–2.

CHAMBERLAIN, Joseph; Mayor of Birmingham in early 1870s, President of the Board of Trade under Gladstone 1880–5, left Liberals in 1886 over home rule. Colonial Secretary 1895–1903, left government to campaign for tariff reform.

CHAMBERLAIN Neville; son of Joseph, director of national service for part of First World War. Succession of posts in Bonar Law and Baldwin governments 1922–4 including Postmaster-General, Minister of Health and Chancellor of the Exchequer. Minister of Health 1924–9, Chancellor of the Exchequer 1931–7, Prime Minister 1937–40, Lord President of the Council 1940.

COOPER Duff; Junior Minister 1928–9 and 1931–5. Secretary of State for War 1935–7, First Lord of the Admiralty 1937–8, resigned over Munich. Minister of Information 1940–1, British representative with De Gaulle 1943–4, ambassador to France 1944–7.

CROOKSHANK Harry; Conservative MP 1924, junior minister 1934–43. Postmaster-General 1943–5. Minister of Health and Leader of the House of Commons 1951–2. Lord Privy Seal and Leader of the House 1952–5.

CURZON George; Junior minister in Conservative governments 1891–2 & 1895–8, Viceroy of India 1899–1905, Lord Privy Seal 1915–6, Lord President of the Council 1916–9, Foreign Secretary 1919–24.

EDEN Anthony; Conservative MP 1924, PPS to Austen Chamberlain as Foreign Secretary. Junior minister at Foreign Office, Foreign Secretary 1935–8. Dominions Secretary 1939–40, Secretary of State for War 1940, Foreign Secretary 1940–5 (Leader of the House 1942–5). Foreign Secretary 1951–5, Prime Minister 1955–7.

ELGIN Victor; Viceroy of India 1894–8, Colonial Secretary 1905–8.

GLADSTONE Herbert, son of William, Liberal MP 1880. Chief Whip 1899–1905, Home Secretary 1905–10, Governor-General of South Africa 1910–14.

GREY Edward; Liberal MP 1886, junior minister 1892–5, Foreign Secretary 1905–16.

HALDANE Richard; Liberal MP 1885, Secretary of State for War 1905–12, Lord Chancellor 1912–5 and in 1924 Labour Government.

HOARE Samuel; Conservative MP 1910. Secretary of State for Air under Bonar Law and Baldwin 1922–9. Secretary of State for India 1931–5. Foreign Secretary resigned 1935 over Hoare-Laval pact. First Lord of the Admiralty 1936–7, Home Secretary 1937–39. Lord Privy Seal 1939–40, briefly Secretary of State for Air in 1940. Ambassador to Spain 1940–4.

HOBHOUSE Henry; Liberal MP, junior minister 1907–11. Chancellor of the Duchy of Lancaster 1911–4. Postmaster-General 1914–May 1915.

HORNE Robert; Conservative MP 1918, Minister of Labour 1919–20, President of Board of Trade 1920–1, Chancellor of the Exchequer 1921–2.

KINGSLEY WOOD James; Conservative MP 1918. Junior minister to Neville Chamberlain at Ministry of Health 1924–9. Postmaster-General 1931–5, Minister of Health 1935–8, Secretary of State for Air 1938–40, briefly Lord Privy Seal. Chancellor of the Exchequer 1940–3.

KITCHENER Horatio Herbert; Sirdar of the Egyptian Army 1892–9, served in South Africa 1899–1900 and as C-in-C 1900–2. C-in-C India 1902–9, British representative in Egypt 1911–4. Secretary of State for War 1914–6.

LAW Andrew Bonar; Conservative MP 1900, leader of the party 1911–21. Colonial Secretary 1915–6, Chancellor of the Exchequer 1916–18, Lord Privy Seal 1919–21, Leader of the House 1916–21. Prime Minister 1922–3.

LINLITHGOW Victor; Junior minister 1922–4, Deputy Chairman of Conservative Party 1924–6, Viceroy of India 1936–43.

LLOYD George (Lord); Conservative MP 1910, Governor of Bombay 1918–23, High Commissioner in Egypt 1925–9, Colonial Secretary 1940–1.

LLOYD GEORGE David; Liberal MP 1890, President of the Board of Trade 1905–8, Chancellor of the Exchequer 1908–15, Minister of Munitions 1915–6, Secretary of State for War 1916. Prime Minister 1916–22. Leader of Liberals after 1926.

LONG Walter; Conservative MP 1880, junior minister 1886–92 & 1895–1905. Colonial Secretary 1916–8, First Lord of the Admiralty 1919–22.

McKENNA Reginald; Liberal MP 1895, junior minister 1905–8, First Lord of the Admiralty 1908–11, Home Secretary 1911–5, Chancellor of the Exchequer 1915–6.

MACMILLAN Harold; Conservative MP 1924. Junior minister at Ministry of Supply and Colonial Office 1940–2. Minister Resident in North Africa and later Italy and Greece 1942–5. Secretary of State for Air in caretaker government 1945. Minister of Housing 1951–4. Minister of Defence 1954–5, Foreign Secretary 1955–6, Chancellor of the Exchequer 1956–7. Prime Minister 1957–63.

MILNER Alfred; civil servant in Egypt and as Chairman of Board of Inland Revenue. High Commissioner for South Africa 1897–1905, member of War Cabinet 1916–8, Secretary of State for War 1918–9, Colonial Secretary 1919–21.

MORLEY John; Liberal MP 1883, biographer of Gladstone, Secretary of State for India 1905–10, Lord President of the Council 1910–4.

ROSEBERY Archibald; Foreign Secretary in Liberal governments of 1886 and 1892–4, leader of the party and Prime Minister 1894–5.

RUNCIMAN Walter; Liberal MP, junior minister 1905–8, President of Board of Education 1908–11, Board of Agriculture 1911–4 and President of Board of Trade 1914–6 and 1931–7.

SALISBURY Robert; (Marquess) Secretary of State for India 1866–7 and 1874–8, Foreign Secretary 1878–80, 1885–6, 1887–92 and 1895–1900. Prime Minister 1885–6, 1886–92 and 1895–1902.

SIMON John; Liberal MP 1906–18, 1922–40. Solicitor-General 1910–3, Attorney-General 1913–5, Home Secretary 1915–6. Foreign Secretary 1931–5, Home Secretary 1935–7, Chancellor of the Exchequer 1937–40, Lord Chancellor 1940–5.

SWINTON, Philip (Cunliffe-Lister); Junior minister in Lloyd George coalition, President of the Board of Trade 1922–3 and 1924–9, Colonial Secretary 1931–5, Secetary of State for Air 1935–8. Chairman of the Security Executive 1940–2. Minister Resident in West Africa 1942–4, Minister of Civil Aviation 1944–5. Chancellor of the Duchy of Lancaster and Minister of Materials 1951–2, Secretary of State for Commonwealth Relations 1952–5.

Index

Index

political flexibility 32, 136, 247, 272, 390–1, 488, 575, 652
poor sense of timing 47
quickness to act 67, 108, 111
smoking 13, 79
temper 123, 125, 173, 579, 597, 621–2, 679
unpopularity 9, 11, 41–2, 55, 68, 96–7, 178–9, 206–7, 208, 267, 432
as Colonial Secretary 70, 225, 248, 249–75
  and coalition government 266–70, 273–5
  and Egyptian nationalism 249, 250–1
  election defeat 275, 276
  and Ireland 260–6
  and Kenya 258–60
  and Lloyd George 267–9
  and Near East 251–8, 743
  and Turkey 270–3
constituencies
  Dundee 75–6, 81, 92–3, 95, 134, 220, 274–5, 489
  Epping 283–4, 356, 402
  Manchester North West 57, 81, 136
  Oldham 38–9, 40–53
  Woodford 810, 812
death 813
early life
  childhood 3
  family background 3–5
  neglected by parents 5–6, 10, 12
early political career
  captured during Boer War 33–4
  defection to Liberals 47–56, 96
  early political speeches 25, 28–9
  maiden speech 41, 61–2
  opposes military expenditure 43–4, 53
  on public expenditure committee 45
  seeks Parliamentary seat 31–2, 34
  selected for Manchester North West 53–4
  selected for Oldham 32, 38
education
  academic performance 8–9, 11–12
  in Army class 12
  bad behaviour 8–9, 11
  at Captain James' crammer 13
  Harrow 11–13, 331
  at Misses Thomson's school 8–10
  preparatory school 8
  and Sandhurst 12, 13–14
  self-education 10, 11, 22–4
finances
  allowance from father 13, 15
  allowance from mother 18, 39
  and commemorative fund 797–8
  directorships 330
  from books and lectures 38–9, 45, 70, 287–8, 330–5, 346–7, 385, 804
  inheritance 17, 287
  investments 39, 287, 330, 386
  post-war 726–7
  problems 18, 39, 45, 334, 385–6, 389

health
  appendicitis 274
  arteriosclerosis 810–13
  breaks hip 812
  contracts paratyphoid 347
  deafness 725, 730, 756, 784
  depression 19, 21, 42, 191–2, 388, 561, 725, 782, 802, 804–6, 808–12
  heart problems 617–18
  pneumonia attacks 529, 598, 617, 654–5, 810
  speech impediment 43, 467
  suffers strokes 730–1, 756, 779, 780–3, 810–12
  traffic accident 346–7
Home Secretary 96–113
  and aliens 112
  and intelligence services 112–13
  on mental degenerates 101–5
  and prison service 105–10, 111
  and Sidney Street siege 111–12
  and suffragettes 105–6, 107–8, 110
  and trades disputes 98–100
  and William Hozier 147
interests
  Army 12, 13, 150–1
  bricklaying 288
  butterflies 13, 22
  fencing 13
  freemasonry 43
  gardening 22
  history 11, 13
  horse racing 727
  hunting 30, 43
  painting 192, 201, 598, 686, 726, 727, 730, 802, 805–6
  politics 15–16, 19–20, 21–4, 42–3, 191–2
  polo 18, 43, 55, 289–91, 382
as Junior Minister 56–7, 58–74
  fails to get Board of Education 72–3
  and Colonial Governors 66–7
  and Local Government Board 73–4, 96
  Privy Councillor 73
  and South Africa 58–65, 67–9
as Minister of Munitions 207, 208–21
  and aircraft 212
  and coalition government 219–20
  and development of tanks 211–12
  and financing of imports 215–17, 299, 409
  labour relations 212–15
  reduced production 211
  reorganisation of ministry 210
in opposition 725–53
  advocates nuclear diplomacy 735–6
  and domestic policy 743–5, 747
  finances 726–30
  General Election 1950 749–50
  General Election 1951 752–3
  health 725–6, 730–1
  and India 739–42
  'Iron Curtain' speech 731–5

882